The first all-new Latin-English dictionary compiled in the United States in the last 60 years—
The first Latin dictionary ever to be compiled on the basis of modern lexicographical principles.

THE NEW COLLEGE
LATIN & ENGLISH DICTIONARY

COMPREHENSIVE: More than 40,000 words and phrases.

DEFINITIVE: Based on the foremost Classical authorities and organized to achieve the utmost clarity, precision, and convenience.

MODERN: Obsolete definitions have been replaced by fresh translations that correspond to current English usage.

A NEW LANDMARK
IN LATIN-ENGLISH DICTIONARIES
FOR THE MODERN STUDENT!

John C. Traupman, author of *The New College Latin & English Dictionary,* is Chairman of the Classics Department of St. Joseph's College, Philadelphia. Professor Traupman took his A.B. at Moravian College and his Ph.D. at Princeton. He served as President of the Philadelphia Classical Society and of the Pennsylvania Classical Association.

THE BANTAM NEW
COLLEGE DICTIONARY SERIES
Edwin B. Williams, General Editor

Edwin B. Williams, A.B., A.M., Ph.D., Doct. d'Univ., LL.D., L.H.D. has been Chairman of the Department of Romance Languages, Dean of the Graduate School, and Provost of the University of Pennsylvania. He is a member of the American Philosophical Society and the Hispanic Society of America and the author of *THE BANTAM NEW COLLEGE SPANISH & ENGLISH DICTIONARY* and the Holt *Spanish and English Dictionary* and many other works on the Spanish, Portuguese, and French languages.

THE
NEW COLLEGE
LATIN & ENGLISH
DICTIONARY

John C. Traupman, Ph.D.

St. Joseph's College,
Philadelphia

THE NEW COLLEGIATE LATIN & ENGLISH DICTIONARY

Bantam Language Library edition / April 1966

2nd printing	...... May 1966	8th printing	... August 1970
3rd printing	.. September 1967	9th printing	.... August 1971
4th printing	.. September 1968	10th printing	...... June 1973
5th printing	.. December 1968	11th printing	..... April 1974
6th printing	..... August 1969	12th printing	...... July 1975
7th printing	.... May 1970	13th printing	.. February 1977
	14th printing	.... May 1978	

Library of Congress Catalog Card Number: 66-12159

ISBN 0-553-12102-2

Published simultaneously in the United States and Canada

Bantam Books are published by Bantam Books, Inc. Its trade-mark, consisting of the words "Bantam Books" and the por-trayal of a bantam, is registered in the United States Patent Office and in other countries. Marca Registrada. Bantam Books, Inc., 666 Fifth Avenue, New York, New York 10019.

PRINTED IN THE UNITED STATES OF AMERICA

INTRODUCTION

Both Latin and English entry words, as well as illustrative phrases under entry words, are treated in strictly alphabetical order.

Adverbs on the Latin-English side are inserted as separate entries and translated in that position without cross-reference to the corresponding adjective.

Adverbs on the English-Latin side ending in -ly are listed under their adjectives

Compound words are generally given in their assimilated forms, e.g., accurrō rather than adcurrō. Cross-references are provided as guides for those using texts which employ the unassimilated forms.

The letter j has been used in place of consonantal i because some recent texts have begun to use the former again and because students can thus more readily distinguish the consonant from the vowel.

If a feminine substantive, singular or plural, of the first declension, a neuter substantive, singular or plural, of the second declension, or a masculine substantive of the second declension falls alphabetically more than one word before or after the corresponding adjective, it is inserted as a separate entry and translated in that position, and a cross-reference to it is given under the adjective; for example, nāt·a -ae *f* occurs fifteen entries before nāt·us -a -um *adj* ... ; *f* see nata.

If such a substantive does not fall alphabetically more than one word before or after the corresponding adjective, it is treated under the adjective.

Many of the variations in spelling of Latin words are indicated by means of cross-references, e.g., sēpiō see saepio.

Only those past participles are listed as separate entries whose difference in form from the first person singular present indicative warrants such listing, provided they fall alphabetically more than one word before or after the first person singular present indicative.

Only the first person singular present indicative and the present infinitive of regular active verbs of the first conjugation are given; in the case of deponent verbs, the perfect is added. For the other three conjugations and for irregular and defective verbs, all principal parts in use are given.

Discriminations between two or more meanings of the entry word are often shown by means of English words in parentheses.

Transitive and intransitive verbs, with their dependent

constructions, are clearly differentiated and are presented in a fixed order of transitive first and intransitive second.

Centered periods within entry words indicate division points at which inflectional elements are to be added.

All source words and phrases are printed in boldface type.

On the English-Latin side a boldface dash represents the vocabulary entry.

On the Latin-English side, the twofold purpose in marking the quantity of vowels is (1) to indicate accentuation of words and (2) to provide the basis for scansion of Classical Latin verse. Thus, all vowels that are long by nature and occur in open syllables are marked, whereas vowels in closed syllables, whether long or short by nature, are not marked, since the syllable in either case is long. However, since a vowel followed by a mute and a liquid can be open or closed, its quantity is marked when it is long. As a further aid to pronunciation, in words of three or more syllables, the short vowel of the penult is marked.

On the English-Latin side, Latin vowels have been marked to distinguish:

(a) words otherwise spelled alike: lēvis, levis
(b) the genitive singular and the nominative and accusative plural from the nominative singular of the fourth declension
(c) the ablative singular from the nominative singular of nouns of the first declension whenever the distinction is not clear from the context
(d) the nominative and genitive singular from the accusative plural of *i*-stem words of the third declension
(e) the infinitive of verbs of the second conjugation from the infinitive of verbs of the third conjugation.

On the English-Latin side, the genitive of the nouns of the fourth declension is provided in order to distinguish these nouns from nouns of the second declension ending in -us.

John C. Traupman

PRONUNCIATION

Vowels

	CLASSICAL METHOD	ECCLESIASTICAL METHOD
ă	Like *a* in *a*go: compărō	(Generally as in the Classical Method. However, in practice the different values of the vowels are frequently not rigidly adhered to.)
ā	Like *a* in f*a*ther: imāgō	
ĕ	Like *e* in p*e*t: propĕrō	
ē	Like *a* in l*a*te: lēnis	
ĭ	Like *i* in h*i*t: ĭdem	
ī	Like *ee* in k*ee*n: amīcus	
ŏ	Like *o* in *o*ften: mŏdus	
ō	Like *o* in h*o*pe: nōmen	
ŭ	Like *u* in p*u*t: ŭt	
ū	Like *u* in r*u*de: ūtor	
ў	Like *ü* in German H*ü*tte: mўrīca	
ȳ	Like *ü* in German *ü*ber: Tȳdeus	

Diphthongs

	CLASSICAL METHOD	ECCLESIASTICAL METHOD
ae	Like *y* in b*y*: caecus	Like *a* in l*a*te: caecus
au	Like *ow* in n*ow*: nauta	As in the Classical Method
ei	Like *ey* in gr*ey*: deinde	As in the Classical Method
eu	Like *eu* in f*eu*d: Orpheus	Like *eu* in Italian n*eu*tro: euge
oe	Like *oi* in *oi*l: coepit	Like *a* in l*a*te: coepit
ui	Like *uey* in gl*uey*: cui	As in the Classical Method
	After **q**, like *wee* in *wee*k: qui	

Consonants

	CLASSICAL METHOD	ECCLESIASTICAL METHOD
b	As in English	As in English
c	Always like *c* in *c*an: cīvis, cantō, actus	Before **e**, **i**, **ae**, or **oe** like *ch* in *ch*erry; excelsis, cīvis, caelum, coepit, but before other letters like *c* in *c*an: cantō, actus
d	As in English	As in English
f	As in English	As in English
g	Always like *g* in *g*o: genus, gula, gallīna, grātus	Before **e** or **i** like *g* in *g*entle: genus, regīna, but before other letters except **g** and **n** (see under Consonant Groups) like *g* in *g*o: gula, gallīna, fugō, grātus
h	As in English	As in English
j	Like *y* in *y*es: jungō, jam	As in the Classical Method
k	As in English	As in English
l	As in English	As in English
m	As in English, but in verse final **m** before an initial vowel in the following word was presumably not pronounced	As in English
n	As in English	As in English
p	As in English	As in English
q	As in English and used only before consonantal **u**	As in English
r	Trilled as in the Romance languages	As in the Classical Method
s	Always like *s* in *s*ing: miser, mors	Like *s* in *s*ing: salūs, but when standing between two vowels or when final and preceded by a voiced consonant, like *z* in do*z*en: miser, mors
t	Like English *t*, but unaspirated	As in the Classical Method

	CLASSICAL METHOD	ECCLESIASTICAL METHOD
u	Like *w* in *w*ine, when un-accented, preceded by **q**, sometimes by **s**, and sometimes by **g**, and followed by a vowel: **qui·a, suā·vis** (but **su·ō·rum**), **dis·tin·guō** (but **ex·i·gŭ·us**)	As in the Classical Method
v	Like *w* in *w*ine: **vīvō**	As in English
x	Like *x* (= ks) in si*x*: **exactus**	Like *x* (=ks) in si*x*: **pax**; but in words beginning with **ex** and followed by a vowel, **h**, or **s**, like *x* (= gz) in e*x*haust: **exaudī, exhālō, exsolvō**
z	*Like dz in adze:* **zōna**	As in the Classical Method

Consonant Groups

	CLASSICAL METHOD	ECCLESIASTICAL METHOD
bs	Like *ps* in a*ps*e: **obsidĕō, urbs**	Like *bs* in o*bs*ession: **obsidĕō**, but in the final position, like *bs* in o*bs*erve: **urbs**
bt	Like *pt* in ca*pt*ain: **obtinēre**	Like *bt* in o*bt*ain: **obtinēre**
cc	Like *kk* in boo*kk*eeper: **ecce, occīdō, occāsum, occlūdō**	Before **e** or **i** like *tch* in ca*tch*: **ecce, occīdō**; but before other letters, like *kk* in boo*kk*eeper: **occāsum, occlū-dō**
ch	Like *ch* in *ch*aotic: **pulcher**	As in the Classical Method
gg	Like *gg* in le*g g*uard: **agger**	Before **e** or **i** like *dj* in a*dj*ourn: **agger**; but before other letters, like *gg* in le*g g*uard: **aggrĕgō**
gn	As in English	Like *ny* in ca*ny*on: **dignus**
gu	See consonant **u**	As in the Classical Method
ph	Like *p-h* in to*p-h*eavy: **phōca**	Like *ph* in *ph*oenix: **phōca**
qu	See consonant *u*	As in the Classical Method
sc	Like *sc* in *sc*ope: **sciō, scūtum**	Before **e** or **i** like *sh* in *sh*in: **ascendō, sciō**; but before other letters, like *sc* in *sc*ope: **scandō, scūtum**
su	See consonant **u**	As in the Classical Method
th	Like *t* in *t*ake: **theātrum**	As in the Classical Method
ti	Like *ti* in English pa*ti*o: **nātiō**	When preceded by **s**, **t**, or **x** or when followed by a consonant, like *ti* in English pa*ti*o: **hostia, admixtiō, fortiter**; but when unaccented, followed by a vowel, and preceded by any letter except **s**, **t**, or **x**, like *tzy* in ri*tzy*: **nātiō, pretium**

viii

SYLLABIFICATION

1. Every Latin word has as many syllables as it has vowels or diphthongs: **ae·ger, fī·li·us, Bai·ae**

2. When a word is divided into syllables:
   a) a single consonant between two vowels goes with the following syllable (**h** is regarded as a consonant; **ch, ph, th, qu**, and somtimes **gu** and **su** are regarded as single consonants)*: **a·ger, ni·hil, a·qua, ci·cho·rē·um**
   b) the first consonant of a combination of two or more consonants goes with the preceding vowel: **tor·men·tum, mit·tō, mon·strum**
   c) a consonant group consisting of a mute (**b, d, g, p, t, c**) followed by **l** or **r** is generally left undivided and goes with the following vowel: **pa·trēs, a·cris, du·plex.** In Classical poetry this combination is often treated like any other pair of consonants: **pat·rēs, ac·ris, dup·lex**
   d) prefixes form separate syllables even if the division is contrary to above rules: **ab·est, ob·lā·tus, abs·ti·nĕ·ō, ab·stō**

3. A syllable ending in a vowel or diphthong is called *open*; all others are called *closed*

4. The last syllable of a word is called the *ultima*; the next to last is called the *penult*; the one before the penult is called the *antepenult*

---

* The double consonant **x** goes with the preceding vowel: **dix·it**

QUANTITY OF VOWELS

1. A vowel is *long* (**lēvis**) or *short* (**lĕvis**) according to the length of time required for its pronunciation

2. A vowel is long:
   a) before **ns, nf**, (and perhaps **gn**): **ingēns, īnfāns, (māgnus)**
   b) when resulting from a contraction: **nil = nihil, cōgō = cŏăgō, iniquus = inaequus**

3. A vowel is short:
   a) before another vowel or **h**: **dĕa, trăhō**
   b) generally before **nd** and **nt**: **amăndus, amănt**

4. Diphthongs are long: **causae**

QUANTITY OF SYLLABLES

1. Syllables are distinguished as *long* or *short* according to the length of time required for their pronunciation

2. A syllable is long:
   a) if it contains a long vowel or a diphthong: **vĕ·nī, scrī·bō, cau·sae** (such a syllable is said to be *long by nature*)
   b) if it contains a short vowel followed by **x, z**, or any two consonants except a mute (**b, d, g, p, t, c**) followed by **l** or **r**: **sax·um, gaz·a, mit·tō, cur·sor** (such a syllable is said to be *long by position*, but the vowel is pronounced *short*)

3. A syllable is short:
   a) if it contains a short vowel followed by a vowel or by a single consonant (**h** is regarded as a consonant; **ch, ph, th, qu**, and sometimes **gu** and **su** are regarded as single consonants): **me·us, ni·hil, ge·rit, a·qua**
   b) if it contains a short vowel followed by a mute (**b, d, g, p, t, c**) plus **l** or **r**, but it is sometimes long in verse: **flă·grans, ba·ră·thrum, ce·lĕ·brō** (such a syllable is said to be *common*)

NOTE: In this dictionary, long vowels are marked except before **x, z**, or two or more consonants unless the two consonants are a mute plus a liquid. Only the short penult of words of three or more syllables is marked.

ACCENT

1. Words of two syllables are accented on the first syllable: om′nēs, tan′gō, ge′rit

2. Words of more than two syllables are accented on the penult if it is long: a·mī′cus, re·gun′tur and on the antepenult if the penult is short: fa·mi′lĭ·a, ge′rĭ·tur

3. These rules apply to words with enclitics appended (-ce, -dum, -met, -ne, -que, -ve): vos′met, lau·dat′ne, de′ă·que (nominative), de·ā′que (ablative)

4. In the second declension, the contracted genitive and the contracted vocative of nouns in -ius and the contracted genitive of those in -ium retain the accent of the nominative: Vir·gĭ′lī, in·gĕ′nī

5. Certain words which have lost a final -e retain the accent of the complete forms: il·lĭc′ for il·lĭ′ce, tan·tōn′ for tan·tō′ne

6. Certain compounds of faciō, in which a feeling for the individuality of the components was preserved, retain the accent of the simple verb: be·ne·fă′cit

---

ABBREVIATIONS

abbr	abbreviation	*interrog*	interrogative
abl	ablative	*loc*	locative
acc	accusative	*m*	masculine noun
adj	adjective	*masc*	masculine
adv	adverb	*math*	mathematics
astr	astronomy	*med*	medicine
bot	botany	*mil*	military
c.	circa, about	*m pl*	masculine plural noun
cent.	century	*mus*	music
coll	colloquial	*n*	neuter noun
com	commercial	*neut*	neuter
comp	comparative	*nom*	nominative
conj	conjunction	*n pl*	neuter plural noun
d.	died	*p*	participle
dat	dative	*phil*	philosophy
defect	defective	*pl*	plural
eccl	ecclesiastical	*pol*	politics
esp.	especially	*pp*	past participle
f	feminine noun	*prep*	preposition
fem	feminine	*pres*	present
fig	figurative	*pron*	pronoun
fl	floruit	*reflex*	reflexive
f pl	feminine plural noun	*rel*	relative
fut	future	*rhet*	rhetoric
genit	genitive	*s*	substantive
gram	grammar	*singl*	singular
impers	impersonal	*subj*	subjunctive
impv	imperative	*superl*	superlative
indecl	indeclinable	*v defect*	defective verb
indef	indefinite	*vi*	intransitive verb
inf	infinitive	*v impers*	impersonal verb
interj	interjection	*vt*	transitive verb

A

ā *interj* ah!

ā or **ab** *prep* (with *abl*) (of agency) by; (of time) since, after, from; (of space) from, away from; at, on, in; **a latere** on the side; **a tergo** in the rear

abactus *pp* of **abigo**

abăc·us -ī *m* cupboard; game board; abacus, counting board; panel; tray

abaliēnāti·ō -ōnis *f* transfer of property

abaliēn·ō -āre *vt* to alienate, estrange; to sell; to separate

Abantiăd·ēs -ae *m* descendant of Abas

Ab·ās -antis *m* king of Argos, father of Acrisius and grandfather of Perseus

abăv·us -ī *m* great-great-grandfather

abdicāti·ō -ōnis *f* abdication, renunciation, resignation

abdic·ō -āre *vt* to abdicate, renounce, resign; to disinherit; **se magistratu abdicare** to resign from office

ab·dīcō -dīcĕre -dixī -dictum *vt* (in augury) to disapprove of, forbid

abdĭtē *adv* secretly, privately

abdĭt·us -a -um *adj* hidden, secret

ab·dō -dĕre -dĭdī -dĭtum *vt* to hide; to remove, withdraw; to plunge (*e.g., a sword*)

abdōm·en -ĭnis *n* abdomen, belly; (fig) gluttony, greed

ab·dūcō -dūcĕre -duxī -ductum *vt* to lead away, take away; to seduce; to alienate

ab·ĕō -īre -ĭī -ĭtum *vi* to go away, depart; to vanish, disappear; to pass away, die; (of time) to pass, elapse; to change, be changed; to retire

abequit·ō -āre *vi* to ride off

aberrāti·ō -ōnis *f* wandering, escape, relief

aberr·ō -āre *vi* to wander, go astray; to deviate, differ

abesse *inf* of **absum**

abhinc *adv* ago

abhorr·ĕō -ēre -ŭī *vi* to shrink back; (with **ab** + *abl*) **a** to be averse to; **b** to be inconsistent with, differ from; **c** to be free from

abiegn·us -a -um *adj* fir

abĭ·ēs -ĕtis *f* fir; ship; spear; writing tablet

ab·ĭgō -igĕre -ēgī -actum *vt* to drive away, get rid of; to banish, expel

abĭt·us -ūs *m* departure; outlet; end

abjectē *adv* abjectly, meanly

abject·us -a -um *adj* abject, mean; downhearted

ab·jĭcĭō -jĭcĕre -jēcī -jectum *vt* to throw away, throw down; to slight; to give up; to humble, debase

abjūdĭc·ō -āre *vt* to take away (*by judicial decree*)

ab·jungō -jungĕre -junxī -junctum *vt* to unyoke; to detach

abjūr·ō -āre *vt* to deny on oath

ablātīv·us -a -um *adj* & *m* ablative

ablātus *pp* of **aufero**

ablēgāti·ō -ōnis *f* sending away, sending off; banishment

ablēg·ō -āre *vt* to send away; to remove, banish; to dismiss

abligurr·ĭō or **abligūr·ĭō** -īre -īvī or -ĭī -ītum *vt* to squander, waste

ablŏc·ō -āre *vt* to lease, rent out

ab·lŭdō -lūdĕre -lūsī -lūsum *vi* to be unlike; (with **ab** + *abl*) to differ from

ab·lŭō -luĕre -lŭī -lūtum *vt* to wash away, cleanse, remove

ablūti·ō -ōnis *f* washing, cleansing

abnĕg·ō -āre *vt* to refuse, turn down

abnĕp·ōs -ōtis *m* great-great-grandson

abnept·is -is *f* great-great-granddaughter

abnoct·ō -āre *vi* to stay out all night, sleep out

abnorm·is -e *adj* irregular, unorthodox

ab·nŭō -nuĕre -nŭī -nūtum *vt* to refuse, deny

abol·ĕō -ēre -ēvī -ĭtum *vt* to abolish, destroy, annihilate

abol·escō -escĕre -ēvī *vi* to decay, vanish, die out

abolĭti·ō -ōnis *f* abolition

abōmĭn·or -ārī -ātus sum *vt* to detest

aborĭgĭn·ēs -um *m* *pl* aborigines, original inhabitants

ab·orĭor -orīrī -ortus sum *vi* to miscarry; to fail; (of stars, etc.) to set

abortĭ·ō -ōnis *f* miscarriage

abortīv·us -a -um *adj* prematurely born

abort·us -ūs *m* miscarriage

ab·rādō -rādĕre -rāsī -rāsum *vt* to scrape off, shave; (fig) to squeeze out, rob

ab·rĭpĭō -rĭpĕre -rĭpŭī -reptum *vt* to take away by force, carry off; to squander

ab·rōdō -rōdĕre -rōsī -rōsum *vt* to gnaw off

abrogātǐ·ō -ōnis *f* repeal

abrŏg·ō -āre *vt* to repeal, annul

abrotōn·um -ī *n* southernwood (*aromatic, medicinal plant*)

ab·rumpō -rumpĕre -rūpī -ruptum *vt* to break off; to tear, sever

abruptē *adv* abruptly, rashly

abruptǐ·ō -ōnis *f* breaking off; divorce

abrupt·us -a -um *pp* of **abrumpo**; *adj* abrupt, steep; *n* precipice

abs *prep* (with *abl*, confined almost exclusively to the combination **abs te**) by, from

abscessǐ·ō -ōnis *f* diminution

abscess·us -ūs *m* departure, absence, remoteness

abs·cīdō -cīdĕre -cīdī -cīsum *vt* to cut off, chop off; to cut short

ab·scindō -scindĕre -scīdī -scissum *vt* to tear off, break off; to divide

abscīs·us -a -um *pp* of **abscido**; *adj* steep, precipitous; concise; abrupt

abscondītē *adv* secretly; obscurely; profoundly

abs条ondīt·us -a -um *adj* concealed, secret

abs·condō -condĕre -condī or **-condīdī -condītum** *vt* to hide; to lose sight of, leave behind; to bury (*weapon*)

abs·ens -entis *pres p* of **absum**; *adj* absent

absentǐ·a -ae *f* absence

absil·ǐō -īre -ǐī or **-ǔī** *vi* to jump away

absimil·is -e *adj* unlike; (with *dat*) unlike

absinth·ǐum -ǐī or **-ī** *n* wormwood

abs·is -īdis *f* vault, arch; orbit (*of a star*)

ab·sistō -sistĕre -stītī *vi* to withdraw, depart; to cease, lay off

absolūtē *adv* perfectly

absolūtǐ·ō -ōnis *f* acquittal; perfection, completeness

absolūtōri·us -a -um *adj* of acquittal, granting acquittal

absolūt·us -a -um *adj* perfect, complete, unqualified

ab·solvō -solvĕre -solvī -solūtum *vt* to release, set free, detach; to acquit; to finish off; to pay off, discharge

absŏn·us -a -um *adj* discordant, incongruous, incompatible

absorb·ĕō -ēre -ǔī *vt* to swallow, devour; to engross

absque *prep* (with *abl*) without, apart from, but for; **absque me foret** if it had not been for me

abstēmǐ·us -a -um *adj* abstemious, temperate, sober

abs·tergĕō -tergēre -tersī -tersum *vt* to wipe off, wipe dry; to expel, banish

absterr·ĕō -ēre -ǔī -ǐtum *vt* to

scare away, deter

abstǐn·ens -entis *adj* temperate, forbearing; continent, chaste

abstinenter *adv* with restraint

abstinentǐ·a -ae *f* abstinence, self-control

abs·tinĕō -tinēre -tinǔī -tentum *vt* to withhold, keep away; *vi* to abstain, refrain; (with *genit, abl,* or with **ab** + *abl*, with *inf*, with **quin** or **quominus**) to refrain from

abst·ō -āre *vi* to stand at a distance, stand aloof

abs·trahō -trahĕre -traxī -tractum *vt* to pull away, drag away, remove, detach

abs·trūdō -trūdĕre -trūsī -trūsum *vt* to push away; to conceal

abstrūs·us -a -um *adj* hidden, deep, abstruse; reserved

ab·sum abesse afǔī *vi* to be away, be absent, be distant; (with *abl* or **ab** + *abl*) to be removed from, keep aloof from, be disinclined to; (with **ab** + *abl*) **a** to be different from, be inconsistent with; **b** to be free from; **c** to be unsuitable to, be unfit for; (with *dat*) to be of no help to

ab·sūmō -sūmĕre -sumpsī -sumptum *vt* to take away, diminish; to consume, use up, waste; to destroy, ruin

absurdē *adv* out of tune; absurdly

absurd·us -a -um *adj* out of tune; absurd, illogical, senseless, silly

Absyrt·us -ī *m* son of Aeëtes, king of Colchis, killed by his sister Medea when she eloped with Jason

abund·ans -antis *adj* overflowing, abundant; rich, affluent

abundanter *adv* copiously

abundantǐ·a -ae *f* abundance, wealth

abundē *adv* abundantly, amply

abund·ō -āre *vi* to overflow; to abound; to be rich

abūsǐ·ō -ōnis *f* incorrect use (*of figure of speech*)

abusque *prep* (with *abl*) all the way from

ab·ūtor -ūtī -ūsus sum *vi* (with *abl*) **a** to use up; **b** to misuse, abuse

Abȳd·os or **Abȳd·us -ī** *f* town on Hellespont, opposite Sestos

āc *conj* (usually used before consonants) and, and also, and moreover, and in particular; (in comparisons) than, as

Acadēmǐ·a -ae *f* Academy (*where Plato taught*); Platonic philosophy; Cicero's villa near Puteoli

Acadēmǐc·us -a -um *adj* Academic; *m* Academic philosopher; *n pl* Cicero's treatise on Academic philosophy

acalanth·is -īdis *f* thistlefinch

acanth·us -ī *m* acanthus

Acarnānǐ·a -ae *f* district of N.W. Greece

Acast·us -ī *m* son of Pelias

ac·cēdō -cēdĕre -cessī -cessum vi to come near, approach; (with dat or ad + acc) a to assent to, agree with, approve of; b to come near in resemblance, be like, resemble; c to be added to; (with ad or in + acc) to enter upon, undertake; accedit ut or quod there is the additional fact that

accelĕr·ō -āre vt to speed, quicken; vi to hurry

ac·cendō -cendĕre -cendī -censum vt to light up, set on fire; (fig) to kindle, inflame, excite, awaken

accens·ĕō -ēre -ŭī -um vt to reckon, regard

accens·us -ī m attendant, orderly; m pl rear-echelon troops

accent·us -ūs m accent

acceptĭ·ō -ōnis f accepting, receiving

accept·ō -āre vt to accept, receive

accept·or -ōris m recipient, approver

acceptr·ix -īcis f recipient (female)

accept·us -a -um pp of accipio; adj welcome, pleasing; n receipt; credit side (in account books)

accers·ō -ĕre -īvī -ītum vt to call, summon; to bring, procure

accessĭ·ō -ōnis f approach; passage, entrance; admittance

ac·cīdō -cīdĕre -cīdī -cīsum vt to cut down; to impair, weaken; to eat up

ac·cĭdō -cidĕre -cĭdī vi to fall; to happen, occur; (with dat) to happen to, befall; (with in + acc) to fall on, fall upon; (with dat or ad + acc) to fall before, fall at (e.g., someone's feet); aures or auribus or ad aures accidere to reach or strike the ears

ac·cingō -cingĕre -cinxī -cinctum vt to gird; to arm, equip, furnish; to make ready; accingi or se accingere (with dat or with ad or in + acc) to prepare oneself for, to enter upon, to undertake

ac·ciō -cīre -cīvī -cītum vt to call, send for, invite

ac·cipĭō -cipĕre -cēpī -ceptum vt to take, receive, accept; to admit, let in; to welcome, entertain; to hear, learn, understand; to interpret, explain; to undertake, assume, undergo; to approve of, assent to

accipĭt·er -ris m hawk, falcon

accīs·us -a -um pp of accīdo; adj impaired, ruined; troubled, disordered

accīt·us -ūs m summons, call

Acc·ius -iī or -ī m Roman tragic poet (170-85? B.C.)

acclāmātĭ·ō -ōnis f shout, acclamation

acclām·ō -āre vt to hail, acclaim; vi to shout, cry out; (with dat) to shout at

acclār·ō -āre vt to make clear, make known

acclīnāt·us -a -um adj prostrate; sloping; (with dat) sloping toward

acclīn·is -e adj (with dat) a leaning on or against; b inclined toward, disposed to

acclīn·ō -āre vt (with dat or in + acc) to lean or rest (something) against; se acclinare (with ad + acc) (fig) to be inclined toward

acclīv·is -e adj sloping upwards, uphill, steep

acclīvit·ās -ātis f slope, ascent

accŏl·a -ae m neighbor

ac·cŏlō -colĕre -coluī -cultum vt to dwell near

accommodātē adv suitably, fittingly

accommodātĭ·ō -ōnis f adjustment, compliance, accommodation

accommŏdāt·us -a -um adj (with dat or ad + acc) fit for, adapted to, suitable to

accommŏd·ō -āre vt (with dat or ad + acc) to adjust or adapt or apply (something) to; se accommodare (with ad + acc) to apply or devote oneself to

accommŏd·us -a -um adj fit, suitable; (with dat) fit for, adapted to, suitable to

ac·crēdō -crēdĕre -crēdĭdī -crēdĭtum vi (with dat) to believe, give credence to

ac·crescō -crescĕre -crēvī -crētum vi to grow larger, increase, be added

accrētĭ·ō -ōnis f increase

accubitĭ·ō -ōnis f reclining at table

accŭb·ō -āre vi to lie nearby; to recline at table; (with dat) to lie near

accūd·ō -ĕre vt to coin

ac·cumbō -cumbĕre -cubŭī -cubĭtum vi to take one's place at table

accumulātē adv abundantly

accumulāt·or -ōris m hoarder

accumŭl·ō -āre vt to heap up, amass; to load, overwhelm

accūrātē adv carefully, accurately, exactly

accūrātĭ·ō -ōnis f carefulness, accuracy

accūrāt·us -a -um adj careful, accurate, exact, studied

accūr·ō -āre vt to take care of, attend to

ac·currō -currĕre -currī -cursum vi to run up; (with ad or in + acc) to run to

accurs·us -ūs m running, concourse

accūsābĭl·is -e adj blameworthy

accūsātĭ·ō -ōnis f accusation; indictment, bill of indictment

accūsātīv·us -a -um adj & m accusative

accūsāt·or -ōris m accuser, prosecutor; informer

accūsātōriē adv like an accuser or prosecutor

accūsātōrĭ·us -a -um adj accuser's, prosecutor's

accūsātr·ix -īcis f accuser (female)

accūsĭt·ō -āre vt to keep on accusing

accūs·ō -āre *vt* to accuse, prosecute; to reproach, blame

ac·er -ĕris *n* maple tree

ăc·er -ris -re *adj* sharp, pointed; pungent, stinging, penetrating, piercing, shrill; sagacious, keen, judicious; energetic, enthusiastic, ardent, brave; passionate, fierce, violent; severe, vigorous

acerbē *adv* bitterly, harshly

acerbĭt·ās -ātis *f* bitterness, harshness, sharpness, sourness; distress

acerb·ō -āre *vt* to embitter, aggravate

acerb·us -a -um *adj* bitter, harsh, sour; unripe; severe; morose, rough; untimely, premature; painful, troublesome; sad

acern·us -a -um *adj* maple

acerr·a -ae *f* incense box

acersecōm·ēs -ae *m* young man, youth

acervātim *adv* in heaps; briefly

acerv·ō -āre *vt* to heap or pile up

acerv·us -ī *m* heap, pile; multitude; (in logic) sorites

acescō acescĕre acŭī *vi* to turn sour

Acest·ēs -ae *m* mythical king of Sicily

acētābŭl·um -ī *n* vinegar bottle

acēt·um -ī *n* sour wine, vinegar; (fig) pungent wit, shrewdness

Achaemĕn·ēs -is *m* first king of Persia, grandfather of Cyrus

Achaemenī·us -a -um *adj* Persian

Achae·us -a -um *adj & m* Achaean; Greek

Achai·a or Achāi·a -ae *f* province in northern part of the Peloponnesus on Gulf of Corinth; Greece

Achāic·us -a -um *adj & m* Achaean; Greek

Achāt·ēs -ae *m* companion of Aeneas; river in Sicily

Achelō·ŭs -ī *m* river in N.W. Greece; river god

Achĕr·ōn -ontis or Achĕr·os -ī *m* river in Hades

Achill·ēs -is *m* Greek warrior, son of Peleus and Thetis

Achillē·us -a -um *adj* of Achilles

Achillīd·ēs -ae *m* descendant of Achilles

Achīv·us -a -um *adj* Achaean, Greek

Acĭdalĭ·a -ae *f* Venus

acĭd·us -a -um *adj* sour, tart; (of sound) harsh, shrill; sharp, keen, pungent; unpleasant, disagreeable

aci·ēs -ēī *f* sharpness, sharp edge; keenness of vision, glance; eyesight, eye, pupil; mental power; battle line, battle array, battlefield, battle; debate

acīnăc·ēs -is *m* scimitar

acīn·um -ī *n* or acīn·us -ī *m* berry, grape; seed in berry

acĭpens·er -ĕris or acĭpens·is -is *m* sturgeon

Ac·is -ĭdis *m* son of Faunus, loved by Galatea, changed into a river

acl·ys -ўdis *f* small javelin

aconīt·um -ī *n* wolf's-bane; strong poison

ac·or -ōris *m* sour taste, sourness

acqui·escō -escĕre -ēvī -ētum *vi* to become quiet; to rest; to die; (with *abl*, *dat*, or with **in** + *abl*) to find rest in, acquiesce in, be content with, find pleasure in, rejoice in

ac·quīrō -quīrĕre -quīsīvī -quīsītum *vt* to acquire, obtain, gain, win

Acrăg·ās -antis *m* town on S.W. coast of Sicily

acrēdŭl·a -ae *f* bird (*perhaps owl or nightingale*)

ācrĭcŭl·us -a -um *adj* irritable, peevish

ācrĭmōnĭ·a -ae *f* sharpness, pungency; irritation; energy

Acrĭsĭōnĭăd·ēs -ae *m* descendant of Acrisius; Perseus

Acris·ĭus -ĭī or -ī *m* king of Argos, father of Danaë

ācrĭter *adv* sharply, keenly, vehemently, severely

acrŏām·a -ătis *n* entertainment; entertainer

Acroceraunĭ·a -ōrum *n pl* promontory on the Adriatic Sea in Epirus

Acrocorinth·us -ī *f* citadel of Corinth

act·a -ae *f* seashore, beach

act·a -ōrum *n pl* deeds, actions; public acts; proceedings of the senate; records, minutes; journal

Actae·ōn -ōnis *m* grandson of Cadmus, changed into a stag

Actae·us -a -um *adj* Attic, Athenian

actĭ·ō -ōnis *f* doing, performance, action, activity; proceedings; (law) suit, process, action, permission for a suit; delivery, gesticulation; plot, action (*of play*)

actĭt·ō -āre *vt* to plead (*cases*) often; to perform (*plays*) often

Act·ium -ĭī or -ī *n* promontory in Epirus (*where Octavian defeated Antony and Cleopatra in 31 B.C.*)

actīv·us -a -um *adj* (gram) active; practical (*opposite of contemplative*)

act·or -ōris *m* doer, performer; (law) plaintiff, pleader, advocate; agent, manager; player, actor; **actor summarum** cashier, accountant

Act·or -ōris *m* companion of Aeneas

actuārĭŏl·um -ī *n* small barge

actuāri·us -a -um *adj* swift; *m* stenographer; *f* swift ship; *n* swift ship

actuōsē *adv* energetically

actuōs·us -a -um *adj* energetic, very active

actus *pp* of ago

act·us -ūs *m* act, performance; driving, motion, impulse; right of way; public business; presentation, delivery, gesture, recital; act (*of play*)

actūtum *adv* instantly, immediately

acŭl·a -ae *f* rivulet

aculeāt·us -a -um *adj* prickly; (fig) stinging, sharp, subtle

aculĕ·us -ī *m* barb, sting; point; sarcasm

acūm·en -inis *n* point, sharpness; sting (*of insect*); pungency; shrewdness, ingenuity, cunning

acŭō acuĕre acŭī acūtum *vt* to make sharp or pointed; to whet; to exercise; to stimulate; to give an edge to, enhance; to tease

ac·us -ūs *f* needle, pin; **acu rem tangere** to hit the nail on the head

acūtē *adv* acutely, sharply, keenly

acūtŭl·us -a -um *adj* somewhat sharp, rather subtle

acūt·us -a -um *pp* of **acuo**; *adj* sharp, pointed; shrill; intelligent

ad *prep* (with *acc*) (of space) to, towards, near, at; (of time) toward, about, until, at, on, by; (with numbers) about, almost; for the purpose of, to; according to, in consequence of; with respect to; compared with

adactĭ·ō -ōnis *f* enforcing

adactus *pp* of **adigo**

adact·us -ūs *m* bringing together; snapping (*of jaws*)

adaequē *adv* equally

adaequ·ō -āre *vt* to make level; to equal, match; (fig) to put on the same level; *vi* to be on the same level, be equal; (with *dat*) to be level with

adamantē·us -a -um *adj* made of steel

adamantĭn·us -a -um *adj* hard as steel, adamantine

adăm·ās -antis *m* adamant; steel; diamond

adambŭl·ō -āre *vi* (with **ad** + *acc*) to walk about near

adăm·ō -āre *vt* to fall in love with

ad·aperĭō -aperīre -aperŭī -apertum *vt* to uncover, throw open

adăqu·ō -āre *vt* to water; *vi* to fetch water

adauct·us -ūs *m* growth

ad·augĕō -augēre -auxī -auctum *vt* to increase, aggravate

adaugesc·ō -ĕre *vi* to begin to grow

ad·bibō -bibĕre -bĭbī -bibĭtum *vt* to drink in; to listen attentively to

adbīt·ō -ĕre *vi* to come near, approach

adc- = acc-

ad·decet -decēre *v impers* it becomes

addens·ĕō -ēre or **addens·ō -āre** *vt* to close (*ranks*)

ad·dīcō -dīcĕre -dixī -dictum *vt* to assign; to doom; to dedicate, devote; *vi* (in augury) to be favorable

ad·discō -discĕre -didĭcī *vt* to learn in addition

additāment·um -ī *n* addition

ad·dō -dĕre -dĭdī -dĭtum *vt* to add, increase; to impart, bestow

ad·docĕō -docēre -docŭī -doctum *vt* to teach in addition

addubĭt·ō -āre *vt* to call into doubt; *vi* to begin to feel doubt; to hesitate

ad·dūcō -dūcĕre -duxī -ductum *vt* to lead up, bring up; to draw together, wrinkle; to prompt, induce, persuade, move

adduct·us -a -um *adj* drawn tight, strained; narrow, tight (*place*); strict, serious, stern (*character*)

ad·ĕdō -esse -ēdī -ēsum *vt* to nibble at; to eat up, consume; to waste

ademptĭ·ō -ōnis *f* taking away

ad·ĕō -īre -iī or **-īvī -ĭtum** *vt* to approach; to attack; to consult, apply to; to visit; to undertake, set about, undergo; *vi* to go up, come up; (with **ad** + *acc*) **a** to go to, approach; **b** to enter upon, undertake, set about, submit to

adĕō *adv* to such a degree, so; (following pronouns and numerals, to give emphasis) precisely, exactly, quite, just, chiefly; (at the beginning of sentence) thus far, to such an extent; even, indeed, truly

ad·eps -ipis *m* or *f* fat; corpulence

adeptĭ·ō -ōnis *f* obtaining, attainment

adeptus *pp* of **adipiscor**

adequit·ō -āre *vi* to ride up; (with *dat* or **ad** + *acc*) to ride up to, ride towards

adesse *inf* of **adedo** or of **adsum**

adēsur·ĭō -īre -īvī *vi* to be very hungry

adēsus *pp* of **adedo**

ad·haerĕō -haerēre -haesī -haesum *vi* (with *dat* or *abl* or with **in** + *abl*) **a** to cling to, stick to; **b** to keep close to, hang on to

ad·haerescō -haerescĕre -haesī -haesum *vi* to stick; to falter; (with *dat* or *abl*, with **ad** + *acc*, or with **in** + *abl*) **a** to stick to, cling to; **b** to be devoted to; **c** to correspond to, accord with

adhaesĭ·ō -ōnis *f* clinging, adhesion

adhaes·us -ūs *m* adhering, adherence

ad·hibĕō -ēre -ŭī -ĭtum *vt* to bring, put, add; to summon, invite; to apply; to use, employ; to consult; to handle, treat

ad·hinnĭō -īre -iī or **-īvī -ĭtum** *vt* to whinny after, lust after; *vi* (with *dat* or with **ad** or **in** + *acc*) **a** to whinny after, lust after, crave; **b** to whinny in delight at

adhortātĭ·ō -ōnis *f* exhortation, encouragement

adhortāt·or -ōris *m* cheerer, supporter

adhort·or -ārī -ātus sum *vt* to cheer on, encourage

adhūc *adv* thus far, hitherto; till now; as yet, still; besides, in addition, moreover

ad·ĭgō -ĭgĕre -ēgī -actum *vt* to drive; to drive home, thrust; to compel; to inflict; to bind (*by oath*)

ad·ĭmō -imĕre -ēmī -emptum *vt* to withdraw, take away; to carry off

adipāt·us -a -um *adj* fatty, greasy; gross, bombastic; *n* pastry (*made in fat*)

ad·ipiscor -ipiscī -eptus sum *vt* to reach, get, obtain, win

aditiāl·is -e *adj* inaugural

aditī·ō -ōnis *f* approach

adīt·us -ūs *m* approach, access; entrance; admittance, audience, interview; beginning, commencement; chance, opportunity

adjac·ĕō -ēre -ŭī *vt* to adjoin; *vi* (with *dat* or **ad** + *acc*) **a** to lie near or at; **b** to border on, be contiguous with

adjectī·ō -ōnis *f* addition, annexation

adjectīv·us -a -um *adj* adjectival

ad·jiciō -jicĕre -jēcī -jectum *vt* to add, increase; (with *dat* or **ad** + *acc*) **a** to throw (*weapon*) at; **b** to add (*something*) to; **c** to turn or direct (*eyes, mind, etc.*) to; (with **in** + *acc*) to hurl (*weapon*) at

adjūdic·ō -āre *vt* to adjudge, award; to ascribe, assign

adjūment·um -ī *n* aid, help, support

adjunct·a -ōrum *n pl* accessory circumstances

adjunctī·ō -ōnis *f* joining, union; addition; (rhet) repetition

ad·jungō -jungĕre -junxī -junctum *vt* (with *dat*) to yoke or harness (*animal*) to; (with *dat* or **ad** + *acc*) **a** to add, attach, join (*something*) to; **b** to apply, direct (*mind, attention, etc.*) to

adjūr·ō -āre *vt* to swear to, confirm by oath; *vi* to swear

adjūtābil·is -e *adj* helpful

adjūt·ō -āre *vt* to help, assist; *vi* (with *dat*) to be of assistance to

adjūt·or -ōris *m* helper, assistant, promoter; aide, adjutant, deputy, secretary; supporting actor

adjūtōr·ium -iī or **-ī** *n* help, support

adjūtr·ix -īcis *f* helper, assistant (*female*)

ad·jŭvŏ -juvāre -jūvī -jūtum *vt* to help, encourage, sustain; *vi* to be of use, be profitable

adl- = all-

admātūr·ō -āre *vt* to bring to maturity; to hasten, expedite

ad·mētĭor -mētīrī -mensus sum *vt* to measure out

Admēt·us -ī *m* king of Pherae in Thessaly, husband of Alcestis

admigr·ō -āre *vi* (with **ad** + *acc*) **a** to go to; **b** to be added to

adminicŭl·ō -āre or **adminicŭl·or -ārī -ātus sum** *vt* to prop, support

adminicŭl·um -ī *n* prop, support, stake, pole; rudder; aid; assistant

administ·er -rī *m* assistant, attendant

administr·a -ae *f* assistant, attendant (*female*)

administrātī·ō -ōnis *f* help, aid; administration, management, government

administrāt·or -ōris *m* administrator, manager, director

administr·ō -āre *vt* to administer, manage, direct

admīrābil·is -e *adj* admirable, wonderful; strange, surprising, paradoxical

admīrābilīt·ās -ātis *f* admiration, wonder, wonderfulness

admīrābilĭter *adv* admirably; astonishingly, paradoxically

admīrātĭ·ō -ōnis *f* admiration, wonder, surprise

admīrāt·or -ōris *m* admirer

admīr·or -ārī -ātus sum *vt* to admire, wonder at, be surprised at

ad·miscĕō -miscēre -miscŭī -mixtum *vt* to mix, add; to involve, implicate; to join, mingle; (with *dat*, with **ad** or in + *acc*, or with **cum** + *abl*) to add (*something*) to, to mix or mix up (*something*) with; **se ad-miscere** to get involved, to meddle

admissār·ius -iī or **-ī** *m* stallion, stud; lecherer

admissĭ·ō -ōnis *f* interview, audience

admiss·um -ī *n* crime

ad·mittō -mittĕre -mīsī -missum *vt* to let in, admit; to let go, let loose; to put at a gallop; to allow; to commit (*crime*)

admixtĭ·ō -ōnis *f* admixture

admixtus *pp* of **admisceo**

admoderātē *adv* appropriately

admŏdum *adv* to the limit; very, quite, fully; (with numbers) just about; (with negatives) at all; (in answers) quite so, yes

admoen·ĭō -īre *vt* to besiege, blockade

admōl·ior -īrī -ītus sum *vt* to bring up, move up; **admoliri** (with *inf*) to strive to, struggle to

admon·ĕō -ēre -ŭī -ĭtum *vt* to admonish, remind, suggest; to warn; to urge

admonitĭ·ō -ōnis *f* admonition, reminder, suggestion

admonit·or -ōris *m* admonisher, reminder

admonitr·ix -īcis *f* admonisher, reminder (*female*)

admonit·um -ī *n* admonition

admonit·us -ūs *m* suggestion; reproof

ad·mordĕō -mordēre -momordī -morsum *vt* to bite at, gnaw at; (fig) to fleece

admōtĭ·ō -ōnis *f* moving, movement

ad·movĕō -movēre -mōvī -mōtum *vt* to move up, bring up, bring near; to lead on, conduct; (with *dat* or **ad** + *acc*) **a** to move or bring (*something*) to; **b** to apply (*something*) to; **c** to direct (*attention, etc.*) to; *vi* to draw near, approach

admūg·ĭō -īre *vi* (with *dat*) to low to, bellow to

admurmurātĭ·ō -ōnis *f* murmuring

admurmur·ō -āre *vi* to murmur (in approval or disapproval)

admutĭl·ō -āre *vt* to clip close; (fig) to clip, cheat

adn- = ann-

ad·olēo -olēre -oluī -ultum vt to magnify; to honor, worship; to sacrifice, burn; to pile up (altars); to sprinkle (altars)

adol·ĕō -ēre vi to smell

adolesc·ens -entis m young man; f young woman

adol·esco -escĕre -ēvī vi to grow, grow up; to be kindled, burn

Adōn·is -is or -ĭdis m son of Cinyras, king of Cyprus, loved by Venus

adoper·iō -īre -uī -tum vt to cover up; to close

adopīn·or -ārī vi to suppose, conjecture

adoptātī·ō -ōnis f adopting (of child)

adoptī·ō -ōnis f adoption (of child)

adoptīv·us -a -um adj adoptive, by adoption

adopt·ō -āre vt to adopt; to select; to graft (plants)

ad·or -ōris or -ōris n spelt

adōrātī·ō -ōnis f adoration, worship

adōrĕ·a -ae f reward for valor; praise, glory

adōrĕ·us -a -um adj of spelt

ad·orior -orīrī -ortus sum vt to rise up against, attack, assault; to attempt; to undertake

adorn·ō -āre vt to equip, get ready; to adorn

adōr·ō -āre vt to implore, entreat; to ask for; to adore, worship

adp- = app-

ad·rādō -rādĕre -rāsī -rāsum vt to scrape, shave; to lop off

Adrast·us -ī m king of Argos, father-in-law of Tydeus and Polynices

adr- = arr-

adsc- = asc-

adse- = ass-

adsi- = assi-

adso- = asso-

adsp- = asp-

adst- = ast-

adsu- = assu-

ad·sum -esse -fuī vi to be near, be present; to appear; to be at hand; to be of assistance; (with dat) to share in, participate in, stand by, assist; animo or animis adesse to pay attention; to cheer up

adt- = att-

adūlātī·ō -ōnis f fawning, cringing, servility, flattery

adūlāt·or -ōris m flatterer

adūlātōrī·us -a -um adj flattering

adulesc·ens -entis adj young

adulesc·ens -entis m young man; f young woman

adulescenti·a -ae f youth, young people

adulescentŭl·a -ae f little girl

adulescentŭl·us -ī m young man

adūl·ō -āre vi to fawn

adūl·or -ārī -ātus sum vt to flatter (in a servile manner); vi (with dat) to kowtow to

adult·er -ĕra -ĕrum adj adulterous,

unchaste; m adulterer; f adulteress

adulterīn·us -a -um adj adulterous; forged, counterfeit

adulter·ium -iī or -ī n adultery; adulteration

adultĕr·ō -āre vt to defile, corrupt; to falsify; vi to commit adultery

adult·us -a -um adj grown, mature, adult

adumbrātim adv in outline

adumbrātī·ō -ōnis f sketch, outline

adumbrāt·us -a -um adj shadowy, sketchy, unreal, fictitious, dim, imperfect

adumbr·ō -āre vt to shade, overshadow; to sketch; to represent

aduncīt·ās -ātis f curvature

adunc·us -a -um adj curved, hooked

adurg·ĕō -ēre vt to pursue closely

ad·ūrō -ūrĕre -ussī -ustum vt to set on fire; to scorch; to nip, freeze; (fig) to inflame

adusque adv entirely, throughout

adusque prep (with acc) all the way to, as far as, right up to

adustī·ō -ōnis f burning

adust·us -a -um pp of aduro; adj scorched; sunburned

advectīcī·us -a -um adj imported, foreign

advectī·ō -ōnis f transportation

advect·ō -āre vt to keep on conveying

advect·us -ūs m conveyance

ad·vĕhō -vehĕre -vexī -vectum vt to carry, convey, transport; (equo) advehi (with ad or in + acc) to ride to; (nave) advehi (with ad + acc) to sail to

advēl·ō -āre vt to veil; to wreathe

advĕn·a -ae m or f stranger, foreigner

ad·veniō -venīre -vēnī -ventum vi to arrive; (with ad or in + acc or with acc of limit of motion) to arrive at, come to, reach

adventīcī·us -a -um adj foreign, strange, extraneous; unusual, extraordinary; unearned

advent·ō -āre vi to keep coming closer, approach

advent·or -ōris m visitor, guest; customer

advent·us -ūs m arrival, approach

adversārī·us -a -um adj (with dat) turned towards, opposed to, opposite; m & f adversary, enemy, rival; n pl journal, notebook, memoranda; assertions (of opponent)

adversātr·ix -īcis f opponent (female)

adversī·ō -ōnis f directing, direction

advers·ō -āre vt to direct (attention)

advers·or -ārī -ātus sum vi (with dat) to oppose, resist

adversum or adversus adv in the opposite direction; prep (with acc) facing, opposite, towards; compared with, contrary to

advers·us -a -um adj opposite, in front; facing; unfavorable, hostile;

adverso flumine upstream; *n* misfortune; opposite

ad·vertō or **ad·vortō -vertĕre -vertī -versum** *vt* (with *dat* or **in** + *acc*) **a** to turn or direct (*something*) to; **b** to steer (*ship*) to; **animum** or **animos advertere** to pay attention; **animum** or **animos advertere** (with *dat* or **ad** + *acc*) to give attention to, attend to, heed, observe; *vi* to land; (with **in** + *acc*) to punish

advesper·ascit -ascĕre -āvit *v impers* evening approaches

advigil·ō -āre *vi* to be vigilant, keep watch; (with *dat*) to keep watch over, bestow attention on; (with **pro** + *abl*) to watch out for

advocātĭ·ō -ōnis *f* legal assistance; legal counsel; the bar; period of time allowed to procure legal assistance; delay, adjournment

advocāt·us -ī *m* witness; advocate, counsel; helper, friend

advŏc·ō -āre *vt* to call, summon; to consult

advŏl·ō -āre *vi* (with *dat* or with **ad** or **in** + *acc*) **a** to fly to; **b** to dash to

ad·volvō -volvĕre -volvī -volūtum *vt* (with *dat* or **ad** + *acc*) to roll (*something*) to or toward; **advolvi** or **se advolvere genua** or **genibus** (with *genit*) to fall prostrate before

advor- = adver-

adўt·um -ī *n* sanctuary; tomb

Aeacĭd·ēs -ae *m* descendant of Aeacus

Aeāc·us -ī *m* king of Aegina, father of Peleus, Telamon, and Phocus, and judge of the dead

aed·ēs or **aed·is -is** *f* shrine, temple; building; *f pl* rooms, apartments; house

aedicŭl·a -ae *f* chapel, shrine; small room, closet; small house; *f pl* small house

aedificātĭ·ō -ōnis *f* constructing, building; structure, building

aedificātiuncŭl·a -ae *f* tiny building

aedificāt·or -ōris *m* builder, architect

aedific·ĭum -ĭī or **-ī** *n* building

aedific·ō -āre *vt* to build, construct, establish

aedilīcĭ·us -a -um *adj* aedile's; *m* ex-aedile

aedil·is -is *m* aedile

aedīlit·ās -ātis *f* aedileship

aedis see **aedēs**

aeditŭ·us or **aeditĭm·us** or **aeditūm·us -ī** *m* temple attendant, sacristan

Aeēt·ēs -ae *m* king of Colchis and father of Medea

Aegae·us -a -um *adj* Aegean; *n* Aegean Sea

Aegāt·ēs -um *f pl* three islands W. of Sicily

aeg·er -ra -rum *adj* sick, infirm,

unsound; dejected; painful

Aeg·eus -ĕī *m* king of Athens, father of Theseus

Aegīd·ēs -ae *m* Theseus

Aegīn·a -ae *f* island off Attica; mother of Aeacus

aeg·is -ĭdis *f* shield of Minerva and of Jupiter; aegis, protection

Aegisth·us -ī *m* son of Thyestes, seducer of Clytemnestra, and murderer of Agamemnon

aegrē *adv* painfully; with difficulty; reluctantly; hardly, scarcely

aegr·ĕō -ēre *vi* to be sick

aegr·escō -escĕre *vi* to become sick; to be aggravated, get worse; to be troubled

aegrimōnĭ·a -ae *f* sorrow, anxiety, trouble

aegritūd·ō -ĭnis *f* sickness; sorrow

aegr·or -ōris *m* illness

aegrōtātĭ·ō -ōnis *f* sickness, disease

aegrōt·ō -āre *vi* to be sick; to languish

aegrōt·us -a -um *adj* sick

Aegypt·us -ī *f* Egypt; *m* mythical king of Egypt, whose 50 sons married the 50 daughters of his brother Danaüs

aelīn·os -ī *m* dirge

aemŭl·a -ae *f* rival (*female*)

aemulātĭ·ō -ōnis *f* emulation, rivalry

aemulāt·or -ōris *m* rival, imitator

aemulāt·us -ūs *m* rivalry

aemŭl·or -ārī -ātus sum *vt* to emulate, rival; *vi* (with *dat*) to be envious of, be jealous of

aemŭl·us -a -um *adj* (with *genit* or *dat*) emulous of, envious of, jealous of, striving after; *m* rival

Aenĕād·ēs -ae *m* descendant of Aeneas; Trojan; Roman; Augustus

Aenē·ās -ae *m* son of Venus and Anchises, and hero of Virgil's epic

Aenē·is -ĭdis or **-ĭdos** *f* Aeneid (*Virgil's epic*)

aēnĕ·us or **ahēnĕ·us -a -um** *adj* bronze

aenigm·a -ătis *n* riddle, mystery

aēnĭp·ēs -ĕdis *adj* bronze-footed

aēn·us or **ahēn·us -a -um** *adj* bronze; (fig) firm, invincible; *n* cauldron

Aeolĭ·a -ae *f* realm of Aeolus, king of winds; group of islands near Sicily

Aeolĭ·ī -ōrum or **Aeŏl·ēs -um** *m pl* Aeolians (*inhabitants of N.W. Asia Minor*)

Aeŏl·is -ĭdis *f* Aeolia, N.W. part of Asia Minor

Aeŏl·us -ī *m* god of winds

aequābĭl·is -e *adj* equal, alike; consistent, uniform; fair, impartial

aequābĭlit·ās -ātis *f* equality; uniformity; impartiality

aequābĭlĭter *adv* equally; uniformly

aequaev·us -a -um *adj* of the same age

aequāl·is -e *adj* equal; even, level; of the same age, contemporary

aequāl·is -is *m* or *f* comrade; contemporary

aequālit·ās -ātis *f* equality; evenness; smoothness

aequāliter *adv* equally; evenly

aequanimit·ās -ātis *f* calmness, patience; kindness; impartiality

aequāti·ō -ōnis *f* equal distribution; **aequatio bonorum** communism

aequē *adv* equally; justly, fairly; **aeque ... ac** or **atque** or **et** just as, as much as, as; **aeque ... ac si** just as if; **aeque ... quam** as ... as, in the same way as

Aequ·ī -ōrum *m pl* people of central Italy

aequilībrit·ās -ātis *f* balance

aequilibr·ium -iī or **-ī** *n* horizontal position; equilibrium

aequinoctiāl·is -e *adj* equinoctial

aequinoct·ium -iī or **-ī** *n* equinox

aequiperābil·is -e *adj* (with *dat* or **cum** + *abl*) comparable to

aequiper·ō or **aequipar·ō -āre** *vt* to compare; to equal, rival, come up to; (with *dat*, with **ad**+ *acc*, or **cum** + *abl*) to compare (*something*) to; *vi* (with *dat*) a to become equal to, be equal to; **b** to attain to

aequit·ās -ātis *f* evenness, conformity, symmetry, equity; calmness

aequ·or -ōris *n* level surface; sea, ocean

aequorē·us -a -um *adj* of the sea, marine

aequ·us -a -um *adj* level, even, flat; favorable, friendly; fair, just; calm; *n* level, plain; justice, fairness

ā·ēr -ēris *m* air, atmosphere, sky; weather; mist

aerāment·um -ī *n* bronze vessel or utensil

aerāri·us -a -um *adj* copper, bronze; of mines; financial, fiscal; *m* coppersmith; low-class Roman citizen; *f* mine; smelting furnace; *n* treasury

aerāt·us -a -um *adj* bronze; rich

āĕrē·us -a -um *adj* aerial, airy, lofty, high

aerē·us -a -um *adj* bronze

aerif·er -ĕra -ĕrum *adj* carrying cymbals

aerip·ēs -ĕdis *adj* bronze-footed

āĕri·us -a -um *adj* aerial, airy, lofty, high

Āĕrŏp·ē -ēs or **Āĕrŏp·a -ae** *f* wife of Atreus, mother of Agamemnon and Menelaus

aerūginōs·us -a -um *adj* rusty

aerūg·ō -inis *f* copper rust, verdigris; corroding passion, envy, greed

aerumn·a -ae *f* need, want, trouble, hardship, calamity

aerumnābil·is -e *adj* full of troubles, calamitous

aerumnōs·us -a -um *adj* full of troubles, wretched, distressed

aes aeris *n* crude metal, copper, bronze; bronze object; armor, statue, utensil, trumpet; money; payment; reward; *n pl* wages, soldier's pay; **aes alienum** debt

Aeschȳl·us -ī *m* Athenian tragic poet (525-456 B.C.)

Aesculāp·ius -iī or **-ī** *m* god of medicine, son of Apollo and Coronis

aesculēt·um -ī *n* oak forest

aesculē·us -a -um *adj* oak

aescŭl·us -ī *f* Italian oak

Aes·ōn -ōnis *m* Thessalian prince, father of Jason, restored to youth by Medea

aest·ās -ātis *f* summer; summer heat

aestif·er -ĕra -ĕrum *adj* heat-bearing, sultry

aestimābil·is -e *adj* valuable

aestimāti·ō -ōnis *f* appraisal, assessment; esteem

aestimāt·or -ōris *m* appraiser

aestim·ō -āre *vt* to appraise, rate, value, estimate; to esteem, judge, hold

aestīv·a -ōrum *n pl* summer camp; campaign season, campaign; summer pastures

aestīv·ō -āre *vi* to pass the summer

aestīv·us -a -um *adj* summer

aestuār·ium -iī or **-ī** *n* tidal waters, lagoon, estuary, marsh; air shaft

aestŭ·ō -āre *vi* to boil, seethe; to burn, glow; to undulate, swell, be tossed, heave; to waver, hesitate; to be excited

aestuōsē *adv* hotly, impetuously

aestuōs·us -a -um *adj* sultry; billowy

aest·us -ūs *m* agitation; glow, heat, sultriness; surge, billows, ebb and flow; tide; raging, seething, passion; uncertainty, irresolution

aet·ās -ātis *f* lifetime, age, generation

aetātŭl·a -ae *f* tender age

aeternit·ās -ātis *f* eternity, immortality

aetern·ō -āre *vt* to perpetuate, immortalize

aeternum *adv* forever; constantly, perpetually

aetern·us -a -um *adj* eternal, everlasting, immortal, imperishable

aeth·ēr -ĕris or **-ĕros** *m* upper air, sky, heaven

aetheri·us -a -um *adj* ethereal, heavenly, celestial; of the upper world

Aethi·ops -ŏpis *m* Ethiopian; Negro; blockhead

aethr·a -ae *f* ether, pure air, serene sky; air, sky, heavens

Aetn·a -ae or **Aetn·ē -ēs** *f* volcano in Sicily

Aetōlī·a -ae *f* district in N. Greece

aevit·ās -ātis *f* age, lifetime

aev·um -ī *n* or **aev·us -ī** *m* age, lifetime, life; time, period; generation; eternity

Āf·er -ra -rum *adj* & *m* African

affābil·is -e *adj* affable, courteous, kind

affābilit·ās -ātis *f* affability, courtesy

affăbrē *adv* in a workmanlike manner, cunningly

affătim *adv* sufficiently, enough, satisfactorily

affāt·us -ūs *m* address, discourse

affectātĭ·ō -ōnis *f* eager desire; affectation, conceit

affectāt·or -ōris *m* affected person

affectāt·us -a -um *adj* choice, select; farfetched, studied

affectĭ·ō -ōnis *f* disposition, state of mind; inclination, partiality; affection, love

affect·ō -āre *vt* to grasp, seize; to pursue, strive after, aim at; to try to win over; to affect, feign

affect·us -a -um *adj* furnished, provided, gifted; weakened, impaired, sick; affected, moved, touched

affect·us -ūs *m* state, disposition, mood; feeling, passion, emotion; affection

affĕrō afferre attŭlī allātum *vt* to bring, carry, convey; to report, announce; to introduce, apply, employ, exert, exercise; to produce, cause, occasion, impart; to allege, assign; to contribute, help; **manus afferre** (with *dat*) to lay hands on, attack, do violence to, rob, plunder

af·fĭcĭō -ficĕre -fēcī -fectum *vt* to treat, handle, manage; to affect, move, influence, impress; to attack, afflict; to impair, weaken; (*abl* and verb may be rendered by the verb corresponding to the *abl*): **cruce afficere** to crucify; **honoribus afficere** to honor; **supplicio afficere** to punish

af·fīgō -fīgĕre -fīxī -fixum *vt* (with *dat* or *ad* + *acc*) to fasten, attach, affix, annex (*something*) to; (with *dat*) to impress (*something*) upon (*mind*)

af·fingō -fingĕre -finxī -fictum *vt* to form, fashion besides; to make up, invent; (with *dat*) to attach, affix, add, join, contribute (*something*) to

affīn·is -e *adj* adjoining, neighboring; related by marriage; (with *dat* or *ad* + *acc*) taking part in, privy to, associated with

affīn·is -is *m* or *f* in-law

affīnĭt·ās -ātis *f* relationship by marriage

affirmātē *adv* with solemn assurance, positively, certainly

affirmātĭ·ō -ōnis *f* affirmation, assertion, declaration

affirm·ō -āre *vt* to strengthen; to confirm, encourage; to aver, assert

afflāt·us -ūs *m* breeze, blast, breath; inspiration

afflĕ·ō -ēre *vi* to weep

afflictātĭ·ō -ōnis *f* physical pain, torture

afflictō -āre *vt* to shatter, damage, harass, injure; to trouble, vex, distress, torment

afflict·or -ōris *m* destroyer, subverter

afflict·us -a -um *adj* damaged, shattered; cast down, downhearted; vile

af·flīgō -flīgĕre -flīxī -flictum *vt* to knock, strike down; (fig) to crush

afflŏ·ō -āre *vt* (with *dat*) **a** to breathe (*something*) upon; **b** to impart (*something*) to; *vi* (with *dat*) **a** to breathe upon; **b** to be favorable to

afflŭ·ens -entis *adj* flowing; rich, affluent; abounding, numerous

affluenter *adv* lavishly, abundantly

affluentĭ·a -ae *f* abundance

af·fluō -fluĕre -fluxī -fluxum *vi* (with *dat* or *ad* + *acc*) **a** to flow to, flow towards, glide by; **b** to hasten to, flock to; (with *dat*) to abound in

af·for -fārī -fātus sum *vt* to address, accost, pray to

affōre = adfutūrus esse

affōrem = adessem

afformīd·ō -āre *vi* to be afraid

af·fulgĕō -fulgēre -fulsī *vi* to shine, beam, dawn, appear; (with *dat*) to shine on

af·fundō -fundĕre -fūdī -fūsum *vt* (with *dat*) **a** to pour, sprinkle, scatter (*something*) on; **b** to send or despatch (*someone*) to; **affundi** or **se affundere** (with *dat*) to throw oneself at, prostrate oneself before

Afrĭc·us -a -um *adj* African; *m* S.W. Wind; *f* originally the district of Carthage, made a Roman province in 146 B.C.; continent of Africa

Agamemn·ōn -ŏnis *m* king of Mycenae, son of Atreus and of Aërope, brother of Menelaus, and commander in chief of Greek forces at Troy

Aganipp·ē -ēs *f* fountain on Mount Helicon, sacred to the Muses

agās·ō -ōnis *m* driver, groom; lackey

agĕdum *interj* come on!; well!

agell·us -ī *m* little field, plot

agēm·a -ătis *n* corps or division (*of soldiers*)

Agēn·or -ŏris *m* son of Belus, king of Phoenicia, father of Cadmus and Europa, and ancestor of Dido

Agēnorĭd·ēs -ae *m* descendant of Agenor; Cadmus; Perseus

ag·er -rī *m* field, ground, arable land, farm, estate; territory, district

agg·er -ĕris *m* fill dirt, rubbish, soil, mound; rampart, dike, dam, pier; fortification; causeway; funeral pile

aggĕr·ō -āre *vt* to pile up, fill up, amass, increase; stimulate

ag·gĕrō -gĕrĕre -gessī -gestum *vt* to bring forward, utter; (with *dat* or *ad* + *acc*) to bring, convey (*something*) to

aggest·us -ūs *m* accumulation

agglomĕr·ō -āre *vt* to wind up (*as on a ball*); to annex; **se agglomerare** (with *dat*) to attach oneself to, join

agglūtĭn·ō -āre *vt* to glue, paste, solder, cement

aggravesc·ō -ĕre *vi* to grow heavy

aggrăv·ō -āre *vt* to make heavier; to make worse, aggravate

ag·gredĭor -grĕdī -gressus sum *vt* to approach; to address; to attack; to undertake, begin

aggrĕg·ō -āre vt to assemble, collect; to attach, join, include, implicate

aggressĭ·ō -ōnis f attack, assault; introduction

agĭl·is -e adj easily moved, agile, nimble, quick; busy, active

agĭlĭt·ās -ātis f mobility, agility, nimbleness, quickness, activity

agĭtābĭl·is -e adj easily moved, light

agĭtātĭ·ō -ōnis f motion, movement, agitation; activity, pursuit; prosecution

agĭtāt·or -ōris m driver, charioteer

agĭt·ō -āre vt to set in motion, drive on, impel; to hunt, chase, pursue; to drive, urge, support, insist on; to practice, exercise; to observe, keep, celebrate; to obey, carry out; to spend, pass (time); to shake, toss, disturb; to vex, distress; to stimulate, excite; to deride, insult; to criticize; to consider, deliberate on; to discuss, debate; vi to live, dwell, be

Aglaur·ŏs -ī f daughter of Cecrops, changed by Mercury into a stone

agm·en -ĭnis n herd, flock, troop, crowd; body, mass; army (on march), procession, train

agn·a -ae f ewe, lamb (female)

ag·nascor -nascī -nātus sum vi to be born (after the father has made his will)

agnātĭ·ō -ōnis f blood relationship (on father's side)

agnāt·us -ī m relative (on father's side)

agnell·us -ī m little lamb

agnīn·a -ae f mutton

agnĭtĭ·ō -ōnis f recognition, acknowledgment, admission; knowledge

ag·noscō -noscĕre -nōvī -nĭtum vt to recognize, identify, acknowledge

agn·us -ī m lamb

agŏ agĕre ēgī actum vt to drive, lead, conduct; to chase, hunt; to drive away, steal; to spend (time); to do, act, perform; to manage, administer, carry on; to plead, transact, discuss, propose; to play, act the part of; to accuse, impeach; to exercise, practice, perform, deliver, pronounce; to treat; **agī** to be at stake; **se agere** to behave, deport oneself

ag·ōn -ōnis m contest, combat (in public games)

agrārĭ·us -a -um adj agrarian; m pl land-reform party

agrest·is -e adj rustic; boorish, wild, savage

agrĭcŏl·a -ae m farmer, peasant

Agrĭcŏl·a -ae m father-in-law of Tacitus

agrĭcultūr·a -ae f agriculture

Agrĭgent·um -ī n city on south coast of Sicily (sometimes called Acragas)

agrĭpĕt·a -ae m colonist, settler

Agrĭpp·a -ae m son-in-law of Augustus, husband of Julia, and father of Agrippina

Agrippīn·a -ae f wife of Tiberius; daughter of Agrippa and Julia, and mother of Caligula

āh interj ah!, ha!, oh!

aha interj aha!

ai interj (denoting grief) alas!

āĭn = aisne (see aio)

aĭō vt & vi (used mainly in present and imperfect indicative) I say; I say yes, I say so; I affirm, assert, tell, relate; **ain** (= **aisne**) **tandem?, ain tu?, ain tute?**, or **ain vero?** (colloquial phrase, expressing surprise) do you really mean it?, you don't say!, really?

Aj·ax -ācis m son of Telamon, king of Salamis; son of Oileus, king of the Locri

āl·a -ae f wing; armpit; squadron (of cavalry); flank (of battle line)

alăc·er -ris -re adj lively, brisk, quick, eager, active, cheerful

alacrĭt·ās -ātis f liveliness, briskness, eagerness, cheerfulness

alăp·a -ae f slap; emancipation (of slave)

ālārĭ·ī -ōrum m pl auxiliaries, allies

ālārĭs -e adj (mil) on the flank, of the flank

ālārĭ·us -a -um adj (mil) on the flank, of the flank

ālāt·us -a -um adj winged

alaud·a -ae f lark

alāz·ōn -ōnis m boaster

Alb·a -ae f town, also called Alba Longa, mother city of Rome, founded by Ascanius, son of Aeneas

albāt·us -a -um adj dressed in white

alb·ĕō -ēre -ŭī vi to be white

albesc·ō -ĕre vi to become white, whiten; to dawn

albĭc·ō -āre vt to make white, whiten vi to be white

albĭd·us -a -um adj white, whitish

Albĭ·ōn -ōnis f Britain

albĭtūd·ō -ĭnis f whiteness

Albŭl·a -ae f Tiber River

albŭl·us -a -um adj whitish

alb·um -ī n white; white tablet, record, list, register

Albunĕ·a or **Albūn·a -ae** f fountain at Tibur; nymph of the fountain

alb·us -a -um adj dead white, white, bright; favorable

Alcae·us -ī m Greek lyric poet of Lesbos, contemporary with Sappho (610 B.C.)

alcēd·ō -ĭnis f kingfisher, halcyon

alcēdōnĭ·a -ōrum n pl halcyon days; (fig) deep calm, tranquillity

alc·ēs -is f elk

Alcĭbĭăd·ēs -is m Athenian politician, disciple of Socrates (450?-404 B.C.)

Alcīd·ēs -ae m Hercules

Alcĭmĕd·ē -ēs f wife of Aeson and mother of Jason

Alcĭnŏ·ŭs -ī m king of the Phaeacians, by whom Ulysses was entertained

Alcmēn·a or **Alcumēn·a** -ae or **Alcmēn·ē** -ēs *f* wife of Amphitryon and mother of Hercules by Jupiter

ălĕ·a -ae *f* dice game; chance, risk, venture

ăleāt·or -ōris *m* dice player, gambler

āleātōrĭ·us -a -um *adj* of dice, gambling

ălĕ·ō -ōnis *m* gambler

āl·es -ĭtis *adj* winged; swift

āl·es -ĭtis *m* or *f* winged creature, fowl, bird; *m* poet; *f* augury, omen, sign

al·escō -escĕre *vi* to grow up, increase

Alexand·er -rī *m* Paris, son of Priam and Hecuba; Alexander the Great, king of Macedon

Alexandrē·a or **Alexandrī·a** -ae *f* city in Egypt, founded by Alexander the Great

alg·a -ae *f* seaweed

al·gĕō -gēre -sī *vi* to be cold, feel cold

al·gescō -gescĕre -sī *vi* to catch cold; to become cold

algĭd·us -a -um *adj* cold

alg·or -ōris *m* cold, chilliness

alg·us -ūs *m* cold

aliā *adv* by another way

aliās *adv* at another time; **alias . . . alias** at one time . . . at another, sometimes . . . sometimes

alibī *adv* elsewhere; otherwise, in other respects; **alibi . . . alibi** in one place . . . in another, here . . . there

alioūbī *adv* at any place, somewhere, anywhere

alicunde *adv* from somewhere, from any place, from someone else

aliēnātĭ·ō -ōnis *f* transfer (*of property*); separation, alienation; aversion, dislike

aliēnigĕn·a -ae *m* foreigner, alien, stranger

aliēn·ō -āre *vt* to make strange, transfer, sell; to alienate, set at variance; to remove, separate; to make insane, drive mad

aliēn·us -a -um *adj* another's; foreign; contrary, hostile; strange, unsuitable, incongruous, inconsistent, inconvenient; *m* stranger, foreigner

āli·ger -gĕra -gĕrum *adj* wearing wings, winged

alimentārĭ·us -a -um *adj* alimentary

aliment·um -ī *n* nourishment, food, provisions; fuel

alimōnĭ·a -ae *f* or **alimōn·ĭum** -ĭī or -ī *n* nourishment, food, support

aliō *adv* to another place, elsewhere

alĭoquī or **alĭoquīn** *adv* otherwise, in other respects, for the rest; besides; in general; in any case

aliorsum or **aliorsus** *adv* in another direction; in another manner, in a different sense

ālĭp·ēs -ĕdis *adj* wing-footed, swift-footed

alipt·ēs or **alipt·a** -ae *m* wrestling trainer

aliquā *adv* somehow, in any direction

aliquam *adv* in some degree

aliquamdĭū *adv* for some time

aliquandō *adv* sometime or other, once; at any time, ever; sometimes, now and then; for once, now; finally, now at last

aliquantisper *adv* for a while, for a time

aliquantō *adv* somewhat, a little, rather

aliquantŭlum *adv* somewhat

aliquantŭl·us -a -um *adj* little, small

aliquantum *adv* somewhat, a little, rather

aliquant·us -a -um *adj* considerable

aliquātĕnus *adv* for some distance, to a certain extent, somewhat; in some respects, partly

alī·quī -qua -quod *adj* some, any

aliquid *adv* to some extent, at all

alī·quid -cūjus *pron* something, anything; something important

alī·quis -cūjus *pron* someone, somebody, anyone; someone important

aliquō *adv* to some place, somewhere

aliquot (indecl) *adj* some, several, a few

aliquotĭens *adv* several times

aliquōvorsum *adv* to some place, one way or another

aliter *adv* otherwise, else, differently

aliŭbī *adv* elsewhere; **aliubi . . . aliubi** here . . . there

āl·ĭum -ĭī or -ī *n* garlic

aliunde *adv* from another source, from elsewhere

ali·us -a -ud *adj* another, other, different; *pron* another; **alii . . . alii** some . . . others; **alius . . . alius** one . . . another, the one . . . the other; **alius ex alio** one after another

al·lābor -lābī -lapsus sum *vi* to glide, slide, slip; to flow

allabōr·ō -āre *vi* to work hard

allacrĭmō -āre *vi* to weep, shed tears

allaps·us -ūs *m* stealthy approach

allātr·ō -āre *vt* to revile; (*of sea*) to break against, dash against

allātus *pp* of **affero**

allaud·ō -āre *vt* to praise highly

all·ēc -ēcis *n* fish sauce

Allectō (indecl) *f* one of the three Furies

allect·ō -āre *vt* to allure, entice

allēgātĭ·ō -ōnis *f* sending, despatching

allēg·ō -āre *vt* to commission, deputize, despatch; to allege; to instigate

al·lēgō -legĕre -lēgī -lectum *vt* to select, elect

allevāment·um -ī *n* alleviation, relief

allevātǐ·ō -ōnis f raising, elevating; easing

allěv·ō -āre vt to lift up, raise; to alleviate; to comfort; to lighten

all·ex -ǐcis m (the) big toe; midget

al·lǐcǐō -licěre -lexī -lectum vt to attract

al·līdō -līděre -līsī -līsum vt (with dat or with **ad** or **in** + acc) to dash (something) against; **allīdī** to be wrecked

allǐg·ō -āre vt to bind, fetter; to bandage; to hinder, detain; to impugn, accuse; (with **ad** + acc) to bind (something) to

al·lǐnō -liněre -lēvī -lǐtum vt to smudge; (with dat) to smear (something) on

all·ǐum -ǐī or **-ī** n garlic

Allobrǒg·ēs -um m pl Gallic tribe living between the Rhone and the Isère

allocūtǐ·ō -ōnis f address; consoling, comforting

alloqu·ǐum -ǐī or **-ī** n address, conversation; encouragement, consolation

al·lǒquor -lǒquī -locūtus sum vt to speak to, address; to exhort, rouse; to console, comfort

allūdǐ·ō -āre vi to play, jest

al·lūdō -lūděre -lūsī -lūsum vi to play, joke; (of waves) (with dat) to play against

al·lǔō -luěre -lǔī vt to wash

alluvǐ·ēs -ēī f inundation, pool (left by flood waters); alluvial land

alluvǐ·ō -ōnis f inundation; alluvial land

alm·us -a -um adj nourishing; genial, kind, propitious, indulgent, bountiful

aln·us -ī f alder tree; ship

al·ō -ěre -ǔī -tum or **-ǐtum** vt to feed, nourish, rear; to support, maintain; to promote; to increase, strengthen

alǒ·ē -ēs f aloe; bitterness

alogǐ·a -ae f pl Alps

Alp·ēs -ǐum f pl Alps

alpha (indecl) n alpha (first letter of Greek alphabet)

Alphē·us or **Alphē·os -ī** m chief river of the Peloponnesus

Alpǐc·us -a -um adj Alpine

Alpīn·us -a -um adj Alpine

alsǐ·us or **als·us -a -um** adj chilly, cool, cold

altār·ǐa -ǐum n pl altar top, altar, high altar

altē adv high, on high, highly, deeply, far, remotely; loftily, profoundly

alt·er -ěra -ěrum adj one (of two); a second, the second, the next; pron one (of two), the one, the other; a second one, the second one, the next one; another (one's fellow man); **alter . . . alter** the one . . . the other, the former . . . the latter

altercātǐ·ō -ōnis f debate, dispute, discussion

alterc·ō -āre or **alterc·or -ārī**

-ātus sum vi to quarrel, wrangle, bicker

alternīs adv by turns, alternately

altern·ō -āre vt to do by turns; to exchange; vi to alternate

altern·us -a -um adj one after another, alternate, mutual, every other

alterǔt·er -ra -rum (f also: **altěra utra;** n also: **altěrum utrum**) adj one (of two), either, one or the other; pron one, either one, one or the other

Althae·a -ae f daughter of Thestius̄, wife of Oeneus, king of Calydon, and mother of Meleager

alticinct·us -a -um adj active, busy, energetic

altil·is -e adj fattened, fat, full; rich

altisǒn·us -a -um adj high-sounding; sounding from on high

altitǒn·ans -antis adj thundering on high

altitūd·ō -ǐnis f height; depth; (fig) depth, reserve, secrecy

altivǒl·ans -antis adj high-flying

alt·or -ōris m foster father

altrinsěcus adv on the other side

altr·ix -ǐcis f nourisher, foster mother

altrōvorsum adv on the other side

alt·us -a -um adj high; deep, profound; ancient, remote (lineage); n high seas, the deep; heaven; **ab alto** from on high, from heaven; **ex alto** farfetched

ālūcǐn·or -ārī vi to indulge in small talk, ramble

alumn·a -ae f foster daughter; pupil

alumn·us -ī m foster son; pupil

alūt·a -ae f soft leather; shoe; purse

alveār·ǐum -ǐī or **ī** n beehive

alvěǒl·us -ī m tray, basin; bed of a stream; game board

alvě·us -ī m hollow, cavity; tub; bathtub; riverbed; hull of boat, boat; game board; beehive

alv·us -ī m belly, bowels, stomach; womb; boat; beehive

amābil·is -e adj lovable, lovely, attractive, pleasant

amābilǐt·ās -ātis f charm

amābilǐter adv lovingly, delightfully

Amalthē·a -ae f nymph who fed infant Jupiter with goat's milk; sibyl at Cumae

āmandātǐ·ō -ōnis f sending away

āmand·ō -āre vt to send away, remove

am·ans -antis adj loving, affectionate; **amans patriae** patriotic; m lover

amanter adv lovingly, affectionately

amārǎc·us -ī m or f marjoram

amarant·us -ī m amaranth

amārē adv bitterly

amārǐtǐ·ēs -ēī f bitterness

amārǐtūd·ō -ǐnis f bitterness; sadness, sorrow, trouble

amār·or -ōris m bitterness

amār·us -a -um adj bitter; n pl disappointments

amās·ǐus -ǐī or **-ī** m lover

amātī·ō -ōnis *f* love affair

amāt·or -ōris *m* lover, friend; **amator patriae** patriot

amātorcŭl·us -ī *m* poor little lover

amātōrĭ·us -a -um *adj* erotic; love; *n* love charm

amātr·ix -īcis *f* mistress, girl friend

Amāz·ōn -ŏnis *or* **Amāzōn·is -ĭdis** *f* Amazon (*member of mythical female warrior tribe dwelling in the Caucasus*)

ambact·us -ī *m* vassal

ambāg·ēs -is *f* winding, labyrinth; double-talk, evasion, digression; ambiguity, obscurity; **per ambages** enigmatically

amb·ĕdō -esse -ēdī -ēsum *vt* to eat up; (*of fire*) to char; to waste

ambĭg·ō -ĕre *vt* to go around, avoid; *vi* to waver, hesitate, be undecided; to argue, debate, wrangle; **ambigitur** it is uncertain

ambiguē *adv* doubtfully, indecisively

ambiguĭt·ās -ātis *f* ambiguity, double meaning

ambigŭ·us -a -um *adj* wavering, changeable; uncertain, doubtful; disputed; unreliable, untrustworthy; ambiguous, dark, obscure; *n* doubt, uncertainty, paradox

amb·ĭō -īre *vt* to go around, encircle; (*pol*) or canvass; to entreat, solicit, court

ambĭtĭ·ō -ōnis *f* (*pol*) campaigning (*by lawful means*); popularity, flattery; ambition (*in good or bad sense*); partiality, favoritism; pomp, ostentation

ambĭtĭōsē *adv* ostentatiously; from a desire to please

ambĭtĭōs·us -a -um *adj* winding, entwining; publicity-conscious, eager for popularity, ambitious; ostentatious

ambĭt·us -ūs *m* winding, revolution; circuit, circumference, border, orbit; (*pol*) illegal campaigning, bribery; pomp, ostentation; circumlocution; (*rhet*) period

amb·ŏ -ae -ō *adj* both, two; *pron* both, the two

Ambracĭ·a -ae *f* district of Epirus in N.W. Greece

ambrosĭ·us -a -um *adj* ambrosial, divine, immortal; *f* food of the gods

ambūbāĭ·a -ae *f* Syrian flute player

ambulācr·um -ī *n* walk, avenue

ambulātĭ·ō -ōnis *f* (*act*) walk; (*place*) walk

ambulātiuncŭl·a -ae *f* short walk; (*place*) small promenade

ambulāt·or -ōris *m* peddler; idler

ambŭl·ō -āre *vt* to traverse, travel; *vi* to walk, take a walk; to march, travel; to strut

amb·ūrō -ūrĕre -ussī -ustum *vt* to burn up, scorch, singe; to consume; to numb, nip

amell·us -ī *m* wild aster

ām·ens -entis *adj* out of one's mind, mad; foolish, stupid

āmentĭ·a -ae *f* madness; folly

āment·ō -āre *vt* to fit (*a javelin*) with a strap

āment·um -ī *n* strap

am·es -ĭtis *m* pole for fowler's net

amethystĭn·us -a -um *adj* dressed in purple; *n pl* purple garments

amethyst·us -ī *f* amethyst

amīc·a -ae *f* girl friend, lady friend

amīcē *adv* in a friendly manner

amic·ĭō -īre -ŭī -tum *vt* to wrap around; to cover, clothe, wrap

amīcĭter *adv* in a friendly way

amīcitĭ·a -ae *f* friendship

amict·us -ūs *m* wrap, cloak; style, fashion (*in dress*)

amīcŭl·a -ae *f* girl friend

amīcŭl·um -ī *n* wrap, mantle

amīcŭl·us -ī *m* pal, buddy

amīc·us -a -um *adj* friendly; *m* friend; patron

āmigr·ō -āre *vi* to move away, emigrate

āmissĭ·ō -ōnis *f* loss

amĭt·a -ae *f* aunt (*father's sister*)

ā·mittō -mittĕre -mīsī -missum *vt* to lose, let slip; **fidem amittere** to break one's word

amnicŏl·a -ae *m or f* riverside plant (*e.g., willow tree*)

amnicŭl·us -ī *m* brook

amn·is -is *m* river; **secundo amni** downstream

am·ō -āre *vt* to love, like, be fond of; to fall in love with; **amabo** *or* **amabo te** (*coll*) please

amoenē *adv* charmingly

amoenĭt·ās -ātis *f* charm

amoen·us -a -um *adj* charming, pleasant; *n pl* charming sights

amōl·ĭor -īrī *vt* to remove; to put aside, put away; **se amoliri** to remove oneself, clear out

amōm·um -ī *n* amomum plant (*aromatic shrub*)

am·or *or* **am·ōs -ōris** *m* love, affection; object of affection, love; Cupid; *m pl* love affair

āmōtĭ·ō -ōnis *f* removal

ā·moveō -movēre -mōvī -mōtum *vt* to remove, withdraw, put away, put aside; to steal; **se amovere** to retire, withdraw

Amphiarā·us -ī *m* famous Greek seer

amphĭbolĭ·a -ae *f* (*rhet*) ambiguity

Amphī·ōn -ŏnis *m* son of Antiope by Jupiter, twin brother of Zethus, king of Thebes, and husband of Niobe

amphĭtheātr·um -ī *n* amphitheater

Amphĭtrȳ·ō *or* **Amphĭtrȳ·ōn -ōnis** *m* husband of Alcmena

Amphĭtrȳōnĭăd·ēs -is *m* Hercules

amphŏr·a -ae *f* amphora; liquid measure (*about 7 gallons*)

amplē *adv* largely, abundantly, broadly, spaciously; splendidly

am·plector -plectī -plexus sum *vt* to embrace, entwine, enclose, encircle; to grab, get hold of; to understand, comprehend; to embrace, include, comprise; to sum up; to embrace affectionately, esteem, cling to; (mil) to occupy, cover

amplex·ō -**āre** or **amplex·or** -**ārī** -**ātus sum** *vt* to embrace; to honor, esteem

amplex·us -**ūs** *m* circuit; embrace, caress

amplificātĭ·ō -**ōnis** *f* extension, enlargement; (rhet) amplification, development

amplificāt·or -**ōris** *m* enlarger, amplifier

amplificē *adv* splendidly

amplific·ō -**āre** *vt* to enlarge, extend, widen; to increase; (rhet) to enlarge upon, develop

amplĭ·ō -**āre** *vt* to widen, enlarge; to enhance; to postpone (*judgment*), adjourn (*court, in order to gather further evidence*); to remand

amplĭter *adv* splendidly

amplitūd·ō -**ĭnis** *f* width, size, bulk, extent; greatness, dignity, importance, high rank; (rhet) development, amplification

amplĭus *adv* any further, any more, any longer, besides; further, more, longer; **amplius uno die** one day longer; longer than one day; **nec amplius** no longer

amplĭus *adj* (neuter comparative of **amplus**) more, further, else; (with numerals) more than; **hoc amplius** this further point; **nihil amplius** nothing further, no more; **quid amplius** what more, what else; *n* more, a larger amount; **amplius negoti** more trouble

ampl·us -**a** -**um** *adj* ample, large, wide, spacious; strong, great, powerful; grand, imposing, splendid; eminent, prominent, illustrious, distinguished

ampull·a -**ae** *f* bottle, jar, flask; bombast

ampullār·ĭus -**ĭī** or -**ī** *m* flask maker

ampull·or -**ārī** -**ātus sum** *vi* to be bombastic

amputātĭ·ō -**ōnis** *f* pruning

amput·ō -**āre** *vt* to lop off, prune; to curtail, shorten; **amputata loqui** to speak disconnectedly

Amūl·ĭus -**ĭī** or -**ī** *m* king of Alba Longa, brother of Numitor, and granduncle of Romulus and Remus

amurc·a -**ae** *f* dregs of oil

amygdăl·a -**ae** *f* almond tree

amygdăl·um -**ī** *n* almond

amyst·is -**ĭdis** *f* drinking bottoms up

an *conj* (introducing the latter clause of a disjunctive direct or indirect question) or

anabăthr·a -**ōrum** *n pl* bleachers

Anăcrĕ·ōn -**ontis** *m* famous lyric poet of Teos (*fl* 540 B.C.)

anadēm·a -**ătis** *n* fillet, headband

anagnost·ēs -**ae** *m* reader, reciter

analectr·is -**ĭdis** *f* shoulder pad (*to improve the figure*)

anapaest·us -**a** -**um** *adj* anapestic; *m* anapest; *n* poem in anapestic meter

an·as -**ătis** *f* duck; **anas fluvialis** wild duck

anaticŭl·a -**ae** *f* duckling

anatĭn·us -**a** -**um** *adj* duck's

anatocism·us -**ī** *m* compound interest

Anaxagŏr·ās -**ae** *m* Greek philosopher of Clazomenae, teacher of Pericles and Euripides (500?-428 B.C.)

Anaximand·er -**rī** *m* Greek philosopher of Miletus (610-547 B.C.)

Anaximĕn·ēs -**is** *m* Greek philosopher of Miletus (*fl* 544 B.C.)

an·ceps -**cipĭtis** *adj* two-headed; two-edged; twin-peaked; amphibious; double, twofold; doubtful, undecided, ambiguous; hazardous, critical; *n* danger, peril

Anchīs·ēs -**ae** *m* son of Capys and father of Aeneas

Anchīsiăd·ēs -**ae** *m* son of Anchises, Aeneas

ancīl·e -**is** *n* oval shield said to have fallen from heaven in reign of Numa, second king of Rome

ancill·a -**ae** *f* maidservant

ancillār·is -**e** *adj* maidservant's

ancillŭl·a -**ae** *f* young slave (*female*)

ancŏr·a -**ae** *f* anchor

ancorāl·e -**is** *n* cable

ancorārĭ·us -**a** -**um** *adj* of an anchor

Ancўr·a -**ae** *f* Ankara, capital of Galatia

andabăt·a -**ae** *m* blindfold gladiator

And·ēs -**ĭum** *f pl* village near Mantua, birthplace of Virgil

androgўn·us -**ī** *m* or **androgўn·ē** -**ēs** *f* hermaphrodite

Andromăch·a -**ae** or **Andromăch·ē** -**ēs** *f* Hector's wife

Andromĕd·a -**ae** *f* daughter of Cepheus and Cassiope, rescued from a sea monster by Perseus

andr·ōn -**ōnis** *m* corridor

Andronīc·us -**ī** *m* Lucius Livius Andronicus (*fl* 241 B.C., *first epic and dramatic poet of the Romans*)

Andr·os -**ī** *f* Aegean island

ānell·us -**ī** *m* little ring

anēth·um -**ī** *n* anise, dill

anfract·us -**ūs** *m* curve, bend (*of road*); orbit; digression, prolixity

angell·us -**ī** *m* small corner

angīn·a -**ae** *f* tonsillitis, inflamation of the throat

angiport·us -**ūs** *m* or **angiport·um** -**ī** *n* alley

ang·ō -**ĕre** *vt* to choke, throttle; to distress, tease, trouble

ang·or -**ōris** *m* strangling, suffocation; anguish

anguicŏm·us -**a** -**um** *adj* snake-haired

anguicŭl·us -**ī** *m* small snake

anguif·er -**ĕra** -**ĕrum** *adj* snaky

anguigĕn·a -**ae** *m* offspring of a dragon; Theban

anguill·a -**ae** *f* eel

anguĭn·us -**a** -**um** *adj* snaky; serpent-like

anguīn·us -**a** -**um** *adj* snaky

anguip·ēs -ĕdis adj serpent-footed

angu·is -is m or f snake, serpent

Angu·is -is m or f Dragon, Hydra (constellation)

Anguitĕn·ens -entis m Ophiuchus (constellation)

angulār·is -e adj angular

angulāt·us -a -um adj angular

angŭl·us -ī m angle, corner; nook, recess; **ad parīs angulos** at right angles

angustē adv within narrow limits, closely, hardly, scarcely; briefly, concisely

angusti·ae -ārum f pl narrow place, defile; narrow passage, strait; (fig) shortness; scarcity, want, deficiency; difficulty, tight spot, perplexity; distress, straits; narrow-mindedness

angusticlāvi·us -a -um adj wearing a narrow purple stripe

angust·ō -āre vt to make narrow

angust·us -a -um adj narrow, close, short, brief (time); scanty (means); difficult, critical; narrow-minded; base, mean; n narrowness; critical condition, danger

anhēlĭt·us -ūs m panting, difficulty in breathing, puffing; breath, breathing; vapor

anhēl·ō -āre vt to breathe out; to pant after; vi to pant, puff; to exhale; (of fire) to roar

anhēl·us -a -um adj panting, puffing

anicŭl·a -ae f little old woman, silly old woman

Aniēns·is -e or **Aniēn·us -a -um** adj of the Anio (tributary of the Tiber)

anīl·is -e adj of an old woman

anilĭt·ās -ātis f old age (of women)

anilĭter adv like an old woman

anĭm·a -ae f air, wind, breeze; breath; breath of life, life; soul (as the principle of life, opposed to **animus** as the principle of thought and feelings); spirit, ghost

animadversi·ō -ōnis f attention, observation; reproach, criticism; punishment

animadvers·or -ōris m observer

animad·vertō or **animad·vortō -vertĕre -vertī -versum** vt to pay attention to, attend to; to notice, observe, realize; to reproach, criticize; to punish

anim·al -ālis n animal; living creature

animāl·is -e adj consisting of air, animate, living

anim·ans -antis adj living, animate; m & f & n living being; animal

animātĭ·ō -ōnis f living being

animāt·us -a -um adj courageous, inclined, disposed; (with **erga** or **in** + acc) disposed toward

anim·ō -āre vt to make alive, to animate; to encourage

animōsē adv courageously; eagerly

animōs·us -a -um adj full of air,

airy; full of life, living, animate; blowing violently; full of courage, bold, spirited, undaunted; proud

animŭl·a -ae f little soul, life

animŭl·us -ī m darling

anim·us -ī m soul (as principle of intellection and sensation, whereas **anima** is soul as principle of life); intellect, understanding, mind, thought, reason; memory; knowledge; sense, consciousness; judgment, opinion; imagination; heart, feelings, passions; spirit, courage, morale; disposition, character; pride, haughtiness; will, purpose, desire, inclination; pleasure, delight; confident hope; **aequo animo** patiently, calmly; **animi causā** for amusement; **bono animo esse** to take heart; **ex animo** from the bottom of the heart, sincerely; **ex animo effluere** to slip one's mind; **in animo habere** (with inf) to intend to; **meo animo** in my opinion

Anĭ·ō -ēnis m tributary of the Tiber

An·ĭus -ĭī or **-ī** m king and priest on Delos who welcomed Aeneas

annāl·is -e adj lasting a year, annual; **lex annalis** law fixing minimum age for holding public offices; m pl annals, chronicle

annăt·ō -āre vi (with dat or **ad** + acc) to swim to

anne conj (pleonastic form of **an**) or

an·nectō -nectĕre -nexŭī -nexum vt (with dat or **ad** + acc) to tie, connect, annex (something) to; (with dat) to apply (something) to

annex·us -ūs m connection

annicŭl·us -a -um adj one year old, yearling

an·nītor -nītī -nīsus sum or **nixus sum** vi (with dat or **ad** + acc) to press against, lean on; (with **ut** or inf) to strive to

anniversāri·us -a -um adj annual, yearly

ann·ō -āre vi (with dat, with **ad** + acc, or with acc of limit of motion) to swim to or towards; (with dat) to swim with or along with

annōn conj or not

annōn·a -ae f year's crop; grain; price of grain; cost of living; high price

annōs·us -a -um adj aged, old

annotātĭ·ō -ōnis f notation, remark

annōtīn·us -a -um adj last year's

annŏt·ō -āre vt to write down, note down; to comment on; to observe, perceive

annŭmĕr·ō -āre vt (with dat) to count out (money) to; (with dat or **in** + acc) to add (something) to, to include (someone) among

annuntĭ·ō -āre vt to announce, make known, proclaim

an·nŭō -nŭĕre -nŭī -nūtum vt to designate by a nod; to indicate, declare; (with dat) to promise, grant (something) to; vi to nod, nod assent; (with *dat*) to nod assent to, to be favorable to, smile on

ann·us -ī *m* year; season; age, time of life; year of office; **ad annum** for the coming year, a year hence; **annum** or **in annum** for a year; **per annos** year to year

annŭ·us -a -um *adj* lasting a year; annual, yearly; *n pl* yearly pay, pension

an·quīrō -quīrĕre -quīsīvī -quīsītum *vt* to search carefully; to examine, inquire into; (with *genit* or *abl* of the charge) to accuse (*someone*) of; *vi* to hold an inquest

ans·a -ae *f* handle; opportunity

ansāt·us -a -um *adj* having handles; **homo ansatus** man with arms akimbo

ans·er -ĕris *m* gander

ante *adv* before, previously; in front, forwards

ante *prep* (with *acc*) before; more than, above

anteā *adv* before, previously, formerly

ante·capiō -capĕre -cēpī -ceptum *vt* to receive beforehand; to take possession of beforehand, preoccupy; to anticipate

ante·cēdō -cēdĕre -cessī -cessum *vt* to precede; to excel, surpass; *vi* (with *dat*) **a** to have precedence over; **b** to excel, surpass

antecessi·ō -ōnis *f* antecedent cause

antecess·or -ōris *m* (mil) scout; *m pl* advance guard

antecurs·or -ōris *m* (mil) scout; *m pl* advance guard

ante·ĕō -īre -iī *vt* to precede; to excel, surpass; to anticipate, prevent; *vi* to precede; to take the lead; (with *dat*) **a** to go before; **b** to excel, surpass

ante·fĕrō -ferre -tŭlī -lātum *vt* to prefer; to anticipate

antefix·us -a -um *pp* of **antefīgo**; *n pl* images, statues, etc., affixed to roofs and gutters of homes or temples

ante·gredĭor -grĕdī -gressus sum *vt* to precede

antehab·ĕō -ēre *vt* to prefer

antehāc *adv* before this time, before now, formerly

antelātus *pp* of **antefero**

antelūcān·us -a -um *adj* before dawn

antemerīdiān·us -a -um *adj* before noon

ante·mittō -mittĕre -mīsī -missum *vt* to send out ahead

antenn·a -ae *f* yardarm, sail yard

Antēn·or -ōris *m* Trojan who after the fall of Troy went to Italy and founded Patavium

antepīlān·ī -ōrum *m pl* front ranks, front line

ante·pōnō -pōnĕre -posŭī -posītum *vt* to prefer; to serve (*food*)

antepŏt·ens -entis *adj* very wealthy

antĕquam or **ante ... quam** *conj* before

Antēr·ōs -ōtis *m* avenger of unrequited love

ant·ēs -ium *m pl* rows (*e.g., of vines*)

antesignān·us -ī *m* soldier who fought in front of the standards to defend them; leader, commander

ante·stō or **anti·stō -stāre -stĕtī** *vi* to excel, be distinguished; (with *dat*) to be superior to

antest·or -ārī -ātus sum *vt* to call as witness

ante·veniō -venīre -vēnī -ventum *vt* to anticipate, thwart; to surpass, excel; *vi* to become more distinguished; (with *dat*) **a** to anticipate; **b** to surpass, excel

ante·vertō -vertĕre -vertī -versum *vt* to go or come before, precede; to anticipate; to prefer

antevŏl·ō -āre *vi* to dash out ahead

anticipātĭ·ō -ōnis *f* preconception, foreknowledge

anticĭp·ō -āre *vt* to anticipate

antīc·us -a -um *adj* front, foremost

Antigŏn·ē -ēs *f* daughter of Theban king Oedipus; daughter of Trojan king Laomedon

Antilŏch·us -ī *m* son of Nestor, killed by Hector at Troy

Antiphăt·ēs -ae *m* king of the Laestrygones, who sank the fleet of Greeks returning from Troy with Ulysses

antiquārĭ·us -a -um *adj* & *m* antiquarian

antīquē *adv* in former times; in the good old style

antīquit·ās -ātis *f* antiquity; men of former times, the ancients; the good old days

antīquĭtus *adv* in former times, of old; from ancient times; in the old style

antīqu·ō -āre *vt* to reject (*law, bill*)

antīqu·us -a -um *adj* old, ancient; oldfashioned, venerable; *m pl* ancients, ancient authors; *n* antiquity; old custom

antist·es -ĭtis *m* priest presiding over temple, high priest

antist·es -ĭtis or **antistĭt·a -ae** *f* priestess presiding over temple, high priestess

Antisthĕn·ēs -is or **-ae** *m* pupil of Socrates and founder of Cynic philosophy

antithĕt·on -ī *n* (rhet) antithesis

antr·um -ī *n* cave, cavern

ānulār·ĭus -ĭī or **-ī** *m* ring maker

ānulāt·us -a -um *adj* wearing a ring

ānŭl·us -ī *m* ring, signet ring

ān·us -ī *m* anus, rectum; ring

an·us -ūs *f* old woman; hag

anxiē *adv* uneasily

anxiĕt·ās -ātis *f* anxiety, trouble

anxif·er -ĕra -ĕrum *adj* causing anxiety

anxi·us -a -um *adj* worried, troubled; disquieting

apăge *interj* go on!; scram!

apēliōt·ēs -ae *m* east wind

Apell·ēs -is *m* famous Greek painter (*fl 4th cent.* B.C.)

ap·er -rī *m* boar

aper·iō -īre -uī -tum *vt* to uncover, open, lay bare, disclose, reveal; to prove, demonstrate; to explain, recount

apertē *adv* openly, frankly, candidly

apert·ō -āre *vt* to keep on laying bare

apert·us -a -um *pp* of **aperio**; *adj* bare, uncovered, exposed; without decks; clear (*style*); frank, candid (*character*); manifest, plain, evident; accessible, unobstructed; in open space; **in aperto** in the open; **in aperto esse** to be clear, evident, well known, notorious

ap·ex -īcis *m* point, top, summit; hat, cap, crown; crowning glory

aphract·us -ī *f* or **aphract·um -ī** *n* ship without deck

apiār·ius -iī *or* **-ī** *n* beekeeper

apicŭl·a -ae *f* little bee

ap·is -is *f* bee

ap·iscor -iscī -tus sum *vt* to pursue; to take, reach, gain, get

ap·ium -iī *or* **-ī** *n* celery

aplustr·e -is *n* stern

apoclēt·ī -ōrum *m pl* select committee (*of Aetolian League*)

apodytēr·ium -iī *or* **-ī** *n* dressing room (*at a bath*)

apolactiz·ō -āre *vt* to kick aside, scorn

Apoll·ō -īnis *m* son of Jupiter and Latona, twin brother of Diana, god of the sun, divination, archery, healing, poetry, and music

Apollodōr·us -ī *m* famous rhetorician, teacher of Augustus; famous Athenian grammarian and author of an extant work on mythology (*fl 140* B.C.)

apolŏg·us -ī *m* story, fable

apophorēt·a -ōrum *n pl* presents for house guests

aposphrāgism·a -ătis *n* device on signet ring, seal

apothēc·a -ae *f* warehouse, storehouse, magazine

apparātē *adv* with much preparation, sumptuously

apparāti·ō -ōnis *f* preparation

apparāt·us -a -um *adj* prepared, well prepared; sumptuous

apparāt·us -ūs *m* getting or making ready, preparing; providing; equipment, apparatus, paraphernalia; pomp, magnificence

appăr·ĕō -ēre -uī -ĭtum *vi* to appear, become visible; to be seen, show oneself; (*with dat*) to wait on, serve; **apparet** it is evident, clear, certain

apparīti·ō -ōnis *f* attendance, service; *f pl* household servants

apparīt·or -ōris *m* servant; attendant of public official (*e.g.*, aide, lictor, secretary)

appăr·ō -āre *vt* to prepare, make ready, provide

appellāti·ō -ōnis *f* addressing; appeal; naming, calling by name; name, title; pronunciation

ap·pellō -pellĕre -pŭlī -pulsum *vt* (*with dat* or **ad** + *acc*) to drive (*something*) to, steer (*ship*) to; *vi* (*of ship*) to land

appell·ō -āre *vt* to accost, address; to appeal to; (law) to sue; to name, call; to mention by name; to pronounce

appendicŭl·a -ae *f* small addition

append·ix -īcis *f* addition, supplement

ap·pendō -pendĕre -pendī -pensum *vt* to weigh; to pay out; (fig) to weigh, consider

appēt·ens -entis *adj* greedy, avaricious; (with *genit*) eager for, craving

appetenter *adv* eagerly, greedily

appetenti·a -ae *f* craving, desire; (with *genit*) craving for, desire for

appetīti·ō -ōnis *f* grasping, craving; (with *genit*) grasping at, craving for

appetīt·us -ūs *m* craving, desire; *m pl* appetites, passions

appĕt·ō -ĕre -īvī -ītum *vt* to try to reach; to lay hold of; to make for, head for; to attack, assail, assault; *vi* to approach, draw near

apping·ō -ĕre *vt* to paint; to write

ap·plaudō -plaudĕre -plausī -plausum *vt* (with *dat*) to strike (*something*) against; *vi* to applaud

applicāti·ō -ōnis *f* applying, application

applicăt·us -a -um *adj* (with **ad** + *acc*) inclined to; (with *dat*) lying close to, attached to

applic·ō -āre -āvī *or* **-uī -ātum** *or* **ĭtum** *vt* to bring in close contact; (with *dat* or **ad** + *acc*) **a** to apply, attach, add, join (*something*) to; **b** to steer (*ship*) toward; **c** to devote (*attention*, *mind*) to

applōr·ō -āre *vt* to deplore, lament

ap·pōnō -pōnĕre -posŭī -positum *vt* to serve (*food*); (with *dat* or **ad** + *acc*) to put or lay (*something*) near, at, or beside; (with *dat*) **a** to set (*food*) before; **b** to appoint or designate (*someone*) to (a *duty*, *task*); **c** to reckon (*something*) as

apporrect·us -a -um *adj* stretched out

apport·ō -āre *vt* to carry or bring up; to cause; (with *dat*) to carry (*something*) to

apposc·ō -ĕre *vt* to demand in addition

appositē *adv* appropriately, pertinently

apposit·us -a -um *pp* of **appono**; *adj* fit, suitable, appropriate; (with *dat*) situated near, contiguous with, bordering on; (with **ad** + *acc*) suited to, fit for

appōt·us -a -um *adj* drunk

apprĕc·or -ārī -ātus sum *vt* to pray to, worship

appre·hendō -hendĕre -hendī -hensum *vt* to seize, take hold of; (mil) to occupy

apprīmē *adv* chiefly, especially

ap·prīmō -prīmĕre -pressī -pressum *vt* (with *dat*) to press (*something*) close to

approbātī·ō -ōnis *f* approbation, approval; proof

approbāt·or -ōris *m* one who seconds or approves

approbē *adv* very well

approb·ō -āre *vt* to approve; to prove

appromitt·ō -ĕre *vt* to promise in addition

app/roper·ō -āre *vt* to hasten, speed up; *vi* to hurry

appropinquātī·ō -ōnis *f* approach

appropinqu·ō -āre *vi* to approach; (with *dat* or **ad** + *acc*) to come near to, approach

appugn·ō -āre *vt* to fight, attack

appuls·us -ūs *m* landing, approach

aprīcātī·ō -ōnis *f* basking in the sun

aprīc·or -ārī *vi* to bask, sun oneself

aprīc·us -a -um *adj* sunny; *n* sunny spot

Aprīl·is *adj* of April; **mensis Aprīlis** April, month of April

aprugn·us -a -um *adj* of a wild boar

aps- = abs-

apsūmēd·ō -īnis *f* devouring

aptē *adv* closely; suitably

apt·ō -āre *vt* to fasten, fit, adjust; to make ready, equip

apt·us -a -um *adj* suitable, adapted, appropriate, proper

apud *prep* (with *acc*) at, by, near, among; at the house of; before, in the presence of; in the writings of; over, (with influence) over

Āpūlī·a -ae *f* district in S.W. Italy

aqu·a -ae *f* water; *f pl* baths, spa; **aquā et igni interdicere** to outlaw; **aquam praebere** (with *dat*) to entertain (*guests*)

aquaeduct·us -ūs *m* aqueduct

aquālicŭl·us -ī *m* belly, stomach

aquāl·is -e *adj* of water; *m & f* washbasin

aquāri·us -a -um *adj* of water; *m* water-conduit inspector

Aquāri·us -ī or **-ī** *m* Aquarius (*constellation; sign of the Zodiac*)

aquātic·us -a -um *adj* growing in water; watery, moist, humid

aquātil·is -e *adj* living or growing in water, aquatic

aquātī·ō -ōnis *f* fetching water; water hole

aquāt·or -ōris *m* water carrier

aquĭl·a -ae *f* eagle (*bird; Roman legionary standard*); (fig) legion; gable of house

aquīl·ex -ēgis *m* water finder, dowser; water-conduit inspector

aquīlĭf·er -ĕrī *m* standard-bearer

aquilīn·us -a -um *adj* eagle's

aquil·ō -ōnis *m* north wind; north

aquilōnĭ·us -a -um *adj* northerly

aquĭl·us -a -um *adj* swarthy

Aquīn·um -ī *n* town of the Volsci, birthplace of Juvenal

Aquītāni·a -ae *f* province in S.W. Gaul

aqu·or -ārī -ātus sum *vi* to fetch water

aquōs·us -a -um *adj* rainy, humid, full of water

aquŭl·a -ae *f* small stream, brook

ār·a -ae *f* altar

Ār·a -ae *f* Altar (*constellation*)

arabarch·ēs -ae *m* customs officer in Egypt

Arabi·a -ae *f* Arabia

Arabĭc·us or **Arabĭ·us** or **Arăb·us -a -um** *adj* Arabian

Arachn·ē -ēs *f* Lydian girl whom Minerva changed into a spider

arānĕ·a -ae *f* spider; cobweb

arānĕŏl·a -ae *f* small spider

arānĕŏl·us -ī *m* small spider

arānĕōs·us -a -um *adj* full of cobwebs

arānĕ·us -a -um *adj* spider's; *m* spider; *n* spider web

Ar·ar -ăris *m* tributary of the Rhone

arātĭ·ō -ōnis *f* cultivation, tilling, agriculture; arable land

arātiuncŭl·a -ae *f* small plot, small farm

arāt·or -ōris *m* farmer; *m pl* farmers on state-owned land

arātr·um -ī *n* plow

Arāt·us -ī *m* Greek author of poem on astronomy (*fl* 270 B.C.)

arbĭt·er -rī *m* eyewitness; arbiter, judge, umpire; ruler, director, controller

arbĭtr·a -ae *f* eyewitness (*female*)

arbĭtrāriō *adv* uncertainly

arbĭtrāri·us -a -um *adj* uncertain

arbĭtrāt·us -ūs *m* decision; inclination, pleasure; direction, guidance

arbĭtr·ium -iī or **-ī** *n* decision, judgment; mastery, power, control, authority

arbĭtr·or -ārī -ātus sum *vt & vi* to decide or judge (*as an arbiter*); to testify; to think, suppose

arb·or or **arb·ōs -ōris** *f* tree; mast, oar, ship; gallows

arbŏrĕ·us -a -um *adj* of a tree; treelike

arbust·us -a -um *adj* wooded, planted with trees; *n* orchard; vineyard planted with trees; *n pl* trees

arbutĕ·us -a -um *adj* of arbutus

arbŭt·um -ī *n* fruit of arbutus

arbŭt·us -ī *f* arbutus, strawberry tree

arc·a -ae *f* chest, box, safe; coffin; prison cell

Arcadĭ·a -ae *f* district of central Peloponnesus

arcānō *adv* in secret, privately

arcān·us -a -um *adj* secret, concealed, private; *n* secret; sacred mystery

arc·eō -ēre -ŭī *vt* to shut up, enclose; to keep at a distance, keep off; to hinder, prevent; (with *abl* or **ab** + *abl*) to keep (*someone*) off, away from

arcessīt·us -a -um *pp* of **arcesso;** *adj* farfetched

arcessīt·us -ūs *m* summons

arcess·ō -ĕre -īvī -ītum *vt* to send for, fetch, summon; (law) to arraign; to derive

archetȳp·us -a -um *adj & n* original

Archilŏch·us -ī Greek iambic poet of Paros (*c.* 714-676 B.C.)

archimagīr·us -ī *m* chief cook

Archimēd·ēs -is *m* scientist and mathematician of Syracuse (287-212 B.C.)

archipīrāt·a -ae *m* pirate captain

architect·ōn -ōnis *m* architect, master builder; master in cunning

architect·or -ārī -ātus sum *vt* to build, construct

architectūr·a -ae *f* architecture

architect·us -ī *m* architect; deviser, author, inventor, contriver

arch·ōn -ōntis *m* archon (*chief magistrate in Athens*)

arcitĕn·ens -entis *adj* holding a bow, wearing a bow

Arcitĕn·ens -entis *m* Archer (*constellation*)

Arctophȳl·ax -ăcis *m* Boötes (*constellation*)

Arct·os -ī *m* the Great and Little Bear (*double constellation*)

arct·os -ī *m* North Pole; North; north wind; night

Arctūr·us -ī *m* brightest star in Boötes

arcŭl·a -ae *f* small box, jewelry box; (rhet) ornament

arcŭ·ō -āre *vt* to curve

arc·us -ūs *m* bow; rainbow; curve; arch, triumphal arch

Ardĕ·a -ae *f* town in Latium

ardĕ·a -ae *f* heron

ardeli·ō -ōnis *m* busybody

ard·ens -entis *adj* blazing, burning, hot, fiery; gleaming, glittering; smarting, burning; (of emotions) glowing, hot, ardent

ardenter *adv* ardently, eagerly, passionately

ardĕō ardēre arsī *vi* to be on fire, burn, blaze; to flash, glow; to smart, burn

ardesc·ō -ĕre *vi* to catch fire; to gleam, glitter; (of passions) to become more intense, increase in violence

ard·or -ōris *m* heat, flame; flashing, brightness; heat (*of passions*); loved one, flame

ardŭ·us -a -um *adj* steep, high; difficult; *n* difficulty

ărĕ·a -ae *f* open space; park, playground; building site; threshing floor

arēna see **harena**

ăr·ĕō -ēre *vi* to be dry; to be thirsty

āreŏl·a *f* small open space

Arēopăg·us -ī *m* criminal court in Athens; hill where criminal court met

Ar·ēs -is *m* Greek god of war

āresc·ō -ĕre *vi* to become dry; to wither

aretālŏg·us -ī *m* braggart

Arethūs·a -ae *f* nymph pursued by river god Alpheus in Peloponnesus and changed by Diana into a fountain; fountain near Syracuse

Argē·ī -ōrum *m* *pl* consecrated places in Rome ascribed to Numa; figures of men, made of rushes and thrown annually into the Tiber

argentāri·us -a -um *adj* silver; financial, pecuniary; *m* banker; *f* banking; bank; silver mine

argentāt·us -a -um *adj* plated or ornamented with silver

argenteŏl·us -a -um *adj* made of pretty silver

argentĕ·us -a -um *adj* silver, silvery

argent·um -ī *n* silver; silver plate; money

Argē·us or **Argīv·us** or **Argolic·us -a -um** *adj* Argive; Greek

Arg·ī -ōrum *m* *pl* Argos, town in N.E. Peloponnesus

Argīlēt·um -ī *n* district in Rome between the Quirinal and Capitoline

argill·a -ae *f* clay

Arg·ō -ūs *f* Jason's ship

Argŏl·is -ĭdis *f* district around Argos

Argonaut·ae -ārum *m* *pl* argonauts

Argos *n* (only *nom* and *acc*) Argos

argūmentāti·ō -ōnis *f* argumentation; proof

argūment·or -ārī -ātus sum *vt* to adduce as proof; (with **de** + *abl*) to conclude from; *vi* to bring evidence

argūment·um -ī *n* evidence, proof, argument; theme, plot; topic; subject, motif (*of artistic representation*)

arg·ŭō -uĕre -ŭī -ūtum *vt* to prove; to reveal, betray; to accuse, charge, impeach (*person*), find fault with (*thing*)

Arg·us -ī *n* many-eyed monster set over Io and killed by Mercury

argūtē *adv* subtly; craftily

argūti·ae -ārum *f* *pl* subtlety; brightness, genius, cunning, shrewdness

argūtŭl·us -a -um *adj* somewhat subtle

argūt·us -a -um *adj* clearcut, clear, bright, distinct; penetrating, piercing; chatty; acute, subtle; bright, smart, witty; cunning, sly

argyrasp·is -ĭdis *adj* wearing a silver shield

Ariadn·a -ae *f* daughter of Minos, king of Crete, who extricated Theseus from the labyrinth

Aricī·a -ae *f* town in Latium on the Via Appia

āridŭl·us -a -um *adj* somewhat dry

ắrĭd·us -a -um *adj* dry, parched; withered; meager; (of style) dry, dull

arĭ·ēs -ĕtis *m* ram; battering ram; beam (*used as breakwater*)

Arĭ·ēs -ĕtis *m* Aries (*sign of the Zodiac*)

arĭĕt·ō -āre *vt & vi* to butt, ram

Ariobarzăn·ēs -is *m* king of Cappadocia

Arĭ·ōn -ŏnis *m* early Greek poet and musician, rescued from drowning by dolphin

arist·a -ae *f* ear of grain

Aristarch·us -ī *m* Alexandrine critic and scholar (*fl* 156 B.C.); stern critic

aristolochĭ·a -ae *f* birthwort

Aristophăn·ēs -is *m* the most famous Greek comic poet (*c.* 444-380 B.C.)

Aristotĕl·ēs -is *m* Aristotle (384-322 B.C.)

arithmĕtĭc·a -ōrum *n pl* arithmetic

ārĭtūd·ō -ĭnis *f* dryness

arm·a -ōrum *n pl* armor, defensive arms, arms; warfare; camp life; armed men; equipment, tools

armāment·a -ōrum *n pl* ship's gear

armāmentār·ium -ĭī or **-ī** *n* arsenal, armory

armārĭŏl·um -ī *n* little chest, little closet

armār·ium -ĭī or **-ī** *n* cupboard, chest

armātūr·a -ae *f* outfit, equipment, armor; light-armed troops

armāt·us -a -um *adj* armed, equipped; *m* armed man

Armenĭ·a *f* country in N.E. Asia Minor

armenĭăc·um -ī *n* apricot

armenĭăc·us -ī *f* apricot tree

armentāl·is -e *adj* of a herd

armentār·ius -ĭī or **-ī** *m* herdsman

arment·um -ī *n* herd

armĭf·er -ĕra -ĕrum *adj* armed

armĭg·er -ĕra -ĕrum *adj* armed; producing warriors; *m* armed person; armor-bearer

armill·a -ae *f* armlet, bracelet

armillāt·us -a -um *adj* wearing a bracelet

armĭpŏt·ens -entis *adj* powerful in arms, warlike

armĭsŏn·us -a -um *adj* reverberating with arms

arm·ō -āre *vt* to furnish with arms, to arm; to rouse to arms

arm·us -ī *m* shoulder, shoulder blade, upper arm; flank (*of animal*)

ar·ō -āre *vt* to plow, till

Arpīn·um -ī *n* town in Latium, birthplace of Marius and Cicero

arquāt·us -a -um *adj* jaundiced

arrect·us -a -um *pp* of **arrigo**; *adj* upright; steep, precipitous

arrēp·ō -ĕre -sī *vi* (with *dat* or **ad** + *acc*) to creep towards, steal up on

arrhāb·ō -ōnis *m* deposit (*of money*)

ar·rīdĕō -rīdēre -rīsī -rīsum *vt* to smile at; *vi* (with *dat*) **a** to smile at

or on, laugh with; **b** to be favorable to; **c** to be pleasing to, please

ar·rĭgō -rigĕre -rexī -rectum *vt* to erect, raise; to rouse, excite

ar·rĭpĭō -rĭpĕre -rĭpuī -reptum *vt* to snatch, seize; (fig) to grasp quickly; (law) to arrest, arraign; to satirize

ar·rōdō -rōdĕre -rōsī -rōsum *vt* to gnaw at

arrŏg·ans -antis *adj* arrogant

arroganter *adv* arrogantly

arrogantĭ·a -ae *f* assumption, presumption; arrogance

arrŏg·ō -āre *vt* to question; to associate; to assume for oneself, claim

ars artis *f* skill; craft, trade; method, way, manner, means; artificial means; work of art; science, theory; manual, textbook; *f pl* cunning; moral qualities, character

artē *adv* closely, tightly; (to love) deeply, dearly; (to sleep) soundly

Artĕm·is -ĭdis *f* Greek counterpart of Diana

artērĭ·a -ae *f* artery; windpipe

arthrĭtĭc·us -a -um *adj* arthritic

artĭculātim *adv* piecemeal; (to speak) articulately, distinctly

artĭcŭl·ō -āre *vt* to utter distinctly, articulate

artĭcŭl·us -ī *m* joint, knuckle; finger; limb; (gram) clause; turning point; **in ipso articulo temporis** in the nick of time

artĭf·ex -ĭcis *adj* skillful, ingenious; artistic; broken, trained (*horse*); *m* craftsman, artist, master; originator, contriver, author

artĭfĭcĭōsē *adv* skillfully

artĭfĭcĭōs·us -a -um *adj* skillful, ingenious, accomplished; artificial

artĭfĭc·ium -ĭī or **-ī** *n* skill, workmanship; artistic work, work of art; art, profession; cleverness, cunning; theory

art·ō -āre *vt* to pack closely; to compress, contract; to limit

artolagăn·us -ī *m* cake

artopt·a -ae *m* baker; bread pan (*to bake in*)

art·us -a -um *adj* close, tight; confined, restricted; dense, firm; scanty, small, needy; strict, severe; sound, deep (*sleep*); stingy; *n* narrow space; tight spot, difficulty

art·us -ūs *m* joint; *m pl* joints, limbs

ārŭl·a -ae *f* small altar

arund·ō -ĭnis *f* reed; shaft, arrow; pipe, flute; pen; fishing rod; hobbyhorse; (in weaving) comb

arvīn·a -ae *f* grease

arv·us -a -um *adj* arable; *n* arable land, soil, land, plain, region; grain

arx arcis *f* fortress, stronghold, citadel, castle, protection, refuge, mainstay; height, summit; **arcem facere e cloaca** to make a mountain out of a molehill

ās assis *m* pound (*divisible into twelve ounces*); bronze coin; **heres ex asse** sole heir

Ascān·ius -iī or **-ī** *m* son of Aeneas and Creusa and founder of Alba Longa

ascendō ascendĕre ascendī ascensum *vt* to climb; to mount (*horse*); to board (*ship*); *vi* to climb up, ascend; (of voice) to rise; (with **ad** or **in** + *acc*) to climb, climb up to; (with **super** or **supra** + *acc*) to rise above, surpass

ascensi·ō -ōnis *f* climbing up, ascent

ascens·us -ūs *m* climbing up, ascent; means of ascending, approach; step, degree; (fig) climb, rise

ascī·a -ae *f* ax; mason's trowel

asc·iō -īre *vt* to associate with oneself, admit

asc·iscō -iscĕre -īvī -ītum *vt* to adopt, approve (*bill*); to adopt (*custom*); to assume, claim, arrogate; to receive, admit (*e.g., as ally, citizen, etc.*); (with **in** + *acc*) to admit (*someone*) to

ascīt·us -a -um *adj* acquired (*as opposed to innate*)

Ascr·a -ae *f* birthplace of Hesiod in Boeotia

a·scrībō -scrībĕre -scripsī -scriptum *vt* to add (*by writing*); to impute, ascribe, attribute; to enroll, register; to reckon, number, class

ascriptīci·us -a -um *adj* enrolled, registered

ascripti·ō -ōnis *f* addition (*in writing*)

ascriptīv·us -ī *m* (mil) reserve

ascript·or -ōris *m* supporter

asell·a -ae *f* little ass

asell·us -ī *m* little ass

Āsi·a -ae *f* Roman province; Asia Minor; Asia

asīl·us -ī *m* gadfly

asīn·us -ī *m* ass; fool

Ās·is -ĭdis *f* Asia

asōt·us -ī *m* playboy

asparăg·us -ī *m* asparagus

aspargō see **aspergo**

aspectābĭl·is -e *adj* visible

aspect·ō -āre *vt* to look at, gaze at; to look with respect at; to face, lie in the direction of; to observe

aspect·us -ūs *m* look, sight, glance; sense of sight; manner of appearance, appearance, countenance

aspell·ō -ĕre *vt* to drive away

asp·er -ĕra -ĕrum *adj* rough, uneven; harsh, severe, stormy (*climate*); harsh, grating, hoarse (*sound*); pungent, strong (*smell*); rough, hard, unkind, rude (*character*); austere, rigid (*person*); wild fierce, savage (*animal*); rough, annoying, adverse (*circumstances*) rugged (*style*)

asperē *adv* roughly; (fig) harshly, sternly, severely

a·spergō -spergĕre -spersī -spersum *vt* to sprinkle, scatter, taint; (with *dat*) to sprinkle (*something*) on

asperg·ō -ĭnis *f* sprinkling; spray

asperĭt·ās -ātis *f* uneveness, roughness; severity, fierceness; difficulty, trouble

aspernātĭ·ō -ōnis *f* disdain, contempt

aspern·or -ārī -ātus sum *vt* to disdain, despise, reject

aspĕr·ō -āre *vt* to make rough or uneven, roughen; to make fierce, exasperate; to excite

aspersĭ·ō -ōnis *f* sprinkling; laying on of colors

a·spiciō -spicĕre -spexī -spectum *vt* to catch sight of, spot; to look at; to examine closely, inspect; to observe, consider

aspīrātĭ·ō -ōnis *f* breathing, blowing; evaporation, exhalation; (gram) aspiration

aspīr·ō -āre *vi* to breathe, blow; (with *dat* or with **ad** or **in** + *acc*) to aspire to, desire to reach or obtain, come near to obtaining; (with *dat*) to favor

asp·is -ĭdis *f* asp

asportātĭ·ō -ōnis *f* removal

asport·ō -āre *vt* to carry away

asprēt·a -ōrum *n pl* rough terrain

assēcl·a -ae *m* hanger-on

assectātĭ·ō -ōnis *f* (respectful) attendance

assectāt·or -ōris *m* attendant, escort; disciple

assect·or -ārī *vt* to follow, tail after

assecŭl·a -ae *m* hanger-on

assensĭ·ō -ōnis *f* assent, approval; *m pl* expressions of approval; (phil) realism

assens·or -ōris *m* backer, supporter

assens·us -ūs *m* assent, approval; *m pl* expressions of approval; (phil) realism; echo

assentātĭ·ō -ōnis *f* assent, agreement; flattery

assentātiuncŭl·a -ae *f* base flattery

assentāt·or -ōris *m* flatterer

assentātōriē *adv* flatteringly

assentātr·ix -īcis *f* flatterer (*female*)

as·sentiō -sentīre -sensī -sensum *vi* to agree; (with *dat*) to assent to, agree with, approve

as·sentĭor -sentīrī -sensus sum *vi* to agree; (with *dat*) to assent to, agree with, approve

assent·or -ārī -ātus sum *vi* to agree always; (with *dat*) to agree with always, to flatter

as·sĕquor -sĕquī -secūtus sum *vt* to pursue, catch up to, reach; to gain, obtain, procure; to come up to, equal, match; to comprehend, understand

ass·er -ĕris *m* pole, stake, post

as·sĕrō -serĕre -sēvī -situm *vt* (with *dat*) to plant (*something*) near

assĕr·ō -ĕre -uī -tum *vt* to set free, liberate (*slave*); to protect, defend; to claim, appropriate; **in servitutem asserere** to claim (*someone*) as one's slave

assertĭ-ō -ōnis f declaration of civil status

assert-or -ōris m defender, champion

asserv-ĭō -īre vi (with dat) to serve, assist

asserv-ō -āre vt to preserve, keep, watch over, guard

assessĭ-ō -ōnis f company, companionship

assess-or -ōris m companion, assistant; (law) assistant to a judge, counselor

assess-us -ūs m company, companionship

assevēranter adv emphatically

assevērātĭ-ō -ōnis f assertion, protestation; firmness, earnestness

assevēr-ō -āre vt to assert strongly, affirm, insist on

as-sĭdĕō -sĭdēre -sēdī -sessum vi to seat nearby; (with dat) **a** to sit near, stand by, attend upon, take care of, keep (someone) company; **b** to be busily engaged in; **c** to attend to, mind; **d** to be near (in some respect), be like, resemble

as-sĭdō -sĭdĕre -sēdī vi to sit down; (with acc) to sit down beside

assidŭē adv assiduously, continually, incessantly

assidŭĭt-ās -ātis f constant presence or attendance; persistence; frequent recurrence

assidŭō adv continually

assidŭ-us -a -um adj continually present; persistent, tireless, incessant, busy; m taxpayer; rich man

assignātĭ-ō -ōnis f allotment (of land)

assign-ō -āre vt to mark out, allot, assign (land); to assign, confer; to ascribe, attribute; to consign; to seal

as-sĭlĭō -sĭlīre -sĭlŭī -sultum vi to jump; (with dat) to jump upon, leap at; (with acc) **a** to jump to; **b** to have recourse to

assimĭlĭter adv in like manner

assimĭl-is -e adj similar; (with dat) like

assimŭlātĭ-ō -ōnis f likeness, similarity

assimŭlāt-us -a -um adj similar; counterfeit

assimŭl-ō -āre vt to consider as similar, compare; to imitate, counterfeit

as-sĭstō -sĭstĕre -stĭtī vi to stand nearby; (with ad + acc) to stand at or by; (with dat) to assist, defend

assĭtus pp of assero

assol-ĕō -ēre vi to be usual

assŏn-ō -āre vi to echo; (with dat) to sound in response to, to echo (a sound)

assuē-facĭō -facĕre -fēcī -factum vt to train; (with dat, with ad + acc, or with inf) to accustom (someone) to

assu-escō -escĕre -ēvī -ētum vt (with dat) to accustom (someone) to, make (someone) familiar with, familiarize (someone) with; vi (with dat, with ad + acc, or with inf) to become used to

assuētūd-ō -ĭnis f habit, custom

assuēt-us -a -um pp of assuesco; adj accustomed, customary, usual; (with abl) trained in; (with dat, with ad or in + acc, or with inf) accustomed to, used to

as-sūgō -ĕre — -suctum vt to suck in

assūl-a -ae f splinter, chip, shaving

assūlātim adv in splinters, in fragments, piecemeal

assult-ō -āre vt to assault, attack; vi to jump; (with dat) to jump to, jump at

assult-us -ūs m assault, attack

as-sūmō -ĕre -sumpsī -sumptum vt to take up, adopt, accept; to usurp, claim, assume; to receive, obtain, derive

assumptĭ-ō -ōnis f taking, receiving, assumption; adoption; (in logic) minor premise

assumptīv-us -a -um adj resting on external evidence, extrinsic

assŭ-ō -ĕre vt (with dat) to sew (e.g., patch) on (e.g., clothes)

as-surgō -surgĕre -surrexī -surrectum vi to rise up, rise, stand up; to mount up, increase, swell; (with dat) to yield to, stand up for (out of respect)

ass-us -a -um adj roasted; n roast; n pl steam bath, sweat bath

ast conj (older form of at) but

Astart-ē -ēs f Syro-Phoenician goddess, counterpart of Venus

a-stern-ō -sternĕre vt (with dat) to strew (something) on; **asterni** (with dat) to throw oneself down upon

astĭpŭlāt-or -ōris m legal assistant; supporter

astĭpŭl-or -ārī -ātus sum vi (with dat) to agree with

a-stō -stāre vi to stand erect, stand up, stand nearby; (with dat) to assist

Astrae-a -ae f goddess of justice

astrĕp-ō -ĕre -ŭī -ĭtum vi to roar; to make a noise; to applaud; (with dat) to assent loudly to, applaud

astrictē adv concisely; strictly

astrict-us -a -um pp of astringo; drawn together, tight; stingy, tight; concise

a-stringō -stringĕre -strinxī -strictum vt to tighten, bind fast; to put under obligation, obligate, oblige; (fig) to draw closer; to compress, abridge; to occupy (attention); to embarrass

astrologĭ-a -ae f astronomy

astrolŏg-us -ī m astronomer; astrologer

astr-um -ī n star; constellation; n pl stars, sky, heaven; immortality

astū (indecl) n city

astup-ĕō -ēre vi (with dat) to be amazed at

ast-us -ūs m cunning, cleverness

astutē adv slyly

astūti·a -ae f skill, dexterity; cunning, astuteness

astūt·us -a -um adj clever; sly, cunning

Astyãn·ax -actis m son of Hector and Andromache

asȳl·um -ī n refuge, sanctuary, asylum

at conj but; (in a transition) but, but on the other hand; (in anticipation of an opponent's objection) but, it may be objected; (in an ironical objection) but really, but after all; (after a negative clause, to introduce a qualification) but at least; **at contra** but on the contrary; **at tamen** and yet, but at least

Atābŭl·us -ī m sirocco, southeast wind

Atalant·a -ae f daughter of King Schoeneus, defeated by Hippomenes in a famous footrace; daughter of Iasius and participant in the Calydonian boar hunt

atat interj (expressing surprise, pain, warning) oh!

atāv·us -ī m great-great-great-grandfather; ancestor

Atell·a -ae f Oscan town in Campania

Atellān·us -a -um adj Atellan; **Atellana** or **fabula Atellana** comic farce which originated in Atella

āt·er -ra -rum adj (opposed to **niger** glossy black) dead black, black; dark, gloomy, eerie; black, unlucky; malicious; poisonous

Athăm·ās -antis m king of Thessaly, father of Helle and Phrixus by Nephele, and of Learchus and Melecerta by Ino

Athēn·ae -ārum f pl Athens

athĕ·os -ī m atheist

athlēt·a -ae m athlete, wrestler

athlēticē adv athletically

athlētic·us -a -um adj athletic

Atl·ās -antis m giant supporting the sky, son of Iapetus and Clymene

atŏm·os -ī f indivisible particle, atom

atque conj (denotes closer internal connection than is implied by **et** and gives prominence to what follows) and, as well as, together with, and even, and . . . too; (after words of comparison) as, than; **atque . . . atque** both . . . and; **atque adeo** and in fact

atquī conj but yet, but anyhow, however, rather, and yet

ātrāment·um -ī n ink

ātrāt·us -a -um adj clothed in black

Atr·eus -eī m son of Pelops, brother of Thyestes, father of Agamemnon and Menelaus

Atrīd·ēs -ae m descendant of Atreus

ātriēns·is -is m butler

ātriŏl·um -ī n small hall, anteroom

ātrīt·ās -ātis f blackness

ātr·ium -iī or **-ī** n main room, entrance room (of Roman house); hall (of temples or public buildings)

atrōcit·ās -ātis f hideousness, repulsiveness (of form, appearance); fierceness, brutality, cruelty (of character); severity, rigidity (of law)

atrōciter adv horribly, fiercely, cruelly, grimly

Atrŏp·os -ī f one of the three Fates

atr·ox -ōcis adj horrible, hideous, frightful; savage, cruel, fierce; harsh, stern, unyielding, grim

attactus pp of **attingo**

attact·us -ūs m touch, contact

attăg·ēn -ēnis m woodcock

attagēn·a -ae f woodcock

Attalic·us -a -um adj of Attalus; Pergamean; rich, splendid; n pl gold-brocaded garments

Attăl·us -ī m king of Pergamum in Asia Minor, who bequeathed his kingdom to Rome

attămen conj but still, but yet

attat or **attătae** interj (indicating surprise, joy, dismay) oh!

attegi·a -ae f hut, cottage

attemperātē adv on time, in the nick of time

attempt·ō -āre vt to try, attempt; to test; to tempt, try to corrupt; to attack

at·tendō -tendĕre -tendī -tentum vt to notice, mark; to pay attention to, mind, consider; (with **dat** or **ad** + acc) to direct (mind, attention) to; vi to pay attention, listen

attentē adv attentively

attentī·ō -ōnis f attention, attentiveness

attentō see **attempto**

attent·us -a -um pp of **attendo**; adj attentive; careful, frugal, industrious

attenuātē adv (rhet) without flowery language, simply

attenuāt·us -a -um adj weak, weakened; shortened, brief; over-refined, affected; plain, bald (style)

attenŭ·ō -āre vt to make weak, weaken; to thin, attenuate; to lessen, diminish; to humble

at·tĕrō -terĕre -trīvī -trītum vt to rub, wear away, wear out, weaken, exhaust; to waste, destroy

attest·or -ārī -ātus sum vt to attest, confirm, corroborate, prove

attex·ō -ĕre -uī -tum vt to weave; to add

Atth·is -ĭdis f Attica

Attic·a -ae f district of Greece, of which Athens was the capital

atticē adv in the Attic or Athenian style

atticiss·ō -āre vi to speak in the Athenian manner

Attic·us -a -um adj Attic, Athenian; m T. Pomponius Atticus (friend of Cicero, 109-32 B.C.)

attigō see **attingo**

at·tineō -tinēre -tinŭī -tentum vt to hold tight, hold on to, hold, detain, hold back; to reach for; *vi* (with **ad** + *acc*) to pertain to, relate to, refer to, concern; **quod ad me attinet** as far as I am concerned

at·tingō -tingĕre -tĭgī -tactum *vt* to touch, come in contact with; to reach, arrive at; to touch (*food*), taste; to touch, lie near, border; to touch upon, mention lightly; to touch, strike, attack; to touch, affect; to undertake, engage in, take in hand, manage; to resemble; to concern, belong to

Att·is -ĭdis *m* priest of Phrygian goddess Cybele

attoll·ō -ĕre *vt* to lift up, raise; to exalt, extol

at·tondĕō -tondēre -tondī -tonsum *vt* to clip, shave, shear; to prune; to crop; to clip, fleece, cheat

attonĭt·us -a -um *adj* thunderstruck, stunned, amazed, dazed, astonished; inspired; frantic

attorquĕō -ēre *vt* to hurl up

at·trahō -trahĕre -traxī -tractum *vt* to attract, draw, drag by force

attrect·ō -āre *vt* to touch, handle; to appropriate to oneself

attrepĭd·ō -āre *vi* to hobble along

attrib·uō -uĕre -uī -ūtum *vt* to allot, assign, bestow, give, annex; to impose (*taxes*)

attribūtĭ·ō -ōnis *f* payment of a debt; (gram) predicate

attribūt·us -a -um *pp* of **attribuo**; *n* (gram) predicate

attrīt·us -a -um *pp* of **attero**; *adj* worn away, wasted; shameless

au *interj* ouch!

au·ceps -cŭpis *m* fowler, bird catcher; spy, eavesdropper

auctār·ium -iī or **-ī** *n* addition

auctĭfĭc·us -a -um *adj* increasing

auctĭ·ō -ōnis *f* increase; auction

auctĭōnārĭ·us -a -um *adj* auction

auctĭōn·or -ārī -ātus sum *vi* to hold an auction

auctĭt·ō -āre *vt* to increase greatly

auct·ō -āre *vt* to increase, augment

auct·or -ōris *m* originator, author; writer, historian; reporter, informant (*of news*); authority (*for statement or theory*); proposer, backer, supporter; progenitor (*of race*); founder (*of city*); model, example; adviser, counselor; teacher; guarantor, security; leader, statesman

auctōrāment·um -ī *n* contract; pay, wages

auctōrĭt·ās -ātis *f* origination, source, cause; view, opinion, judgment; advice, counsel, encouragement; might, power, authority, weight, influence, leadership; importance, significance, worth, consequence; example, model, precedent; authority (*for establishing a fact*); document, record; decree (*of senate*); right of possession

auctōr·ō -āre *vt* to bind; **auctorari** or **se auctorare** to hire oneself out

auctus *pp* of **augeo**

auct·us -ūs *m* increase, growth, abundance

aucup·ium -iī or **-ī** *n* fowling; trap; eavesdropping; **aucupia verborum** quibbling

aucŭp·ō -āre or **aucŭp·or -ārī -ātus sum** *vt* to lie in wait for, watch for, chase, strive after, catch; *vi* to catch birds

audācĭ·a -ae *f* (in good sense) boldness, courage, daring; (in bad sense) recklessness, effrontery, audacity; bold deed; *f pl* adventures

audacter *adv* boldly, audaciously

aud·ax -ācis *adj* (in good sense) bold, daring; (in bad sense) reckless, rash, foolhardy

aud·ens -entis *adj* bold, daring, courageous

audentĭ·a -ae *f* daring, boldness

audĕō audēre ausus sum *vt* to dare, venture, risk; **vix ausim** (*old perf subj*) **credere** I could scarcely dare to believe; *vi* to dare, be bold

audĭ·ens -entis *m* hearer, listener; *m pl* audience

audientĭ·a -ae *f* hearing, attention; **audientiam facere** to command attention, to command silence

aud·ĭō -īre -īvī or **-ĭī ĭtum** *vt* to hear, listen to, give attention to; to hear, be taught by, learn from; to hear, listen to, grant; to accept, agree with, approve, yield to, grant, allow; to listen to, obey; to be called, be named, be reported, be regarded

audītĭ·ō -ōnis *f* hearsay, rumor, report, news

audītōr·ium -iī or **-ī** *n* lecture hall; the audience

audīt·us -ūs *m* sense of hearing; a hearing; report, rumor

aufĕrō auferre abstŭlī ablātum *vt* to bear or take away, bear off, remove, withdraw; to snatch away, steal, rob; to sweep away, kill, destroy; to gain, obtain, receive, get; to learn, understand; to mislead, lead into a digression; **auferri e conspectu** to disappear from sight

Aufĭd·us -ī *m* river in Apulia

au·fugĭō -fugĕre -fūgī *vt* to escape, flee from; *vi* to escape, run away

Augĕ·ās -ae *m* king of Elis whose stables Hercules cleaned by diverting the River Alpheus through them

augĕō augēre auxī auctum *vt* to increase, enlarge, augment, spread; to magnify, extol, exalt; to exaggerate; to enrich; to honor, advance, promote; to feed (*flame*)

augesc·ō -ĕre *vi* to begin to grow; to become larger, increase

aug·ur -ŭris *m* or *f* augur (*priest who foretold the future by observing the flight of birds, lightning, etc.*), prophet, seer

augurāl·is -e *adj* of divination; augur's; *n* area in Ròman camp where the general took auspices

augurātĭ·ō **-ōnis** *f* prophesying

augurātō *adv* after taking the auguries

augurāt·us **-ūs** *m* office of augur

augur·ĭum **-ĭī** or **-ī** *n* observation of omens, interpretation of omen, augury; sign, omen; prophesy, prediction, forecast; foreboding

auguri·us **-a** **-um** *adj* of augurs; **jus augurĭum** the right to take auguries

augŭr·ō **-āre** or **augur·or** **-ārī** **-ātus sum** *vt* to consult by augury; to consecrate by augury; to conjecture, imagine; to foretell, predict, prophesy; *vi* to act as augur; to take auspices; to play augur

August·a **-ae** *f* (*in imperial period*) mother, wife, daughter, or sister of the emperor

Augustāl·is **-e** *adj* of Augustus; *n pl* games in honor of Augustus; **sodales Augustales** priests of deified Augustus

Augustān·us **-a** **-um** *adj* Augustan; imperial

augustē *adv* reverently

august·us **-a** **-um** *adj* august, sacred, venerable; majestic, magnificent

August·us **-a** **-um** *adj* Augustan, imperial; cognomen of Octavius Caesar and of subsequent emperors; **mensis Augustus** August

aul·a **-ae** *f* inner court, hall (*of house*); palace; royal court; people of the royal court, the court

aulae·um **-ī** *n* curtain, canopy; theater curtain; bed cover, sofa cover, tapestry

aulic·us **-a** **-um** *adj* courtly, princely; *n pl* courtiers

Aul·is **-is** or **-ĭdis** *f* port in Boeotia from which the Greeks sailed for Troy

auloed·us **-ī** *m* singer (*accompanied by flute*)

aur·a **-ae** *f* breeze, breath of air, wind; air, atmosphere; heights, heaven; upper world; odor, exhalation; daylight, publicity; **ad auras ferre** to make known, publicize; **ad auras venire** to come to the upper world; **auram captare** to sniff the air; **aura popularis** popular favor; **auras fugere** to hide; **aura spei** breath of hope

aurāri·us **-a** **-um** *adj* of gold, golden, gold; *f* gold mine

aurāt·us **-a** **-um** *adj* decorated with gold, made of ʼgold, gold-plated, golden; glittering

aureŏl·us **-a** **-um** *adj* gold; splendid

aurĕ·us **-a** **-um** *adj* of gold, golden; gilded; beautiful, magnificent, splendid; *m* gold coin

auricŏm·us **-a** **-um** *adj* golden-haired; with golden foliage

auricŭl·a *f* external ear, ear

aurif·er **-ĕra** **-ĕrum** *adj* producing or containing gold; (of tree) bearing golden apples

aurif·ex **-ĭcis** *m* goldsmith

aurīg·a **-ae** *m* or *f* charioteer, driver; (fig) pilot

Aurīg·a **-ae** *m* Auriga, Wagoner (*constellation*)

aurigĕn·a **-ae** *m* offspring of gold (*i.e., Perseus*)

aurīg·er **-ĕra** **-ĕrum** *adj* gold-bearing; gilded

aurīg·ō **-āre** *vi* to drive a chariot, compete in chariot race

aur·is **-is** *f* ear; *f pl* listeners; critical ears; **aurem admovere** to listen; **auribus servire** to flatter; **auris adhibere** to be attentive, pay attention; **in aurem dextram** or **in aurem utramvis dormire** to sleep soundly, i.e., to be unconcerned

aurītŭl·us **-ī** *m* ass

aurīt·us **-a** **-um** *adj* long-eared; attentive; nosey; **testis aurītus** witness by hearsay only; *m* rabbit

aurōr·a **-ae** *f* morning, dawn, daybreak; the Orient, the East

Aurōr·a **-ae** *f* goddess of dawn

aur·um **-ī** *n* gold; color of gold, golden luster; gold cup; gold necklace; gold jewelry; gold plate; golden fleece; gold money; Golden Age

auscultātĭ·ō **-ōnis** *f* obedience

auscultāt·or **-ōris** *m* listener

auscult·ō **-āre** *vt* to hear (*with attention*), listen to; to overhear; *vi* (with *dat*) to obey, listen to

ausim see **audeo**

Ausŏn·ēs **-um** *m pl* Ausonians (*ancient inhabitants of central Italy*)

Ausonĭd·ae **-ārum** *m pl* Italians

Ausonĭ·us **-a** **-um** *adj* Ausonian, Italian; *m pl* Ausonians, Italians; *f* Ausonia, Italy

ausp·ex **-ĭcis** *m* augur, soothsayer; author, founder, leader, director, protector; *m pl* witnesses (*at marriage ceremony*)

auspicātō *adv* after taking the auspices; under good omens, at a fortunate moment

auspicāt·us **-a** **-um** *adj* consecrated (*by auguries*); auspicious, favorable, lucky

auspic·ium **-ĭī** or **-ī** *n* divination (*through observation of flight of birds*), auspices; sign, omen, premonition; command, leadership, guidance, authority; right, power, will, inclination; **auspicium habere** to have the right to take auspices; **auspicium facere** (of birds) to give a sign, to yield an omen

auspic·or **-ārī** **-ātus sum** *vt* to begin, take up; *vi* to take auspices; to make a start

aust·er **-rī** *m* south wind; the South

austērē *adv* austerely, severely

austērĭt·ās **-ātis** *f* austerity

austēr·us **-a** **-um** *adj* austere, stern, harsh (*person*); pungent (*smell*); harsh (*taste*); drab, dark (*color*); serious (*talk*); gloomy, sad, hard (*circumstances*)

austrāl·is -e *adj* southern; **cingulus, regio,** or **ora australis** torrid zone

austrīn·us -a -um *adj* from the south, southerly; southern

aus·us -a -um *pp* of **audeo**; *n* daring attempt, enterprise, adventure

aut *conj* or; (correcting what precedes) or, or rather, or else; (adding emphatic alternative) or at least; **aut . . . aut** either . . . or

autem *conj* (regularly follows an emphatic word) but, on the other hand, however; (in a transition) but, and now

autheps·a -ae *f* cooker, boiler (*utensil*)

autogrāph·us -a -um *adj* written with one's own hand, autograph

Autolўc·us -ī *m* father of Anticlea, maternal grandfather of Ulysses, and famous robber

automăt·on -ī *n* automaton

automăt·us -a -um *adj* automatic, spontaneous, voluntary

Automĕd·ōn -ontis *m* charioteer of Achilles

Autonŏ·ē -ēs *f* daughter of Cadmus, wife of Aristaeus, and mother of Actaeon

autumnāl·is -e *adj* autumn, autumnal

autumn·us -a -um *adj* autumn, autumnal; *m* autumn

autŭm·ō -āre *vt* to assert, affirm, say

auxiliār·ēs -ĭum *m pl* auxiliary troops

auxiliār·is -e *adj* auxiliary

auxiliărĭ·us -a -um *adj* auxiliary

auxiliāt·or -ōris *m* helper, assistant

auxiliāt·us -ūs *m* aid

auxil·or -ārī -ātus sum *vi* (with *dat*) **a** to help, aid, assist; **b** to relieve, heal, cure

auxil·ium -iī or -ī *n* help, aid, assistance; *n pl* auxiliary troops, auxiliaries; military force, military power; **auxilio esse** (with *dat*) to be of assistance to

avārē *adv* greedily

avārĭter *adv* greedily

avăritĭ·a -ae *f* greed, selfishness, avarice; gluttony

avăritĭ·ēs -ēī *f* avarice

avār·us -a -um *adj* greedy, covetous, avaricious; (with *genit*) desirous of, eager for

avē see **aveo**

ā·vĕhō -vehĕre -vexī -vectum *vt* to carry away; **avehi** to ride away, sail away

ā·vellō -vellĕre -vellī (or -vulsī or -volsī) -vulsum (or -volsum) *vt* to pull or pluck away; to tear off; to separate, remove; **avelli** or **se avellere** (with **ab** + *abl*) to tear oneself away from, withdraw from

avēn·a -ae *f* oats; reed, stalk, a straw; shepherd's pipe

Aventīn·us -a -um *adj* Aventine; *m & n* Aventine Hill (*one of the seven hills of Rome*)

av·ĕō -ēre *vt* to wish, desire, long for, crave; (with *inf*) to wish to, long to; *vi* to say good-bye; **avel** or **avetel** haill, hello!; good morning!; farewell!, good-bye!

Avernāl·is -e *adj* of Lake Avernus

Avern·us -a -um *adj* without birds; of Lake Avernus; *m* Lake Avernus (*near Cumae, said to be an entrance to the lower world*)

āverrunc·ō -āre *vt* to avert

āversābĭl·is -e *adj* abominable

āvers·or -ārī -ātus sum *vt* to repulse, reject, refuse, decline, shun, avoid, send away; *vi* to turn away (*in displeasure, contempt, shame, etc.*)

āvers·or -ōris *m* embezzler

āvers·us -a -um *adj* turned away (*in flight*); rear, in the rear; disinclined, alienated, unfavorable, hostile; (with *dat* or **ab** + *abl*) averse to, hostile to, opposed to, estranged from; *n* the back part, the back; *n pl* the back parts, the back; hinterland; **in adversum** backwards

ā·vertō (or **ā·vortō**) -vertĕre -vertī -versum *vt* to turn away, avert; to embezzle, misappropriate; to divert; to alienate; **se avertere** to retire; *vi* to withdraw, retire

avĭ·a -ae *f* grandmother; old wives' tale

āvĭ·a -ōrum *n pl* pathless, lonely places

aviārĭ·us -a -um *adj* of birds, bird; *n* aviary; haunt of wild birds

avĭdē *adv* eagerly, greedily

avidĭt·ās -ātis *f* eagerness, longing, great desire; avarice

avĭd·us -a -um *adj* eager, earnest, greedy; hungry, greedy, voracious, gluttonous, insatiable; (with *genit* or *dat* or with **in** + *acc*) desirous of, eager for

av·is -is *f* bird; sign, omen; **avis alba** rarity

avīt·us -a -um *adj* grandfather's, ancestral; old

āvĭ·us -a -um *adj* out-of-the-way, lonely; trackless, pathless, untrodden; wandering, straying; going astray

āvocāment·um -ī *n* diversion, recreation

āvocātĭ·ō -ōnis *f* distraction, diversion

āvŏc·ō -āre *vt* to call away; to divert, remove, withdraw; to divert, amuse

āvŏl·ō -āre *vi* to fly away; to hasten away, dash off

āvulsus *pp* of **avello**

avuncŭl·us -ī *m* mother's brother, maternal uncle; **avunculus magnus** great-uncle; **avunculus major** great-great-uncle

av·us -ī *m* grandfather; forefather, ancestor

Axěl·on -ŏnis *f* city on Euphrates

Babylōni·a -ae *f* country between Tigris and Euphrates — *wait this belongs to B*

Axěn·us -ī *m* Black Sea

axicl·a -ae *f* scissors

axill·a -ae *f* armpit

ax·is -is *m* axle; chariot, wagon; axis, pole; North Pole; sky; the heavens; region, country; board, plank

B

babae *interj* wonderful!, strange!

Babȳl·ōn -ōnis *f* city on Euphrates

Babylōni·a -ae *f* country between Tigris and Euphrates

bāc·a -ae *f* berry; olive; fruit; pearl

bācāt·us -a -um *adj* adorned with pearls

bacc·ar -āris *n* cyclamen (*plant whose root yields fragrant oil*)

Bacch·a -ae *f* bacchante, maenad

bacchābund·us -a -um *adj* raving, riotous

Bacchān·al -ālis *n* place sacred to Bacchus; *n pl* bacchanalian orgies

bacchāti·ō -ōnis *f* orgy; revelry

bacch·or -ārī -ātus sum *vi* to celebrate the festival of Bacchus; to revel, rave, rage

Bacch·us -ī *m* god of wine; (fig) vine; (fig) wine

bācif·er -ěra -ěrum *adj* bearing berries or olives

bacill·um -ī *n* small staff, wand; lictor's staff

bacŭl·um -ī *n* or **bacŭl·us -ī** *m* stick; staff; scepter

badiss·ō -āre *vi* to go, walk

Baetic·us -a -um *adj* of the Baetis; *f* Baetica (*Roman province*)

Baet·is -is *m* river in Spain

Bāi·ae -ārum *f pl* resort town at northern extremity of Bay of Naples

bājŭl·ō -āre *vt* to carry, bear

bājŭl·us -ī *m* porter; day laborer

bālaen·a -ae *f* whale

balanāt·us -a -um *adj* anointed with balsam; embalmed

balăn·us -ī *m* or *f* acorn; date; balsam; shell-fish

balătr·ō -ōnis *m* jester, buffoon

bālāt·us -ūs *m* bleating

balb·us -a -um *adj* stammering

balbūti·ō -īre *vt & vi* to stammer, stutter

balině·um -ī *n* bath

ballist·a -ae *f* large military device for hurling stones; heavy artillery

ballistār·ium -iī or **-ī** *n* artillery emplacement

balně·ae -ārum *f pl* baths

balneāri·us -a -um *adj* of a bath; *n pl* baths

balneāt·or -ōris *m* bath superintendent

balneŏl·ae -ārum *f pl* baths

balneŏl·um -ī *n* small bath

balně·um -ī *n* bath

bāl·ō -āre *vi* to bleat

balsăm·um -ī *n* balsam; balsam tree

baltě·us -ī *m* belt; baldric; girdle

baptister·ium -iī or **-ī** *n* bath; swimming pool

barăthr·um -ī *n* abyss, chasm, pit; lower world

barb·a -ae *f* beard

barbărē *adv* in a foreign language; barbarously, cruelly

barbari·a -ae or **barbarī·ēs -ēī** *f* foreign country, strange land; rudeness, want of culture

barbaric·us -a -um *adj* foreign, outlandish

barbariēs see **barbaria**

barbăr·us -a -um *adj* foreign; barbarous, savage, uncivilized, rude; *m* foreigner; barbarian

barbātŭl·us -a -um *adj* wearing a small beard

barbāt·us -a -um *adj* bearded; adult; old-time; *m* old-timer; philosopher, longhair; goat

barbig·er -ěra -ěrum *adj* wearing a beard, bearded

barbĭt·os -ī *m* lyre; lute

barbŭl·a -ae *f* small beard

bard·us -a -um *adj* stupid, dull

bard·us -ī *m* bard

băr·ō -ōnis *m* dunce, blockhead

barr·us -ī *m* elephant

bāsiāti·ō -ōnis *f* kissing; kiss

basilic·us -a -um *adj* royal; splendid; *f* public building, basilica (*used as law court and exchange*); portico

bāsi·ō -āre *vt* to kiss

bas·is -is *f* base, foundation, support; pedestal

bās·ium -iī or **-ī** *n* kiss

Bassăr·eus -ĕī *m* Bacchus

batill·um -ī *n* brazier

battŭ·ō -ěre -ī *vt* to beat, pound

beātē *adv* happily

beātĭt·ās -ātis *f* happiness

beātitūd·ō -inis *f* happiness

beāt·us -a -um *adj* happy; prosperous, rich; fertile; abundant; *n* happiness

Bēlid·ēs -um *f pl* descendants of Belus, the Danaids, who killed their husbands on their wedding night

bellāri·a -ōrum *n pl* dessert

bellăt·or -ōris *adj* warlike; valorous; spirited; *m* warrior

bellātr·ix -īcis *adj* warlike, skilled in war; *f* warrior (*female*)

bellē *adv* prettily, neatly, nicely, well

Bellerŏph·ōn -ontis *m* slayer of Chimaera and rider of Pegasus

bellicōs·us -a -um *adj* warlike, martial, valorous

bellĭc·us -a -um *adj* war, military; warlike, fierce; *n* bugle; bugle call

bellĭg·er -ĕra -ĕrum *adj* belligerent, warlike, aggressive; martial; valiant

bellĭgĕr·ō -āre or **belligĕr·or -ārī -ātus sum** *vi* to wage war, fight

bellĭpŏt·ens -entis *adj* mighty or valiant in war; *m* Mars

bell·ō -āre or **bell·or -ārī -ātus sum** *vi* to wage war, fight

Bellōn·a -ae *f* Roman goddess of war

bellŭl·us -a -um *adj* pretty, lovely, cute, fine

bell·um -ī *n* war; battle

bēlŭ·a -ae *f* beast, monster, brute

bēluōs·us -a -um *adj* full of monsters

Bēl·us -ī *m* Baal; king of Tyre and father of Dido; king of Egypt, father of Danaus and Aegyptus

bene *adv* well; thoroughly; very, quite

bene·dīcō -dīcĕre -dīxī -dictum *vt* to speak well of, praise; (eccl) to bless

beneficentĭ·a -ae *f* beneficence, kindness

beneficiārī·ī -ōrum *m pl* soldiers exempt from menial tasks

benefĭc·ium -iī or **-ī** *n* kindness, favor, benefit, service; help, support; promotion; right, privilege

benefĭc·us -a -um *adj* generous, liberal, obliging

Benevent·um -ī *n* town in Samnium in S. Italy

benevŏlē *adv* kindly

benevŏl·ens -entis *adj* kind-hearted, obliging

benevolentĭ·a -ae *f* benevolence, kindness, goodwill; favor

benevŏl·us -a -um *adj* kind, friendly; devoted, faithful

benignē *adv* in a friendly manner, kindly, courteously; mildly, indulgently; liberally, generously

benignit·ās -ātis *f* kindness, friendliness, courtesy; liberality, bounty

benign·us -a -um *adj* kind-hearted; mild, affable; liberal; favorable; bounteous, fruitful

be·ō -āre *vt* to make happy; to bless; to enrich; to refresh

Berecynt·us -ī *m* mountain in Phrygia sacred to Cybele

bēryll·us -ī *m* precious stone, beryl

bēs bessis *m* two thirds

bestĭ·a -ae *f* beast, wild beast

bestiārĭ·us -a -um *adj* of wild beasts; *m* wild-beast fighter

bestiŏl·a -ae *f* little beast

bēt·a -ae *f* beet

bēta (indecl) *n* second letter of Greek alphabet

bibliopōl·a -ae *m* bookseller

bibliothēc·a -ae *f* library

bibliothēcār·ius -iī or **-ī** *m* librarian

bib·ō -ĕre -ī *vt* to drink; to visit, reach, live near (*river*); (fig) to take in, absorb, listen eagerly to

bibŭl·us -a -um *adj* fond of drinking; absorbent; thirsty

bi·ceps -cĭpĭtis *adj* two-headed; twin-peaked

biclīn·ium -iī or **-ī** *n* table for two

bicŏl·or -ōris *adj* two-colored

bicorn·is -e *adj* two-horned; two-pronged

bid·ens -entis *adj* with two teeth; with two points; two-pronged; *m* hoe, mattock; sacrificial animal; sheep

bident·al -ālis *n* place struck by lightning

bīdŭ·um -ī *n* period of two days; two days

bienn·ium -iī or **-ī** *n* period of two years; two years

bifārĭam *adv* on both sides, twofold, double, in two parts, in two directions

bifārĭ·us -a -um *adj* double, twofold

bif·er -ĕra -ĕrum *adj* bearing fruit twice a year; of twofold form

bifĭd·us -a -um *adj* split in two, forked, cloven

bifŏr·is -e *adj* having two doors; having two holes or openings; double

biformāt·us -a -um *adj* double, having two forms

biform·is -e *adj* double, having two forms

bifr·ons -ontis *adj* two-headed; two-faced

bifurc·us -a -um *adj* two-pronged; forked

bīg·a -ae *f* or **bīg·ae -ārum** *f pl* span of horses, team; two-horse chariot

bijŭg·ī -ōrum *m pl* team of horses; two-horse chariot

bijŭg·is -e *adj* yoked two together; drawn by a pair of horses

bijŭg·us -a -um *adj* yoked two together; two-horse

bilĭbr·is -e *adj* two-pound

bilingu·is -e *adj* two-tongued; bilingual; hypercritical, deceitful, false

bīl·is -is *f* gall, bile; wrath, anger; **bīlis atra** melancholy; madness

bimăr·is -e *adj* situated between two seas

bimarīt·us -ī *m* bigamist

bimāt·er -ris *adj* having two mothers

bimembr·is -e *adj* half man, half beast

bimembr·is -is *m* centaur

bimestr·is -e *adj* two-month-old; lasting two months

bimŭl·us -a -um *adj* two-year-old

bīm·us -a -um *adj* two-year-old; for two years

bīn·ī -ae -a *adj* two by two; two to each, two each; two at a time; a pair of

binoct·ium -iī or **-ī** *n* two nights

binōmin·is -e *adj* having two names

bipalm·is -e *adj* two spans long

bipart·iō -īre — -ītum *vt* to divide into two parts; to bisect

bipartītō *adv* in two parts

bipăt·ens -entis *adj* open in two directions

bipedāl·is -e *adj* two feet long, broad, thick, or high

bipennif·er -ĕra -ĕrum *adj* wielding a two-edged ax

bipenn·is -e *adj* two-edged; *f* two-edged ax

bip·ēs -ĕdis *adj* two-footed, biped

birēm·is -e *adj* two-oared; with two banks of oars; *f* ship with two banks of oars

bis *adv* twice

Bistŏn·ēs -um *m pl* fierce tribesmen in Thessaly

bisulc·us -a -um *adj* split, cloven; forked

bīt·ō -ĕre *vi* to go

bitūm·en -ĭnis *n* bitumen, asphalt

bivi·us -a -um *adj* two-way; *n* crossroads, intersection

blaes·us -a -um *adj* lisping; indistinct

blandē *adv* flatteringly; courteously

blandiloquentĭ·a -ae *f* flattery

blandiloquentŭl·us -a -um *adj* smooth-tongued

blandiment·um -ī *n* flattery, compliment; charm

bland·ior -īrī -ītus sum *vt* to flatter; to coax; to allure; to please

blandĭter *adv* flatteringly

blanditĭ·a -ae *f* caress, flattery, compliment; charm

blandītim *adv* flatteringly

bland·us -a -um *adj* smooth; flattering, fawning; alluring, charming, winsome, pleasant

blatĕr·ō -āre *vi* to talk foolishly, to babble

blatt·a -ae *f* cockroach; moth

blenn·us -ī *m* idiot, blockhead

blitĕ·us -a -um *adj* silly; tasteless

blit·um -ī *n* tasteless vegetable, kind of spinach

boārī·us -a -um *adj* cattle

Boeotĭ·a -ae *f* district north of Attica in central Greece, the capital of which was Thebes

bōlēt·us -ī *n* mushroom

bol·us -ī *m* throw (*of the dice*); cast (*of the net*); (fig) haul, piece of good luck, gain; choice morsel

bombax *interj* strange!; indeed!

bomb·us -ī *m* booming; buzzing, humming

bombўcīn·us -a -um *adj* silk, silken

bomb·ўx -ўcis *m* silkworm; silk; silk garment

Bon·a De·a (*genit:* **Bon·ae De·ae**) *f* goddess of chastity and fertility

bonĭt·ās -ātis *f* goodness, integrity; kindness, benevolence

bon·us -a -um *adj* good; honest, virtuous; faithful, patriotic; fit, suitable; able, clever; brave; noble; auspicious, favorable; useful, advantageous; *n* good; profit, advantage; *n pl* goods, property

bo·ō -āre *vi* to cry aloud; to roar

Boŏt·ēs -ae *m* constellation containing the bright star Arcturus

borĕ·as -ae *m* north wind

borĕ·us -a -um *adj* north, northern

bōs bovis *m* or *f* ox, bull; cow

Bospŏr·us -ī *m* strait between Thrace and Asia Minor, connecting Propontis and Black Sea

botŭl·us -ī *m* sausage

bovīl·e -is *n* ox stall

bovill·us -a -um *adj* cattle

brāc·ae -ārum *f pl* pants, trousers

brācāt·us -a -um *adj* wearing trousers; foreign, barbarian; effeminate

bracchiāl·is -ē *adj* of the arm

bracchiŏl·um -ī *n* dainty arm

bracch·īum -īī or **-ī** *n* arm, lower arm; claw; bough; tendril; arm of the sea; sail yard

bractĕ·a -ae *f* gold leaf; gold foil

bractĕŏl·a -ae *f* very thin gold leaf

brassĭc·a -ae *f* cabbage

breviār·ium -ĭī or **-ī** *n* summary, abridgement; statistics

brevicŭl·us -a -um *adj* rather short

brevilŏqu·ens -entis *adj* brief (*in speech*)

breviloquentĭ·a -ae *f* brevity

brevī *adv* briefly, in a few words; shortly, in a short time

brĕv·is -e *adj* short, little, brief; concise; small; shallow; narrow; *n pl* shoals, shallows

brevĭt·ās -ātis *f* brevity; smallness; shortness

brevĭter *adv* shortly, briefly

Britannĭ·a -ae *f* Britain; British Isles

Brom·ĭus -ĭī or **-ī** *m* Bacchus

brūm·a -ae *f* winter solstice; winter; winter's cold

brūmāl·is -e *adj* wintry

Brundis·ium -ĭī or **-ī** *n* port in S.E. Italy on Adriatic Sea

Bruttĭ·ī -ōrum *m pl* inhabitants of toe of Italy

Brūt·us -ī *m* Lucius Junius Brutus (*credited with having driven out the last Roman king, Tarquinius Superbus*); Marcus Junius Brutus (*one of the murderers of Julius Caesar*)

brūt·us -a -um *adj* heavy, unwieldy; dull, stupid

būbīl·e -is *n* ox stall

būb·ō -ōnis *m* owl

būbŭl·a -ae *f* beef

bubulcĭt·or -ārī -ātus sum *vi* to be a herdsman; to ride herd

bubulc·us -ī *m* cowherd; plowman

būbŭl·us -a -um *adj* of cows or oxen

būcaed·a -ae *m* flogged slave

bucc·a -ae *f* cheek; loudmouthed person; trumpeter; parasite; mouthful

buccell·a -ae *f* small mouthful; morsel

buccŭl·a -ae *f.* little cheek; visor

buccŭlent·us -a -um *adj* loudmouthed

būcĕr(ĭ)·us -a -um *adj* horned

būcĭn·a -ae *f* (curved) trumpet; war trumpet; shepherd's horn

būcĭnāt·or -ōris *m* trumpeter

būcolĭc·us -a -um *adj* pastoral, bucolic

būcŭl·a -ae *f* heifer

būf·ō -ōnis m toad

bulb·us -ī m onion

būl·ē -ēs f (Greek) council, senate

būleut·a -ae m councilor

būleutēr·ium -iī or **-ī** n meeting place of Greek council

bull·a -ae f bubble; boss, stud, knob; amulet; badge (*symbol of boyhood*)

bullāt·us -a -um adj inflated, bombastic; studded; wearing a bulla, i.e., still a child

būmast·us -ī f species of grape with large clusters

būr·is -is m curved handle of plow

bustirăp·us -ī m ghoul, grave robber

bustuārī·us -a -um adj of a tomb or pyre

bust·um -ī n pyre; tomb, sepulcher

buxif·er -ĕra -ĕrum adj producing boxwood trees

bux·um -ī n boxwood; (spinning) top; comb; writing tablet (*made of boxwood*)

bux·us -ī f boxwood tree

Byzant·ium -iī or **-ī** n city on the Bosporus, later named Constantinople

C

caball·us -ī m pack horse, nag, hack

cachinnātī·ō -ōnis f loud or immoderate laughter

cachinn·ō -āre vi to laugh loud; to roar (*with laughter*)

cachinn·ō -ōnis m scoffer

cachinn·us -ī m loud laugh; jeering; rippling, roaring

cac·ō -āre vt to defile; vi to defecate

cacoēth·es -is n malignant disease; itch

cacūm·en -ĭnis n point, tip, top, peak

cacūmĭn·ō -āre vt to make pointed; to sharpen

Căc·us -ī m son of Vulcan, a giant who lived on the Aventine Hill, killed by Hercules

cadāv·er -ĕris n corpse, carcass

cadāverōs·us -a -um adj cadaverous, ghastly

Cadmē·us -a -um adj Cadmean; Theban; f citadel of Thebes

Cadm·us -ī m son of Phoenician king Agenor, brother of Europa, and founder of Thebes

cadō cadĕre cecĭdī cāsum vi to fall, sink, drop; to be slain, die, be sacrificed; to happen; to belong, refer, be suitable, apply; to abate, subside, flag, decline, decay, vanish, fail, cease; to end, close

cadūceāt·or -ōris m herald

cadūcĕ·us -ī m herald's staff, caduceus

cadūcif·er -ĕra -ĕrum adj with herald's staff

cadūc·us -a -um adj falling, fallen; inclined to fall; frail, perishable, transitory; vain, futile, ineffectual; (law) lapsed, without heir

cad·us -ī m jar, flask, jug

caecigĕn·us -a -um adj born blind

caecĭt·ās -ātis f blindness

caec·ō -āre vt to make blind; to make obscure

Caecŭb·um -ī n famous wine from S. Latium

caec·us -a -um adj blind; invisible; vague, random, aimless, uncertain, unknown; making invisible, blinding; dark, gloomy, obscure

caed·ēs -is f murder, slaughter, massacre; bloodshed, gore; the slain

caed·ō caedĕre cecīdī caesum vt to hack at, chop; to strike, beat; to fell, cut down, cut off, cut to pieces; to kill, murder

caelām·en -ĭnis n engraving, basrelief

caelāt·or -ōris m engraver

caelātūr·a -ae f engraving

cael·ebs -ĭbis adj unmarried, single (*whether bachelor or widower*)

cael·es -ĭtis adj heavenly, celestial

caelest·ia -ium n pl heavenly bodies

caelest·is -e adj heavenly, celestial; divine, supernatural

caelest·is -is m deity

caelibāt·us -ūs m celibacy

caelicŏl·a -ae m god

caelif·er -ĕra -ĕrum adj supporting the sky

caelipŏt·ens -entis adj powerful in heaven

caelĭt·ēs -um m pl inhabitants of heaven, gods

Cael·ius Mon·s (*genit:* **Cael·iī** or **-ī Mon·tis**) m Caelian Hill in Rome

cael·ō -āre vt to engrave in relief, to emboss, to carve; to cast; to fashion, compose; to adorn

cael·um -ī n sky, heaven, heavens; air, climate, weather; engraver's chisel, burin

caement·um -ī n quarry stone; rubble; cement

caenōs·us -a -um adj dirty, filthy, muddy

caen·um -ī n dirt, filth, mud, mire

caep·a -ae f or **caep·e -is** n onion

Caere (indecl) n city in Etruria

caerimōnī·a -ae f rite; ritual, religious ceremony; sanctity, sacredness; awe, reverence, veneration

caerŭl·a -ōrum n pl sea

caerŭlĕ·us or **caerŭl·us -a -um** adj blue, azure, dark-blue, green, dark-green; dark, gloomy

Caes·ar -ăris m C. Julius Caesar (102?-44 B.C.)

caesariāt·us -a -um *adj* long-haired

caesari·ēs -ēī *f* hair

caesici·us -a -um *adj* bluish, dark blue

caesim *adv* by cutting; in short clauses, in a clipped style

caesī·us -a -um *adj* bluish-grey; blue-eyed; gray-eyed; cat-eyed

caesp·es -ĭtis *m* sod, turf, grass; altar of sod

caest·us -ūs *m* boxing glove

caetr·a -ae *f* short Spanish shield

caetrāt·us -a -um *adj* armed with a shield

Caiēt·a -ae *f* nurse of Aeneas; town on coast of Latium

Caius see Gaius

Calǎb·er -ra -rum *adj* Calabrian

Calabri·a -ae *f* S.W. peninsula of Italy

Calǎ·is -is *m* son of Boreas and Orithyia, and brother of Zetes

calamist·er -rī *m* hair curler, curling iron; (rhet) flowery language

calamistrāt·um -a -um *adj* curled (*with a hair curler*)

calamistr·um -ī *n* curling iron

calamit·ās -ātis *f* loss, injury, damage; misfortune, calamity, disaster; military defeat

calamitōsē *adv* unfortunately

calamitōs·us -a -um *adj* disastrous, ruinous, destructive; exposed to injury, suffering great damage, unfortunate

calǎm·us -ī *m* reed, stalk, pen; arrow; fishing rod; pipe

calathisc·us -ī *m* small wicker basket

calǎth·us -ī *m* wicker basket; milk pail; wine cup

calāt·or -ōris *m* servant, attendant

calc·ar -āris *n* spur; stimulus

calcǎrě·um -ī *n* heel

calceāment·um -ī *n* shoe

calceāt·us -ūs *m* sandal, shoe

calcě·ō -āre *vt* to furnish with shoes, to shoe

calceolār·ĭus -ĭī or -ī *m* shoemaker

calcěŏl·us -ī *m* small shoe, half-boot

calcě·us -ī *m* shoe, half-boot

Calch·ās -antis *m* Greek prophet at Troy

calcītr·ō -āre *vi* to kick; to resist; to be stubborn; to kick up one's heels

calcītr·ō -ōnis *m* blusterer

calc·ō -āre *vt* to tread, tread under foot; to trample on, oppress; to scorn, abuse

calculāt·or -ōris *m* arithmetic teacher; accountant, bookkeeper

calcŭl·us -ī *m* pebble, stone; kidney stone; counter of an abacus; stone used in games; stone used in voting; vote, sentence, decision

caldāri·us -a -um *adj* warm-water; *n* hot bath

caldus see calidus

Calēdoni·a -ae *f* Highlands of Scotland

cale·faciō or cal·faciō -facěre

-fēcī -factum *vt* to warm, heat; to rouse up, excite, make angry

calefact·ō -āre *vt* to warm, heat

Calend·ae -ārum *f pl* first day of Roman month, calends

calendār·ĭum -ĭī or -ī *n* account book

cal·ěō -ēre -ŭī *vi* to be warm, hot; to feel warm; to glow; to be hot with passion; to be troubled, be perplexed; to be zealously pursued; to be new or fresh

Cal·ēs -ĭum *f pl* Campanian town famous for its wine

cal·escō -escěre -ŭī *vi* to get warm or hot; to become excited, be inflamed

calĭd·a or cald·a -ae *f* warm water

calĭdē *adv* quickly, promptly

calĭd·us or cald·us -a -um *adj* warm, hot; eager, rash, hasty, hotheaded, vehement; quick, ready, prompt; *n* warm drink; *f* see calida

caliendr·um -ī *n* wig (*for women*)

calĭg·a -ae *f* shoe, soldier's boot; soldier

calĭgāt·us -a -um *adj* wearing soldier's boots; (of a peasant) wearing clodhoppers

cālĭg·ō -ĭnis *f* mist, vapor, fog; gloom, darkness, obscurity; mental blindness; calamity, affliction

cālĭg·ō -āre *vt* to veil in darkness, to obscure; to make dizzy; *vi* to steam, reek; to be wrapped in mist or darkness; to be blind, grope

calĭgŭl·a -ae *f* small military boot

Calĭgŭl·a -ae *m* pet name given by the soldiers to Gaius Caesar when he was a small boy

cal·ix -ĭcis *m* cup; pot; (fig) wine

callaĭn·us -a -um *adj* turquoise

call·ěō -ēre -ŭī *vt* to know by experience or practice, to understand; (with *inf*) to know how to; *vi* to be callous, to be thick-skinned; to be insensible; to be experienced, clever, skillful

callĭdĭt·ās -ātis *f* skill; shrewdness; cunning, craft

callĭdē *adv* skillfully, expertly, shrewdly; well; cunningly

callĭd·us -a -um *adj* expert, adroit, skillful; ingenious, prudent, dexterous; clever, shrewd; sly, cunning, crafty, calculating

Callĭmǎch·us -ī *m* famous Alexandrine poet and grammarian (*c.* 270 B.C.)

Calliŏp·ē -ēs or Calliopē·a -ae *f* Calliope (*muse of epic poetry*)

call·is -is *m* stony, uneven footpath; mountain path; cattle trail; mountain pasture; mountain pass, defile

Callist·ō -ūs *f* daughter of Lycaon, king of Arcadia, who was changed into the constellation Helice or Ursa Major

callōs·us -a -um *adj* hard-skinned; thick-skinned, callous; solid, hard, thick

call·um -ī *m* hard or thick skin; insensibility, stupidity

cal·ō -āre *vt* to call out, proclaim; to convoke

cāl·ō -ōnis *m* soldier's servant; menial servant, drudge

cal·or -ōris *m* warmth, heat, glow; passion, love; fire, zeal, impetuosity, vehemence

calth·a -ae *f* marigold

calthŭl·a -ae *f* yellow robe

calumni·a -ae *f* trickery; pretense, evasion; false statement, misrepresentation, fallacy; false accusation, malicious charge; conviction for malicious prosecution

calumniāt·or -ōris *m* malicious prosecutor, perverter of the law, pettifogger

calumni·or -ārī -ātus sum *vt* to accuse falsely; to misrepresent, calumniate; to blame unjustly; to put in a false light

calv·a -ae *f* scalp, bald head

calvit·ium -iī or **-ī** *n* baldness

calv·us -a -um *adj* bald

cal·x -cis *f* heel; (fig) foot, kick; **calcibus caedere** to kick

cal·x -cis *f* pebble; limestone, lime; finish line (*marked with lime*), goal; **ad calcem pervenire** to reach the goal; **ad carceres a calce revocari** to be recalled from the finish line to the starting gate; to have to start all over again

Calȳd·ōn -ōnis *f* town in Aetolia, scene of the famous boar hunt led by Meleager

Calyps·ō -ūs *f* nymph, daughter of Atlas, who entertained Ulysses on the island of Ogygia

camell·a -ae *f* drinking cup

camēl·us -ī *m* camel

Camēn·a -ae *f* Muse; poem; poetry

camēr·a -ae *f* vault, arched roof, arch; houseboat

Camerīn·um -ī *n* town in Umbria

Camill·a -ae *f* Volscian female warrior who assisted Turnus against Aeneas

Camill·us -ī *m* M. Furius Camillus, who freed Rome from the Gauls

camīn·us -ī *m* fireplace; furnace; forge; **oleum addere camino** to pour oil on the fire

cammăr·us -ī *m* lobster

Campāni·a -ae *f* district on E. coast of central Italy

campest·er -ris -re *adj* flat, level; overland (*march*); (of city) situated in a plain; (of army) fighting in a plain; (of sports, elections, etc.) held in the Campus Martius; *n* shorts (*worn in sports*); *n pl* flat lands

camp·us -ī *m* flat space, plain; sports field; level surface, surface (*of sea*); **Campus Martius** field near the Tiber used for sports, elections, military exercises, etc.

cam·ur -ŭra -ŭrum *adj* crooked, concave

canāl·is -is *m* pipe, conduit, gutter

cancell·ī -ōrum *m pl* railing, grating; barrier (*at sports, public events*); boundaries, limits

canc·er -rī *m* crab; the South; tropical heat; cancer (*disease*)

Canc·er -rī *m* Cancer (*northern zodiacal constellation; sign of the zodiac*)

cande·faciō -facĕre -fēcī -factum *vt* to make dazzling white; to make glow, make red-hot

candēl·a -ae *f* candle, torch, taper; waxed cord; **candelam apponere valvis** to set the house on fire

candelābr·um -ī *n* candlestick, candelabrum, chandelier; lamp stand

cand·ens -entis *adj* shining white, glittering, dazzling, glowing

cand·eō -ēre *vi* to be shining white, glitter, shine; to be white-hot

cand·escō -escĕre -ŭī *vi* to become white, begin to glisten; to get red-hot

candidātōri·us -a -um *adj* of a candidate, candidate's

candidāt·us -a -um *adj* clothed in white; *m* candidate for office

candidē *adv* in dazzling white; clearly, simply, sincerely

candidŭl·us -a -um *adj* pretty white

candid·us -a -um *adj* (*cf* **albus**) shiny white, white, bright, dazzling, gleaming, sparkling; fair, radiant (*complexion*); candid, open, sincere, frank (*person*); bright, cheerful (*circumstances*); clear, bright (*day*); (of winds) bringing clear weather; white, silvery (*poplar, hair, etc.*); clear, unaffected (*style*); clothed in white; **candida sententia** vote of acquittal

cand·or -ōris *m* glossy whiteness, brightness, radiance; candor, sincerity; naturalness (*of style*); brilliance (*of discourse*)

cān·ens -entis *adj* grey, white

cān·eō -ēre -ŭī *vi* to be grey, be white

cānesc·ō -ĕre *vi* to grow white, become grey; to grow old; (of discourse) to lose force, grow dull

can·ī -ōrum *m pl* grey hair

canīcŭl·a -ae *f* small dog, pup; (as term of abuse) little bitch

Canīcŭl·a -ae *f* Canicula, Sirius, Dog Star (*brightest star in Canis Major*)

canīn·us -a -um *adj* canine; snarling, spiteful, caustic; **canina littera** letter R

can·is -is *m* or *f* dog, hound; (term of reproach to denote vile person, enraged person, hanger-on, etc.) dog; worst throw (*in dice*)

Can·is -is *m* Canis Major (*constellation, of which the brightest star is Canicula*)

canistr·um -ī *n* wicker basket (*for bread, fruit, flowers, etc.*)

cānitĭ·ēs (*genit* not in use) *f* greyness; grey hair; old age

cann·a -ae *f* reed; reed pipe, flute
cannăb·is -ae *f* or **cannăb·um -ī** *n* hemp
Cann·ae -ārum *f pl* village in Apulia where Hannibal won great victory over Romans in 216 B.C.
canō canĕre cecĭnī cantum *vt* to sing; to play; to speak in a singsong tone; to sing the praises of, celebrate; to prophesy, predict, foretell; (mil) to blow, sound; **signa canĕre** to sound the signal for battle; *vi* to sing; to play; (of birds) to sing; (of roosters) to crow; (of frogs) to croak; **receptuī canĕre** to sound retreat; **tibiā canĕre** to play the flute
can·or -ōris *m* tune, sound, melody, song; tone (*of instruments*)
canōr·us -a -um *adj* melodious, musical; singsong, jingling; *n* melody, charm (*in speaking*)
Cantăbr·a -ae *f* district in N.W. Spain
cantăm·en -ĭnis *n* incantation, spell
cantăt·or -ōris *m* singer
canthăr·is -ĭdis *f* beetle; Spanish fly
canthăr·us -ī *m* wide-bellied drinking vessel with handles, tankard
canthēr·ius or **cantēr·ius -iī** or **-ī** *m* gelding; eunuch
canth·us -ī *m* iron tire; wheel
cantĭc·um -ī *n* song; aria in Roman comedy; (in delivery of speech) singsong
cantilēn·a -ae *f* old song, gossip; **cantilēnam eandem canĕre** to sing the same old song, harp on the same theme
cantĭ·ō -ōnis *f* singing; incantation, charm, spell
cantĭt·ō -āre *vt* to keep on singing or playing, to sing or play repeatedly
cantiuncŭl·a -ae *f* catchy tune
cant·ō -āre *vt* to sing; to play; to sing of, celebrate, praise in song; to harp on, keep repeating; to predict; to drawl out; (of actor) to play the part of; *vi* to sing; to play; (of instruments) to sound; to drawl; (of rooster) to crow; **ad surdas aures cantare** to preach to deaf ears
cant·or -ōris *m* singer, poet; eulogist; actor, player; musician
cantr·ix -īcis *f* musician, singer (*female*)
cant·us -ūs *m* tune, melody, song, playing; incantation; prediction; magic spell
cān·us -a -um *adj* white, grey; aged, old venerable
capăcĭt·ās -ātis *f* capacity
cap·ax -ācis *adj* capacious, spacious, wide, roomy; (of mind) able to grasp, receptive, capable
capēd·ō -ĭnis *f* cup or bowl used in sacrifices
capēduncŭl·a -ae *f* small cup or bowl used in sacrifices
capell·a -ae *f* she-goat, nanny goat
Capell·a -ae *f* Capella (*star of the*

first magnitude in Auriga)
Capēn·a -ae *f* Porta Capena (*a gate in the Servian Wall which marked the start of the Via Appia*)
cap·er -rī *m* he-goat, billy goat
caperr·ō -āre *vt & vi* to wrinkle
capess·ō -ĕre -īvī or **-iī -ītum** *vt* to try to reach, make for, seize, get hold of, snatch at; to take up, undertake, engage in; **capessere rem publicam** to be engaged in politics
capillāt·us -a -um *adj* having hair, hairy; **bene capillatus** having a fine head of hair
capill·us -ī *m* hair
capĭō capĕre cēpī captum *vt* (archaic *fut:* **capsō**) to take hold of, grasp, seize; to occupy; to take up, assume (*office*); to catch, capture; to captivate, charm; to cheat, seduce, mislead, delude; to defeat, overcome (*in suite*); to convince (*in a dispute*); to reach, arrive at, land at; to exact, extort, accept as a bribe; to take, obtain, get, enjoy, reap (*profit, advantage*); to acquire, cherish, cultivate, adopt (*habits, etc.*); to form, conceive, come to, reach (*conclusions, plans, thoughts, resolutions, purposes*); to take, derive, draw, obtain (*examples, proofs, instances*); to entertain, conceive, receive, experience (*impressions, feelings*); (of feelings, experiences) to seize, overcome, occupy, take possession of; to suffer, be subjected to (*injury*); to hold, contain, be large enough for; to comprehend, grasp
cap·is -ĭdis *f* bowl (*with one handle, used in sacrifices*)
capistr·ō -āre *vt* to muzzle
capistr·um -ī *n* halter, muzzle
capĭt·al or **capĭt·āle -ālis** *n* capital offense
capitāl·is -e *adj* relating to the head or life; (law) affecting a man's life or civil status; (of crime) punishable by death, punishable by loss of civil rights, capital; dangerous, deadly, mortal; chief, preeminent, distinguished, of first rank
capĭt·ō -ōnis *m* big-head
Capitōlīn·us -a -um *adj* Capitoline; *m* Capitoline Hill; *m pl* persons in charge of the Capitoline games
Capitōl·ium -iī or **-ī** *n* the Capitol (*temple of Jupiter on the summit of Mons Tarpeius*); the Capitoline Hill (*including temple and citadel*); citadel (*of any city*)
capitŭlātim *adv* briefly, summarily
capitŭl·um -ī *n* small head; (as term of endearment) dear fellow
Cappadocĭ·a -ae *f* country in Asia Minor between the Taurus and Pontus
capr·a -ae *f* she-goat, nanny goat; body odor of armpits
caprĕ·a -ae *f* wild goat, roe
Caprĕ·ae -ārum *f pl* island at S. end of Bay of Naples off Sorrento

capreŏl·us -ī *m* roebuck, chamois; prop, support

Capricorn·us -ī *m* Capricorn (*sign of the zodiac*)

caprific·us -ī *f* wild fig tree

caprigĕn·us -a -um *adj* of goats; **caprigenum pecus** herd of goats

caprimulg·us -ī *m* rustic

caprīn·us -a -um *adj* of goats, goat; **de lana caprina rixari** to argue over nothing

caprĭp·ēs -ĕdis *adj* goat-footed

caps·a -ae *f* holder, container, box, case (*esp. for book rolls*)

capsō see **capio**

capsŭl·a -ae *f* small box

capt·a -ae *f* captive, prisoner (*female*)

captātĭ·ō -ōnis *f* hunt, quest; **captatio verborum** verbalism, sophistry

captāt·or -ōris *m* (fig) hound; **aurae popularis captator** publicity hound

captĭ·ō -ōnis *f* taking, catching; fraud; loss, disadvantage; sophism

captiōsē *adv* slyly, insidiously, deceptively

captiōs·us -a -um *adj* deceitful; captious, sophistical; dangerous, harmful

captiuncŭl·a -ae *f* quibble, sophism

captīvĭt·ās -ātis *f* captivity; conquest, capture

captīv·us -a -um *adj* caught, taken captive; prisoner's; captured, conquered; *mf* prisoner of war, captive

capt·ō -āre *vt* to catch at eagerly; to keep reaching for; to try to catch, chase after; to strive after, long for, desire earnestly; to try to hear; to try to trap, entice, allure; to adopt (*plan*); to try to cause (*laughter*); to watch for (*opportunity*); to begin (*conversation*)

captūr·a -ae *f* capture; quarry

capt·us -a -um *pp* of **capio**; *adj* **oculis et auribus captus** blind and deaf; **mente captus** mad, crazy; *m* captive, prisoner

capt·us -ūs *m* mental grasp, mental capacity; notion

Capŭ·a -ae *f* chief city of Campania

capulār·is -e *adj* with one foot in the grave

capŭl·us -ī *m* coffin; hilt, handle

cap·ut -ĭtis *n* head; top, summit, point, extremity; source (*of river*); root (*of plant*); top (*of tree*); head, leader; capital (*of country*); main point (*of discourse*); chapter, principal division, heading; substance, summary; (com) capital; main course; life, civil status; **capitis accusare** to accuse of a capital offense; **capitis damnare** to condemn to death; **capitis res** matter of life and death; **diminutio capitis** loss of civil rights; **diminutio capitis maxima** condemnation to death or slavery; **diminutio capitis media** loss of citizenship; **diminutio capitis minima** change of status (*as by adoption or, in the case of women, by marriage*)

Cap·ys -yos *m* son of Assaracus and father of Anchises; companion of Aeneas; eighth king of Alba Longa

carbasĕ·us -a -um *adj* linen, canvas

carbăs·us -ī *f* (*pl:* **carbăs·a -ōrum** *n*) fine Spanish flax; linen garment; sail, canvas; awning

carb·ō -ōnis *m* charcoal

carbōnār·ius -iī or **-ī** *m* charcoal burner, collier

carbuncŭl·us -ī *m* small piece of coal; grief, sorrow; precious stone, garnet

carc·er -ĕris *m* prison, jail; prisoner; (term of reproach) jailbird; *m pl* starting gate (*at racetrack*); **ad carceres a calce revocari** to have to start all over again

carcerārĭ·us -a -um *adj* prison

carchēs·ĭum -iī or **-ī** *n* drinking cup (*slightly contracted in the middle*); upper part of mast (*similarly formed*)

cardĭăc·us -ī *m* dyspeptic

card·ō -ĭnis *m* hinge; turning point, crisis; (astr) axis, pole; **cardo rerum** critical juncture, crisis

cardŭ·us -ī *m* thistle

cārē *adv* at a high price, dearly; highly

cārect·um -ī *m* sedge

cār·ĕō -ēre -uī *vi* (with *abl* or *genit*) **a** to be without; **b** to miss; **c** to be free from; **d** to keep away from, be absent from; **e** to abstain from

cār·ex -ĭcis *f* sedge

Cārĭ·a -ae *f* province in S.W. Asia Minor

carĭ·ēs (*genit* not in use) *f* decay, rot

carīn·a -ae *f* bottom of ship, keel; ship

Carīn·ae -ārum *f pl* the Keels (*district in Rome Between the Caelian and Esquiline Hills*)

carīnār·ius -iī or **-ī** *m* dyer of yellow

cariōs·us -a -um *adj* rotten, decayed, crumbled; wrinkled

cār·is -ĭdis *f* crab

cārĭt·ās -ātis *f* dearness, costliness, high price, high cost of living; affection, love

carm·en -ĭnis *n* song, tune; lyric poetry, poetry; incantation, charm; oracular utterance; ritual formula, legal formula; adage

Carment·a -ae or **Carment·is -is** *f* Roman goddess of prophecy, the mother of Evander, who came with him from Arcadia to Latium

Carmentāl·is -e *adj* of Carmenta; **Porta Carmentalis** gate at Rome near temple of Carmenta (*also called* **Porta Scelerata,** *i.e., ominous gate*)

carnār·ium -iī or **-ī** *n* meat hook; pantry

Carneăd·ēs -is *m* famous philosopher, born at Cyrene, and founder of the New Academy (215-130 B.C.)

carnif·ex -ĭcis m hangman, executioner; murderer, butcher; scoundrel

carnificīn·a -ae f execution; torture, torment

carnifĭc·ō -āre vt to mutilate, cut to pieces, behead

car·ō -nis or **carn·is -is** f flesh, meat; **caro ferina** venison; **caro putida** carrion; (fig) rotten egg

car·ō -ĕre vt to card (wool)

Carpăth·us -ī f island between Crete and Rhodes

carpatin·us -a -um adj of rough leather; f crude shoe

carpent·um -ī n two-wheeled covered carriage (esp. used by women on holidays)

carp·ō -ĕre -sī -tum vt to pluck, pick, cull; to carp at, criticize, take apart; to enjoy, make use of; to crop, browse on (grass); to pick, gather (fruit); to separate into parts, divide; (mil) to harass, weaken (esp. by repeated attacks); **auras vitales carpere** to breathe the breath of life; **diem carpere** to make the most of the present; **gyrum carpere** to go in a circle; **iter** or **viam carpere** to make one's way, pick one's way, travel; **vellera carpere** to spin

carptim adv piecemeal, separately, in parts; at different times; at different points; gradually

carpt·or -ōris m carver (of food)

Carrh·ae -ārum f pl town in Mesopotamia where Crassus was defeated and killed by the Parthians (53 B.C.)

carrūc·a -ae f four-wheeled carriage

carr·us -ī m four-wheeled wagon

Carthāginiens·is -e adj & mf Carthaginian

Carthāg·ō -ĭnis f Carthage (city in N. Africa, founded as a Phoenician colony in 9th cent. B.C.)

caruncŭl·a -ae f little piece of meat

cār·us -a -um adj dear, high-priced, expensive, costly; dear, beloved, esteemed; loving, affectionate

cas·a -ae f cottage, cabin, hut

casc·us -a -um adj old, primitive

cāseŏl·us -ī m small piece of cheese

cāsĕ·us -ī m cheese

casĭ·a -ae f mezereon (fragrant plant with purple flowers)

Cassandr·a -ae f daughter of Priam and Hecuba who had the gift of prophecy but was believed by no one

cass·ēs -ium m pl hunting net, snare; spider web

cassid·a -ae f metal helmet

Cassiŏp·ē -ēs or **Cassiopē·a -ae** f wife of Cepheus and mother of Andromeda, afterwards made a constellation

Cass·ĭus -ĭī or **-ī** m C. Cassius Longinus (one of the murderers of Caesar)

cass·is -ĭdis f metal helmet

cass·ō -āre vi to totter, trip

cass·us -a -um adj empty, hollow; (fig) empty, groundless, vain, pointless; (with abl) deprived of, devoid of, without; **cassus lumine** without life, dead; **in cassum** to no purpose, pointlessly

Castāl·is -ĭdis adj Castalian; **sorores Castalides** Muses; f Muse

Castalĭ·us -a -um adj Castalian; f fountain on Mt. Parnassus, sacred to Apollo and the Muses

castanĕ·a -ae f chestnut tree; chestnut

castē adv purely, chastely, spotlessly; virtuously; devoutly, piously

castellān·us -a -um adj of a fort, of a castle; m occupant of a castle or fortress; m pl garrison (of a fortress)

castellātim adv one fortress after another; **castellatim dissipati** (troops) stationed in various fortresses

castell·um -ī n fort, fortress, stronghold, castle; (fig) defense, shelter, refuge

castērĭ·a -ae f rowers' quarters

castĭgābĭl·is -e adj punishable

castĭgātĭ·ō -ōnis f correction, punishment; censure, reproof

castĭgāt·or -ōris m corrector, critic

castĭgātōrĭ·us -a -um adj reproving

castĭgāt·us -a -um adj small, contracted, slender

castĭg·ō -āre vt to correct, make right, blame, reprove, censure, chide, find fault with, punish; to correct, amend; to hold in check, restrain

castimōnĭ·a -ae f purity, morality; chastity, abstinence

castĭt·ās -ātis f purity, chastity

cast·or -ōris m beaver

Cast·or -ōris m son of Tyndareus, twin brother of Pollux, brother of Helen and Clytemnestra, and patron of sailors

castorĕ·um -ī m bitter, strong-smelling secretion of beavers

castrens·is -e adj camp, military

castr·ō -āre vt to castrate

castr·um -ī n fort, fortress, castle; n pl military camp; day's march; the service, army life; (pol) party; (phil) school; **bina castra** two camps; **castra facere** or **habere** to encamp; **castra movere** to break camp; **castra munire** to construct a camp; **castra ponere** to pitch camp; **castra una** one camp

cast·us -a -um adj (morally) pure, chaste, spotless, guiltless, virtuous; religious, pious, holy, sacred

casŭl·a -ae f little hut, little cottage

cās·us -ūs m falling; (fig) fall, downfall, overthrow, end; chance, event, happening, occurrence, emergency; occasion, opportunity; misfortune, mishap, accident, calamity; fall, death; fate; (gram) case; **non con-sulto sed casu** not on purpose but by chance

catagelasīm·us -a -um adj bantering, jeering; exposed to ridicule

catagrăph·us -a -um adj painted, colored

cataphract·ēs -ae m coat of mail

cataphract·us -a -um adj mail-clad

catăpl·us -ī m arrival of ship; arriving ship or fleet

catapult·a -ae f catapult; (fig) missile

catapultārī·us -a -um adj catapulted, shot (from catapult)

cataract·a or **catarract·a** or **ca-tarract·a -ae** f waterfall, cataract (esp. on the Nile); floodgate; drawbridge

cataractrī·a -ae f spice

catast·a -ae f stage on which slaves were displayed for sale

catē adv skillfully, wisely

catēl·a -ae f javelin

catell·a -ae f puppy (female); small chain

catell·us -ī m puppy; small chain

catēn·a -ae f chain; series; barrier, restraint, bond

catēnāt·us -a -um adj chained

caterv·a -ae f crowd, throng, band, mob; troop (of actors); (mil) troop, horde

catervātim adv in companies, by troops; in crowds or flocks (of plague-stricken people)

cathědr·a -ae f armchair, cushioned seat; litter, sedan; professional chair

Catilīn·a -ae m L. Sergius Catiline (Roman patrician whose conspiracy was exposed by Cicero in 63 B.C.)

catill·ō -āre vi to lick the plate

catill·us -ī m plate

catīn·us -ī m plate, pot, bowl

Cat·ō -ōnis m M. Porcius Cato (model of Roman aristocratic conservatism, 239-149 B.C.); M. Porcius Cato Uticensis (grandson of Porcius Cato, inveterate enemy of Caesar, 95-45 B.C.)

catōn·ium -iī or **-ī** n lower world

Catull·us -ī m C. Valerius Catullus (lyric and elegiac poet of Verona, 86-54 B.C.)

catŭl·us -ī m puppy; whelp, cub

cat·us -a -um adj sharp, shrewd, keen; sly, cunning

Caucăs·us -ī m Caucasus mountains

caud·a -ae f tail (of animal); penis; **caudam jactare** (with dat) to flatter; **caudam trahere** to be mocked

caudě·us -a -um adj of wood, wooden

caud·ex or **cōd·ex -īcis** m trunk (of tree); block (of wood to which one was tied for punishment); book, ledger; blockhead

caudīcāl·is -e adj of wood cutting

Caud·ium -iī or **-ī** n town in Samnium

caul·ae -ārum f pl hole, opening passage; sheepfold, pen

caul·is -is f stalk, stem; cabbage stalk, cabbage

caup·ō -ōnis m innkeeper

caupōn·a -ae f inn, tavern; retail shop

caupōni·us -a -um adj of a shop or tavern

caupōn·or -ārī -ātus sum vt to trade in or traffic in

caupōnŭl·a -ae f small inn or tavern

caus·a or **causs·a -ae** f (law) lawsuit, case; grounds, cause, motive, purpose, reason; good reason, just cause; pretext, pretense; inducement, occasion, opportunity; side, party, faction, cause; condition, situation, position; (rhet) matter of discussion, subject matter; matter, business, concern; commission, charge; personal relationship, connexion; **causā** (with genit) for the sake of, on account of; **causā ca-dere** to lose a case; **causam agere**, **causam dicere**, or **causam orare** to plead a case; **causam cognos-cere** to examine a case (as judge); **vestrā causā** in your interests; **per causam** (with genit) under the pretext of; **sine causā** without good reason

causārī·us -a -um adj sick; m (mil) malingerer, goldbrick

causi·a -ae f Macedonian hat (with wide brim)

causidĭc·us -ī m pleader, lawyer; shyster

causifĭc·or -ārī -ātus sum vi to make excuses

caus·or -ārī -ātus sum vt to pretend, give as a reason

caussa see **causa**

causŭl·a -ae f petty lawsuit; minor cause

cautē adv cautiously, carefully; with security

cautēl·a -ae f precaution

caut·ēs -is f rock, crag

cautim adv warily, cautiously

cauti·ō -ōnis f caution, wariness; guarantee, provision; (law) bond, security, bail, warranty; **mea cau-tio est** I must see to it; **mihi cau-tio est** I must take care

caut·or -ōris m wary person; bondsman, surety

caut·us -a -um adj cautious, careful; safe, secure

cavaed·ium -iī or **-ī** n inner court of Roman house

cavě·a -ae f cavity; enclosure for animals: cage, den, stall, beehive, bird cage; auditorium, theater; **pri-ma cavea** section of auditorium for nobility; **ultima cavea** section for lower classes

cavě·ō cavēre cāvī cautum vt to guard against, beware of; to keep clear of; to stipulate, decree, order; to guarantee; vi to be careful, look out, be on one's guard; (with abl or

ab + *abl*) to be on one's guard against; (with **ab** + *abl*) to get a guarantee from; (with *dat*) **a** to guarantee, give a guarantee to; **b** to provide for, take care of; **cave tangere** (= **noli tangere**) do not touch

cavern·a -ae *f* hollow, cavity, cave, cavern; vault; hold (*of ship*)

cavill·a -ae *f* jeering, scoffing

cavillāti·ō -ōnis *f* banter, scoffing, raillery; sophistry, quibbling

cavillāt·or -ōris *m* scoffer; quibbler, sophist

cavill·or -ārī -ātus sum *vt* to scoff at, mock, criticize, satirize; *vi* to scoff, jeer; to quibble

cav·ō -āre *vt* to hollow out, excavate; to pierce, run through

cav·us -a -um *adj* hollow, hollowed; concave, vaulted; deep-channeled (*river*); *m & n* hole, cavity, hollow

-ce demonstrative enclitic appended to pronouns and adverbs (like colloquial English *here*, *there*, with *this* or *that*); **hice** (for **hicce**) this (*here*); **hujusce** of this (*here*); (when followed by the enclytic **-ne**, the form becomes **-ci: hicine, sicine**)

Cecropid·ae -ārum *m pl* descendants of Cecrops, Athenians

Cecrŏp·is -ĭdis *f* female descendant of Cecrops (*esp. Aglauros*); Procne; Philomela; Athenian woman

Cecr·ops -ōpis *m* first king of Athens

cēdō cēdĕre cessī cessum *vt* to grant, concede, yield, give up; *vi* to go, move, walk, walk along; to go away, depart, withdraw; (*of time*) to pass; (*of events*) to turn out; to pass away, die; (*mil*) to retreat; (with *dat*) **a** to befall, fall to the lot of, accrue to; **b** to yield to, submit to, give in to; **c** to yield (*in rank*) to, be inferior to; **d** to comply with, conform to, obey; (with **in** + *acc*) to be changed into, become; (with **pro** + *abl*) to pass for, be the equivalent of, be the price of; **bonis** or **possessionibus alicui cedere** to give up or cede one's property to someone; **foro cedere** to go bankrupt

cedo (*pl:* **cette**) (old *impv*) here with, bring here, give here; let's hear, tell, out with; look at; **cedo dum!** all right!; come now!; **cedo ut inspiciam** let me look

cedr·us -ī *f* cedar, juniper; cedar wood; cedar oil

Celaen·ō -ūs *f* daughter of Atlas and one of the Pleiades; one of the Harpies; greedy woman

cēlāt·um -ī *n* secret

celĕb·er -ris -re *adj* crowded, populous, frequented; well-attended; famous; well-known, common, usual; solemn, festive; numerous, repeated, frequent

celebrāti·ō -ōnis *f* large assembly; festival, celebration; *f pl* throngs

celebrāt·us -a -um *adj* much-frequented, much-visited, crowded, populous; celebrated, famous, renowned; customary, usual, frequent; solemn, festive; trite, familiar, often-repeated

celebrĭt·ās -ātis *f* throng, crowd, multitude, large assembly; publicity; repetition, frequency; fame, renown; celebration

celĕbr·ō -āre *vt* to frequent, crowd, fill, visit in crowds; to repeat, practice, exercise; to publicize, advertise, honor, glorify; to escort, attend; to cause to resound

cel·er -ĕris -ĕre *adj* swift, speedy, quick, rapid, hurried; rash, hasty

celĕrĕ *adv* quickly

Celĕr·ēs -um *m pl* mounted bodyguards of Roman kings

celerĭp·ēs -ĕdis *adj* swift-footed

celerĭt·ās -ātis *f* speed, quickness, rapidity

celerĭter *adv* quickly, speedily

celĕr·ō -āre *vt* to quicken, speed up, accelerate; *vi* to be quick, rush, speed

cell·a -ae *f* storeroom, storehouse, grain elevator, silo; cheap apartment, garret; sanctuary (*of temple, where the cult image stood*); cell (*of beehive*)

cellāri·us -a -um *adj* of a storeroom; *m* storekeeper, butler

cellŭl·a -ae *f* small storeroom, small apartment

cēl·ō -āre *vt* to hide, conceal; to veil (*feelings*); to keep (*something*) secret, keep quiet about; (with *acc* of thing and *acc* of person from whom one conceals) to keep (*someone*) in the dark about, hide (*something*) from (*someone*); **celari** (with **de** + *abl*) to be kept in ignorance of

cel·ox -ōcis *adj* swift, quick; *f* swift-sailing ship, cutter, speedboat

cels·us -a -um *adj* high, lofty, towering, prominent, erect; lofty, elevated (*thoughts*); high (*rank*); proud, haughty

Celt·ae -ārum *m pl* Celts (*who occupied most of W. Europe*); (in more restricted sense) inhabitants of central Gaul

Celtibĕr·ī -ōrum *m pl* Celtiberians (*early people of Central Spain*)

cēn·a -ae *f* principal meal, dinner; dish, course; company at dinner

cēnācŭl·um -ī *n* dining room (*usually on an upper floor*); attic

cēnātĭc·us -a -um *adj* dinner

cēnātĭ·ō -ōnis *f* dining room

cēnāt·us -a -um *adj* having dined; spent in feasting

cēnĭt·ō -āre *vi* to dine habitually, dine often

cēn·ō -āre *vt* to make a meal of, dine on, eat; *vi* to dine, eat dinner

cens·ĕō -ēre -ŭī -um *vt* to assess, rate, estimate, tax; to esteem, appreciate, value; (*of senate*) to decree, resolve; to propose, move, vote, argue, suggest, advise; to think, believe, hold, suppose, imagine, expect

censi·ō -ōnis f rating, assessment, taxation; opinion

cens·or -ōris m censor (one of two Roman magistrates who took the census and exercised general control over morals, etc.); severe judge of morals, critic

censōri·us -a -um adj of the censors; subject to censure; rigid, stern, austere; **homo censorius** ex-censor; **lex censoria** contract (drawn up by censors) for leasing buildings

censūr·a -ae f office of censor, censorship; criticism

cens·us -ūs m census; register of the census; income bracket; wealth, property; rich presents, gifts; **censum agere** or **habere** to hold a census; **censu prohibere** to exclude from citizenship, disenfranchise

centaurē·um -ī n centaury (medical herb)

Centaur·us -ī m centaur (creature fabled to be half man and half horse); Centaurus (southern constellation between the Southern Cross and Hydra)

centēn·ī -ae -a adj one hundred each; **deciens centena milia passum** ten hundred thousand paces, one million paces

centēsim·us -a -um adj hundredth; f hundredth part, one percent; (com) 1% monthly (12% per annum)

centi·ceps -cipĭtis adj hundred-headed

centiēs or **centiēns** adv a hundred times; (fig) a great many times

centimān·us -a -um adj hundred-handed

cent·ō -ōnis m patchwork, quilt

centum (indecl) adj hundred

centumgemin·us -a -um adj hundredfold

centumpl·ex -ĭcis adj hundredfold

centumpond·ium -iī or -ī n hundred pounds, hundred-pound weight

centumvirāl·is -e adj of the centumviri

centumvir·ī -ōrum m pl panel of one hundred (jurors chosen annually to try civil suits under a quaestor, esp. concerning inheritances)

centuncul·us -ī m piece of patchwork, cloth of many colors, saddle cloth

centuri·a -ae f (mil) company, century (theoretically composed of one hundred men); (pol) century (one of the 193 groups into which Servius Tullius divided the Roman people)

centuriātim adv by companies, by centuries

centuriāt·us -a -um adj divided into companies or centuries; **comitia centuriata** centuriate assembly

(legislative body which met in the Campus Martius to elect high magistrates, decree war, etc.)

centuri·ō -ōnis m centurion (commander of an infantry company)

centuri·ō -āre vt to divide into centuries

centuriōnāt·us -ūs m election of centurions

centuss·is -is m a hundred aces (bronze coins)

cēnŭl·a -ae f little dinner

Cephăl·us -ī m husband of Procris, whom he unintentionally shot

Ceph·eus -ĕī m king of Ethiopia, husband of Cassiope and father of Andromeda

Cephīs·us -ī m river in Attica; river in Phocis and Boeotia

cēr·a -ae f wax; writing tablet (covered with wax); wax seal; wax bust of an ancestor; cell (of beehive)

Ceramīc·us -ī m cemetery of Athens

cērār·ĭum -iī or -ī n fee for affixing a seal

cerast·ēs -ae m horned serpent

ceras·us -ī f cherry tree; cherry

cērāt·us -a -um adj waxed

Cerber·us -ī m three-headed dog which guarded the entrance to the lower world

cercopithēc·us -ī m long-tailed monkey

cercūr·us -ī m swift-sailing ship, cutter

cerd·ō -ōnis m workman, laborer

Cereāl·ĭa -ĭum n pl festival of Ceres (April 10th)

Cereāl·is -e adj of Ceres; of grain; **arma Cerealia** utensils for grinding and baking

cerebrōs·us -a -um adj hot-headed

cerĕbr·um -ī n brain; head, skull; understanding; hot temper

Cer·ēs -ĕris f goddess of agriculture and mother of Proserpine; grain bread, food

cērĕ·us -a -um adj of wax, waxen; wax-colored; soft, pliant; m candle

cērinth·a -ae f wax flower

cērĭn·us -a -um adj wax-colored; n pl wax-colored clothes

cernō cernĕre crēvī crētum vt (of sight) to discern, distinguish, make out, see; (of mind) to discern, see, understand; to decide, decree, determine; **hereditatem cernere** to formally declare oneself heir to an inheritance, accept an inheritance

cernŭ·us -a -um adj with face turned toward the earth, stooping forwards

cērōm·a -ātis n wrestler's oil

cērōmatic·us -a -um adj smeared with oil, oily, greasy

cerrīt·us -a -um adj crazy, frantic

certām·en -ĭnis n contest, match; rivalry; (mil) battle, combat

certātim adv with a struggle, in rivalry

certātĭ·ō -ōnis f contest; rivalry, discussion, debate

certē adv surely, certainly, unquestionably, undoubtedly, of course; (in answers) yes, certainly; (to restrict an assertion) at least, at any rate

certō *adv* for certain, for sure; surely, in fact, really

cert·ō -āre *vi* to fight, contend, struggle, do battle; to compete; (law) to debate; (with *inf*) to strive to

cert·us -a -um *adj* certain, determined, resolved, fixed, settled; specific, particular, certain, precise, definite; faithful, trusty, dependable; sure of aim, unerring; unwavering, inexorable; **certiorem facere** to inform; **certum est mihi** (with *inf*) I am determined to; **certum habere** to regard as certain; **pro certo** for sure; **pro certo habere** to be assured

cērūl·a -ae *f* piece of wax; **cerula miniata** red pencil (*of a critic*)

cēruss·a -ae *f* ceruse, white paint

cērussāt·us -a -um *adj* painted white

cerv·a -ae *f* hind, deer

cervīc·al -ālis *n* pillow, cushion

cervīcŭl·a -ae *f* slender neck

cervīn·us -a -um *adj* of a stag or deer

cerv·ix -īcis *f* neck; nape of the neck; **in cervicibus nostris esse** to be on our necks, i.e., to have (*something or someone unpleasant*) on our hands; **a cervicibus nostris avertere** to get (*someone*) off our neck, get rid of (*someone*); **cervicibus sustinere** to shoulder (*responsibility*)

cerv·us -ī *m* stag, deer; (mil) palisade

cessātĭ·ō -ōnis *f* letup, delay; inactivity, idleness, cessation

cessāt·or -ōris *m* idler, loafer

cessĭ·ō -ōnis *f* surrendering, relinquishment

cess·ō -āre *vi* to let up, slack off, become remiss, stop; to be inactive, be idle, do nothing; to lie fallow

cestrosphendŏn·ē -ēs *f* artillery piece for hurling stones

cest·us or **cěst·os -ī** *m* girdle (*esp. of Venus*)

cētār·ĭum -ĭī or **-ī** *n* fish pond

cētār·ĭus -ĭī or **-ī** *m* fish dealer

cětěra *adv* otherwise, in all other respects, for the rest

cēterōquī or **cēterōquīn** *adv* otherwise, in all other respects, for the rest

cětěrum *adv* otherwise, in all other respects, for the rest; but, yet, still, on the other hand

cětěr·us -a -um *adj* the other, the remaining, the rest of; *pron m pl & f pl* the others, all the rest, everybody; *n* the rest

Cethēg·us -ī *m* C. Cornelius Cethegus (*fellow conspirator of Catiline*)

cette see **cedo**

cēt·us -ī (*pl:* **cēt·ē**) *m* sea monster: whale, shark, seal, dolphin

ceu *conj* (in comparisons) as, just as; (in comparative conditions) as if, just as if; **ceu cum** as when

cēv·ĕō -ēre *vi* (*cf* **criso**) (of a male) to move the haunches

Cē·yx -ȳcis *m* king of Trachis, who was changed into a kingfisher, as was his wife Alcyone

Chaldae·us -a -um *adj* Chaldaean; *m* astrologer, fortune-teller

chalybēi·us -a -um *adj* steel

Chalȳb·es -um *m pl* people of Pontus in Asia Minor noted as steelworkers

chal·ybs -ȳbis *m* steel

Chāŏn·es -um *m pl* a tribe in Epirus

Chāonĭ·us -a -um *adj* Chaonian; of Epirus; *f* Chaonia (*district of Epirus*)

Cha·os -ī *n* chaos, the unformed world, empty space, shapeless mass from which the world was formed; **a Chao** from the beginning of the world

char·a -ae *f* wild cabbage

charistĭ·a -ōrum *n pl* Roman family festival

Charĭt·es -um *f pl* the Graces

Char·ōn -ontis *m* ferryman of the lower world

chart·a -ae *f* sheet of papyrus; sheet of paper; writing, letter, poem; book; record

chartŭl·a -ae *f* sheet of paper; letter, note

Charybd·is -is *f* whirlpool between Italy and Sicily, personified as a female monster

Chatt·ī -ōrum *m pl* people of central Germany

Chēl·ae -ārum *f pl* the Claws (*of Scorpio*); Libra (*constellation into which Scorpio extends*)

chelȳdr·us -ī *m* water snake

chely·s (*genit* not in use; *acc:* **chelyn**) *f* tortoise; lyre

cheragr·a -ae *f* arthritis in the hand

chīliarch·ēs -ae or **chīliarch·us -ī** *m* commander of 1000 men; Persian chancellor (*highest office next to the king*)

Chimaer·a -ae *f* fire-breathing monster, with lion's head, goat's body, and dragon's tail

Chi·os -ī *f* island off coast of Asia Minor, famous for its wine

chīrogrăph·um -ī *n* handwriting; autography; document; **falsa chirographa** forgeries

Chīr·ōn -ōnis *m* Chiron (*centaur, tutor of Aesculapius, Hercules, and Achilles, and famous for his knowledge of medicine and prophecy*)

chīronŏm·os -ī or **chīronŏm·ōn -untis** *m* pantomimist

chīrurgī·a -ae *f* surgery

Chi·us -a -um *adj & mf* Chian; *n* Chian wine; *n pl* Chian cloth

chlamydāt·us -a -um *adj* wearing a military uniform

chlam·ys -ȳdis *f* military cloak; gold-brocaded mantle

Choeril·us -ī *m* incompetent Greek panegyrist of Alexander the Great

chorāg·ium -iī or -ī *n* choreography

chorāg·us -ī *m* choragus (*man who finances the chorus*)

choraul·ēs -ae *m* flute player who accompanied the choral dance

chord·a -ae *f* gut string, string (*of musical instrument*); cord, rope

chorē·a -ae *f* dance

chorē·us -ī *m* trochee

chor·us -ī *m* chorus; choir

Chrem·ēs -ētis or -is or -ī *m* miserly old man (*in Roman comedy*)

Christiān·us -ī *m* Christian

Christ·us -ī *m* Christ

Chrȳsē·is -ĭdis *f* Agamemnon's slave girl, daughter of Chryses

Chrȳs·ēs -ae *m* priest of Apollo

Chrȳsipp·us -ī *m* famous Stoic philosopher (290-210 B.C.)

chrȳsolith·os -ī *m* chrysolite, topaz

chrȳs·os -ī *m* gold

cibāri·us -a -um *adj* of food; common, coarse (*food of slaves*); *n pl* rations, provisions, food allowance

cibāt·us -ūs *m* food

cib·ō -āre *vt* to feed

cibōr·ium -iī or -ī *n* drinking cup

cib·us -ī *m* food; feed; (fig) food, nourishment

cicād·a -ae *f* locust, harvest fly

cicātrīcōs·us -a -um *adj* scarred, covered with scars

cicātr·ix -īcis *f* scar

cicc·us -ī *m* core of pomegranate; something worthless, trifle

cic·er -ĕris *n* chick-pea

Cicĕr·ō -ōnis *m* M. Tullius Cicero (*orator and statesman*, 106-43 B.C.)

cīchorē·um -ī *n* endive

Cicŏn·es -um *m pl* Thracian tribe

cicōni·a -ae *f* stork

cic·ur -ŭris *adj* tame

cicūt·a -ae *f* hemlock tree; hemlock poison; pipe, flute (*carved from hemlock tree*)

ciĕō ciēre cīvī citum *vt* to set in motion, move; to stir, agitate; to call for, send for; to summon for help; to invoke, appeal to; to call on by name, mention by name; to start, bring about; to renew (*combat*)

Cilici·a -ae *f* country in S. Asia Minor

Cilici·us -a -um *adj* Cilician; *n* garment of goat's hair

Cil·ix -īcis *adj* & *m* Cilician

Cimbr·ī -ōrum *m pl* Germanic tribe (*defeated by Marius in 101 B.C.*)

cīm·ex -ĭcis *m* bug

Cimmeri·ī -ōrum *m pl* people in the Crimea; mythical people living in perpetual darkness in caves at Cumae

cinaedĭc·us -a -um *adj* lewd

cinaed·us -ī *m* sodomite; lewd dancer

cincinnāt·us -a -um *adj* curly-haired

Cincinnāt·us -ī *m* L. Quinctius Cincinnatus (*famous Roman hero, dictator in 458 B.C.*)

cincinn·us -ī *m* curled hair, artificial curl (*of hair*); (rhet) highly artificial expression

cinctĭcŭl·us -ī *m* small belt or sash

cinctūr·a -ae *f* belt, sash

cinct·us -ūs *m* tucking up; belt, sash; cinctus Gabinius Gabinian style of wearing toga (*usually employed at religious festivals*)

cinctūt·us -a -um *adj* wearing a belt or sash; old-fashioned

cinefact·us -a -um *adj* reduced to ashes

cinerār·ius -iī or -ī *m* curling iron, hair curler

cingō cingĕre cinxī cinctum *vt* to surround, encircle; to wreathe (*head*); to tuck up (*garment*); (mil) to beleaguer, invest; to cover, protect; cingi in proelia to prepare oneself for battle, get ready for battle; ferrum cingi to put on one's sword

cingŭl·a -ae *f* belt; sash (*worn by women*); girth (*worn by horses, etc.*); sword belt; chastity belt

cingŭl·um -ī *n* belt; sword belt; sash (*worn by women*); girdle, chastity belt

cingŭl·us -ī *m* zone (*of the earth*)

cinĭfl·ō -ōnis *m* hair curler

cin·is -ĕris *m* ashes; ruin, death

Cinn·a -ae *m* L. Cornelius Cinna (*consul 87-84 B.C. and supporter of Marius, d. 84 B.C.*)

cinnamōm·um or cinnăm·um -ī *n* cinnamon; *n pl* cinnamon sticks

Cinȳr·ās -ae *m* father of Myrrha and Adonis

cipp·us -ī *m* stake, post, pillar; gravestone; (mil) palisade

circā *adv* around, round about, all around, in the vicinity; *prep* (with *acc*) (of place) around, surrounding, about, among, through, in the neighborhood of, near; attending, escorting (*persons*); (of time) at about, around, towards; (with numerals) about, nearly, almost; concerning, in respect to

circamoer·ium -iī or -ī *n* area on both sides of a city wall

Circ·ē -ēs or -ae *f* daughter of Helios and Perse, famous for her witchcraft

circens·is -e *adj* of the racetrack; *m pl* races

circĭn·ō -āre *vt* to make round; to circle

circĭn·us -ī *m* (geometer's) compass, pair of compasses

circĭter *adv* (of time and number) nearly, about, approximately; *prep* (with *acc*) about, near

circlus see circulus

circueō see circumeo

circuitĭō see circumitio

circuĭt·us or circumĭt·us -ūs *m* circuit; going round, revolution; de-

tour; circumference; circumlocution; (rhet) period
circulāt·or -ōris *m* peddler, vendor
circŭl·or -ārī -ātus sum *vi* to
gather around (*for conversation*);
to stroll about
circŭl·us or **circl·us -ī** *m* circle, circuit; ring, hoop; social circle; (astr)
orbit
circum *adv* about, all around; *prep*
(with *acc*) around, about; in the
neighborhood of
circum·ăgō -ăgĕre -ēgī -actum *vt*
to turn around; to sway (*emotionally*); **circumagi** or **se circumage-
re** to go out of one's way, go in a
round about way; (of time) to pass
away, roll around
circumăr·ō -āre *vt* to plow around
circumcaesūr·ā -ae *f* contour, outline
circum·cīdō -cīdĕre -cīdī -cīsum
vt to cut around, trim; to cut short,
cut down on; to abridge, shorten;
to circumcise
circumcircā *adv* all around
circumcīs·us -a -um *pp* of **cir-
cumcīdo**; *adj* steep; inaccessible;
abridged, short
**circum·clūdō -clūdĕre -clūsī -clū-
sum** *vt* to shut in, hem in, enclose,
surround
circumcŏl·ō -ĕre *vt* to live near
circumcurs·ō -āre *vt* & *vi* to run
around
circum·dō -dăre -dĕdī -dătum *vt*
to surround, enclose, encircle; (with
dat) to place or put (*something*)
around
**circum·dūcō -dūcĕre -duxī -duc-
tum** *vt* to lead around, draw
around; (with double *acc*) to lead
(*someone*) around to; **aliquem omnia praesidia circumdūcĕre** to
take someone around to all the gar-
risons
circum·ĕō or **circu·ĕō -īre -īvī** or
iī -ĭtum *vt* to go around, go around
to, visit, make the rounds of; to
surround, encircle, enclose, encompass; to get around, circumvent, deceive, cheat; *vi* to go around, make
a circuit
circumequĭt·ō -āre *vt* to ride
around
circum·fĕrō -ferre -tŭlī -lātum
vt to carry around, hand around; to
publicize, spread abroad; to purify;
circumferri to revolve; **oculos
circumferre** to look around,
glance about
**circum·flectō -flectĕre -flexī -flex-
um** *vt* to turn around, wheel about
circumfl·ō -āre *vt* to blow around;
(fig) to buffet
circum·flŭō -flŭĕre -fluxī *vt* to flow
around; to surround; to overflow;
vi to be overflowing, abound
circumflŭ·us -a -um *adj* flowing
around; surrounded (*by water*)
circumforānĕ·us -a -um *adj* strolling about from market to market,

itinerant; around the forum
**circum·fundō -fundĕre -fūdī -fū-
sum** *vt* to pour around; to surround, cover, envelop; **circumfundī** or **se circumfundĕre** to crowd
around; **circumfundī** (with *dat*) to
cling to
circumgĕm·ō -ĕre *vt* to growl
around (*e.g., a sheepfold*)
circumgest·ō -āre *vt* to carry
around
**circum·grĕdior -grĕdī -gressus
sum** *vt* to surround
circumitĭ·ō or **circuitĭ·ō -ōnis** *f*
going round; patrolling; circumlocution
circumĭtus see **circuĭtus**
circumjăc·ĕō -ēre *vi* (with *dat*) to
lie near, border on, be adjacent to
circum·jiciō -jicĕre -jēcī -jectum
vt to throw or place around; to surround; (with *dat*) to throw (*something*) around (*someone or something*); **fossam circumjicĕre** to
dig a trench all around
circumject·us -a -um *adj* surrounding, adjacent; (with *dat*) adjacent
to; *n pl* neighborhood
circumject·us -ūs *m* surrounding;
embrace
circumlātus *pp* of **circumfero**
circumlĭg·ō -āre *vt* to bind; (with
dat) to bind or fasten (*something*)
over
circum·lĭnō -linĕre — -lĭtum *vt* to
smear all over; to anoint
circumlŭ·ō -ĕre *vt* to flow around
circumluvĭ·ō -ōnis *f* island (*formed
by a river flowing in a new channel*)
**circum·mittō -mittĕre -mīsī
-missum** *vt* to send around
circummūn·ĭō or **circummoen·ĭō
-īre** *vt* to fortify
circummūnĭtĭ·ō -ōnis *f* investment
(*of town*); circumvallation
circumpadān·us -a -um *adj* situated along the Po River
circumpend·ĕō -ēre *vi* to hang
around
circumplaud·ō -ĕre *vt* to applaud
from every direction
**circum·plector -plectī -plexus
sum** *vt* to clasp, embrace, surround
circumplĭc·ō -āre *vt* to wind; (with
dat) to wind (*something*) around
**circum·pōnō -pōnĕre -posŭī -po-
sĭtum** *vt* (with *dat*) to place or set
(*something*) around
circumpōtātĭ·ō -ōnis *f* round of
drinks
circumrēt·ĭō -īre -īvī -ītum *vt* to
snare
circum·rōdō -rōdĕre -rōsī *vt* to
nibble all around; to hesitate to say;
to slander, backbite
circumsaep·ĭō or **circumsēp·ĭō
-īre -sī -tum** *vt* to fence in, enclose
circumscind·ō -ĕre *vt* to strip off
**circum·scrībō -scrībĕre -scripsī
-scriptum** *vt* to draw a line
around, mark the boundary of; to

limit, restrict; to set aside; to defeat the purpose of; to trap, defraud

circumscriptē *adv* comprehensively; (rhet) in periods

circumscriptǐ·ō -ōnis *f* encircling; circle; circuit, limit, boundary; comprehensive statement; cheating, deceiving; (rhet) period

circumscript·or -ōris *m* cheat

circumscript·us -a -um *pp* of **circumscribo**; *adj* restricted, limited; (rhet) periodic

circumsěc·ō -āre *vt* to cut around

circum·seděō -sedēre -sēdī -sessum *vt* to beset, besiege, invest, blockade

circumsēpǐō see **circumsaepio**

circumsessǐ·ō -ōnis *f* besieging, blockading

circumsǐd·ō -ěre *vt* to besiege

circumsǐl·ǐō -īre *vi* to hop around, dance around

circum·sǐstō -sistěre -stětī *vt* to stand around, surround

circumsǒn·ō -āre *vt* to make resound, fill with sound; *vi* to resound everywhere; (with *dat*) to resound to

circumsǒn·us -a -um *adj* noisy

circumspectātr·ix -ǐcis *f* spy (female)

circumspectǐ·ō -ōnis *f* looking around; circumspection, caution

circumspect·ō -āre *vt* to search attentively, watch for; *vi* to keep looking around, look around anxiously

circumspect·us -a -um *pp* of **circumspicio**; *adj* well-considered; guarded (*words*); circumspect, cautious (*person*)

circumspect·us -ūs *m* consideration; view

circum·spicǐō -spicěre -spexī -spectum *vt* to look around for, survey, see; to consider, examine; *vi* to be circumspect, be cautious, be on the watch; **se circumspicere** to think highly of oneself

circumstant·ēs -ǐum *m pl* bystanders

circum·stō -stāre -stětī *vt* to surround, envelop; (of terror, etc.) to grip, confront, overwhelm; *vi* to stand around

circumstrěp·ō -ěre *vt* to surround with noise or shouts

circumsurg·ō -ěre *vi* (of mountains) to rise all around

circumtent·us -a -um *adj* tightly covered

circumtěr·ō -ěre *vt* to rub shoulders with, crowd around

circumtext·us -a -um *adj* with embroidered border

circumtǒn·ō -āre -ǔī *vt* to crash around (*someone*)

circumtons·us -a -um *adj* clipped

circum·vādō -vāděre -vāsī *vt* to attack on every side; (of terror, etc.) to grip, confront

circumvǎg·us -a -um *adj* flowing around, encircling

circumvall·ō -āre *vt* to blockade, invest

circumvectǐ·ō -ōnis *f* carting around (*of merchandise*); revolution (*of sun*)

circumvect·ō -āre *vt* to carry around

circumvect·or -ārī -ātus sum *vt* to ride or cruise around; to describe; *vi* to ride about, cruise about

circum·věhor -věhī -vectus sum *vt* to ride or cruise around; to describe, express by circumlocution; *vi* to ride about, cruise about

circumvēl·ō -āre *vt* to veil, envelop, cover

circum·venǐō -venīre -vēnī -ventum *vt* to encircle, surround; to go around to; to surround (*in a hostile manner*), invest; to distress, afflict, oppress; to circumvent, cheat, deceive

circumvert·ō -ěre *vt* to turn (*something*) around; **circumverti** to turn oneself around, turn 'around; **circumverti axem** to turn around an axle

circumvest·ǐō -īre *vt* to clothe, wrap

circumvinc·ǐō -īre *vt* to bind, tie up

circumvīs·ō -ěre *vt* to look around, glare around at

circumvolǐt·ō -āre *vt & vi* to fly around, dash about, rove around; to hover around

circumvǒl·ō -āre *vt* to fly around, hover about, flit about

circum·volvō -volvěre — volūtum *vt* to wind, roll around; **circumvolvi** or **se circumvolvere** (with *dat* or *acc*) to revolve around, wind oneself around

circ·us -ī *m* circle; racetrack; (astr) orbit

Circ·us Maxǐm·us (*genit:* **Circ·ī Maxǐm·ī**) *m* oldest racetrack in Rome, between the Palatine and Aventine, alleged to have been built by Tarquinius Priscus

cirrāt·us -a -um *adj* curly-haired

Cirrh·a -ae *f* town near Delphi, sacred to Apollo

cirr·us -ī *m* lock, curl; forelock; fringe

cis *prep* (with *acc*) on this side of; within

Cisalpīn·us -a -um *adj* Cisalpine, on the Roman side of the Alps

cis·ǐum -ǐī or **-ī** *n* light two-wheeled carriage

Cissē·is -ǐdis *f* Hecuba

Ciss·eus -ěī *m* king of Thrace and father of Hecuba

cist·a -ae *f* box, chest

cistell·a -ae *f* small box

cistellātr·ix -ǐcis *f* female slave in charge of a money box

cistellǔl·a -ae *f* small box

cistern·a -ae *f* cistern, reservoir

cistophǒr·us -ī *m* Asiatic coin

cistǔl·a -ae *f* small box

citātim *adv* quickly, hastily

citāt·us -a -um *adj* quick, speedy, rapid; citato equo at full gallop

citeri·or -us *adj* on this side; nearer to earth, more down to earth, more mundane

Cithaer·ŏn -ōnis *m* mountain range dividing Attica from Boeotia

cithăr·a -ae *f* zither, lyre, lute; art of playing the zither, lyre, or lute

citharist·a -ae *m* zither player, lute player

citharistri·a -ae *f* zither player, lutist (*female*)

cithariz·ŏ -āre *vt* to play the zither, lyre, or lute

citharoed·us -ī *m* singer accompanied by zither, lyre, or lute

citĭm·us -a -um *adj* nearest

citĭus *adv* sooner, rather; dicto citius no sooner said than done; se- rius aut citius sooner or later

cito *adv* quickly; soon

cit·ŏ -āre *vt* to excite, rouse; to call, summon, cite; to call to witness, appeal tŏ

citrā *adv* on this side, on the near side; citra cadere to fall short; *prep* (with *acc*) on this side of, on the near side of; (of time) since, before; short of, less than

citrĕ·us -a -um *adj* of citrus wood

citrŏ *adv* to this side, this way; ultro citro, ultro citroque, or ultro et citro to and fro, up and down; mutually

citr·us -ī *f* citrous tree; citron tree

cit·us -a -um *pp* of cieo; *adj* quick, rapid, swift

cīvic·us -a -um *adj* civil; civic; co- rona civica oak-leaf crown awarded for saving a fellow soldier's life

cīvīl·is -e *adj* civil; civic; political; civilian; democratic; polite; jus ci- vile rights as a citizen, civil rights; civil law; ratio civilis political science

cīvīlit·ās -ātis *f* politics; courtesy

cīvīliter *adv* like a citizen; as an ordinary citizen would; politely

cīv·is -is *m* or *f* citizen; fellow citizen; private citizen

cīvit·ās -ātis *f* citizenship; state, commonwealth, community

clād·ēs -is *f* disaster, ruin, damage, loss; (mil) defeat; (fig) scourge

clam *adv* secretly, privately, in secret; stealthily; *prep* (with *abl* or *acc*) without the knowledge of, unknown to; clam habere aliquem to keep someone in the dark; neque clam me est nor is it unknown to me

clāmāt·or -ōris *m* loudmouth

clāmitātĭ·ŏ -ōnis *f* bawling, noise, racket

clāmĭt·ŏ -āre *vt & vi* to cry out, yell

clām·ŏ -āre *vt* to call out, call upon; to proclaim, declare; to invoke; *vi* to cry out, yell, shout

clām·or -ōris *m* shout, cry, call; acclamation, applause; outcry, complaint; war cry; noise, sound, echo

clāmōs·us -a -um *adj* clamorous, noisy

clancŭlum *adv* secretly, privately; *prep* (with *acc*) unknown to

clandestīnŏ *adv* secretly

clandestīn·us -a -um *adj* clandestine, secret, hidden

clang·or -ōris *m* clang, din, shrill cry

clārē *adv* distinctly, clearly; brightly; with distinction

clār·ĕŏ -ēre *vi* to be clear, be bright, be distinct; to be evident; to be famous

clār·escŏ -escĕre -ŭī *vi* to become clear, become distinct, become bright; to become obvious; to become famous

clārigātĭ·ŏ -ōnis *f* demand for satisfaction, ultimatum; fine

clārig·ŏ -āre *vi* to give an ultimatum

clārisŏn·us -a -um *adj* clear-sounding, loud

clārit·ās -ātis *f* clarity, distinctness; clearness (of *style*); celebrity, distinction

clāritūd·ŏ -ĭnis *f* brightness; distinction, fame

clār·ŏ -āre *vt* to make clear, explain, illustrate; to make famous; to illuminate

Clar·os -ī *f* town in Asia Minor near Colophon, famous for a temple and an oracle of Apollo

clār·us -a -um *adj* clear, distinct, bright; plain, manifest; famous, renowned; notorious

classiāri·us -a -um *adj* naval; *m pl* marines

classicŭl·a -ae *f* flotilla

classĭc·us -a -um *adj* first-class; naval; *m pl* marines; *n* battle signal; bugle

class·is -is *f* fleet; army; (pol) class

clāthr·ī or clātr·ī -ōrum *m pl* bars, cage, lattice

clātrāt·us -a -um *adj* barred

claud·ĕŏ -ēre or claud·ŏ -ĕre *vi* to limp; to falter, hesitate, waver

claudicātĭ·ŏ -ōnis *f* limping

claudĭc·ŏ -āre *vi* to be lame, limp; to waver; to be defective

Claud·ius -iī or -ī *m* Appius Claudius Caecus (censor in 312 B.C. and builder of the Appian aqueduct and the Appian Way); Roman emperor, 41-54 A.D.

claudŏ claudĕre clausī clausum *vt* to bolt, bar, shut, close; to bring to a close, conclude; to lock up, imprison; to blockade, hem in; to limit, restrict; to cut off, block; agmen claudere to bring up the rear; nu- meris or pedibus claudere to put into verse; transitum claudere to block traffic

claud·us -a -um *adj* lame, limping; crippled, imperfect, defective; wavering, untrustworthy

claustr·a -ōrum *n pl* lock, bar, bolt; gate, dam, dike; barrier, barricade; cage, den; fortress, defenses

clausŭl·a -ae f close, conclusion, end; (rhet) close of a period

claus·us -a -um pp of **claudo**; n enclosure

clāv·a -ae f cudgel, club, knotty branch

clāvār·ium -iī or **-ī** n allowance to soldiers for shoe nails

clāvicŭl·a -ae f tendril

clāvig·er -ĕra -ĕrum adj carrying a club; carrying keys; m club bearer (Hercules); key bearer (Janus)

clāv·is -is f key; **clavīs adimere uxori** to take the keys away from a wife, get a divorce

clāv·us -ī m nail; rudder, helm; purple stripe (on a tunic, broad for senators, narrow for knights); **clavus anni** beginning of the year; **clavus trabalis** spike; **trabali clavo figere** to nail down, clinch

Cleanth·ēs -is m Stoic philosopher, pupil of Zeno (300?-220 B.C.)

clēm·ens -entis adj gentle, mild, merciful, kind, compassionate; mitigated, qualified, toned down

clēmenter adv gently, mildly, mercifully, kindly, compassionately; by degrees, gradually

clēmenti·a -ae f mildness, mercy, clemency, compassion

Cle·ōn -ōnis m Athenian demagogue after death of Pericles in 429 B.C.

Cleopātr·a -ae f queen of Egypt (68-31 B.C.)

clep·ō -ĕre -sī -tum vt to steal

clepsydr·a -ae f water clock; (fig) time (allotted to speakers); **clepsydram dare** (with dat) to give (someone) the floor; **clepsydram petere** to ask for the floor

clept·a -ae m thief

cli·ens -entis m client, dependant (freeman protected by a patron); follower, retainer; companion, favorite; vassal

client·a -ae f client (female)

clientēl·a -ae f clientele; patronage, protection; f pl allies, dependants; clienteles

clientŭl·us -ī m poor client

clīnām·en -inis n swerve

clīnāt·us -a -um adj bent, inclined

Clī·ō -ūs f Muse of history

clipeāt·us -a -um adj armed with a shield

clipĕ·um -ī n or **clipĕ·us -ī** m round bronze Roman shield; medallion; disc (of sun)

clītell·a -ae f saddlebag; f pl packsaddle

clītellārī·us -a -um adj carrying a packsaddle

clīvōs·us -a -um adj hilly, full of hills; steep

clīv·us -ī m slope, ascent, hill; slope, pitch; **adversus clivum** uphill; **primi clivi** foothills

Clīv·us Sac·er (genit: **Clīv·ī Sac·rī**) m part of the Via Sacra ascending the Capitoline Hill, also called Clivus Capitolinus

cloāc·a -ae f sewer, drain; **cloaca maxima** main sewer (draining the valley between the Capitoline, Palatine, and Esquiline)

Cloācīn·a -ae f Venus

Clōdi·a -ae f sister of Publius Clodius Pulcher and thought to be the person called Lesbia in Catullus' poems

Clōd·ius -iī or **-ī** m Publius Clodius Pulcher (notorious enemy of Cicero who caused the latter to be exiled in 58 B.C. and was himself killed by Milo in 52 B.C.)

Cloeli·a -ae f Roman girl who was given as hostage to Porsenna and escaped by swimming the Tiber

Clōth·ō (genit not in use; acc: **-ō**) f one of the three Fates

clu·ĕō -ēre or **clu·ĕor -ērī** vi to be named, be spoken of, be reputed, be famous

clūn·is -is m or f buttock

clūrīn·us -a -um adj of apes

Clūs·ium -iī or **-ī** n ancient Etruscan town

Clūs·ius -iī or **-ī** m Janus

Clymĕn·ē -ēs f wife of Merops and mother of Phaëthon

Clytaemnestr·a -ae f wife of Agamemnon, sister of Helen, Castor, and Pollux, and mother of Electra, Iphigenia, and Orestes, the latter of whom killed her

Cnid·us -ī f town in Caria, famous for worship of Venus

coacervātī·ō -ōnis f piling up, accumulation

coacerv·ō -āre vt to pile up, accumulate

coac·escō -escĕre -ŭī vi to become sour

coact·ō -āre vt to force

coact·or -ōris m collector (of money); **agminis coactores** rearguard elements

coactus pp of **cogo**; adj forced, unnatural, hypocritical; n felt

coact·us -ūs m coercion, compulsion

coaedific·ō -āre vt to build up (an area), fill with buildings; **loci coaedificati** built-up areas

coaequ·ō -āre vt to level off, make level, bring down to the same level

coagmentātī·ō -ōnis f combination, union

coagment·ō -āre vt to join, glue, cement

coagment·um -ī n joint

coāgŭl·um -ī n rennet

coal·escō -escĕre -ŭī -itum vi to grow firm, take root; to increase, become strong, become established, thrive

coangust·ō -āre vt to contract, compress; to limit, restrict

coarct- = coart-

coargŭ·ō -ĕre -ī vt to prove conclusively, demonstrate; to refute, prove wrong or guilty; (with genit of the charge) to prove (someone) guilty of

coartāti·ō -ōnis *f* crowding together

coart·ō -āre *vt* to crowd together, confine; to shorten, abridge

coccināt·us -a -um *adj* clothed in scarlet

coccinē·us or **coccin·us -a -um** *adj* scarlet

cocc·um -ī *n* scarlet

coclě·a or **cochlě·a -ae** *f* snail

cocleār·e -is *n* spoon

cocl·es -ĭtis *m* person blind in one eye

Cocl·es -ĭtis *m* Horatius Cocles (*famous for defending the Pons Sublicius against Porsenna's army*)

coctĭl·is -e *adj* baked; brick

coct·us -a -um *pp* of **coquo**; *adj* well-considered

Cōcўt·us -ī *m* river of the lower world

cōdex see **caudex**

cōdicill·ī -ōrum *m pl* small trunks of trees, fire logs; note; petition; codicil

Codr·us -ī *m* last king of Athens, who sacrificed his life for an Athenian victory (1160-1132 B.C.)

coel- = cael-

co·ēmō -ēmere -ēmī -emptum *vt* to buy up

coēmptĭ·ō -ōnis *f* marriage (*contracted by fictitious sale of contracting parties*); fictitious sale of an estate (*to relieve it of religious obligations*)

coēmptĭōnāl·is -e *adj* of a fictitious marriage; used in a mock sale; worthless

coen- = caen-

co·ěō -īre -ĭvī or **-ĭī -ĭtum** *vt* societatem coire to enter an agreement, form an alliance; *vi* to come or go together; to meet, assemble; to be united, combine; to mate, copulate; to congeal, curdle; to agree; to conspire; to clash (*in combat*); (*of wounds*) to close, heal up

coep·ĭō -ĕre -ī -tum *vt & vi* to begin

coept·ō -āre *vt* to begin eagerly; to try; (*with inf*) to try to; *vi* to begin, make a beginning

coept·us -a -um *pp* of **coepio**; *n* beginning; undertaking

coept·us -ūs *m* beginning

coēpulōn·us -ī *m* dinner guest

coērc·ěō -ēre -ŭī -ĭtum *vt* to enclose, confine, hem in; to limit; to restrain, check, control

coērcĭtĭ·ō -ōnis *f* coercion; right to punish

coēt·us -ūs *m* coming together, meeting; crowd, company

Coe·us -ī *m* Titan, father of Latona

cōgitātē *adv* deliberately

cōgitātĭ·ō -ōnis *f* thinking, deliberating; reflection, meditation; thought, plan, design; reasoning power, imagination

cōgĭt·ō -āre *vt* to consider, ponder, reflect on; to imagine; (*with inf*) to intend to; *vi* to think, reflect, meditate

cōgitāt·us -a -um *adj* well-considered, deliberate; *n pl* thoughts, ideas

cognātĭ·ō -ōnis *f* relationship by birth; agreement, resemblance, affinity; relatives, family

cognāt·us -a -um *adj* related by birth; related, similar, connected; *mf* relative

cognitĭ·ō -ōnis *f* learning, acquiring knowledge; notion, idea, knowledge; recognition; (law) inquiry, investigation, trial; (*with genit*) knowledge of, acquaintance with

cognĭt·or -ōris *m* advocate, attorney; defender, protector; witness

cognĭtus *pp* of **cognosco**; *adj* acknowledged

cognōm·en -ĭnis *n* surname, family name (*e.g., Caesar*)

cognōment·um -ī *n* surname; name

cognōmināt·us -a -um *adj* synonymous

cognōmĭn·is -e *adj* like-named, of the same name

co·gnoscō -gnoscěre -gnōvī -gnĭtum *vt* to become acquainted with, get to know, learn; to recognize, identify; to inquire into, investigate; to criticize, appreciate; to reconnoiter; **cognovisse** to know

cō·gěre -ēgī -actum *vt* to gather together, collect, convene; to thicken, condense, curdle; to pressure, bring pressure upon; to compel, force; to coax; to exact, extort; to infer, conclude; **agmen cogere** to bring up the rear

cohaer·ens -entis *adj* adjoining, continuous; consistent; harmonious

cohaerentĭ·a -ae *f* coherence, connection

co·haerěō -haerēre -haesī -haesum *vi* to stick or cling together, cohere; to be consistent, be in agreement; (*with abl*) to consist of, be composed of; (*with cum + abl*) to be closely connected with, be in harmony with, be consistent with; **inter se cohaerere** to be consistent

co·haerescō -haerescěre -haesī *vi* to cling together, cohere

cohēr·ēs -ēdis *m* or *f* coheir

cohĭb·ěō -ēre -ŭī *vt* to hold together, hold close, confine; to hold back, repress, check, stop

cohonest·ō -āre *vt* to do honor to, celebrate

cohorr·escō -escěre -ŭī *vi* to shiver all over

cohor·s -tis *f* yard (*esp. for cattle or chickens*); train, retinue, escort; (mil) cohort (*comprising 3 maniples or 6 centuries and forming one tenth of a legion*)

cohortātĭ·ō -ōnis *f* encouragement

cohortĭcŭl·a -ae *f* small cohort

cohort·or -ārī -ātus sum *vt* to encourage, cheer up, urge on

coĭtĭ·ō -ōnis *f* conspiracy, coalition; agreement

coĭt·us -ūs *m* meeting; sexual union

colăph·us -ī *m* slap, blow with a fist

Colch·is -**ĭdis** *f* country on E. end of the Black Sea; Medea

cōlĕ·us -**ī** *m* sack, scrotum

cōl·is -**is** *m* stalk, cabbage

collabasc·ō -**ĕre** *vi* to waver, totter

collabefact·ō -**āre** *vt* to shake hard

collabe·fīō -**fĭĕrī** -**factus sum** *vi* to collapse, be ruined, fall to pieces

col·lābor -**lābī** -**lapsus sum** *vi* to collapse, fall to pieces

collacerāt·us -**a** -**um** *adj* torn to pieces

collacrĭmātĭ·ō -**ōnis** *f* weeping

collacrĭm·ō -**āre** *vt* to cry bitterly over; *vi* to cry together

collactĕ·a -**ae** *f* foster sister

collār·e -**is** *n* collar

Collātĭ·a -**ae** *f* old town in Latium

Collātīn·us -**ī** *m* husband of Lucretia

collātĭ·ō -**ōnis** *f* bringing together; contribution of money, collection; comparison, analogy; **signorum collatio** clash of troops

collāt·or -**ōris** *m* contributor

collātus *pp* of **confero**

collandātĭ·ō -**ōnis** *f* warm praise

colland·ō -**āre** *vt* to praise highly

collax·ō -**āre** *vt* to make loose

collect·a -**ae** *f* contribution of money

collectīcĭ·us -**a** -**um** *adj* hastily-gathered

collectĭ·ō -**ōnis** *f* gathering; summing up, recapitulation; inference

collectus *pp* of **colligo**

collect·us -**ūs** *m* collection

collēg·a -**ae** *m* colleague, partner (*in office*); associate, companion; fellow member (*of a club*)

collēg·ĭum -**ĭī** or -**ī** *n* association in office; official body, board, college, guild, company, corporation, society

collībert·us -**ī** *m* fellow freedman

collĭb·et or **collŭb·et** -**ēre** -**ŭit** -**ĭtum** *v impers* it pleases

col·līdō -**līdĕre** -**līsī** -**līsum** *vt* to smash to pieces, shatter, crush; to cause to clash, set at variance

colligātĭ·ō -**ōnis** *f* binding together, connection

collĭg·ō -**āre** *vt* to tie together, connect; to unite, combine; to fasten, chain; to stop, hinder

col·lĭgō -**lĭgĕre** -**lēgī** -**lectum** *vt* to pick up, gather together, collect; to contract, compress, concentrate; to acquire gradually; to infer, conclude, gather; to assemble, bring together; to enumerate; to gather, repair; to check, control (*horse*); **animum colligere, mentem colligere,** or **se colligere** to collect or compose oneself, muster one's courage, rally, come to, come around; **vasa colligere** to pack up (*for the march*)

Collīn·a Port·a (*genit:* **Collīn·ae Port·ae**) *f* Colline Gate (*near the Quirinal Hill*)

collīnĕ·ō -**āre** *vt* to aim straight; *vi* to hit the mark

col·lĭnō -**lĭnĕre** -**lēvī** -**lĭtum** *vt* to smear; to defile

colliquefact·us -**a** -**um** *adj* dissolved, melted

coll·is -**is** *m* hill

collocātĭ·ō -**ōnis** *f* arrangement; giving in marriage

collŏc·ō -**āre** *vt* to place, put in order, arrange; to station, deploy; to give in marriage; to lodge, quarter; to occupy, employ; **se collocare** to settle, settle down (*in a place*)

collocuplēt·ō -**āre** *vt* to enrich, make quite rich

collocūtĭ·ō -**ōnis** *f* conversation, conference

colloqu·ĭum -**ĭī** or -**ī** *n* conversation, conference

col·lŏquor -**lŏquī** -**locūtus sum** *vt* to talk to; *vi* to talk together, converse, hold a conference

collŭbet see **collĭbet**

collūc·ĕō -**ēre** *vi* to shine brightly, be entirely illuminated; (fig) to be resplendent

col·lūdō -**lūdĕre** -**lūsī** -**lūsum** *vi* to play together; to be in collusion; (with *dat*) to play with

coll·um -**ī** *n* neck

col·lŭō -**luĕre** -**lŭī** -**lūtum** *vt* to wash out, rinse, moisten; **ora colluere** to wet the mouth, quench the thirst

collūsĭ·ō -**ōnis** *f* collusion

collūs·or -**ōris** *m* playmate; fellow-gambler

collustr·ō -**āre** *vt* to light up; to survey, inspect; (in painting) to represent in bright colors

collutulent·ō -**āre** *vt* to soil, defile

colluvĭ·ō -**ōnis** or **colluvĭ·ēs** (*genit not in use*) *f* dregs, impurities, filth; rabble

collȳb·us -**ī** *m* conversion of currency; rate of exchange

collȳr·a -**ae** *f* noodles, macaroni

collȳr·ĭum -**ĭī** or -**ī** *n* eyewash

colō colĕre colŭī cultum *vt* to till, cultivate, work; to live in (*a place*); to guard, protect; to honor, cherish, revere, worship; to adorn, dress; to practice, follow; to experience, live through, spend

colocāsĭ·a -**ae** *f* lotus, water lily

colōn·a -**ae** *f* peasant woman

colōnĭ·a -**ae** *f* colony, settlement; colonists, settlers

colōnĭc·us -**a** -**um** *adj* colonial

colōn·us -**ī** *m* settler; farmer

col·or or **col·ōs** -**ōris** *m* color, hue, tint; external condition; complexion; tone, style; luster; grace; colorful pretext

colōrāt·us -**a** -**um** *adj* colored, tinted; healthily tanned

colōr·ō -**āre** *vt* to color, tan; (fig) to give a certain tone to

colossē·us -**a** -**um** *adj* colossal

coloss·us -**ī** *m* gigantic statue, colossus

colostr·a -**ae** *f* or **colostr·um** -**ī** *n* first milk after delivery, colostrum

colŭb·er -rī *m* snake, adder

colŭbr·a -ae *f* snake, adder (*female*)

colubrĭf·er -ĕra -ĕrum *adj* snaky

colubrīn·us -a -um *adj* snaky; wily, sly

cōl·um -ī *n* strainer

columb·a -ae *f* pigeon, dove (*female*)

columb·ar -āris *n* collar

columbār·ium -iī *or* **-ī** *n* pigeonhole; (fig) vault with niches for cinerary urns

columbīn·us -a -um *adj* of a dove or pigeon; *m* little dove

columb·us -ī *m* pigeon, dove

columell·a -ae *f* small column

colŭm·en -ĭnis *n* height, summit, peak; gable; pillar; head, leader; support, prop

column·a -ae *f* column, pillar, post; (fig) pillar, support; waterspout; **ad columnam** (i.e., **Maeniam**) **pervenire** *or* **ad columnam adhaerescere** to be brought to punishment (*because at the Columna Maenia in the Roman forum criminals and debtors were tried*); *f pl* display columns (*in bookshop*); bookshop

Column·a Maeni·a (*genit:* **Column·ae Maeni·ae**) *f* column in the Roman forum, possibly of the Basilica Porcia supporting a projecting balcony (**maenianum**), at which thieves and slaves were whipped and to which debtors were summoned for trial; whipping post

columnār·ium -iī *or* **-ī** *n* tax on house pillars

columnār·ius -iī *or* **-ī** *m* criminal debtor (*punished at the Columna Maenia*)

colŭrn·us -a -um *adj* made of hazel wood

col·us -ī *or* **-ūs** *m or f* distaff

cōlўphĭ·a -ōrum *n pl* choice cuts of meat, loin cuts

com·a -ae *f* hair (*of the head*); mane (*of horse or lion*); fleece; foliage; grass; sunbeams

com·ans -antis *adj* hairy, long-haired; plumed (*helmet*); leafy; **comans stella** comet

cōmarch·us -ī *m* chief burgess

comāt·us -a -um *adj* long-haired; leafy

combĭb·ō -ĕre -ī *vt* to drink up; to absorb; to swallow, engulf; to repress, conceal (*tears*); to imbibe, acquire (*knowledge*)

combĭb·ō -ōnis *m* drinking partner

comb·ūrō -ūrĕre -ussī -ustum *vt* to burn up, consume; (fig) to ruin

com·ĕdō -edĕre (*or* **-esse**) **-ēdī -ēsum** (*or* **-estum**) *vt* to eat up, consume, devour; to waste, squander, dissipate, spend; **se comedere** to pine away

com·es -ĭtis *m or f* companion, fellow traveler; associate, comrade; attendant, retainer, dependant; concomitant, consequence

comēt·ēs -ae *m* comet

cōmĭcē *adv* like a comedy

cōmic·us -a -um *adj* of comedy, comic; **comicum aurum** stage money; *m* actor (*of comedy*); playwright (*of comedy*)

cōm·is -e *adj* courteous, polite; kind, friendly; (with *dat* or with **erga** or **in** + *acc*) friendly toward

cōmissābund·us -a -um *adj* parading in a riotous bacchanalian procession; carousing

cōmissātĭ·ō -ōnis *f* riotous bacchanalian procession; wild drinking party

cōmissāt·or -ōris *m* drinking partner, reveler, guzzler

cōmiss·or *or* **cōmis·or -ārī -ātus sum** *vi* to join in a bacchanalian procession; to revel, guzzle

cōmĭt·ās -ātis *f* politeness, courteousness; kindness, friendliness

comĭtāt·us -ūs *m* escort, retinue; imperial retinue, court; company (*traveling together*), caravan

cōmĭter *adv* politely, courteously; kindly

comĭtĭ·a -ōrum *n pl* comitia, popular assembly; elections; **comitia consularia** *or* **comitia consulum** election of consuls; **comitia praetoria** election of praetors

comĭtĭāl·is -e *adj* of the assembly; of the elections, election

comĭtĭāt·us -ūs *m* assembly of the people in the comitia

comĭt·ium -iī *or* **-ī** *n* comitium, assembly place

comĭt·ō -āre *or* **comĭt·or -ārī -ātus sum** *vt* to accompany, attend, follow

commacŭl·ō -āre *vt* to spot, stain; to defile

commanipulār·is -is *m* comrade in the same brigade

commarīt·us -ī *m* fellow husband

commeāt·us -ūs *m* passage, thoroughfare; leave of absence, furlough; transport, passage, convoy; (mil) lines of communication; (mil) supplies; **in commeatu esse** to be on a furlough

commedĭt·or -ārī -ātus sum *vt* to practice; to imitate

commemĭn·ī -isse *vt & vi* to remember well

commemorābĭl·is -e *adj* memorable, worth mentioning

commemorātĭ·ō -ōnis *f* recollection, remembrance; mentioning, reminding

commemŏr·ō -āre *vt* to keep in mind, remember; to bring up (*in conversation*), to mention, recount, relate; *vi* (with **de** + *abl*) to be mindful of

commendābĭl·is -e *adj* commendable, praiseworthy

commendātĭcĭ·us -a -um *adj* of recommendation, of introduction; **litterae commendaticiae** letter of introduction or of recommenda-

commendātĭ·ō -ōnis f recommendation, recommending; commendation, praise; excellence, worth

commendāt·or -ōris m backer, supporter

commendātr·ix -īcis f backer, supporter (female)

commendāt·us -a -um adj commended, recommended, acceptable, approved

commend·ō -āre vt to entrust, commit; to recommend; to render acceptable

commentārĭŏl·um -ī n short treatise

commentār·ĭum -ĭī or **-ī** n or **commentār·ĭus -ĭī** or **-ī** m notebook, journal, diary, notes, memorandum; (law) brief; pl memoirs

commentātĭ·ō -ōnis f careful study, deep reflection; preparation; essay, treatise

commentīcĭ·us -a -um adj thought out; invented, fictitious, imaginary; ideal; forged, false; legendary

comment·or -ārī -ātus sum vt to think over, consider well, study; to invent, contrive, make up; to prepare, produce (writings); to discuss, write about; to imitate, adopt the language of; vi to meditate, deliberate, reflect; to experiment in speaking, attempt to speak

comment·or -ōris m inventor

comment·us -a -um pp of **comminiscor**; adj fictitious, feigned, invented, pretended; n invention, fiction, fabrication; device, contrivance

commē·ō -āre vi to come and go; to go back and forth; to travel repeatedly; to make frequent visits

commerc·ĭum -ĭī or **-ī** n trade, commerce; right to trade; dealings, business; communication, correspondence; **belli commercia** ransom

commerc·or -ārī vt to deal in, purchase

commer·ĕo -ēre -ŭī -ĭtum or **commer·ĕor -ērī -ĭtus sum** vt to earn, merit, deserve fully; to be guilty of

com·mētĭor -mētīrī -mensus sum vt to measure; (with **cum** + abl) to measure (something) in terms of

commēt·ō -āre vi to go often

commigr·ō -āre vi to move, migrate

commīlit·ĭum -ĭī or **-ī** n comradeship, companionship, fellowship

commīlit·ō -ōnis m fellow soldier, army buddy

comminātĭ·ō -ōnis f threatening, menacing; f pl violent threats

com·mingō -mingĕre -minxī -mictum vt to urinate on; to wet (bed); to defile, pollute; **commictum caenum** (term of reproach) dirty skunk

com·miniscor -miniscī -mentus sum vt to contrive, invent, devise

commin·or -ārī -ātus sum vt to threaten violently

commin·ŭō -ŭĕre -ŭī -ūtum vt to lessen considerably, diminish; to break up, shatter; to weaken, impair; to humble, crush, humiliate

commĭnus adv hand to hand, at close quarters; near at hand, near; **comminus conferre signa** to engage in hand-to-hand fighting

com·miscĕō -miscēre -miscŭī -mixtum vt to mix together, mix up, join together; to unite, bring together, mingle

commiserātĭ·ō -ōnis f pitying; (rhet) appeal to compassion

commiseresc·ō -ĕre vi (with genit) to feel pity for; v impers (with genit) **me commiserescit ejus** I pity him

commisĕr·or -ārī -ātus sum vt to feel sympathy for; vi (rhet) to try to evoke sympathy

commissĭ·ō -ōnis f beginning (of fight, game, etc.)

commissūr·a -ae f connection; joint

commiss·us -a -um pp of **committō**; n offense, crime; secret; undertaking

commītĭg·ō -āre vt to soften up

com·mittō -mittĕre -mīsī -missum vt to connect, unite; to match (for a fight, dance); to start, commence; to undertake; to commit, perpetrate; to entrust, commit; to engage in (battle); to incur (penalty); **se committere** (with dat or in + acc) to venture into

commodĭt·ās -ātis f proportion, symmetry; aptness of expression; convenience, comfort; right time; pleasantness (of personality); courtesy, kindness

commŏd·ō -āre vt to adjust, adapt; to bestow, supply, lend, give; vi to be obliging; (with dat) to adapt oneself to, be obliging to

commodŭlē or **commodŭlum** adv nicely, conveniently

commŏdum adv at a good time, in the nick of time; **commodum cum** just at the time when

commŏd·us -a -um adj adapted, suitable, fit, convenient; opportune (time); convenient, comfortable, advantageous; agreeable, obliging, pleasant (person); **quod commodum est** just as you please; n convenience, opportunity; profit, advantage; privilege, favor; loan; pay, reward; **commodo tuo** at your convenience

commŏl·ĭor -īrī -ītus sum vt to set in motion

commone·facĭō -facĕre -fēcī -factum vt to recall, call to mind; (with acc of person and genit of thing) to remind (someone) of

common·ĕō -ēre -ŭī -ĭtum vt to remind, warn; (with genit or de + abl) to remind (someone) of

commonstr·ō -āre vt to point out clearly

commorātĭ·ō -ōnis f delaying, staying; residence, sojourn; (rhet) dwelling (*on some point*)

com·mŏrĭor -**mŏrī** -**mortŭus sum** *vi* (with *dat* or with **cum** + *abl*) to die with, die at the same time as

commŏr·or -**ārī** -**ātus sum** *vt* to stop, detain; *vi* to linger, stay, stop off; (with **apud** + *acc*) to stay at the house of; **in sententia commorari** to stick to an opinion

commŏtĭ·ō -**ōnis** *f* commotion; **animi commotio** excitement

commŏtĭuncŭl·a -**ae** *f* minor inconvenience

commŏt·us -**a** -**um** *adj* excited, angry; deranged, insane; impassioned, lively (*style*)

com·mŏvĕō -**movēre** -**mōvī** -**mōtum** *vt* to stir up, agitate, shake; to disturb, unsettle, disquiet, excite, shake up; to arouse, provoke; to stir up, generate, produce; to start, introduce (*novelties*); to displace, dislodge (*enemy*); to refute

commūn·e -**is** *n* community, state; **in commune** for general use, for all; in general

commūnĭcātĭ·ō -**ōnis** *f* imparting, communicating

commūnĭc·ō -**āre** or **commūnĭc·or** -**ārī** *vt* to make common; to communicate, impart; share; to share in, take part in; to unite, connect, join

commūnĭ·ō -**ōnis** *f* sharing in common

commūn·ĭō -**īre** -**īvī** or -**iī** -**ītum** *vt* to fortify, strengthen, barricade

commūn·is -**e** *adj* common, public, universal, general; familiar; courteous, affable; democratic; **loca communia** public places; **loci communes** commonplaces, general topics; **sensus communis** common sense; *n* see **commune**

commūnĭter *adv* in common, together

commūnītĭ·ō -**ōnis** *f* road building; (rhet) introduction

commurmŭr·ō -**āre** or **commurmŭr·or** -**ārī** *vi* to murmur, grumble

commūtābĭl·is -**e** *adj* changeable, subject to change; interchangeable

commūtātĭ·ō -**ōnis** *f* changing, change, alteration

commūtāt·us -**ūs** *m* change, alteration

commūt·ō -**āre** *vt* to change, alter; to interchange, exchange; (with *abl* or **cum** + *abl*) to exchange (*something*) for

cōm·ō -**ĕre** -**psī** -**ptum** *vt* to comb, arrange, braid; to adorn, deck out

cōmoedĭ·a -**ae** *f* comedy

cōmoedĭcē *adv* as in comedy

cōmoed·us -**ī** *m* comic actor

cŏmōs·us -**a** -**um** *adj* with long hair, hairy; leafy

compact·us -**a** -**um** *pp* of **compingo**; *adj* compact, well built; *n* agreement

compāg·ēs -**is** *f* joining together, joint, structure, framework

compāg·ō -**ĭnis** *f* connection

compar·ār -**ăris** *adj* equal, on an equal level; (with *dat*) matching

compar·ăris *m* or *f* comrade; playmate; perfect match; spouse

comparābĭl·is -**e** *adj* comparable

comparātĭ·ō -**ōnis** *f* comparison; arrangement; acquisition, preparation, provision; relative position (*of planets*)

comparātīv·us -**a** -**um** *adj* comparative

compār·ĕō -**ēre** -**ŭī** *vi* to be visible, be plain, be evident, appear; to be at hand, be present

compăr·ō -**āre** *vt* to put together, get together, provide; to prepare, arrange; to match; to compare; to procure, get, obtain, collect; to appoint, establish, constitute; **se comparare** (with **ad** or **in** + *acc*) to prepare oneself for, get ready for

comp·ascō -**ascĕre** — -**astum** *vt* & *vi* to feed together

compascŭ·us -**a** -**um** *adj* of public grazing

compec·iscor -**iscī** -**tus sum** *vi* to come to an agreement

compect·us -**a** -**um** *adj* in agreement, agreed; *n* agreement; **compecto** by agreement, according to the agreement

comped·ĭō -**īre** — -**ītum** *vt* to shackle

compellātĭ·ō -**ōnis** *f* rebuke, reprimand

compell·ō -**āre** *vt* to summon, call; to call to account, bring to book; to reproach; (law) to arraign

com·pellō -**pellĕre** -**pŭlī** -**pulsum** *vt* to drive together; to crowd, concentrate; to compel, force, urge, drive on

compendĭārĭ·us -**a** -**um** *adj* short, abridged; **via compendiaria** shortcut

compend·ĭum -**ĭī** or -**ī** *n* careful weighing; saving (*of money*); profit; shortening, abridging; shortcut; **compendi facere** to save; **compendi fieri** to be brief; **suo privato compendio servire** to serve one's own private interests

compensātĭ·ō -**ōnis** *f* compensation, recompense

compens·ō -**āre** *vt* to compensate, make up for

com·percō -**percĕre** -**persī** *vt* to save, hoard up

comperendinātĭ·ō -**ōnis** *f* or **comperendināt·us** -**ūs** *m* (law) two-day adjournment

comperendin·ō -**āre** *vt* to adjourn (*court*) for two days; to put off (*defendant*) for two days

comper·ĭō -**īre** -**ī** -**tum** or **comper·ĭor** -**īrī** -**tus sum** *vt* to find out, ascertain, learn; **compertum habeo** or **compertum mihi est**

I have ascertained, I know for certain

compert·us -a -um *adj* discovered, well authenticated; (with *genit*) convicted of

comp·ēs -ĕdis *f* shackle (*for the feet*); (fig) bond

compesc·ō -ĕre -ŭī *vt* to confine, restrain, suppress, check, chain down

competīt·or -ōris *m* competitor, rival

competītr·ix -īcis *f* competitor, rival (*female*)

competĕ·ō -ĕre -īvī or **-iī -ītum** *vi* to coincide, come together, meet; to be adequate, be suitable; (with **ad** + *acc*) to be capable of

compīlātī·ō -ōnis *f* pillaging, plundering; (contemptuously said of a collection of documents) compilation

compīl·ō -āre *vt* to pillage, plunder

com·pingō -pingĕre -pēgī -pactum *vt* to put together, frame, compose; to confine, lock up, put (*in jail*)

compitāl·ia -ium or **-iōrum** *n pl* festival celebrated annually at the crossroads in honor of the Lares of the crossroads on a day appointed by the praetor

compitālici·us -a -um *adj* of the crossroads

compitāl·is -e *adj* of the crossroads

compīt·um -ī *n* crossroads, intersection

complac·ĕō -ēre -ŭī or **-ĭtus sum** *vi* (with *dat*) to be quite pleasing to, suit just fine

complān·ō -āre *vt* to make even or level; to raze to the ground, pull down

com·plector -plectī -plexus sum *vt* to embrace, clasp; to comprise; (of writings) to include; to grasp, understand; to display affection for, display esteem for; to enclose (*an area*); to seize, take possession of

complēment·um -ī *n* complement

compl·ĕō -ēre -ēvī -ētum *vt* to fill, fill up; (mil) to bring (*legion, etc.*) to full strength; (mil) to man; to complete; to impregnate; to fill with sound, make resound; to supply fully, furnish

complēt·us -a -um *adj* complete; perfect

complexi·ō -ōnis *f* combination, connection; conclusion in a syllogism; dilemma; (rhet) period

complex·us -ūs *m* embrace; (fig) love, affection; close combat; in **complexum alicujus venīre** to come to close grips with someone

complicāt·us -a -um *adj* complicated, involved

complic·ō -āre *vt* to fold up

complōrātī·ō -ōnis *f* or **complōrāt·us -ūs** *m* groaning, lamentation, wailing

complōr·ō -āre *vt* to mourn for

complūr·ēs -ium *adj* several; a good many

complūriēns or **complūriēs** *adv* several times, a good many times

compluscŭl·ī -ae -a *adj* a fair number of

compluv·ium -iī or **-ī** *n* rain trap (*quadrangular open space in middle of Roman house towards which the roof sloped so as to direct the rain into a basin, called impluvium, built into the floor*)

com·pōnō -pōnĕre -posŭī -positum *vt* to put together, join; to construct, build; to compose, write; to arrange, settle, agree upon, fix, set; to match, pair, couple; to compare, contrast; to put away; take down, lay aside; to lay out, bury (*the dead*); to compose, pacify, allay, calm, appease, quiet, reconcile; to feign, invent, concoct, contrive

comport·ō -āre *vt* to carry together, bring in, collect, gather, accumulate

comp·os -ŏtis *adj* (with *genit* or *abl*) in possession of, master of, having control over; having a share in, participating in; **compos animi** or **compos mentis** sane; **compos sui** self-controlled; **compos voti** having one's prayer answered

composité *adv* in an orderly manner, orderly, regularly; **composite dicere** to speak logically

compositi·ō -ōnis *f* putting together, connecting, arranging, composition; matching (*of gladiators, etc.*); reconciliation (*of friends*); orderly arrangement (*of words*)

composit·or -ōris *m* composer, author

compositūr·a -ae *f* connection

composit·us -a -um *pp* of **compono**; *adj* compound (*words, etc.*); prepared, well arranged, orderly; made-up, feigned, false; adapted; composed, calm, settled; *n* agreement, compact; **composito** or **ex composito** by agreement, as agreed, as had been arranged

compotātī·ō -ōnis *f* drinking party

compot·iō -īre -īvī -ītum *vt* (with *acc* of person and *abl* of thing) to make (*someone*) master of, put (*someone*) in possession of

compōt·or -ōris *m* drinking partner

compōtr·ix -īcis *f* drinking partner (*female*)

comprans·or -ōris *m* dinner companion, fellow guest

comprecātī·ō -ōnis *f* public supplication

comprĕc·or -ārī -ātus sum *vt* to pray earnestly to, implore, supplicate

compre·hendō -hendĕre -hendī -hensum or **compren·dō -dĕre -dī -sum** *vt* to bind together, unite; to take hold of, grasp, seize, catch, apprehend; to attack, seize, arrest, capture, apprehend; to detect, discover; to occupy (*places*); to grasp, perceive, comprehend, take in; to express, describe, narrate, recount; **ignem comprehendere** to catch fire; **memoriā comprehendere** to remember; **numero comprehendere** to enumerate, count

comprehensibil·is -e *adj* comprehensible, conceivable, intelligible

comprehensi·ō -ōnis *f* seizing, laying hold of; arrest; comprehension, perception; combining; (rhet) period

comprendō see **comprehendo**

compressi·ō -ōnis *f* pressing closely; embrace; (rhet) compression

compress·us -ūs *m* compression; embrace

com·primō -primĕre -pressī -pressum *vt* to press together, bring together, compress, close; to embrace; to check, curb, restrain; to keep back, suppress, withhold, conceal; **animam comprimere** to hold the breath; **compressis manibus sedere** to sit on folded hands, to not lift a hand; **ordines comprimere** to close ranks

comprobāti·ō -ōnis *f* approbation, approval

comprobāt·or -ōris *m* enthusiastic backer

comprŏb·ō -āre *vt* to approve, sanction, acknowledge; to prove, establish, make good, confirm, verify

comprōmiss·um -ī *n* mutual agreement to abide by arbiter's decision

comprō-mittō -mittĕre -mīsī -missum *vi* to agree to abide by an arbiter's decision

compt·us -a -um *pp* of **como**; *adj* neat, elegant

compt·us -ūs *m* hairdo

com·pungō -pungĕre -punxī -punctum *vt* to puncture, prick; to tattoo; to prod

compūt·ō -āre *vt* to compute, count

computresc·ō -ĕre *vi* to become putrid, rot

Cōm·um -ī *n* Como (*town N. of the Po and birthplace of Pliny the Younger*)

cōnām·en -ĭnis *n* effort, struggle; support, prop; **conamen mortis** attempt at suicide

cōnāt·um -ī *n* effort, exertion; attempt, undertaking, venture

cōnāt·us -ūs *m* effort; endeavor; impulse, inclination, tendency; undertaking

concăc·ō -āre *vt* to defile with excrement

concaed·ēs -ĭum *f pl* log barricade

concale·faciō -facĕre -fēcī -factum *vt* to warm up

concall·escō -escĕre -uī *vi* to grow hard; to become insensible; to become shrewd

concastīg·ō -āre *vt* to punish severely

concăv·ō -āre *vt* to curve, bend

concăv·us -a -um *adj* concave, hollow; curved, arched, bent, vaulted; deep (*valley*)

con·cēdō -cēdĕre -cessī -cessum *vt* to give up, relinquish, cede; to pardon, overlook; to allow, grant; *vi* to go away, give way, depart, withdraw, retire; (with *dat*) **a** to yield to, submit to, give way to, succumb to; **b** to submit to, comply with; **c** to make allowance for, pardon; **d** to be inferior to; (with **in** + *acc*) to pass over to, be merged in; **fato concedere, naturae concedere,** or **vitā concedere** to die

concelĕbr·ō -āre *vt* to frequent, fill; to pursue (*studies*); to fill with life, enliven; to celebrate; to make widely known, proclaim, publish

concēnāti·ō -ōnis *f* dining together

concenti·ō -ōnis *f* singing together, harmony

concenturi·ō -āre *vt* to marshal by the hundreds; (with *dat*) to bring (*fear*) to

concent·us -ūs *m* concert, symphony; harmony; choir; concord, agreement, harmony

concepti·ō -ōnis *f* conception (*becoming pregnant*); (law) composing legal formulas

conceptīv·us -a -um *adj* movable (*holidays*)

concept·us -ūs *m* conception (*becoming pregnant*), pregnancy

concerp·ō -ĕre -sī -tum *vt* to tear up, tear to shreds; (fig) to cut up, abuse, revile

concertāti·ō -ōnis *f* controversy, dispute

concertāt·or -ōris *m* rival

concertātōri·us -a -um *adj* controversial

concert·ō -āre *vi* to fight it out; to quarrel, debate

concessi·ō -ōnis *f* concession; admission (*of guilt with plea for mercy*)

concess·ō -āre *vt* (with *inf*) to stop (*doing something*)

concess·us -a -um *pp* of **concedo**; *n* concession (*thing allowed*)

concess·us -ūs *m* permission, leave

conch·a -ae *f* clam, oyster, mussel, murex; clam shell, oyster shell, mussel shell; pearl; purple dye; trumpet (*of Triton*); vessel (*containing ointments, etc.*); vulva

conch·is -is *f* bean

conchĭt·a -ae *m* clam digger, conch digger

conchÿliāt·us -a -um *adj* purple

conchÿl·ium -iī or **-ī** *n* shellfish, clam, oyster; murex; purple dye, purple; purple garments

concĭd·ō -ĕre -ī *vi* to collapse; to fall (*in battle*); (fig) to decline, fail, fall, decay, perish, go to ruin; (of winds) to subside

con·cīdō -cīdĕre -cīdī -cīsum *vt* to cut up, cut to pieces, kill; to beat severely; (fig) to crush (*with arguments*); (rhet) to chop up (*sentences*)

con·ciĕō -ciĕre -cīvī -cītum or **-ciō**

-cīre -cīvī -cītum *vt* to assemble; to shake, stir up; (fig) to rouse, stir up, provoke

conciliābŭl·um -ī *n* public meeting place

conciliātĭ·ō -ōnis *f* union, bond; conciliating, winning over; inclination, bent, disposition

conciliāt·or -ōris *m* mediator, promoter

conciliātrīcŭl·a -ae *f* procuress, madame

conciliātr·ix -īcis *f* mediator, promoter, match maker (*female*)

conciliāt·us -a -um *adj* (with ad + *acc*) endeared to, favorable to

conciliāt·us -ūs *m* union, connection, combination

concilĭ·ō -āre *vt* to bring together, unite, connect; to unite (*in feeling*), make friendly, win over; to bring about (*by mediation*); to acquire, win

concil·ĭum -ĭī *or* -ī *n* gathering, meeting, assembly; council; combination, union

concinnē *adv* nicely, elegantly

concinnit·ās -ātis *or* concinnĭtūd·ō -ĭnis *f* finish, elegance, symmetry (*of style*)

concinn·ō -āre *vt* to make symmetrical, get right, adjust; to bring about, produce, cause; to make (*e.g., insane*)

concinn·us -a -um *adj* symmetrical; neat, elegant; courteous, agreeable, nice; polished (*style*)

concin·ō -ĕre -ŭī *vt* to sing, celebrate; to prophesy; *vi* to sing or play together, harmonize; (fig) to agree, harmonize

concĭō *see* concieo

concĭō *see* contio

concipĭl·ō -āre *vt* to carry off

con-cipĭō -cipĕre -cēpī -ceptum *vt* to take hold of, take up, take, receive; to take in, absorb; to imagine, conceive, think; to understand, comprehend, perceive; to catch (*fire*); to entertain (*hope*); to draw up in formal language; to announce in formal language

concīsē *adv* concisely

concīsĭ·ō -ōnis *f* (rhet) dividing a sentence into short phrases

concīs·us -a -um *pp of* concido; *adj* cut up, short, concise

concitātē *adv* vigorously, vividly

concitātĭ·ō -ōnis *f* rapid movement; excitement; sedition, agitation

concitāt·or -ōris *m* instigator, ringleader; rabble-rouser

concitāt·us -a -um *adj* rapid, swift; excited

concĭt·ō -āre *vt* to stir up, rouse, urge; to cause, occasion

concĭt·or -ōris *m* instigator, ringleader; rabble-rouser

conclāmātĭ·ō -ōnis *f* loud shouting, yell; acclamation

conclāmĭt·ō -āre *vi* to keep on shouting, keep on yelling

conclām·ō -āre *vt* to shout, yell; to call to (*for help*); to call repeatedly by name, bewail (*the dead*); to exclaim; jam conclamatum est all's lost; vasa conclamare to give the signal to pack up (*for the march*); *vi* to shout, yell, cry out; ad arma conclamare to sound the alarm (*for an attack*)

conclāv·e -is *n* room; bedroom; dining room; cage, stall, coop

con-clūdō -clūdĕre -clūsī -clūsum *vt* to shut up, enclose; to include, comprise; to round off, conclude (*letter, speech*); to end rhythmically; to deduce, infer, conclude

conclūsē *adv* (rhet) in rhythmical cadence

conclūsĭ·ō -ōnis *f* blockade; end, conclusion; conclusion (*of a speech*), peroration; conclusion (*of syllogism*); (rhet) period

conclūsĭuncŭl·a -ae *f* false conclusion

conclūs·us -a -um *pp of* concludo; *adj* confined; *n* logical conclusion

concŏl·or -ōris *adj* of the same color

concomitāt·us -a -um *adj* escorted

con-cŏquō -cŏquĕre -coxī -coctum *vt* to cook thoroughly; to boil down; to digest; to stomach, put up with; to cook up, concoct (*plans*); to weigh seriously, reflect upon, consider well; to prepare, ripen

concordĭ·a -ae *f* concord, harmony, good rapport; union

concordĭter *adv* harmoniously

concord·ō -āre *vi* to be of one mind, be in harmony, agree

concor·s -dis *adj* of the same mind, concordant, agreeing, harmonious

concrēbr·escō -escĕre -ŭī *vi* to grow strong

concrēd·ō -ĕre -idī -itum *vi* to entrust, commit, consign

concrĕm·ō -āre *vt* to burn to ashes, burn up

concrep·ō -āre -ŭī -itum *vi* to rattle, creak, grate, clash, sound, make noise; digitis concrepare to snap the fingers

con-crescō -crescĕre -crēvī -cretum *vi* to grow together; to congeal, curdle, clot; to stiffen; to take shape, grow, increase

concrētĭ·ō -ōnis *f* condensing, congealing; matter, substance

concrēt·us -a -um *pp of* concresco; *adj* grown together, compounded; condensed, congealed, curdled, thick, stiff, hard; frozen; inveterate; dim (*light*); *n* hardness, solid matter

concrīmin·or -ārī *vi* to make bitter charges

concrucĭ·ō -āre *vt* to torture

concubīn·a -ae *f* concubine

concubīnāt·us -ūs *m* concubinage, free love

concubīn·us -ī *m* adulterer

concubit·us -ūs *m* reclining together (*at table*); sexual intercourse

concubĭ·us -a -um *adj* used only in

the expression **concubiā nocte** early in the night, at bedtime; *n* bedtime

conculc·ō -āre *vt* to trample under foot, despise, treat with contempt

con·cumbō -cumbĕre -cubŭī -cubĭtum *vi* to lie together; (with **cum** + *abl*) to sleep with, have intercourse with

concup·iscō -iscĕre -īvī -ītum *vt* to long for, covet; to aspire to, strive after

concūr·ō -āre *vt* to take good care of

con·currō -currĕre -currī or **-cucurrī -cursum** *vi* to run together, flock together; to unite; to strike one another, crash; (mil) to clash, engage in combat; (mil) to happen at the same time, coincide; (with **ad** + *acc*) to have recourse to, run for help to; **concurritur** the armies meet, there is a clash

concursāti·ō -ōnis *f* running together; rushing about; (mil) skirmishing

concursāt·or -ōris *m* (mil) skirmisher

concursi·ō -ōnis *f* meeting, concurrence; (rhet) repetition for emphasis

concurs·ō -āre *vt* to run around to; **domos concursare** to run from house to house; *vi* to rush about excitedly, dash up and down; (mil) to skirmish

concurs·us -ūs *m* running together, concourse, assembly; union, combination; collision; (mil) rush, charge, clash

concuss·us -ūs *m* shaking, concussion

con·cutiō -cutĕre -cussī -cussum *vt* to strike together, bang together; to convulse; to strike, shake, shatter; to shock; to wave (*the hand*); to brandish (*weapon*); to shake out, ransack, examine; to shake, alarm, trouble, terrify

condal·ium -iī or **-ī** *n* slave's ring

condēc·et -ēre *v impers* it befits, it becomes

condecŏr·ō -āre *vt* to grace, honor, adorn

condemnāt·or -ōris *m* accuser, prosecutor

condemn·ō -āre *vt* to condemn, convict, find guilty, sentence, doom; to blame, condemn; to prosecute successfully, bring a conviction against

condens·ō -āre *vt* to press close together, condense

condens·us -a -um *adj* close together, thick, crowded

condici·ō -ōnis *f* arrangement, settlement, agreement; stipulation, terms, condition; state, situation; circumstances, rank, place; marriage contract, marriage; **ea condicione ut** on condition that; **sub condicione** conditionally; **vitae condicio** way of life, living conditions

con·dīcō -dīcĕre -dixī -dictum *vt*

to talk over, arrange together; to promise; **cenam condicere** (with *dat*) or **ad cenam condicere** (with *dat*) to make a dinner engagement with (*someone*)

condignē *adv* very worthily

condign·us -a -um *adj* fully deserving; (with *abl*) fully worthy of

condiment·um -ī *n* seasoning, spice

cond·iō -īre -īvī or **-iī -ītum** *vt* to preserve, pickle (*fruits, vegetables*); to season; to embalm (*the dead*); (fig) to spice, give spice to

condiscipulāt·us -ūs *m* companionship at school

condiscipŭl·us -ī *m* schoolmate, school companion, fellow student

con·discō -discĕre -didicī *vt* to learn by heart

conditĭō see **condicio**

conditī·ō -ōnis *f* preserving (*of fruits, etc.*); seasoning, spicing

condĭt·or -ōris *m* founder, builder; author, composer

conditōr·ium -iī or **-ī** *n* coffin, cinerary urn; tomb

condīt·us -a -um *pp* of **condio**; *adj* seasoned, spicy; polished (*style*)

con·dō -dĕre -didī -ditum *vt* to build, found; to write, compose (*poetry*); to establish (*an institution*); to store, treasure, hoard; to preserve, pickle; to bury; to conceal, hide, suppress; to shut (*eyes*); to sheathe (*sword*); to place (*soldiers*) in ambush; to plunge, bury (*sword*); to imprison; to memorize; to store up

condoce·faciō -facĕre -fēcī -factum *vt* to train well

condoc·eō -ēre -ŭī -tum *vt* to teach, instruct thoroughly

condol·escō -escĕre -ŭī *vi* to begin to ache, get very sore

condōnātĭ·ō -ōnis *f* donating, donation

condōn·ō -āre *vt* to give, present, deliver, abandon, surrender; to adjudge; (with double *acc*) to make (*someone*) a present of; (with *acc* of thing and *dat* of person) to forgive, pardon (*someone an offense*); **condonare alicui pecunias creditas** to remit someone's debt

condorm·iō -īre *vi* to sleep soundly

condorm·iscō -iscĕre -īvī *vi* to fall sound asleep

condūcibil·is -e *adj* advantageous, profitable; (with **ad** + *acc*) just right for

con·dūcō -dūcĕre -duxī -ductum *vt* to draw together, collect, assemble; to connect, unite; to hire, rent, borrow; to bribe; to employ; to induce; to contract for; *vi* to be of use; (with *dat*) to be useful to, profitable to; (with **ad** or **in** + *acc*) to be conducive to

conductīcĭ·us -a -um *adj* hired, mercenary

conductĭ·ō -ōnis *f* bringing together; recapitulation; hiring, renting

conduct·or -ōris *m* contractor; lessee, tenant

conduct·us -a -um *pp* of **conduco**; *m pl* hired men; (mil) mercenaries; *n* rented apartment, rented house

conduplicāti·ō -ōnis *f* doubling; (humorously) embrace

conduplĭc·ō -āre *vt* to double; **corpora conduplicare** (humorously) to embrace

condūr·ō -āre *vt* to harden, make very hard

cond·us -ī *m* storeroom manager

cō·nectō -nectĕre -nexŭī -nexum *vt* to tie; to connect, join, link; to state as a conclusion; (with *dat*) to implicate (*someone or something*) in; (with *dat* or **cum** + *abl*) to join (*something*) to, connect (*something*) with

cōnexi·ō -ōnis *f* logical conclusion

cōnex·us -a -um *pp* of **conectō**; *adj* connected, joined; **per affinitatem conexus** (with *dat*) related by marriage to; *n* necessary inference, logical connection, necessary consequence

cōnex·us -ūs *m* combination

confābŭl·or -ārī -ātus sum *vt* to discuss; *vi* to converse, have a talk

confarreāti·ō -ōnis *f* solemn marriage ceremony in the presence of the Pontifex Maximus and ten witnesses

confarrĕ·ō -āre *vt* to marry with solemn rites

confātāl·is -e *adj* bound by the same fate

confecti·ō -ōnis *f* completion, successful completion; chewing, mastication

confect·or -ōris *m* finisher, executor; destroyer, consumer

con·ferciō -fercīre — -fertum *vt* to stuff, cram, pack together; to stuff full

con·fĕrō -ferre -tŭlī -lātum *vt* to bring together; to contribute (*money, etc.*); to condense, compress; to bring together (*plans, ideas, etc.*), discuss, talk over; to bear, convey, direct; to devote, apply, confer, bestow, give, lend, grant; to ascribe, attribute, impute, assign; to put off, defer, postpone; (with **in** + *acc*) to change or transform (*someone or something*) into; to compare, contrast; **capita conferre** to put heads together, confer; **gradum conferre** (with **cum** + *abl*) to walk together with; **lites conferre** to quarrel; **pedem cum pede conferre** to fight toe to toe; **se conferre** (with **in** + *acc*) a to go to, head for; **b** to have recourse to; **c** to join (*a group, etc.*); **sermones conferre** (with **cum** + *abl*) to engage in conversation with, to engage (*someone*) in conversation; **signa conferre** to engage in combat, begin fighting

confertim *adv* (mil) shoulder to shoulder

confert·us -a -um *pp* of **conferciō**; *adj* crowded, packed, thick, dense; (mil) shoulder to shoulder

confervēfac·iō -ĕre *vt* to make glow, make melt

con·fervescō -fervescĕre -ferbŭī *vi* to begin to boil, grow hot

confessi·ō -ōnis *f* confession, acknowledgment

confess·us -a -um *pp* of **confiteor**; *adj* acknowledged, incontrovertible, certain; *m* self-acknowledged criminal; *n* admission; **ex confesso** admittedly, beyond doubt; **in confessum venire** to be generally admitted

confestim *adv* immediately, without delay, suddenly

confici·ens -entis *adj* productive, efficient; (with *genit*) productive of; efficient in; *n pl* (with *genit*) sources of

con·ficiō -ficĕre -fēcī -fectum *vt* to make, manufacture, construct; to make ready, prepare, bring about, complete, accomplish, execute, fulfill; to bring about, cause; to bring together, collect; to get together, secure, obtain; to use up, wear out, exhaust; to finish off, weaken, sweep away, destroy, kill; to run through (*money, inheritance*); to chew (*food*); to complete, finish, spend, pass (*time*)

conficti·ō -ōnis *f* fabrication, invention (*of an accusation*)

confid·ens -entis *adj* trustful; self-confident; presumptuous, smug

confidenter *adv* confidently; smugly

confidenti·a -ae *f* confidence; self-confidence, smugness

confīdentilŏqu·us -a -um *adj* speaking confidently

con·fīdō -fīdĕre -fīsus sum *vi* to have confidence, be confident, be sure; (with *dat*) to confide in, rely on, trust, believe; **sibi confidere** to rely on oneself, have self-confidence

con·fīgō -fīgĕre -fixī -fixum *vt* to fasten, join together; to pierce, transfix; (fig) to paralyze

con·fingō -fingĕre -finxī -fictum *vt* to make up, invent, fabricate

confin·is -e *adj* having common boundaries, adjoining; (fig) closely related, akin

confīn·ium -iī or **-ī** *n* common boundary, frontier; (fig) borderline; *n pl* neighbors; confines

confirmāti·ō -ōnis *f* confirmation, encouragement; affirmation, verification, corroboration; (rhet) presentation of evidence

confirmāt·or -ōris *m* guarantor, surety

confirmāt·us -a -um *adj* resolute, confident, courageous; established, certain

confirmit·ās -ātis *f* firmness; stubbornness

confirm·ō -āre vt to strengthen, reinforce; to confirm, sanction, ratify; to encourage; to corroborate; to assert positively; **se confirmare** to recover, get back one's strength

confisc·ō -āre vt to deposit in a bank; to confiscate

confisi·ō -ōnis f confidence, assurance

con·fiteor -fitērī -fessus sum vt to confess, acknowledge, admit; to reveal; vi to confess

conflāgr·ō -āre vi to burn, be on fire; (fig) to burn

conflicti·ō -ōnis f conflict

conflict·ō -āre vt to beat down, strike down; to ruin; **conflictari** to be afflicted, be tormented; vi to contend, struggle, fight

conflict·or -ārī -ātus sum vi to struggle, wrestle

conflict·us -ūs m striking together; wrestling, struggle

con·flīgō -flīgĕre -flīxī -flīctum vt to throw or knock together; (with **cum** + abl) to contrast (something) with, compare (something) with; vi to come into conflict, clash, fight, battle; (with **cum** + abl) to come into conflict with, clash with; (with **adversus** + acc or **contra** + acc) to fight against; **inter se confligere** to collide, collide with one another

confl·ō -āre vt to kindle, ignite; to inflame (passions); to melt down (metals); to bring together, get up, raise (army, money, etc.); to forge, invent (accusation); to bring about, cause, occasion, produce

conflu·ens -entis m confluence, junction (of rivers); m pl confluence

con·fluō -fluĕre -fluxī vi to flow or run together; (fig) to pour in together, come together in crowds

con·fodiō -fodĕre -fōdī -fossum vt to dig up (soil); to stab; (fig) to stab

conformāti·ō -ōnis f shape, form, fashion; idea, notion; arrangement (of words); expression (in the voice); (rhet) figure of speech

conform·ō -āre vt to shape, fashion, put together; to modify, educate

confoss·us -a -um pp of **confodio**; adj full of holes

confractus pp of **confringo**

confragōs·us -a -um adj rough, rugged (terrain); n pl rough terrain

confrĕm·ō -ĕre -ŭī vi to grumble

confric·ō -āre vt to rub vigorously, rub in; **genua confricare** to nag, pester

con·fringō -fringĕre -frēgī -fractum vt to smash, crush; to break down, destroy

con·fugiō -fugĕre -fūgī vi to flee, take refuge, run for help; (with **ad** + acc) (fig) a to resort to, have recourse to; **b** to appeal to

confug·ium -ĭī or **-ī** n place of refuge, shelter

confulg·ĕō -ēre vi to glitter, sparkle

con·fundō -fundĕre -fūdī -fūsum vt to pour together, blend, mingle; to mix up, jumble together, confuse, bewilder, perplex; to spread, diffuse

confūsē adv in disorder, in confusion

confūsi·ō -ōnis f mixing, blending; confusion, mixup, trouble; **confusio oris** blush

confūs·us -a -um pp of **confundo**; adj confused, perplexed; troubled, confused (look)

confūt·ō -āre vt to prevent (water, etc.) from boiling over; to repress, stop; to silence, confute

congĕl·ō -āre vt to cause to freeze up, freeze, harden; **in lapidem congelare** to petrify; vi to freeze, freeze up

congemināti·ō -ōnis f doubling

congemin·ō -āre vt to double

congĕm·ō -ĕre -ŭī vt to deplore deeply; vi to gasp, sigh, or groan deeply

cong·er -rī m eel

congeri·ēs -ēī f heap, pile, mass; funeral pile; accumulation

con·gĕrō -gerĕre -gessī -gestum vt to bring together; to heap up, build up; to keep up, multiply, repeat (arguments); (with **in** + acc) a to shower (weapons) upon, send a barrage of (weapons) upon; **b** to heap (curses, favors, etc.) upon

congĕr·ō -ōnis m thief

congerr·ō -ōnis m playmate

congestīci·us -a -um adj piled up

congest·us -ūs m heap, mass, accumulation

congiāl·is -e adj holding a gallon

congiāri·us -a -um adj holding a gallon; n gift of one gallon (e. g., of oil) apiece to the people; bonus to the army; gift of money to the Roman people; gift of money among private friends

cong·ius -ĭī or **-ī** m Roman liquid measure equaling six sextarii, i.e., about six pints

conglaci·ō -āre vi to freeze up

conglisc·ō -ĕre vi to blaze up

conglobāti·ō -ōnis f massing together

conglŏb·ō -āre vt to make round, form into a ball, roll up

conglomĕr·ō -āre vt to roll up, group together, crowd together; **se in forum conglomerare** to crowd into the forum

conglūtināti·ō -ōnis f gluing together; (fig) combining (of words)

conglūtin·ō -āre vt to glue, cement; (fig) to weld together, cement

congraec·ō -āre vt to squander like the Greeks

congrātūl·or -ārī -ātus sum vi to offer congratulations

con·gredior -grĕdī -gressus sum vt to meet, accost, address, associate with; to fight; vi to come together, meet; to fight; (with **cum** + abl) a to meet with; **b** to associate with; **c** to fight against

congregăbĭl·is -e *adj* gregarious

congregātĭ·ō -ōnis *f* flocking together, congregation, union, association

congrĕg·ō -āre *vt* to herd together; to unite, associate

congressĭ·ō -ōnis *f* meeting, conference

congressus *pp of* **congredior**

congress·us -ūs *m* meeting, association, society, union; hostile encounter, contest, fight

congrŭ·ens -entis *adj* coinciding, corresponding; suitable, consistent; self-consistent, uniform, harmonious

congruenter *adv* consistently; (with *dat* or **ad** + *acc*) in conformity with; **congruenter naturae vivere** to live in conformity with nature

congruentĭ·a -ae *f* consistency, symmetry

congrŭ·ō -ĕre -ŭī *vi* to coincide; to correspond, agree, be consistent; (with **ad** + *acc* or with **cum** + *abl*) to coincide with; (with *dat* or **cum** + *abl*) to correspond to, agree with, be consistent with; (with *dat* or **in** + *acc*) to agree (*in feeling, opinion*) with

congrŭ·us -a -um *adj* agreeing, agreeable

cōnicĭō or **cŏĭcĭō** see **conjicio**

cōnĭf·er -ĕra -ĕrum *adj* coniferous

cōnĭg·er -ĕra -ĕrum *adj* coniferous

cō·nītor -nītī -nixus sum or **-nīsus sum** *vi* to make a great effort, struggle, exert oneself; (with **in** + *acc*) to struggle toward, press on toward, try to reach

cōnīv·ĕō -ēre -ī *vi* to close the eyes (*in sleep, from light, from fear, etc.*), to blink; (of sun or moon) to be darkened, be eclipsed; (fig) to be drowsy; (with **in** + *abl*) to connive at, wink at, overlook

conjectĭ·ō -ōnis *f* throwing, barrage (*of missiles*); conjecture, interpretation

conject·ō -āre *vt* to conjecture, infer, conclude, guess

conject·or -ōris *m* interpreter of dreams, seer

conjectr·ix -īcis *f* interpreter of dreams, seer (*female*)

conjectūr·a -ae *f* conjecture, guess, inference; interpretation

conjectūrāl·is -e *adj* conjectural

conject·us -ūs *m* throwing together; crowding together; connecting; heap, crowd, pile; throwing, casting, hurling; turning, directing (*eyes*); casting (*a glance*); barrage (*of stones, weapons*); **ad** or **intra teli conjectum venire** to come within range of a weapon

con·jicĭō -jicĕre -jēcī -jectum *vt* to pile together (*e.g., baggage*); to

conclude, infer, conjecture; to interpret (*omen*); to throw, fling, cast; to throw in (*e.g., words in a letter or speech*); **se in fugam** or **se in pedes conjicere** to take to one's heels

conjugāl·is -e *adj* conjugal

conjugātĭ·ō -ōnis *f* etymological relationship (*of words*)

conjugāt·or -ōris *m* uniter (*said of Hymen, god of marriage*)

conjugiāl·is -e *adj* marriage

conjug·ium -iī or **-ī** *n* union (*e.g., of body and soul*); marriage, wedlock; mating (*of animals*); (fig) husband, wife, spouse

conjŭg·ō -āre *vt* to form (*friendship*); **verba conjugata** cognates

conjunctē *adv* conjointly; at the same time; (in logic) conditionally, hypothetically; **conjuncte vivere** to live intimately together

conjunctim *adv* jointly

conjunctĭ·ō -ōnis *f* combination, union; association, connection; friendship; intimacy; marriage; relationship (*by blood or by marriage*); sympathy, affinity; (gram) conjunction

conjunct·us -a -um *adj* (with *dat* or *abl*) bordering upon, near; (with *dat* or *abl*, or with **cum** + *abl*) a connected with; **b** agreeing with, conforming with; *n* connection

con·jungō -jungĕre -junxī -junctum *vt* to join together, connect, unite; to unite in making (*war*); to unite or join in marriage; to unite (*by bonds of friendship*); (with *dat*) to add (*e.g., words*) to (*e.g., a letter*)

con·junx or **con·jux -jŭgis** *m* married person, spouse, husband; *m pl* married couple; *f* married person, spouse, wife; fiancee; bride; the female (*of animals*)

conjūrātĭ·ō -ōnis *f* conspiracy, plot; alliance

conjūrāt·us -a -um *adj* bound together by an oath, allied, associate; (mil) sworn in; *m pl* conspirators

conjūr·ō -āre *vi* to take an oath together; to plot, conspire

conjux see **conjunx**

conl- = **coll-**

conm- = **comm-**

Con·ōn -ōnis *m* famous Athenian admiral (*fl* 400 B.C.); famous mathematician and astronomer of Samos (283-222 B.C.)

cōnōpē·um or **cōnōpē·um -ī** *n* mosquito net

cōn·or -ārī -ātus sum *vt* to try, endeavor, venture, attempt

conquassātĭ·ō -ōnis *f* severe shaking; disturbance

conquass·ō -āre *vt* to shake hard; (fig) to shatter, upset, disturb

con·quĕror -quĕrī -questus sum *vt* to complain bitterly about, deplore; *vi* to complain, complain bitterly

conquestĭ·ō -ōnis *f* complaining, complaint; (rhet) appeal for sympathy; (with *genit*, with **de** + *abl*, or with **adversus** + *acc*) complaint about

conquest·us -ūs *m* loud complaint

conqui·escō -escĕre -ēvī -ētum *vi* to rest, take a rest; to find rest, find recreation; to keep quiet, remain inactive; to slacken, flag; to lie dormant; to take a nap; to stop, pause

conquinisc·ō -ĕre *vi* to squat, stoop down

con·quīrō -quīrĕre -quīsīvī -quīsītum *vt* to search for, look for; to procure, bring together, collect; (fig) to search for, go after (*pleasures, etc.*)

conquīsītī·ō -ōnis *f* search; procuring, collection; (mil) conscription, draft, recruitment

conquīsīt·or -ōris *m* recruiting officer

conquīsīt·us -a -um *pp* of **conquīro**; *adj* chosen, select

conr- = corr-

consaep·iō or **consēp·iō -īre -sī -tum** *vt* to fence in, hedge in, enclose

consaept·um -ī *n* enclosure

consalūtātī·ō -ōnis *f* exchange of greetings

consalūt·ō -āre *vt* to greet (*as a group*), greet cordially; *vi* **inter se consalūtāre** to greet one another, exchange greetings

consān·escō -escĕre -uī *vi* to heal up; to recover

consanguinē·us -a -um *adj* related by blood; *m* brother; *m pl* relatives; *f* sister

consanguinit·ās -ātis *f* blood relationship; **consanguinitate propinquus** closely related

consauci·ō -āre *vt* to wound severely

conscelerāt·us -a -um *adj* wicked, depraved, criminal; (fig) rotten to the core

conscelĕr·ō -āre *vt* to stain with guilt, dishonor, disgrace

con·scendō -scendĕre -scendī -scensum *vt* to climb up, mount, ascend; to board (*ship*); **aequor navibus conscendere** to go to sea; *vi* to climb; to go aboard, board; (with **in** + *acc*) to go aboard (*ship*)

conscensi·ō -ōnis *f* embarkation; **in navīs conscensio** boarding the ships

conscienti·a -ae *f* joint knowledge; consciousness, knowledge; moral sense, conscience; good conscience; bad conscience; scruple; sense of guilt, remorse

con·scindō -scindĕre -scīdī -scissum *vt* to tear up, tear to pieces; (fig) to tear to pieces, abuse

consc·iō -īre *vt* to become conscious of (*wrong*)

consc·īscō -īscĕre -īvī or **-iī -ītum** *vt* to approve or decide upon; (sibi) **mortem consciscere** to decide

upon death for oneself, commit suicide

consci·us -a -um *adj* sharing knowledge with another; cognizant, conscious, aware; (with *genit* or *dat*) having knowledge of, aware of, privy to; *mf* partner, accomplice, confidant(e), confederate

conscrē·or -ārī -ātus sum *vi* to clear the throat

con·scrībō -scrībĕre -scripsī -scriptum *vt* to enlist, enroll; to write, write up, compose; to prescribe

conscriptī·ō -ōnis *f* document, draft; record, report

conscript·us -a -um *pp* of **conscribo**; *m* senator; **patres conscripti** members of the senate

consĕc·ō -āre -uī -tum *vt* to cut up into small pieces, dismember

consecrātī·ō -ōnis *f* consecration; deification (*of emperors*)

consĕcr·ō -āre *vt* to make holy, consecrate, dedicate to a god; to dedicate to the gods below, doom to destruction, execrate; to immortalize, deify

consectāri·us -a -um *adj* logic; *n pl* conclusions, inferences

consectātī·ō -ōnis *f* eager pursuit

consectātr·ix -īcis *f* pursuer (*female*)

consecti·ō -ōnis *f* cutting up

consect·or -ārī -ātus sum *vt* to follow eagerly, go after; to follow up, pursue, chase, hunt; to overtake; to imitate, follow

consecūtī·ō -ōnis *f* effect, consequences; (rhet) order, sequence

consen·escō -escĕre -uī *vi* to grow old, grow old together; to become gray; to become obsolete; to waste away, fade, decline; to degenerate, sink

consensi·ō -ōnis *f* agreement, unanimity; harmony; plot, conspiracy

consens·us -ūs *m* agreement, unanimity; agreement, harmony; plot, conspiracy; **consensū** with one accord; **in consensum vertere** to become a general custom; **omnium vestrum consensu** with the agreement of all of you, as you all agree

consentānē·us -a -um *adj* (with *dat* or **cum** + *abl*) agreeing with, according to, in accord with, proper for; **consentaneum est** it is reasonable; *n pl* concurrent circumstances

consenti·ens -entis *adj* unanimous

con·sentiō -sentīre -sensī -sensum *vt* **bellum consentire** to agree to war, vote for war; *vi* to agree; (with *inf*) to agree, plot, conspire to; (with **cum** + *abl*) to harmonize with, fit in with, be consistent with

consēp- = consaep-

consĕqu·ens -entis *adj* reasonable;

corresponding, logical, fit, suitable; *n* consequence, conclusion

consequenti·a -ae *f* consequence, natural sequence

con·sĕquor -sĕquī -secūtus sum *vt* to follow, follow up, pursue, go after; to catch up with, catch, reach, attain to, arrive at; (fig) to follow, copy, imitate; to obtain, get, acquire; to understand, perceive, learn; (of speech) to be equal to, do justice to; (of time) to come after, follow; to result from, be the consequence of, arise from

con·sĕrō -serĕre -serŭī -sertum *vt* to entwine, tie, join, string together; **manum** or **manūs conserere** to fight hand to hand, engage in close combat; **proelium conserere** to begin fighting

con·sĕrō -serĕre -sēvī -situm *vt* to sow, plant

consertē *adv* in close connection, connectedly

conserv·a -ae *f* fellow slave (*female*)

conservātī·ō -ōnis *f* keeping, preserving

conservāt·or -ōris *m* preserver, defender

conservit·ĭum -iī or **-ī** *n* servitude

conserv·ō -āre *vt* to keep safe, preserve, maintain; (fig) to keep intact

conserv·us -ī *m* fellow slave

consess·or -ōris *m* table companion; fellow spectator; (law) assessor

consess·us -ūs *m* assembly, court

considerātē *adv* with caution, deliberately

considerātī·ō -ōnis *f* contemplation, consideration

considerāt·us -a -um *adj* circumspect, cautious; well considered, deliberate

considĕr·ō -āre *vt* to look at closely, inspect, examine, survey; to consider, contemplate; reflect upon

con·sīdō -sīdĕre -sēdī -sessum *vi* to sit down, be seated, settle; (of assemblies) to hold sessions, be in session; (mil) to encamp, take up a position; to settle, stay (*in residence*); to settle, sink down, subside; (fig) to settle, sink, be buried; to diminish, subside, abate, die out

consign·ō -āre *vt* to seal, sign; to certify, attest, vouch for; to note, register, record

consil·escō -escĕre -ŭī *vi* to become still, calm down

consiliāri·us -a -um *adj* counseling; *m* counselor, adviser; interpreter, spokesman

consiliāt·or -ōris *m* counselor

consiliō *adv* intentionally, purposely

consili·or -ārī -ātus sum *vi* to take counsel, consult; (with *dat*) to give counsel to, advise

consil·ĭum -iī or **-ī** *n* consultation, deliberation; deliberative body, council; council of war; plan, measure, stratagem; decision; purpose, intention, design, policy; judgment, wisdom, prudence, discretion, sense;

cabinet; advice, counsel; **consilium capere** or **consilium inire** or **consilium suscipere** to form a plan, come to a decision, decide, determine; **consilium est mihi** (with *inf*) I intend to; **non est consilium mihi** (with *inf*) I don't mean to; **privato consilio** for one's own purposes

consimil·is -e *adj* quite similar; (with *genit* or *dat*) completely similar to, just like

consip·ĭō -ĕre *vi* to be sane

con·sistō -sistĕre -stitī -stitum *vi* to come to a stop, come to rest, stop, pause, halt, take a stand, stand still; to grow hard, become solid, set; (mil) to take up a position, be posted, make a stand; (of ships) to come to anchorage, to ground; (of travelers) to halt on a journey; to be firm, be steadfast, continue, endure; to be, exist, occur, take place; (with *abl* or with **in +** *abl*) to consist of, depend on

consitĭ·ō -ōnis *f* sowing, planting

consit·or -ōris *m* sower, planter

consitūr·a -ae *f* sowing, planting

consōbrīn·a -ae *f* first cousin (*daughter of a mother's sister*)

consōbrīn·us -ī *m* first cousin (*son of mother's sister*)

consociātĭ·ō -ōnis *f* association, society

consociāt·us -a -um *adj* held in common, shared

consocĭ·ō -āre *vt* to associate, join, unite, connect, share

consōlābil·is -e *adj* consolable

consōlātĭ·ō -ōnis *f* consolation, comfort; encouragement; alleviation

consōlāt·or -ōris *m* comforter

consōlātōrĭ·us -a -um *adj* comforting; **litterae consolatoriae** letter of condolence

consōl·or -ārī -ātus sum *vt* to console, comfort, reassure, soothe, encourage, cheer up; to relieve, alleviate, mitigate

consomnĭ·ō -āre *vt* to dream about

consŏn·ō -āre -ŭī *vi* to sound together, ring, resound, reecho; (with *dat* or with **cum +** *abl*) to harmonize with, agree with; **inter se consonare** to agree, harmonize

consŏn·us -a -um *adj* harmonious; (fig) fit, suitable

consōp·ĭō -īre *vt* to put to sleep

consor·s -tis *adj* having a common lot, of the same fortune; common; shared in common; *mf* partner, associate; *m* brother; *f* wife; sister

consortĭ·ō -ōnis *f* partnership, association, fellowship

consort·ĭum -iī or **-ī** *n* partnership; participation; (with *genit*) partnership in

conspect·us -a -um *pp* of **conspicio**; *adj* visible; in full sight; conspicuous, striking

conspect·us -ūs *m* look, sight, view; sight (*power of seeing*); mental view;

being seen, appearance on the scene; **conspectu in medio** before all eyes

con·spergō -spergĕre -spersī -spersum *vt* to sprinkle, splatter

conspiciend·us -a -um *adj* worth seeing; distinguished

conspicill·um -ī *n* (with *genit*) keeping an eye on

con·spiciō -spicĕre -spexī -spectum *vt* to look at attentively, observe, fix the eyes upon; to catch sight of, spot; to look at with admiration; to face (*e.g.*, *the forum*); to perceive, see, discern; **conspici** to be conspicuous, be noticed, be admired, attract attention

conspic·or -ārī -ātus sum *vt* to catch sight of, spot, see

conspicŭ·us -a -um *adj* visible, in sight; conspicuous, striking, remarkable, distinguished

conspīrāti·ō -ōnis *f* agreement, unanimity, harmony, concord; plot, conspiracy

conspīrāt·us -a -um *adj* conspiring, in conspiracy

conspīr·ō -āre *vi* to breathe together, blow together, sound together; to act in unison, to agree; to plot together, conspire

conspons·or -ōris *m* coguarantor

con·spŭō -spuĕre — -spūtum *vt* to spit on; **nive conspuere** to sprinkle with snow

conspurc·ō -āre *vt* to defile, mess up

conspūt·ō -āre *vt* to spit on in contempt

constabil·iō -īre -īvī -ītum *vt* to establish, confirm

const·ans -antis *adj* constant, uniform, steady, fixed, stable, regular, invariable, persistent; consistent, harmonious; (fig) faithful, constant, trustworthy

constanter *adv* constantly, steadily, uniformly, invariably; consistently; calmly

constanti·a -ae *f* steadiness, firmness, constancy, perseverance; harmony, symmetry, consistency; steadfastness; self-possession

consternāti·ō -ōnis *f* consternation, dismay, alarm; disorder, disturbance; mutiny; wild rush, stampede

con·sternō -sternĕre -strāvī -strātum *vt* to spread, cover; to pave; to thatch; **constrata navis** ship with deck

constīp·ō -āre *vt* to crowd together

constit·ŭō -uĕre -ŭī -ūtum *vt* to set up, erect, establish; to settle (*e.g.*, *a people in a place*); to set up, establish (*authority*); to settle, determine, fix (*date, price, penalty*); to arrange, set in order, organize; to construct, erect; to designate, select, assign, appoint; to decide, arbitrate, decree, judge; (mil) to station, post, deploy

constitūti·ō -ōnis *f* constitution, nature; disposition; regulation, or-

dinance, order; definition; (rhet) issue, point of discussion

constitūt·us -a -um *pp* of **constituo**; *adj* ordered, arranged; **bene constitutum corpus** good constitution; *n* agreement, arrangement

con·stō -stāre -stĭtī -stātum *vi* to stand together; to agree, correspond; to stand firm, remain unchanged, be constant; to stand still, stand firm; to be in existence; (of facts) to be established, be undisputed, be well known; (com) to tally, be correct; (with *abl* of price) to cost; **non mihi satis constat** I have not quite made up my mind; **ratio constat** the account tallies, is correct

constrāt·us -a -um *pp* of **consterno**; *n* flooring

con·stringō -stringĕre -strinxī -strictum *vt* to tie up; to shackle, chain; (fig) to bind, restrain; (rhet) to condense, compress

constructi·ō -ōnis *f* building, construction; arrangement (*of words*)

con·strŭō -struĕre -struxī -structum *vt* to heap up, pile up; to construct, build up; (gram) to construct

constuprāt·or -ōris *m* rapist

constŭpr·ō -āre *vt* to rape

consuād·ĕō -ēre *vi* (with *dat*) to advise strongly

Consuāl·ia -ĭum *n pl* feast of Consus, ancient Italian god of fertility, celebrated on August 21st

consuās·or -ōris *m* adviser

consūcĭd·us -a -um *adj* very juicy

consūd·ō -āre *vi* to sweat profusely

consuē·faciō -facĕre -fēcī -factum *vt* to accustom, inure

consu·escō -escĕre -ēvī -ētum *vt* to accustom, inure; *vi* to become accustomed; (with *inf*) to become accustomed to; (with **cum** + *abl*) to cohabit with

consuētĭ·ō -ōnis *f* sexual intercourse

consuētūd·ō -ĭnis *f* custom, habit; usage, idiom; social intercourse, social ties; sexual intercourse; **ad consuetūdinem** (with *genit*) according to the custom of; **consuetudine** or **ex consuetudine** according to custom, from habit; **pro consuetudine mea** according to my habit, as is my habit; **ut fert consuetudo** as is usual

consuēt·us -a -um *pp* of **consuesco**; *adj* usual, regular, customary

con·sul -sŭlis *m* consul (*one of the two highest magistrates of the Roman republic*); **consul designatus** consul-elect; **consulem creare, dicere**, or **facere** to elect a consul; **consul ordinarius** consul who entered office on the first of January; **consul suffectus** consul chosen in the course of the year to fill a vacancy in the consulship

consulār·is -e *adj* consular; **aetas**

consularis minimum legal age for election to consular office; **comitia consularia** consular elections; *m* ex-consul

consulāriter *adv* like a consul, in a manner worthy of a consul

consulāt·us -ūs *m* consulship; **consulatum petere** to run for the consulship; **se consulatu abdicare** to resign from the consulship

consŭl·ō -ĕre -ŭī -tum *vt* to consult, ask advice of; to consider; to advise (*something*), offer as advice; **boni consulere** to regard favorably; *vi* to deliberate, reflect; (with **ad** or **in** + *acc*) to reflect on, take into consideration; (with *dat*) to look after; (with **in** + *acc*) to take measures against; (with **de** + *abl*) to pass sentence on

consultātĭ·ō -ōnis *f* mature deliberation, consideration; consulting, inquiry; subject of consultation, case

consultē *adv* deliberately, after due consideration

consultō *adv* deliberately, on purpose

consult·ō -āre *vt* to reflect on, consider maturely; to ask (*someone*) for advice, consult; *vi* to deliberate, reflect; (with *dat*) to take into consideration, look after, care for; **in medium consultare** to look after the common good

consult·or -ōris *m* counselor, adviser; advisee, client

consultr·ix -īcis *f* protectress

consult·us -a -um *pp* of **consulo;** *adj* skilled, experienced; *m* expert; **juris consultus** legal expert, lawyer; *n* deliberation, consideration; decree, decision, resolution; response (*from an oracle*)

consummāt·us -a -um *adj* consummate, perfect

consumm·ō -āre *vt* to sum up; to finish, complete, accomplish, perfect

con·sūmō -sūmĕre -sumpsī -sumptum *vt* to use up, consume, exhaust; to devour; to squander; to wear out, destroy; to spend, waste (*money, time, effort*)

consumptĭ·ō -ōnis *f* consumption, wasting

consumpt·or -ōris *m* destroyer

con·sŭō -suĕre -suī -sūtum *vt* to stitch together, sew up

con·surgō -surgĕre -surrexī -surrectum *vi* to stand up; to rise in a body; (with **ad** or **in** + *acc*) to aspire to

consurrectĭ·ō -ōnis *f* rising up, standing up in a body

Cons·us -ī *m* ancient Italian deity of agriculture and fertility

consusurr·ō -āre *vi* to whisper together

contābefac·ĭō -ĕre *vt* to wear out completely, consume, waste

contāb·escō -escĕre -ŭī *vi* to waste away

contabulātĭ·ō -ōnis *f* flooring; story

contābŭl·ō -āre *vt* to cover with boards; to build with (*several*) stories

contact·us -ūs *m* touch, contact; contagion; (fig) contagion, infection

contāg·ēs -is *f* touch, contact

contāgĭ·ō -ōnis *f* touching; touch; contact; contagion, infection; moral contagion, bad example

contāg·ium -ĭī or **-ī** *n* touch, contact; contagion; moral contamination

contāmināt·us -a -um *adj* polluted, contaminated, impure, vile, degraded; *m pl* perverted youths

contāmin·ō -āre *vt* to bring into contact, mingle, blend; to corrupt, defile; (fig) to corrupt, stain, taint, spoil

contechn·or -ārī -ātus sum *vi* to devise plots, think up tricks

con·tĕgō -tegĕre -texī -tectum *vt* to cover up; to hide; to protect

contemĕr·ō -āre *vt* to defile

con·temnō -temnĕre -tempsī -temptum *vt* to think little of, depreciate, slight, belittle, disregard; to despise, defy

contemplātĭ·ō -ōnis *f* viewing, surveying, contemplation

contemplāt·or -ōris *m* contemplator, observer

contemplāt·us -ūs *m* contemplation

contempl·ō -āre or **contempl·or -ārī -ātus sum** *vt* to observe, survey, gaze upon, contemplate

contemptim *adv* contemptuously

contemptĭ·ō -ōnis *f* belittling, despising; **in contemptionem venire** (with *dat*) to become an object of contempt to

contempt·or -ōris *m* or **contemptr·ix -īcis** *f* scorner, despiser

contempt·us -a -um *pp* of **contemno;** *adj* contemptible, despicable

contempt·us -ūs *m* belittling, despising, scorn; **contemptui esse** to be an object of contempt

con·tendō -tendĕre -tendī -tentum *vt* to stretch, draw tight; to tune (*instrument*); to aim, shoot, hurl; (fig) to strain, stretch, exert; to hold, assert, maintain; to compare, contrast; to direct (*course*); *vi* to exert oneself; to compete, contend, fight; to travel, march; (with *inf*) to be in a hurry to; (with **in** + *acc*) to rush to, head for; (with **ad** + *acc*) to strive for, aspire to

contentē *adv* with great effort, earnestly; closely, scantily, sparingly

contentĭ·ō -ōnis *f* competition, struggle, dispute; straining, exertion, effort; contrast, comparison, antithesis

content·us -a -um *pp* of **contendo;** *adj* tense, tight, taut, strained; eager, intense

content·us -a -um *pp* of **contineo;** *adj* content, satisfied

contermin·us -a -um *adj* (with *dat*) bordering upon

con·tĕrō -terĕre -trīvī -trītum *vt* to grind to powder, pulverize, crumble; (fig) to wear away, wear out, use up; to consume, waste (*time*)

conterr·ĕō -ēre -ŭī -ĭtum *vt* to frighten, scare the life out of

contest·or -ārī -ātus sum *vt* to call to witness; (fig) to prove, attest; **lītem contestārī** to open a lawsuit by calling witnesses

contex·ō -ĕre -ŭī -tum *vt* to weave together; to brace together; to connect; to devise, build; to compose (*writings*); to dream up (*a charge*)

contextē *adv* in a coherent manner

context·us -a -um *pp* of **contexo**; *adj* connected

context·us -ūs *m* connection, coherence

contic·escō or **contic·iscō -escĕre -ŭī** *vi* to become quite still, fall completely silent, hush; to keep silence; (fig) to cease, abate

conticinnō *adv* in the evening

contignātĭ·ō -ōnis *f* floor, story

contign·ō -āre *vt* to lay a floor on

contigŭ·us -a -um *adj* touching, adjoining; within reach; (with *dat*) bordering on, near

contin·ens -entis *adj* contiguous, adjacent; unbroken, uninterrupted; self-controlled, continent; (with *dat*) bordering on, contiguous with, adjacent to

contin·ens -entis *f* continent, mainland

contin·ens -entis *n* chief point, main point (*of a speech*)

continenter *adv* in unbroken succession; without interruption; (sitting) close together; moderately, temperately

continentĭ·a -ae *f* self-control; continence

con·tinĕō -tinēre -tinŭī -tentum *vt* to hold or keep together; to keep within bounds, confine; to contain, comprise, include; to control, repress

con·tingō -tingĕre -tĭgī -tactum *vt* to come into contact with; (fig) to touch, affect; to touch, border on; to reach, reach to; to contaminate; *vi* to happen, turn out, come to pass; (with *dat*) **a** to touch, border on; **b** to happen to, befall

continuātĭ·ō -ōnis *f* unbroken series, succession; (rhet) period

continŭ·ō -āre *vt* to make continuous, join together, connect; to extend; to continue, carry on, draw out, prolong; to pass, occupy (*time*); **continuārī** (with *dat*) **a** to be contiguous with, adjacent to; **b** to follow closely upon

continŭō *adv* immediately, without delay; as a necessary consequence, necessarily

continŭ·us -a -um *adj* continuous, unbroken; successive; **dies con-** tinuos quinque for five successive days

contĭ·ō -ōnis *f* meeting, rally; public meeting (*of the people or of soldiers*); speech, pep talk, harangue

contiōnābund·us -a -um *adj* haranguing

contiōnāl·is -e *adj* typical of a public assembly; demagogic

contiōnārĭ·us -a -um *adj* mob-like

contiōnāt·or -ōris *m* demagogue, public agitator, rabble-rouser

contiōn·or -ārī -ātus sum *vi* to hold forth at a rally, to harangue; to come to a rally; to make a statement at a rally

continncŭl·a -ae *f* short harangue, trifling speech

contoll·ō -ĕre *vt* to bring together

contŏn·at -āre *v impers* it is thundering hard

contor·quĕō -quēre -sī -tum *vt* to whirl, twist; to throw hard; to twist (*words*) around

contortē *adv* intricately

contortĭōn·ēs -um *f pl* intricacies (*of language*)

contort·or -ōris *m* perverter; **contortor legum** pettifogger

contortŭl·us -a -um *adj* rather complicated

contortuplicāt·us -a -um *adj* all twisted up

contort·us -a -um *pp* of **contorqueo**; *adj* involved, intricate; vehement (*speech*)

contrā *adv* in opposition, opposite, in front, face to face; in turn, in return, on the other hand, on the other side; reversely, in the opposite way, the other way; on the contrary, conversely; **contra atque** or **ac** contrary to, otherwise than; **contra dicere** to reply, say in reply; to raise objections; **contra dicitur** the objection is raised; **contra ferire** to make a counterattack; **contra qua fas est** contrary to divine law; **contra quam senatus consuluisset** contrary to what the senate would have decided, contrary to the senate resolution; **quin contra** nay on the contrary, in fact it's just the opposite

contrā *prep* (with *acc*) opposite, opposite to, facing, towards, against; in answer to, in reply to; (in hostile sense) against, with, in opposition to, as the opponent of; against, injurious to, unfavorable to; contrary to, the reverse of; in violation of; against, in defiance of; **contra ea putare** to think otherwise; **quod contra** whereas, while; **valere contra** to counterbalance

contractĭ·ō -ōnis *f* drawing together, contraction; shortening (*of syllable*); despondency

contractiuncŭl·a -ae *f* slight mental depression

contract·us -a -um *pp* of **contraho**; *adj* contracted; narrow, limited (place); brief; pinching (poverty); in seclusion; **res contracta** contract

contract·us -ūs m shrinking

contrā·dīcō -dīcĕre -dixī -dictum vi (with dat) to contradict, speak against

contrādictī·ō -ōnis f objection, refutation

con·trāhō -trahĕre -traxī -tractum vt to draw together, collect, assemble; to contract, shorten, narrow, abridge, lessen, diminish; to wrinkle; (fig) to bring about, accomplish, cause, produce, incur; to conclude (bargain); to transact (business); to settle (an account); to complete (business arrangements)

contrāriē adv in opposite ways, in a different way

contrārī·us -a -um adj opposite; contrary, conflicting; hostile, antagonistic; from the opposite direction; (with dat) opposed to, contrary to; n the opposite, the contrary, the reverse; antithesis; **ex contrario** on the contrary, on the other hand; **in contraria** in opposite directions; **in contraria versus** changed into its opposite

contrectābiliter adv appreciably, tangibly

contrectātī·ō -ōnis f handling, touching

contrect·ō -āre vt to touch, handle; (fig) to defile; (fig) to dwell upon, consider

contrem·iscō -iscĕre -ŭī vt to shudder at; vi to tremble all over; to waver

contrĕm·ō -ĕre -ŭī vi to tremble all over; to quake

contrib·ŭō -uĕre -ŭī -ūtum vt to bring together, enroll together, associate, unite, incorporate; to contribute, add

contrist·ō -āre vt to sadden, cover with gloom; (fig) to darken, cloud

contrīt·us -a -um pp of **contero**; adj worn out, common, trite

contrōversi·a -ae f controversy, quarrel, dispute, debate; civil lawsuit, litigation; subject of litigation; contradiction; question; **sine controversia** indisputably

contrōversiōs·us -a -um adj much disputed, controversial

contrōvers·us -a -um adj disputed, controversial, questionable, undecided

contrucīd·ō -āre vt to cut down, cut to pieces, massacre; (fig) to wreck, make a mess of

con·trūdō -trūdĕre -trūsī -trūsum vt to crowd together

contrunc·ō -āre vt to hack to pieces

contubernāl·is -is m army comrade, army buddy; junior staff officer; (coll) husband (of slave); personal attendant; comrade, companion, associate; colleague; f (coll) wife (of slave)

contubern·ium -iī or **-ī** n military companionship; common war tent; concubinage; marriage (of slaves); hovel (of slaves)

con·tuĕor -tuērī -tuītus sum vt to look at attentively, regard, survey

contuit·us or **contūt·us -ūs** m sight, observation

contumācī·a -ae f stubbornness, defiance, willfulness; constancy, firmness

contumācīter adv stubbornly, defiantly

contūm·ax -ācis adj stubborn, defiant

contumēlī·a -ae f mistreatment, rough treatment; outrage, insult, abuse, affront

contumēliōsē adv abusively

contumēliōs·us -a -um adj bringing dishonor; insulting, abusive; reproachful, insolent

contumŭl·ō -āre vt to bury

con·tundō -tundĕre -tŭdī -tūsum vt to crush, grind, pound, bruise; (fig) to crush, destroy, break, subdue; to baffle

conturbātī·ō -ōnis f confusion, consternation

conturbāt·us -a -um adj confused, distracted, disordered, in confusion

conturb·ō -āre vt to confuse, throw into confusion; to disquiet, disturb; to upset (plans); **rationes** or **rationem conturbare** to be bankrupt; vi to be bankrupt

cont·us -ī m pole

cōnūbiāl·is -e adj marriage, connubial

cōnūb·ium -iī or **-ī** n intermarriage; right to intermarry according to Roman law; marriage; sexual intercourse; **jus conubi** right to intermarry

cōn·us -ī m cone; apex (of helmet)

convăd·or -ārī -ātus sum vt to subpoena

conval·escō -escĕre -ŭī vi to grow strong; to regain strength, convalesce; (fig) to improve

convall·is -is f valley

convās·ō -āre vt to pack up, pack

convect·ō -āre vt to heap together; to bring home

convect·or -ōris m fellow passenger

con·vĕhō -vehĕre -vexī -vectum vt to collect, bring in (esp. the harvest)

con·vellō -vellĕre -vellī -vulsum vt to tear away, pull off, pluck, wrest; to tear to pieces, dismember; to break, shatter; (fig) to turn upside down, subvert, overthrow; **convellere signa** to break camp

convĕn·ae -ārum m pl or f pl strangers; refugees, vagabonds

conveni·ens -entis adj agreeing, harmonious, consistent; appropriate; (with dat or with **cum + abl**) consistent with, appropriate to; (with **ad + acc**) appropriate for, suitable for

convenienter *adv* consistently; suitably; **(with cum** + *abl* or with **ad** + *acc*) in conformity with

convenienti·a -ae *f* agreement, accord, harmony; conformity

con·venĭō -venīre -vēnī -ventum *vt* to meet, go to meet; to interview; *vi* to come together, meet, gather, come in a body; to coincide; to unite, combine; to come to an agreement, agree; (with **ad** + *acc*) to fit (*as a shoe fits the foot*); (with *dat*, with **ad** or **in** + *acc*, or with **cum** + *abl*) to be applicable to, appropriate to, fit; **convenit** it is fitting, proper; **convenit inter se** (with *dat*) there is harmony among

conventīcĭ·us -a -um *adj* coming together, gathering together; *n* fee for attending the assembly

conventĭcŭl·um -ī *n* small gathering; meeting place

conventĭ·ō -ōnis *f* agreement, contract

convent·us -a -um *pp* of **convenio;** *n* agreement, contract

convent·us -ūs *m* gathering, assembly; congress; district court; company, corporation; agreement; **ex conventu** by agreement; of one accord; **conventum agere** to hold court

con·verrō or **con·vorrō -verrēre -verrī -versum** *vt* to sweep together, sweep up; to brush thoroughly; (fig) to scoop up (*e.g.*, *an inheritance*)

conversātĭ·ō -ōnis *f* social intercourse; conversation

conversĭ·ō -ōnis *f* revolving, revolution; (fig) alteration, change; (rhet) repetition of word at end of clause; (rhet) balancing of phrases

convers·ō -āre *vt* to turn around; **se conversare** to revolve

con·vertō or **con·vortō -vertēre -vertī -versum** *vt* to cause to turn, turn back, reverse; (fig) to convert, transform; to translate; to attract (*attention*); (mil) **sese convertere** to retreat; *vi* to return; to change, be changed, turn; (with **in** + *acc*) to be changed into, turn into

convest·ĭō -īre *vt* to clothe, cover

convex·us -a -um *pp* of **conveho;** *adj* rounded off; arched, convex, concave; sloping down; *n* vault, arch

convĭcĭāt·or -ōris *m* reviler

convĭcĭ·or -ārī -ātus sum *vt* to revile

convīc·ĭum -ĭī or **-ī** *n* noise, chatter; wrangling; jeers, invective, abuse; cry of protest; reprimand; **conviciis consectari aliquem** to keep after someone with abuses

convictĭ·ō -ōnis *f* companionship; companions

convict·or -ōris *m* bosom friend

convict·us -ūs *m* association, socializing; close friends; feast, banquet

con·vincō -vincĕre -vīcī -victum *vt* to refute, prove wrong; to convict, prove guilty; to prove true, demonstrate clearly

convĭs·ō -ĕre *vt* to examine, search; to shine on

convīv·a -ae *m* guest, table companion

convīvāl·is -e *adj* convivial, festive

convīvāt·or -ōris *m* master of ceremonies; host

convīv·ĭum -ĭī or **-ī** *n* banquet, dinner; dinner party; *n pl* dinner guests; **convivium agitare** to throw a party

con·vīvō -vīvĕre -vixī *vi* to live together; (with **cum** + *abl*) to feast with

convīv·or -ārī -ātus sum *vi* to feast together, have a party

convocātĭ·ō -ōnis *f* calling together

convŏc·ō -āre *vt* to call together, assemble

convŏl·ō -āre *vi* to flock together; (fig) to flock together, gather hastily

con·volvō -volvĕre -volvī -volūtum *vt* to roll together; to roll up (*a scroll*); to fasten together, interweave; to wrap; **se convolvere** to roll along; to go in a circle

convŏm·ō -ĕre *vt* to vomit on, vomit all over

convortō see **converto**

convulnĕr·ō -āre *vt* to wound seriously

convulsus *pp* of **convello**

coöper·ĭō -īre -ŭī -tum *vt* to cover; to overwhelm

coöptātĭ·ō -ōnis *f* cooption, election of a colleague by vote of incumbent members

coöpt·ō -āre *vt* to coopt

coör·ĭor -īrī -tus sum *vi* to rise, rise suddenly; (fig) (of war) to break out; (of wind) to arise

coört·us -ūs *m* rising, originating

cōp·a -ae *f* barmaid

cophĭn·us -ī *m* basket

cōpĭ·a -ae *f* abundance, supply, store, plenty; multitude, large number; wealth, prosperity; opportunity, means; command of language, fluency, richness of expression; (with *genit*) power over; (with *dat*) access to; **pro copia** according to opportunity, according to ability; *f pl* troops, armed forces; provisions, supplies

cōpĭŏl·ae -ārum *f pl* small contingent of troops

cōpĭōsē *adv* abundantly, plentifully; (rhet) fully, at length

cōpĭōs·us -a -um *adj* plentiful; well supplied, rich, wealthy; eloquent, fluent (*speech*); (with *abl*) abounding in, rich in

cōp·is -e *adj* rich, well supplied

cōpŭl·a -ae *f* cord, string, rope, leash; (fig) tie, bond

cŏpŭlātĭ·ō -ōnis f coupling, joining, union; combining (of words)

cŏpŭl·ō -āre vt to couple, join; (fig) to unite; (with dat or with cum + abl) to couple with, join to, combine with

cŏpŭl·or -ārī -ātus sum vt to join, clasp; **dexteras copulari** to shake hands

coqu·a -ae f cook (female)

coquīn·ō -āre vi to be a cook

co·quō -quĕre -xī -ctum vt to cook; to fry, roast, bake, boil; to prepare (a meal); to burn, parch; to ripen, mature; to digest; to disturb, worry, disquiet; to plan, concoct, dream up

coqu·us or coc·us -ī m cook

cor cordis n heart; mind, judgment; (as seat of feelings) heart, soul; dear friend; n pl persons, souls; **cordi esse** (with dat) to please, be dear to, be agreeable to

cōram adv in person, personally; publically, openly; in someone's presence, face to face; prep (coming before or after abl) before, in the presence of, face to face with

corb·is -is m or f wicker basket

corbīt·a -ae f slow-sailing merchant ship

corbŭl·a -ae f small basket

corcŭl·um -ī n little heart; sweetheart; poor fellow

Corcȳr·a -ae f island off the coast of Epirus, identified with Scheria, the island of Alcinous

cordātē adv wisely, prudently

cordŏl·ĭum -lī or -ī n heartache

Corfīn·ĭum -lī or -ī n town in Central Italy which served as headquarters of Italian allies during the Social War against Rome in 90-89 B.C.

coriandr·um -ī n coriander

Corinthĭ·us -a -um adj Corinthian; **aes Corinthium** alloy of gold, silver, and copper, used in making expensive jewelry, etc.; m pl Corinthians; n pl costly Corinthian products

Corinth·us -ī f Corinth

Coriŏl·ī -ōrum m pl town in Latium, capital of the Volsci, from the capture of which, in 493 B.C., C. Marcius received the surname of Coriolanus

cor·ĭum -ĭī or -ī n or cor·ĭus -ĭī or -ī m skin, hide; bark; leather

Cornēlĭ·us -a -um adj Cornelian; **gens Cornelia** Cornelian tribe (famous Roman tribe, especially for the Scipios, the Gracchi, and Sulla); f Cornelia (daughter of Scipio Africanus Major and mother of the Gracchi)

corneŏl·us -a -um adj horny

cornĕ·us -a -um adj horny; of the cornel tree; of cornel wood

cornĭc·en -ĭnis m horn blower

cornĭc·or -ārī -ātus sum vi to caw

cornĭcŭl·a -ae f poor little crow

cornĭcŭlār·ĭus -ĭī or -ī m soldier

decorated with a horn-shaped medal for bravery; adjutant to a centurion

cornĭcŭl·um -ī n little horn; horn-shaped decoration, awarded for bravery

cornĭg·er -ĕra -ĕrum adj horn-bearing, horned

cornĭp·ēs -ĕdis adj hoofed

corn·ix -īcis f crow (whose appearance on one's left side was considered a favorable omen and whose cries were regarded as a sign of rain)

corn·ū -ūs or **corn·um -ī** n horn; horn, trumpet; lantern; funnel; oil cruet; hoof; bill (of bird); horn (of moon); branch (of river); arm (of bay); tongue (of land); crest socket (of helmet); roller end (of book); (mil) wing, flank; **cornua addere** (with dat) to give courage to, add strength to; **cornua sumere** to gain strength

corn·um -ī n cornel cherry

corn·us -ī f cornel cherry tree; dogwood tree; spear, shaft, javelin

coroll·a -ae f small garland

corollar·ĭum -ĭī or -ī n garland; gilt wreath given as reward to actors; gift, gratuity

corōn·a -ae f crown, garland; circle of bystanders; (mil) cordon of besiegers; ring of defense; **corona civica** decoration for saving a life; **corona muralis** decoration for being the first to scale an enemy wall; **corona navalis** decoration for naval victory; **sub corona vendere** to sell (captives) as slaves; **sub corona venire** (of captives) to be sold at public auction

Corōn·a -ae f Ariadne's crown, Corona Borealis (constellation)

corōnārĭ·us -a -um adj for a crown; **aurum coronarium** gold collected in the provinces for a victorious general

Corōnē·a -ae f town in Boeotia

Corōn·eus -ĕī m king of Phocis whose daughter was changed into a crow

Corōnīd·ēs -ae m Aesculapius, the son of Coronis

Corōn·is -ĭdis f daughter of Phlegyas and mother of Aesculapius

corōn·ō -āre vt to crown, wreathe; to enclose, encircle, shut in

corporĕ·us -a -um adj physical, of the body; corporeal, substantial; of flesh

corpulent·us -a -um adj corpulent

corp·us -ŏris n body; matter, substance; flesh; trunk; corpse; person, individual; body, frame, structure; framework; community; corporation; particle, grain

corpuscŭl·um -ī n puny body; particle, atom; (as term of endearment) little fellow

cor·rādō -rādĕre -rāsī -rāsum vt to scrape together, rake up; (fig) to scrape (e.g., money) together

correctĭ·ō -ōnis f correction, improvement, amendment; rhetorical restatement

correct·or -ōris m reformer; censor, critic

correctus pp of **corrigo**

cor·rēpō -rēpĕre -repsī vi to creep, slink; **in dumeta correpere** (fig) to beat around the bush, indulge in jargon

correptius adv more briefly; **correptius exire** to end in a short vowel, have a short vowel

correptus pp of **corripio**

corrīd·ĕō -ēre vi to laugh out loud

corrigĭ·a -ae f shoelace

cor·rigō -rigĕre -rexī -rectum vt to make straight, straighten out; to smooth out; to correct, improve, reform; to make up for (delay); to make the best of

cor·ripĭō -ripĕre -ripŭī -reptum vt to seize, snatch up, carry off; to speed up, rush; to steal, carry off; to attack; to shorten, contract; to reprove, accuse, reproach; to cut (a period of time) short

corrōbŏr·ō -āre vt to strengthen, invigorate, corroborate; (fig) to fortify, encourage

cor·rōdo -rōdĕre -rōsī -rōsum vt to gnaw, chew up

corrŏg·ō -āre vt to go asking for, collect, drum up, solicit

corrōsus pp of **corrodo**

corrūg·ō -āre vt to wrinkle, corrugate; **nares corrugare** (with dat) to cause (someone) disgust

cor·rumpō -rumpĕre -rūpī -ruptum vt to burst; to break to pieces, smash; to destroy completely, ruin, waste; to mar, corrupt, adulterate; to falsify, tamper with (documents); to bribe; to seduce, corrupt

corrŭ·ō -ĕre -ī vt to shatter, wreck, ruin; vi to fall down, tumble, sink; (fig) to fall, fail, sink, go down

corruptē adv corruptly, perversely; in a lax manner

corruptēl·a -ae f corruption, seduction; bribery; seducer, misleader

corruptĭ·ō -ōnis f corrupting, ruining, breaking up; corrupt condition

corrupt·or -ōris m or **corruptr·ix -īcis** f corrupter, seducer, briber

corrupt·us -a -um pp of **corrumpo**; adj corrupt, spoiled, bad, ruined

cort·ex -ĭcis m or f bark, shell, hull, rind; cork; **nare sine cortice** to swim without a cork life preserver; to be on one's own

cortīn·a -ae f kettle, caldron; tripod; (fig) vault of heaven

corŭlus see **corylus**

corusc·ō -āre vt to shake, brandish; vi to flit, flutter, to oscillate; to tremble; to flash, gleam

corusc·us -a -um adj oscillating, vibrating, tremulous; flashing, gleaming, glittering

corv·us -ī m raven; (mil) grapnel

Corybant·ēs -ĭum m pl Corybantes (priests of Cybele)

Corybantĭ·us -a -um adj of the Corybantes

cōrўc·us -ī m punching bag

corylēt·um -ī n cluster of hazel trees

corýl·us or **corŭl·us -ī** f hazel tree

corymbĭf·er -ĕra -ĕrum adj wearing or bearing clusters of ivy berries; m Bacchus

corymb·us -ī m cluster (esp. of ivy berries)

coryphae·us -ī m leader, head

cōrўt·os or **cōrўt·us -ī** m quiver (for arrows)

cōs cōtis f flint; grindstone, whetstone

Cō·s or **Co·ūs -ī** f small island in the Aegean Sea, famous for its wine and fine linen

cosmēt·a -ae m slave in charge of the wardrobe

cost·a -ae f rib; (fig) side, wall

cost·um -ī n perfume

cothurnāt·us -a -um adj wearing the tragic buskin; suitable to tragedy; tragic, of tragedy

cothurn·us -ī m high boot; hunting boot; buskin (worn by tragic actors); subject of tragedy; tragedy; lofty style of Greek tragedy

cōtĭd- = **cottid-**

cottăb·us -ī m game which consisted in flicking drops of wine on a bronze vessel

cottăn·a or **cottŏn·a -ōrum** n pl Syrian figs

cottīdiānō adv daily

cottīdiān·us or **cotīdiān·us -a -um** adj daily; everyday, ordinary

cottīdĭē or **cōtīdĭē** adv daily, every day

coturn·ix -īcis f quail

Cotyttĭ·a -ōrum n pl festival of Cotytto

Cotytt·o -ūs f Thracian goddess of lewdness

Coŭs see **Cos**

Cō·us -a -um adj Coan; n Coan wine; n pl Coan garments

covinnăr·ĭus -ĭī or **-ī** m soldier who fought from a chariot

covinn·us -ī m war chariot of the Britons and the Belgae; coach

cox·a -ae f hipbone

coxend·ix -īcis f hip

crābr·ō -ōnis m hornet; **irritare crabrones** (fig) to stir up a hornet's nest

cramb·ē -ēs f cabbage; **crambe repetita** warmed-over cabbage; same old story

Crant·or -ōris m Greek Academic philosopher of Soli in Cilicia (fl 300 B.C.)

crāpŭl·a -ae f drunkenness; hangover

crāpulārĭ·us -a -um adj for (i.e., to prevent) a hangover

crās adv tomorrow; (fig) in the future

crassē *adv* thickly; rudely; confusedly; dimly

crassitūd·ō -ĭnis *f* thickness, density; dregs

crass·us -a -um *adj* thick, dense; dense, dull, stupid

Crass·us -ī *m* L. Licinius Crassus (*famous orator, d 90 B.C.*); M. Licinius Crassus (*triumvir, together with Caesar and Pompey, 112?-53 B.C.*)

crastĭn·us -a -um *adj* tomorrow's; (*old abl* form) **diē crastĭnī** tomorrow; *n* tomorrow; **in crastĭnum differre** to put off till tomorrow

crāt·ēr -ēris *m* or **crātēr·a -ae** *f* mixing bowl; bowl; crater

Crāt·ēr -ēris *m* Bowl (*constellation*)

crāt·is -is *f* wickerwork; harrow; ribs of shield; (*mil*) faggots (*for filling trenches*); joint, rib (*of body*); honeycomb

creātĭ·ō -ōnis *f* election

creāt·or -ōris *m* creator; procreator, father; founder

creātr·ix -īcis *f* creatress; mother

crēb·er -ra -rum *adj* luxuriant, prolific (*growth*); numerous, crowded; repeated; frequent

crēbr·escō or **crēb·escō -escĕre -uī** *vi* to increase, become frequent; to gain strength

crēbrĭt·ās -ātis *f* frequency

crēbrō *adv* repeatedly, frequently, again and again

crēdĭbĭl·is -e *adj* credible, trustworthy

crēdĭbĭlĭter *adv* credibly

crēdĭt·or -ōris *m* creditor, lender

crēd·ō -ĕre -ĭdī -ĭtum *vt* to lend, loan; to entrust, consign; to believe; to think, believe, suppose, imagine; *vi* (*with dat*) to believe, put faith in, have trust or confidence in; **crēdās** one would image; **satis crēdĭtum est** it is believed on good evidence

crēdŭlĭt·ās -ātis *f* credulity, trustfulness

crēdŭl·us -a -um *adj* credulous, trustful; gullible; (*with dat* or **in** *with acc*) trusting in

crem·ō -āre *vt* to burn to ashes; to cremate

Cremōn·a -ae *f* town in N. Italy, which became a Roman colony in 209 B.C.

crem·or -ōris *m* juice obtained from animal or vegetable substances; broth

cre·ō -āre *vt* to create, produce; to elect to office; to cause, occasion; to beget, bear

Cre·ō or **Cre·ōn -ontis** *m* brother of Jocaste and brother-in-law of Oedipus; king of Corinth who gave his daughter in marriage to Jason

crep·er -ĕra -ĕrum *adj* dark; (*fig*) uncertain, doubtful

crepĭd·a -ae *f* slipper, sandal

crepĭdāt·us -a -um *adj* sandal-wearing

crepĭd·ō -ĭnis *f* base, pedestal; quay, pier; dam, dike, causeway

crepĭdŭl·a -ae *f* small sandal

crepĭt·ō -āre *vi* to make noise, rattle, crackle, creak, chatter, rumble, rustle

crepĭt·us -ūs *m* noise, rattle, creak, chatter, rumble, rustle

crep·ō -āre -ŭī -ĭtum *vt* to make rattle; to talk noisily about, chatter about; *vi* to make noise, rattle, crackle, creak, chatter, rumble, rustle

crepundĭ·a -ōrum *n pl* rattle; toys

crepuscŭl·um -ī *n* dusk, twilight; dimness, obscurity; *n pl* darkness

crescō crescĕre crēvī crētum *vi* to come into being, arise; to grow, grow up; to increase, swell; to prosper, thrive; to become great, attain honor

crēt·a -ae *f* chalk; white clay; cosmetic

Crēt·a -ae *f* Crete

crētāt·us -a -um *adj* chalked; dressed in white (*as candidate for office*)

crētě·us -a -um *adj* of chalk, of clay

crētĭ·ō -ōnis *f* (*law*) formal acceptance of an inheritance

crētōs·us -a -um *adj* abounding in chalk or clay

crētŭl·a -ae *f* white clay (*used for seals*)

crētus *pp* of **cerno**; *pp* of **cresco**

Creūs·a -ae *f* daughter of Priam and wife of Aeneas; daughter of Creon, king of Corinth and wife of Jason

crībr·um -ī *n* sieve; **imbrem in crībrum gerere** to carry coals to Newcastle

crīm·en -ĭnis *n* charge, accusation; reproach; guilt, crime; **esse in crimĭne** to be accused

crīmĭnātĭ·ō -ōnis *f* accusation; slander, false charge

crīmĭnāt·or -ōris *m* accuser

crīmĭn·ō -āre or **crīmĭn·or -ārī -ātus sum** *vt* to accuse; to slander; to complain of, denounce

crīmĭnōsē *adv* by way of accusation, accusingly, reproachfully

crīmĭnōs·us -a -um *adj* accusing, reproachful, slanderous

crīnāl·is -e *adj* for the hair; *n* hairpin

crīn·is -is *m* hair; (*fig*) tail of a comet

crīnīt·us -a -um *adj* long-haired; **stella crinita** comet

crīs·ō -āre *vi* (*of women*) to wiggle the buttocks

crisp·ans -antis *adj* curled, wrinkled

crisp·ō -āre *vt* to curl, wave (*hair*); to swing, wave, brandish (*a weapon*)

crisp·us -a -um *adj* curled, waved (*hair*); curly-headed; curled, wrinkled; tremulous, quivering

crist·a -ae *f* cock's comb; crest, plume

cristāt·us -a -um adj crested, plumed

critīc·us -ī m critic

croce·us -a -um adj of saffron; saffron-colored, yellow, golden

crocīn·um -ī n saffron

crōc·iō -īre vi to croak

crocodīl·us -ī m crocodile

crocōtāri·us -a -um adj of saffron-colored clothes

crocōtūl·a -ae f saffron-colored dress

croc·us -ī m or **croc·um -ī** n crocus; saffron; saffron color

Croes·us -ī m king of Lydia, famous for his wealth (590?-546 B.C.)

crotalistri·a -ae f castanet dancer

crotăl·um -ī n castanet

cruciābilitāt·ēs -um f pl torments

cruciābiliter adv with torture

cruciāment·um -ī n torture

cruciāt·us -ūs m torture; mental torment; instrument of torture; (humorously) calamity

crucĭ·ō -āre vt to put to wrack, torture, torment; (fig) to grieve, torment

crūdēl·is -e adj cruel, hardhearted; (with in + acc) cruel toward

crūdēlit·ās -ātis f cruelty

crūdēliter adv cruelly

crūd·escō -escĕre -ŭī vi to grow violent, grow worse

crūdĭt·ās -ātis f indigestion

crūd·us -a -um adj bloody, bleeding; uncooked, raw; unripe, green; undressed (hide); undigested; suffering from indigestion; hoarse; fresh, vigorous (old age); cruel, merciless

cruent·ō -āre vt to bloody, stain with blood; (fig) to wound

cruent·us -a -um adj gory, bloodstained; bloodthirsty, cruel; bloodred

crumēn·a or **crumīn·a -ae** f purse, pouch; (fig) money

crumill·a -ae f purse

cru·or -ōris m gore, blood; m pl bloodshed, murder

cruppellāri·ī -ōrum m pl mail-clad combatants

crūrifrag·ius -iī or **-ī** m slave with broken shins

crūs crūris n leg, shin

crust·a -ae f crust, shell, rind, bark; inlaid work, mosaic; stucco

crustŭl·um -ī n cooky

crust·um -ī n pastry

crux crucis f cross, gallows; trouble, misery; gallows bird; tormentor; **i in malam crucem** (coll) go hang yourself

crypt·a -ae f underground passage, covered gallery

cryptoportĭc·us -ūs f covered walk

crystallīn·us -a -um adj made of crystal; n pl crystal vases

crystall·us -ī f or **crystall·um -ī** n crystal

cubiculār·is -e adj bedroom

cubiculāri·us -a -um adj bedroom; m chamberlain

cubicŭl·um -ī n bedroom; emperor's box in the theater

cubīl·e -is n bed, couch; marriage bed; lair, nest, hole; kennel; **avaritiae cubilia** (fig) den of greediness

cubĭt·al -ālis n elbow cushion

cubĭtāl·is -e adj of the elbow; one cubit long

cubĭt·ō -āre vi to be in the habit of lying down; (with **cum** + abl) to go to bed with, have intercourse with

cubĭt·um -ī n elbow; cubit

cubĭt·us -ūs m lying down; intercourse

cub·ō -āre -ŭī or **-āvī -ĭtum** vi to lie, lie down; to recline at table; to lie in bed; to lie sick; (of roof) to slope; (of towns, etc.) to lie on a slope

cucull·us -ī m cowl, hood

cucŭl·us -ī m cuckoo; lazy farmer

cucŭm·is -ĕris m cucumber

cucurbĭt·a -ae f gourd; (med) cupping glass

cūd·ō -ĕre vt to strike, beat, pound; thresh; to forge; to coin, stamp

cuicuimŏdī or **quoiquoimŏdī** adj any kind of

cuj·ās -ātis pron from what country

culcĭt·a -ae f mattress, feather tick; cushion, pillow

culcitell·a -ae f little cushion

cūlĕus see **culleus**

cul·ex -ĭcis m or f gnat

culīn·a -ae f kitchen; cuisine

cullĕ·us or **cūlĕ·us -ī** m leather bag (for holding liquids); scrotum

culm·en -ĭnis n stalk; top, summit; roof; (fig) height, pinnacle, zenith

culm·us -ī m stalk, stem; straw, thatch

culp·a -ae f fault, blame; immorality; **in culpa esse** or **in culpa versari** to be at fault

culpĭt·ō -āre vt to blame, find fault with

culp·ō -āre vt to blame, reproach, censure, find fault with, complain of

cult·a -ōrum n pl plantation; grain fields

cultē adv elegantly, sophisticatedly, with refinement

cultell·us -ī m small knife

cult·er -rī m knife; razor; plowshare

cultĭ·ō -ōnis f cultivation; tilling of the ground, agriculture

cult·or -ōris m tiller, planter, cultivator, farmer; inhabitant; supporter; worshiper

cultr·ix -īcis f cultivator (female); inhabitant (female); (fig) nurse

cultūr·a -ae f tilling, cultivating; agriculture; care, cultivation (of the mind); (with genit) playing up to (e.g., influential friends)

cult·us -a -um pp of **colo**; adj tilled, cultivated; neat, well dressed, prim; cultivated, refined, civilized (person); cultured, refined (mind)

cult·us -ūs m tilling, cultivation (of land); care, tending, keeping (of flocks, etc.); care (of body); training, education; culture, refinement, civilization; high style of living; luxury;

style of dress, fancy clothes; fancy outfit; worship, reverence, veneration

culull·us -ī *m* drinking cup

cūl·us -ī *m* buttock

cum *prep* (with *abl*) (accompaniment) with, together with, in company with; (time) at the same time with, at the time of, at, with; (circumstance, manner, etc.) with, under, in, in the midst of, among, in connection with; **cum eo quod** or **cum eo ut** on condition that; **cum pace** peacefully; **cum prima luce** at dawn; **cum primis** especially, particularly; **mecum** at my house

cum, quum, or **quom** *conj* when, at the time when; whenever; when, while, as; since, now that, because; although; **cum maxime** just when; especially when, just while; just then, just now; **cum primum** as soon as; **cum . . . tum** both . . . and, not only . . . but also, while . . . so too; **praesertim cum** or **cum praesertim** especially since, especially as; **quippe cum** since of course; **utpote cum** seeing that

Cūm·ae -ārum *f pl* town on coast of Campania and oldest Greek colony in Italy, famous as the residence of its Sibyl

Cūmān·us -a -um *adj* Cumaean; *n* Cicero's estate near Cumae

cumb·a or **cymb·a -ae** *f* boat, skiff

cumēr·a -ae *f* bin

cumīn·um -ī *n* cumin (*medicinal plant, said to produce paleness*)

cunque, cunque, or **quomque** *adv* at any time

cumulātē *adv* fully, completely, abundantly, copiously

cumulāt·us -a -um *adj* increased, augmented; filled, full, perfect, complete

cumul·ō -āre *vt* to heap up, pile up; to amass, accumulate; to overload; to make complete, make perfect, crown

cumul·us -ī *m* heap, pile; increase, addition

cūnābŭl·a -ōrum *n pl* cradle

cūn·ae -ārum *f pl* cradle; nest

cunctābund·us -a -um *adj* hesitant, loitering, delaying

cunct·ans -antis *adj* hesitant, reluctant, dilatory

cunctanter *adv* hesitantly, slowly

cunctāti·ō -ōnis *f* hesitation, reluctance, delay

cunctāt·or -ōris *m* dawdler, slowpoke

cunct·or -ārī -ātus sum *vi* to hesitate, delay, linger, be in doubt; **cunctatus brevi** after a moment's hesitation

cunct·us -a -um *adj* all together, the whole, all, entire

cuneātim *adv* in the form of a wedge

cuneāt·us -a -um *adj* wedge-shaped

cuneō -āre *vt* to fasten with a wedge; (fig) to wedge in, squeeze in

cunĕ·us -ī *m* wedge; wedge-form sections of seats in the theater; (mil) troops formed up in the shape of a wedge

cunīcŭl·us -ī *m* rabbit; burrowing underground; (mil) mine

cunque see **cumque**

cūp·a -ae *f* vat

cuped- = **cupped-**

cupīdē *adv* eagerly

cupidit·ās -ātis *f* eagerness, enthusiasm, desire; passion, lust; ambition; greed, avarice; partisanship

cupīd·ō -inis *m* eagerness, desire, longing; passion, lust; greed, avarice

Cupīd·ō -inis *m* Cupid (*son of Venus*)

Cupīdinĕ·us -a -um *adj* Cupid's

cupĭd·us -a -um *adj* eager, enthusiastic, desirous, longing; ambitious; (with *genit*) desirous of, longing for, fond of, attached to

cupi·ens -entis *adj* eager, enthusiastic; (with *genit*) desirous of, longing for, fond of, enthusiastic about

cupienter *adv* eagerly, enthusiastically

cup·iō -ĕre -īvī or **-iī -ītum** *vt* to wish, be eager for, long for, desire

cupīt·or -ōris *m* daydreamer

cuppēdĭ·a -ōrum *n pl* or **cupēdĭ·a -ae** *f* delicacies; sweet tooth

cuppēdinār·ius or **cupēdinār·ius -iī** or **-ī** *m* confectioner

cuppēd·ō -inis *f* desire, longing

cupp·ēs -ēdis *adj* fond of delicacies

cupressēt·um -ī *n* cypress grove

cupressĕ·us -a -um *adj* cypress

cupressif·er -ĕra -ĕrum *adj* cypress-bearing

cupress·us -ī or **-ūs** *f* cypress tree; box of cypress

cūr or **quor** *adv* why

cūr·a -ae *f* care, concern, worry; care, pains, attention; heartache; object of concern; sweetheart; administration, management, charge; trusteeship, guardianship; means of healing, cure, treatment; guardian, keeper; study, reflection; literary effort, literary work; **curae esse** (with *dat*) to be of concern to

cūrābil·is -e *adj* troublesome

cūral·ium -iī or **-ī** *n* coral

cūrāti·ō -ōnis *f* management, administration; office; treatment, cure

cūrātius *adv* more carefully

cūrāt·or -ōris *m* superintendent, manager; (law) guardian, keeper

cūrātūr·a -ae *f* care, attention; dieting

cūrāt·us -a -um *adj* cared-for, attended-to; anxious, earnest

curcul·iō -ōnis *m* weevil

curculiuncŭl·us -ī *m* little weevil; (fig) trifle

Cur·ēs -ium *m pl* ancient Sabine town

Cūrēt·ēs -um *m pl* mythical people of Crete who attended Jupiter at his birth

cūri·a -ae *f* curia, ward (*one of the thirty parts into which Romulus divided the Roman people*); meeting place of a curia; senate building

cūriāl·is -is *m* member of a curia or ward

cūriātim *adv* by curiae, by wards

cūriāt·us -a -um *adj* composed of curiae or wards; passed by the assembly of curiae; **comitia curiata** assembly of the curiae

cūri·ō -ōnis *m* ward boss; **curio maximus** chief ward boss

cūri·ō -ōnis *adj* lean, emaciated

cūriōsē *adv* carefully; curiously; (of style) affectedly

cūriōsit·ās -ātis *f* curiosity

cūriōs·us -a -um *adj* careful, diligent; curious, prying, inquisitive; careworn

cur·is or **quir·is -ītis** *f* spear

cūr·ō -āre *vt* to take care of, look after, attend to, trouble oneself about; to take charge of, see to; to provide for the payment of, settle up; to attend to (*the body with food, washing, etc.*); to cure; to worry about; **cura ut** see to it that; (at the end of a letter) **cura ut valeas** take care of yourself

curriculō *adv* at full speed, quickly

curricul·um -ī *n* race; lap (*of race*); racetrack; racing chariot; (fig) career

currō currĕre cucurrī cursum *vt* to run over, skim over, traverse; *vi* to run, dash, hurry; to sail; to move quickly, flow along; to fly; (of a speech) to move along; (of night, day) to pass away

curr·us -ūs *m* chariot, car; war chariot; triumphal car; triumph; racing chariot; plow wheel; ship

cursim *adv* on the double

cursit·ō -āre *vi* to keep running around, run up and down; to vibrate

curs·ō -āre *vi* to run around, run up and down

curs·or -ōris *m* runner, racer; courier; errand boy

cursūr·a -ae *f* running; haste, speed

curs·us -ūs *m* running, speeding, speed; trip; course, direction; suitable time or weather for travel; rapid movement, speed, flow; flow, progress; **magno cursu** at top speed; **cursus honorum** political career

curt·ō -āre *vt* to shorten; to circumcise

curt·us -a -um *adj* shortened; gelded, castrated; circumcised; broken; defective

cūrūl·is -e *adj* official, curule; **aedilis curulis** patrician aedile; **sella curulis** curule chair, official chair (*used by consuls, praetors, and patrician aediles*)

curvām·en -inis *n* curve, bend

curvātūr·a -ae *f* curvature; **curvatura rotae** rim of a wheel

curv·ō -āre *vt* to curve, bend, arch; (fig) to affect, move, stir

curv·us -a -um *adj* curved, bent; crooked; concave, arched, hollow; winding (*stream, shore*); (fig) crooked; *n* wrong, crookedness

cusp·is -idis *f* point, pointed end; bayonet; spearhead; spear, javelin; trident; scepter; sting (*of scorpion*)

custōdēl·a -ae *f* watch, guard, care

custōdi·a -ae *f* watch, guard, care; sentry, guard; sentry post; custody, prison; **custodiam agitare** to keep guard, be on guard; **in libera custodia** under surveillance, under house arrest

custōd·iō -īre -īvī or **-iī -ītum** *vt* to guard, watch over, protect, defend; to hold in custody; to keep an eye on; to keep carefully, preserve; **memoriā custodire** to keep in mind, remember well

cust·ōs -ōdis *m* guard, guardian, watchman; protector, bodyguard; jailer, warden; (mil) sentinel; spy; *m pl* garrison; *f* guardian; protectress; box, container

cuticul·a -ae *f* skin, cuticle

cut·is -is *f* skin; **cutem curare** (fig) to look after one's own skin

Cyān·ē -ēs *f* nymph who was changed into a fountain

cyathiss·ō -āre *vi* to serve wine

cyăth·us -ī *m* ladle; liquid measure (*one-twelfth of a sextarius, i.e., a half pint*)

cybae·a -ae *f* merchant ship

Cybĕl·ē or **Cybĕl·ē -ēs** *f* originally a Phrygian goddess of fertility, later worshiped in Rome as Ops or Mater Magna

Cyclăd·es -um *f pl* Cyclades (*group of islands in Aegean Sea*)

cycl·as -ădis *f* woman's formal gown

cyclĭc·us -a -um *adj* cyclic; **poeta cyclicus** cyclic poet (*one of a group of poets treating the epic sagas revolving around the Trojan War*)

Cycl·ops -ōpis *m* mythical one-eyed giant of Sicily, esp. Polyphemus

cycnē·us -a -um *adj* swan's

cycn·us or **cygn·us -ī** *m* swan; (fig) poet

Cycn·us or **Cygn·us -ī** *m* king of the Ligurians, son of Sthenelus, changed into a swan, and placed among the stars; son of Neptune, changed into a swan

Cydōni·us -a -um *adj* Cretan; *n* quince

cygnus see **cycnus**

cylindr·us -ī *m* cylinder; roller (*for rolling ground*)

Cyllēn·ē -ēs or **-ae** *f* mountain in Arcadia where Mercury was born

Cyllēni·us -a -um *adj* of Mt. Cyllene; *m* Mercury

cymb·a -ae *f* boat, skiff

cymbăl·um -ī *n* cymbal

cymb·ium -iī or **-ī** *n* small cup

Cynicē *adv* like the Cynics

Cynic·us -a -um *adj* Cynic, relating to the Cynic philosophy; *m* Cynic philosopher, esp. Diogenes, its founder (412-323 B.C.)

cynocephăl·us -ī *m* dog-headed ape

Cynosūr·a -ae *f* Cynosure (*the northern constellation Ursa Minor*)

Cynthĭ·us -a -um *adj* of Mt. Cynthus; Cynthian; *m* Apollo; *f* Diana

Cynth·us -ī *m* mountain of Delos, famous as the birthplace of Apollo and Diana

cypariss·us -ī *f* cypress tree

Cyprĭ·us -a -um *adj* Cypriote; *f* Venus

Cypr·us or **Cypr·os -ī** *f* Cyprus (*island off the coast of Asia Minor*)

Cypsĕl·us -ī *m* despot of Corinth (655-625 B.C.)

Cyrēn·ē -ēs *f* or **Cyrēn·ae -ārum** *f pl* chief city of Greek settlement in N.E. Africa

Cyr·us -ī *m* founder of the Persian monarchy in 559 B.C. (*d.* 529 B.C.); Cyrus the Younger (*under whom Xenophon served, d.* 401 B.C.)

Cyt·ae -ārum *f pl* town in Colchis, birthplace of Medea

Cytae·is -ĭdis *f* Medea

Cythēr·a -ōrum *n pl* island off the S. coast of the Peloponnesus, famous for worship of Venus

Cythērē·is -ĭdis *f* Venus

Cytherē·us -a -um *adj* Cytherean; heros **Cythereius** Aeneas; *f* Venus

Cythērē·us -a -um *adj* Cytherean; *f* Venus

cytĭs·us -ī *m* or *f* clover

Cytōrĭăc·us -a -um *adj* of Cytorus, Cytorian; **pecten Cytoriacus** comb made of boxwood

Cytōr·us or **Cytōr·os -ī** *m* mountain of Paphlagonia, famous for its boxwood

Cyzĭc·um -ī *n* or **Cyzĭc·us** or **Cyzĭc·os -ī** *f* town on Sea of Marmora

D

Dāc·ī -ōrum *m pl* Dacians (*people of the lower Danube*)

dactylĭc·us -a -um *adj* dactylic

dactyl·us -ī *m* dactyl

daedăl·us -a -um *adj* skillful, artistic, artfully constructed

Daedăl·us -ī *m* mythical builder of the labyrinth in Crete and the first to build wings and fly

Damascēn·us -a -um *adj* of Damascus

Damasc·us -ī *f* Damascus (*capital of Coele-Syria*)

damm·a or **dām·a -ae** *f* deer; venison

damnātĭ·ō -ōnis *f* condemnation

damnātōrĭ·us -a -um *adj* guilty (*verdict*)

damnāt·us -a -um *adj* criminal; hateful

damnifĭc·us -a -um *adj* harmful, injurious, pernicious

damnigerŭl·us -a -um *adj* harmful, injurious

damn·ō -āre *vt* to find guilty, sentence, condemn; to disapprove of, reject, blame; to consecrate, offer as a sacrifice, doom to the gods below; (with *genit* or *abl* of charge or punishment) to find (*someone*) guilty of; **capite** or **capitis damnare** to condemn to death; **de majestate damnare** to find guilty of treason; **voti damnare** to oblige (*someone*) to fulfill a vow

damnōsē *adv* destructively, so as to bring ruin

damnōs·us -a -um *adj* damaging, injurious, destructive, pernicious; prodigal; **canes damnosi** crap (*worst throw of the dice*); *m* spendthrift

damn·um -ī *n* loss, damage, harm, injury; misfortune; fine, penalty; fault; defect

Dană·ē -ēs *f* daughter of Acrisius and mother of Perseus

Danaĭd·ēs -um *f pl* daughters of Danaus who killed their husbands on their wedding night, with the exception of Hypermnestra, and as punishment were made to carry water in the lower world

Dană·us -ī *m* king of Argos and father of fifty daughters; *m pl* Greeks

danist·a -ae *m* money lender, banker

danistĭc·us -a -um *adj* money-lending, banking, of bankers

danō see **dō**

Dānuv·ĭus -ĭī or **-ī** *m* Danube

Daphn·ē -ēs *f* nymph pursued by Apollo and changed into a laurel tree

Daphn·is -ĭdis *m* handsome young Sicilian shepherd, the inventor of pastoral song

dapĭn·ō -āre *vt* to serve (*food*)

dap·s -is *f* ceremonial feast; sumptuous meal, banquet; simple food, poor meal

dapsĭl·is -e *adj* sumptuous, costly

Dardăn·us -a -um *adj* Dardanian, Trojan; Roman (*descendant of Aeneas*); *m* son of Jupiter and Electra and ancestor of the Trojan race; *m pl* people of Upper Moesia (*on Danube*)

Darē·us -ī *m* Darius (*king of Persia,* 521-485 B.C.); Darius Ochus or

Nothus (*king of Persia*, 424-405 B.C.); Darius Codomanus (*last king of Persia*, 336-331 B.C.)

datāri·us -a -um *adj* to be handed out, to give away

datātim *adv* giving in turn, passing from one to another

datǐ·ō -ōnis *f* giving, alloting; (*law*) right of alienation

datīv·us -a -um *adj & m* dative

dat·ō -āre *vt* to keep giving away, be in the habit of giving

dat·or -ōris *m* giver

dat·us -ūs *m* giving

Daul·is -ǐdis *f* town in Phocis, famous for the fable of Procne and Philomela

Daun·us -ī *m* king of Apulia and ancestor of Turnus, the opponent of Aeneas

dē *prep* (*with abl*) (of space) down from, from, away from, out of; (of origin) from, of, descended from, derived from; (of separation) from among, out of; (of time) immediately after; about, concerning, of, in respect to; for, on account of, because of; according to, in imitation of; **de improviso** unexpectedly; **de industria** on purpose; **de integro** afresh, all over again; **de novo** anew

de·a -ae *f* goddess

dealb·ō -āre *vt* to whiten, whitewash, plaster

deambulātǐ·ō -ōnis *f* strolling, walking about, stroll, walk

deambŭl·ō -āre *vi* to go for a walk, take a stroll

deǎm·ō -āre *vt* to be in love with; to be much obliged to

dearm·ō -āre *vt* to disarm

deartǔ·ō -āre *vt* to tear limb from limb, dismember; (*fig*) to waste, wreck

deascǐ·ō -āre *vt* to smooth with an ax; (*coll*) to cheat, con

dēbacch·or -ārī -ātus sum *vi* to rant and rave

dēbellāt·or -ōris *m* conqueror

dēbell·ō -āre *vt* to fight it out with, wear down, subdue; *vi* to fight it out to the end; to bring a war to an end

dēb·ěō -ēre -ǔī -ǐtum *vt* to owe; to be responsible for; (*with inf*) a to have to, be bound to, be obliged to; **b** to be destined to, be fated to; (*with dat*) to owe (*e.g., a favor*) to, be indebted to (*someone*) for; **deberi** (*with dat*) to be due to

dēbǐl·is -e *adj* lame, crippled, frail, feeble, paralyzed

dēbilit·ās -ātis *f* lameness, debility, weakness, helplessness

dēbilitātǐ·ō -ōnis *f* disabling, paralyzing

dēbilit·ō -āre *vt* to lame; to disable, debilitate, weaken; to unnerve; to paralyze

dēbitǐ·ō -ōnis *f* debt

dēbit·or -ōris *m* debtor; person under obligation

dēbĭt·um -ī *n* debt; obligation

dēblatěr·ō -āre *vt* to blurt out

dēcant·ō -āre *vt* to repeat monotonously; *vi* to sing on to the end; to stop singing

dē·cēdō -cēděre -cessī -cessum *vi* to withdraw, clear out, depart; to retire, retreat, fall back, abandon a position; to give place, make way, make room, yield; to depart, disappear, die; to abate, subside, cease; to go wrong, go awry; (*with dat*) to yield to, give in to; (*with de + abl*) to give up, relinquish, abandon

decem (*indecl*) *adj* ten; (*fig*) large number of

December·er -ris *adj & m* December

decemjŭg·is -is *m* ten-horse chariot

decempěd·a -ae *f* ten-foot measuring rod, ten-foot rule

decempedāt·or -ōris *m* surveyor

decempl·ex -ǐcis *adj* tenfold

decemprīm·ī or **decem prīm·ī -ōrum** *m pl* board of ten (*governing Italian towns*)

decemscalm·us -a -um *adj* tenoared

decemvirāl·is -e *adj* decemviral; **leges decemvirales** laws passed by the decemviri

decemvirāt·us -ūs *m* decemvirate

decemvir·ī -ōrum *m pl* decemviri, ten-man commission (*appointed in Rome at different times and for various purposes*); **decemviri legibus scribundis** commission to codify the laws (451 B.C.); **decemviri sacris faciundis** commission for attending to religious matters

decenn·is -e *adj* ten-year, lasting ten years

dec·ens -entis *adj* proper, becoming; handsome, pretty; decent, proper

decenter *adv* becomingly, decently, properly, with propriety

decentǐ·a -ae *f* propriety, decency

dē·cernō -cerněre -crēvī -crētum *vt* to sift, separate; to decide, settle, determine, decree, resolve, vote; to decide by combat, fight out; to fight, combat; *vi* to contend, compete, struggle; to put forward a proposal; (*with de or pro + abl*) to fight over, fight for (*in court*)

dēcerp·ō -ěre -sī -tum *vt* to pluck off, tear away, break off, gather, crop; to derive, enjoy (*e.g., benefits, satisfaction*); **aliquid de gravitate decerpere** to detract somewhat from the dignity

dēcertātǐ·ō -ōnis *f* decision, decisive struggle

dēcert·ō -āre *vi* to fight it out, decide the issue

dēcessǐ·ō -ōnis *f* withdrawing; retirement, departure (*from a province*); decrease; disappearance

dēcess·or -ōris *m* retiring official, predecessor in office

dēcess·us -ūs *m* withdrawal; retirement (*of official from a province*); decease, death

dec·et -ēre -ŭit (used only in 3d *sing & pl*) *vt* to befit, be becoming to; (with *inf*) it is fitting to (*someone*) to, it is proper for (*someone*) to; *vi* to be fitting, be proper; (with *dat & inf*) it is fitting to (*someone*) to, it is proper for (*someone*) to

dēcĭd·ō -ēre -ī *vi* to fall down; to fall dead, die; to fall, drop, sink, fail, perish

dē-cīdō -cīdĕre -cīsī -cīsum *vt* to cut off, cut away; to cut short, terminate, put an end to, decide, settle; **pennas decidĕre** (fig) to clip (*someone's*) wings

decĭens or **decĭēs** *adv* ten times; **decĭens centena milia** or **decĭens** million

decimānus see **decumanus**

decĭm·us or **decŭm·us -a -um** *adj* the tenth; **cum decimo** tenfold; **cum decimo effecit ager** the field produced a tenfold return; **decimum** for the tenth time

dē-cĭpĭō -cĭpĕre -cēpī -ceptum *vt* to deceive, cheat; to snare, mislead, beguile; to escape the notice of; **aliquem laborum decipere** to make one forget his troubles; **laborum decipi** to be freed of troubles, forget one's troubles

dēcĭsĭ·ō -ōnis *f* decision, settlement

decīsum *pp* of **decīdo**

Dec·ĭus -ĭī or **-ī** *m* P. Decius Mus (*Roman hero who voluntarily gave his life in battle during the Latin War in 340 B.C. to bring victory to the Roman army; his son who likewise gave his life in Samnite War in 295 B.C.*)

dēclāmātĭ·ō -ōnis *f* practice in public speaking; theme or subject matter in rhetorical exercise; loud talking, shouting, hubbub

dēclāmāt·or -ōris *m* elocutionist, declaimer; ranter

dēclāmātōrĭ·us -a -um *adj* rhetorical

dēclāmĭt·ō -āre *vt* to plead (*cases*); *vi* to practice public speaking; to bluster

dēclām·ō -āre *vt* to recite; *vi* to practice public speaking

dēclārātĭ·ō -ōnis *f* disclosure, declaration

dēclār·ō -āre *vt* to make clear, make evident, disclose; to proclaim, announce officially; to show, prove, demonstrate; to mean, express, signify; to declare (*as chosen for office*)

dēclīnātĭ·ō -ōnis *f* leaning away, bending aside, swerving; shunning, avoiding; digression; (gram) declension

dēclīn·ō -āre *vt* to deflect; to parry, avoid; to decline, conjugate; *vi* to deviate; to digress

dēclīv·e -is *n* declivity, slope

dēclīv·is -e *adj* sloping, steep, downhill

dēclīvĭt·ās -ātis *f* sloping terrain

dēcoct·a -ae *f* cold drink

dēcoct·or -ōris *m* bankrupt; (coll) old rake

dēcoct·us -a -um *pp* of **decoquo;** *adj* boiled down; mellow (*style*)

dēcoll·ō -āre *vt* to behead

dēcōl·ō -āre *vi* to trickle away, come to naught, fail

dēcōl·or -ōris *adj* off-color, faded; dark, tanned; degenerate

dēcolōrātĭ·ō -ōnis *f* discoloring

dēcolōr·ō -āre *vt* to discolor, stain, deface

dē-cŏquō -coquĕre -coxī -coctum *vt* to boil down, boil thoroughly; to bring to ruin; *vi* to go bankrupt

dec·or -ōris *m* beauty, grace, elegance, charm; ornament

decōrē *adv* beautifully, gracefully; suitably, properly

decŏr·ō -āre *vt* to beautify, adorn, embellish; to decorate, honor

decōr·us -a -um *adj* beautiful, graceful, adorned; decorous, proper, suitable; fine, handsome; noble; *n* grace, propriety

dēcrepĭt·us -a -um *adj* decrepit, broken down, worn out

dē-crescō -crescĕre -crēvī -crētum *vi* to grow less, become fewer, diminish, subside, wane

dēcrēt·us -a -um *pp* of **decerno;** *n* decision, decree; principle, doctrine

decŭm·a or **decĭm·a -ae** *f* tenth part, tithe, land tax; largess to the people

decumān·us or **decimān·us -a -um** *adj* paying tithes; of the tenth cohort, of the tenth legion; *m* tax collector; *m pl* men of the tenth legion; *f* tax collector's wife; **porta decumana** main gate of a Roman camp on the side turned away from the enemy

decumāt·ēs -ĭum *adj* subject to tithes

dē-cumbō -cumbĕre -cubŭī *vi* to lie down; to recline at table; to fall (*in battle*)

decŭm·ō or **decĭm·ō -āre** *vt* to decimate

decurĭ·a -ae *f* decuria, group of ten; tenth part (*of a curia*); division, class (*without reference to number*); panel (*of judges*); social club

decurĭātĭ·ō -ōnis *f* dividing into decuries

decurĭāt·us -ūs *m* dividing into decuries

decurĭ·ō -āre *vt* (pol) to divide into groups of ten; (fig) to divide into groups

decurĭ·ō -ōnis *m* decurion (*head of a decuria*); (mil) cavalry officer (*in charge of ten men*); senator of a municipality or colony

dē-currō -currĕre -cucurrī or **-currī -cursum** *vt* to pass over, run over, traverse; to pass through (*life*); to get over (*troubles*); to discuss, treat; *vi* to run down; (mil) to parade, maneuver; (of river, ship) to run down to the sea; to run for help; to sail; to land; **eo decursum est ut** it got to the point where

dēcursǐ·ō -ōnis f (mil) dress parade; maneuvers; raid, descent

dēcurs·us -ūs m running down; downward course; (mil) dress parade; (mil) maneuvers; (mil) raid; end of course, completion; **decursus honōrum** completion of political career

dēcurtāt·us -a -um adj cut down, cut off short, mutilated; clipped (style)

dec·us -ŏris n beauty, glory, honor, dignity; virtue, worth; source of glory; n pl great deeds, distinctions

dēcuss·ō -āre vt to divide crosswise (in the form of an X)

dē·cutǐō -cutĕre -cussī -cussum vt to shake off, beat off, strike down; to chop off (head); to break down (wall with battering ram)

dē·dĕcet -decĕre -decuit (used only in 3d sing & pl) vt it ill becomes, ill befits; (with inf) it is a disgrace to

dēdĕcŏr·ō -āre vt to disgrace, dishonor, bring shame to; to make a sham of

dēdĕcŏr·us -a -um adj disgraceful, dishonorable, unbecoming

dēdĕc·us -ŏris n disgrace, dishonor, shame; vice, crime, outrage; (mil) disgraceful defeat; **dedecori esse** (with dat) to be a source of disgrace to; **dedecus admittere** to incur disgrace; **per dedecus** disgracefully

dēdĭcātǐ·ō -ōnis f dedication, consecration

dēdĭc·ō -āre vt to dedicate, consecrate, set aside; to declare (property in a census return)

dēdignor -ārī -ātus sum vt to scorn, disdain, look down on; (with double acc) to scorn (someone) as; **aliquem maritum dedignari** to regard someone as an unworthy husband

dē·discō -discĕre -didĭcī vt to forget

dēditĭc·ǐus -ǐī or **-ī** m captive; m pl prisoners of war

dēditĭ·ō -ōnis f surrender, capitulation

dēdĭt·us -a -um pp of dedo; adj (with dat) given to, devoted to, addicted to; (with in + abl) absorbed in; m pl prisoners of war, captives

dē·dō -dĕre -dĭdī -dĭtum vt to give up, surrender; to devote; to apply; to abandon; **aliquem hostibus in cruciatum dedere** to hand someone over to the enemy to be tortured; **deditā operā** on purpose, intentionally; **neci** or **ad necem dedere** to put to death

dēdoc·ĕō -ēre -ŭī -tum vt to cause to forget; (with inf) to teach (someone) not to

dēdŏl·ĕō -ēre -ŭī vi to grieve no more

dēdŏl·ō -āre vt to chop away; to chop smooth

dē·dūcō -dūcĕre -duxī -ductum vt to lead or draw down; to launch (ship); to accompany, escort; to lead out (colonists to new colony); to conduct (bride to her husband), give away (bride); to evict; to subtract, deduct, diminish; to summon (as witness); to divert, mislead; to derive (name); to compose (poetry); to dissuade; to spin out (thread); to comb out (hair)

dēductǐ·ō -ōnis f leading or drawing off; settling (of colonists); (law) eviction; reduction; inference; **rationis deductio** train of reasoning

dēduct·us -a -um pp of deduco; adj drawn down; bent inwards, concave; lowered, modest; subtle, well wrought (poem)

dēerr·ō -āre vi to go astray, wander away; **a vero deerrare** (fig) to stray from the truth

dēfaec·ō -āre vt to cleanse of dregs; to wash; (fig) to clear up, make clear

dēfatīgātǐ·ō -ōnis f exhaustion

dēfatīg·ō -āre vt to wear out, exhaust

dēfatiscor see defetiscor

dēfectǐ·ō -ōnis f failure; defection, desertion; weakening, exhaustion; eclipse; **defectio animi** mental breakdown; **in defectione esse** to be up in revolt

dēfect·or -ōris m defector, deserter; rebel

dēfect·us -a -um pp of deficio; adj weak, worn out

dēfect·us -ūs m failing, failure; desertion; revolt; eclipse

dē·fendō -fendĕre -fendī -fensum vt to repel, beat off, avert; to defend, protect, guard; to keep off (the cold); to answer (a charge); to champion (a cause); to support, uphold, maintain (an argument); to play the part of (a character); (law) to defend

dēfensǐ·ō -ōnis f defense

dēfensǐt·ō -āre vt to defend often; **causas defensitare** to be a lawyer

dēfens·ō -āre vt to defend, protect

dēfens·or -ōris m defender, protector; (law) defense lawyer; (law) guardian; champion (of people); m pl garrison

dēfensus pp of defendo

dē·fĕrō -ferre -tŭlī -lātum vt to bring or carry down; to bear off, carry away; to throw (ship) off course; to offer, confer, grant; to inform against, indict; to give an account of, announce, report; to recommend; to register; **ad aerarium deferre** to recommend (someone) for a monetary reward (because of outstanding service to the State); **ad consilium deferre** to take into consideration

dē·fervescō -fervescĕre -fervī or **-ferbŭī** vt & vi to cool off, calm down; (of a speech) to lose momentum; (of passions) to die out

dēfess·us -a -um *adj* weary, worn out, exhausted

dē·fetiscor or **dē·fatiscor -fetiscī -fessus sum** *vi* to become weary, tired

dē·ficiō -ficĕre -fēcī -fectum *vt* to fail, disappoint; to desert, abandon; *vi* to fail, be a failure; to defect, desert; to secede; (of arms, food, etc.) to run short, run out; (of strength, morale, etc.) to fail, grow weak, droop, sink; (of sun, moon) to be eclipsed; (of fire) to die out; (com) to be bankrupt

dē·fīgō -fīgĕre -fīxī -fīxum *vt* to fix, fasten down; to drive down; to fix, concentrate (*eyes, attention*); to root to the spot, astound, stupefy; to bewitch, enchant; **in terra defīgere** to stick, plant, set up (*something*) in the ground

dē·fingō -fingĕre -finxī *vt* to form, mold; to portray; to disfigure, deface

dēfīn·iō -īre -īvī -ītum *vt* to set bounds to, limit; (fig) to limit, define, explain; to fix, determine, appoint; to delimit, bring to a finish, end; to assign, prescribe

dēfīnītē *adv* precisely

dēfīnītĭ·ō -ōnis *f* boundary; (fig) marking out, prescribing; definition

dēfīnītīv·us -a -um *adj* explanatory

dēfīnīt·us -a -um *adj* definite, precise

dē·fīō -fĭerī *vi* to fail, be lacking

dēflagrātĭ·ō -ōnis *f* conflagration

dēflăgr·ō -āre *vt* to burn down; *vi* to burn down, go up in flames; to perish, be destroyed; (of passions) to cool off, be allayed, subside

dē·flectō -flectĕre -flexī -flexum *vt* to deflect, bend aside, turn away, divert; (fig) to turn away, lead astray; *vi* to turn away, digress, deviate

defl·ĕō -ēre -ēvī -ētum *vt* to cry bitterly for; to mourn as lost; *vi* to cry bitterly

dēfloccāt·us -a -um *adj* stripped of wool, shorn; bald (*head*)

dēflōr·escō -escĕre -ŭī *vi* to shed blossoms; (fig) to fade, droop

dēflŭ·ō -ĕre -xī *vi* to flow or float down; to glide down, slide, fall; to flow out, run dry; to vanish, pass away, disappear, cease; to go out of style, become obsolete

dē·fodiō -fodĕre -fōdī -fossum *vt* to dig down; to hollow out; to bury, hide, conceal

dēfŏre = dēfutūrum esse

dēform·is -e *adj* shapeless, amorphous; misshapen, disfigured, ugly; degrading; degraded; unbecoming, humiliating

dēformĭt·ās -ātis *f* deformity, ugliness, hideousness; vileness, turpitude

dēformĭter *adv* without grace, without beauty

dēform·ō -āre *vt* to form from a pattern; to sketch, delineate; to deform, disfigure, mar

dēfossus *pp* of **defodio**

defraud·ō or **defrūd·ō -āre** *vt* to defraud, rob; to cheat; **genium suum defraudare** to deny oneself some pleasure

defrēnāt·us -a -um *adj* unbridled, uncontrolled

defric·ō -āre -ŭī -ātum *vt* to rub down; to brush (*teeth*); (fig) to satirize

de·fringō -fringĕre -frēgī -fractum *vt* to break off, break to pieces

defrūdo see **defraudo**

defrŭt·um -ī *n* new wine

dē·fugiō -fugĕre -fūgī *vt* to run away from, avoid, shirk; to evade (*e.g., authority, law*); *vi* to run off, escape

dēfunct·us -a -um *pp* of **defungor**; *adj* finished; dead

dē·fundō -fundĕre -fūdī -fūsum *vt* to pour out; to empty (*e.g., bucket*)

dē·fungor -fungī -functus sum *vi* (with *abl*) a to perform, finish, be done with; **b** to have done with, get rid of; **defunctus jam sum** I'm safe now; **defungi vitā** or **defungi** to die; **parvo victu defungi** to do with or be content with little food

dēfūsus *pp* of **defundo**

dēgĕn·er -ĕris *adj* degenerate; unworthy; ignoble

dēgĕner·ō -āre *vt* to disgrace, dishonor, fall short of; *vi* to be inferior to one's ancestors, be degenerate; (fig) to fall off, degenerate, decline

dēgĕr·ō -ĕre *vt* to carry off, carry away

dēg·ō -ĕre -ī *vt* to spend, pass (*time, life*); **aetatem degere** to live; *vi* to live

dēgrandĭnat *v impers* it is hailing hard

dēgrăv·ō -āre *vt* to weigh down; (fig) to burden, distress, inconvenience, overpower

dē·gredior -grĕdī -gressus sum *vi* to march down, go down, walk down, descend; **ad pedes degredi** to dismount

dēgrunn·iō -īre *vi* to grunt hard, grunt out loud

dēgust·ō -āre *vt* to taste; (fig) to taste, sample, try, experience; (of weapon) to graze

dehinc *adv* from here; from now on; then, next; hereafter

dehisc·ō -ĕre *vi* to part, divide, gape, yawn

dehonestāment·um -ī *n* blemish, disfigurement, dishonor, disgrace

dehonest·ō -āre *vt* to dishonor, disgrace

dehort·or -ārī -ātus sum *vt* to advise to the contrary, dissuade

Dēianīr·a -ae *f* daughter of Oeneus and wife of Hercules

dein see **deinde**

deinceps *adv* one after another, in succession, in order; in regular order, without interruption

deinde or **dein** *adv* (of place) from that place, from there; (of time) then, thereafter, thereupon, afterwards; (in enumerating facts, presenting arguments) secondly, next in order, in the next place

Dēiŏtăr·us -ī *m* king of Galatia (*defended by Cicero before Caesar in the latter's house*)

Dēiphŏb·us -ī *m* son of Priam and Hecuba, and husband of Helen after Paris' death

dējectĭ·ō -ōnis *f* (law) eviction

dēject·us -a -um *pp* of **dejicio;** *adj* low, depressed, sunken (*place*); discouraged, downhearted, despondent

dēject·us -ūs *m* felling (*of trees*); steep slope

dējĕr·ō or **dējūrō** -āre *vi* to swear solemnly

dē·jiciŏ -jicĕre -jēcī -jectum *vt* to throw down, fling down; to fell, bring low, kill; to depose (*from office*); to lower (*eyes*); to drive off course; (law) to evict; (mil) to dislodge, drive out; to deprive; (with *abl* or **de** + *abl*) to deprive (*someone*) of, prevent (*someone*) from obtaining, rob (*someone*) of; **oculos dejicere** (with **ab** + *abl*) to divert the eyes from; to turn away from

dējung·ō -ĕre *vt* to unyoke; to sever

dējūrō see **dejero**

dējŭv·ō -āre *vt* to fail to help

dē·lābor -lābī -lapsus sum *vi* to slip down, fall down, sink down; to glide down, float down; (fig) to come down, sink; (fig) to stoop, condescend; (with **ad** + *acc*) to be inclined toward, be partial to, tend toward; (with **in** + *acc*) to sneak in among

dēlacĕr·ō -āre *vt* to tear to pieces

dēlāment·or -ārī -ātus sum *vt* to grieve deeply for

delass·ō -āre *vt* to tire out, weary

dēlātĭ·ō -ōnis *f* reporting; informing, denouncing; **nominis delatio** indicting of a person

dēlāt·or -ōris *m* reporter; informer, denouncer

dēlātus *pp* of **defero**

dēlectābĭl·is -e *adj* delightful, enjoyable

dēlectāment·um -ī *n* delight, amusement, pastime

dēlectātĭ·ō -ōnis *f* delight, pleasure, charm, amusement, satisfaction

dēlect·ō -āre *vt* to delight, amuse, charm; to attract, allure; **delectari** (with *abl*) to be delighted by, delight in; *v impers* **me ire delectat** I like to go, I enjoy going

dēlect·us -a -um *pp* of **deligo;** *adj* picked, choice, select

dēlect·us -ūs *m* choosing, choice

dēlēgātĭ·ō -ōnis *f* substitution, dele-

gation (*of one person for another*); payment (*of debt*)

dēlēg·ō -āre *vt* to assign, transfer; to attribute, impute, ascribe

dēlēnĭfĭc·us -a -um *adj* soothing, seductive

dēlēnĭment·um -ī *n* palliative, solace, comfort; allurement, bait

dēlēn·ĭō or **dēlīn·ĭō** -īre -īvī -ītum *vt* to soothe, calm down, console, appease; to allure, seduce, win over

dēlēnīt·or -ōris *m* charmer, cajoler

dēl·ĕō -ēre -ēvī -ētum *vt* to destroy, annihilate, overthrow, extinguish, raze; to blot out, erase, obliterate (*writing*); to annul, put an end to, abolish, finish

dēlētr·ix -īcis *f* destroyer

Dēlĭăc·us -a -um *adj* Delian, of or from Delos

dēlīberābund·us -a -um *adj* deliberating maturely

dēlīberātĭ·ō -ōnis *f* considering, weighing; deliberation, consultation; **habet res deliberationem** the matter requires thought, needs consideration

dēlīberātīv·us -a -um *adj* deliberative; requiring deliberation

dēlīberāt·or -ōris *m* thoughtful person

dēlīberāt·us -a -um *adj* resolved upon, determined

dēlībĕr·ō -āre *vt* to weigh well, ponder; to resolve, determine; to consult (*oracle*); *vi* to reflect, deliberate; (with **de** + *abl*) to think seriously about, think over well

dēlīb·ō -āre *vt* to sip, take a sip of; to taste, take a taste of, nibble at; to take away, detract, subtract, remove

dēlibr·ō -āre *vt* to strip the bark off (*trees*); to peel

dēlibūt·us -a -um *adj* anointed; defiled, stained, smeared; steeped

dēlĭcātē *adv* delicately, softly, luxuriously

dēlĭcāt·us -a -um *adj* delicate, dainty, tender, soft; pampered, spoiled; dainty, fastidious

dēlĭcĭ·ae -ārum *f pl* allurements, enticements, delights; whims, pet ideas, fanciful ideas; voluptuousness; favorite, sweetheart, darling; **delicias facere** to play tricks; **delicias facere** (with *dat*) to play around with (*a girl*); **esse in deliciis** (with *dat*) to be the pet or favorite of; **habere in deliciis** to have as a pet or favorite

dēlĭcĭŏl·ae -ārum *f pl* darling

delic·ĭum -ĭī or -ī *n* sweetheart; favorite

dēlĭc·ō -āre *vt* to make clear, explain

dēlict·um -ī *n* fault, offense, wrong, transgression, defect

dēlĭcŭ·us -a -um *adj* lacking, wanting

dēlĭg·ō -āre *vt* to tie up, bind together, bind fast

dē·lĭgō -lĭgĕre -lēgī -lectum *vt* to

choose, select, pick out, single out,
elect; to gather, gather in

dē·lingō -lingĕre -linxī vt to lick
off; to have a lick of

dēlīni- = deleni-

dē·linquō -linquĕre -līquī -lictum
vi to fail, be wanting, fall short; to
do wrong, commit a fault or crime

dē·liquescō -liquescĕre -licŭī vi
to melt, melt away, dissolve; to pine
away

dēliquī·ō -ōnis f failure; (with
genit) failure to get

dēliqu·ium -iī or -ī n failure

dēliqu·ō or dēlīc·ō -āre vt to clear
up, explain

dēlīrāment·um -ī n nonsense, absurdity

dēlīrātī·ō -ōnis f silliness, folly,
madness; infatuation; dotage

dēlīr·ō -āre vi to be off the beam,
be crazy, be mad; to drivel

dēlīr·us -a -um adj crazy, demented,
silly; in dotage

dēlit·escō -escĕre -ŭī vi to conceal
oneself, lie hidden, lurk

dēlītīg·ō -āre vi to rant

Dēli·us -a -um adj Delian, of Delos

Dēl·os -ī f sacred island in the Cyclades, where Apollo was born

Delph·ī -ōrum m pl town in Phocis,
in Central Greece, famous for the
shrine and oracle of Apollo; inhabitants of Delphi

delphīn·us -ī or delph·īn -īnis m
dolphin

Delphīn·us -ī m Dolphin (constellation)

Deltōt·on -ī n Triangulum (constellation)

dēlūbr·um -ī n shrine, temple, sanctuary

dēluct·ō -āre or dēluct·or -ārī
-ātus sum vi to wrestle

dēlūdific·ō -āre vt to make fun of

dē·lūdō -lūdĕre -lūsī -lūsum vt to
dupe, mock, deceive, delude

dēlumb·is -e adj enervated, enfee-
bled, weakened

dēmad·escō -escĕre -ŭī vi to become drenched; to be moistened

dēmand·ō -āre vt to hand over, entrust

dēmarch·us -ī m demarch (chief of
a village in Attica); (fig) tribune of
the people

dēm·ens -entis adj out of one's
mind, demented, distracted, mad;
senseless, wild, reckless

dēmensus pp of dēmetior; n ration, allowance

dēmenter adv insanely

dēmenti·a -ae f insanity, madness;
f pl follies

dement·iō -īre vi to be mad

dēmer·eō -ēre -ŭī -ĭtum or dēmer·
ĕor -ērī -ĭtus sum vt to earn,
merit, deserve; to serve well, do a
service to

dē·mergō -mergĕre -mersī -mer-
sum vt to sink, plunge, submerge;
(fig) to plunge, cast down, overwhelm

dēmessus pp of dēmeto

dē·mētior -mētīrī -mensus sum
vt to measure off, measure out

dē·mětō -metĕre -messŭī -mes-
sum vt to mow, reap, cut off, cut
down, harvest

dēmigrātī·ō -ōnis f emigration

dēmigr·ō -āre vi to migrate, emigrate, move, depart; (fig) to depart,
die

dēmin·ŭō -uĕre -ŭī -ūtum vt to
make smaller, lessen, diminish; (fig)
to remit, reduce, lessen; capite de-
minuere to deprive of citizenship

dēminūtī·ō -ōnis f lessening, diminution, abridging; (law) right of
disposing of property; capitis diminutio loss of civil rights; provinciae diminutio shortening of
term of office

dēmīr·or -ārī -ātus sum vt to be
surprised at, be amazed at

dēmissē adv low; humbly, modestly;
abjectly, meanly

dēmissīci·us -a -um adj allowed to
hang down, flowing

dēmissi·ō -ōnis f letting down, sinking, lowering; demissio animi
low morale

dēmiss·us -a -um pp of dēmitto;
adj low, low-lying (place); drooping
(lips, etc.); bent (head); allowed to
hang down, flowing, loose (hair);
downhearted, dejected; shy, unassuming, retiring, humble; poor,
humble

dēmītīg·ō -āre vt to make mild; dē-
mitigari to grow more lenient

dē·mittō -mittĕre -mīsī -missum
vt to drop, let drop, let sink, lower;
to bring downstream; to land (ship);
to grow (beard); to move down
(troops from higher place); se dē-
mittere to descend; to stoop, bend
down

dēmiurg·us or dāmiurg·us -ī m
chief magistrate in a Greek state

dēm·ō -ĕre -psī -ptum vt to take
away, remove, withdraw, subtract;
(with dat or with de + abl) to take
away from, subtract from, withhold from

Dēmocrīt·us -ī m famous philosopher of Abdera, in Thrace, founder
of the atomic theory (460-361 B.C.)

dēmōl·ior -īrī -ītus sum vt to demolish, pull down

dēmōlītī·ō -ōnis f pulling down (of
statues)

dēmonstrātī·ō -ōnis f pointing out;
explanation

dēmonstrātīv·us -a -um adj showy

dēmonstrāt·or -ōris m indicator

dēmonstr·ō -āre vt to point out
clearly; to state precisely, explain,
describe; to mention, speak of; to
demonstrate, prove, establish

dē·morior -mŏrī -mortŭus sum
vi to die, die off

dēmŏr·or -ārī -ātus sum vt to delay, detain; to hinder, block; vi to
wait

Dēmosthĕn·ēs -is m greatest Greek orator (384-322 B.C.)

dē-movĕō -movēre -mōvī -mōtum vt to remove, move away, dispossess, expel; to remove, discharge (from office); (fig) to divert, turn away

demptus pp of demo

dēmūgīt·us -a -um adj bellowing, lowing

dē-mulcĕō -mulcēre -mulsī vt to stroke lovingly, to caress

dēmum adv at last, finally; not till then; (to give emphasis) precisely, exactly, just; (to give assurance) in fact, certainly, to be sure, as a matter of fact; **decimo dēmum anno** not till the tenth year; **modo dēmum** only now, not till now; **nunc dēmum** now at last, not till now; **post dēmum** not till after; **sic dēmum** thus finally; **tum dēmum** then at length, not till then

dēmurmŭr·ō -āre vt to grumble right through (e.g., a performance)

dēmūtātī·ō -ōnis f changing, perversion, degeneracy

dēmūt·ō -āre vt to change, alter; to make worse; vi to change one's mind

dēnār·ius -iī or **-ī** m Roman silver coin, originally containing ten aces, later eighteen, approximately equivalent to twenty-five cents; money

dēnarr·ō -āre vt to recount in detail

dēnās·ō -āre vt to bite the nose off (the face)

dēnāt·ō -āre vi to swim downstream

dēnĕg·ō -āre vt to deny, refuse, turn down; vi to say no, give a flat refusal

dēn·ī -ae -a adj in sets of ten, ten each, in tens; ten; tenth

dēnicāl·is -e adj purifying from death; **feriae dēnicāles** purification service (after death in the household)

dēnique adv finally, at last; in short, in a word, briefly; (for emphasis) just, precisely; (ironical) of course; **octāvo dēnique mēnse** not till after the eighth month; **tum dēnique** then at last, only then, not till then

dēnōmin·ō -āre vt to name, designate

dēnorm·ō -āre vt to make crooked or irregular; to disfigure, spoil

dēnŏt·ō -āre vt to mark down, specify; to take careful note of, observe closely

dēn·s -tis m tooth; ivory; point, prong, fluke; (fig) tooth (of envy, hatred, time, etc.); **albis dentibus deridēre aliquem** to laugh heartily at someone; **dēns Indus** elephant's tusk

dēnsē adv closely, thickly; in quick succession, repeatedly

dēnsit·ās -ātis f closeness, thickness

dēns·ō -āre or **dēns·ĕō -ēre —** **-ētum** vt to make thick, thicken; to press close together; to close

(ranks); to condense (a speech)

dēns·us -a -um adj dense, close, crowded, thick; frequent, continuous; intense (love, cold); concise (style)

dentāl·ia -ium n pl plow beam

dentāt·us -a -um adj toothed, having teeth; serrated; polished (paper)

dentifrangibŭl·us -a -um adj tooth-breaking; m thug; n fist

dentilĕg·us -ī m toothpicker (one who picks up teeth after they have been knocked out)

dent·iō -īre vi to teethe, cut one's teeth

dē-nūbō -nūbĕre -nupsī -nuptum vi (of a woman) to marry beneath one's rank

dēnūd·ō -āre vt to denude, strip naked, strip bare; (fig) to lay bare (facts)

dēnuntiātī·ō -ōnis f intimation, warning, threat; announcement, proclamation; **senātūs dēnuntiātio** senate ordinance; **testimōni dēnuntiātio** summons to testify

dēnuntī·ō -āre vt to intimate; to give notice of; to announce officially; to give official warning to; (mil) to report to, give an official report to; to warn, threaten; **dēnuntiāre testimōnium** (with dat) to give (someone) a summons to testify

dēnŭō adv anew, afresh, once more, all over again

deonĕr·ō -āre vt to unload

deorsum or **deŏrsus** adv downwards, down; (of position) down, below

deoscŭl·or -ārī -ātus sum vt to kiss warmly, kiss up and down

dēpac·iscor see depeciscor

dēpact·us -a -um adj lashed down; driven tight

dēparc·us -a -um adj very stingy

dē-pascō -pascĕre -pāvī -pastum or **dē-pascor -pascī -pastus sum** vt to feed off, graze on; to consume; to destroy, waste; (fig) to prune off (excesses of style)

dēpec·iscor or **dēpac·iscor -iscī -tus sum** vt to agree upon, bargain for, settle by bargaining

dē-pectō -pectĕre — -pexum vt to comb, curry; to curry (one's hide), flog

dēpeculāt·or -ōris m embezzler, plunderer

dēpecŭl·or -ārī -ātus sum vt to embezzle, plunder

dē-pellō -pellĕre -pŭlī -pulsum vt to drive off, drive away, drive out, expel; to avert; (mil) to dislodge; (with quin or with dē or ab + abl) to avert, deter, dissuade, wean from; (with abl) to dislodge from; vi to deviate

dēpend·ĕō -ēre vi to hang down; (with abl) to be derived from; (with dē + abl) to depend upon; (with ex + abl) to hang down from

dē-pendō -pendĕre -pendī -pen-

sum *vt* to pay up; **poenam depen-dere** (with *dat*) to pay the penalty to

dēper·dō -děre -dĭdī -dĭtum *vt* to lose completely; to ruin, destroy

dēper·ĕō -īre -ĭī *vt* to be hopelessly in love with; *vi* to go to ruin, perish; to be lost, finished

dē·pingō -pingěre -pinxī -pictum *vt* to paint, portray; to embroider; to portray, describe, represent (*in words or thoughts*)

dē·plangō -plangěre -planxī *vt* to grieve over, cry one's heart out over

dēplex·us -a -um *adj* gripping firmly, grasping

dēplōrābund·us -a -um *adj* weeping bitterly, sobbing

dēplōr·ō -āre *vt* to cry over, mourn; to despair of; *vi* to take it hard, cry bitterly

dēplŭ·it -ěre -it *v impers* it is raining hard, pouring down

dē·pōnō -pōněre -posŭī -positum *vt* to lay down; to put down, put aside, get rid of; to bet, wager; to deposit; (with **apud** + *acc*) to entrust to, commit to the care of; **bellum deponere** to give up war; **imperium deponere** to relinquish power, renounce power

dēpopulātĭ·ō -ōnis *f* ravaging, pillaging

dēpopulāt·or -ōris *m* pillager, marauder

dēpopŭl·ō -āre or **depopŭl·or -ārī -ātus sum** *vt* to ravage, pillage, lay waste; to depopulate; (fig) to waste, destroy, wreck

dēport·ō -āre *vt* to carry down; to carry away; to bring home (*victory*); to transport; to banish; (fig) to win

dē·poscō -poscěre -poposcī *vt* to demand, require; to request earnestly; to challenge; **sibi deposcere** to claim (*something*) for oneself

dēposĭt·us -a -um *pp* of **depono**; *adj* despaired of; *n* deposit (*of money as first payment*); deposit (*for safe keeping*)

dēprāvātē *adv* perversely

dēprāvātĭ·ō -ōnis *f* distorting; (fig) distortion

dēprāv·ō -āre *vt* to make crooked, distort; to pervert, corrupt, seduce; to misrepresent

dēprecābund·us -a -um *adj* imploring

dēprecātĭ·ō -ōnis *f* supplication; deprecation, averting by prayer; invocation, earnest entreaty; (with *genit*) intercession against (*danger, etc.*)

dēprecāt·or -ōris *m* intercessor (*generally against rather than for*)

dēprěc·or -ārī -ātus sum *vt* to pray against, avert by prayer; to pray for, beg for; to intercede in behalf of; to plead in excuse

dēpre·hendō -henděre -hendī -hensum or **dēpren·dō -děre -dī**

-sum *vt* to get hold of; to arrest, intercept; to surprise, catch in the act; to detect, discover, find out; to perceive, understand; to embarrass

dēprehensĭ·ō -ōnis *f* detection

dēpress·us -a -um *pp* of **deprimo**; *adj* low, suppressed (*voice*); low (*land*)

dē·prīmō -prīměre -pressī -pressum *vt* to depress, press down, weigh down; to plant deep; to dig (*e.g., a trench*) deep; to sink (*a ship*)

dēproelĭ·or -ārī -ātus sum *vi* to fight it out, battle fiercely

dē·prōmō -prōměre -prompsī -promptum *vt* to take down; to bring out, produce

dēproper·ō -āre *vt* to make in a hurry; *vi* to hurry

deps·ō -ěre -ŭī -tum *vt* to knead

dōpŭd·et -ēre -ŭit *v impers* **eum depudet** he has no sense of shame

dēpūg·is or **dēpȳg·is -is** *adj* without buttocks, with thin buttocks

dēpugn·ō -āre *vi* to fight hard; to fight it out; (with **cum** + *abl*) to be in a death struggle with

dēpulsĭ·ō -ōnis *f* averting; (rhet) defense

dēpuls·ō -āre *vt* to push aside; **de via depulsare** to push out of the way

dēpuls·or -ōris *m* averter

dēpulsus *pp* of **depello**

dēpung·ō -ěre *vt* to mark off, designate

dēpurg·ō -āre *vt* to clean

dēpūt·ō -āre *vt* to prune; to reckon, consider

dēpȳgis see **depugis**

dēque *adv* down, downwards

dērect·us -a -um *pp* of **derigo**; *adj* straight, direct, level, upright, perpendicular; (fig) straightforward, direct, simple, right

dērelictĭ·ō -ōnis *f* dereliction, disregarding, neglecting

dēre·linquō -linquěre -līquī -lictum *vt* to leave behind, forsake, abandon

dērepente *adv* suddenly

dērēp·ō -ěre -sī *vi* to creep down

dēreptus *pp* of **deripio**

dē·rīděō -rīdēre -rīsī -rīsum *vt* to deride

dērīdĭcŭl·us -a -um *adj* quite ridiculous; *n* derision, mockery; absurdity; **deridiculo esse** to be the object of derision, be the butt of ridicule

dērig·escō -escěre -ŭī *vi* to grow stiff, grow rigid; to curdle

dē·rĭgō -rigěre -rexī -rectum *vt* to direct, aim; to steer (*ship*); to draw up in battle line; (fig) to direct, guide, regulate; (with *dat* or with **ad** or **in** + *acc*) to direct or aim at, guide to; (with **ad** + *acc*) to regulate (*e.g., life*) according to

dē·ripĭō -ripěre -ripŭī -reptum *vt* to tear down, tear off, pull down

dērīs·or -ōris *m* scoffer, cynic

dērīs·us -ūs m derision

dērīvātī·ō -ōnis f diversion, diverting (*of river from its course*)

dērīv·ō -āre vt to draw off, divert; to derive

dērŏg·ō -āre vt to propose to repeal in part; to restrict, modify; to take away, diminish, impair

dērōs·us -a -um adj gnawed away, nibbled

dēruncīn·ō -āre vt to plane off; to cheat

dēru̇·ō -ĕre -ŭī vt to throw down, overthrow, demolish; to detract

dērupt·us -a -um adj rough, steep, broken; n pl crevasses

dēsaev·iō -īre -īī vi to rage furiously; to run wild

dēsalt·ō -āre vi to dance

dē·scendō -scendĕre -scendī -scensum vi to climb down, descend, come or go down; to dismount; to fall, sink, sink down, penetrate; (fig) to go down, sink, sink down, penetrate; (fig) to lower oneself, stoop, yield; (mil) to march down

descensi·ō -ōnis f going down; **descensio Tiberina** sailing down the Tiber

descens·us -ūs m climbing down, descent; slope, descent

desc·iscō -iscĕre -īvī or **-īī -ītum** vi to revolt, desert; (fig) to depart, deviate, fall off; (with **ab** + abl) **a** to revolt from, break allegiance with; **b** to deviate from, fall away from

dē·scrībō -scrībĕre -scrīpsī -scrīptum vt to write out, transcribe, copy; to describe, represent, portray, draw, design, sketch

descriptē see **discriptē**

descriptī·ō -ōnis f copy; representation, diagram, sketch, map; description

descriptus pp of **describo**

dēsĕc·ō -āre -ŭī -tum vt to cut off

dēsĕr·ō -ĕre -ŭī -tum vt to desert, abandon, forsake; (law) to forfeit

dēsert·or -ōris m deserter

dēsert·us -a -um pp of **desero;** adj deserted; unpopulated, uninhabited; n pl wilderness, desert

dēserv·iō -īre vi (with dat) to be a slave to, serve devotedly

dēs·es -ĭdis adj sitting down, sitting at ease; lazy; apathetic, lifeless, idle

dēsicc·ō -āre vt to dry up; to drain

dē·sīdĕō -sidĕre -sēdī vi to sit idle, remain inactive

dēsīderābĭl·is -e adj desirable

dēsīderātī·ō -ōnis f missing, feeling the absence; **desideratio voluptatum** the missing of pleasures, yearning for pleasures

dēsīder·ĭum -ī or **-ī** n longing, missing, feeling of loss; want, need, necessity; request, petition; **ex desiderio laborare** to be homesick; **me desiderium tenet** (with genit)

I miss, am homesick for

dēsīdĕr·ō -āre vt to miss, long for, feel the want of; (mil) to lose (*men*) as casualties; **desiderari** (mil) to be missing, be lost, be a casualty

dēsidĭ·a -ae f idleness, inactivity; laziness; apathy

dēsidiābŭl·um -ī n place to lounge, hangout

dēsidiōsē adv idly

dēsidiōs·us -a -um adj idle, indolent, lazy; causing idleness or laziness; spent in idleness

dē·sīdō -sīdĕre -sēdī vi to sink, settle down; (fig) to sink, deteriorate

dēsignātī·ō -ōnis f specification; designation, election to office

dēsignātor see **dissignator**

dēsign·ō -āre vt to mark out, point out, designate, define, trace; to denote, describe, represent; to appoint, choose, elect; **consul designatus** consul-elect

dē·silĭō -silīre -silŭī -sultum vi to jump down, alight; **ab equo desilire** to dismount; **de nave desilire** to jump overboard; (fig) to venture forth

dē·sinō -sinĕre -sīī -sītum vt to give up, abandon; **furere desinere** to stop raging; vi to stop, come to a stop, end; (with **in** + acc) to end in; **similiter desinere** to have similar endings

dēsipĭ·ens -entis adj foolish, silly

dēsipienti·a -ae f folly, foolishness

dēsip·iō -ĕre vi to be silly, act foolishly

dē·sistō -sistĕre -stĭtī -stĭtum vi to stop, desist; to get stuck, stick; (with abl or with **ab** or **de** + abl) to desist from, abandon, give up (*an action begun*); **desistere a defensione** to give up the defense

dēsitus pp of **desino**

dēsōl·ō -āre vt to leave desolate, leave alone, forsake, abandon; **desolatus** (with abl) deprived of

despect·ō -āre vt to look down on, overlook, command a view of; to look down on, despise

despect·us -a -um pp of **despicio;** adj contemptible

despect·us -ūs m commanding view, view

despēranter adv hopelessly

despērātī·ō -ōnis f desperation, despair

despērāt·us -a -um adj despaired of; hopeless; desperate, hopeless

despēr·ō -āre vt to despair of; vi to despair, give up hope; (with **de** + abl) to despair of

despicātī·ō -ōnis f contempt; f pl feelings of contempt

despicāt·us -a -um adj despicable; **aliquem despicatum habere** to hold someone in contempt

despicĭ·ens -entis adj contemptuous; (with genit) contemptuous of

despicienti·a -ae f despising, contempt

**de·spiciō -spicĕre -spexī -spec-
tum** *vt* to despise, look down on,
express contempt for; *vi* to look
down; (with **in** + *acc*) to look down
on, have a view of

despic·or -ārī -ātus sum *vt* to despise, disdain

despoliāt·or -ōris *m* robber, plunderer, marauder

despoli·ō -āre *vt* to strip, rob, plunder

**de·spondĕō -spondĕre -spondī
-sponsum** *vt* to pledge, promise
solemnly; to promise in marriage;
to give up, lose; **animum despondere** or **animos despondere** to
lose heart

despūm·ō -āre *vt* to skim off, skim;
vi to stop foaming

despŭ·ō -ĕre *vt* to spit upon, show
contempt for; *vi* to spit (on the
ground)

desquām·ō -āre *vt* to take the
scales off, to scale (fish); (fig) to
peel off

destill·ō -āre *vt* to drip, distil; *vi* to
trickle down, drip

destimŭl·ō -āre *vt* to goad on, stimulate

destinātī·ō -ōnis *f* establishing; resolution, determination, purpose, design

destināt·us -a -um *adj* fixed, determined; **destinatum est mihi**
(with *inf*) I have made up my mind
to; *n pl* designs, intentions

destin·ō -āre *vt* to lash down, secure; (fig) to fix, determine, resolve;
to design, destine; to appoint, designate; to take aim at

destit·ŭō -uĕre -ŭī -ūtum *vt* to set
apart; to set down, place; to forsake, abandon; to leave in the lurch,
leave high and dry, betray, desert;
(with **ab** + *abl*) to rob of, leave
destitute of

destitūtī·ō -ōnis *f* forsaking, abandonment; disappointment

district·us -a -um *adj* severe, rigid

**de·stringō -stringĕre -strinxī
-strictum** *vt* to strip; to unsheathe;
to give (someone) a rubdown; to
brush gently against, skim; (of
weapon) to graze; (fig) to criticize,
satirize

destructī·ō -ōnis *f* pulling down
(e.g., of walls); destruction, demolition; refutation

**de·struō -struĕre -struxī -struc-
tum** *vt* to pull down, demolish, destroy; (fig) to ruin

dēsubitō or **dē subitō** *adv* suddenly

dēsūdasc·ō -ĕre *vi* to begin to sweat
all over

dēsūd·ō -āre *vi* to sweat; (with *dat*)
(fig) to sweat over, work hard at

dēsuē·fīō -fĭĕrī -factus sum *vi* to
become unused or unaccustomed

dēsu·escō -escĕre -ēvī -ētum *vi* to
become unaccustomed

dēsuētūd·ō -ĭnis *f* disuse, lack of
use

dēsuēt·us -a -um *pp* of **desuesco**;
adj unused, out of use, obsolete;
out of practice; (with *dat*) unused
to, unfamiliar with

dēsult·or -ōris *m* circus rider who
leaps from one horse to another;
amoris desultor (fig) fickle lover

dēsultōri·us -a -um *adj* of a circus
rider; **equus desultorius** show
horse

dēsultūr·a -ae *f* leaping down (from
horse), dismounting

dē·sum -esse -fŭī -futūrus *vi* to
fall short, fail; to fail in one's duty;
to be absent, be missing; (with *dat*)
to be absent from, be missing from,
be lacking from; **sibi deesse** to
cheat oneself, sell oneself short;
tempori deesse or **occasioni
temporis deesse** to pass up the
opportunity, pass up the chance

**dē·sūmo -sūmĕre -sumpsī -sump-
tum** *vt* to pick out, choose; to assume, undertake; **sibi hostem de-
sumere** to take on an enemy

dēsŭper *adv* from above, from overhead

dēsurg·ō -ĕre *vi* to rise; **cenā de-
surgere** to get up from the table

dē·tĕgō -tegĕre -texī -tectum *vt*
to detect, uncover, expose, lay bare;
to reveal, disclose, betray; **formi-
dine detegi** to be betrayed by fear

dē·tendō -tendĕre - -tensum *vt*
to unstretch; to take down (tent)

dētentus *pp* of **detineo**

dē·tergĕō -tergĕre -tersī -tersum
vt to wipe off, wipe away, wipe
clean; (fig) to wipe clean; **mensam
detergere** to eat up everything on
the table

dēteri·or -us *adj* inferior, worse,
poorer, meaner; less favorable,
worse (time); degenerate (person);
(mil) weaker (e.g., in cavalry)

dēterius *adv* worse

dētermināti·ō -ōnis *f* boundary;
conclusion, end; end (of speech)

dētermin·ō -āre *vt* to bound, limit,
prescribe; to determine, settle

dē·tĕrō -terĕre -trīvī -tritum *vt*
to rub away, wear away; to wear
out; to lessen, weaken, detract from;
calces alicujus deterere to tread
on someone's heels

dēterr·ĕō -ēre -ŭī -itum *vt* to deter,
frighten away, discourage; (with
abl, or with **ab** or **de** + *abl*, or with
ne, quin, or **quominus**) to deter
or discourage from; **deterruit
quominus hostes persequeren-
tur** he discouraged them from pursuing the enemy

dētersus *pp* of **detergeo**

dētestābil·is -e *adj* detestable,
abominable

dētestāti·ō -ōnis *f* execration, curse;
averting (by sacrifices or prayers)

dētest·or -ārī -ātus sum *vt* to
curse, execrate; to invoke (the gods);
to avert; to plead against; to detest,
loathe, abhor; (with **in** + *acc*) to

call down (*e.g.*, *vengeance*) upon; **invidiam detestari** to avert envy, avoid unpopularity

dē·tex·ō -ĕre -ŭī -tum *vt* to weave, finish weaving; (fig) to finish, finish off

dē·tinĕō -tinēre -tinŭī -tentum *vt* to hold back, keep back; to hold up, detain; to occupy, keep occupied; (with **ab** or **dē** + *abl*) to keep back from; (with *abl* or with **in** + *abl*) to occupy (*e.g.*, *day*, *mind*) with, keep (*someone*) busied with

dē·tondĕō -tondēre -totondī or **-tondī -tonsum** *vt* to cut off, clip off, shear off (*hair*, *wool*); (fig) to strip

dētŏn·ō -āre -ŭī *vi* to stop thundering; (of Jupiter) to thunder down

dētonsus *pp* of detondeo

dē·torquĕō -torquēre -torsī -tortum *vt* to twist or bend aside; to twist out of shape; to turn aside; to turn, direct; to avert (*eyes*); to divert, pervert; to distort, misrepresent (*words*)

dētractĭ·ō -ōnis *f* taking away, wresting; removal; (rhet) ellipsis

dētractō see detrecto

detract·or -ōris *m* detractor

dē·trăhō -trahĕre -traxī -tractum *vt* to drag down, drag away, pull down, pull away; to remove, withdraw; to take away, deprive, rob, strip; to induce to come down, draw down (*e.g.*, *an enemy from a strong position*); to disparage, detract, slander; (with *dat* or **dē** + *abl*) to take away from (*someone*), rob (*someone*) of

dētrectātĭ·ō -ōnis *f* drawing back, avoidance; **militiae detrectatio** draft dodging

dētrectāt·or -ōris *m* detractor, disparager

dētrect·ō or **detract·ō -āre** *vt* to draw back from, shirk, decline, reject, refuse; to disparage, depreciate; to demean; **militiam detrectare** to dodge the draft

dētrīmentōs·us -a -um *adj* detrimental, harmful

dētrīment·um -ī *n* detriment, loss, damage; **detrimentum accipere** or **detrimentum capere** to incur or suffer harm; **detrimentum inferre** or **detrimentum afferre** to cause harm

dētrītus *pp* of detero

dē·trūdō -trūdĕre -trūsī -trūsum *vt* to push down, push away, push off; (mil) to dislodge; (law) to evict; to postpone, put off; **aliquem de sua sententia detrudere** to force someone to change his mind

detrunc·ō -āre *vt* to cut off, chop off; (fig) to mutilate, behead

dēturb·ō -āre *vt* to beat down, expel, tear down, strike down; (mil) to dislodge, force to come down; to eject, dispossess; **aliquem de sani-**

tate **deturbare** to drive a person mad

Deucalĭ·ōn -ōnis *m* son of Prometheus, who, together with his wife Pyrrha, was the sole survivor of the Deluge

de·unx -uncis *m* eleven twelfths; **heres ex deunce** heir to eleven twelfths

de·ūrō -ūrĕre -ussī -ustum *vt* to burn up, destroy; (of frost) to nip

de·us -ī (*nom pl*: **deī** or **dī**; *genit pl*: **deōrum** or **deum**) *m* god, deity; (of a person) god, divine being; *m pl* (of persons in high places) the powers that be; **dī bonī!** good heavens!; **dī hominesque** all the world; **dī meliora!** Heaven forbid!; **dis volentibus** with the help of the gods; **dī te ament!** bless your little heart!

deustus *pp* of deuro

de·ūtor -ūtī -ūsus sum *vi* (with *abl*) to mistreat

dēvast·ō -āre *vt* to devastate, lay waste

dē·vĕhō -vehĕre -vexī -vectum *vt* to carry down, carry away, carry off; **devehi** to ride down, sail down

dē·vellō -vellĕre -vellī or **-volsī -vulsum** *vt* to pluck off

dēvēl·ō -āre *vt* to unveil

dēvenĕr·or -ārī -ātus sum *vt* to reverence, worship; to avert by prayer

dē·veniō -venīre -vēnī -ventum *vi* to come down, arrive; (with *acc* of extent of motion or with **ad** or **in** + *acc*) to arrive at, reach; (with **ad** + *acc*) to happen to, befall

dēverbĕr·ō -āre *vt* to thrash soundly

dēvers·or -ārī -ātus sum *vi* to stay as a guest; (with **apud** + *acc*) to stay at the house of

dēvers·or -ōris *m* guest

dēversōriŏl·um -ī *n* small inn, motel

dēversōrĭ·us or **dēvorsorĭ·us -a -um** *adj* of an inn; fit to stay at; **taberna deversoria** inn; *n* inn, hotel

dēverticŭl·um or **dēvorticŭl·um -ī** *n* side road, detour; digression; inn, hotel, tavern; low haunt, dive; refuge

dē·vertō (or **dē·vortō**) **-vertĕre -vertī -versum** or **dē·vertor -vertī -versus sum** *vi* to turn aside, turn away; to stay as guest, spend the night; (with **ad** or **apud** + *acc*) to stay with or at the house of; (with **ad** + *acc*) to have recourse to, resort to

dēvex·us -a -um *adj* inclining, sloping, steep; (with **ad** + *acc*) prone to, inclined to

dē·vinciō -vincīre -vinxī -vinctum *vt* to tie up, clamp; (fig) to bind fast, obligate, unite closely; **se vino devincire** (coll) to get tight

dē·vincō -vincĕre -vīcī -victum *vt* to conquer, subdue

dēvinct·us -a -um pp of devincio;
adj (with dat) strongly attached to

dēvītātǐ·ō -ōnis f avoidance

dēvīt·ō -āre vt to avoid

dēvǐ·us -a -um adj out of the way,
off the beaten track; devious; living
apart, solitary, sequestered; inconsistent

dēvŏc·ō -āre vt to call down; to call
off, recall, call away; to allure, seduce; **deos ad auxilium devocare** to invoke the gods for help

dēvŏl·ō -āre vi to fly down; to fly
away; to hasten down, hasten
away

**dē·volvō -volvěre -volvī -volū-
tum** vt to roll down; **ad spem
inanem pacis devolvi** to fall back
on false hopes of peace; **devolvi** to
roll down, go tumbling down, sink
down

dēvŏr·ō -āre vt to devour, gulp
down; to consume, waste, squander
(money, etc.); (of the sea) to engulf,
swallow up; to swallow, mumble
(words); to repress (tears); to bear
with patience

dēvor- = dever-

dēvortǐ·a -ōrum n pl side roads, detour

dēvōtǐ·ō -ōnis f self-sacrifice; cursing, outlawing; incantation, spell;
capitis devotio or **vitae devotio**
sacrifice of one's life

dēvŏt·ō -āre vt to lay a spell on, bewitch, jinx

dēvōt·us -a -um pp of devoveo;
adj devoted, faithful; accursed;
(with dat) a devoted to, faithful to;
b addicted to, given to (wine, drinking)

dē·voveō -vovēre -vōvī -vōtum vt
to devote, vow, sacrifice, dedicate;
to mark out, doom, destine; to curse,
execrate; to bewitch; **se devovere
dis** to devote oneself to death

dēvulsus pp of devello

dext·ans -antis m five sixths

dextell·a -ae f little right hand;
right-hand man

dext·er -ěra -ěrum or **-ra -rum**
adj right, on the right side; handy,
dexterous; lucky, propitious, favorable; opportune, right; f right
hand; right side, the right; **a dextra laevaque** to the right and left,
right and left, everywhere; **dextrā**
with the right hand; (fig) with val-
or; **dextrā** (with acc) to the right
of; **dextram dare** or **dextram
tendere** to give a pledge of friendship; **dextram renovare** to renew
a solemn pledge

dextěrē or **dextrē** adv dexterously,
skillfully; **dextre fortunā uti** (fig)
to play the cards right

dexterǐt·ās -ātis f dexterity, adroitness; readiness

dextrorsum or **dextrorsus** or **dex-
trōvorsum** adv to the right, towards the right side

dī see deus

Dī·a -ae f ancient name of the island
of Naxos; mother of Mercury

diabathrār·ǐus -ǐī or **-ǐ** m shoemaker

diadēm·a -ătis n diadem

diaet·a -ae f diet; living room

dialectǐcē adv logically

dialectǐc·us -a -um adj dialectical;
m dialectician; f dialectics, logic; n
pl dialectics, logical discussions

dialect·os -ī f dialect

Diāl·is -e adj of Jupiter; of Jupiter's
high priest; **apex Dialis** high
priest's miter; **conjux Dialis** high
priest's wife; **flamen Dialis** high
priest of Jupiter

dialŏg·us -ī m dialogue, conversation

Diān·a or Diān·a -ae f Diana (goddess of hunting, patroness of virginity, of the moon as Luna, of
childbirth as Lucina, and of incan-
tations and magic as Hecate); (fig)
Diana's temple; (fig) moon; **ira-
cunda Diana** lunacy

diārǐ·a -ōrum n pl daily ration

dibăph·us -ī f crimson robe; official
robe of magistrate

dic·a -ae f lawsuit, case, judicial
process, judicial proceedings; **dicam scribere** (with dat) to sue
(someone); **sortiri dicas** to select a
jury

dicācǐt·ās -ātis f wittiness, sarcasm

dicăcŭl·us -a -um adj quick-witted,
sharp

dicātǐ·ō -ōnis f declaration of intent
of becoming a citizen

dic·ax -ācis adj witty, sharp, sarcastic, caustic; pert

dichorē·us -ī m double trochee

dicǐ·ō -ōnis f jurisdiction, sway, authority, control, rule, dominion, sovereignty; **in dicione esse** (with
genit) or **sub dicione esse** (with
genit) to be under the control of,
be subject to, be under the jurisdiction of; **in dicionem redigere**
(with genit) or **dicioni subjicere**
(with genit) to bring (someone) under the control of

dicis causā or **grātiā** adv for show,
for the sake of appearances

dic·ō -āre vt to dedicate, consecrate;
to deify; to inaugurate; to set apart,
devote; (with dat) to devote (e.g.,
time, energy) to; **se dicare** (with
dat or **in** + acc) to dedicate oneself
to

dīcō dīcěre dixī dictum vt to say,
tell; to indicate, mention, specify;
point out; to nominate, appoint; to
fix, set, appoint (day or date); to
speak, deliver, recite; to pronounce,
utter, articulate; to call, name; to
assert, affirm; to describe, relate;
celebrate; to tell, predict; (with
double acc) to appoint (someone) as;
causam dicere to plead or defend
a case; **diem dicere** (with dat) to
set a date for; **facete dictum!**
well put!; **sententiam dicere** to

express an opinion; **testimonium dicere** to give evidence

dicrŏt·um -ī n bireme

dictamn·us -ī f dittany (wild marjoram, growing in abundance on Mt. Dicte in Crete)

dictāt·a -ōrum n pl lessons, rules; dictation

dictāt·or -ōris m dictator (emergency magistrate in Rome with absolute authority, legally appointed for a maximum six-month term); chief magistrate (of Italic town)

dictātōri·us -a -um adj dictatorial

dictātr·ix -īcis f mistress of ceremonies

dictātūr·a -ae f dictatorship

Dict·ē -ēs f mountain in Crete where Jupiter was hidden in a cave from his father Saturn

dicti·ō -ōnis f saying, speaking, uttering; diction, style; conversation; oracular response, prediction; **dictio causae** defense of a case; **dictio testimoni** right to give testimony; **juris dictio** administration of justice; jurisdiction

dictit·ō -āre vt to keep saying, to state emphatically; **causas dictitare** to practice law; **ut dictitabat** as he used to say, as he continually alleged

dict·ō -āre vt to say repeatedly, reiterate; to dictate; to compose; to suggest, remind

dict·us -a -um pp of **dīco;** n saying word, statement; witticism; maxim, proverb; prediction, prophecy; order, command, instruction; promise, assurance

Dictynn·a -ae f Diana

dī·dō or **dis·dō -děre -dīdī -dītum** vt to publicize, broadcast, disseminate; to distribute, hand out

Dīd·ō -ūs (acc: **Dīdō**) f daughter of Tyrian king Belus, sister of Pygmalion, foundress and queen of Carthage, also called Elissa

dī·dūcō -dūcěre -duxī -ductum vt to draw apart, part, sever, separate, split; to undo, untie; to divide, distribute; to scatter, disperse; (in mathematics) to divide; **animus diductus** (with abl) the mind torn between (alternatives)

diēcŭl·a -ae f little while

diērect·us -a -um adj (coll) finished, done for; **i dierectus** or **abi dierectus!** go to the devil!

di·ēs -ēī m or f day; time, period, space of time, interval; daylight, light of day; anniversary; daybreak; season; **dicere diem** (with dat) to impeach, bring an accusation against; **diem ex die** from day to day, day after day; **diem noctemque** day and night, uninterruptedly; **dies meus** my birthday; **in diem** for the moment; for a future day; **in dies** (more and more) every day; **multo denique die** not till

late in the day; **postridie ejus diei** the day after that; **post tertium ejus diei** two days after that

Diespĭt·er -ris m Jupiter

diffām·ō -āre vt to divulge (something); to defame (someone)

differenti·a -ae f difference, diversity; specific difference, species

differit·ās -ātis f difference

differō differre distŭlī dīlātum vt to carry in different directions; to scatter, disperse; to publicize, spread around, divulge; to defer, postpone, delay; to humor; to get rid of, put off; to distract, disquiet; vi to differ, be different, be distinguished; (with **ab + abl**) to differ from

differt·us -a -um adj stuffed, crowded, overcrowded

diffĭcĭl·is -e adj difficult, hard; surly, cantankerous; hard to manage, hard to please

diffĭcĭliter adv with difficulty, barely

diffĭcult·ās -ātis f difficulty, hardship, trouble, distress; surliness; poverty, financial embarrassment

diffĭculter adv with difficulty, barely

diffīd·ens -entis adj diffident, anxious, nervous

diffīdenter adv without confidence, distrustfully

diffīdenti·a -ae f diffidence, mistrust, distrust

dif·fīdō -fīděre -fīsus sum vi (with dat) to distrust, despair of

dif·findō -fiňděre -fīdī -fissum vt to split, split apart, divide; (law) **diem diffindere** to cut short the business day; (fig) to detract

dif·fingō -ěre vt to form differently, remodel; to alter

diffissus pp of **diffindo**

diffit·ěor -ērī vt to disavow, disown

diffl·ō -āre vi to blow away; to disperse

diffĭŭ·ō -ěre vi to flow in different directions, flow away; to dissolve, melt away, disappear; (with abl) to wallow in (luxury, vice)

dif·fringō -fringěre — fractum vt to shatter, break apart, smash

dif·fugiō -fugěre -fūgī vi to flee in different directions; to disperse; to disappear

diffug·ĭum -ĭī or **-ī** n dispersion

diffundĭt·ō -āre vt to pour out, scatter; to waste

dif·fundō -funděre -fūdī -fūsum vt to pour, pour out; to scatter, diffuse, spread, extend; to give vent to; to cheer up, gladden

diffūsē adv diffusely; fully, at length, in detail

diffūsĭl·is -e adj diffusive, expanding

diffūs·us -a -um pp of **diffundo;** adj spread out, spread abroad; wide; prolix; protracted

diffutūt·us -a -um adj exhausted by excessive sexual indulgence

Dīgentī·a -ae *f* small stream on Horace's Sabine farm

dī·gĕrō -gĕrĕre -gessī -gestum *vt* to spread about, distribute, divide; to arrange, assort, catalogue; to interpret; to digest

dīgestī·ō -ōnis *f* arrangement; (rhet) enumeration

dīgestus *pp* of **dīgero**

dīgitŭl·us -ī *m* little finger

dīgit·us -ī *m* finger; inch (*one sixteenth of a Roman foot*); toe; **caelum dīgitō attingere** to reach the heights of happiness, be thrilled; **dīgitīs concrepāre** to snap the fingers; **dīgitō unō attingere** to touch lightly, touch tenderly; **dīgitum intendere** (with **ad** + *acc*) to point the finger at; **dīgitus pollex** thumb; **in dīgitos arrectus** on tiptoe; **minimus dīgitus** little finger

dīgladĭ·or -ārī -ātus sum *vi* to fight hard

dīgnātī·ō -ōnis *f* esteem, respect; dignity, honor

dīgnē *adv* worthily, fitly

dīgnĭt·ās -ātis *f* worth, worthiness; dignity; authority, rank, reputation, distinction, majesty; self-respect; dignitary; political office; dignity (*of style*)

dīgn·ō -āre or **dīgn·or -ārī -ātus sum** *vt* to think worthy; (with *abl*) to think worthy of; (with double *acc*) to think (*someone*) worthy of being (*e.g., a son*)

dīgnōsc·ō or **dīnōsc·ō -ĕre** *vt* to distinguish; (with *abl*) to distinguish (*someone*) from; **dominum ac servum dīgnoscere** to know the difference between master and slave

dīgn·us -a -um *adj* worthy, deserving (*person*); fit, adequate, suitable, deserved, proper; (with *abl*) worthy of

dī·gredior -grĕdī -gressus sum *vi* to move apart, separate; to deviate; to digress

dīgressī·ō -ōnis *f* parting, separation; deviation; digression

dīgressus *pp* of **dīgredior**

dīgress·us -ūs *m* departure; digression

dījūdicātī·ō -ōnis *f* decision

dījūdĭc·ō -āre *vt* to decide, settle; **vera et falsa dijudicare** or **vera a falsis dijudicare** to distinguish between truth and falsehood

dījun = **disjun**

dī·lābor -lābī -lapsus sum *vi* to fall apart, break up; (of ice, etc.) to break up, dissolve; to disperse; to break up, decay; (of time) to slip away; (of water) to flow in different directions

dīlacĕr·ō -āre *vt* to tear to pieces

dīlāmĭn·ō -āre *vt* to split in two; **nuces dilaminare** to crack nuts

dīlanĭ·ō -āre *vt* to tear to pieces

dīlapĭd·ō -āre *vt* to demolish (a

structure of stone); to squander

dīlapsus *pp* of **dīlabor**

dīlarg·ior -īrī -ītus sum *vt* to hand out generously, lavish

dīlātī·ō -ōnis *f* postponement, delay

dīlāt·ō -āre *vt* to dilate, stretch, broaden, extend, enlarge; (fig) to amplify, spread, extend; to drawl out

dīlāt·or -ōris *m* procrastinator, slowpoke

dīlātus *pp* of **differo**

dīlaud·ō -āre *vt* to praise enthusiastically

dīlect·us -a -um *pp* of **diligo**; *adj* beloved

dīlect·us -ūs *m* selection; (mil) selective service, draft; draftees; recruitment; **dilectum habere** to conduct a draft; **legiones ex novo dilectu conficere** to bring the legions to full strength with new draftees

dīlĭg·ens -entis *adj* careful, conscientious, accurate; exacting, strict; thrifty, industrious; (with *genit*) observant of; (with **ad** + *acc* or with **in** + *abl*) careful in, careful to, conscientious about

dīligenter *adv* carefully, diligently, industriously

dīligentī·a -ae *f* diligence, care, industry, attentiveness, faithfulness; economy, frugality; (with *genit*) regard for

dī·līgō -līgĕre -lexī -lectum *vt* to single out; to esteem, love, value, prize; to approve, be content with, appreciate

dīlōric·ō -āre *vt* to tear open

dīlūc·ĕō -ēre *vi* to be clear, be evident; (with *dat*) to be obvious to

dī·lūcescō -lūcescĕre -luxī *vi* to grow light, dawn

dīlūcĭdē *adv* clearly, distinctly, plainly

dīlūcĭd·us -a -um *adj* clear, distinct, plain, evident

dīlūcŭl·um -ī *n* daybreak, dawn

dīlūd·ĭum -ĭī or **-ī** *n* intermission

dīl·ŭō -ŭĕre -ŭī -ūtum *vt* to wash away, break up, separate; to dilute; to get rid of (*worries, annoyances*); to atone for; to explain, solve

dīluvĭ·ēs -ēī *f* inundation, flood, deluge

dīluvĭ·ō -āre *vt* to inundate, flood, deluge

dīluv·ĭum -ĭī or **-ī** *n* flood, deluge; (fig) destruction

dīmān·ō -āre *vi* to flow in different directions; (fig) to spread around

dīmensĭ·ō -ōnis *f* measurement

dī·mētĭor -mētīrī -mensus sum *vt* to measure out, measure off; to count off

dīmēt·ō -āre or **dīmēt·or -ārī -ātus sum** *vt* to measure out, mark out (*area*)

dīmicātī·ō -ōnis *f* fight, combat, struggle; contest, rivalry dīmĭc·ō -āre vi to fight, struggle; to be in conflict, run a risk, be in peril; (with **cum** + *abl*) to fight against; **de capite dimicare** or **de vita dimicare** to fight for one's life

dīmĭdĭāt·us -a -um *adj* half, in half

dīmĭdĭ·us -a -um *adj* half; broken in two, broken; **dimidius patrum, dimidius plebis** half patrician, half plebeian; *n* half; **dīmidium militum quam** half as many soldiers as

dīmīssĭ·ō -ōnis *f* dismissal, discharging, sending out

dī·mittō -mittĕre -mīsī -missum vt to send away, send around, send out, scatter, distribute; to break up, dismiss, disband; (mil) to discharge; to let loose; to divorce (*wife*); to leave, desert, abandon, give up, relinquish; to let go, let slip, forgo, forsake, renounce; to remit

dīmmĭnŭ·ō or dīminŭ·ō -ĕre vt to break to pieces, smash, shatter

dī·movĕō -movēre -mōvī -mōtum vt to move apart, part, separate; to disperse, dismiss, scatter; to lure away

Dindymēn·ē -ēs *f* Cybele (*also called Magna Mater by the Romans*)

Dindym·us -ī *m* or Dindym·a -ōrum *n pl* mountain in Asia Minor, sacred to Cybele

dīnoscō see dignosco

dīnumerātĭ·ō -ōnis *f* enumeration, counting up

dīnumĕr·ō -āre vt to enumerate, count up, compute; to count out, pay

dĭōbolār·is -e *adj* costing two obols

Dĭodŏt·us -ī *m* Stoic philosopher and tutor of Cicero (*d.* 59 B.C.)

dĭoecēs·is -is *f* district, governor's jurisdiction

dĭoecēt·ēs -ae *m* treasurer; secretary of revenue

Dĭogĕn·ēs -is *m* famous Ionic philosopher and pupil of Anaximenes (*5th cent.* B.C.); Cynic philosopher, born at Sinope, in Pontus (412?-323 B.C.)

Dĭomēd·ēs -is *m* son of Tydeus and king of Argos; hero at Troy

Dĭōn·ē -ēs or Dĭōn·a -ae *f* mother of Venus

Dĭonȳsĭ·a -ōrum *n pl* Greek festival of Bacchus

Dĭonȳsĭ·us -ī *m* tyrant of Syracuse (430-367 B.C.); Dionysus the Younger (397-330?)

Dĭonȳs·us or Dĭonȳs·os -ī *m* Bacchus

dĭōt·a -ae *f* two-handled wine jar

dĭplōm·a -ătis *n* official letter of recommendation

Dĭpȳl·on -ī *n* N.W. gate at Athens

Dīr·a -ae *f* a Fury; *f pl* the Furies (*goddesses of revenge and remorse*)

dīr·ae -ārum *f pl* curse, execration

Dīrcae·us -a -um *adj* Dircean, Boeotian; **cycnus Dircaeus** Dir-

cean or Boeotian swan (*i.e., Pindar, famous lyric poet from Boeotia,* 522?-442 B.C.)

Dirc·ē -ēs *f* famous fountain in Boeotia

dīrect·us -a -um *pp* of **dirigo;** *adj* straight, direct; straightforward

dīremptus *pp* of **dirimo**

dīrempt·us -ūs *m* separation

dīreptĭ·ō -ōnis *f* plundering, pillaging; *f pl* acts of pillage

dīrept·or -ōris *m* plunderer

dīreptus *pp* of **diripio**

dirĭb·ēō -ēre — -ĭtum vt to sort (*votes taken out of the ballot box*)

dīrĭbĭtĭ·ō -ōnis *f* sorting

dīrĭbĭt·or -ōris *m* sorter (*of ballots*)

dīrĭbĭtōr·ĭum -ĭī or -ĭ *n* sorting room

dī·rĭgō -rĭgĕre -rēxī -rectum vt to put in order, arrange, line up, deploy

dir·ĭmō -ĭmĕre -ēmī -emptum vt to take apart, part, separate, divide; to break off, disturb, interrupt; to separate, dissolve; to put off, delay; to break off, end, bring to an end; to nullify, bring to naught

dī·rĭpĭō -rĭpĕre -rĭpŭī -reptum vt to tear apart, tear to pieces; to lay waste, pillage, plunder, ravage; to snatch away, tear away; to whip out (*sword*); to steal

dīrĭt·ās -ātis *f* mischief; misfortune; cruelty

dī·rumpō or dis·rumpō -rumpĕre -rūpī -ruptum vt to break to pieces, smash, shatter; to break off (*friendship*); to sever (*ties*); **dirumpi** to burst (*with laughter, envy, indignation, etc.*)

dī·rŭ·ō -ĕre -ī -tum vt to pull apart, demolish, destroy, overthrow; to scatter, disperse; (mil) to break up (*enemy formation*); to bankrupt

dīr·us -a -um *adj* fearful, awful; ominous, ill-omened; dreadful, awful, abominable; cruel, relentless, fierce; **temporibus diris** in the reign of terror; **venena dira** deadly poisons

dī·s -tis *adj* rich, wealthy; rich, fertile (*land*); rich, generous, expensive (*offerings*); (with *abl*) abounding in

Dī·s -tis *m* Pluto (*king of the lower world*)

dis·cēdō -cēdĕre -cessī -cessum vi to go away, depart; to separate, be severed; to disperse, scatter, be dissipated, disappear; (mil) to march off, break camp; to come off (*victorious, etc.*); to deviate; to swerve; to pass away, vanish, cease; (with **ab** + *abl*) **a** to forsake (*e.g., friends*); **b** to deviate from, swerve from; **c** to abandon, give up; (with **ex** or **de** + *abl*) to go away from, depart from; (with **ad** + *acc*) to depart for; (with **in** + *acc*) to vote for; **discedere in Catonis sen-**

tentiam to vote for Cato's proposal

disceptāti·ō -ōnis f dispute, difference of opinion: discussion, debate

disceptāt·or -ōris m or **disceptā-tr·ix -īcis** f arbitrator

discept·ō -āre vt to debate, dispute, discuss, treat; to decide, settle (controversies, wars); vi to act as umpire; to be at stake

dis·cernō -cernĕre -crēvī -crētum vt to separate, mark off, divide; to keep apart; to distinguish between; to discern, make out, distinguish

dis·cerpō -cerpĕre -cerpsī -cerp-tum vt to tear to pieces, mangle, mutilate; (fig) to tear apart (with words, arguments)

discessi·ō -ōnis f separation, division; separation, divorce; (in the senate) division, formal vote; **dis-cessio sine ulla varietate** unanimous vote

discess·us -ūs m separation, parting; going away, departure; banishment; marching away, marching off

discid·ium -iī or **-ī** n parting, separation; discord, dissension, disagreement; divorce

discīd·ō -ĕre vt to cut to pieces, cut up

discinct·us -a -um pp of discingo; adj without a girdle; dissolute, loose; effeminate, voluptuous

di·scindō -scindĕre -scīdī -scis-sum vt to tear apart, tear open, rend, tear; **amicitias discindere** to break off ties of friendship

dis·cingō -cingĕre -cinxī -cinc-tum vt to take off, ungird; to loose; (fig) to relax

disciplīn·a -ae f instruction, training, teaching, education; learning, knowledge, science; discipline; custom, habit; system; **militaris disciplina** basic training; **rei publicae disciplina** statesmanship

discipŭl·us -ī m or **discipŭl·a -ae** f pupil, student; disciple, follower

discissus pp of discindo

dis·clūdō -clūdĕre -clūsī -clūsum vt to keep apart, divide, shut off; **iram et cupiditatem locis discludere** to assign anger and passion to their proper places

discō discĕre didĭcī vt to learn, learn to know, become acquainted with; to be told (e.g., the truth); (with inf) to learn how to

discobŏl·us -ī m discus thrower

discŏl·or -ōris adj of a different color; different; (with dat) different from

disconduc·ō -ĕre vi to be unprofitable

disconven·iō -īre vi to disagree; to be inconsistent

discordābil·is -e adj discordant, disagreeing

discordi·a -ae f discord, dissension, disagreement; mutiny

discordiōs·us -a -um adj prone to

discord, seditious

discord·ō -āre vi to quarrel, disagree; (with dat or ab + abl) to be out of harmony with, be opposed to

discor·s -dis adj discordant, inharmonious; disagreeing, at variance; contradictory, inconsistent; warring (winds, etc.); (with abl) inconsistent with, at variance with, different from

discrepanti·a -ae f discrepancy, dissimilarity, difference

discrepāti·ō -ōnis f disagreement, dispute

discrepit·ō -āre vi to be completely different

discrĕp·ō -āre -ŭī vi to be different in sound, sound different; to be out of tune; to disagree, be different, be inconsistent, vary, differ; to be disputed; (with dat or abl or with ab or cum + abl) to disagree with, be different from, be inconsistent with; v impers there is a difference of opinion, it is undecided, it is a matter of dispute; **discrepat inter scriptores rerum** there is a difference of opinion among historians

di·scrībō -scrībĕre -scripsī -scriptum vt to distribute, classify, divide; to assign, apportion; (with in + acc) to distribute among, divide among

discrīm·en -ĭnis n dividing line; interval, intervening space, division, distance, separation; discrimination, difference, distinction; critical moment, turning point; decision, determination; crisis, jeopardy, peril, danger, risk; decisive battle

discrīmin·ō -āre vt to divide, separate; to apportion

discriptē adv orderly, lucidly, distinctly

discripti·ō -ōnis f distribution, classification

discript·us -a -um pp of discribo; adj well arranged; secluded

discruci·ō -āre vt to torture; to distress, torment

dis·cumbō -cumbĕre -cubŭī -cu-bĭtum vi to take their places at the table; (of several) to go to bed

discup·iō -ĕre vt (coll) to want badly; (with inf) (coll) to be dying to

dis·currō -currĕre -cucurrī or **-currī -cursum** vi to run in different directions, scamper about, run up and down, dash around

discurs·us -ūs m running up and down, running about; (mil) pincer movement

discus·us -ī m discus

dis·cutiō -cutĕre -cussī -cussum vt to knock apart; to smash to pieces, shatter; to break up, disperse, scatter, dispel; to frustrate, bring to naught; to suppress, destroy

disertē or **disertim** adv eloquently

disert·us -a -um adj fluent, well-spoken; clear, articulate

disject·ō -āre *vt* to toss about

disject·us -a -um *pp* of **disjicio**; *adj* scattered; dilapidated

disject·us -ūs *m* scattering

dis-jiciō -jicĕre -jēcī -jectum *vt* to drive apart, scatter, break up; to tear to pieces; to ruin, destroy; to thwart, frustrate, wreck; (mil) to break up (*enemy formation*)

disjunctĭ·ō or **dijunctĭ·ō -ōnis** *f* separation, alienation; diviation, variation; dilemma; asyndeton (*succession of clauses without conjunctions*)

disjunct·us -a -um *adj* separate, distinct; distant, remote; disjointed, disconnected, incoherent (*speech*); logically opposed; *n pl* opposites

dis-jungō or **dī-jungo -jungĕre -junxi -junctum** *vt* to unyoke; to sever, divide, part, remove; to separate, part, estrange, disunite, alienate

dispālesc·ō -ĕre *vi* to be divulged, spread

dispāl·or -ārī -ātus sum *vi* to wander about, straggle

dis-pandō (or **dis-pendō) -pandĕre — -pansum** (or **dis-pennō -pennĕre — -pessum**) *vt* to stretch out, extend; to spread out, expand

dis-pār -păris *adj* different, unlike; unequal, ill-matched; unequal, of different lengths

disparĭl·is -e *adj* different, dissimilar

disparīlĭter *adv* differently

dispăr·ō -āre *vt* to separate, segregate

dispartĭō or **dispartĭor** see **dispertio**

dispectus *pp* of **dispicio**

dis-pellō -pellĕre -pŭlī -pulsum *vt* to disperse, scatter; to drive away, dispel

dispend·ium -iī or **-ī** *n* expense, cost; loss

dispendō see **dispando**

dispennō see **dispando**

dispensātĭ·ō -ōnis *f* weighing out, doling out; management, superintendence, direction, administration; position of superintendent or treasurer

dispensāt·or -ōris *m* household manager, chief butler; cashier, treasurer

dispens·ō -āre *vt* to weigh out, pay out; to distribute, manage (*household stores*); to regulate, manage, superintend

dispercut·ĭō -ĕre *vt* to knock out; **cerebrum dispercutere** (with *dat*) (coll) to knock out (*someone's*) brains

disper·dō -dĕre -dĭdī -dĭtum *vt* to spoil, ruin; to squander

disper·ĕō -īre -ĭī *vi* to go to ruin; to go to waste; to be undone, perish; **disperiī** (coll) I'm finished; **dispeream si** (coll) I'll be darned if

di-spergō -spergĕre -spersī -sper-

sum *vt* to scatter about, disperse; to splatter; to distribute, scatter (*e.g., men*) without organization; to spread, extend (*war, rumor, etc.*)

dispersē *adv* here and there; occasionally

dispersus *pp* of **dispergo**

dispert·ĭō -īre -īvī or **-ĭī -ītum** or **dispert·ĭor** or **dispart·ĭor -īrī -ītus sum** *vt* to distribute, divide; to assign (*e.g., gates, areas*) as posts to be guarded

dispessus *pp* of **dispando**

di-spiciō -spicĕre -spexī -spectum *vt* to see clearly, make out, distinguish, detect; to consider carefully, perceive, detect, discern, discover, reflect on

displic·ĕō -ēre -ŭī -ĭtum *vi* to be unpleasant, be displeasing; (with *dat*) to displease; **sibi displicere** to be dissatisfied with oneself; to be in a bad humor

dis-plōdō -plōdĕre — -plōsum *vi* to explode

dis-pōnō -pōnĕre -posŭī -positum *vt* to place here and there; to distribute, arrange, set in order; to station, post, assign; to adjust, order, dispose; **diem disponere** to arrange the day's schedule

dispositē *adv* orderly, methodically

dispositĭ·ō -ōnis *f* orderly arrangement, development (*of theme, essay*)

dispositūr·a -ae *f* orderly arrangement

disposĭt·us -a -um *pp* of **dispono**; *adj* well arranged; methodical, orderly

disposĭt·us -ūs *m* orderly arrangement

dispŭd·et -ēre -ŭit *v impers* (with *inf*) it is a great shame to

dispulsus *pp* of **dispello**

dis-pungō -pungĕre -punxī -punctum *vt* to check, balance, audit (*an account*)

disputātĭ·ō -ōnis *f* arguing; argument, debate

disputāt·or -ōris *m* disputant, debater

dispŭt·ō -āre *vt* to dispute, discuss; (com) to estimate, compute; to examine, treat, explain

disquīr·ō -ĕre *vt* to examine in detail

disquīsĭtĭ·ō -ōnis *f* inquiry, investigation

disrumpō see **dirumpo**

dissaep·ĭō -īre -sī -tum *vt* to separate, wall off, fence off

dissaept·um -ī *n* partition, barrier

dissāvĭ·or or **dissuāvĭ·or -ārī -ātus sum** *vt* to kiss passionately

dissĕc·ō -āre -ŭī -tum *vt* to cut apart, dissect

dissēmĭn·ō -āre *vt* to disseminate

dissensĭ·ō -ōnis *f* difference of opinion, disagreement; dissension; conflict, incompatibility

dissens·us -ūs *m* dissension, discord

dissentānĕ·us -a -um *adj* disagreeing, contrary

dis·sentiō -sentīre -sensī -sensum *vi* to differ in opinion, disagree, dissent; to differ, be in conflict, be inconsistent; (with *dat* or with **ab** or **cum** + *abl*) to differ with, disagree with; (with **ab** + *abl*) to differ from, be opposed to

disserēn·at -āre *v impers* it is clearing up

dis·sērō -serĕre -sēvī -sĭtum *vt* to scatter; to sow here and there; to stick in the ground at intervals

disser·ō -ŭī -tum *vt* to arrange; to examine; to discuss, argue, treat

disserp·ō -ĕre *vi* to creep about; to spread gradually

dissertĭ·ō -ōnis *f* gradual abolition, severance

dissert·ō -āre *vt* to discuss, treat

dissertus *pp* of **dissero** (to arrange)

dis·sĭdĕō -sidēre -sēdī -sessum *vi* to be located far apart, be distant, be remote; to disagree, be at variance; to differ, be unlike; (of a garment) to be on crooked; (with **ab** or **cum** + *abl*) to disagree with

dissignātĭ·ō -ōnis *f* arrangement

dissignāt·or -ōris *m* master of ceremonies; usher (*at the theater*); undertaker

dissign·ō -āre *vt* to regulate, arrange; to contrive

dissil·ĭō -īre -ŭī *vi* to fly apart, split, break up, burst; to be dissolved

dissimĭl·is -e *adj* dissimilar, unlike, different; (with *genit* or *dat* or with **atque** or **ac**) to be dissimilar to, different from

dissimĭlĭter *adv* differently

dissimilitūd·ō -ĭnis *f* difference

dissimulanter *adv* secretly, slyly

dissimulantĭ·a -ae *f* faking, hiding, dissembling

dissimulātĭ·ō -ōnis *f* concealing, disguising; Socratic irony

dissimulāt·or -ōris *m* dissembler, faker

dissimŭl·ō -āre *vt* to dissemble, conceal, disguise; to keep secret; to pretend not to see, ignore

dissipābĭl·is -e *adj* diffusible, dispersible

dissipātĭ·ō -ōnis *f* scattering, dispersal, dissipation; destruction

dissĭp·ō or **dissŭp·ō -āre** to scatter, disperse; to break up (*enemy formation*); to demolish, overthrow; to squander, dissipate; to circulate, spread; to drive away (*worries*)

dissĭt·us *pp* of **dissero** (to scatter)

dissociābĭl·is -e *adj* separating, estranging; incompatible

dissociātĭ·ō -ōnis *f* separation

dissocĭ·ō -āre *vt* to dissociate, separate; to ostracize; to set at variance, estrange; to divide into factions; to detach

dissolūbĭl·is -e *adj* dissoluble, separable

dissolūtē *adv* disconnectedly, loosely; carelessly

dissolūtĭ·ō -ōnis *f* dissolution, dissolving, breaking up; abolishing, destruction; refutation; looseness, dissoluteness; asyndeton (*succession of clauses without conjunctions*)

dissolūt·us -a -um *adj* disconnected, loose; careless, negligent, remiss; loose, licentious, dissolute; *n* asyndeton (*succession of clauses without conjunctions*)

dis·solvō -solvĕre -solvī -solūtum *vt* to dissolve, break up, loosen; to free, release; (fig) to break up; to pay; to refute; to unite; **animam dissolvere** to die; **legem dissolvere** to abrogate or annul a law; **poenam dissolvere** to pay the penalty

dissŏn·us -a -um *adj* dissonant, discordant, jarring, confused (*sounds, voices*); different; (with *abl*) differing from, different from

dissor·s -tis *adj* having a different fate; unshared

dis·suādĕō -suādēre -suāsī -suāsum *vt* to advise against, dissuade, object to, oppose

dissuāsĭ·ō -ōnis *f* dissuasion; (with *genit*) opposition to, objection to

dissuās·or -ōris *m* objector, opponent

dissuāvior *see* **dissavior**

dissult·ō -āre *vi* to fly apart, burst

dis·suō -suĕre — -sūtum *vt* to unstitch; to untie, undo, unfasten

dissŭpō *see* **dissipo**

distaed·et -ēre *v impers* it makes (one) tired; (with *genit*) it makes (one) tired of; **me distaedet loqui** I'm sick and tired of speaking

distantĭ·a -ae *f* distance, remoteness; difference, diversity

dis·tendō (or **dis·tennō**) **-tendĕre -tendī -tentum** *vt* to stretch apart, stretch out; to distend, swell; to distract, perplex

distent·us -a -um *pp* of **distendo**; *adj* distended; *pp* of **distineo**; *adj* busy, occupied, distracted

distermĭn·ō -āre *vt* to separate by a boundary, divide, limit

distĭch·on -ī *n* couplet

distinctē *adv* distinctly, clearly, with precision

distinctĭ·ō -ōnis *f* distinction, differentiation, discrimination; difference; (gram) punctuation

distinct·us -a -um *pp* of **distinguo**; *adj* distinct, separate; studded, adorned; varied, diversified; lucid (*speaker*); eminent

distinct·us -ūs *m* difference, distinction

dis·tinĕō -tinēre -tinŭī -tentum *vt* to keep apart, separate; to detain, hold back, hinder; to employ, engage, divert; to put off, delay; (mil) to keep (*troops*) from meeting; to keep divided; to stand in the way of (*peace, victory, etc.*); to distract

di·stinguŏ -stinguĕre -stinxī -stinctum *vt* to mark off; to separate, part; to set off (*with colors, gold, etc.*); to distinguish, specify; to punctuate

dist·ŏ -āre *vi* to stand apart, be separate, be distant; to differ, be different; (*with dat or ab + abl*) to differ from; *v impers* there is a difference, it is important, makes a difference

dis·torquĕŏ -torquĕre -torsī -tortum *vt* to twist, distort; to curl (*lips*); to roll (*eyes*)

distortĭ·ŏ -ōnis *f* twisting; contortion

distort·us -a -um *pp* of **distorqueo**; *adj* distorted, misshapen, deformed; perverse

distractĭ·ŏ -ōnis *f* pulling apart; dividing; discord, dissension

distract·us -a -um *adj* severed, separate

dis·trāhŏ -trahĕre -traxī -tractum *vt* to pull or drag apart, separate forcibly; to tear away, drag away, remove; to distract; to sever, break up; to estrange, alienate; to prevent, frustrate; to end, settle (*e.g., disputes*); to sell at retail, sell (*e.g., land*) in lots

distrib·ŭŏ -uĕre -ŭī -ūtum *vt* to distribute

distribŭtē *adv* methodically

distribūtĭ·ŏ -ōnis *f* distribution, apportionment, division

district·us -a -um *adj* drawn in opposite directions; distracted, busied, engaged

di·stringŏ -stringĕre -strinxī -strictum *vt* to draw apart; to distract, draw the attention of.

distrunc·ŏ -āre *vt* to cut in two, hack apart

disturbātĭ·ŏ -ōnis *f* destruction

disturb·ŏ -āre *vt* to throw into confusion; to smash up, demolish; to break up (*a marriage*); to frustrate

dītesc·ŏ -ĕre *vi* to grow rich

dīthyrambĭc·us -a -um *adj* dithyrambic; *m* dithyramb (*song in honor of Bacchus*)

dīthyramb·us -ī *m* dithyramb

dītĭ·ae -ārum *f pl* wealth

dīt·ŏ -āre *vt* to make rich, enrich; **ditari** to get rich

diū *adv* by day, in the daytime; long, for a long time; in a long time; **diū noctuque** by day and by night, continually; **iam diu** this long; **satis diu** long enough

diurn·us -a -um *adj* of the day, by day, day, daytime; daily, of each day; day's, of one day; **acta diurna** daily newspaper; **merum diurnum** daytime drinking; *n* account book; *n pl* record, journal, diary

di·us -a -um *adj* godlike, divine, noble

diūtĭnē *adv* for a long time

diūtĭn·us -a -um *adj* long, lasting

diūtissĭmē *adv* for a very long time; longest; **iam diutissime** long, long ago

diūtĭus *adv* longer, still longer; **paulum diutius** a little too long

diūturnĭt·ās -ātis *f* length of time, long duration; durability

diūturn·us -a -um *adj* long, longlasting

dīv·a -ae *f* goddess

dīvārĭc·ŏ -āre *vt* to stretch out, spread

dī·vellŏ -vellĕre -vellī -vulsum *vt* to tear apart, tear to pieces; to tear away; to untie; to wrest, remove, separate; to estrange

dī·vendŏ -vendĕre ‒ -vendĭtum *vt* to sell piecemeal, retail

dīverbĕr·ŏ -āre *vt* to zip through, fly through

dīverb·ĭum -ĭī *or* **-ĭ n** dialogue, verbal exchange

dīversē *or* **dīvorsē** *adv* in different directions; differently

dīversĭt·ās -ātis *f* diversity, difference; contradiction, direct opposite

dīvers·us *or* **dīvors·us -a -um** *pp* of **diverto**; *adj* in different directions; apart, separate; different; remote, opposite, diametrically opposed; hostile; unsettled, irresolute; dissimilar, distinct; *m pl* individuals; *n* opposite direction, different quarter, opposite side, opposite view

dī·vertŏ *or* **dī·vortŏ -vertĕre -vertī -versum** *vi* to go different ways; to turn off; to stop off, stay

dīv·es -ĭtis *adj* rich, wealthy; costly, precious, sumptuous; plentiful, abundant; (*with genit or abl*) rich in, abounding in

dīvex·ŏ -āre *vt* to plunder; to violate

dīvidĭ·a -ae *f* worry, trouble, nuisance; dissension, antagonism

dī·vidŏ -vidĕre -vīsī -vīsum *vt* to divide, force apart; to divide, distribute, share; to break up, destroy; to arrange, apportion; to separate, distinguish; to separate, segregate, keep apart; to accompany (*songs with music*); **sententiam dividere** to break down a proposal (*so as to vote on each part separately*)

dīvidŭ·us -a -um *adj* divisible; divided, separated

dīvīnātĭ·ŏ -ōnis *f* clairvoyance; forecasting, predicting, divination; (*law*) selection of the most suitable prosecutor

dīvīnē *adv* through divine power; prophetically, by divine inspiration; divinely, gorgeously

dīvīnĭt·ās -ātis *f* divinity, godhead; prophetic power, clairvoyance; excellence

dīvīnĭtus *adv* from heaven, from god; providentially; prophetically; divinely, in a godlike manner; excellently

dīvīn·ō -āre vt to divine, predict, prophesy, foresee, dread

dīvīn·us -a -um adj divine, heavenly; divinely inspired, prophetic; godlike, superhuman, excellent, gorgeous; **dīvīnum jūs** natural law; **dīvīnum jūs et hūmānum** natural and positive law; **dīvīnum scelus** sacrilege; **rērum dīvīnārum et hūmānārum scientia** physics and ethics; **rem dīvīnam facere** to worship; to sacrifice; **rēs dīvīna** worship; sacrifice; **rēs dīvīnae** religious affairs, religion; m prophet; n offering; n pl divine matters; religious duties; **agere dīvīna hūmānaque** to perform religious and secular duties; **dīvīna hūmānaque** things divine and human, the whole world

dīvīsiō -ōnis f division, distribution

dīvīs·or -ōris m distributer; person hired by a candidate to distribute bribes

dīvīs·us -a -um pp of **dīvīdo**; adj separate, distinct

dīvīs·us -ūs m distribution; **dīvīsui facilis** easily divided, easy to divide

dīvitī·ae -ārum f pl riches, wealth; richness (of soil); costly things

dīvolg- = dīvulg-

dīvor- = dīver-

dīvort·ium -iī or **-ī** n separation; divorce; fork (of road or river); **dīvortium facere cum aliquā** to divorce some woman

dīvulgāt·us -a -um adj common, widespread

dīvulg·ō -āre vt to divulge, spread among the people; to publish (a book); to spread, publicize, advertise

dīvulsus pp of **dīvello**

dīv·us -a -um adj divine; deified; m god, deity; n sky; the open; **sub dīvo** out in the open, under the open sky; **sub dīvum rapere** to bring out in the open

dō dare dedī datum (danit = dat; danunt = dant; dane = dasne; duim = dem) vt to give; to offer; to offer, dedicate; to give out, pay (money); to bestow, confer; to permit, grant, concede, allow; to give up, hand over; to communicate, tell; to ascribe, impute, assign; to cause, produce, make; to furnish, afford, present; to grant, admit; to administer (medicine); to utter, give expression to, announce; **legem dare** to enact a law; **locum dare** (with dat) to make way for; **nomen dare** to enlist; **operam dare** to pay attention; **operam dare** (with dat) to pay attention to, give or devote attention to, look out for; **poenam** or **poenas dare** to pay the penalty; **se dare** to present oneself; to plunge, rush; **velum dare** to set sail; **veniam dare** to grant pardon

doc·ĕō -ēre -ŭī -tum vt to teach, instruct; to instruct, give instructions

to; (with double acc) to teach (someone something); **fabulam docere** to teach a play (to the actors), produce a play, put on a play

dochm·ius -iī or **-ī** m dochmaic foot (consisting of a trochee and a cretic)

docil·is -e adj docile, easily taught, teachable; docile, tractable

docilĭt·ās -ātis f docility, aptitude for learning

doctē adv learnedly, skillfully; shrewdly, cleverly

doct·or -ōris m teacher

doctrīn·a -ae f teaching, instruction, education, training; lesson; erudition, learning; science

doct·us -a -um pp of **doceo**; adj learned, skilled, experienced, clever, trained; cunning, shrewd; (with abl, with **ad** + acc, or **in** + abl) skilled in, experienced in, clever at

document·um -ī or **docŭm·en -ĭnis** n example, model, pattern; object lesson, warning; evidence, proof

Dōdōn·a -ae f town in Epirus, famous for the oracular oak tree sacred to Jupiter

Dōdōnae·us -a -um adj of Dodona

dodr·āns -antis m three fourths; **heres ex dodrante** heir entitled to three fourths of the estate

dogm·a -ătis n doctrine, tenet

dolābr·a -ae f pickax, mattock

dol·ens -entis adj painful, smarting; distressing

dolenter adv painfully; with sorrow

dol·ĕō -ēre -ŭī -ĭtum vt to give pain to, hurt; vi to feel pain, be sore, ache, smart; to grieve, be sorry, be hurt; take offense; (with dat) to give pain to, afflict, hurt; **caput mihi dolet** I have a headache

dōliăr·is -e adj fat, tubby

dōliŏl·um -ī n small barrel

dōl·ium -iī or **-ī** n large wine jar

dol·ō -āre vt to chop; to beat, beat up, drub; (fig) to hack out (e.g., a poem)

dol·ō or **dol·ōn -ōnis** m pike; string; fore topsail

Dol·ō -ōnis m Dolon (Trojan spy)

Dolŏp·es -um m pl a people of Thessaly

dol·or -ōris m pain, ache, smart; pain, grief, distress, anguish; indignation, resentment, chagrin; pathos; object of grief; **capitis dolor** headache; **dentis dolor** toothache; **esse dolori** (with dat) to be a cause of grief or resentment to

dolōsē adv shrewdly, slyly

dolōs·us -a -um adj wily, cunning, deceitful

dol·us -ī m trick, device; deceit, cunning, trickery; **dolus malus** (law) intentional deceit, willful wrong, fraud, malice

domābil·is -e adj tameable

domesticātim adv at home

domestic·us -a -um adj of the house or home; domestic, household;

familiar, private, personal; domestic, native, of one's own country; **bellum domesticum** civil war; *m pl* members of the household or family

domi *adv* at home

domicil·ium -iī or **-ī** *n* residence, home

domin·a or **domn·a -ae** *f* lady of the house; mistress, owner; lady; sweetheart; wife

domin·ans -antis *adj* ruling, holding sway; **nomen dominans** word in its literal sense; *m* ruler

dominātī·ō -ōnis *f* mastery; tyranny, despotism, absolute power; *f pl* control, supremacy; rulers

domināt·or -ōris *m* ruler, lord

dominātr·ix -īcis *f* ruler, mistress

domināt·us -ūs *m* absolute rule, sovereignty, tyranny; control, mastery

dominic·us -a -um *adj* of a lord, lord's, master's

Dominic·us -a -um *adj* (eccl) the Lord's

domin·ium -iī or **-ī** *n* absolute ownership; banquet, feast

domin·or -ārī -ātus sum *vi* to be master, be lord, have dominion; to play the master, domineer; (with **in** + *acc* or **in** + *abl*) to lord it over, tyrannize

domin·us -ī *m* owner, proprietor, possessor, master, ruler, lord; ruler, despot, tyrant; commander, chief; entertainer, host

Domin·us -ī *m* (eccl) Lord, Master

domiport·a -ae *f* snail

Domitiān·us -ī *m* T. Flavius Domitianus (*son of Vespasian, brother of Titus, and Roman emperor, 81-96 A.D.*)

domit·ō -āre *vt* to train, break in

domit·or -ōris *m* or **domitr·ix -īcis** *f* tamer

domit·us -ūs *m* taming

dom·ō -āre -uī -itum *vt* to tame, break in; to domesticate; to master, subdue, vanquish, conquer

dom·us -ūs or **-ī** (*dat:* **domuī** or **domō**; *abl:* **domō** or **domū**; *locat:* **domī** rarely **domō** or **domuī**; *genit pl:* **domŭum** or **domōrum**) *f* house, building, mansion, palace; home, residence, family; native country; philosophical sect; **domī** at home; **domī militiaeque** at home and in the field, in peace and in war; **domum** homewards, home

dōnābil·is -e *adj* worthy of a gift

dōnār·ium -iī or **-ī** *n* gift repository of a temple; sanctuary; altar; votive offering

dōnātī·ō -ōnis *f* donation

dōnātīv·um -ī *n* (mil) bonus

dōnec *conj* while; as long as; until

dōn·ō -āre *vt* to present, bestow, grant, confer; to forgive, pardon; to give up, sacrifice; **aliquem civitate donare** to present someone with citizenship; **civitatem ali-**

cui donare to bestow citizenship on someone

dōn·um -ī *n* gift, present; votive offering, sacrifice; **ultima dona** funeral rites, obsequies

dorc·as -ādis *f* gazelle

Dōr·ēs -um *m pl* Dorians (*one of the four Hellenic tribes*)

Dōric·us or **Dōrici·us -a -um** *adj* Dorian; Greek

Dōr·is -idis *f* daughter of Oceanus, wife of Nereus, and mother of fifty sea nymphs

dorm·iō -īre -īvī or **-iī -ītum** *vi* to sleep; to be inactive, be idle, be lazy

dormītāt·or -ōris *m* dreamer

dormīt·ō -āre *vi* to be sleepy, be drowsy; to nod, fall asleep

dormītōri·us -a -um *adj* for sleeping; **cubiculum dormitorium** bedroom

dors·um -ī *n* back; ridge; reef

dōs dōtis *f* dowry

Dossenn·us -ī *m* hunchback, clown (*well-known character in early Italic comedy*)

dōtāl·is -ē *adj* of a dowry, given as a dowry, dotal

dōt·ō -āre *vt* to endow

drachm·a or **drachŭm·a -ae** *f* drachma (*Greek coin approximately the value of a denarius*)

drac·ō -ōnis *m* dragon; huge serpent

Drac·ō -ōnis *m* Dragon (*constellation*); Draco (*Athenian lawgiver, notorious for his severity, c. 621 B.C.*)

dracōnigĕn·us -a -um *adj* sprung from a dragon; **urbs draconigena** Thebes

drāpĕt·a -ae *m* runaway slave

drom·as -ādis *m* dromedary, camel

drom·os -ī *m* Spartan racetrack

Druïd·ēs -um or **Druïd·ae -ārum** *m pl* Druids (*priests and sages of the Gauls and Britons*)

Drūsill·a -ae *f* Livia Drusilla (*second wife of Augustus and mother of Tiberius, 63 B.C.-29 A.D.*)

Drūs·us -ī *m* Livius Drusus (*tribune of the people with C. Gracchus in 122 B.C.*); M. Livius Drusus (*former's son, famous orator and tribune of the people in 91 B.C.*); Nero Claudius Drusus (*son of Livia, brother of Tiberius, 38-9 B.C.*)

Dry·ad -ădis *f* dryad (*wood nymph*)

Dryŏp·es -um *m pl* people of Epirus

dubiē *adv* doubtfully; **haud dubie** undoubtedly, indubitably

dubitābil·is -e *adj* doubtful

dubitanter *adv* doubtingly, hesitantly

dubitātī·ō -ōnis *f* doubt, uncertainty; wavering, hesitancy, irresolution; hesitation, delay; (rhet) pretended embarrassment (*to win over the sympathy of the audience*)

dubit·ō -āre *vt* to doubt; to consider, ponder; *vi* to be doubtful, be in doubt, be uncertain, be perplexed;

to deliberate; to waver, hesitate, delay

dubi·us -a -um adj wavering, doubtful, dubious, uncertain, irresolute; dubious, undermined; precarious, critical, adverse, difficult; dim (light); overcast (sky); indecisive (battle); n doubt, question; **haud pro dubio habere** to regard as beyond doubt; **in dubium venire** to come in question; **in dubium vocare** to call in question; **procul dubio** beyond doubt, undoubtedly

ducēnāri·us -a -um adj receiving a salary of 200,000 sesterces

ducēn·ī -ae -a adj two hundred each

ducentēsim·a -ae f half percent

ducent·ī -ae -a adj two hundred

ducentiens or **ducentiēs** adv two hundred times

dūcō dūcēre duxī ductum vt to lead, guide, direct, conduct; to lead, command; to lead, march; to draw, pull, haul; to draw out, protract, prolong; to put off, stall (someone); to pass, spend (time); to pull at (oars); to mislead, take in, fool, trick; to draw, attract; to draw (lots); to draw in, breathe in, inhale; to suck in, drink; to draw, trace; to construct, form, fashion, shape; to run (a wall from one point to another); to assume, get (name); to lead home, marry (a woman); to calculate, compute; to regard, consider, hold, account; to derive, trace (lineage); to spin (wool); (of a road) to lead, take (someone)

ductim adv in a continuous stream

ductit·ō -āre vt to take home, marry (a woman); to lead on, trick, deceive, cheat

duct·ō -āre vt to lead; to draw; to accompany, escort

duct·or -ōris m leader, commander, general; guide, pilot

duct·us -ūs m drawing, conducting; line, row; leadership, command; **oris ductus** facial expression

dūdum adv a short time ago, a little while ago; just now; once, formerly; **cum dudum** just as; **haud dudum** not long ago, just now; **jam dudum** for some time; **jam dudum eum exspecto** I have been expecting him; **quam dudum** how long; **ut dudum** just as

Duill·ius or **Duil·ius -iī** or **-ī** m Roman consul who won Rome's first naval engagement against the Carthaginians off Sicily in 260 B.C.

duim see **do**

dulcēd·ō -inis f sweetness; pleasantness, charm, delightfulness

dulc·escō -escēre -uī vi to become sweet

dulcicūl·us -a -um adj rather sweet

dulcif·er -ēra -ērum adj full of sweetness, sweet

dulc·is -e adj pleasant, charming,

delightful; dear, friendly, kind; sweet

dulcīter adv agreeably, pleasantly, sweetly

dulcitūd·ō -inis f sweetness

dūlicē adv like a slave

Dūlich·ium -iī or **-ī** n or **Dīlichi·a -ae** f island in the Ionian Sea, belonging to the realm of Ulysses

dum adv up to now, yet, as yet; now; **age dum!** or **agite dum!** come now!; all right!; **nemo dum** no one yet, no one as yet; **non dum** not yet, not as yet

dum conj while, during the time in whieh; as long as; until; provided that, if only; **dum modo** or **dummodo** provided that, if only; **exspectabam dum rediret** I was waiting for him to return

dūmēt·um -ī n thicket, underbrush

dummōdo conj provided that, if only

dūmōs·us -a -um adj overgrown with bushes, bushy

dumtaxat adv strictly speaking, at least; only, simply, merely

dūm·us -ī m bush, bramble

du·o -ae -o adj two

duodeciens or **duodeciēs** adv twelve times

duodĕcim (indecl) adj twelve

duodecim·us -a -um adj twelfth

duodēn·ī -ae -a adj twelve each, twelve apiece, twelve; a dozen; **duodenis assibus** at twelve percent

duodēquadrāgēsim·us -a -um adj thirty-eighth

duodēquadrāgintā (indecl) adj thirty-eighth

duodēquinquāgēsim·us -a -um adj forty-eighth

duodētriciens or **duodētriciēs** adv twenty-eight times

duodētrigintā (indecl) adj twenty-eight

duodēvicēn·ī -ae -a adj eighteen each

duodēvigintī (indecl) adj eighteen

duoetvicēsimān·ī -ōrum n pl soldiers of the twenty-second legion

duoetvicēsim·us -a -um adj twenty-second

duovirī see **duumviri**

dupl·a -ae f double the price

dupl·ex -icis adj twofold, double; divided into two; in double rows; double, twice as big, twice as long; complex, compound; two-faced, double-dealing, false

duplicār·ius -iī or **-ī** m soldier receiving double pay

dupliciter adv doubly, on two accounts

duplic·ō -āre vt to double; to bend double; to enlarge, lengthen, increase

dupl·us -a -um adj double, twice as much, twice as large; n double price; **in duplum** twice the amount, double; **in duplum ire** to pay twice as much, pay double

dupond·ius -iī or -ī *m* or **dupond·ium** -iī or -ī *n* two-ace coin, worth about five cents

dūrābil·is -e *adj* durable, lasting

dūrām·en -ĭnis *n* hardness

dūratĕ·us -a -um *adj* wooden

dūrē or **dūrĭter** *adv* hard, sternly, rigorously, roughly; stiffly, awkwardly

dūr·escō -escĕre -ŭī *vi* to grow hard, harden

dūrĭt·ās -ātis *f* hardness, toughness, harshness

dūrĭter see **dūre**

dūritĭ·a -ae or **dūritĭ·ēs** -ēī *f* hardness; austerity; strictness, harshness, rigor; oppressiveness; insensibility, callousness

dūriuscŭl·us -a -um *adj* somewhat hard, rather harsh

dūr·ō -āre *vt* to make hard, harden, solidify; (fig) to harden, inure, toughen up; to make insensible, to dull, blunt; to bear, endure; *vi* to be inured, be tough; to endure, last, remain, continue, hold out; (of hills) to continue unbroken, extend

dūr·us -a -um *adj* hard; lasting; rough (*to the senses*); tough, hardy, hale; rough, rude, uncouth; shameless, brazen; harsh, cruel, callous, insensible; severe, oppressive; parsimonious, miserly

duum·vir -vĭrī *m* member of a commission or board of two

duumvirāt·us -ūs *m* duumvirate, office of a duumvir

duumvir·ī -ōrum or **duovir·ī** -ōrum *m pl* two-man commission; **duumviri ad aedem faciendam** two-man commission for the construction of a temple; **duumviri juri dicundo** two-man board of colonial magistrates; pair of judges; **duumviri navales** two-man commission to equip the navy; **duumviri perduellionis** criminal court; **duumviri sacrorum** two-man commission in charge of the Sibylline books

dux ducis *m* or *f* conductor, guide; leader, head, author, ringleader; general

Dym·ās -antis *m* father of Hecuba, the queen of Troy

dynăm·is -is *f* store, plenty

dynast·ēs -ae *m* ruler, prince, petty monarch

Dyrrach·ium -iī or -ī *n* Adriatic port in Illyria which served as landing place for those who sailed from Italy

E

ē see **ex**

eā *adv* there, that way

ea ejus *f pron* she

eādem *adv* by the same way, the same way; at the same time; likewise, by the same token

eāpropter *adv* therefore

eapse see **ipse**

eātĕnus *adv* to such a degree, so far

ebĕnus see **hebenus**

ēbĭb·ō -ĕre -ī *vt* to drink up, drain; to absorb; to spend in drinks, squander

ēbland·ior -īrī -ītus sum *vt* to coax out, obtain by flattery

Ēborāc·um or **Ēburāc·um** -ī *n* town of the Brigantes in Britain, York

ēbriĕt·ās -ātis *f* drunkenness

ēbriŏl·us -a -um *adj* tipsy

ēbriōsĭt·ās -ātis *f* habitual drunkenness, heavy drinking

ēbriōs·us -a -um *adj* & *m* drunk

ēbri·us -a -um *adj* drunk; drunken (*acts, words*), of a drunk; (fig) intoxicated (*e.g., with love, power*)

ēbull·iō -īre *vt* to brag about; *vi* to bubble up, boil over

ebŭl·um -ī *n* or **ebŭl·us** -ī *m* danewort, dwarf elder

eb·ur -ŏris *n* ivory; ivory objects; statue, flute, scabbard; elephant

eburāt·us -a -um *adj* inlaid with ivory

eburneŏl·us -a -um *adj* ivory

eburnĕ·us or **eburn·us** -a -um *adj* ivory; white as ivory; **ensis eburneus** sword with ivory hilt; **dentes eburnei** tusks (*of elephant*)

ēcastor *interj* by Castor!

ecca see **ecce**

eccam see **ecce**

ecce *interj* see!, look!, look here!, here!; **ecce me** here I am; (colloquially combined with the pronouns **is, ille,** and **iste**): **ecca** (i.e., **ecce** + **ea**) or **eccam** (i.e., **ecce** + **eam**) here she is; **eccilla** or **eccistam** there she is; **eccillum** or **eccum** here he is; **eccos** here they are

eccĕrē *interj* there!

eccheum·a -ătis *n* pouring out

ecclēsĭ·a -ae *f* Greek assembly of people; (eccl) church, congregation

ecdĭc·us -ī *m* legal representative of a community

ecf- = **eff-**

echĭdn·a -ae *f* viper

Echĭdn·a -ae *f* hydra; **Echĭdna Lernaea** Lernaean hydra; monstrous mother of Cerberus, half woman and half serpent

Echĭnăd·es -um *f pl* cluster of small islands off Acarnania

echīn·us -ī *m* sea urchin; dishpan

Echī·ōn -ŏnis *m* hero who sprang from the dragon's teeth sown by

Cadmus, married Agave, and became father of Pentheus

Ech·ō -ūs *f* nymph who was changed by Hera into an echo

eclŏg·a -ae *f* literary selection; eclogue

eclogāri·ī -ōrum *m pl* excerpted literary passages

ecquandŏ *adv* ever, at any time; (in indirect questions) whether ever

ecquī *conj* whether

ecqu·ī -ae or **-od** *adj* any

ec·quid -cūjus *pron* anything; (in indirect questions) whether, if at all

ec·quis -cūjus *pron* any, anyone; (in indirect questions) whether anyone

ecquŏ *adv* anywhere

ecule·us -ī *m* foal, colt; small equestrian statue; wooden torture rack

edācit·ās -ātis *f* gluttony

ed·ax -ācis *adj* gluttonous; (fig) devouring, destructive

ēdent·ō -āre *vt* to knock the teeth out of

ēdentŭl·us -a -um *adj* toothless, old

edĕpol *interj* by Polluxl, gad!

edĕra see **hedera**

ē·dīcō -dīcĕre -dixī -dictum *vt* to proclaim, announce, decree, ordain, appoint

ēdictĭ·ō -ōnis *f* edict, order

ēdict·ō -āre *vt* to proclaim, publish

ēdict·um -ī *n* decree, edict, proclamation; edict of a praetor listing rules he would follow in his capacity as judge; order, command

ē·discō -discĕre -didicī *vt* to learn by heart, learn thoroughly

ēdissĕr·ō -ĕre -ŭī -tum *vt* to explain in detail, analyze fully

ēdissert·ō -āre *vt* to explain fully, explain in all details

ēditicĭ·us -a -um *adj* set forth, proposed; **judices editicii** panel of jurors (*subject to challenge by the defendant*)

ēditĭ·ō -ōnis *f* statement, account, published statement; publishing, publication; edition (*of a book*); (law) declaration (*of the form of judicial procedure to be followed*)

ēdit·us -a -um *adj* high; (with *abl*) descended from; *n* height; command, order

e·dō -dĕre -dĭdī -dĭtum *vt* to give out, put forth, bring forth, emit; to give birth to, bear; to publish; to tell, announce, declare, disclose; to show, display, produce, perform; to bring about, cause; to promulgate

edō edĕre (or **esse**) **ēdī ēsum** *vt* to eat; (fig) to devour, consume, destroy; **pugnos edere** to eat fists, to get a good beating

ēdoc·ĕō -ēre -ŭī -tum *vt* to teach thoroughly; to instruct clearly; to inform; to show clearly; (with double *acc*) to teach (*someone something*) well

ēdŏl·ō -āre *vt* to chop out, hack out; to finish, prepare

ēdŏm·ō -āre -ŭī -ĭtum *vt* to conquer, subdue

Ēdŏn·ī -ōrum *m pl* Thracian tribe noted for its heavy drinking

Ēdŏn·is -ĭdis *adj* Edonian; *f* bacchante

ēdorm·ĭō -īre -īvī or **ĭī** *vt* to sleep off; **crapulam edormire** to sleep off a hangover; *vi* to sleep soundly

ēdormisc·ō -ēre *vt* to sleep off; **crapulam edormiscere** to sleep off a hangover

ēducātĭ·ō -ōnis *f* rearing; education

ēducāt·or -ōris *m* foster father; tutor, instructor

ēducātr·ix -īcis *f* nurse

ēdŭc·ō -āre *vt* to bring up; to train, educate, develop; to produce

ē·dūcō -dūcĕre -duxī -ductum *vt* to draw out; to take away; to draw (*sword*); to draw out, spend (*time*); to lead out, march out (*army*); to summon (*to court*); to hatch; to rear, bring up, educate, train; to raise, erect

edŭl·is -e *adj* edible

ēdūr·ō -āre *vi* to last, continue

ēdūr·us -a -um *adj* hard, tough; (fig) tough

Ēetĭ·ōn -ōnis *m* father of Andromache and king of Thebe in Cilicia

effarciō see **effercio**

effāt·us -a -um *pp* of **effor**; *adj* solemnly pronounced; solemnly dedicated; *n* axiom; prediction

effectĭ·ō -ōnis *f* accomplishment, performing; efficient cause

effectīv·us -a -um *adj* producing, practical

effect·or -ōris *m* or **effectr·ix -īcis** *f* producer, author

effect·us -a -um *pp* of **efficio**; *adj* finished, complete; *n* effect

effect·us -ūs *m* effecting, completion; operation; effect, result, consequence

effēmināt·ē *adv* effeminately, like a woman

effēmināt·us -a -um *adj* effeminate

effēmin·ō -āre *vt* to make a woman of; to represent as a woman; to effeminate, enervate

efferāt·us -a -um *adj* wild, brutal, savage

ef·ferciō or **ec·ferciō** or **ef·farciō -fercīre — -fertum** *vt* to stuff; to fill in (*e.g., a ditch*)

efferĭt·ās -ātis *f* wildness, barbarism

effĕr·ō -āre *vt* to make wild, brutalize; to exasperate

effĕrō or **ecfĕrō efferre extŭlī ēlātum** *vt* to carry out, bring out, bring forth; to utter, express; to publish, spread (*news*); to carry out for burial, bury; to produce, bear; to name, designate; to lift up, raise; to promote, advance; to bring out, expose; to praise, extol; to sweep off one's feet; **efferri** (fig) to be carried away; **se efferre** to be haughty, be proud, be conceited

effert·us -a -um *pp* of **effercio**; *adj* full, crammed, bulging

effer·us -a -um *adj* wild, fierce, savage

ef·fervescō -fervescĕre -fervī *vi* to boil, boil over; to burst forth

efferv·ō -ĕre *vi* to boil over; (of bees) to swarm out; (of volcano) to erupt

effēt·us -a -um *adj* effete, spent; vain, delusive; (with *genit*) incapable of

efficācit·ās -ātis *f* efficiency

efficāciter *adv* efficiently, effectively

effic·ax -ācis *adj* efficient, effective, efficacious

effici·ens -entis *adj* efficient, effective; **res efficientes** causes

efficienter *adv* efficiently

efficienti·a -ae *f* efficiency, efficacy, influence

ef·ficiō -ficĕre -fēcī -fectum *vt* to bring about, bring to pass, effect, cause, produce; to make, form; to finish, complete, accomplish; (of a field) to yield, produce; (of numbers) to amount to; to prove, show; **ita efficitur ut** thus it follows that

effictus *pp* of **effingo**

effigi·ēs -ēī or **effigi·a -ae** *f* effigy, likeness, semblance; opposite number; copy, imitation; image; statue, figure, portrait; ghost, phantom

ef·fingō -fingĕre -finxī -fictum *vt* to mold, form, fashion; to imitate; to wipe out, wipe clean; to represent, portray; to imagine

effiō passive of **efficio**

efflāgitāti·ō -ōnis *f* urgent demand

efflāgitāt·us -ūs *m* urgent request; **efflāgitatu meo** at my insistence

efflāgit·ō -āre *vt* to demand, insist upon

efflictim *adv* (to love, desire) desperately

efflict·ō -āre *vt* to strike dead

ef·flīgō or **ecf·flīgō -flīgĕre -flixī -flictum** *vt* to strike dead, exterminate

effl·ō or **ecfl·ō -āre** *vt* to breathe out; **animam efflare** to expire

efflōr·esco -escĕre -uī *vi* to bloom, blossom, flourish

efflu·ō or **ecflu·ō -ĕre -xī** *vi* to flow out, flow forth, run out; to slip away, drop out, disappear; (of a rumor) to get out, circulate; **ex pectore effluere** to be forgotten

effluv·ium -iī or **-ī** *n* outlet; **effluvium lacūs** outlet of a lake

ef·fodiō or **ecf·fodiō -fodĕre -fōdī -fossum** *vt* to dig up; to gouge out (*eyes*); to root out, gut; to excavate

ef·for or **ecf·for -fārī -fātus sum** *vt* to speak out, say out loud, tell; (in augury) to mark off, consecrate (*area*); *vi* to state a proposition

effossus *pp* of **effodio**

effrēnātē *adv* without restraint, out of control

effrēnāti·ō -ōnis *f* impetuosity

effrēnāt·us -a -um *adj* unbridled; (fig) unbridled, unrestrained

ef·fringō or **ec·fringō -fringĕre -frēgī -fractum** *vt* to break open, smash, break off; to break in (*door*)

ef·fugiō -fugĕre -fūgī *vt* to escape; to escape the notice of; *vi* to escape; (with *abl* or with **ab** or **ex** + *abl*) to escape from

effug·ium -iī or **-ī** *n* escape, flight; means of escape; avoidance

ef·fulgeō -fulgēre -fulsī *vi* to shine forth, gleam, glitter

effult·us -a -um *adj* propped up, supported

ef·fundō or **ec·fundō -fundĕre -fūdī -fūsum** *vt* to pour out, pour forth; to fling (*weapon*); to give up, let go, abandon, resign; to throw down; to produce in abundance; to lavish, waste, squander, run through; to empty out (*bags, etc.*); to given vent to, pour out; **effundi** or **se effundere** to pour out, rush out; to yield, indulge

effūsē *adv* far and wide; at random, in disorder; lavishly; immoderately

effūsi·ō -ōnis *f* outpouring, rushing out; shedding; effusion; profusion, lavishness, extravagance; *f pl* excesses

effūs·us -a -um *pp* of **effundo**; *adj* spread out, extensive, broad, wide; relaxed, loose; disheveled; lavish; straggly, disorderly; lavish; loose, dissolute

effūt·iō -īre — -itum *vt* & *vi* to blab, babble, chatter

ef·futuō or **ec·futuō -futuĕre -futuī -futūtum** *vt* to exhaust through excesses

ēgelid·us -a -um *adj* chilly, cool; lukewarm

eg·ens -entis *adj* needy, poor; (with *genit*) in need of

egēn·us -a -um *adj* needy, destitute; (with *genit* or *abl*) in need of

eg·eō -ēre -uī *vi* to be needy, suffer want; (with *genit* or *abl*) **a** to be in need of; **b** to lack, be without; **c** to want, desire, miss

Egeri·a -ae *f* nymph whom King Numa visited at night for advice

ē·gerō -gerĕre -gessī -gestum *vt* to carry out, take away, remove; to discharge, vomit, emit

egest·ās -ātis *f* need, want, poverty; (with *genit*) lack of

ēgesti·ō -ōnis *f* squandering

ēgestus *pp* of **egero**

ego *pron* I

egŏmet *pron* I personally, I and nobody else

ē·gredior -grĕdī -gressus sum *vt* to go beyond, pass; to quit; (fig) to go beyond, surpass; *vi* to go out, come out; to march out; to set sail, put out to sea; to disembark, land; to go up, climb; to digress

ēgregiē *adv* exceptionally, singularly, uncommonly, splendidly

ēgrēgǐ·us -a -um *adj* exceptional, singular, uncommon; distinguished, illustrious; *n* honor, distinction

ēgrēssus *pp* of egredior

ēgrēss·us -ūs *m* departure; way out, exit; disembarking, landing; mouth (*of river*); digression; *m pl* comings and goings

ēgurgǐt·ō -āre *vt* to pour out, lavish

ehem *interj* (expressing pleasant surprise) ha!, aha!

eheu *interj* (expressing pain) oh!

eho *interj* (expressing rebuke) look here!, see here!; eho dum! look here now!

ei *interj* (expressing fear or dismay) golly!

ēia or hēia *interj* (expressing joy or surpise) ah!, ah ha!; good!; (expressing haste) quick!, come on!

ējācǔl·or -ārī -ātus sum *vt* to squirt (*e.g., water*); se ejaculari to squirt

ējectāment·a -ōrum *n pl* refuse; jetsam

ējectǐ·ō -ōnis *f* ejection; banishment, exile

ēject·ō -āre *vt* to spout forth; to keep throwing up (*e.g., blood*)

eject·us -ūs *m* emission

ējēr·ō or ējūr·ō -āre *vt* to refuse upon oath, abjure, forswear; to deny on oath; to resign, abdicate; to disown, abandon

ē·jicǐō -jicěre -jēcī -jectum *vt* to throw out, drive out, put out, eject, expel; to banish, drive into exile; to utter; to run aground; to reject, disapprove; to boo (*someone*) off the stage; ejici to be stranded; se ejicere (of passions) to break out, come to the fore

ējulātǐ·ō -ōnis *f* wailing, lamenting

ējǔl·ō -āre *vi* to wail, lament

ējūrō see ejero

ē·lābor -lābī -lapsus sum *vi* to glide off; to slip away, escape; to pass away, disappear; (with *abl* or with super + *acc*) to glance off

ēlabōrāt·us -a -um *adj* studied, overdone; elaborate, finished

ēlabōr·ō -āre *vt* to work out, elaborate; to produce; *vi* to make a great effort, take great pains; (with *inf*) to strive to

ēlāmentābǐl·is -e *adj* pathetic

ēlangu·escō -escěre -ī *vi* to slow down, slacken, let up

ēlapsus *pp* of elabor

ēlātē *adv* proudly

ēlātǐ·ō -ōnis *f* elation, ecstasy

ēlātr·ō -āre *vt* to bark out

ēlāt·us -a -um *pp* of effero; *adj* high, elevated; exalted; haughty, proud

ē·lāvō -lavāre -lāvī -lautum or -lōtum *vt* to wash out; (coll) to clean out, rob

Elě·a -ae *f* town in Lucania in S. Italy, birthplace of Eleatic philosophy

Ēleātǐc·ī -ōrum *m pl* Eleatics, Eleatic philosophers

ēlecēbr·a -ae *f* snare; seductress

ēlectē *adv* tastefully

ēlectǐl·is -e *adj* choice, dainty

ēlectǐ·ō -ōnis *f* choice; *f pl* selection

ēlect·ō -āre *vt* to select, choose; to wheedle out, coax out (*a secret*)

Ēlectr·a -ae *f* Pleiad, daughter of Atlas and Pleione and the mother of Dardanus by Jupiter; daughter of Agamemnon and Clytemnestra

ēlectr·um -ī *n* amber; electrum (*alloy of gold and silver*); *f pl* amber beads

ēlect·us -a -um *pp* of eligo; *adj* select, picked, choice; (mil) elite

ēlect·us -ūs *m* choice

ēlěg·ans -antis *adj* fine, elegant, refined; choosy; fine, choice, select

ēleganter *adv* tastefully, neatly, elegantly

ēlegantǐ·a -ae *f* elegance, refinement, taste, propriety

ēlěg·ī -ōrum *m pl* elegiac verses

elegī·a or elegē·a -ae *f* elegy

Ēlěl·ĕus -ĕī *m* (epithet of) Bacchus

elementārǐ·us -a -um *adj* elementary; senex elementarius old schoolteacher

element·um -ī *n* first principle, element; *n pl* elements, rudiments; beginnings; ABC's

elench·us -ī *m* pearl

elephantomǎch·a -ae *m* fighter mounted on an elephant

elephant·us -ī or ēlěph·ās -antis *m* elephant; (fig) ivory

Eleus·īn -īnis *f* Eleusis (*sacred city in Attica, famous for its cult of Demeter*)

Eleusīn·us -a -um *adj* Eleusinian; Eleusīna mater Ceres

ēlěv·ō -āre *vt* to lift up, raise; to alleviate; to lessen, diminish; to make light of, disparage

ē·licǐō -licěre -licuī -licitum *vt* to elicit, draw out; to lure out, entice; to conjure up

Elǐc·ǐus -ǐī or -ī *m* (epithet of) Jupiter

ē·līdō -līděre -līsī -līsum *vt* to knock out, strike out, tear out, force out; to shatter, smash to pieces, crush; to force out, stamp out; (fig) to stamp out

ē·lǐgō -lǐgěre -lēgī -lectum *vt* to pluck out; to pick out, choose

ēlīmǐn·ō -āre *vt* to carry outside; to spread abroad

ēlīm·ō -āre *vt* to file; to finish off, perfect

ēlingu·is -e *adj* without tongue, speechless; (fig) inarticulate

ēlingu·ō -āre *vt* (coll) to tear out the tongue of

Ēl·is or Āl·is -ǐdis *f* district and town on the W. coast of the Peloponnesus in which Olympia is located

Eliss·a or Elīs·a -ae *f* Dido

ēlīsus *pp* of elido

ēlix·us -a -um *adj* wet through and through, soaked

ellam = **ecce + illam**

elleborōs·us -a -um *adj* crazy

ellebŏr·us or **hellebŏr·us -ī** *m* or **ellebŏr·um -ī** *n* hellebore (*plant used for mental illness*)

ellips·is -is *f* ellipsis

ellum = **ecce + illum**

ēlŏc·ō -āre *vt* to lease out, rent out

ēlocūtī·ō -ōnis *f* style of speaking, delivery

ēlog·ium -iī or **-ī** *n* saying, maxim; inscription, epitaph; clause (*in a will*)

ēlŏqu·ens -entis *adj* eloquent

ēloquenter *adv* eloquently

ēloquenti·a -ae *f* eloquence

ēlŏqu·ium -iī or **-ī** *n* eloquence

ē·lŏquor -lŏquī -locūtus sum *vt* to speak out, declare; *vi* to give a speech

ēlōtus *pp* of **elavo**

ē·lūcĕō -lūcēre -luxī *vi* to shine forth; to glitter

ēluct·or -ārī -ātus sum *vt* to struggle out of, struggle through (*e.g., deep snow*); to surmount; *vi* to force a way out

ēlūcŭbr·ō -āre or **ēlūcŭbr·or -ārī -ātus sum** *vt* to compose by lamp light

ē·lūdō -lūdĕre -lūsī -lūsum *vt* to elude, parry, avoid; to escape, shun; to delude, deceive; to make fun of; to get the better of, outmaneuver; *vi* to end the game

ē·lūgĕō -lūgĕre -luxī *vt* to mourn for; to cease to mourn

ēlumb·is -e *adj* loinless; bland (*style*)

ē·lŭō -lŭĕre -luī -lūtum *vt* to wash off, wash clean; to wash away; (fig) to wash away, remove, get rid of

ēlūsus *pp* of **eludo**

ēlūt·us -a -um *pp* of **eluo**; *adj* washed out, watery, insipid

ēluvĭ·ēs -ēī *f* inundation, overflow; sewage

ēluvĭ·ō -ōnis *f* deluge

Ēlys·ium -iī or **-ī** *n* realm of the blessed in the lower world

em *interj* (expressing wonder or emphasis) there!

emācĭt·ās -ātis *f* fondness for shopping

ēmancĭpātĭ·ō or **ēmancupātĭ·ō -ōnis** *f* emancipation; transfer of property

ēmancĭpāt·us -a -um *adj* made over, sold

ēmancĭp·ō or **ēmancŭp·ō -āre** *vt* to transfer; to declare (*a son*) free and independent, emancipate; to surrender, abandon

ēmān·ō -āre *vi* to flow out; to trickle out, leak out; to become known

Ēmathĭ·a -ae *f* Macedonia

Ēmath·is -ĭdis *adj* Macedonian; *f pl* the Pierides (*daughters of the Macedonian king Pierus*)

ēmātūr·escō -escĕre -uī *vi* to begin to ripen; to soften; (fig) to soften

em·ax -ācis *adj* fond of shopping

emblēm·a -ātis *n* mosaic, inlaid wood

embol·ium -iī or **-ī** *n* interlude

ēmendābĭl·is -e *adj* capable of correction

ēmendātē *adv* faultlessly

ēmendātĭ·ō -ōnis *f* emendation, correction

ēmendāt·or -ōris *m* or **ēmendātr·ix -īcis** *f* corrector

ēmendāt·us -a -um *adj* faultless

ēmendīc·ō -āre *vt* to obtain by begging

ēmend·ō -āre *vt* to emend, correct; to reform, improve, revise; to atone for

ēmensus *pp* of **emetior**

ēment·ior -īrī -ītus sum *vt* to falsify, fabricate, feign; *vi* to tell a lie

ēmerc·or -ārī -ātus sum *vt* to buy up; to bribe

ēmer·ĕō -ēre or **ēmer·ĕor -ērī -ĭtus sum** *vt* to merit fully; to lay under obligation; (mil) to serve out (*term of service*); **aliquem emerere** to do someone a favor or favors

ē·mergō -mergĕre -mersī -mersum *vt* to raise (*from the water*); **emergi** or **se emergere** to raise oneself up, rise; *vi* to emerge; to rise (*in power*); to extricate oneself; (with **ex + abl**) to get clear of

ēmerĭt·us -a -um *pp* of **emereor**; *adj* worn out, unfit for service; *m* veteran

ēmersus *pp* of **emergo**

emetĭc·a -ae *f* emetic

ē·mētĭor -mētīrī -mensus sum *vt* to measure out; to traverse, travel over; to live through; to impart, bestow

ēmĕt·ō -ĕre *vt* to mow down

ēmic·ō -āre -ŭī -ātum *vi* to dart out, shoot out, dash out; to flash out; (fig) to shine, be prominent

ēmigr·ō -āre *vi* to move out, depart; **e vita migrare** to pass on, die

ēmin·ens -entis *adj* projecting out, prominent, high; eminent

ēminentĭ·a -ae *f* projection, prominence; (in painting) highlights

ēmin·ĕō -ēre -ŭī *vi* to stand out, project; to be conspicuous, stand out; (in painting) to be highlighted

ēmin·or -ārī -ātus sum *vt* to threaten

ēminus *adv* out of range, at a distance; from afar

ēmīr·or -ārī -ātus sum *vt* to be greatly surprised at, stand aghast at

ēmissār·ium -iī or **-ī** *n* drain, outlet

ēmissār·ius -iī or **-ī** *m* scout, spy

ēmissīcĭ·us -a -um *adj* prying, spying

ēmissĭ·ō -ōnis *f* discharge, hurling, shooting; releasing; letting off

ēmissus *pp* of **emitto**

ēmiss·us -ūs *m* emission

ē·mittō -mittĕre -mīsī -missum *vt* to sound out; to hurl, discharge, shoot; to let go, let slip, let loose, drop, release, let out; to send out, publish; to allow to escape; to emancipate, set at liberty; to utter; to pass up (*an opportunity*); **animam emittere** to give up the ghost; **emitti** or **se emittere** (with **ex** + *abl*) to break out of (*e.g., jail*)

emō emĕre ēmī emptum *vt* to buy; to pay for; to gain, obtain, acquire; to bribe; **bene emere** to buy cheap; **in diem emere** to buy on credit; **male emere** to pay dearly for

ēmŏdĕr·or -ārī -ātus sum *vt* to moderate

ēmŏdŭl·or -ārī -ātus sum *vt* to sing the praises of, celebrate in song

ēmŏl·ior -īrī -ītus sum *vt* to accomplish

ēmoll·iŏ -īre -īvī or **-iī -ītum** *vt* to soften; to make mild; to enervate

ēmŏl·ō -ĕre — -ītum *vt* to grind up; to consume

ēmolument·um -ī *n* profit, gain, advantage

ēmon·ĕŏ -ēre *vt* to advise, admonish

ē·morior -mŏrī -mortŭus sum *vi* to die, die off; (fig) to die out

ēmortŭāl·is -e *adj* of death; **dies emortualis** day of one's death

ēmortŭus *pp* of **emorior**

ē·movĕŏ -movēre -mōvī -mōtum *vt* to move out, remove, expel; to dislodge; to shake (*e.g., foundations of wall*)

Empĕdŏcl·ēs -is *m* philosopher of Sicily who is said to have jumped into the crater of Mt. Aetna (*fl* 444 B.C.)

emphăs·is -is *f* emphasis, stress

empīric·us -ī *m* self-trained physician

empor·ium -iī or **-ī** *n* market town, market, mart

empti·ŏ -ōnis *f* buying, purchase; thing purchased, purchase

emptit·ŏ -āre *vt* to be in the habit of buying

empt·or -ōris *m* buyer, purchaser

emptus *pp* of **emo**

ēmūg·iŏ -īre *vt* to bellow out

ē·mulgĕŏ -mulgēre — -mulsum *vt* to drain out; to exhaust

ēmunct·us -a -um *adj* discriminating; **naris emunctae esse** to have discriminating tastes

ē·mungŏ -mungĕre — -munxī -munctum *vt* to blow the nose of; to swindle; (with *abl*) to cheat (*someone*) of; **emungi** to blow one's nose

ēmūn·iŏ -īre -īvī or **-iī -ītum** *vt* to build up; to fortify; to make a road through (*woods*)

ēn *interj* (in questions) really?; (in commands) come on!; (to call attention) look!, see!

ēnarrābil·is -e *adj* describable, intelligible

ēnarrāti·ŏ -ōnis *f* description; analysis

ēnarr·ŏ -āre *vt* to explain in detail, describe; to interpret

ē·nascor -nascī -nātus sum *vi* to grow out, sprout, arise

ēnăt·ŏ -āre *vi* to swim away, escape by swimming; (fig) to get away with it

ēnātus *pp* of **enascor**

ēnāvig·ŏ -āre *vt* to sail over, traverse; *vi* to sail away; (fig) to escape

Encelăd·us -ī *m* one of the giants whom Jupiter buried under Aetna

endrōm·is -idis *f* athlete's bathrobe

Endymi·ōn -ōnis *m* handsome young man with whom Luna fell in love and who was doomed to everlasting sleep on Mt. Patmos in Caria

ē·nĕcŏ (or **ē·nĭcŏ**) **-necāre -necŭī** (or **-nicāvī**) **-nectum** (or **-necātum**) *vt* to kill, kill off; to exhaust, wear out; (coll) to kill, pester to death

ēnervāt·us -a -um *adj* without sinews; without energy or force

ēnerv·is -e *adj* weak, feeble

ēnerv·ŏ -āre *vt* to weaken, enervate, render impotent

ēnĭcŏ see **eneco**

enim *conj* namely, for instance; yes, indeed, certainly; in fact, to be sure; (in replies) of course, no doubt; for, because

enimvērŏ *adv* yes indeed, to be sure, certainly; (ironical) of course

Enīp·eus -ĕī *m* tributary of the Peneus in Thessaly

ēnīsus *pp* of **enitor**

ēnit·ĕŏ -ēre -ŭī *vi* to shine out, sparkle; to be distinguished or conspicuous

ēnitesc·ŏ -ĕre *vi* to begin to shine, begin to brighten, become conspicuous

ē·nītor -nītī -nīsus or **nixus sum** *vt* to work one's way up, climb; to give birth to; *vi* to exert oneself, make an effort; (with *inf*) to struggle to, strive to

ēnixē *adv* strenuously, earnestly

ēnix·us -a -um *pp* of **enitor;** *adj* strenuous, earnest

Enn·ius -ī *m* father of Latin literature, writer of tragedy, comedy, epic, and satire, born at Rudiae in Calabria (239-169 B.C.)

Ennosigae·us -ī *m* (epithet of Neptune) Earthshaker

ēn·ŏ -āre *vi* to swim out, swim away, escape by swimming

ēnōdātē *adv* without knots; plainly, clearly

ēnōdāti·ŏ -ōnis *f* solution, explanation

ēnōd·is -e *adj* without knots; plain, clear

ēnōd·ŏ -āre *vt* to explain, clarify

ēnorm·is -e *adj* irregular; enormous

ēnormĭt·ās -ātis *f* irregular shape

ēnōt·escŏ -escĕre -ŭī *vi* to become known

ēnŏt·ŏ -āre *vt* to take notes of, note down

ensicŭl·us -ī *m* small sword

ensĭf·er -ĕra -ĕrum *adj* with a sword, wearing a sword

ensĭg·er -ĕra -ĕrum *adj* with a sword, wearing a sword

ens·is -is *m* sword

enthȳmēm·a -ătis *n* thought, reflection; condensed syllogism

ē·nūbō -nūbĕre -nupsī *vi* (said of a woman) to marry out of one's rank

ēnucleātē *adv* plainly

ēnucleāt·us -a -um *adj* pure, clean; straightforward; simple, clear (*style*)

ēnuclĕ·ō -āre *vt* (fig) to give in a nutshell, explain to the point

ēnumerātĭ·ō -ōnis *f* enumeration

ēnumĕr·ō -āre *vt* to count up; to pay; to recount, relate, detail, describe

ēnuntiātĭ·ō -ōnis *f* (in logic) proposition

ēnuntĭ·ō -āre *vt* to disclose, reveal, betray; to say, assert, express

ēnuptĭ·ō -ōnis *f* right to marry outside the clan

ēnutrĭ·ō -īre -īvī or **-iī -ītum** *vt* to nourish, raise, bring up (*children*)

eō īre īvī or **iī ītum** *vi* to go; to go, walk, sail, ride; (mil) to march; (of time) to pass; (of events) to go on, happen, turn out; **in sententiam īre** to vote for a bill

eō *adv* there, to that place; to that end, to that purpose; so far, to such an extent, to such a pitch; on that account, for that reason, with that in view; **eo ero brevior** I will be all the briefer; **eo magis** all the more; **eo maxime quod** especially because; **eo quo** to the place to which; **eo . . . quo** the . . .; **eo quod** because; **eo . . . ut** to such an extent . . . that

eōdem *adv* to the same place, purpose, or person

Ēōs (*nom only*) *f* Dawn

Ēō·us -ī *m* morning star; inhabitant of the East, Oriental; one of the horses of the sun

Epaminond·ās -ae *m* famous Theban general who fought against the Spartans (*d.* 362 B.C.)

Epaph·us -ī *m* son of Jupiter and Io

ēpast·us -a -um *adj* eaten up

Epē·us or **Epi·us -ī** *m* builder of the Trojan horse

ephēb·us -ī *m* young man (18 *to* 20 *years of age*)

ephēmĕr·is -ĭdis *f* diary, journal

Ephĕs·us -ī *f* city in Asia Minor with famous temple of Diana

ephippiāt·us -a -um *adj* riding a saddled horse

ephipp·ium -iī or **-ī** *n* saddle

ephŏr·us -ī *m* ephor (*Spartan magistrate*)

Ephr̄·a -ae or **Ephȳr·ē -ēs** *f* ancient name of Corinth

Epicharm·us -ī *m* Greek philosopher and writer of early comedy (540-450 B.C.)

epichȳs·is -is *f* jug

epicrŏc·us -a -um *adj* transparent, thin

Epicūr·us -ī *m* Greek philosopher, born on Samos (342-270 B.C.)

epic·us -a -um *adj* epic

epidictĭc·us -a -um *adj* for display

epidipn·is -ĭdis *f* dessert

epigramm·a -ătis *n* inscription; short poem, epigram

epilŏg·us -ī *m* epilogue, peroration

epimēnĭ·a -ōrum *n pl* month's rations

Epimēth·eus -ĕī *m* son of Iapetus and brother of Prometheus

epirēd·ium -iī or **-ī** *n* trace

epistol·ium -iī or **-ī** *n* note

epistŭl·a -ae *f* letter

epitaph·ium -iī or **-ī** *n* eulogy

epithalam·ium -iī or **-ī** *n* wedding song

epithēc·a -ae *f* addition, increase

epitŏm·a -ae or **epitŏm·ē -ēs** *f* epitome, abridgment

epitȳr·um -ī *n* olive salad

epŏd·es -um *m pl* seafish

ep·ops -ōpis *m* hoopoe

epos (*nom & acc only*) *n* epic

ēpōt·us or **expōt·us -a -um** *adj* drained to the dregs; drunk dry

epŭl·ae -ārum *f pl* courses, dishes; sumptuous meal, banquet; **epulae regum** dinner fit for a king

epŭlār·is -e *adj* at dinner, of a dinner; **sermo epularis** talk at dinner

epŭl·ō -ōnis *m* dinner guest, guest at a banquet; **Tresviri** or **Septemvirī Epulones** college of priests who superintended the state dinner to the gods

epŭl·or -ārī -ātus sum *vt* to feast on; *vi* to attend a dinner; (with *abl*) to feast on

epŭl·um -ī *n* banquet, feast

equ·a -ae *f* mare

equ·es -ĭtis *m* rider; (mil) trooper, cavalryman; cavalry; *m pl* cavalry

Equ·es -ĭtis *m* knight; capitalist (*member of Roman middle class*); equestrian order, bourgeoisie

equest·er -ris -re *adj* cavalry; equestrian; middle class, bourgeois, capitalist

equĭdem *adv* truly, indeed, in any event; (with first person) for my part, as far as I am concerned; of course, to be sure

equīn·us -a -um *adj* horse's

equīrĭ·a -ōrum *n pl* horse race

equitāt·us -ūs *m* cavalry

equĭt·ō -āre *vi* to ride, ride a horse

equŭlĕ·us -ī *m* foal, colt; small equestrian statue; torture rack

equ·us -ī *m* horse; **equis virisque** or **equis viris** (fig) with might and main; **equo merere** to serve in the cavalry; **equo vehi** to ride, to ride a horse; **equus bipes** sea horse; **in equo** mounted; *m pl* (fig) chariot

er·a -ae *f* mistress of the house

ērādīc·ō or **exrādīc·ō -āre** *vt* to root out, uproot, destroy

ē·rādō -rādēre -rāsī -rāsum *vt* to scratch out, erase, obliterate

erăn·us -ī *m* mutual insurance society

Ērătō (*nom* only) *f* Muse of erotic poetry; Muse

Eratosthĕn·ēs -is *m* famous Alexandrine geographer, poet, and philosopher (276-196 B.C.)

erc- see **herc-**

Ĕrĕb·us -ī *m* god of darkness, son of Chaos and brother of Night; lower world

Erechth·eus -ĕī *m* mythical king of Athens, son of Hephaestus

ērect·us -a -um *pp* of **erigo**; *adj* erect, upright; noble, elevated, lofty; haughty; attentive, alert, tense; resolute, courageous

ē·rēpō -rēpĕre -repsī *vt* to crawl through (*field*); to crawl up (*mountain*); *vi* to crawl out

ēreptī·ō -ōnis *f* robbery

ērept·or -ōris *m* robber

ēreptus *pp* of **eripio**

ergā *prep* (with *acc*) to, towards; against

ergastŭl·um -ī *n* prison; *n pl* inmates

ergō *adv* therefore, consequently; (resumptive) well then, I say, as I was saying; (with *imperatives*) then, now; **quid ergo?** why then?; *prep* (with preceding *genit*) for the sake of; **illius ergo** for his sake

Erichthon·ius -iī or **-ī** *m* mythical king of Athens; son of Dardanus, father of Tros, and king of Troy

ēric·ius -iī or **-ī** *m* hedgehog; (mil) beam with iron spikes

Ĕridăn·us -ī *m* Po river (*so called by the Greeks*)

erifŭg·a -ae *m* runaway slave

ē·rigō -rigĕre -rexī -rectum *vt* to set up straight, straighten out (*e.g., tree*); to set up, erect; to cheer up, encourage; to arouse, excite; (mil) to deploy troops on a slope; **erigi** or **se erigere** to raise oneself, arise

Ĕrigŏn·ē -ēs *f* Virgo (*constellation*)

eril·is -e *adj* master's, mistress's

Ĕrīn·ys -ўos *f* Fury; (fig) frenzy

Eriphȳl·a -ae or **Eriphȳl·ē -ēs** *f* wife of the seer Amphiaraus and the mother of Alcmaeon, who killed her for betraying Amphiaraus

ē·ripiō -ripĕre -ripuī -reptum *vt* to snatch away, pull out, tear out; to deliver, rescue; to rob; (with *dat* or with **ab** or **ex** + *abl*) to take away from, wrest from, rescue from; **se eripere** to escape

ērogāti·ō -ōnis *f* paying out, payment

ērogit·ō -āre *vt* to try to find out

ērŏg·ō -āre *vt* to allocate, expend; to bequeath; (with **in** + *acc*) **a** to allocate to, expend on; **b** to bequeath to

Ĕr·ōs -ōtis *m* Cupid

errābund·us -a -um *adj* wandering, straggling

errātic·us -a -um *adj* erratic, roving, wandering

errāti·ō -ōnis *f* wandering

errāt·um -ī *n* error, mistake

errāt·us -ūs *m* roving, wandering about

err·ō -āre *vi* to wander, lose one's way, stray, roam; to waver; to err, make a mistake, be mistaken; (with **in** + *abl*) to be mistaken about

err·ō -ōnis *m* vagrant, vagabond

err·or -ōris *m* wandering, wavering, uncertainty; error; cause of error, deception; maze, winding, intricacy

ērub·escō -escĕre -uī *vt* to blush at; to be ashamed of; to respect; *vi* to grow red, redden; to blush

ērūc·a -ae *f* colewort

ēruct·ō -āre *vt* to belch, vomit, throw up; (fig) to belch

ērud·iō -īre -iī -ītum *vt* to educate, teach, instruct

ērudītē *adv* learnedly

ērudītī·ō -ōnis *f* instructing, instruction; erudition

ērudītŭl·us -a -um *adj* somewhat experienced, somewhat skilled

ērudīt·us -a -um *adj* educated, learned, accomplished

ē·rumpō -rumpĕre -rūpī -ruptum *vt* to cause to break out; to give vent to; **iram in hostes erumpere** to vent one's wrath on the enemy; *vi* to burst out, break out

ē·ruō -ruĕre -ruī -rūtum *vt* to root up, uproot, dig out; to undermine, demolish, destroy; to draw out, elicit; to rescue; to plow up

ērupti·ō -ōnis *f* eruption; (mil) sortie, sally

ēruptus *pp* of **erumpo**

er·us -ī *m* master of the house, head of the family; lord, owner, proprietor

ērūt·us *pp* of **eruo**

erv·um -ī *n* pulse, vetch

Ĕrycīn·us -a -um *adj* of Mt. Eryx (*in Sicily*); of Venus; Sicilian; *f* Venus

Ĕrymanth·is -īdis *f* Callisto (*changed into a bear and made a constellation*)

Ĕrymanth·us -ī *m* mountain range in Arcadia, where Hercules killed a boar

Ĕrysichth·ōn -ōnis *m* son of Thessalian king Triopas, punished with insatiable hunger for having cut down a grove sacred to Ceres

erythīn·us -ī *m* red mullet

Ĕr·yx -ўcis or **Ĕrȳc·us -ī** *m* mountain on W. coast of Sicily, famous for its temple to Venus

esc·a -ae *f* dish; food; bait

escāri·us -a -um *adj* of food; of bait; *n pl* dishes, courses

e·scendō -scendĕre -scendī -scensum *vt & vi* to climb, climb up

escensi·ō or **exscensi·ō -ōnis** *f* climb, climbing

esculent·us -a -um *adj* edible; *n pl* edibles

esculētum see **aesculetum**

esculus see **aesculus**

ēsĭt·ō -āre *vt* to be accustomed to eating

Esquili·ae -ārum *f pl* Esquiline Hill in Rome

Esquilin·us -a -um *adj* Esquiline; *f* Esquiline gate

essedār·ius -īi or **-ī** *m* soldier fighting from a chariot

esse *inf* of **sum**; *inf* of **edo**

essĕd·um -ī *n* combat chariot (*used by Gauls and Britons*)

essenti·a -ae *f* essence

estr·ix -īcis *f* glutton (*female*)

essĭt·ō -āre *vt* to be accustomed to eating

ēsuriāl·is -e *adj* of hunger

ēsur·iō -īre — -ītum *vt* to be hungry for; *vi* to be hungry

ēsurītī·ō -ōnis *f* hunger

ēsus *pp* of **edo**

et *adv* besides, also; even, I mean

et *conj* and; (for emphasis) and even, yes and; (antithetical) however, but; **et . . . et** both . . . and, not only . . . but also

etēnim *conj* for, and as a matter of fact

etēsi·ae -ārum *m pl* periodic winds (*on the Aegean Sea*)

ēthĭc·ē -ēs *f* ethics

ēthologī·a -ae *f* portrayal of character

ētholŏg·us -ī *m* impersonator

etiam *conj* also, and also, besides, likewise; (of time) yet, as yet, still, even now; (in affirmation) yes, yes indeed, certainly, by all means; (emphatic) even, rather; (with emphatic imperatives) but just; **etiam atque etiam** again and again, repeatedly

etiamnunc or **etiamnum** *adv* even now, even at the present time, still

etiamsi *conj* even if, although

etiamtum or **etiamnunc** *adv* even then, till then, still

Etrūri·a -ae *f* district N. of Rome

Etrusc·us -a -um *adj & mf* Etruscan

etsī *conj* even if, although

etymologī·a -ae *f* etymology

eu *interj* well done!, bravo!

Euan or **Euhan** *m* Bacchus

Euand·er or **Euandr·us -rī** *m* Evander (*Arcadian who founded Pallanteum at the foot of the Palatine hill*)

eu·ans or **euh·ans -antis** *adj* crying Euan or Euhan (*Bacchic cry*)

euax *interj* hurray!

Euboe·a -ae *f* island off the E. coast of Attica and Boeotia

Euĕn·us -ī *m* river in Aetolia

euge or **eugĕpae** *interj* well done!, terrific!

euh·ans -antis *adj* shouting Euan (*Bacchic cry*)

Euhēmĕr·us -ī *m* Greek writer who attempted to prove that all the ancient myths were actually historical events (*fl* 316 B.C.)

Euh·ius -ĭi or **-ī** *m* Bacchus

Euhoe or **Euoe** *interj* ecstatic cry of revelers at festival of Bacchus

Eu·ius -ĭi or **-ī** *m* Bacchus

Eumenid·es -um *f pl* Erinyes or Furies (*goddesses of vengeance*)

eunūch·us -ī *m* eunuch

Euoe see **Euhoe**

Euphorb·us -ī *m* brave Trojan warrior whose soul Pythagoras asserted had transmigrated to himself

Euphrāt·ēs -is *m* Euphrates River

Eupŏl·is -idis *m* famous Athenian comic poet (446?-411 B.C.)

Eurīpĭd·ēs -is *m* Athenian tragic poet (485-405 B.C.)

Eurīp·us -ī *m* strait between Boeotia and Euboea; channel, canal

Eurōp·a -ae or **Eurōp·ē -ēs** *f* daughter of Agenor and mother of Sarpedon and Minos by Jupiter; he, in the shape of a bull, carried her off to Crete

Eurōt·as -ae *m* chief river in Laconia

Eur·us -ī *m* S.E. wind; east wind; wind

Eurydĭc·ē -ēs *f* wife of Orpheus

Eurypўl·us -ī *m* Greek warrior who fought at Troy

Eurysth·eus -ĕī *m* son of Sthenelus, grandson of Perseus, and king of Nycenae, who imposed the twelve labors of Hercules

Eurŷt·is -ĭdis *f* Iole (*with whom Hercules fell in love*)

Eurŷt·us -ī *m* king of Oechalia and father of Iole

euschēmē *adv* gracefully

Euterp·ē -ēs *f* Muse of lyric poetry

Euxīn·us Pont·us or **Euxīn·us -ī** *m* or **Pont·us -ī** *m* Black Sea

ē·vādō -vādĕre -vāsī -vāsum *vt* to pass, pass by; to pass through, escape; *vi* to go out; to turn out, become, prove to be, turn out to be; to get away, escape; to rise, climb

ēvāg·or -ārī -ātus sum *vt* to stray beyond, transgress; *vi* (mil) to maneuver; (fig) to spread

ēval·escō -escĕre -ŭī *vi* to grow strong; to increase; (of a word or expression) to gain currency; (with *inf*) to be able to; (with **in** + *acc*) to develop into

ēvān·escō -escĕre -ŭī *vi* to vanish, pass away, die away; (of wine) to become vapid; to be forgotten, perish

ēvānĭd·us -a -um *adj* vanishing

ēvast·ō -āre *vt* to devastate, wreck completely

evasus *pp* of **evado**

ē·věhō -vehĕre -vexī -vectum *vt* to carry out, convey out; to carry abroad, spread abroad; to lift up, raise; **evehi** to ride, sail, drift

ē·vellō -vellĕre -vellī or -vulsī -vulsum *vt* to tear or pluck out; to eradicate

ē·veniō -venīre -vēnī -ventum *vi* to come out, come forth; to come to pass, happen; to follow, result, turn out, end; *v impers* it happens

ēvent·um -ī *n* event, occurrence; result, effect, consequence; fortune, experience

ēvent·us -ūs *m* event, accident, fortune, lot, fate; good fortune, success; issue, consequence, result

ēverbĕr·ō -āre *vt* to strike hard; to beat violently

ēverricŭl·um -ī *n* broom; dragnet

ē·verrō -verrĕre -verrī -versum *vt* to sweep out; (fig) to clean out, strip

ēversi·ō -ōnis *f* overthrow, subversion, destruction

ēvers·or -ōris *m* subverter, destroyer

ēversus *pp* of everro; *pp* of everto

ē·vertō or ē·vortō -vertĕre -vertī -versum *vt* to overturn, turn upside down; to overthrow, upset; to turn out, expel, eject; to subvert, destroy, ruin

ēvestīgāt·us -a -um *adj* tracked down

ēvictus *pp* of evinco

ēvĭd·ens -entis *adj* evident, visible, plain

ēvidenter *adv* evidently, plainly, clearly

ēvidentĭ·a -ae *f* distinctness, clearness (*in speech*)

ēvigĭl·ō -āre *vt* to watch through (*the night*); to work through the night writing (*e.g., books*); *vi* to be wide-awake; (fig) to be on one's toes

ēvīl·escō -escĕre -ŭī *vi* to depreciate, become worthless

ē·vinciō -vincīre -vinxī -vinctum *vt* to tie up; to crown, wreathe

e·vincō -vincĕre -vīcī -victum *vt* to conquer completely, trounce; to prevail over

ēvinctus *pp* of evincio

ēvīr·ō -āre *vt* to unman, castrate

ēviscĕr·ō -āre *vt* to disembowel; to mangle

ēvītābĭl·is -e *adj* avoidable

ēvītātĭ·ō -ōnis *f* avoidance

ēvīt·ō -āre *vt* to avoid, escape

ēvocāt·ī -ōrum *m pl* veterans called up again; reenlisted veterans

ēvocāt·or -ōris *m* recruiter

ēvŏc·ō -āre *vt* to call out, summon; to challenge; (mil) to call up (*for service*); to evoke, excite, stir

ēvolgō see evulgo

ēvŏl·ō -āre *vi* to fly out, fly away; to rush out, dash out; (fig) to soar

ēvolūtĭ·ō -ōnis *f* unrolling a book; (fig) reading

ē·volvō -volvĕre -volvī -volūtum *vt* to roll out, unroll, unfold; to spread; to unroll, read, study; to unfold, disclose; to free, extricate; to repel; to evolve, develop

ē·vŏmō -vomĕre -vomŭī -vomĭtum *vt* to vomit, spew out, disgorge

ēvulg·ō or ēvolg·ō -āre *vt* to divulge, make public

ēvulsĭ·ō -ōnis *f* pulling out, extraction (*of a tooth*)

ēvulsus *pp* of evello

ex or ē *prep* (with *abl*) (of space) out of, from; down from; up from, above; (of time) from, from . . . onward, immediately after, following, since; (cause or origin) from, through, by, on account of, by reason of; (transition) from, out of; from being; (conformity) after, according to, in conformity with; (means) with, by means of; (partitive) out of, from among, among; made of, out of

exacerb·ō -āre *vt* to exasperate, provoke

exactĭ·ō -ōnis *f* driving out, expulsion; supervision; exaction, collection; tax, tribute

exact·or -ōris *m* expeller; supervisor; tax collector

exact·us -a -um *pp* of exigo; *adj* exact, precise

exac·ŭō -ŭĕre -ŭī -ūtum *vt* to sharpen; to sharpen, stimulate, excite, inflame

exadversum or exadvorsum or exadversus or exadvorsus *adv* on the opposite side; *prep* (with *dat* or *acc*) across from, right opposite

exaedificātĭ·ō -ōnis *f* construction

exaedific·ō -āre *vt* to finish building, build, construct; (fig) to complete

exaequātĭ·ō -ōnis *f* leveling; uniformity

exaequ·ō -āre *vt* to level, make level; (fig) to equal, regard as equal; **exaequari** (with *dat*) to be put on the same level with

exaestŭ·ō -āre *vi* to seethe, boil; to ferment

exaggerātĭ·ō -ōnis *f* (fig) elevation, enlargement; **animi exaggeratio** broadening of the mind

exaggĕr·ō -āre *vt* to pile up; to enlarge; to enhance

exagitāt·or -ōris *m* critic

exagĭt·ō -āre *vt* to stir up, keep on the move; to scare away; to criticize, satirize; to irritate; to excite, stir up (*feelings*)

exagōg·a -ae *f* exportation

exalb·escō -escĕre -ŭī *vi* to turn pale

exām·en -ĭnis *n* swarm; crowd; tongue of scale; weighing, consideration; examination

exāmĭn·ō -āre *vt* to weigh; to consider; to try, test, examine

examussim *adv* exactly

exancl·ō -āre vt to draw off, drain; to drain to the dregs

exanimāl·is -e adj dead, lifeless; deadly

exanimātī·ō -ōnis f breathlessness; terror, panic

exanim·is -e or **exanim·us -a -um** adj breathless, terrified; dead, lifeless; fainting (e.g., from fear)

exanim·ō -āre vt to knock the breath out of; to wind, tire, weaken; to deprive of life, kill; to scare out of one's wits; to dishearten; to agitate

exanimus see **exanimis**

ex·ardescō -ardescĕre -arsī -arsum vi to catch fire; to flare up; (fig) to flare up, be provoked, be exasperated

exār·escō -escĕre -ŭī vi to become quite dry, dry up

exarm·ō -āre vt to disarm

exăr·ō -āre vt to plow up; to raise, produce; to write (on wax with a stylus), write down, note; to furrow, wrinkle; **frontem rugis exarare** to knit one's brow

exasciāt·us -a -um adj hewn out; properly planned, properly worked out

exaspĕr·ō -āre vt to make rough, roughen; to exasperate

exauctōr·ō -āre vt (mil) to discharge, cashier

exaud·iō -īre -īvī -ītum vt to hear clearly; to discern; to perceive, understand; to listen to; to grant

exaug·ĕō -ēre vt to increase; to confirm

exaugurātī·ō -ōnis f desecration, profaning

exaugŭr·ō -āre vt to desecrate, profane

exauspic·ō -āre vi to find the omens good

exballist·ō -āre vt to put an end to, finish off

exbĭbō see **ebibo**

excaec·ō -āre vt to blind; to stop up (a river, pipe, etc.); to darken

excandescenti·a -ae f mounting anger, outburst of anger

excand·escō -escĕre -ŭī vi to grow white hot; to reach a pitch (of emotion)

excant·ō -āre vt to charm away

excarnific·ō -āre vt to tear to pieces, torture to death

excăv·ō -āre vt to hollow out

ex·cēdō -cēdĕre -cessī -cessum vt to exceed, pass, surpass; vi to go out, go away, withdraw, depart, disappear; to die; **e medio excedere** or **e vita excedere** to depart from life, die

excell·ens -entis adj excellent, outstanding, distinguished, superior

excellenter adv excellently

excellenti·a -ae f excellence, superiority

ex·cellō -cellĕre vi to excel, be superior

excelsē adv high, loftily

excelsit·ās -ātis f loftiness

excels·us -a -um adj high, lofty; eminent; n height; high social status; **in excelso aetatem** or **vitam agere** to be in the limelight

exceptī·ō -ōnis f exception, restriction, limitation; (law) objection raised by a defendant against an accuser's statement

except·ō -āre vt to catch, catch up to

exceptus pp of **excipio**

ex·cernō -cernĕre -crēvī -crētum vt to sift out, separate

ex·cerpō -cerpĕre -cerpsī -cerptum vt to pick out, extract; to pick out, choose, gather; to leave out, omit, except

excerpt·um -ī n excerpt

excess·us -ūs m departure; death; digression

excĕtr·a -ae f snake

excidī·ō -ōnis f destruction

excid·ium -iī or **-ī** n overthrow, destruction; cause of destruction

ex·cĭdō -cidĕre -cidī vi to fall out; (of an utterance) to slip out, escape; to pass away, perish; to degenerate; to disappear; to be forgotten; (with **in** + acc) to degenerate into; (with abl or **ex** + abl) a to be deprived of, lose; b to forget, miss; (with dat or **de** + abl) a to fall from; b to escape from (lips); **e memoria excidere** to slip the memory

ex·cĭdō -cidĕre -cidī -cīsum vt to cut out, cut off, cut down; to raze, demolish; (fig) to banish, eliminate

exciĕō see **excio**

exc·iō -īre -īvī or **-iī -ītum** or **exci·ĕō -ēre** vt to call (someone) out, summon; to awaken (from sleep); to disturb; to frighten; to stir up, excite; to produce, occasion

ex·cipiō -cipĕre -cēpī -ceptum vt to take out, remove; to rescue; to exempt; to take, receive, catch, capture; to follow, succeed; to catch, intercept; to be exposed to; to incur; to receive, welcome; to take up eagerly; to listen to, overhear; to except, make an exception of; to reach (a place); to mention in particular; to take on, withstand

excīsī·ō -ōnis f destruction

excīsus pp of **excīdo**

excitāt·us -a -um adj excited, lively, vigorous; loud

excit·ō -āre vt to wake, rouse; to raise, stir up; to erect, construct, produce; to cause, occasion; (fig) to arouse, awaken, incite, inspire, stimulate, enliven, encourage; to startle

excītus pp of **excio**

exclāmātī·ō -ōnis f exclamation

exclām·ō -āre vt to exclaim; vi to shout, yell

ex·clūdō -clūdĕre -clūsī -clūsum vt to exclude, shut out, shut off; to remove, separate; to hatch; (coll) to knock out (an eye); to prevent

exclūsi·ō -ōnis f exclusion

exclūsus pp of **excludo**

excoctus pp of **excoquo**

excōgitāti·ō -ōnis f thinking out, inventing, contriving

excōgitāt·us -a -um adj choice

excōgit·ō -āre vt to think out, devise, contrive

ex·cōlō -colěre -colŭī -cultum vt to tend, cultivate, work carefully; to refine, ennoble, perfect, improve; to worship

ex·cŏquō -coquěre -coxī -coctum vt to cook out, boil away; to dry up, bake thoroughly; to harden, temper (steel)

excor·s -dis adj senseless, silly, stupid

excrēment·um -ī n excretion

excrēō see **exscreo**

ex·crescō -crescěre -crēvī -crētum vi to grow out; to grow up, rise up

excruciābil·is -e adj deserving torture

excruci·ō -āre vt to torture, torment; to trouble, harass, distress

excubi·ae -ārum f pl standing guard; sentry; watchfire

excubit·or -ōris m sentry

excŭb·ō -āre -ŭī -ĭtum vi to sleep out of doors; to stand guard; to be attentive, be on the alert

ex·cūdō -cūděre -cūdī -cūsum vt to beat or strike out; to hammer out; to forge; (fig) to hatch (eggs); (fig) to hammer out, write up, hammer into shape

exculc·ō -āre vt to kick out; to tread down on; to stomp

excultus pp of **excolo**

excūrāt·us -a -um adj carefully attended to

ex·currō -currěre -cucurrī or **-currī -cursum** vi to run or dash out; (mil) to sally forth, make an incursion; to project, extend; (fig) to fan out, expand

excursi·ō -ōnis f sally, sortie; inroad, invasion; outset, opening (of a speech)

excurs·or -ōris m skirmisher, scout

excurs·us -ūs m reconnoitering, running out ahead; raid, charge, attack, invasion; digression

excūsābil·is -e adj excusable

excūsātē adv excusably, without blame

excūsāti·ō -ōnis f excuse

excūsāt·us -a -um adj free from blame, exempt

excūs·ō -āre vt to free from blame, excuse; to exempt; to make excuses for, apologize for; to allege in excuse, plead as an excuse

excussus pp of **excutio**

excūsus pp of **excudo**

ex·cutiō -cutěre -cussī -cussum vt to shake out, shake off, shake loose; to knock out (e.g., teeth); (of horse) to throw, throw off; to shake out (garment); to jilt, give a cold shoulder to; to toss, throw; to shake out, search; to examine, investigate; (fig) to shake off, discard, banish

exdorsŭ·ō -āre vt to fillet

exec- see **exsec-**

ex·ědō -esse -ēdī -ēsum vt to eat up, consume; to destroy; to prey on; to hollow; to wear away, corrode

exědr·a -ae f sitting room; lecture room; hall

exedr·ium -ĭī or **-ī** n sitting room, parlor, living room

exempl·ar or **exempl·āre -āris** n copy; likeness; pattern, model, ideal

exemplār·is -e adj following a model

exempl·um -ī n sample, example, typical instance; precedent; pattern, make, character; model, pattern (of conduct); object lesson; warning; copy, transcript; portrait

exemptus pp of **eximo**

exentěr·ō -āre vt to disembowel; to empty, exhaust; to torture, torment

ex·ěō -īre -ĭī -ĭtum vt to pass beyond, cross; to parry, ward off, avoid; (fig) to exceed; vi to go out, go forth; to go away, withdraw, depart, retire; to march out; to disembark; to pour out, gush out, flow out; to escape, be freed; to pass away, perish; (of time) to run out, expire; to get out, become public; to burgeon forth; (of hills) to rise; **ex urna exire** to come out of, fall out of the urn (said of lots)

exeq- = **exseq-**

exerc·ěō -ēre -ŭī -ĭtum vt to exercise, train; (mil) to drill, exercise, train; to keep (someone) busy, keep (someone) going; to supervise; to cultivate, work (the soil); to engage, occupy (the mind); to practice, follow (a trade, occupation); to carry into effect; to disturb, worry

exercitāti·ō -ōnis f exercise, practice, experience, training; (with genit) practice in

exercitāt·us -a -um adj experienced, trained, disciplined; troubled, worried, disturbed

exercit·ium -ĭī or **-ī** exercise, training

exercit·ō -āre vt to keep in training, exercise

exercit·or -ōris m trainer

exercit·us -a -um pp of **excerceo**; adj disciplined; experienced; trying, tough, harassing; harassed, vexed

exercit·us -ūs m army; infantry; (pol) assembly of the people; army of followers; swarm, flock, multitude

exěrō see **exsero**

exēs·or -ōris m corrosive factor, underminer

exēsus pp of **exedo**

exhālāti·ō -ōnis f exhalation, vapor

exhāl·ō -āre vt to exhale, breathe out; vi to steam; to breathe one's last, expire

ex·haurĭō -haurīre -hausī -haustum *vt* to draw out, empty, exhaust; to take away, remove; to drain dry; to bring to an end; to undergo, endure (*troubles*); to discuss fully

exhērēd·ō -āre *vt* to disinherit

exhēr·ēs -ēdis *adj* disinherited

exhĭb·ĕō -ēre -ŭī -ĭtum *vt* to hold out; to present, produce; to display, exhibit; to cause, occasion; to render, make

exhĭlăr·ō -āre *vt* to cheer up

exhorr·escō -escĕre -ŭī *vt* to shudder at; *vi* to be terrified

exhortātĭ·ō -ōnis *f* encouragement; *f pl* words of encouragement

exhort·or -ārī -ātus sum *vt* to encourage

ex·ĭgō -igĕre -ēgī -actum *vt* to drive out, push out, thrust out, expel; to demand, exact, collect, require; to pass, spend, complete, close (*life, time*); to finish, complete, conclude; to ascertain, determine; to weigh, consider, estimate, examine, try, test; to dispose of

exigŭē *adv* briefly, slightly, sparingly, barely

exigŭĭt·ās -ātis *f* shortness, smallness, meagerness, scantiness, scarcity

exigŭ·us -a -um *adj* short, small, meager, scanty, poor, paltry, inadequate; a little, a bit of

exilĭō see exsilio

exĭl·is -e *adj* thin, small, meager, feeble, poor; cheerless, dreary; depleted (*ranks*); worthless, insincere; dry, flat (*style*)

exĭlĭt·ās -ātis *f* thinness; meagerness, dreariness

exĭlĭter *adv* drily, drearily, jejunely

exilĭum see exsilĭum

exim see exinde

eximĭē *adv* exceptionally

eximĭ·us -a -um *adj* taken out, exempted; exempt; select, special, exceptional

ex·ĭmō -imĕre -ēmī -emptum *vt* to take out, take away, remove; to exempt; to free, release, let off; to make an exception of; to waste, lose (*time*); to banish (*e.g., worries*)

exin see exinde

exĭnān·ĭō -īre -īī -ītum *vt* to empty completely; to plunder; (fig) to clean out, fleece

exinde or exim or exin *adv* from that place, from that point; (in enumerating) after that, next, then; (of time) from that point, after that, then, furthermore, next; accordingly

existimātĭ·ō -ōnis *f* appraisal, judgment, estimate, opinion, decision, verdict; reputation, good name, character; (com) credit; **vulgi existimatio** public opinion

existimăt·or -ōris *m* critic, judge

existĭm·ō or existŭm·ō -āre *vt* to appraise, evaluate, value, estimate;

to think, judge, consider, regard; **in hostium numero existimare** to regard as an enemy

existō see exsisto

exitĭābĭl·is -e *adj* deadly, fatal, destructive; (with *dat*) fatal to

exitĭāl·is -e *adj* deadly, fatal

exitĭ·ō -ōnis *f* going out, exit

exitĭōs·us -a -um *adj* deadly, destructive

exit·ĭum -ĭī or -ī *n* destruction, ruin; cause of destruction

exĭt·us -ūs *m* going out, exit, departure; way out, outlet, exit; end, close, conclusion; **ad exitum adducere** to bring to a close

exlecēbra see elecebra

ex·lex -lēgis *adj* without law, bound by no law; lawless, heedless of laws

exobsĕcr·ō or exopsĕcr·ō -āre *vi* to make an earnest entreaty

exocŭl·ō -āre *vt* to knock the eyes out of

exod·ĭum -ĭī or -ī *n* farce (*presented after the main feature*)

exol·escō -escĕre -ēvī -ētum *vi* to decay, fade; to become obsolete

exolēt·us -a -um *adj* full-grown; *m* (fig) old rake

exonĕr·ō -āre *vt* to unload; (fig) to relieve, free, exonerate

exoptābĭl·is -e *adj* highly desirable, long-awaited

exoptāt·us -a -um *adj* longed-for, welcome, desired

exopt·ō -āre *vt* to long for, wish earnestly, desire greatly

exōrābĭl·is -e *adj* accessible, sympathetic, placable

exōrābŭl·a -ōrum *n pl* enticements, bait, arguments

exōrāt·or -ōris *m* lucky petitioner

ex·ordĭor -ordīrī -orsus sum *vt & vi* to begin, start, commence

exord·ĭum -ĭī or -ī *n* beginning, start, commencement, origin; introduction

ex·orĭor -orīrī -ortus sum *vi* to come out, come forth, rise, appear; to begin, arise, be caused, be produced

exornātĭ·ō -ōnis *f* embellishment

exorn·ō -āre *vt* to fit out, furnish, equip, provide, supply; to adorn, embellish, decorate, set off, give luster to

exōr·ō -āre *vt* to prevail upon, win over; to gain or obtain by entreaty; to appease

exorsus *pp* of **exordior**; *n pl* beginning, commencement; introduction, preamble

exors·us -ūs *m* beginning, commencement; introduction

exortus *pp* of **exorior**

exort·us -ūs *m* rising; the East, the Orient

ex·os -ossis *adj* boneless

exoscŭl·or -ārī -ātus sum *vt* to kiss lovingly, kiss tenderly

exoss·ō -āre *vt* to bone, take the bones out of

exostr·a -ae *f* movable stage; **in exostra** in public

exōs·us -a -um *adj* hating, detesting; hated, detested

exōtic·us -a -um *adj* foreign, exotic

expall·escō -escĕre -ŭī *vt* to turn pale at, dread; *vi* to turn pale

expalliāt·us -a -um *adj* robbed of one's cloak

expalp·ō -āre *vt* to coax out

ex·pandō -pandĕre -pandī -pansum *vt* to spread out, unfold, expand

expătr·ō -āre *vt* to waste, squander

expav·escō -escĕre -ŭī *vt* to panic at; *vi* to panic

expect- = **exspect-**

expecŭliāt·us -a -um *adj* stripped of property

exped·iō -īre -ĭī or **-īvī -ītum** *vt* to unfetter, extricate, disentangle; to get out, get ready; to clear for action; to clear (*roads of obstacles*); to free, extricate (*from troubles*); to put in order, arrange, settle, adjust, set right; to explain, unfold, clear up, disclose, recount, relate; **expedit** *v impers* it is expedient, useful, advantageous

expedītē *adv* without obstacles, without difficulty, quickly, promptly

expedĭtĭ·ō -ōnis *f* expedition, campaign, special mission

expedīt·us -a -um *adj* unencumbered, unhampered, unobstructed; (*mil*) lightly equipped; ready, prompt; ready at hand, convenient; **in expedito habere** to have at hand

ex·pellō -pellĕre -pŭlī -pulsum *vt* to drive out, eject, expel; to disown

ex·pendō -pendĕre -pendī -pensum *vt* to weigh out; to pay out, pay down, lay out, expend; to rate, estimate; to ponder, consider; to pay (*penalty*)

expens·us -a -um *adj* paid out, spent; *n* payment, expenditure

expergē·faciō -facĕre -fēcī -factum *vt* to awaken, wake up; to arouse, excite

exper·giscor -giscī -rectus sum *vi* to wake up; to be alert

expergō -gĕre -ī -ītum *vt* to awaken, wake up

experi·ens -entis *adj* enterprising, active; (with *genit*) ready to undergo

experientĭ·a -ae *f* test, trial, experiment; experience, practice; effort

experiment·um -ī *n* test, experiment, proof; experience

exper·ior -īrī -tus sum *vt* to test, try, prove; to experience, endure, find out; to try to do, attempt; to measure strength with; *vi* to go to court

experrectus *pp* of **expergiscor**

exper·s -tis *adj* (with *genit*) having no share in, devoid of, free from, without

expert·us -a -um *pp* of **experior;**

adj tried, proved, tested; (with *genit*) experienced in

expetess·ō -ĕre *vt* to desire, long for

expĕt·ō -ĕre -īvī or **-ĭī -ītum** *vt* to ask for, demand; to aim at, head for; to desire, long for, wish; *vi* (with **in** + *acc*) to befall; to fall upon, assail

expiātĭ·ō -ōnis *f* expiation, atonement; satisfaction

expictus *pp* of **expingo**

expĭlātĭ·ō -ōnis *f* pillaging, plundering, ransacking

expīlāt·or -ōris *m* plunderer, robber

expīl·ō -āre *vt* to pillage, plunder, rob, ransack; to plagiarize

ex·pingō -pingĕre -pinxī -pictum *vt* to paint up; to depict; to paint true to life

expĭ·ō -āre *vt* to purify, cleanse ritually; to atone for, expiate; to avert (*curse, bad omen*)

expīrō see **exspiro**

expisc·or -ārī -ātus sum *vt* to fish for (*information*), ferret out, try to find out

explānātē *adv* plainly, clearly, distinctly

explānātĭ·ō -ōnis *f* explanation; clear pronunciation

explānāt·or -ōris *m* explainer; interpreter

explānāt·us -a -um *adj* plain, distinct

explān·ō -āre *vt* to explain, make clear; to pronounce clearly

ex·plaudō -plaudĕre -plausī -plausum *vt* to boo at, hiss at; to reject

explēment·um -ī *n* filling, stuffing

ex·plēō -ēre -ēvī -ētum *vt* to fill out, fill up; to complete; to satisfy (*desires*); to make good, repair (*losses*); to fulfill, perform, accomplish, discharge

explētĭ·ō -ōnis *f* satisfying

explēt·us -a -um *adj* full, complete, perfect

explicātē *adv* clearly, plainly

explicātĭ·ō -ōnis *f* unfolding, uncoiling; analysis; interpretation

explicāt·or -ōris *m* or **explicātr·ix -īcis** *f* explainer

explicāt·us -a -um *adj* pláin, clearcut

explicāt·us -ūs *m* unfolding; explanation, interpretation

explicĭt·us -a -um *adj* disentangled; simple, easy

explic·ō -āre -āvī or **-ŭī -ātum** or **-ĭtum** *vt* to unfold, unroll; to spread out; to loosen, undo; (*mil*) to exceed, deploy; to set free, release; to set in order, arrange, adjust, settle; to set forth, exhibit, explain

ex·plōdō or **ex·plaudō -plōdĕre -lōsī -plōsum** *vt* to drive off by clapping; to boo (*off the stage*); to disapprove, discredit

explōrātē *adv* after careful examination; for sure, for certain

explōrātĭ·ō -ōnis *f* exploration, examination

explōrāt·or -ōris *m* scout, spy

explōrāt·us -a -um *adj* sure, certain

explōr·ō -āre *vt* to explore, investigate; (mil) to reconnoiter; to probe, search; to test, try, try out

explōsĭ·ō -ōnis *f* booing (*of an actor*)

expol·ĭō -īre -īvī or **-ĭī -ītum** *vt* to polish; (fig) to polish, refine, adorn

expolītĭ·ō -ōnis *f* polishing, finishing off, embellishing

expolīt·us -a -um *adj* polished, lustrous; refined

ex·pōnō -pōnĕre -posŭī -posĭtum or **-postum** *vt* to put out; to expose, abandon; to expose, lay open; to reveal, publish; to exhibit, relate, explain; to offer, tender; to set on shore, disembark, land

expor·rĭgō -rigĕre -rexī -rectum *vt* to stretch out, spread, spread out; **exporge frontem** (coll) smooth out your brow, quit frowning

exportātĭ·ō -ōnis *f* exportation

export·ō -āre *vt* to carry out; to export

ex·poscō -poscĕre -poposcī *vt* to demand, beg, insist upon; to demand the surrender of

expositīcĭ·us -a -um *adj* foundling

expositĭ·ō -ōnis *f* exposing; (rhet) narration, explanation (*of details of a case*)

exposĭt·us -a -um *pp* of **expono**; *adj* accessible; accessible, affable

expostulātĭ·ō -ōnis *f* insistent demand; complaint

expostŭl·ō -āre *vt* to demand, insist on; to complain of; (with **cum** + *abl* of person) to complain of (*something*) to (*someone*); *vi* to lodge a complaint; (with **cum** + *abl*) to lodge a complaint with

expostus *pp* of **expono**

expōtus see **epotus**

express·us -a -um *adj* distinct, clear, express; distinct, real

ex·primō -primĕre -pressī -pressum *vt* to press out, squeeze out; (fig) to squeeze out, wring, extort; to model, form, portray; to represent, imitate, copy, describe, express; to translate; to pronounce, articulate

exprobrātĭ·ō -ōnis *f* reproach

exprŏbr·ō -āre *vt* to reproach, find fault with; (with *dat*) to cast (*something*) up to, put the blame for (*something*) on; *vi* (with *dat*) to complain to

ex·prōmō -prōmĕre -prompsī -promptum *vt* to bring out, fetch out; to give vent to; to disclose, display, exhibit; to give utterance to, utter, express, state

expugnābĭl·is -e *adj* vulnerable to attack, pregnable

expugnācĭ·or -us *adj* more potent

expugnātĭ·ō -ōnis *f* assault; (with *genit*) assault on

expugnāt·or -ōris *m* attacker; **expugnator pudicitiae** assailant

expugn·ō -āre *vt* to assault, storm; to conquer (*persons*) in war; (fig) to conquer, overcome; (fig) to achieve, accomplish; (fig) to wrest, extort

expulsĭ·ō -ōnis *f* expulsion

expuls·ō -āre *vt* to drive out, expel

expuls·or -ōris *m* expeller

expulsus *pp* of **expello**

expultr·ix -īcis *f* expeller (*female*)

ex·pungō -pungĕre -punxī -punctum *vt* to expunge; to cancel; to remove

expurgātĭ·ō -ōnis *f* justification, excuse

expurg·ō -āre *vt* to cleanse, purify; to cure; to vindicate, excuse, justify

expūtescō·ō -ĕre *vi* to rot away

expūt·ō -āre *vt* to prune, lop off; to consider; to comprehend

ex·quīrō -quīrĕre -quīsīvī -quīsītum *vt* to investigate, scrutinize; to search for, look for; to ransack; to devise

exquīsītē *adv* carefully, accurately; exquisitely

exquīsīt·us -a -um *pp* of **exquiro**; *adj* carefully considered, choice, exquisite

exrādīcĭtus *adv* from the very roots

exsaev·ĭō -īre *vi* to cease raging, calm down

exsangu·is -e *adj* bloodless; pale; feeble; causing paleness

ex·sarcĭō or **ex·sercĭō -sarcīre — -sartum** *vt* to patch up; (fig) to repair

exsatĭ·ō -āre *vt* to satiate, satisfy fully, glut

exsaturābĭl·is -e *adj* appeasable

exsatūr·ō -āre *vt* to satiate, satisfy completely

exsce- = **esce**

ex·scindō -scindĕre -scĭdī -scissum *vt* to annihilate, destroy

exscrĕ·ō -āre *vt* to cough up, spit out

ex·scrībō -scrībĕre -scripsī -scriptum *vt* to write down; to write out in full; to copy; (fig) to copy, take after, resemble

exsculp·ō -ĕre -sī -tum *vt* to carve out; to scratch out, erase; (fig) to extort

exsĕc·ō or **exsĭc·ō -āre -ŭī -tum** *vt* to cut out, cut away, cut off; to castrate; to deduct

exsecrābĭl·is -e *adj* accursed; bitter, merciless, deadly; execrating, cursing

exsecrātĭ·ō -ōnis *f* curse, execration; solemn oath

exsecrāt·us -a -um *adj* accursed, detestable

exsĕcr·or -ārī -ātus sum *vt* to curse, execrate; *vi* to take a solemn oath

exsectĭ·ō -ōnis *f* cutting out

exsecūtǐ·ō -ōnis *f* execution, performance; discussion

exsecūtus *pp* of exsequor

exsequǐ·ae -ārum *f pl* funeral procession, funeral rites

exsequǐāl·is -e *adj* funeral; **carmina exsequialia** dirges

ex·sěquor -sěquī -secūtus sum *vt* to follow out; to accompany to the grave; to perform, execute, accomplish, carry out; to follow up, investigate: to pursue, go after; to avenge, punish; to say, tell, describe, relate

exsěr·ō -ěre -ǔī -tum *vt* to untie, disconnect; to stretch out (*one's arms*); to stick out (*the tongue in disdain*); to bare, uncover

exsert·ō -āre *vt* to keep on stretching or sticking out

exsertus *pp* of exsero; *adj* uncovered, bare; protruding

exsǐbǐl·ō -āre *vt* to hiss off the stage

exsiccāt·us -a -um *adj* dry, uninteresting

exsicc·ō -āre *vt* to dry up; to drain dry

exsǐcō see exseco

exsign·ō -āre *vt* to mark down exactly, write down in detail

ex·silǐō -silǐre -silǔī *vi* to jump out, leap up; to start; **exsilire gaudǐo** to jump for joy

exsil·ǐum -ǐī or **-ǐ** *n* exile, banishment (*voluntary or involuntary*); place of exile

ex·sistō -sistěre -stǐtī -stǐtum *vi* to come out, come forth; to appear, emerge; to exist, be; to arise, proceed; to turn into, become; to be visible

ex·solvō -solvěre -solvī -solūtum *vt* to loosen, untie; to release, free, set free; to discharge, pay; to keep, fulfill; to satisfy (*hunger*); to break open, wound; to solve, explain; to throw off, get rid of; to repay, requite; to give out (*awards, punishment*)

exsomn·is -e *adj* sleepless

exsorb·ěō -ēre -ǔī *vt* to suck up, drain; to drain, exhaust; to grasp at eagerly, welcome

exsor·s -tis *adj* without lots; chosen specially; (with *genit*) having no share in, free from

exspatǐ·or -ārī -ātus sum *vi* to go off course; to digress

exspectābǐl·is -e *adj* expected, anticipated

exspectātǐ·ō -ōnis *f* expectation, suspense; **exspectationem facere** to cause suspense

exspectāt·us -a -um *adj* expected, awaited, desired

exspect·ō -āre *vt* to await, wait for, look out for; to hope for, long for, anticipate

ex·spergō -spergěre — -spersum *vt* to sprinkle, scatter

exspēs *adj* hopeless, forlorn; (with *genit*) without hope of

exspīrātǐ·ō -ōnis *f* breathing out, exhalation

exspīr·ō -āre or **expīr·ō -āre** *vt* to breathe out, exhale, emit; *vi* to expire, breathe one's last; (fig) to come to an end, cease

exsplend·escō -escěre -ǔī *vi* to glitter, shine

exspolǐ·ō -āre *vt* to strip; to pillage

es·spǔō -spuěre -spǔī -spūtum *vt* to spit out; (fig) to banish (*e.g., worries*)

exstern·ō -āre *vt* to startle, scare; to terrify; to stampede (*horses*)

exstill·ō -āre *vi* to drop, trickle out; to melt

exstimulāt·or -ōris *m* instigator

exstimǔl·ō -āre *vt* to instigate, goad on

exstinctǐ·ō -ōnis *f* extinction

exstinct·or -ōris *m* extinguisher; suppressor; destroyer

ex·stinguō -stinguěre -stinxī -stinctum *vt* to extinguish, put out; to destroy, kill; to abolish, annul; **exstingui** to die, die out; to be forgotten

exstirp·ō -āre *vt* to extirpate, root out, eradicate

exst·ō -āre *vi* to stand out, protrude, project; to stand out, be prominent, be conspicuous; to be visible; to appear; to exist, be extant

exstructǐ·ō -ōnis *f* erection

ex·strǔō -struěre -struxī -structum *vt* to pile up, heap up; to build, erect

exsuct·us -a -um *pp* of **exsugo**; *adj* dried up

exsūd·ō -āre *vt* to sweat; (fig) to sweat out, sweat over; *vi* to pour out

ex·sūgō -sūgěre -suxī -suctum *vt* to suck out

exs·ul or **ex·ul -ǔlis** *m* or *f* exile, refugee

exsǔl·ō -āre *vi* to be an exile, be a refugee

exsultātǐ·ō -ōnis *f* exultation, jumping for joy

exsultim *adv* friskily

exsult·ō or **exult·ō -āre** *vi* to jump up; to frisk about; (of horses) to rear, prance; to exult, rejoice, jump for joy; to revel, run riot; to boast; (of speech) to range freely

exsuperābǐl·is -e *adj* climbable; superable

exsuperantǐ·a -ae *f* superiority

exsupěr·ō -āre *vt* to surmount; to exceed, surpass; to overpower; *vi* to rise; (of flames) to shoot up; to be superior, excel, be conspicuous, prevail

exsurd·ō -āre *vt* to deafen; (fig) to dull

ex·surgō -surgěre -surrexī *vi* to get up, rise, stand up; (fig) to rise, recover strength; **foras exsurgere** to get up and go out

exsuscǐt·ō -āre *vt* to rouse from sleep; to fan (*fire*); to excite, stir up

ext·a -ōrum *n pl* vital organs (*of sacrificial animals*)

extāb·escō -escĕre -ŭī *vi* to waste away, pine away; to disappear

extār·is -e *adj* used for cooking the sacrificial victim; sacrificial

extemplō or **extempŭlō** *adv* immediately, right away; on the spur of the moment

ex·tendō -tendĕre -tendī -tentum or **-tensum** *vt* to stretch out, spread out, extend; to enlarge, increase; to widen, broaden; to prolong, continue; to pass, spend; to exert, strain; **extendī** to stretch out, extend; **labellum extendere** to pout

extent·ō -āre *vt* to exert, strain

extent·us -a -um *pp* of **extendo**; *adj* extensive, wide; **extentis itineribus** by forced marches

extenuāti·ō -ōnis *f* extenuation; thinning out

extenuāt·us -a -um *adj* thinned, reduced; trifling; weak, faint

extenŭ·ō -āre *vt* to thin out; to lessen, diminish, extenuate, detract from

exter or **extĕr·us -a -um** *adj* external, outward; foreign, strange

exterĕbr·ō -āre *vt* to bore out; to extort

ex·tergĕō -tergēre -tersī -tersum *vt* to wipe out, wipe clean; (fig) to wipe out, plunder

exterǐ·or -us *adj* outer, exterior

exterǐus *adv* on the outside

extermĭn·ō -āre *vt* to drive out, banish; to put aside, put away, remove

extern·us -a -um *adj* external, outward; foreign, strange; *m* foreigner, stranger, foreign enemy; *n pl* foreign goods

ex·tĕrō -terĕre -trīvī -trītum *vt* to rub out, wear away; (fig) to crush

exterr·ĕō -ēre -ŭī -ĭtum *vt* to frighten, terrify

extersus *pp* of **extergeo**

extĕrus see **exter**

extex·ō -ĕre *vt* to unweave; (fig) to cheat

extim·escō -escĕre -ŭī *vt* to become terribly afraid of, dread; *vi* to become afraid

extĭm·us -a -um *adj* outermost, farthest, most remote

extisp·ex -ĭcis *m* soothsayer, diviner (*who makes predictions by inspecting the entrails of animals*)

extoll·ō -ĕre *vt* to lift up; to erect; to postpone; to extol, praise; to raise, exalt; to beautify; **animos extollere** to raise the morale

ex·torquĕō -torquēre -torsī -tortum *vt* to wrench, wrest; to dislocate; to extort

extorr·is -e *adj* driven out of one's country, banished, exiled

extort·or -ōris *m* extorter

extortus *pp* of **extorqueo**; *adj* deformed

extrā *adv* outside, on the outside; **extra quam** except in the case that; **extra quam sī** unless; *prep* (with *acc*) outside, outside of, beyond; apart from, aside from; contrary to; except, besides; without; **extra jocum** all joking aside

ex·trāhō -trahĕre -traxī -tractum *vt* to pull out, drag out; to drag out, prolong; to waste (*time*); to extricate, release, rescue; to remove

extrānĕ·us -a -um *adj* extraneous, external, irrevelant, strange; *m* stranger

extrāordināri·us -a -um *adj* extraordinary

extrārǐ·us -a -um *adj* outward, external; unrelated (*by family ties*)

extrēm·a -ōrum *n pl* end (*e.g., of a marching column, of strip of land, of life*)

extrēmit·ās -ātis *f* extremity, end

extrēmō *adv* finally, at last

extrēmum *adv* finally, at last; for the last time

extrēm·us -a -um *adj* extreme, outermost, on the end; latest, last; (of degree) utmost, extreme; lowest, meanest; **extrema aetas** advanced old age; **extrema cauda** tip of the tail; **extremā lineā amare** to love at a distance; **extrema manus** final touches; **extremis digitis attingere** to touch lightly; to touch lightly on; to hold tenderly; **extremus ignis** flickering flame; **in extremo libro secundo** at the end of the second book; *n* end; extremity; **ad extremum** at last; at the end; utterly; **in extremo** in mortal danger, in a crisis

extrīc·ō -āre or **extrīc·or -ārī -ātus sum** *vt* to extricate; to clear up; to obtain with difficulty

extrīnsĕcus *adv* from outside, from abroad; on the inside, outside

extrītus *pp* of **extero**

ex·trūdō -trūdĕre -trūsī -trūsum *vt* to thrust out, drive out; to get rid of

extum·ĕō -ēre *vi* to swell up

ex·tundō -tundĕre -tūdī -tūsum *vt* to beat out, hammer out; to fashion; to devise; to extort

exturb·ō -āre *vt* to drive out, chase out, drive away; to divorce; to knock out

exūbĕr·ō -āre *vi* to grow luxuriantly; to abound

exulcĕr·ō -āre *vt* to make sore, aggravate; to exasperate

exulŭl·ō -āre *vt* to invoke with cries; *vi* to howl

exunctus *pp* of **exungo**

exund·ō -āre *vi* to overflow; **in lĭtora exundare** to wash up on the shores

ex·ungō -ungĕre — -unctum *vt* to oil down, rub with oil

ex·ŭŏ -ŭĕre -ŭī -ūtum vt to take off, pull off; to shake off; to unclothe; to strip, deprive; to cast aside, cast off; to bare

exurg·ĕŏ -ēre vt to squeeze out

ex·ūrŏ -ūrĕre -ussī -ustum vt to burn out, burn up; to dry up; to consume, destroy; (fig) to inflame

exustĭ·ŏ -ōnis f conflagration

exustus pp of **exuro**

exūtus pp of **exuo**

exuvĭ·ae -ārum f pl clothing; equipment; arms; hide; slough; booty, spoils

F

fab·a -ae f bean

fabāl·is -e adj bean; **stipulae fabales** bean stalks

fābell·a -ae f short story; fable, tale; short play

fab·er -ra -rum adj skilled; m craftsman; smith; carpenter; (mil) engineer; **faber ferrarius** blacksmith; **faber tignarius** carpenter

Fab·ius -iī or **-ī** m Quintus Fabius Maximus Cunctator, elected consul five times and appointed dictator in 217 B.C. to conduct the war against Hannibal (d. 203 B.C.); Quintus Fabius Pictor, first Roman historian to use prose (fl 225 B.C.)

fabrē adv skillfully

fabrĕ·facĭŏ -facĕre -fēcī -factum vt to build, make; to forge

fabrĭc·a -ae f trade, industry; workshop, factory; piece of work, structure, production; **fabricam fingere** (with **ad** + acc) (coll) to pull a trick on

fabricātĭ·ŏ -ōnis f structure, construction

fabricāt·or -ōris m builder, architect, producer, creator

fabrĭc·or -ārī -ātus sum or **fabrĭc·ō -āre** vt to build, construct, produce, forge; to prepare, form; to coin (words)

fabrīl·is -e adj craftman's, carpenter's, sculptor's; n pl tools

fābŭl·a -ae f story; tale; talk, conversation, conversation piece; small talk; affair, matter, concern; myth, legend; drama, play; dramatic poem; **fabulae!** (coll) baloney!; **lupus in fabula!** (coll) speak of the devil!

fābŭlār·is -e adj legendary

fābŭl·or -ārī -ātus sum vt to say, invent; vi to talk, chat, gossip

fābŭlōs·us -a -um adj legendary

fabŭl·us -ī m small bean

facess·ŏ -ĕre -īvī -ītum vt to do eagerly, perform, accomplish; to bring on, cause, create; **negotium alicui facessere** to cause someone trouble; vi to go away, depart

facētē adv facetiously, humorously, wittily, brilliantly

facētĭ·ae -ārum f pl clever thing, clever talk, witticism, humor

facēt·us -a -um adj witty, humorous; fine, polite; elegant; brilliant

facĭ·ēs -ēī f make, form, shape; face, look; look, appearance; nature, character; external appearance, pretense, pretext

facĭl·is -e adj easy; nimble; suitable, convenient; ready, quick; easy, easygoing, good-natured; favorable, prosperous; gentle (breeze); easilyborne, slight (loss); **ex** or **e facili** easily; **in facili esse** to be easy; **facilis victu** prosperous, well-off, well-to-do

facĭle adv easily, without trouble; unquestionably, by far, far; quite, fully; promptly, readily, willingly; pleasantly, well; **non facile** hardly

facĭlĭt·ās -ātis f facility, easiness, ease; readiness; fluency; suitability; good nature, affability, courteousness; levity

facinorōs·us or **facinerōs·us -a -um** adj & m criminal

facĭn·us -ŏris n deed, action; crime, villany

facĭŏ facĕre fēcī factum (**faxim = fēcĕrim; faxō = fēcĕrō**) vt to make, fashion, frame, create, build, erect; to do, perform; to make, produce, compose; to bring about, cause, occasion; to acquire, gain, get, accumulate; to incur, suffer; to render, grant, give, confer; to grant, admit; to assume, suppose; to assert, say, represent, depict; to choose, appoint; to follow, practice; to regard, prize, value; **certiorem facere** to inform; **copiam facere** to afford the opportunity; **fac ita esse** suppose it were so, granted that it is so; **fidem facere** to give one's word; **pecuniam facere** or **stipendium facere** to make money, earn money; **promissum facere** to fulfill a promise; **sacra facere** to sacrifice; **verbum facere** to speak; **viam facere** (with dat) to make way for; vi to do, act; to take part, take sides; (with dat or with **ad** + acc) to be satisfactory for, be fit for, do for

factĕon = faciendum

factĭ·ŏ -ōnis f doing; making; party, faction; partisanship; company, social set, association, class; oligarchy; (with genit) right to make (e.g., a will)

factiōs·us -a -um adj busy; partisan; oligarchical; factious, revolutionary, seditious

factĭt·ō -āre vt to keep doing or making; to practice (e.g., trade); (with double acc) to declare (someone) to be (e.g., heir)

fact·or -ōris m (in playing ball) batter

fact·us -a -um pp of facio; n deed, act; accomplishment, exploit

facŭl·a -ae f little torch

facult·ās -ātis f opportunity, means; feasibility; ability, capacity, mental resources; material resources, means, supplies, abundance

fācundē adv eloquently

fācundĭ·a -ae f eloquence

fācundĭt·ās -ātis f eloquence

fācund·us -a -um adj eloquent, fluent

faecĕ·us -a -um adj morally impure, morally rotten

faecŭl·a -ae f wine lees

faenĕbr·is -e adj of interest, regarding interest; **res faenebris** indebtedness

faenerātĭ·ō -ōnis f lending at interest, investment

faenerātō adv with interest

faenerāt·or -ōris m money lender, investor, capitalist

faenĕr·or -ārī -ātus sum or **faenĕr·ō -āre** vt to lend at interest; to invest; to ruin through high interest rates; vi to bring interest, bring profit; **faeneratum beneficium** (fig) a favor richly repaid

faenĕ·us -a -um adj made of hay

faenīl·ia -ĭum n pl hayloft

faenisĕc·a -ae m peasant

faen·um or **fēn·um -ī** n hay; **faenum habet in cornu** (fig) he's crazy

faen·us or **fēn·us -ōris** n interest; debt (as result of heavy interest); capital; (fig) profit, gain, advantage

faenuscŭl·um or **fēnuscŭl·um -ī** n a little interest

fae·x -cis f dregs, sediments, grounds, lees; (fig) dregs

fāginĕ·us or **fāgĭn·us** or **fāgĕ·us -a -um** adj beech

fāg·us -ī f beech tree

fal·a or **phal·a -ae** f movable wooden siege tower; scaffold

falāric·a or **phalāric·a -ae** f incendiary missile

falcār·ius -ĭī or **-ī** m sickle maker

falcāt·us -a -um adj fitted with scythes, scythed; sickle-shaped, curved

falcĭf·er -ĕra -ĕrum adj scythebearing

Falern·us -a -um adj Falernian; **ager Falernus** district in N. Campania, famous for its wine; n Falernian wine

Falisc·ī -ōrum m pl a people of S.E. Etruria

fallācĭ·a -ae f deception, deceit, trick

fallācĭter adv deceptively, deceitfully, fallaciously

fall·ax -ācis adj deceptive, deceitful, fallacious

fallō fallĕre fefellī falsum vt to cause to fall, trip; to lead into error; to deceive, trick, dupe, cheat; to fail to live up to, disappoint; to wile away; to escape the notice of, slip by; **fidem fallere** to break one's word; **me fallit** I do not know; **nisi** or **ni fallor** unless I'm mistaken; **opinionem fallere** (with genit) to fail to live up to the expectations of

falsē adv falsely

falsidĭc·us -a -um adj speaking falsely, lying

falsific·us -a -um adj acting dishonestly

falsijūrĭ·us -a -um adj swearing falsely

falsilŏqu·us -a -um adj lying

falsimōnĭ·a -ae f trick

falsipār·ens -entis adj bastard

falsō adv mistakenly, wrongly, erroneously; falsely, deceitfully, untruly

fals·us -a -um pp of fallo; adj mistaken, wrong, erroneous; false, untrue; lying, deceitful; vain, groundless, empty; spurious, sham, fictitious; n error; lying, perjury; lie, untruth, falsehood

fal·x -cis f sickle; pruning hook, pruning knife; (mil) hook for pulling down walls

fām·a -ae f talk, rumor, report; saying, tradition; reputation; fame, renown, glory, name; infamy, notoriety; public opinion

famēlic·us -a -um adj famished, starved

fam·ēs -is f hunger, starvation; poverty; famine; greed; (rhet) bald style, poverty of expression

fāmigerātĭ·ō -ōnis f rumor

fāmigerāt·or -ōris m gossip, rumormonger

famĭlĭ·a -ae or **-ās** f household slaves, domestics; household; house, family; family estate; fraternity; sect, school; **familiam ducere** to be the head of a sect; **pater familias** head of the household

familiār·is -e adj domestic, family, household; familiar, intimate; (in augury) one's own (part of the sacrificial animal); m servant, slave; acquaintance, friend, companion

familiārĭt·ās -ātis f familiarity, intimacy; association, friendship

familiārĭter adv on friendly terms

fāmōs·us -a -um adj much talked of; famous, renowned; infamous, notorious; slanderous, libelous; **carmen famosum** lampoon

famŭl·a -ae f slave, maid, maidservant

famulār·is -e adj of slaves, of servants

famulāt·us -ūs m servitude, slavery

famŭl·or -ārī -ātus sum vi to be a slave; (with dat) to serve

famŭl·us -a -um adj serviceable; m servant, attendant

fānătĭc·us -a -um adj fanatic, enthusiastic, inspired; wild, frantic

fān·um -ī n shrine, sanctuary, temple

fār farris n spelt; coarse meal, grits; sacrificial meal; bread; dog biscuit; n pl grain

far·ciō -cīre -sī -tum vt to stuff, cram

farfăr·us or **farfĕr·us -ī** m coltsfoot (plant)

farīn·a -ae f flour; powder; character, quality

farrāg·ō -ĭnis f mash (for cattle); medley, hodgepodge

farrāt·us -a -um adj filled with grain; made with grain

fart·is -is f stuffing, filling, mincemeat; **fartim facere ex hostibus** to make mincemeat of the enemy

fart·or -ōris m fattener of fowls

fartus pp of **farcio**

fās (indecl) n divine law; sacred duty; divine will, fate; right; **fas est** it is right, it is lawful, it is permitted

fascĭ·a -ae f bandage, swathe; girth; fillet; wisp of cloud

fasciātim adv in bundles

fascĭcŭl·us -ī m small bundle

fascĭn·ō -āre vt to cast an evil eye on, bewitch, jinx; to envy

fascĭn·um -ī n or **fascĭn·us -ī** m evil eye; jinx; witchcraft; charm, amulet; penis

fasciŏl·a -ae f small bandage

fasc·is -is m bundle, pack, parcel, fagot; load, burden; baggage; m pl fasces (bundle of rods and ax, carried before high magistrates by lictors as symbols of authority); high office, supreme power, consulship

fassus pp of **fateor**

fast·ī -ōrum m pl calendar, almanac; annals; register of higher magistrates

fastīd·ĭō -īre -īvī or **-ĭī -ītum** vt to disdain, despise, snub, turn up the nose at; vi to feel disgust, feel squeamish; to be snobbish, be haughty

fastīdĭōsē adv fastidiously, squeamishly; disdainfully, snobbishly

fastīdĭōs·us -a -um adj fastidious, squeamish; disdainful, snobbish; refined, delicate

fastīd·ĭum -ĭī or **-ī** n fastidiousness, squeamishness, distaste, disgust, loathing; snobbishness, haughtiness, contempt

fastīgātē adv sloped (like a gable), sloping up, sloping down

fastīgāt·us -a -um adj rising to a point; sloping down

fastīg·ĭum -ĭī or **-ī** n gable; pediment; roof, ceiling; slope; height, elevation, top, edge; depth, depression; finish, completion; rank, dignity; main point, heading, highlight (of story, etc.)

fast·us -a -um adj legal (day); **dies fastus** court day

fast·us -ūs m disdain, contempt, arrogance; m pl brash deeds; calendar

fātāl·is -e adj fateful, destined, preordained; fatal, deadly; **deae fatales** the Fates

fātālĭter adv according to fate, by fate

fatĕor fatērī fassus sum vt to admit, acknowledge; to disclose, reveal

fātĭcăn·us or **fātĭcĭn·us -a -um** adj prophetic

fātĭdĭc·us -a -um adj prophetic

fātĭf·er -ĕra -ĕrum adj fatal, deadly

fatĭgātĭ·ō -ōnis f fatigue, weariness

fatĭg·ō -āre vt to fatigue, weary, tire; to worry, torment, harass, wear down; to importune, pray to constantly

fātĭlŏqu·a -ae f prophetess

fatisc·ō -ĕre or **fatisc·or -ī** vi to split, crack, give way; (fig) to crack, break down, collapse from exhaustion

fatuĭt·ās -ātis f silliness

fāt·um -ī n divine utterance, oracle; fate, destiny, doom; calamity, mishap, ruin; death; **ad fata novissima** to the last; **fato obire** to meet death, die; **fatum proferre** to prolong life

fātus pp of **for**

fatŭ·us -a -um adj silly, foolish; clumsy; m fool

fauc·ēs -ĭum f pl upper part of the throat, throat, gullet; strait, channel; pass, defile, gorge; (fig) jaws; **fauces premere** (with genit) to choke, throttle

Faun·us -ī m mythical king of Latium, father of Latinus, and worshiped as the Italian Pan; m pl Fauns, woodland spirits

faustē adv favorably, auspiciously

faustĭt·ās -ātis f fertility; good fortune, happiness

Faustŭl·us -ī m shepherd who raised Romulus and Remus

faust·us -a -um adj auspicious, favorable, fortunate, lucky

faut·or or **favĭt·or -ōris** m promoter, patron, supporter, fan

fautr·ix -ĭcis f patroness, protectress

favĕ·a -ae f favorite girl, pet slave girl

favĕō favēre fāvī fautum vi (with dat) to be favorable to, favor, support, side with; (with inf) to be eager to; **favere linguis** or **favere ore** to observe a reverent silence

favill·a -ae f ashes, embers; (fig) spark, beginning

favĭtor see **fautor**

Favŏn·ius -ĭī or **-ī** m west wind (also called Zephyrus)

fav·or -ōris *m* favor, support; applause; appreciation (*shown by applause*)

favōrābil·is -e *adj* popular

fav·us -ī *m* honeycomb

fa·x -cis *f* torch; wedding torch; wedding; funeral torch; funeral; meteor, shooting star, comet; firebrand; fire, flame; guiding light; instigator; flame of love; stimulus, incitement; cause of ruin, destruction; **dicendi faces** fiery eloquence; **dolorum faces** pangs of grief

faxim see **facio**

febrīcul·a -ae *f* slight fever

febr·is -is *f* fever

Februă·lia -ōrum *n pl* Roman festival of purification and expiation, celebrated on February 15th

Februări·us -a -um *adj* & *m* February

febru·um -ī *n* purgation, purification

fēcundĭt·ās -ātis *f* fertility, fruitfulness; (rhet) overstatement

fēcund·ō -āre *vt* to fertilize

fēcund·us -a -um *adj* fertile, fruitful; abundant, rich; fertilizing; (with *genit* or *abl*) rich in, abounding in

fe·l -llis *n* gallbladder; gall, bile; bitterness, animosity; poison

fēl·ēs -is *f* cat

fēlīcĭt·ās -ātis *f* fertility; luck, good fortune, piece of luck; felicity, happiness

fēlīcĭter *adv* fruitfully, abundantly; favorably, auspiciously; luckily; happily; successfully

fēl·ix -īcis *adj* fruit-bearing; fruitful, fertile; favorable, auspicious; lucky; happy; successful

fēmell·a -ae *f* girl

fēmĭn·a -ae *f* female; woman

fēminăt·us -a -um *adj* effeminate

fēminĕ·us -a -um *adj* woman's; effeminate, unmanly

fēminīn·us -a -um *adj* (gram) feminine

fem·ur -ŏris or **-ĭnis** *n* thigh

fēn- = faen-

fenestr·a -ae *f* window; hole (*for earrings*); (fig) opening, opportunity; (mil) breach (*in a wall*)

fer·a -ae *f* wild beast, wild animal

ferācĭus *adv* more fruitfully

Fērāl·ia -ium *n pl* festival of the dead, celebrated on February 17th or 21st

fērāl·is -e *adj* funeral; deadly, fatal; gloomy, dismal

fer·ax -ācis *adj* fertile, fruitful; (with *genit*) productive of

fercŭl·um -ī *n* food tray; dish, course; litter for carrying spoils in a victory parade or cult images in religious processions

fercŭl·us -ī *m* litter bearer

ferē or **fermē** *adv* approximately, nearly, almost, about, just about; generally, as a rule, usually; (with negatives) practically; **nemo fere** practically no one

ferentār·ius -iī or **-ī** *m* light-armed soldier; eager helper

Feretr·ius -iī or **-ī** *m* epithet of Jupiter

ferētr·um -ī *n* litter, bier

fēri·ae -ārum *f pl* holidays, vacation; (fig) leisure

fēriăt·us -a -um *adj* vacationing, taking it easy, relaxing, taking time off

ferīn·us -a -um *adj* of wild animals; **caro ferina** venison; *f* game, venison

fer·iō -īre *vt* to strike, hit, shoot, knock; to kill; to slaughter, sacrifice (*an animal*); to coin; (fig) to strike, reach, affect; (fig) to cheat, trick; **cornu ferire** to butt; **foedus ferire** to make a treaty; **securi ferire** to behead; **verba ferire** to coin words

ferĭt·ās -ātis *f* wildness, fierceness

fermē see **fere**

ferment·um -ī *n* yeast; beer; (fig) ferment, provocation, vexation, anger, passion

ferō ferre tulī or **tetŭlī lātum** *vt* to bear, carry; to bear, produce, bring forth; to bear, endure; to lead, drive, conduct, direct; to bring, offer; to receive, acquire, obtain, win; to take by force, carry off, plunder, ravage; to manifest, display, make known, report, relate, say, tell; to propose, bring forward; to allow, permit; to cause, create; to set in motion; to call, name; (in accounting) to enter; **aegre ferre** to be annoyed at; **caelo supinas manus ferre** to raise the hands heavenward in prayer; **ferri** to move, rush; to sail; to fly; to flow along; (fig) to be carried away (*e.g., with ambition, greed*); **ferri** or **se ferre** to rush, flee; **iter ferre** to pursue a course; **laudibus ferre** to extol; **legem ferre** to propose a bill; **moleste ferre** to be annoyed at; **pedem ferre** to come, go, move, get going; **prae se ferre** to display, manifest; **se ferre obviam** (with *dat*) to rush to meet; **repulsam ferre** to experience defeat (*at the polls*); **sententiam ferre** to pass judgment; to cast a vote; **signa ferre** (mil) to begin marching; **ventrem ferre** to be pregnant; *vi* to say, e.g., **ut ferunt** as people say, as they say; to allow, permit, e.g., **si occasio tulerit** if occasion permit; to lead, e.g., **iter ad oppidum ferebat** the road led to the town

ferōci·a -ae *f* courage, bravery, spirit; ferocity, barbarity; presumption

ferōcĭt·ās -ātis *f* courage, spirit, fierceness, aggressiveness; ferocity, barbarity; pride, presumption

ferōcĭter *adv* bravely, courageously, aggressively; defiantly; haughtily

Fērōnĭ·a -ae *f* early Italic goddess of groves and fountains, and patroness of ex-slaves

fer·ox -ōcis *adj* brave, intrepid, warlike; defiant; overbearing, haughty, insolent

ferrāment·um -ī *n* tool, implement

ferrārĭ·us -a -um *adj* iron; **faber ferrarius** blacksmith; *m* blacksmith; *f pl* iron mines, iron works

ferrātĭl·is -e *adj* fit to be chained

ferrāt·us -a -um *adj* iron-plated; iron-tipped; in chains; in armor; **calx ferrata** spur; *m pl* soldiers in armor

ferrĕ·us -a -um *adj* iron, made of iron; hardhearted, cruel; firm, unyielding

ferricrepĭn·us -a -um *adj* (coll) clanking chains

ferrīter·ĭum -ĭī or **-ĭ** *n* (coll) brig, jug

ferrītĕr·ī *m* (coll) glutton for punishment

ferritrīb·ax -ācis *adj* (coll) chainsore (*sore from dragging chains*)

ferrūgĭnĕ·us or **ferrūgĭn·us -a -um** *adj* rust-colored, dark, dusky

ferrūg·ō -ĭnis *f* rust; verdigris; dark red; dark color; gloom

ferr·um -ī *n* iron; tool, implement; iron object: sword, dart, arrowhead, ax, plowshare, crowbar, spade, scissors, curling iron; **ferro atque igni** with fire and sword; **ferro decernere** to decide by force of arms

fertĭl·is -e *adj* fertile, fruitful, productive; fertilizing; (with *genit*) productive of

fertilĭt·ās -ātis *f* fertility, fruitfulness

ferŭl·a -ae *f* reed, stalk; rod, whip

fer·us -a -um *adj* wild; uncultivated, untamed; savage, uncivilized; rude, cruel, fierce; wild, desert (*place*); *m* wild beast, wild horse, lion, stag; *f* wild beast

fervē·faciō -facĕre -fēcī -factum *vt* to heat, boil

ferv·ens -entis *adj* seething, burning, hot; (fig) hot, heated, violent, impetuous

ferventer *adv* (fig) heatedly, impetuously

ferv·ĕō -ēre or **ferv·ō -ĕre -ī** *vi* to boil, seethe, steam; to foam; to swarm; to be busy, bustle about; (fig) to burn, glow, rage, rave

fervesc·ō -ĕre *vi* to become boiling hot, begin to boil, grow hot

fervĭd·us -a -um *adj* boiling, seething, hot; fermenting (*grapes*); hot, highly spiced; (fig) hot, fiery, violent, impetuous, hot-blooded

fervō see **ferveo**

ferv·or -ōris *m* heat, boiling heat; boiling; fermenting; fever; raging (*of the sea*); (fig) heat, vehemence, ardor, passion

Fescennĭ·a -ae *f* town in Etruria

Fescennīn·us -a -um *adj* Fescennine, of Fescennia; *m pl* Fescennine verses (*rude form of dramatic dialogue*)

fess·us -a -um *adj* tired, exhausted, worn out

festīnanter *adv* quickly

festīnātĭ·ō -ōnis *f* hurrying, haste, hurry

festīnātō *adv* hurriedly

festīn·ō -āre *vt & vi* to rush, hurry, accelerate; **jussa festinare** to carry out orders promptly

festīn·us -a -um *adj* hasty, quick, speedy

festīvē *adv* gaily; humorously

festīvĭt·ās -ātis *f* gaiety, fun; humor

festīv·us -a -um *adj* holiday, festal; gay, merry; agreeable, pleasing, pretty; humorous

festūc·a -ae *f* stalk; rod with which slaves were tapped when freed

fest·us -a -um *adj* joyous, festive, in holiday mood; *n* holiday; feast; **festum agere** to observe a holiday

fētĭāl·is -is *m* member of a college of priests who performed the ritual in connection with declaring war and making peace

fetĭāl·is -e *adj* negotiating, diplomatic; fetial, of the fetial priests

fetĭd·us -a -um *adj* fetid, stinking

fētūr·a -ae *f* breeding, bearing; offspring, young

fēt·us -a -um *adj* pregnant, breeding; fruitful, teeming, productive

fēt·us -ūs *m* breeding; (of plants) producing; bearing; offspring, young, brood; fruit, produce; (fig) growth, production

fī *interj* (expressing disgust at a bad smell) phew!

fib·er -rī *m* beaver

fibr·a -ae *f* fiber, filament; *f pl* entrails

fībŭl·a -ae *f* clasp, pin, brooch, buckle; brace, clamp

fīcēdŭl·a or **fīcĕdŭl·a -ae** *f* beccafico (*small bird*)

fictē *adv* falsely, fictitiously

fictĭl·is -e *adj* clay, earthen; *n* jar; clay statue; *n pl* earthenware

fictĭ·ō -ōnis *f* forming, formation; disguising; supposition; fiction

fict·or -ōris *m* sculptor, molder, shaper

fictr·ix -īcis *f* maker, creator (*female*)

fict·um -ī *n* falsehood, fiction, pretense

fictūr·a -ae *f* shaping, fashioning

fict·us -a -um *pp* of **fingo**; *adj* false, fictitious; **vox ficta** falsehood

fīcŭl·us -ī *m* little fig

fīculn·us or **fīculnĕ·us -a -um** *adj* of a fig tree

fīc·us -ī or **-ūs** *f* fig; fig tree

fīdēcommiss·um or **fīdeīcommiss·um -ī** *n* trust fund

fidēlĭ·a -ae *f* earthen pot, pail,

bucket; **duo parietes de eadem fidelia dealbare** to whitewash two walls with one pail, to kill two birds with one stone

fidél·is -e *adj* faithful, loyal; trusty, trustworthy, true, sure, safe (*ship, port, advice, etc.*); (with *dat* or **in** + *acc*) faithful to; *m* confidant

fidélit·ās -ātis *f* faithfulness, loyalty, fidelity

fidéliter *adv* faithfully, loyally; securely, certainly

Fidēn·ae -ārum *f pl* ancient town in Latium

fīd·ens -entis *adj* confident; resolute; bold

fīdenter *adv* confidently; resolutely; boldly

fīdenti·a -ae *f* self-confidence, boldness

fid·ēs -ēī *f* trust, faith, reliance, confidence; credence, belief; trustworthiness, conscientiousness, honesty; promise, assurance, word, word of honor; protection, guarantee; promise of protection, safe conduct; (com) credit; confirmation, proof, fulfilment; **de fide mala** in bad faith, dishonestly; **Di vostram fidem!** for heaven's sake! **ex fide bona** in good faith, honestly; **fidem dare** to give one's word, offer a guarantee; **fidem facere** to inspire confidence; **fidem fallere** to break one's word; **fidem habere** (with *dat*) to have confidence in; to convince; **fidem servare** to keep one's word; **pro fidem deum!** for heaven's sake! **res fidesque** capital and credit

fid·ēs -is *f* string (*of a musical instrument*); *f pl* stringed instrument; lyre, lute, zither

fidic·en -inis *m* lutist, lyre player; lyric poet

fidicin·us -a -um *adj* stringed-instrument; *f* lutist, lyre player (*female*)

fidicul·a -ae *f* or **fidicul·ae -ārum** *f pl* small lute

fīdissimē *adv* most faithfully

Fid·ius -iī *or* **-ī** *m* epithet of Jupiter; **medius fidius!** honest to goodness!

fīdō fidēre fīsus sum *vi* (with *dat* or *abl*) to trust, put confidence in

fīdūci·a -ae *f* trust, confidence, reliance; self-confidence; trustworthiness; (law) deposit, pledge, security, mortgage

fīdūciāri·us -a -um *adj* held in trust

fīd·us -a -um *adj* trusty, dependable; certain, sure, safe

figlīn·us or **figulīn·us -a -um** *adj* potter's

fīgō fīgēre fīxī fīxum *vt* to fix, fasten, affix, attach, nail; to drive in; to pierce; to erect, set up; to build; to post up, hang up

figulār·is -e *adj* potter's

figul·us -ī *m* potter; bricklayer

figūr·a -ae *f* figure, shape, form;

phantom, ghost; nature, kind; figure of speech

figūrāt·us -a -um *adj* figurative

figūr·ō -āre *vt* to shape, form, mold, fashion; to train, educate

fīlātim *adv* thread by thread

fīli·a -ae *f* daughter

filicāt·us -a -um *adj* engraved with fern patterns

fīliŏl·a -ae *f* little daughter

fīliŏl·us -ī *m* little son

fīl·ius -iī or **-ī** *m* son; **terrae filius** a nobody

fil·ix -īcis *f* fern

fīl·um -ī *n* thread; fillet; string, cord; wick; figure, shape (*of a woman*); texture, quality, style (*of speech*)

fimbri·ae -ārum *f pl* fringe, border, end

fim·us -ī *m* dung, manure; mire

findō findēre fidī fissum *vt* to split, split in half

fingō fingēre fīnxī fictum *vt* to shape, form; to mold, model (*in clay, stone, etc.*); to arrange, dress, trim; to imagine, suppose, think, conceive; to contrive, invent, pretend, feign; to compose (*poetry*); to disguise (*looks*); to trump up (*charges*); (with double *acc*) to represent as, depict as; **ars fingendi** sculpture; **linguā fingere** to lick; **se fingere** (with **ad** + *acc*) to adapt oneself to; to be subservient to

fīnient·ēs -ium *m pl* horizon

fīn·iō -īre -īvī *or* **-iī -ītum** *vt* to limit; (fig) to set bounds to, limit, restrain; to mark out, fix, determine; to put an end to, finish complete; **finiri** to come to an end, end; *vi* to come to an end; to die

fīn·is -is *m* or *f* boundary, border, limit; end; purpose, aim; extreme limit, summit, highest degree; starting point; goal; death; **fine** (with *genit*) up to, as far as; **finem facere** (with *genit* or *dat*) to put an end to; **quem ad finem** how long, to what extent; *m pl* boundaries, country, territory, land

fīnītē *adv* to a limited degree

fīnitīm·us or **fīnitŭm·us -a -um** *adj* neighboring, bordering; (with *dat*) a bordering upon; **b** (fig) bordering upon, akin to; *m pl* neighbors

fīnit·or -ōris *m* surveyor

fīnīt·us -a -um *adj* limited; (rhet) rhythmical

fīō fĭērī factus sum *vi* to come into being, arise; to be made, become, get; to happen; **fieri non potest quin** it is inevitable that; **fieri potest ut** it is possible that; **ita fit ut** or **quo fit ut** thus it happens that

firmām·en -inis *n* prop, support

firmāment·um -ī *n* prop, support; support, mainstay; main point

firmāt·or -ōris *m* establisher, promoter

firmē adv firmly, steadily

firmit·ās -ātis f firmness, strength; steadfastness, stamina, endurance

firmiter adv firmly, steadily

firmitūd·ō -inis f firmness, strength, durability; (fig) stability, constancy

firm·ō -āre vt to strengthen, fortify, support; to encourage, strengthen, fortify, assure, reinforce; to establish, prove, confirm; to declare, aver

firm·us -a -um adj firm, strong, hardy, stable; (fig) firm, steadfast, trusty, true, faithful, lasting; **firmus ad bellum** toughened for combat

fiscāl·is -e adj fiscal

fiscell·a -ae f small basket

fiscĭn·a -ae f small basket

fisc·us -ī m basket; money box; state treasury; imperial treasury, emperor's privy purse, imperial revenues

fissĭl·is -e adj easy to split; split

fissĭ·ō -ōnis f dividing, splitting

fiss·us -a -um pp of **findo**; adj cloven; n slit, fissure

fistūc·a -ae f mallet

fistŭl·a -ae f pipe, tube; water pipe; hollow stalk or reed; flute; fistula, ulcer

fīsus pp of **fido**

fix·us -a -um pp of **figo**; adj fixed, immovable; permanent

flābellifer·a -ae f female slave who waved a fan

flābell·um -ī n fan

flābĭl·is -e adj of air

flābr·a -ōrum n pl gusts of wind; breezes, winds

flacc·ĕō -ēre vi to be flabby; to lose heart; (of a speech) to get dull

flacc·escō -escĕre -uī vi to become flabby; to wither, droop

flaccĭd·us -a -um adj flabby; languid, feeble

flacc·us -a -um adj flabby

flagell·ō -āre vt to whip

flagell·um -ī n whip; scourge; riding crop; young shoot, sucker; arm (of a polypus); sting (e.g., of conscience)

flāgitātĭ·ō -ōnis f demand

flāgitāt·or -ōris m persistent demander

flāgitiōsē adv shamefully, disgracefully

flāgitiōs·us -a -um adj shameful, disgraceful, profligate

flāgit·ĭum -ĭī or **-ī** n shame, disgrace, scandalous conduct, scandal; rascal, good-for-nothing

flāgit·ō -āre vt to demand; (with double acc or with acc of thing or **ab** + abl of person) to demand (something) from (someone)

flagr·ans -antis adj blazing, flaming, hot; shining, glowing, glittering; ardent, hot, vehement, eager

flagranter adv vehemently, ardently

flagranti·a -ae f blazing, glow; **flagiti flagrantia** utter disgrace

flagritrib·a -ae m (coll) (said of a slave) victim of constant whipping

flagr·ō -āre vi to blaze, be on fire; (with abl) a to glow with, flare up in; b to be the victim of (e.g., envy)

flagr·um -ī n whip

flām·en -ĭnis m flamen (priest of a specific deity); **flamen Diālis** priest of Jupiter

flām·en -ĭnis n gust, gale; breeze

flāmĭnic·a -ae f wife of a flamen

Flāminīn·us -ī m T. Quintus Flamininus (consul of 198 B.C., and conqueror of Philip of Macedon at Cynoscephalae, in Thessaly, in 197 B.C.)

flāmĭn·ĭum -ĭī or **-ī** n office of flamen, priesthood

Flāminĭ·us -a -um adj Flaminian; **via Flaminia** road leading from Rome to Ariminum; m Gaius Flaminius (conqueror of Insubrian Gauls in 223 B.C., builder of the Circus Flaminius and the Flaminian highway in 220 B.C., and casualty in the battle at Lake Trasimenus in 217 B.C.)

flamm·a -ae f flame, fire, blaze; star; torch; flame of passion, fire of love, glow, passion; sweetheart; danger, destruction; **flamma fumo est proxima** where there's smoke there's fire; **flammam concipere** to catch fire

flammār·ĭus -ĭī or **-ī** m maker of bridal veils

flammeŏl·um -ī n bridal veil

flammesc·ō -ĕre vi to become inflamed, become fiery

flammĕ·us -a -um adj flaming, fiery; flashing (eyes); flame-covered; n bridal veil

flammĭf·er -ĕra -ĕrum adj fiery

flamm·ō -āre vt to set on fire; (fig) to inflame, incense; vi to burn, glow, blaze

flammŭl·a -ae f little flame

flāt·us -ūs m blowing, breathing, breath; breeze, wind; snorting; arrogance

flāv·ens -entis adj yellow, golden

flāvesc·ō -ĕre vi to become yellow, become golden-yellow

Flāvĭ·us -a -um adj Flavian; **gens Flavia** Flavian clan (to which the emperors Vespasian, Titus, and Domitian belonged)

flāv·us -a -um adj yellow, blond, reddish-yellow, golden

flēbĭl·is -e adj pitiful, pathetic, deplorable; crying, tearful

flēbiliter adv tearfully, mournfully

flectō flectĕre flexī flexum vt to bend, curve; to turn, wheel about, turn around; to wind, twist, curl; to direct, avert, turn away (eyes, mind, etc.); to double, sail around (a cape); to modulate (voice); to change (the mind); to persuade, move, appease; **viam** or **iter flectere** (with **ad** + acc) to make one's way toward, head toward; vi to turn, go, march

fēmin·a -um n pl swollen, bloody
ankles

fi·ĕō -ēre -ēvī -ētum vt to cry for,
mourn for; vi to cry

fiēt·us -ūs m crying; m pl tears

flexanĭm·us -a -um adj moving,
touching

flexibĭl·is -e adj flexible; shifty,
fickle

flexil·is -e adj flexible, pliant

flexilŏqu·us -a -um adj ambiguous

flexĭ·ō -ōnis f bending, turning;
modulation (of the voice)

flexĭp·ēs -ēdis adj creeping (ivy)

flexuōs·us -a -um adj winding
(road)

flexŭr·a -ae f bending, winding

flexus pp of flecto

flex·us -ūs m bending, turning,
winding; shift, change, transition,
crisis

fict·us -ūs m clashing, banging together

fl·ō -āre vt to blow, breathe; to coin
(money); vi to blow

flocc·us -ī m lock (of hair, wool);
down; flocci facere to think little
of, disregard, not give a hoot about

Flōr·a -ae f goddess of flowers,
whose festival was celebrated on
April 28th

flōr·ens -entis adj blooming; prosperous; flourishing, in the prime;
(with abl) in the prime of, at the
height of

flōr·ĕō -ēre -ŭī vi to bloom, blossom;
to be in one's prime; (of wine) to
foam, ferment; to be prosperous, be
eminent; (with abl) a to abound in;
b to swarm with, be filled with

flōr·escō -escēre -ŭī vi to begin to
bloom, begin to blossom

flōrĕ·us -a -um adj flowery; made
of flowers

flōrĭd·us -a -um adj flowery; fresh,
pretty; florid (style)

flōrĭf·er -ĕra -ĕrum adj flowery

flōrĭlĕg·us -a -um adj (of bees) going from flower to flower

flōr·us -a -um adj luxuriant

fl·ōs -ōris m flower; bud, blossom;
best (of anything); prime (of life);
youthful beauty, innocence; crown,
glory; nectar; literary ornament

floscŭl·us -ī m little flower, floweret;
flower, pride, glory

fluctifrăg·us -a -um adj wave-
breaking (shore), surging

fluctuātĭ·ō -ōnis f wavering, vacil-
lating

fluctŭ·ō -āre or fluctŭ·or -ārī
-ātus sum vi to fluctuate, undulate, wave; to be restless; to waver,
vacillate, fluctuate

fluctuōs·us -a -um adj running
(sea)

fluct·us -ūs m wave, billow; flowing,
undulating; turbulence, commotion;
disorder, unrest; fluctus in sim-
pulo tempest in a tea cup

flu·ens -entis adj loose, flowing;
(morally) loose; effeminate; fluent

fluent·a -ōrum n pl flow, stream,
river

fluenter adv like a wave

fluĭd·us or fluvĭd·us -a -um adj
flowing, fluid; soft; relaxing

fluĭt·ō or fluĭt·ō -āre vi to float,
swim; to sail; to toss about; to hang
loose, flap; to be uncertain, waver;
to stagger

flūm·en -ĭnis n flowing, stream, river, flood; fluency; (fig) flood (e.g., of
tears, words, etc.); flumine adverso upstream; secundo flumine
downstream

flūmĭnĕ·us -a -um adj river

flu·ō -ĕre -xī -xum vi to flow; to
run down, drip; to overflow; (of
branches) to spread; to sink, drop,
droop; to pass away, vanish, perish;
to be fluent; to be monotonous; to
spring, arise, proceed

flūtō see fluito

fluviāl·is -e adj river, of a river

fluviātĭl·is -e adj river, of a river

flūvĭdus see fluidus

fluv·ĭus -ĭī or -ī m river; running
water, stream

flux·us -a -um adj flowing, loose;
careless; loose, dissolute; frail,
weak; transient, perishable

fōcāl·e -is n scarf

fōcĭll·ō -āre vt to warm, revive

focŭl·um -ī n stove

focŭl·us -ī m brazier; (fig) fire

foc·us -ī m hearth, fireplace; brazier; funeral pile; altar; home, family

fodĭc·ō -āre vt to poke, nudge

fodĭō fodĕre fōdī fossum vt to dig,
dig out; (fig) to prod, goad, prick

foecund- = fecund-

foedē adv foully, cruelly, shamefully

foederāt·us -a -um adj confeder-
ated, allied

foedifrăg·us -a -um adj treacherous, perfidious

foedĭt·ās -ātis f foulness, hideousness

foed·ō -āre vt to make hideous, disfigure; to pollute, defile, disgrace

foed·us -a -um adj foul, filthy, horrible, ugly, disgusting, repulsive;
disgraceful, vile

foed·us -ĕris n treaty, charter,
league; compact, agreement; law;
aequo foedere on equal terms, mutually; foedere certo by fixed law;
foedere pacto by fixed agreement

foen- = faen-

foet·ĕō -ēre vi to stink

foetĭd·us -a -um adj stinking

foet·or -ōris m stink, stench

foetu- = fētu-

foliāt·us -a -um adj leafy; n nard
oil

fol·ium -ĭī or -ī n leaf; folium recitare Sibyllae to tell the gospel
truth

follicŭl·us -ī m small bag, sack;
shell, skin; eggshell

foll·is -is m bag; punching bag; bellows; money bag; puffed-out cheeks

fōment·um -ī n bandage; mitigation, alleviation

fōm·es -itis m tinder

fon·s -tis m spring, fountain; spring water, water; stream; lake; source, origin, fountainhead

fontān·us -a -um adj spring

fonticūl·us -ī m little spring, little fountain

for fārī fātus sum vt & vi to say, speak, utter

forābil·is -e adj vulnerable

forām·en -inis n hole, opening

forās adv out, outside; **forās dare** to publish (writings)

forc·eps -ipis m or f forceps, tongs

ford·a -ae f pregnant cow

fore = futūr·us -a -um esse to be about to be

forem = essem

forens·is -e adj of the forum, in the forum; public, forensic

forf·ex -icis f scissors

for·is -is f door, gate; f pl double doors; opening, entrance; (fig) door

forīs adv outside, out of doors; abroad, in foreign countries; from outside, from abroad

form·a -ae f form, shape, figure; beauty; shape, image; mold, stamp; shoemaker's last; vision, apparition, phantom; species, form, nature, sort, kind; outline, design, sketch, plan

formāment·um -ī n shape

formāt·or -ōris m fashioner

formātūr·a -ae f fashioning, shaping

Formī·ae -ārum f pl town in S. Latium

formīc·a -ae f ant

formīcīn·us -a -um adj ant-like

formīdābil·is -e adj terrifying

formīd·ō -āre vt to fear, dread; vi to be frightened

formīd·ō -inis f fear, dread, awe, terror; scarecrow; threats

formīdolōsē adv dreadfully, terribly

formīdolōs·us -a -um adj dreadful, terrifying, terrible; afraid, terrified

form·ō -āre vt to form, shape, mold, build; to make, produce, invent; to imagine; to regulate, direct

formōsē adv beautifully, gracefully

formōsit·ās -ātis f beauty

formōs·us -a -um adj shapely, beautiful, handsome

formul·a -ae f nice shape, beauty; form, formula, draft; contract, agreement; rule, regulation; (law) regular method, formula, rule; (phil) principle

fornācāl·is -e adj of an oven

fornācul·a -ae f small oven

forn·ax -ācis f oven, furnace, kiln; forge

fornicāt·us -a -um adj arched

forn·ix -icis m arch, vault; arcade; brothel

fornus see **furnus**

for·ō -āre vt to bore, pierce

fors adv perhaps, chances are, there is a chance, possibly

for·s -tis f chance, luck, fortune, accident; **forte** by chance, accidentally, by accident; as it happens, as it happened; perhaps

forsan, forsit, or **forsitan** adv perhaps

fortasse or **fortassis** adv perhaps

forte see **fors**

forticūl·us -a -um adj quite bold, rather brave

fort·is -e adj strong, mighty, powerful; brave, courageous, valiant, resolute, steadfast, firm

fortiter adv strongly, vigorously, firmly, bravely, boldly

fortitūd·ō -inis f strength; bravery, courage, resolution

fortuītō adv by chance, accidentally, casually

fortuīt·us -a -um adj accidental, fortuitous, casual

fortūn·a -ae f chance, luck, fate, fortune; good luck, prosperity; bad luck, misfortune; lot, circumstances, state, rank, position; property, goods, fortune

fortūnātē adv fortunately, prosperously

fortūnāt·us -a -um adj fortunate, lucky, prosperous, happy; rich, well-off

fortūn·ō -āre vt to make happy, make prosperous, bless

forūl·ī -ōrum m pl bookcase

for·um -ī n shopping center, market, marketplace; market town; trade, commerce; forum, civic center; court; public life, public affairs; jurisdiction; **cedere foro** to go bankrupt; **extra suum forum** beyond his jurisdiction; **forum agere** to hold court; **forum attingere** to enter public life; **in foro versari** to be engaged in commerce

For·um Appiī (genit: **For·ī Appiī**) n town in Latium on the Via Appia

For·um Aurēliī (genit: **For·ī Aurēliī**) n town N. of Rome on the Via Aurelia

For·um Juliī (genit: **For·ī Juliī**) n town in S. Gaul, colony of the eighth legion

for·us -ī m gangway; tier of seats; tier of a beehive

foss·a -ae f ditch, trench; **fossam deprimere** to dig a deep trench

fossi·ō -ōnis f digging

foss·or -ōris m digger; lout, clown

fossūr·a -ae f digging

fossus pp of **fodio**

fōtus pp of **foveo**

fově·a -ae f small pit; (fig) pitfall

foveō fovēre fōvī fōtum vt to warm, keep warm; to fondle, caress; to love, cherish; to support, encourage; to pamper

fract·us -a -um pp of **frango**; adj interrupted, irregular; weak, feeble

frāg·a -ōrum n pl strawberries

fragil·is -e adj fragile, brittle;

crackling; weak, frail; unstable, fickle

fragilit·ās -ātis *f* weakness, frailty

fragiō see **fragrō**

fragm·en -inis *n* fragment; *n pl* debris, ruins, wreckage

fragment·um -ī *n* fragment, remnant

frag·or -ōris *m* crash, noise, uproar, din; applause; clap of thunder

fragōs·us -a -um *adj* broken, uneven, rough; crashing, roaring

fragr·ō or **fragl·ō -āre** *vi* to smell sweet, be fragrant; to reek

framē·a -ae *f* German spear

frangō frangĕre frēgī fractum *vt* to break in pieces, smash to pieces, shatter; to grind, crush; (fig) to break down, overcome, crush, dishearten, humble, weaken, soften, move, touch; **diem mero frangere** to break up the day with wine

frāt·er -ris *m* brother; cousin; friend, comrade

frātercŭl·us -ī *m* little brother

frāternē *adv* like a brother

frāternit·ās -ātis *f* brotherhood

frātern·us -a -um *adj* brotherly; brother's; fraternal

frātricīd·a -ae *m* murderer of a brother, a fratricide

fraudāti·ō -ōnis *f* swindling

fraudāt·or -ōris *m* swindler

fraud·ō -āre *vt* to swindle, cheat, defraud; to embezzle; (with *abl*) to defraud (*someone*) of, cheat (*someone*) of

fraudulenti·a -ae *f* tendency to swindle, deceitfulness

fraudulent·us -a -um *adj* fraudulent; deceitful, treacherous

frau·s -dis *f* fraud, deception, trickery; error, delusion; crime, offense; harm, damage; deceiver, fraud, cheat; **sine fraude** without harm

fraxinē·us or **fraxin·us -a -um** *adj* of ash wood, ashen

fraxin·us -ī *f* ash tree; spear (*made of ash wood*)

Fregell·ae -ārum *f pl* ancient Volscan city on the Liris River, in Latium, made a Roman colony in 328 B.C.

fremebund·us -a -um *adj* roaring

fremit·us -ūs *m* roaring, growling, snorting; din, noise

frem·ō -ĕre -ŭī -ĭtum *vt* to grumble at, complain loudly of; to demand angrily; *vi* to roar, growl, snort, howl, grumble, murmur; to resound

frem·or -ōris *m* roaring, grumbling, murmuring

frend·ō -ĕre -ŭī *vi* to gnash the teeth; **dentibus frendere** to gnash the teeth

frēnī see **frenum**

frēn·ō -āre *vt* to bridle, curb; (fig) to curb, control

frēn·um -ī *n* or **frēn·a -ōrum** *n pl* or **frēn·ī -ōrum** *m pl* bridle, bit; (fig) curb, control, restraint

frequ·ens -entis *adj* crowded, in crowds, numerous, filled; frequent, repeated, usual, common; (may be rendered adverbially) often, repeatedly

frequentāti·ō -ōnis *f* piling up

frequenter *adv* frequently, often; in great numbers

frequenti·a -ae *f* crowd, throng; crowded assembly, large attendance

frequent·ō -āre *vt* to visit often, frequent, resort to; to do often, repeat; to crowd, people, stock; to attend (*e.g., games*) in large numbers

fretens·is -e *adj* **fretense mare** Strait of Messina

fret·um -ī *n* strait, channel; sea, waters; (fig) seething flood

frēt·us -a -um *adj* confident; (with *dat* or *abl*) supported by, relying on, depending on

fret·us -ūs *m* strait

fric·ō -āre -ŭī -tum *vt* to rub, rub down

frictus *pp* of **frigo**

frīgefact·ō -āre *vt* to make cold or cool

frīg·ĕō -ēre *vi* to be cold, be chilly; to freeze; (fig) to be numbed, be lifeless, be dull; (fig) to get a cool reception, be snubbed, get a cold shoulder; (fig) to fall flat

frīgesc·ō -ĕre *vi* to become cold, become chilled; to become lifeless

frīgidāri·us -a -um *adj* cooling

frīgidē *adv* feebly

frīgidŭl·us -a -um *adj* rather cold; rather faint

frīgid·us -a -um *adj* cold, cool; numbed, dull, lifeless, indifferent, unimpassioned, feeble; flat, insipid, trivial; *f* cold water

frīg·ō frigĕre frixī frictum *vt* to fry, roast

frīg·us -ōris *n* cold, coldness, chill, coolness; frost; cold of winter, winter; coldness of death, death; chill, fever; cold shudder, chill; cold region; cold reception; coolness, indifference; slowness, inactivity; *n pl* cold spell, cold season

frigutt·iō -īre *vi* to stutter

fri·ō -āre *vt* to crumble

fritill·us -ī *m* dice box

frīvŏl·us -a -um *adj* frivolous, trifling, worthless, sorry, pitiful; *n pl* trifles

frondāt·or -ōris *m* pruner

frond·ĕō -ēre *vi* to have leaves; to become green

frondesc·ō -ĕre *vi* to get leaves

frondĕ·us -a -um *adj* leafy, covered with leaves

frondif·er -ĕra -ĕrum *adj* leafy

frondōs·us -a -um *adj* full of leaves, leafy

fron·s -dis *f* foliage; leafy bough, green bough; chaplet, garland

fron·s -tis *f* forehead, brow; front end, front; countenance, face, look; face, façade, van, vanguard; exterior, appearance; outer end of a scroll; sense of shame; **a fronte** in front; **frontem contrahere** to knit the brow, frown; **frontem ferire** to hit oneself on the head (*in self-annoyance*); **frontem remittere** to smooth the brow, to cheer up; **in fronte** (in measuring land) in breadth, frontage; **salvā fronte** without shame; **tenuis frons** low forehead

frontāl·ia -ium *n pl* frontlet (*ornament for forehead of a horse*)

front·ō -ōnis *m* one with a large forehead

fructuāri·us -a -um *adj* productive; subject to land tax

fructuōs·us -a -um *adj* fruitful, productive

fructus *pp of* **fruor**

fruct·us -ūs *m* produce, fruit; proceeds, profit, income, return, revenue; enjoyment, satisfaction; benefit, reward, results, consequence

frūgāl·is -e *adj* frugal; honest; worthy

frūgālit·ās -ātis *f* frugality, economy; temperance; honesty; worth

frūgāliter *adv* frugally, economically; temperately

frūgēs see **frux**

frūgī (indecl) *adj* frugal; temperate; honest, worthy; useful, proper

frūgif·er -ēra -ērum *adj* fruitful, productive, fertile; profitable

frūgifer·ēns -entis *adj* fruitful

frūgilĕg·us -a -um *adj* (of ants) food-gathering

frūgipār·us -a -um *adj* fruitful

fruitus *pp of* **fruor**

frūmentāri·us -a -um *adj* of grain, grain; grain-producing; of provisions; **res frumentaria** (mil) supplies, quartermaster corps; *m* grain dealer

frūmentātǐ·ō -ōnis *f* (mil) foraging

frūmentāt·or -ōris *m* grain merchant; (mil) forager

frūment·or -ārī -ātus sum *vi* (mil) to forage

frūment·um -ī *n* grain; wheat; *n pl* grain fields, crops

frūn·iscor -iscī -ītus sum *vt* to enjoy

fruor fruī frūctus sum or **fruī·tus sum** *vt* to enjoy; *vi* (with *abl*) **a** to enjoy, delight in; **b** to enjoy the company of; **c** (law) to have the use and enjoyment of

frustillātim *adv* in bits

frustrā *adv* in vain, uselessly, for nothing; without reason, groundlessly; **frustra discedere** to go away disappointed; **frustra esse** to be mistaken; **frustra habere** to have (*someone*) confused or baffled

frustrām·en -inis *n* deception

frustrātǐ·ō -ōnis *f* deception; frustration

frustrāt·us -ūs *m* deception; **frustratui habere** (coll) to take for a sucker

frustr·or -ārī -ātus sum or **frustr·ō -āre** *vt* to deceive, trick; to

disappoint; to frustrate

frustulent·us -a -um *adj* crumby, full of crumbs

frust·um -ī *n* crumb, bit, scrap; **frustum puerī** (coll) whippersnapper

frut·ex -icis *m* shrub, bush; (coll) blockhead

fruticēt·um -ī *n* thicket, shrubbery

frutic·ō -āre or **frutic·or -ārī -ātus sum** *vi* to sprout; to become bushy; (fig) (of the hair) to become bushy

fruticōs·us -a -um *adj* bushy, overgrown with bushes

frux frūgis *f* or **frūg·ēs -um** *f pl* fruit, produce, grain, vegetables; barley meal (*for sacrifice*); fruits, benefit, result; **se ad frugem bonam recipere** to turn over a new leaf; **expers frugis** worthless

fūcāt·us -a -um *adj* dyed, colored, painted; artificial, spurious

fūc·ō -āre *vt* to dye red, redden, paint red; to disguise, falsify

fūcōs·us -a -um *adj* painted, colored; spurious, phoney

fūc·us -ī *m* red paint; rouge; drone; bee glue; disguise, pretense, deceit

fue or **fu** *interj* phui!

fug·a -ae *f* flight, escape; avoidance; exile; speed, swift passage; disappearance; (with *genit*) avoidance of, escape from; **fugae sese mandare, fugam capere, fugam capessere, fugam facere, se in fugam conferre, se in fugam conjicere,** or **sese in fugam dare** to flee, take flight; **in fugam conferre, in fugam conjicere, in fugam dare,** or **in fugam impellere** to put to flight

fugācius *adv* more cautiously, with one eye on flight

fug·ax -ācis *adj* apt to flee, fleeing; shy, timid; swift; passing, transitory; (with *genit*) shy of, shunning, avoiding, steering clear of, averse to

fugi·ēns -entis *adj* fleeing, retreating; (with *genit*) avoiding, averse to

fugiō fugĕre fūgī fugitum *vt* to escape, escape from, run away from, shun, avoid; to leave (*esp. one's country*); to be averse to, dislike; to escape the notice of, escape, be unknown to; **fuge** (with *inf*) do not; **fugit me scribere** I forgot to write; *vi* to flee, escape, run away; to go into exile; to speed, hasten; to vanish, disappear; to pass away, perish

fugit·ans -antis *adj* fleeing; (with *genit*) averse to

fugitīv·us -a -um *adj* & *m* runaway, fugitive

fugit·ō -āre *vt* to run away from

fugit·or -ōris *m* deserter

fug·ō -āre *vt* to put to flight, drive away, chase away; to exile, banish; to avert

fulcim·en -inis *n* support, prop, pillar

fulcĭŏ fulcīre fulsī fultum vt to prop up, support; to secure, sustain

fulcr·um -ī n bed post; couch, bed

fulgĕŏ fulgēre fulsī or **fulg·ŏ -ēre** vi to gleam, flash, blaze, shine, glare; to shine, be conspicuous, be illustrious

fulgĭd·us -a -um adj flashing, shining

fulgŏ see **fulgeo**

fulg·or -ōris m flash of lightning, lightning; brightness; thing struck by lightning

fulgurāl·is -e adj of lightning; **libri fulgurales** books on lightning

fulgurāt·or -ōris m interpreter of lightning

fulgurīt·us -a -um adj struck by lightning

fulgŭr·ŏ -āre vi to lighten, send lightning; v impers it is lightning

fulĭc·a -ae or **ful·ix -ĭcis** f coot (waterfowl)

fūlīg·ŏ -ĭnis f soot; black paint

fulix see **fulica**

full·ŏ -ōnis m fuller

fullōnĭc·a -ae f fuller's craft, fulling

fullōnĭc·us -a -um adj fuller's

fulm·en -ĭnis n thunderbolt, lightning bolt; (fig) bolt, bolt out of the blue

fulment·a -ae f heel

fulmĭnĕ·us -a -um adj of lightning; lightning; shine, sparkling, flashing

fulmĭn·ŏ -āre vi to lighten; (fig) to flash

fultūr·a -ae f support, prop

fultus pp of **fulcio**

fulv·us -a -um adj yellow, yellowish brown, reddish yellow, tawny; blond

fūmĕ·us -a -um adj smoky

fūmĭd·us -a -um adj smoking, smoky

fūmĭf·er -ĕra -ĕrum adj smoking

fūmĭfĭc·ŏ -āre vi to smoke; to burn incense

fūmĭfĭc·us -a -um adj smoking, steaming

fūm·ŏ -āre vi to smoke, fume, steam, reek

fūmōs·us -a -um adj smoked, smoky

fūm·us -ī m smoke, steam, fume

fūnāl·e -is n rope; torch; chandelier, candelabrum

fūnambŭl·us -ī m tightrope walker

functĭ·ŏ -ōnis f performance

functus pp of **fungor**

fund·a -ae f sling; sling stone; dragnet

fundām·en -ĭnis n foundation

fundāment·um -ī n foundation; (fig) basis, ground, beginning; **a fundamentis** utterly, completely; **fundamenta agere, jacere,** or **locare** to lay the foundations

fundāt·or -ōris m founder

fundāt·us -a -um adj well-founded, established

fundĭt·ŏ -āre vt to sling, shoot with a sling; (fig) to sling (e.g., words) around

fundĭt·or -ōris m slinger

fundĭtus adv from the bottom, utterly, entirely

fund·ŏ -āre vt to found, build, establish; to secure to the ground, make fast

fundŏ fundĕre fūdī fūsum vt to pour, pour out; to melt (metals); to cast (in metal); to pour in streams, shower, hurl; (mil) to pour in (troops); (mil) to rout; to pour out, empty; to spread, extend, diffuse; to bring forth, bear, yield in abundance; to throw to the ground, bring down; to give up, lose, waste; to utter, pour out (words)

fund·us -ī m bottom; farm, estate; (law) sanctioner, authority

fūnĕbr·is -e adj funeral; deadly, murderous

fūnerāt·us -a -um adj done in, killed

fūnerĕ·us -a -um adj funeral; deadly, fatal

fūner·ŏ -āre vt to bury; **prope funeratus** almost sent to my (his, etc.) grave

fūnest·ŏ -āre vt to defile with murder, desecrate

fūnest·us -a -um adj deadly, fatal, calamitous; sad, dismal, mournful; **annales funesti** obituary column

fungīn·us -a -um adj of a mushroom

fungor fungī functus sum vi (with abl) **a** to perform, execute, discharge, do; **b** to busy oneself with, be engaged in; **c** to finish, complete; **morte fungi** to suffer death, die

fung·us -ī m mushroom, fungus; candle snuff; (fig) clown

fūnĭcŭl·us -ī m cord

fūn·is -is m rope, cable, cord; rigging; **funem ducere** (fig) to command; **funem reducere** (fig) to change one's mind; **funem sequi** (fig) to serve, follow

fūn·us -ĕris n funeral rites, funeral, burial; corpse; death, murder; havoc; ruin, destruction; **sub funus** on the brink of the grave; n pl shades of the dead

fūr fūris m or f thief; (fig) rogue, rascal

fūrācissĭmē adv quite like a thief

fūr·ax -ācis adj thievish

furc·a -ae f fork; fork-shaped prop (for supporting vines, bleachers, etc.); wooden yoke (put around slave's neck as punishment)

furcĭf·er -ĕrī m rogue, rascal

furcill·a -ae f little fork

furcill·ŏ -āre vt to support, prop up

furcŭl·a -ae f fork-shaped prop; f pl narrow pass, defile

Furcŭl·ae Caudĭn·ae (genit: **Furcŭl·ārum Caudīn·ārum**) f pl Caudine Forks (mountain pass near Caudium, in Samnium, where the Roman army was trapped in 321 B.C. by the Samnites and made to pass under the yoke)

furenter *adv* furiously

furf·ur -ŭris *m* chaff; bran

Furi·a -ae *f* Fury (one of the three goddesses of frenzy and vengeance, who were named Megaera, Tisiphone, and Alecto)

furi·a -ae *f* frenzy, madness, rage; remorse; madman

furiāl·is -e *adj* of the Furies; frenzied, frantic, furious; infuriated

furiāliter *adv* frantically

furibund·us -a -um *adj* frenzied, frantic, mad; inspired

fūrĭn·us -a -um *adj* of thieves

furĭ·ō -āre *vt* to drive mad, infuriate

furiōsē *adv* in a rage, in a frenzy

furiōs·us -a -um *adj* frenzied, frantic, mad, furious; maddening

furn·us or forn·us -ī *m* oven; bakery

fur·ō -ĕre *vi* to be crazy, be out of one's mind, rage, rave

fūr·or -ārī -ātus sum *vt* to steal, pilfer; to pillage; to plagiarize; to obtain by fraud; to withdraw in secret; to impersonate

fur·or -ōris *m* madness, rage, fury, passion; furor, excitement; prophetic frenzy, inspiration; passionate love

furtific·us -a -um *adj* thievish

furtim *adv* secretly, by stealth, clandestinely

furtīvē *adv* secretly, stealthily

furtīv·us -a -um *adj* stolen; secret, hidden, furtive

furt·um -ī *n* theft, robbery; trick, stratagem; secret action, intrigue; secret love; *n pl* intrigues; secret love affair; stolen goods

fūruncŭl·us -ī *m* petty thief

furv·us -a -um *adj* black, dark, gloomy, eerie

fuscĭn·a -ae *f* trident

fusc·ō -āre *vt* to blacken

fusc·us -a -um *adj* dark, swarthy; low, muffled, indistinct (sound)

fūsē *adv* widely; in great detail

fūsĭl·is -e *adj* molten, liquid

fūsĭ·ō -ōnis *f* outpouring, effusion

fust·is -is *m* club, stick, cudgel; beating to death (as a military punishment)

fustitudĭn·us -a -um *adj* (coll) whip-happy (jail)

fustuār·ium -iī or -ī *n* beating to death (as a military punishment)

fūs·us -a -um *pp* of **fundo**; *adj* spread out; broad, wide; diffuse (style)

fūs·us -ī *m* spindle

futtĭl·is or fūtĭl·is -e *adj* brittle; futile, worthless, untrustworthy

futtĭlĭt·ās or fūtĭlĭt·ās -ātis *f* futility, worthlessness

fut·ŭō -ŭĕre -ŭī -ūtum *vt* to have sexual intercourse with (a woman)

futūr·us -a -um *fut p* of **sum**; *adj* & *n* future

Gabĭ·ī -ōrum *m pl* ancient town in Latium

Gad·ēs -ĭum *f pl* Cadiz (town in S. Spain)

gaes·um -ī *n* Gallic spear

Gaetūl·ī -ōrum *m pl* a people in N.W. Africa along the Sahara Desert

Gā·ĭus -ī *m* Roman praenomen (the names of Gaius and Gaia were formally given to the bridegroom and bride at the wedding ceremony)

Galăt·ae -ārum *m pl* Galatians (a people of central Asia Minor)

Galatĭ·a -ae *f* Galatia (country in central Asia Minor)

Galb·a -ae *m* Servius Sulpicius Galba, the Roman emperor from June, 68 A.D.–69 A.D. to January, 69 A.D. (5 B.C.–69 A.D.)

galbanĕ·us -a -um *adj* of galbanum

galban·um -ī *n* galbanum (resinous sap of a Syrian plant)

galbĭn·us -a -um *adj* chartreuse; (fig) effeminate; *n pl* pale green clothes

galĕ·a -ae *f* helmet

galeāt·us -a -um *adj* helmeted

galērĭcŭl·um -ī *n* cap

galērīt·us -a -um *adj* wearing a farmer's cap, countryish

galēr·um -ī *n* or **galēr·us -ī** *m* cap; (fig) wig

gall·a -ae *f* gallnut

Gall·ī -ōrum *m pl* Gauls (inhabitants of modern France and N. Italy)

Gallĭ·a -ae *f* Gaul

Gallĭc·us -a -um *adj* Gallic

gallĭn·a -ae *f* chicken, hen; (as term of endearment) chick

gallīnācĕ·us or gallīnācĭ·us -a -um *adj* poultry

gallīnār·ĭus -iī or -ī *m* poultry farmer

Gallograec·ī -ōrum *m pl* Galatians (Celts who migrated from Gaul to Asia Minor in the 3rd cent. B.C.)

Gall·us -a -um *adj* Gallic; *m* Gaul; priest of Cybele; C. Cornelius Gallus, lyric poet and friend of Virgil (69–27 B.C.)

gall·us -ī *m* rooster, cock

gănĕ·a -ae *f* or **gănĕ·um -ī** *n* brothel, dive; cheap restaurant

gănĕ·ō -ōnis *m* glutton

gănĕum see **ganea**

Gangarĭd·ae -ārum *m pl* an Indian people on the Ganges

Gang·es -is *m* Ganges River

gann·ĭō -īre *vi* to snarl, growl

gannīt·us -ūs *m* snarling, growling

Ganymēd·ēs -is *m* Ganymede (*handsome youth carried off to Olympus by the eagle of Jupiter to become the cupbearer of the gods*)

Garamant·es -um *m pl* tribe in N. Africa

Gargaphī·ē -ēs *f* valley in Boeotia sacred to Diana

Gargān·us -ī *m* mountain in S.E. Italy

garr·ĭō -īre *vt* to chatter, prattle, talk; **nugas garrire** to talk nonsense; *vi* to chatter, chat; (of frogs) to croak

garrŭlĭt·ās -ātis *f* talkativeness; chattering

garrŭl·us -a -um *adj* talkative, babbling, garrulous

gar·um -ī *n* fish sauce

gaud·ens -entis *adj* cheerful

gaudĕō gaudēre gāvīsus sum *vt* to rejoice at; **gaudium gaudere** to feel joy; *vi* to rejoice, be glad, feel pleased; (with *abl*) to delight in; **in se gaudere** or **in sinu gaudere** to be secretly glad

gaud·ium -iī or **-ī** *n* joy, gladness, delight; sensual pleasure, enjoyment; joy, cause of joy; **mala mentis gaudia** gloating

gaul·us -ī *m* bucket

gausăp·e -is or **gausăp·um -ī** *n* felt; (fig) shaggy beard

gāvīsus *pp* of gaudeo

gaz·a -ae *f* royal treasure; treasure, riches

gelĭdē *adv* coldly, indifferently

gelĭd·us -a -um *adj* cold, icy, frosty; icy cold, stiff, numbed; *f* cold water

gel·ō -āre *vt & vi* to freeze

Gelōn·ī -ōrum *m pl* Scythian tribe

gel·u -ūs *n* or **gel·um -ī** *n* or **gel·us -ūs** *m* coldness, cold, frost, ice; chill, coldness (*of death, old age, fear*)

gemebund·us -a -um *adj* sighing, groaning

gemellipăr·a -ae *f* mother of twins

gemell·us -a -um *adj & m* twin

gemināti·ō -ōnis *f* doubling; compounding

gemin·ō -āre *vt* to double; to join, unite, pair; to repeat, reproduce

gemin·us -a -um *adj* twin; double, twofold, two, both; similar; *m pl* twins

gemit·us -ūs *m* sigh, groan

gemm·a -ae *f* bud; gem, jewel; jeweled goblet; signet ring, signet; eye of a peacock's tail; literary gem

gemmāt·us -a -um *adj* set with jewels, jeweled

gemmĕ·us -a -um *adj* set with jewels, jeweled; brilliant, glittering, sparkling

gemmĭf·er -ĕra -ĕrum *adj* gemproducing

gemm·ō -āre *vi* to sprout, bud; to sparkle

gem·ō -ĕre -ŭī -ĭtum *vt* to sigh

over, lament; *vi* to sigh, groan, moan; to creak

Gemōni·ae -ārum *f pl* steps on the Capitoline slope from which criminals were thrown

gen·a -ae *f* or **gen·ae -ārum** *f pl* cheek; cheekbone; eye socket; eye

geneălŏg·us -ī *m* genealogist

gen·er -ĕrī *m* son-in-law; daughter's boyfriend or fiancé

generāl·is -e *adj* of a species, generic; general, universal

generālĭter *adv* in general, generally

generasc·ō -ĕre *vi* to be generated

generātim *adv* by species, by classes; in general, generally

generāt·or -ōris *m* producer, breeder

genĕr·ō -āre *vt* to beget, procreate, produce, engender

generōsĭus *adv* more nobly

generōs·us -a -um *adj* of good stock, highborn, noble; noble, nobleminded

genĕs·is -is *f* birth, creation; horoscope

genesta *see* genista ..

genetīv·us -a -um *adj* inborn, innate; (gram) genitive; *m* genitive case

genĕtr·ix -īcis *f* mother, ancestress

geniāl·is -e *adj* nuptial, bridal; genial; joyous, festive, merry

geniālĭter *adv* merrily

geniculāt·us -a -um *adj* knotted, having knots, jointed

genist·a or **genest·a -ae** *f* broom plant; broom

genitābĭl·is -e *adj* productive

genitāl·is -e *adj* generative, productive; of birth; **dies genitalis** birthday

genitālĭter *adv* fruitfully

genitīvus *see* genetivus

genit·or -ōris *m* father, creator

genitrix *see* genetrix

genĭtus *pp* of gigno

gen·ius -iī or **-ī** *m* guardian spirit; taste, appetite, natural inclination; talent, genius

gen·s -tis *f* clan; stock; tribe; folk, nation, people; species; breed; descendant, offspring; *f pl* foreign nations; **longe gentium** abīre to be far, far away; **minime gentium** by no means; **ubi gentium** where in the world, where on earth

gentic·us -a -um *adj* tribal; national

gentīlici·us -a -um *adj* family

gentīl·is -e *adj* family, hereditary; tribal; national; *m* clansman, kinsman

gentīlĭt·ās -ātis *f* clan relationship

gen·ū -ūs *n* knee; **genibus minor** kneeling; **genibus nixus** on one's knees; **genuum junctura** knee joint

genuāl·ia -ium *n pl* garters

genuīn·us -a -um *adj* innate, natural; of the cheek; jaw, of the jaw; *m pl* back teeth

gen·us -ĕris n race, descent, lineage, breed, stock, family; noble birth; tribe; nation, people; descendant, offspring, posterity; kind, sort, species, class; rank, order, division; fashion, way, style; matter, respect; genus; sex; gender; **aliquid id genus** (*acc of description instead of genit* of quality) something of that sort; **in omni genere** in every respect

geŏgraphi·a -ae f geography

geōmĕtr·ēs -ae m geometer, mathematician

geōmetri·a -ae f geometry

geōmetric·us -a -um adj geometrical; n pl geometry

georgic·us -a -um adj agricultural; n pl Georgics (*poems on farming by Virgil*)

ger·ens -entis adj (with genit) managing (*e.g., a business*)

germān·a -ae f full sister, real sister

germānē adv sincerely

Germān·ī -ōrum m pl Germans

Germāni·a -ae f Germany

Germānic·us -a -um adj Germanic; m cognomen of Tiberius' nephew and adoptive son (15 B.C.-19 A.D.)

germānit·ās -ātis f brotherhood, sisterhood (*relationship between brothers and sisters of the same parents*); relationship between colonies of the same mother-city

germān·us -a -um adj having the same parents; brotherly; sisterly; genuine, real, true; m full brother, own brother; f see **germana**

germ·en -ĭnis n sprout, bud, shoot, offspring; embryo

germĭn·ō -āre vt to put forth, grow (*hair, wings, etc.*); vi to sprout

gerō gerĕre gessī gestum vt to bear, carry, wear, have, hold; to bring; to display; exhibit, assume; to bear, produce; to carry on, manage, govern, regulate, administer; to carry out, transact, do, accomplish; **bellum gerere** to fight, carry on war; **dum ea geruntur** while that was going on; **gerere morem** (with dat) to gratify, please, humor; **personam gerere** (with genit) to play the part of; **rem gerere** to run a business, conduct an affair; **se gerere** to behave; **se gerere** (with pro + abl) to claim to be for; **se medium gerere** to remain neutral

ger·ō -ōnis m porter

gerr·ae -ārum f pl trifles, nonsense

gerr·ō -ōnis m (coll) loafer

gerulifĭgŭl·us -ī m accomplice; (with genit) accomplice in

gerŭl·us -ī m porter

Gērў·ōn -ōnis or **Gērўŏn·ēs -ae** m mythical three-headed king of Spain who was slain by Hercules

gestām·en -ĭnis n that which is worn or carried, load; vehicle, litter; n pl ornaments; accouterments; arms

gestātĭ·ō -ōnis f drive (*place where one drives*)

gestāt·or -ōris m bearer, carrier

gestĭ·ō -ōnis f performance

gest·ĭō -īre -īvī or **-iī -ītum** vi to be delighted, be thrilled, be excited; to be eager; (with inf) to be itching to, long to

gestĭt·ō -āre vt to be in the habit of carrying or wearing

gest·ō -āre vt to bear, wear, carry; to carry about, blab, tell; to cherish; **gestari** to ride, drive, sail (*esp. for pleasure*)

gest·or -ōris m tattler

gestus pp of **gero**; adj **res gestae** accomplishments, exploits

gest·us -ūs m gesture; gesticulation; posture, bearing, attitude

Get·ae -ārum m pl Thracian tribe of the lower Danube

gibb·us -ī m hump

Gīgant·es -um m pl Giants (*race of gigantic size, sprung from Earth as the blood of Uranus fell upon her. They tried to storm heaven but were repelled by the gods with the aid of Hercules and placed under various volcanoes*)

gignō gignĕre genŭī genĭtum vt to beget, bear, produce; to cause, occasion, create, begin

gilv·us -a -um adj pale-yellow; **equus gilvus** palomino

gingīv·a -ae f gum (*of the mouth*)

glab·er -ra -rum adj hairless, bald, smooth; m young slave, favorite slave

glaciāl·is -e adj icy, frozen

glaci·ēs -ēī f ice; f pl ice fields

glaci·ō -āre vt to turn into ice, freeze

gladiāt·or -ōris m gladiator; m pl gladiatorial combat, gladiatorial show; **gladiatores dare** or **gladiatores edere** to stage a gladiatorial show

gladiātōrĭ·us -a -um adj gladiatorial; n gladiator's pay

gladiātūr·a -ae f gladiatorial profession

glad·ĭus -ĭī or **-ī** m sword; murder, death; **gladium educere** or **gladium stringere** to draw the sword; **gladium recondere** to sheathe the sword

glaeb·a -ae f lump of earth, clod; soil, land; lump, piece

glaebŭl·a -ae f small lump; bit of land, small farm

glaesum see **glesum**

glandif·er -ĕra -ĕrum adj acorn-producing

glandiōnĭd·a -ae f choice morsel

gland·ĭum -ĭī or **-ī** n choice cut (*of meat*)

glan·s -dis f mast; nut; acorn; chestnut; bullet

glārĕ·a -ae f gravel

glăreōs·us -a -um *adj* full of gravel, gravelly

glaucōm·a -ătis *n* cataract; **glaucomam ob oculos objicere** (with *dat*) to throw dust into the eyes of

glauc·us -a -um *adj* grey-green, greyish; bright, sparkling

Glauc·us -ī *m* leader of the Lycians in the Trojan War; fisherman of Anthedon, in Euboea, who was changed into a sea deity

glēba see **glaeba**

glēs·um or **glaes·um -ī** *n* amber

glī·s -ris *m* dormouse

glīscō -ĕre *vi* to grow, swell up, spread, blaze up; to grow, increase

globōs·us -a -um *adj* spherical

glob·us -ī *m* ball, sphere, globe; crowd, throng, gathering; clique

glomerām·en -inis *n* ball, globe

glomĕr·ō -āre *vt* to form into a ball, gather up, roll up; to collect, gather together, assemble

glom·us -ĕris *n* ball of yarn

glōrĭ·a -ae *f* glory, fame; glorious deed; thirst for glory, ambition; pride, boasting, bragging

glōrĭātĭ·ō -ōnis *f* boasting, bragging

glōrĭŏl·a -ae *f* bit of glory

glōrĭ·or -ārī -ātus sum *vt* (only with *neut pron* as object) to boast about, e.g., **haec gloriari** to boast about this; **idem gloriari** to make the same boast; *vi* to boast, brag; (with *abl* or with **de** or **in** + *abl*) to take pride in, boast about; (with **adversus** + *acc*) to boast or brag to (*someone*)

glōrĭōsē *adv* gloriously; boastfully, pompously

glōrĭōs·us -a -um *adj* glorious, famous; boastful

glossēm·a -ătis *n* word to be glossed

glūt·en -inis *n* glue

glūtināt·or -ōris *m* bookbinder

glūtĭn·ō -āre *vt* to glue together

glutt·iŏ or **glūt·iŏ -īre** *vt* to gulp down

glutt·ō -ōnis *m* glutton

Gnae·us or **Gnē·us -ī** *m* Roman praenomen

gnār·us -a -um or **gnārŭr·is -e** *adj* skillful, expert; known; (with *genit*) familiar with, versed in, expert in

gnātus see **natus**

gnāv- = **nav-**

gnōbilis see **nobilis**

Gnōsĭ·a -ae or **Gnōsĭ·as -ădis** or **Gnōs·is -ĭdis** *f* Ariadne (*daughter of King Minos*)

gnoscō see **nosco**

Gnoss·us or **Gnōs·us -ī** *f* Cnossos (*ancient capital of Crete and residence of Minos*)

gnōtus see **nosco**

gōb·ĭus or **cōb·ĭus -ĭī** or **-ī** or **gōbĭ·ō -ōnis** *m* goby (*small fish*)

Gorgĭ·as -ae *m* famous orator and sophist of Leontini, in Sicily (*c. 480-390 B.C.*)

Gorg·ō -ōnis *f* Gorgon (*a daughter of Phorcys and Ceto*); *f pl* Gorgons (*Stheno, Medusa, and Euryale*)

Gorgōn·us -a -um *adj* Gorgonian; **Gorgoneus equus** Pegasus; **Gorgoneus lacus** fountain Hippocrene on Mount Helicon

grabāt·us -ī *m* cot

Gracch·us -ī *m* Tiberius Sempronius Gracchus (*social reformer and tribune in 133 B.C.*); Gaius Sempronius Gracchus (*younger brother of Tiberius and tribune in 123 B.C.*)

gracĭl·is -e or **gracĭl·us -a -um** *adj* slim, slender; thin, skinny; poor; slight, insignificant; plain, simple (*style*)

gracĭlĭt·ās -ātis *f* slenderness; thinness, leanness, meagerness

grācŭl·us or **graccŭl·us -ī** *m* jackdaw

gradātim *adv* step by step, gradually, little by little

gradātĭ·ō -ōnis *f* climax

gradĭor gradī gressus sum *vi* to go, walk, step

Grādīv·us or **Grādīv·us -ī** *m* epithet of Mars

grad·us -ūs *m* step, pace, walk, gait; step, degree, grade, stage; approach, advance, progress; status, rank; station, position; step, rung, stair; footing; **concito gradu** on the double; **de gradu dejicere** (fig) to throw off balance; **gradum celerare** or **gradum corripere** to pick up the pace, speed up the pace; **gradum conferre** (mil) to come to close quarters; **gradūs ferre** (mil) to charge; **pleno gradu** on the double; **suspenso gradu** on tiptoe

Graecē *adv* Greek, in Greek; **Graece loqui** to speak Greek; **Graece scire** to know Greek

Graecĭ·a -ae *f* Greece; **Magna Graecia** southern Italy

graecissŏ -āre *vi* to ape the Greeks

graec·or -ārī -ātus sum *vi* to go Greek, act like a Greek

Graecŭl·us -a -um *adj* (in contemptuous sense) Greek through and through, hundred-percent Greek; *mf* Greekling, dirty little Greek

Graec·us -a -um *adj* & *mf* Greek; *n* Greek, Greek language

Grā·iī or **Grā·ī -ōrum** *m pl* Greeks

Grāiugĕn·a -ae *m* Greek, Greek by birth

grall·ae -ārum *f pl* stilts

grallāt·or -ōris *m* stilt walker

grām·en -inis *n* grass; meadow, pasture; plant, herb

grāminĕ·us -a -um *adj* grassy, of grass; of bamboo

grammatĭc·us -a -um *adj* grammatical, of grammar; *m* teacher of literature and language; philologist; *f* & *n pl* grammar; philology

grānārĭ·a -ōrum *n pl* granary

grandaev·us -a -um *adj* old, aged

grandescŏ -ĕre *vi* to grow, grow big

grandicŭl·us -a -um *adj* rather large; pretty tall

grandĭf·er -ĕra -ĕrum *adj* productive

grandĭlŏqu·us -ī *m* braggart

grandĭn·at -āre *v impers* it is hailing

grand·ĭō -īre *vt* to enlarge, increase

grand·is -e *adj* full-grown, grown up, tall; large, great; aged; important, powerful, strong; grand, lofty, dignified (*style*); loud, strong (*voice*); heavy (*debt*); dignified (*speaker*)

grandĭt·ās -ātis *f* grandeur

grand·ō -ĭnis *f* hail

grānĭf·er -ĕra -ĕrum *adj* (of ants) grain-carrying

grān·um -ī *n* grain, seed

graphĭcē *adv* masterfully

graphĭc·us -a -um *adj* masterful

graph·ĭum -ĭī *or* **-ī** *n* stilus

grassāt·or -ōris *m* vagabond, tramp; bully; prowler

grass·or -ārī -ātus sum *vi* to walk about, prowl around; to hang around, loiter; to go, move, proceed; (with **adversus** *or* **in** + *acc*) to attack, waylay

grātē *adv* willingly, with pleasure; gratefully

grātēs (*genit* not in use) *f pl* thanks, gratitude; **grates agere** (with *dat*) to thank, give thanks to; **grates habere** (with *dat*) to feel grateful to

grātĭ·a -ae *f* grace, charm, pleasantness, loveliness; influence, prestige; love, friendship; service, favor, kindness; thanks, gratitude, acknowledgment; cause, reason, motive; **cum gratia** (with *genit*) to the satisfaction of; with the approval of; **eā gratiā ut** for the reason that; **exempli gratiā** for example; **gratiā** (with *genit*) for the sake of, on account of; **gratiam facere** (with *dat* of person and *genit* of thing) to pardon (*someone*) for (*a fault*); **gratias agere** (with *dat*) to thank, give thanks to; **gratias habere** (with *dat*) to feel grateful to; **in gratiam** (with *genit*) in order to win the favor of, in order to please; **in gratiam habere** to regard (*something*) as a favor; **meā gratiā** for my sake; **quā gratiā** why

Grātĭ·a -ārum *f pl* Graces (*Aglaia, Euphrosyne, and Thalia, daughters of Jupiter by Eurynome*)

grātĭfĭcātĭ·ō -ōnis *f* kindness

grātĭfĭc·or -ārī -ātus sum *vt* to give up, surrender, sacrifice; *vi* (with *dat*) **a** to do (*someone*) a favor; **b** to gratify, please

grātĭīs *adv* gratis, free, for nothing, gratuitously

grātĭōs·us -a -um *adj* popular, influential; obliging

grātis *adv* gratis, free, for nothing, gratuitously

grāt·or -ārī -ātus sum *vi* to rejoice; to express gratitude; (with *dat*) to congratulate; **invicem inter se gratari** to congratulate one another

grātuītō *adv* gratuitously, gratis, for nothing; for no particular reason

grātuīt·us -a -um *adj* gratuitous, free, spontaneous; voluntary; unprovoked

grātulābund·us -a -um *adj* congratulating

grātulātĭ·ō -ōnis *f* congratulation; rejoicing, joy; public thanksgiving

grātulāt·or -ōris *m* congratulator, well-wisher

grātŭl·or -ārī -ātus sum *vi* to be glad, rejoice, manifest joy; (with *dat*) **a** to congratulate; **b** to render thanks to

grāt·us -a -um *adj* pleasing, pleasant, agreeable, welcome; thankful, grateful; deserving thanks, earning gratitude; *n* favor; **gratum facere** (with *dat*) to do (*someone*) a favor

gravanter *adv* reluctantly

gravātē *adv* with difficulty; unwillingly, grudgingly

gravātim *adv* with difficulty; unwillingly

gravēdĭnōs·us -a -um *adj* prone to catch colds

gravēd·ō -ĭnis *f* cold, head cold

gravesc·ō -ĕre *vi* to grow heavy; (fig) to become worse

gravĭdĭt·ās -ātis *f* pregnancy

gravĭd·ō -āre *vt* to impregnate

gravĭd·us -a -um *adj* loaded, filled, full; pregnant; (with *abl*) teeming with

grav·is -e *adj* heavy, weighty; burdensome; troublesome, oppressive, painful, harsh, hard, severe, unpleasant; unwholesome, indigestible; important, influential, venerable, grave, serious; pregnant; hostile; low, deep, bass; flat (*note*); harsh, bitter, offensive (*smell or taste*); impressive (*speech*); stormy (*weather*); oppressive (*heat*)

gravĭt·ās -ātis *f* weight; severity, harshness, seriousness; importance; dignity, influence; pregnancy; violence, vehemence

gravĭter *adv* heavily, ponderously; hard, violently, vehemently; severely, harshly, unpleasantly, disagreeably; sadly, sorrowfully; with dignity, with propriety, with authority; (to feel) deeply; (to smell) offensive, strong; (to speak) impressively; **graviter ferre** to take (*something*) hard

grav·ō -āre *vt* to weigh down, load, load down; to burden, be oppressive to; to aggravate; to increase

grav·or -ārī -ātus sum *vt* to feel annoyed at, object to, refuse, decline; to bear with reluctance, regard as a burden; *vi* to feel annoyed, be vexed

gregāl·is -e *adj* of the herd or flock; common; **sagulum gregale** uniform of a private; *m pl* comrades, companions

gregāri·us -a -um *adj* common; (mil) of the same rank; **miles gregarius** private

gregātim *adv* in flocks, in herds, in crowds

grem·ium -iī or **-ī** *n* lap, bosom; womb

gressus *pp* of **gradior**

gress·us -ūs *m* step; course, way

gre·x -gis *m* flock, herd; swarm; company, group, crowd, troop, set, clique, gang; theatrical cast

gruis see **grus**

grunn·iō or **grund·iō -īre -īvī** or **-iī -ītum** *vi* to grunt

grunnit·us -ūs *m* grunt, grunting

grū·s or **gru·is -is** *m* or *f* crane

grȳ (indecl) *n* scrap, crumb

gryps grȳpis *m* griffin

gubernācul·um or **gubernācl·um -ī** *n* rudder, tiller, helm; *n pl* (fig) helm

gubernātĭ·ō -ōnis *f* navigation

gubernāt·or -ōris *m* navigator, pilot; governor

gubernātr·īx -īcis *f* directress

gubern·ō -āre *vt* to navigate, pilot; to direct, govern

gul·a -ae *f* gullet, throat; palate, appetite, gluttony

gulōs·us -a -um *adj* appetizing, dainty

gurg·es -itis *m* abyss, gulf, whirl-pool; waters, flood, depths, sea; spendthrift

gurguli·ō -ōnis *m* gullet, windpipe

gurgust·ium -iī or **-ī** *n* dark hovel; (fig) hole in the wall

gustātōr·ium -iī or **-ī** *n* appetizer

gustāt·us -ūs *m* sense of taste; flavor, taste

gust·ō -āre *vt* to taste; (fig) to enjoy; to overhear; *vi* to have a snack

gust·us -ūs *m* tasting; appetizer

gutt·a -ae *f* drop; spot, speck

guttātim *adv* drop by drop

guttŭl·a -ae *f* tiny drop

gutt·ur -ŭris *n* gullet, throat, neck; *n pl* throat, neck

gūt·us or **gutt·us -ī** *m* cruet, flask

Gy·ās -ae *m* hundred-armed giant

Gȳg·ēs -is or **-ae** *m* king of Lydia (716-678 B.C.)

gymnasiarch·us -ī *m* manager of a gymnasium

gymnas·ium -iī or **-ī** *n* gymnasium

gymnastic·us -a -um *adj* gymnastic

gymnĭc·us -a -um *adj* gymnastic

gymnosophist·ae -ārum *m pl* Hindu Stoics

gynaecē·um or **gynaecī·um -ī** *n* women's apartments

gypsāt·us -a -um *adj* covered with plaster

gyps·um -ī *n* gypsum, plaster

gȳr·us -ī *m* circle, cycle, ring, orbit, course

H

ha, hahae, hahahae *interj* expression of joy, satisfaction, or laughter

habēn·a -ae *f* strap; *f pl* reins; (fig) reins, control; **habenae rerum** reins of the state; **habenas adducere, dare, effundere,** or **immittere** (with *dat*) to give free rein to

hab·ēō -ēre -uī -itum *vt* to have, hold, keep; to retain, detain; to contain; to possess, own; to wear; to treat, handle, use; to hold, conduct (*meeting*); to deliver (*speech*); to occupy, inhabit; to pronounce, utter (*words*); to hold, manage, govern, wield; to hold, think, consider, believe; to occupy, engage, busy; to occasion, produce, render; to know, be informed of, be acquainted with; to take, accept, endure, bear; **in animo habere** to have on one's mind; **in animo habere** (with *inf*) to intend to; **pro certo habere** to regard as certain; **secum** or **sibi habere** to keep (*something*) to oneself, keep secret; **se habere** (with *adv*) to be,feel (*well, etc.*); *vi* **bene habet** it is well, all is well; **sic habet** that's how it is

habil·is -e *adj* handy; suitable, convenient; active, nimble; skillful

habilit·ās -ātis *f* aptitude

habitābil·is -e *adj* habitable, fit to live in

habitāti·ō -ōnis *f* dwelling, house

habitāt·or -ōris *m* inhabitant, tenant

habit·ō -āre *vt* to inhabit; *vi* to dwell, live, stay, reside; (with **in + abl**) **a** to live in, reside at; **b** to be always in (*a certain place*); **o** (fig) to dwell upon

habitūd·ō -ĭnis *f* condition, appearance

habit·us -a -um *adj* well-kept, fat, stout

habit·us -ūs *m* condition (*of the body*); character, quality; style, style of dress, attire; disposition, state of feeling; habit

hāc *adv* this way, in this way

hactĕnus *adv* to this place, thus far; up till now, hitherto, so far; to this extent, so far, so much

Hadrĭ·a -ae *f* city in Picenum, the birthplace of Hadrian; city in the country of the Veneti, on the coast of the sea named after it; *m* Adriatic Sea

Hadrián·us -ī *m* Hadrian (*Roman emperor,* 117-138 A.D.)

haec hōrum (*neut pl* of **hoc**) *adj & pron* these

haec hūjus (older form; **haece;** *gen-it:* **hujusce**) (*fem* of **hic**) *adj* this; the present, the actual; the latter; (occasionally) the former; **haec . . . haec** one . . . another; *pron* this one, she; the latter; (occasionally) the former; **haec . . . haec** one . . . another one; **haecine** (**haec** with *interrog* enclitic **-ne**) is this . . .?

haece see **haec**

haecīne see **haec**

Haed·ī -ōrum *m pl* pair of stars in the constellation Auriga

haedili·a -ae *f* little kid

haedill·us -ī *m* (term of endearment) little kid or goat

haedín·us -a -um *adj* kid's, goat's

haedúl·us -ī *m* little kid, little goat

haed·us -ī *m* young goat, kid

Haemoni·a -ae *f* Thessaly

Haem·us or **Haem·os -ī** *m* mountain range in Thrace

haerēō haerēre haesī haesum *vi* to cling, stick; to hang around, linger, stay, remain fixed, remain in place; to be rooted to the spot, come to a standstill, stop; to be embarrassed, be at a loss, hesitate, be in doubt; (with *dat* or *abl* or with *in* + *abl*) **a** to cling to, stick to, adhere to, be attached to; **b** to loiter in, hang around in, waste time in (*a place*) or at (*an activity*); **c** to adhere to, stick by (*an opinion, purpose*); **d** to gaze upon; **e** to keep close to; **in terga, in tergis,** or **tergis hostium haerere** to pursue the enemy closely

haeresc·ō -ĕre *vi* to adhere

haerĕs·is -is *f* sect, school of thought

haesitábund·us -a -um *adj* hesitating, faltering

haesitanti·a -ae *f* stammering

haesitátĭ·ō -ōnis *f* hesitation, indecision; stammering

haesitát·or -ōris *m* hesitator

haesit·ō -āre *vi* to get stuck; to stammer; to hesitate, be undecided, be at a loss

hahae hahahae *interj* expression of joy, satisfaction, or laughter

halagŏra -ae *f* salt market

hāl·ans -antis *adj* fragrant

hāl·ēc -ēcis *n* fish sauce

haliaeĕt·os -ī *m* sea eagle, osprey

hālít·us -ūs *m* breath; steam, vapor

hall·ex -ícis *m* big toe

hallūcín·or or **hālūcín·or -ārī -ātus sum** *vi* to daydream, have hallucinations, talk wildly

hāl·ō -āre *vt* to exhale; *vi* to exhale; to be fragrant

halophant·a -ae *m* scoundrel

hālūcinor see **hallucinor**

ham·a or **am·a -ae** *f* bucket, pail

Hamādrý·as -ádis *f* wood nymph

hāmātíl·is -e *adj* with hooks

hāmāt·us -a -um *adj* hooked, hook-shaped

Hamílc·ar -āris *m* famous Carthaginian general in the First Punic War, surnamed Barca, and father of Hannibal (d. 228 B.C.)

hāmiŏt·a -ae *m* angler

hāmúl·us -ī *m* small hook

hām·us -ī *m* hook, fishhook

Hannĭb·al -ális *m* son of Hamilcar Barca and famous general in the Second Punic War (246-172 B.C.)

har·a -ae *f* pen, coop, stye

harēn·a -ae *f* sand; seashore, beach; arena; *f pl* desert

harēnōs·us -a -um *adj* sandy

hariŏl·or -ārī -ātus sum *vi* to foretell the future; to talk gibberish

hariŏl·us -ī *m* or **hariŏl·a -ae** *f* soothsayer

harmoni·a -ae *f* harmony

harpăg·ō -āre *vt* to steal

harpăg·ō -ōnis *m* hook, harpoon, grappling hook; greedy person

Harpalýc·ē -ēs *f* daughter of a Thracian king, brought up as a warrior

harp·ē -ēs *f* scimitar

Harpȳ·ae -árum *f pl* Harpies (*mythical monsters, half woman, half bird*)

harundĭf·er -ĕra -ĕrum *adj* reed-bearing

harundinĕ·us -a -um *adj* made of reed

harundinōs·us -a -um *adj* overgrown with reeds

harund·ō -ĭnis *f* reed, cane; fishing rod; pen; shepherd's pipe; arrow shaft, arrow; fowler's rod; weaver's comb; hobbyhorse (*toy*)

harusp·ex -ĭcis *m* soothsayer who foretold the future from the inspection of the vital organs of animals; prophet

haruspíc·a -ae *f* soothsayer (*female*)

haruspicín·us -a -um *adj* of divination; *f* art of divination

haruspíc·ĭum -ĭī *n* divination

Hasdrŭb·al or **Asdrŭb·al -ális** *m* brother of Hannibal (d. 207 B.C.); son-in-law of Hamilcar Barca (d. 221 B.C.)

hast·a -ae *f* spear; **sub hasta vendere** to sell at auction, auction off

hastāt·us -a -um *adj* armed with a spear; *m pl* soldiers in first line of a Roman battle formation

hastíl·e -is *n* shaft; spear, javelin

hau or **au** *interj* cry of pain or grief

haud or **haut** or **hau** *adv* not, hardly, not at all, by no means

hauddum *adv* not yet

haudquáquam *adv* not at all, by no means

hauriō haurīre hausī haustum *vt* to draw, draw up, draw out; to drain, drink up; to spill, shed; to swallow, devour, consume, exhaust; to derive; (fig) to drink in, seize upon, imbibe

haustr·um -ī *n* scoop, bucket

haustus *pp* of **haurio**

haust·us -ūs *m* drawing (*of water*); drinking, swallowing; drink, draught; handful; stream (*of blood*)

haut see **hand**

havĕō see **aveo**

hebdŏm·as -ădis *f* week

Hēb·ē -ēs *f* goddess of youth, daughter of Juno, and cupbearer of the gods

hebĕn·us -ī *f* ebony

heb·ĕō -ēre *vi* to be blunt, be dull; (fig) to be inactive, be sluggish

heb·es -ĕtis *adj* blunt, dull; faint, dim; dull, obtuse, stupid

hebesc·ō -ĕre *vi* to grow blunt, grow dull; to become faint or dim; to lose vigor

hebĕt·ō -āre *vt* to blunt, dull, dim

Hebr·us -ī *m* principal river in Thrace

Hecăt·ē -ēs *f* goddess of magic and witchcraft and often identified with Diana

hecatomb·ē -ēs *f* hecatomb

Hect·or -ŏris *m* son of Priam and Hecuba, husband of Andromache, and bravest Trojan warrior in fighting the Greeks

Hecŭb·a -ae or **Hecŭb·ē -ēs** *f* wife of Priam who, after the destruction of Troy, became a captive of the Greeks and was eventually changed into a dog

hedĕr·a -ae *f* ivy

hederig·er -ĕra -ĕrum *adj* wearing ivy

hederōs·us -a -um *adj* overgrown with ivy

hēdўchr·um -ī *n* perfume

hei hēia see **ei, ēia**

Helĕn·a -ae or **Helĕn·ē -ēs** *f* Helen (*wife of Menelaus, sister of Clytemnestra, Castor, and Pollux, who was abducted by Paris*)

Helĕn·us -ī *m* prophetic son of Priam and Hecuba

Hēliăd·es -um *f pl* daughters of Helios and sisters of Phaëthon, who were changed into poplars and whose tears were changed to amber

Helĭc·ē -ēs *f* Big Bear (*constellation*)

Helĭc·ōn -ōnis *m* mountain in Boeotia sacred to the Muses and to Apollo

Helicōniăd·es or **Helicōnid·es -um** *f pl* Muses

Hell·as -ădis *f* Greece

Hell·ē -ēs *f* daughter of Athamas and Nephele who, while riding the golden-fleeced ram, fell into the Hellespont and drowned

hellĕbor- = ellebor-

Hellespont·us -ī *m* Dardanelles

hellŭ·ō -ōnis *m* glutton, squanderer

hellŭ·or -ārī -ātus sum *vi* to be a glutton

hel·ops or **el·ops** or **ell·ops -ŏpis** *m* highly-prized fish (*perhaps the sturgeon*)

helvell·a -ae *f* delicious herb

Helvĕtĭ·ī -ōrum *m pl* people of Gallia Lugdunensis (*modern Switzerland*)

helv·us -a -um *adj* light-bay

hem *interj* (expression of surprise) well!

hēmerodrŏm·us -ī *m* courier

hēmicill·us -ī *m* mule

hēmicycl·ium -iī or **-ī** *n* semicircle of seats

hēmin·a -ae *f* half of a sextarius (*half a pint*)

hendecasyllăb·ī -ōrum *m pl* hendecasyllabics (*verses with eleven syllables*)

hēpatārĭ·us -a -um *adj* of the liver

hepter·is -is *f* galley with seven banks of oars

hera see **era**

Hēr·a -ae *f* Greek goddess identified with Juno

Hēraclīt·us -ī *m* early Greek philosopher of Ephesus who believed that fire was the primary element of all matter (*fl* 513 B.C.)

herb·a -ae *f* blade, stalk; herb, plant; grass, lawn; weed

herbesc·ō -ĕre *vi* to sprout

herbĕ·us -a -um *adj* grass-green

herbĭd·us -a -um *adj* grassy

herbif·er -ĕra -ĕrum *adj* grassy, grass-producing; made of herbs

herbōs·us -a -um *adj* grassy; made with herbs

herbŭl·a -ae *f* little herb

hercisc·ō -ĕre *vi* to divide an inheritance

herct·um or **erct·um -ī** *n* inheritance

Herculānĕ·um -ī *n* town on the seacoast of Campania which was destroyed with Pompeii in an eruption of Vesuvius in 79 A.D.

Hercŭl·ēs -is or **-ī** *m* son of Jupiter and Alcmena, husband of Deianira, and after his death and deification, husband of Hebe

hercŭlēs or **hercŭle** or **hercle** *interj* by Hercules!

here *adv* yesterday

hērēdĭtārĭ·us -a -um *adj* of or about an inheritance; inherited; hereditary

hērēdĭt·ās -ātis *f* inheritance

hērēd·ium -iī or **-ī** *n* inherited estate

hēr·ēs -ēdis *m* heir; (fig) heir, successor; *f* heiress

herī or **here** *adv* yesterday

herif- heril- = erif- eril-

Hermāphrodīt·us -ī *m* son of Hermes and Aphrodite who combined with the nymph Salmacis to become one person

Herm·ēs or **Herm·a -ae** *m* Greek god identified with Mercury

Hermĭŏn·ē -ēs or **Hermĭŏn·a -ae** *f* daughter of Helen and Menelaus and wife of Orestes

Hērŏdŏt·us -ī *m* father of Greek history, born at Halicarnassus on coast of Asia Minor (484-425 B.C.)

hērōĭc·us -a -um adj heroic, epic

hērōĭn·a -ae f demigoddess

hērō·ĭs -ĭdis f demigoddess

hēr·ōs -ōĭs m demigod, hero (*rarely used of men born of human parents*)

hērō·us -a -um adj heroic, epic

herus see **erus**

Hēsĭŏd·us -ī m Hesiod (*early Greek poet, born in Boeotia, 8th cent. B.C.*)

Hēsĭŏn·ē -ēs or **Hēsĭŏn·a -ae** f daughter of Laomedon, king of Troy, whom Hercules rescued from a sea monster

Hespĕr·us or **Hespĕr·os -ī** m evening star

hestern·us -a -um adj yesterday's

hetairĭ·a -ae f secret society

hetairĭc·ē -ēs f Macedonian mounted guard

heu! interj (expression of pain or dismay) oh!, ah!

heus! interj (to draw attention) say there!, hey!

hexamĕt·er -rī m hexameter verse

hexēr·is -is f ship with six banks of oars

hiāt·us -ūs m opening; open or gaping mouth; mouthing, bluster; basin (*of fountain*); chasm; (gram) hiatus

Hibēr·es -um m pl Spaniards

hibern·a -ōrum n pl winter quarters

hībernācŭl·a -ōrum n pl winter bivouac; winter residence

hībern·ō -āre vi to spend the winter; to stay in winter quarters; (fig) to hibernate

hībern·us -a -um adj winter, in winter, wintry

hibiscum -ī n hibiscus

hibrĭd·a or **hybrĭd·a -ae** m or f hybrid, mongrel, half-breed

hīc (or **hic**) **hūjus** (older form: **hīce hūjusce**) adj this; the present, the actual; the latter; (occasionally) the former; **hic . . . hic** one . . . another; **pron** this one, he; this man, myself, your's truly (*i.e., the speaker or writer*); the latter; (occasionally) the former; (in court) the defendant, my defendant; **hic . . . hic** one . . . another; **hicine** (**hic** with interrog enclitic **-ne**) is this . . . ?

hīc adv here, in this place; at this point; in this affair, in this particular, herein

hīce see **hic**

hicine see **hic**

hiemāl·is -e adj winter, wintry; stormy

hiĕm·ō -āre vi to spend the winter, pass the winter; to be wintry, be cold, be stormy

hiem·s or **hiem·ps -is** f winter; cold; storm

Hiĕr·ō -ōnis m ruler of Syracuse and patron of philosophers and poets (?-466 B.C.); friend of the Romans in the First Punic War (306?-215 B.C.)

Hierosolўm·a ōrum m pl Jerusalem

hĭĕt·ō -āre vi to keep yawing

hĭlăr·e adv cheerfully, merrily, gaily

hĭlăr·is -e or **hĭlăr·us -a -um** adj cheerful, merry, gay

hĭlarĭt·ās -ātis f cheerfulness, gaiety

hĭlarĭtūd·ō -ĭnis f cheerfulness

hĭlăr·ō -āre vt to cheer up

hĭlarŭl·us -a -um adj merry little

hĭlărus see **hilaris**

hill·ae -ārum f pl smoked sausage

Hīlŏt·ae or **īlŏt·ae -ārum** m pl Helots (*slaves of the Spartans*)

hĭl·um -ī n something, trifle

hinc adv from here, from this place; on this side, here; for this reason; from this source; after this, henceforth, from now on

hinn·ĭō -īre vi to whinny, neigh

hinnīt·us -ūs m neighing

hinnŭlĕ·us -ī m fawn

hĭ·ō -āre vt to sing; vi to open, be open; to gape; to yawn; to make eyes (*in surprise or greedy longing*)

hippagōg·ī -ōrum f pl ships for transporting horses and cavalry

Hipparch·us -ī m son of Pisistratus, the tyrant of Athens, who was slain by Harmodius and Aristogiton in 514 B.C.

Hippĭ·ās -ae m son of Pisistratus, the tyrant of Athens, and tyrant of Athens himself, 527-510 B.C.

hippocentaur·us -ī m centaur

Hippocrăt·ēs -is m famous physician, founder of scientific medicine (c. 460-380 B.C.)

Hippocrēn·ē -ēs f spring on Mt. Helicon, sacred to the Muses and produced when the hoof of Pegasus hit the spot

Hippodăm·ē -ēs or **Hippodamē·a** or **Hippodamī·a -ae** f daughter of Oenamaus, the king of Elis, and wife of Pelops; daughter of Adrastus and wife of Pirithous

hippodrŏm·os -ī m racetrack

Hippolўt·ē -ēs or **Hippolўt·a -ae** f Amazonian wife of Theseus; wife of Acastus, king of Magnesia

Hippolўt·us -ī m son of Theseus and Hippolyte

hippomăn·es -is n membrane of the head of a new-born foal; discharge of a mare in heat

Hippomĕn·ēs -ae m son of Megareus who competed with Atalanta in a race and won her as his bride

Hippōn·ax -actis m Greek satirist (fl 540 B.C.)

hippotoxŏt·ae -ārum m pl mounted archers

hippūr·us -ī m goldfish

hīr·a -ae f empty gut

hircĭn·us or **hirquīn·us -a -um** adj goat, of a goat

hircōs·us -a -um adj smelling like a goat

hirc·us -ī m goat

hirnĕ·a -ae f jug

hirsūt·us -a -um adj hairy, shaggy, bristly; prickly; rude

Hirt·ius -iī or **-ī** m Aulus Hirtius (consul in 43 B.C. and author of the eighth book of Caesar's Memoirs on the Gallic War)

hirt·us -a -um adj hairy, shaggy; uncouth

hirūd·ō -ĭnis f bloodsucker, leech

hirundinīn·us -a -um adj swallow's

hirund·ō -ĭnis f swallow

hisc·ō -ēre vt to murmur, utter; vi to open, gape, yawn; to open the mouth

Hispān·ī -ōrum m pl Spaniards

Hispāni·a -ae f Spain

Hispāniens·is -e adj Spanish

hispĭd·us -a -um adj hairy, shaggy, rough

Hist·er or **Ist·er -rī** m lower Danube

histori·a -ae f history; account, story; theme (of a story)

historic·us -a -um adj historical; m historian

histric·us -a -um adj theatrical

histri·ō -ōnis m actor

histriōnāl·is -e adj theatrical; histrionic

histriōni·a -ae f dramatics, art of acting

hiulcē adv with frequent hiatus

hiulc·ō -āre vt to split open

hiulc·us -a -um adj split, split open; open, gaping; with hiatus

hōc hūjus (older form: **hōce**; genit: **hūjusce**) (neut of **hic**) adj this; the present, the actual; the latter (occasionally) the former; pron this one, it; the latter; (occasionally) the former; (with genit) this amount of, this degree of, so much; **hoc erat quod** this was the reason why; **hoc est** that is, I mean, namely; **hōcine** (hoc with interrog enclitic **-ne**) is this . . . ?; **hoc facilius** all the more easily

hōce see **hoc**

hōcine see **hoc**

hodiē adv today; now, nowadays; still, to the present; at once, immediately; **hodie mane** this morning; **numquam hodie** (coll) never at all, never in the world

hodiern·us -a -um adj today's; **hodiernus dies** this day, today

holĭt·or -ōris m grocer

holĭtōri·us -a -um adj vegetable

hol·us -ĕris n vegetables

Homēr·us -ī m Homer

homicīd·a -ae m or f murderer, killer

homicīd·ium -iī or **-ī** n murder, manslaughter

hom·ō -ĭnis m or f human being, man, person, mortal; mankind, human race; fellow; fellow creature; (coll) this one; m pl persons, people; infantry; bodies, corpses; members (of the senate); **inter homi-**

nes esse to be alive; to see the world

homull·us -ī or **homucĭ·ō -ōnis** or **homuncŭl·us -ī** m poor man, poor creature

honest·a -ae f lady

honestāment·um -ī n ornament

honest·ās -ātis f good reputation, respectability; sense of honor, respect; beauty, grace; honesty, integrity, uprightness; decency; f pl respectable persons, decent people

honestē adv honorably, respectably, decently, virtuously

honest·ō -āre vt to honor, dignify, embellish, grace

honest·us -a -um adj honored, respected; honorable, decent, respectable, virtuous; handsome; m gentleman; n virtue, good

hon·or or **hon·ōs -ōris** m honor, esteem; position, office, post; mark of honor, reward, acknowledgment; offering, rites (to the gods or the dead); beauty, grace, charm; glory, fame, reputation; **honoris causā** out of respect, with all respect

honōrābĭl·is -e adj honorable

honōrāri·us -a -um adj honored, respected, highly esteemed; honorary, conferring honor

honōrātē adv with honor, honorably

honōrāt·us -a -um adj honored, respected; in high office; honorable, respectable; **honoratum habere** to hold in honor

honōrificē adv honorably, respectfully

honōrific·us -a -um adj honorable, complimentary

honōr·ō -āre vt to honor, respect; to embellish, decorate

honōr·us -a -um adj honorable, complimentary

honōs see **honor**

hoplomăch·us -ī m gladiator

hōr·a -ae f hour; time; season; **in diem et horam** continually; **in horam vivere** to live from hand to mouth; **quota hora est?** what time is it?; f pl clock; **in horas** from hour to hour, every hour

Hōr·a -ae f wife of Quirinus (i.e., of deified Romulus), called Hersilia before her death

Hōr·ae -ārum f pl Hours (daughters of Jupiter and Themis and goddesses who kept watch at the gates of heaven)

hōrae·us -a -um adj pickled

Horāt·ius -iī or **-ī** m Quintus Horatius Flaccus (65-8 B.C.); Horatius Cocles (defender of the bridge across the Tiber in the war with Porsenna)

hordĕ·um -ī n barley

hori·a -ae f fishing boat

horĭŏl·a -ae f small fishing boat

hornō adv this year, during this year

hornōtĭn·us -a -um adj this year's

horn·us -a -um adj this year's

hŏrolog·ĭum -ĭī or -ī *n* clock; water clock; sundial

horrend·us -a -um *adj* horrendous, horrible, terrible; awesome

horr·ens -entis *adj* bristling, bristly, shaggy

horr·ĕō -ēre -ŭī *vt* to dread; to shudder at, shrink from; to be amazed at; *vi* to stand on end, stand up straight; to get gooseflesh; to shiver, tremble, quake, shake; to look frightful, be rough

horr·escō -escĕre -ŭī *vt* to dread, become terrified at; *vi* to stand on end; (of the sea) to become rough; to begin to shake or shiver; to start (*in fear*)

horrĕ·um -ī *n* barn, shed; silo, granary; wine cellar; beehive

horribĭl·is -e *adj* horrible, terrifying; amazing

horridē *adv* roughly, rudely, sternly

horridŭl·us -a -um *adj* rather shaggy; somewhat shabby; somewhat unsophisticated (*style*)

horrĭd·us -a -um *adj* bristling, bristly, shaggy, prickly; rude, uncouth, rough, rugged, wild; disheveled; blunt, unpolished, course (*manner*); frightful, frightened, awful

horrĭf·er -ĕra -ĕrum *adj* causing shudders; freezing, chilling; terrifying

horrĭficē *adv* awfully

horrĭfic·ō -āre *vt* to make rough, ruffle; to terrify, appall

horrĭfic·us -a -um *adj* frightful, terrifying

horrĭsŏn·us -a -um *adj* frightening (*sound*), frightening to hear

horr·or -ōris *m* bristling; shivering, shuddering, quaking; dread, horror; awe, reverence; chill; thrill

horsum *adv* this way, here

hortām·en -ĭnis *n* injunction; encouragement

hortāment·um -ī *n* encouragement

hortātĭ·ō -ōnis *f* exhortation, encouragement

hortāt·or -ōris *m* backer, supporter, rooter, instigator

hortāt·us -ūs *m* encouragement, cheering, cheer

Hortens·ĭus -ĭī or -ī *m* Quintus Hortensius (*famous orator and friendly competitor of Cicero*, 114-50 B.C.)

hort·or -ārī -ātus sum *vt* to encourage, cheer, incite, instigate; to give a pep talk to (*soldiers*)

hortŭl·us -ī *m* little garden, garden plot

hort·us -ī *m* garden; *m pl* park

hosp·es -ĭtis *m* host, entertainer; guest, visitor; friend; stranger, foreigner

hospĭt·a -ae *f* hostess; guest, visitor; friend; stranger, foreigner

hospĭtāl·is -e *adj* host's; guest's; hospitable

hospĭtālĭt·ās -ātis *f* hospitality

hospĭtālĭter *adv* hospitably, as a guest

hospĭt·ĭum -ĭī or -ī *n* hospitality, friendship; welcome; guest room; lodging; inn

hostĭ·a -ae *f* victim, sacrifice

hostĭāt·us -a -um *adj* bringing offerings

hostĭc·us -a -um *adj* hostile; foreign, strange; *n* enemy territory

hostĭl·is -e *adj* enemy's, enemy, hostile

hostīlĭter *adv* hostilely, like an enemy

Hostīl·ĭus -ĭī or -ī *m* Tullus Hostilius (*third king of Rome*)

hostĭment·um -ī *n* compensation, recompense

host·ĭō -īre *vi* to return like for like

host·is -is *m or f* enemy

hūc *adv* here, to this place; to this, to this point, so far; to such a pitch; for this purpose; **huc atque illuc** here and there, in different directions; **hucine?** (**huc** + *interrog* enclitic) so far?

huī *interj* (expressing surprise or admiration) wow!

hūjusmŏdī or **hūjuscemŏdī** *adj* of this sort, such

humānē or **hūmānĭter** *adv* like a man; politely, gently, with compassion

hūmānĭt·ās -ātis *f* human nature; mankind; kindness, compassion; courtesy; culture, refinement, civilization

hūmānĭtus *adv* humanly; humanely, kindly, compassionately

hūmān·us -a -um *adj* of man, human; humane, kind, compassionate; courteous; cultured, refined, civilized, well educated

humātĭ·ō -ōnis *f* burial

hūme- = **ume-**

humī *adv* on or in the ground

hūmĭd· = **umĭd-**

humĭl·is -e *adj* low, low-lying, low-growing; shallow; stunted; low, common, colloquial; lowly, humble, poor, obscure, insignificant; base, mean, small-minded, cheap

humĭlĭt·ās -ātis *f* lowness; lowliness, insignificance; smallness of mind, meanness, cheapness

humĭlĭter *adv* low, deeply; meanly, abjectly

hum·ō -āre *vt* to bury

hum·us -ī *f* ground, earth; land, region, country

hyacinthĭn·us -a -um *adj* of the hyacinth; crimson

hyacinth·us or **hyacinth·os** -ī *m* hyacinth

Hyacinth·us or **Hyacinth·os** -ī *m* Spartan youth, who was accidently killed by his friend Apollo and from whose blood flowers of the same name sprang

Hyăd·es -um *f* Hyads (*group of sev-*

en stars in the head of the constellation Taurus whose rising with the sun was accompanied by rainy weather)

hyaen·a -ae *f* hyena

hyăl·us -ī *m* glass

Hybl·a -ae or **Hybl·ē -ēs** *f* Sicilian mountain, famous for its honey

hybrĭd·a -ae *m* or *f* hybrid, mongrel, half-breed

Hydasp·ēs -is *m* tributary of the Indus River

Hȳdr·a -ae *f* Hydra *(seven-headed dragon killed by Hercules)*; Hydra or Anguis *(constellation)*; fifty-headed monster at the gates of the lower world

hydraulĭc·us -a -um *adj* hydraulic

hydraul·us -ī *m* water organ

hydrĭ·a -ae *f* jug, urn

Hydrochŏ·us ͓ī *m* Aquarius *(constellation)*

hydrōpĭc·us -a -um *adj* dropsical

hydr·ops -ōpis *m* dropsy

hydr·us or **hydr·os -ī** *m* serpent

Hyl·ās -ae *m* youthful companion of Hercules who was carried off by the nymphs as he was drawing water

Hyll·us or **Hūl·us -ī** *m* son of Hercules and husband of Iole

Hym·ēn -ĕnis or **Hymenae·us** or

Hymenae·os -ī *m* Hymen *(god of marriage)*; wedding ceremony; wedding; wedding song

Hymett·us or **Hymett·os -ī** *m* mountain in E. Attica, famous for its honey

Hypăn·is -is *m* river in Sarmatia *(modern Bug)*

hyperbăt·on -ī *n* (rhet) transposition of words

hyperbŏl·ē -ēs *f* hyperbole

Hyperborĕ·ī -ōrum *m* *pl* legendary people in the land of the midnight sun

Hyperī·ōn -ŏnis *m* son of Titan and Earth, father of the Sun

Hypermestr·a -ae or **Hypermestr·ē -ēs** *f* the only one of the fifty daughters of Danaus who did not kill her husband on her wedding night

hypocaust·um or **hypocaust·on -ī** *n* sweat bath

hypodidascăl·us -ī *m* instructor

hypomnēm·a -ătis *n* memorandum, note

Hypsipȳl·ē -ēs *f* queen of Lemnos at the time of the Argonauts

Hyrcān·ī -ōrum *m* *pl* a people on the Caspian Sea

I

ia- = ja-

Iacch·us -ī *m* Bacchus; wine

iambē·us -a -um *adj* iambic

iamb·us -ī *m* iamb; iambic poem, iambic poetry

ianthĭn·a -ōrum *n* *pl* violet-colored garments

Iapĕt·us -ī *m* Titan, father of Prometheus, Epimetheus, and Atlas

Iāpȳd·es -um *m* *pl* Illyrian tribe

Iāp·yx -ȳgis *m* son of Daedalus who ruled in S. Italy; wind that blew from Apulia to Greece

Iăs·ius -iī or **-ī** *m* son of Jupiter and Electra and brother of Dardanus

Iăs·ōn -ŏnis *m* Jason *(son of Aeson, leader of the Argonauts, and husband of Medea and afterwards of Creusa)*

iasp·is -ĭdis *f* jasper

Ībēr- = Hiber-

ibi or **ibī** *adv* there, in that place; then, on that occasion; therein

ibīdem *adv* in the same place, just there; at that very moment; at the same time; in the same matter

Ib·is -is or **-ĭdis** *f* ibis *(bird sacred to the Egyptians)*

Īcăr·us -ī *m* son of Daedalus, who, on his flight from Crete with his father, fell into the sea; father of Penelope

ichneum·ōn -ŏnis *m* ichneumon

(Egyptian rat that eats crocodile eggs)

īcō īcĕre īcī īctum *vt* to hit, strike, shoot

īc·ōn -ŏnis *f* image

icterĭc·us -a -um *adj* jaundiced

ict·is -ĭdis *f* weasel

īctus *pp* of **īcō**

ict·us -ūs *m* stroke, blow, hit; cut, sting, bite, wound; range; stress, beat; **sub īctum** within range

id *adv* for that reason, therefore

id ejus *(neut* of **is)** *adj* this, that, the said, the aforesaid; *pron* it; a thing, the thing; **ad id** for that purpose; **aliquid id genus** something of that sort, something like that; **cum eo ... ut** on condition that, with the stipulation that; **eo plus** the more; **ex eo** from that time on; as a result of that, consequently; **id consili** some sort of plan, some plan; **id quod** a thing which, the thing which; **id temporis** at that time; of that age; **in id** to that end; **in eo esse** to depend on it; **in eo esse ... ut** to be so far gone that, to get to the point where

Īd·a -ae or **Īd·ē -ēs** *f* mountain near Troy; mountain in Crete where Jupiter was brought up

Īdal·ium -iī or **-ī** *n* city in Cyprus dear to Venus

idcircō *adv* on that account, for that reason, therefore

īdem eădem īdem *adj* the same, the very same, exactly this; (often equivalent to a mere connective) also, likewise; *pron* the same one

identĭdem *adv* again and again, continually, habitually; now and then, at intervals

idĕō *adv* therefore

idiōt·a -ae *m* uneducated person, ignorant person, layman

īdōl·on -ī *n* apparition, ghost

idōnēē *adv* suitably

idōnĕ·us -a -um *adj* suitable, fit, proper; (with *dat* or with **ad** or **in** + *acc*) fit for, capable of, suited for, convenient for, sufficient for

Īd·ūs -ŭum *f pl* Ides (*fifteenth day of March, May, July, and October, and thirteenth of the other months; interest, debts, and tuition were often paid on the Ides*)

ie- = **je-**

iens euntis *pres p* of **eo**

igĭtur *adv* then, therefore, accordingly; (resumptive after parenthetical matter) as I was saying; (in summing up) so then, in short

ignār·us -a -um *adj* ignorant, unaware, inexperienced; unsuspecting; senseless; unknown, strange, unfamiliar; (with *genit*) unaware of, unfamiliar with

ignāvē *adv* listlessly, lazily

ignāvĭ·a -ae *f* listlessness, laziness; cowardice

ignāvĭter *adv* listlessly

ignāv·us -a -um *adj* listless, lazy, idle, inactive; relaxing; cowardly, bastardly; unproductive (*field, etc.*)

ignescō·ō -ĕre *vi* to catch fire, become inflamed, burn; (fig) to flare up

ignĕ·us -a -um *adj* of fire, on fire, fiery; red-hot, fiery

ignicŭl·us -ī *m* small fire, little flame, spark

ignĭf·er -ĕra -ĕrum *adj* fiery

ignĭgĕn·a -ae *m* son of fire (*epithet of Bacchus*)

ignĭp·ēs -ĕdis *adj* fiery-footed

ignĭpŏt·ens -entis *adj* lord of fire (*epithet of Vulcan*)

ign·is -is *m* fire; conflagration; watch fire, signal fire; torch; lightning, bolt of lightning; funeral pyre; star; brightness, glow, brilliancy, splendor; (fig) fire, rage, fury, love, passion; flame, sweetheart; agent of destruction, fanatic; *m pl* love poems

ignōbĭl·is -e *adj* insignificant, obscure, unknown, undistinguished; low-born, ignoble

ignōbĭlit·ās -ātis *f* obscurity; humble birth

ignōmĭnĭ·a -ea *f* ignominy, dishonor, disgrace; **ignōminiā afficere** to dishonor, disgrace; **ignōminia senatūs** public censure imposed by the senate

ignōminiōs·us -a -um *adj* disgraced, degraded; disgraceful, shameful, ignominious; *m* infamous person

ignōrābĭl·is -e *adj* unknown

ignōrantĭ·a -ae *f* ignorance

ignōrātĭ·ō -ōnis *f* ignorance

ignōr·ō -āre *vt* to not know, be ignorant of, be unfamiliar with; to mistake, misunderstand; to ignore, disregard, take no notice of

ignosc·ens -entis *adj* forgiving

ig·nōscō -nōscĕre -nōvī -nōtum *vt* (with *dat* of person and *acc* of the offense) to pardon, forgive, excuse (*someone a fault*); *vi* (with *dat*) to pardon, forgive, excuse

ignōt·us -a -um *adj* unknown, unfamiliar, strange; inglorious; unnoticed; low-born, ignoble; vulgar; ignorant

īl·ex -ĭcis *f* holm oak

Īlĭ·a -ae *f* Rhea Silvia (*mother of Romulus and Remus*)

īl·ĭa -ium *n pl* guts, intestines; groin, belly

Īlĭăc·us -a -um *adj* Trojan

Īlĭ·as -ădis *f* Iliad; Trojan woman

īlĭcet *adv* (ancient form for adjourning an assembly) let us go; all is lost, kaput; at once, immediately, instantly

īlĭcō *adv* on the spot, right then and there; immediately

īlign·us or **īlĭgnĕ·us -a -um** *adj* of holm oak, oak

Īl·ĭos -iī or **-ī** *f* Troy

Īlĭthȳĭ·a -ae *f* goddess who aided women in childbirth

Īl·ĭum -iī or **-ī** or **Īl·ĭon -ī** *n* Troy

Īlĭ·us -a -um *adj* Trojan

illā *adv* that way

ill·a -īus *adj fem* that; that famous; *pron* that one; she

illabefact·us -a -um *adj* unbroken, uninterrupted

il·lābor -lābī -lapsus sum *vi* to flow; to sink, fall; fall in, cave in; to slip; (with *dat* or with **ad** or **in** + *acc*) to flow into, enter into, penetrate

illabōr·ō -āre *vi* (with *dat*) to work at, work on

illāc *adv* that way

illacessīt·us -a -um *adj* unprovoked

illacrimābĭl·is -e *adj* unlamented, unwept; inexorable

illacrĭm·ō -āre or **illacrĭm·or -ārī -ātus sum** *vi* (with *dat*) to cry over

ill·aec (*acc:* **-anc**; *abl:* **-āc**) *adj fem* that; *pron* she

illaes·us -a -um *adj* unhurt, unharmed

illaetābĭl·is -e *adj* sad, melancholy

illapsus *pp* of **illabor**

illaquĕ·ō -āre *vt* to trap

illātus *pp* of **infero**

illaudāt·us -a -um *adj* without fame, obscure; detestable

ill·e -īus *adj masc* that; that famous; the former; **ille aut ille** this or that, such and such; *pron* that one; he; the former one

illecĕbr·a -ae *f* attraction, allurement

illecebrōs·us -a -um *adj* alluring, seductive

illect·us -a -um *adj* unread

illect·us -ūs *m* allurement

illepĭdē *adv* inelegantly, rudely, impolitely

illepĭd·us -a -um *adj* inelegant, impolite, churlish

ill·ex -ĭcis *m* or *f* lure, decoy

ill·ex -ēgis *adj* lawless

illibāt·us -a -um *adj* undiminished, unimpaired

illiberāl·is -e *adj* ungenerous, stingy

illiberālĭt·ās -ātis *f* stinginess

ill·ic (*acc:* -**unc**; *abl:* -**ōc**) *adj masc* that; *pron* he

illic *adv* there, yonder, in that place; in that matter, therein

il·liciō -licĕre -lexī -lectum *vt* to allure, attract, seduce, mislead, lead astray

illicitāt·or -ōris *m* fake bidder (*one who bids at an auction to make others bid higher*)

illicĭt·us -a -um *adj* unlawful

il·līdō -līdĕre -līsī -līsum *vt* to smash to pieces, crush; (*with dat or with ad or in + acc*) to smash (*something*) against

illig·ō -āre *vt* to attach, connect; to tie, bind; to oblige; to impede, hamper

illim *adv* from there

illim·is -e *adj* unmuddied, clear

illinc *adv* from there; on that side; **hinc illinc** from one side to another

il·līnō -linĕre -lēvī -lĭtum *vt* to cover; to smear; (*with dat*) to smear or spread (*something*) on

illiquefact·us -a -um *adj* melted

illĭsus *pp* of **illīdo**

illiterāt·us -a -um *adj* uneducated, illiterate

illĭtus *pp* of **illino**

illō or **illōc** *adv* there, to that place; to that point

illōt·us -a -um *adj* unwashed, dirty

illūc *adv* to that place, in that direction; to that person, to him, to her; to that matter; to that place

ill·ūc (*acc:* -**ūc**; *abl:* -**ōc**) *adj neut* that; *pron* it

illuc·ēō -ēre *vt* to shine on; *vi* to blaze

il·lucescō -lucescĕre -luxī *vi* to grow light, dawn, to begin to shine

ill·ud -īus *adj neut* that; the former; *pron* it

il·lūdō -lūdĕre -lūsī -lūsum *vt* to make fun of, ridicule; to waste, abuse; *vi* (*with dat*) to play around with, do mischief to

illūminātē *adv* clearly

illūmin·ō -āre *vt* to light up, make bright, illuminate; to illustrate

illūsi·ō -ōnis *f* irony

illustr·is -e *adj* bright, clear, brilliant; plain, distinct, evident; distinguished, famous, illustrious, noble

illustr·ō -āre *vt* to light up, illuminate; to make clear, clear up, explain, illustrate; to adorn, embellish; to make famous

illūsus *pp* of **illūdo**

illuvĭ·ēs -ēī *f* inundation; offscouring, filth, dirt

Illyrĭc·us -a -um *adj* Illyrian; *n* Illyria

Illyrĭ·us -a -um *adj & m* Illyrian; *f* Illyria (*country on the E. coast of the Adriatic Sea*)

Il·us -ī *m* son of Tros, father of Laomedon, and founder of Ilium; Ascanius

imāginārĭ·us -a -um *adj* imaginary

imāginātĭōn·ēs -um *f pl* imaginings

imāgin·or -ārī -ātus sum *vt* to imagine

imāg·ō -ĭnis *f* image, likeness, picture, bust; bust of ancestor; ghost, vision; echo; appearance, semblance, shadow; mental picture, image, conception, thought, idea; figure of speech, simile, metaphor

imbēcillĭt·ās -ātis *f* weakness, feebleness; helplessness

imbēcillĭus *adv* more weakly, more faintly

imbēcill·us -a -um *adj* weak, feeble; helpless

imbell·is -e *adj* anti-war, pacifistic; peaceful; unfit for war, soft, cowardly; peaceful, quiet

imb·er -ris *m* rain, shower, rain storm; rain cloud; water; stream of tears; shower (*of gold, spears, etc.*)

imberb·is -e or **imberb·us -a -um** *adj* beardless

im·bibō -bibĕre -bĭbī *vt* to imbibe, drink in; to resolve on; **animo imbibere** to conceive, form (*e.g., an opinion*)

imbr·ex -ĭcis *f* tile

imbric·us -a -um *adj* rainy

imbrĭf·er -ĕra -ĕrum *adj* rainy

im·buō -buĕre -buī -būtum *vt* to wet, soak, saturate; to stain, taint, infect, imbue, fill, steep; to instruct, train, educate

imitābil·is -e *adj* imitable

imitām·en -ĭnis *f* imitation; *n pl* likeness, image

imitāment·a -ōrum *n pl* pretense

imitātĭ·ō -ōnis *f* imitation; pretense

imitāt·or -ōris *m* or **imitātr·ix -ĭcis** *f* imitator

imitāt·us -a -um *adj* fictitious, copied

imĭt·or -ārī -ātus sum *vt* to imitate, copy, portray; to ape

immad·escō -escĕre -uī *vi* to become wet

immānē *adv* savagely

immān·is -e *adj* huge, enormous, monstrous; inhuman, savage, monstrous

immānĭt·ās -ātis *f* vastness, enormity; savageness, cruelty, monstrousness, barbarity

immansuēt·us -a -um adj wild, savage

immātūrit·ās -ātis f overanxiousness

immātūr·us -a -um adj immature, unripe, premature

immedicābil·is -e adj incurable

immēm·or -ōris adj forgetful, forgetting; negligent

immemorābil·is -e adj not worth mentioning; untold

immemorāt·a -ōrum n pl novelties

immensit·ās -ātis f immensity; f pl immense stretches

immens·us -a -um adj immense, unending; n infinite space, infinity

immēr·ens -entis adj undeserving, innocent

im·mergō -mergĕre -mersī -mersum vt to immerse, dip, plunge; (with **in** + acc) to dip (something) into; **se immergere** (with **in** + acc) a to plunge into; b to insinuate oneself into

immeritō adv undeservedly, innocently

immerit·us -a -um adj undeserving, innocent; undeserved, unmerited; **immerito meo** through no fault of mine

immersābil·is -e adj unsinkable

immersus pp of **immergo**

immētāt·us -a -um adj unmeasured

immigr·ō -āre vi to immigrate; (with **in** + acc) a to move into; b (fig) to invade

immin·ĕō -ēre vi to project, stick out; to be near, be imminent, be near at hand; to threaten, menace; (with dat) a to jut out over; b to look out over, overlook (a view); c to hover over, loom over, threaten; (with dat or **in** + acc) to be intent on, be eager for

immin·ŭō -ŭĕre -ŭī -ūtum vt to lessen, curtail; to weaken, impair; to infringe upon, encroach upon, violate, subvert, destroy

imminūti·ō -ōnis f lessening; mutilation; understatement

im·miscĕō -miscēre -miscŭī -mixtum vt to mix in, intermix, blend; (fig) to mix up, confound; **immisceri** or **se immiscere** (with dat) a to join, join in with, mingle with, get lost in (e.g., a crowd); b to blend with, disappear in (e.g., night, cloud, etc.); **manūs manibus immiscere** (of boxers) to mix it up

immiserābil·is -e adj unpitied

immisericordĭter adv unmercifully

immisericor·s -dis adj merciless, pitiless

immissi·ō -ōnis f letting grow, letting alone

immissus pp of **immitto**

immīt·is -e adj unripe, sour, green; rude, harsh, stern, severe; pitiless, inexorable

im·mittō -mittĕre -mīsī -missum vt to insert; to let in, let go in, admit; let go of, let drop; to let go, let fly, launch; to set on, incite, egg on; **immitti** or **se immittere** (with dat or **in** + acc) a to plunge or dive into; b to rush against, attack; **in terram immittere** to ground

immixtus pp of **immisceo**

immo or **immō** adv (in contradiction or correction of preceding words) no, on the contrary, or rather; (in confirmation of preceding words) quite so, yes indeed; **immo vero** yes and in fact

immōbil·is -e adj motionless, unshaken; immovable; clumsy

immoderātē adv without limit; immoderately, extravagantly

immoderāti·ō -ōnis f lack of moderation, excess

immoderāt·us -a -um adj unmeasured, limitless; immoderate, uncontrolled, excessive

immodestē adv immoderately, shamelessly

immodesti·a -ae f excesses; insubordination

immodest·us -a -um adj immoderate, uncontrolled

immodicē adv excessively

immodic·us -a -um adj huge, enormous; immoderate, excessive; (with genit or abl) given to, excessive in

immodulāt·us -a -um adj unrhythmical

immolāti·ō -ōnis f sacrifice

immolāt·or -ōris m sacrificer

immōlīt·us -a -um adj constructed, erected; n pl buildings

immŏl·ō or **inmŏl·ō -āre** vt to immolate, sacrifice, offer

im·morior -mŏrī -mortŭus sum vi (with dat) to die in, die upon; (fig) to get sick over

immŏr·or -ārī -ātus sum vi (with dat) to dwell upon

immors·us -a -um adj bitten into; excited

immortāl·is -e adj immortal

immortālit·ās -ātis f immortality

immortālĭter adv infinitely

immortŭus pp of **immorior**

immōt·us -a -um adj unmoved, immovable; unshaken, undisturbed, steadfast

immūg·ĭō -īre -īvī or **-ĭī -ītum** vi to bellow, roar

immulg·ĕō -ēre vt to milk

immundĭti·a -ae f dirtiness, filth

immund·us -a -um adj dirty, filthy, foul

immūn·ĭō -īre -īvī vt to reinforce, fortify

immūn·is -e adj without duty or office; tax-exempt, free, exempt; pure, innocent; (with abl or **ab** + abl) free from, exempt from; (with genit) free of, free from, devoid of, without

immūnit·ās -ātis f immunity, exemption, exemption from taxes

immūnit·us -a -um adj unfortified, undefended; unpaved (street)

immurmur·ō -āre vi to grumble; (with dat) (of the wind) to whisper among

immūtābil·is -e adj immutable, unchangeable

immūtābilit·ās -ātis f immutability

immūtāti·ō -ōnis f exchange, substitution; metonymy

immūtāt·us -a -um adj unchanged

immūt·ō -āre vt to change, alter; to substitute

impācāt·us -a -um adj restless; aggressive

impactus pp of impingo

impall·escō -escĕre -uī vi (with abl) to turn pale at

im·pār -āris adj uneven, odd (numbers); uneven (in size or length); not matching, unlike (in color or appearance); unequal; unfair; ill-matched; uneven, crooked; (with dat) not a match for, inferior to, unable to cope with

imparāt·us -a -um adj unprepared

impariter adv unequally

impast·us -a -um adj unfed, hungry

impati·ens -entis adj impatient; (with genit) unable to stand, endure, tolerate

impatienter adv impatiently; intolerably

impatienti·a -ae f impatience; (with genit) inability to stand or endure

impavidē adv fearlessly

impavid·us -a -um adj fearless, dauntless

impediment·um -ī n impediment, hindrance; difficulty; n pl baggage, luggage; mule train

imped·iō -īre -īvī or **-iī -ītum** vt to entangle; to hamper, hinder; to entwine, encircle; to clasp, embrace; to block up (road); to hinder, prevent; to embarrass; **impedīre** (with ne, quin, or quominus) to prevent (someone) from

impedīti·ō -ōnis f obstacle, obstruction

impedīt·us -a -um adj hampered, obstructed, blocked; difficult, intricate; impassable; busy, occupied

im·pellō -pellĕre -pulī -pulsum vt to strike against, strike, reach; to push, drive, drive forward, impel, propel; to urge, persuade, stimulate, induce; to force, compel; to put to rout; to swell (sails)

impend·eō -ēre vi to be near, be at hand, be imminent, threaten; (with dat) to hang over; (with dat or in + acc) to hover or loom over, threaten

impendiōs·us -a -um adj extravagant

impend·ium -iī or **-ī** n expense, cost, outlay; interest (paid out); loss

im·pendō -pendĕre -pendī -pen- sum vt to weigh out, pay out; to expend, devote, apply, employ; (with in + acc) a to spend (money) on; b to expend (effort) on, pay (attention) to

impenetrābil·is -e adj impenetrable

impens·a -ae f expense, cost, outlay; waste; contribution; **meis impensis** at my expense

impensē adv at a high cost, expensively; with great effort

impens·us -a -um pp of impendo; adj high, costly, expensive; strong, vehement, earnest; n high price

impĕr·ans -antis m master, ruler, conqueror

imperāt·or -ōris m commander, general; commander in chief; emperor; director, master, ruler, leader

imperātōri·us -a -um adj of a general, general's; imperial

imperātr·ix -īcis f controller, mistress

imperāt·um -ī n command, order

impercept·us -a -um adj unperceived, unknown

impercuss·us -a -um adj noiseless

imperdīt·us -a -um adj unscathed

imperfect·us -a -um adj unfinished, imperfect

imperfoss·us -a -um adj unpierced, not stabbed

imperiōs·us -a -um adj imperial; magisterial; tyrannical, overbearing, domineering, imperious

imperītē adv unskillfully, clumsily, ignorantly

imperīti·a -ae f inexperience, awkwardness, ignorance

imperīt·ō -āre vt & vi to command, rule, govern

imperīt·us -a -um adj inexperienced, unfamiliar, ignorant, unskilled; (with genit) inexperienced in, unacquainted with, ignorant of

imper·ium -iī or **-ī** n command, order; right to command; exercise of authority; military commission, supreme command; mastery, sovereignty; realm, empire, dominion, supremacy, authority; public office, magistracy; term of office

imperjūrāt·us -a -um adj sacrosanct, inviolable

impermiss·us -a -um adj forbidden, unlawful

impĕr·ō -āre vt to requisition, give orders for, order, demand; (with acc of thing demanded and dat of source demanded from) to demand (e.g., hostages) from; vi to be in command, rule, be master; (with dat) to give orders to, order, command, govern, master

imperterrit·us -a -um adj undaunted, unterrified

impert·iō -īre vt (with dat) to impart, communicate, bestow, assign, direct (something) to, share (something) with; (with acc of person and abl of thing) to present (someone) with

imperturbāt·us -a -um adj unperturbed, unruffled

impervi·us -a -um adj impassable; (with dat) impervious to

impetibil·is -e adj intolerable

impět·ō -ēre vt to make for; to attack

impetrābil·is -e adj obtainable; successful

impetrātī·ō -ōnis f obtaining, procurement

impetr·iō -īre vt to try to obtain through favorable omens

impětr·ō -āre vt to obtain, procure (by asking); to achieve, accomplish, bring to pass

impět·us -ūs m attack, assault; rush; impetus, impetuosity, vehemence, vigor, violence, fury, force; impulse, passion

impex·us -a -um adj uncombed; unpolished

impiē adv wickedly

impiět·ās -ātis f impiety, irreverence; disloyalty; treason

impĭg·er -ra -rum adj diligent, active, energetic

impĭgrē adv energetically, actively, quickly

impĭgrĭt·ās -ātis f energy, activity

im-pingō -pingěre -pēgī -pactum vt (with dat or in + acc) a to fasten to; b to pin against, force against, dash against; c to press or force (something) on; d to fling at

impĭ·ō -āre vt to make irreverent

impĭ·us -a -um adj impious, irreverent; disobedient, undutiful; disloyal, unpatriotic; wicked, unscrupulous, shameless

implācābĭl·is -e adj implacable, unappeasable

implācāt·us -a -um adj unappeased, unsatisfied

implācĭd·us -a -um adj fierce, savage

impl·ěō -ēre -ēvī -ētum vt to fill up; to satisfy; to fatten; to impregnate, make pregnant; to enrich; to cover with writing, fill up (a book); to discharge, fulfill, execute, implement; to complete, finish, end; to spend (time)

implex·us -a -um adj enfolded, entwined; involved

implicātĭ·ō -ōnis f entanglement; incorporation; embarrassment

implicāt·us -a -um adj entangled, involved, complicated, confused

implĭcisc·or -ī vi to become confused

implĭcĭtē adv intricately

implĭcĭtus pp of **implico**; adj confused, confounded; **implicitus morbo** disabled by sickness, sick

implĭc·ō -āre -āvī -ātum or **-āre -ŭī -ĭtum** vt to entangle, involve, enfold, envelop; to embrace, clasp, grasp; to connect, unite, join; to involve, implicate, engage; to embarrass; **se dextrae implicāre** to embrace, shake hands

implōrātĭ·ō -ōnis f begging, imporing

implōr·ō -āre vt to implore, appeal to, call upon for aid; (with double acc) to beg (someone) for; (with **ab** + abl) to ask for (something) from

implūm·is -e adj without feathers, unfledged

impl·ŭō -uěre -ŭī -ūtum vi (with dat) to rain on

impluviāt·us -a -um adj shaped like an impluvium, square

impluv·ĭum -ī or **-ī** n skylight, impluvium (opening in the roof of the atrium of the Roman house to get rid of smoke and let in light); builtin basin in the atrium to catch the rain water; uncovered space in the atrium

impolītē adv simply, without fancy words

impolīt·us -a -um adj unpolished, rough; unrefined, inelegant; unfinished

impollūt·us -a -um adj unsullied

im-pōnō -pōněre -posŭī -positum or **-postum** vt to impose; to establish, introduce; to place, set; to inflict, impose, dictate; to assign; to apply, give; to impose, assess, exact; to put (someone) in charge; (with dat, with **in** + acc, **in** + abl, or **supra** + acc) to place, put, set, lay (someone or something) on or in; (with dat) a to impose (taxes, etc.) upon; b to put (someone) in charge of; vi (with dat) to impose upon, trick, cheat

import·ō -āre vt to bring in, import; to introduce

importūnĭt·ās -ātis f importunity, rudeness, insolence; unfitness

importūn·us -a -um adj inconvenient, unsuitable; troublesome, annoying; lacking consideration for others, rude, ruthless, churlish; stormy; ill-omened

importuōs·us -a -um adj without a harbor

imp·os -ōtis adj without control; (with genit) without control of

impositus pp of **impono**

impossibĭl·is -e adj impossible

impostus pp of **impono**

impŏt·ens -entis adj impotent, powerless; having no control of oneself, wild, uncontrollable, impetuous, violent

impotenter adv impotently, weakly

impotentĭ·a -ae f weakness, helplessness; lack of self-control, violence, fury, passion

impraesentĭārum adv for the present, under present circumstances

imprans·us -a -um adj without breakfast, fasting

imprecātĭ·ō -ōnis f imprecation, curse

imprěc·or -ārī -ātus sum vt to call down (a curse); to invoke

impressĭ·ō -ōnis f pressure; assault, attack, charge; rhythmical beat;

emphasis; impression (*on the mind*)

impressus *pp* of **imprimo**

imprīmīs or **in prīmīs** *adv* in the first place, chiefly, especially

im·primō -primĕre -pressī -pressum *vt* to press down; to impress, imprint, stamp; (*fig*) to impress, engrave, mark

improbātĭ·ō -ōnis *f* disapprobation, blame

imprōbē *adv* badly, wickedly, wrongfully; recklessly; persistently

improbĭt·ās -ātis *f* wickedness, depravity; roguishness

imprōb·ō -āre *vt* disapprove, condemn, blame, reject

improbŭl·us -a -um *adj* naughty

imprōb·us -a -um *adj* below standard, poor, inferior, bad, shameless; rebellious, unruly; restless, indomitable, self-willed; cruel, merciless; persistent

imprōcēr·us -a -um *adj* undersized

imprōdict·us -a -um *adj* not postponed

imprompt·us -a -um *adj* slow

improperāt·us -a -um *adj* slow, deliberate

impropri·us -a -um *adj* unsuitable

imprōsp·er -ĕra -ĕrum *adj* unfortunate

imprōspĕrē *adv* unfortunately

imprōvĭdē *adv* without foresight, thoughtlessly

imprōvĭd·us -a -um *adj* not foreseeing, not anticipating; (with *genit*) indifferent to

imprōvīs·us -a -um *adj* unexpected; **de imprōvīso, ex imprōvīso** or **imprōvīso** unexpectedly; *n pl* emergencies

imprūd·ens -entis *adj* not foreseeing, not anticipating, unsuspecting, off one's guard; inconsiderate; (with *genit*) unaware of, ignorant of, heedless of, not experienced in

imprūdenter *adv* without foresight, thoughtlessly, inconsiderately, imprudently

imprūdentĭ·a -ae *f* thoughtlessness; ignorance, imprudence

impūb·es -ĕris or **-is** *adj* youthful, young; innocent, chaste, celibate, virgin

impūd·ens -entis *adj* shameless

impudenter *adv* shamelessly

impudentĭ·a -ae *f* shamelessness

impudīcitĭ·a -ae *f* immodesty, lewdness, shamelessness

impudīc·us -a -um *adj* immodest, lewd, shameless

impugnātĭ·ō -ōnis *f* assault, attack

impugn·ō -āre *vt* to assault, attack; (*fig*) to impugn

impulsĭ·ō -ōnis *f* pressure; impulse

impuls·or -ōris *m* instigator

impulsus *pp* of **impello**

impuls·us -ūs *m* push, pressure, impulse, shock; instigation, incitement

impūne or **inpūne** *adv* with impunity, unpunished, scot-free; safely, unscathed

impūnīt·ās -ātis *f* impunity

impūnītē *adv* with impunity

impūnīt·us -a -um *adj* unpunished; unrestrained

impūrē *adv* impurely

impūrĭt·ās -ātis *f* impurity

impūr·us -a -um *adj* impure, unclean, filthy; (morally) impure, filthy, vile

imputāt·us -a -um *adj* unpruned, untrimmed

imput·ō -āre *vt* to charge to someone's account, enter in an account; (with *dat*) to charge to, ascribe to, give credit for (*something*) to, put the blame for (*something*) on

īmŭl·us -a -um *adj* cute little

īm·us -a -um *adj* deepest, lowest; last; the bottom of, the foot of, the tip of; *n* bottom, depth; **ab imo** utterly; **ab imo ad summum** from top to bottom; **ex imo** utterly, completely; *n pl* lower world

in *prep* (with *abl*) in, on, upon, among, at; before; under; during, within, in, at, in the course of, on the point of, in case of, in relation to; subject to, affected by, engaged in, involved in; (with *acc*) into, up to, towards; till, to, for; in relation to, about, respecting, against; for, with a view to, according to, after

inaccess·us -a -um *adj* inaccessible

inac·escō -escĕre -ŭī *vi* to turn sour

Īnachĭd·ēs -ae *m* descendant of Inachus; Perseus; Epaphus

Īnäch·is -ĭdis *f* female descendant of Inachus (*esp. Io*)

Īnăch·us or **Īnăch·os -ī** *m* first king or Argos and father of Io

inadsc- = inasc-

inadt- = inatt-

inadust·us -a -um *adj* unburned

inaedificĭ·ō -āre *vt* to build on, build as an addition, erect, construct; to wall up, barricade; (with **in** + *abl*) to build (*something*) on top of

inaequābĭl·is -e *adj* uneven

inaequābĭlĭter *adv* unevenly, unequally

inaequāl·is -e *adj* uneven, unequal; unlike, changeable, inconstant

inaequālĭt·ās -ātis *f* unevenness

inaequālĭter *adv* unevenly

inaequāt·us -a -um *adj* unequal

inaequ·ō -āre *vt* to level off

inaestimābĭl·is -e *adj* inestimable; invaluable; valueless

inaestŭ·ō -āre *vi* bilis inaestuat anger flares up

inaffectāt·us -a -um *adj* unaffected, natural

inamābĭl·is -e *adj* hateful, revolting

inamārescō -ĕre *vi* to become bitter

inambitĭōs·us -um *adj* unambitious

inambulātĭ·ō -ōnis *f* walking about, strutting about

inambŭl·ō -āre *vi* to walk up and down

inamoen·us -a -um *adj* unpleasant

inānī·ae -ārum *f pl* emptiness

inānilogist·a -ae *m* chatterbox

inānīment·um -ī *n* empty space

inanim·us -a -um *adj* inanimate

inān·e -is *n* empty space, vacuum; emptiness; worthlessness

inān·is -e *adj* empty, void; deserted, abandoned, unoccupied; hollow; worthless, idle; lifeless, unsubstantial; penniless, poor; unprofitable; groundless, unfounded

inānit·ās -ātis *f* empty space, emptiness; uselessness, worthlessness

inānĭter *adv* uselessly, vainly

inarāt·us -a -um *adj* untilled, fallow

in·ardescō -ardescĕre -arsī *vi* to catch fire, burn, glow

ināresc·ō -ĕre *vi* to become dry, dry up

inascens·us -a -um *adj* not climbed

inassuēt·us -a -um *adj* unaccustomed

inattenuāt·us -a -um *adj* undiminished; unappeased

inaud·ax -ācis *adj* timid, cowed

inaud·ĭō -īre -īvī or **-ĭī -ītum** *vt* to hear, learn

inaudīt·us -a -um *adj* unheard-of, unusual; without a hearing in court

inaugurātō *adv* after taking the auspices

inaugŭr·ō -āre *vt* to inaugurate, consecrate, install; *vi* to take the auspices

inaurāt·us -a -um *adj* gilded, gilt

inaur·ēs -ium *f pl* earrings

inaur·ō -āre *vt* to goldplate, gild; to line the pockets of (*someone*) with gold, to make rich

inauspicātō *adv* without consulting the auspices

inauspicāt·us -a -um *adj* undertaken without auspices; unlucky

inaus·us -a -um *adj* unattempted

inb- = imb-

inbīt·ō -ĕre *vt* enter

incaedŭ·us -a -um *adj* uncut

incal·escō -escĕre -ŭī *vi* to grow warm or hot; to get excited

incalfac·ĭō -ĕre *vt* to warm, heat

incallĭdē *adv* unskillfully

incallĭd·us -a -um *adj* unskillful; stupid, simple, clumsy

incand·escō -escĕre -ŭī *vi* to become white; to get white-hot

incān·escō -escĕre -ŭī *vi* to get grey

incantāt·us -a -um *adj* enchanted

incān·us -a -um *adj* grown grey

incassum *adv* in vain

incastigāt·us -a -um *adj* unscolded, unpunished

incautē *adv* incautiously, recklessly

incaut·us -a -um *adj* incautious, inconsiderate, thoughtless, reckless; unforeseen, unexpected; unguarded

in·cēdō -cēdĕre -cessī -cessum *vi* to go, step, move, walk, stalk; to proceed, go forward; to come along, happen, occur, appear, arrive; to advance, go on

incelebrāt·us -a -um *adj* unheralded

incēnāt·us -a -um *adj* supperless

incendiār·ĭus -iī or **-ī** *m* agitator

incend·ĭum -iī or **-ī** *n* fire; heat

in·cendō -cendĕre -cendī -censum *vt* to light, set on fire, burn; to light up, make bright; (*fig*) to inflame, fire, excite, enrage

incēn·is -e *adj* dinnerless, without dinner

incensĭ·ō -ōnis *f* burning

incensus *pp* of **incendo**

incens·us -a -um *adj* not registered (*with the censor*)

inceptĭ·ō -ōnis *f* beginning; undertaking

incept·ō -āre *vt* to begin; to undertake

incept·or -ōris *m* beginner, originator

incept·us -a -um *pp* of **incipio**; *n* beginning; undertaking, attempt, enterprise; subject, theme

in·cernō -cernĕre -crēvī -crētum *vt* to sift

incēr·ō -āre *vt* to wax, cover with wax

incertō *adv* not for certain

incert·ō -āre *vt* to render doubtful, make uncertain

incert·us -a -um *adj* uncertain, vague, obscure; doubtful, dubious; unsure, hesitant; *n* uncertainty, insecurity; contingency; **in incertum** for an indefinite time

incess·ō -ĕre -īvī *vt* to fall upon, assault, reproach, accuse, attack; (*fig*) to attack

incess·us -ūs *m* walk, gait, pace; tread, trampling; invasion, attack

incestē *adv* impurely, sinfully; indecently

incest·ō -āre *vt* to pollute, defile; to violate (*a girl*)

incest·us -a -um *adj* polluted, defiled, unclean, impure, sinful; lewd, unchaste, incestuous

incest·us -ūs *m* indecency, incest

in·cĭdō -cidĕre -cĭdī -cāsum *vi* to happen, occur; (*with* in *or* ad + *acc*) to fall into, fall upon; (*with* in + *acc*) **a** to come upon unexpectedly, fall in with; **b** to attack; (*with* dat *or* in + *acc*) **a** to occur to (*mentally*); **b** to fall on (*a certain day*); **c** to befall; **d** to agree with

in·cīdō -cīdĕre -cīdī -cīsum *vt* to carve, engrave, inscribe; to cut, sever; (*fig*) to cut into, cut short, put an end to, break off, interrupt

incīl·e -is *n* ditch, trench

in·cingō -cingĕre -cinxī -cinctum *vt* to drape; to wreathe; to invest, surround

incīn·ō -ĕre *vt* to sing; to play

incipessō *see* **incipisso**

in·cipĭō -cipĕre -cēpī -ceptum *vt & vi* to begin, start

incipiss·ō -ĕre vt to begin

incīsē or **incīsim** adv in short phrases

incīsi·ō -ōnis f or **incīs·um -ī** n clause

incīsus pp of **incido**

incitāment·um -ī n incitement, incentive

incitāti·ō -ōnis f inciting, rousing; speed

incitātius adv rather impetuously

incitāt·us -a -um adj rapid, speedy; **equo incitato** at full gallop

incit·ō -āre vt to incite, urge on, spur on, drive on; to stimulate; to inspire; to stir up, arouse; to increase, augment; **currentem incitare** (fig) to spur a willing horse; **se incitare** to rush

incīt·us -a -um adj rapid, swift; immovable; **ad incita redigere** to bring to a standstill

inclāmit·ō -āre vt to cry out against, abuse

inclām·ō -āre vt to shout at, scold, chide; vi to yell

inclār·escō -escĕre -uī vi to become famous

inclēm·ens -entis adj inclement, harsh, unmerciful

inclēmenter adv harshly, severely

inclēmenti·a -ae f harshness, severity, rigor

inclīnāti·ō -ōnis f leaning; inclination, tendency, bias; change; inflection

inclīnāt·us -a -um adj inclined, prone; sinking; low, deep

inclīn·ō -āre vt to bend, turn, to turn back, drive back, repulse; (fig) to divert, shift (e.g., blame); to change, alter; **inclinari** (mil) to fall back, give way; **inclinari** or **se inclinare** to lean, bend, turn; to change (esp. for the worse); vi to bend, turn, lean, dip, sink, (mil) to fall back, give way; (fig) to change, deteriorate; (fig) to change for the better

inclit·us -a -um adj famous

in·clūdō -clūdĕre -clūsī -clūsum vt to shut in, confine, lock up; to include, insert; to block, obstruct, shut off, stop up; (fig) to include, embrace, comprehend; to restrain, control; to close, end (e.g., day)

inclūsi·ō -ōnis f locking up, confinement

inclŭt·us or **inclĭt·us -a -um** adj famous

incoct·us -a -um pp of **incoquo;** adj uncooked, raw

incōgitābil·is -e adj thoughtless, inconsiderate

incōgit·ans -antis adj unthinking, thoughtless

incōgitanti·a -ae f thoughtlessness

incōgitāt·us -a -um adj thoughtless, inconsiderate

incōgit·ō -āre vt to think up

incognit·us -a -um adj not investigated; unknown, unrecognized, unidentified; unparalleled

incohāt·us -a -um adj unfinished

incŏh·ō -āre vt to begin, start

incŏl·a -ae m & f inhabitant, resident

incŏl·ō -ĕre -uī vt to live in, inhabit, occupy; vi to live, reside

incolŭm·is -e adj unharmed, safe and sound, unscathed, alive; (with abl) safe from

incolumit·ās -ātis f safety

incomitāt·us -a -um adj unaccompanied

incommendāt·us -a -um adj unprotected

incommŏdē adv at the wrong time; inconveniently; unfortunately

incommodestic·us -a -um adj (coll) ill-timed, inconvenient

incommodit·ās -ātis f inconvenience; unsuitableness; disadvantage

incommŏd·ō -āre vi (with dat) to be inconvenient to, to be annoying to, to inconvenience

incommŏd·us -a -um adj inconvenient, annoying; n inconvenience; trouble, setback, disaster

incommūtābil·is -e adj unchangeable

incomparābil·is -e adj unequaled, incomparable

incompert·us -a -um adj unknown, forgotten

incompositē adv in disorder

incomposit·us -a -um adj disordered, confused, unstudied, uncouth; irregular

incomprehensibil·is -e adj incomprehensible

incompt·us -a -um adj unkempt, messy; primitive, rude (discourse)

inconcess·us -a -um adj forbidden, unlawful

inconcili·ō -āre vt to deceive, trick, to rob, fleece

inconcinn·us -a -um adj clumsy, awkward; absurd

inconcuss·us -a -um adj unshaken

incondītē adv confusedly

incondīt·us -a -um adj unorganized, disorderly, confused, irregular; rough, undeveloped (style); raw (jokes)

inconsīderātē adv thoughtlessly

inconsīderāt·us -a -um adj thoughtless

inconsōlābil·is -e adj incurable

inconst·ans -antis adj inconsistent, fickle, shifty

inconstanter adv inconsistently

inconstanti·a -ae f inconsistency, fickleness

inconsultē adv indiscreetly

inconsult·us -a -um adj indiscreet, ill-advised, imprudent; not consulted

inconsult·us -ūs m **inconsultu meo** without consulting me

inconsumpt·us -a -um adj unconsumed

incontāmināt·us -a -um adj untainted

incontent·us -a -um *adj* loose, untuned (*string*)

incontin·ens -entis *adj* incontinent

incontinenter *adv* without self-control, incontinently

incontinenti·a -ae *f* lack of self-control

inconveni·ens -entis *adj* unsuitable, dissimilar

in·cŏquŏ -cŏquĕre -coxī -coctum *vt* to boil, cook; to dye

incorrect·us -a -um *adj* uncorrected, unrevised

incorruptē *adv* justly, fairly

incorrupt·us -a -um *adj* untainted; uncorrupted, unspoiled; genuine, pure

incrēbr·escŏ or **incrēb·escŏ -escĕre -ŭī** *vi* to grow, rise, increase, spread

incrēdibil·is -e *adj* incredible

incrēdibiliter *adv* incredibly

incrēdŭl·us -a -um *adj* incredulous

incrēment·um -ī *n* growth, increase; increment, addition; addition to the family, offspring

increpit·ŏ -āre *vt* to scold, rebuke

increp·ŏ -āre -ŭī (or **-āvī**) **-ĭtum** (or **-ātum**) *vt* to cause to make noise; to rattle; (*of Jupiter*) to thunder at; to scold, rebuke; *vi* to make a noise, to rustle, rattle, clatter, clash; to speak angrily

incr·escŏ -escĕre -ēvī *vi* to grow, increase; (with *dat* or *abl*) to grow in or upon

incrētus *pp* of **incerno**

incruentāt·us -a -um *adj* unbloodied

incruent·us -a -um *adj* bloodless, without bloodshed

incrust·ŏ -āre *vt* to cover with a coat, encrust

incŭb·ŏ -āre -ŭī -ĭtum *vi* (with *dat*) **a** to lie in or upon; **b** to lean on; **c** to brood over; **d** to watch jealously over

inculc·ŏ -āre *vt* to impress, inculcate; (with *dat*) to force (*something*) upon

inculpāt·us -a -um *adj* blameless

incultē *adv* uncouthly, roughly

incult·us -a -um *adj* untilled, uncultivated; neglected, slovenly; rough, uneducated, uncivilized; *n pl* desert, wilderness

incult·us -ūs *m* neglect; dirt, squalor

in·cumbŏ -cumbĕre -cubŭī -cubĭtum *vi* (with *dat* or **in** + *acc*) **a** to lean on or against; **b** to lie down on (*a couch, bed*); **c** to bend to (*the oars*); **d** to light on, fall on; **e** (*fig*) to press upon, burden, oppress, weigh down; **f** to apply onself to, take pains with, pay attention to; (with **ad** or **in** + *acc*) to be inclined towards, lean towards

incūnābŭl·a -ōrum *n pl* baby clothes, swaddling clothes; (*fig*) cradle, infancy, birthplace, source, origin

incūrāt·us -a -um *adj* neglected; uncured

incūri·a -ae *f* carelessness, negligence

incūriōsē *adv* carelessly

incūriōs·us -a -um *adj* careless, unconcerned, indifferent; neglected

in·currŏ -currĕre -currī or **-cucurrī -cursum** *vt* to attack; *vi* (with *dat* or **in** + *acc*) **a** to run into, rush at, charge, attack, invade; **b** to extend to; **c** to meet, run into; **d** to fall on, coincide with

incursĭ·ŏ -ōnis *f* incursion, invasion, raid; assault, attack, collision

incurs·ŏ -āre *vt* to assault, attack; to invade; *vi* (with *dat* or **in** + *acc*) **a** to assault, attack; **b** to run into, bump against; **c** to strike, meet (*e.g., the eyes*); **d** to affect, touch, move

incurs·us -ūs *m* assault, attack; invasion; impulse

incurv·ŏ -āre *vt* to bend, curve

incurv·us -a -um *adj* bent, crooked

inc·ūs -ūdis *f* anvil

incūsātĭ·ŏ -ōnis *f* accusation

incūs·ŏ -āre *vt* to blame, find fault with, accuse

incuss·us -ūs *m* shock

incussus *pp* of **incutio**

incustōdīt·us -a -um *adj* unguarded; unconcealed; imprudent

incūs·us -a -um *adj* forged; **lapis incusus** indented millstone

in·cutĭŏ -cutĕre -cussī -cussum *vt* to throw; to produce; (with *dat* or **in** + *acc*) to strike (*something*) on or against; (with *dat*) **a** to strike into, instill in; **b** to throw at, to fling upon; **metum incutere** (with *dat*) to inspire fear in, strike fear in; **scipionem in caput alicujus incutere** to beat someone over the head with a stick

indāgātĭ·ŏ -ōnis *f* investigation, search

indāgāt·or -ōris *m* or **indāgātr·ix -īcis** *f* investigator

indāg·ŏ -āre *vt* to track down, hunt; (*fig*) to track down, investigate, explore

indāg·ŏ -ĭnis *f* dragnet; **indagine agere** to ferret out

indaudĭŏ see **inaudio**

inde *adv* from there; from that source, therefrom; from that time on, after that, thereafter; then; from that cause

indēbit·us -a -um *adj* not owed, not due

indĕc·ens -entis *adj* unbecoming, improper, indecent

indecenter *adv* improperly, indecently

indec·eŏ -ēre *vt* to be improper for

indēclīnāt·us -a -um *adj* unchanged, constant

indĕc·or -ōris or **indecŏr·is -e** *adj* disgraceful, dishonorable, cowardly indecōrē adv indecently, improperly

indecŏr·ō -āre vt to disgrace

indecŏr·us -a -um adj unsightly, improper, disgraceful

indēfens·us -a -um adj undefended

indēfess·us -a -um adj tireless; not tired

indēflēt·us -a -um adj unwept

indēject·us -a -um adj undemolished

indēlēbil·is -e adj indestructible, indelible

indēlībāt·us -a -um adj undiminished

indemnāt·us -a -um adj unconvicted

indēplōrāt·us -a -um adj unwept

indēprens·us -a -um adj undetected

ineptus pp of indipiscor

indēsert·us -a -um adj unforsaken

indēspect·us -a -um adj unfathomable

indestrict·us -a -um adj unscathed

indētons·us -a -um adj unshorn

indēvītāt·us -a -um adj unerring (e.g., arrow)

ind·ex -icis m index, sign, mark, indication, proof; title (of book); informer, spy; index finger

Indi·a -ae f India

indicātī·ō -ōnis f value; price

indīc·ens -entis adj not speaking; me indicente without a word from me

indic·ium -iī or -ī n information, disclosure, evidence; indication, proof, permission to give evidence; reward for giving evidence

indĭc·ō -āre vt to point out; to reveal, disclose, make known; to betray, inform against, accuse; to put a price on; vi to give evidence

in·dīcō -dīcere -dīxī -dictum vt to proclaim, announce, publish; to summon, convoke; to impose (a fine); bellum indicere to declare war; diem indicere to set a date

indict·us -a -um adj unsaid; causā indictā without a hearing

Indic·us -a -um adj Indian; m Indian; n indigo

indīdem adv from the same place; from the same source, from the same thing

indiffĕr·ens -entis adj (morally) indifferent; unconcerned, indifferent

indigĕn·a -ae adj masc & fem native

indĭg·ens -entis adj indigent; (with genit) in need of

indigentĭ·a -ae f indigence, want, need; craving

indĭg·ĕō -ēre -uī vi (with genit or abl) to need, be in need of, require; (with genit) to crave, desire

indĭg·es -ĕtis adj indigenous, native; m native god; national hero

indĭgest·us -a -um adj unarranged, confused

indignābund·us -a -um adj indignant, highly indignant

indign·ans -antis adj indignant; impatient, reluctant

indignātī·ō -ōnis f indignation, displeasure; provocation, occasion for indignation; f pl expressions of indignation

indignē adv unworthily, undeservedly; indignantly

indignit·ās -ātis f unworthiness; indignation; indignity, shameful treatment; enormity, shamefulness

indign·or -ārī -ātus sum vt to be indignant at, displeased at, angry at, offended at

indign·us -a -um adj unworthy, undeserving; undeserved; (with abl) a unworthy of; b not deserving; c not worth; (with genit) unworthy of, undeserving of; indignum! shame!

indĭg·us -a -um adj (with genit or abl) in need of, needing

indīlig·ens -entis adj careless

indīligenter adv carelessly

indīligentĭ·a -ae f carelessness

ind·ipiscor -ipiscī -eptus sum or indipisc·ō -ĕre vt to obtain, get; to attain, reach

indīrept·us -a -um adj unplundered

indiscrēt·us -a -um adj closely connected; indiscriminate, undistinguishable; confused

indisertē adv without eloquence

indisert·us -a -um adj not eloquent; at a loss for words

indisposit·us -a -um adj confused, disorderly

indissolūbil·is -e adj imperishable, indestructible

indistinct·us -a -um adj indistinct, obscure; confused

inditus pp of indo

indivīdu·us -a -um adj indivisible; inseparable; n atom, indivisible particle

in·dō -dĕre -dĭdī -dĭtum vt to put, place; to introduce; to impart, give; (with in + acc) to put or place (something) into or on, insert in

indocil·is -e adj difficult to teach, slow to learn; hard to learn; untaught

indoctē adv unskillfully

indoct·us -a -um adj untaught, untrained, unschooled; illiterate, ignorant

indolentĭ·a -ae f freedom from pain, insensibility

indŏl·ēs -is f inborn quality, natural quality; nature, character, disposition; natural ability, talent, genius

indol·escō -escĕre -uī vi to feel sorry; to feel resentment

indomābil·is -e adj untameable

indomit·us -a -um adj untamed, wild; (fig) wild, unmanageable

indorm·iō -īre -īvī or -iī -ītum vi to fall asleep; to grow careless; (with dat or abl or with in + abl) a to fall asleep at or on; b to fall asleep over; c to become careless about

indōtāt·us -a -um adj without dowry; poor; without funeral rites

or funeral honors; **ars indotata**
unadorned style; **corpora indotata** bodies that have not been accord-
ed the usual honors paid to the dead
indubitābil·is -e adj indubitable
indubitāt·us -a -um adj undoubted
indubit·ō -āre vi (with dat) to begin
to distrust, begin to doubt
indubi·us -a -um adj undoubted,
certain
indūcī·ae -ārum f pl armistice,
truce
in·dūcō -dūcĕre -dūxī -ductum vt
to lead or bring in; to bring in, introduce; to induce, persuade, seduce, move; to overlay, drape, wrap,
cover, put on, clothe; to strike out,
erase; to repeal, cancel; to present,
exhibit; to mislead, delude; (with **in**
+ acc) **a** to lead to, lead into, lead
against; **b** to bring into, introduce
into; **c** (fig) to introduce (e.g., a
new custom) into; **d** to enter into
(account books), charge to (someone's account); (with dat or **super**
+ acc) to put (item of apparel) on,
spread over, wrap around, draw
over; **animum inducere** or **in
animum inducere** to make up
one's mind, convince oneself, be convinced, conclude, suppose, imagine
inducti·ō -ōnis f bringing in, introduction, admission; resolution, determination; intention; induction,
generalization; **animi inductio** inclination; **erroris inductio** deception
induct·or -ōris m (referring to a
whip) persuader
induct·us -ūs m persuasion, inducement
indūcŭl·a -ae f skirt, petticoat
indulg·ens -entis adj indulgent,
lenient; (with dat or **in** + acc) lenient toward, kind toward
indulgenter adv indulgently, lenient-
ly, kindly
indulgenti·a -ae f indulgence, leniency, kindness
in·dulgĕō -dulgĕre -dulsī vt (with
dat) to grant, concede (something)
to; **veniam indulgere** (with dat)
to make allowances for; vi (with
dat) **a** to be lenient toward, be kind
to, be tender to; **b** to yield to, give
way to; **c** to indulge in, be addicted
to; **sibi indulgere** to be self-indulgent, take liberties
ind·ŭō -ŭĕre -ŭī -ūtum vt to put
on (e.g., a tunic); to cover, wrap,
clothe, array, envelop; to engage in;
to assume, put on; to assume the
part of; to involve, entangle; (with
dat) to put (e.g., a tunic) on (someone)
indup- = imp-
indūr·escō -escĕre -ŭī vi to become
hard, harden
indūr·ō -āre vt to harden
Ind·us -a -um adj Indian; m Indian;
Ethiopian; mahout
industri·a -ae f industry, diligence;

industriā or **de** or **ex industriā**
or **ob industriam** on purpose
industriē adv industriously, diligently
industri·us -a -um adj industrious,
diligent, painstaking
indūti·ae -ārum f pl clothes
indūt·us -ūs m wearing; clothing
induvi·ae -ārum f pl clothes
inebri·ō -āre vt to make drunk; (fig)
to fill (e.g., ear with gossip)
inedi·a -ae f fasting; starvation
inēdit·us -a -um adj not made
known, unknown, unpublished
inēlĕg·ans -antis adj inelegant, undistinguished
inēleganter adv without distinction
inēluctābil·is -e adj inescapable
inēmor·ior -ī vi (with dat) to die in
or at
inempt·us -a -um adj unpurchased;
without ransom
inēnarrābil·is -e adj indescribable
inēnarrābiliter adv indescribably
inēnōdābil·is -e adj inexplicable
in·ĕō -īre -īī -ĭtum vt to enter; to
enter upon, undertake, form; to begin, engage in; **consilium inire**
to form a plan; **consilium inire
ut, qua,** or **quemadmodum** to
plan how to (do something); **inire
numerum** (with genit) to go into
an enumeration of, enumerate;
inire rationem (with genit) to
form an estimate of; **inire rationem ut, qua,** or **quemadmodum**
to consider, find out, or figure out
how to (do something); **viam inire**
to begin a trip; to find a way, devise a means
ineptē adv foolishly, absurdly, inap-
propriately, pointlessly
inepti·a -ae f foolishness; f pl nonsense; trifles
inept·ĭō -īre vi to be absurd, make
a fool of oneself
inept·us -a -um adj foolish, silly;
inept, awkward, absurd; unsuitable, out of place; tactless, tasteless
inerm·is -e or **inerm·us -a -um**
adj unarmed, defenseless; undefended; toothless (gums); harmless
inerr·ans -antis adj not wandering,
fixed
inerr·ō -āre vi to wander about
iner·s -tis adj unskillful, incompetent; inactive, sluggish; weak, soft,
helpless; stagnant, motionless; ineffective, dull, insipid; numbing
(cold); expressionless (eyes); un-
eventful, leisurely (time)
inerti·a -ae f lack of skill, ignorance,
rudeness; inactivity, laziness
inērudīt·us -a -um adj uneducated;
crude, inconsiderate
inesc·ō -āre vt to bait; (fig) to bait,
trap, deceive
inēvect·us -a -um adj mounted

inēvītābil·is -e *adj* inevitable, inescapable

inexcīt·us -a -um *adj* unexcited, calm

inexcūsābil·is -e *adj* without excuse; admitting no excuse

inexercitāt·us -a -um *adj* untrained

inexhaust·us -a -um *adj* unexhausted, not wasted; inexhaustible

inexōrābil·is -e *adj* inexorable, relentless; unswerving, strict

inexperrect·us -a -um *adj* unawakened

inexpert·us -a -um *adj* untried, untested; novel (with *abl*, or with **in** or **adversus** + *acc*) inexperienced in, unaccustomed to

inexpiābil·is -e *adj* inexpiable, not to be atoned for; irreconcilable, implacable

inexplēbil·is -e *adj* insatiable

inexplēt·us -a -um *adj* unsatisfied, unfilled

inexplicābil·is -e *adj* inextricable; inexplicable; impassable (*road*); involved, unending (*war*)

inexplōrātō *adv* without reconnoitering

inexplōrāt·us -a -um *adj* unexplored; unfamiliar

inexpugnābil·is -e *adj* impregnable, unassailable; invincible

inexspectāt·us -a -um *adj* unexpected

inexstinct·us -a -um *adj* unextinguished; insatiable

inexsuperābil·is -e *adj* insuperable, insurmountable

inextrīcābil·is -e *adj* inextricable

infābrē *adv* unskillfully

infabricāt·us -a -um *adj* unshaped, untrimmed

infacētē *adv* witlessly

infacēti·ae -ārum *f pl* coarse jokes

infacēt·us -a -um *adj* not witty, not funny, dull, stupid

infācund·us -a -um *adj* ineloquent

infāmi·a -ae *f* bad reputation, bad name; disrepute, disgrace, scandal; embarrassment

infām·is -e *adj* infamous, notorious, disreputable, disgraceful

infām·ō -āre *vt* to defame, dishonor, disgrace

infand·us -a -um *adj* unspeakable, shocking

inf·ans -antis *adj* speechless, unable to speak; baby, infant, young; childish, silly; (fig) incapable of speaking, tongue-tied; *m* or *f* infant

infanti·a -ae *f* infancy; childishness; inability to speak; lack of eloquence

infar- = infer-

infatu·ō -āre *vt* to make a fool of

infaust·us -a -um *adj* ill-omened, unpropitious; unfortunate

infect·or -ōris *m* dyer

infect·us -a -um *pp* of **inficio**; *adj* not made, not done, undone, unfinished, unachieved; unfeasible; impossible

infēcundit·ās -ātis *f* unfruitfulness

infēcund·us -a -um *adj* unfruitful

infēlīcit·ās -ātis *f* bad luck, misfortune

infēlīciter *adv* unhappily; unluckily, unsuccessfully

infēlīc·ō -āre *vt* to make unhappy

infēl·ix -īcis *adj* unfruitful; unhappy, unfortunate; causing misfortune, ruinous; ill-omened; pessimistic

infensē *adv* hostilely, aggressively

infens·ō -āre *vt* to antagonize; to make dangerous; *vi* to be hostile

infens·us -a -um *adj* hostile, antagonistic; dangerous; (with *dat* or **in** + *acc*) a hostile to, antagonistic toward; b dangerous to

in·ferciō or **infarciō -fercīre -fersī -fersum** or **-fertum** *vt* to stuff, cram

infer·a -ōrum *n pl* lower world

infer·ī -ōrum *m pl* the dead; the world below

inferi·ae -ārum *f pl* rites and offerings to the dead

inferi·or -us *adj* lower, farther down; (fig) inferior, lower; subsequent, later

inferius *adv* lower, too low

infernē *adv* below, beneath

infern·us -a -um *adj* lower; infernal, of the lower world

inferō inferre intulī illātum *vt* to bring in, introduce, carry in; to import; to bring forward, adduce, produce, make, occasion, incite, cause; to offer, render, sacrifice; to bury, inter; **arma, bellum, gradum, pedem,** or **signa inferre** to make an attack, make an advance, begin hostilities; **arma, bellum, pedem** or **signa inferre** (with *dat* or with **in** or **contra** + *acc*) to attack, advance against, invade; **conversa signa inferre** (with *dat*) to turn around and attack; **ignem inferre** (with *dat*) to set fire to; **se inferre** to go, march, rush, charge, plunge; **se in periculum inferre** to expose oneself to danger; *vi* to infer, conclude

infer·us -a -um *adj* lower; southern

in·fervescō -fervescēre -ferbuī *vi* to simmer, boil

infestē *adv* hostilely, violently, outrageously

infest·ō -āre *vt* to annoy; to infest; to attack

infest·us -a -um *adj* infested, molested, disturbed, unsafe; hostile, aggressive; dangerous; threatening

inficēt- = infacēt-

in·ficiō -ficěre -fēcī -fectum *vt* to dip, dye, tint; to infect; to stain; to corrupt, spoil; to imbue, instruct; (fig) to poison, infect

infidēl·is -e *adj* unfaithful, untrue, disloyal

infidēlit·ās -ātis *f* infidelity, unfaithfulness, disloyalty

infidēliter *adv* disloyally

infīd·us -a -um *adj* untrustworthy, treacherous

in·fīgō -fīgĕre -fīxī -fīxum *vt* to drive in, nail, thrust; to imprint, fix, impress; (with *dat*) **a** to drive into, thrust into; **b** to impale on; **c** to imprint on or in

infīmātis see **infumātis**

infīm·us or **infŭm·us -a -um** (*superl* of **inferus**) *adj* lowest, last; lowest, worst, humblest; **ab infimo colle** at the foot of the hill; **infimum mare** the bottom of the sea; *n* bottom

in·findō -findĕre -fīdī -fissum *vt* (with *dat*) to cut (*e.g., furrows*) into

infīnit·ās -ātis *f* endlessness, infinity

infīnitē *adv* without bounds, without end, infinitely; without exception

infīnitī·ō -ōnis *f* boundlessness, infinity

infīnit·us -a -um *adj* unlimited, boundless; without end, endless, infinite; countless; indefinite

infirmātī·ō -ōnis *f* invalidation; refutation

infirmē *adv* weakly, faintly, feebly

infirmit·ās -ātis *f* weakness, feebleness; infirmity, sickness; inconstancy

infirm·ō -āre *vt* to weaken, enfeeble; to refute, disprove; to annul

infirm·us -a -um *adj* weak, faint, feeble; infirm, sick; trivial; inconstant

infissus *pp* of **infindo**

infit *v defect* he, she, it begins

infīti·ae -ārum *f pl* denial; **infītias ire** (with *acc*) to deny

infītiāl·is -e *adj* negative

infītiātī·ō -ōnis *f* denial

infītiāt·or -ōris *m* repudiator

infīti·or -ārī -ātus sum *vt* to deny, repudiate, contradict, disown

infixus *pp* of **infīgo**

inflammātī·ō -ōnis *f* setting on fire; **inflammationem inferre** (with *dat*) to set on fire

inflamm·ō -āre *vt* to set on fire, kindle, light up; (fig) to inflame, excite

inflātī·ō -ōnis *f* swelling up; **habet inflationem faba** beans cause gas

inflātius *adv* too pompously

inflāt·us -a -um *adj* blown up, swollen, inflated; haughty; turgid (*style*)

inflāt·us -ūs *m* puff, blast; inspiration

in·flectō -flectĕre -flexī -flexum *vt* to bend, curve, bow, turn aside; to change; to influence; to inflect

inflēt·us -a -um *adj* unwept

inflexibil·is -e *adj* inflexible

inflexī·ō -ōnis *f* bending

inflexus *pp* of **inflecto**

inflex·us -ūs *m* curve

in·flīgō -flīgĕre -flīxī -flictum *vt* to strike, smash, dash, swing; to inflict (*wound*); to bring (*e.g., disgrace*)

infl·ō -āre *vt* to blow (*horn*), play (*flute*); to inspire; to inflate, puff up, fill

in·fluō -fluĕre -fluxī *vi* (with **in** + *acc*) **a** to flow into; **b** (fig) to spill over into, stream into, pour into

in·fodiō -fodĕre -fōdī -fossum *vt* to dig; to bury

informātī·ō -ōnis *f* sketch; idea

inform·is -e *adj* unformed, shapeless; ugly, hideous

inform·ō -āre *vt* to form, shape

infor·ō -āre *vt* to bring into court

infortūnāt·us -a -um *adj* unfortunate

infortūn·ium -iī or **-ī** *n* misfortune, calamity; punishment

infossus *pp* of **infodio**

infrā *adv* below, underneath; down south, down the coast; *prep* (with *acc*) below, beneath, under; later than

infractī·ō -ōnis *f* weakening; **animi infractio** discouragement

infract·us -a -um *pp* of **infringo**; *adj* broken, weakened, exhausted; **infractos animos gerere** to feel down and out

infragil·is -e *adj* unbreakable, strong

infrĕm·ō -ĕre -uī *vi* to growl, bellow, roar; to rage

infrēnāt·us -a -um *adj* unbridled

infrend·ĕō -ĕre or **infrend·ō -ĕre** *vi* **dentibus infrendere** to gnash the teeth

infrēn·is -e or **infrēn·us -a -um** *adj* unbridled

infrēn·ō -āre *vt* to put a bridle on; to harness; (fig) to curb

infrēnus see **infrenis**

infrĕqu·ens -entis *adj* uncrowded, not numerous; poorly attended; thinly populated; inconstant, irregular

infrequenti·a -ae *f* small number, scantiness; poor attendance; emptiness

in·fringō -fringĕre -frēgī -fractum *vt* to break, break in; to impair, affect, subdue, weaken, break down

infr·ons -ondis *adj* leafless

infructuōs·us -a -um *adj* unfruitful; pointless

infūcāt·us -a -um *adj* painted over, varnished; hidden

infūl·a -ae *f* bandage; fillet; mark of distinction, badge of honor

infumāt·is or **infimāt·is -is** *m* one of the lowest (*in rank*)

infūmus see **infimus**

in·fundō -fundĕre -fūdī -fūsum *vt* to pour in, pour on, pour out; (with *dat* or **in** + *acc*) **a** to pour into, pour upon; **b** to administer to; **infundi** or **se infundere** (with *dat*) to lay on, spread out on

infusc·ō -āre *vt* to darken, obscure; to stain, corrupt, sully

infūsus *pp* of **infundo**; *adj* diffused, permeating; fallen (*snow*); crowded

ingemin·ō -āre vt to redouble; to repeat, reiterate; vi to redouble

ingem·iscō or **ingem·escō -iscĕre -uī** vi to groan, heave a sigh; (with dat or **in** + abl) to groan over, sigh over

ingĕm·ō -ĕre -uī vt to groan over, sigh over; vi (with dat) to sigh over

ingenĕr·ō -āre vt to engender, generate, produce, create

ingeniāt·us -a -um adj naturally endowed, talented

ingeniōsē adv ingeniously

ingeniōs·us -a -um adj ingenious, clever, talented; (with dat or ad + acc) naturally suited to

ingenĭt·us -a -um adj inborn, natural

ingen·ĭum -ĭī or **-ī** n innate or natural quality; nature, temperament, character, bent, inclination; natural ability, talent, genius; clever person, genius

ing·ens -entis adj huge, vast; great, mighty, powerful

ingenŭē adv liberally; frankly

ingenuĭt·ās -ātis f noble birth; noble character; frankness

ingenŭ·us -a -um adj native, indigenous; natural; free-born; like a freeman, noble; frank

in·gĕrō -gerĕre -gessī -gestum vt to carry in, throw in, heap; to hurl, shoot (weapon); to pour out (angry words), heap (abuse)

inglōri·us -a -um adj inglorious, without glory, inconspicuous

ingluvĭ·ēs -ēī f crop, maw; gluttony

ingrātē adv unpleasantly; unwillingly; ungratefully

ingrātĭfic·us -a -um adj ungrateful

ingrātĭīs or **ingrātīs** adv without thanks; unwillingly

ingrāt·us -a -um adj unpleasant, unwelcome; ungrateful; receiving no thanks, unappreciated; thankless

ingravesc·ō -ĕre vi to grow heavier; to become pregnant; to grow worse; to become more serious; to become weary; to become dearer (in price); to become more important

in·gredior -grĕdī -gressus sum vt to enter; to undertake; to begin; to walk in, follow (footsteps); vi to go in, enter; to go, walk, walk along; to begin, commence; to begin to speak; (with **in** + acc) **a** to go in, enter; **b** to enter upon, begin, take up, undertake; **in rem publicam ingredi** to enter politics, enter public life

ingressĭ·ō -ōnis f entering; walking; gait, pace; beginning

ingress·us -ūs m entering; (mil) inroad; walking; gait; beginning

ingrŭ·ō -ĕre -ī vi to come, come on, rush on; (of war) to break out; (of rain) to pour down; (with dat or **in** + acc) to fall upon, attack

ingu·en -ĭnis n groin; swelling, tumor; n pl private parts

ingurgĭt·ō -āre vt to gorge, stuff; **se ingurgitare** to stuff oneself; **se ingurgitare** (with **in** + acc) to steep oneself in, devote oneself to

ingustāt·us -a -um adj untasted

inhabĭl·is -e adj clumsy, unhandy; (with dat or **ad** + acc) unfit for

inhabitābĭl·is -e adj uninhabitable

inhabĭt·ō -āre vt inhabit

in·haerĕō -haerēre -haesī -haesum vi to stick, cling; (fig) to cling, adhere; to be inherent; (with dat, with **ad** + acc, or with **in** + abl) **a** to cling to; **b** to be closely connected with; **c** to gaze upon

in·haerescō -haerescĕre -haesī vi to stick fast, take hold

inhāl·ō -āre vt (with dat) to breathe (e.g., bad breath) on (someone)

inhĭb·ĕō -ēre -uī -ĭtum vt to hold back, curb, check, control; to use, practice, perform; to apply, inflict; **retro navem inhibere** to back up the ship; vi to row backwards, backwater

inhibitĭ·ō -ōnis f backing up

inhĭ·ō -āre vt to gape at; to covet; vi to stand open-mouthed, be amazed

inhonestē adv dishonorably, disgracefully; dishonestly

inhonest·ō -āre vt to dishonor, disgrace

inhonest·us -a -um adj dishonorable, disgraceful, shameful, inglorious; indecent; ugly, degrading

inhonōrāt·us -a -um adj unhonored, disregarded, unrewarded

inhonōr·us -a -um adj defaced

inhorr·ĕō -ēre -uī vi to stand on end, bristle

inhorr·escō -escĕre -uī vi to stand on end, bristle; to vibrate; to shiver, tremble, shudder

inhospitāl·is -e adj inhospitable, unfriendly

inhospitālĭt·ās -ātis f inhospitality

inhospĭt·us -a -um adj inhospitable

inhūmānē adv inhumanly, savagely

inhūmānĭt·ās -ātis f inhumanity, barbarity; churlishness; extreme stinginess

inhūmānĭter adv impolitely

inhūmān·us -a -um adj inhuman, savage; brutal; crude, impolite

inhumāt·us -a -um adj unburied

inĭbī or **inĭbĭ** adv there, in that place; near at hand

inimīc·a -ae f (personal) enemy (female)

inimīcē adv hostilely, in an unfriendly way

inimīcĭtĭ·a -ae f unfriendliness, enmity; f pl feuds

inimīc·ō -āre vt to make into enemies, set at odds

inimīc·us -a -um adj unfriendly, hostile; harmful; m (personal) enemy; **inimicissimus suus** his bitterest enemy

inīquē adv unequally, unevenly; unfairly

inīquĭt·ās -ātis f unevenness; inequality; disadvantage; unfairness

iniqu·us -a -um *adj* uneven, unequal; not level, sloping; unfair; adverse, harmful; dangerous, unfavorable; prejudiced; excessive; impatient, discontented; **iniquo animo** impatiently, unwillingly; *m* enemy, foe

initi·ō -āre *vt* to initiate, begin; to initiate (*into mysteries*)

init·ium -iī or **-ī** *n* entrance; beginning; *n pl* elements; first principles; sacred rites, sacred mysteries

initus *pp* of **ineo**

init·us -ūs *m* entrance; beginning

in·jiciō -jicĕre -jēcī -jectum *vt* to throw, inject; to impose, apply; to inspire, infuse; to cause, occasion; to furnish (*a cause*); to bring up, mention (*a name*); (with *dat* or **in** + *acc*) to throw or fling into, on or over; (with *dat* or **in** + *acc*) **a** to throw oneself into, rush into, expose oneself to; **b** to fling oneself down on; **c** (*of the mind*) to turn itself to, concentrate on, reflect on; **manum injicere** (with *dat*) to lay hands on, take possession of

injūcundit·ās -ātis *f* unpleasantness

injūcundius *adv* rather unpleasantly

injūcund·us -a -um *adj* unpleasant

injūdicāt·us -a -um *adj* undecided

in·jungō -jungĕre -junxī -junctum *vt* to join, attach, fasten; to inflict, impose; (with *dat*) **a** to join, attach, fasten to; **b** to inflict on, impose (*e.g., taxes, obligations*) on

injūrāt·us -a -um *adj* not under oath

injūri·a -ae *f* injury, wrong, outrage, injustice; insult, affront; harshness, severity; revenge; damage, harm; ill-gotten goods; **injuriā** unjustly, undeservedly, innocently; **per injuriam** unjustly, outrageously

injūriōsē *adv* unjustly, wrongfully

injūriōs·us -a -um *adj* unjust, wrongful; harmful

injūri·us -a -um *adj* unjust, wrong

injūr·us -a -um *adj* wrongful

injussū (*abl only*) *m* without orders; **injussu meo** without my orders

injuss·us -a -um *adj* unasked, unbidden, voluntary

injustē *adv* unjustly

injustiti·a -ae *f* injustice

injust·us -a -um *adj* unjust

inl- = **ill-**

inm- = **imm-**

innābil·is -e *adj* unswimmable

in·nascor -nascī -nātus sum *vi* (with *dat*) to be born in, grow in or on; (with **in** + *abl*) (fig) to originate in

innăt·ō -āre *vt* to swim; *vi* (with *dat*) to swim around in, float on; (with **in** + *acc*) to swim into

innăt·us -a -um *pp* of **innascor**; *adj* inborn, natural

innāvigābil·is -e *adj* unnavigable

in·nectō -nectĕre -nexŭī -nexum *vt* to entwine; to tie, fasten together; to join, attach, connect; (fig) to devise, invent, plan

in·nītor -nītī -nixus sum or **-nīsus sum** *vi* (with *abl*) to lean on, rest on, be supported by

inn·ō -āre *vt* to swim; to sail, sail over; *vi* (with *abl*) **a** to swim in, float on; **b** to sail on; **c** (*of the sea*) to wash against (*a shore*)

innŏc·ens -entis *adj* harmless; guiltless, innocent; upright; unselfish; (with *genit*) innocent of

innocenter *adv* blamelessly

innocenti·a -ae *f* innocence; integrity; unselfishness

innocŭē *adv* harmlessly; innocently

innocŭ·us -a -um *adj* harmless, innocuous; innocent; unharmed

innōt·escō -escĕre -ŭī *vi* to become known; to become notorious

innŏv·ō -āre *vt* to renew, restore; **se innovare** (with **ad** + *acc*) to return to

innoxi·us -a -um *adj* harmless; safe; innocent; unhurt; (with *genit*) innocent of

innūbil·us -a -um *adj* cloudless

innūb·a -ae (*fem only*) *adj* unmarried

in·nūbō -nūbĕre -nupsī *vi* (with *dat*) to marry into

innumerābil·is -e *adj* innumerable

innumerābilit·ās -ātis *f* countless number

innumerābiliter *adv* innumerably

innumerāl·is -e *adj* innumerable

innumĕr·us -a -um *adj* countless

in·nŭō -nŭĕre -nŭī -nūtum *vi* to give a nod; (with *dat*) to nod to

innupt·a -ae (*fem only*) *adj* unmarried; *f* unmarried girl, maiden

innutr·iō -īre -īvī or **-iī -ītum** *vt* (with *dat*) to bring up in

In·ō -ūs *f* daughter of Cadmus and Harmonia, wife of Athamas, mother of Learchus and Melicerta, and stepmother of Phrixus and Helle; pursued by mad Athamas, she and Melicerta hurled themselves into the sea, whereupon they were changed into sea deities

inoblīt·us -a -um *adj* unforgetful

inobrŭt·us -a -um *adj* not overwhelmed

inobservābil·is -e *adj* unnoticed

inobservanti·a -ae *f* inattention

inobservāt·us -a -um *adj* unobserved

inoccidŭ·us -a -um *adj* never setting

inodōr·us -a -um *adj* odorless

inoffens·us -a -um *adj* unobstructed, uninterrupted, unhindered

inofficiōs·us -a -um *adj* irresponsible; not obliging

inŏl·ens -entis *adj* odorless

inol·escō -escĕre -ēvī *vi* to become inveterate; (with *dat*) to grow on or in inōmināt·us -a -um *adj* ill-omened, inauspicious

inopi·a -ae *f* lack, want, need, poverty; scarcity; barrenness (*of style*); helplessness

inopīn·ans -antis *adj* unsuspecting, taken by surprise

inopīnanter *adv* unexpectedly

inopīnātō *adv* unexpectedly, by surprise

inopīnāt·us -a -um *adj* not expected, unexpected, unsuspected, surprising; *n* surprise; **ex inopinato** by surprise

inopīn·us -a -um *adj* unexpected

inopiōs·us -a -um *adj* (with *genit*) in need of

in·ops -ōpis *adj* without means or resources; poor, needy, destitute; helpless, weak, forlorn; bald (*style*); poor (*expression*); pitiful, wretched, contemptible; (with *genit*) destitute of, stripped of, without; (with *abl*) lacking in, deficient in, poor in

inōrāt·us -a -um *adj* not presented; **re inorata** without presenting one's case

inordināt·us -a -um *adj* disordered

inōrnāt·us -a -um *adj* unadorned; plain (*style*); unheralded

inp- = imp-

inpendiōs·us -a -um *adj* extravagant

inperc·ō -ĕre *vi* (with *dat*) to spare

inpluviāt·us -a -um *adj* square, shaped like an impluvium

inpūrāt·us -a -um *adj* (morally) defiled

inpūriti·ae -ārum *f pl* (moral) impurity

inquam *v defect* say; after one or more words of direct quotation, e.g., **Desilite, inquit, milites et . . .** "Jump down, fellow soldiers", he says, "and . . ."; in emphatic repetition, e.g., **tuas, tuas inquam suspiciones . . .** your suspicions, yes I say yours . . . ; **inquit** it is said, one says

inqui·ēs -ētis *adj* restless

inquiēt·ō -āre *vt* to disquiet, disturb

inquiēt·us -a -um *adj* restless, unsettled

inquilīn·us -ī *m* tenant, inhabitant

inquinātē *adv* filthily

inquināt·us -a -um *adj* filthy, foul

inquīn·ō -āre *vt* to mess up, defile, contaminate

in·quīrō -quīrĕre quīsīvī -quīsītum *vt* to search for, inquire into, examine, pry into; *vi* to hold an investigation; to hold a preliminary hearing

inquīsīti·ō -ōnis *f* search, inquiry, investigation; preliminary hearing; (with *genit*) search for, inquiry into, investigation of

inquīsīt·or -ōris *m* inspector, examiner; spy; (*law*) investigator

inquīsīt·us -a -um *pp* of **inquiro**; *adj* not investigated

inquit *see* **inquam**

inr- = irr-

insalūbr·is -e *adj* unhealthy

insalūtāt·us -a -um *adj* ungreeted

insānābil·is -e *adj* incurable

insānē *adv* crazily, madly

insāni·a -ae *f* insanity, madness, frenzy; rapture; mania; excess; inspiration

insān·iō -īre -īvī or -iī -ītum *vi* to be crazy, be mad, be insane; to be absurd, be wild

insānit·ās -ātis *f* unsoundness, disease

insān·us -a -um *adj* insane, mad, crazy; absurd, foolish; excessive, extravagant; monstrous, outrageous; inspired; maddening

insatiābil·is -e *adj* insatiable; that cannot cloy, uncloying

insatiābiliter *adv* insatiably

insatiēt·ās -ātis *f* insatiety

insaturābil·is -e *adj* insatiable

insaturābiliter *adv* insatiably

in·scendō -scendĕre -scendī -scensum *vt & vi* to climb up, mount

inscensi·ō -ōnis *f* mounting; **in navem inscensio** boarding a ship

inscensus *pp* of **inscendo**

insci·ens -entis *adj* unaware; silly, stupid

inscienter *adv* ignorantly, inadvertently

inscienti·a -ae *f* ignorance; inexperience; foolishness; awkwardness

inscīt·us -a -um *adj* ignorant, clumsy, stupid

insci·us -a -um *adj* ignorant, unaware

in·scrībō -scrībĕre -scripsī -scriptum *vt* to inscribe; to ascribe; to title (*a book*); to assign, attribute, ascribe; to advertise; to address (*a letter*); (with *dat* or **in** + *abl*) to write (*something*) on or in

inscripti·ō -ōnis *f* inscribing

inscript·us -a -um *pp* of **inscribo**; *adj* unwritten

in·sculpō -sculpĕre -sculpsī -sculptum *vt* to cut, carve, engrave; (with *abl* or **in** + *abl*) to cut, carve, or engrave upon

insectāti·ō -ōnis *f* hot pursuit

insectāt·or -ōris *m* persecutor

insect·or -ārī -ātus sum or insect·ō -āre *vt* to pursue, attack; to attack with words, criticize

insect·us -a -um *adj* indented, notched

insecūtus *pp* of **insequor**

insēdābiliter *adv* incessantly

insen·escō -escĕre -uī *vi* (with *dat*) to grow old amidst, grow old over

insensil·is -e *adj* imperceptible

insepult·us -a -um *adj* unburied

insēqu·ens -entis *adj* next, following, succeeding

in·sēquor -sēquī -secūtus sum *vt* to follow, follow after; to succeed, to follow up; to attack; to prosecute; to pass, overtake; to reproach;

to strive after; *vi* to follow, come next

in·sĕrŏ -serĕre -sēvī -sĭtum *vt* to graft; (fig) to implant

in·sĕrŏ -serĕre -serŭī -sertum *vt* to insert; to introduce; to involve; to join, enroll, associate; to mingle, blend; to let in

insert·ŏ -āre *vt* to insert

inserv·ĭŏ -īre -īvī or **-ĭī -ītum** *vt* to serve, obey; *vi* to be a slave, be a subject; (with *dat*) to serve, be subservient to, be devoted to

insessus *pp* of **insido**

insībil·ŏ -āre *vi* (of the wind) to whistle, hiss

in·sīdŏ -sīdĕre -sēdī -sessum *vt* to hold, occupy; *vi* to sit down; to settle down; to be deep-seated; (with *abl* or *in* + *abl*) **a** to sit on; **b** to settle down on or in; **c** (fig) to be fixed in, stamped in

insidĭ·ae -ārum *f pl* ambush; plot, trap; **insidias dare, comparare, collocare, parare,** or **struere** (with *dat*) to lay a trap for

insidĭāt·or -ōris *m* soldier in ambush; (fig) plotter, subversive

insidĭ·or -ārī -ātus sum *vi* to lie in wait; (with *dat*) **a** to lie in wait for; **b** (fig) to plot against; **c** (fig) to watch for (*an opportunity*)

insidĭōsē *adv* insidiously, by underhand means

insidĭōs·us -a -um *adj* insidious, treacherous, tricky

in·sīdŏ -sīdĕre -sēdī -sessum *vt* to occupy, keep possession of, possess; *vi* (with *dat*) to settle in or on; (with *in* + *abl*) (fig) to become fixed in

insign·e -is *n* insignia, mark, token; (mil) decoration, medal; standard; coat of arms; signal; honor, distinction; brilliant passage, gem; *n pl* insignia, regalia, uniform, attire, accouterments

insign·ĭŏ -īre -īvī or **-ĭī -ītum** *vt* to make conspicuous, distinguish

insign·is -e *adj* conspicuous, distinguished; prominent, eminent, extraordinary, singular

insignītē *adv* extraordinarily, notably

insignĭter *adv* remarkably

insignīt·us -a -um *adj* marked, conspicuous, clear, glaring; distinguished, striking, notable

insīl·a -ium *n pl* treadle (*of a loom*)

insil·ĭŏ -īre -ŭī or **-īvī** *vt* to jump up on, mount; *vi* (with *dat*) to jump on; (with *in* + *acc*) **a** to jump into or on; **b** to jump on, mount, climb aboard

insimulātĭ·ŏ -ōnis *f* charge, accusation

insimŭl·ŏ -āre *vt* to accuse, accuse falsely, allege

insincēr·us -a -um *adj* mixed, spoiled, not pure

insinuātĭ·ŏ -ōnis *f* winning sympathy

insinŭ·ŏ -āre *vt* to bring in secretly, sneak in; **se insinuare** (with *inter* + *acc*) to wriggle in between, work one's way between or among; **se insinuare in familiaritatem** (with *genit*) to ingratiate oneself with

insipĭ·ens -entis *adj* foolish

insipĭenter *adv* foolishly

insipientĭ·a -ae *f* foolishness

in·sistŏ -sistĕre -stĭtī *vt* to stand on, trample on; to set about, keep at (*a task, etc.*); to follow, chase after, pursue; **iter insistere** or **viam insistere** to enter upon a course, pursue a course; *vi* to stand, stop, come to a standstill; to pause; (with *dat*) **a** to tread on the heels of, pursue closely; **b** to press on with; **c** (fig) to dwell upon; (with *dat* or *in* + *acc*) to set foot on or in, step on, tread on, stand on; (with *dat* or *in* + *abl*) to persist in; (with *ad* or *in* + *acc*) to keep at, keep after, keep the pressure on, pursue vigorously

insitĭ·ŏ -ōnis *f* grafting; grafting time

insitīv·us -a -um *adj* grafted; (fig) spurious

insĭt·or -ōris *m* grafter

insĭt·us -a -um *pp* of **insero**; *adj* inborn, innate; incorporated

insocĭābil·is -e *adj* incompatible

insōlābĭlĭter *adv* unconsolably

insŏl·ens -entis *adj* unaccustomed, unusual; immoderate, excessive; extravagant, insolent; (with *genit* or *in* + *abl*) unaccustomed to, inexperienced in; **in aliena re insolens** free with someone else's money

insolenter *adv* unusually; excessively; insolently

insolentĭ·a -ae *f* unusualness, strangeness, novelty; inexperience; affectation; insolence, arrogance

insolesc·ŏ -ĕre *vi* to become strange; to become insolent; to become elated

insolĭd·us -a -um *adj* soft

insolĭt·us -a -um *adj* unaccustomed, inexperienced; unusual, strange, uncommon; *n* the unusual

insomnĭ·a -ae *f* insomnia, sleeplessness

insomn·is -e *adj* sleepless

insomn·ĭum -ĭī or **-ī** *n* nightmare; dream

insŏn·ŏ -āre -ŭī *vi* to make noise; to sound, resound, roar; **calamis insonare** to make music with a reed pipe; **flagello insonare** to crack the whip; **pennis insonare** to flap the wings

ins·ons -ontis *adj* innocent; harmless

insōpīt·us -a -um *adj* sleepless

insŏp·or -ōris *adj* sleepless

inspect·ŏ -āre *vt* to look at, view, observe

inspectus *pp* of **inspicio**

inspēr·ans -antis *adj* not expecting

insperāt·us -a -um *adj* unhoped for, unexpected, unforeseen; unwelcome; **ex insperato** unexpectedly

in·spergō -spergĕre -spersī -spersum *vt* to sprinkle

in·spiciō -spicĕre -spexī -spectum *vt* to inspect, look into, examine, consider; to inspect, review; to look at, consult (*books*)

inspīc·ō -āre *vt* to make pointed; to sharpen

inspīr·ō -āre *vt* to inspire, infuse, enkindle; *vi* (with *dat*) to blow on, breathe on

inspoliāt·us -a -um *adj* undespoiled

inspūt·ō -āre *vt* to spit on

instābil·is -e *adj* unstable, unsteady; (fig) unsteady, changeable

inst·ans -antis *adj* present; immediate, threatening, urgent

instanter *adv* vehemently

instanti·a -ae *f* presence; vehemence

instar (indecl) *n* image, likeness, appearance, resemblance; (with *genit*) like, equal to, as large as, worth, as good as

instaurātī·ō -ōnis *f* renewal, repetition

instaurātīv·us -a -um *adj* begun anew, repeated

instaur·ō -āre *vt* to set up; to renew, repeat, start all over again (*esp. games and celebrations*); to repay, requite

in·sternō -sternĕre -strāvī -strātum *vt* to cover

instīgāt·or -ōris *m* or **instīgātr·īx -īcis** *f* instigator, ringleader

instīg·ō -āre *vt* to instigate, goad on, stimulate, incite

instill·ō -āre *vt* (with *dat*) to pour (*something*) on, instill (*something*) in

instimulāt·or -ōris *m* instigator

instimūl·ō -āre *vt* to stimulate, urge on

instinct·or -ōris *m* instigator

instinct·us -a -um *adj* incited, inspired

instinct·us -ūs *m* inspiration, impulse

instipūl·or -ārī -ātus sum *vi* to bargain

instit·a -ae *f* border, flounce; (fig) lady

institī·ō -ōnis *f* standing still

instit·or -ōris *m* salesman, huckster, hawker

instit·ŭō -uĕre -ŭī -ūtum *vt* to set, fix, plant; to set up, erect, establish; to arrange; to build, make, construct; to prepare, make ready; to provide, furnish; to institute, organize, set up; to appoint, designate; to undertake, begin; to decide, determine; to control, direct, govern; to teach, train, instruct, educate

institūtī·ō -ōnis *f* arrangement; custom; instruction, education; *f pl* principles of education

institūt·um -ī *n* practice, custom,

usage; precedent; principle; decree, regulation, stipulation, terms; purpose, intention; **ex instituto** according to custom

in·stō -stāre -stitī *vt* to follow, pursue; to work hard at; to menace, threaten; *vi* to be at hand, approach, be impending; to insist; (with *dat* or **in** + *abl*) to stand on or in; (with *dat*) **a** to be close to; **b** to be on the heels of, pursue closely; **c** to harass

instrātus *pp* of **insterno**

instrēnū·us -a -um *adj* lethargic

instrēp·ō -āre -ŭī -ĭtum *vi* to creak, rattle

instructī·ō -ōnis *f* construction; array

instructĭus *adv* with better preparation

instruct·or -ōris *m* supervisor

instruct·us -a -um *pp* of **instruo**; *adj* provided, equipped, furnished; prepared, arranged; instructed, versed

instruct·us -ūs *m* equipment; stock-in-trade (*of an orator*)

instrūment·um -ī *n* instrument, tool, utensil; equipment; dress, outfit; repertory, stock-in-trade; means, supply, provisions; document

in·strŭō -struĕre -struxī -structum *vt* to build up, construct; to furnish, prepare, provide, fit out; to instruct; (mil) to deploy

insuās·um -ī *n* dark-orange color

insuāv·is -e *adj* unpleasant, disagreeable

insūd·ō -āre *vi* (with *dat*) to sweat on, drip sweat on

insuēfact·us -a -um *adj* accustomed

in·suescō -suescĕre -suēvī -suētum *vt* to accustom, familiarize; *vi* (with *dat*, with **ad** + *acc*, or with *inf*) to get used to

insuēt·us -a -um *adj* unusual; (with *genit* or *dat*, with **ad** + *acc*, or with *inf*) unused to

insŭl·a -ae *f* island; apartment building

insulān·us -ī *m* islander

insulsē *adv* in poor taste; insipidly, absurdly

insulsit·ās -ātis *f* lack of taste; silliness, absurdity

insuls·us -a -um *adj* unsalted, without taste; coarse, tasteless, insipid; silly, absurd; bungling; *f pl* silly creatures (*i.e., women*)

insult·ō -āre *vt* to insult, scoff at, taunt; (of votaries) to dance about in; *vi* to jump, gambol, prance; to gloat; (with *abl*) **a** to jump in, cavort in, gambol on, jump upon; **b** to gloat over; (with *dat* or **in** + *acc*) to scoff at, gloat over

insultūr·a -ae *f* jumping in

insum inesse infŭī *vi* to be there; (with *dat* or **in** + *abl*) **a** to be in, be on; **b** to be implied in, be contained in, be in, belong to

in·sūmō -sūmĕre -sumpsī -sump-
tum *vt* to spend, devote, waste;
(with *dat* or in + *acc*) to devote to,
apply to; (with *abl* or in + *abl*)
to expend on; **operam insumere**
(with *dat*) to devote effort to, waste
effort on

in·sŭō -sŭĕre -sŭī -sūtum *vt* to
sew up; (wth *dat*) a to sew up in;
b to embroider (*something*) on

insŭper *adv* above, overhead, on the
top; from above; moreover, besides,
in addition; *prep* (with *acc*) above,
over, over and above; (with *abl*) in
addition to, besides

insuperābĭl·is -e *adj* insurmountable; unconquerable

in·surgō -surgĕre -surrexī -sur-
rectum *vi* to rise, stand up; to rise,
stand high, tower; to rise, increase,
grow, grow intense; to rise to power; (with *dat*) a to rise up against;
b to strain at (*e.g.*, oars)

insusurr·ō -āre *vt* (with *dat*) to
whisper (*something*) to; **insusurrare in aurem** (with *genit*) to
whisper into the ear of; **sibi can-
tilenam insusurrare** to hum a
tune to oneself; *vi* to whisper; (of
wind) to blow gently

intāb·escō -escĕre -ŭī *vi* to melt
away gradually, dissolve gradually;
(fig) to waste away, pine away

intactĭl·is -e *adj* intangible

intact·us -a -um *adj* untouched; uninjured, intact; unpolluted; untried; unmarried; virgin, chaste

intact·us -ūs *m* intangibility

intāmĭnāt·us -a -um *adj* unsullied

intect·us -a -um *pp* of intego; *adj*
uncovered; naked; open, frank

integell·us -a -um *adj* fairly pure
or chaste; in fair condition

intĕg·er -ra -rum *adj* whole, complete, intact, unimpaired; unhurt,
unwounded; healthy, sound, fresh;
new, fresh; pure, chaste; untouched,
unaffected; unbiased, unprejudiced;
unattempted; unsubdued, unconquered; unbroken (*horse*); not worn,
unused; inexperienced, ignorant;
virtuous, honest, blameless, irreproachable; healthy, sane; **ab integro** or **de integro** anew, all over
again; **in integrum restituere** to
restore to a former condition; to
pardon; **integrum alicui esse**
(with *inf*) to be in someone's power to

in·tĕgō -tegĕre -texī -tectum *vt*
to cover up; to protect

integrasc·ō -ĕre *vi* to break out
fresh, start all over again

integrātĭ·ō -ōnis *f* renewal, new beginning

intĕgrē *adv* wholly, entirely; honestly; correctly

integrĭt·ās -ātis *f* soundness; integrity; innocence; purity, chastity;
correctness

intĕgr·ō -āre *vt* to make whole; to
heal, repair; to renew, begin again;

to refresh

integument·um -ī *n* covering; lid;
protection

intellectus *pp* of intelligo

intellect·us -ūs *m* perception; comprehension, understanding; intellect

intellĕg·ens -entis *adj* intelligent;
(with *genit*) appreciative of; (with
in + *abl*) versed in

intellegenter *adv* intelligently

intellegentĭ·a -ae *f* intelligence; understanding, knowledge; perception,
judgment, discrimination, taste,
skill; concept, notion; (with *genit*)
knowledge or understanding of;
(with in + *abl*) judgment in

intel·lĕgō -legĕre -lexī -lectum
vt to understand, perceive, discern,
comprehend, gather; to realize, recognize; to have an accurate knowledge of, be an expert in; *vi* intel-
lego (in answers) I understand, I
get it

intemĕrāt·us -a -um *adj* undefiled,
pure; pure, undiluted

intempĕr·ans -antis *adj* intemperate, without restraint; profligate;
excessive

intemperanter *adv* intemperately

intemperantĭ·a -ae *f* intemperance,
lack of self-control; extravagance,
excess

intemperātē *adv* intemperately

intemperāt·us -a -um *adj* excessive

intemperĭ·ae -ārum *f pl* wild
outbursts, wildness

intemperĭ·ēs -ēī *f* wildness, excess;
outrageous conduct, excesses; **intemperies aquarum** heavy rain;
intemperies caeli stormy weather

intempestīvē *adv* at a bad time, in-
opportunely

intempestīv·us -a -um *adj* untimely, unseasonable; poorly timed

intempest·us -a -um *adj* unseasonable; dark, dismal; unhealthy; **nox
intempesta** dead of night

intemptāt·us or intentāt·us -a
-um *adj* unattempted

in·tendō -tendĕre -tendī -tentum
or -tensum *vt* to stretch, stretch
out, extend, spread out; to stretch,
bend (*e.g.*, bow); to aim, direct, shoot
(*weapon*); to increase, magnify, intensify; to intend; to urge, incite;
to aim at, intend; to assert, maintain; to aim, turn, direct; to raise
(*voice*); to stretch (*truth*); to direct,
turn, focus (*mind, attention*); **to
pitch** (*tent*)

intentātus see intemptatus

intentē *adv* intently, attentively

intentĭ·ō -ōnis *f* stretching, straining, tension; attention; effort, exertion; accusation

intent·ō -āre *vt* to stretch out; to
aim, direct; to threaten

intent·us -a -um *pp* of intendo;
adj taut, tense; intent, attentive;
eager, waiting, tense; strict (*discipline*); vigorous, tense, nervous
(*speech*)

intent·us -ūs *m* stretching out, extending (*of the palms*)

intep·ĕō -ēre -ŭī *vi* to be lukewarm

intep·escō -pescĕre -ŭī *vi* to grow warm, be warmed

inter *prep* (with *acc*) between, among, amidst; during, within, in the course of; in spite of; (in classifying) among, in, with; **inter se** each other, one another, mutual, mutually

interaestŭ·ō -āre *vi* to retch

interāment·a -ōrum *n pl* framework of a ship

Interamn·a -ae *f* town in Latium, on the Liris; town in Umbria, birthplace of Tacitus

interapt·us -a -um *adj* joined together

interāresc·ō -ĕre *vi* to dry up

interātim *adv* meanwhile

interbĭb·ō -ĕre *vt* to drink up

interbĭt·ō -ĕre *vi* to come to nothing

intercalār·is -e *adj* intercalary, inserted

intercalārĭ·us -a -um *adj* intercalary, inserted

intercăl·ō -āre *vt* to intercalate, insert

intercapĕd·ō -ĭnis *f* interruption, break, pause

inter·cēdō -cēdĕre -cessī -cessum *vi* to come or go in between; (of time) to intervene, pass, occur; to act as an intermediary; to intercede; (of tribunes) to exercise the veto; (with *dat*) **a** to veto, protest against; **b** to interfere with, obstruct, hinder

intercepti·ō -ōnis *f* interception

intercept·or -ōris *m* embezzler

interceptus *pp* of **intercipio**

intercessĭ·ō -ōnis *f* intercession, mediation; (tribune's) veto

intercess·or -ōris *m* intercessor, mediator; interferer, obstructor; tribune exercising the veto

inter·cĭdō -cĭdĕre -cĭdī *vi* to fall short, miss the mark; to happen in the meantime; to drop out, be lost

inter·cĭdō -cĭdĕre -cĭdī -cīsum *vt* to cut through, sever, cut down

intercĭn·ō -ĕre *vt* to interrupt with song or music

inter·cĭpĭō -cĭpĕre -cēpī -ceptum *vt* to intercept; to cut off (*the enemy*); to interrupt, cut off, preclude; to appropriate; to misappropriate; to receive by mistake (*e.g., poison*)

intercīsē *adv* piecemeal

intercīsus *pp* of **intercido**

inter·clūdō -clūdĕre -clūsī -clūsum *vt* to shut off, shut out, cut off; to stop, block up; to hinder, prevent; to blockade, shut in; to cut off, intercept, separate, divide

interclūsĭ·ō -ōnis *f* stopping; parenthesis; **animae interclusio** shortwindedness

interclūsus *pp* of **intercludo**

intercolumn·ĭum -ĭī or **-ī** *n* space between columns, intercolumniation

inter·currō -currĕre -cucurrī -cursum *vi* to intervene, mediate; to mingle; to rush in

intercurs·ō -āre *vi* to crisscross; to infiltrate; **inter se intercursare** to crisscross each other

intercurs·us -ūs *m* intervention

interc·us -ūtis *adj* between the skin and flesh; **aqua intercus** dropsy

inter·dīcō -dīcĕre -dīxī -dictum *vt* to forbid, prohibit; *vi* to make a provisional decree; **aquā et igni interdicere** (with *dat*) to outlaw, banish

interdictĭ·ō -ōnis *f* prohibiting; **aquae et igni interdictio** banishment

interdict·um -ī *n* prohibition; contraband; provisional decree (*of a praetor*)

interdictus *pp* of **interdico**

interdĭū or **interdĭūs** *adv* by day, in the daytime

interd·ō -āre *vt* to give intermittently; to distribute

interduct·us -ūs *m* punctuation

interdum *adv* sometimes, now and then, occasionally; meanwhile

interdŭ·ō -āre *vt* floccum interduo or **nihil interduo** I don't give a hoot

intereā *adv* meanwhile, in the interim; meanwhile, anyhow, nevertheless

interemptus *pp* of **interimo**

inter·ĕō -īre -ĭī -ĭtum *vi* to be done for, be finished, perish, be lost; to become extinct

ride in between

interequĭt·ō -āre *vt* to ride between (*e.g., the ranks or columns*); *vi* to

interfātĭ·ō -ōnis *f* interruption

interfectĭ·ō -ōnis *f* killing

interfect·or -ōris *m* or **interfec-trīx -īcis** *f* killer

inter·ficĭō -ficĕre -fēcī -fectum *vt* to destroy; to kill

inter·fīō -fĭĕrī *vi* to pass away, be destroyed

inter·flŭō -fluĕre -fluxī *vt* to flow between; *vi* to flow in between

inter·fodĭō -fodĕre -fōdī -fossum *vi* to pierce

interf·or -ārī -ātus sum *vt & vi* to interrupt

interfug·ĭō -ĕre *vi* to scatter

interfulg·ĕō -ēre *vi* (with *abl*) to shine amidst or among

interfūs·us -a -um *adj* spread here and there; (with *acc*) flowing between

interĭbī *adv* in the meantime

interĭm *adv* meanwhile; for the moment; sometimes; however, anyhow

inter·imō -imĕre -ēmī -emptum *vt* to do away with, abolish; to kill

inter·ĭor -ĭus *adj* inner, interior; inner side of; secret, private; deeper, more profound; more intimate, more personal, more confidential

interitĭ·ō -ōnis *f* ruin, destruction

interĭt·us -ūs *m* ruin; death

interius *adv* on the inside, in the middle; too short; (to listen) closely

interjac·ĕō -ēre *vi* (with *dat*) to lie between

interjaciō see **interjicio**

interjecti·ō -ōnis *f* interjection; parenthesis

interject·us -a -um *pp* of **interjicio; adj** (with *dat* or **inter +** *acc*) set or lying between

interject·us -ūs *m* interposition; interval

inter·jiciō -jicĕre -jēcī -jectum *vt* to interpose; (with *dat* or **inter +** *acc*) **a** to throw or set (*something*) between; **b** to intermingle (*something*) with, intermix (*something*) with

inter·jungō -jungĕre -junxī -junctum *vt* to join together; to clasp

inter·lābor -lābī -lapsus *vi* to glide or flow in between

inter·lĕgō -legĕre -lēgī -lectum *vt* to pick or pluck here and there

inter·linō -linĕre -lēvī -litum *vt* to smear; to alter by erasing

inter·lŏquor -lŏquī -locūtus sum *vi* to interrupt; (with *dat*) to interrupt (*someone*)

inter·lūcĕo -lūcĕre -luxī *vi* to shine through; to lighten now and then; to be transparent; to be plainly visible

interlūni·a -ōrum *n pl* new moon

interlŭ·ō -ĕre *vt* to flow between, wash

intermenstrū·us -a -um *adj* of the new moon; *n* new moon

intermināt·us -a -um *adj* endless

intermin·or -ārī -ātus sum *vt* (with *dat*) to threaten (*someone*) with (*something*); *vi* to threaten

inter·miscĕō -miscēre -miscŭī -mixtum *vt* to intermingle

intermissi·ō -ōnis *f* interruption

inter·mittō -mittĕre -mīsī -missum *vt* to interrupt, break off, suspend, omit, neglect; to leave gaps in, leave unoccupied, leave undefended; to allow (*time*) to pass; *vi* to pause, stop

intermixtus *pp* of **intermiscĕo**

inter·morior -mŏrī -mortŭus sum *vi* to die suddenly; to faint

intermortŭ·us -a -um *adj* dead; unconscious; (fig) half-dead, moribund

intermundi·a -ōrum *n pl* outer space

intermūrāl·is -e *adj* intermural, between two walls

internāt·us -a -um *adj* (with *dat*) growing among or between

internecīn·us -a -um *adj* internecine, exterminating, of extermination

internecī·ō -ōnis *f* massacre, extermination

internecīv·us -a -um *adj* exterminating; **bellum internecivum** war of extermination

internĕc·ō -āre *vt* to kill off, exterminate

internect·ō -ĕre *vt* to intertwine

internit·ĕō -ēre *vi* to shine out

internōd·ium -iī *or* **-ī** *n* space between two joints

inter·noscō -noscĕre -nōvī -nōtum *vt* to distinguish, recognize; (with **ab +** *abl*) to distinguish (*one thing*) from (*another*)

internuntiō -āre *vi* to exchange messages

internunt·ius -iī *or* **-ī** *m* or **internunti·a -ae** *f* messenger, courier, mediator, go-between

intern·us -a -um *adj* internal; civil, domestic

in·terō -terĕre -trīvī -trītum *vt* to rub in, mash together

interpellāti·ō -ōnis *f* interruption

interpellāt·or -ōris *m* interrupter, disturber

interpell·ō -āre *vt* to interrupt, break in on; to disturb, obstruct, hinder; to raise as an objection

interpŏl·is -e *adj* patched up

interpŏl·ō -āre *vt* to polish, dress up; to interpolate, falsify

inter·pōnō -pōnĕre -posŭī -posĭtum *vt* to insert, interpose, intersperse; to introduce, insert; to introduce, admit (*a person*); to let (*time*) pass or elapse; to alter, falsify (*writings*); to allege, use as pretext; **operam** or **studium interponere** to apply effort; **se interponere** (with *dat* or **in +** *acc*) to interfere with, meddle with, get mixed up with

interpositi·ō -ōnis *f* insertion; introduction; parenthesis

interpositus *pp* of **interpono**

interposit·us -ūs *m* interposition

interpr·es -ĕtis *m & f* mediator, negotiator; middleman, broker; interpreter; expounder; translator

interpretāti·ō -ōnis *f* interpretation, explanation; meaning; translation

interprĕt·or -ārī -ātus sum *vt* to interpret, put a construction on, construe; to understand, infer, conclude; to decide, determine; to translate

inter·prīmō -primĕre -pressī -pressum *vt* to squeeze

interpunct·a -ōrum *n pl* pauses, punctuation

interpuncti·ō -ōnis *f* punctuation

interpunct·us -a -um *adj* well-divided

inter·quiescō -quiescĕre -quiēvī *vi* to rest awhile; to pause awhile

interregn·um -ī *n* interregnum (*time between death of one king and election of another or similar interval between consuls*)

inter·rex -rēgis *m* interrex, regent

interrĭt·us -a -um *adj* undaunted

interrogāti·ō -ōnis *f* question; interrogation, cross-examination; syllogism

interrogāt·um -ī n question.

interrŏg·ō -āre vt to ask, question; to interrogate, cross-examine; to indict, sue

inter·rumpō -rumpĕre -rūpī -ruptum vt to break apart, break in half, break up, smash; to divide, scatter; to interrupt, break off

interruptē adv with interruptions

interruptus pp of **interrumpo**

inter·saepiō -saepīre -saepsī -saeptum vt to fence off, enclose; to stop up, close, cut off

inter·scindō -scindĕre -scĭdī -scissum vt to tear apart, tear down; to cut off, separate

inter·scrībō -scrībĕre -scripsī -scriptum vt to write (something) in between

inter·sĕrō -serĕre -serŭī vt to interpose; to allege as an excuse

interspīrātĭ·ō -ōnis f breathing pause, correct breathing (in delivering a speech)

interstinct·us -a -um adj blotchy

inter·stinguō -stinguĕre — -stinctum vt to spot, blotch; to extinguish

interstring·ō -ĕre vt to strangle

inter·sum -esse -fŭī vi to be present, assist, take part; to differ; to be of interest; (with dat) to be present at, attend, take part in; (with **in** + abl) to be present at; v impers there is a difference; it makes a difference; it is of importance; it is of interest; (with **inter** + acc) there is a difference between; (with **in** + abl) there is a difference among; (with genit or with fem of possessive pronouns **meā, tuā, nostrā,** etc.) it make a difference to, it is of importance to, it concerns (me, you, us, etc.); (with genit of value, e.g., **magni, permagni, tanti,** or with adv **multum, plurimum, maxime**) it makes a (great, very great, such a great) difference, it is of (great, very great, such great) importance, it is of (great, very great, such great) concern; **ne minimum quidem interest** there is not the slightest difference; **nihil omnino interest** there is no difference whatever

intertext·us -a -um adj interwoven

inter·trăhō -trahĕre -traxī vt (with dat) to take (something) away from

intertrīment·um -ī n wear and tear; loss, wastage

interturbātĭ·ō -ōnis f confusion, turmoil

interturb·ō -āre vt to confuse

intervall·um -ī n interval, space, distance; interval of time, spell, pause, intermission; contrast, difference

inter·vellō -vellĕre -vulsī -vulsum vt to pluck here and there

inter·veniō -venīre -vēnī -ventum vt to interfere with; vi to hap-

pen along; to intervene, intrude; to happen, occur; (with dat) to interfere with, interrupt, put a stop to, come in the way of, oppose, prevent

intervent·or -ōris m intruder, untimely visitor

intervent·us -ūs m intervention, intrusion; mediation

inter·vertō or **inter·vortō -vertĕre -vertī -versum** vt to divert, embezzle; (with acc of person and abl of thing) to rob or cheat (someone) of

inter·vīsō -vīsĕre -vīsī -vīsum vt to visit from time to time; to look after

intervolĭt·ō -āre vi to flit about

intervŏm·ō -ĕre -ŭī -ĭtum vt (with **inter** + acc) to throw up amongst

intervulsus pp of **intervello**

intestābĭl·is -e adj infamous, notorious; wicked

intestātō adv intestate

intestāt·us -a -um adj intestate; unconvicted by witnesses

intestāt·us -a -um adj castrated

intestīn·us -a -um adj internal; n & n pl intestines

in·texō -texĕre -texŭī -textum vt to interweave, interlace; to weave; to embroider; to surround, envelop

intĭb·um -ī n endive

intĭmē adv intimately, cordially

intĭm·us or **intŭm·us -a -um** adj innermost; deepest, most profound; most secret, most intimate; m intimate friend

in·tingō or **in·tinguō -tingĕre -tinxī -tinctum** vt to dip, soak

intolerābĭl·is -e adj intolerable; irresistible

intolerand·us -a -um adj intolerable

intolĕr·ans -antis adj intolerable, insufferable; (with genit) unable to stand, unable to put up with

intoleranter adv intolerably, immoderately, excessively

intolerantĭ·a -ae f unbearableness, insolence

intŏn·ō -āre -ŭī -ātus vt to thunder out; vi to thunder

intons·us -a -um adj unshorn, untrimmed; long-haired; rude

in·torquĕō -torquēre -torsī -tortum vt to twist, turn, roll; (with **circum** + acc) to wrap (something) around; (with dat or **in** + acc) to aim, cast, throw (a weapon) at

intort·us -a -um adj twisted; tangled; (fig) crooked

intrā adv on the inside, inside, within; inward; prep (with acc) inside, within; during, within, in the course of, in less than; less than, fewer than, within the limits of

intrābĭl·is -e adj inaccessible

intractābĭl·is -e adj intractable, unmanageable; formidable, dangerous

intractāt·us -a -um adj untamed, wild; unbroken (horse); unattempted

intrem·iscō -iscĕre -ŭī *vi* to begin to shake or tremble

intrĕm·ō -ĕre -ŭī *vi* to shake, tremble, shiver

intrepĭdē *adv* calmly, intrepidly

intrepĭd·us -a -um *adj* calm, intrepid, not nervous

intrīc·ō -āre *vt* to entangle, involve

intrinsĕcus *adv* on the inside

intrīt·us -a -um *adj* not worn away; (fig) not worn out

intrō *adv* inwards, inside, in

intr·ō -āre *vt & vi* to enter; to penetrate

intrō·dūcō -dūcĕre -duxī -ductum *vt* to introduce

intrōductĭ·ō -ōnis *f* introduction

intrō·eō -īre -ĭī -ĭtum *vt & vi* to enter

intrō·fĕrō -ferre -tŭlī -lātum *vt* to carry in

intrō·gredĭor -grĕdī -gressus sum *vi* to step inside

intrŏĭt·us -ūs *m* entrance; beginning, prelude

intrōlātus *pp* of introfero

intrō·mittō -mittĕre -mīsī -missum *vt* to let in, admit

introrsum or **introrsus** *adv* inwards, towards the inside; (fig) inwardly, inside

intrō·rumpō -rumpĕre -rūpī -ruptum *vi* to break in, enter by force

introspect·ō -āre *vt* to look in on

intrō·spicĭō -spicĕre -spexī -spectum *vt* to look into, look at; (fig) to inspect, examine, observe; *vi* (with **in** + *acc*) to look into; (fig) to look into, inspect, examine

intŭb·um -ī *n* endive

in·tŭĕor -tŭērī -tŭĭtus sum *vt* to look at, gaze upon; to contemplate, consider; to look up to, have regard for, admire; to keep an eye on

intum·escō -escĕre -ŭī *vi* to swell up, rise; (of voice) to grow louder; (of river) to rise; to become angry; to get a big head, swell with pride

intumulāt·us -a -um *adj* unburied

in·tŭor -tŭī *vt* to look at, gaze at; to consider

inturbĭd·us -a -um *adj* undisturbed, quiet

intus *adv* inside, within; at home, in; to the inside; from within

intūt·us -a -um *adj* unguarded; unsafe

inŭl·a -ae *f* elecampane (*plant*)

inult·us -a -um *adj* unavenged; unpunished, without being punished

inumbr·ō -āre *vt* to shade; to cover

inundātĭ·ō -ōnis *f* inundation

inund·ō -āre *vt* to flood, inundate; *vi* to overflow; **sanguine inundare** to run red with blood

in·ungō -ungĕre -unxī -unctum *vt* to anoint

inurbānē *adv* impolitely, rudely; without wit

inurbān·us -a -um *adj* impolite, rude, rustic

in·urgĕō -urgēre -ursī *vi* to butt

in·ūrō -ūrĕre -ussī -ustum *vt* to burn in, brand, imprint; (with *dat*) **a** to brand upon, imprint upon, affix to; **b** to inflict upon

inūsĭtātē *adv* unusually, strangely

inūsĭtāt·us -a -um *adj* unusual, strange, uncommon, extraordinary

inustus *pp* of inuro

inūtĭl·is -e *adj* useless, unprofitable; impractical; injurious, harmful

inūtĭlĭt·ās -ātis *f* uselessness; harmfulness

inūtĭlĭter *adv* uselessly, unprofitably

in·vādō -vādĕre -vāsī -vāsum *vt* to come or go into, enter; to enter upon, undertake, attempt; to invade, attack, assault, rush upon; (fig) to seize, take possession of; *vi* to come or go in; to invade; (with **in** + *acc*) **a** to assail, attack, invade; **b** to seize, get possession of, usurp

inval·escō -escĕre -ŭī *vi* to grow stronger

invalĭd·us -a -um *adj* weak, feeble, impotent; inadequate, unsuitable

invāsus *pp* of invado

invectĭ·ō -ōnis *f* importing, importation; arrival by boat

in·vĕhō -vehĕre -vexī -vectum *vt* to carry in, bring in (*by cart, horse, boat, etc.*); (with *dat*) to bring (*e.g., evils*) upon; **invehi** (with *acc* or **in** + *acc*) **a** to ride into, sail into; **b** to attack; **c** to inveigh against, attack (*with words*); **invehi equo** to ride a horse; **invehi nave** to sail; **se invehere** (with *acc* or **in** + *acc*) to rush against, attack

invendibĭl·is -e *adj* unsalable

in·venĭō -venīre -vēnī -ventum *vt* to come upon, find, come across, discover; to find out, invent, devise; to learn, ascertain; to acquire, get, reach, earn

inventĭ·ō -ōnis *f* inventiveness; inventing, invention

invent·or -ōris *m* or **inventr·ix -īcis** *f* inventor, author, discoverer

invent·us -a -um *pp* of invenio; *n* invention, discovery

invenust·us -a -um *adj* having no sex appeal; homely, unattractive; unlucky in love

inverēcund·us -a -um *adj* disrespectful, immodest, shameless

inverg·ō -ĕre *vt* to pour upon

inversĭ·ō -ōnis *f* inversion (*of words*); irony; allegory

invers·us -a -um *adj* turned upside down; turned inside out

in·vertō -vertĕre -vertī -versum *vt* to invert, turn upside down, upset, reverse, turn inside out; to transpose, reverse; to pervert, abuse, misrepresent; to use ironically

invesperasc·it -ĕre *v impers* evening is approaching, twilight is falling

investīgātĭ·ō -ōnis *f* investigation

investigāt·or -ōris *m* investigator, researcher

investig·ō -āre *vt* to track, trace, search after; to investigate, search into, search after

inveter·ascō -ascĕre -āvī *vi* to begin to grow old, grow old; to become fixed, become established; to become rooted, grow inveterate; to become obsolete

inveterāti·ō -ōnis *f* chronic illness

inveterāt·us -a -um *adj* inveterate, long-standing

invĭcem or **in vĭcem** *adv* in turn, taking turns, one after another, alternately; mutually, each other

invīct·us -a -um *adj* unconquered; invincible

invĭd·ens -entis *adj* envious, jealous

invidentĭ·a -ae *f* enviousness, jealousy

in·vidĕō -vidēre -vīdī -vīsum *vt* to cast an evil eye on; to envy, begrudge; *vi* (with *dat*) to envy, begrudge; (with *dat* of person and *abl* of cause or **in** + *abl*) to begrudge (*someone something*), envy (*someone because of something*)

invidĭ·a -ae *f* envy, jealousy; unpopularity; **invidiae esse** (with *dat*) to be a cause of envy to; **invidiam habēre** to be unpopular, be hated

invidiōsē *adv* spitefully

invidiōs·us -a -um *adj* envious, spiteful; envied; causing envy

invĭd·us -a -um *adj* envious, jealous; (with *dat*) hostile to, unfavorable to

invigĭl·ō -āre *vi* to be alert, be on one's toes; (with *dat*) to be on the lookout for, keep an eye on, pay attention to, watch over; (with **pro** + *abl*) to watch over

inviolābĭl·is -e *adj* inviolable; invulnerable, indestructible

inviolātē *adv* inviolately

inviolāt·us -a -um *adj* inviolate, unhurt; inviolable

invīsitāt·us -a -um *adj* rarely seen; not seen before, unknown, strange

in·vīsō -vīsĕre -vīsī -vīsum *vt* to visit, get to see; to look into, inspect; to look after; to get sight of

invīs·us -a -um *pp* of **invideo**; *adj* unseen; hateful, detested; hostile

invītāment·um -ī *n* attraction, allurement, inducement

invītātĭ·ō -ōnis *f* invitation; challenge

invītāt·us -ūs *m* invitation

invītē *adv* unwillingly, against one's wish

invīt·ō -āre *vt* to invite; to entertain; to summon, challenge; to ask, request; to allure, attract; to encourage, court

invīt·us -a -um *adj.* reluctant, unwilling, against one's will; **invītā Minervā** against one's better judgment, against the grain

invĭ·us -a -um *adj* without a road, trackless, impassable; *n pl* rough terrain

invocātĭ·ō -ōnis *f* invocation

invocāt·us -a -um *adj* unbidden

invŏc·ō -āre *vt* to invoke, call upon, appeal to

involāt·us -ūs *m* flight

involgō see **invulgo**

involĭt·ō -āre *vi* (with *dat*) (of long hair) to float over, trail over

invŏl·ō -āre *vt* to swoop down upon, pounce upon; *vi* to swoop down; (with **in** + *acc*) to swoop down upon, pounce upon

involūcr·e -is *n* smock

involūcr·um -ī *n* wrapper, cover, case, envelope; (fig) cover-up, front

involūt·us -a -um *adj* complicated

in·volvō -volvĕre -volvī -volūtum *vt* to wrap up, involve, envelop; to cover completely, overwhelm; (with *dat* or **in** + *acc*) to pile (*something*) on; **se involvĕre** (with *dat*) (fig) to get all wrapped up in

involvŏl·us -ī *m* caterpillar

invulg·ō -āre *vi* to give evidence

invulnerāt·us -a -um *adj* unwounded

iō *interj* ho!

io- = jo-

Ĭ·ō -ūs or **Ĭ·ōn -ōnis** *f* Io (*daughter of Argive King Inachus, changed by Jupiter into a heifer, and driven by Juno in this form over the world under the surveillance of hundred-eyed Argus*)

Ĭocast·a -ae or **Ĭocast·ē -ēs** *f* wife of Laius and mother as well as wife of Oedipus

Ĭŏla·us -ī *m* son of Iphicles and companion of Hercules

Ĭŏl·ē -ēs *f* daughter of Eurytus, the king of Oechalia, who fell in love with Hercules

Ĭōn see **Io**

Ĭōn·es -um *m pl* Ionians (*Greek inhabitants of the W. coast of Asia Minor*)

Ĭŏnĭc·us -a -um *adj* Ionic; *m* Ionic dancer; *n pl* Ionic dance

Ĭŏnĭ·us -a -um *adj* Ionian; *f* Ionia (*coastal district of Asia Minor*); *n* Ionian Sea (*off the W. Coast of Greece*)

Ĭōta (*indecl*) *n* iota (*ninth letter of the Greek alphabet*)

Ĭphianass·a -ae *f* Iphigenia

Ĭphigenĭ·a -ae *f* daughter of Agamemnon and Clytemnestra, who was to have been sacrificed at Aulis but was saved by Diana and conveyed to the Tauric Chersonese, where .she became priestess of Diana

Ĭphĭt·us -ī *m* Argonaut, son of Eurytus and Antiope

ips·a -īus or **-īus** *adj* self, very, just, mere, precisely; in person; by herself, alone; of herself, of her own accord; *pron* she herself; mistress of the house

ips·e (or **ips·us**) **-īus** (or **-īus**) *adj* self, very, just, mere, precisely; in person; by himself, alone; of himself, of his own accord; *pron* he himself; master; host

ips·um -īus or **-īus** *adj* self, very, just, mere, precisely; by itself, alone; of itself, spontaneously; **nunc ipsum** just now; **tunc ipsum** just then; *pron* it itself, that itself; **ipsum quod . . .** the very fact that . . .

ipsus see **ipse**

īr·a -ae *f* ire, wrath, resentment

īrācundē *adv* angrily; passionately

īrācundi·a -ae *f* quick temper; anger, wrath, violence, passion; resentment

īrācund·us -a -um *adj* hot-tempered, quick-tempered, irritable; angry; resentful

īrasc·or -ī *vi* to get angry, fly into a rage; (with *dat*) to get angry at

īrātē *adv* angrily

īrāt·us -a -um *adj* angry, irate, enraged; (with *dat*) angry at

Ir·is -idis *f* goddess of the rainbow and messenger of the gods

īrōni·a -ae *f* irony

irrās·us -a -um *adj* unshaven

irrātiōnāl·is -e *adj* irrational

ir·raucescō -raucescĕre -rausī *vi* to become hoarse

irredivīv·us -a -um *adj* irreparable

irrēd·ux -ūcis *adj* one-way (*road*)

irreligāt·us -a -um *adj* not tied

irreligiōsē *adv* impiously

irreligiōs·us -a -um *adj* impious, irreligious

irremeābil·is -e *adj* not to be traversed; one-way

irreparābil·is -e *adj* irretrievable

irrepert·us -a -um *adj* undiscovered, not found

ir·rēpō -rēpĕre -repsī -reptum *vi* to creep in; (fig) to sneak in; (with **ad** or **in** + *acc*) to creep toward or into; to sneak up on

irreprehens·us -a -um *adj* blameless

irrequiēt·us -a -um *adj* restless

irresect·us -a -um *adj* untrimmed

irresolūt·us -a -um *adj* not loosened, still tied

irrēt·iō -īre -īvī or **-iī -ītum** *vt* to trap

irretort·us -a -um *adj* not turned back

irrevĕr·ens -entis *adj* irreverent, disrespectful

irreverenter *adv* irreverently, disrespectfully

irreverenti·a -ae *f* irreverence, disrespect

irrevocābil·is -e *adj* irrevocable; implacable, relentless

irrevocāt·us -a -um *adj* not called back, not asked back

ir·rīdeō -rīdēre -rīsī -rīsum *vt* to

ridicule, laugh at, mock; *vi* to laugh, joke; (with *dat*) to laugh at

irrīdiculē *adv* with no sense of humor

irrigāti·ō -ōnis *f* irrigation

irrig·ō -āre *vt* to irrigate, water; to inundate; (fig) to diffuse; (fig) to flood, steep, soak

irrigu·us -a -um *adj* wet, soaked, well-watered; refreshing

irrīsi·ō -ōnis *f* ridicule, mockery

irrīs·or -ōris *m* reviler, mocker

irrīsus *pp* of **irrideo**

irrīs·us -ūs *m* mockery, derision; laughing stock, object of derision

irrītābil·is -e *adj* easily excited, easily enraged, irritable, sensitive

irrītām·en -inis *n* incentive; provocation

irrītāment·um -ī *n* incentive; provocation

irrītāti·ō -ōnis *f* incitement; irritation, provocation; stimulant

irrīt·ō -āre *vt* to incite, excite, provoke, enrage

irrit·us -a -um *adj* invalid, null and void; futile, pointless, useless; unsuccessful (*person*)

irrogāti·ō -ōnis *f* imposing (*e.g., of a fine*)

irrog·ō -āre *vt* to impose, inflict; to object to (*proposals*)

irrōr·ō -āre *vt* to wet, moisten, sprinkle

irruct·ō -āre *vi* to belch

ir·rumpō -rumpĕre -rūpī -ruptum *vt* to rush into, break down; *vi* to rush in; (with *dat* or **in** + *acc*) **a** to rush into, rush through; **b** (fig) to intrude upon

ir·ruŏ -ruĕre -ruī *vi* to rush in, force one's way in; to make a slip (*in speaking*); (with **in** + *acc*) to rush into, rush on, invade, attack; **inruere in odium** (with *genit*) to incur the anger of

irrupti·ō -ōnis *f* invasion

irrupt·us -a -um *pp* of **irrumpo**; *adj* unbroken

Īr·us -ī *m* beggar in the palace of Ulysses in Ithaca

is ejus *adj* this, that, the said, the aforesaid; *pron* he; **is qui** he who, the person who, the one who

Īs·is -is or **-īdis** *f* Egyptian goddess

Ismari·us -a -um *adj* of Mt. Ismarus in Thrace; Thracian

Īsocrăt·ēs -is *m* famous orator and teacher of rhetoric at Athens (436-338 B.C.)

ista see **iste**

istāc *adv* that way

istactĕnus *adv* thus far

istaec see **istic**

ist·e -a -ud *adj* that of yours; this, that, the very, that particular; such, of such a kind; that terrible, that despicable; *pron* that one; (in court) your client

Isthm·us or **Isthm·os -ī** *m* Isthmus of Corinth

ist·ic -aec -oc or **-uc** *adj* that, that of yours; *pron* the one, that one

istic *adv* there, in that place; herein; on this occasion

istinc *adv* from there, from where you are

istiusmodī or **istimōdī** or **istīus modī** or **istī modī** *adj* that kind of, such

istō *adv* where you are; therefore; in that matter

istōc *adv* there, to where you are, yonder

istorsum *adv* in that direction

istūc *adv* there, to that place, to where you are, that way; **istuc veniam** I'll come to that matter

istūcīne see **istic**

istud see **iste**

ita *adv* thus, so, in this manner, in this way; (of natural consequence) thus, accordingly, therefore, under these circumstances; (in affirmation) yes, true, exactly; (in questions) really?, truly?; **ita . . . ut** (in comparisons) just as, although . . . nevertheless; (as correlatives) both . . . and, both . . . as well as; (in restriction) on condition that, in sofar as, on the assumption that; (of degree) to such a degree . . . that, so much . . . that, so . . . that; **non ita** not very, not especially; **quid ita?** how so?, what do you mean?

Ïtalī·a -ae *f* Italy

Ïtalic·us -a -um *adj* Italian

Ïtăl·is -ĭdis *adj* Italian; *f pl* Italian women

Ïtalī·us -a -um *adj* Italian; *f* see **Italia**

Ïtăl·us -a -um *adj* Italian

ităque *conj* and so, and thus, accordingly, therefore, consequently

item *adv* likewise, besides, moreover, also

it·er -ĭnĕris *n* journey, trip, march, walk; day's march, day's journey; route; right of way; passage (*of voice, etc.*); method, course, way, road; **ex itinere** or **in itinere en** route; **iter flectere** to change course; **iter terrestre** overland route; **maximis itineribus** by marching at top speed

iterātī·ō -ōnis *f* repetition

iter·ō -āre *vt* to repeat, renew; to plow again

iterum *adv* again, a second time; **iterum atque iterum** repeatedly, again and again

Ithăc·a -ae or **Ithăc·ē -ēs** *f* island off the W. coast of Greece in the Ionian Sea and home of Odysseus

itĭdem *adv* in the same way

itĭ·ō -ōnis *f* going, walking

it·ō -āre *vi* to go

it·us -ūs *m* going; going away, departure

It·ys -ўos *m* son of Tereus and Procne, who was killed by Procne and served up as food to Tereus

iu- = ju-

Ïxī·ōn -ōnis *m* son of Antion or of Jupiter, king of the Laipthae in Thessaly, and father of Pirithous; he was allowed into heaven by Jupiter after killing his father-in-law, but for trying to seduce Juno, was tied to a wheel and sent flying into Tartarus

J

jac·ĕō -ēre -uī *vi* to lie, lie down; to lie ill, be sick; to lie dead, to have fallen; to lie in ruins; to hang loose; to lie idle, rest; to lie, be situated; to lie flat, lie low; to feel low, be despondent; to lie prostrate, be powerless; to fall, fail, be refuted; to be low in someone's pinion; to linger, stay

jaciō jacĕre jēcī jactum *vt* to lay, build, establish, set, found, construct; to throw, cast, fling; to emit, produce; to sow, scatter; to throw away; to mention, utter, declare, intimate

jact·ans -antis *adj* boasting, bragging, showing off

jactanter *adv* boastfully

jactantī·a -ae *f* boasting, showing off

jactātī·ō -ōnis *f* tossing to and fro; swaying; shaking; writhing; boasting, bragging, showing off; gesticulation; **jactatio animi** agitation; **jactatio maritima** seasickness

jactāt·us -ūs *m* tossing, waving

jactĭt·ō -āre *vt* to display, show off

jact·ō -āre *vt* to throw, hurl; to toss about, shake; to throw away, throw out, throw overboard; to disturb, disquiet, stir up; to consider, discuss; to throw out, mention; to brag about, show off; **jactari** to toss, rock; (of money) to fluctuate in value; **se jactare** to boast, show off, throw one's weight around

jactūr·a -ae *f* throwing away, throwing overboard; loss, sacrifice

jactus *pp* of **jacio**

jact·us -ūs *m* toss, throw, cast

jaculābĭl·is -e *adj* missile

jaculāt·or -ōris *m* thrower, shooter; light-armed soldier; spearman

jaculātr·ix -īcis *f* huntress

jacŭl·or -ārī -ātus sum *vt* to throw; to shoot at; (fig) to aim at, strive after

jacŭl·us -a -um *adj* throwing, casting; *n* dart, javelin; casting net

jājūn- = jejun-

jam *adv* (present) now, already; (past) already, by then; (future) very soon, right away; (in transition) now, next, moreover; (for emphasis) actually, precisely, quite; (in a conclusion) then surely; **jam dudum** long ago, long since; **jam inde** immediately; **jam jam** even now, at every moment; **jam** . . . **jam** at one time . . . at another; **jam nunc** even now; **jam pridem** long since; **jam tum** even then, even at that time

Jānĭcŭl·um -ī *n* Roman hill on the right bank of the Tiber

jānĭt·or -ōris *m* doorman

jānĭtr·īx -īcis *f* portress

jānŭ·a -ae *f* door, house door; entrance; (fig) entrance, approach

Jānŭārĭ·us -a -um *adj & m* January

jān·us -ī *m* covered passage, arcade

Jān·us -ī *m* Janus (*old Italian deity, represented as having two faces*); temple of Janus (*at the bottom of the Argiletum in the Forum*)

jec·ur -ŏris *n* liver; (as the seat of emotions) anger, lust

jecuscŭl·um -ī *n* little liver

jējūnē *adv* (fig) drily

jējūnĭōs·ĭor or **jājūnĭōs·ĭor -ĭus** *adj* fasting, hungry

jējūnĭt·ās or **jājūnĭt·ās -ātis** *f* fasting; dryness (*of style*)

jējūn·ĭum -ĭī or **-ī** *n* fasting, fast; hunger; leanness

jējūn·us or **jājūn·us -a -um** *adj* fasting; hungry; poor (*land*); thin; insignificant, paltry, contemptible; low; dry (*style*)

jentācŭl·um -ī *n* breakfast

joc·or -ārī -ātus sum or **joc·ō -āre** *vt* to say in jest; *vi* to joke, crack a joke, be joking

jocōsē *adv* humorously, as a joke, jokingly

jocōs·us -a -um *adj* humorous, funny, clowning

joculār·is -e *adj* humorous, funny

joculār·ĭus -a -um *adj* ludicrous

joculāt·or -ōris *m* joker

jocul·or -ārī -ātus sum *vi* to joke

jocŭl·us -ī *m* joke

joc·us -ī (*pl*: **joc·ī -ōrum** *m* or **joc·a -ōrum** *n*) *m* joke; laughingstock; child's play; **joco remoto** all joking aside; **per jocum** as a joke, jokingly

jub·a -ae *f* mane; crest

jub·ar -ăris *n* radiance, brightness; sunshine

jubāt·us -a -um *adj* crested

jubēō jubēre jussī jussum *vt* to order; (pol) to order, decree, enact, ratify; to designate, appoint, assign; (med) to prescribe; **jube fratrem tuum salvere** (in letters) best regards to your brother

jūcundē *adv* pleasantly, delightfully, agreeably

jūcundĭt·ās -ātis *f* pleasantness, delight, enjoyment, agreeableness; *f pl* favors

jūcund·us -a -um *adj* pleasant, delightful, agreeable

Jūdae·us -a -um *adj* Jewish; *m* Jew; *f* Jewess; Judaea, Palestine

jūd·ex -ĭcis *m* judge; juror; arbitrator; umpire; critic; scholar; **judex morum** censor; **me judice** in my judgment

jūdĭcātĭ·ō -ōnis *f* judicial investigation; (fig) judgment, opinion

jūdĭcāt·us -a -um *adj* decided, determined; *m* condemned person; *n* decision, precedent; fine; **judicatum facere** to carry out a decision; **judicatum solvere** to pay a fine

jūdĭcāt·us -ūs *m* judgeship

jūdĭcĭāl·is -e *adj* judicial, forensic

jūdĭcĭārĭ·us -a -um *adj* judiciary

jūdĭc·ĭum -ĭī or **-ī** *n* trial, court, court of justice; sentence; jurisdiction; opinion, decision; faculty of judging, judgment, good judgment, taste, tact, discretion

jūdĭc·ō -āre *vt* to judge; to examine; to sentence, condemn; to form an opinion of; to conclude; to declare, proclaim; (with *dat* of person and *acc* of the offense) to convict (*someone*) of; (with *genit*) to find (*someone*) guilty of; (with *dat* of person and *genit* of the offense) to convict (*someone*) of

jugāl·is -e *adj* yoked together; nuptial

jugātĭ·ō -ōnis *f* tying up

jūger·um -ī *n* jugerum (*land measure: about two thirds of an acre*)

jūg·is -e *adj* continual, perennial, inexhaustible

jugl·ans -andis *f* walnut tree

jugōs·us -a -um *adj* hilly

Jugŭl·ae -ārum *f pl* Orion's belt (*three stars in the constellation Orion*)

jugŭl·ō -āre *vt* to cut the throat of, kill, murder; to destroy; to silence

jugŭl·um -ī *n* or **jugŭl·us -ī** *m* throat

jug·um -ī *n* yoke, collar; pair, team; (mil) yoke (*consisting of a spear laid crosswise on two upright spears, under which the conquered had to pass*); crossbar (*of a loom*); thwart (*of a boat*); common bond, union; wedlock; pair, couple; mountain ridge; *n pl* heights

Jugurth·a -ae *m* king of Numidia (160-104 B.C.)

Jūlĭ·a -ae *f* aunt of Julius Caesar and wife of Marius; daughter of Julius Caesar and wife of Pompey (*d.* 54 B.C.); daughter of Augustus by Scribonia (39 B.C.-14 A.D.)

Jūlĭ·us -a -um *adj* Julian; of July; *m* Roman praenomen; July

jūment·um -ī *n* beast of burden, horse, mule

junce·us -a -um *adj* of reeds; slim, slender

juncōs·us -a -um *adj* overgrown with reeds

junctĭ·ō -ōnis *f* joining

junctūr·a -ae *f* joining, uniting, joint, juncture; connection, relationship; combination

junct·us -a -um *pp* of **jungo**; *adj* connected, associated, united, attached

junc·us -ī *m* reed

jungō jungĕre junxī junctum *vt* to join, join together, unite, connect; to yoke, harness; to couple, pair, mate; to bridge (*a river*); to bring together, unite, associate, ally; to add; to compose (*poems*); to combine (*words*)

jūni·or -ōris *adj* younger

jūnipĕr·us -ī *f* juniper

Jūni·us -a -um *adj* June, of June; *m* Roman praenomen; June

jūn·ix -īcis *f* heifer

Jūn·ō -ōnis *f* daughter of Saturn and wife and sister of Jupiter

Juppĭter (or **Jupĭter** or **Diespĭter**) **Jovis** *m* son of Saturn, brother and husband of Juno, and chief god of the Romans

jūrāt·or -ōris *m* judge; assistant censor

jūreconsult·us -ī *m* legal expert, lawyer

jūrejūr·ō -āre *vi* to swear

jūreperītus see **jurisperītus**

jurg·ium -ī or **-ī** *n* quarrel; *n pl* reproaches

jurg·ō -āre *vi* to quarrel

jūridiciāl·is -e *adj* juridical

jūrisconsult·us or **jūreconsult·us -ī** *m* legal expert, lawyer

jūrisdicti·ō -ōnis *f* administration of justice; jurisdiction

jūrisperīt·us or **jūreperīt·us -ī** *m* legal expert, lawyer

jūr·ō -āre *vt* to swear; to swear by, attest, call to witness; to swear to, attest; *vi* to swear, take an oath; to conspire; (with **in** + *acc*) to swear allegiance to, swear to observe, vow obedience to; **in haec verba jurare** to swear according to the prescribed form; to conspire against; **jurare calumniam** to swear that the accusation is not false

jū·s -ris *n* juice, broth, gravy, soup; law (*as established by society and custom rather than statute law*); right, justice; law court, court of justice; legal right, authority, permission, prerogative; jurisdiction; **in jus ire** to go to court; **jure** by right, rightfully, in justice; **jus dicere** to sit as judge, hold court; **jus gentium** international law; **jus publicum** common right; **summum jus** strict letter of the law

jūs jūrand·um (*genit:* **jūr·is jūrand·ī**) *n* oath

jussū (*abl* only) *m* by order; **meo jussū** by my order

juss·us -a -um *pp* of **jubeo**; *n* order, command, bidding

justē *adv* justly, rightly

justific·us -a -um *adj* just-dealing

justiti·a -ae *f* justice, fairness

justit·ium -ī or **-ī** *n* suspension of legal business; (fig) standstill

just·us -a -um *adj* just, fair; justified, well-founded; formal; in due order, according to protocol, regular; *n* justice; due measure; **plus quam justo** more than due measure, too much; *n pl* rights; formalities; ceremonies, due ceremony; funeral rites, obsequies

Jūturn·a -ae *f* nymph, sister of Turnus, the king of the Rutuli

jūtus *pp* of **juvo**

juvenāl·is -e *adj* youthful; juvenile

Juvenāl·is -is *m* Juvenal (*D. Junius Juvenalis, Roman satirist in the time of Domitian and Trajan, c. 62-142 A.D.*)

juvenc·us -a -um *adj* young; *m* bullock; young man; *f* heifer; girl

juven·escō -escĕre -uī *vi* to grow up; to get young again

juvenīl·is -e *adj* youthful; juvenile; cheerful

juvenīliter *adv* youthfully, boyishly

juvĕn·is -e *adj* young; *m* young man (*between the ages of twenty and forty-five*); warrior; *f* young lady

juvĕn·or -ārī -ātus sum *vi* to act like a kid

juvent·a -ae *f* youth

juvent·ās -ātis *f* youth, prime of life, manhood; (collectively) young people, youth

juvent·ūs -ūtis *f* youth, prime of life, manhood; (collectively) young people, youth

juvō juvāre jūvī jūtum *vt* to help; to please, delight; **juvat** (with *inf*) it helps to; **juvat me** it delights me, I am glad

juxtā *adv* nearby, in close proximity; alike, in like manner, equally; (with **ac, atque, et, quam,** or **cum**) as well as, just the same as; *prep* (with *acc*) close to, near to, next to; next to, immediately after; near, bordering upon; next door to

juxtim *adv* near; equally

K

Kalend·ae or **Calend·ae -ārum** *f pl* Kalends (*first day of the Roman month*); **tristes Kalendae** gloomy Kalends (*because interest was due on the Kalends*)

Kalendār·ium -ī or **-ī** *n* account book

Karthāginiens·is -e *adj* Carthaginian

Karthāg·ō -ĭnis *f* Carthage (*city of N. Africa*)

L

labasc·ō -ĕre *vi* to waver; to give in, yield

lābēcŭl·a -ae *f* blemish, spot, stain (*e.g., on someone's reputation*)

labe·faciō -facĕre -fēcī -factum *vt* to cause to totter, to shake, to weaken; (fig) to weaken, ruin, destroy

labefact·ō -āre *vt* to shake; (fig) to weaken, ruin, destroy

labell·um -ī *n* lip

labell·um -ī *n* small basin

lāb·ēs -is *f* fall, falling down; stroke, blow, ruin, destruction; blemish, spot, defect; disgrace, discredit

labī·a -ae *f* lip

Labiēn·us -ī *m* Caesar's officer who defected to Pompey

labiōs·us -a -um *adj* thick-lipped

lab·ium -iī or -ī *n* lip

lab·ō -āre *vi* to totter, wobble; to waver, hesitate, be undecided; to fall to pieces, go to ruin

lābor lābī lapsus sum *vi* to glide, slide, slip; to slip, fall, sink; to slip away, disappear, escape; (of time) to slip by, pass, elapse; (fig) to fade

lab·or or lab·ōs -ōris *m* effort; trouble, distress, suffering; work, task

labōrif·er -ĕra -ĕrum *adj* struggling

labōriōs·us -a -um *adj* full of troubles, troublesome; energetic, industrious

labōr·ō -āre *vt* to work out, make, produce; *vi* to work; to suffer, be troubled; to be in danger; (with *inf*) to try to

labōs see labor

labr·um -ī *n* lip, edge

lābr·um -ī *n* basin, tub, bathtub

labrusc·a -ae *f* wild vine

labrusc·um -ī *n* wild grape

labyrinthē·us -a -um *adj* labyrinthine

labyrinth·us -ī *m* labyrinth

lac lactis *n* milk; milk of plants

Lacaen·a -ae *f* Spartan woman

Lacedaem·ōn -ŏnis *f* Sparta

Lacedaemŏni·us -a -um *adj* Spartan

lac·er -ĕra -ĕrum *adj* mangled, torn, lacerated, mutilated; lacerating, tearing

lacerāti·ō -ōnis *f* tearing, laceration, mangling

lacern·a -ae *f* coat, topcoat, overcoat

lacernāt·us -a -um *adj* wearing an overcoat

lacĕr·ō -āre *vt* to lacerate, tear, mangle; to slander, abuse; to waste, squander, destroy; to wreck (*ship*)

lacert·us -a -um *adj* muscular, brawny; *m* lizard; upper arm, muscle; *m pl* muscles, strength, brawn; *f* lizard

lacess·ō -ĕre -īvī or -iī -ītum *vt* to provoke, exasperate; to challenge; to move, arouse

Lachĕs·is -is *f* one of the three Fates

lacini·a -ae *f* flap (*of a garment*)

Lacīn·ium -iī or -ī *n* promontory in Bruttium with a temple to Juno

Lac·ō or Lac·ōn -ōnis *m* Spartan; Spartan dog

Lacōni·a -ae *f* district of the Peloponnesus of which Sparta was the chief city

Lacōnic·us -a -um *adj* Spartan; *n* sweat bath

lacrĭm·a or lacrŭm·a -ae *f* tear; gumdrop (*plant*)

lacrimābĭl·is -e *adj* worthy of tears, deplorable

lacrimābund·us -a -um *adj* tearful, about to break into tears

lacrĭm·ō or lacrŭm·ō -āre *vt* to cry for, shed tears over; (of trees) to drip; *vi* to cry, shed tears

lacrimōs·us -a -um *adj* crying, tearful; causing tears, bringing tears to the eyes

lacrimŭl·a -ae *f* teardrop, little tear; (fig) crocodile tear

lacrum· = lacrim·

lact·ans -antis *adj* milk-giving

lactāri·us -a -um *adj* milky

lactāti·ō -ōnis *f* allurement

lact·ens -entis *adj* suckling; milky, juicy, tender; full of milk; *m* suckling

lacteŏl·us -a -um *adj* milk-white

lact·ēs -ium *f pl* intestines; laxae lactēs empty stomach

lactesc·ō -ĕre *vi* to turn to milk

lactĕ·us -a -um *adj* milky, full of milk, milk-colored; milk-white

lact·ō -āre *vt* to cajole, wheedle

lactūc·a -ae *f* lettuce

lacūn·a -ae *f* ditch, hole, pit; pond, pool; (fig) hole, gap

lacūn·ar -āris *n* paneled ceiling

lacūn·ō -āre *vt* to panel

lacūnōs·us -a -um *adj* sunken

lac·us -ūs *m* vat; tank, pool, reservoir, cistern; lake

laedō laedĕre laesī laesum *vt* to knock, strike; to hurt, rub open; to wound; to break (*promise, pledge*); to offend, outrage, violate; (with ad + *acc*) to smash (*something*) against

laen·a -ae *f* lined coat

Lāërt·ēs -ae *m* father of Ulysses

Lāërtĭăd·ēs -ae *m* Ulysses

laesi·ō -ōnis *f* attack, provocation

Laestrȳg·ōn -ŏnis *m* Laestrygonian (*one of the mythical race of cannibals in Italy, founders of Formiae*)

laes·us *pp* of laedo

laetābĭl·is -e *adj* cheerful, glad

laet·ans -antis *adj* joyful, glad

laetāti·ō -ōnis *f* rejoicing, joy

laetē *adv* joyfully, gladly

laetific·ans -antis *adj* joyous

laetific·ō -āre *vt* to gladden, cheer up; laetificari to rejoice

laetific·us -a -um *adj* joyful, cheerful

laetiti·a -ae *f* joyfulness, gladness, exuberance

laet·or -ārī -ātus sum *vi* to rejoice, be glad

laet·us -a -um *adj* rejoicing, glad, cheerful; happy, fortunate, auspicious; fertile, rich, smiling (*grain*); sleek, fat (*cattle*); bright, cheerful (*appearance*); cheering, welcome (*news*)

laevē *adv* awkwardly

laev·us -a -um *adj* left, on the left side; awkward, stupid; ill-omened; lucky, propitious; *f* left hand, left side; *n* the left; *n pl* the area on the left

lagăn·um -ī *n* pancake

lagē·os -ī *f* Greek vine

lagoen·a or lagōn·a -ae *f* jug

lagō·is -ĭdis *f* grouse

laguncŭl·a -ae *f* flask

Laïăd·ēs -ae *m* son of Laius (*Oedipus*)

Laï·us -ī *m* Laius (*father of Oedipus*)

lall·ō -āre *vi* to sing a lullaby

lām·a -ae *f* swamp, bog

lambĕr·ō -āre *vt* to tear to pieces

lamb·ō -ĕre -ī *vt* to lick, lap; (of a river) to wash, flow by; (of ivy) to cling to

lāment·a -ōrum *n pl* wailing, moaning, lamentation

lāmentābĭl·is -e *adj* pitiable: doleful; mournful, sorrowful

lāmentārĭ·us -a -um *adj* sorrowful, pitiful

lāmentātĭ·ō -ōnis *f* lamentation

lāment·or -ārī -ātus sum *vt* to cry over, lament; *vi* to wail, cry

lami·a -ae *f* witch, sorceress

lāmĭn·a or lammĭn·a or lamn·a -ae *f* plate, leaf (*of metal or wood*); blade; coin; peel, shell

lamp·as -ādis *f* torch; brightness; day; meteor; lamp

Lam·us -ī *m* mythical king of the Laestrygonians; son of Hercules and Omphale

lān·a -ae *f* wool; working in wool, spinning, lana aurea golden fleece; lanam trahere to card wool; lanas ducere to spin wool; rixari de lana caprina to argue over nothing

lānār·ius -a -um *adj* wool; *m* wool worker

lānăt·us -a -um *adj* woolly; *f pl* sheep

lancĕ·a -ae *f* lance, spear

lancĭn·ō -āre *vt* to squander, waste

lānĕ·us -a -um *adj* woolen; soft

langue·faciō -facĕre -fēcī -factum *vt* to make tired

langu·ens -entis *adj* languid, drooping, listless

langu·ĕō -ēre *vi* to be tired, be weary; to be weak, feeble (*from disease*); (fig) to be dull, languid, listless; to be without energy

langu·escō -escĕre -ŭī *vi* to become weak, grow faint; (fig) to become listless; to decline, decrease; to relax

languidē *adj* weakly, faintly, without energy

languidŭl·us -a -um *adj* languid; withered, faded

languĭd·us -a -um *adj* weak, faint, languid, sluggish; listless; enervating

langu·or -ōris *m* weakness, faintness, languor; dullness, listlessness, sluggishness

laniăt·us -ūs *m* mangling; *f pl* mental anguish

laniēn·a -ae *f* butcher shop

lānific·ĭum -ĭī or -ī *n* weaving

lānĭfĭc·us -a -um *adj* spinning, weaving, of spinning, of weaving

lānĭg·er -ĕra -ĕrum *adj* fleecy; *m* sheep (*ram*); *f* sheep (*ewe*)

lani·ō -āre *vt* to tear to pieces, mangle

lanist·a -ae *m* gladiator trainer, fencing master; (*in derision*) ringleader

lānĭt·ĭum -ĭī or -ī *n* wool

lan·ĭus -ĭī or -ī *m* butcher; (*in derision*) executioner, butcher

lantern·a -ae *f* lantern

lanternār·ius -ĭī or -ī *m* guide

lānūg·ō -ĭnis *f* down (*of plants, cheeks, etc.*)

Lānŭv·ĭum -ĭī or -ī *n* town in Latium on the Appian Way

lan·x -cis *f* dish, platter; scale

Lāocŏ·ōn -ontis *m* son of Priam and priest of Apollo, who, with his two sons, was killed by two serpents from the sea

Lāomĕd·ōn -ontis *m* king of Troy and father of Priam and Ganymede

Lāomedontē·us or Lāomedontĭ·us -a -um *adj* Trojan

Lāomedontĭăd·ēs -ae *m* son of Laomedon; Priam; *m pl* Trojans

lapăth·um -ī *n* or lapăth·us -ī *f* sorrel (*plant*)

lapicīd·a -ae *m* stonecutter, quarry worker

lapicīdīn·ae -ārum *f pl* stone quarry

lapidār·ius -a -um *adj* stone; latomiae lapidariae stone quarries

lapidātĭ·ō -ōnis *f* throwing stones

lapidăt·or -ōris *m* stone thrower

lapĭdĕ·us -a -um *adj* of stones, stone, stony; lapideus sum (fig) I am petrified

lapĭd·ō -āre *vt* to throw stones at; *v impers* it is raining stones, it is hailing stones

lapĭdōs·us -a -um *adj* full of stones, stony; hard as stone; gritty (*bread*)

lapill·us -ī *m* pebble; precious stone, gem, jewel; *m pl* small stones (*esp. for mosaics*)

lap·is -ĭdis *m* stone; milestone; platform; boundary stone, landmark; tombstone; precious stone, gem, pearl, jewel, stone statue; marble table; **lapides loqui** to speak harsh words

Lapĭth·ae -ārum m pl mountain tribe in Thessaly that fought the centaurs at the marriage of their king Pirithous

lapp·a -ae f burr

lapsĭ·ō -ōnis f sliding, slipping; (fig) tendency

laps·ō -āre vi to keep slipping, stumble

laps·us -a -um pp of **labor**; adj fallen

laps·us -ūs m falling, fall, sliding, slipping, gliding, flow, flight; blunder, error, fault, slip

laqueār·ia -ium n pl paneled ceiling

laqueāt·us -a -um adj paneled, having a paneled ceiling

laquě·us -ī m noose; snare; (fig) snare, trap; m pl (fig) subtleties

Lār Laris m tutelary deity, household god; hearth, home; m pl hearth, home, house, household, family

lard·um -ī n lard, fat

Larentĭ·a -ae f wife of Faustulus who reared Romulus and Remus

largē adv liberally, generously

largĭfic·us -a -um adj bountiful

largĭflŭ·us -a -um adj gushing

largĭlŏqu·us -a -um adj talkative

larg·ior -īrī -ītus sum vt to give generously, bestow freely; to lavish; to bestow, confer; to grant, concede; vi to give bribes, bribe

largĭt·ās -ātis f generosity, bounty

largĭtĭ·ō -ōnis f generosity; bribery

largĭt·or -ōris m generous donor; spendthrift; briber

larg·us -a -um adj abundant, plentiful, large, much; generous, liberal, bountiful, profuse

lārĭd·um -ī n lard, bacon fat

Lārīss·a -ae f town in Thessaly on the Peneus River

Lār·ius -ĭī or **-ī** m Lake Como

lar·ix -ĭcis f larch tree

larv·a -ae f mask; ghost

larvāt·us -a -um adj bewitched

lasăn·um -ī n chamber pot

lasarpīcĭf·er -ěra -ěrum adj producing asafetida (used as an antispasmodic)

lascīvĭ·a -ae f playfulness; petulence; lewdness

lascīvībund·us -a -um adj petulant, roguish

lascīv·ĭō -īre -ĭī -ītum vi to frolic, be frisky; to run riot, run wild

lascīv·us -a -um adj playful, frisky; brash, impudent, petulant; licentious, lustful; luxuriant (growth)

lāserpīc·ium -ĭī or **-ī** n silphium (plant which yielded asafetida)

lassĭtūd·ō -ĭnis f physical weariness, lassitude

lass·ō -āre vt to fatigue, exhaust

lassŭl·us -a -um adj somewhat tired

lass·us -a -um adj tired, weary, fatigued, exhausted

lātē adv widely, extensively; profusely; **late longeque** far and wide

latěbr·a -ae f hiding place, hideaway, hideout; (fig) loophole

latebrĭcŏl·a -ae m or f person who hangs around dives or brothels

latebrōsē adv secretly

latebrōs·us -a -um adj full of holes; hidden, secret; porous

lat·ens -entis adj hidden, secret

latenter adv in secret

lat·ěō -ēre -ŭī vi to lie hidden, lie concealed, lurk; to keep out of sight, sulk; to live a retired life, remain in obscurity, remain unknown, escape notice; to be in safety; to avoid a summons, lie low; to be obscure

lat·er -ěris m brick, tile; **laterem lavare** to waste effort

laterām·en -ĭnis n earthenware

latercŭl·us -ī m small brick; tile; biscuit

laterĭcĭ·us -a -um adj brick, made of brick; n brickwork

lātern·a -ae f lantern

latesc·ō -ěre vi to hide

lat·ex -ĭcis m liquid, fluid; water; spring; wine; oil

latĭbŭl·um -ī n hiding place, hideout, lair, den; (fig) refuge

lātĭclāvĭ·us -a -um adj having a broad crimson stripe (distinctive mark of senators, military tribunes of the equestrian order, and of sons of distinguished families)

Latīnē adv Latin, in Latin; in proper Latin; in plain Latin; **Latine loqui** to speak Latin; to speak correct Latin; **Latine reddere** to translate into Latin; **Latine scire** to understand Latin

Latīnĭt·ās -ātis f pure Latin, Latinity; Latin rights and privileges

Latīn·us -a -um adj Latin; possessing Latin rights and privileges; m Latinus (king of the Laurentians, who gave his daughter Lavinia in marriage to Aeneas); n Latin language; **in Latinum convertere** to translate into Latin

lātĭ·ō -ōnis f bringing, rendering; proposing

latĭt·ō -āre vi to keep hiding oneself; to be concealed, hide, lurk; to lie low (in order to avoid a summons)

lātĭtūd·ō -ĭnis f breadth, width; size, extent; broad pronunciation; richness of expression

lātĭus adv of late

Latĭ·us -a -um adj of Latium, Latin, Roman; n Latium (district in W. central Italy, in which Rome was situated); **jus Lati** or **Latium** Latin political rights and privileges

Lātō·is -ĭdis f Diana

lātom- = lautom-

Lātōn·a -ae f daughter of the Titan Coeus and Phoebe, and mother of Apollo and Diana

Lātōnigen·a -ae m or f child of Latona; m pl children of Latona, i.e., Apollo and Diana

Lătōnĭ·us -a -um adj of Latona; f Diana

lāt·or -ōris m bringer, bearer; proposer (of a law)

Lătō·us -ī m Apollo

lātrāt·or -ōris m barker; dog

lātrāt·us -ūs m barking

lātrīn·a -ae f wash room, toilet

lātr·ō -āre vt to bark at, snarl at; to clamor for; vi to bark; (fig) to rant

latr·ō -ōnis m mercenary; freebooter; brigand, bandit; (in chess) pawn

latrōcĭn·ĭum -ĭī or **-ī** n military service (as a mercenary); freebooting; brigandage, banditry, vandalism, piracy, robbery, highway robbery; villany, outrage; band of robbers

latrōcĭn·or -ārī -ātus sum vi to serve as a mercenary, be a mercenary soldier; to be a bandit, be a highwayman, be a pirate

latruncŭl·us -ī m small-time bandit

lātumĭ·ae -ārum f pl stone quarry; prison

lātus pp of **fero**

lāt·us -a -um adj wide, broad; extensive; widespread; broad (pronunciation); diffuse (style)

lat·us -ĕris n side, flank; body, person; lungs; lateral surface; coast; (mil) flank, wing; **a latere** (mil) on the flank; **a latere** (with genit) a at the side of, in the company of; **b** from among the friends of; **aperto latere** (mil) on the exposed flank; **latere tecto** scot free; **latus dare** to expose oneself; **latus tegere** (with genit) to walk by the side of, to escort (someone)

latuscŭl·um -ī n small side

laudābĭl·is -e adj laudable, praiseworthy

laudābĭlĭter adv laudably

laudātĭ·ō -ōnis f commendation; eulogy, panegyric, funeral oration; (in court) testimony by a character witness

laudāt·or -ōris m praiser; eulogist, panegyrist; (law) character witness

laudāt·us -a -um adj praiseworthy, commendable, excellent

laud·ō -āre vt to praise, commend; to name, quote, cite; to pronounce a funeral oration over

laurĕ·a -ae f laurel tree; laurel, laurel branch, laurel crown, bay wreath; triumph

laureāt·us -a -um adj laureate, laureled, crowned with laurel; **litterae laureatae** communiqué announcing victory

Laurent·ēs -um m pl Laurentians (people of Lanuvium)

Laurentīn·us or **Laurentĭ·us -a -um** adj Laurentian

laureŏl·a -ae f little laurel crown; triumph

laurĕ·us -a -um adj laurel, of laurel; f see **laurea**

lauricŏm·us -a -um adj laurel-covered (mountain)

laurĭf·er -ĕra -ĕrum adj crowned with laurel

laurĭg·er -ĕra -ĕrum adj wearing laurel

laur·us -ī f laurel tree, bay tree; triumph, victory

laus laudis f praise, commendation; fame, glory; approval, praiseworthy deed; merit, worth

Laus·us -ī m son of Numitor and brother of Rhea Silvia; son of Mezentius, killed by Aeneas

lautē adv sumptuously, splendidly; excellently

lantĭ·a -ōrum n pl state banquet (given to foreign ambassadors and official guests)

lautitĭ·a -ae f luxury, high living

lautumĭ·ae or **lātomĭ·ae** or **lātumĭ·ae -ārum** f pl stone quarry; prison

laut·us -a -um adj expensive, elegant, fine; well-heeled; refined, fashionable

lavābr·um -ī n bath

lavātĭ·o -ōnis f washing, bathing, bath; bathing kit

Lāvīnĭ·us -a -um adj Lavinian, of Lavinium; n town in Latium founded by Aeneas; f wife of Aeneas

lavō lavāre (or **lavĕre**) **lāvī lautum** (or **lavātum** or **lōtum**) vt to wash, bathe; to wet, drench; to wash away; **lavi** to wash, wash oneself, bathe; vi to wash, wash oneself, bathe

laxāment·um -ī n relaxation, respite, letup, mitigation

laxāt·us -a -um adj loose, extended (e.g., ranks)

laxē adv loosely, widely; freely

laxĭt·ās -ātis f roominess, extent

lax·ō -āre vt to extend, widen, expand, open; to open, undo, release; to relax, slacken; to mitigate; (fig) to release, relieve; vi (of price) to go down

lax·us -a -um adj roomy, wide; loose, slack; prolonged, extended (time); (fig) relaxed, easygoing, free; low (price)

le·a -ae f lioness

leaen·a -ae f lioness

Lēand·er -rī m youth of Abydos who swam across the Hellespont every night to his lover Hero of Sestos

Learch·us -ī m son of Athamas and Ino, killed by his mad father

leb·ēs -ētis m pan, cauldron, basin

lectĭc·a -ae f litter; sofa, couch

lectĭcār·ĭus -ĭī or **-ī** m litter bearer

lectĭcŭl·a -ae f small litter; small bier

lectĭ·ō -ōnis f selection; reading, reading aloud; perusal; **lectio senatūs** revision of the senate roll (by the censor)

lectisterniāt·or -ōris m slave who arranged the seating at table

lestistern·ium -ĭī or **-ī** n ritual feast (at which images of the gods were placed on couches at the table)

lectĭt·ō -āre *vt* to read and reread; to like to read

lectiuncŭl·a -ae *f* light reading

lect·or -ōris *m* reader (*esp. slave who read aloud to his master*)

lectŭl·us -ī *m* cot; small couch, settee; humble bier

lect·us -ī *or* **-ūs** *m* bed, couch; bier

lect·us -a -um *pp of* lego; *adj* select, choice, special, elite

Lēd·a -ae *or* **Lēd·ē -ēs** *f* Tyndarus's wife, whom Jupiter visited in the form of a swan and who bore Helen, Clytemnestra, Castor, and Pollux

lēgātĭ·ō -ōnis *f* embassy, mission, legation; members of an embassy; work or report of work of a mission; nominal staff appointment; command of a legion; **legatio lībera** junket (*all-expenses-paid trip, a privilege granted to senators, nominally in an official capacity, to visit the provinces to transact private business*)

lēgāt·um -ī *n* bequest, legacy

lēgāt·us -ī *m* deputy, representative; ambassador, envoy; adjutant (*of a consul, proconsul, or praetor*); commander of a legion

lēgĭf·er -ĕra -ĕrum *adj* law-giving

legĭ·ō -ōnis *f* legion (*divided into 10 cohorts and numbering between 4,200 and 6,000 men*); army

legiōnārĭ·us -a -um *adj* legionary

lēgirŭp·a -ae *or* **lēgirup·iō -ōnis** *m* lawbreaker

lēgitĭmē *adv* legitimately, lawfully; properly

lēgitĭm·us -a -um *adj* legitimate, lawful; regular, right, just, proper; *n pl* legal formalities

legiuncŭl·a -ae *f* under-manned legion

lēg·ō -āre *vt* to commission; to send on a public mission, despatch; to delegate, deputize; to bequeath, will; (fig) to entrust

legō legĕre lēgī lectum *vt* to gather, collect, pick; to pick out, choose; to pick one's way through, cross; to sail by, coast along; to read, peruse; to recite, read out loud; to pick up, steal; to pick up (*news, rumor*); **fīla legĕre** to wind up the thread of life; **senatum legĕre** to read off the senate roll

lēgŭlē·ĭus -iī *or* **-ī** *pettifogger**

legūm·en -ĭnis *n* leguminous plant; vegetable; pulse; bean

lemb·us -ī *m* cutter, yacht (*built for speed*), speedboat

lemm·a -ătis *n* theme, subject matter; epigram

Lemnicŏl·a -ae *m* inhabitant of Lemnos, i.e., Vulcan

lemniscāt·us -a -um *adj* heavily decorated (*with combat ribbons*)

lemnisc·us -ī *m* ribbon which hung down from a victor's wreath

Lemnĭ·us -a -um *adj* Lemnian; *m* Lemnian; Vulcan

Lemn·os *or* **Lemn·us -ī** *f* large island in the Aegean

Lemŭr·ēs -um *m pl* ghosts

Lemŭrĭ·a -ōrum *n pl* night festival to drive ghosts from the house

lēn·a -ae *f* procuress, madame; seductress

Lēnae·us -a -um *adj* Lenaean, Bacchic; *m* Bacchus

lēnē *adv* gently

lēnīm·en -ĭnis *n* consolation, comfort, compensation, reward

lēnīment·um -ī *n* alleviation

lēn·iō -īre -īvī *or* **-iī -ītum** *vt* to soften, alleviate, soothe, calm; *vi* to calm down

lēn·is -e *adj* soft, gentle, mild, smooth, calm; gradual (*slope*); (fig) gentle, mild, kind

lēnĭt·ās -ātis *f* softness, gentleness, mildness, smoothness; (fig) gentleness, mildness, tenderness, clemency

lēnĭter *adv* softly, gently, mildly; (fig) mildly, quietly, calmly; (of style) smoothly; halfheartedly

lēnĭtūd·ō -ĭnis *f* softness, mildness, gentleness, smoothness

lēn·ō -ōnis *m* pander, procurer, pimp; seducer

lēnōcĭn·ĭum -iī *or* **-ī** *n* pandering, pimping; allurement, attraction; bawdy or gaudy clothes; flattery

lēnōcĭn·or -ārī -ātus sum *vi* to be a pimp; (with *dat*) **a** to play up to, humor, pander to; **b** to stimulate, promote

lēnōnĭ·us -a -um *adj* pimp's

len·s -tis *f* lentil

lentē *adv* slowly; indifferently, halfheartedly; calmly, leisurely, deliberately

lent·escō -ĕre *vi* to get sticky, soften; (fig) to soften, weaken; (with ad + *acc*) to stick to

lentiscĭf·er -ĕra -ĕrum *adj* (of a region) producing mastic trees

lentisc·us -ī *f* mastic tree; toothpick (*made of mastic wood*)

lentĭtūd·ō -ĭnis *f* slowness; insensibility, apathy, dullness

lent·ō -āre *vt* to bend

lentŭl·us -a -um *adj* somewhat slow

lent·us -a -um *adj* sticky, clinging; pliant, limber; slow, sluggish; lingering; irresponsive, reluctant, indifferent, backward; slow-moving; tedious; drawling; at rest, at leisure, lazy; calm, unconcerned

lēnŭl·us -ī *m* little pimp

lēnuncŭl·us -ī *m* little pimp; small sailboat, skiff

le·ō -ōnis *m* lion

Le·ō -ōnis *m* Lion (*constellation*)

Leōnĭd·ās -ae *m* king of Sparta (487-480 B.C.), who fell at Thermopylae in 480 B.C. after a gallant stand

leōnīn·us -a -um *adj* lion's, of a lion

Leontīn·ī -ōrum *m pl* town in E. Sicily

lep·as -ădis *f* limpet

lepĭdē *adv* pleasantly, charmingly,

neatly; (as affirmative answer) yes, indeed; (of approval) bravo!

lepĭd·us -a -um *adj* pleasant, charming, neat; effeminate

lep·ōs or **lep·or -ōris** *m* pleasantness, charm, attractiveness

lep·us -ŏris *m* hare

Lep·us -ŏris *m* Hare (*constellation*)

lepuscŭl·us -ī *m* little hare

Lern·a -ae or **Lern·ē -ēs** *f* marsh near Argos, where Hercules slew the Hydra

Lernae·us -a -um *adj* Lernaean

Lesbĭ·us -a -um *adj* Lesbian; *f* pseudonym for the girl friend of the poet Catullus; *n* Lesbian wine

Lesb·os or **Lesb·us -ī** *f* large island in the N. Aegean, the birthplace of the lyric poets Alcaeus and Sappho

less·us (only *acc:* **lessum** in use) *m* wailing

lētāl·is -e *adj* lethal, fatal, mortal

Lēthae·us -a -um *adj* of Lethe; infernal; causing drowsiness

lēthargic·us -ī *m* lazy fellow

lētharg·us -ī *m* lethargy

Lēth·ē -ēs *f* Lethe (*river of oblivion in the lower world*); forgetfulness

lētĭf·er -ĕra -ĕrum *adj* deadly, fatal; **locus letifer** mortal spot

lēt·ō -āre *vt* to kill

lēt·um -ī *n* death; ruin, destruction; **leto dare** to put to death

Leuc·as -ādis *f* island off W. Greece

leucasp·is -ĭdis *adj* armed with a white shield

Leucipp·us -ī *m* philosopher, teacher of Democritus, and one of the founders of Atomism (5th cent. B.C.)

Leucothĕ·a -ae or **Leucothĕ·ē -ēs** *f* name of Ino, daughter of Cadmus, after she was changed into a sea deity

Leuctr·a -ōrum *n pl* small town in Boeotia where Epaminondas defeated the Spartans in 371 B.C.

levām·en -ĭnis *n* alleviation, comfort, consolation

levāment·um -ī *n* alleviation, comfort, consolation

levāti·ō -ōnis *f* lightening; relief, comfort; lessening

levicŭl·us -a -um *adj* somewhat vain

levidens·is -e *adj* poor, inferior

levifĭd·us -a -um *adj* untrustworthy

lēv·is -e *adj* light, not heavy; light-armed; lightly dressed; light, easily digested; thin, poor (*soil*); light, nimble; flitting; slight, small; unimportant, trivial; unfounded (*rumor*); easy, simple; mild; gentle, easygoing; capricious, unreliable, fickle

lēv·is -e *adj* smooth; slippery; smooth, hairless, beardless; delicate, tender; effeminate; smooth (*style*)

levisomn·us -a -um *adj* light-sleeping

levit·ās -ātis *f* lightness; mobility, nimbleness; levity, frivolity; (fig) shallowness

lēvit·as -ātis *f* smoothness; (fig) smoothness, fluency

levĭter *adv* lightly; slightly, a little, somewhat; easily, without difficulty; nimbly

lĕv·ō -āre *vt* to lift up, raise; to lighten, relieve, ease; to console, comfort; to lessen, weaken; to release, free; to take away; to avert

lēv·ō -āre *vt* to make smooth, polish; to soothe

lēv·or -ōris *m* smoothness

lex lēgis *f* motion, bill; law, statute; rule, regulation, principle, precept; condition, stipulation; **eā lege ut** with the stipulation that, on condition that; **lege** or **legibus** legally; **lege agere** to proceed legally; **legem abrogare** to repeal a law; **legem ferre** to propose a bill; **legem derogare** to amend a bill or law; **legem jubere** to sanction a law; **legem perferre** to pass a law; **sine legibus** without restraint, without control

libām·en -ĭnis *n* libation; firstfruits

libāment·um -ī *n* libation; firstfruits

libāti·ō -ōnis *f* libation

libell·a -ae *f* small silver coin, ace; small sum; level (*instrument*); **ad libellam** to a tee, exactly; **heres ex libella** sole heir

libell·us -ī *m* small book, pamphlet; notebook; journal, diary; program; handbill, advertisement; petition; answer to a petition; letter; written accusation, indictment, libel; satirical verse

lib·ens or **lub·ens -entis** *adj* willing, ready, glad; merry, cheerful

libenter or **lubenter** *adv* willingly, gladly, with pleasure

lib·er -rī *m* bark of a tree; book; work, treatise; catalog, list, register; letter, rescript

līb·er -ĕra -ĕrum *adj* free; open, unoccupied; unrestricted; unprejudiced; outspoken, frank; uncontrolled, unrestricted; (not slave) free; (of states or municipalities) independent, autonomous; exempt; free of charge; (with *abl* or **ab +** *abl*) free from, exempt from; (with *genit*) free of; *m pl* see **liberi**

Līb·er -ĕrī *m* Italian fertility god, later identified with Bacchus; wine

Lībĕr·a -ae *f* Proserpina; Ariadne, the wife of Bacchus

Līberāl·ia -ium *n pl* festival of Liber, held on March 17th, at which young men received the toga virilis

līberāl·is -e *adj* relating to freedom, relating to civil status, of free citizens; worthy of a freeman, honorable, gentleman's; courteous; liberal, generous; handsome

līberālit·ās -ātis *f* courtesy, politeness; liberality, generosity; grant, gift

līberālĭter *adv* like a freeman, nobly; liberally (*e.g.*, *educated*); courteously; liberally, generously

līberātī·ō -ōnis *f* liberation, delivery, freeing, release; acquittal

līberāt·or -ōris *m* liberator

līberē *adv* freely; frankly, outspokenly; ungrudgingly; like a freeman, liberally

līber·ī -ōrum *m pl* children

līber·ō -āre *vt* to set free, free, release; to acquit, discharge; to cancel, get rid of (*e.g.*, *debts*); to exempt; to manumit, set free; (with *abl* or with *ab* or *ex* + *abl*) to free or release from, acquit of; **fidem līberāre** to keep one's promise; **nomina līberāre** to cancel debts; **se aere aliēno līberāre** to pay up a debt

lībert·a -ae *f* freedwoman, ex-slave

lībert·ās -ātis *f* liberty, freedom; status of a freeman; political freedom; freedom of speech, freedom of thought; frankness

lībertīn·us -a -um *adj & mf* ex-slave; *m* freedman; *f* freedwoman

lībert·us -ī *m* freedman, ex-slave

lib·et (or **lub·et**) **-ēre -uit** (or **libitum est**) *v impers* (with *dat*) it pleases, is pleasant, is agreeable to, is nice for (*someone*); (with *inf*) it is nice, pleasant to (*do something*); **sī lubet** if you please; **ut lubet** as you please

lībidin·or -ārī -ātus sum *vi* to gratify lust

lībidinōsē *adv* willfully; arbitrarily

lībidinōs·us -a -um *adj* willful; arbitrary; lustful, sensual

lībid·ō or **lubīd·ō -inis** *f* desire, longing, inclination, pleasure; will, willfulness, arbitrariness, caprice, fancy; lust, rut, heat; **ex lībidine** arbitrarily

lībit·a -ōrum *n pl* will, pleasure, liking

Libitīn·a -ae *f* burial goddess; implements for burial; grave, death

līb·ō -āre *vt* to taste, sip; to pour as a libation, offer, consecrate; to touch lightly, barely touch, graze; to spill, waste; to extract, collect, compile

lībr·a -ae *f* balance, scales; plummet, level; pound (*of twelve ounces*)

lībrāment·um -ī *n* weight; balance, ballast; plane surface; gravity

lībrāri·a -ae *f* forelady (*who weighed out wool for slaves to spin*)

lībrāriōl·us -ī *m* copyist, scribe

lībrāri·us -a -um *adj* book, of books; **taberna lībrāria** bookstore; *m* copyist, scribe; *n* bookcase

lībrāt·us -a -um *adj* poised; hurled; powerful

lībrīl·is -e *adj* one-pound, weighing a pound

lībrit·or -ōris *m* artilleryman

lībr·ō -āre *vt* to balance; to poise, level, hurl, launch; to sway

līb·um -ī *n* cake; birthday cake

Liburni·a -ae *f* district of Illyria between Istria and Dalmatia

Liburn·us -a -um *adj & mf* Liburnian; *f* Liburnian galley

Libў·a -ae or **Libў·ē -ēs** *f* Libya (*Africa*)

Libў·es -um *m pl* Libyans

Libў·us or **Libyss·us** or **Libystīn·us** or **Libў·us -a -um** or **Libyst·is -idis** *adj* Libyan; (in general) African

lic·ens -entis *adj* free, bold

licenter *adv* freely, boldly, without restraint, licentiously

licenti·a -ae *f* license, liberty, freedom; lawlessness, licentiousness

lic·eō -ēre *vi* to cost; to be for sale

lic·eor -ērī -itus sum *vt* to bid on, bid for, make an offer for; *vi* to bid, make a bid

lic·et -ēre -uit or **-itum est** *v impers* it is permitted or lawful; (with *dat & inf*) it is all right for (*someone*) to; **licet** (to express assent) yes, all right

licet *conj* granted that, even if, although

Lich·ās -ae *m* companion of Hercules

līch·ēn -ēnis *m* ringworm

licitātī·ō -ōnis *f* bidding (*at auction*); haggling

licit·or -ārī -ātus sum *vt* to bid for

licit·us -a -um *adj* permissible, lawful

līc·ium -iī or **-ī** *n* thread

līct·or -ōris *m* lictor (*attendant and bodyguard of a magistrate, of whom twenty-four attended a dictator, twelve a consul, and six a praetor*)

li·ēn -ēnis *m* spleen

liēnōs·us -a -um *adj* splenetic

ligām·en -inis *n* bandage

ligāment·um -ī *n* bandage

lignār·ius -iī or **-ī** *m* carpenter

lignātī·ō -ōnis *f* gathering of lumber

lignāt·or -ōris *m* woodcutter, lumberjack

ligneōl·us -a -um *adj* wooden

ligne·us -a -um *adj* wooden

lign·or -ārī -ātus sum *vi* to gather wood

lign·um -ī *n* wood; timber, firewood, log, plank; writing tablet; tree; **in silvam ligna ferre** to carry coals to Newcastle

lig·ō -āre *vt* to tie, tie up, bandage; to close (*a deal*)

lig·ō -ōnis *m* mattock, hoe; farming

ligŭl·a -ae *f* shoe strap

Lig·ur or **Lig·us -uris** *m* or *f* Ligurian

Liguri·a -ae *f* Liguria (*district along the N.W. coast of Italy*)

ligūr·iō or **ligurr·iō -īre -īvī** or **-iī -ītum** *vt* to lick, pick at; to eat daintily; (fig) to prey on; (fig) to be dying for

ligūrītī·ō -ōnis *f* daintiness

Ligus see **Ligur**

Ligusc·us or **Ligustīc·us** or **Ligustīn·us -a -um** *adj* Ligurian

ligustr·um -ī *n* privet

līl·ium -iī or -ī n lily; (mil) trench lined with sharp stakes

līm·a -ae f file; (fig) polishing, revision

līmātius adv in a more polished manner

līmātul·us -a -um adj (fig) rather sharp (judgment)

līmāt·us -a -um adj (fig) polished, refined

līm·ax -ācis m or f snail

līmbolāri·us -a -um adj textores līmbolarii tassel makers, hemmers

līmb·us -ī m fringe, hem, tassel

līm·en -inis n lintel, threshold; doorway, entrance; threshold, outset, beginning; starting gate (at racetrack); house, home

līm·es -itis m country trail; path; road along a boundary; boundary, frontier; channel, course, way; zodiac

līm·ō -āre vt to file; (fig) to polish, refine; to file down, take away from, lessen; to get down to (the truth)

līmōs·us -a -um adj muddy; mud, growing in mud

līmpid·us -a -um adj limpid, clear

līmūl·us -a -um adj squinting

līm·us -a -um adj squinting; sidelong, askance; m mud; dirt; grime; ceremonial apron (worn by priests at sacrifice)

līne·a -ae f line, string, thread; fishing line; plumb line; outline; boundary line, limit; ad lineam or rectā lineā in a straight line, vertically; horizontally; extremā lineā amare to love at a distance; lineas transire to go out of bounds

līneāment·um -ī n line; characteristic, feature; outline

līne·ō -āre vt to make straight, make perpendicular

līne·us -a -um adj flaxen, linen

līngō līngere līnxī līnctum vt to lick up, lap up

līngu·a -ae f tongue; speech, language, dialect; (of animals) note, song, bark; tongue of land; eloquence; linguā promptus insolent; utraque lingua Greek and Latin

līngul·a -ae f tongue of land

līngulāc·a -ae m or f gossip, chatterbox

līnig·er -ěra -ěrum adj wearing linen

līnō līnēre lēvī or līvī lītum vt to smear; to erase; to cover, overlay; (fig) to mess up

līnquō līnquěre līquī vt to leave, forsake, depart from; to leave or let alone; to leave in a pinch; līnquī animo or līnqui to faint; līnquitur (with ut) it remains to (do something)

līnteāt·us -a -um adj canvas

līntě·ō -ōnis m linen weaver

līnteōl·um -ī n small linen cloth

līnt·er -ris f skiff; tub, vat

līntě·us -a -um adj linen; n linen,

linen cloth; canvas, sail; kerchief

līntricūl·us -ī m small boat

līn·um -ī n flax; linen; thread, rope, line; fishing line; net

Līn·us -ī m son of Apollo and instructor of Orpheus and Hercules

Lipār·a -ae or Lipār·ē -ēs f island off the N. coast of Sicily; f pl the Aeolian islands

Liparae·us -a -um or Liparens·is -e adj of Lipara

līpp·iō -īre -īvī or -iī -ītum vi to have sore eyes; (of eyes) to burn, ache

līppitūd·ō -inis f running eyes, inflammation of the eyes

līpp·us -a -um adj with sore eyes, sore-eyed; burning (eyes); (fig) blind

līque·faciō -facěre -fēcī -factum (passive: līque·fīō -ferī -factus sum) vt to melt, dissolve; to decompose; to waste, weaken

līqu·ens -entis adj clear, limpid; flowing, gliding; liquid, fluid

līquěō līquēre līcuī vi to be liquid; v impers it is clear, is apparent, is evident; liquet mihi (with inf) I am free to; non liquet (law) it is not clear (legal formula used by a hung jury)

līquescō līquescěre līcuī vi to melt; to decompose; to grow soft, grow effeminate; (fig) to melt away; to become clear

līquidē adv clearly; (fig) clearly, plainly

līquidiuscul·us -a -um adj somewhat softer

līquidō adv clearly, plainly, certainly

līquid·us -a -um adj liquid, fluid, flowing; clear, transparent; pure (pleasure); clear (voice); calm (mind); clear, evident, certain; n liquid, water; clearness, certainty

līqu·ō -āre vt to melt, dissolve; to strain, filter

līqu·or -ī vi to flow; to melt, dissolve; (fig) to melt away, waste away

līqu·or -ōris m fluidity; liquid, fluid; sea

Līr·is -is m river between Campania and Latium

līs lītis f lawsuit, litigation; matter of dispute; quarrel, wrangling; charge, accusation; lītem intendere or lītem inferre (with dat) to sue (someone); lītem aestimare to assess damages; līs capitis criminal charge

lītāti·ō -ōnis f success in sacrificing, efficacious sacrifice

lītātō adv with favorable omens

lītěra see lìttera

lītic·en -inis m clarion player

lītigāt·or -ōris m litigant

lītigiōs·us -a -um adj quarrelsome, litigious; contested, disputed

lītig·ium -iī or -ī n quarrel, dispute

lītig·ō -āre vi to quarrel, squabble; to go to court

lit·ō -āre vt to offer duly or acceptably; *vi* to offer acceptable sacrifice; to receive a good omen; (with *dat*) to propitiate, satisfy, appease

litorāl·is -e *adj* shore, of the shore

litorĕ·us -a -um *adj* seashore, at or along the seashore

littĕr·a or **lītĕr·a -ae** *f* letter (*of the alphabet*); handwriting; *f pl* epistle, letter, dispatch; edict, ordinance; literature, books, literary works; learning, liberal education, scholarship; records, accounts; **littera salutaris** (*i.e.*, **A = absolvo**) vote of acquittal; **littera tristis** (*i.e.*, **C = condemno**) vote of guilty; **litteras discere** to learn to read and write; **litteras scire** to know how to read and write

litterāri·us -a -um *adj* of reading and writing; **ludus litterarius** elementary school

litterātē *adv* legibly, in a clear handwriting; literally; learnedly

litterāt·or -ōris *m* elementary-school teacher; grammarian, philologist

litterātūr·a -ae *f* alphabet

litterāt·us -a -um *adj* marked with letters, engraved; learned, scholarly; liberally educated; devoted to literature

litterŭl·a -ae *f* small letter; *f pl* short letter, note; slight literary endeavors

litūr·a -ae *f* erasure; erased passage; correction, emendation; blot, smear; wrinkle

litus *pp* of **lino**

līt·us -ōris *n* seashore, beach, coast; river bank; **in litus harenas fundere** to carry coals to Newcastle; **litus arare** to waste effort

litŭ·us -ī *m* cavalry trumpet, clarion; (fig) signal; augur's wand (*crooked staff carried by an augur*); **lituus meae profectionis** signal for my departure

līv·ens -entis *adj* black-and-blue, livid

līv·ĕō -ēre *vi* to be black and blue, be livid; to be envious; (with *dat*) to be jealous of

līvesc·ō -ĕre *vi* to turn black and blue

Līvi·a -ae *f* second wife of Augustus (58 B.C.-29 A.D.)

līvidŭl·us -a -um *adj* inclined to be jealous, somewhat envious

līvid·us -a -um *adj* leaden (*in color*); blue; black and blue; jealous, envious, spiteful

Līv·ius -iī or **-ī** *m* T. Livius Patavinus or Livy (*famous historian*, 59 B.C.-17 A.D.)

līv·or -ōris *m* leaden color; bluish color; black-and-blue mark; jealousy, envy, spite

lix·a -ae *m* camp follower

locāti·ō -ōnis *f* arrangement, placement; renting out, contract, lease

locāt·um -ī *n* lease, contract

locĭt·ō -āre *vt* to lease out

loc·ō -āre *vt* to place, put, set, lay; to establish, constitute, lay, set; to give in marriage, marry off; to let, rent out; to contract for; to invest

locŭl·us -ī *m* little place, spot; pocket

locŭpl·ēs -ētis *adj* rich; reliable, responsible

locŭplēt·ō -āre *vt* to make rich, enrich

loc·us -ī (*pl*: **loc·ī -ōrum** *m*; **loc·a -ōrum** *n*) *m* place, site, spot, locality, district; place, seat; period, period of time; opportunity, room, occasion; situation, position, category; rank, degree, birth; passage in a book; topic, subject, point, division; (mil) position, post, station; **adhuc locorum** till now; **ad id locorum** till then; **ex aequo loco dicere** to speak in the senate; to hold a conversation; **ex or de loco superiore dicere** to speak from the rostrum; **ex loco inferiore dicere** to speak before a judge, speak in court; **inde loci** since then; **in eo loci** in such a condition; **interea loci** meanwhile; **loci communes** general topics; public places, parks; **loco** (with *genit*) instead of; **loco** or **in loco** at the right time; **loco cedere** to give way, yield; **postea loci** afterwards; **post id locorum** afterwards; **ubicumque loci** whenever

lōcust·a -ae *f* locust

Lōcust·a -ae *f* woman notorious as poisoner in the time of Claudius and Nero

locūti·ō -ōnis *f* speech; way of speaking, pronunciation

locūtus *pp* of **loquor**

lōd·ix -īcis *f* blanket

logic·us -a -um *adj* logical; *n pl* logic

log·os or **log·us -ī** *m* word; witticism; *m pl* mere words, empty talk

lōlīgō see **lolligo**

lol·ium -iī or **-ī** *n* darnel

lollīg·ō or **lōlig·ō -inis** *f* cuttlefish

lollīguncŭl·a -ae *f* small cuttlefish

lōment·um -ī *n* face cream

Londīn·ium -iī or **-ī** *n* London

longaev·us -a -um *adj* aged

longē *adv* far, far off, long way off; away, distant; out of reach, of no avail; long, for a long period; (to speak) at greater length; (with comparatives) far, by far, much; **longe lateque** far and wide, everywhere

longinquit·ās -ātis *f* length, extent; remoteness, distance; length, duration

longinqu·us -a -um *adj* long, extensive; far off, distant, remote; from afar, foreign; long, prolonged, continued, tedious; **ex** or **e longinquo** from far away

longĭter *adv* far

longitūd·ō -inis *f* length; **in longitudinem** lengthwise

longiuscŭl·us -a -um *adj* pretty long

longur·ius -iī or **-ī** *m* long pole

long·us -a -um *adj* long; spacious; long, protracted, drawn-out; tedious; *n* length; **in longum** for a long while; **ne longum faciam** in short

loquācit·ās -ātis *f* talkativeness

loquācĭter *adv* long-windedly; at length, in detail

loquācŭl·us -a -um *adj* rather talkative

loqu·ax -ācis *adj* talkative, loquacious

loquell·a -ae *f* speech, language

loquĭt·or -ārī -ātus *vi* to chatter away

loquor loquī locūtus sum *vt* to say; to talk of, speak about; to tell, tell of, mention; (fig) to declare, show, indicate; *vi* to speak; to rustle, murmur

lōrār·ius -iī or **-ī** *m* flogger, slave driver

lōrāt·us -a -um *adj* tied with thongs

lōrĕ·us -a -um *adj* striped

lōrĭc·a -ae *f* breastplate; parapet; **libros mutare loricis** to exchange books for arms

lōrīcāt·us -a -um *adj* wearing a breastplate

lōrĭp·ēs -ĕdis *adj* bowlegged

lōr·um -ī *n* strip of leather, thong, strap; whip, scourge; leather badge; *n pl* reins

lōt·os or **lōt·us -ī** *f* lotus; flute (*of lotus wood*)

lōtus *pp* of lavo

lub- = lib-

lŭbenti·a -ae *f* pleasure

lŭbrĭc·ō -āre *vt* to oil, grease, make smooth

lŭbrĭc·us -a -um *adj* slippery; smooth; slimy; gliding; deceitful, tricky; precarious; *n* precarious situation, critical period

Lūc·a bōs (genit: **Lūc·ae bovis**) *f* elephant

Lūcāni·a -ae *f* district in S.W. Italy

Lūcānĭc·us -a -um *adj* Lucanian; *f* Lucanian sausage

Lūcān·us -a -um *adj* Lucanian; *m* Lucanian; Lucan (*M. Annaeus Lucanus, epic poet, 39-65 A.D.*)

lūc·ar -āris *n* forest tax

lucell·um -ī *n* slight profit

lūcĕō lūcēre luxī *vi* to shine, be light, glow, glitter, be clear; (fig) to be clear, be apparent, be conspicuous; *v impers* it is light, day is dawning

Lūcĕr·ēs -um *m pl* one of the three original Roman tribes

lucern·ae -ae *f* lamp; (fig) midnight oil

lūcescō or **lūciscō lūcescĕre luxī** *vi* to begin to shine; *v impers* it is getting light

lūcĭdē *adv* clearly, distinctly

lūcĭd·us -a -um *adj* shining, bright, clear; lucid, clear

lūcĭf·er -ĕra -ĕrum *adj* shiny

Lūcĭf·er -ĕrī *m* morning star; planet Venus; son of Aurora and Cephalus; day

lūcĭfŭg·us -a -um *adj* light-shunning; *n* length; **in longum** for a long

Lūcil·ius -iī or **-ī** *m* C. Lucilius (*first Roman satiric poet, c. 180-102 B.C.*)

Lūcīn·a -ae *f* goddess of childbirth; childbirth

lūciscō see **lucesco**

Lucrēti·a -ae *f* daughter of Spurius Lucretius and wife of Collatinus, who, having been raped by Sextus Tarquinius, committed suicide in 509 B.C.

Lucrēt·ius -iī or **-ī** *m* Spurius Lucretius (*father of Lucretia and consul in 509 B.C.*); Titus Lucretius Carus (*philosophical poet, 94?-55? B.C.*)

lucrĭfĭcābĭl·is -e or **lucrĭfĭc·us -a -um** *adj* profitable

lucrĭfŭg·a -ae *m* or *f* person not out for gain, disinterested person

Lucrīn·us -a -um *adj* Lucrine; *m* Lake Lucrine (*small lake near Baiae, famous for its oysters*)

lucrĭpĕt·a -ae *m* profiteer

lucr·or -ārī -ātus sum *vt* to gain, win, get

lucrōs·us -a -um *adj* profitable

lucr·um -ī *n* profit, gain; wealth; greed, love of gain; **lucri facere** to gain; **lucri fieri** to be gained; **lucro esse** (with *dat*) to be advantageous for (*someone*); **ponere in lucro** or **in lucris** to regard as gain

luctām·en -ĭnis *n* wrestling; struggle, effort

luct·ans -antis *adj* reluctant

luctātĭ·ō -ōnis *f* wrestling; struggle, contest

luctāt·or -ōris *m* wrestler

luctĭfĭc·us -a -um *adj* causing sorrow, doleful, woeful

luctĭsŏn·us -a -um *adj* sad-sounding

luct·or -ārī -ātus sum or **luct·ō -āre** *vi* to wrestle; (with *inf*) to struggle to

luctuōsĭus *adv* more pitifully

luctuōs·us -a -um *adj* causing sorrow, sorrowful; sad, feeling sad

luct·us -ūs *m* sorrow, mourning, grief, distress; signs of sorrow, mourning clothes; source of grief, affliction

lūcŭbrātĭ·ō -ōnis *f* moonlighting, working by lamp light; evening gossip; nighttime writing

lūcŭbr·ō -āre *vt* to compose at night; *vi* to moonlight, burn the midnight oil

lūcŭlentē *adv* splendidly, well; (to beat) soundly

lūcŭlenter *adv* brilliantly, smartly, very well

lŭculent·us -a -um *adj* bright, brilliant; (fig) brilliant, smart, excellent; considerable (*wealth*); sound (*beating*); trustworthy (*sources*)

Lŭcull·us -ī *m* Lucius Licinius Lucullus (*Roman general and politician*, 117-56 B.C.)

Lŭcŭm·ō or **Lucm·ō -ōnis** *m* Etruscan prince, Etruscan priest

lūc·us -ī *m* sacred grove; woods

lūdi·a -ae *f* actress; gladiator (*female*)

lūdibr·ium -iī or **-ī** *n* derision; subject of derision, butt of ridicule; (fig) plaything, sucker; **ludibrio esse** (with *dat*) to be made a fool of by (*someone*), be taken in by (*someone*); **ludibrio habere** to take for a sucker, make fun of

lūdibund·us -a -um *adj* playful, playing around; without effort, without danger

lūdic·er -ra -rum *adj* for sport, in sport; **ludicra exercitatio** sports; athletics; **ludicrum praemium** sports award; **ludicra res** drama; *n* sport, game; toy; show, public game; stage play

lūdificābil·is -e *adj* used in mockery

lūdificāti·ō -ōnis *f* ridiculing, mocking; fooling, tricking

lūdificāt·or -ōris *m* mocker

lūdificāt·us -ūs *m* mockery

lūdific·ō -āre or **lūdific·or -ārī -ātus sum** *vt* to make a fool of, fool, take for a sucker; to fool, trick, baffle

lūdi·ō -ōnis or **lūd·ius -iī** or **-ī** *m* actor

lūdō lūdĕre lūsī lūsum *vt* to play; to spend in play; to amuse oneself with, do for amusement, practice as a pastime; to imitate, mimic, mock, do a takeoff on, ridicule; to deceive, delude; *vi* to play; to frisk, frolic; to play around, make love; **aleā ludere** to shoot craps; **pilā ludere** to play ball, play tennis

lūd·us -ī *m* play, game, sport, pastime, diversion; school; mere child's play; joke, fun; playing around, fooling around, lovemaking; public show, public game; **amoto ludo** all joking aside; **in ludum ire** to go to school; **per ludum** as a joke, for fun; *m pl* public games, public exhibition; games, tricks; **ludos facere** or **ludos reddere** (with *dat*) to play tricks on, make fun of

luell·a -ae *f* expiation, atonement

lu·ēs -is *f* infection, contagion, plague, pestilence; calamity

Lugdūnens·is -e *adj* of Lyons

Lugdūn·um -ī *n* Lyons (*town in E. Gaul*)

lūgĕō lugēre luxī *vt* to mourn, lament, deplore; *vi* to mourn, be in mourning; to be in mourning clothes

lūgubr·ia -ium *n pl* mourning clothes

lūgubr·is -e *adj* mourning; doleful; disastrous

lumbifrag·ium -iī or **-ī** *n* physical wreck

lumbric·us -ī *m* worm; (as term of reproach) worm

lumb·us -ī *m* loin; *m pl* loins; genital organs

lūm·en -inis *n* light; lamp, torch; brightness, sheen, gleam; daylight; light of the eye, eye; light of life, life; window, window light; distinguished person, luminary, celebrity; glory, pride

lūmīnār·e -is *n* window

lūmīnōs·us -a -um *adj* luminous; (fig) bright, conspicuous

lūn·a -ae *f* moon; month; night; crescent (*worn as ornament by senators on their shoes*); **luna laborans** moon in eclipse, eclipse of the moon; **luna minor** waning moon

lūnār·is -e *adj* lunar, of the moon

lūnāt·us -a -um *adj* crescent-shaped

lūn·ō -āre *vt* to make crescent-shaped, to shape like a crescent

lūnŭl·a -ae *f* little crescent (*ornament worn by women*)

lu·ō -ĕre -ī *vt* to wash; to cleanse, purge; to set free, let go; to pay (*debt of penalty*); to suffer, undergo; to atone for, expiate; to satisfy, appease; to avert by expiation or punishment

lup·a -ae *f* she-wolf; flirt, prostitute

lupān·ar -āris *n* brothel

lupāt·us -a -um *adj* jagged (*like wolf's teeth*); *m pl* or *n pl* jagged bit

Luperc·al -ālis *n* shrine on the Palatine hill sacred to Pan

Lupercāl·ia -ium *n pl* festival of Lycaean Pan, celebrated in February

Luperc·us -ī *m* Pan

lupill·us -ī *m* small lupine (*plant*)

lupīn·us -a -um *adj* lupine, wolf's; *m & n* lupine, wolf's-bane (*plant*); stage money

lup·us -ī *m* wolf; (fish) pike; jagged bit; grapnel

lurc·ō -ōnis *m* glutton

lūrĭd·us -a -um *adj* pale-yellow, wan, ghastly, lurid; making pale

lūr·or -ōris *m* sallowness

luscīnī·a -ae *f* nightingale

lusciniŏl·a -ae *f* little nightingale

luscin·ius -iī or **-ī** *m* nightingale

lusciōs·us -us or **luscitiōs·us -a -um** *adj* purblind, partly blind

lusc·us -a -um *adj* one-eyed

lūsi·ō -ōnis *f* play, game

Lūsītān·ī -ōrum *m pl* Lusitanians

Lūsītāni·a -ae *f* Lusitania (*modern Portugal and W. part of Spain*)

lūsit·ō -āre *vi* to like to play

lūs·or -ōris *m* player, gambler; humorous writer; joker

lustrāl·is -e *adj* lustral, propitiatory; quinquennial

lustrāti·ō -ōnis *f* purification, lustration; wandering

lustr·ō -āre *vt* to purify; to travel

over, traverse; to check, examine; to go around, encircle; to survey; (mil) to review (troops); to light up, make bright, illuminate; to scan (with the eyes); to consider, review

lustr·or -ārī -ātus sum vi to frequent brothels

lustr·um -ī n haunt, den, lair; wilderness; brothel; sensuality; purificatory sacrifice, lustration; lustrum, period of five years; period of years; **ingens lustrum** one hundred years, century

lūsus pp of **ludo**

lūs·us -ūs m play, game, sport, amusement; playing around (amorously)

lūteŏl·us -a -um adj yellowish

lūtě·us -a -um adj of mud, of clay; muddy; dirty, grimy; (fig) dirty; mud-colored; golden-yellow, yellow, orange

lutĭt·ō -āre vt to splatter with mud; (fig) to throw mud at

lut·ō -āre vt to make dirty

lutulent·us -a -um adj muddy, filthy; (fig) filthy; turbid (style)

lut·um -ī n mud, mire; clay; yellow

lux lūcis f light; light of day, daylight; light of day, life; public view, publicity; the public, the world; light of hope, encouragement; glory; elucidation; **luce** or **luci** by daylight, in the daytime; **lux aestiva** summer; **lux brumalis** winter

lux·ō -āre vt to put out of joint, dislocate

lux·or -ārī -ātus sum vi to live riotously, have a ball

luxurĭ·a -ae or **luxurĭ·ēs -ēī** f luxurience; luxury, extravagance, excess

luxurĭ·ō -āre or **luxurĭ·or -ārī -ātus sum** vi to grow luxuriantly; to luxuriate; (of the body) to swell up; (of animals) to be frisky; to run riot, lead a wild life

luxurĭōsē adv luxuriously, voluptuously

luxurĭōs·us -a -um adj luxuriant; exuberant; extravagant, voluptuous

lux·us -ūs m extravagance, excess, luxury; splendor, pomp, magnificence

Lyae·us -a -um adj Bacchic; m Bacchus; wine

Lycae·us -a -um adj Lycaean (esp. applied to Pan); m mountain in Arcadia where Jupiter and Pan were worshiped

Lycā·ōn -ŏnis m king of Arcadia, the father of Callisto, who was changed into a wolf

Lycāŏn·is -ĭdis f Callisto, who was changed into the Great Bear

Lycē·um or **Lycī·um -ī** n Aristotle's school at Athens

Lycĭ·us -a -um adj & m Lycian; f country in S.W. Asia Minor

lychnūch·us -ī m lamp stand; chandelier

lychn·us -ī m lamp

Lyctĭ·us -a -um adj Cretan

Lycurg·us -ī m Thracian king who prohibited the worship of Bacchus and was punished with madness and death; Spartan lawgiver (date unknown); Athenian orator and friend of Demosthenes (390-324 B.C.)

Lyc·us or **Lyc·os -ī** m husband of Antiope, who divorced her to marry Dirce

Lўdĭ·us -a -um adj & m Lydian; Etruscan; f country of Asia Minor, whose capital was Sardis

Lўd·us -a -um adj & m Lydian; Etruscan

lymph·a -ae f water, spring water; water nymph

lymphātĭc·us -a -um adj crazy, frantic; n craziness

lymphāt·us -a -um adj crazy, mad

Lynce·us -a -um adj sharp-eyed; m Argonaut, famous for keen vision; son of Egyptus and Hyperraestra

lyn·x -cis m or f lynx

lyr·a -ae f lyre; lyric poetry, lyric

Lyr·a -ae f Lyra (constellation)

lyrĭc·us -a -um adj lyric (of the lyre; m pl lyric poets; n pl lyric poems

lyrist·ēs -ae m lyrist

Lyrnēs·is or **Lyrness·is -ĭdis** f Briseis

Lyrnēs·us -ī f town in the Troad, the birthplace of Briseis

Lysĭ·ās -ae m Athenian orator in the time of Socrates (c. 450-370 B.C.)

M

Macăr·eus -ĕī or **-ĕos** m son of Aeolus, who lived in incest with his sister Canace

Macěd·ō -ŏnis m Macedonian

Macedonĭc·us -a -um adj Macedonian

Macedonĭ·us -a -um adj Macedonian; f Macedonia (country lying between Thessaly and Thrace)

macell·um -ī n butcher shop, meat market

mac·ĕō -ēre vi to be lean, be skinny

mac·er -ěra -ěrum adj lean; skinny; thin, poor (soil)

Mac·er -rī m C. Licinius Macer (Roman historian and orator who was impeached by Cicero and committed suicide in 66 B.C.); C. Licinius Macer Calvus (*son of the former, and distinguished orator and poet*, 82-46 B.C.)

măcĕrī·a -ae *f* brick or stone wall; garden wall

măcĕr·ō -āre *vt* to knead, soften, make tender; to weaken, waste; to distress, vex, torment

macesc·ō -ēre *vi* to grow thin

machaer·a -ae *f* sword

machaerophŏr·us -ī *m* soldier armed with sword

Machā·ōn -ŏnis *m* famous physician of the Greeks in the Trojan War and son of Aesculapius

Machāonī·us -a -um *adj* surgical

māchĭn·a -ae *f* machine; engine; crane; pulley, windlass, winch; (*fig*) scheme, stratagem

māchinānent·um -ī *n* machine, engine, contrivance

māchinātī·ō -ōnis *f* mechanism; machine; trick

māchināt·or -ōris *m* engineer, machinist; (*fig*) contriver

māchĭn·or -ārī -ātus sum *vt* to engineer, design, contrive; to scheme, plot

maci·ēs -ēī *f* leanness, thinness; barrenness; poverty (*of style*)

macilent·us -a -um *adj* skinny

macresc·ō -ēre *vi* to grow thin, get skinny

macritūd·ō -ĭnis *f* leanness, skinniness

macrocoll·um -ī *n* large-size sheet of paper

mactābĭl·is -e *adj* deadly

mactāt·us -ūs *m* sacrifice

mactē *interj* well done!; good luck!

mact·ō -āre *vt* to magnify, glorify, honor; to sacrifice; to slaughter, put to death; to destroy, ruin, overthrow; to trouble, afflict

mact·us -a -um *adj* glorified, honored, adored; **macte virtute (esto)** (*congratulatory exclamation*) good luck!; well done!

macŭl·a -ae *f* spot, stain, blemish; mesh (*of a net*); (*fig*) stigma, blemish, disgrace, defect

macŭl·ō -āre *vt* to spot; to stain; to defile, pollute; to dishonor

maculōs·us -a -um *adj* spotted; stained

made·faciō -facĕre -fēcī -factus (*passive*: **made·fĭō -fĭĕrī -factus sum**) *vt* to wet, moisten, drench, soak, steep

mad·ens -entis *adj* wet, moist; flowing (*hair*); melting (*snow*); reeking (*with blood*)

mad·ĕō -ēre -ŭī *vi* to be wet, be moist, be soaked, be drenched; to drip; to flow; to be soused; to be full, overflow

mad·escō -escĕre -ŭī *vi* to become wet, become moist

madĭdē *adv* drunkenly

madĭd·us -a -um *adj* wet, moist, drenched; dyed, steeped; drunk

mad·or -ōris *m* moisture

madŭls·a -ae *m* souse, drunkard

Maeand·er or **Maeandr·os** or **Maeandr·us -ī** *m* river in Asia Minor, famous for its winding course; winding; winding border; devious course

Maecēn·ās -ātis *m* C. Cilnius Maecenas (*adviser to Augustus and friend of Virgil and Horace*, d. 8 B.C.)

maen·a -ae *f* sprat (*fish*)

Maenăl·is -ĭdis *adj* **Maenalis ursa** Callisto (*who was changed into the Great Bear*)

Maenăl·us or **Maenăl·os -ī** *m* or **Maenăl·a -ōrum** *n pl* Mt. Maenalus (*mountain range in Arcadia, sacred to Pan*)

Maen·as -ădis *f* Bacchante

Maenī·us -a -um *adj* Maenian; **Maenia Columna** pillar in the forum at which thieves, slaves, and debtors were tried and flogged

Maeŏn·es -um *m pl* Maeonians (*ancient name of the Lydians*)

Maeonĭd·ēs -ae *m* native of Maeonia; Homer; Etrurian

Maeŏn·is -ĭdis *f* Maeonian woman (*esp. Arachne or Omphale*)

Maeonī·us -a -um *adj* Lydian; Homeric; Etruscan; *f* Maeonia, Lydia; Etruria

Maeōt·ae -ārum *m pl* Scythian tribe on Lake Maeotis on the N.E. coast of the Black Sea

Maeōt·is -ĭdis *adj* Maeotic; Scythian; **Maeotis lacus** Sea of Azov

maer·ĕō -ēre *vi* to mourn

maer·or -ōris *m* mourning, sadness

maestĭter *adv* like a mourner

maestitī·a -ae *f* sadness, gloom, melancholy

maestitūd·ō -ĭnis *f* sadness

maest·us -a -um *adj* mourning, sad, gloomy

Maev·ius -ĭī or **-ī** *m* poetaster often ridiculed by Virgil and Horace

māgāl·ia -ĭum *n pl* huts

mage see **magis**

magĭc·us -a -um *adj* magic; **artes magicae** magic

magis or **mage** *adv* more, in a higher degree, rather; **eo magis** all the more, the more; **magis magisque** more and more; **magis ... quam** or **magis ... atque** rather ... than; **non magis ... quam** not so much ... as

magist·er -rī *m* chief, master, director; teacher; adviser, guardian; ringleader, author; captain, pilot; (in apposition with another noun) expert; **magister morum** censor; **magister sacrorum** chief priest

magister·ĭum -ĭī or **-ī** *n* directorship, presidency; **magisterium morum** censorship

magistr·a -ae *f* directress, mistress, instructress

magistrāt·us -ūs *m* magisterial office, magistracy; magistrate, official; body of magistrates; military command

magnanimit·ās -ātis f magnanimity; bravery

magnanim·us -a -um adj magnanimous; brave

Magn·ēs -ētis adj & m Magnesian; f city in Caria, near the Meander; city in Lydia near Mt. Sipylus; district in Thessaly on the Aegean Sea

magnidīc·us -a -um adj talking big

magnificē adv magnificently, splendidly; pompously

magnificenti·a -ae f magnificence, grandeur, splendor; pompousness

magnific·ō -āre vt to think much of

magnific·us -a -um adj grand, great, splendid, august; rich, costly, magnificent; pompous

magniloquenti·a -ae f lofty style; pompous language

magniloqu·us -a -um adj sublime; bragging

magnitūd·ō -ĭnis f greatness, magnitude, size; large quantity, large number; vastness, extent

magnopēre or **magnō opēre** adv greatly, very much, particularly; strongly, earnestly, heartily, urgently

magn·us -a -um (comp: **major;** superl: **maximus**) adj big, large, great; long (time); high (price); important, momentous; significant; impressive; high, powerful (in rank); loud (voice); heavy (rain); advanced (age); noble (character); proud, boastful; n great thing; great value; **magni (pretii) aestimare** or **magni habere** to value highly, have a high regard for; **magno emere** to buy at a high price; **magno vendere** to sell at a high price; **vir magno jam natu** aged man, man advanced in years

mag·us -a -um adj magic; **artes magae** magic; m learned man (among the Persians); magician

Māi·us -a -um adj & m May; f daughter of Atlas and Pleione, and mother of Mercury by Jupiter

mājāl·is -is m castrated hog; (as term of abuse) swine

mājest·ās -ātis f majesty, dignity, grandeur; high treason; sovereign power, sovereignty; authority

māj·or -us (comp of **magnus**) adj bigger, larger, greater; **annos natu major quadraginta** forty years older; **in majus ferre** to exaggerate; **majoris (pretii)** at a higher price; more highly; **major natu** elder, older

mājōr·ēs -um m pl ancestors, forefathers

mājuscŭl·us -a -um adj somewhat greater; a little older

māl·a -ae f cheekbone, upper jaw; f pl cheek; (fig) jaws (e.g., of death)

malaci·a -ae f calm at sea, dead calm

malaciss·ō -āre vt to soften, soft-

en up

malăc·us -a -um adj soft; luxurious

male adv badly, wrongly; wickedly, cruelly, maliciously; unfortunately, unsuccessfully, awkwardly; excessively, extremely, very much; (with adjectives having a good sense) not, scarcely, not at all; (with adjectives having a bad sense) very much; terribly; **male audīre** to be ill spoken of; **male dicere** (with dat) to say nasty things to, abuse; **male emere** to buy at a high price; **male facere** (with dat) to treat badly or cruelly; **male habere** to harass; **male metuere** to be terribly afraid of; **male vendere** to sell at a loss; **male vivere** to be a failure in life

maledic·ax -ācis adj abusive, foul-mouthed

maledicē adv abusively, slanderously

maledic·ens -entis adj abusive, foul-mouthed

male·dīcō -dīcĕre -dixī -dictum vi (with dat) to speak ill of, abuse, slander; b to say nasty things to

maledictī·ō -ōnis f abusive language, abuse

maledictĭt·ō -āre vi (with dat) to keep saying nasty things to

maledict·um -ī n curse; abuse

maledĭc·us -a -um adj abusive, scurrilous, foul-mouthed

malefact·or -ōris m malefactor

malefact·um or **malfact·um -ī** n wrong, injury

maleficē adv mischievously

maleficenti·a -ae f harm, wrong, mischief

malefĭc·ĭum -ĭī or **-ī** n evil deed, crime, offense; harm, injury, wrong, mischief; **maleficium admittere** or **committere** to commit an offense or crime

malefĭc·us -a -um adj wicked, vicious, criminal; m mischief-maker

malesuād·us -a -um adj seductive, tempting

malevŏl·ens -entis adj spiteful

malevolenti·a -ae f spitefulness, malice, meanness

malevŏl·us -a -um adj spiteful, malicious, mean; mf enemy; jealous person

malif·er -ĕra -ĕrum adj apple-growing

malignē adv spitefully, jealously, meanly; stingily, grudgingly

malignĭt·ās -ātis f spite, malice, jealousy, meanness; stinginess

malign·us -a -um adj spiteful, malicious, jealous, mean; stingy; (fig) stingy, unproductive (soil); scanty (light)

malĭti·a -ae f malice, ill-will, bad behavior; f pl devilish tricks

malitiōsē adv craftily, wickedly

malitiōs·us -a -um adj crafty, wicked, malicious, devilish

malleŏl·us -ī m small hammer, small mallet; fiery arrow

mallĕ·us -ī m hammer, mallet; pole-ax (for slaughtering animals)

mālō or **māvŏlō malle mālŭī** vt to prefer; vi (with dat) to incline toward, be more favorably disposed to

malobăthr·um -ī n malobathrum oil, betel juice

māl·um -ī n apple; **aureum malum** quince; **felix malum** lemon; **malum Punicum** or **malum granatum** pomegranate

mal·um -ī n evil, ill; harm; punishment; disaster; hardship

māl·us -ī m mast (of ship); pole; f apple tree

mal·us -a -um adj bad; ill, evil; ugly; unpatriotic; adverse, unsuccessful; unlucky; **ī in malam rem** go to hell!; n see **malum**

malv·a -ae f mallow

Mām·ers -ertis m Mars

Māmertīn·ī -ōrum m pl (mercenaries of Agathocles who after his death seized Messana, c. 282 B.C., and precipitated the First Punic War)

mamill·a -ae f breast, teat

mamm·a -ae f breast (of a woman); dug

mammeāt·us -a -um adj large-breasted, full-bosomed

mānābĭl·is -e adj penetrating (cold)

manc·eps -ĭpis m purchaser; contractor

mancĭp·ĭum or **mancŭp·ĭum -ĭī** or **-ī** n formal purchase; possession, right of ownership; slave; **mancipio accipere** to take possession of; **mancipio dare** to turn over possession of; **res mancipī** possessions basic to running a farm (e.g., land, slaves, livestock, farm implements); **res nec mancipī** possessions other than those needed to run a farm

mancĭp·ō or **mancŭp·ō -āre** vt to sell, transfer

manc·us -a -um adj crippled, maimed; (fig) defective, imperfect

mandāt·um -ī n command, order, commission; n pl instructions

mandāt·us -ūs m command, order

mand·ō -āre vt to commit, entrust; to command, order, enjoin, commission

mandō mandĕre mandī mansum vt to chew; to champ; to eat, devour; **humum mandere** to bite the dust (said of those who fall in battle)

mandr·a -ae f stable, stall; drove of cattle; checkerboard

mandūc·us -ī m mask representing a glutton

māne (indecl) n morning; adv early in the morning; **bene mane** very early; **cras mane** tomorrow morning; **heri mane** yesterday morning; **hodie mane** this morning; **postridie ejus diei mane** the following morning

maneō manēre mansī mansum vt to wait for, await; vi to stay, remain; to stop off, pass the night; to last, endure, continue, persist; **in condicione manere** to stick by an agreement; **in sententia manere** to stick to an opinion

mān·ēs -ĭum m pl souls of the dead; ghosts; lower world; last remains (of the body), ashes

mang·ō -ōnis m pushy salesman; slave dealer

manĭc·ae -ārum f pl handcuffs; grappling hook; long sleeves; gloves

manicāt·us -a -um adj long-sleeved

manĭcŭl·a -ae f little hand

manifestē adv plainly, distinctly

manifestō adv manifestly, evidently, plainly

manifest·ō -āre vt to reveal, betray

manifest·us -a -um adj manifest, plain, clear, distinct; exposed, brought to light, detected, caught; (with genit) convicted of, caught in; (with inf) known to

manipl· = manipul·

manipulār·is -e adj of a maniple or company; **miles manipularis** private

manipulār·is -is m private; soldier of the same company; comrade

manipulātim adv by companies

manipŭl·us or **manipl·us -ī** m handful (esp. of hay); (coll) gang; (mil) maniple, company (three of which constituted a cohort)

Manl·ius -ĭī or **-ī** m M. Manlius Capitolinus (consul in 392 B.C., who, in 389 B.C., saved the Capitoline from the invading Gauls); T. Manlius Torquatus (consul in 340 B.C., famous for his military discipline)

mannŭl·us -ī m pony

mann·us -ī m small Gallic horse

mān·ō -āre vi to drip, trickle, flow; to stream; (fig) to spread, emanate

mansĭ·ō -ōnis f stopover

mansĭt·ō -āre vi to stay on

mansuē·facĭō -facĕre -fēcī -factum (passive: **mansuē·fīō -fĭĕrī -factus sum**) vt to tame; (fig) to tame, pacify, civilize

mansu·ēs -is or **-ētis** adj tame, mild

mansu·escō -escĕre -ēvī -ētum vt to tame; vi to grow tame, become tame; (fig) to grow gentle, grow mild

mansuētē adv gently, mildly

mansuētūd·ō -ĭnis f mildness, gentleness

mansuēt·us -a -um adj tame; mild, gentle

mansus pp of **mando** and **maneo**

mantēl·e -is n napkin, towel

mantell·um or **mantēl·um -ī** n mantle

mantĭc·a -ae f knapsack

manticĭn·or -ārī -ātus sum vi to predict, prophesy

mant·ō -āre vt to wait for; vi to stay, remain, wait

Mant·ō -ūs f prophetic daughter of Tiresias

Mantŭ·a -ae f birthplace of Virgil, in N. Italy

manuāl·is -e adj that can be held in hand, hand-sized (e.g., rocks)

manubĭ·ae -ārum f pl money derived from the sale of booty

manubĭārĭ·us -a -um adj (coll) bringing in the loot

manūbr·ium -iī or **-ī** n handle; hilt

manufestārĭ·us -a -um adj plain, obvious

manulĕ·a -ae f long sleeve

manuleār·ĭus -iī or **-ī** m sleeve-maker

manuleāt·us -a -um adj long-sleeved

manūmissĭ·ō -ōnis f manumission, freeing of a slave

manū·mittō or **manū·mittō -mittĕre -mīsī -missum** vt to manumit, emancipate, set free (a slave)

manupret·ium -iī or **-ī** n workman's pay, wages; (fig) pay, reward

man·us -ūs f hand; band, company; gang; force, violence, close combat; finishing touch; handwriting; work; workmanship; elephant's trunk; grappling irons; power; (law) power of the husband over his wife; **ad manum habere** to have at hand, have in readiness; **ad manum venire** to come within reach; **e manu** at a distance, from a distance; **in manibus esse** to be in everyone's hands, be well known; to be near, be at hand; to be present; **in manu esse** (with genit) to be in the power of, be under the jurisdiction of; **in manu esse** (with dat) to be obvious to; **inter manus** under one's hands, with one's care; in one's hands, in one's arms; **manibus pedibusque** (fig) with might and main; **manu by hand**, artificially; (mil) by force of arms; **manu tenere** to know for sure; **manum committere, conserere,** or **conferre** to begin to fight; **manum dare** to lend a hand; **manum injicere** (with dat) to lay hands on, arrest; **manus dare** or **manus dedere** to give oneself up, surrender; **per manus** by hand; by force, by main force; from hand to hand, from mouth to mouth, from father to son; **plenā manu** generously; **prae manibus** or **prae manu** at hand, in readiness; **sub manu** or **sub manum** at hand, near; immediately

mapāl·ia -ium n pl African huts; African village, kraal

mapp·a -ae f napkin; flag (used in starting races at the racetrack)

Marăth·ōn -ōnis f site, in E. Attica, of victory by Miltiades over the Persians (490 B.C.)

Marcell·us -ī m Roman cognomen in the gens Claudia; M. Claudius Marcellus (nephew of Augustus, whose premature death is referred to in the Aeneid, 43-23 B.C.)

marc·ĕō -ēre vi to wither, droop, shrivel; to be weak, be feeble, be decrepit, be run-down; to slack off

marcesc·ō -ēre vi to begin to wither, begin to droop; to become weak, become run-down; to become lazy

marcĭd·us -a -um adj withered, drooping; groggy

Marc·ius -iī or **-ī** m Ancus Marcius (fourth king of Rome)

marcŭl·us -ī m small hammer

mar·e -is n sea; seawater, saltwater; **mare inferum** Tyrrhenian Sea; **mare nostrum** Mediterranean Sea; **mare superum** Adriatic Sea

Mareōt·a -ae f town and lake near Alexandria in Egypt

Mareōtĭc·us -a -um adj Mareotic; Egyptian

margarīt·a -ae f or **margarīt·um -ī** n pearl

margĭn·ō -āre vt to furnish with a border; to curb (a street)

marg·ō -ĭnis f margin, edge, border; frontier

Marĭān·ī -ōrum m pl partisans of Marius

Marĭc·a -ae f nymph of Minturnae, mother of Latinus

marīn·us -a -um adj sea, of the sea, marine

marisc·a -ae f fig; **tumidae mariscae** the piles

marīt·a -ae f wife, married woman

marītāl·is -e adj marital, nuptial, matrimonial

marītĭmus or **marītŭm·us -a -um** adj sea, of the sea; seafaring, maritime; (fig) changeable (like the sea); **ora maritima** seacoast; n pl seacoast

marīt·ō -āre vt to marry; to train (a vine to a tree)

marīt·us -a -um adj matrimonial nuptial; m husband, married man; lover; f see **marita**

Mar·ius -iī or **-ī** m C. Marius (conqueror of Jugurtha and of the Cimbri and Teutons, and seven times consul, 157-86 B.C.)

marm·or -ŏris n marble; marble statue, marble monument; smooth surface of the sea

marmorĕ·us -a -um adj marble, made of marble; marble-like

Mar·ō -ōnis m cognomen of Virgil

marr·a -ae f hoe, weeding hook

Mar·s -tis m god of war and father of Romulus and Remus; battle, war; engagement; planet; **aequo Marte** on an equal footing; **suo Marte** by one's own exertions, independently

Mars·ī -ōrum m pl Marsians (a people of S. central Italy, regarded as tough warriors)

marsupp·ium -iī or **-ī** n pouch, purse

Marsў·ās or **Marsў·a -ae** m satyr who challenged Apollo with the flute and was flayed alive upon his defeat; statue in the Roman forum of Marsyas

Martiāl·is -is *m* M. Valerius Martialis (*commonly called Martial and famous for his epigrams, c.* 40-120 A.D.)

Marticŏl·a -ae *m* worshiper of Mars

Marti·us -a -um *adj* Martian, of Mars; sacred to Mars; descended from Mars; March; *m* March, month of March

mās maris *adj* male, masculine; manly, masculine, brave; *m* male

masculīn·us -a -um *adj* male, masculine

mascŭl·us -a -um *adj* male, masculine; manly, vigorous; *m* male

mass·a -ae *f* mass, lump; (coll) chunk of money

Massĭc·us -a -um *adj* Massic; *m* Mt. Massicus (*between Latium and Campania, famous for its wine*); *n* Massic (*wine*)

Massīli·a -ae *f* Greek colony on S. coast of Gaul (*modern Marseilles*)

Massyl·ī -ōrum *m pl* tribe of E. Numidia

mastigi·a ae *m* rascal

mastrūc·a -ae *f* sheepskin; (as term of abuse) ninny

mastrūcāt·us -a -um *adj* clothed in sheepskin

matār·a -ae or **matăr·is -is** *f* Celtic javelin

matell·a -ae *f* chamber pot

matell·ō -ōnis *m* pot

māt·er -ris *f* mother; matron; **mater familiās** lady of the house; (of animals) dam; cause, origin, source

mātercŭl·a -ae *f* a little mother, poor mother

māt·erfamiliās -risfamiliās *f* lady of the house, mistress of the household

māteri·a -ae or **māterĭ·ēs -ēī** *f* matter, stuff, material; lumber, wood, timber; fuel; subject, subject matter, theme, topic; cause, source, occasion, opportunity; capacity, natural ability, disposition

māteriār·ius -iī or **-ī** *m* timber merchant

māteriāt·us -a -um *adj* built with lumber; **male materiatus** built with poor lumber

māteriēs see **materia**

māteri·or -ārī -ātus sum *vi* to fetch or gather wood

mātern·us -a -um *adj* maternal, mother's, of a mother

mātertĕr·a -ae *f* aunt, mother's sister

mathēmatĭc·us -ī *m* mathematician; astrologer

Matīn·us -ī *m* mountain in Apulia, near Horace's birthplace

mātricīd·a -ae *m* matricide, mother's murderer

mātricīd·ium -iī or **-ī** *n* matricide, murder of one's mother

mātrimōn·ium -iī or **-ī** *n* matrimony, marriage; **in matrimonium ire** to enter matrimony, get mar-

ried; **in matrimonium aliquam dūcere** to marry some girl

mātrīm·us -a -um *adj* having a mother still living

mātrōn·a -ae *f* married woman, matron, wife; woman of quality, lady

Mātrōnāl·ia -ium *n pl* festival celebrated by matrons on March 1 in honor of Mars

mātrōnāl·is -e *adj* matronly, womanly, wifely

matt·a -ae *f* straw mat

matŭl·a -ae *f* pot; chamber pot

mātūrātē *adv* in good time

mātūrē *adv* at the right time; in time; betimes, in good time, promptly, quickly; prematurely

mātūr·escō -escĕre -ŭī *vi* to get ripe, ripen, mature

mātūrit·ās -ātis *f* ripeness, maturity; (fig) maturity, height, perfection

mātūr·ō -āre *vt* to ripen, bring to maturity; to accelerate, speed up; (with *inf*) to be too quick in doing; *vi* to hasten

mātūr·us -a -um *adj* ripe, mature, full-grown; opportune, at the right time; early, coming early (*e.g.*, winter); advanced in years; marriageable; mellow (*with age*)

Mātūt·a -ae *f* goddess of the dawn

mātūtin·us -a -um *adj* morning, early; **tempora matutina** morning hours

Mauritāni·a -ae *f* country of N.W. Africa

Maur·us -a -um *adj* Moorish; African

Maurūsĭ·us -a -um *adj* Moorish, Mauretanian

Māvor·s -tis *m* Mars

Māvorti·us -a -um *adj* Martian, of Mars

maxill·a -ae *f* jaw

maximē or **maxŭmē** *adv* very, most, especially, particularly; just, precisely, exactly; (in sequences) in the first place, first of all; (in affirmations) by all means, certainly, yes; **immo maxime** certainly not; **nuper maxime** just recently; **quam maxime** as much as possible; **tum cum maxime** at the precise moment when; **tum maxime** just then, precisely at that time; **ut maxime . . . ita maxime** the more . . . so much the more

maximit·ās -ātis *f* magnitude

maximus or **maxŭmus** (*superl of* **magnus**) see **magnus**

mazonŏm·us -ī *m* large dish

meāmet = **meā**, *abl fem sing of* **meus**, strengthened by **-met**

meapte = **mea**, *nom fem sing of* **meus**, strengthened by **-pte**

meāt·us -ūs *m* motion, movement; course, channel

mecastor *interj* by Castor!

mēd = **me**

mēcum = **cum me**

medd·ix or **med·ix -īcis** *m* magistrate (*among the Oscans*); **meddix tuticus** senior magistrate (*among the Oscans*)

Mēdē·a -ae f daughter of Aeetes, the king of Colchis, and wife of Jason, famous for her magic

Mēdē·is -ĭdis adj magic

med·ens -entis m physician

med·ĕor -ērī vt to heal; vi (with dat) to heal, cure, be good for, remedy

Mēd·ī -ōrum m pl Medes; Persians; Parthians

Mēdī·a -ae f Asian country between Armenia, Parthia, Hyrcania, and Assyria

mediastīn·us -ī m servant, drudge

mēdĭc·a -ae f alfalfa

medicābĭl·is -e adj curable

medicām·en -ĭnis n medicine, remedy, drug, antidote; tincture; cosmetic; (fig) cure, remedy

medicāment·um -ī n medication, medicine; potion; (fig) relief, antidote; (rhet) embellishment

medicāt·us -ūs m magic charm

medicīn·a -ae f medicine, medical science; medicine, remedy; doctor's office; (with genit) (fig) cure for, remedy for

medĭc·ō -āre vt to medicate, cure; to dye

medĭc·or -ārī -ātus sum vt to cure; vi (with dat) to heal, cure

medĭc·us -a -um adj medical; healing; m doctor, surgeon

Mēdĭc·us -a -um adj Median, of the Medes

mediē adv moderately

mediĕt·ās -ātis f mean

medimn·um -ī n or **medimn·us -ī** m bushel, medimnus (containing six modii)

mediŏcr·is -e adj medium, average, ordinary; mediocre; narrow, small

mediocrĭt·ās -ātis f mean; moderation; mediocrity; f pl moderate passions

mediocrĭter adv moderately, fairly; not particularly, not very, not much; calmly

Mediolān·um -ī n Milan

medioxŭm·us -a -um adj (coll) in the middle

meditāment·um -ī n practice, drill

meditātē adv purposely

meditāti·ō -ōnis f reflection, contemplation; practice; rehearsal; (with genit) reflection on, contemplation of

meditāt·us -a -um adj premeditated

mediterrāně·us -a -um adj inland

medĭt·or -ārī -ātus sum vt to think over, reflect on; to practice; to plan, design

medĭ·us -a -um adj middle, central, the middle of, in the middle; intervening (time); middling, ordinary, common; undecided, neutral, ambiguous; meddling; **in mediā insulā** in the middle of the island; **media pars** half, one half; m mediator; n middle, center; commu-

nity, common good; public, publicity; **e medio abire** to disappear; **in medio relinquere** to leave undecided, leave hanging in the air; **in medium** into the center; on behalf of the public; for the common good; **in medium proferre** to publish

medius fidĭus interj by Heaven!

med·ix -ĭcis m magistrate (among the Oscans); **medix tuticus** senior magistrate

medull·a -ae f marrow; middle, center

medullĭtus adv (fig) with all one's heart

Medūs·a -ae f one of the three Gorgons, the daughter of Phorcys, whose eyes turned everything they looked upon into stone

Medūsae·us -a -um adj Medusan; **equus Medusaeus** Pegasus

Megaer·a -ae f one of the three Furies

Megalens·ĭa or **Megalēs·ĭa -ĭum** n pl festival of Cybele, celebrated on the 4th of April

Megăr·a -ae f or **Megăr·a -ōrum** n pl town near Athens

Megarē·us or **Megarĭc·us -a -um** adj Megarean

megistān·es -um m pl grandees

mehercle or **mehercŭle** or **mehercŭles** interj by Hercules!

mēi·ō -ĕre vi to urinate

mel mellis n honey; **meum mel** (as term of endearment) my honey!; n pl drops of honey

melancholĭc·us -a -um adj melancholy

melandr·yum -ī n piece of salted tuna

Melanth·ĭus -ĭī or **-ī** m goatherd of Ulysses

melcŭl·um -ī n (term of endearment) little honey

Meleăg·er or **Meleăg·ros -rī** m son of King Oeneus of Calydon and participant in the famous Calydonian boar hunt

Meleagrĭd·es -um f pl sisters of Meleager, who were changed into birds

Melicert·a or **Melicert·ēs -ae** m son of Ino and Athamas, who was changed into a sea god, called by the Greeks Palaemon and by the Romans Portunus

melĭc·us -a -um adj musical; lyric

melĭlōt·os -ī m clover

melimēl·a -ōrum n pl honey apples

mellĭn·a -ae f mead

mēlĭn·a -ae f leather wallet

Mēlĭn·um -ī n pigment; Melian white

melĭ·or -us (comp of bonus) adj better

melisphyll·um -ī n balm

Melĭt·a or **Melĭt·ē -ēs** f Malta

Melĭtens·is -e adj Maltese

mellĭus (comp of bene) adv better

meliuscŭlē adv pretty well

meliuscŭl·us -a -um *adj* a little better

mell·a -ae *f* mead

mellicŭl·us -a -um *adj* sweet as honey

mellif·er -ĕra -ĕrum *adj* honey-producing

mellill·a -ae *f* (term of endearment) little honey

mellīn·a -ae *f* sweetness, delight

mellīn·a -ae *f* leather wallet

mellīt·us -a -um *adj* honeyed, sweetened with honey; sweet as honey

mel·os -ī (Greek *pl*: **mel·e**) *n* tune, melody, song

Melpomēn·ē -ēs *f* Muse of tragic poetry

membrān·a -ae *f* membrane, skin; slough; parchment; film

membrānŭl·a -ae *f* small piece of parchment

membrātim *adv* limb by limb; piecemeal, singly; in short sentences

membr·um -ī *n* limb, member; part, division; clause

mēmet *pron* (emphatic form of **me**) me

memĭn·ī -isse *vt* to remember; *vi* (with *genit*) to be mindful of, remember

Memn·ōn -ŏnis *m* son of Tithonus and Aurora, king of the Ethiopians, and ally of the Trojans, who was killed by Achilles

Memnŏnĭd·es -um *f pl* birds that rose from the pyre of Memnon

Memnŏnĭ·us -a -um *adj* Memnonian; Oriental, Moorish, black

mem·or -ŏris *adj* mindful, remembering; having a good memory; reminding; (with *genit*) mindful of, remembering

memorābĭl·is -e *adj* memorable, remarkable

memorand·us -a -um *adj* worth mentioning, notable

memorāt·us -ūs *m* mention

memorĭ·a -ae *f* memory; remembrance; period of recollection, recollection, time, lifetime; a memory, past event, history; historical account; **memoriae prodere** to hand down to posterity; **paulo supra hanc memoriam** not long ago; **post hominum memoriam** within the memory of man; **superiore memoriā** in earlier times

memorĭŏl·a -ae *f* weak memory

memorĭter *adv* from memory, by heart; accurately, correctly

memŏr·ō -āre *vt* to mention, bring up, relate; to name, call; *vi* (with **de** + *abl*) to speak of

Memph·is -is or **-idos** *f* city in central Egypt

Memphĭtĭc·us -a -um *adj* Egyptian

Menand·er or **Menand·ros -rī** *m* Greek comic playwright, the most important representative of the Attic New Comedy (342-291 B.C.)

Menandrē·us -a -um *adj* of Menander

mend·a -ae *f* fault, blemish

mendācilŏqu·ior -us *adj* more false, more mendacious

mendāc·ĭum -ĭī or **-ī** *n* lie

mendāciuncŭl·um *n* white lie, fib

mend·ax -ācis *adj* mendacious, given to lying, false; *m* liar

mendicābŭl·um -ī *n* beggar

mendicĭt·ās -ātis *f* beggary

mendic·ō -āre or **mendic·or -ārī -ātus sum** *vt* to beg, beg for; *vi* to beg, go begging

mendicŭl·us -a -um *adj* beggarly

mendĭc·us -a -um *adj* needy, poor, poverty-stricken; (fig) poor, sorry, paltry; *m* beggar

mendōsē *adv* faultily, carelessly

mendōs·us -a -um *adj* full of physical defects; full of faults, faulty, incorrect, erroneous; blundering

mend·um -ī *n* defect, fault; blunder

Menelā·us -ī *m* son of Atreus, brother of Agamemnon, and husband of Helen

Menen·ĭus -ĭī or **-ī** *m* Menenius Agrippa (*patriotic Roman who told the plebs the fable of the belly and the limbs during the secession of the plebs in 494 B.C.*)

Menoec·eus -ĕī or **-ĕos** *m* son of Theban king Creon, who hurled himself off the city walls to save the city

Menoetĭăd·ēs -ae *m* Patroclus

Menoet·ĭus -ĭī or **-ī** *m* father of Patroclus

mens idea; feeling, heart, soul; purpose, intention, plan; courage, boldness; passion, impulse; **addere mentem** to give courage; **captus mente** crazy; **demittere mentem** to lose heart; **in mentem venire** to come to mind; **mentis suae esse** to be in one's right mind

men·s -tis *f* mind, intellect; understanding, reason; thought, opinion, intention, plan; courage, boldness; passion, impulse; **addere mentem** to give courage; **captus mente** crazy; **demittere mentem** to lose heart; **in mentem venire** to come to mind; **mentis suae esse** to be in one's right mind

mens·a -ae *f* table; meal, course, dinner; guests at table; counter; bank; sacrificial table, altar; **mensa secunda** dessert

mensār·ĭus -ĭī or **-ī** *m* banker; treasurer, treasury-board member

mensĭ·ō -ōnis *f* measure, measuring; quantity (*of a syllable*)

mens·is -is *m* month; **primo mense** at the beginning of the month

mens·or -ōris *m* surveyor

menstruāl·is -e *adj* for a month

menstru·us -a -um *adj* monthly; lasting for a month; *n* rations for a month; month's term of office

mensŭl·a -ae *f* little table

mensūr·a -ae *f* measuring, measurement; standard of measure; amount, size, proportion, capacity, extent, limit, degree

mensus *pp* of **metior**

ment·a or **menth·a -ae** *f* mint

menti·ens -entis *m* sophism, fallacy

mentĭ·ō -ōnis *f* mention; **mentio-**

nem facere (with *genit* or **de** + *abl*) to make mention of; **mentiones serere** (with **ad** + *acc*) to throw hints to

ment·ior -īrī -ītus sum *vt* to invent, fabricate; to feign, imitate, fake; *vi* to lie; to act deceitfully

Ment·or -ōris *m* friend of Ulysses; famous artist in metalwork; ornamental cup

ment·um -ī *n* chin

mē·ō -āre *vi* to go, pass

mephīt·is -is *f* malaria

mepte *pron* (emphatic form of **mē**) me, me myself

merācul·us or **merācl·us -a -um** *adj* pretty pure, rather pure

merāc·us -a -um *adj* pure, unmixed, undiluted, straight

mercābil·is -e *adj* buyable

mercāt·or -ōris *m* merchant, trader, dealer, wholesale dealer

mercātōri·us -a -um *adj* merchant, trading; **navis mercatoria** merchant ship

mercātūr·a -ae *f* trading, trade, commerce; purchase; *f pl* goods

mercāt·us -ūs *m* trade, traffic; market, marketplace; fair

mercēdul·a -ae *f* poor pay; low rent, low income

mercēnāri·us -a -um *adj* hired, paid, mercenary; *m* common laborer, servant

merc·ēs -ēdis *f* pay, wages, salary; bribe; reward, recompense; cost; injury, detriment; stipulation, condition, retribution, punishment; rent, income, interest

mercimōn·ium -iī or **-ī** *n* merchandise

mer·cor -ārī -ātus sum *vt* to deal in, trade in, purchase

Mercuriāl·is -e *adj* of Mercury; *m pl* corporation of merchants in Rome

Mercur·ius -iī or **-ī** *m* Mercury (*son of Jupiter and Maia, messenger of the gods, patron of commerce, diplomacy, lying, gambling, and conductor of departed souls to the world below*); Mercury (*planet*)

merd·a -ae *f* droppings, excrement

merend·a -ae *f* lunch, snack

mer·eo -ēre -uī -itum or **mer·eor -ērī -itus sum** *vt* to deserve, merit, be entitled to; to win, earn, acquire, merit; *vi* to serve; to serve in the army; (with **de** + *abl*) to serve, render service to, do a favor for; **bene de re publica merere** or **mereri** to serve one's country well; **de te merui** I have done you a favor, I have treated you well; **equo merere** to serve in the cavalry

meretrīci·us -a -um *adj* prostitute's

meretrīcul·a -ae *f* cute little wench

meretr·ix -īcis *f* prostitute, harlot, wench, strumpet

merg·ae -ārum *f pl* pitchfork

merg·es -ītis *f* sheaf

mergō mergĕre mersī mersum *vt* to dip, plunge, sink; to engulf, swallow up; to swamp, overwhelm, bury, drown; **mergi** to sink, drown; to go bankrupt

merg·us -ī *m* diver (*bird*)

merīdiān·us -a -um *adj* midday, noon; southern, southerly

merīdiātī·ō -ōnis *f* siesta

merīdi·ēs -ēī *m* midday, noon; south; **spectare ad merīdiem** to face south

merīdi·ō -āre *vi* to take a siesta

Mēriŏn·ēs -ae *m* charioteer of Idomeneus

meritō *adv* deservedly, rightly

merit·ō -āre *vt* to earn regularly

meritōr·ius -a -um *adj* rented, hired; *n pl* rented apartment

merit·us -a -um *adj* deserved, just, right, proper, deserving; guilty; *n* service, favor, kindness; blame, fault, offense; merit, worth

merobib·us -a -um *adj* drinking unmixed wine

Merŏp·ē -ēs *f* one of the Pleiades, the daughter of Atlas and Pleione

Mer·ops -ŏpis *m* king of Ethiopia, husband of Clymene, and reputed father of Phaethon

mer·ops -ŏpis *f* bee eater (*bird*)

mers·ō -āre *vt* to keep dipping or plunging, to immerse; (fig) to engulf; **mersari** (with *dat*) to plunge into

mersus *pp* of **mergo**

merūl·a -ae *f* blackbird

mer·us -a -um *adj* pure, unmixed, undiluted, unadulterated; (fig) undiluted; (fig) nothing but, mere; *n* wine

mer·x -cis *f* merchandise, wares; **mala merx** (fig) bad lot

Messallīn·a -ae *f* wife of the Emperor Claudius; wife of Nero

Messān·a -ae *f* town in N.E. Sicily

Messāpi·us -a -um *adj* Apulian; *f* town and district in S.E. Italy, named after the mythical founder Messapus

mess·is -is *f* harvest; harvest time; **adhuc tua messis in herba est** (fig) don't count your chickens before they are hatched

mess·or -ōris *m* reaper, mower

messōr·ius -a -um *adj* reaper's

messus *pp* of **meto**

mēt·a -ae *f* marker for measuring the distance at a racetrack; (fig) goal, end; (fig) turning point, critical moment

metall·um -ī *n* metal; *n pl* mine

metamorphōs·is -is *f* transformation

metaphŏr·a -ae *f* metaphor

mētāt·or -ōris *m* planner; **metator urbis** city planner

Metaur·us -ī *m* small river in Umbria, at the banks of which Hasdrubal was defeated in 207 B.C.

Metell·us -ī *m* Roman surname; Q. Caecilius Metellus Numidicus (*commander of the Roman forces against Jugurtha from 109 B.C. until replaced by Marius in 107 B.C.*)

Methymn·a -ae *f* town on the island of Lesbos

mētior mētīrī mensus sum *vt* to measure; to traverse, travel; to judge, estimate; (with *dat*) to measure (*something*) out to, distribute (*something*) among; (with *abl*) to judge (*someone*) by the standard of

metō metēre messuī messum *vt* to reap, mow, gather, collect, harvest; (fig) to mow down (*e.g., with the sword*)

mēt·or -ārī -ātus sum *vt* to measure off; to lay out (*e.g., a camp*)

metrēt·a -ae *f* liquid measure (*about nine gallons*)

metuculōs·us -a -um *adj* fearful; scary

metū·ens -entis *adj* afraid, apprehensive, anxious

metū·ō -ēre *vt* to fear, be afraid of; *vi* to be afraid, be apprehensive

met·us -ūs *m* fear, anxiety, apprehension

me·us -a -um *adj* my; *pron* mine; **meā interest** it is of importance to me; **meum est** (with *inf*) it is my duty to; **meus est** (coll) I've got him

Mezent·ius -iī or **-ī** *m* Etruscan tyrant of Caere, slain by Aeneas

mī = mihi

mīc·a -ae *f* crumb, morsel

Micips·a -ae *m* son of Masinissa and king of Numidia (148-118 B.C.); *m pl* (fig) Numidians, Africans

mic·ō -āre *vi* to vibrate, quiver, twinkle, sparkle, flash

mictur·iō -īre *vi* to have to urinate

Mid·ās -ae *m* king of Phrygia, at whose touch everything turned to gold (*8th cent. B.C.*)

migrāti·ō -ōnis *f* moving, changing residence; metaphorical use

migrāt·us -ūs *m* transporting

migr·ō -āre *vt* to transport; (fig) to transgress, violate; *vi* to move, change residence, depart, migrate; (fig) to go away, change, turn

mīl·es -itis *m* soldier; infantryman; private; army

Mīlēsi·us -a -um *adj* Milesian, of Miletus

Mīlēt·us -ī *f* Miletus (*town on the W. coast of Asia Minor*)

mīl·ia -ium *n pl* thousands; see **mille**

mīliār·ium -iī or **-ī** *n* milestone

mīliār·is -e *adj* military

mīlitār·iter *adv* in a military manner, like a soldier

mīlitār·is -a -um *adj* soldierly, military

mīliti·a -ae *f* army; war; the military; military discipline; **mīlitiae** in war, on the battlefield, in the army; **mīlitiae domique** abroad

and at home, on the war front and on the home front

mīlit·ō -āre *vt* to carry on (*war*); *vi* to serve as a soldier, be in the service

mil·ium -iī or **-ī** *n* millet

mille (indecl) *adj* thousand; *n* thousand; **mille homines** a thousand men; **milia** *n pl* thousands; **duo milia passuum** two miles

millēsim·us or **millensim·us -a -um** *adj* thousandth

milliār·ium -iī or **-ī** *n* milestone

milliens or **milliēs** *adv* a thousand times; innumerable times

Mil·ō -ōnis *m* T. Annius Milo (*friend of Cicero and enemy of Clodius, defended by Cicero on a charge of having murdered Clodius in 52 B.C.*)

Miltiad·ēs -is *m* Athenian general victorious at Marathon (490 B.C.)

mīluīn·us -a -um *adj* rapacious

mīlu·us or **mīlv·os -ī** *m* kite (*bird of prey*); gurnard (*fish*)

Mīlv·us -ī *m* Kite (*constellation*)

mīm·a -ae *f* actress

Mimallōn·is -idis *f* Bacchante

Mim·ās -antis *m* one of the giants

mīmicē *adv* like a mime actor

mīmic·us -a -um *adj* suitable for the mime, farcical

Mimnerm·us -ī *m* Greek elegiac poet of Colophon (*fl. 560 B.C.*)

mīmul·a -ae *f* miserable little actress

mīm·us -ī *m* mime, farce; actor of a mime; (fig) farce

min·a -ae *f* Greek coin (*about 100 denarii*)

mināci·ae -ārum *f pl* menaces, threats

mināciter *adv* threateningly

min·ae -ārum *f pl* menaces, threats; projecting points of a wall

minanter *adv* threateningly

mināti·ō -ōnis *f* threatening

min·ax -ācis *adj* threatening, menacing; projecting, jutting out

min·eō -ēre *vi* to project, jut out

Minerv·a -ae *f* goddess of wisdom and of the arts and sciences, identified with Pallas Athene; (fig) skill, genius; spinning and weaving; **invītā Minervā** against one's better judgment

mingō mingěre minxī mictum *vi* to urinate

miniān·us -a -um *adj* vermilion

miniātul·us -a -um *adj* reddish

minimē or **minumē** *adv* least of all, least, very little; by no means, certainly not, not in the least; **minume gentium** (coll) by no means

minim·us or **minum·us -a -um** (*superl* of **parvus**) *adj* smallest, least, very small; slightest, very insignificant; youngest; shortest (*time*); **minimus natū** youngest; *n* the least, minimum; lowest price; **minimo emere** to buy at a very low price; **minimo provocare** to provoke for the least thing or on the flimsiest pretext

mini·ō -āre *vt* to color red, paint red

minist·er -rī *m* servant, attendant, helper; agent, tool, instrument

minister·ium -iī or **-ī** *n* office, ministry, service, occupation, work, employment; retinue

ministr·a -ae *f* servant, attendant, helper; waitress; handmaid

ministrāt·or -ōris *m* or **ministrātr·ix -īcis** *f* assistant, helper

ministr·ō -āre *vt* to serve, wait on; to tend; to execute, carry out (*orders*); (with *dat*) to hand out (*something*) to; (with *abl*) to supply (*someone or something*) with

minitābund·us -a -um *adj* threatening

minit·ō -āre or **minit·or -ārī -ātus sum** *vt* to make threats of (*e.g.*, *war*); (with *acc* of thing and *dat* of person) to threaten to bring (*e.g.*, *evil*, *death*) upon, hold (*something* threateningly over (*someone*); *vi* to make threats; (with *dat* of person threatened and *abl* of means) to threaten (*somone*) with

min·ium -iī or **-ī** *n* vermilion; red lead

Mīnō·is -idis *f* Ariadne

Mīnō·us or **Mīnō·us -a -um** *adj* of Minos, Cretan

min·or -ārī -ātus sum *vt* to threaten; to promise boastfully; (with *dat* of person and *acc* of thing) to threaten (*someone*) with (*something*), to hold (*something*) over (*someone*) as a threat; *vi* to jut out, project; to be menacing, make threats; (with *dat*) to threaten, make threats to

min·or -us (*comp* of **parvus**) *adj* smaller, less; less, shorter (*time*); younger; inferior, less important; (with *abl*) **a** (of time) too short for; **b** inferior to; **c** unworthy of; (with *inf*) unfit to, incapable of; **dimidio minor quam** half as small as; **minores facere filios quam** to think less of the sons than of; **minor natu** younger; *m pl* descendants, posterity; *n* less, smaller amount; **minoris emere** to buy at a lower price; **minus praedae** less booty

Mīn·ōs -ōis or **-ōnis** *m* son of Zeus and Europa, king of Crete, and, after his death, judge in the lower world; grandson of the former, likewise king of Crete, husband of Pasiphaë, and father of Ariadne and Phaedra

Mīnōtaur·us -ī *m* monstrous offspring of Pasiphaë, half man and half bull, and kept in the labyrinth

minūmē see **minime**

minūmus see **minimus**

min·uō -uěre -uī -ūtum *vt* to diminish, lessen, reduce; to weaken, lower; to modify (*plans*); to settle (*controversies*); to limit, restrict (*authority*); to offend against, try to cheapen (*e.g.*, *the majesty of the*

Roman *people*); *vi* to diminish, abate, ebb; **minuente aestu** at ebbtide

minus *adv* less; not; by no means, not at all

minuscŭl·us -a -um *adj* rather small, smallish

minūt·al -ālis *n* hamburger, hash

minūtātim *adv* piecemeal; bit by bit

minūtē *adv* in a small-minded way

minūtŭl·us -a -um *adj* tiny

minūt·us -a -um *adj* small, minute; petty, narrow-minded

Minÿ·ae -ārum *m pl* Argonauts, the companions of Jason

Minÿ·ās -ae *m* mythical king of Thessaly

mīrābĭl·is -e *adj* wonderful, marvelous, amazing, extraordinary

mīrābiliter *adv* wonderfully, amazingly

mīrābund·us -a -um *adj* full of amazement, astonished

mīrācŭl·um -ī *n* wonder, marvel; surprise, amazement

mīrand·us -a -um *adj* fantastic

mīrātĭ·ō -ōnis *f* admiration, wonder

mīrāt·or -ōris *m* admirer

mīrātr·ix -īcis *adj fem* admiring

mīrē *adv* wonderfully, uncommonly, strangely; **mire quam** it is strange how, strangely

mīrĭficē *adv* wonderfully

mīrĭfic·us -a -um *adj* causing wonder, wonderful

mīrimŏdīs *adv* in a strange way

mirmill·ō -ōnis *m* gladiator (*who fought with Gallic arms*)

mir·or -ārī -ātus sum *vt* to be amazed at, be surprised at; to look at with wonder, admire

mīr·us -a -um *adj* amazing, surprising, astonishing; wonderful; **mirum est** (with *acc & inf*) it is surprising that; **mirum quam** or **mirum quantum** it is amazing how, it is amazing to what extent

miscellānĕ·a -ōrum *n pl* hash

miscĕō miscēre miscŭī mixtum *vt* to mix, blend, mingle; to combine, associate, share; to mix up, confuse, turn upside down; to mix, prepare, brew

misell·us -a -um *adj* poor little

Mīsēn·um -ī *n* promontory and town near the bay of Naples

mis·er -ěra -ěrum *adj* poor; wretched, miserable, unhappy; sorry, worthless

miserābĭl·is -e *adj* miserable, pitiable; piteous

miserābiliter *adv* pitiably; piteously

miserand·us -a -um *adj* pitiful, deplorable

miserātĭ·ō -ōnis *f* pity, compassion, sympathy; appeal for sympathy

miserē *adv* wretchedly, miserably, unhappily; pitifully; desperately

miser·ĕō -ēre -uī -ĭtum or **miserĕor -ērī -ĭtus sum** *vi* (with *genit*) to pity, feel sorry for, sympathize with; *v impers* (with *acc* of person who feels pity and *genit* of object of pity), e.g., **miseret** or **miseretur me aliorum** I feel sorry for the others

miseresc·ō *-ěre vi* to feel pity, feel sympathetic; (with *genit*) to pity, feel sorry for; *v impers* (with *acc* of person who feels pity and *genit* of object of pity), e.g., **me miserescit tuī** I feel sorry for you, I pity you

miseri·a *-ae f* poverty; misery, unhappiness, distress, trouble

misericordi·a *-ae f* pity, sympathy, compassion; mercy

misericor·s *-dis adj* sympathetic, merciful

miseriter *adv* sadly

miser·or *-ārī* *-ātus sum vt* to deplore; to pity; *vi* to feel pity

missicŭl·ō *-āre vt* to keep sending

missĭl·is *-e adj* missile, flying; *n pl* missiles

missi·ō *-ōnis f* release, liberation; sending off, despatching; military discharge; dismissal from office; cessation, end; **sine missione** without letup, to the death

missĭt·ō *-āre vt* to keep sending

missus *pp* of **mittō**

miss·us *-ūs m* letting go, throwing, hurling; sending

mītesc·ō *-ěre vi* to grow mild, grow mellow, become ripe; (fig) to get soft; (fig) to become gentle, become tame

Mithr·ās *-ae m* Mithra (*sun-god of the Persians*)

Mithridāt·ēs *-is m* Mithridates the Great (*king of Pontus from 120 B.C. to 63 B.C.*)

Mithridātē·us or **Mithridātĭc·us** *-a -um adj* Mithridatic

mītigātĭ·ō *-ōnis f* mitigation, soothing

mītig·ō *-āre vt* to mellow, ripen; to soften; to calm down, appease, pacify

mīt·is *-e adj* mellow, ripe, soft; calm, placid; mild, gentle

mitr·a *-ae f* miter, turban

mittō mittěre mīsī missum vt to send; let fly, throw, fling, launch; to emit, shed; to let out, utter; to let go of, drop; to free, release, discharge, dismiss; to pass over in silence, omit; to send for, invite; to pass up, forego; to dedicate (*a book*); to yield, produce, export; to dismiss, forget; **sanguinem mittere** to bleed; **sanguinem provinciae mittere** (fig) to bleed a province dry

mītŭl·us *-ī m* limpet

mixtim *adv* promiscuously

mixtūr·a *-ae f* mixing, blending

Mnēmosўn·ē *-ēs f* mother of the Muses

mnēmosўn·on *-ī n* souvenir

mōbĭl·is *-e adj* mobile, moveable, portable; nimble, active, shifty, changing; impressionable, excitable

mōbĭlĭt·ās *-ātis f* mobility; agility, quickness; shiftiness

mōbĭlĭter *adv* quickly, rapidly

mōbĭlĭt·ō *-āre vt* to impart motion to, endow with motion

moderābĭl·is *-e adj* moderate

moderām·en *-ĭnis n* control

moderanter *adv* under control

moderātē *adv* with moderation

moderātim *adv* gradually

moderātĭ·ō *-ōnis f* controlling, control, regulation, guidance; moderation, self-control; rules, regulation

moderāt·or *-ōris m* or **moderātr·ix** *-īcis f* controller, director, guide

moderāt·us *-a -um adj* controlled, well regulated, orderly, restrained

moděr·ō *-āre* or **moděr·or** *-ārī* *-ātus sum vt* to control, direct, guide; *vi* (with *dat*) **a** to moderate, restrain, put restraint upon; **b** to allay, mitigate

modestē *adv* with moderation, discreetly; modestly

modesti·a *-ae f* moderation, restraint; discretion; modesty, sense of shame, sense of honor, dignity; propriety; mildness (*of weather*)

modest·us *-a -um adj* moderate, restrained; modest, discreet; orderly, obedient

modiāl·is *-e adj* containing a modius or peck

modicē *adv* moderately, with restraint; in an orderly manner; only slightly

modĭc·us *-a -um adj* moderate; small; modest, unassuming; ordinary, puny, trifling

modificāt·us *-a -um adj* regulated (*in length*)

mod·ius *-ĭī* or *-ī m* modius, peck (*one sixth of a medimnus*); measure; **plēno modio** in full measure

modo *adv* only, merely, simply, solely; (of time) just now, just recently, lately; presently, in a moment; **modo ... deinde** (or **tum** or **postea** or **interdum**) first ... then, at one time ... next time; **modo ... modo** now ... now, sometimes ... sometimes, at one moment ... at another; **non modo ... sed etiam** or **verum etiam** not only ... but also; *conj* if only, provided that

modulātē *adv* according to measure, in time; melodiously

modulāt·or *-ōris m* director, musician

modŭl·or *-ārī* *-ātus sum vt* to regulate the time of, measure rhythmically; to modulate; to sing; to play

modŭl·us *-ī m* small measure, small stature

mod·us *-ī m* standard of measurement, measure; time, rhythm; size; limit, boundary; rule, regulation; way, manner, mode; **ad modum** (with *genit*) or **in modum** (with *genit*) or **modo** (with *genit*) in the manner of, according to the style of, like; **ejus modi homo** that kind of man; **hujus modi homo** this kind of man

moech·a -ae *f* adultress

moechiss·ō -āre *vt* to ravish, rape

moech·or -ārī -ātus sum *vi* to have an affair, commit adultery

moech·us -ī *m* adulterer

moen·ia -ium *n pl* town walls, ramparts, fortifications; fortified town; castle, stronghold; defenses

moeniō see **munio**

moerus see **murus**

Moes·ī -ōrum *m pl* a people on the lower Danube

mol·a -ae *f* millstone; mill; flour; *f pl* mill

molār·is -is *m* millstone; molar (*tooth*)

mōl·ēs -is *f* mass, bulk, pile; massive structure, dam, mole, pier; mass (*of people, etc.*); burden, effort, trouble; calamity; might, greatness

molestē *adv* with annoyance; with difficulty, with trouble; **moleste ferre** to be annoyed at, be disgruntled at, just about stand

molesti·a -ae *f* annoyance, trouble; worry; affectation (*in style*)

molest·us -a -um *adj* annoying, troublesome, distressing; labored, affected (*style*)

mōlīm·en -inis *n* great exertion, great effort; attempt, undertaking

mōliment·um -ī *n* great exertion, great effort

mōl·ior -īrī -ītus sum *vt* to do with great effort, strain at, exert oneself over; to wield, heave, hurl; to work hard at; to build, erect; to rouse; to displace; to undertake, attempt; to perform; to cause, occasion; *vi* to exert oneself, struggle, take great pains

mōlīti·ō -ōnis *f* building, erection; demolition

mōlīt·or -ōris *m* builder

molītus *pp* of **molo**

molītus *pp* of **molior**

mollescō -ēre *vi* to become soft; to become gentle; to become effeminate

mollicul·us -a -um *adj* tender, dainty

moll·iō -īre -īvī or **-iī -ītum** *vt* to make soft, soften; (fig) to soften, mitigate; to demoralize

mollip·ēs -ēdis *adj* soft-footed

moll·is -e *adj* soft; springy; flexible; flabby; mild, calm; easy; gentle (*slope*); sensitive, impressionable; tender, touching; weak, effeminate; amatory (*verses*); complaint; changeable, untrustworthy

molliter *adv* softly; gently, smoothly; effeminately; voluptuously; patiently, with fortitude

mollīti·a -ae or **mollīti·ēs -ēī** *f* softness; flexibility; tenderness; sensitivity; weakness, irresolution; effeminacy, voluptuousness

mollitūd·ō -inis *f* softness; flexibility; susceptibility

mol·ō -ēre -uī -itum *vt* to grind

Moloss·us -a -um *adj* Molossian; *m* Molossian hound; *m pl* Molossians (*a people of Epirus*)

mōl·y -yos *n* magic herb

mōm·en -inis *n* movement, motion; momentum

mōment·um -ī *n* movement, motion; alteration; turn, critical time; moment; impulse; momentum; influence, importance; motive

Mon·a -ae *f* Isle of Man

monēdūl·a -ae *f* jackdaw

mon·eō -ēre -uī -itum *vt* to call to mind, remind, advise, point out; to warn; to foretell; to teach, instruct, inform

monēr·is -is *f* galley

Monēt·a -ae *f* Juno Moneta, in whose temple on the Capitoline Hill money was kept; coin, money; stamp or die (*for money*)

monētāl·is -e *adj* of the mint; *m* (coll) money man

monīl·e -is *n* necklace

monim- = monum-

monit·a -ōrum *n pl* warnings; prophecies

moniti·ō -ōnis *f* reminder

monit·or -ōris *m* reminder, counselor; teacher

monit·us -ūs *m* reminder, warning

monogramm·us -a -um *adj* sketchy, shadowy

monopod·ium -iī or **-ī** *n* table with a single central leg

monotrop·us -a -um *adj* single, alone

mon·s -tis *m* mountain, mountain range; mass, heap; hill; **montis auri polliceri** to make wild promises; **summus mons** mountain top

monstrāti·ō -ōnis *f* pointing out

monstrāt·or -ōris *m* displayer; inventor

monstr·ō -āre *vt* to show, to point out, exhibit, make known, advise, teach; to appoint, institute, ordain; to advise, urge

monstr·um -ī *n* sign, portent, wonder; warning; monster, monstrosity; miracle, marvel

monstruōsē *adv* unnaturally

monstruōs·us -a -um *adj* unnatural, strange, monstrous

montān·us -a -um *adj* mountain, of a mountain; mountainous; *m pl* mountaineers; *n pl* mountainous regions

monticol·a -ae *m* mountaineer, highlander

montivăg·us -a -um *adj* wandering over the mountains

montōs·us or **montuōs·us -a -um** *adj* mountainous

monument·um -ī *n* reminder; monument, memorial; record (*written or oral*); token of identification

Mopsopi·us -a -um *adj* Athenian; *f* Attica, Athens

mor·a -ae *f* delay; pause; spell, period of time; stop-off; division of the Spartan army consisting of from three to seven hundred men

mōrāl·is -e *adj* moral

morāt·or -ōris *m* obstructionist; (in court) lawyer who spoke only to gain time

mōrāt·us -a -um *adj* -mannered; -natured; in character; **bene morātus** well-mannered; **male morātus** ill-mannered, rude

morbĭd·us -a -um *adj* sickly; causing sickness, unwholesome

morbōs·us -a -um *adj* debauched

morb·us -ī *m* sickness, disease; fault, vice; distress; **in morbum cadere** or **in morbum incidere** to fall sick

mordācĭus *adv* more bitingly; (fig) more radically

mord·ax -ācis *adj* biting, snapping; (fig) sharp, stinging, caustic, snarling; pungent (*taste*)

mordĕō mordēre momordī morsum *vt* to bite; to eat, devour; to bite, grip, (of cold) to nip; (of words) to cut, hurt; (of a river) to bite its way through

mordĭc·ēs -um *m pl* bites

mordĭcus *adv* by biting, with the teeth; (fig) tightly, doggedly

mōrē *adv* foolishly

morēt·um -ī *n* salad

moribund·us -a -um *adj* dying, at the point of death; mortal; deadly

mōrĭgĕr·ō -āre or **mōrĭgĕr·or -ārī -ātus sum** *vi* (with *dat*) to humor, pamper, yield to, comply with

mōrĭgĕr·us -a -um *adj* obedient, obsequious

morĭor morī mortŭus sum *vi* to die; (fig) to die out, wither, decay, pass away

morm·yr -ўris *f* Pontic fish

mōrŏlŏg·us -a -um *adj* speaking nonsense, foolish

mor·or -ārī -ātus sum *vt* to delay, detain; to entertain, hold the attention of; to hinder, prevent; **nihil morari** (with *acc*) **a** to disregard, care nothing for, not value; **b** to have nothing against, have nothing to say against; *vi* to delay, linger, tarry, loiter; to stay, remain, wait; **quid moror?** or **quid multis morer?** why should I drag out the point?, to make a long story short

mōrōsē *adv* morosely, crabbily

mōrōsĭt·ās -ātis *f* moroseness, peevishness, crabbiness

mōrōs·us -a -um *adj* morose, peevish, crabby; fastidious, particular; (fig) stubborn (*disease*)

Morph·eus -ĕos *m* god of dreams

mors mortis *f* death; destruction; corpse; **mortem obire** to meet death; **mortis poena** death penalty; **sibi mortem consciscere** to commit suicide

mors·a -ōrum *n pl* bits, little pieces

morsiuncŭl·a -ae *f* peck, kiss

morsus *pp* of **mordeo**

mors·us -ūs *m* bite; pungency; grip; corrosion; gnawing pain; sting, vicious attack

mortāl·is -e *adj* mortal, subject to death; human, mortal; transient; man-made; *m* mortal, human being

mortālĭt·ās -ātis *f* mortality; mortals, mankind

morticīn·us -a -um *adj* dead; corpse-like, rotting

mortif·er or **mortif·ĕrus -ĕra -ĕrum** *adj* lethal, deadly

mortĭfĕrē *adv* mortally

mortuāl·ĭa -ĭum *n pl* dirges

mortŭ·us -a -um *pp* of **morior;** *adj* dead, deceased; withered, decayed; scared to death; *m* corpse

mōrŭl·us -a -um *adj* dark, black

mōr·um -ī *n* blackberry, mulberry

mōr·us -ī *f* mulberry tree

mōr·us -a -um *adj* foolish; *mf* fool

mōs mōris *m* caprice, mood; nature, manner; custom, usage, practice; fashion, style; rule, regulation, law; **de more** or **ex more** according to custom; **morem gerere** (with *dat*) to humor (*someone*); *m pl* morals, character, behavior; customs; laws

Mōs·ēs or **Moys·ēs -is** *m* Moses

mōtĭ·ō -ōnis *f* motion

mōt·ō -āre *vt* to keep moving, keep shifting

mōtus *pp* of **moveo**

mōt·us -ūs *m* motion, movement; gesture; dancing; change (*e.g.*, of fortune); impulse, inspiration; emotion, passion; rebellion, riot; **motus animi** emotion; **motus terrae** earthquake

mov·ens -entis *adj* movable; **res moventes** personal property; *n pl* motives

movĕō movēre mōvī mōtum *vt* to move; to stir, shake, disturb; to dislodge (*the enemy*); to eject, expel; to degrade; to remove, take away; to plow; to cause, occasion, promote; to begin; to undertake; to trouble, torment; to move, influence, affect; to dissuade; to exert, exercise; to turn over in the mind, ponder; **se ex loco movere** to budge from the spot; **se movere** to dance; *vi* to move

mox *adv* soon, presently; hereafter; next, then, later on

Moys·ēs -is *m* Moses

mūcĭd·us -a -um *adj* sniveling, driveling; moldy, musty

Mūc·ĭus -ĭī or **-ī** *m* Roman family name

mūcr·ō -ōnis *m* sharp point, sharp edge; sword; edge, boundary; keenness

mūc·us -ī *m* nasal mucus

mūgient·ēs -ĭum *m pl* oxen

mūgĭl or **mūgĭl·is -is** *m* mullet

mugin·or -ārī -ātus sum *vi* to dillydally

mŭg·ĭō **-īre** **-īvī** or **-ĭī** **-ītum** *vi* to bellow, low; to rumble, roar

mūgīt·us **-ūs** *m* bellowing, lowing; rumbling, roaring

mūl·a **-ae** *f* mule

mulcĕō **mulcēre** **mulsī** **mulsum** *vt* to stroke, pet; to stir gently; to soothe, alleviate; to appease; to flatter, delight

Mulcĭb·er **-ērī** or **-ĕris** *m* Vulcan; fire

mulc·ō **-āre** *vt* to beat, cudgel; to mistreat, injure

mulctr·a **-ae** *f* milk pail

muctrār·ium **-iī** or **-ī** or **muctr·um** **-ī** *n* milk pail

mulgĕō **mulgēre** **mulsī** **mulsum** or **mulctum** *vt* to milk

muliĕbr·is **-e** *adj* woman's, womanly, feminine; womanish, effeminate

muliebriter *adv* like a woman; effeminately

muli·er **-ĕris** *f* woman; wife

mulierāri·us **-a** **-um** *adj* woman's; *m* woman chaser, wolf

muliercŭl·a **-ae** *f* little woman; little hussy

mulierōsit·ās **-ātis** *f* weakness for women

mulierōs·us **-a** **-um** *adj* woman-crazy

mūlīn·us **-a** **-um** *adj* mulish

mūl·ō **-ōnis** *m* mule driver

mūliōnī·us **-a** **-um** *adj* mule driver's

mullŭl·us **-ī** *m* little mullet

mull·us **-ī** *m* mullet

muls·us **-a** **-um** *pp* of **mulceo**; *adj* honeyed, sweet as honey; *f* (term of endearment) honey; *n* mead (*wine mixed with honey*)

mult·a **-ae** *f* fine; penalty; loss of money; **multam certare** to contest a fine; **multam committere** to incur a fine; **multam dicere** (with *dat* of person and *acc* of the fine) to fine (*someone a certain amount*); **multam subire** to incur a fine, be fined

multa *adv* much, very, greatly, earnestly

mult·a **-ōrum** *n pl* many things; much; **ne multa** in short, to be brief

multangŭl·us **-a** **-um** *adj* many-angled

multātici·us **-a** **-um** *adj* fine, of a fine; **multaticia pecunia** fine

multātĭ·ō **-ōnis** *f* fine, penalty

multēsĭm·us **-a** **-um** *adj* trifling, negligible

mult·ī **-ōrum** *m pl* many men, many; multitude, mass, common people

multibĭb·us **-a** **-um** *adj* heavy-drinking

multicăv·us **-a** **-um** *adj* porous

multĭcĭ·a **-ōrum** *n pl* diaphanous garments

multifāriam *adv* in many places

multifĭd·us **-a** **-um** *adj* divided into many parts; (of a river) having many tributaries; **dens multifida** comb

multiform·is **-e** *adj* multiform, manifold

multifŏr·us **-a** **-um** *adj* many-holed; (flute) having many stops

multigener·is **-e** or **multigĕn·us** **-a** **-um** *adj* of many kinds, various, complex

multijŭg·is **-e** or **multijŭg·us** **-a** **-um** *adj* yoked together; (fig) various, complex

multilŏqu·ax **-ācis** *adj* talkative

multilŏqu·ium **-iī** or **-ī** *n* talkativeness

multilŏqu·us **-a** **-um** *adj* talkative

multimŏdīs *adv* in many ways

multĭpl·ex **-ĭcis** *adj* with many folds; winding, labyrinthine, serpentine; manifold; many; (in implied comparisons) many times as great, far greater; varied, complicated; changeable, versatile, many-sided; sly, cunning; *n* manifold return

multiplicābĭl·is **-e** *adj* manifold, many

multiplicĭter *adv* in various ways

multiplĭc·ō **-āre** *vt* to multiply, increase, enlarge

multipŏt·ens **-entis** *adj* mighty, powerful

multitūd·ō **-ĭnis** *f* great number, multitude, crowd, throng; rabble, common people

multivŏl·us **-a** **-um** *adj* passionate

multō *adv* (with comparatives) much, far, by far, a great deal; **multo aliter ac** far otherwise than, much different from; **multo ante** long before; **multo post** long after; **non multo secus fieri** to turn out just about the same

mult·ō **-āre** *vt* to punish, fine

mult·us **-a** **-um** (*comp*: **plures**; *superl*: **plurimus**) *adj* many a, much, great; abundant, considerable, extensive; tedious, long-winded; full, numerous, thick, loud, heavy, constant; **ad multum diem** till late in the day; **multā nocte** late at night; **multo die** late in the day; (with plural nouns) many; *m pl* see **multi**; *n* much; **multi** of great value, highly; **multi facere** to think highly of, make much of, think much of; **multum est** it is of great importance; **multum temporis** a great deal of time, much time; *n pl* see **multa**

multum *adv* much, greatly, very, often, frequently, far; (with comparatives) much, far; **multum valere** to have considerable influence

mūl·us **-ī** *m* mule

Mulvī·us **-a** **-um** *adj* Mulvian; **Mulvius pons** Mulvian bridge (*across the Tiber, above Rome, on the Via Flaminia*)

Mumm·ius **-iī** or **-ī** *m* L. Mummius Achaicus (*conqueror of Corinth*, 146 B.C.)

mundān·us **-ī** *m* world citizen

mundē or mundĭter *adv* neatly, cleanly

mundĭtĭ·a -ae or mundĭtĭ·ēs -ēī *f* neatness, cleanness; elegance; politeness

mundŭl·us -a -um *adj* trim, neat, sharp

mund·us -a -um *adj* neat, clean, nice; fine, smart, sharp, elegant; choice (*words*); *m* neat person; world, universe, heavens; earth, mankind; beauty aids

mūnerigerŭl·us -ī *m* bearer of presents

mūnĕr·ō -āre or mūnĕr·or -ārī -ātus sum *vt* to reward, honor, present; (with *acc* of thing and *dat* of person) to present to

mūnĭ·a -ōrum *n pl* official duties or functions

mūnĭc·eps -ĭpis *m* or *f* citizen of a municipality; fellow citizen, fellow countryman

mūnĭcĭpāl·is -e *adj* municipal; (as term of contempt) provincial, country

mūnĭcĭp·ium -ĭī or -ī *n* municipality, town (*whose people were Roman citizens, but otherwise autonomous*)

mūnĭfĭcē *adv* generously

mūnĭfĭcentĭ·a -ae *f* generosity

mūnĭfĭc·ō -āre *vt* to treat generously

mūnĭfĭc·us -a -um *adj* generous; splendid

mūnīm·en -ĭnis *n* defense

mūnīment·um -ī *n* defense, protection, fortification, rampart; (fig) shelter, defense

mūn·ĭō or moen·ĭō -īre -īvī or -ĭī -ītum *vt* to wall, defend with a wall, fortify, strengthen, defend, protect, guard, secure; to build (*road*); (fig) to guard, shelter, protect, support

mūn·is -e *adj* obliging

mūnītĭ·ō -ōnis *f* building, fortifying, defending; fortification, rampart, trenches, lines; munitio fluminum bridging of rivers; munitio viae road construction

mūnīt·ō -āre *vt* to open up (*a road*)

mūnīt·or -ōris *m* builder, engineer

mūnīt·us -a -um *adj* fortified; (fig) protected, safe

mūn·us or moen·us -ĕris *n* service, function, duty; gift; service, favor, kindness; duty, tribute; public entertainment, gladiatorial show, extravaganza; tribute (*to the dead*), rite, sacrifice; public office

mūnuscŭl·um -ī *n* small present

mūraen·a -ae *f* moray (*eel-like fish*)

mūrāl·is -e *adj* wall; wall-destroying; wall-defending; corona mūralis mural crown (*award for being the first to scale the enemy walls*)

mūr·ex -ĭcis *m* murex, mollusk (*yielding purple dye*); purple dye, purple; jagged rock; spiked trap (*as defense against cavalry attack*)

murĭ·a -ae *f* brine

murĭātĭc·um -ī *n* pickled fish

mūrĭcīd·us -ī *m* mouse killer; (fig) coward

murmill·ō -ōnis *m* gladiator with Gallic arms, who fought against a retarius

murm·ur -ŭris *n* murmur, murmuring; buzz, hum; roar, crash; growling, grumbling; rumbling; hubbub

murmurill·um -ī *n* low murmur

murmŭr·ō -āre *vi* to murmur; to mutter, grumble; to rumble, roar

murr·a or murrh·a or myrrh·a -ae *f* myrrh tree; myrrh

murrĕ·us or myrrhĕ·us -a -um *adj* made of myrrh; perfumed with myrrh; myrrh-colored, yellowish

murrĭn·us or myrrhĭn·us -a -um *adj* of myrrh; *f* drink flavored with myrrh; *n pl* vases

murt- = myrt-

mūr·us -ī *m* wall, city wall; dam, dike; rim (*of dish or pot*); (fig) wall, protection

mūs mūris *m* or *f* mouse, rat

Mūs·a -ae *f* Muse (*patron goddess of poetry, song, dance, literature, astronomy, etc.*); poem, song; talent, genius, taste; *f pl* studies

Mūsae·us -ī *m* mythical pre-Homeric bard and musician in the time of Orpheus

musc·a -ae *f* fly

muscār·ium -ĭī or -ī *n* fly swatter

muscĭpŭl·a -ae *f* or muscĭpŭl·um -ī *n* mousetrap

muscōs·us -a -um *adj* mossy

muscŭl·us -ī *m* little mouse; muscle; (mil) mantelet

musc·us -ī *m* moss

Mūsē·us or Mūsae·us -a -um *adj* of the Muses, musical, poetic

mūsĭc·a -ae or mūsĭc·ē -ēs *f* or mūsĭc·ā -ōrum *n pl* music, art of music (*including poetry*)

mūsĭcē *adv* pleasantly

mūsĭc·us -a -um *adj* musical; poetic; cultural; *m* musician

mussĭt·ō -āre *vt* to bear in silence; *vi* to be silent; to mutter, grumble

muss·ō -āre *vt* to bear in silence, bear silently; to brood over; *vi* to mutter, murmur; (of bees) to hum; to hesitate

mustācĕ·us -ī *m* or mustācĕ·um -ī *n* cake, wedding cake

mustell·a or mustēl·a -ae *f* weasel

mustellĭn·us or mustēlĭn·us -a -um *adj* of a weasel

must·um -ī *n* fresh grape juice, unfermented wine, must; vintage

mūtābĭl·is -e *adj* changeable; fickle

mūtābĭlĭt·ās -ātis *f* mutability; fickleness

mūtātĭ·ō -ōnis *f* mutation, change, alteration; exchange, interchange

mutĭl·ō -āre *vt* to cut off, lop off, crop; to mutilate; to reduce, shorten, lessen; to rob

mutĭl·us -a -um *adj* maimed, mutilated; defective

Mutīn·a -ae f town of N. central Italy, S. of the Po, which played a role in the civil war after the death of Julius Caesar

mūtīō see **muttio**

mūtītiō see **muttitio**

mūt·ō -āre vt to move, shift, change, alter; to exchange, interchange, barter, sell; to modify, transform, vary; to change for the better; to change for the worse; (with abl or **pro + abl**) to exchange or substitute (something or someone) for; vi to change

mūt·ō -ōnis m penis

mutt·iō or **mūt·iō -īre -īvī -ītum** vi to mutter, mumble

muttīti·ō or **mūtīti·ō -ōnis** f muttering, mumbling

mūtuātī·ō -ōnis f borrowing

mūtuē adv mutually; in return

mūtuīt·ō -āre vt to wish to borrow

mūtuō adv mutually, in return

mūtŭ·or -ārī -ātus sum vt to borrow; to derive, obtain, get

mūt·us -a -um adj mute, speechless; silent, still; n pl brutes

mūtŭ·us -a -um adj mutual, reciprocal, interchangeable; borrowed, lent; n reciprocity; loan; **mutuum dare** (with **cum + abl**) to lend to (someone); **mutuas pecunias sumere** (with **ab + abl**) to borrow money from (someone); **mutuum argentum rogare** to ask for a loan of cash

Mycēn·ae -ārum f pl or **Mycēn·ē -ēs** f Mycene (city of Agamemnon in Argolis)

Mycēnae·us -a -um or **Mycēnens·is -e** adj Mycenean

Mycēn·is -ĭdis f Mycenaean girl (Iphigenia)

Mygdŏn·es -um m pl a people of Thrace, some of whom later migrated to Phrygia

Mygdonĭ·us -a -um adj Phrygian

myopăr·ō -ōnis m pirate ship

myrīc·a -ae or **myrīc·ē -ēs** f tamarisk

Myrmidŏn·es -um m pl Myrmidons (people of Thessaly whom Achilles led in battle)

Myr·ōn -ōnis m famous Greek sculptor, whose most famous work is the Discus Thrower, 5th cent. B.C.

myropōl·a -ae m perfumer

myropōl·ium -iī or **-ī** n perfume shop

myrrh- = murr-

myrtēt·um or **murtēt·um -ī** n myrtle grove

myrtĕ·us or **murtĕ·us -a -um** adj myrtle; crowned with myrtle

Myrtō·um mar·e (genit: **Myrtō·ī mar·is**) n sea between the Peloponnesus and the Cyclades

myrt·um -ī n myrtle berry

myrt·us -ūs or **-ī** f myrtle

Mўsĭ·us -a -um adj Mysian; f Mysia (country in N.W. Asia Minor)

myst·a or **myst·ēs -ae** m priest of the mysteries of Ceres; an initiate

mystagōg·us -ī m initiator

mystēr·ium -iī or **-ī** n secret religion, secret service, secret rite or worship, divine mystery; secret; **mysteria facere** to hold service; **mysteria Romana** festival of Bona Dea

myst·ēs -ae m priest of the mysteries of Ceres

mystic·us -a -um adj mystic

Mytilēn·ae -ārum f pl or **Mytilēn·ē -ēs** f capital of the island of Lesbos

N

Nabatae·us -a -um adj Nabataean; Arabian, Eastern, Oriental; m pl Nabataeans; f Nabataea (ancient Arab kingdom S.E. of Palestine)

nablĭ·ium -iī or **-ī** n Phoenician harp (an instrument of ten or twelve strings, played with both hands)

nactus pp of **nanciscor**

Naevĭān·us -a -um adj of Naevius

Naev·ius -iī or **-ī** m Cn. Naevius (early Roman dramatic and epic poet, c. 270-200 B.C.)

naev·us -ī m body mole

Nāi·as -ădis or **Nā·is -ĭdis** or **-ĭdos** f Naiad, water nymph

nam conj for; for instance; (transitional) now, but now, on the other hand

namque conj for, for in fact, for no doubt, for surely

nanciscor nanciscī nanctus sum or **nactus sum** vt to get by accident (esp. by good luck), obtain, chance upon, find

nān·us -ī m dwarf, midget

Napae·ae -ārum f pl dell nymphs

nāp·us -ī m turnip

Narb·ō -ōnis m town in S. Gaul, from which the province of Narbonese Gaul took its name

Narbōnens·is -e adj Narbonese

narciss·us -ī m narcissus

Narciss·us -ī m son of Cephisus and the nymph Liriope, who was changed into a flower of the same name; powerful freedman of Claudius

nard·um -ī n or **nard·us -ī** f nard, spikenard (fragrant ointment)

nār·is -is f nostril; f pl nostrils, nose; **acutae nares** keen perception; **homo naris obesae** dimwit;

naribus dūcere to smell; **naribus uti** (with **ad** + *acc*) to turn up the nose at

narrābil·is -e *adj* to be told

narrāti·ō -ōnis *f* narration, narrative

narrātiuncŭl·a -ae *f* short story

narrāt·or -ōris *m* narrator, historian

narrāt·um -ī *n* account, statement, narrative

narrāt·us -ūs *m* narration, narrative

narr·ō -āre *vt* to tell, relate, narrate, recount; to describe; *vi* to speak, tell; **bene narrare** (with **dē** + *abl*) to tell good news about (*someone*); **male narrare** (with **dē** + *abl*) to tell bad news about (*someone*); **ti- bi narro** I'm telling you, I assure you

narthēc·ium -iī or **-ī** *n* medicine chest

narus see **gnarus**

Nārycī·us -a -um *adj* of Naryx (*city of the Opuntian Locrians and birthplace of Ajax Oileus*)

nascor nascī nātus sum or **gnā- tus sum** *vi* to be born; to rise, begin, originate, be produced, spring forth, proceed, grow, be found; **post homines natos** since the beginning of the world

Nās·ō -ōnis *m* Publius Ovidius Naso (*Roman poet, born in Sulmo, in central Italy, 43 B.C.-c. 17 A.D.*)

nass·a -ae *f* wicker trap (*for catching fish*); (fig) trap

nassitern·a -ae *f* large water jug

nastur·cium -ciī or **-ī** *n* garden cress

nās·us -ī *m* or **nās·um -ī** *n* nose; sense of smell; sagacity; anger; scorn; nozzle, spout

nāsūtē *adv* sarcastically

nāsūt·us -a -um *adj* big-nosed; satirical, sarcastic

nāt·a or **gnāt·a -ae** *f* daughter

nātālicī·us -a -um *adj* birthday, natal; *n pl* birthday party

nātāl·is -e *adj* of birth, natal; *m* birthday; *m pl* birth, origin, lineage

nat·ans -antis *m* or *f* fish

natātī·ō -ōnis *f* swimming

natāt·or -ōris *m* swimmer

nat·ēs -ium *f pl* buttocks, rear, rear end

nāti·ō -ōnis *f* race, stock; tribe, nation, people; (in contemptuous sense) breed, set

nat·is -is *f* buttock, rump; *f pl* se- nates

nātīv·us -a -um *adj* born; inborn, innate, original; produced by nature, natural; primitive (*words*)

nat·ō -āre *vi* to swim, float; to flow; to swim, overflow, be flooded; (of the eyes) to be glassy; (of birds) to fly, glide; to waver, fluctuate, be uncertain; to hover, move to and fro

nātr·ix -īcis *f* water snake

nātūr·a -ae *f* blood relationship,

natural affinity, birth; nature, natural constitution, quality, property; nature, natural disposition, character; physical nature, world, universe; order of the world, course of things; element, substance; reproductive organs

nātūrāl·is -e *adj* natural; by birth, one's own (*e.g., father, son*); produced by nature; according to nature

nātūrāliter *adv* naturally, by nature

nāt·us or **gnāt·us -a -um** *pp* of **nascor**; *adj* born, made, destined, fit; (with *dat* or with **ad** or **in** or **propter** + *acc*) born for, made for, naturally suited to; (with **annos**) at the age of . . , . . . years old; *e.g.,* **annos vigintī natus** at the age of twenty, twenty years old; **non amplius novem annos na- tus** no more than nine years old; **pro** or **e re nata** under the existing circumstances, as matters stand; *m* son; *m pl* children; *f* see **nata**

nauarch·us -ī *m* captain of a ship, skipper

nauclēric·us -a -um *adj* ship owner's, skipper's

nauclēr·us -ī *m* ship owner, skipper

nauc·um -ī *n* trifle; (mostly in genitive of value with a negative) **non nauci esse** to be of no value, be good for nothing; **non nauci fa- cere** or **non nauci habere** to regard as worthless, regard as good for nothing

naufrag·ium -iī or **-ī** *n* shipwreck; wreck, ruin, destruction; wreckage; **naufragium facere** to be shipwrecked

naufrăg·us -a -um *adj* shipwrecked, wrecked, of the shipwrecked; causing shipwreck, dangerous to shipping; (fig) ruined; *m* shipwrecked person

naul·um -ī *n* fare

naumachi·a -ae *f* simulated sea engagement (*staged as an exercise or for amusement*)

nause·a -ae *f* seasickness; vomiting, nausea

nause·ō -āre *vt* to make (*someone*) throw up; (fig) to belch forth, throw up, utter; *vi* to be seasick; to vomit; to feel squeamish, feel disgust; to cause disgust

nauseŏl·a -ae *f* slight squeamishness

Nausică·a -ae *f* daughter of Alcinous, king of the Phaeacians

naut·a or **nāvit·a -ae** *m* sailor, seaman, mariner; captain

nautē·a -ae *f* nausea; stinking liquid

nautic·us -a -um *adj* nautical, sailors'; *m pl* sailors, seamen

nāvāl·is -e *adj* naval, of ships, of a ship; **castra navalia** camp for the protection of ships; **forma navalis** shape of a ship; *n* tackle, rigging; *n pl* dock, dockyard, shipyard; rigging

nāvicŭl·a -ae f small ship

nāviculārĭ·us -a -um adj of a small ship; m skipper; ship owner; f shipping business

nāvifrăg·us -a -um adj dangerous, treacherous, causing shipwreck

nāvigābĭl·is -e adj navigable

nāvigātĭ·ō -ōnis f sailing, navigation, voyage

nāvig·er -ĕra -ĕrum adj navigable

nāvig·ĭum -ĭī or -ī n ship

nāvig·ō -āre vt to sail across, navigate; vi to sail, put to sea; (fig) to swim

nāv·is -is f ship; navem appellere or navem terrae applicare to land a ship; navem deducere to launch a ship; navem solvere to set sail; navem subducere to beach a ship; navis aperta ship without a deck; navis longa battleship; navis mercatoria merchant vessel; navis oneraria transport, cargo ship; navis praetoria flagship; navis tecta ship with a deck

nāvĭt·a -ae m sailor, seaman; captain

nāvĭt·ās -ātis f energy, zeal

nāviter adv energetically, zealously, actively, busily; utterly, completely

nāv·ō -āre vt to do or perform energetically, conduct or prosecute with vigor; operam navare to act energetically; operam navare (with dat) to render assistance to

nāv·us or gnāv·us -a -um adj energetic, busy

Nax·os -ī f largest island of the Cyclades, famous for its wine and as the place where Theseus abandoned Ariadne

nē interj (always with a personal or demonstrative pronoun) indeed, certainly, surely; adv not; ne . . . quidem (to negate emphatically the words placed between) not even; (in negative commands) not; ne time-te do not fear; conj that not, lest; (after verbs and nouns denoting fear) lest, that

-ne enclitic (introducing a question and added to the first important word of a clause)

nebŭl·a -ae f mist, fog, vapor; cloud; smoke; darkness, obscurity

nebŭl·ō -ōnis m loafer, good-for-nothing

nebulōs·us -a -um adj foggy

nec or neque adv not; conj nor, and not; nec . . . et not only not . . . but also; nec . . . nec or neque . . . neque neither . . . nor; nec non (introducing an emphatic affirmative) and certainly, and besides

necdum or neque dum conj and not yet, nor yet

necessārĭē or necessārĭō adv necessarily, of necessity

necessārĭ·us -a -um adj necessary, indispensable, needful, requisite; necessary, inevitable; pressing, urgent; connected by blood or friend-

ship, related, closely connected; mf relative, kinsman; friend; n pl necessities

necesse (indecl) adj necessary; unavoidable, inevitable; requisite; necesse esse to be necessary; necesse habere to regard as necessary, regard as inevitable

necessĭt·ās -ātis f necessity, inevitableness, compulsion, urgency; requirement; privation, want; relationship, friendship, connection

necessitūd·ō -ĭnis f necessity, need, want, distress; relationship, bond, connection, relationship, friendship; f pl ties of friendship; relatives, friends, personal connections

necessum (indecl) adj necessary, requisite; inevitable

necne adv or not

necnōn adv also, besides, moreover

nec·ō -āre vt to kill, murder, slay, destroy

necopīn·ans -antis adj unaware

necopīnātō adv unexpectedly, by surprise

necopīnāt·us -a -um adj unexpected

necopīn·us -a -um adj unexpected; unsuspecting, careless, off guard

nect·ar -ăris n nectar (drink of the gods); nectar (as term for honey, milk, wine, poetry, sweetness, etc.)

nectarĕ·us -a -um adj of nectar, sweet or delicious as nectar

nectō nectĕre nexŭī or nexī nexum vt to tie, connect, fasten together, join; to weave; to clasp; to imprison, fetter; to devise, contrive; (fig) to attach, affix

nēcŭbi conj lest anywhere, so that nowhere

nēcunde conj lest from anywhere

nēdum adv (after an expressed or implied negative) much less, still less; (after an affirmative) not to say, much more

nefand·us -a -um adj unspeakable, impious, abominable

nefārĭē adv impiously, abominably

nefārĭ·us -a -um adj impious, abominable, criminal; n crime, criminal act

nefās (indecl) n crime, wrong, wickedness, act contrary to divine law, sin; criminal, monster; per omne fas ac nefas by hook or by crook

nefast·us -a -um adj forbidden, unlawful; impious, irreligious; criminal; unlucky, inauspicious; n crime, outrage

negātĭ·ō -ōnis f denial

negĭt·ō -āre vt to deny, refuse, turn down

neglectĭ·ō -ōnis f neglect

neglectus pp of neglego

neglect·us -ūs m neglect

neglĕg·ens -entis adj negligent, careless, indifferent

neglegenter adv carelessly

neglegentĭ·a -ae f negligence, carelessness, neglect

neg·lĕgō -legĕre -lexī -lectum vt

to be unconcerned about; to neglect, disregard, overlook; to slight, despise

neg·ō -āre vt to deny, refuse, decline; vi to say no; to refuse

negōtiāl·is -e adj business

negōtĭ·ans -antis m business man

negōtiātĭ·ō -ōnis f banking, banking business

negōtiāt·or -ōris m business man; banker; salesman, dealer

negōtĭŏl·um -ī n minor matter

negōti·or -ārī -ātus sum vi to do business, do banking; to trade

negōtiōs·us -a -um adj business; busy

negōt·ium -iī or **-ī** n business, occupation, employment; matter, thing, affair; situation; trouble; banking, money lending; trade, commerce; **negotium suum** private affairs; **quid negoti est?** what's the matter?; **quid negoti tibi est?** what business is it of yours?

Nēl·eus -ĕī or **-ĕos** m son of Neptune and the nymph Tyro, king of Pylos, and father of Nestor

Nemae·us -a -um adj Nemean

Nemĕ·a -ae or **Nemĕ·ē -ēs** f town in Argolis, where Hercules slew the Nemean lion and founded the Nemean games

Nemĕ·a -ōrum n pl Nemean games (held every two years at Nemea)

Nemĕs·is -is or **-ios** f goddess of vengeance

nēm·ō -ĭnis m or f no one, nobody; **nemo quisquam** nobody at all; **nemo unus** no single person, no one by himself; **non nemo** someone, many a one

nemorāl·is -e adj sylvan

nemorens·is -e adj of a grove; of Diana's grove

nemoricultr·ix -īcis f denizen of the forest

nemorivăg·us -a -um adj roaming the woods

nemorōs·us -a -um adj wooded; covered with foliage

nempe adv (in confirmation or in sarcasm) certainly, to be sure, of course, naturally; (in questions) do you mean?

nem·us -ŏris n grove; sacred grove; plantation

nēnĭ·a or **naenĭ·a -ae** f funeral dirge; doleful song; incantation; ditty

neō nēre nēvī nētum vt to spin; to weave

Neoptolĕm·us -ī m Pyrrhus, the son of Achilles

nep·a -ae f scorpion; crab

Nephelē·is -idos f Helle (daughter of Nephele and Athamas)

nep·ōs -ōtis m grandson; nephew; descendant; spendthrift

Nep·ōs -ōtis m Cornelius Nepos (Roman biographer and friend of Cicero, c. 100- c. 25 B.C.)

nepōtŭl·us -ī m little grandson

nept·is -is f granddaughter

Neptūnĭ·us -a -um adj of Neptune

Neptūn·us -ī m Neptune (god of the sea and brother of Jupiter)

nēquam (indecl) adj worthless, bad, good for nothing

nēquāquam adv by no means, not at all

neque see nec

nequēdum see necdum

nequ·ĕō -īre -īvī or **-ĭ -ĭtum** vi to be unable; (with inf) to be unable to, not to be able to, be incapable of; **nequit** (with quin) it is impossible to

nēquĭ·or -us adj (comp of nequam) worse, more worthless

nēquiquam or **nēquicquam** adv pointlessly, for nothing, to no purpose; without good reason; with impunity

nēquissĭm·us -a -um adj (superl of nequam) worst, most worthless

nēquĭter adv worthlessly, wretchedly, miserably, vilely, wrongly

nēquitĭ·a -ae or **nēquitĭ·ēs -ēī** f worthlessness, vileness, wickedness

Nērē·is -ĭdis f sea nymph, Nereid (daughter of Nereus, of whom there were 50)

Nēr·eus -ĕī or **-ĕos** m son of Oceanus and Tethys, husband of Doris and father of the Nereids; sea

Nērīn·ē -ēs f daughter of Nereus

Nēritĭ·us -a -um adj of Neritos; **Neritius dux** Ulysses

Nērĭt·os or **Nērĭt·us -ī** m island near Ithaca

Nēr·ō -ōnis m Nero Claudius Caesar (Roman emperor 38-68 A.D.; reigned 54-68 A.D.)

Nērōniān·us -a -um adj Nero's, Neronian

Nerv·a -ae m M. Cocceius Nerva (Roman emperor 30-98 A.D., reigned 96-98 A.D.)

nervōsē adv strongly, vigorously

nervōs·us -a -um adj sinewy, brawny, strong

nervŭl·us -ī m a little vigor

nerv·us -ī m sinew, tendon, muscle; string, wire; bowstring; thong, strap; penis; leather covering of a shield; prison; power, vigor, strength, nerve, force, energy

nesc·ĭō -īre -īvī or **-ĭ -ĭtum** vt not to know, be ignorant of, be unacquainted with; (with inf) a not to know how to; b to be unable to; **nescio modo** somehow or other; **nescio quando** sometime or other; **nescio quid** something or other; **nescio quis** someone or other

nescĭ·us -a -um adj unaware, not knowing, ignorant; unknown; (with genit or de + abl) ignorant of, unaware of; (with inf) not knowing how to, unable to, incapable of; (with acc & inf) unaware that, not knowing that

Ness·us -ī m centaur who was slain by Hercules with a poisoned arrow for trying to molest his wife

Nest·or -ōris m son of Neleus, king

of Pylos, and wise counselor of the Greeks at Troy

neu see **neve**

neut·er -ra -rum *adj* neither (*of two*); neuter; of neither sex; *pron* neither one (*of two*)

neutiquam or **ne utiquam** *adv* on no account, in no way

neutrō *adv* to neither side

neutrŭbi *adv* in neither the one place nor the other

nēve or **neu** *conj* or not, and not; **neve . . . neve** or **neu . . . neu** neither . . . nor

nex necis *f* death, murder, slaughter

nexil·is -e *adj* tied up, bound together

nex·um -ī *n* slavery for debt; voluntary servitude for debt

nex·us -a -um *pp* of **necto**; *m* free person who has pledged his person as security for a debt

nex·us -ūs *m* grip; bond; enslavement for debt

nī *adv* not; **quid nī?** why not?; *conj* (in prohibition or negative purpose) that not; (in negative condition) if not, unless

nīcētēr·ium -ĭī or **-ī** *n* prize

nic·ō -ĕre -ī *vi* to beckon

nict·ō -āre *vi* to wink; (with *dat*) to wink at

nīdāment·um -ī *n* material for a nest

nīd·or -ōris *m* steam, vapor, smell

nīdŭl·us -ī *m* little nest

nīd·us -ī *m* nest; (*fig*) home; *m pl* nestlings, brood

nig·er -ra -rum *adj* black; swarthy, dark; dismal; unlucky, ill-omened; black, bad (*character*); malicious

nigr·ans -antis *adj* black, dusky

nigr·escō -escĕre -ŭī *vi* to grow black, grow dark

nigr·ō -āre *vi* to be black

nigr·or -ōris *m* blackness, darkness

nihil or **nīl** (indecl) *n* nothing; (with *genit*) no, not a bit of; **nihil boni** no good, not a bit of good; **nil est** it is pointless, it's no good

nihil or **nīl** *adv* not, not at all, in no respect

nihilōmĭnus *adv* nonetheless, nevertheless, just the same; no less

nihil·um or **nīl·um -ī** *n* nothing; **de nihilo** for nothing, for no reason; **nihil est quod, cur,** or **quam ob rem** there is no reason why; **nihili esse** to be worthless, be of no value; **nihili facere** or **nihili pandere** to consider as worthless; **nihilo minus** nonetheless, nevertheless; **nihil quicquam** nothing whatever, nothing at all; **pro nihilo putare** to regard as worthless

nīl see **nihil**

Nīliăc·us -a -um *adj* Nile, of the Nile, Egyptian

Nīligĕn·a -ae *masc & fem adj* born on the Nile, Egyptian

nīlum see **nihilum**

Nīl·us -ī *m* Nile River; god of the Nile

nimbāt·us -a -um *adj* light, frivolous

nimbĭf·er -ĕra -ĕrum *adj* stormy

nimbōs·us -a -um *adj* stormy, rainy

nimb·us -ī *m* cloud; storm cloud, black rain cloud; rainstorm, heavy shower, pouring rain; (fig) storm

nimiō *adv* far, much; **nimio plus** far more, much more

nimīrum *adv* no doubt, certainly; surely; (ironically) doubtless, of course

nimis *adv* very, very much, too much; **non nimis** not particularly

nimium *adv* too, too much; very, very much; **nimium quam** or **nimium quantum** very much indeed, ever so much, very; **nimium quam es barbarus** you are as barbarous as can be; **non nimium** not particularly, not very much

nimi·us -a -um *adj* very much, very great; too great, excessive; *n* excess, abundance

ningit (or **ninguit**) **ningĕre ninguit** (or **ninxit**) *v impers* it is snowing

ningu·ēs -ium *f pl* snowflakes, snow

Nin·us -ī *m* son of Belus, the first king of Assyria, husband of Semiramis, and builder of Nineveh; Nineveh

Nĭŏb·a -ae or **Nĭŏb·ē -ēs** *f* daughter of Tantalus and wife of Amphion, who was turned into a weeping mountain after Apollo and Diana had slain her seven sons and seven daughters

Nīr·eus -ĕī or **-ĕos** *m* handsomest Greek at Troy

Nīsē·is -ĭdis *f* Scylla (*daughter of Nisus*)

nisi *conj* unless, if not; except, but

nīsus *pp* of **nitor**

nīs·us or **nix·us -ūs** *m* pressure, effort; labor pain (*of childbirth*); soaring, flight; posture; **nisu immotus eodem** immobile in the same posture

Nīs·us -ī *m* king of Megara, father of Scylla, who betrayed her country by cutting off his purple lock of hair; friend of Euryalus in the Aeneid

nītēdŭl·a -ae *f* dormouse

nit·ens -entis *adj* shining; bright; brilliant; beautiful, glowing with beauty, glamorous; sleek (*cattle*); greasy

nit·ĕō -ēre -ŭī *vi* to shine, gleam, glisten; to be glamorous; to glow with health; (of animals) to be sleek; to be greasy; to be flashy

nit·escō -escĕre -ŭī *vi* to become shiny, become bright; to begin to glow (*with health or beauty*); to grow sleek

nitĭdē *adv* brightly

nitidiuscŭlē *adv* somewhat more sprucely

nitidiuscŭl·us -a -um *adj* a little more shiny

nitid·us -a -um *adj* shining, bright; glowing (*with health or beauty*); shiny, greasy; glamorous, flashy; smart, spruce, handsome; cultivated, refined; sleek (*cattle*)

nit·or -ōris *m* brightness, sheen; luster; glamour, beauty, healthy glow; elegance (*of style*); dignity (*of character*)

nitor nītī nixus sum (usually in the literal sense) or **nīsus sum** (usually in the figurative sense) *vi* to make an effort, struggle, strain, strive; to be in labor; to push forward, advance, climb, fly; to contend, insist; (with *abl* or **in** + *acc*) to lean on, support oneself on; (with *abl* or **in** + *abl*) (fig) to depend on, rely on, trust to; (with **ad** + *acc*) to aspire to; (with *inf*) to try to, endeavor to, struggle to

nitr·um -ī *n* soda; soap, cleanser

nivāl·is -e *adj* snowy; covered with snow; cold, wintry; (fig) cold, chilly

nivĕ·us -a -um *adj* of snow, snowy, snow; covered with snow; snow-white

nivōs·us -a -um *adj* snowy

nix nivis *f* snow; *f pl* (fig) grey hair

nix·or -ārī -ātus sum *vi* to struggle hard; (with *abl*) to lean upon, rest on

nixus *pp* of **nitor**

nix·us -ūs see **nisus**

nō nāre *vi* to swim, float; to sail; to fly; (of eyes) to be glazed

nōbil·is -e *adj* known; noted; notable, famous; notorious; noble; thorough-bred (*horse*); fine, excellent; *m pl* notables, nobles

nōbilit·ās -ātis *f* fame, renown; noble birth; the nobility; excellence

nōbilit·ō -āre *vt* to make famous; to make notorious

noc·ens -entis *adj* harmful; guilty criminal

noc·ĕō -ēre -uī -itum *vi* (with *dat*) to harm, injure

nocīv·us -a -um *adj* harmful, injurious

noctif·er -ĕrī *m* evening star

noctilūc·a -ae *f* moon

noctivāg·us -a -um *adj* night-wandering

noctū *adv* by night, at night

noctŭ·a -ae *f* owl

noctuābund·us -a -um *adj* traveling by night

noctuīn·us -a -um *adj* of owls

nocturn·us -a -um *adj* nocturnal, of night, at night, by night, night

noctuvigil·us -a -um *adj* awake at night

nocŭ·us -a -um *adj* harmful, injurious

nōd·ō -āre *vt* to tie in a knot, knot, tie

nōdōs·us -a -um *adj* knotty

nōd·us -ī *m* knot; knob, knot (*in wood*); girdle; bond, tie; obligation; knotty point, difficulty, crisis

nōlō nolle nōluī *vt* (with *inf*) to be unwilling to, wish not to, refuse to; *vi* to be unwilling

nom·as -ădis *m* or *f* nomad; Numidian

nōm·en -ĭnis *n* name; gentile name (*e.g., Julius, as distinct from the praenomen*); race, stock; title; noun; bond, claim, debt; debtor; name, fame, reputation; title, pretext, pretense, excuse, account, reason, responsibility, authority, sake, behalf; mere name (*as opposed to reality*); **aetātis nomine** on the pretext of age, on account of age; **eo nomine** on that account; **nomen dare** or **nomen profiteri** to enlist (*in the army*); **nomen deferre** (with *genit*) to bring an accusation against, accuse (*someone*); **nomen dissolvere** or **nomen expedire** or **nomen solvere** to liquidate an account, pay a debt; **nomina sua exigere** to collect one's debt

nōmenclāt·or -ōris *m* name caller (*slave who accompanied his master and identified those whom they met, esp. during a political campaign*)

nōminātim *adv* by name, expressly

nōminātĭ·ō -ōnis *f* nomination for office

nōminātīv·us -a -um *adj & m* nominative

nōmināt·us -a -um *adj* renowned

nōminit·ō -āre *vt* to usually call

nōmin·ō -āre *vt* to name, call by name; to mention by name; to make famous; to nominate for an office; to denounce, arraign

nomism·a -ătis *n* coin

nōn *adv* not; no; by no means

Nōn·ae -ārum *f pl* Nones (*fifth day in all months, except March, May, July, and October, in which they occurred on the seventh*)

nōnāgēnsĭm·us or **nōnāgēsĭm·us -a -um** *adj* ninetieth

nōnāgĭens or **nōnāgĭēs** *adv* ninety times

nōnāgintā (indecl) *adj* ninety

nōnān·us -a -um *adj* of the ninth legion; *m* soldier of the ninth legion

nōnārĭ·a -ae *f* prostitute

nondum *adv* not yet

nongent·ī -ae -a *adj* nine hundred

nonne *adv* is it not?; (in indirect questions) whether not; **nonne vidēs?** don't you see?, you see, don't you?; **quaeritur nonne ire statim velis** the question is whether you do not wish to go at once

nonnull·us -a -um *adj* some, many a; **nonnulli** some, some people

nonnunquam *adv* sometimes

nonnusquam *adv* in some places

nōn·us -a -um *adj* ninth; *f* ninth hour

nōn·us decĭm·us -a -um *adj* nineteenth

Nōric·us -a -um *adj* of Noricum; *n* region between the Danube and the Alps

norm·a -ae *f* square (*carpenter's tool*); (fig) rule, standard

nōs *pron* we; us

noscĭt·ō -āre *vt* to examine closely, observe; to recognize, know

noscō noscĕre nōvī nōtum or **gnoscō — gnōvī gnōtum** *vt* to get to know, become acquainted with, recognize, learn; to examine, inquire into; to approve of; **novisse** to have become acquainted with, (*and therefore*) to know

nosmet *pron* (emphatic form of **nōs**) we ourselves; us

nost·er -ra -rum *adj* our, our own; *pron* ours; **noster** our friend; **nostri** our men, our soldiers, our side

nostr·ās -ātis *adj* native, of our country

not·a -ae *f* note, mark, sign; letter, character; note, short letter; punctuation mark; brand (*of wine*); marginal note, critical mark; tattoo marks, brand; distinctive mark, distinctive quality; stamp (*on coin*); brand, stigma; nickname; black mark (*against one's name*); reproach, disgrace; nod, sign, beck; *f pl* letters of the alphabet; shorthand notes; memoranda

notābĭl·is -e *adj* notable, noteworthy, memorable; notorious

notābĭlĭter *adv* notably, remarkably; perceptibly

notār·ĭus -ĭī or **-ī** *m* stenographer; secretary

notātĭ·ō -ōnis *f* notation, mark; black mark (*of a censor*); choice; observation; etymology

notāt·us -a -um *adj* noted, distinguished

nŏt·escō -escĕre -ŭī *vi* to become known

noth·us -a -um *adj* bastard, illegitimate; mongrel; not genuine, phoney

nōtĭ·ō -ōnis *f* acquaintance; (law) investigation; (fig) notion, idea

nōtĭtĭ·a -ae or **nōtĭtĭ·ēs -ēī** *f* acquaintance; fame; notion, conception

not·ō -āre *vt* to mark; to mark out; to note, mark, observe; to write down; to record; to take down in shorthand; to mark critically; to brand; to indicate, denote; to brand, reproach

not·us or **not·os -ī** *m* south wind; wind

nōt·us -a -um *pp* of **nosco**; *adj* known, well known; notorious; familiar, customary; *m pl* acquaintances

novācŭl·a -ae *f* razor

novāl·is -is *f* or **novāl·e -is** *n* field plowed for the first time, reclaimed land; cultivated field; fallow land; crops

novātr·ix -īcis *f* renovator, renewer (*female*)

novē *adv* newly, in an unusual manner

novell·us -a -um *adj* new, fresh, young, newly acquired

novem (indecl) *adj* nine

Novemb·er or **Novemb·ris -re** *adj* & *m* November

novendĕcim or **novemdĕcim** (indecl) *adj* nineteen

novendĭāl·is or **novemdĭāl·is -e** *adj* nine-day; occurring on the ninth day

novensĭl·ēs -ĭum *m pl* new gods (*introduced from abroad*)

novēn·ī -ae -a *adj* in groups of nine, nine each, nine

noverc·a -ae *f* stepmother

novercāl·is -e *adj* stepmother's, of a stepmother, like a stepmother

novīcĭ·us -a -um *adj* new, brand new

novĭens or **novĭēs** *adv* nine times

novissĭmē *adv* very recently, of late

novissĭm·us -a -um *adj* latest, last, most recent; **novissimum agmen** (mil) the rear; **novissima verba** parting words; *m pl* (mil) rear guard

novĭt·ās -ātis *f* newness, novelty; rareness, strangeness, unusualness; novelty of high rank, recently acquired rank

nov·ō -āre *vt* to make new, renovate, renew; to repair, fix; to refresh; to change, alter; to invent, coin (*words*); **res novare** to bring about a revolution

nov·us -a -um *adj* new, young, fresh, novel; strange, unusual, unheard-of; recent, modern; new, unused; inexperienced; renewed, revived; **homo novus** self-made man (*first man of a family to reach a curule office*); **res novae** political innovations, revolution; *n* news

nox noctis *f* night; night activity; sleep; death; darkness, blindness; mental darkness, ignorance; gloom; **ad multam noctem** till late at night; **nocte** or **de nocte** at night, by night; **noctem et dies** night and day; **sub noctem** at nightfall

nox·a -ae *f* harm, injury; offense, fault, guilt, responsibility; punishment

noxĭ·us -a -um *adj* harmful, noxious; guilty; (with *genit* or *abl*) guilty of; *f* harm, damage, injury; blame, guilt; fault, offense; **in noxia esse** to be at fault

nūbēcŭl·a -ae *f* little cloud; gloomy expression

nūb·ēs -is *f* or **nūb·is -is** *m* cloud; gloom; veil

nūbĭf·er -ĕra -ĕrum *adj* cloudy; cloud-capped (*mountain*); cloud-bringing (*wind*)

nūbĭgĕn·a -ae *adj masc* or *fem* born of clouds

nūbĭl·is -e *adj* marriageable

nūbĭl·us -a -um *adj* cloudy; cloud-bringing (*wind*); troubled; dark, gloomy, melancholy

nūbō nūbĕre nupsī nuptum *vi* (of women) to marry; (with *dat*) to marry (*a man*), be married to (*a man*)

nucifrangĭbŭl·um -ī n (colloquially of teeth) nutcracker

nuclĕ·us -ī m nut; kernel, stone (of fruit)

nudĭus adv it is now the . . . day since, e.g., nudĭus tertĭus dedĭ ad tē epistolam it is now the third day since I mailed you a letter; ago, e.g., nudĭus tertĭus decĭmus twelve days ago

nūd·ō -āre vt to strip, bare; to lay bare, uncover; (mil) to leave undefended; (with abl) to divest of

nūd·us -a -um adj nude, naked; lightly clothed; bare, empty; defenseless; poor, needy; bare, mere, simple, sole, only; (with genit or abl or with ab + abl) bare of, without, stripped of, destitute of, deprived of

nūg·ae -ārum f pl trifles, nonsense; good-for-nothing, a nobody

nūgāt·or -ōris m joker; fibber, babbler, braggart

nūgātōrĭ·us -a -um adj worthless, useless, nonsensical

nūg·ax -ācis adj nonsensical

nūgĭvend·us -ī m dealer in women's apparel

nūg·or -ārī -ātus sum vi to talk nonsense; (with dat) to trick, cheat

null·us -a -um adj no; (coll) not, not at all; non-existent, of no account; pron none

num adv (of time, used only with etiam) now, e.g., etiam num now, even now, still; interrog particle (expecting negative answer) surely not, really, actually, e.g., num ista est nostra culpa? is that really our fault?, that isn't our fault, is it?; conj (in indirect questions) whether

Num·a -ae m Numa Pompilius (second king of Rome)

numcŭbī adv ever?, at any time?

numell·a -ae f shackle

nūm·en -ĭnis n nod; will, consent; divine will; divine power, divinity; deity, godhead

numerābĭl·is -e adj easily counted, few in number

numerāt·um -ī n ready cash

numĕrō adv at the right time, just now; too soon

numĕr·ō -āre vt to number, count; to pay out (money); to consider; to enumerate, mention; to relate, recount; to reckon as one's own, possess, own

numerōsē adv rhythmically

numerōs·us -a -um adj numerous; rhythmical

numĕr·us -ī m member; (mil) division, troop; mere cipher; class, category; rank, position; estimation, regard; rhythm, meter, verse; quantity, measure; portion (of work), part, function; aliquo numero esse to be of some account; in numero haberī (with genit) to be regarded as, be ranked among; nul-

lo numero esse to be of no account; m pl mathematics, astronomy

Numĭd·a -ae m Numidian

Numidĭ·a -ae f Numidia (a country of N. Africa)

Numidĭc·us -a -um adj Numidian

Numĭt·or -ōris m king of Alba, brother of Amulius, father of Ilia, and grandfather of Romulus and Remus

nummārĭ·us -a -um adj financial; mercenary

nummāt·us -a -um adj rich; bene nummatus well-off, well-to-do

nummulār·ĭus -ĭī or -ī m banker

nummŭl·ī -ōrum m pl petty cash

numm·us -ī m coin, cash, money; sesterce (small silver coin, worth about a nickel); small sum, trifle, mere nothing; in nummis habere to have in ready cash

numquam or nunquam adv never; non numquam sometimes

numquid adv (to introduce direct question): numquid meministī? do you remember?; (to introduce indirect question): whether

nunc adv now; nowadays, today; now, in view of this, but as matters now stand; nunc . . . nunc at one time . . . at another, once . . . once

nuncupātĭ·ō -ōnis f name, appellation; public pronouncing (of vows)

nuncŭp·ō -āre vt to name, call; to take or make (a vow) publicly; to proclaim publicly

nundĭn·ae -ārum f pl market day; marketplace, market town; trade, sale

nundināl·is -e adj market

nundinātĭ·ō -ōnis f trading, bargaining, buying and selling

nundĭn·or -ārī -ātus sum vt to buy; vi to hold a market, attend a market; to trade; to gather in large numbers

nundĭn·um -ī n market time; trinum nundinum period of three market times, i.e., seventeen days

nunq- = numq-

nuntĭātĭ·ō -ōnis f announcement (by an augur)

nuntĭ·ō -āre vt to announce, declare, report, relate

nuntĭ·us -a -um adj bringing news; m messenger, courier; news, message; order, injunction; nuntium remittere (with dat) to send a letter of divorce to, to divorce (a wife); n pl message, news

nūper adv recently

nūpĕr·us -a -um adj recent

nupt·a -ae f bride, wife

nuptĭ·ae -ārum f pl marriage, wedding

nuptĭāl·is -e adj nuptial, wedding

nur·us -ūs f daughter-in-law; young lady, young married woman

nusquam adv nowhere; on no occasion; for nothing, to nothing; nusquam alibī nowhere else; **nusquam esse** to not exist; **nusquam gentium** nowhere in the world

nūt·ō -āre *vi* to keep nodding; to sway to and fro, totter; to hesitate, waver

nūtrīcāt·us -ūs *m* nursing (*of babies*)

nūtrīc·ius -iī or **-ī** *m* tutor

nūtrīc·ō -āre or **nūtrīc·or -ārī -ātus sum** *vt* to nurse, suckle; to rear, bring up

nūtrīcŭl·a -ae *f* nurse

nūtrīm·en -inis *n* nourishment

nūtrīment·um -ī *n* nutriment, nourishment, support; fuel (*for fire*)

nūtr·iō -īre -īvī or **-iī -ītum** *vt* to nurse, suckle, nourish, feed; to rear, bring up, support, maintain, foster; to take care of, attend to; to cherish, cultivate

nūtr·īx -īcis *f* nurse; *f pl* breasts

nūt·us -ūs *m* nod; hint, intimation; will, pleasure, command; gravity

nux nucis *f* nut; nut tree, almond tree; **nuces relinquere** (fig) to put away childish things

Nyctē·is -ĭdis *f* Antiope (*wife of Lycus, the king of Thebes, and mother of Amphion and Zethus*)

Nyct·eus -ĕī or **-ĕos** *m* father of Antiope

nymph·a -ae or **nymph·ē -ēs** *f* bride; nymph (*demi-goddesses who inhabit fountains, rivers, sea, woods, and mountains*); water

Nȳs·a -ae *f* mythical birthplace of Bacchus

Nȳsae·us or **Nȳsī·us -a -um** *adj* of Nysa, Nysaean

Nȳs·eus -ĕī or **-ĕos** *m* Bacchus

Nȳsigĕn·a -ae *m* native of Nysa

O

ō *interj* oh!

Oax·ēs or **Oax·is -is** *m* river in Crete

ob *prep* (with *acc*) before, in front of; on account of, because of; for the sake of, in the interest of; in return for, instead of; in proportion to, balanced against; **ob rem** to the purpose, usefully, profitably; **quam ob rem** wherefore, accordingly

obaerāt·us -a -um *adj* deeply in debt; *m* debtor

obambŭl·ō -āre *vt* to prowl all over, prowl about (*e.g., the city*); *vi* to walk about, wander, prowl about; (with *dat*) to prowl about near; (with **ante** + *acc*) to wander around in front of

obarm·ō -āre *vt* to arm

obăr·ō -āre *vt* to plow up, plow over

obbrūtesc·ō -ĕre *vi* to grow dull

obc- = occ-

ob·dō -dĕre -dĭdī -dĭtum *vt* to close, lock; to expose

obdorm·īo -īre -īvī or **-iī -ītum** *vi* to fall asleep

obdorm·īscō -īscĕre -īvī — vi to fall asleep

ob·dūcō -dūcĕre -duxī -ductum *vt* to put on (*clothes*); to cover, veil, surround, envelop; to hide; to swallow; to pass (*time*); to bring forward as a candidate; to run or dig (*ditch*); (with *dat* of thing protected) to draw or place (*something*) over; (with *dat* or **ad** + *acc*) to pit (*someone or something*) against

obductī·ō -ōnis *f* veiling

obduct·ō -āre *vt* to introduce as a rival

obdūr·escō -escĕre -ŭī *vi* to grow hard, harden; to become insensitive

obdūr·ō -āre *vi* to persist, stick it out

ob·ĕō -īre -īvī or **-iī -ītum** *vt* to go to meet; to travel, travel to, travel over, wander through, traverse, encircle, visit; to run over, review, enumerate (*in a speech*); to undertake, engage in; **diem edictī obīre** to meet one's death; *vi* to go; to pass away, die; to fade, disappear; (*of heavenly bodies*) to go down, set

obequit·ō -āre *vi* to ride up; (with *dat*) to ride up to

oberr·ō -āre *vi* to ramble about, wander around; (with *abl*) **a** to wander about, wander among; **b** to make a mistake on or at

obēs·us -a -um *adj* fat, plump; swollen; crude, coarse

ob·ex -icis *m* or *f* bar, bolt; barrier; obstacle, hindrance

obf- = off-

obg- = ogg-

ob·haerescō -haerescĕre -haesī *vi* to get stuck

obīr·ascor -ascī -ātus sum *vi* (with *dat*) to get angry at

obīter *adv* on the way, as one goes along; (fig) in passing, incidentally

obitus *pp* of **obeo**

obit·us -ūs *m* approach, visit; death, passing, ruin, downfall; setting (*of heavenly bodies*)

objac·ĕō -ēre -ŭī *vi* (with *dat*) to lie before, lie at

objectāti·ō -ōnis *f* reproach

object·ō -āre *vt* to oppose; to expose, endanger; to throw in the way; to cause (*delay*); (with *dat*) **a** to expose, to abandon to; **b** to impute to, throw up (*faults*) to, bring a charge of (*e.g., madness*) against, fling (*charges, abuse*) at; (with *dat* & *acc* & *inf*) to throw a hint to (*someone*) that

object·us -a -um *adj* lying in the

way, lying in front; (with *dat*) a opposite; **b** exposed to; *n pl* charges, accusations

object·us -ūs *m* interposition; obstacle, hindrance; protection; (with *genit*) protection afforded by

ob·jiciō -jicĕre -jēcī -jectum *vt* to cast, hurl; to present, offer, expose; to hold up as an example; to set up as a defense, use as a defense; (with *dat*) **a** to cast before, throw to, offer to, expose to, set up as a defense against; **b** to throw up (*faults, weaknesses, etc.*) to; **c** to bring upon, inflict on, inspire in; **objici** (with *dat*) to happen to, befall, occur to; **se objicere** (with *dat*) to expose oneself to

objurgāti·ō -ōnis *f* scolding, rebuke

objurgāt·or -ōris *m* critic

objurgātōri·us -a -um *adj* scolding, reproachful

objurgĭt·ō -āre *vt* to keep on scolding

objurg·ō -āre *vt* to scold, rebuke, blame, reprimand; to chastise, correct; to deter

oblangu·escō -escĕre -ŭī *vi* to taper off

oblātrātr·ix -īcis *f* nagging woman, nag

oblātus *pp* of **offero**

oblectām·en -inis *n* delight

oblectāment·um -ī *n* delight, amusement, pastime

oblectāti·ō -ōnis *f* delight, amusement; attraction; (with *genit*) diversion from

oblect·ō -āre *vt* to attract, delight, amuse, divert; to spend (*time*) pleasantly; **se oblectare** to amuse oneself, enjoy oneself

ob·līdō -līdĕre -līsī -līsum *vt* to crush; to squeeze together, strangle

obligāti·ō -ōnis *f* binding, pledging, obligation

obligāt·us -a -um *adj* obliged, under obligation; (with *dat*) (vow) made to

oblĭg·ō -āre *vt* to tie up, bandage; to bind, oblige, put under obligation, make liable; to hamper, tie down; to embarrass; to mortgage; **fidem obligare** to pledge one's word; **obligari** (with *abl*) **a** to be guilty of; **b** to be obliged to, compelled to

oblĭm·ō -āre *vt* to cover with mud; to dissipate, squander

ob·līnō -linĕre -lēvī -litum *vt* to smear; (fig) to smear, defile; (fig) to overload

oblīquē *adv* sideways; (fig) indirectly

obliqu·ō -āre *vt* to turn aside, twist, shift, slant

obliqu·us -a -um *adj* slanting, crosswise; from the side; indirect; sly; envious; downhill (*road*); **obliquus oculus** disapproving look, envious look; *n* side; **ab obliquo** from the side; **per obliquum** across

oblīsus *pp* of **oblīdo**

oblit·escō -escĕre -ŭī *vi* to hide

oblittĕr·ō -āre *vt* to erase; to cancel; (fig) to blot out; **nomina oblitterare** to cancel debts

oblītus *pp* of **oblino**

oblītus *pp* of **obliviscor**

oblivi·ō -ōnis *f* oblivion; forgetting; forgetfulness

obliviōs·us -a -um *adj* forgetful, oblivious; (wine) causing forgetfulness

ob·līviscor -līviscī -lītus sum *vt* to forget; *vi* to forget; (with *genit*) to forget, neglect, disregard, be indifferent to

obliv·ium -iī or **-ī** *n* forgetfulness, oblivion

oblocūt·or -ōris *m* contradictor

oblong·us -a -um *adj* oblong

ob·lŏquor -lŏquī -locūtus sum *vt* (with *dat*) **a** to interrupt; **b** to answer (*in argument*), contradict; **c** to speak against, abuse, rail at; **d** to accompany (*in music*), sing to

obluct·or -ārī -ātus sum *vi* (with *dat*) to struggle with, fight against, struggle against

oblūd·ō -ĕre *vt* to play jokes on

obmōl·ior -īrī -ītus sum *vt* to make a barricade of

obmurmŭr·ō -āre *vi* (with *dat*) to roar in answer to

obmūt·escō -escĕre -ŭī *vi* to become silent, hush up; to cease

obnāt·us -a -um *adj* growing on (*e.g., the bank of a river*)

ob·nitor -nitī -nixus sum *vi* to strain, struggle, put on the pressure; (with *dat*) **a** to press against, lean against; **b** to resist, oppose

obnīxē *adv* with all one's might, obstinately

obnix·us -a -um *pp* of **obnitor**; *adj* steadfast, firm, resolute

obnoxiē *adv* guiltily; timidly

obnoxiōsius *adv* more slavishly

obnoxiōs·us -a -um *adj* submissive

obnoxi·us -a -um *adj* liable, addicted, guilty; submissive, servile, obedient; weak, timid; obliged, under obligation, indebted; answerable, responsible; liable, subject, exposed; **obnoxium est** (with *inf*) it is dangerous to

ob·nūbō -nūbĕre -nupsī -nuptum *vt* to veil, cover

obnuntiāti·ō -ōnis *f* announcement (of omens)

obnunti·ō -āre *vi* to make an announcement; to make an announcement that the omens are adverse; to announce bad news

oboedi·ens -entis *adj* obedient; (with *dat* or **ad** + *acc*) obedient to

oboedienter *adv* obediently

oboedienti·a -ae *f* obedience

oboed·iō -īre -īvī or **-iī -ītum** *vi* (with *dat*) to give ear to, listen to, obey

obol·ĕō -ēre -ŭī *vt* to smell of; *vi* to smell

ob·orior -orīrī -ortus sum *vi* to rise, appear

obp- = opp-

ob·rēpō -rēpere -repsī -reptum *vt* to creep up on, sneak up on; *vi* to creep up; (with *dat*) **a** to creep up on, sneak up on, take by surprise; **b** to trick, cheat; (with **in** + *acc*) to steal over; **obrepere ad honorēs** to worm one's way into high positions

obreptō -āre *vi* to sneak up

obrēt·iō -īre -īvī or **-iī -ītum** *vt* to entangle

obrig·escō -escēre -uī *vi* to stiffen; to freeze

obrōd·ō -ēre *vt* to gnaw at

obrōg·ō -āre *vi* (with *dat*) to supersede (*a law*)

ob·ruō -ruere -ruī -rūtum *vt* to cover up, cover, hide, bury; to overwhelm, overthrow; to sink, cover with water, swamp, overflow; to overpower, surpass, obscure, eclipse; *vi* to fall to ruin

obruss·a -ae *f* test, proof

obsaep·iō -īre -sī -tum *vt* to fence in; to block (*road*); (fig) to close, block

obsatur·ō -āre *vt* to sate, cloy; **istius obsaturari** to have enough of him

obscaen- = obscen-

obscaev·ō -āre *vi* to give a bad omen

obscēnē *adv* obscenely

obscēnit·ās -ātis *f* obscenity

obscēn·us -a -um *adj* dirty, filthy; indecent, obscene; ominous

obscūrāti·ō -ōnis *f* obscuring, darkening; disappearance

obscūrē *adv* indistinctly; secretly, imperceptibly

obscūrit·ās -ātis *f* obscurity

obscūr·ō -āre *vt* to obscure, darken; to cover, hide; to veil (*words*); (of love) to blind; to hide, suppress

obscūr·us -a -um *adj* obscure, dark, shady; obscure, lowly, mean; dim, indistinct, unintelligible; secret; reserved; vague, uncertain; gloomy; *n* the dark, darkness; obscurity

obsecrāti·ō -ōnis *f* entreaty; public appeal to the gods

obsecr·ō -āre *vt* to entreat, appeal to, implore

obsecund·ō -āre *vi* (with *dat*) to comply with, humor

obsecūtus *pp* of **obsequor**

obsēp- = obsaep-

obsequ·ens -entis *adj* compliant, obedient; indulgent, gracious (*gods*); (with *dat*) obedient to

obsequenter *adv* compliantly, obsequiously

obsequenti·a -ae *f* obsequiousness

obsequiōs·us -a -um *adj* obsequious

obsequ·ium -iī or **-ī** *n* compliance, indulgence; obedience, allegiance

ob·sequor -sequī -secūtus sum *vi* (with *dat*) to comply with, yield to, give into, gratify, humor

obser·ō -āre *vt* to bolt, bar, lock up

ob·serō -serere -sēvī -situm *vt* to sow or plant thickly; to fill, cover

observ·ans -antis *adj* attentive, respectful; (with *genit*) respectful of, attentive to, careful about

observanti·a -ae *f* regard, respect; (with *genit* or **in** + *acc*) regard for, respect for

observāti·ō -ōnis *f* observation; caution, care

observāt·or -ōris *m* observer

observit·ō -āre *vt* to watch carefully, note carefully

observ·ō -āre *vt* to watch, watch out for, take careful note of; to guard; to observe, keep, obey, comply with; to pay attention to, pay respect to

obs·es -idis *m* or *f* hostage; guarantee

obsessi·ō -ōnis *f* blockade

obsess·or -ōris *m* frequenter, regular visitor; blockader

ob·sīdeō -sīdēre -sēdī -sessum *vt* to sit near or at, remain by or near; to frequent; (mil) to besiege, invest, blockade; to block, choke; to occupy, fill; to look out for, watch closely; to keep guard over

obsidiāl·is -e *adj* for breaking a blockade; **corona obsidiālis** decoration for breaking a blockade

obsidi·ō -ōnis *f* blockade, siege; imminent danger

obsid·ium -iī or **-ī** *n* blockade, siege; imminent danger, great peril; status of hostage

ob·sīdō -sīdere -sēdī -sessum *vt* to besiege, invest, beset, blockade; to take possession of, occupy

obsignāt·or -ōris *m* sealer; witness; **obsignator testamenti** witness to a will

obsign·ō -āre *vt* to seal, seal up; to sign and seal; (fig) to stamp, impress

ob·sistō -sistere -stitī -stitum *vi* (with *dat*) to stand in the way of, block, resist, oppose, disapprove of, forbid

obsitus *pp* of **obsero** (to sow)

obsole·fīō -fīerī -factus sum *vi* to wear out, become spoiled; to become worthless

obsol·escō -escere -ēvī -ētum *vi* to wear out, go out of style, become obsolete, get shabby, lose value

obsolētius *adv* rather shabbily

obsolēt·us -a -um *adj* out of date, old, obsolete, worn out; shabby, threadbare; low, mean, poor

obsōnāt·or -ōris *m* shopper

obsōnāt·us -ūs *m* shopping

obsōn·ium -iī or **-ī** *n* shopping items, food

obsōn·ō -āre or **obsōn·or -ārī -ātus sum** *vt* to shop for; **famem obsonare** to work up an appetite; *vi* to go shopping; to provide food; (with **de** + *abl*) to provide a feast for

obsōn·ō -āre *vi* (with *dat*) to drown out

obsorb·eō -ēre -uī *vt* to gulp down

obstant·ia -ĭum *n pl* obstacles, obstructions

obstĕtr·ix -īcis *f* midwife

obstĭnātē *adv* resolutely, with determination; obstinately, stubbornly

obstĭnātĭ·ō -ōnis *f* resolution, determination; obstinacy, stubbornness

obstĭnāt·us -a -um *adj* resolute, determined, fixed; obstinate, stubborn

obstĭn·ō -āre *vt* to be resolved on, resolve, determine; (with *inf*) to resolve to, determine to; *vi* to be determined, be resolved; (with **ad +** *acc*) to be set on

obstĭpescō see **obstupesco**

obstĭp·us -a -um *adj* bent, bent to one side; bent forwards, bowed; **capite obstipo stare** to stand with head bowed

ob·stō -stāre -stĕtī *vi* to stand in the way, be in the way, raise opposition; (with *dat*) to stand in the way of, oppose, object to, resist, hinder, obstruct; (with **ne, quin, quominus,** or **cur non**) to prevent (*someone*) from

obstrĕp·ō -ĕre -ŭī -ĭtum *vt* to fill with noise, drown out; *vi* to make a racket, make noise; **a** (with *dat*) to shout at, drown out with shouts, interrupt with shouts; **b** (*of the sea*) to resound against

ob·stringō -stringĕre -strinxī -strictum *vt* to shut in, confine, tie up; (fig) to tie up, involve, put under obligation, oblige; **fidem obstringere** (with *dat*) to pledge one's word to; **obstringi** or **se obstringere** (with *abl*) to get involved in, be guilty of

obstructĭ·ō -ōnis *f* obstruction

obstructus *pp of* **obstruo**

obs·trūdō or **ob·trūdō -trūdĕre -trūsī -trūsum** *vt* to gulp down; (with *dat*) to force (*something*) upon, thrust (*something*) upon

ob·strŭō -strŭĕre -struxī -structum *vt* to pile up, block up, stop up; (with *dat*) to block or close (*e.g.*, *the road*) against

obstrūsus *pp of* **obstrudo**

obstŭpe·facĭō -facĕre -fēcī -factum *vt* to astound, astonish, paralyze, stupefy

obstŭp·escō or **obstĭp·escō -escĕre -ŭī** *vi* to be astounded, be struck dumb, be paralyzed

obstŭpĭd·us -a -um *adj* stupefied

ob·sum -esse -fŭī *vi* (with *dat*) to be opposed to, be against; to be prejudicial to, harm; **nihil obest dicere** there is no harm in saying

ob·sŭō -sŭĕre -sŭī -sūtum *vt* to sew on; to sew up

obsurd·escō -escĕre -ŭī *vi* to become deaf; (fig) to turn a deaf ear

ob·tĕgō -tegĕre -texī -tectum *vt* to cover up; to protect; (fig) to conceal, keep secret; **animus sui obtegens** secretive mind

obtemperātĭ·ō -ōnis *f* compliance, obedience

obtempĕr·ō -āre *vi* (with *dat*) to comply with, submit to, obey

ob·tendō -tendĕre -tendī -tentum *vt* to spread, stretch out; to offer as an excuse; to envelop, conceal; **obtendi** (with *dat*) to lie opposite; **obtentā nocte** under cover of darkness

obtentus *pp of* **obtineo**

obtent·us -ūs *m* screen, cover; pretext, pretense

ob·tĕrō -terĕre -trīvī -trītum *vt* to trample on, trample down, crush; (fig) to trample on, crush, degrade, destroy

obtestātĭ·ō -ōnis *f* adjuring, adjuration; solemn entreaty, supplication

obtest·or -ārī -ātum sum *vt* to call as witness; to make an appeal to, implore, entreat

obtex·ō -ĕre -ŭī *vt* to cover, veil

obtĭc·ĕō -ēre *vi* to be silent

obtĭc·escō -escĕre -ŭī *vi* to fall silent, be dumbstruck

ob·tĭnĕō -tĭnēre -tĭnŭī -tentum *vt* to get hold of; to hold on to, keep, maintain, preserve, uphold; to assert, maintain; to obtain, gain, acquire; *vi* to continue

ob·tingō -tingĕre -tĭgī *vi* to happen, occur; (with *dat*) to happen to, befall, occur to

obtorp·escō -escĕre -ŭī *vi* to become numb, become stiff, become insensible

ob·torquĕō -torquēre -torsī -tortum *vt* to twist

obtrectātĭ·ō -ōnis *f* detraction, disparagement

obtrectāt·or -ōris *m* detractor, disparager

obtrect·ō -āre *vt* to treat spitefully, mistreat, disparage; to carp at; *vi* (with *dat*) to detract from, disparage, belittle

obtrītus *pp of* **obtero**

obtrūdō see **obstrudo**

obtrunc·ō -āre *vt* to cut off, cut down; (in battle) to cut down, kill

ob·tŭĕor -tŭērī -tŭĭtus sum *vt* to gaze at, gaze upon; to see clearly

ob·tundō -tundĕre -tŭdī -tūsum or **-tunsum** *vt* to beat, beat on, thump on; to blunt; (fig) to pound away at, stun, deafen, annoy, molest, importune

obturb·ō -āre *vt* to throw into disorder; (fig) to disturb, confuse, distract

obturgesc·ō -ĕre *vi* to begin to swell up

obtūr·ō -āre *vt* to block up, stop up, plug up; **aures obturare** to refuse to listen

obtūsus or **obtunsus** *pp of* **obtundo**; *adj* blunt, dull; (fig) dulled, blurred

obtūt·us -ūs *m* stare, gaze

obumbr·ō -āre *vt* to overshadow, shade; to darken, obscure; to cover, screen

obunc·us -a -um *adj* hooked

obust·us -a -um *adj* singed; hardened in the fire; nipped (*by cold*)

obvāg·ĭō -īre *vi* to whimper

obvall·ō -āre *vt* to fortify

ob·venĭō -venīre -vēnī -ventum *vi* to come up, happen, occur; (*with* *dat*) to fall to the lot of, be alloted to

obvers·or -ārī -ātus sum *vi* to make an appearance, show oneself; (fig) hover

obvers·us -a -um *adj* (*with ad +* *acc*) a turned toward, facing; b inclined to; (*with dat*) engaged in; *m* *pl* opponents

ob·vertō or **ob·vortō -vertĕre** **-vertī -versum** *vt* (*with dat or ad* + *acc*) to turn (*something*) towards or in the direction of; (*with* **in** + *acc*) to turn (*e.g., the soldiers*) to face (*e.g., the enemy*); **obvertī** (*with* **ad** + *acc*) to turn toward

obviam or **ob viam** *adv* (*with dat*) a to meet, in order to meet, in the way of; b (fig) opposed to; **effundī obviam** (*with dat*) to pour out to meet, go out in great numbers to meet; **obviam esse** (*with dat*) a to meet; b to oppose, resist; **obviam ire** (*with dat*) or **obviam procedere** (*with dat*) to go to meet; **obviam obsistere** (*with dat*) to stand in the way of (*someone*); **obviam prodire** or **obviam proficisci** or **obviam progredī** (*with dat*) to go out to meet; **obviam venire** (*with dat*) to go to meet, come to meet

obvigilāt·um -ī *n* vigilance

obvĭ·us -a -um *adj* in the way; exposed, open; accessible (*person*); ready, at hand; (*with dat*) a to meet, so as to meet; b opposed to; c exposed or open to; **obvius esse** (*with dat*) to meet, encounter; **obvius venire** (*with dat*) to come to meet

ob·volvō -volvĕre -volvī -volūtum *vt* to wrap up, cover up

occaecō -āre *vt* to blind, make blind; to darken, obscure; to hide; to numb

occall·escō -escĕre -ŭī *vi* to become thick-skinned; (fig) to become callous

occăn·ō -ĕre -ŭī *vi* to sound the charge

occāsĭ·ō -ōnis *f* occasion, opportunity, good time, chance; pretext; (mil) surprise, raid; **occasionem amittere** to lose the opportunity; **occasionem arripere** to seize the opportunity; **per occasionem** at the right time

occāsiuncŭl·a -ae *f* nice little opportunity

occās·us -ūs *m* setting; sunset; west; (fig) downfall, ruin, death

occātĭ·ō -ōnis *f* harrowing

occāt·or -ōris *m* harrower

oc·cēdō -cēdĕre -cessī -cessum *vi* to go up; **obviam occedere** (*with dat*) to go to meet

occent·ō -āre *vt* to serenade; to satirize in verse

occept·ō -āre *vt* to begin

occĭd·ens -entis *m* the setting sun; west

occīdĭ·ō -ōnis *f* massacre, annihilation; **occidione occidere** to massacre, annihilate, wipe out

oc·cīdō -cīdĕre -cīdī -cīsum *vt* to knock down; to cut down, slay, kill; to murder; to ruin; to pester to death; **se occidere** to commit suicide

oc·cĭdō -cĭdĕre -cĭdī -cāsum *vi* to fall, fall down; (of the sun) to go down, set; to fall, be slain, perish; (of hope, etc.) to fade, die; (fig) to be ruined, be lost; **occidī** I'm finished!

occidŭ·us -a -um *adj* setting; western; (fig) sinking, fading, dying

occill·ō -āre *vt* to smash

oc·cĭnō -cĭnĕre -cecĭnī or **-cinŭī** *vi* to sound ominous

oc·cipĭō -cipĕre -cēpī -ceptum *vt* & *vi* to begin

occipit·ĭum -iī or **-ī** or **occĭp·ut -ĭtis** *n* back of the head

occīsĭ·ō -ōnis *f* massacre; **occisionem facere** to cause a massacre

occīs·or -ōris *m* killer, murderer

occīsus *pp* of **occīdō**

occlāmĭt·ō -āre *vt* to shout at; *vi* to cry out, bawl

oc·clūdō -clūdĕre -clūsī -clūsum *vt* to close up, shut up, lock up; to check, control

occ·ō -āre *vt* to harrow

occŭb·ō -āre *vi* to lie; to rest

occulc·ō -āre *vt* to trample down

occŭl·ō -ĕre -ŭī -tum *vt* to cover; to cover up, hide

occultātĭ·ō -ōnis *f* concealment, hiding

occultāt·or -ōris *m* hideout

occultē *adv* secretly, in concealment

occult·ō -āre *vt* to hide

occult·us -a -um *adj* hidden, secret; reserved (*person*); *n* concealment; secret; **ex occulto** from a place of concealment; secretly

oc·cumbō -cumbĕre -cubŭī -cubĭtum *vt* to fall to, meet; **mortem occumbere** to meet death; *vi* to sink down in death, fall dying; **certae morti occumbere** to meet certain death; **morti occumbere** to fall prey to death; **occumbere** (*with* **per** + *acc*) to die at the hands of

occupātĭ·ō -ōnis *f* occupation (*e.g.,* *of a town*); occupation, employment, business; business engagement, task; job; involvement, concern

occupāt·us -a -um *adj* occupied, busied, engaged, involved

occŭp·ō -āre *vt* to occupy, seize; to win, gain; to attack, strike down; to outstrip, overtake; to fill, take up; to invest, loan, lend; (*with inf*) to be the first to

oc·currō -currĕre -currī or **-cu-**

currī -cursum *vi* to run up; (with *dat*) a to run up to, run to meet, meet; b to rush against, attack; c to resist, oppose, counteract; d to meet, answer, reply to, object to; e to relieve, remedy; f to occur to, suggest itself to, present itself to; g (fig) to run into, run up against, get involved in

occursātĭ·ō -ōnis *f* hustle and bustle; excited welcome; officiousness

occurs·ō -āre *vt* to run to meet; *vi* (with *dat*) a to run to meet, go or come to meet, meet; b to go to meet (*the enemy*), attack, charge, oppose; c (of thoughts) to occur to

occurs·us -ūs *m* meeting; (with *genit*) running into (*someone or something*)

ōceanīt·is -ĭdis *f* ocean nymph

ōcĕăn·us -ī *m* ocean; Oceanus (*son of Caelus and Terra, husband of Tethys, and father of rivers and of ocean nymphs*)

ocell·us -ī *m* eye; gem; darling

ōcĭm·um -ī *n* basil

ōcĭ·or -us *adj* swifter, quicker

ōcĭus *adv* more swiftly, more quickly; sooner; more easily; immediately, on the spot; (with *abl*) rather than; ocius serius sooner or later; quam ocissime as quickly as possible

ocrĕ·a -ae *f* greave, shin guard

ocreāt·us -a -um *adj* wearing shin guards

Octāvĭ·a -ae *f* sister of Augustus, wife of C. Marcellus, and later of M. Antony (64-11 B.C.); daughter of Claudius and wife of Nero (*murdered in 62 A.D.*)

Octāv·ĭus -ĭī or -ī *m* C. Octavius (*Emperor Augustus, who, upon adoption by Julius Caesar, became C. Julius Caesar Octavianus, 63 B.C.-14 A.D.*)

octāvum *adv* for the eighth time

octāv·us -a -um *adj* eighth; octava pars one eighth; *f* eighth hour of the day (*i.e., 2 p.m.*); *n* cum octavo efficere to produce eightfold

octāv·us decĭm·us -a -um *adj* eighteenth

octĭens or octĭēs *adv* eight times

octingentēsĭm·us or octingentensĭm·us -a -um *adj* eight hundredth

octingent·ī -ae -a *adj* eight hundred

octĭp·ēs -ēdis *adj* eight-footed

octō (indecl) *adj* eight

Octōb·er -ris *adj* & *m* October

octōdĕcim (indecl) *adj* eighteen

octōgēnārĭ·us -a -um *adj* & *m* octogenarian

octōgēn·ī -ae -a *adj* eighty each

octōgēsĭm·us or octōgensĭm·us -a -um *adj* eightieth

octōgĭēs or octōgĭens *adv* eighty times

octōgintā (indecl) *adj* eighty

octōjŭg·is -e *adj* eight-team

octōn·ī -ae -a *adj* eight at a time, eight each

octōphŏr·os -on *adj* carried by eight carriers; *n* eight-man litter

octuplicāt·us -a -um *adj* eightfold

octŭpl·us -a -um *adj* eightfold; *n* eightfold fine

octuss·is *m* sum of eight aces

oculāt·us -a -um *adj* having eyes; exposed to view, conspicuous; oculātus testis eyewitness

oculĕ·us -a -um *adj* many-eyed

oculissĭm·us -a -um *adj* dearest

ocŭlĭtus *adv* like one's own eyes, dearly

ocŭl·us -ī *m* eye; eye, bud (*in plants*); sight, vision; mind's eye; apple of the eye; aequis oculis contentedly; altero oculo captus blind in one eye; ante oculos in full view; (fig) obvious; ante oculos ponere to imagine; ex oculis abire to go out of sight, disappear; in oculis in view, in public, in the limelight; in oculis ferre or gestare to hold dear, value; oculos adjicere (with ad + *acc*) to eye; to covet; oculos dejicere (with ab + *abl*) to take one's eyes off; (fig) to lose sight of; oculos pascere (with *abl*) to feast one's eyes on; sub oculis (with *genit*) in the presence of, under the very nose of

ōd·ī -isse *vt* to have taken a dislike to, dislike, hate, be disgusted at

ōdĭōsē *adv* hatefully; unpleasantly

ōdĭōsĭc·us -a -um *adj* odious, unpleasant, annoying

ōdĭōs·us -a -um *adj* odious, unpleasant, annoying

ōd·ĭum -ĭī or -ī *n* dislike, hatred, aversion; object of hatred, nuisance; dissatisfaction, disgust; offensive conduct, insolence; odĭo esse (with *dat*) to be hateful to, be disliked by, be hated by; *n pl* feelings of hatred

od·or or od·ōs -ōris *m* odor, smell, scent; stench, stink; pleasant smell, fragrance, perfume; inkling, suggestion, hint; *m pl* perfume

odōrātĭ·ō -ōnis *f* smell, smelling

odōrāt·us -a -um *adj* fragrant, scented

odōrāt·us -ūs *m* smell, smelling; sense of smell

odōrĭf·er -ĕra -ĕrum *adj* fragrant

odōr·ō -āre *vt* to make fragrant

odōr·or -ārī -ātus sum *vt* to sniff at, scent; to aspire to, aim at; to be sniffing after, search for, investigate; to get a smattering of

odōr·us -a -um *adj* smelly, fragrant; keen-scented

odōs see odor

Odrysĭ·us -a -um *adj* & *m* Thracian

Odyssē·a or Odyssĭ·a -ae *f* the Odyssey

Oeăg·er -rī *m* king of Thrace and father of Orpheus

Oeagrĭ·us -a -um *adj* Thracian

Oebalĭd·ēs -ae *m* male descendant of Oebalus; *m pl* Castor and Pollux

Oebali·us -a -um *adj* Spartan; Tarentine; Sabine; *f* Tarentum (*Spartan colony in S. Italy*)

Oebăl·us -ī *m* king of Sparta, father of Tyndareus, and grandfather of Helen and Clytemnestra

Oedīp·us -ŏdis or **-ī** *m* Oedipus

Oen·eus -ĕī or **-ĕos** *m* king of Calydon, husband of Althaea, and father of Meleager and Deianira

Oenīd·ēs -ae *m* descendant of Oeneus; Meleager; Diomedes (*son of Tydeus*)

Oenomă·us -ī *m* king of Pisa in the Peloponnesus and father of Hippodamia

oenophŏr·um -ī *n* wine-bottle basket

Oenopī·a -ae *f* ancient name of Aegina (*island between Attica and Argolis*)

oenopōl·ium -iī or **-ī** *n* wine shop, tavern

Oenōtri·us -a -um *adj* Oenotrian, Italian; *f* ancient name of S.E. Italy; Italy

oestr·us -ī *m* horsefly, gadfly; fancy, inspiration

oesȳp·um -ī *n* lanolin

Oet·a -ae or **Oet·ē -ēs** *f* Mt. Oete (*mountain in S. Thessaly, on which Hercules died*)

Oetae·us -a -um *adj* Oetean; *m* Hercules

ofell·a -ae *f* bit, morsel

off·a -ae *f* pellet, lump, dumpling; swelling; shapeless mass

offātim *adv* in bits, in little lumps

offectus *pp* of **officio**

of·fendō -fendĕre -fendī -fensum *vt* to bump, bump against, stub, strike, hit; to hit upon, come upon, meet with, bump into, stumble upon, find; to offend, shock, vex, disgust; to hurt (*feelings*); to injure (*reputation*); **nihil offendere** to suffer no damage, receive no injury; *vi* to make a blunder, make a mistake, blunder; to give offense, be offensive; to fail, take a loss, be defeated, come to grief; to run aground; (with *dat* or **in** + *abl*) to hit against, bump against; (with *dat*) to give offense to; (with **in** + *acc*) to take offense at; **terrae offendere** to run aground

offens·a -ae *f* offense, affront, injury; displeasure, resentment, hatred; crime; **offensā** (with *genit*) out of hatred for

offensi·ō -ōnis *f* stubbing; tripping, stumbling; dislike, displeasure, hatred, digust, aversion; discredit, bad reputation, mishap, failure, disaster, accident, defeat; *f pl* offensive acts; feelings of displeasure

offensiuncŭl·a -ae *f* slight displeasure; minor setback; disappointment

offens·ō -āre *vt & vi* to bump

offens·us -a -um *pp* of **offendo**; *adj* offensive, odious; offended, displeased, annoyed

offens·us -ūs *m* bump; shock; offense

offĕrō offerre obtŭlī oblātum *vt* to offer, bring forward, present, show; to cause, occasion; to confer, bestow, inflict; **se offerre** (with *dat*) **a** to meet, encounter; **b** to expose oneself to

offerūment·a -ae *f* (*said humorously of a blow or welt*) present

officīn·a or **opificīn·a -ae** *f* shop, workshop, factory, office

of·ficiō -ficĕre -fēcī -fectum *vi* (with *dat*) to get in the way of, interfere with, oppose, obstruct, be detrimental to, hinder

officiōsē *adv* obligingly, courteously

officiōs·us -a -um *adj* ready to serve, obliging; dutiful, obligatory

offic·ium -iī or **-ī** *n* service, favor, kindness, courtesy; obligation, duty, function, office, part; social obligation, social call, social visit; ceremony, ceremonial observance, attendance; official duty; employment, business, job; sense of duty, conscience; allegiance

of·fīgō -fīgĕre -fīxī -fixum *vt* to fasten down, nail down, drive in

offirmāt·us -a -um *adj* determined, resolute

offirm·ō -āre *vt* **se offirmare** to steel oneself, be determined; *vi* to be determined

offlect·ō -ĕre *vt* to turn (*something*) around

offrēnāt·us -a -um *adj* curbed

offūci·a -ae *f* cosmetic; (*fig*) trick

of·fulgĕō -fulgĕre -fulsī -fulsum *vi* (with *dat*) to shine on

of·fundō -fundĕre -fūdī -fūsum *vt* to pour out; to cover, fill; to eclipse; **offundi** (with *dat*) to pour out over, spread over

oggan·iō -īre -īvī or **-iī -ītum** *vt & vi* to growl

og·gĕrō -gerĕre *vt* to bring, offer, give

Ōgȳg·ēs -is or **Ōgȳg·us -ī** *m* mythical king of Thebes, in whose reign the Deluge occurred

Ōgȳgi·us -a -um *adj* Theban

oh *interj* oh!

ōhē or **ŏhē** *interj* whoa!

oi *interj* (*express complaint*) oh no!

Oïl·eus -ĕī or **-ĕos** *m* king of Locris and father of Ajax the archer

olĕ·a -ae *f* olive; olive tree

oleāgin·us -a -um *adj* olive, of an olive tree

oleāri·us -a -um *adj* oil, of oil; *m* oil merchant

oleast·er -rī *m* oleaster, wild olive tree

ōleni·us -a -um *adj* of Olenus (*town in Achaia and Aetolia*); Achaian, Aetolian

ol·ens -entis *adj* smelling; fragrant; smelly, stinking; musty

ol·ĕō -ēre -ŭī *vt* to smell of, smell like; (*fig*) to betray; *vi* to smell; (with *abl*) to smell of

olĕ·um -ī *n* olive oil, oil; (*fig*) palaestra; **oleum addĕre camino** (*fig*) to pour oil on the fire; **oleum**

et operam perdere to waste time and effort

ol·facĭō -facĕre -fēcī -factum *vt* to smell

olfact·ō -āre *vt* to sniff at

olĭd·us -a -um *adj* smelly

ōlim *adv* once, once upon a time; at the time; for a good while; someday, in the future, hereafter; now and then, at times; ever, at any time

olit- = holit-

olīv·a -ae *f* olive; olive tree; olive wreath; olive branch; olive staff

olīvēt·um -ī *n* olive grove

olīvíf·er -ĕra -ĕrum *adj* olive-producing, olive-growing

olīv·um -ī *n* oil; ointment; (fig) palaestra

oll·a -ae *f* pot, jar

olle or **ollus = ille**

ol·or -ōris *m* swan

olōrīn·us -a -um *adj* swan, of a swan

olus see **holus**

Olympĭ·a -ae *f* Olympia (*region in Elis, in the Peloponnesus, where the Olympian games were held*)

Olympĭ·a -ōrum *n pl* Olympian games

Olympĭăc·us -a -um *adj* Olympian

Olympĭ·as -ădis *f* Olympiad (*period of four years between Olympian games, starting in the year 776 B.C., according to which the Greeks reckoned time*); wife of Philip V of Macedon and mother of Alexander the Great

Olympĭc·us or **Olympĭ·us -a -um** *adj* Olympian

Olympionīc·ēs -ae *m* Olympic victor

Olymp·us -ī *m* Mt. Olympus (*mountain on the boundary of Macedonia and Thessaly, regarded as the home of the gods or heaven*)

omās·um -ī *n* tripe; (fig) paunch, belly

ōm·en -ĭnis *n* omen, sign, token, foreboding; solemn assurance

ōment·um -ī *n* fat; bowels

ōmĭnāt·or -ōris *m* diviner

ōmĭn·or -ārī -ātus sum *vt* to forebode, predict, prophesy

ōmĭnōs·us -a -um *adj* ominous

omiss·us -a -um *adj* remiss, negligent

omitto omittĕre omīsī omissum *vt* to let go, let fall, let go of; to give up, abandon; to omit, pass over, say nothing of; to overlook, disregard

omníf·er -ĕra -ĕrum *adj* all-sustaining

omnigĕn·us -a -um *adj* of every kind

omnimŏdīs or **omnimŏdo** *adv* by all means, wholly

omnīnō *adv* altogether, entirely, wholly; (with numerals) in all; (in generalizations) in general; (in concessions) no doubt, to be sure, yes, by all means, certainly; **haud om-**

nino or **non omnino** not quite, not entirely; absolutely not, not at all; not expressly; **omnino nemo** no one at all

omnipăr·ens -entis *adj* all-producing (*earth*)

omnipŏt·ens -entis *adj* almighty

omn·is -e *adj* all, every; every kind of, every sort of; the whole; *m pl* all, all men, everybody; *n* the universe; *n pl* all things, everything, all nature, all the world

omnitŭ·ens -entis *adj* all-seeing

omnivăg·us -a -um *adj* roving everywhere

omnivŏl·us -a -um *adj* all-craving

Omphăl·ē -ēs *f* Lydian queen whom Hercules had to serve

onăg·er or **onagr·us -ī** *m* wild ass

onăg·os -ī *m* ass driver

Onchesmīt·ēs -ae *m* wind blowing from Onchesmus (*harbor in Epirus*)

onerārĭ·us -a -um *adj* carrying freight; **jumenta oneraria** beasts of burden; **oneraria** or **navis oneraria** freighter, transport

onĕr·ō -āre *vt* to load, load down, burden; (fig) to overload, oppress; (fig) to pile on, aggravate

onerōs·us -a -um *adj* onerous, burdensome, oppressive, heavy

on·us -ĕris *n* load, burden; freight, cargo; burden, difficulty; trouble; tax expense; foetus, embryo; **oneri esse** (with *dat*) to be a burden to

onust·us -a -um *adj* loaded, burdened; filled, full

on·yx -ўchis *m* or *f* onyx; onyx box

opăcĭt·ās -ātis *f* shade, darkness

opăc·ō -āre *vt* to shade

opăc·us -a -um *adj* shady; dark, obscure; *n pl* **per opaca locorum** through shady places

opell·a -ae *f* light work

opĕr·a -ae *f* effort, pains, exertion, work, labor; care, attention; service, assistance; leisure, spare time; laborer, workman, artisan; **operae esse** or **operae pretium esse** to be worthwhile; **operam dare** to take pains, exert oneself, be busied, pay attention, give attention; **operam funeri dare** to attend a funeral; **operam sermoni dare** to listen to a conversation; **operam tonsori dare** to see a barber, get a haircut; **operā meā (tuā,** etc.**)** through my (*your, etc.*) agency, thanks to me (*you, etc.*)

operārĭ·us -a -um *adj* working; *m* working man, workman, laborer; *f* working woman

opercŭl·um -ī *n* lid, cover

operīment·um -ī *n* lid, cover

opĕr·ĭō -īre -ŭī -tum *vt* to cover, cover up; to shut, close; to hide; to overwhelm

opĕr·or -ārī -ātus sum *vi* to work, work hard, take pains; (with *dat*) **a** to work hard at, be busied with, be engaged in; **b** to perform (*religious services*); **c** to attend; **d** to worship

operōsē *adv* with great effort, at great pains

operōs·us -a -um *adj* active, busy, painstaking; troublesome, difficult, elaborate; efficacious, powerful (*drugs*)

opert·us -a -um *pp* of **operio**; *adj* closed; hidden; secret; *n* secret; secret place; **in operto** inside, in secret; *n pl* depths; veiled oracles

opēs see **ops**

ophit·ēs -ae *m* serpentine (*type of marble*)

Ophiūsi·us -a -um *adj* Cyprian; *f* old name of Cyprus

ophthalmi·ās -ae *m* a fish

opīc·us -a -um *adj* boorish

opīf·er -ĕra -ĕrum *adj* helpful

opīf·ex -icis *m* maker, framer, creator; craftsman, mechanic

opificīn·a -ae *f* workshop

ōpili·ō -ōnis *m* shepherd

opīmē *adv* richly, splendidly

opīmit·ās -ātis *f* abundance

opīm·us -a -um *adj* fat, plump; fertile, fruitful; rich, enriched; abundant, copious, plentiful; sumptuous, splendid; lucrative; noble; **spolia opima** armor stripped from one general by another on the field of battle

opīnābil·is -e *adj* conjectural, imaginary

opīnāti·ō -ōnis *f* mere opinion, conjecture, supposition, hunch

opīnāt·or -ōris *m* guesser

opīnāt·us -a -um *adj* supposed, imagined

opīnāt·us -ūs *m* supposition

opīni·ō -ōnis *f* opinion, conjecture, supposition, guess, belief, expectation; general impression, estimation; rumor; reputation, bad reputation; **amplius opinione** beyond expectation, beyond all hopes; **celerius opinione** sooner than expected; **hac opinione ut** under the impression that; **in opinione esse** (with *acc & inf*) to be of the opinion that; **praebere opinionem timoris** to convey the impression of fear; **praeter opinionem** contrary to expectation, sooner than expected; **ut opinio mea est** as I suppose

opīniōs·us -a -um *adj* opinionated

opīn·ō -āre or **opīn·or -ārī -ātus sum** *vt* to suppose, imagine, conjecture; *vi* (parenthetical) to suppose, imagine

opipārē *adv* splendidly, sumptuously

opipăr·us -a -um *adj* splendid, sumptuous, ritzy

opisthogrăph·us -a -um *adj* written on the back

opitŭl·or -ārī -ātus sum *vi* (with *dat*) to bring help to, assist

oport·et -ēre -ŭit *v impers* it is right, it is proper; **me ire oportet** I ought to go, should go

op·pangō -pangĕre -pēgī -pactum *vt* to affix, imprint

oppect·ō -ĕre *vt* to comb off; (coll) to pluck, pick, eat

oppēd·ō -ĕre *vi* (with *dat*) **a** to break wind at; **b** (fig) to deride, mock

opper·ior -īrī -tus sum *vt* to wait for, await; (with **num**) to wait and see whether; *vi* to wait

oppĕt·ō -ĕre -īvī or **-iī -ītum** *vt* to go to meet; **mortem oppetere** to go to meet death, perish, die; *vi* to perish, die

oppidān·us -a -um *adj* of a town, in a town; (disparagingly) provincial; *m pl* townsfolk, townspeople

oppidō *adv* absolutely, quite, completely; (as affirmative answer) exactly

oppidŭl·um -ī *n* small town

oppĭd·um -ī *n* town

oppignĕr·ō -āre *vt* to pledge

oppĭl·ō -āre *vt* to shut up, shut off

op·plĕō -plēre -plēvī -plētum *vt* to fill up, choke up

op·pōnō -pōnĕre -posŭī -positum *vt* to put, place, station; to oppose; to expose, lay bare, open; to wager, mortgage; to bring forward, present, adduce, allege; to reply, respond, object; to compare

opportūnē *adv* opportunely, at the right time

opportūnit·ās -ātis *f* suitableness, fitness, convenience; opportunity, right time; advantage

opportūn·us -a -um *adj* suitable, fit, convenient; advantageous, useful; exposed; **tempore opportunissimo** in the nick of time; *n pl* exposed parts

oppositi·ō -ōnis *f* opposition

opposit·us -a -um *pp* of **oppono**; *adj* opposite; (with *dat*) opposite, across from

opposĭt·us -ūs *m* opposing, opposition

oppressi·ō -ōnis *f* force, violence; violent seizure; suppression, overthrow

oppressiuncŭl·a -ae *f* slight pressure

oppressus *pp* of **opprimo**

oppress·us -ūs *m* pressure

op·prīmō -prīmĕre -pressī -pressum *vt* to press down, weigh down; to pressure, put pressure on; to close, shut; to overwhelm; to put down, suppress, quell; to sink (*a ship*); to subvert, overthrow, crush, subdue, overpower; to conceal, suppress; to seize, catch, surprise

opprobrāment·um -ī *n* disgrace, scandal

opprobr·ium -iī or **-ī** *n* disgrace, scandal, reproach; cause of disgrace; taunt, abuse, abusive word

opprŏbr·ō -āre *vt* to taunt

oppugnāti·ō -ōnis *f* assault; (fig) attack, assault, accusation

oppugnāt·or -ōris *m* assailant, attacker

oppugn·ō -āre *vt* to assault, assail, attack, storm; (fig) to attack, assail

ops opis *f* power, might; help, aid; influence, weight; **opem ferre** (with *dat*) to bring help to, help; *f pl* wealth, resources, means; military or political resources

Ops Opis *f* goddess of abundance, sister and wife of Saturn, and identified with Earth

ops- = obs-

optābil·is -e *adj* desirable

optātī·ō -ōnis *f* wishing, wish

optātō *adv* according to one's wish

optāt·us -a -um *adj* longed-for, desired, welcome; *n* wish, desire

optigō see **obtegō**

optim·ās -ātis *m* aristocrat; *m pl* aristocracy, aristocratic party

optimē or **optŭmē** (*superl* of **bene**) *adv* very well, thoroughly, best; most opportunely, just in time

optim·us or **optŭm·us -a -um** (*superl* of **bonus**) *adj* very good, best; excellent

optī·ō -ōnis *m* helper, assistant; (mil) adjutant

optīv·us -a -um *adj* chosen

opt·ō -āre *vt* to choose, select; to wish for, desire

optum- = optim-

opŭl·ens -entis *adj* opulent, rich

opulentē or **opulenter** *adv* richly, splendidly

opulenti·a -ae *f* opulence, wealth; resources; power

opulentit·ās -ātis *f* opulence; power

opulent·ō -āre *vt* to make rich, enrich

opulent·us -a -um *adj* opulent, rich, wealthy; powerful; sumptuous

op·us -ĕris *n* work; product of work, structure, building; literary work, composition, book; work of art, workmanship; deed, achievement; (mil) offensive works, siege works; (mil) defensive works, fortifications; **magno opere** greatly; **quanto opere** how much, how greatly; **tanto opere** so much, so greatly; **opus est** (with *inf*) it is useful or beneficial to; **opus est** (with *dat* of person in need and *abl* of person or thing needed) to need, e.g., **vobis duce opus est** you need a leader

opuscŭl·um -ī *n* little work, minor work

ōr·a -ae *f* boundary, border, edge; coastline, coast; region, district; cable, hawser; (fig) people of the coast, people of the region; **ora maritima** seacoast

ōrācŭl·um or **ōrācl·um -ī** *n* oracle; prophesy

ōrāri·us -a -um *adj* coasting; **navis oraria** coaster, coasting vessel

ōrāt·a -ōrum *n pl* prayers, requests

ōrātī·ō -ōnis *f* faculty of speech; speech, language; style of speech, manner of speaking, style, expression; oration, speech; theme, subject; prose; eloquence; imperial rescript; **orationem habere** to give a speech

ōrātiuncŭl·a -ae *f* short speech, insignificant speech

ōrāt·or -ōris *m* orator, speaker; spokesman; suppliant

ōrātōriē *adv* oratorically

ōrātōri·us -a -um *adj* orator's, oratorical

ōrātr·ix -īcis *f* suppliant (*female*)

ōrāt·us -ūs *m* request

orb·a -ae *f* orphan; widow

orbāt·or -ōris *m* murderer (*of someone's children or parents*)

Orbīl·ius -iī or **-ī** *m* Horace's teacher in Venusia

orb·is -is *m* circle; disk, ring, orbit; quoit; hoop; wheel; round shield; eye socket, eye; globe, earth, world, universe; region, territory, country; circuit, round; rotation; cycle, period; (rhet) balance; zodiac; **orbis lacteus** Milky Way; **orbis terrae** or **terrarum** earth, world, universe

orbit·a -ae *f* rut, wheel track; (fig) rut, routine

orbit·ās -ātis *f* childlessness, widowhood, orphanhood

orbitōs·us -a -um *adj* full of ruts

orb·ō -āre *vt* to bereave of parents, father, mother, children, husband, or wife; to strip, rob, deprive, make destitute

orb·us -a -um *adj* bereaved, bereft; destitute; orphaned, fatherless; childless; widowed; (with *genit* or *abl* or with **ab + abl**) bereft of, deprived of, without; *m* orphan; *f* see **orba**

orc·a -ae *f* vat, barrel

Orcăd·es -um *f pl* islands N. of Scotland (*modern Orkneys*)

orch·as -ădis *f* olive

orchestr·a -ae *f* senatorial seats (*in the theater*); (fig) senate

Orc·us -ī *m* lower world; Pluto (*king of the lower world*); death

orde- = horde-

ordināri·us -a -um *adj* ordinary, usual, regular

ordinātim *adv* in order, in good order, in succession; regularly, properly

ordinātī·ō -ōnis *f* orderly arrangement; orderly government

ordināt·us -a -um *adj* regular; appointed

ordin·ō -āre *vt* to set in order, arrange, regulate; to govern, rule; to record chronologically

ordior ordīrī orsus sum *vt* to begin, undertake; to describe; *vi* to begin, begin to speak

ord·ō -ĭnis *m* line, row, series; row of seats (*in a theater*); order, methodical arrangement; (pol) rank, order, class; (mil) line, file (*of soldiers*), company, century, command of a company or century; *m pl* officers of a company; promotions; **amplissimus ordo** senatorial order; **ex ordine** in succession, without a break; **extra ordinem** extraordinarily, especially, uncommonly; **ordine, in ordine,** or **per ordinem** in order, in sequence, in detail, with regularity, regularly

Ore·as -ădis f Oread, mountain nymph

Orest·ēs -is or **-ae** m son of Agamemnon and Clytemnestra who avenged his father's death by killing his mother

orex·is -is f longing, appetite

organic·us -ī m organist

organ·um -ī n instrument, implement; musical instrument, organ

orgi·a -ōrum n pl Bacchic revels; orgies

orichalc·um -ī n copper ore; brass

ōricill·a -ae f lobe

ori·ens -entis m rising sun, morning sun; morning; day; land of the rising sun, Orient, the East

orīg·ō -inis f origin, source, beginning, start; birth, lineage, descent; race, stock, family; founder, progenitor

Ōrī·ōn or **Orī·ōn -ŏnis** or **-ŏnis** m mythical hunter, turned into a constellation

orĭor orīrī ortus sum vi to rise, get up; to become visible, appear; to be born, originate, be descended; to proceed, begin, start

Ōrithyī·a -ae f daughter of Erechtheus and mother of Calais and Zetes by Boreas

oriund·us -a -um adj descended, sprung, born

ornāment·um -ī n equipment, trappings, apparatus; ornament, adornment, decoration; trinket, jewel; (fig) distinction; rhetorical ornament; pride and joy

ornātē adv ornately, elegantly

ornātr·ix -īcis f hairdresser (female)

ornātŭl·us -a -um adj fancy

ornāt·us -a -um adj equipped, fitted out, furnished, dressed, harnessed; adorned, decorated, embellished; handsome; illustrious, excellent

ornāt·us -ūs m equipment; attire, apparel, outfit; furniture; decoration, ornament; world, universe

orn·ō -āre vt to equip, fit out, furnish, dress; to set off, decorate, adorn; to honor, praise, commend

orn·us -ī f mountain ash

ōr·ō -āre vt to beg, entreat, implore, plead with; to ask for; to plead (a case); (with double acc) to ask (someone) for; vi to plead, beg, pray; (with **cum** + abl) to plead or argue with

Oront·ēs -is or **-ae** m chief river of Syria; companion of Aeneas

Orontē·us -a -um adj Syrian

Orph·eus -ěī or **-ěos** m son of Oeagrus and Calliope, husband of Eurydice, and famous musician and poet

Orphē·us or **Orphic·us -a -um** adj Orphic

ors·us -a -um pp of ordior; n pl beginnings; utterance, words; attempt

ors·us -ūs m beginning; attempt, undertaking

ortus pp of orior

ort·us -ūs m rising; the East; birth, origin; source

Ortygĭ·a -ae or **Ortygĭ·ē -ēs** f Delos; island in the port of Syracuse

or·yx -ygis m gazelle

oryz·a -ae f rice

os ossis n bone; marrow, innermost parts; n pl skeleton

ōs ōris n mouth; beak; voice, speech, expression; lip, face, countenance, look; sight, presence (of a person); impudence; mask, mouth, opening, orifice, front; **habere aliquid in ore** to be talking about something continually; **in ore omnium esse** to be on the lips of everyone, be talked about

osc·en -inis m bird of augury (e.g., crow, raven, owl)

oscill·um -ī n small mask

oscĭt·ans -antis adj yawning; (fig) indifferent, bored

oscĭt·ō -āre or **oscĭt·or -ārī -ātus sum** vi to gape; to yawn

osculāti·ō -ōnis f kissing

oscŭl·or -ārī -ātus sum vt to kiss; (fig) to make a fuss over

oscŭl·um -ī n little mouth; kiss; **breve osculum** peck

Osc·us -a -um adj Oscan; m pl Oscans (ancient people of Campania and Samnium)

Osīr·is -is or **-ĭdis** m Egyptian god, the husband of Isis

ōs·or -ōris m hater

Oss·a -ae f mountain in N.E. Thessaly

ossĕ·us -a -um adj bony

ossifrăg·a -ae f osprey

ostendō ostendĕre ostendī ostentum vt to stretch out, stretch forth; to expose; to show, exhibit, display, present; to reveal, disclose; to declare, make known

ostentāti·ō -ōnis f display; ostentation, showing off; mere show, pretense

ostentāt·or -ōris m show-off

ostent·ō -āre vt to show, exhibit; to show off, display, parade, boast of; to declare, point out, set forth

ostent·um -ī n portent, prodigy

ostent·us -ūs m display, show; **ostentui** for appearances, in pretense

Ostĭ·a -ae f or **Ostĭ·a -ōrum** n pl Ostia (port and town at the mouth of the Tiber)

ostiār·ium -ĭī or **-ī** n tax on doors

ostiātim adv from door to door

ost·ium -ĭī or **-ī** n door; entrance, mouth

ostrĕ·a -ae f or **ostrĕ·um -ī** n oyster

ostreāt·us -a -um adj covered with oyster shells; (fig) black and blue

ostreōs·us -a -um *adj* abounding in oysters

ostrif·er -ĕra -ĕrum *adj* oyster-growing

ostrīn·us -a -um *adj* purple

ostr·um -ī *n* purple; purple dress, purple covering

ōsus *pp* of **odi**

Oth·ō -ōnis *m* L. Roscius Otho (*author of the law in 67 B.C. reserving fourteen rows in the theaters for the equestrian order*); M. Salvius Otho (*Roman emperor in 69 A.D.*)

Othr·ys -yos *m* mountain in S. Thessaly

ōtiŏl·um -ī *n* bit of leisure

ōti·or -ārī -ātus sum *vi* to take it easy

ōtiōsē *adv* at leisure; leisurely, without haste; calmly, fearlessly

ōtiōs·us -a -um *adj* at leisure, relaxing; free from official obligations; quiet, calm; unconcerned, in-

different, neutral; passionless; *m* private person (*not holding public office*); *m pl* civilians, non-combatants

ōt·ium -iī or **-ī** *n* leisure, free time, relaxation; freedom from public affairs, retirement; peace, quiet; ease, idleness, inactivity

Ovid·ius -iī or **-ī** *m* P. Ovidius Naso or Ovid (*Latin poet, born at Sulmo, 43 B.C.-17 A.D.*)

ovīl·e -is *n* sheepfold; voting enclosures in the Campus Martius

ovīl·is -e *adj* sheep, of sheep

ovill·us -a -um *adj* sheep, of sheep

ov·is -is *f* sheep; wool; simpleton

ov·ō -āre *vi* to rejoice; to hold a celebration; to celebrate a minor triumph

ōv·um -ī *n* egg; *n pl* wooden balls used to mark the laps at the racetrack

P

pābulātĭ·ō -ōnis *f* foraging

pābulāt·or -ōris *m* forager

pābŭl·or -ārī -ātus sum *vi* to forage; (coll) to make a living

pābŭl·um -ī *n* food, fodder; pasturage, grass; (fig) nourishment

pācāl·is -e *adj* of peace

pācāt·us -a -um *adj* peaceful, quiet, calm; *n* friendly country

Pachўn·um -ī *n* S.E. point of Sicily

pācif·er -ĕra -ĕrum *adj* peace-bringing, peaceful

pācificātĭ·ō -ōnis *f* pacification

pācificāt·or -ōris *m* peacemaker

pācificātōrĭ·us -a -um *adj* peace-making

pācific·ō -āre *vt* to pacify, appease; *vi* to make peace, conclude peace

pācific·us -a -um *adj* peace-making; peaceable

paciscor pascisci pactus sum *vt* to bargain for, agree upon; to stipulate; to barter; to betroth; *vi* to come to an agreement, agree, make a bargain, make a contract; (with *inf*) to agree to, pledge oneself to

pac·ō -āre *vt* to pacify, soothe, subdue

pact·a -ae *f* fiancee; bride

pactĭ·ō -ōnis *f* pact, contract, agreement, treaty; condition, stipulation; collusion

Pactōl·us -ī *m* river in Lydia famous for its gold

pact·or -ōris *m* contractor, negotiator, party (*in a contract*)

pact·us -a -um *pp* of **paciscor** and of **pango**; *n* pact, contract, agreement; way, manner; **aliquo pacto** somehow; **hoc pacto** in this way; **in pacto manere** to stick to the agreement; **quo pacto** how, in what way

Pācuv·ius -iī or **-ī** *m* Roman tragic poet, native of Brundisium, and nephew of Ennius (*c. 220-130 B.C.*)

Pad·us -ī *m* Po River (*in N. Italy*)

pae·ān -ānis *m* epithet of Apollo as the god of healing; paean, hymn of praise, victory song

paedagōg·ium -iī or **-ī** *n* training school for pages

paedagōg·us -ī *m* slave in charge of school children; (fig) guide, leader

paedīc·ō -āre *vt* to have abnormal relations with (*young boys*)

paed·or -ōris *m* filth

pael·ex -ĭcis *f* concubine, mistress

paelicāt·us -ūs *m* concubinage

Paelign·ī -ōrum *m pl* a people of central Italy

paenē *adv* almost, nearly

paeninsŭl·a -ae *f* peninsula

paenitend·us -a -um *adj* regrettable

paenitentĭ·a -ae *f* repentance, regret

paenit·ĕŏ -ēre -ŭī *vt* to cause to regret; to displease; *vi* (with *genit*) to regret; *v impers* (with *acc* of person), e.g., **me paenitet** I am sorry; (with *acc* of person and *genit* of thing), e.g., **me paenitet consilī** I regret the plan, I am dissatisfied with the plan; (with *acc* of person and *inf* or *quod*), e.g., **eos paenitet animum tuum offendisse** or **eos paenitet quod animum tuum offenderint** they regret having offended your feelings

paenŭl·a -ae *f* traveling coat; raincoat

paenulāt·us -a -um *adj* wearing a traveling coat

pae·ōn -ōnis *m* metrical foot containing one long and three short syllables

paeŏni·us -a -um *adj* healing, medicinal

Paest·um -ī *n* town in Lucania in S. Italy

paetŭl·us -a -um *adj* slightly squint-eyed

paet·us -a -um *adj* squinting, squint-eyed; leering

pāgān·us -a -um *adj* of a village, rustic; ignorant, untaught; *m* villager, peasant; (as term of contempt) yokel

Pagăs·a -ae *f* or **Pagăs·ae -ārum** *f pl* town on the coast of Thessaly, from which the Argonauts sailed

Pagasae·us -a -um *adj* Pagasaean; *m* Jason

pāgātim *adv* by villages, in every village

pāgell·a -ae *f* small page

pāgin·a -ae *f* page (*of book*)

pāginŭl·a -ae *f* small page

pāg·us -ī *m* village; canton, province; country people, villagers

pāl·a -ae *f* spade

palaestr·a -ae *f* palaestra, wrestling school, gymnasium; school of rhetoric; rhetorical training; school; wrestling; exercise; brothel

palaestrĭcē *adv* as at the palaestra

palaestrĭc·us -a -um *adj* of the palaestra, gymnastic; *f* gymnastics

palaestrīt·a -ae *m* professional wrestler; director of a palaestra

palam *adv* openly, publicly, plainly; **palam esse** to be public, be well known; **palam facere** to make public, disclose; *prep* (with *abl*) before, in the presence of, face to face with

Palātīn·us -a -um *adj* Palatine; imperial

Palāt·ium -iī or **-ī** *n* Palatine Hill (*residential area of distinguished Romans and several Roman emperors*); palace

palāt·um -ī *n* or **palāt·us -ī** *m* palate; taste; literary taste

palē·a -ae *f* chaff

paleār·ia -ium *n pl* dewlap

Pal·ēs -is *f* Italic goddess of shepherds and flocks

Palĭc·ī -ōrum *m pl* twin sons of Jupiter and the nymph Thalia

Palīl·is -e *adj* of Pales; *n pl* festival of Pales celebrated on April 21st

palimpsest·us -ī *m* palimpsest

Palinūr·us -ī *m* pilot of Aeneas who fell overboard and drowned; promontory named after him

paliūr·us -ī *m* Christ's thorn (*plant*)

pall·a -ae *f* ladies' long robe; outer garment, mantle; tragic actor's costume

Palladĭ·us -a -um *adj* of Pallas; *n* statue of Pallas, Palladium

Pall·as -ădis or **-ădos** *f* Athene; olive oil, oil; olive tree; Palladium (*Trojan statue of Pallas*)

pall·ens -entis *adj* pale, sallow;

grey-green, yellow-green, chartreuse, yellowish, sickly-looking

pall·ĕō -ēre -uī *vi* to be pale, look pale; to be yellow, look yellow; to change color, fade; (with *dat*) to grow pale over, worry about

pall·escō -escĕre -uī *vt* to turn pale at; *vi* to turn pale; to turn yellow; to fade

palliāt·us -a -um *adj* wearing a Greek cloak; **fabula palliata** Latin play with Greek setting and characters

pallidŭl·us -a -um *adj* somewhat pale

pallĭd·us -a -um *adj* pale, sallow; grey-green, yellow-green, chartreuse

palliolātim *adv* in a mantle

palliolāt·us -a -um *adj* wearing a short mantle, wearing a hood

palliŏl·um -ī *n* short cloak; cape, hood

pall·ium -iī or **-ī** *n* coverlet, cover; Greek cloak

pall·or -ōris *m* paleness, pallor; **pallorem ducere** to turn pale

pallŭl·a -ae *f* short cloak

palm·a -ae *f* palm of the hand; hand; palm tree, date; palm branch, palm wreath; palm of victory, prize, victory, honor, distinction; blade of an oar

palmār·is -e *adj* excellent, deserving the palm or prize

palmāri·us -a -um *adj* prize-winning, excellent; *n* masterpiece

palmāt·us -a -um *adj* embroidered with palm branches; **tunica palmata** palm-embroidered tunic (*worn by a general*)

palm·es -ītis *m* vine sprout, vine branch; branch, bough

palmēt·um -ī *n* palm grove

palmĭf·er -ĕra -ĕrum *adj* palm-growing, full of palm trees

palmōs·us -a -um *adj* full of palm trees

palmŭl·a -ae *f* oar blade

pāl·or -ārī -ātus sum *vi* to roam about, wander aimlessly

palpāti·ō -ōnis *f* stroking; *f pl* flattering

palpāt·or -ōris *m* flatterer

palpĕbr·a -ae *f* eyelid

palpĭt·ō -āre *vi* to throb, palpitate, quiver

palp·ō -āre or **palp·or -ārī -ātus sum** *vt* to stroke, pat; to wheedle, coax; to flatter; *vi* (with *dat*) **a** to coax; **b** to flatter

palp·us -ī *m* palm of the hand; coaxing

palūdāment·um -ī *n* military coat; general's coat

palūdāt·us -a -um *adj* wearing a general's coat

palūdōs·us -a -um *adj* swampy, marshy

palumb·ēs -is *m* or *f* pigeon, dove

pāl·us -ī *m* stake, post; wooden post used in sword practice pal·us -ūdis f swamp, marsh; sedge

palust·er -ris -re adj swampy, marshy, in the swamps

pampinė·us -a -um adj of vine tendrils, made of vine leaves; odor pampineus bouquet of wines

pampĭn·us -ī m vine shoot, tendril; vine leaf; tendril (of any plant)

Pān Pānos m Pan (Greek god of flocks, shepherds, and woods, often identified with Faunus)

panacē·a -ae f or panăc·es -is n panacea

Panaetōlĭc·us -a -um adj Pan-Aetolian

pānār·ĭum -ĭī or -ī n bread basket

Panchāī·a -ae f region in Arabia famous for its frankincense

panchrest·us or panchrist·us -a -um adj good for everything, universally useful

pancratĭcē adv (coll) fine, splendidly; pancratice valere to get along splendidly

pancrat·ĭum or pancrat·ĭon -iī or -ī n contest which included both boxing and wrestling

Pandăr·us -ī m famous Lycian archer in the Trojan army; companion of Aeneas, killed by Turnus

pandĭcŭl·or -ārī -ātus sum vi to stretch oneself

Pandĭ·ōn -ōnis m king of Athens and father of Procne and Philomela

Pandīonĭ·us -a -um adj of Pandion

pandō pandēre pandī pansum or passum vt to spread out, extend, expand, unfold; to open, lay open, throw open; to reveal, make known, publish

pand·us -a -um adj crooked, bent, curved

pangō pangĕre panxī or pepĕgī -pactum vt to fasten, fix, drive in; to fix, settle, agree upon, determine; to write, compose, celebrate, record; to promise in marriage; indutias pangere (with cum + abl) to conclude an armistice with

pānĭcē·us -a -um adj made of bread; milites panicei (coll) Breadville brigade

pānĭcŭl·a -ae f tuft

pānĭc·um -ī n millet

pān·is -is m bread, loaf; panis cibarius coarse bread; panis secundus stale bread

Pānisc·us -ī m little Pan

pannĭcŭl·us -ī m rag

Pannonĭ·us -a -um adj Pannonian; f Pannonia (country on the Danube)

pannōs·us -a -um adj tattered, ragged; shriveled, wrinkled, sad-looking

pannūce·us or pannūcĭ·us -a -um adj ragged; shriveled, wrinkled

pann·us -ī m patch; rag

Panŏp·ē -ēs or Panopē·a -ae f a sea nymph

pans·a -ae masc & fem adj flat-footed, splayfooted

pansus pp of pando

panthēr·a -ae f panther

Panthoīd·ēs -ae m Euphorbus (Trojan warrior)

Panth·us -ī m priest of Apollo at Troy and father of Euphorbus

pantĭc·ēs -um m pl bowels; sausages

papae interj great!, wonderful!

pāp·as -ae or -ātis m tutor

papāv·er -ĕris n poppy

papāverĕ·us -a -um adj of poppies

Paphĭ·ē -ēs f Venus

Paphĭ·us -a -um adj Paphian, of Paphos

Paph·us -ī f town in Cyprus sacred to Venus

pāpĭlĭ·ō -ōnis m butterfly

papill·a -ae f nipple, teat; breast

papp·ō -āre vi to eat baby food, eat pap

papp·us -ī m hairy seed (of certain plants)

papŭl·a -ae f pimple

papȳrĭf·er -ĕra -ĕrum adj papyrus-producing

papȳr·us -ī m & f or papȳr·um -ī n papyrus; paper; garment (made of papyrus)

pār paris adj equal, like, on a par, equally matched, well matched; suitable, adequate; of equal size; (with dat or cum + abl) equal to, comparable to, similar to, as large as; (with limiting abl, ad + acc, or in + abl) equal, similar, alike in; par est it is right, it is proper; par proelium indecisive battle; ut par est (used parenthetically) as is only right; m companion, comrade; equal; mate, spouse; pares cum paribus facillime congregantur birds of a feather flock together; n pair, couple; the like; par pari like for like, tit for tat

parābĭl·is -e adj available

parasīt·a -ae f parasite (female)

parasītast·er -rī m poor parasite

parasītātĭ·ō -ōnis f sponging

parasītĭc·us -a -um adj parasitical

parasīt·or -ārī -ātus sum vi to sponge, freeload, be a parasite

parasīt·us -ī m parasite, sponger, freeloader

parātē adv with preparation; carefully; readily; promptly

parātĭ·ō -ōnis f preparing, procuring, acquisition

paratragoed·ō -āre vi to talk in a tragic style, be melodramatic

parāt·us -a -um adj prepared, ready; well prepared, furnished, equipped; learned, well versed, skilled; (with dat or ad + acc) a ready for; b equipped to; (with inf) prepared to, ready to; (with abl or in + abl) versed in, experienced in

parāt·us -ūs m preparation, provision, equipment, outfit; clothing, apparel

Parc·a -ae f goddess of Fate, Fate

parcē adv sparingly, thriftily; moderately, with restraint; stingily; rarely, seldom parceprōm·us -ī m stingy person

parcō parcĕre pepercī parsum vt to spare, use sparingly; vi to be sparing, economize; (with dat) a to spare, use carefully; b to show mercy to; c to abstain from, refrain from; d to refuse (help); (with inf) to cease, stop (e.g., doing, talking)

parc·us -a -um adj thrifty, economical, frugal; niggardly, stingy; moderate, conservative; slight, little, scanty, paltry (thing given)

pard·us -ī m panther

par·ens -entis adj obedient; m parent, father; ancestor, grandparent; founder, inventor; m pl subjects; ancestors; f parent, mother

parentāl·is -e adj parental; diēs parentalis memorial day; n pl festival in honor of dead ancestors and relatives

parent·ō -āre vi to hold memorial service in honor of dead parents or relatives; (with dat) a to offer sacrifice to (the dead); b to avenge (a dead person) with the death of another person; c to appease, satisfy

pār·ĕō -ēre -uī vi to appear, be visible, be evident, be at hand; (with dat) a to obey, be obedient to, comply with, be subject to, be subservient to; b to yield to, gratify, satisfy (pleasures, etc.); c to fulfill (promises)

pari·ēs -ĕtis m wall (esp. partition in a house or building)

parietin·ae -ārum f pl tumbled-down walls; ruins; (fig) ruins

Paril·ia -ium n pl festival of Pales (celebrated on April 21st)

paril·is -e adj equal, like; aetas parilis same age, like age

pariō parĕre pepĕrī partum vt to bear, bring forth, give birth to; (of animals) to lay, spawn, produce; (fig) to produce, create, devise, cause, effect, accomplish, acquire, obtain

Par·is -idis m son of Priam and Hecuba, also called Alexandros; famous pantomime actor in the reign of Nero; famous pantomime actor in the reign of Domitian, the freedman of Domitia

pariter adv equally, in like manner, as well, alike; at the same time, simultaneously, together, at once; pariter ac (or atque), pariter ut as well as; pariter ac si just as if; pariter (with cum + abl) together with, at the same time as

parit·ō -āre vt (with inf) to get ready to

Pari·us -a -um adj & mf Parian

parm·a -ae f small round shield; shield

parmāt·us -a -um adj armed with a shield, light-armed

parmŭl·a -ae f small shield

Parnās·is -idis or Parnāsi·us -a -um adj of Parnassus, Parnassian

Parnās·us or Parnās·os -ī m mountain in Phocis, in central Greece, sacred to Apollo and the Muses, on whose slopes Delphi was located

par·ō -āre vt to prepare, make ready, provide, furnish; to get, procure, acquire, gather, purchase; se parare to prepare oneself, get ready; vi to get ready, make preparations, make arrangements; (with dat or ad + acc) to get ready for

paroch·a -ae f room and board (required of provincials for traveling Roman officials)

paroch·us -ī m official host (local official who provided accommodations for traveling Roman dignitaries); host

parops·is -idis f dish, dessert dish

Par·os or Par·us -ī f island of the Cyclades, famous for its white marble

parr·a -ae f owl

Parrhās·is -idis f Arcadian woman; Callisto

Parrhāsi·us -a -um adj Arcadian; Parrhasia virgo Callisto; f district in Arcadia

parricīd·a -ae m or f parricide (murder of a parent or close relative); assassin of a high magistrate; murderer, assassin; traitor, outlaw, criminal

parricīd·ium -iī or -ī n parricide (murderer of a parent or close relative); murder, assassination; treason, high treason

par·s -tis f part, portion, share, section, fraction; side, direction, region; part, function, duty; part of body, member (esp. genital organs); f pl part, role, character; political party; ab omni parte in all respects; ex altera parte on the other hand; ex magna parte to a great extent; ex parte partly; in eam partem in that direction; in that sense; in such a manner; in perjorem partem rapere to put a worse construction on; in utramque partem in both directions; major pars populi the majority; maximam partem for the most part; minor pars populi the minority; omnibus partibus in all respects; pars ... pars, pars ... alii some ... others; parte in part, partly; pro mea parte to the best of my abilities; tres partes three fourths

parsimōni·a -ae f parsimony

parsus pp of parco

parthenic·ē -ēs f parthenium (plant)

Parthenopae·us -ī m son of Meleager and Atalanta and one of the Seven who fought against Thebes

Parthenōp·ē -ēs f one of the Sirens, after whom Naples was originally named

Parthi·a -ae f Parthia (country located S.E. of the Caspian)

Parthic·us -a -um adj Parthian

Parth·us -a -um adj & m Parthian

partic·eps -ipis *adj* (with *genit*) sharing in, taking part in; *m* partner, confederate

particĭp·ō -āre *vt* to make (*someone*) a partner; to share (*something*)

particŭl·a -ae *f* bit, particle, grain

partim *adv* partly, in part, to some extent; for the most part, mostly; (with *genit* or **ex** + *abl*) some of; **partim . . . partim** some . . . others

partĭ·ō -ōnis *f* bringing forth, producing

part·ĭō -īre -īvī or **-iī -ītum** or **part·ĭor -īrī -ītus sum** *vt* to share, distribute, apportion, divide

partītē *adv* with proper divisions, methodically

partītĭ·ō -ōnis *f* division, distribution, sharing; division of a speech

partĭtūd·ō -ĭnis *f* bearing (*of young*)

partŭr·ĭō -īre -īvī or **-iī** *vt* to teem with; to be ready to produce; to bring forth, yield; (fig) to brood over; *vi* to be in labor

partus *pp* of **pario**; *adj* acquired; *n* acquisition, gain, store

part·us -ūs *m* birth; young, offspring; (fig) beginnings

parum *adv* a little, too little, insufficiently; **parum est** it is not enough, it does not suffice; **parum habere** to regard as unsatisfactory; **satis eloquentiae sapientiae parum** enough eloquence but too little wisdom

parumper *adv* for a little while, a moment; **operire parumper** wait a moment

parvĭt·ās -ātis *f* smallness

parvŭl·us or **parvŏl·us -a -um** *adj* tiny; slight, petty; young; *n* childhood, infancy; **ab parvulis** from childhood, from infancy

parv·us -a -um (*comp* **minor**; *superl* **minimus**) *adj* small, little, puny; short; young; brief, short (*time*); small, insignificant, unimportant; low, cheap (*price*); *n* a little, trifle; childhood, infancy; **a parvis** or **a parvo** from childhood, from infancy; **parvi esse** to be of little importance; **parvi facere, aestimare, habere**, or **ducere** to think little of, care little for; **parvi refert** it makes little difference, it matters little

pascĕŏl·us -ī *m* money bag

pascō pascĕre pāvī pastum *vt* to feed, pasture, keep, raise (*animals*); to cultivate, cherish; to feed (*flames, passions*); to pile up (*debts*); to grow (*beard*); to lay waste, ravage (*fields*); to feast, gratify (*the eyes*); to cherish (*hope*)

pascor pascī pastus sum *vi* to graze, browse, be fed; (with *abl*) a to graze on; **b** (fig) to feed on, feast on, thrive on

pascŭ·us -a -um *adj* grazing, pasture; *n* pasture

Pāsiphă·ē -ēs or **Pāsiphă·a -ae** *f* daughter of Helios, sister of Circe,

husband of Minos, and mother of Androgeos, Ariadne, Phaedra, and the Minotaur

pass·er -ĕris *m* sparrow; plaice, flounder; **passer marinus** ostrich

passercŭl·us -ī *m* little sparrow

passim *adv* here and there, all over, at random; without order, indiscriminately, promiscuously

passus *pp* of **pando** and of **patior**; *adj* spread out, extended, open; disheveled; dried, dry; *n* wine made from dried grapes, raisin wine

pass·us -ūs *m* step, pace; footstep, track; **mille passūs** mile; **tria milia passuum** three miles

pastill·us -ī *m* lozenge

pastĭ·ō -ōnis *f* pasture, grazing

past·or -ōris *m* shepherd

pastōrāl·is -e *adj* shepherd's, pastoral

pastōricĭ·us or **pastōrĭ·us -a -um** *adj* shepherd's, pastoral

pastus *pp* of **pasco**

past·us -ūs *m* pasture, fodder, food; (fig) food

patagiār·ĭus -ĭī or **-ī** *m* fringe maker

patagiāt·us -a -um *adj* (tunic) with fringes

Patăr·a -ae *f* town in Lycia with an oracle of Apollo

Patăr·eus -ĕī or **-ĕos** *m* Apollo

Patavīn·us -a -um *adj* of Patavium

Patav·ĭum -ĭī or **-ī** *n* city in N. Italy, the birthplace of Livy (*modern Padua*)

pate·facĭō -facĕre -fēcī -factus (*passive*: **pate·fĭō -fĭĕrī**) *vt* to throw open; to open up, make accessible; to bring to light

patefactĭ·ō -ōnis *f* disclosure

patell·a -ae *f* pan, dish, plate

pat·ens -entis *adj* open, accessible; extensive; exposed; evident

patentius *adv* more openly, more clearly

pat·ĕō -ēre -ŭī *vi* to stand open, be open; to be accessible; to be exposed; to open, stretch out, extend; to be clear, be plain, be well known; to be accessible, be attainable, be free; (of the mind) to be open, be receptive

pat·er -ris *m* father; **pater cenae** host; **pater familias** head of the household, head of the family; *m pl* forefathers; senators

patĕr·a -ae *f* flat dish (*used esp. in making libations*)

pat·erfamilĭās -risfamilĭās *m* head of the household, head of the family

patern·us -a -um *adj* father's, paternal; ancestral; of a native country, native

pat·escō -escĕre -ŭī *vi* to be opened, be open; to stretch out, extend; to be disclosed, be divulged, become evident

pathĭc·us -a -um *adj* lustful

patibĭl·is -e *adj* tolerable, endurable; sensitive

patibulāt·us -a -um adj gibbeted; wearing a yoke

patibŭl·um -ī n fork-shaped yoke (tied around the neck of a criminal); fork-shaped gibbet

pati·ens -entis adj hardy, tough; hard; stubborn, unyielding, patient, tolerant; (with genit or **ad** + acc) able to endure, inured to, able to take; **amnis patiens navium** navigable river

patienter adv patiently

patienti·a -ae f patience, endurance; resignation, forbearance; submissiveness; sexual submission

patin·a -ae f dish, pan

patināri·us -a -um adj of pans; in a pan; **strues patinaria** pile of dishes

patior pātī passus sum vt to experience, undergo, suffer; to put up with, allow; to submit to sexually; **aequo animo pati** to suffer patiently; **aegre pati** to resent, be displeased with

patrāt·or -ōris m perpetrator

patrāt·us adj masc **pater patratus** plenipotentiary

patri·a -ae f native land, native city, home

patricē adv paternally

patrici·us -a -um adj of patrician status, patrician; m pl patricians, patrician class

patrimōn·ium -iī or **-ī** n patrimony, inheritance

patrīm·us -a -um adj having a father living

patriss·ō -āre vi to take after one's father

patrīt·us -a -um adj father's, inherited from one's father

patri·us -a -um adj father's, of a father, fatherly, paternal; ancestral, traditional, heriditary; native; f see **patria**

patr·ō -āre vt to bring about, effect, achieve, accomplish, perform, finish, conclude; **bellum patrare** to bring the war to an end; **jus jurandum patrare** to take an oath (confirming a treaty); **pacem patrare** to conclude a peace

patrōcin·ium -iī or **-ī** n patronage, protection, legal defense, legal representation

patrōcin·or -ārī -ātus sum vi to be a patron, afford protection; (with dat) to serve (someone) as patron, protect, defend

Patrŏcl·us -ī m son of Menoetius and friend of Achilles, who wearing the armor of Achilles, was killed by Hector

patrōn·a -ae f legal protectress, patroness; advocate; defender, safeguard

patrōn·us -ī m legal protector, patron; advocate (in court); defender

patruēl·is -e adj of or descended from a father's brother, cousin's; m cousin

patrŭ·us -a -um adj uncle's; m (paternal) uncle

patŭl·us -a -um adj open, standing open; spreading, spread out, broad

pauciloqu·ium -iī or **-ī** n reticence

paucĭt·ās -ātis f paucity, scarcity, small number

paucŭl·ī -a -a adj just a few, very few; n pl few words

pauc·us -a -um adj few, little; pron masc pl few, a few; the select few, elite; **inter paucos (paucas)** or **in paucis** especially; pron neut pl a few things, a few words; **paucis** in a few words, briefly

paulātim adv little by little, gradually, by degrees; a few at a time

paulisper adv for a little while

paulō adv (as abl of degree of difference in expressions of comparison) by a little, a little, somewhat; **paulo antea** a little before; **paulo post** a little later

paulŭlō adv somewhat, a little; cheaply, at a low price

paulŭlum adv somewhat, a little

paulŭl·us -a -um adj very little; n a bit; **paululum pecuniae** a bit of money

paulum adv a little, to some extent, to some degree

paul·us -a -um adj small, little; n bit, trifle; **post paulum** after a bit, after a while

Paul·us -ī m L. Aemilius Paulus (conqueror of Macedonia through the victory at Pydna in 168 B.C.)

paup·er -ĕris adj poor; scanty, meager; (with genit) poor in; m poor man, pauper

paupercŭl·us -a -um adj poor

pauperi·ēs -ēī f poverty

paupĕr·ō -āre vt to impoverish; (with abl) to rob (someone) of

paupert·ās -ātis f poverty

paus·a -ae f pause, stop, end

pausi·a -ae f plump olive

pauxillātim adv bit by bit, little by little

pauxillisper adv by degrees

pauxillŭlum adv a little, a bit

pauxillŭl·us -a -um adj very little, tiny; n bit

pauxillum adv a little, a bit

pauxill·us -a -um adj very little, tiny; n small amount

pavefact·us -a -um adj frightened, scared

pavĕō pavēre pāvī vt to be scared of; vi to be terrified, tremble, or shiver with fear

pavesc·ō -ĕre vt to get scared of; vi to begin to be alarmed

pavidē adv in panic

pavid·us -a -um adj panicky, alarmed, shivering or trembling with fear, startled; with beating heart, nervous; causing alarm

paviment·ō -āre vt to pave

paviment·um -ī n pavement; floor

pav·iō -īre -īvī or **-iī -ītum** vt to strike, beat

pavīt·ō -āre vt to be panicky over; vi to quake with fear, be scared to death; to shiver (with fever)

pāv·ō -ōnis m peacock

pav·or -ōris m panic, terror, dismay, quaking, shivering; **pavorem injicere** (with dat) to throw the fear of the Lord into, to terrify

pax pācis f peace; peace treaty, reconciliation, compact, agreement; harmony, tranquility; favor, pardon (from the gods); **pace tua** with your permission, with your leave

peco·ans -antis m offender, sinner

peccāt·um -ī n fault, mistake, slip, transgression, sin

pecc·ō -āre vi to make a mistake, commit a fault, sin

pecorōs·us -a -um adj rich in cattle

pect·en -inis m comb; plectrum (for strumming a lyre); scallop (sea food)

pectō pectĕre pexī pexum vt to comb; to card (wool); (coll) to clobber (with stick or fist)

pect·us -ōris n breast; heart, feeling; soul, conscience, mind, understanding; character, person

pecū (genit not in use) n flock; n pl cattle; pastures

pecuārī·us -a -um adj of sheep, of cattle; **res pecuaria** livestock; m cattle man, cattle breeder, rancher; f livestock; n pl herds of cattle, herds of sheep

pecūlāt·or -ōris m embezzler

pecūlāt·us -ūs m embezzlement

pecūliār·is -e adj one's own, as one's own private property; special

pecūliāt·us -a -um adj rich, well off

pecūli·ō -āre vt to give away for good

pecūliōs·us -a -um adj owning private property

pecūl·ium -iī or **-ī** n small savings (esp. accumulated by slaves); private property

pecūni·a -ae f money; **pecunia praesens** ready cash

pecūniārī·us -a -um adj pecuniary, financial, money

pecūniōs·us -a -um adj rich, wealthy, loaded with money; profitable, bringing in money

pec·us -ōris n cattle, herd, flock; sheep; head of cattle; **pecus equinum** stud; (as term of scorn) cattle

pec·us -ŭdis f head of cattle; beast; sheep; domestic animal; land animal (as opposed to birds); (as term of abuse) brute, beast, swine

pedāl·is -e adj one-foot-long

pedār·ius -iī or **-ī** m inferior senator (who let others step all over him)

ped·es -ītis m infantryman; pedestrian; infantry

pedest·er -ris -re adj infantry; pedestrian; on land, by land; written in prose; prosaic, plain

pedetemptim adv by feeling one's

way, step by step, slowly, cautiously

pedīc·a -ae f foot chain; trap, snare

pedīculōs·us -a -um adj lousy

ped·is -is m or f louse

pedisĕqu·a -ae f attendant, handmaid

pedisĕqu·us -ī m footman, page, lackey

peditastell·us -ī m poor infantryman

peditāt·us -ūs m infantry

pedīt·um -ī n wind, gas

pēdō pēdĕre pepēdī vi to break wind

ped·um -ī n shepherd's hook

Pēgasĕ·us or **Pēgasei·us -a -um** adj of Pegasus, Pegasean

Pēgasīd·es -um f pl Muses

Pēgās·us -ī m winged horse which sprang from the blood of Medusa and whose hoof, as it hit Mt. Helicon, caused Hippocrene, a fountain dear to the Muses, to flow

pegm·a -ātis n bookcase; scaffolding

pējerātiuncŭl·a -ae f petty oath

pējerāt·us or **pējurāt·us -a -um** adj offended by false oaths; **jus pejeratum** false oath

pējer·ō or **perjūr·ō -āre** vt to swear falsely by; vi to swear a false oath; (coll) to lie

pējerōs·us -a -um adj perjured

pēj·or -us (comp of malus) adj worse

pējus (comp of male) adv worse

pelagi·us -a -um adj of the sea

pelăg·us -ī n sea, open sea

pēlăm·is -idis or **pēlăm·ys -ỹdis** f young tuna fish

Pelasg·ī -ōrum m pl aborigines of Greece

Pēl·eus -ĕī or **-ĕos** m king of Thessaly, son of Aeacus, husband of Thetis, and father of Achilles

Peli·ās -ae m king of Iolcos in Thessaly and uncle of Jason

Pēlīd·ēs -ae m descendant of Peleus; Achilles; Neoptolemus

Pēli·on -ī n mountain in E. Thessaly

Pēli·us or **Pēliăc·us -a -um** adj of Mt. Pelion

Pell·a -ae or **Pell·ē -ēs** f city of Macedonia and birthplace of Alexander the Great

pellāci·a -ae f charm, allurement

Pellae·us -a -um adj of or from Apella; **Pellaeus juvenis** Alexander

pell·ax -ācis adj seductive, alluring

pellĕcti·ō -ōnis f perusal

pel·liciō -licĕre -lexī -lectum vt to allure, entice, coax, wheedle

pellicŭl·a -ae f small hide, skin, fleece

pelli·ō -ōnis m furrier

pell·is -is f skin, hide; leather; felt; tent; shield cover; **detrahere pellem** to expose one's true character

pellīt·us -a -um adj clothed in skins, wearing leather coat

pellō pellĕre pepŭlī pulsum vt to push, beat, strike, knock, hurl; to drive out or away, expel, banish; to repel, drive back, rout; to play or strum (lyre, etc.); to affect, impress, move, strike; to stamp (the earth)

pellūc- = **perl-**

Pelopēi·as -ădis or **Pelopē·is -ĭdis** adj Peloponnesian

Pelopēi·us or **Pelopē·us -a -um** adj Pelopian; Mycenaean; Phrygian

Pelopĭd·ae -ārum m pl descendants of Pelops

Peloponnēns·is -e adj Peloponnesian

Peloponnēsiăc·us or **Peloponnēsi·us -a -um** adj Peloponnesian

Peloponnēs·us -ī f the Peloponnesus (modern Morea)

Pel·ops -ŏpis m son of Tantalus, father of Atreus and Thyestes, and grandfather of Agamemnon and Menelaus

pelōr·is -ĭdis f large shellfish

Pelōr·us or **Pelōr·os -ī** m N.E. promontory of Sicily

pelt·a -ae f small leather shield

peltast·ēs or **peltast·a -ae** m soldier armed with a small leather shield

peltāt·us -a -um adj armed with a small leather shield

Pēlūs·ium -ĭī or **-ī** n city on the E. mouth of the Nile

pelv·is -is f bucket, basin

penāri·us -a -um adj food, supply, storage

Penāt·ēs -ium m pl Penates, household gods; hearth, home, house; cells (of bees)

penātĭg·er -ĕra -ĕrum adj carrying the household gods

pendĕō pendēre pependī vi to hang, hang down, be suspended; to hang loose; to hang down, be flabby, be weak; to depend, be dependent; to be in suspense, be uncertain, hesitate; to hang around, loiter; to hang in the air, be suspended, hover, float, overhang; (with abl or with **ab, dē** or **ex** + abl) **a** to hang down from, hang by; **b** to depend on, be dependent upon; **c** to hang on to, be devoted to; (with **in** + abl) to be poised on, hover in, hover over

pendō pendĕre pependī pensum vt to weigh, weigh out; to pay, pay out; to weigh, ponder, consider, value, esteem; to pay (penalty); **flocci pendere** to think little of; **magni pendere** to think much of, value highly; vi to weigh, have weight

pendŭl·us -a -um adj hanging, hanging down; doubtful, uncertain

Pēnē·is -ĭdis or **Pēnēi·us -a -um** adj of Peneus

Pēnelŏp·a -ae or **Pēnelŏp·ē -ēs** f daughter of Icarius and Periboea and wife of Ulysses

penes prep (with acc of person only) in the possession of, in the power of, belonging to, resting with; at the house of, with; **penes se esse** to be in one's senses

penetrābĭl·is -e adj penetrating, piercing; penetrable

penetrāl·is -e adj penetrating, piercing; inner, internal, interior; n pl the interior, center; inner chambers; sanctuary; the interior, hinterlands

penĕtr·ō -āre vt & vi to penetrate, enter

Pēnē·us -a -um adj of Peneus, of the Peneus River; m Peneus River (largest river in Thessaly); river god, the father of Cyrene and Daphne

pēnicill·us -ī m paint brush, pencil

pēnicŭl·us -ī m brush; sponge

pēn·is -is m tail; penis; lechery

penĭtē adv inwardly

penĭtus adv internally, inside, deep within, deeply; from within; thoroughly, completely, through and through; heartily

penĭt·us -a -um adj inner, inward

penn·a -ae f feather; wing; flight

pennāt·us -a -um adj feathered

pennĭg·er -ĕra -ĕrum adj winged, feathered

pennĭpŏt·ens -entis adj winged, able to fly

pennŭl·a -ae f little wing

pensĭl·is -e adj hanging; **uva pensilis** grape hung out to dry

pensĭ·ō -ōnis f payment, instalment

pensĭt·ō -āre vt to pay; to weigh, ponder, consider; vi to be taxable

pens·ō -āre vt to weigh out; to weigh, ponder, consider, examine; to compare, contrast; to pay, atone for; to repay, compensate, requite

pens·um -ī n work quota; duty, task; consideration, scruple; **pensi esse** to be of value, be of importance; **pensi habere** to value, consider of importance

pensus pp of **pendo**

pentēr·is -is f galley, quinquereme

Penthesilē·a -ae f Amazon, warrior queen who was killed by Achilles at Troy

Penth·eus -ĕi or **-ĕos** m king of Thebes, son of Echion and Agave, grandson of Cadmus, and opponent of the Bacchic cult

pen·um -ī n supplies, provisions, food

pēnūri·a -ae f want, need, dearth

pen·us -ūs or **-ī** m or **pen·us -ŏris** n supplies, provisions, food

pepl·um -ī n or **pepl·us -ī** m robe for the statue of Athena

per prep (with acc) (of space) through, throughout, all over, along; (of time) through, during, for, in the course of, at, at the time of; (of agency) through, by, by means of, at the hands of; (of means or manner) through, by, under pretense of; for the sake of, with a view to; (in oath) by

pēr·a -ae f wallet

perabsurd·us -a -um adj completely absurd

peraccommodāt·us -a -um *adj* very convenient

perāc·er -ris -re *adj* very sharp

peracerb·us -a -um *adj* very harsh, very sour

perac·escō -escĕre -ŭī *vi* to become completely sour

peractī·ō -ōnis *f* conclusion, last act (*of a play*)

peractus *pp* of **perago**

peracūtē *adv* very acutely

peracūt·us -a -um *adj* very sharp; very clear (*voice, intellect*)

peradulesc·ens -entis *adj* very young

peradulescentŭl·us -ī *m* very young man

peraequē *adv* quite evenly, uniformly

peragĭt·ō -āre *vt* to harass

per·agō -agĕre -ēgī -actum *vt* to carry through to the end, complete, accomplish; to pierce; to travel through; to harass, disturb, trouble; to describe, relate, go over; to work over, till, cultivate; to deliver (*speech*); (law) to prosecute to a conviction

peragrātī·ō -ōnis *f* traveling

perāgr·ō -āre *vt* to travel through, travel, traverse; *vi* (fig) to spread, penetrate

peralt·us -a -um *adj* very high

perām·ans -antis *adj* (with *genit*) very fond of

peramanter *adv* very lovingly

perambŭl·ō -āre *vt* to travel, traverse, walk through

peramoen·us -a -um *adj* very pleasant, very charming

perampl·us -a -um *adj* very large, very spacious

perangustē *adv* very narrowly

perangust·us -a -um *adj* very narrow

perantīqu·us -a -um *adj* very ancient, very old

perapposit·us -a -um *adj* very suitable

perardŭ·us -a -um *adj* very difficult

perargūt·us -a -um *adj* very clear; very sharp, very witty

perarmāt·us -a -um *adj* heavily armed

per·arō -āre *vt* to plow through; to furrow; to write on (*a wax tablet*); to write

pērātim *adv* bag by bag

perattentē *adv* very attentively

perattent·us -a -um *adj* very attentive

peraudiend·us -a -um *adj* that must be heard to the end

perbacch·or -ārī -ātus sum *vt* to carouse through (*e.g., many days*)

perbeāt·us -a -um *adj* very happy

perbellē *adv* very prettily

perbĕne *adv* very well

perbenevŏl·us -a -um *adj* very friendly

perbenignē *adv* very kindly

perbĭb·ō -ĕre -ī *vt* to drink up, drink in, imbibe

perbīt·ō -ĕre *vi* to go to ruin

perbland·us -a -um *adj* very attractive, very charming

perbŏn·us -a -um *adj* very good, excellent

perbrĕv·is -e *adj* very short, very brief; **perbrevi** or **perbrevī tempore** in a very short time

perbrevĭter *adv* very briefly

perc·a -ae *f* perch

percalefact·us -a -um *adj* warmed through and through

percal·escō -escĕre -ŭī *vi* to become quite hot

percall·escō -escĕre -ŭī *vt* to become thoroughly versed in; *vi* to become very hardened

percār·us -a -um *adj* very dear, very costly; very dear, much loved

percaut·us -a -um *adj* very cautious

percelĕbr·or -ārī -ātus sum *vi* to be quite famous

percĕl·er -ĕris *adj* very quick

percelerĭter *adv* very quickly

per·cellō -cellĕre -cŭlī -culsum *vt* to knock down, beat down, overthrow; to scare to death; to overthrow, ruin; to send scurrying; to hit hard

percens·ĕō -ēre -ŭī *vt* to count up; to review, survey; to travel through, traverse

perceptĭ·ō -ōnis *f* harvesting; comprehension; *f pl* concepts

percept·us -a -um *pp* of **percipio**; *n* precept, rule, doctrine

per·cīdō -cīdĕre -cīdī -cīsum *vt* to smash to pieces

perci·ĕō -ēre or **perc·iō -īre -īvī or -iī -itum** *vt* to stir up, excite

per·cipiō -cipĕre -cēpī -ceptum *vt* to get a good hold of; to catch; to occupy, seize; to gather in, harvest, reap; (of the senses) to take in, perceive, feel; (of feelings) to get hold of, get the better of; to learn, know, comprehend, understand, perceive

percĭt·us -a -um *pp* of **percieo**; *adj* aroused, provoked; impetuous, excitable

percoctus *pp* of **percoquo**

percōl·ō -āre *vt* to strain, filter

per·cōlō -colĕre -colŭī -cultum *vt* to reverence, revere, worship; to beautify; to crown, complete

percōm·is -e *adj* very courteous

percommŏdē *adv* very conveniently, very well, very suitably

percommŏd·us -a -um *adj* very convenient, very suitable

percontātĭ·ō -ōnis *f* thorough investigation

percontāt·or -ōris *m* inquisitive fellow

percont·or -ārī -ātus sum *vt* to question, investigate, interrogate; (with double *acc*) to ask (*someone something*)

percontŭm·ax -ācis *adj* very stubborn

per·cŏquō -coquĕre -coxī -coctum
vt to cook through and through,
cook thoroughly; to heat thoroughly; to ripen; to scorch, blacken

percrēb·escō or percrēbr·escō
-escĕre -ŭī vi to become prevalent,
be spread abroad

percrēp·ō -āre -ŭī -ĭtum vi to resound, ring

percruci·or -ārī -ātus sum vi to
torment oneself

perculsus pp of percello

percult·us -a -um pp of percolo;
adj decked out; (coll) dolled up
(woman)

percupĭd·us -a -um adj (with genit)
very fond of

percupĭ·ō -ĕre vt (with inf) to be
eager to, desire very much to, be
dying to

percūrĭōs·us -a -um adj very curious

percūr·ō -āre vt to heal completely

per·currō -currĕre -cucurrī or
currī -cursum vt to run through,
run along, run over, pass over,
speed over; (fig) to scan briefly, look
over; (in a speech) to treat in succession, go over, run over; (of feelings) to run through, penetrate,
pierce; vi to run fast, hurry along;
(with ad + acc) to dash to (e.g.,
the Forum); (with per + acc) a to
run through or across, travel
through; b (fig) to run through,
mention quickly, treat in succession

percursātĭ·ō -ōnis f traveling; per-
cursatio Italiae traveling through
Italy

percursĭ·ō -ōnis f quick survey

percurs·ō -āre vi to roam about,
range about

percussĭ·ō -ōnis f hitting, striking;
snapping (of fingers); (mus) beat,
time

percuss·or -ōris m assailant; assassin

percussus pp of percutio

percuss·us -ūs m beating, striking

per·cutĭō -cutĕre -cussī -cussum
vt to beat or hit hard; to pierce,
transfix, run through; to shoot, kill;
to shock, impress, move, astound;
to cut through; to dig (ditch); to
coin, stamp (money); to cheat, trick

perdecŏr·us -a -um adj very pretty

perdēlir·us -a -um adj very silly,
quite mad

perdeps·ō -ĕre -ŭī vt to knead thoroughly; (fig) to seduce

perdifficĭl·is -e adj very difficult

perdifficĭlĭter adv with great difficulty

perdign·us -a -um adj (with abl)
quite worthy of

perdīlĭg·ens -entis adj very diligent, very conscientious

perdīlĭgenter adv very diligently,
very conscientiously

per·discō -discĕre -didĭcī vt to
learn thoroughly, learn by heart

perdisertē adv very eloquently

perdĭtē adv recklessly, desperately

perdĭt·or -ōris m destroyer

perdĭt·us -a -um adj ruined, lost;
profligate, degenerate, infamous,
reckless, incorrigible, hopeless

perdiū adv for a very long time

perdiūturn·us -a -um adj longlasting, protracted

perdīv·es -itis adj very rich

perd·ix -īcis m partridge

per·dō -dĕre -dĭdī -dĭtum vt to
wreck, ruin, destroy; to waste,
squander; to lose

perdoc·ĕō -ēre -ŭī -tum vt to teach
thoroughly

perdoctē adv very skillfully

perdoct·us -a -um pp of perdoceo;
adj very learned, very skillful

perdol·escō -escĕre -ŭī vi to become resentful

perdŏm·ō -āre -ŭī -ĭtum vt to tame
completely, subdue, subjugate

perdormisc·ō -ĕre vi to sleep on,
keep on sleeping

per·dūcō -dūcĕre -duxī -ductum
vt to lead, guide; to cover, spread;
to prolong, drag out; to induce; to
seduce; (with ad + acc) a to lead,
bring, guide, escort to; b to build,
run (wall, ditch, road, etc.) to; c
to prolong, protract, drag out, continue (something) to or till; d to
win over to, convince of

perduct·ō -āre vt to lead, conduct

perduct·or -ōris m guide; pimp

perdūdum adv long long ago

perduellĭ·ō -ōnis f treason, high
treason

perduell·is -is m enemy

perdūr·ō -āre vi to hold out, last,
endure

per·ĕdō -esse -ēdī -ēsum vt to eat
up, devour

perēgrē adv abroad, away from
home; from abroad; peregre abire
or peregre exire to go abroad

peregrīnābund·us -a -um adj traveling around

peregrīnātĭ·ō -ōnis f living abroad,
travel, touring; roaming, ranging
(said of animals)

peregrīnāt·or -ōris m traveler,
wanderer

peregrīnĭt·ās -ātis f foreign manners, strange ways

peregrīn·or -ārī -ātus sum vi to
live abroad, travel abroad, travel
around; (fig) to be a stranger

peregrīn·us -a -um adj foreign,
strange, alien, exotic; (fig) strange,
inexperienced; amores peregrī-
nī love affairs with foreign wom-
en; praetor peregrinus praetor
who tried cases involving foreigners
and Roman citizens; terror pere-
grīnus fear of a foreign enemy;
mf foreigner, alien

perēlĕg·ans -antis adj very elegant

perēleganter adv very elegantly

perēlŏqu·ens -entis adv very eloquent

peremn·ia -ium *n pl* auspices taken before crossing a river

peremptus *pp of* **perimo**

perendiē *adv* the day after tomorrow

perendin·us -a -um *adj* **dies perendinus** the day after tomorrow; *m* the day after tomorrow

perenn·is -e *adj* perennial, continual, everlasting

perenniserv·os -ī *m* slave for life

perennit·ās -ātis *f* continuance, perpetuity

perenn·ō -āre *vi* to last

perenticīd·a -ae *m* (coll) crook

per·eō -īre -iī -itum *vi* to pass away, pass on, die; to go to waste, perish, be destroyed; to be lost, be ruined, be undone; to be desperately in love, pine away; (of snow) to melt away; (of iron) to rust away; **periī** I'm ruined!, I'm finished!, I'm washed up!

perequit·ō -āre *vt* to ride up through; *vi* to ride around

pererr·ō -āre *vt* to roam around, wander through; to survey, look (*someone*) over

pererudit·us -a -um *adj* very learned

perēsus *pp of* **peredo**

perexcels·us -a -um *adj* very high, exalted

perexiguē *adv* very sparingly

perexigu·us -a -um *adj* tiny; insignificant; very short (*day*)

perfacētē *adv* very wittily

perfacēt·us -a -um *adj* very witty, very sharp

perfacile *adv* very easily, very readily

perfacil·is -ē *adj* very easy; very courteous

perfamiliār·is -e *adj* very close, intimate; *m* very close friend

perfectē *adv* completely, perfectly

perfectī·ō -ōnis *f* completion; perfection

perfect·or -ōris *m* perfecter; **dicendi perfector** stylist

perfect·us -a -um *pp of* **perficio**; *adj* complete, finished, perfect, excellent

per·ferō -ferre -tulī -lātum *vt* to carry through; to endure to the end, bear with patience, put up with; to pass (*a law*); to bring, announce, report (*news*)

per·ficiō -ficere -fēcī -fectum *vt* to complete, finish, accomplish, carry out, perform, execute, bring to an end; to bring to completion, finish, perfect; to bring about, cause

perfic·us -a -um *adj* perfecting; **natura perfica** nature which perfects

perfidēl·is -e *adj* very faithful, very trusty

perfidi·a -ae *f* perfidy, treachery

perfidiōsē *adv* treacherously

perfidiōs·us -a -um *adj* treacherous, faithless

perfīd·us -a -um *adj* treacherous, untrustworthy, dishonest, sneaky; *m* sneak

per·fīgō -fīgere -fixī -fixum *vt* to pierce

perfiābil·is -e *adj* airy; invisible (*gods*)

perfiāgitiōs·us -a -um *adj* utterly disgraceful

perfi·ō -āre *vt* to blow through, blow across

perfluctū·ō -āre *vt* to surge through

per·fodiō -fodere -fōdī -fossum *vt* to dig through; to pierce

perfor·ō -āre *vt* to bore through, pierce; to make by boring

perfortiter *adv* very bravely

perfoss·or -ōris *m* **perfossor parietum** burglar

perfossus *pp of* **perfodio**

perfractus *pp of* **perfringo**

perfrēm·ō -ere -uī *vi* to snort loud

perfrequ·ens -entis *adj* very crowded, over-crowded

perfric·ō -āre -uī -ātum or **-tum** *vt* to rub well, rub all over; **os perfricare** to rub away blushes, put on a bold front

perfrigefac·iō -ere *vt* (fig) to send a chill over, make shudder

per·frigescō -frigescere -frixī *vi* to catch a bad cold

perfrigid·us -a -um *adj* very cold, ice-cold

per·fringō -fringere -frēgī -fractum *vt* to break through; to break to pieces, batter in, smash; (fig) to break (*laws, etc.*), break up (*conspiracy*)

per·fruor -fruī -fructus sum *vi* (with *abl*) to experience to the full, fully enjoy, be delighted by, perform gladly

perfug·a -ae *m* military deserter; political turncoat

per·fugiō -fugere -fūgī *vi* (with **ad** or **in** + *acc*) **a** to flee to for refuge; **b** to desert to; **c** (fig) to have recourse to, find comfort in

perfunctī·ō -ōnis *f* performance, performing, discharge

perfunctus *pp of* **perfungor**

per·fundō -fundere -fūdī -fūsum *vt* to drench, bathe; to sprinkle; to dye; (fig) to fill, flood, steep, inspire

per·fungor -fungī -functus sum *vt* to enjoy; *vi* (with *abl*) **a** to perform, discharge, fulfill; **b** to go through, endure, undergo; **c** to get rid of; **d** to be finished with, be done with; **e** to enjoy

perfūr·ō -ere *vi* to rage wildly, rage on

perfūsus *pp of* **perfundo**

Pergam·a -ōrum *n pl* or **Pergăm·us -ī** *f* citadel of Troy, Troy

Pergamē·us -a -um *adj* Trojan; *m pl* Trojans

Pergăm·um -ī *n* Troy; Pergamum (*city in Mysia, the capital of the Attalid kingdom, famous for its library*)

pergaud·ĕō -ēre *vi* to be very glad

per·gō -gĕre -rexī -rectum *vt* to go on uninterruptedly with, continue; (with *inf*) to continue to; *vi* to go straight on, continue, proceed; (with **ad** + *acc*) to pass on to, proceed to (*esp. in speaking*)

pergraec·or -ārī -ātus sum *vi* to go completely Greek, have a ball

pergrand·is -e *adj* very large, huge; **pergrandis natu** very old

pergraphic·us -a -um *adj* very cunning

pergrāt·us -a -um *adj* very pleasant; *n* distinct pleasure

pergrāv·is -e *adj* very heavy; very important; very impressive

pergravĭter *adv* very seriously

pergŭl·a -ae *f* veranda, balcony; school; brothel

Perg·us -ī *m* lake in Sicily, near Henna, where Pluto carried off Proserpina

perhib·ĕō -ēre -ŭī -ĭtum *vt* to hold, assert, maintain; to call, name; to adduce, cite

perhīlum *adv* very little

perhonōrificē *adv* very respectfully, with all due respect

perhonōrific·us -a -um *adj* very honorable, very complimentary; very respectful

perhorr·escō -escĕre -ŭī *vt* to begin to shudder at; to develop a terror of; *vi* to begin to quake, begin to tremble violently

perhorrĭd·us -a -um *adj* horrible, dreadful

perhūmānĭter *adv* very kindly

perhūmān·us -a -um *adj* very courteous

Pericl·ēs -is or **-ī** *m* Athenian statesman, son of Xanthippus and political leader of Athens during the city's most flourishing period (c. 495-429 B.C.)

perīclĭtātĭ·ō -ōnis *f* test, experiment

perīclĭt·or -ārī -ātus sum *vt* to test, put to the test, try; to jeopardize; to risk; *vi* to be in danger, be in jeopardy; to run a risk; (with *abl*) to be in danger of losing (*e.g., life, reputation*); **capite periclĭtāri** to be in danger of losing one's life, risk one's life

perīculōsē *adv* dangerously

perīculōs·us -a -um *adj* dangerous, perilous, risky

perīcŭl·um or **perīcl·um -ī** *n* danger, peril, risk; trial, attempt, experiment, test; literary venture; (law) trial, case, lawsuit, legal record, writ, sentence

perīdōnĕ·us -a -um *adj* very suitable; (with *dat* or **ad** + *acc*) well adapted to, well suited to

perillustr·is -e *adj* very clear; very illustrious, very distinguished

perimbēcill·us -a -um *adj* very weak, very feeble

per·imō -imĕre -ēmī -emptum *vt*

to take away completely; to destroy; to slay, kill

perimpedīt·us -a -um *adj* rough (*terrain*), full of obstacles

perincommŏdē *adv* very inconveniently

perincommŏd·us -a -um *adj* very inconvenient

perinde *adv* in the same manner, equally, just as, quite as; (with **atque, ac, ut,** or **quam**) just as, exactly as; (with **ac si, quasi, tamquam,** or **quam si**) just as if

perindulg·ens -entis *adj* very tender; (with **ad** + *acc*) very tender toward

perinfirm·us -a -um *adj* very weak

peringeniōs·us -a -um *adj* very clever

periniqu·us -a -um *adj* very unfair; very upset, very annoyed, very impatient, very reluctant; **periniquo animo ferre** or **ferre** to be quite upset at, be quite annoyed at, be very reluctant about

perinsign·is -e *adj* very remarkable

perinvīt·us -a -um *adj* very unwilling

perĭŏd·us -ī *f* sentence, rhetorical period

peripatētĭc·us -a -um *adj* peripatetic, Aristotelian; *m pl* peripatetics, Aristotelians

peripetasmăt·a -um *n pl* curtains, drapes

perīrāt·us -a -um *adv* very angry; (with *dat*) very angry with

periscĕl·is -ĭdis *f* anklet

peristrōm·a -ătis *n* carpet

peristŷl·ium -iī or **-ī** *n* peristyle (*open court surrounded by a colonnade*)

peristŷl·um -ī *n* colonnade around a building, peristyle

perītē *adv* skillfully, expertly

perītĭ·a -ae *f* experience, practical knowledge, skill; (with *genit*) experience in, familiarity with, knowledge of

perīt·us -a -um *adj* experienced, skillful, expert, familiar; (with *genit* or *abl*, with **in** + *abl*, or with **ad** + *acc*) experienced in, skillful in, expert in or at, familiar with; (with *inf*) skilled in, expert at, e.g., **peritus cantare** skilled in singing, expert at singing

perjūcundē *adv* very pleasantly

perjūcund·us -a -um *adj* very pleasant

perjūr·ium -iī or **-ī** *n* perjury, false oath

perjūrō see **pejero**

perjūr·us or **pejēr·us -a -um** *adj* perjured, oath-breaking; lying, dishonest

per·lābor -lābī -lapsus sum *vi* to glide along, skim across or over; (with **per** + *acc*) to slip through; (with **ad** + *acc*) to come, move, glide, or slip toward; (with **in** + *acc*) to glide into, slip into

perlaet·us -a -um *adv* very glad, most joyful

perlapsus *pp* of **perlabor**

perlātē *adv* very extensively

perlat·ĕō -ēre -uī *vi* to be completely hidden

perlātus *pp* of **perfero**

perlecti·ō -ōnis *f* thorough perusal

per·lĕgō -legĕre -lēgī -lectum *vt* to scan, survey thoroughly; to read through

perlepidē *adv* very nicely

perlĕv·is -e *adj* very light, very slight

perlevĭter *adv* very lightly, very slightly

perlīb·ens or **perlŭb·ens** -entis *adj* very willing

perlibenter or **perlubenter** *adv* very gladly

perlīberāl·is -e *adj* very genteel

perlīb·et or **perlŭb·et** -ēre *v impers* (with *inf*) I should very much like to

perliciō see **pellicio**

perlīt·ō -āre *vi* to sacrifice with favorable omens

perlongē *adv* a long way off, very far

perlonginqu·us -a -um *adj* very long; very tedious

perlub- = **perlib-**

per·lūcĕō or **pel·lūcĕō** -lūcēre -luxī *vi* to shine clearly, be bright; to be clearly visible; to be transparent; to be clear, be intelligible

perlūcidŭl·us -a -um *adj* somewhat transparent

perlūcid·us or **pellūcid·us** -a -um *adj* very bright; transparent

perluctuōs·us -a -um *adj* very sad

per·lŭō -luĕre -luī -lūtum *vt* to wash thoroughly, wash off, bathe

perlustr·ō -āre *vt* to traverse; to scan, survey, review

permadefac·iō -ĕre *vt* to soak through and through, drench

permagn·us -a -um *adj* very great; very important; *n* great thing; **permagno** at a very high price, very dearly; **permagnum aestimare** (with *inf*) to think it quite something to

permānanter *adv* by flowing through

permānasc·ō -ĕre *vi* (*of a report*) to begin to spread

per·manĕō -manēre -mansī -mansum *vi* to last, continue, hold out, remain, persist, endure

permān·ō -āre *vt* to seep through, penetrate; *vi* to penetrate; (with **ad** or **in** + *acc*) **a** to seep through to, seep into, penetrate; **b** (fig) to reach, extend to, penetrate

permansi·ō -ōnis *f* persistence, continuance

permarīn·us -a -um *adj* sea-going

permātūr·escō -escĕre -uī *vi* to become fully ripe

permediōcr·is -e *adj* completely normal

permeditāt·us -a -um *adj* well rehearsed, well trained

permensus *pp* of **permetior**

permĕ·ō -āre *vt* to go through, cross over, cross; *vi* (with **in** + *acc*) to penetrate; (with **per** + *acc*) to penetrate, permeate

Permess·us -ī *m* river in Boeotia sacred to Apollo and the Muses

per·mētior -mētīrī -mensus sum *vt* to measure out, measure; to traverse, travel, travel over

per·mingō -mingĕre -minxī *vt* to soak with urine; to pollute

permīr·us -a -um *adj* very surprising, truly amazing

per·miscĕō -miscēre -miscuī -mixtum *vt* to mix together, intermingle; (fig) to mix together, mix up, confuse

permissi·ō -ōnis *f* unconditional surrender; permission

permiss·us -a -um *pp* of **permitto**; *n* permission

permiss·us -ūs *m* permission, leave

permitiāl·is -e *adj* destructive, deadly

permitĭ·ēs -ēī *f* wasting away; ruin, decay

per·mittō -mittĕre -mīsī -missum *vt* to let through, let go through; to throw, hurl; to give up, surrender; to concede, relinquish; to let loose, let go; to let, permit, allow, grant; (with *dat*) to give up to, surrender (*something*) to, entrust (*something*) to, grant (*something*) to; (with **in** + *acc*) to send flying at, hurl or throw at

permixtē or **permixtim** *adv* confusedly, promiscuously

permixti·ō -ōnis *f* mixture; confusion, bedlam

permixt·us -a -um *pp* of **permisceo**; *adj* confused, promiscuous

permodest·us -a -um *adj* very modest, very moderate

permolestē *adv* with much trouble; **permoleste ferre** to be quite annoyed at

permolest·us -a -um *adj* very troublesome, very annoying

permŏl·ō -ĕre *vt* to grind up; **alienas uxores permolere** (fig) to seduce other men's wives

permōti·ō -ōnis *f* excitement; **animi permotio** or **mentis permotio** excitement, deep emotion

per·movĕō -movēre -mōvī -mōtum *vt* to stir up, churn up (*the sea*); to move deeply, make a deep impression upon; to excite, agitate, rouse; to influence, induce, prevail on

per·mulcĕō -mulcēre -mulsī -mulsum *vt* to stroke, pet, caress; to soothe, charm; to delight, flatter; to appease, tame, mitigate, allay

permultō *adv* (with *comparatives*) by far, far, much

permultum *adv* very much; **permultum ante** very often before; **permultum interest** it makes a world of difference

permult·us -a -um *adj* very much,
very many; *n* a lot, much

permūn·iō -īre -īvī or **-iī -ītum** *vt*
to fortify thoroughly; to finish fortifying

permūtātī·ō -ōnis *f* permutation,
complete change; change, alteration; crisis, revolution; exchange,
barter; substitution

permūt·ō -āre *vt* to change completely, alter completely; to exchange, interchange

pern·a -ae *f* ham

pernecessāri·us -a -um *adj* very
necessary; very closely related; *m*
close friend; close relative

pernecesse (indecl) *adj* very necessary, indispensable

pernĕg·ō -āre *vt* to deny flatly; to
turn down flat

per·nĕō -nēre -nēvī -nētum *vt* (of
the Fates) to spin out

perniciābil·is -e *adj* ruinous

pernici·ēs -ēī *f* ruin, destruction,
disaster, calamity; pest, curse

perniciōsē *adj* perniciously, ruin-
ously

perniciōs·us -a -um *adj* pernicious,
ruinous

pernicit·ās -ātis *f* agility, nimbleness, swiftness

perniciter *adv* nimbly, swiftly

pernig·er -ra -rum *adj* jet black

pernimi·us -a -um *adj* much too
much

pern·ix -īcis *adj* agile, nimble, active, swift

pernōbil·is -e *adj* famous, illustrious

pernoct·ō -āre *vi* to spend the night

per·nōscō -nōscĕre -nōvī -nōtum
vt to examine thoroughly; to become
fully acquainted with, get an accurate knowledge of

pernōt·ēscō -ēscĕre -uī *vi* to become generally known

pern·ox -octis *adj* all-night; **luna
pernox** full moon

pernumĕr·ō -āre *vt* to count up

pēr·ō -ōnis *m* clodhopper, brogue
(*worn by peasants and soldiers*)

perobscūr·us -a -um *adj* very obscure

perodiōs·us -a -um *adj* very annoying

perofficiōsē *adv* with devotion, with
attention

perol·ĕō -ēre *vi* to have a strong
odor

pērōnāt·us -a -um *adj* wearing
clodhoppers

peropportūnē *adv* very opportunely,
very conveniently

peropportūn·us -a -um *adj* very
opportune, very convenient, well
timed

peroptātō *adv* very much to one's
wish

perŏpus (indecl) *n* great need; **per-
opus est** it is absolutely essential

perōrātī·ō -ōnis *f* peroration, conclusion of a speech

perōrnāt·us -a -um *adj* very flow-

ery (*style*)

perorn·ō -āre *vt* to enhance the prestige of (*e.g., the senate*)

perōr·ō -āre *vt* to plead (*a case*) all
by oneself; to wind up, conclude (*a
speech, case*), rest (*a case*); *vi* to
give the summation

perōs·us -a -um *adj* hating, detesting

perpāc·ō -āre *vt* to silence completely; to pacify thoroughly

perparcē *adv* very stingily

perparvŭl·us -a -um *adj* tiny

perparv·us -a -um *adj* very small

perpast·us -a -um *adj* well fed

perpauc·ī -ae -a *adj* very few; *n pl*
very few words; **perpauca dicere**
to speak very briefly

perpaucŭl·ī -ae -a *adj* very few

perpaulum *adv* somewhat, slightly

perpaul·um -ī *n* small bit

perpaup·er -ĕris *adj* very poor

perpauxill·um -ī *n* little bit

perpavefac·iō -ĕre *vt* to frighten
the daylight out of

per·pellō -pellĕre -pulsī -pulsum
vt to push hard; to urge strongly,
force

perpendicŭl·um -ī *n* plumb line,
plummet; **ad perpendiculum** per-
pendicularly

**per·pendō -pendĕre -pendī -pen-
sum** *vt* to weigh carefully, consider; to value, judge

perpĕram *adv* incorrectly, falsely

perp·es -ĕtis *adj* continuous, uninterrupted

perpessi·ō -ōnis *f* suffering, endurance

per·petior -pĕtī -pessus sum *vt* to
endure, put up with, stand; to allow, permit

perpĕtr·ō -āre *vt* to accomplish, go
through with, carry out, achieve,
perform; to perpetrate, commit

perpetuĭt·ās -ātis *f* perpetuity

perpetŭō *adv* constantly, without interruption, forever

perpetŭ·ō -āre *vt* to perpetuate

perpetŭ·us -a -um *adj* perpetual,
continuous, uninterrupted; general,
universal; whole, entire; **quaestio-
nes perpetuae** standing courts;
permanent committee; *n* **in perpetuum** without a break, continuously; for all time, forever

perplac·ĕō -ēre -uī *vi* (with *dat*) to
please immensely

perplexābil·is -e *adj* obscure, perplexing

perplexābiliter *adv* perplexingly

perplexē or **perplexim** *adv* confusedly, unintelligibly

perplex·or -ārī -ātus sum *vi* to
cause confusion

perplex·us -a -um *adj* intricate,
confused; ambiguous, obscure; *n*
ambiguity, confusion

perplicāt·us -a -um *adj* entangled

perplŭ·ō -ĕre *vt* (fig) to rain, pour;
vi (of roof, etc.) to leak, let the
rain in

perpol·iŏ -īre -īvī or **-iī -ītum** vt to polish well, bring to a high polish; (fig) to polish up, perfect

perpolīt·us -a -um adj polished, refined

perpopŭl·or -ārī -ātus sum vt to ravage, devastate

perpōtātĭ·ŏ -ōnis f heavy drinking; drinking party

perpōt·ō -āre vt to drink off; vi to drink heavily, drink constantly

per·prīmō -prīmĕre -pressī vt to press hard, squeeze hard; to lie on

perpropinqu·us -a -um adj very near

perprūrisc·ō -ĕre vi to begin to itch all over

perpugn·ax -ācis adj very belligerent

perpulch·er -ra -rum adj very beautiful, very handsome

perpulsus pp of **perpello**

perpurg·ō -āre vt to cleanse thoroughly, clean up; (fig) to clear up, explain

perpusill·us -a -um adj puny

perpŭt·ō -āre vt to prune back hard; to clear up, explain in detail

perquam adv very, extremely

per·quīrō -quīrĕre -quīsīvī -quīsītum vt to search carefully for; to examine carefully

perquīsītius adv more accurately, more critically

perquīsīt·or -ōris m enthusiast; **auctiōnum perquisitor** auction enthusiast

perrārō adv very rarely, very seldom

perrār·us -a -um adj very rare, quite uncommon

perrecondīt·us -a -um adj recondite, abstruse

perrectus pp of **pergo**

per·rēpō -rēpĕre -repsī -reptum vt to crawl over, crawl along

perrept·ō -āre vt to creep through, sneak through; vi to creep around

perrīdĭcŭlē adv most absurdly

perrīdicŭl·us -a -um adj utterly absurd

perrogātĭ·ō -ōnis f passage (of a law)

perrŏg·ō -āre vt to ask in succession; to poll (opinions); **sententias perrogare** to have roll call (in the senate)

per·rumpō -rumpĕre -rūpī -ruptum vt to break through, force one's way through; to break in two, shatter, smash; to offend against, violate; vi to break through, make a breakthrough

Pers·a or **Pers·ēs -ae** m Persian

persaepe adv very often

persalsē adv very wittily

persals·us -a -um adj very witty

persalūtātĭ·ō -ōnis f round of greetings, greeting all in turn

persalūt·ō -āre vt to salute one after another

persanctē adv very solemnly

persapĭ·ens -entis adj very wise

persapienter adv very wisely

perscienter adv very wisely, very discreetly

per·scindō -scindĕre -scīdī -scissum vt to tear to pieces; to scatter (e.g., clouds)

perscīt·us -a -um adj very clever, very smart

per·scrībō -scrībĕre -scripsī -scriptum vt to write out; to describe fully, give in detail; to record, register; to enter (into an account book); to make over by writing; to pay by check

perscriptĭ·ō -ōnis f entry, official record; check, payment by check

perscript·or -ōris m bookkeeper, accountant

perscriptus pp of **perscribo**

perscrūt·ō -āre or **perscrūt·or -ārī -ātus sum** vt to search or examine thoroughly, scrutinize

per·sĕcō -secāre -secŭī -sectum vt to dissect, cut into pieces; (fig) to cut through, cut out, eliminate

persect·or -ārī -ātus sum vt to follow eagerly, investigate

persecūtĭ·ō -ōnis f prosecution, suing, lawsuit

persecūtus pp of **persequor**

per·sedĕō or **per·sidĕō -sedēre -sēdī -sessum** vi to remain seated

persegn·is -e adj very slow-moving, dull, tedious

per·sentiō -sentīre -sensī -sensum vt to perceive clearly; to feel deeply

persentisc·ō -ĕre vt to detect; to feel deeply

Persephŏn·ē -ēs f daughter of Demeter and queen of the lower world, called Proserpina by the Romans

persĕqu·ens -entis adj pursuing; (with genit) given to the practice of

per·sĕquor -sĕquī -secūtus sum vt to follow persistently, follow up; to be in hot pursuit of, be on the heels of; to chase after, catch up to; to follow verbatim; to imitate, copy; to prosecute; to take vengeance on; to follow out, execute, perform; to describe, explain

Pers·ēs -ae or **Pers·eus -ēī** m last king of Macedonia, conquered by Aemilius Paulus at Pydna (169 B.C.)

Pers·eus -ēī or **-ĕos** m son of Jupiter and Danae, who killed Medusa and slew the sea monster who was about to devour Andromeda

Persĕ·us or **Persēĭ·us -a -um** adj of Perseus

persevēr·ans -antis adj persevering, persistent, relentless

persevēranter adv persistently, relentlessly

persevērantĭ·a -ae f perseverance, persistence

persevēr·ō -āre vt to persist in; vi to persist

persevēr·us -a -um adj very strict

Persi·a -ae or **Pers·is -ĭdis** *f* Persia

Persic·us -a -um *adj* Persian; (fig) luxurious, soft; of Perses (*king of Macedonia*); *m pl* Persians; *f* peach tree; *n* peach; *n pl* Persian history

per·sīdō -sīdĕre -sēdī -sessum *vi* to sink down, penetrate

persign·ō -āre *vt* to record in detail

persimil·is -e *adj* very similar; (with *genit* or *dat*) very similar to, very much like

persimpl·ex -ĭcis *adj* very plain, very simple

Pers·is -ĭdis *adj* Persian; *f* Persia; Persian woman

Pers·ĭus -ĭī or **-ī** *m* A. Persius Flaccus (*famous satirist in the reign of Nero,* 34-62 A.D.)

persoll·a -ae *f* little mask; (as term of abuse) you ugly little thing!

persōl·us -a -um *adj* completely alone

per·solvō -solvĕre -solvī -solūtum *vt* to solve, explain; to pay up; to pay (*a penalty*); to fulfill (*a vow*); to render (*thanks*); to offer (*sacrifice*); **poenas persolvere** (with *dat*) to suffer at the hands of

persōn·a -ae *f* mask; part, character; mask, pretense; personality, person, character

personāt·us -a -um *adj* wearing a mask, masked; under false pretenses; **pater personatus** father on the stage

persŏn·ō -āre *vt* to make resound, make ring; to shout; **aurem personare** to make the ear ring; *vi* to resound, reecho; **citharā personare** to play the zither loudly

perspectē *adv* intelligently

perspect·ō -āre *vt* to look all around

perspect·us -a -um *pp* of **perspicio**; *adj* well known, clear, evident

perspecŭl·or -ārī -ātus sum *vt* to examine thoroughly, explore thoroughly

perspergō -ĕre *vt* to sprinkle

perspĭc·ax -ācis *adj* sharp-sighted; keen, penetrating, perspicacious

perspicienti·a -ae *f* clear perception

per·spiciō -spicĕre -spexī -spectum *vt* to see through; to look closely at, examine, inspect, observe

perspĭcŭē *adv* clearly

perspicuit·ās -ātis *f* clarity

perspĭcŭ·us -a -um *adj* clear, transparent; clear, evident, perspicuous

per·sternō -sternĕre -strāvī -strātum *vt* to pave

perstimŭl·ō -āre *vt* to stimulate violently

per·stō -stāre -stĭtī -stātum *vi* to stand firm, hold one's ground; to keep standing; to remain unchanged, last; to be firm, persevere, persist; hold out

perstrātus *pp* of **persterno**

perstrĕp·ō -ĕre -ŭī -ĭtum *vi* to make a loud noise, make a lot of noise

per·stringō -stringĕre -strinxī -strictum *vt* to ' tie, tie up; to blunt, deaden (*the senses*), dazzle (*the eyes*), deafen (*the ears*); to touch lightly, graze, graze against; to glance over, touch lightly on; to belittle, slight

perstudiōsē *adv* enthusiastically

perstudiōs·us -a -um *adj* very eager, enthusiastic; (with *genit*) very fond of, enthusiastic about

per·suādēō -suādēre -suāsī -suāsum *vi* (with *dat*) to persuade, convince; **sibi persuasum habere** to convince oneself, be convinced

persuāsĭ·ō -ōnis *f* convincing

persuastr·ix -īcis *f* seductress

persuāsus *pp* of **persuadeo**

persuās·us -ūs *m* persuasion

persubtīl·is -e *adj* very subtle, very ingenious

persult·ō -āre *vt* to gambol about, prance about; to scour (*woods*); *vi* to gambol, prance, run around

per·taedet -taedĕre -taesum est *v impers* (with *acc* of person = subject in English and *genit* of thing = object in English) to be weary of, be sick and tired of, be bored with, e.g., **me negotii pertaedet** I am sick and tired of this business

per·tĕgō -tegĕre -texī -tectum *vt* to cover, cover up

pertemptō -āre *vt* to test thoroughly; to sound (*someone*) out; to consider well; (fig) to pervade, fill, overwhelm; **gaudia pertemptant pectus** joy fills (*their*) hearts

per·tendō -tendĕre -tendī -tensum or **-tentum** *vt* to press on with, continue, carry out; *vi* to press on, continue, persevere, persist, keep going

pertenŭ·is -e *adj* very thin, very slight, very small, very fine

perterĕbr·ō -āre *vt* to bore through

per·tergēō -tergēre -tersī -tersum *vt* to wipe off; (of air) to brush lightly against

perterre·faciō -facĕre -fēcī -factum *vt* to scare the life out of

perterr·ĕō -ēre -ŭī -ĭtum *vt* to frighten, terrify; (with **ab** + *abl*) to frighten (*someone*) away from

perterricrĕp·us -a -um *adj* terrible-sounding, rattling frightfully

per·texō -texĕre -texŭī -textum *vt* to bring to an end, go through with, accomplish

pertĭc·a -ae *f* pole, rod, staff; measuring pole; (fig) measure

pertim·escō -escĕre -ŭī *vt* to be alarmed at, become afraid of; *vi* to become very frightened, become alarmed

pertināci·ā -ae *f* stubbornness; perseverance, determination

pertināciter *adv* stubbornly, tenaciously; perseveringly, constantly

pertin·ax -ācis *adj* very tenacious; persevering, steadfast; unyielding, stubborn, obstinate

pertin·ĕō -ēre -ŭī *vi* to reach, extend; (with **per** + *acc*) to pervade, reach; (with **ad** + *acc*) **a** to extend to, reach; **b** to pertain to, relate to, concern; **c** to apply to, be applicable to, suit, be suitable to; **d** to tend toward, be conducive to; **e** to belong to; **quod pertinet** (with **ad** + *acc*) as regards, as far as concerns

perting·ō -ĕre *vi* to extend

pertolĕr·ō -āre *vt* to put up with, endure to the end

pertorqu·ĕō -ēre *vt* to twist, distort

pertractātē *adv* systematically

pertractātī·ō -ōnis *f* handling, treatment

pertract·ō -āre *vt* to handle, fondle; (fig) to handle carefully, treat systematically; to influence

per·trăhō -trahĕre -traxī -tractum *vt* to drag; to allure, lead on, decoy

pertrect- = **pertract-**

pertrist·is -e *adj* very sad, very gloomy

pertumultuōsē *adv* very excitedly, hysterically

per·tundō -tundĕre -tŭdī -tūsum *vt* to punch a hole through, perforate

perturbātē *adv* confusedly, in confusion

perturbātī·ō -ōnis *f* confusion, disorder; political disturbance, revolution; mental disturbance; disturbing emotion

perturbātr·ix -īcis *f* disturbing element

perturbāt·us -a -um *adj* disturbed, troubled; excited, alarmed; embarrassed

perturb·is -e *adj* downright shameful

perturb·ō -āre *vt* to throw into confusion, confuse, disturb; to embarrass; to upset, alarm

pertūs·us -a -um *pp* of **pertundō**; *adj* perforated; tattered (*clothes*)

per·ungō -ungĕre -unxī -unctum *vt* to oil thoroughly, anoint thoroughly

perurbān·us -a -um *adj* very urbane, very sophisticated; *m* sophisticate

per·ūrō -ūrĕre -ussī -ustum *vt* to burn up; to consume; to inflame, rub sore; to scorch; (of cold) to nip, bite; (fig) to fire, inflame

Perusi·a -ae *f* town in Etruria

perustus *pp* of **peruro**

perūtil·is -e *adj* very useful, very practical

per·vādō -vādĕre -vāsī -vāsum *vt* to pass through, go through; to spread throughout, pervade; to penetrate, reach; *vi* to spread, permeate; (with **ad** or **in** + *acc*) to go as far as, spread to, reach, arrive at, penetrate; (with **per** + *acc*) to spread through or over

pervagāt·us -a -um *adj* widespread,

prevalent, well known; general, common

pervăg·or -ārī -ātus sum *vt* to spread through or over, pervade; *vi* to wander all over, range about; (with **ad** + *acc*) to spread to, extend to, be known as far as

pervăg·us -a -um *adj* wandering about

pervariē *adv* in various versions

pervast·ō -āre *vt* to devastate

pervāsus *pp* of **pervado**

per·vĕhō -vehĕre -vexī -vectum *vt* to bring, carry, convey; to bring (*e.g., supplies*) through; **pervehi** to ride, drive, sail; to reach; **in portum pervehi** to sail into port, reach port

per·vellō -vellĕre -vellī *vt* to pull hard; to pinch hard; to excite, arouse; (fig) to tear apart (*with words*), disparage

per·veniō -venīre -vēnī -ventum *vt* to come to, reach; *vi* to come up, arrive; (with **ad** or **in** + *acc*) **a** to arrive at, reach; **b** (fig) to attain to

pervēn·or -ārī -ātus sum *vt* to search through (*e.g., all the city*)

perversē or **pervorsē** *adv* wrongly, perversely

perversit·ās -ātis *f* perversity, distortion

pervers·us or **pervors·us -a -um** *adj* turned the wrong way, awry, crooked; cross-eyed; (fig) crooked, wrong, perverse; spiteful, malicious

per·vertō or **per·vortō -vertĕre -vertī -versum** *vt* to overturn, upset, knock down; (fig) to abuse, misuse, undo, destroy, pervert

pervespĕrī *adv* late in the evening

pervestīgātī·ō -ōnis *f* thorough search, examining, investigation

pervestīg·ō -āre *vt* to track down, hunt down; (fig) to trace, detect

pervĕt·us -ĕris *adj* very old, ancient

pervetust·us -a -um *adj* outdated, antiquated

perviam *adv* **perviam facere** to make accessible

pervĭcācĭ·a -ae *f* persistence; stubbornness

pervĭcācĭus *adv* more obstinately, more stubbornly

pervĭc·ax -ācis *adj* persistent, determined; headstrong, stubborn, obstinate

pervīctus *pp* of **pervinco**

per·vĭdĕō -vĭdēre -vīdī -vīsum *vt* to look over, overlook, survey; to see through; to examine, investigate; to realize

pervĭg·ĕō -ēre -ŭī *vi* to continue to thrive

pervĭg·il (*genit*: **-ĭlis**) *adj* wide awake, ever watchful

pervĭgĭlātĭ·ō -ōnis *f* religious vigil

pervĭgĭl·ĭum -ĭī or **-ī** *n* all-night vigil

pervĭgĭl·ō -āre *vt* to spend or pass (*nights, days*) without sleep; *vi* to stay awake all night, keep an all-night vigil

pervil·is -e *adj* very cheap

per·vincō -vincĕre -vīcī -victum *vt* to defeat completely, completely overcome, completely get the better of; to outdo, surpass, exceed; to outbid; to convince; to prove; *vi* to win, succeed; to carry a point; (with **ut**) to succeed in, bring it about that; **non pervicit ut referrent consules** he did not succeed in having the consuls make a formal proposal

pervīsus *pp* of **pervideo**

pervi·us -a -um *adj* crossable, passable, accessible; *n* passage, thoroughfare

per·vīvō -vīvĕre -vixī *vi* to live on; **pervivere usque ad summam aetatem** to live on to a ripe old age

pervolgō see **pervulgo**

pervolit·ō -āre *vt & vi* to fly about, flit about

pervŏl·ō -āre *vt* to fly through or about, flit about; to dart through, pass quickly over; *vi* to fly about, flit about; (with **in** + *acc*) to fly through to, arrive at, reach

per·vŏlō -velle -volŭī *vt* to want badly, wish very much; (with *inf*) to wish very much to; (with *acc & inf*) to eagerly wish (*someone*) to

pervolūt·ō -āre *vt* to turn over often, read through (*books*)

per·volvō -volvĕre -volvī -volūtum *vt* to roll (*someone*) over; to keep reading, read through (*books*); **pervolvi** to be busy, be engaged

pervor- see **perver-**

pervulgāt·us or **pervolgāt·us -a -um** *adj* widely known, very common

pervulg·ō or **pervolg·ō -āre** *vt* to make known, make public, publicize; to frequent; **se pervulgare** to prostitute oneself, become a prostitute

pēs pedis *m* foot; foot (*measure*); foot, meter (*in verse*); leg (*of table, couch, etc.*); sail rope, sheet; **ad pedes descendere** to dismount (*in order to fight on foot*); **aequis pedibus labi** to sail on an even keel; **ante pedes** in plain view; **pede dextro, felice, or secundo** auspiciously; **pedem conferre** to come to close quarters; **pedem ferre** to come; to go; **pedem ponere** (with **in** + *abl*) to set foot on; **pedem referre** to go back, retreat; **pedibus** on foot; **pedibus claudere** to set to verse, put in meter; **pedibus ire in sententiam** (with *genit*) to vote in favor of the proposal of; **pedibus itur in sententiam** the proposal is put to a vote, a vote is taken on the proposal; **pedibus merere or pedibus mereri** to serve in the infantry; **pedibus vincere** to win a footrace; **pugna ad pedes** infantry battle; **se in pedes conjicere** to take to one's heels; **servus a pedibus** footman; **sub pedibus** under one's sway

pessĭmē (*superl* of **male**) *adv* very badly, most wretchedly

pessĭm·us -a -um (*superl* of **malus**) *adj* worst; *m* scoundrel

pessŭl·us -ī *m* bolt (*of a door*)

pessum *adv* down, to the ground, to the bottom; **pessum dare** to send to the bottom, sink, drown, ruin, destroy; **pessum ire** to go down, sink, go to ruin

pestĭf·er -ĕra -ĕrum *adj* pestilential; destructive, pernicious; *m* trouble maker

pestifĕrē *adv* balefully

pestĭl·ens -entis *adj* pestilential, unhealthful; (fig) destructive, pernicious

pestilentĭ·a -ae *f* unhealthful atmosphere, unhealthful climate; pestilence, plague; destruction, death

pestĭlĭt·ās -ātis *f* pestilence, plague

pest·is -is *f* contagious disease, plague; destruction, death; trouble maker, anarchist, subversive

petasāt·us -a -um *adj* wearing a hat; (fig) ready to travel

petasĭ·ō or **petās·ō -ōnis** *m* ham

petasuncŭl·us -ī *m* little ham

petās·us -ī *m* hat

petaur·um -ī *n* springboard

petess·ō or **petiss·ō -ĕre** *vt* to be eager for, pursue; **pugnam petessere** to be spoiling for a fight

petītĭ·ō -ōnis *f* attack, blow, thrust, aim; petition, request, application; candidacy, political campaign; claim, suit, suing; right to sue; **petitioni se dare** to become a candidate

petīt·or -ōris *m* applicant; political candidate; plaintiff

petĭtur·ĭō -īre *vi* to be eager for office

petīt·us -a -um *pp* of **peto**; *n* request, desire

petĭt·us -ūs *m* (with *genit*) heading for

pet·ō -ĕre -īvī or **-iī -ītum** *vt* to make for, head for; to attack; to strive for, aim at; to demand, require, exact; to claim, sue for; to beg, desire, entreat; to look for, go in search of, search for; to run after, chase, court (*girls*); to fetch, bring, obtain, draw; to run for (*office*); to refer to, relate to

petorrīt·um -ī *n* open four-wheeled carriage

petr·a -ae *f* rock, crag

petr·ō -ōnis *m* yokel

Petrōn·ius -iī or **-ī** *m* Petronius Arbiter (*author and master of ceremonies at the court of Nero*)

petŭl·ans -antis *adj* pert, impudent, smart-alecky, petulant, forward

petulanter *adv* pertly, impudently, petulantly

petulantĭ·a -ae f pertness, impudence, forwardness; carelessness

petulc·us -a -um adj butting, apt to butt

pex·us -a -um pp of pecto; adj combed; new, still having the nap on

Phaeāc·es -um m pl Phaeacians (people described in the Odyssey as living on a utopian island)

Phaeācĭ·us -a -um adj Phaeacian; f Phaeacia

Phaeāc·us -a -um adj Phaeacian

Phaedr·a -ae f daughter of Minos and Pasiphae and wife of Theseus

Phaedr·us -ī m pupil of Socrates; freedman of Augustus and famous writer of Latin fables

Phaest·um -ī n town in Crete

Phaëth·ōn -ontis m son of Helios and Clymene who was killed trying to drive his father's chariot

Phaëthontē·us -a -um adj of Phaethon

Phaëthontĭăd·es -um f pl sisters of Phaethon

phalang·ae -ārum f pl wooden rollers

phalangīt·ae -ārum m pl soldiers belonging to a Macedonian phalanx

phal·anx -angis f phalanx, battalion (compact body of heavy-armed men in battle array first developed by the Macedonians)

phalārĭc·a or falārĭc·a -ae f firebrand, fiery missile (shot by a catapult or thrown by hand)

phalēr·ae -ārum f pl military medals; medallions (worn by horses on forehead and chest)

phalerāt·us -a -um adj wearing medals, decorated; ornamental

Phalērĭc·us -a -um adj of Phaleron

Phalēr·um -ī n Athenian harbor

pharētr·a -ae f quiver

pharetrāt·us -a -um adj wearing a quiver

pharmaceutrĭ·a -ae f witch, sorceress

pharmacopōl·a -ae m druggist; quack

Pharsālĭc·us -a -um adj of Pharsalus

Pharsālĭ·us -a -um adj Pharsalian; f district of Pharsalia

Pharsāl·os or Pharsāl·us -ī f town in Thessaly near which Caesar defeated Pompey (48 B.C.)

Phar·os or Phar·us -ī m or f island in the harbor at Alexandria famous for its lighthouse; lighthouse

phasēl·us -ī m or f kidney bean; pinnace (light boat); yacht

Phāsĭăc·us -a -um adj Colchian

Phāsĭān·a -ae f pheasant (female)

Phāsĭān·us -ī m pheasant

Phāsĭ·as -ădis adj Colchian

Phās·is -ĭdis or -ĭdos m river in Colchis

phasm·a -ătis n ghost

Pher·ae -ārum f pl city in Thessaly, the home of Admetus

Pherae·us -a -um adj of Pherae

phiăl·a -ae f saucer

Phīdĭ·ās -ae m famous Greek sculptor and friend of Pericles (fl 440 B.C.)

philēm·a -ătis n kiss

Philēm·ōn -ŏnis m pious rustic who was changed into an oak tree while his wife Baucis was changed into a linden tree

Philipp·ī -ōrum m pl city in Macedonia where Octavian and Antony defeated Brutus and Cassius (42 B.C.)

Philippĭc·ae -ārum f pl series of vitriolic speeches directed at Antony by Cicero

Philipp·us -ī m name of several kings of Macedon (esp. Philip II, son of Amyntas, and father of Alexander the Great, c. 382-336 B.C.)

philitĭ·a or phiditĭ·a -ōrum n pl communal meals at Sparta

Phil·ō or Phil·ōn -ōnis m Academic philosopher and teacher of Cicero

Philoctēt·ēs -ae m Greek warrior and famous archer who was abandoned by the Greek army on the island of Lemnos

philologĭ·a -ae f love of study, study of literature

philolŏg·us -a -um adj learned, scholarly

Philomēl·a -ae f daughter of Pandion and sister of Procne, who was changed into a nightingale

philosŏphē adv philosophically

philosophĭ·a -ae f philosophy

philosŏph·or -ārī vi to pursue philosophy

philosŏph·us -a -um adj philosophical; mf philosopher

phĭtr·um -ī n love potion

philўr·a -ae f inner bark of the lime tree; linden tree

phĭm·us -ī m dice box

Phīn·eus -ĕī or -ĕos m king of Salmydessus in Thrace, whom the Argonauts rescued from the torments which the Harpies visited upon him

Phlegĕth·ōn -ontis m river of fire in the lower world

Phlegethont·is -ĭdis adj of Phlegethon

Phlegў·ās -ae m king of the Lapiths and father of Ixion

Phlĭ·ūs -untis f city in N.E. Peloponnesus

phōc·a -ae or phōc·ē -ēs f seal

Phōcaĭc·us or Phōcē·us or Phōcĭ·us -a -um adj & mf Phocian

Phōc·is -ĭdis f a country of Greece W. of Boeotia

Phoeb·as -ădis f prophetess, priestess of Apollo

Phoeb·ē -ēs f moon goddess, the sister of Phoebus; night

Phoebigĕn·a -ae m son of Phoebus (i.e., Asculapius)

Phoeb·us -ī m Apollo as sun god; sun

Phoenīc·ē -ēs f Phoenicia

Phoenīc·es -um *m pl* Phoenicians

phoenicoptěr·us -ī *m* flamingo

Phoeniss·a -ae *f* Phoenician woman (*esp. Dido*)

phoen·ix -īcis *m* phoenix (*famous Arabian bird which was said to live 500 years and from whose ashes a young phoenix would be born*)

Phoen·ix -īcis *m* son of Amyntor and companion of Achilles

Phorc·is -ĭdos *f* female descendant of Phorcus; Medusa

Phorc·us -ī *m* son of Neptune and father of Medusa and the other Gorgons

Phorcȳn·is -ĭdis or **-ĭdos** *f* Medusa

Phraāt·ēs or **Phrahāt·ēs -ae** *m* king of Parthia

phrenēs·is -is *f* frenzy, delirium

phrenētĭc·us -a -um *adj* frenetic, frantic, delirious

Phrix·us -ī *m* son of Athamas and Nephele and brother of Helle, with whom he fled to Colchis along on the ram with the golden fleece

Phryg·es -um *m pl* Phrygians (*a people of Asia Minor*)

phrygi·ō -ōnis *m* embroiderer

Phrygi·us -a -um *adj* & *mf* Phrygian; Trojan; *f* Phrygia (*a country of Asia Minor*)

Phthī·a -ae *f* home of Achilles in Thessaly

Phthīōt·a or **Phthīōt·ēs -ae** *m* native of Phthia

phthis·is -is *f* consumption, tuberculosis

phy *interj* bah!

phylăc·a -ae *f* jail

phylacist·a -ae *m* jailer; overanxious creditor

phylarch·us -ī *m* tribal chief

physic·a -ae or **physic·ē -ēs** *f* physics

physic·us -a -um *adj* natural, physical, belonging to natural philosophy or physics; *m* natural philosopher, physicist, scientist; *n pl* physics

physiognōm·ōn -ŏnis *m* physiognomist

physiologĭ·a -ae *f* natural philosophy, natural science

piābil·is -e *adj* expiable

piăculār·is -e *adj* expiatory, atoning; *n pl* expiatory sacrifices

piăcŭl·um -ī *n* propitiatory sacrifice; victim; atonement, expiation; remedy; crime, sacrilege; punishment

piām·en -ĭnis *n* atonement

pic·a -ae *f* magpie

picāri·a -ae *f* place where pitch is made

picě·a -ae *f* pine tree

Pic·ens -entis *adj* Picene, of Picenum

Pīcēn·us -a -um *adj* & *m* Picene; *n* district of Central Italy on the Adriatic coast

picě·us -a -um *adj* made of pitch; pitch-black

pict·or -ōris *m* painter

Pict·or -ōris *m* Q. Fabius Pictor (*earliest Roman historian, who wrote a history of Rome in Greek, fl 225 B.C.*)

pictūr·a -ae *f* painting, art of painting; a painting, picture; embroidery

pictūrāt·us -a -um *adj* painted; embroidered

pict·us -a -um *pp* of **pingo**; *adj* decorated, colored; tattooed; ornate (*style*); false, unreal

pīc·us -ī *m* woodpecker; griffin (*fabulous bird*)

Pīc·us -ī *m* son of Saturn and grandfather of Latinus, who was changed by Circe into a woodpecker

piē *adv* dutifully, affectionately

Pierĭ·a -ae *f* district in Macedonia

Pīěr·is -ĭdis or **-ĭdos** *f* daughter of Pieros; Muse; *f pl* the nine Muses

Pīěrĭ·us -a -um *adj* Pierian; poetic; musical; *f see* **Pieria**; *f pl* Muses

Pīěr·os or **Pīěr·us -ī** *m* father of the nine Muses

piět·ās -ātis *f* responsibility, sense of responsibility, sense of duty; devotion, piety; kindness, tenderness; loyalty, patriotism

pig·er -ra -rum *adj* reluctant, unwilling; apathetic, slow, lazy; numbing (*cold*); slow-moving, tedious, dull (*war, etc.*); backward, slow, dull (*person*)

pig·et -ēre -ŭit or **-ĭtum est** *v impers* it irks, pains, annoys, makes regretful; (*with genit* of cause of feeling), e.g., **piget stultitiae meae** I am irked by my foolishness; (*with inf*), e.g., **illa me composuisse piget** I repent having written those verses

pigmentār·ius -ĭī or **-ī** *m* paint dealer

pigment·um -ī *n* pigment, paint, color; coloring, color (*of style*)

pignerāt·or -ōris *m* mortgagee

pigněr·ō -āre *vt* to pledge, mortgage, pawn; (fig) to pledge

pigněr·or -ārī -ātus sum *vt* to take as pledge, accept in good faith; to claim to

pign·us -ŏris or **-ŏris** *n* pledge, security, guarantee; hostage; mortgage; income from mortgages; wager, stake; (fig) pledge, assurance, proof; *n pl* children

pigrē *adv* slowly, sluggishly

pigritĭ·a -ae or **pigritĭ·ēs -ēī** *f* sluggishness, laziness

pigr·ō -āre or **pigr·or -ārī -ātus sum** *vi* to be slow, be sluggish, be lazy

pīl·a -ae *f* a mortar; pillar; pier

pĭl·a -ae *f* ball; ball game; ballot (*used by jury*); **mea pila est** the ball is mine, I've won; **pĭlā ludere** to play ball

pīlān·us -ī *m* soldier in the third rank in battle

pīlāt·us -a -um *adj* armed with javelin

pīlent·um -ī *n* ladies' carriage

pilleāt·us -a -um _adj_ wearing a felt skullcap (_as a symbol of free status_)

pilleŏl·us -ī _m_ skullcap

pillě·um -ī _n_ or **pillě·us -ī** _m_ felt cap or hat (_worn by Romans at festivals, esp. at the Saturnalia, and given to a slave when freed as a symbol of his freedom_); freedom, liberty

pilōs·us -a -um _adj_ hairy

pīl·um -ī _n_ javelin

pīl·us -ī _m_ maniple or company of the triarii, company of veteran reserves; **primi pili centuriō** chief centurion of a legion (_centurion of the first century of the triarii_); **prīmus pilus** chief centurion of the triarii and therefore of the legion

pīl·us -ī _m_ hair; (fig) whit; **nōn pilī facere** to care not a whit for

Pimpl·a -ae _f_ town in Pieria sacred to the Muses

Pimplē·a -ae or **Pimplē·is -īdis** _f_ Muse

Pindaric·us -a -um _adj_ Pindaric

Pindăr·us -ī _m_ Pindar (_famous lyric poet from Thebes in Boeotia, 518-438 B.C._)

Pind·us -ī _m_ mountain range separating Thessaly from Epirus

pīnēt·um -ī _n_ pine forest

pīně·us -a -um _adj_ pine, of pine

pingō pingĕre pinxī pictum _vt_ to draw, paint; to embroider; to depict, represent, portray; to stain, color; to decorate; to color, embellish (_style_)

pingu·e -is _n_ fat, grease

pinguescō -ĕre _vi_ to get fat; to become fertile

pingu·is -e _adj_ fat; oily, greasy; juicy; rich, fertile; thick, dense; stupid, dull; quiet, comfortable

pīnif·er -ĕra -ĕrum _adj_ pine-producing, pine-covered

pīnig·er -ĕra -ĕrum _adj_ pine-producing, pine-covered

pinn·a -ae _f_ feather; wing; flight; fin; feathered arrow; pinnacle, battlement

pinnāt·us -a -um _adj_ feathered, winged

pinnig·er -ĕra -ĕrum _adj_ winged; having fins, finny

pinnip·ēs -ĕdis _adj_ wing-footed

pinnirăp·us -ī _m_ crest-snatcher (_gladiator who tried to get his opponent's helmet crest_)

pinnūl·a -ae _f_ little wing

pīnotēr·ēs -ae _m_ hermit crab

pins·ō -ĕre -ī (or **-ŭi**) **-um** (or **-ĭtum**) _vt_ to pound

pīn·us -ūs or **-ī** _f_ pine tree, fir tree; pine forest; ship; torch; wreath of pine

pi·ō -āre _vt_ to appease by sacrifice, propitiate; to honor with religious rites, worship; to purify with religious rites; to atone for, expiate; to avert

pip·er -ĕris _n_ pepper

pīpil·ō -āre _vi_ to chirp

pīpŭl·um -ī _n_ or **pīpŭl·us -ī** _m_ shrieking, yelling

Pīrae·eus or **Pīrae·us -ī** _m_ or **Pī-rae·a -ōrum** _n pl_ principal harbor of Athens

pīrāt·a -ae _m_ pirate

pīrātic·us -a -um _adj_ pirate; _f_ piracy; **pirāticam facere** to practice piracy

Pīrēn·ē -ēs _f_ fountain on the citadel of Corinth near which Bellerophon caught Pegasus

Pīrithŏ·us -ī _m_ son of Ixion and king of the Lapiths

pir·um -ī _n_ pear

pir·us -ī _f_ pear tree

Pīs·a -ae _f_ of **Pīs·ae -ārum** _f pl_ Pisa (_city in Elis on the Alpheus River near which the Olympic games were held_)

Pīs·ae -ārum _f pl_ Pisa (_ancient city of N. Etruria_)

Pīsae·us -a -um _adj_ of Pisa; _f_ Hippodamia

piscāri·us -a -um _adj_ fish, of fishing or fish; **forum piscarium** fish market

piscāt·or -ōris _m_ fisherman; fishmonger

piscātōrĭ·us -a -um _adj_ fishing; fish

piscāt·us -ūs _m_ fishing; fish; (fig) good haul

piscicŭl·us -ī _m_ little fish

piscīn·a -ae _f_ fish pond; swimming pool

piscīnār·ius -iī or **-ī** _m_ person fond of swimming pools or fish ponds

pisc·is -is _m_ fish

Pisc·is -is _m_ Piscis (_constellation_)

pisc·or -ārī -ātus sum _vi_ to fish

piscōs·us -a -um _adj_ full of fish

pisculent·us -a -um _adj_ well stocked with fish

Pīsistratĭd·ae -ārum _m pl_ sons of Pisistratus (_i.e., Hippias and Hipparchus_)

Pīsistrăt·us -ī _m_ enlightened tyrant of Athens (560-527 B.C.)

pistill·um -ī _n_ pestle

pist·or -ōris _m_ miller; baker

pistrīll·a -ae _f_ little mill

pistrīn·um -ī _n_ flour mill; bakery; drudgery

pistr·is -is or **pistr·ix -īcis** _f_ sea monster (_of any kind_); whale, shark; swift ship

pithēc·ium -iī or **-ī** _n_ little ape

Pitth·eus -ĕī or **-ĕos** _m_ king of Troezen and father of Aethra, the mother of Theseus

pītuīt·a -ae _f_ phlegm; rheum; head cold

pītuītōs·us -a -um _adj_ full of phlegm, phlegmatic

pi·us -a -um _adj_ conscientious; godfearing, godly, holy; fatherly, motherly, brotherly, sisterly; affectionate; patriotic; good; sacred, holy (_objects connected with religion_)

pix picis _f_ pitch; _f pl_ chunks of pitch

plācābil·is -e _adj_ easily appeased; pacifying, appeasing

plācābilit·ās -ātis _f_ readiness to forgive, conciliatory disposition

plăcām·en -ĭnis *n* means of appeasing, peace offering

plăcāment·um -ī *n* means of appeasing, peace offering

plăcātē *adv* calmly, quietly

plăcātĭ·ō -ōnis *f* pacifying, propitiating

plăcāt·us -a -um *adj* calm, quiet; appeased, reconciled

plac·ens -entis *adj* pleasing

placent·a -ae *f* cake

plac·ĕō -ēre -ŭī -ĭtum *vi* (with *dat*) to please, satisfy, give pleasure to, be acceptable to; **sibi placere** to be satisfied with oneself, pride oneself; *v impers* it seems right, seems proper; it is settled, is agreed; it is resolved, is decided; **eis placitum est ut considerent** they decided to consider; **senatui placuit** the senate decreed

placidē *adv* calmly, placidly, gently, quietly

placĭd·us -a -um *adj* calm, placid, gentle, quiet

placĭt·ō -āre *vi* to be very pleasing

placĭt·us -a -um *adj* pleasing, acceptable; agreed upon; in principle, belief, tenet; **ultra placitum laudare** to praise excessively

plāc·ō -āre *vt* to calm, quiet; to appease; to reconcile

plāg·a -ae *f* blow; wound; (fig) blow

plāg·a -ae *f* region, tract, zone; hunting net; mesh of a net; curtain; (fig) trap

plagiār·ĭus -ĭī or **-ī** *n* plunderer; kidnapper; plagiarist

plăgĭg·er -ĕra -ĕrum *adj* covered with welts

plāgĭgerŭl·us -a -um *adj* covered with welts

plāgĭpatĭd·a -ae *m* whipping boy

plāgōs·us -a -um *adj* quick to use the rod

plagŭl·a -ae *f* curtain

plagŭsĭ·a -ae *f* a fish

planctus *pp* of **plango**

planct·us -ūs *m* beating

plānē *adv* clearly, distinctly; legibly; completely, entirely, quite; certainly, to be sure

plangō plangĕre planxī planctum *vt* to strike, beat; to beat (*breast, head as sigh of grief*); to lament, bewail; *vi* to wail, lament; (fig) to wring the hands

plang·or -ōris *m* striking, beating; beating of the breast; wailing

plānĭlŏqu·os -a -om *adj* speaking clearly

plānĭp·ēs -ĕdis *m* ballet dancer

plānĭt·ās -ātis *f* distinctness

plānĭtĭ·ēs -ēī or **plānĭtĭ·a -ae** *f* flat surface, level ground, plain

plant·a -ae *f* sprout, shoot; young plant, slip; sole (*of the foot*)

plantār·ĭa -ĭum *n pl* slips; young trees; hair

plān·us -a -um *adj* flat, level, even; plain, clear; *n* level ground, plain

plan·us -ī *m* tramp; imposter, cheat

plasm·a -ătĭs *n* phoney accent

Platae·ae -ārum *f pl* Plataea (*town in Boeotia near which the Greeks defeated the Persians in 479 B.C.*)

platălĕ·a -ae *f* waterfowl, spoonbill

platăn·us -ī or **-ūs** *f* plane tree

platĕ·a or **platĕ·a -ae** *f* street

Plat·ō or **Plat·ōn -ōnis** *m* Plato (*famous Greek philosopher, 429-348 B.C.*)

Platŏnĭc·us -a -um *adj* Platonic; *m pl* Platonists

plaudō plaudĕre plausī plausum *vt* to slap, clap, beat; *vi* to flap, beat, clap; (with *dat*) to applaud, approve of; **alis plaudere** to flap the wings; **manibus plaudere** to clap the hands

plausĭbĭl·is -e *adj* deserving applause

plaus·or -ōris *m* applauder

plaustr·um -ī *n* wagon, cart

Plaustr·um -ī *n* the Great Bear (*constellation*)

plausus *pp* of **plaudo**

plaus·us -ūs *m* clapping, flapping; clapping of the hands; applause

Plaut·us -ī *m* T. Maccius Plautus (*famous Roman writer of comedies, born at Sarsina in Umbria, c. 254-184 B.C.*)

plēbēcŭl·a -ae *f* rabble

plēbēi·us or **plēbēj·us -a -um** *adj* plebeian, of the common people; common, low, vulgar

plēbĭcŏl·a -ae *m* democrat; demagogue

plēbiscīt·um -ī *n* decree of the commons

pleb·s -is or **plēb·ēs -ēī** or **-ī** *f* plebeians, common people; the masses, proletariat

plectĭl·is -e *adj* plaited

plectō plectĕre plexī or **plexŭī plexum** *vt* to plait, braid

plect·ō -ĕre *vt* to punish

Plēï·as -ădis *f* Pleiad; *f pl* Pleiades (*seven daughters of Atlas and Pleione, who were placed among the stars*)

Plēïŏn·ē -ēs *f* daughter of Oceanus and Tethys, wife of Atlas, and mother of the Pleiades

plēnē *adv* fully, completely

plēn·us -a -um *adj* full; stout, plump; pregnant; filled, satisfied; full, packed; full, strong, loud (*voice*); full-length, unabridged, uncontracted; abundant, plentiful; advanced, mature (*years*); complete, finished

plērumque *adv* generally, mostly; often, frequently

plēr·usque -ăque -umque *adj* a very great part of, the greater part of, most; very many, a good many; *n* the greatest part

plex·us -a -um *pp* of **plecto**; *adj* plaited

plicātr·ix -ĭcis *f* woman who folds clothes, folder

plic·ō -āre -āvī or -ŭī -ātum or -ĭtum *vt* to fold, wind, coil up

Plīn·ius -iī or -ī *m* C. Plinius Secundus (*author of a work on natural history, who perished in the eruption of Vesuvius in 79 A.D.*); C. Plinius Caecilius (*his nephew, author of Letters and a Panegyric to Trajan, 62 A.D.-c. 114 A.D.*)

plōrābil·is -e *adj* deplorable

plōrāt·or -ōris *m* mourner

plōrāt·us -ūs *m* wailing, wail

plōr·ō -āre *vt* to cry over; *vi* to cry aloud, wail

plostell·um -ī *n* cart

ploxēm·um -ī *n* wagon frame

pluit pluĕre pluit *vt* it is raining (*stones, blood, etc.*); *vi* it is raining; (*with abl*) it is raining (*stones, etc.*)

plūm·a -ae *f* down, soft feather; (collectively) feathers, down

plūmātīl·e -is *n* dress embroidered with feathers

plūmāt·us -a -um *adj* covered with feathers

plumbĕ·us -a -um *adj* lead, of lead; leaden, oppressive (*weather*); dull, stupid

plumb·um -ī *n* lead; bullet; pipe; ruler (*for drawing lines*); **plumbum album** tin

plūmĕ·us -a -um *adj* downy, filled with down; like feathers

plūmĭp·ēs -ĕdis *adj* with feathered feet

plūmōs·us -a -um *adj* downy, feathered

plūrĭmum *adv* very much, especially, commonly, generally, most

plūrĭm·us -a -um (*superl of multus*) *adj* many a; most; very much; very many; very great, very intense; **plurimam salutem dare** to send warmest greetings; *n* a great deal; **plurimi facere** to think very highly of, think a great deal of; **quam plurimum** as much as possible

plūs *adv* more; **multo plus** much more; **paulo plus** a little more

plūs plūris (*comp of multus*) *adj* more; *n* more; too much; **et, quod plus est, Romani estis** and what is more, you are Romans; **plus animi** more courage; **plus nimio** much too much; **plus plusque** more and more; **uno viro plus habere** to have one man too much; **pluris esse** (*genit* of value) to be of more value, of a higher price, worth more, be higher, be dearer; *n pl* more words; **quid plura?** why should I say more?, in short

pluscŭl·us -a -um *adj* a little more, somewhat more; *n* a little more; **plusculum negoti** a little more business

plutĕ·us -ī *m* or plutĕ·um -ī *n* (mil) movable mantlet or shed used to protect soldiers in siege work; parapet; couch, dining couch; book shelf; book case; board, slab

Plūt·ō or Plūt·ōn -ōnis *m* king of the lower world, husband of Proserpina, and brother of Jupiter and Neptune

pluvĭ·a -ae *f* rain

pluvĭāl·is -e *adj* rain, of rain, rainy; **fungi pluviales** mushrooms brought out by the rain

pluvĭ·us -a -um *adj* rain, of rain, rainy; **pluvia aqua** rain water; **pluvius arcus** rainbow; *f see* pluvia

pōcill·um -ī *n* small drinking cup

pōcŭl·um -ī *n* drinking cup; drink, draught; **poculum ducere** or **exhaurire** to drain a cup

podāgr·a -ae *f* arthritis

podagrōs·us -a -um *adj* arthritic

pōd·ex -ĭcis *m* anus, rectum

pod·ĭum -iī or -ī balcony; box seat (*for the emperor*)

Poeantĭăd·ēs -ae *m* Philoctetes

Poe·ās -antis *m* father of Philoctetes

poēm·a -ătis *n* poem

poēmat·ĭum -iī or -ī *n* short poem

poen·a -ae *f* compensation, recompense, retribution, satisfaction, penalty, fine, punishment; hardship, loss, pain; (in games) penalty; **poenam** or **poenas dare, dependere, pendere, persolvere, reddere, solvere, suscipere,** or **sufferre** to pay the penalty, make restitution, give satisfaction; **poenam** or **poenas capere, persequi, petere, repetere,** or **reposcere** to exact a penalty, demand satisfaction; **poena mortis** capital punishment, death penalty

poenĭō *see* punio

Poen·us -a -um *adj & m* Carthaginian

poēs·is -is *f* art of poetry; poetry, poems

poēt·a -ae *m* maker, contriver; poet

poētĭc·a -ae or poētĭc·ē -ēs *f* art of poetry; poetics

poētĭcē *adv* poetically

poētĭc·us -a -um *adj* poetic, poetical; *f see* poetica

poētrĭ·a -ae *f* poetess

poētr·is -ĭdis or -ĭdos *f* poetess

pol *interj* by Pollux!; Lord!

polent·a -ae *f* pearl barley

polentārĭ·us -a -um *adj* caused by eating barley

pol·ĭō -īre -īvī or -iī -ītum *vt* to polish, smooth; (fig) to polish, improve, perfect

polītē *adv* in a polished manner, with taste, smoothly, elegantly

polītĭc·us -a -um *adj* political

polīt·us -a -um *adj* polished, smooth; (fig) polished, smooth, smooth-spoken, smooth-mannered, refined, cultivated

poll·en -ĭnis *n* or poll·is -ĭnis *m* or *f* flour

poll·ens -entis *adj* strong, powerful, thriving, able

pollentĭ·a -ae *f* might, power

poll·ĕō -ēre vi to be strong, be powerful; to be capable, be able; (of medicines) to be powerful, be efficacious; to have influence; **in re publica plurimum pollere** to have tremendous influence in politics

poll·ex -ĭcis m thumb; big toe

pollic·ĕor -ērī -ĭtus sum vt to promise

pollicitātĭ·ō -ōnis f promise

pollicit·or -ārī -ātus sum vt to keep promising

pollicit·us -a -um pp of **polliceor**; n promise

pollināri·us -a -um adj flour, for flour

pollinct·or -ōris m embalmer

pol·lingō -lingĕre -linxī -linctum vt to lay out, embalm

Pollĭ·ō -ōnis m C. Asinius Pollio (distinguished orator, poet, historian, patron of literature, and statesman, 76 B.C.-4 A.D.)

poll·is -ĭnis m or f flour

pol·lūcĕō -lūcēre -luxī -luctum vt to offer, offer up as sacrifice; to serve (meal); to entertain

pollūcibĭlĭter adv sumptuously, in grand style

polluctūr·a -ae f sumptuous dinner

polluct·us -a -um pp of **polluceo**; n offering, sacrificial meal

pol·lŭō -luĕre -luī -lūtum vt to pollute, defile, soil, mess up; to defile, violate

Poll·ux or **Poll·ūcēs -ūcis** m son of Tyndareus and Leda, twin brother of Castor, and famous boxer

pol·us -ī m end of an axis, pole; North Pole; **polus australis** South Pole

Polyb·ius -iī or **-ī** m Greek historian and friend of Scipio Aemilianus (c. 203-120 B.C.)

Polydăm·ās -antis m son of Panthus and friend of Hector

Polydōr·us -ī m son of Priam and Hecuba, murdered by Polymestor the king of Thrace

Polyhymnĭ·a -ae f one of the nine Muses

Polymest·or -ōris m king of the Thracian Chersonese, husband of Ilione the daughter of Priam

Polynĭc·ēs -is m son of Oedipus and Jocasta and brother of Eteocles

Polyphēm·us -ī m son of Neptune and one of the Cyclops of Sicily

pōlyp·us -ī m polyp (sea animal; tumor)

Polyxĕn·a -ae f daughter of Priam whom Pyrrhus, the son of Achilles, sacrificed at his father's tomb

pōmāri·us -a -um adj fruit, of fruit trees; m fruit vendor; n orchard

pōmerīdiān·us -a -um adj afternoon

pōmēr·ium or **pōmoer·ium -iī** or **-ī** n space kept free of buildings inside and outside a city wall

pōmĭf·er -ĕra -ĕrum adj fruit-bearing

pōmōs·us -a -um adj loaded with fruit

pomp·a -ae f solemn or religious procession; retinue; pomp, ostentation

Pompēĭ·us or **Pompēj·us -ī** m Pompey the Great (Roman general and statesman, 106-48 B.C.)

Pompējān·us -a -um adj Pompeian; m pl inhabitants of Pompeii; soldiers or followers of Pompey

Pompēj·ī -ōrum m pl city south of Naples, destroyed by the eruption of Vesuvius in 79 A.D.

Pompil·ius -iī or **-ī** m Numa Pompilius (second king of Rome and traditional founder of Roman state religion)

Pomptīn·us -a -um adj Pomptine; **Pomptinae paludes** Pomptine Marshes in Latium

pōm·um -ī n fruit; fruit tree

pōm·us -ī f fruit tree

pondĕr·ō -āre vt to weigh; to consider, ponder

ponderōs·us -a -um adj weighty, heavy; full of meaning

pondō adv in weight

pondō (indecl) n pound, pounds; **auri quinque pondo** five pounds of gold

pond·us -ĕris n weight; mass; burden; importance; stability of character; n pl balance, equilibrium

pōne adv behind, after, back; prep (with acc) behind

pōnō pōnĕre posŭī posĭtum or **postum** vt to put, place, put down, set down, set, fix, deposit; to lay aside, lay down; to lay out, spend; to stake; to place, station, post; to set up, erect, build, found; to regard, consider; to cite, assert; to suppose, assume; to lay out for burial; to smooth, calm; to arrange, smooth (hair); vi to abate, calm down

pons pontis m bridge; gangway; drawbridge; deck

pontĭcŭl·us -ī m small bridge

pontĭf·ex -ĭcis m pontiff, pontifex, priest (one of a board of fifteen); **pontifex maximus** chief pontiff

pontĭfĭcāl·is -e adj pontifical

pontĭfĭcāt·us -ūs m pontificate

pontĭfĭc·us -a -um adj pontifical

pont·ō -ōnis m ferry

pont·us -ī m sea; sea water

Pont·us -ī m Euxine or Black Sea; region around the Black Sea; kingdom of Mithridates between Bithynia and Armenia, subsequently a Roman province

pop·a -ae m priest's assistant (attendant who slew the victim)

popăn·um -ī n sacrificial cake

popell·us -ī m rabble, mob

popīn·a -ae f restaurant; food sold at a restaurant

popīn·ō -ōnis m diner at a restaurant

popl·es -ĭtis m hollow of the knee;

knee; **duplicato poplite** on bended knee; **contento poplite** with a stiff knee

Pŏplicŏla see **Publicola**

poppysm·a -ătis n clicking with the tongue (as sign of approval)

populābil·is -e adj destructible

populābund·us -a -um adj ravaging, laying waste

populār·ēs -ium m pl people's party, democrats

populār·ia -ium n pl general-admission seats

populār·is -e adj of the people, by the people, for the people, people's, popular; approved by the people, popular; favoring the people, democratic; demagogic; of the same country, native; common, coarse

populār·is -is m or f fellow countryman; party member; fellow member, associate; (with genit) partner or associate in

populārit·ās -ātis f fellow citizenship; popularity

populāriter adv like the people; like a demagogue; **populariter loqui** to use slang

populāti·ō -ōnis f ravaging, devastation

populāt·or -ōris m ravager, destroyer

populāt·us -ūs m devastation

pōpulĕ·us -a -um adj of poplars, poplar

pōpulif·er -ĕra -ĕrum adj filled with poplar trees

pōpuln·us -a -um adj of poplars, poplar

pōpŭl·ō -āre or **pōpŭl·or -ārī -ātus sum** vt to ravage, devastate, lay waste; (fig) to pillage, ruin, destroy, spoil

pōpŭl·us -ī m people (as a political community), nation; people, crowd, public; citizens (as opposed to soldiers), civilians; region, district

pōpŭl·us -ī f poplar tree

porc·a -ae f sow

porcell·a -ae f little sow

porcell·us -ī m little hog

porcīnār·ius -ĭī or **-ī** m pork seller

porcīn·us -a -um adj hog's, pig's; f pork

Porc·ius -ĭī or **-ī** m M. Porcius Cato the Censor (235-149 B.C.); M. Porcius Cato Uticensis (95-46 B.C.)

porcŭl·a or **porculĕn·a -ae** f little sow

porcŭl·us -ī m little pig

porc·us -ī m pig, hog

porgō see **porrigo**

Porphyri·ōn -ōnis m a Giant

porrect·a -ōrum n pl offering; **inter caesa et porrecta** (fig) at the eleventh hour

porrecti·ō -ōnis f extending, stretching out

porrect·us -a -um pp of **porrigo**; adj stretched out, extended, extensive, long; protracted (delay); laid out, dead; (fig) wide-spread

porric·iō -ĕre vt to offer up, make an offering of

por·rĭgō or **porg·ō -rigĕre -rexī -rectum** vt to reach out, stretch out, extend; to offer, present, hand; to lengthen (a syllable); **se porrigere** to extend

porrig·ō -ĭnis f dandruff

porrō adv forwards, farther on, on; far off, at a distance; long ago; in the future, hereafter; again, in turn; next, furthermore, moreover, on the other hand

porr·um -ī n leek; chive

Porsenn·a or **Porsĕn·a** or **Porsinn·a -ae** m king of Clusium in Etruria who sided with Tarquin in a war against Rome

port·a -ae f city gate; gate; entrance; outlet; camp gate (of which there were always four)

portāti·ō -ōnis f carrying, conveyance

por·tendō -tendĕre -tendī -tentum vt to indicate, foretell, portend, predict

portentific·us -a -um adj monstrous, abnormal

portentōs·us -a -um adj monstrous, abnormal, unnatural, portentous

portent·um -ī n portent, omen, sign; monstrosity, monster; fantasy, farfetched fiction; (as term of contempt) monster, demon

portentus pp of **portendo**

porthm·eus -ĕī or **-ĕos** m ferryman (i.e., Charon, who piloted the ferry across the Styx)

porticŭl·a -ae f small portico

portic·us -ūs f colonnade, portico; (mil) gallery (formed by placing vineae end to end); Stoicism

porti·ō -ōnis f portion, share; ratio, portion; instalment, payment; **pro portione** proportionally, relatively

portiscŭl·us -ī m gavel

portit·or -ōris m customs officer; ferryman, boatman

port·ō -āre vt to carry; to bring

portōr·ium -ĭī or **-ī** n port duty, customs duty; tax (on peddlers)

portŭl·a -ae f small gate

Portūn·us -ī m tutelary deity of harbors

portuōs·us -a -um adj having good harbors

port·us -ūs m port, harbor; haven, refuge; mouth of a river

posc·a -ae f sour drink

poscō poscĕre poposcī vt to ask, request, beg, demand; (of things) to require, demand, need, call for, make necessary; (with **ab + abl**) to ask for (something) from, demand (something) of; (with double acc) to demand (something) of, ask (someone) for

Posīdōn·ius -ĭī or **-ī** m Stoic philosopher at Rhodes, teacher of Cicero

positi·ō -ōnis f putting, placing, setting; position, posture; situation

posĭt·or -ōris m builder

positūr·a -ae f posture; formation

posĭt·us -a -um pp of **pono**; adj situated, located

posĭt·us -ūs m position; arrangement

possessī·ō -ōnis f possession; getting possession, occupation, possession, estate

possessiuncŭl·a -ae f small estate

possess·or -ōris m possessor, occupant; (law) defendant

possibĭl·is -e adj possible

pos·sĭdĕō -sĭdēre -sēdī -sessum vt to possess, occupy; to have, own; to dwell in, live in; (fig) to take hold of

pos·sīdo -sīdĕre -sēdī -sessum vt to take possession of, occupy, seize

possum posse potŭī vi to be able; **multum (plus, plurimum) posse** to have much (more, very great) influence; **non possum quin exclamem** I can't help exclaiming; **quantum** or **ut fieri potest** as far as is possible

post adv (of place) behind, back, backwards; (of time) later, afterwards; (of order) next; **aliquanto post** somewhat later; **multis post annis** many years later; prep (with acc) (of place) behind; (of time) after, since

posteā adv afterwards, after this, after that, hereafter, thereafter

posteāquam conj after

posterĭ·or -us adj later, next, following; latter, posterior; inferior, worse; hind

posterĭt·ās -ātis f the future, afterages, posterity, later generations; offspring (of animals); **in posteritatem** in the future

posterĭus adv later, at a later date

poster·us -a -um adj following, ensuing, next, subsequent, future; m pl future generations, posterity, descendants; n future time; next day; consequence; **in posterum** till the next day; for the future

post·fĕrō -ferre vt to put after; to esteem less; to sacrifice

postgenĭt·us -a -um adj born later; m pl later generations

posthab·ĕō -ēre -ŭī -ĭtum vt to consider of secondary importance; to slight, neglect; (with dat) to think (something) less important than

posthāc adv hereafter, in the future

posthinc or **post hinc** adv from here, from this place, next

posthōc or **post hōc** adv after this, afterwards

postĭbī adv afterwards, then

postĭcŭl·um -ī n small building in the rear

postĭc·us -a -um adj hind, back, rear; n back door

postĭdĕā adv afterwards, after that

postilēn·a -ae f crupper; buttocks

postillā adv afterwards

post·is -is m door post; door; m pl double doors

postlimĭn·ĭum -ĭī or **-ī** n right to return home and resume one's former rank and privileges, right of recovery; **postlimĭnĭo** by the right of recovery

postmerīdĭān·us -a -um adj afternoon

postmŏdo or **postmŏdum** adv after a bit, a little later, afterwards

postpart·or -ōris m successor, heir

post·pōnō -pōnĕre -posŭī -posĭtum or **-postum** vt to consider of secondary importance; to neglect, disregard; (with dat) to consider (something) of less importance than, set (something) aside in favor of

postprincipĭ·a -ōrum n pl sequel

postpŭt·ō -āre vt to consider of secondary importance; (with **prae +** abl) to consider (something) less important than

postquam conj after, when

postrēmō adv at last, finally; **primo ... deinde ... postremo** first ... then ... finally

postrēmum adv for the last time, last of all

postrēm·us -a -um (superl of **posterus**) adj last, last in line, rear; lowest, worst

postrīdĭē adv on the day after, on the following day; **postridie mane** the next morning; prep (with genit), e.g., **postridie ejus diei** on the day after that; (with acc), e.g., **postridie ludos** on the day after the games

postrīdŭō adv on the day after

postscaen·ĭum -ĭī or **-ī** n backstage

post·scrībō -scrībĕre -scrīpsī scrīptum vt (with dat) to add (e.g., a name) to; **Tiberi nomen suo postscribere** to add the name of Tiberius to his own name

postulāt·a -ōrum n pl demands, claims, requests

postulātĭ·ō -ōnis f demand, request, desire; complaint; (law) application for permission to present a claim

postulāt·us -ūs m claim, suit

postŭl·ō -āre vt to demand, claim; to arraign, prosecute; to apply for (a writ from the praetor to prosecute)

postŭm·us -a -um adj last, latest-born

postus pp of **pono**

pōtātĭ·ō -ōnis f drinking, drinking party

pōtāt·or -ōris m drinker

pot·ens -entis adj capable; mighty, powerful, strong; efficacious, potent; fit, capable, equal; influential; (with genit) a capable of, equal to, fit for; **b** having power over; **c** presiding over; **d** having obtained (one's wish); **e** having carried out (an order)

potentāt·us -ūs *m* political power, rule, dominion

potenter *adv* powerfully, mightily, effectually, vigorously; according to one's ability

potentī·a -ae *f* force, power; political power (*esp. unconstitutional power*)

potēr·ium -iī *or* **-ī** *n* goblet

potest·ās -ātis *f* power, ability, capacity; efficacy, force; public authority, rule, power, sway, dominion, sovereignty, empire, rule; magisterial power, magistracy, office; possibility, opportunity, permission; person in office, magistrate, ruler; property, quality

potin *or* **potin'** = **potisne** can you?, are you able?

pōtī·ō -ōnis *f* drinking; drink, draught; magic potion

pot·ior -īrī -ītus sum *vt* to acquire, get possession of; *vi* (*with genit or abl*) to acquire, get possession of, become master of, get hold of, get

pōti·or -us (*comp of* **potis**) *adj* better, preferable, superior; more important

potis *or* **pote** (*indecl*) *adj* able, capable; possible

potissimum *adv* chiefly, especially, eminently

potissim·us -a -um *adj* chief, principal, most important

potius *adv* rather, more, by preference; **potius quam** more than, rather than

pōt·ō -āre *vt* to drink; to absorb

pōt·or -ōris *m* drinker

pōtr·ix -īcis *f* drinker (*female*)

pōtulent·us -a -um *adj* drinkable; *n pl* drinks

pōt·us -a -um *adj* drunk

pōt·us -ūs *m* drink

prae *adv* before, in front; in preference; *prep* (*with abl*) before, in front of; compared with, in comparison with; in view of; because of; by reason of, on account of, through; **prae manu** at hand; **prae se** publicly, openly, plainly; **prae se ferre** to display, manifest, exhibit, profess

praeacu·ō -ēre *vt* to sharpen to a point

praeacūt·us -a -um *adj* pointed

praealt·us -a -um *adj* very high; very deep

praeb·eō -ēre -uī -itum *vt* to hold out, offer, present; to supply, give; to exhibit, represent, show; to give up, yield, surrender; to cause, occasion; to permit, allow; **se praebere** to show oneself, behave

praebib·ō -ēre -ī *vt* (*with dat*) to drink (*e.g., a toast*) to

praebit·or -ōris *m* supplier

praecalid·us -a -um *adj* very warm, hot

praecantr·ix -īcis *f* witch, enchantress

praecān·us -a -um *adj* prematurely grey

prae·caveō -cavēre -cāvī -cautum *vt* to guard against, try to avoid; *vi* to take precautions, be on one's guard; (*with dat*) to look out for, look after; (*with abl*) to guard against, be on one's guard against

prae·cēdō -cēdēre -cessī -cessum *vt* to precede, go out before, lead; to surpass, excel; *vi* to excel, be superior; (*with dat*) to excel, be superior to

praecell·ens -entis *adj* superior, excellent, preeminent

praecell·ō -ēre *vt* to surpass, outdo; *vi* to distinguish oneself, excel; (*with dat*) to rule over

praecels·us -a -um *adj* towering

praecentī·ō -ōnis *f* musical prelude (*before a sacrifice*)

praecent·ō -āre *vi* (*with dat*) to sing to

praecentus *pp of* **praecino**

praec·eps -ipitis *adj* headfirst; downhill, steep, precipitous; sinking (*sun*); swift, rushing, violent; hasty, rash, inconsiderate; dangerous; *n* edge of a cliff, cliff, precipice; danger, critical situation

praeceps *adv* headfirst

praeceptī·ō -ōnis *f* preconception; precept, rule; priority

praecept·or -ōris *m* or **praeceptr·ix -īcis** *f* teacher, preceptor

praecept·um -ī *n* rule, maxim; order, command, direction

prae·cerpō -cerpēre -cerpsī -cerptum *vt* to pick or gather before time; (*with dat*) (fig) to snatch away from

prae·cīdō -cīdēre -cīdī -cīsum *vt* to lop off, cut short; to cut, cut through; to damage, mutilate; to break off, finish abruptly, end suddenly (*a speech, etc.*); to end, destroy (*hopes, etc.*); to refuse, decline

prae·cingō -cingēre -cinxī -cinctum *vt* to gird; to surround, ring; to dress; **ense cingi** to wear a sword; **male cinctus** improperly dressed; **recte cinctus** properly dressed

prae·cinō -cinēre -cinuī -centum *vt* to predict; (*with dat*) to predict (*something*) to; *vi* to make predictions; (*with dat*) to sing or play before or at (*e.g., dinner, sacrifice*)

prae·cipiō -cipere -cēpī -ceptum *vt* to take or receive in advance; to grasp beforehand, anticipate; to teach, instruct, direct, warn; to prescribe; **animo praecipere** *or* **cogitatione praecipere** to imagine beforehand, reckon on, anticipate, expect; **oculis praecipere** to see beforehand, get a preview of; **opinione praecipere** to suspect in advance; **pecuniam mutuam praecipere** to get an advance loan

praecipitanter *adv* at a high speed

praecipit·ō -āre *vt* to throw down

head first; to hasten, hurry, precipitate; **se praecipitare** to throw oneself down, throw oneself down headfirst, jump down, dive; to sink; *vi* to rush headfirst, rush at top speed, rush thoughtlessly; to fall, sink; to be ruined

praecipŭē *adv* especially, chiefly

praecipŭ·us -a -um *adj* special, peculiar, particular; chief, principal; distinguished, excellent, extraordinary; *n* excellence, superiority; *n pl* outstanding or important elements; **praecipua rerum** highlights

praecisē *adv* briefly, concisely; absolutely

praecīs·us -a -um *pp* of **praecido**; *adj* abrupt, precipitous ; rugged, rough; brief, abrupt (*speech*)

praeclārē *adv* very clearly; excellently; (to express agreement) very good, splendid

praeclār·us -a -um *adj* very clear; very nice; splendid, noble, distinguished, excellent; famous, distinguished; notorious

prae·clūdō -clūdĕre -clūsī -clūsum *vt* to shut, shut off, obstruct; to hinder, stop, impede; **portas consuli praecludere** to shut the gates on the consul, shut the gates in the consul's face; **vocem praecludere alicui** to shut someone up, to hush someone up

praec·ō -ōnis *m* crier, herald; auctioneer; (fig) pangyrist

precōgĭt·ō -āre *vt* to premeditate

praecognĭt·us -a -um *adj* known beforehand, foreseen

prae·cōlō -colĕre — -cultum *vt* to cultivate prematurely; (fig) to embrace prematurely

praecomposĭt·us -a -um *adj* arranged beforehand; studied, self-conscious

praecōnĭ·us -a -um *adj* of a public crier, of an auctioneer; *n* crier's office; proclamation, announcement; praising, praise

praecon·sūmō -sumĕre -sumpsī -sumptum *vt* to spend or use up beforehand

praecontrect·ō -āre *vt* to consider in advance

praecordĭ·a -ōrum *n pl* diaphragm, midriff; insides, stomach; breast, heart

praecor·rumpō -rumpĕre -rūpī -ruptum *vt* to bribe in advance

praec·ox -ōcis *adj* premature, hasty, rash

praecurrent·ĭa -ĭum *n pl* antecedents

prae·currō -currĕre -cucurrī or -currī -cursum *vt* to precede, anticipate; to outdo, surpass; *vi* to run out ahead, take the lead; (with **ante** + *acc*) to run out ahead of; (with *dat*) to outdo

praecursĭ·ō -ōnis *f* previous occurrence; (mil) skirmish; (rhet) warm-up (*of the audience*)

praecurs·or -ōris *m* forerunner; spy; (mil) scout; advance guard

praecursōrĭ·us -a -um *adj* sent in advance

prae·cutĭō -cutĕre -cussī -cussum *vt* to wave, brandish in front

praed·a -ae *f* booty, spoils, plunder; prey; **praedae esse** (with *dat*) to fall prey to

praedābund·us -a -um *adj* pillaging, plundering

praedamn·ō -āre *vt* to condemn beforehand; **spem praedamnare** to give up hope too soon

praedātĭ·ō -ōnis *f* pillaging, plunder

praedāt·or -ōris *m* marauder, looter, vandal; hunter; greedy man

praedātōrĭ·us -a -um *adj* marauding, looting; graspy, greedy

praedēlass·ō -āre *vt* to tire out, weaken beforehand

praedestĭn·ō -āre *vt* to predetermine

praediāt·or -ōris *m* real-estate agent

praediātōrĭ·us -a -um *adj* real-estate; **jus praediatorium** mortgage law

praedicābĭl·is -e *adj* praiseworthy, laudable

praedicātĭ·ō -ōnis *f* announcement, publication; praising

praedicāt·or -ōris *m* appreciator; eulogist

praedĭc·ō -āre *vt* to announce, proclaim; to report; to assert; to praise

prae·dīcō -dīcĕre -dixī -dictum *vt* to mention beforehand or earlier; to prearrange; to predict; to order, command beforehand

praedictĭ·ō -ōnis *f* prediction

praedict·um -ī *n* prediction, prophecy; command, order; **velut ex praedicto** as if by prearrangement

praedĭŏl·um -ī *n* small estate, small farm

praedisc·ō -ĕre *vt* to learn beforehand, find out in advance

praedisposĭt·us -a -um *adj* previously arranged

praedĭt·us -a -um *adj* endowed, gifted, provided, furnished; (with *abl*) endowed with, provided with, furnished with

praed·ĭum -ĭī or **-ī** *n* estate, farm; **praedia urbana** city lots

praedīv·es -ĭtis *adj* very rich

praedīvīn·ō -āre *vt* to know in advance, have a presentiment of

praed·ō -ōnis *m* marauder, looter, robber, pirate

praedoct·us -a -um *adj* instructed beforehand

praed·or -ārī -ātus sum *vt* to raid, plunder, loot, rob; (fig) to rob, ravish; **amores alicujus praedari** to steal away someone's sweetheart; *vi* to plunder, loot, make a raid; (with **ex** + *abl*) to prey on, profit by, take advantage of, e.g., **ex al-**

terius inscientiā praedari to prey on someone else's ignorance

prae-dūcō -dūcĕre -dūxī -ductum *vt* to run or construct (*trench, wall*) out in front (*for defensive purposes*)

praedulc·is -e *adj* very sweet; (fig) very satisfying (*honor, reward*)

praedūr·us -a -um *adj* very tough (*skin*); tough, brawny

praeēmin·ĕō -ēre *vt* to surpass, excel; *vi* to project forward, stick out

prae·ĕō -īre -īvī or **-iī -ĭtum** *vt* to lead, precede; to read out, dictate, lead (*prayers*); *vi* to go out ahead, take the lead; (with *dat*) to walk in front of

praefātĭ·ō -ōnis *f* preface, introduction; formula

praefātus *pp* of **praefor**

praefectūr·a -ae *f* supervision, superintendence; prefectship, office of prefect, superintendency; government of a district; prefecture (*Italian city governed by a Roman prefect*); territory of a prefecture, district

praefect·us -ī *m* prefect, supervisor, superintendent; commander; governor; (with *genit* or *dat*) supervisor of, commander of, prefect or governor of

prae·fĕrō -ferre -tŭlī -lātum *vt* to hold out, carry in front; to prefer; to anticipate; to display, reveal, betray; to offer, present; to offer as a model; **praeferri** to ride past, ride by, march past, outflank; **praeferri** or **se praeferri** (with *dat*) to surpass

praefĕr·ox -ōcis *adj* very belligerent, very defiant

praeferrāt·us -a -um *adj* iron-tipped; (coll) chained (*slave*)

praefervĭd·us -a -um *adj* boiling; (fig) boiling; **ira praefervida** boiling anger

praefestin·ō -āre *vt* to hurry past; (with *inf*) to be in a hurry to

praefĭc·a -ae *f* hired mourner (*female*)

prae·ficĭō -ficĕre -fēcī -fectum *vt* to put (*someone*) in charge; (with double *acc*) to appoint (*someone*) as; (with *dat*) to put (*someone*) in charge of, set (*someone*) over, appoint (*someone*) to command

praefĭd·ens -entis *adj* too trustful, overconfident; (with *dat*) too trustful of; **homines sibi praefidentes** overconfident men

prae·fĭgō -fīgĕre -fixī -fixum *vt* to fix, fasten, set up in front, fasten on the end; to tip, point; to transfix; **capistris praefigere** to muzzle; **cuspidibus praefixus** pointed; **ferro praefixus** iron-tipped

praefin·iō -īre -īvī or **-iī -ĭtum** *vt* to determine in advance; to prescribe, appoint; to limit

praefīnītō *adv* in the prescribed manner

praefiscinē or **praefiscinī** *adv* meaning no offense

praefiōr·ō -āre *vt* to deflower, deprive of its bloom; (fig) to tarnish, spoil

praefiŭ·ō -ĕre *vt* & *vi* to flow by

praefōc·ō -āre *vt* to choke, choke up, strangle

prae·fodĭō -fodĕre -fōdī *vt* to bury beforehand; to dig in front of; **portas praefodire** to dig trenches in front of the gates

prae·for -fārī -fātus sum *vt* to say beforehand, utter in advance, preface; to address in prayer beforehand; to foretell; to invoke; *vi* to pray beforehand; (with *dat*) to pray before

praefractē *adv* obstinately

praefract·us -a -um *pp* of **praefringo**; resolute, determined; abrupt

praefrīgĭd·us -a -um *adj* very cold, freezing

prae·fringō -fringĕre -frēgī -fractum *vt* to break off at the tip or end, break to pieces, smash

prae·fulciō -fulcīre -fulsī -fultum *vt* to prop up, support in front; (with *dat*) to use (*someone*) as a prop or support for; **illud praefulci ut** make sure that

prae·fulgĕō -fulgēre -fulsī *vi* to shine forth, glitter, sparkle

praegelĭd·us -a -um *adj* very cold

praegest·ĭō -īre *vi* to be very eager

praegn·ans -antis or **praegn·ās -ātis** *adj* pregnant; (with *abl*) full of, swollen with

praegracĭl·is -e *adj* very lean or slender

praegrand·is -e *adj* huge, very great; very powerful

praegrăv·is -e *adj* very heavy; very fat; oppressive; very tiresome

praegrăv·ō -āre *vt* to weigh down; to outweigh; (fig) to burden

prae·gredior -grĕdī -gressus sum *vt* to go in advance of, go ahead of; to go by, go past; *vi* to walk out in front; (with *dat*) to precede, lead

praegressĭ·ō -ōnis *f* procession; (fig) precedence

praegustāt·or -ōris *m* taster, sampler

praegust·ō -āre *vt* to taste beforehand, get a sample of

praehib·ĕō -ēre *vt* to offer, furnish, supply; to utter, speak (*words*); **praehibere operam** (with *dat*) to offer to help

praejac·ĕō -ēre *vt* to lie before, be located in front of; *vi* (with *dat*) to lie before

praejūdĭcāt·us -a -um *adj* decided beforehand; prejudiced; *n* prejudged matter; prejudice; **id pro praejudicato ferre** to take it as a foregone conclusion

praejūdĭc·ĭum -ĭī or **-ī** *n* preliminary hearing; prejudgment; precedent, example

praejūdĭc·ō -āre vt to decide beforehand, prejudge

prae·jŭvō -juvāre -jūvī vt to help in advance

prae·lābor -lābī -lapsus sum vt & vi to glide along, glide by, float by

praelamb·ō -ĕre vt to pretaste

praelarg·us -a -um adj very ample

praelātus pp of **praefero**

prae·lēgō -legĕre -lēgī -lectum vt to sail past

praelĭg·ō -āre vt to tie up; (with dat) to tie (something) to

praelong·us -a -um adj very long

prae·lŏquor -lŏquī -locūtus sum vt to make (a speech) before someone else; to present (a case) first; to say by way of preface; vi to speak first

prae·lūcĕō -lūcēre -luxī vi (with dat) a to throw light on; b to outshine, outdo, surpass

praelūsĭ·ō -ōnis f prelude

praelustr·is -e adj magnificent

praemandāt·a -ōrum n pl warrant for arrest

praemand·ō -āre vt to order in advance

praemātūrē adv too soon, prematurely

praemātūr·us -a -um adj premature

praemedicāt·us -a -um adj protected by charms

praemeditātĭ·ō -ōnis f premeditation, prior consideration

praemedĭt·or -ārī -ātus sum vt to think over beforehand; to practice, practice on (a musical instrument)

praemer·or -ārī -ātus sum vt to buy in advance

praemetŭ·ens -entis adj apprehensive

praemetuenter adv anxiously

praemetŭ·ō -ĕre vt to fear beforehand; vi (with dat) to be apprehensive about

prae·mittō -mittĕre -mīsī -missum vt to send out ahead, send in advance; vi to send word

praem·ĭum -ĭī or **-ī** n prize, reward, recompense; exploit (worthy of reward); gift, bribe

praemolestĭ·a -ae f apprehension, presentiment of trouble

praemŏl·ĭor -īrī vt to prepare beforehand

praemon·ĕō -ēre -ŭī -ĭtum vt to forewarn; to warn of; to foreshadow, presage, predict

praemonĭt·us -ūs m forewarning, premonition

praemonstrāt·or -ōris m director, guide

praemonstr·ō -āre vt to point out the way to, guide, direct; to predict

prae·mordĕō -mordēre -mordī or **morsī -morsum** vt to bite the tip off of; (fig) to crib, pilfer

prae·morĭor -mŏrī -mortŭus sum vi to die too soon, die prematurely

praemūn·ĭō -īre -īvī -ītum vt to fortify, protect, secure

praemūnītĭ·ō -ōnis f (rhet) preparation, conditioning (of the minds of the hearers)

praenarr·ō -āre vt to relate beforehand

praenăt·ō -āre vt to float past, flow by

Praenest·e -is n or f ancient town in Latium (modern Palestrina)

Praenestīn·us -a -um adj & m Praenestine

praenit·ĕō -ēre -ŭī vi (with dat) a to outshine; b to appear more attractive to

praenōm·en -ĭnis n first name

praenosc·ō -ĕre vt to find out beforehand, foreknow

praenōtĭ·ō -ōnis f innate idea, preconception

praenūbĭl·us -a -um adj heavily clouded; dark, gloomy

praenuntĭ·a -ae f harbinger, foreteller, omen

praenuntĭ·ō -āre vt to foretell

praenuntĭ·us -a -um adj foreboding; m forecaster, harbinger, omen

praeoccupātĭ·ō -ōnis f seizing beforehand, advance occupation

praeoccŭp·ō -āre vt to occupy before another; to preoccupy; to anticipate, prevent

praeŏl·it -ĕre v impers a smell is emitted, there is a strong smell; **praeolit mihi quod tu velis** I scent your wishes before you express them

praeopt·ō -āre vt to prefer

praepand·ō -ĕre vt to spread, extend

praeparātĭ·ō -ōnis f preparation

praeparāt·us -a -um adj prepared, supplied, furnished, ready; n stores; **ex ante preparato** from the stores; (fig) by previous arrangement

praepăr·ō -āre vt to get ready, prepare, prepare for; to gather together

praepedīment·um -ī n impediment, hindrance

praeped·ĭō -īre -īvī or **-ĭī -ĭtum** vt to shackle, chain; to hinder, obstruct, hamper; to embarrass

praepend·ĕō -ēre vi to hang down in front

praep·es -ĕtis adj nimble, fast; winged; of good omen, favorable; m or f bird of good omen; bird, large bird

praepilāt·us -a -um adj tipped with a ball; **missile prapilatum** blunted missile

praepingu·is -e adj very fat; very fertile

praepoll·ĕō -ēre vi to be powerful; to be superior; (with dat) to surpass in power

praepondĕr·ō -āre vt to outweigh; to regard as superior

prae·pōnō -pōnĕre -posŭī -posi-

tum *vt* (with *dat*) **a** to place, set, put (*something*) in front of or before; **b** to entrust (*someone*) with, put (*someone*) in command of, in charge of; **c** to prefer (*someone or something*) to

praeport·ō -āre *vt* to carry before oneself

praepositi·ō -ōnis *f* preference; prefixing

praeposĭt·us -a -um *pp* of **praepono**; *adj* preferred, preferable; *m* prefect, commander; *n* that which is desirable, a desirable good

prae·possum -posse -potŭī *vi* to get the upper hand, have the better of it

praepostĕrē *adv* in reversed order, out of order

praepostĕr·us -a -um *adj* inverted, in reverse order; absurd, preposterous

praepŏt·ens -entis *adj* very powerful; (with *genit*) in full control of, fully controlling

praeproperanter or **praepropĕrē** *adv* very quickly

praepropĕr·us -a -um *adj* very quick; overhasty, sudden

praepūt·ium -iī or **-ī** *n* foreskin

praequam *conj* in comparison to; **nihil hoc est, praequam alios sumptus facit** this is nothing in comparison to the other expenses that he runs up

praequest·us -a -um *adj* complaining beforehand; **multa praequestus** having first raised many complaints

praeradi·ō -āre *vt* to outshine

praerapĭd·us -a -um *adj* very swift

praereptus *pp* of **praeripio**

praerig·escō -escĕre -ŭī *vi* to become very stiff

prae·ripĭō -ripĕre -ripŭī -reptum *vt* to snatch away, carry off; to anticipate, forestall; to count on too soon, presume upon; (with *dat*) to snatch from, steal from

prae·rōdō -rōdĕre -rōsī -rōsum *vt* to bite the ends of, nibble at; **digitos praerodere** to bite the fingernails

praerogatīv·us -a -um *adj* asked before others; voting first, privileged; *f* first tribe or century to vote; vote of the first tribe or century; previous election; sure sign, omen

praerōsus *pp* of **praerodo**

prae·rumpō -rumpĕre -rūpī -ruptum *vt* to break off, tear away (*something*) in front

praerupt·us -a -um *adj* broken off, broken up; broken up, rough (*terrain*); steep; hasty, impetuous

praes praedis *m* bondsman, surety; collateral

praesaep- = **praesep-**

praesāg·iō -īre -īvī or **praesāg·ior -īrī** *vt* to have forebodings of, feel beforehand; to cause

praesāgītī·ō -ōnis *f* presentiment, strange feeling, foreboding, prophetic power

praesāg·ium -iī or **-ī** *n* presentiment, presage, prediction

praesāg·us -a -um *adj* divining, prophetic

praesc·iō -īre -īvī *vt* to know beforehand

praescisc·ō -ĕre *vt* to find out or learn beforehand

praesci·us -a -um *adj* prescient; (with *genit*) foreseeing; **praescius venturi** foreseeing the future

prae·scrībō -scrībĕre -scripsī -scriptum *vt* to prefix in writing; to describe beforehand; to determine in advance, prescribe, ordain; to dictate; to outline, map out; to put forward as an excuse

praescripti·ō -ōnis *f* heading, title; preface; pretext; rule, law; limit, restriction

praescript·um -ī *n* regulation, rule, proviso

praesĕc·ō -āre -ŭī -tum *vt* to cut off, cut out, cut short

praesegmĭn·a -um *n pl* clippings

praes·ens -entis *adj* present, in person, at hand; existing, contemporary; prompt, immediate, impending; efficacious, powerful, effective; influential; resolute; propitious; **sermo praesens** a face-to-face talk; *n* present time; **ad praesens** or **in praesens** for the present

praesensi·ō -ōnis *f* presentiment; preconception

praesensus *pp* of **praesentio**

praesentāri·us -a -um *adj* ready, at hand

praesentĭ·a -ae *f* presence; efficacy, effect; **animi praesentia** presence of mind; **in praesentia** at the present time, just now, for the present

praesent·ia -ium *n pl* present circumstances, present state of affairs

prae·sentiō -sentīre -sensī -sensum *vt* to feel beforehand, to realize in advance, have strange feelings about, divine

praesēp·e or **praesaep·e -is** *n* or **praesēp·is** or **praesēp·es -is** *f* stall, stable; crib, manger; room, lodgings; tavern; hovel; beehive

praesēp·iō or **praesaep·iō -īre -sī -tum** *vt* to fence in, barricade

praesertim *adv* especially, particularly, principally; **praesertim cum** especially because

praeserv·iō -īre *vi* (with *dat*) to serve as a slave to

praes·es -idis *m* guard, guardian, protector, defender; president, superintendent; captain, pilot; *f* guardian, protectress

praesĭd·ens -entis *m* president, ruler

prae·sidĕō -sidēre -sēdī *vt* to guard, protect, defend; to command, be in command of; *vi* to be in charge, be in command; (with *dat*) **a** to watch over, guard, protect; **b** to preside over, direct, manage, command

praesidiāri·us -a -um *adj* on garrison duty

praesid·ium -iī or **-ī** *n* protection, defense; help, assistance; guard, garrison; convoy, escort; garrison post, defensive position

praesignific·ō -āre *vt* to indicate in advance, foretoken

praesign·is -e *adj* outstanding

praesŏn·ō -āre -uī *vi* to sound beforehand

praesparg·ō -ĕre *vt* to strew, scatter

praestābĭl·is -e *adj* excellent, outstanding

praest·ans -antis *adj* outstanding, eminent, exceptional

praestanti·a -ae *f* excellence, superiority, preeminence

praestern·ō -ĕre *vt* to strew

praest·es -ĭtis *adj* guardian, protecting, presiding

praestigi·ae -ārum *f pl* sleight of hand, juggling, tricks, illusion, deception

praestigiāt·or -ōris *m* or **praestīgiātr·ix -īcis** *f* juggler, magician; imposter

praestin·ō -āre *vt* to buy, shop for

prae·stituō -stituĕre -stituī -stitūtum *vt* to fix or set up beforehand, prescribe

praestĭtus *pp* of **praesto**

praestō *adv* at hand, ready, present; **praesto esse** (with *dat*) **a** to be on hand for, attend, serve, be helpful to, aid; **b** to be in the way of, resist, oppose

prae·stō -stāre -stĭtī -stĭtum *vt* to excel, be superior to; to show, exhibit, give evidence of, display; to answer for, be responsible for, take upon oneself; to perform, discharge, fulfill; to keep, maintain, retain; **fidem praestare** to keep one's word; **impetūs populi praestare** to be responsible for popular outbreaks; **nihil praestare** to be answerable for nothing; **officia praestare** to perform duties; **se praestare** to show oneself, behave; **socios salvos praestare** to keep the allies safe; **terga hosti praestare** to show one's back to the enemy, retreat; **virtutem praestare** to display courage; *vi* to stand out, be outstanding, be preeminent, be superior; *v impers* it is preferable, it is better

praestŏl·or -ārī -ātus sum *vt* to wait for, expect; *vi* (with *dat*) to wait for

prae·stringō -stringĕre -strinxī -strictum *vt* to draw together, squeeze; to blunt (*an edge*); to blind, dazzle (*the eyes*); to dazzle, baffle, confuse

prae·struō -struĕre -struxī -structum *vt* to build up, block up,

block, stop up; to build up (*e.g.*, *confidence*) beforehand

praes·ul -ŭlis *m* or *f* public dancer

praesult·ō -āre *vi* (with *dat*) to jump around in front of

prae·sum -esse -fuī *vi* to preside, be in charge, be in command; (with *dat*) **a** to preside over, be in charge of, be in command of; **b** to protect; (with **in** + *abl*) to be governor in

prae·sūmō -sūmĕre -sumpsī -sumptum *vt* to take in advance; to anticipate, take for granted, presume

praesumptĭ·ō -ōnis *f* anticipation

praesūt·us -a -um *adj* sewed up; covered

praetĕg·ō -ĕre *vt* to protect

praetempt·ō -āre *vt* to try out in advance, test in advance; to grope for

prae·tendō -tendĕre -tendī -tentum *vt* to hold or stretch in front of oneself; to present; to offer as an excuse, give as pretext, allege, pretend; (with *dat*) to hold or draw (*e.g.*, *a toga*) in front of (*e.g.*, *the eyes*); **praetendī** (of places) to lie to the front or opposite; **praetendī** (with *dat*) to lie or be situated opposite or over against

praetentō see **praetempto**

praetentus *pp* of **praetendo**

praetep·escō -escĕre -uī *vi* (of love) to glow

praeter *conj* besides, other than; *prep* (with *acc*) of place) past, by, along, before, in front of; (in comparison) above, beyond, more than; against, contrary to, aside from; besides, apart from, except; besides, in addition to

praeterǎg·ō -ĕre *vt* (with double *acc*) to drive (*e.g.*, *a horse*) past (*a place*)

praeterbĭt·ō -ĕre *vt & vi* to go by or past

praeterĕā *adv* besides, moreover; hereafter, thereafter

praeter·eō -īre -īvī or **-iī -ĭtum** *vt* to go past, pass by; to skip, pass over in silence, neglect; to escape the notice of; to go beyond; to surpass

praeterequĭt·ans -antis *adj* riding by

praeter·fĕrō -ferre -tŭlī -lātum *vt* (with double *acc*) to carry or take (*someone*) past (*something*); **praeterferri** to move or sweep by (*a place*)

praeterflŭ·ō -ĕre *vt & vi* to flow by

praeter·gredĭor -grĕdī -gressus sum *vt* to march by, go past; to surpass

praeterhāc *adv* in addition

praeterĭt·us -a -um *pp* of **praetereo**; *adj* past, past and gone, bygone; *n pl* bygone events, the past

praeter·lābor -lābī -lapsus sum *vt* to glide by; *vi* to glide by, slip away

praeterlātus *pp* of **praeterfero**

praetermĕ·ō **-āre** *vt* & *vi* to go past or by

praetermissĭ·ō **-ōnis** *f* leaving out, omission; passing over, neglecting; (with *genit*) omission of, neglecting of

praeter·mittō **-mittĕre** **-mīsī** **-missum** *vt* to let pass, let go by; to leave undone; to pass over, omit, disregard, overlook, neglect

praetĕr·ō **-ĕre** *vt* to wear down in front

praeterquam *adv* besides, other than; **praeterquam quod** apart from the fact that

praetervectĭ·ō **-ōnis** *f* passing by

praeter·vĕhor **-vĕhī** **-vectus sum** *vt* & *vi* to ride by; to sail by; to march or go by

praetervŏl·ō **-āre** *vt* & *vi* to fly by; (of opportunity) to slip by; to escape

praetex·ō **-ĕre** **-ŭī** **-tum** *vt* to border, edge, fringe; to adorn in front; (fig) to cloak, conceal, disguise; to allege as a pretext

praetextāt·us **-a** **-um** *adj* wearing the toga praetexta (*crimson-bordered toga*); underage, juvenile; **mores praetextati** loose morals

praetext·us **-a** **-um** *pp* of **praetexo**; *adj* bordered; wearing the crimson-bordered toga; **fabula praetexta** Roman tragic drama; *f* toga praetexta (*crimson-bordered toga which was worn by higher magistrates and by freeborn boys*); tragedy; **praetextas docere** to put on tragedies; *n* pretext, pretense, excuse

praetext·us **-ūs** *m* outward show, splendor; pretense, pretext

praetim·ĕō **-ēre** *vi* to be apprehensive

praetinct·us **-a** **-um** *adj* previously dipped

praet·or **-ōris** *m* praetor (*judicial magistrate, accompanied by six lictors*); commander; (during the early years of the republic) chief magistrate, chief executive; (in Italian municipalities) chief magistrate; **praetor peregrinus** praetor who had jurisdiction over cases involving foreigners; **praetor urbanus** or **praetor urbis** praetor who had jurisdiction over cases involving Roman citizens

praetōriān·us **-a** **-um** *adj* praetorian, belonging to the emperor's bodyguard; *m pl* praetorian guard, soldiers of the praetorian guard

praetōricĭ·us **-a** **-um** *adj* received from the praetor (*at public games*)

praetōri·us **-a** **-um** *adj* of the commander in chief, of the commander or general; praetor's, of the praetor; propraetor's; **cohors praetoria** general's bodyguard; **comitia praetoria** praetorian elections; **navis praetoria** flagship; **porta praetoria** camp gate nearest the general's tent; **turba praetoria**

crowd around the praetor; *n* general's quarters, headquarters; official residence of the governor in a province; council of war; emperor's bodyguard; palace, mansion

praetorqu·ĕō **-ēre** *vt* to twist beforehand; to strangle first

praetrepĭd·ans **-antis** *adj* very nervous

praetrepĭd·us **-a** **-um** *adj* very nervous, trembling

praetrunc·ō **-āre** *vt* to cut off, cut short

praetūr·a **-ae** *f* praetorship; **praeturā se abdicare** to resign the praetorship

praeumbr·ans **-antis** *adj* casting a shadow; (fig) overshadowing

praeust·us **-a** **-um** *adj* burnt at the tip; hardened by fire at the point; frost-bitten

praeut *conj* as compared with, when compared with

praeval·ĕō **-ēre** **-ŭī** *vi* to be stronger, have more power; to have greater influence; to have the upper hand

praevalĭd·us **-a** **-um** *adj* of superior strength, unusually strong, unusually powerful, imposing; too strong

praevāricātĭ·ō **-ōnis** *f* collusion

praevāricāt·or **-ōris** *m* phoney accuser, prosecutor in collusion, prevaricator

praevāric·or **-ārī** **-ātus sum** *vi* to make a sham defense or prosecution; (with *dat*) to favor because of collusion

prae·vĕhor **-vĕhī** **-vectus sum** *vt* (of a river) to flow past; *vi* to ride in front, ride by; to sail by

prae·venio **-venīre** **-vēnī** **-ventum** *vt* to come before, precede, get the jump on, anticipate; to prevent; *vi* to come before, precede

praeverr·ō **-ĕre** *vt* to sweep before

praevert·ō **-ĕre** **-ī** or **prae·vertor** **-vertī** *vt* to go before, precede, outrun, outstrip; to turn to first, attend to first; to prefer; to come before, anticipate, prevent; to preoccupy; (with *dat* or **prae** + *abl*) to prefer (*someone or something*) to; *vi* (with *dat* or **ad** + *acc*) to go to first, turn to first, attend to first

prae·vidĕō **-vidēre** **-vīdī** **-vīsum** *vt* to foresee

praevitĭ·ō **-āre** *vt* to taint or pollute beforehand

praevĭ·us **-a** **-um** *adj* going before, leading the way

praevŏl·ō **-āre** *vi* to fly out in front

pragmatic·us **-a** **-um** *adj* experienced; *m* lawyer, attorney

prandĕō **prandēre** **prandī** **pransum** *vt* to eat for breakfast, eat for lunch; *vi* to have breakfast, have lunch

prand·ium **-ĭī** or **-ī** *n* breakfast, lunch

pransĭt·ō **-āre** *vt* to usually eat for lunch

prans·or **-ōris** *m* guest at lunch

prans·us -a -um *pp* of **prandeo;** *adj* having had breakfast, after eating; well fed; **pransus potus** having been wined and dined

prasin·us -a -um *adj* green; **factio prasina** the Greens (*one of the stables of horses at the racetrack in Rome*)

prātens·is -e *adj* meadow, growing in the meadow

prātŭl·um -ī *n* small meadow

prāt·um -ī *n* meadow; (*fig*) plain (*of the sea*); *n pl* meadow grass

prāvē *adv* crookedly; improperly, wrongly, badly, poorly; **prave facti versus** poorly written verses

prāvit·ās -ātis *f* crookedness, distortion; impropriety, irregularity; perverseness, depravity

prāv·us -a -um *adj* crooked, distorted, deformed; irregular, improper, wrong, bad; perverse, vicious

Praxitĕl·ēs -is *m* famous Greek Athenian sculptor (*4th cent. B.C.*)

precāriō *adv* upon request

precāri·us -a -um *adj* obtained by prayer; dependent on another's will, uncertain, precarious

precāti·ō -ōnis *f* prayer; **precationes facere** to say prayers

precāt·or -ōris *m* intercessor, suppliant

precēs = *pl* of **prex**

preci·ae -ārum *f pl* grapevine

prec·or -ārī -ātus sum *vt* to entreat, supplicate, pray to; to pray for; to wish for; (*with double acc*) to pray to (*someone*) for; (*with acc* of thing and *abl* of person) to request (*something*) from; (*with* **pro** + *abl*) to entreat (*e.g., the gods*) on behalf of; (*with* **ut** or **ne**) to pray that, pray that not; **longum Augusto diem precari** to wish Augustus long life; *vi* to pray; (*with* **ad** + *acc*) to pray to, e.g., **di ad quos precantur** the gods to whom they pray; **male precari** to curse, utter curses

pre·hendō -hendĕre -hendī -hensum or **prendō prendĕre prendī prensum** *vt* to take hold of, grasp, seize; to detain; to arrest; to occupy; to catch, surprise; to reach, arrive at; to grasp, understand

prēl·um -ī *n* wine press, oil press; clothes press

premō premĕre pressī pressum *vt* to press, squeeze; to lie down on; to hug (*shore*); to suppress, hide; to cover, crown; to press hard, bear down on; to chase, attack; to weigh down, load; to press together, close; to curb, stop; to depress, lower; to mark, impress; to prune; to pressure, urge, importune; to degrade, humble, disparage; to abridge; to subjugate

prensāti·ō -ōnis *f* campaigning (*for office*)

prens·ō or **prehens·ō -āre** *vt* to take hold of, clutch at, grab; to stop, detain; *vi* to campaign, be a candidate

prensus *pp* of **prendo**

pressē *adv* distinctly, with articulation; concisely; accurately; simply

pressi·ō -ōnis *f* fulcrum; leverage

press·ō -āre *vt* to press

press·us -a -um *pp* of **premo;** *adj* closed, shut tight; suppressed; slow; lowered, low, subdued; concise, precise, accurate; articulate

press·us -ūs *m* pressing, pressure; expression (*of the face*)

prest·ēr -ēris *m* waterspout

pretiōsē *adv* at great cost, expensively

pretiōs·us -a -um *adj* previous, valuable; expensive; extravagant

pret·ium -iī or **-ī** *n* price; value, worth; reward, return, recompense; bribe; pay, wages; **in pretio esse** to be prized; to be held in high esteem; **in pretio habere** to prize, hold in high esteem; **pretium curae esse** to be worth the trouble; **pretium habere** to have value, be worth something; **pretium facere** to set a price; **pretium operae esse** to be worth the effort, be worthwhile

prex precis *f* prayer, request; curse, imprecation; intercession

Priamē·is -idis *f* daughter of Priam

Priamēl·us -a -um *adj* Priam's, of Priam

Priamĭd·ēs -ae *m* son of Priam

Priăm·us -ī *m* Priam (*son of Laomedon, husband of Hecuba, father of Hector, Paris, etc., king of Troy at the time of its fall*)

prīdem *adv* long ago, long, since; **haud ita prīdem** not so long ago; not long before; **quam prīdem** how long ago

prīdiē *adv* the day before, the previous day

prīm·a -ōrum *n pl* first part, beginning; first principles or elements; **cum primus** among the first, especially; **in primis** above all, chiefly, particularly, especially, principally

prīm·ae -ārum *f pl* lead, first rank, highest place, highest importance; **primas dare** (*with dat*) to attach supreme importance to

prīmaev·us -a -um *adj* young, youthful

prīmān·ī -ōrum *m pl* soldiers of the first legion

prīmāri·us -a -um *adj* first in rank; first-rate

prīmigĕn·us -a -um *adj* original

prīmipīl·us -ī *m* first-ranking centurion of a legion

prīmiti·ae -ārum *f pl* firstfruits

prīmĭtus *adv* originally, at first; for the first time

prīmō *adv* first, in the first place; at first, at the beginning

prīmord·ium -iī or **-ī** *n* origin, beginning; commencement; beginning of a new reign

prīmōr·ēs -um *m pl* chiefs, nobles, leaders; (mil) front line

prīmōr·is -e *adj* first, foremost, extreme, tip of; first, principal; **digitāli primores** fingertips; **primori in acie** all the way up front

prīmŭlum *adv* first of all, at first

prīmŭl·us -a -um *adj* very first

prīmum *adv* first, in the first place, before all else; at first; for the first time; **cum primum, ubi primum, ut primum** as soon as; **primum dum** in the first place; **quam primum** as soon as possible

prīm·us -a -um *adj* first, foremost; principal; eminent, distinguished; earliest; **primas partes agere** to play the lead role; **primis digitis** with or at the fingertips; **primo anno** at the beginning of the year or season; **primus in provinciam introiit** he was the first to enter the province; **primus quisque** the very first, the first possible; *f pl see* **primae;** *n* beginning, front; **a primo** from the first, from the beginning; **in primo** in the beginning; (mil) at the head of the column; *n pl see* **prima**

prīnc·eps -ĭpis *adj* first, in front; foremost, chief; *m* leader, chief; emperor; (mil) maniple, company; captain, company commander, centurion; captaincy, centurionship; *m pl* soldiers of the second line (*between the hastati and triarii*), second line

prīncipāl·is -e *adj* first, foremost; original, primitive; chief, principal; of the emperor; **via principalis** (mil) main street of a camp; **porta principalis** (mil) main gate of a camp

prīncipāt·us -ūs *m* first place; post of commander in chief; principate, rule, sovereignty; origin, beginning

prīncipi·a -ōrum *n pl* first principles; foundations; front line, front-line troops; headquarters

prīncipiāl·is -e *adj* initial

prīncip·ium -ĭī or **-ī** *n* start, commencement, origin; beginner, originator; first to vote; right to vote first; **a principio** or **principio** at the beginning, at first

pri·or -us *adj* previous, preceding, prior, former; first; better, superior, preferable

priōr·ēs -um *m pl* forefathers, ancestors, ancients; *f pl* (only *acc*) lead, preference

priscē *adv* in the old-fashioned style

prisc·us -a -um *adj* old, ancient; old-time, old-fashioned; former, previous

pristǐn·us -a -um *adj* former, earlier; pristine, primitive, original; preceding, previous, yesterday's; *n* former condition; **in pristinum restituere** to restore to its former condition

pristis *see* **pistrix**

prius *adv* earlier, before, previously,

sooner, first; sooner, rather

priusquam *conj* before

prīvātim *adv* privately, in private, in a private capacity, as a private citizen; at home

prīvāti·ō -ōnis *f* removal

prīvātō *adv* at home

prīvāt·us -a -um *adj* private; personal, individual, peculiar; isolated, withdrawn; ordinary (*language*); *m* private citizen, civilian; *n* privacy, retirement; private property, private land; **ex privato** out of one's own pocket; **in privato** in private; **in privatum** for private use

prīvign·a -ae *f* stepdaughter

prīvign·us -ī *m* stepson; *m pl* stepchildren

prīvilēg·ium -ĭī or **-ī** *n* special bill directed against an individual; special bill in favor of an individual

prīv·ō -āre *vt* to deprive, rob, strip; to free, release

prīv·us -a -um *adj* every, each single; own, private; (with *genit*) deprived of

prō *adv* (with **quam** or **ut**) just as, according as; *prep* (with *abl*) before, in front of, in, on, in the presence of; for, in behalf of, in favor of, in the service of, on the side of; instead of, in place of, for; in return for, in exchange for; for; just as, as, the same as, for; in proportion to, according to, in comparison with, by virtue of; **pro eo** just the same; **pro eo atque** or **ac** just as, the same as; **pro eo quod** in view of the fact that; **pro se quisque** each one for himself, individually; **pro ut** or **pro eo quantum** as, in proportion as; *interj* oh!; **pro di immortales!** Oh, heavens above!

proāgŏr·us -ī *m* chief magistrate in some provincial towns

proavi·a -ae *f* great-grandmother

proavīt·us -a -um *adj* great-grandfather's, ancestral

proäv·us -ī *m* great-grandfather; ancestor, forefather

probābil·is -e *adj* worthy of approval, commendable, acceptable, pleasing, agreeable; probable, plausible, credible, likely

probābilit·ās -ātis *f* probability, plausibility

probābiliter *adv* probably

probāti·ō -ōnis *f* approval, approbation, assent; test, trial; proof

probāt·or -ōris *m* approver, supporter, backer

probāt·us -a -um *adj* approved, acceptable; tried, tested, good; esteemed

probē *adv* well, properly, correctly; well, thoroughly, very, very much

probǐt·ās -ātis *f* probity, honesty, worth, goodness

prob·ō -āre *vt* to approve, commend, esteem; to make good, represent as good, make acceptable; to pronounce judgment on; to pronounce approval of; to make credible, prove, show, demonstrate; to test, try, inspect; **probare pro** (with *abl*) to pass (*someone*) off for; **probari pro** (with *abl*) to pass for, be taken for

probriperlecēbr·ae -ārum *f pl* temptations

probrōs·us -a -um *adj* scandalous, shameful, abusive

probr·um -ī *n* abuse, invective, reproach; shameful act, vile deed; lewdness, indecency; shame, disgrace; charge of disgraceful conduct

prob·us -a -um *adj* good, honest, upright, virtuous, decent; (coll) real, proper, downright

Proc·a or **Proc·ās -ae** *m* king of Alba and father of Numitor and Amulius

procācit·ās -ātis *f* brashness

procāciter *adv* brashly

proc·ax -ācis *adj* brash

prō·cēdō -cēdĕre -cessī -cessum *vi* to proceed, go forward, advance; to make progress, advance; to come out (*in public*), show oneself, appear; to come forth, arise; (of time) to pass, elapse; to turn out, result, succeed; to continue

procell·a -ae *f* violent wind, squall, hurricane, storm; (fig) violence, commotion, storm; (mil) charge, sudden attack

prōcell·ō -ĕre *vt* to throw down; **se procellere in mensam** to lie down at the table

procel·lōs·us -a -um *adj* gusty

proc·er -ēris *m* chief, noble, prince, leader

prōcērit·ās -ātis *f* height, tallness; length; *f pl* the different heights

prōcērius *adv* farther, to a greater extent, more

prōcēr·us -a -um *adj* tall; long; **palmae procerae** upraised palms

prōcessi·ō -ōnis *f* advance

prōcessus *pp* of **procedo**

prōcess·us -ūs *m* advance, progress

Prochyt·a -ae or **Prochyt·ē -ēs** *f* small island off the Campanian coast

prō·cīdō -cidĕre -cīdī *vi* to fall forwards, fall over, fall down, fall prostrate

prōcinctū (*abl* only) *m* **in procinctu** under arms, ready for combat

prōclāmāt·or -ōris *m* loudmouth

prōclām·ō -āre *vi* to yell

prōclīn·ō -āre *vt* to bend forward, bend; **res proclinata** critical situation, crisis

prōclīv·e -is *n* slope, descent; **in proclivi esse** to be easy

prōclive *adv* downward, downhill; rapidly

prōclīv·is -e or **prōclīv·us -a -um** *adj* sloping forward; downhill; easy; inclined, disposed, subject, ready, willing

prōclīvit·ās -ātis *f* proclivity, tendency, predisposition

prōclīvus see **proclivis**

Procn·ē or **Progn·ē -ēs** *f* daughter of Pandion, sister of Philomela, wife of Tereus, and mother of Itys, who was changed into a swallow; swallow

proc·ō -āre *vt* to require, demand

prōcons·ul -ŭlis *m* vice-consul, proconsul; governor of a province; military commander

prōconsulār·is -e *adj* proconsular

prōconsulāt·us -ūs *m* proconsulship, proconsulate

prōcrāstināti·ō -ōnis *f* procrastination

prōcrāstin·ō -āre *vt* to postpone, put off from day to day

prōcreāti·ō -ōnis *f* procreation, breeding

prōcreāt·or -ōris *m* procreator, sire, parent, father

prōcreātr·ix -īcis *f* mother

prōcrĕ·ō -āre *vt* to procreate, beget, produce

prōcresc·ō -ĕre *vi* to spring forth, be produced; to continue to grow, grow up

Procr·is -is or **-ĭdis** *f* wife of Cephalus who mistook her for a wild beast and shot her

Procrust·ēs -ae *m* notorious robber in Attica who stretched his victims to the length of his bed or mutilated them if they were too tall

prōcŭb·ō -āre *vi* to lie stretched out

prō·cūdō -cūdĕre -cūdī -cūsum *vt* to forge, fashion; to bring forth, produce

procul *adv* at a distance, in the distance, far; from a distance, from far; **haud procul afuit quin legatos violarent** they came close to outraging the ambassadors

prōcŭlc·ō -āre *vt* to trample upon, trample down

prō·cumbō -cumbĕre -cubŭī -cubitum *vi* to fall down, sink down; to lean forward, bend over, be broken down; to extend, spread; (fig) to go to ruin

prōcūrāti·ō -ōnis *f* management, administration, superintendence; expiation, expiatory sacrifice

prōcūrāt·or -ōris *m* procurator, manager, administrator, superintendent, agent, deputy; governor of a province

prōcūrātr·ix -īcis *f* governess, protectress

prōcūr·ō -āre *vt* to manage, administer; to take care of, attend to; to avert by sacrifice; to expiate; *vi* to serve as procurator

prō·currō -currĕre -cucurrī or **-currī -cursum** *vi* to run out ahead, dash forward; to jut out, project

prōcursāti·ō -ōnis *f* sally, charge

prōcursātōr·ēs -um *m pl* skirmishers

prŏcurs·ō -āre vi to keep charging out, continue to skirmish

prŏcurs·us -ūs m sally, charge, onset

prŏcurv·us -a -um adj curving forwards; curving, winding (shore)

proc·us -ī m noble; gigolo; **impudentes proci** shameless candidates

Procy·ōn -ōnis m Lesser Dog Star, Sirius

prōdactus pp of **prodigo**

prōdeambŭl·ō -āre vi to go out for a walk

prōd·ĕō -īre -ĭī -ĭtum vi to go out, come out, go forth, come forth; (of a cliff) to project; (of plants) to come out, appear; to appear in public; to go ahead, advance, proceed

prō·dīcō -dīcĕre -dīxī -dictum vt to put off, defer, postpone; **diem prodicere** to adjourn a case to a later date

prōdictāt·or -ōris m vice-dictator

prōdĭgē adv lavishly

prōdigenti·a -ae f profusion, extravagance; openhandedness

prōdigiālĭter adv to a fantastic degree

prōdigiōs·us -a -um adj prodigious; freakish

prōdig·ium -ĭī or **-ī** n portent; unnatural crime, monstrous crime; monster, freak

prōd·Igō -igĕre -ēgī -actum vt to squander, waste

prōdig·us -a -um adj wasteful; lavish, openhanded; (with genit) free with; **animae prodigus** free with or careless with one's life; **herbae prodigus locus** spot with luxuriant growth of grass

prōditĭ·ō -ōnis f betrayal, treason; **proditionem agere** (with dat) to commit treason against, betray

prōdĭt·or -ōris m betrayer, traitor

prō·dō -dĕre -dĭdī -dĭtum vt to bring out, bring forth, produce; to reveal, disclose; to record, relate, report, hand down, transmit; to proclaim, appoint, elect; to give up, surrender; to forsake, betray; to prolong, protract; (fig) to display, exhibit

prōdoc·ĕō -ēre vt to preach publicly

prodrŏm·us -ī m forerunner, advance messenger

prō·dūcō -dūcĕre -duxī -ductum vt to bring out, bring forth; to produce; to promote, advance; to bring to light, reveal; to bring into the world, produce, raise, bring up; to educate; to drag out, protract, stretch out, lengthen; to lead on, induce; to put off, adjourn; to put (a slave) up for sale; to produce (on the stage), perform; to bring to court

prōductē adv long; **producte litteram dicere** to lengthen the letter or vowel

prōductĭ·ō -ōnis f lengthening

prōduct·ō -āre vt to drag out, delay

prōduct·us -a -um pp of **produco**; adj lengthened, prolonged, long

proēgmĕn·on -ī n preference

proeliār·is -e adj battle, of battle

proeliāt·or -ōris m combatant

proeli·or -ārī -ātus sum vi to battle, fight

proel·ium -ĭī or **-ī** n battle, combat, fight; n pl fighting men, warriors

Proet·us -ī m king of Tiryns

prŏfān·ō -āre vt to profane, desecrate

prŏfān·us -a -um adj unconsecrated, ordinary, common; impious, wicked; ill-omened

prŏfātus pp of **profor**

profectĭ·ō -ōnis f setting out, departure; source (of money)

profectō adv really, actually

profectus pp of **proficiscor**

prŏfectus pp of **proficio**

prŏfect·us -ūs m progress, advance, success; increase, profit

prō·fĕrō -ferre -tŭlī -lātum vt to bring forward, advance, bring out; to extend, enlarge; to put off, postpone, defer; to produce, discover, invent; to make known, reveal, publish; to mention, cite, quote; **pedem proferre** to advance; **signa proferre** to march forward

profess·ae -ārum f pl professional prostitutes, professionals

professĭ·ō -ōnis f public acknowledgment, profession, declaration; registration (at which property, etc., was declared); profession, business

profess·or -ōris m professor, teacher

professōrĭ·us -a -um adj professorial; professional, expert

professus pp of **profiteor**

profest·us -a -um adj non-holiday, ordinary; **dies profestus** working day

prō·ficĭō -ficĕre -fēcī -fectum vi to make progress, make headway, advance, have success, succeed; to be useful, do good, help, be conducive; **nihil proficere** to do no good

prō·ficiscor -ficiscī -fectus sum vi to set out, start, go, depart; to originate, proceed, arise

prō·fitĕor -fitērī -fessus sum vt to declare publicly, acknowledge, confess, profess; to offer freely, promise, volunteer; to follow as a profession, practice (e.g., law); to make a declaration of, register (property, etc.) before a public official; **indicium profiteri** to volunteer evidence, testify freely; **nomen profiteri** to put one's name in as a candidate, announce oneself a candidate; **se adjutorem profiteri** (with **ad** + acc) to volunteer to help (someone); **se amicum profiteri** to avow oneself a friend, profess to be a friend; vi to make a confession, make an admission; to be a professor, be a teacher

prōflīgāt·or -ōris *m* big spender

prōflīgāt·us -a -um *adj* profligate, dissolute

prōflīg·ō -āre *vt* to knock to the ground, knock down; to defeat, conquer; to bring to an end, do away with, finish off; to ruin, crush; to debase, degrade

prōfl·ō -āre *vt* to breathe out

prōflŭ·ens -entis *adj* flowing along; fluent (*speech*); *f* running water

prōflŭenter *adv* easily, effortlessly

prōflŭenti·a -ae *f* fluency

prō·flŭō -flŭĕre -flūxī *vi* to flow out; to flow along; (fig) to proceed

prōflŭv·ĭum -ĭī or **-ĭ n** flow

prof·or -ārī -ātus sum *vt* to say, declare; *vi* to speak out

pro·fŭgĭō -fŭgĕre -fūgī *vt* to run away from, escape from; *vi* to run away, escape; (with *ad* + *acc*) to take refuge with, take refuge at the house of

profŭg·us -a -um *adj* fugitive; banished, exile; nomadic; *m* fugitive, refugee

pro·fundō -fundĕre -fūdī -fūsum *vt* to pour, pour out; to shed; to utter; to give vent to; to spend freely, waste, squander; **se profundere** (of things) to come pouring out; (of persons) to come pouring out, come charging out, break out

profund·us -a -um *adj* deep; boundless, vast; dense (*forest, cloud*); high (*heaven*); infernal; (fig) bottomless, boundless; *n* depth; the deep, deep sea; (fig) abyss

profūsē *adv* in disorder, helter-skelter, haphazardly; extravagantly

profūsĭ·ō -ōnis *f* profusion

profūs·us -a -um *pp* of **profundo**; *adj* extravagant, lavish, profuse; excessive, expensive

prōgĕn·er -ĕrī *m* granddaughter's husband

prōgenĕr·ō -āre *vt* to beget, produce

prōgenĭ·ēs -ēī *f* line, lineage; progeny, descendants, offspring, posterity

prōgenĭt·or -ōris *m* progenitor, founder, ancestor

prō·gignō -gignĕre -genŭī -genĭtum *vt* to beget, produce

prognārīter *adv* precisely, exactly

prognāt·us -a -um *adj* born, descended; (with *abl* or with *ab* or **ex** + *abl*) born of, descended from; *m* child; grandson

Prognē see **Procne**

prognōstic·on or **prognostic·um -ī n** sign of the future, prognostic

prō·gredĭor -grĕdī -gressus sum *vi* to go forward, march forward, proceed, advance; to go on, make headway, make progress; to go forth, go out

prōgressĭ·ō -ōnis *f* progress, advancement; increase, growth; (rhet) climax

prōgressus *pp* of **progredior**

prōgress·us -ūs *m* progress, advance; march (*of time or events*)

prōh *interj* oh!, O!

prohib·ĕō -ēre -ŭī -ĭtum *vt* to hold back, check, hinder, prevent, avert, keep off; to prohibit, forbid; to keep away; to defend, protect

prohibitĭ·ō -ōnis *f* prohibition

proinde or **proin** *adv* consequently, accordingly; **proinde atque** (or **ac**), **proinde ut**, or **proinde quam** just as, exactly as; **proinde atque si** (or **ac si**), **proinde quasi** just as if

prōjectīcĭ·us -a -um *adj* exposed (*child*)

prōjectĭ·ō -ōnis *f* stretching out; **projectio bracchii** stretching out of the arm

prōject·ō -āre *vt* to accuse, blame

prōject·us -a -um *pp* of **projicio**; *adj* jutting out, projecting; prostrate, stretched out; inclined; prone; abject, contemptible; downcast

prōject·ūs -ūs *m* projection, extension

prō·jicĭō -jicĕre -jēcī -jectum *vt* to throw down, throw out, throw; to throw away, abandon, forsake; to hold out, extend; to throw out, banish, exile; to neglect, desert; to blurt out; to throw away, give up, sacrifice; to put off, delay; to throw overboard; **se projicere** (with *genit*) to throw oneself at the feet of, fall prostrate before; **se projicere ex nave** to jump overboard; **se projicere in forum** to rush into the forum

prō·lābor -lābī -lapsus sum *vi* to glide forward, slip or move forward; to fall forwards, fall on one's face; to slip out; (of words) to slip out, escape; to be led on, led astray (*by greed, fear, etc.*); (fig) to fail, go to ruin, collapse

prōlapsĭ·ō -ōnis *f* falling, collapse

prōlapsus *pp* of **prolabor**

prōlātĭ·ō -ōnis *f* expansion, extension (*of territory*); adducing, mentioning (*of precedents*); delay, postponement

prōlāt·ō -āre *vt* to extend; to put off, delay

prōlātus *pp* of **profero**

prōl·ēs -is *f* offspring, progeny, children, descendants; race, stock; child; young man

prōlētārĭ·us -ĭī or **-ĭ** *m* proletarian; *m pl* proletariat

prō·licĭō -licĕre -lixī *vt* to entice, bring out, incite

prōlixē *adv* freely, wildly; readily, cheerfully, freely

prōlix·us -a -um *adj* long, freely growing, wild (*beard, hair, etc.*); obliging, ready and unwilling; favorable (*circumstances*)

prōlocūtus *pp* of **proloquor**

prōlŏg·us -ī *m* prologue (*of a play*); actor who gives the prologue

prō·lŏquor -lŏquī -locūtus sum *vt & vi* to speak out

prōlŭb·ium -iī or -ī *n* desire, inclination, yen

prō·lūdō -lūdĕre -lūsī -lūsum *vi* to practice; (of boxers) to spar, shadowbox

prō·lŭō -luĕre -lŭī -lūtum *vt* to wash out, flush, wash off, wash away; to wet, drench

prōlūsi·ō -ōnis *f* sparring, shadowboxing

prōlūtus *pp* of **proluo**

prōluvi·ēs -ēī *f* flood; refuse, sewage

prōmer·ĕō -ēre -uī -ĭtum or **prōmer·ĕor** -ērī -ĭtus sum *vt* to deserve, merit, earn; *vi* to be deserving; (with **de** + *abl*) to deserve the gratitude of; **bene de multis promerere** or **promereri** to deserve the full gratitude of many people

prōmerĭt·um -ī *n* reward, due; merit; guilt

Prōmĕth·eus -ĕī or -ĕos *m* son of Iapetus and Clymene, brother of Epimetheus, and father of Deucalion, who by teaching men the use of fire, incurred the wrath of Jupiter

Prōmēthē·us -a -um *adj* Promethean, of Prometheus

Prōmēthĭd·ēs -ae *m* son of Prometheus, Deucalion (*who, with his wife Pyrrha, was the sole survivor of the Deluge*)

prōmĭn·ens -entis *adj* projecting, prominent; *n* headland

prōmin·ĕō -ēre -uī *vi* to jut out, hang forward, bend forward, extend; (with **in** + *acc*) to reach down to

prōmiscam or **prōmiscē** *adv* in common, without distinction, indiscriminately

prōmiscŭē *adv* indiscriminately, promiscuously

prōmiscŭ·us or **prōmiscŭ·us** -a -um *adj* promiscuous, haphazard, indiscriminate, in common, open to all; common, ordinary

prōmissĭ·ō -ōnis *f* promise

prōmiss·or -ōris *m* promiser, fourflusher

prōmiss·us -a -um *adj* allowed to grow, long, hanging down; *n* promise

prō·mittō -mittĕre -mīsī -missum *vt* to let (*e.g., the hair*) grow; to promise; to give promise of, give hope of; *vi* to promise to go; **ad cenam promittere** to promise to go to dinner, make a dinner engagement

prōmō prōmĕre prompsī promptum *vt* to bring out, draw out; to produce (*arguments*); to bring to light, reveal; to bring out, express (*feelings, ideas, emotions*)

prōmontōr·ium -iī or -ī *n* promontory

prōmōt·a -ōrum *n pl* second choice

(*things preferred next after absolute good*)

prō·movĕō -movēre -mōvī -mōtum *vt* to move (*something*) forward, cause to advance; to enlarge, extend; to effect, accomplish; to promote (*to higher office*); to bring to light, reveal; to put off, postpone; **nihil promovere** to accomplish nothing, do no good, make no progress

promptē *adv* readily, quickly; easily; frankly

prompt·ō -āre *vt* to give out, distribute

promptū (only *abl*) *m* **in promptu** in readiness, ready, at hand; public, visible, manifest; **in promptu gerere, habere,** or **ponere** to display

promptuārĭ·us -a -um *adj* of a storehouse, storage; **cella promptuaria** (coll) jail

prompt·us -a -um *pp* of **promo**; *adj* prompt, ready; easy; brought to light, evident; bold, enterprising; (with *dat* or with **ad** or **in** + *acc*) a ready or prepared for, set for; b inclined to, disposed to; (with **in** + *abl*) quick at, prompt at; (with **adversus** + *acc*) ready for, prepared against; (with *inf*) ready to, quick to

prōmulgātĭ·ō -ōnis *f* promulgation, publication

prōmulg·ō -āre *vt* to promulgate, publish

prōmuls·is -ĭdis *f* hors d'oeuvres

prōmuntūr·ium -iī or -ī *n* promontory

prōm·us -ī *m* butler

prōmūtŭ·us -a -um *adj* on credit, advanced, given in advance

prōnē *adv* downwards

prōnĕp·ōs -ōtis *m* great-grandson

prōnept·is -is *f* great-granddaughter

prōnoe·a -ae *f* providence

prōnŭb·a -ae *f* patroness of marriage

prōnuntiātĭ·ō -ōnis *f* proclamation, declaration; announcement (*of the jury's verdict*); delivery (*of a speech*); proposition (*in logic*)

prōnuntiāt·or -ōris *m* narrator

prōnuntiāt·um -ī *n* proposition (*in logic*)

prōnuntĭ·ō -āre *vt* to proclaim, announce; to utter, pronounce, express (*opinion, judgment*); to hold out, promise, offer; to recite, deliver, narrate, relate; (in the senate) to formulate, announce, put to a vote

prōnŭr·us -ūs *f* grandson's wife

prōn·us -a -um *adj* leaning, inclined, bending, stooping, bent over, bent forwards; swift, rushing, dashing, moving swiftly along; sloping, steep (*hill, road*); sinking, setting (*sun, etc.*); downhill; easy; inclined, disposed, prone; *n* downward tendency, gravity; *n pl* slopes

prooemi·or -ārī *vi* to make an introduction or preface

prooem·ium -iī or **-ī** *n* preface; prelude; (fig) prelude (*e.g., to a fight*)

propāgātī·ō -ōnis *f* propagation; extension, prolongation; **nominis propagatio** perpetuation of the name

propāg·ō -āre *vt* to propagate (*race*); to extend (*territory*); to prolong (*life*)

prōpālam *adv* openly, publicly

prōpatul·us -a -um *adj* open; *n* open space; **in propatulo habere** to display

prope *adv* near, nearby; (of time) near, at hand; (of degree) nearly, almost, practically, just about; (with **ab** + *abl*) close by, near to; **prope est cum** the time has come when; *prep* (with *acc*) near, near to; **prope diem** very soon, presently

prō·pellō -pellĕre -pŭlī -pulsum *vt* to drive forward, push forward; to drive away, drive out

propemŏdo or **propemŏdum** *adv* nearly, practically, almost

prō·pendĕo -pendĕre -pendī -pensum *vi* to hang down; to preponderate; (with **in** + *acc*) to be inclined to, be favorably disposed to

prōpensē *adv* readily, willingly

prōpensi·ō -ōnis *f* propensity, inclination, tendency

prōpens·us -a -um *pp* of **propendeo**; *adj* important; coming near, approaching; inclined, disposed, ready, willing; **propenso animo** with a ready mind, willingly; **propensus in alteram partem** inclined toward the other point of view

properanter *adv* quickly, hastily

properanti·a -ae *f* haste

properāti·ō -ōnis *f* haste

properātō *adv* quickly, speedily

properāt·us -a -um *adj* hurried, quick, speedy; *n* haste, speed; **properato opus est** speed is required

properē *adv* quickly, in haste, hastily

properip·ēs -ēdis *adj* quick-moving

proper·ō -āre *vt* to speed up, accelerate; to prepare hastily, do in haste; *vi* to be quick; to go or move quickly

Ᵽropert·ius -iī or **-ī** *m* Sextus Propertius (*Latin elegiac poet, c. 50-15 B.C.*)

prōper·us -a -um *adj* quick, speedy

prōpex·us -a -um *adj* combed forward

prōpīnātī·ō -ōnis *f* toast

propīn·ō or **prōpīn·ō -āre** *vt* to drink (*e.g., a cup of wine*) as a toast; to drink a toast to, toast; (with *dat*) **a** to drink (*e.g., a cup of wine*) as a toast to; **b** to pass on (*a cup*)

propinqu·a -ae *f* relative (*female*)

propinquē *adv* near at hand

propinquit·ās -ātis *f* proximity, nearness, vicinity; (fig) relationship, affinity; friendship

propinqu·ō -āre *vt* to bring on; to accelerate, hasten; *vi* to draw near, approach; (with *dat*) to draw near to, approach

propinqu·us -a -um *adj* near, neighboring; (of time) near, at hand; related; *m* relative; *f* see **propinqua**; *n* neighborhood, vicinity

propi·or -us *adj* nearer, closer; later, more recent; more closely related, more like, more nearly resembling; more intimate, closer; of more concern, of greater import; (with *dat*) **a** nearer to, closer to; **b** closer to in resemblance, more like; (with *acc* or with **ab** + *abl*) closer to

propiŏr·a -um *n pl* closer side (*e.g., of a river*); more recent events

propitī·ō -āre *vt* to propitiate, appease

propiti·us -a -um *adj* propitious, well-disposed, favorable

propnigē·um -ī *n* room where the bath was heated

propōl·a -ae *m* retailer

prōpollŭ·ō -ĕre *vt* to pollute further

prō·pōnō -pōnĕre -posŭī -positum *vt* to put or place forward, expose to view, display; to propose; to imagine; to offer, propose; to say, report, relate, publish; to threaten; to denounce; to design, determine, intend

Propont·is -idis or **-idos** *f* Sea of Marmora

prōporrō *adv* furthermore; wholly, completely

prōportī·ō -ōnis *f* proportion, symmetry; analogy

prōpositī·ō -ōnis *f* proposition; intention, purpose; theme; basic assumption (*in logic*)

prōposit·us -a -um *pp* of **propono**; *adj* exposed, open; accessible; impending, at hand; *n* intention, design, purpose, resolution; main point, theme; first premise (*in logic*)

prōpraet·or -ōris *m* propraetor (*ex-praetor who was made governor of a province*)

propriē *adv* in the strict sense; strictly for oneself, personally; peculiarly, especially

propriet·ās -ātis *f* property, peculiarity, quality

propritim *adv* specifically, properly

propri·us -a -um *adj* own; very own; special, peculiar, individual, particular, personal; lasting, permanent

propter *adv* near, near at hand

propter *prep* (with *acc*) near, close to, next to; on account of, because of, for the sake of; through, by means of

propterĕā *adv* for that reason, therefore, on that account; **propterea quod** for the very reason that

prōpudiōs·us -a -um *adj* shameful, disgraceful

prōpud·ium -iī or **-ī** *n* shameful act; (said of a person) disgrace

prōpugnācŭl·um -ī *n* rampart, battlement; defense; (fig) safeguard

prōpugnātǐ·ō -ōnis *f* defense, vindication

prōpugnāt·or -ōris *m* defender, champion

prōpugn·ō -āre *vt* to defend; *vi* to come out and fight; to fight a defensive action, repel an assault; (fig) to put up a defense

prōpulsātǐ·ō -ōnis *f* repulse

prōpuls·ō -āre *vt* to drive back, repel, repulse; (fig) to ward off, repel

prōpulsus *pp* of **propello**

Prōpylae·a -ōrum *n pl* entrance to the Athenian Acropolis

prōquam *conj* according as

prōr·a -ae *f* prow; (fig) ship; **mihi prora et puppis est** my intention from first to last is

prō·rēpō -rēpĕre -repsī *vi* to creep ahead, crawl out

prōrēt·a -ae *m* look-out at the prow

prōrĕ·us -ī *m* look-out at the prow

prō·ripiō -ripĕre -ripŭī -reptum *vt* to drag forth, drag out; to rush; **se proripere** to rush, dash

prōrogātǐ·ō -ōnis *f* extension, prolongation (*of a term of office*); postponement

prōrŏg·ō -āre *vt* to prolong, extend; to put off, postpone

prorsum *adv* forwards; (with a negative) absolutely, at all, e.g., **prorsum nihil** absolutely nothing, nothing at all

prorsus *adv* forward; by all means, certainly; in short, in a word; (with a negative) absolutely, at all, e.g., **nullo prorsus modo assentior** I don't agree in any way at all

prō·rumpō -rumpĕre -rūpī -ruptum *vt* to make (*something*) break forth, fling forth; **prorumpi** to burst forth; *vi* to break out, rush out, make an attack

prō·ruō -ruĕre -ruī -rutum *vt* to overthrow, demolish; *vi* to rush forth; to tumble

prōrupt·us -a -um *pp* of **prorumpo**; *adj* unrestrained

prōsāpǐ·a -ae *f* stock, race, line

proscaen·ium -iī or **-ī** *n* front part of a stage; *n pl* stage; theater

prō·scindō -scindĕre -scĭdī -scissum *vt* to plow up, break up; (fig) to criticize harshly, satirize, cut to pieces

prō·scrībō -scrībĕre -scripsī -scriptum *vt* to publish in writing; to proclaim, announce; to advertise (*for sale, etc.*); to confiscate (*property*); to punish with confiscation of property, deprive of property; to proscribe, outlaw

proscriptǐ·ō -ōnis *f* advertisement; proscription, notice of confiscation, notice of outlawry

proscriptur·iō -īre *vi* to be anxious to hold a proscription

proscript·us -a -um *pp* of **proscribo**; *m* proscribed person, outlaw

prōsĕc·ō -āre -ŭī -tum *vt* to cut off (*esp. parts of a sacrificial victim*)

prōsecūtus *pp* of **prosequor**

prōsēd·a -ae *f* prostitute

prōsēmĭn·ō -āre *vt* to sow, scatter about, plant; to propagate, raise (*family*)

prō·sentiō -sentīre -sensī *vt* to sense or realize beforehand

prō·sĕquor -sĕquī -secūtus sum *vt* to escort, attend; to pursue (*enemy*); to chase, follow; to pursue, go on with, continue (*a topic*); to describe in detail; to follow, imitate; to attend, honor

Proserpĭn·a -ae *f* daughter of Ceres and wife of Pluto

prōserp·ō -ĕre *vi* to creep or crawl forwards, creep along

proseuch·a -ae *f* synagogue

prōsil·iō -īre -ŭī *vi* to jump forward, jump up; to jump to one's feet; (of blood) to spurt; (of sparks) to shoot out; to rush, dash

prōsŏc·er -ĕrī *m* wife's grandfather

prospect·ō -āre *vt* to view, look out at, gaze upon; (of places) to look towards, command a view of; to look for, hope for, expect, await

prospectus *pp* of **prospicio**

prospect·us -ūs *m* distant view; sight, view; faculty of sight; sight (*thing seen*)

prospecŭl·or -ārī -ātus sum *vt* to look out for, watch for; *vi* to look around, reconnoiter

prosp·er see **prosperus**

prospĕrē *adv* favorably, luckily, as desired, successfully

prosperĭt·ās -ātis *f* success, good fortune, prosperity; **prosperitas valetudinis** good health

prospĕr·ō -āre *vt* to cause to succeed, make happy, make fortunate

prosp·ĕrus or **prosp·er -ĕra -ĕrum** *adj* successful, fortunate, lucky, favorable, prosperous

prospicientǐ·a -ae *f* foresight, precaution

prō·spiciō -spicĕre -spexī -spectum *vt* to see far off, see in the distance; to spot; to command a view of; to watch for; to look out for, provide for; to foresee; *vi* to look forward; to look into the distance, have a distant view, have a view; to be on the lookout, exercise foresight; (with **in** + *acc*) to command a view of, overlook; **ex superioribus in urbem prospicere** to have a view of the city from a vantage point; **parum prospiciunt ocŭli** the eyes are nearsighted

prō·sternō -sternĕre -strāvī -strātum *vt* to throw to the ground, throw down, knock down; to wreck, ruin, overthrow, subvert; to debase; **se prosternere** to debase oneself; **se prosternere ad**

pedes (with *genit*) to throw oneself at the feet of, fall down before

prostibil·is -is *f* prostitute

prostibŭl·um -ī *n* prostitute

prostit·ŭō -ŭĕre -ŭī -ūtum *vt* to expose for sale; to prostitute

pro·stō -stāre -stĭtī *vi* to project; (of wares) to be set out for sale; to prostitute oneself, be a prostitute

prostrātus *pp* of **prosterno**

prōsubīg·ō -ĕre *vt* to dig up, root up

prō·sum -desse -fŭī *vi* to be useful, be of use, do good, be profitable; **multum prodesse** to do a lot of good

Prōtagŏr·ās -ae *m* Greek sophist, contemporary of Socrates, born at Abdera (*c.* 485-415 B.C.)

prō·tĕgō -tĕgĕre -texī -tectum *vt* to cover in front, cover, cover up; to cover with a roof; to shelter, protect; (fig) to cover, defend, protect

prōtēl·ō -āre *vt* to chase away, drive off

prōtēl·um -ī *n* team of oxen; (fig) row, series

prō·tendō -tendĕre -tendī -tentum *vt* to stretch forth, stretch out, extend

prōtent·us -a -um *adj* extended

prōtĕnus see **protinus**

prō·tĕrō -terĕre -trīvī -trītum *vt* to wear down, rub out; to trample down, trample under foot; (fig) to trample upon, rub out, crush

prōterr·ĕō -ĕre -ŭī -ĭtum *vt* to scare away

protervē *adv* boldly, brashly, impudently, brazenly

protervĭt·ās -ātis *f* brashness, brazenness

proterv·us -a -um *adj* bold, brash, brazen, impudent

Prōtesĭlā·us -ī *m* first Greek casualty in the Trojan War

Prōt·eus -ĕī or **-ĕos** *m* god of the sea with power to assume various forms

prothȳmē *adv* willingly, readily

prothymĭ·a -ae *f* willingness, readiness

prōtĭnam *adv* immediately

prōtinus or **prōtĕnus** *adv* straight on, forward, farther on; continuously, right on, without pause; immediately, at once, on the spot

prōtoll·ō -ĕre *vt* to stretch out (*hand*); to put off, postpone

prōtopraxĭ·a -ae *f* priority (*among creditors in receiving payment*)

prō·trăhō -trahĕre -traxī -tractum *vt* to drag forward, drag out; to produce; to reveal, expose, disclose, bring to light

prōtrītus *pp* of **protero**

prō·trūdō -trūdĕre -trūsī -trūsum *vt* to push forwards, push out; to push off, postpone

prōturb·ō -āre *vt* to drive ahead, drive on, drive away, repel; to knock down

proŭt *conj* as, just as

prōvect·us -a -um *adj* advanced; **aetate provectus** advanced in years; **nox provecta erat** the night had been far advanced

prō·vĕhō -vehĕre -vexī -vectum *vt* to carry forwards; to transport, convey; to lead, lead on; to promote, advance, raise; **provehi** to ride, drive, move, or sail ahead

prō·veniō -venīre -vēnī -ventum *vi* to go on, proceed; to succeed; to come out, appear; to come out, grow, be produced; to come about, happen

prōvent·us -ūs *m* result, outcome; success; yield, produce; harvest

prōverb·ium -iī or **-ī** *n* proverb

prōvĭd·ens -entis *adj* prudent

prōvĭdenter *adv* prudently, with foresight

prōvĭdentĭ·a -ae *f* foresight, foreknowledge; precaution; **providentia deorum** providence

prō·vĭdĕō -vĭdēre -vīdī -vīsum *vt* to. see in the distance; to see coming; to foresee; to provide for; to provide against, guard against, avert, avoid; to look after, look out for, care for; to prepare, make ready

prōvĭd·us -a -um *adj* foreseeing; prudent, cautious; provident; (with *genit*) providing

prōvincĭ·a -ae *f* sphere of administration; sphere of jurisdiction; office, duty, charge; public office, commission, command, administration; sphere of action; province

prōvincĭāl·is -e *adj* provincial, of a province, in a province; **bellum provinciale** war in a province; **molestia provincialis** annoyance of administering a province; *m* provincial

prōvīsĭ·ō -ōnis *f* foresight; precaution; (with *genit*) precaution against

prōvīsō *adv* with forethought

prōvīs·ō -ĕre *vt* to go out to see; to be on the lookout for

prōvīs·or -ōris *m* lookout (*person*); provider

prōvīsū (only *abl*) *m* by looking forward; (with objective *genit*) **a** by foreseeing (*e.g., danger*); **b** by providing, providing for

prōvīsus *pp* of **provideo**

prō·vīvō -vīvĕre -vixī *vi* to live on

prōvocātĭ·ō -ōnis *f* appeal (*to a higher court*); challenge

prōvocāt·or -ōris *m* challenger; type of gladiator

prōvŏc·ō -āre *vt* to challenge; to provoke; to exasperate; to stir, stimulate; **bellum provocare** to provoke a war; **beneficio provocatus** touched or stirred by an act of kindness; **in aleam provocare** to challenge to a game of dice; **provocare maledictis** to provoke or exasperate with nasty remarks

prōvŏl·ō -āre *vi* to fly out, rush out, dash out

prō·volvō -volvĕre -volvī -volū-
tum *vt* to roll forward, roll along;
to roll over, overturn; to humble,
ruin; **se provolvere** to prostrate
oneself, fall down, grovel, humble
oneself

prōvŏm·ō -ĕre *vt* to vomit, throw
up

proximē or proxŭmē *adv* (of place)
nearest, next; (of time) most recently, just recently; (with *acc*)
close to, next to, at the side of, very
much like, closely resembling; (with
dat) (of place) next to; **proxime
atque** almost as much as, nearly
the same as; **proxime Pompeium
sedebam** I was sitting next to
Pompey; **quam proxime** (with
dat or *acc*) as close as possible to

proxĭmĭt·ās -ātis *f* proximity, vicinity; resemblance, similarity; close
relationship

proxĭmō *adv* very recently, just recently

proxĭm·us or proxŭm·us -a -um
adj nearest, next; next, following,
ensuing; previous, most recent, latest, last; closely related; adjoining;
most direct (*route*); *m* close relative,
next of kin; *n* neighborhood; next
door, next-door neighbor

prūd·ens -entis *adj* foreseeing, fore-
knowing; conscious, aware; skilled,
skillful, experienced, versed; prudent, discreet, sensible, intelligent;
(with *genit* or *abl* or with **in** + *abl*)
aware of, conscious of, familiar
with, skilled in, experienced in

prūdenter *adv* prudently, cautiously;
skillfully

prūdentĭ·a -ae *f* foreseeing; prudence, discretion, good sense; **prudentia juris publici** knowledge of
or experience in public law

pruīn·a -ae *f* frost; winter

pruīnōs·us -a -um *adj* frosty

prūn·a -ae *f* live coal

prūnĭtĭ·us -a -um *adj* of plum-tree
wood

prūn·um -ī *n* plum

prūn·us -ī *f* plum tree

prūrīg·ō -ĭnis *f* itching, itch; yen

prūr·ĭō -īre *vi* to itch; to have an
itch; (with **in** + *acc*) to be itching
for

prytanē·um -ī *n* state dining hall
(*where the Prytanes dined*)

prytăn·is -is *m* prytane (*member of
the executive body in some Greek
states*)

psall·ō -ĕre *vi* to play the lyre or
lute

psaltēr·ĭum -ĭī or -ī *n* stringed instrument, lute

psaltrĭ·a -ae *f* lutist, musician (*female*)

psec·as -ădis *f* female slave who
perfumed her lady's hair

psēphism·a -ătis *n* plebiscite of the
Greek assembly

pseudocăt·ō -ōnis *m* a make-believe
Cato

pseudomĕn·os or pseudomĕn·us -ī
m fallacious syllogism

pseudothȳr·um -ī *n* back door

psittăc·us -ī *m* parrot

Psych·ē -ēs *f* maiden loved by Cupid
and made immortal by Jupiter

psychomantī·um or psychoman-
tē·um -ī *n* place where people attempted to communicate with the
dead

-pte *enclitic* (added to pronouns) self,
own

ptisanār·ĭum -ĭī or -ī *n* gruel

Ptolemae·us -ī *m* Ptolemy (*name
of a series of Egyptian kings descended from Lagus, a general of
Alexander the Great*)

pūb·ens -entis *adj* mature; juicy
(*plant*)

pūber see pubes

pūbert·ās -ātis *f* puberty; manhood,
virility; sign of maturity, beard

pūb·ēs or pūb·er -ĕris *adj* grown
up, adult; downy, covered with
down; *m pl* grown-ups, adults, men;
pūb·ēs -is *f* pubic hair; groin;
youth, young men, grown-up males;
throng, people; bullocks

pūb·escō -escĕre -ŭī *vi* to reach the
age of puberty, arrive at maturity;
(of plants) to grow up, ripen; (of
meadows, etc.) to be clothed, covered (*e.g., with flowers*)

pūblĭcān·us -a -um *adj* of public
revenues; *m* revenue agent

pūblĭcātĭ·ō -ōnis *f* confiscation

pūblĭcē *adv* publicly, officially, in behalf of the state, for the state;
at public expense; generally, universally; **publice dicere** to speak
officially

pūblĭcĭtus *adv* at public expense, at
the expense of the state; publicly

pūblĭc·ō -āre *vt* to confiscate; to
throw open to the general public;
to prostitute

Pūblĭcŏl·a -ae or Pōplĭcŏl·a -ae *m* Publius Valerius Publicola (*fl 509 B.C.*)

pūblĭc·us -a -um *adj* of the people,
public, common; of the state, state,
federal, national; common, ordinary, vulgar; common, general,
public; **causa publica** affair of national importance; (law) federal
case (*i.e., criminal case*); **res publica** state, government, politics,
public life, country; *m* public official; *n* public, publicity; public
property, national treasury, federal
revenue; **de publico** at public expense; **in publico** in public, publicly; **in publicum prodire** to go
out in public; **in publicum redigere** to hand over to the national
treasury

pudend·us -a -um *adj* shameful,
scandalous

pud·ens -entis *adj* modest, bashful

pudenter *adv* modestly, bashfully

pud·ĕō -ēre -ŭī or pudĕum est *vt*
to make ashamed; *v impers* (with
acc of person and *genit* or *abl* of

cause of feeling), e.g., **me tui pu-det** I am ashamed of you

pudibund·us -a -um *adj* modest, bashful

pudīcē *adv* chastely, modestly, virtuously

pudīcitī·a -ae *f* chastity, modesty, purity

pudīc·us -a -um *adj* chaste, modest, virtuous, pure

pud·or -ōris *m* shame, decency, modesty, sense of shame; sense of honor, propriety; cause for shame, shame, disgrace; blush

puell·a -ae *f* girl; girl friend, sweetheart; young wife

puellār·is -e *adj* young girl's, girlish, youthful

puellāriter *adv* girlishly

puellŭl·a -ae *f* little girl; little sweetheart

puell·us -ī *m* little boy, lad

pu·er -ērī *m* boy, lad, young man; servant, slave, page; bachelor; a **pueris** or a **puero** from boyhood, from childhood; **ex pueris excedere** to outgrow childhood

puerīl·is -e *adj* boyish, childish, youthful, puerile

puerīliter *adv* like a child, childishly

pueritī·a or **puertī·a -ae** *f* childhood, boyhood

puerper·ium -iī or **-ī** *n* childbirth, lying-in, giving birth

puerper·us -a -um *adj* helping childbirth, easing labor pains; *f* woman in labor

puertia see **pueritia**

puerŭl·us -ī *m* little boy, little slave

pūg·a or **pȳg·a -ae** *f* rump, rear, buttocks

pug·il -ilis *m* boxer

pugilātī·ō -ōnis *f* boxing

pugilāt·us -ūs *m* boxing

pugilīcē *adv* like a boxer

pugillār·is -e *adj* hand-size; *m pl* & *n pl* notebook

pugillātōri·us -a -um *adj* boxing, punching; **follis pugillatorius** punching bag

pugi·ō -ōnis *m* dagger

pugiuncŭl·us -ī *m* small dagger

pugn·a -ae *f* fist fight, brawl; fight, combat, battle

pugnācit·ās -ātis *f* pugnacity, aggressiveness

pugnāciter *adv* pugnaciously, doggedly

pugnācŭl·um -ī *n* fortress

pugnant·ēs -ium *m pl* fighters, warriors

pugnant·ia -ium *n pl* contradictions, inconsistencies

pugnāt·or -ōris *m* fighter, combatant

pugn·ax -ācis *adj* pugnacious, scrappy, aggressive; quarrelsome; dogged, obstinate

pugnĕ·us -a -um *adj* of the fist; **mergae pugneae** punches

pugn·ō -āre *vt* to fight; *vi* to fight; to contend, dispute; (with *dat* or

cum + *abl*) a to fight, fight against, struggle with, oppose; **b** to contradict

pugn·us -ī *m* fist

pulchell·us -a -um *adj* cute little

pulch·er -ra -rum *adj* beautiful, fair, handsome

pulchrē *adv* beautifully; (as exclamation of applause) fine!; **pulchre mihi est** I am fine

pulchritūd·ō -inis *f* beauty; excellence, attractiveness

pūlē·ium or **pūleg·ium -iī** or **-ī** *n* pennyroyal, mint; (fig) fragrance, pleasantness

pūl·ex -icis *m* flea

pullār·ius -iī or **-ī** *m* keeper of the sacred chickens

pullāt·us -a -um *adj* wearing black, in black, in mourning

pullŭl·ō -āre *vi* to sprout; (of animals) to produce young

pull·us -a -um *adj* dark-grey, dark, blackish; mourning; **toga pulla** mourning toga; *n* dark-grey garment

pull·us -ī *m* young (*of animals*), foal, offspring, chick, chicken

pulmentār·ium -iī or **-ī** *n* relish, appetizer

pulment·um -ī *n* relish; food, rations

pulm·ō -ōnis *f* lung

pulmōnĕ·us -a -um *adj* of the lungs, pulmonary

pulp·a -ae *f* meat, flesh

pulpāment·um -ī *n* meat; game

pulpīt·um -ī *n* platform; stage

puls pultis *f* pulse, porridge, mush

pulsātī·ō -ōnis *f* knock

puls·ō -āre *vt* to batter, keep hitting; to knock at; to strum (*lyre*); to beat on, strike against; (fig) to jolt, disquiet; *vi* to throb

pulsus *pp* of **pello**

puls·us -ūs *m* push, pushing; beat, beating, striking, stamping, blow, stroke; trample; (fig) impression, influence

pultātī·ō -ōnis *f* knocking (*at the door*)

pultiphagōnīd·ēs -ae *m* porridge eater

pultiphăg·us -ī *m* porridge eater

pult·ō -āre *vt* to knock at

pulverĕ·us -a -um *adj* dust, of dust; dusty; fine as dust; raising dust

pulverulent·us -a -um *adj* dusty; raising dust; covered with dust

pulvill·us -ī *m* small cushion

pulvīn·ar -āris *n* cushioned couch; couch; sacred couch for the images of the gods; seat of honor; shrine, temple

pulvīnār·ium -iī or **-ī** *n* cushioned seat of a god; dry dock

pulvīn·us -ī *m* pillow, cushion; seat of honor

pulv·is -ĕris *m* dust, powder; scene of action, arena, field; effort, work

pulviscŭl·us -ī *m* fine dust, fine powder

pŭm·ex -ĭcis *m* pumice stone; porous stone, lava

pŭmĭcĕ·us -a -um *adj* pumice, lava

pŭmĭc·ō -āre *vt* to smooth or polish with pumice stone

pūmĭlĭ·ō -ōnis *m* or *f* midget, dwarf, pygmy

punctim *adv* with the point, with the pointed end

punct·um -ī *n* prick, puncture; point, mathematical point; point, spot; vote, ballot; clause, phrase; moment; **puncto temporis eodem** at the same instant; **punctum temporis** moment, instant, point of time

pungō pungĕre pupŭgī punctum *vt* to prick, puncture, dent; to sting, bite; to cause (*a wound*); to stab; (fig) to sting, annoy, trouble, disturb

Pūnĭcān·us -a -um *adj* Punic, Carthaginian, in the Carthaginian style

Pūnĭcē *adv* Puᴺic, in the Punic language

pŭnĭcĕ·us -a -um *adj* reddish, red, crimson, pink

Pūnĭc·us -a -um *adj* Punic, Carthaginian; red, crimson, reddish, pink; *n* pomegranate

pūn·ĭō -īre -īvī or **-ĭī -ītum** or **pūn·ĭor -īrī -ītus sum** *vt* to punish, chastise; to avenge, revenge

pūnīt·or -ōris *m* avenger

pūp·a -ae *f* doll, puppet; girl, lass

pūpill·a¹ -ae *f* orphan girl, ward; minor; pupil (*of the eye*)

pūpillār·is -e *adj* of an orphan, belonging to an orphan

pūpill·us -ī *m* orphan boy, orphan, ward

pupp·is -is *f* stern; ship; (coll) back; **a puppi** astern

pūpŭl·a -ae *f* pupil; eye

pūpŭl·us -ī *m* little boy

pūrē *adv* clearly, brightly; plainly, simply; purely, chastely

purgām·en -ĭnis *n* dirt, filth; means of expiation, purification

purgāment·a -ōrum *n pl* offscourings, refuse, dirt, filth, garbage; (term of abuse) trash, dregs, garbage

purgātĭ·ō -ōnis *f* cleansing, cleaning, cleanup; apology, justification

purgāt·us -a -um *adj* cleansed, clean, pure

purg·ō -āre *vt* to clean, cleanse, clear, clear away, remove; to clear of a charge, exculpate, excuse, justify; to refute; to cleanse, purify ritually; to purge (*the body*)

pūrĭfic·ō -āre *vt* to purify

pūrĭter *adv* purely, cleanly; **vitam pūriter agere** to lead a clean life

purpŭr·a -ae *f* purple, deep-red, dark-red; purple or deep-red cloth or garment; royal-purple robe; royalty; consular dignity, imperial dignity

purpŭrāt·us -a -um *adj* wearing royal purple; *m* courtier

purpurĕ·us -a -um *adj* deep-red, crimson, pink, violet, royal-purple (*and various shades, as applied to* roses, poppies, lips, flesh, blood, wine, dawn, hair)

purpurissāt·us -a -um *adj* rouged

purpuriss·um -ī *m* rouge; red dye

pūr·us -a -um *adj* pure, clear, clean; cleared, cleansed; cleansing, purifying; pure, chaste; plain, naked, unadorned, natural; plain (*toga*), without crimson border; pure, accurate, faultless (*style*); (law) unconditional, absolute; subject to no religious claims; *n* clear sky

pūs pūris *n* pus; (fig) venom, malice

pusill·us -a -um *adj* petty, puny; *n* bit, trifle

pūsĭ·ō -ōnis *m* little boy

pustŭl·a -ae *f* pimple; blister

pustŭlāt·us or **pusŭlāt·us -a -um** *adj* refined, purified

pūtām·en -ĭnis *n* clipping, peeling, shell, husk

pŭtātĭ·ō -ōnis *f* pruning

pŭtāt·or -ōris *m* pruner

pŭtĕ·al -ālis *n* low wall (*around a well or sacred spot*), stone enclosure; **pŭteal Lĭbōnis** stone enclosure in the Roman Forum near which much business was transacted

pŭteāl·is -e *adj* well, of a well

pŭt·ĕō -ēre *vi* to stink; to be rotten, be putrid

Pŭteolān·us -a -um *adj* of Puteoli

Pŭteŏl·ī -ōrum *m pl* commercial city on the coast of Campania (*modern Pozzuolo*)

put·er or **put·ris -e** *adj* putrid, rotting; crumbling; flabby

pūt·escō -escĕre -ŭī *vi* to become rotten

pŭtĕ·us -ī *m* well; pit; dungeon

pūtĭdē *adv* disgustingly, disagreeably

pūtĭdiuscŭl·us -a -um *adj* rather tedious

pūtĭd·us -a -um *adj* stinking, rotten; affected, unnatural (*style*)

pŭtill·us -a -um *adj* tiny

put·ō -āre *vt* to trim, prune; to think, ponder, consider, judge, suppose, imagine; to reckon, estimate, value; to believe in, recognize (*gods*); to clear up, settle (*accounts*); **magni putare** to think highly of; **pro certo putare** to regard as certain; *vi* to think, imagine, suppose

pūt·or -ōris *m* stench

putre·faciō -facĕre -fēcī -factum *vt* to make rotten, rot; to cause to crumble, soften

putresc·ō -ĕre *vi* to become rotten, get moldy

putrĭd·us -a -um *adj* rotten; flabby

putris see **puter**

put·us -a -um *adj* pure, bright, perfectly pure; splendid; unmixed; unmitigated; *m* boy

pyct·a or **pyct·ēs -ae** *m* boxer

Pydn·a -ae *f* city in Macedonia near which Aemilius Paulus defeated

Perseus, the Macedonian king (169 B.C.)

pyg·a -ae *f* rump, rear, buttocks

Pygmali·on -ōnis *m* son of Belus the king of Cyprus and brother of Dido; king of Cyprus who fell in love with a statue

Pylăd·ēs -ae *m* son of Strophius and friend of Orestes

Pyl·ae -ārum *f pl* Thermopylae (*narrow pass in E. Thessaly*)

Pylĭ·us -a -um *adj* of Pylos

Pyl·os -ī *f* Pylos (*home of Nestor in S.E. Peloponnesus*)

pyr·a -ae *f* pyre

pyrăm·is -ĭdis *f* pyramid; cone

Pyrăm·us -ī *m* neighbor and boy friend of Thisbe

Pȳrēnae·us -a -um *adj* of the Pyrenees

Pȳrēn·ē -ēs *f* the Pyrenees Mountains

pyrĕthr·on or **pyrĕthr·um -ī** *n* Spanish camomile (*plant*)

pyrŏp·us -ī *m* bronze

Pyrrh·a -ae or **Pyrrh·ē -ēs** *f* daughter of Epimetheus, wife of Deucalion, and survivor of the Deluge

Pyrrh·ō -ōnis *m* philosopher of Elis, contemporary of Aristotle, and founder of the philosophical school of Skepticism (*c.* 360-270 B.C.)

Pyrrh·us -ī *m* son of Achilles and founder of Epirus (*also called Neoptolemus*); king of Epirus who invaded Italy to assist the Tarentines against the Romans in 280 B.C. (319-272 B.C.)

Pȳthagŏr·ās -ae *m* Greek philosopher and mathematician (6*th cent.* B.C.)

Pȳthagorē·us or **Pȳthagorĭc·us -a -um** *adj* Pythagorean

Pȳthĭ·us -a -um *adj* Pythian, Delphic; *m* Apollo; *f* Pythia (*priestess of Apollo at Delphi*); *n pl* Pythian games (*held in honor of Apollo every four years*)

Pȳth·ō -ūs *f* Delphi

Pȳth·ōn -ōnis *m* dragon slain by Apollo near Delphi

pȳtism·a -ătis *n* spit, squirt of wine

pȳtiss·ō -āre *vt* to spit, spit out (*wine*)

pyx·is -ĭdis *f* powder box, cosmetic box

Q

quā *adv* where, in what direction, by what way; to what extent, as far as; whereby, how, by what means; in any way, to any degree; **qua . . . qua** partly . . . partly, both . . . and

quācumque *adv* wherever, by whatever way, in whatever way; by whatever means, howsoever

quādam tenus *adv* to a certain point, only so far and no farther

quadr·a -ae *f* square table, dining table; square crust; square morsel, square bit (*of cheese, etc.*)

quadrāgēn·ī -ae -a *adj* forty each

quadrāgēsĭm·us or **quadrāgen-sĭm·us -a -um** *adj* fortieth; *f* one fortieth; 2½ percent tax

quadrāgiēs or **quadrāgiens** *adv* forty times

quadrāgintā (indecl) *adj* forty

quadr·ans -antis *m* fourth part, a fourth, a quarter; cent (*smallest coin, worth one sixth of an ace*); quarter of a pound; quarter pint (*quarter of a sextarius*); **quadrante lavatum īre** take a bath for one cent (*usual price of a bath*)

quadrant·al -ālis *n* five-gallon jar

quadrantāri·us -a -um *adj* quarter; **mulier quadrantaria** two-bit wench (*woman who sold herself for a pittance*); **tabulae quadrantariae** record of debts reduced to a fourth

quadrāt·us -a -um *adj* squared, square; *n* square

quadrīdŭ·um -ī *n* four-day period, four days

quadrienn·ĭum -ĭī or **-ī** *n* four-year period, four years

quadrifāriam *adv* in four parts

quadrifĭd·us -a -um *adj* split into four parts

quadrīg·ae -ārum *f pl* four-horse team; four-horse chariot

quadrīgār·ĭus -ĭī or **-ī** *m* chariot racer

quadrīgāt·us -a -um *adj* stamped with a four-horse chariot

quadrīgŭl·ae -ārum *f pl* little four-horse team

quadrijŭg·is -e *adj* four-horse-team

quadrijŭg·us -a -um *adj* four-horse-team; *m pl* four-horse team

quadrilībr·is -e *adj* four-pound

quadrīmŭl·us -a -um *adj* only four years old

quadrīm·us -a -um *adj* four-year-old

quadringēnāri·us -a -um *adj* consisting of four hundred men each

quadringēn·ī -ae -a *adj* four hundred each

quadringentēsĭm·us -a -um *adj* four-hundredth

quadringentiēs *adv* four hundred times

quadripertīt·us -a -um *adj* four-fold

quadrirēm·is -e *adj* having four banks of oars; *f* quadrireme

quadriv·ĭum -ĭī or **-ī** *n* crossroads

quadr·ō -āre vt to make square; to complete; to round out, give rhythmic finish to (a speech); vi to make a square; to be exact; (of accounts) to agree, come out right, tally; (with dat or in + acc) to suit, fit, seem proper to

quadr·um -ī n square; **in quadrum redigere sententias** to balance sentences

quadrupĕd·ans -antis adj galloping; m pl horses

quadrŭp·ēs -ĕdis adj four-footed; on all fours; mf quadruped

quadruplāt·or -ōris m informer (who received one fourth of the forfeiture); corrupt judge

quadrŭpl·ex -icis adj quadruple, fourfold

quadruplic·ō -āre vt to quadruple, increase fourfold

quadrŭpl·or -ārī -ātus sum vi to be an informer

quadrŭpl·us -a -um adj quadruple, fourfold; n four times the amount

quaerīt·ō -āre vt to keep looking for; to keep asking

quaerō quaerĕre quaesīvī quaesītum vt to look for, search for; to try to get; to get, obtain; to try to gain, earn, acquire; to miss, lack; to require, demand, call for; to ask, interrogate; to examine, investigate; to plan, devise, aim at; (with inf) to try to, wish to; (with ab or de or ex + abl) to ask (something) of or from (someone); vi to hold an examination; (with de + abl) to ask about, inquire about; **si quaeris** or **si quaerimus** (coll) to tell the truth

quaesītī·ō -ōnis f questioning under torture

quaesīt·or -ōris m judge (praetor or other official who presided over a criminal trial)

quaesīt·us -a -um pp of quaero; adj select, special; far-fetched, artificial, affected; n question; n pl gains, earnings, acquisitions, store

quaes·ō -ĕre vt to beg, ask; **quaeso** (usually parenthetical) please

quaesticŭl·us -ī m slight profit

quaestī·ō -ōnis f inquiry, investigation, questioning, examination; judicial investigation, criminal trial; court of inquiry, court; questioning under torture, third degree; question, subject of investigation, case; court record; (with de + abl of the nature of the charge) court investigating a charge of (e.g., forgery, etc.); **in quaestione versare** to be under investigation; **quaestio extraordinaria** investigation by a special board; **quaestio inter sicarios** murder trial, court investigating a murder; **quaestio perpetua** standing court; **quaestioni praeesse** to preside over a case, be judge at a trial; **servos in quaestionem dare** or **ferre** to hand over

slaves for questioning under torture

quaestiuncŭl·a -ae f minor or trifling question

quaest·or -ōris m quaestor; financial officer; treasury official; public prosecutor of criminal offenses

quaestōrī·us -a -um adj quaestor's, of a quaestor; m ex-quaestor; n quaestor's tent in a camp; quaestor's residence in a province

quaestuōs·us -a -um adj profitable, lucrative, productive; acquiring wealth; eager to make a profit, acquisitive; enriched, wealthy

quaestūr·a -ae f quaestorship; quaestor's safe, public funds

quaest·us -ūs m gain, profit; acquisition; way of making money, job, occupation, business, trade; (fig) profit, gain, benefit, advantage; **ad quaestum** for profit, to make a profit; **quaestui rem publicam habere** to use public office for personal profit; **quaestum facere** to make money

quālĭbet or **quālŭbet** adv anywhere, everywhere; in any way, as you please

quāl·is -e adj what sort of, what kind of; of such a kind, such as, as; (with quotations and citations) as, as for example; **in hoc bello, quale** in this war, the likes of which; **qualis erat!** what a man he was!

quāl·iscumque -ecumque adj of whatever kind; of any kind whatever, any at all; **homines, qualescumque sunt** men, no matter what kind they are

quāl·islibet -ēlibet adj of whatever kind, of whatever sort

quālĭt·ās -ātis f quality, nature, property

quālĭter adv as, just as

quāl·us -ī m wicker basket, straw basket

quam adv (in questions and exclamations) to what extent, how, how much; (in comparisons) as, than; (with superlatives) as . . . as possible, e.g., **quam celerrime** as fast as possible; **quam plurimo vendere** to sell at the highest price possible; **quam primum** as soon as possible; (after verbs implying preference) rather than

quamdiū or **quam diū** adv how long; conj as long as, until

quamlĭbet or **quamlŭbet** adv as much as you please

quamōbrem or **quam ob rem** adv for what reason, why; for which reason, wherefore, why

quamquam conj though, although

quamvīs adv (with adj or adv) however; ever so; conj although

quānam adv by what route, by what way

quandō adv (in questions) when, at what time; (indefinite, after si, ne,

num) ever, at any time; *conj* when; because, since

quandōcumque or **quandōcunque** *adv* at some time or other, some day; *conj* whenever; as often as, no matter when

quandōque *adv* at some time, at one time or other, some day; *conj* whenever; as often as; since

quandōquidem *conj* in as much as, whereas, seeing that

quantill·us -a -um *adj* how much, how little

quantĭt·ās -ātis *f* quantity

quantō *adv* by how much, how much; **quanto ante** how much earlier; **quanto ... tanto** the ... the

quantopĕre *adv* how much, how greatly; with how great effort, how carefully

quantŭlum *adv* how little; **quantulum interest utrum** how little difference it makes whether

quantŭl·us -a -um *adj* how great, how much, how little, how small, how insignificant

quantŭl·uscumque -acumque -umcumque *adj* however small, however unimportant

quantum *adv* as much as, so much as, as great an extent; how much, how far, to what extent; (with comparatives) the more, the greater; **quantum in me fuit** as much as I could, to the best of my ability; **quantum maxĭmā voce potuī** at the the top of his voice; **quantum potest** as much (*or* fast, quickly, soon, long, *etc.*) as possible

quantumcumque *adv* as much as

quantumlĭbet *adv* however much

quantumvīs *adv* however; **quantumvīs rusticus** however unsophisticated, although unsophisticated

quant·us -a -um *adj* how great, how much; **quantus quantus** however great, however much; *pron neut* what amount; (with *genit*) how much; **in quantum** to whatever extent, as far as; **quanti** (*genit* of price) at what price, how much, how dearly, how high; **quanto** (*abl* of price) at what price, for how much; **quantum frumenti** how much grain

quant·uscumque -acumque -umcumque *adj* however great; of whatever size; however small, however trifling, however unimportant

quant·uslĭbet -alĭbet -umlĭbet *adj* however great; ever so great

quant·usvīs -āvīs -umvīs *adj* however great

quāpropter *adv* wherefore, why

quāquā *adv* by whatever route, whatever way

quāquam *adv* by any way

quārē or **quā rē** *adv* by what means, how; from what cause, why; whereby; wherefore

quartadecumān·ī -ōrum *m pl* sol-

diers of the fourteenth legion

quartān·us -a -um *adj* occurring every fourth day; *f* quartan fever; *m pl* soldiers of the fourteenth legion

quartār·ius -ĭī or **-ī** *m* quarter pint

quartō *adv* for the fourth time

quartum *adv* for the fourth time

quart·us -a -um *adj* fourth

quart·us decĭm·us -a -um *adj* fourteenth

quasī *conj* as if, just as if, as though

quasī *adv* as it were, so to speak; about, nearly, almost

quasill·um -ī *n* or **quasill·us -ī** *m* small basket

quassātĭ·ō -ōnis *f* shaking

quass·ō -āre *vt* to keep shaking, keep tossing, keep waving; to batter, shatter, smash to pieces; (fig) to shake, weaken

quass·us -a -um *pp* of **quatio;** *adj* shattered, broken; **vox quassa** weak voice

quate·facĭō -facĕre -fēcī -factum *vt* to shake; (fig) to weaken

quātĕnus *adv* how far, to what point; as far as; till when, how long; to what extent; **est quatenus** there is an extent to which; *conj* as far as; insofar as, inasmuch as, seeing that, since, as

quater *adv* four times

quater deciens or **quater deciēs** *adv* fourteen times

quatern·ī -ae -a *adj* four together, four in a group, four each

quatĭō quatĕre — -quassum *vt* to shake, cause to tremble, cause to vibrate; to brandish, wave about; to beat, strike, drive; to batter, crush; (fig) to touch, move, affect; (fig) to plague, harass

quattŭor (indecl) *adj* four

quattuordĕcim (indecl) *adj* fourteen

quattuorvirāt·us -ūs *m* membership on the board of four

quattuorvir·ī -ōrum *m pl* board of four officials (*executive board of municipalities and colonies*)

-que *conj* and

quemadmŏdum or **quem ad mŏdum** *adv* in what way, how; *conj* just as, as

qu·ĕō -īre -īvī or **-ĭī -ĭtum** *vi* to be able; (with *inf*) to be able to

quercēt·um -ī *n* oak forest

quercĕ·us -a -um *adj* oak, of oak

querc·us -ūs *f* oak tree; oak-leaf crown (*awarded to a soldier who saved citizen in battle*); acorns

querell·a or **querēl·a -ae** *f* complaint

queribund·us -a -um *adj* complaining; **vox queribunda** whining voice

querimōnĭ·a -ae *f* complaint, grievance; elegy

querĭt·or -ārī -ātus sum *vi* to keep complaining

quern·us -a -um *adj* oak, of oak

queror querī questus sum *vt* to

complain of, complain about; to lament; *vi* to complain; (of birds) to sing, warble, sing sadly, coo mournfully

querquetulān·us -a -um *adj* oak, covered with oak trees

querŭl·us -a -um *adj* complaining, full of complaints, querulous; plaintive; warbling, cooing

questus *pp* of **queror**

quest·us -ūs *m* complaint; plaintive note (*of the nightingale*)

qui quae quod *adj* (interrog) which, what, what kind of; (indefinite) any; *pron* (rel) who, that; (indef, after **si, nisi, num, ne**) anyone

qui *adv* how; why; at what price; whereby; in some way, somehow

quia *conj* because

quiănam *adv* why

quicquam cūjusquam *pron* anything

quicque cūjusque *pron* each, each one

quidquid (*genit* not in use) *pron* whatever

quicum (old *abl* + **cum**) *pron* with whom, with which

quicumque quaecumque quodcumque or **quīcunque quaecunque quodcunque** *pron* (rel) whoever, whosoever, everyone who, whatever, whatsoever, everything that, all that; (indef) any whatsoever, any possible, every possible

quid *adv* why

quid cūjus *pron* (interrog) what; (indef, after **si, nisi, num,** or **ne**) anything

quidam quaedam quiddam *pron* a certain one, a certain person, a certain thing

quidam quaedam quoddam *adj* a certain; (to soften an expression) a kind of, what one might call

quidem *adv* (emphasizing the word that is placed before it) indeed, in fact; (qualifying or limiting) at least, at any rate; (concessive) it is true; of course; all right; (exemplifying) for example; **ne . . . quidem** (emphasizing the intervening word) not even, e.g., **ne tu quidem** not even you

quidnam cūjusnam *pron* (interrog) what

quidnam *adv* why, why in the world

quidnī *adv* why not

quidpĭam cūjuspĭam *pron* anything, something

quidquid (*genit* not in use; *abl:* **quoquo**) *pron* whatever, whatsoever, everything which; **per quiquid deorum** by all the gods

quidquid *adv* to whatever extent, the further

qui·ēs -ētis *f* quiet, peace, rest; calm, lull; neutrality; sleep; dream; sleep of death, death

qui·escō -escĕre -ēvī -ētum *vt* to stand by and watch, quietly allow; *vi* to rest, keep quiet, be inactive;

to rest, sleep, be asleep; to lie still, be still, be undisturbed; to pause, make a pause; to be calm, be unruffled; to be neutral, keep neutral; (with *inf*) to cease to, stop; (with **ab** + *abl*) to be free from

quiētē *adv* quietly, calmly

quiēt·us -a -um *adj* at rest, resting, free from exertion, inactive; quiet, peaceful, undisturbed; neutral; calm, quiet; still, silent; idle; *n pl* period of peace

quīlĭbet quaelĭbet quidlĭbet *pron* anyone, any you wish, no matter who, anything, anything you wish, not matter what, everything

quīlĭbet quaelĭbet quodlĭbet *adj* any, any at all, any you wish

quīn *adv* (interrog) why not; (corroborative) in fact, as a matter of fact; *conj* so that not, without; **facere non possum, quin ad te mittam librum** I can't help sending you the book; **nullo modo introire possem, quin vidĕrent me** I just couldn't walk in without their seeing me; (after verbs of preventing, opposing) from: **milites aegre sunt retenti quin oppidum oppugnarent** the soldiers could barely be kept from assaulting the town; (after verbs of hesitation, doubt, suspicion): **non dubito quin** I do not doubt that; (esp. representing a nominative of a relative pronoun with a negative) that . . . not, without: **nemo aspicere potest quin dicat** no one can look on without saying; **nemo est quin velit** there is no one who does not prefer

quīnam quaenam quodnam *adj* which, what, just which, just what

Quint- = Quint-

quinc·unx -uncis *m* five twelfths; five percent (*interest*); the figure five (*as arranged on dice or cards*)

quindecĭens or **quindecĭēs** *adv* fifteen times

quindĕcim (indecl) *adj* fifteen

quindecimprĭm·ī -ōrum *m pl* executive board of fifteen (*magistrates of a municipality*)

quindecimvirāl·is -e *adj* of the board of fifteen

quindecimvir·ī -ōrum *m pl* board of fifteen; **quindecimviri Sibyllini** board of fifteen in charge of the Sibylline Books

quingēnārĭ·us -a -um *adj* of five hundred each, consisting of five hundred men

quingēn·ī -ae -a *adj* five hundred each

quingentēsĭm·us -a -um *adj* five-hundredth

quingent·ī -ae -a *adj* five hundred

quingentĭens or **quingentĭēs** *adv* five hundred times

quīn·ī -ae -a *adj* five each; **quini deni** fifteen each; **quini viceni** twenty-five each

quinquāgēn·ī -ae -a *adj* fifty each

quinquāgēsim·us -a -um *adj* fiftieth; *f* two-percent tax

quinquāginta (indecl) *adj* fifty

Quinquātr·ūs -ūum *f pl* or **Quinquātr·ia -ium** *n pl* festival in honor of Minerva (*celebrated from March 19th to 23rd*)

quinque (indecl) *adj* five

quinquennāl·is -e *adj* quinquennial, occurring every five years; five-year, lasting five years

quinquenn·is -e *adj* five years old, of five years

quinquenn·ium -iī or **-ī** *n* five-year period, five years

quinquepartīt·us -a -um *adj* fivefold, divided into five parts

quinqueprīm·ī -ōrum *m pl* fiveman board of magistrates

quinquerēm·is -e *adj* having five banks of oars; *f* quinquereme

quinquĕ·vir -virī *m* member of a five-man board

quinquevirāt·us -ūs *m* membership on a board of five

quinquevir·ī -ōrum *m pl* five-man board (*created at various times to serve various purposes*)

quinquiēns or **quinquiēs** *adv* five times

quinquiplic·ō -āre *vt* to multiply by five

quintadecimān·ī -ōrum *m pl* soldiers of the fifteenth legion

quintān·us -a -um *adj* of the fifth; *m pl* members of the fifth legion; *f* camp street running between the fifth and sixth maniple (*used as the market street of the camp*)

Quintiliān·us or **Quinctiliān·us -ī** *m* M. Fabius Quintilianus (*Quintilian, famous orator and rhetoric teacher, c.* 35-*c.* 95 A.D.)

Quintīl·is or **Quinctīl·is -e** *adj* & *m* July

quintō or **quintum** *adv* for the fifth time

quint·us -a -um *adj* fifth

Quint·us -ī *m* Roman first name

quint·us decim·us -a -um *adj* fifteenth

quippe *adv* of course, naturally, obviously, by all means; *conj* since, for; **quippe qui** since he (*is, was, will be one who*), inasmuch as he; **multa Caesar questus est quippe qui vidisset** Caesar complained a lot since he had seen

quippiam = **quidpiam**

quippinī *adv* why not?; of course, to be sure

Quirīnāl·ia -ium *n pl* festival in honor of Romulus (*celebrated on the 17th of February*)

Quirīnāl·is -e *adj* of Quirinus; **collis Quirinalis** Quirinal Hill (*one of the seven hills of Rome*)

Quirīn·us -a -um *adj* of Quirinus; *m* Quirinus (*epithet applied to Romulus after his deification, to Janus, to Augustus, and to Antony*)

Quir·īs -ītis *m* Roman citizen; inhabitant of Cures (*Sabine town*)

quirītāti·ō -ōnis *f* shrieking, shriek

quirītāt·us -ūs *m* scream, shriek

Quirītēs = *pl* of **Quiris**

quirīt·ō -āre *vi* to scream, shriek

quis cūjus *pron* (interrog) who, which one; (indef) anyone

quīs = **quibus**

quisnam quaenam (see **quidnam**) *pron* (interrog) who

quispiam cūjuspiam *pron* someone

quispiam quaepiam quodpiam *adj* any

quisquam cūjusquam *pron* anyone, anybody, any person

quisque cūjusque *pron* each, each one, everybody, every one; **doctissimus quisque** every one of great learning, all the most learned; **optimus quisque** all the best ones

quisque quaeque quodque *adj* each

quisquili·ae -ārum *f pl* refuse, trash, junk, rubbish, odds and ends

quisquis (*genit* not in use; *abl:* **quōquo**) *pron* whoever, whosoever, every one who; every one, each

quīvīs quaevīs quidvīs *pron* anyone, anyone you please, anyone at all; **quīvīs unus** any one person

quīvīs quaevīs quodvīs *adj* any, any you please, any at all

quō *adv* (interrog) where, to what place; what for, to what purpose; (after **si, nisi,** or **ne**) to any place, anywhere; **quo . . . eo** the . . . the; **quo magis . . . eo magis** the more . . . the more; *conj* where, to which place; whereby, wherefore; (replacing **ut** when the clause contains a comparative) in order that, so that

quoad *adv* how far; how long; *conj* as long as; as far as; until

quōcircā *adv* for which reason, wherefore, therefore, that's the reason why

quōcumque *adv* to whatever place, wherever

quod *conj* because; as for the fact that; for the fact that; insofar as; as far as; **quod si** or **quodsi** but if

quōdammŏdo or **quōdam modo** *adv* in a way

quoi = **cui**

quōjus = **cujus**

quōlĭbet *adv* anywhere you please

quom see **cum**

quōmĭnus *conj* that not; (after verbs of hindering) from, e.g., **deterrere aliquem quominus habeat** to keep someone from having

quōmŏdo *adv* (interrog) in what way, how; (rel) just as, as

quōmodocumque *adv* in whatever way, however

quōmodŏnam *adv* in just what way, how then

quōnam *adv* where, where to; to what purpose, to what end

quondam *adv* once, at one time, formerly; at times, sometimes, once in a while; some day, one day (*in the future*)

quōnĭam *conj* because, seeing that, now that

quōpĭam *adv* to any place, anywhere

quŏque *adv* too, also

quōquō *adv* to whatever place, wherever

quōquōmŏdo *adv* in whatever way, however

quōquōversum or **quōquōversus** *adv* in every direction, every way

quorsum or **quorsus** *adv* in what direction, where to; to what end, why

quot (indecl) *adj* (interrog) how many; (correlative) as many; **quot Kalendis** every first of the month; **quot mensibus** every month

quotannīs *adv* every year

quotcumque (indecl) *adj* however many

quotēn·ī -ae -a *adj* how many each

quotīdĭē *adv* daily

quotiens or **quotiēs** *adv* (interrog) how many times; (correlative) as often as

quotienscumque or **quotienscun-que** *adv* however often, as often as

quotquot (indecl) *adj* however many, no matter how many

quotŭm·us -a -um *adj* which in number, which in order

quot·us -a -um *adj* which, what; what a small, what a trifling; **quota hora est?** what time is it?; **quota pars** what part; **quot erit iste liber qui . . .** which will be the book which . . .; **quotus quisque philosophorum invenitur** how rarely is one of the philosophers found, how few philosophers are found

quot·uscumque -acumque -um-cumque *adj* just what, just which; **quotacumque pars** just what part

quōusque *adv* how far, how long

quōvīs *adv* to any place whatsoever, anywhere; **quovis gentium** anywhere in the world

quum see **cum** *conj*

R

rabĭdē *adv* rabidly, madly, furiously

rabĭd·us -a -um *adj* rabid, mad, furious, raving, uncontrolled

rabĭ·ēs (*genit* not in use) *f* rage, madness; (fig) rage, anger, fury, wild passion, eagerness

rabĭōsē *adv* furiously, ravingly

rabĭōsŭl·us -a -um *adj* half-crazy

rabĭōs·us -a -um *adj* rabid, mad, raving, crazy

rabŭl·a -ae *m* ranting lawyer

racēmĭf·er -ěra -ěrum *adj* clustered; covered with grape clusters

racēm·us -ī *m* cluster, bunch (*esp. of grapes*); (fig) wine

radĭ·ans -antis *adj* shining, beaming, radiant

radĭāt·us -a -um *adj* spoked; having rays, radiant

rādīcĭtus *adv* by the roots, root and all; completely

rādīcŭl·a -ae *f* small root

radĭ·ō -āre or **radĭ·or -ārī -ātus sum** *vt* to radiate; *vi* to radiate, shine, gleam

radĭōs·us -a -um *adj* radiant

rad·ĭus -ĭī or **-ī** *m* stake, stick; spoke; ray, beam; shuttle; radius; measuring rod; elongated olive

rād·ix -īcis *f* root; radish; foot (*of hill or mountain*); base, foundation; basis, origin

rādō rādĕre rāsī rāsum *vt* to scrape, scratch; to shave; to scratch out, erase; to graze, touch in passing; to strip off; (of the wind) to lash

raed·a -ae *f* four-wheeled carriage, coach

raedār·ĭus -ĭī or **-ī** *m* coach driver

Raetĭ·us -a -um *adj* Raetian; *f* Raetia (*Alpine country between Germany and Italy*)

Raet·us -a -um *adj* & *m* Raetian

rall·us -a -um *adj* thin, threadbare

rāmāl·ĭa -ĭum *n pl* brushwood, undergrowth

rāment·um -ī *n* or **rament·a -ae** *f* chip, shaving

rāmĕ·us -a -um *adj* of branches, of boughs

rām·ex -ĭcis *m* hernia, rupture; blood vessel of the lung

Ramn·ēs or **Ramnens·ēs -ĭum** *m pl* one of the three original Roman tribes; (fig) blue bloods

rāmōs·us -a -um *adj* branchy, branching; branch-like

rāmŭl·us -ī *m* twig

rām·us -ī *m* branch, bough; branch (*of an antler*); stick, club

rān·a -ae *f* frog; **rana marina** frog fish

ranc·ens -entis *adj* putrid, stinking

rancidŭl·us -a -um *adj* rank, stinking; disgusting

rancĭd·us -a -um *adj* rancid, rank, stinking; disgusting

rānuncŭl·us -ī *m* little frog, tadpole

rapācĭd·a -ae *m* son of a thief

rapācĭt·ās -ātis *f* rapacity, greediness

rap·ax -ācis *adj* rapacious, grasping, grabby, greedy for plunder; insatiable

raphăn·us -ī *m* radish

rapĭdē *adv* rapidly; (to burn) fiercely

rapĭdĭt·ās -ātis *f* rapidity, velocity, swiftness, rush

rapĭd·us -a -um *adj* tearing away,

seizing; fierce, consuming, white-hot (*fire*); rapid, swift, rushing, hurrying, impetuous

rapīn·a -ae *f* rapine, pillage; prey, booty

rapīō rapĕre rapŭī raptum *vt* to seize and carry off, to snatch, tear, pluck; to drag off; to hurry, drive, cause to rush; to carry off by force, rob, ravish, ravage, lay waste; to lead on hurriedly; **flammam rapere** to catch fire; **in jus rapere** to drag off to court, hale before a court; **se rapere** to hurry, dash, take off

raptim *adv* hurriedly, speedily, suddenly

raptĭ·ō -ōnis *f* abduction, ravishing, rape

rapt·ō -āre *vt* to seize and carry off, drag away; to drag along; to plunder; to hale, arraign

rapt·or -ōris *m* plunderer, robber; rapist

rapt·us -a -um *pp* of **rapio**; *n* plunder, loot

rapt·us -ūs *m* snatching away; looting, robbery; rape, abduction

rāpŭl·um -ī *n* little turnip

rāp·um -ī *n* turnip

rārē *adv* rarely, seldom

rārē·facĭō -facĕre -fēcī -factum *vt* to rarefy, thin out

rāresc·ō -ĕre *vi* to grow thin, lose density, become rarefied; to grow wider, widen out, open up; to become fewer; to disappear, die away

rārĭt·ās -ātis *f* looseness of texture; thinness; small number

rārō *adv* rarely, seldom

rār·us -a -um *adj* wide apart, of loose texture, thin; far apart, scattered far apart; scarce, sparse; few; (mil) in open rank; uncommon, rare, unusual

rāsĭl·is -e *adj* shaved smooth, scraped, polished

rastr·um -ī *n* rake; mattock

rāsus *pp* of **rado**

ratĭ·ō -ōnis *f* calculation, computation, reckoning, account; matter, affair, business, transaction; consideration, respect, regard; grounds; scheme, system, method, procedure; theory, doctrine; science; relation, connection, reference; fashion, way, style; reasoning, reason, judgment, understanding; reasonableness, order, law, rule; view, opinion; **propter rationem** (with *genit*) out of regard for; **ratio aeraria** rate of exchange; **ratio atque usus** theory and practice; **ratio constat** the accounts tally; **rationem conferre, referre,** or **deferre** (with *genit*) to render or give an account of, account for; **rationem ducere** to make a calculation, reckon; **rationem habere** (with **cum** + *abl*) to have to do with; **rationem inire** to calculate, make a calculation

ratĭōcĭnātĭ·ō -ōnis *f* (rhet) exercise

of the reasoning powers, reasoning; syllogism

ratĭōcĭnātīv·us -a -um *adj* syllogistic

ratĭōcĭnāt·or -ōris *m* accountant

ratĭōcĭn·or -ārī -ātus sum *vt & vi* to calculate, reckon; to reason, argue, conclude, infer

rat·is -is *f* raft; boat; *f pl* pontoons

ratiuncŭl·a -ae *f* small account; trifling reason; petty syllogism

rat·us -a -um *pp* of **reor**; *adj* reckoned, calculated; fixed, established, settled, certain, sure, approved; **pro rata parte** or **pro rata** in proportion, proportionately; **ratum facere** or **ratum efficere** to confirm, ratify, approve; **ratum habere** or **ducere** to consider valid, regard as certain or sure

raucĭsŏn·us -a -um *adj* hoarse

rauc·us -a -um *adj* raucous, hoarse; screaming, strident; scraping; deep, deep-voiced

raud·us or **rūd·us -ĕris** *n* copper coin

rauduscŭl·um or **rūduscŭl·um -ī** *n* bit of money

rāv·ĭō -īre *vi* to talk oneself hoarse

rāv·is -is *f* hoarseness

rāv·us -a -um *adj* greyish

re·a -ae *f* defendant, guilty woman

reapse *adv* in fact, actually, really

Reāt·e -is *n* Sabine town

Reātīn·us -a -um *adj & m* Reatine

rebellātĭ·ō -ōnis *f* rebellion

rebellātr·ix -īcis *f* rebel; **Germania rebellatrix** rebel Germany

rebellĭ·ō -ōnis *f* rebellion

rebell·is -e *adj* rebellious; *m pl* rebels

rebell·ĭum -ĭī or **-ī** *n* rebellion

rebell·ō -āre *vi* to rebel

rebĭt·ō -ĕre *vi* to go back

rebŏ·ō -āre *vt* to make reecho; *vi* to reecho, bellow back

recalcĭtr·ō -āre *vi* to kick back

recal·ĕō -ēre *vi* to be warmed; (of a river) to run warm (*e.g., with blood*)

recal·escō -escĕre -ŭī *vi* to grow warm again

recal·facĭō -facĕre -fēcī *vt* to make warm again, warm up again

recalv·us -a -um *adj* bald in front, with receding hairline

recand·escō -escĕre -ŭī *vi* to grow white; to grow hot, glow; (with *dat*) to grow white, grow hot, glow in response to

recant·ō -āre *vt* to recant; to charm back, charm away; *vi* to reecho

re·cēdō -cēdĕre -cessī -cessum *vi* to go back, go away, withdraw, recede, give ground, fall back; to depart; to vanish, disappear; to stand back, be distant

recell·ō -ĕre *vi* to spring back, recoil

rec·ens -entis *adj* recent, fresh, young; newly arrived, just arrived; modern; fresh, rested; *n pl* recent events

recens *adv* just, recently, lately, newly

recens·ĕō -ēre -ŭī -um *vt* to count, enumerate, number, survey; to review, hold a review of (*the army*); (of a censor) to revise the roll of, review, enroll; to recount, go over again, retell

recensi·ō -ōnis *f* revision

recensus *pp* of **recenseo**

recens·us -ūs *m* review

receptācŭl·um -ī *n* receptacle, container; reservoir; place of refuge, shelter; hiding place

recepti·ō -ōnis *f* reception

recept·ō -āre *vt* to take back; to welcome frequently into the home, entertain; to tug at; **se receptare** to beat a hasty retreat

recept·or -ōris *m* or **receptr·ix -īcis** *f* shelterer; concealer

recept·us -a -um *pp* of **recipio**; *n* obligation

recept·us -ūs *m* taking back, recantation; (mil) retreat; way of escape; refuge, place of retreat; return; **(signum) receptui canere** to sound retreat

recessim *adv* backwards

recess·us -ūs *m* retreat, withdrawal; departure; secluded spot, retreat; inner room, central chamber; recess; background

recharmĭd·ō -āre *vi* to stop being a Charmides (*character in Roman comedy*)

recidīv·us -a -um *adj* recurring, returning; rebuilt

re·cĭdō -cĭdĕre -cĭdī -cīsum *vt* to cut back, cut away, cut off, cut down; to abridge, cut short

re·cĭdō -cĭdĕre -cĭdī -cāsum or **rec·cĭdō -cĭdĕre** *vi* to fall back; to jump back, recoil; to suffer a relapse; (fig) to fall back, fall, sink, relapse; to turn out, result; (with **ad** or **in** + *acc*) to pass to, be handed over to

re·cingō -cingĕre — -cinctum *vt* to loosen, undo, take off

recĭn·ō -ĕre *vt* to repeat, reecho; *vi* to sound a warning

reciper- = recuper-

re·cĭpĭō -cĭpĕre -cēpī -ceptum *vt* to keep back, keep in reserve; to take back, withdraw, bring back, carry back, retake, recover, regain; to take in, accept, receive, welcome; to gain, collect, take in, make (*money*); to take up, assume, undertake; to guarantee, pledge; (mil) to retake, reoccupy, recapture, seize, take, occupy; **ad se** or **in se recipere** to take upon oneself, take responsibility for, promise, guarantee; **se recipere** to get hold of oneself again, regain self-composure, recover, come to again; to retreat, escape; **se recipere** (with **ad** or **in** + *acc*) to retreat to, escape to, find refuge in

reciprŏc·ō -āre *vt* to move back and forth; to turn back; to back (*e.g.*, *a ship*) about, reverse the direction of; to reverse, convert (*a proposition*); *vi* (of the tide) to ebb and flow, rise and fall

reciprŏc·us -a -um *adj* ebbing and flowing, going backwards and forwards

recisus *pp* of **recīdo**

recitātĭ·ō -ōnis *f* reading aloud, recitation

recitāt·or -ōris *m* reader, reciter

recĭt·ō -āre *vt* to read out, read aloud, recite; to name in writing, appoint, constitute; **senatum recitare** to have roll call in the senate

reclāmātĭ·ō -ōnis *f* cry of disapproval

reclāmĭt·ō -āre *vi* to voice disapproval

reclām·ō -āre *vt* to protest; *vi* to raise a protest, voice disapproval, shout objections; to reverberate; (with *dat*) to express disapproval to, contradict

reclīn·is -e *adj* reclining, leaning back

reclīn·ō -āre *vt* to bend back, lean back, rest; (with **ab** + *abl*) to distract (*someone*) from; **se reclinare** to lean

re·clūdō -clūdĕre -clūsī -clūsum *vt* to open; to lay open, disclose; to draw (*sword*); to break up (*the soil*)

recoctus *pp* of **recoquo**

recŏgĭt·ō -āre *vi* (with **de** + *abl*) to think again about, reconsider, reflect on

recognitĭ·ō -ōnis *f* reinvestigation

reco·gnoscō -gnoscĕre -gnōvī -gnitum *vt* to call to mind again, review; to recognize; to look over, examine, inspect, investigate; to certify, authorize

recol·lĭgō -lĭgĕre -lēgī -lectum *vt* to gather again, gather up, collect; **te recollige** get hold of yourself, pluck up your courage

re·cŏlō -cŏlĕre -cŏlŭī -cultum *vt* to till again; to honor again; to recall to mind, think over, consider; to cultivate once more, practice again, resume

recomminisc·or -ī *vt* to call to mind again, recall

recomposĭt·us -a -um *adj* rearranged

reconciliātĭ·ō -ōnis *f* winning back again, reestablishment, restoration; reconciling, reconciliation

reconcĭl·ō -āre *vt* to bring back, regain, recover; to restore, reestablish; to win over again, conciliate; to bring together again, reconcile

reconcinn·ō -āre *vt* to set right again, repair

recondĭt·us -a -um *adj* hidden, concealed; recondite, abstruse, profound; reserved (*person*)

recon·dō -dĕre -dĭdī -dĭtum *vt* to put back again, put away, hoard; to hide, conceal; to plunge (*sword*); to close (*eyes*) again; to store up (*in the mind*)

reconfl·ō -āre *vt* to blow up again, rekindle

re·cŏquō -coquĕre -coxī -coctum *vt* to cook, boil, or bake again; to recast, remold

recordāti·ō -ōnis *f* recollection, remembrance

record·or -ārī -ātus sum *vt* to recall, recollect, remember

recrĕ·ō -āre *vt* to recreate, restore, renew; (fig) to revive, refresh

recrĕp·ō -āre *vt & vi* to reecho

re·crescō -crescĕre -crēvī *vi* to grow again; to be renewed

recrūd·escō -escĕre -ŭī *vi* to become raw again; (of a wound) to open up again; (of a revolt) to break out again

rectā *adv* by a direct route, right on, directly

rectē *adv* in a straight line; rightly, correctly, suitably, properly, well; quite; (in answers) well, right, quite well, fine

recti·ō -ōnis *f* direction, controlling

rect·or -ōris *m* guide, controller, leader, ruler, master, pilot

rect·us -a -um *pp* of **rego**; *adj* in a straight line, straight, direct; correct, right, proper, appropriate; just, upright, conscientious, virtuous; *n* right; uprightness, rectitude, virtue

recūb·ō -āre *vi* to lie on one's back, lie down, rest

recŭl·a -ae *f* little thing

recultus *pp* of **recolo**

re·cumbō -cumbĕre -cubŭī *vi* to lie down again, lie down; to recline (*esp. at table*); to sink down (*e.g., in a swamp*); to fall; (of fog) to settle down

recuperāti·ō -ōnis *f* recovery

recuperāt·or or **reciperāt·or -ōris** *m* recoverer, regainer; (law) arbiter (*member of a bench of from three to five men who expedited cases needing speedy decisions*)

recuperātōrī·us or **reciperātōrī·us -a -um** *adj* of the special court for summary civil suits

recupĕr·ō or **recipĕr·ō -āre** *vt* to regain, recover, get back; to win over again

recūr·ō -āre *vt* to restore, refresh, restore to health

re·currō -currĕre -currī *vi* to run back, hurry back; to return, recur, come back

recurs·ō -āre *vi* to keep running back; to keep recurring

recurs·us -ūs *m* return; retreat

recurv·ō -āre *vt* to curve, bend back

recurv·us -a -um *adj* curving, curved, bent, crooked

recusāti·ō -ōnis *f* refusal; (law) objection, protest; counterplea

recūs·ō -āre *vt* to raise objections to, reject, refuse; (with *inf*) to be

reluctant to, refuse to; *vi* to raise an objection, object; to make a rebuttal

recuss·us -a -um *adj* reverberating

recutīt·us -a -um *adj* with the foreskin cut back, circumcised; Jewish

redactus *pp* of **redigo**

redambŭl·ō -āre *vi* to walk back

redăm·ō -āre *vt* to love in return

redargu·ō -ĕre -ī *vt* to disprove, contradict, refute

redauspic·ō -āre *vi* to take the return auspices; (coll) to return

red·dō -dĕre -didī -ditum *vt* to give back, return, restore, replace; to repay; to repeat, recite (*words*); to translate; to render, make; to give as due, pay, deliver; to reflect, reproduce, imitate; **se reddere** to return, come back

redempti·ō -ōnis *f* ransoming; bribing; revenue collection

redempt·ō -āre *vt* to ransom, repeatedly

redempt·or -ōris *m* contractor; revenue agent

redemptūr·a -ae *f* revenue collection

redemptus *pp* of **redimo**

red·eō -īre -iī -itum *vi* to go or come back, return; (of a speaker) to return (*to the main theme*); (with **ad** + *acc*) **a** to return to, revert to; **b** to fall back on, have recourse to, be reduced to; **c** (of power, inheritances, etc.) to revert to, devolve upon; **ad se redire** to come to again, regain consciousness; to control oneself

redhāl·ō -āre *vt* to exhale

redhib·eō -ēre — -itum *vt* to take back

red·igō -igĕre -ēgī -actum *vt* to drive back, lead back, bring back; to call in, collect, raise (*money, revenues*); to reduce, diminish (*numbers*); to force, compel, subdue, reduce; (with double *acc*) to render, make; (with **in** or **sub** + *acc*) to bring under the power of; **ad vanum et irritum redigere** to make meaningless; **in memoriam redigere** to remember, recall; **in provinciam redigere** to reduce to the rank of a province

redimicŭl·um -ī *n* band, chaplet, fillet; chain, fetter

redim·iō -īre -iī -ītum *vt* to crown, wreathe

red·imō -imĕre -ēmī -emptum *vt* to buy back; to ransom, redeem; to buy off, rescue by payment, rescue, release, set free; to buy up; to buy off, ward off, avert; to pay for, compensate for, atone for; to get by contract, collect under contract

redintĕgr·ō -āre *vt* to make whole again, restore, refresh; (mil) to bring to full strength

redipisc·or -ī *vt* to get back

reditī·ō -ōnis *f* return

redĭt·us -ūs *m* return; revenue, proceeds, returns; (of heavenly bodies) revolution, orbit; (fig) restoration

redivia see **reduvia**

redivīv·us -a -um *adj* second-hand (*building materials*)

redol·ĕō -ēre -ŭī *vt* to smell of; *vi* to smell, be redolent

redomĭt·us -a -um *adj* retamed, broken in again

redŏn·ō -āre *vt* to restore, give back again; to give up, abandon

redorm·ĭō -īre *vi* to go to sleep again

re·dūcō -dūcĕre -dūxī -ductum *vt* to draw back; to lead back, bring back; to escort (*official as mark of honor to his home*); to remarry (*after a separation*); to restore to normal; to withdraw (*troops*); **in gratiam reducere** to restore to favor

reductĭ·ō -ōnis *f* restoration

reduct·or -ōris *m* restorer

reduct·us -a -um *pp* of **reduco**; remote, secluded, aloof, removed

redunc·us -a -um *adj* bent backwards, curved backwards

redundantĭ·a -ae *f* excess; redundancy

redund·ō -āre *vi* to overflow; to be too numerous, be too large; to be soaked (*e.g., with blood*); (with *abl*) to abound in; (with **de** or **ex** + *abl*) to stream from, overflow with

reduvĭ·a or **redivĭ·a -ae** *f* hangnail, loose fingernail

red·ux -ūcis *adj* guiding back, rescuing; brought back, restored

refectus *pp* of **reficio**

refell·ō -ĕre -ī *vt* to refute, disprove

re·fercĭō -fercīre -fersī -fertum *vt* to stuff, cram, choke, crowd

refer·ĭō -īre *vt* to strike back, hit back

refĕrō referre rettŭlī relātum *vt* to bring back, carry back; to give back, return, restore, pay back, repay; to bring back, return, echo (*a sound*); to renew, revive, repeat; to bring back, direct, focus, turn (*mind, attention*); to present again, represent; to say in turn, answer, reply; to announce, report, relate, tell; to note down, enter, register, record; to reckon, consider, regard; to refer, attribute, ascribe; to bring up, spit out, vomit; **gradum referre** to go back, retreat; **gratiam** or **gratias referre** to return thanks, show gratitude; **in rationibus referendis** in accounting; **pedem referre** to go back, retreat, withdraw, retire; **pedes fertque refertque** he walks up and down; **rationes referre ad aerarium** to make an accounting to the treasury; **se referre** to go back, return; **vestigia referre** to retrace footsteps, return; *vi* to make a motion, make a proposal; **ad senatum referre** (with **de** + *abl*) to bring be-

fore the senate the matter of, make a proposal to the senate about; *v impers* it is of importance, it is of consequence; **meā** (**tuā, nostrā**) **refert** it is of importance, of consequence, of advantage to me (*you, us*); **non refert utrum** it makes no difference whether; **parvi refert** (with *inf*) it is of little importance, of little advantage to; **quid refert?** what's the difference?

refert·us -a -um *pp* of **refercio**; *adj* stuffed, packed, crammed; crowded

referv·ĕō -ēre *vi* to boil over, bubble over

refervesc·ō -ĕre *vi* to begin to boil or bubble

re·ficĭō -ficĕre -fēcī -fectum *vt* to rebuild, repair, restore; to revive (*hope, etc.*); to refresh, invigorate; to get (*e.g., money*) back again; to reappoint, reelect

re·fīgō -fīgĕre -fīxī -fixum *vt* to unfasten, undo; to take down (*pictures, posters, etc.*); to annul (*laws*)

refing·ō -ĕre *vt* to refashion

refixus *pp* of **refigo**

reflāgĭt·ō -āre *vt* to demand again, ask back

reflāt·us -ūs *m* head wind

re·flectō -flectĕre -flexī -flexum *vt* to bend back or backwards, turn around, turn away; (fig) to turn back, bring back, change

refl·ō -āre *vt* to breathe out again; *vi* to blow in the wrong direction

reflŭ·ō -ĕre *vi* to flow back, run back; to overflow

reflŭ·us -a -um *adj* ebbing, receding

refocill·ō -āre *vt* to rewarm; to revive

reformāt·or -ōris *m* reformer

reformīdātĭ·ō -ōnis *f* dread

reformīd·ō -āre *vt* to dread, stand in awe of; to shrink from, shun

reform·ō -āre *vt* to reshape, remold, transform

re·fovĕō -fovēre -fōvī -fōtum *vt* to warm again; to restore, revive, refresh

refractārĭŏl·us -a -um *adj* a bit refractory, somewhat stubborn

refractus *pp* of **refringo**

refrāg·or -ārī -ātus sum *vi* (with *dat*) to oppose, resist, thwart

refrēn·ō -āre *vt* to curb, restrain, keep down, control

refrĭc·ō -āre -ŭī -ātum *vt* to rub open, scratch open; to irritate, reopen, inflame (*a wound*); (fig) to irritate, exasperate; (fig) to renew; *vi* to break out again

refrīgerātĭ·ō -ōnis *f* coolness

refrīgĕr·ō -āre *vt* to cool off, cool, chill; to refresh; to weary, exhaust; **refrigerari** to grow cool, grow weary

re·frīgescō -frīgescĕre -frixī *vi* to grow cool, become cool; (fig) to lose force, flag, abate, fail, grow dull, grow stale, fall flat

re·fringō -fringere -frēgī -fractum vt to break open, break down; to tear off (clothes); (fig) to break, check, destroy, put an end to

re·fugiō -fugere -fūgī vt to run away from; to avoid; vi to run away, escape; to disappear

refug·ium -iī or **-ī** n place of refuge; recourse

refūg·us -a -um adj receding, vanishing; m fugitive

re·fulgeō -fulgēre -fulsī vi to gleam, reflect, reflect light, glitter

re·fundō -fundere -fūdī -fūsum vt to pour back, pour out; **refundi** to flow back, overflow

refūtātiō -ōnis f refutation

refūtāt·us -ūs m refutation

refūt·ō -āre vt to repress, suppress; to refute, disprove

rēgāl·is -e adj kingly, regal; king's, of a king, royal

rēgāliter adv royally, in royal style, splendidly; despotically

regel·ō -āre vt to cool off; to thaw

re·gerō -gerere -gessī -gestum vt to carry back, throw back; (fig) to throw back (remarks)

rēgi·a -ae f palace, castle, court; fortress, residence; (in camp) king's tent; royal family, king and courtiers, court; regia (originally the palace of King Numa on the Sacred Way in the Roman Forum and later the residence of the Pontifex Maximus)

rēgiē adv royally; despotically

Rēgiens·is -e or **Rēgīn·us -a -um** adj of Regium; m pl inhabitants of Regium

rēgific·us -a -um adj royal, kingly, magnificent

regign·ō -ere vt to reproduce

Rēgillān·us -a -um or **Rēgillens·is -e** adj of or at Lake Regillus

rēgill·us -a -um adj royal, magnificent

Rēgill·us -ī m lake in Latium famous for the victory over the Latins won by the Romans under the dictator Postumius (496 B.C.)

rēgim·en -inis n steering, controlling; rudder; government, rule, command, guidance; director, ruler, governor

rēgīn·a -ae f queen; princess; noble woman, lady

regi·ō -ōnis f straight line, line, direction; boundary, boundary line; region, area, quarter, neighborhood; ward (of Rome); district, province (of a country); department, sphere; **ab recta regione** in a straight line; **de recta regione deflectere** to veer off from a straight path; **e regione** in a straight line, directly; **e regione** (with genit) in the opposite direction to, exactly opposite; **rectā regione** by a direct route

regiōnātim adv by wards, by districts

Rēg·ium or **Rhēg·ium -iī** or **-ī** n city on the toe of Italy; town in Cisalpine Gaul

rēgi·us -a -um adj king's, kingly, royal, regal; like a king, worthy of a king, magnificent; m pl the king's troops; f see **regia**

reglūtin·ō -āre vt to unglue

regnāt·or -ōris m ruler, sovereign

regnātr·ix -īcis adj fem imperial

regn·ō -āre vi to be king, reign; to be supreme, hold sway; to domineer; (with genit) to be king of; (with **in** + acc) to rule over; **regnari** to be ruled by a king, be under a king

regn·um -ī n monarchy, royal power, kingship; absolute power, despotism, power; supremacy, control, direction, sovereignty; realm, kingdom; domain, estate

regō regere rexī rectum vt to keep in a straight line; keep in a proper course; to guide, conduct; to govern, rule, command; to manage, direct; **regere finis** (law) to mark out the limits

re·gredior -gredī -gressus sum vi to step or go back; to come back, return; to march back, retreat

regress·us -ūs m return; retreat

rēgul·a -ae f ruler (for measuring); straight stick; straight board; rule, standard, example, model, principle

rēgul·us -ī m petty king, prince, chieftain; prince

Rēgul·us -ī m M. Atilius Regulus (Roman general who was taken prisoner by the Carthaginians in the First Punic War, refused to let himself be ransomed, and was killed in 250 B.C.)

regust·ō -āre vt to taste again; (fig) to delve again into (e.g., literature)

rē·iciō -icere -jēcī -jectum vt to throw back, fling back; to throw over one's shoulders or behind one; to beat back, repel, repulse; to reject, refuse, disdain, scorn; (of judges) to challenge, overrule; to refer, direct, assign; to postpone; **rem reicere** (with **ad** + acc) to turn over or refer the matter to (someone for consideration or decision); **potestas reiciendi** (law) right to challenge

rējectānē·us -a -um adj to be rejected

rējecti·ō -ōnis f rejection; (law) challenging; **rejectio judicum** challenging of the members of the jury

rēject·ō -āre vt to throw back

rējectus pp of **reicio**

re·lābor -lābī -lapsus sum vi to slide or glide back; to sink down (upon a couch); (of rivers) to flow back; to sail back; (fig) to return

relangu·escō -escere -ī vi to faint; to be relaxed, relax; to weaken

relāti·ō -ōnis f report (made by a

magistrate to the senate or empe-
ror); repetition, reiteration; **rela-**
tio criminis (law) answering to a
charge
relāt·or -ōris *m* proposer of a motion
relātus *pp of* **refero**
relāt·us -ūs *m* official report; narration, recital, listing; **relatus car-**
minum recital of poems
relaxāti·ō -ōnis *f* relaxation, easing;
mitigation
relax·ō -āre *vt* to stretch out, widen,
open; to loosen, open; to release, set
free; to ease, ease the tensions of,
relieve, cheer up; to alleviate, mitigate
relectus *pp of* **relego**
relēgāti·ō -ōnis *f* banishment, sending into retirement
relēg·ō -āre *vt* to send away, remove,
send into retirement, retire; to banish; to put aside, reject; to refer
re·lĕgō -legĕre -lēgī -lectum *vt* to
collect again, gather up, gather together, to travel over, sail over
again; to go over, review (*in*
thought, in a speech); to reread
relentesc·ō -ĕre *vi* to slack off, cool
off
relĕv·ō -āre *vt* to lighten; to lift up
or raise again; (fig) to relieve, free,
lighten, soothe, alleviate
relictī·ō -ōnis *f* abandonment
relictus *pp of* **relinquo**
relicŭus *see* **reliquus**
religātī·ō -ōnis *f* tying back, tying
up
religi·ō -ōnis *f* religious scruple,
conscientiousness, sense of right;
misgivings; reverence, awe; religion; superstition; sanctity, holiness; religion, sect, cult, mode of
worship; object of veneration, sacred object, sacred place; divine
service, worship, religious observation
religiōsē *adv* scrupulously, conscientiously, carefully, exactly; reverently, piously, religiously
religiōs·us -a -um *adj* scrupulous,
conscientious, exact, precise, accurate; religious, reverent, pious, devout; superstitious; sacred, holy,
consecrated; subject to religious
claims, under religious liability
relig·ō -āre *vt* to bind back, tie up;
to moor (*a ship);* to unbind, untie,
loosen; (fig) to bind
re·linō -linĕre -lēvī — *vt* to unseal, open
re·linquō -linquĕre -līquī -lictum
vt to leave behind, not take along;
to leave behind, bequeath; to permit to remain, let remain; to leave
alive; to forsake, abandon, desert,
leave in a lurch; to give up, abandon, relinquish, resign; to leave unmentioned; **locum integrum re-**
linquere to leave the place untouched
reliquī·ae -ārum *f pl* remains, rem-
nants

reliqu·us or **relicŭ·us -a -um** *adj*
remaining, left over, left; remaining, subsequent, future (*time);* outstanding (*debt);* *m pl* the others; *n*
remainder, rest, residue; **in reli-**
quum in the future, for the future;
nihil reliqui facere to leave
nothing undone, omit nothing, leave
no stone unturned; **reliqui omnes**
all the rest; **reliquum est** (with
inf or **ut**) it only remains to; **reli-**
quum aliquem facere to leave
someone behind; to spare someone;
reliquum aliquid facere or **ali-**
quid reliqui facere to leave something remaining, leave something
behind, neglect something
rellig- = relig-
relliq- = reliq-
re·lūcĕō -lūcēre -luxī *vi* to reflect
light, gleam, shine out, blaze
re·lūcescō -lūcescĕre -luxī *vi* to
grow bright again, clear
reluct·or -ārī -ātus sum *vi* to fight
back, put up a struggle, resist; to
be reluctant
re·manĕō -manēre -mansī *vi* to
stay behind; to remain, continue (*in*
a certain state)
remān·ō -āre *vi* to flow back
remansī·ō -ōnis *f* staying behind,
stay
remed·ium -iī or **-ī** *n* remedy, cure,
antidote, medicine
remensus *pp of* **remetior**
remĕ·ō -āre *vt* to retrace, relive; *vi*
to go or come back, return
re·mētior -mētīrī -mensus sum
vt to remeasure; to retrace, go back
over
rēm·ex -igis *m* rower, crew member,
oarsman
Rēm·ī -ōrum *m pl* a people of Gaul
(*near modern Rheims)*
rēmigāti·ō -ōnis *f* rowing
rēmig·ium -iī or **-ī** *n* rowing; oars;
oarsmen, rowers
rēmig·ō -āre *vi* to row
remigr·ō -āre *vi* to move back, go
back, return
reminisc·or -ī *vt* to call to mind, remember; *vi* to remember; (with
genit) to be mindful of, conscious of,
remember
re·miscĕō -miscēre — -mixtum
vt to mix up, intermingle; **veris**
falsa remiscere to intermingle
lies with truth
remissē *adv* mildly, gently
remissī·ō -ōnis *f* release; easing,
letting down, lowering; relaxing (*of*
muscles); relaxation, recreation;
mildness, gentleness; submissiveness; abatement, diminishing; remission (*of debts)*
remiss·us -a -um *adj* relaxed, loose,
slack; mild, gentle; negligent, remiss; easy-going, indulgent, yielding; gay, merry, light; low, cheap
(*price)*
re·mittō -mittĕre -mīsī -missum
vt to send back; to release; to slack-
en, loosen; to emit, produce, let out,

yield, send forth, give off; to send back, return, restore; to give up, reject, resign, concede; to relax, relieve (*the mind*); to pardon; to remit, remove (*penalty*); (with *inf*) to stop (*doing something*); *vi* (of wind, rain, etc.) to slack off, abate

remixtus *pp* of **remisceo**

remōl·ior -īrī -ītus sum *vt* to push or move back or away, heave back

remollesc·ō -ĕre *vi* to get soft again, soften; to weaken

remŏr·a -ae *f* hindrance, delay

remorāmin·a -um *n pl* hindrances, delays

re·mordĕō -mordēre — -morsum *vt* to bite back; to attack in return; to disturb, annoy, worry, torture

remŏr·or -ārī -ātus sum *vt* to delay, hinder, hold back, detain; *vi* to loiter, delay, linger, stay behind

remōtē *adv* at a distance, far away

remōti·ō -ōnis *f* removal

remōt·us -a -um *adj* removed, out of the way, far off, remote, distant; (fig) remote, apart, separate, clear, free; dead; (with ab + abl) removed from, separate from, apart from, clear of, free from

re·movĕō -movēre -mōvī -mōtum *vt* to move back, withdraw, put away, remove; to shroud, veil; (fig) put out of sight, set aside, abolish; to subtract

remūg·īō -īre *vi* to bellow back; to resound, reecho

re·mulcĕō -mulcēre -mulsī *vt* to stroke, smooth back; **caudam remulcere** to put the tail between the legs (*in fear*)

remulc·um -ī *n* tow rope, tow line

remūnerāti·ō -ōnis *f* remuneration, reward, recompense, repayment

remūnĕr·or -ārī -ātus sum *vt* to repay, reward

remurmŭr·ō -āre *vi* to murmur back in reply

rēm·us -ī *m* oar; (fig) wing; **remi corporis** hands and feet (*of a swimmer*)

Rem·us -ī *m* brother of Romulus

renarr·ō -āre *vt* to tell over again, recount

re·nascor -nascī -nātus sum *vi* to be born again; to rise again, spring up again, be restored; to reappear; to recur

renāvig·ō -āre *vi* to sail back

ren·ĕō -ēre *vt* to unravel, undo

rēn·ēs -um *m pl* kidneys

renīd·ens -entis *adj* beaming, glad

renīd·ĕō -ēre *vi* to reflect, reflect light, glitter, shine; to smile, grin all over; to beam with joy

renīdesc·ō -ĕre *vi* to begin to reflect light, begin to glitter

renīt·or -ī *vi* to put up a struggle, fight back, resist

ren·ō -āre *vi* to swim back, float back

rēn·ō or **rhēn·ō -ōnis** *m* fur

renōd·ō -āre *vt* to tie back in a knot; to untie

renovām·en -inis *n* renewal, new condition

renovāti·ō -ōnis *f* renovation, renewal; revision; compound interest

renŏv·ō -āre *vt* to make new again; to renovate, repair, restore; to plow up (*a fallow field*); to reopen (*wounds*); to revive (*old customs*, *etc.*); to start (*battles*) all over again; to refresh (*the memory*); to repeat, keep repeating, reaffirm; **faenus renovare in singulos annos** to compound the interest on a yearly basis

renumĕr·ō -āre *vt* to count over again, recount; to pay back, repay

renuntiāti·ō -ōnis *f* formal or official report, announcement

renunti·ō -āre *vt* to report; to announce; to retract (*promise, etc.*); to renounce, call off, reject; (with double *acc*) to announce or declare elected as; (with *acc* & *inf*) to bring back word that

renunt·ius -iī or **-ī** *m* bringer of news, reporter

re·nŭō -nŭĕre -nŭī *vt* to nod refusal to, deny, refuse, turn down, decline, say not to, reject; *vi* to shake the head in refusal, refuse, say no; (with *dat*) to say no to, deny (*a charge*)

renŭt·ō -āre *vt* to refuse emphatically

reor rērī ratus sum *vt* to think, deem; (with *acc* & *inf*) to think that; (with *acc* & *adj* as objective complement) to regard (*something*) as; *vi* to think, suppose

repāgŭl·a -ōrum *n pl* bolts, bars; (fig) restraints, regulations, rules, limits

repand·us -a -um *adj* curved backwards, concave; (*shoes*) with turned-up toes

reparābil·is -e *adj* capable of being repaired, reparable, retrievable

reparc·ō -ĕre *vi* (with *dat*) to be sparing with, take it easy with

repăr·ō -āre *vt* to get again, acquire again; to recover, retrieve, make good; to restore, renew, repair; to recruit (*a new army*); **vīna merce reparare** to get wine in exchange for wares, barter for wine

repastināti·ō -ōnis *f* digging up again

re·pectō -pectĕre — -pexum *vt* to comb back; to comb again, recomb

repellō repellĕre reppŭlī repulsum *vt* to drive back, push back, repel, repulse; to reject; to remove; to refute

re·pendō -pendĕre -pendī -pensum *vt* to repay, pay back; to ransom, redeem; (fig) to repay in kind, requite, recompense, reward; to compensate for; to balance, balance out; **magna rependere** to pay back in full

rep·ens -entis *adj* sudden, unexpected, unlooked-for, hasty

repensus *pp* of **rependo**

repentē *adv* suddenly, unexpectedly, all of a sudden

repentīnō *adv* suddenly, unexpectedly

repentīn·us -a -um *adj* sudden, unexpected, unlooked-for; hasty, impetuous

reperc·ō -ĕre *vi* (with *dat*) **a** to be sparing with; **b** to refrain from

repercussus *pp of* **repercutio**; *adj* rebounding; reflected, reflecting; echoed, echoing

repercuss·us -ūs *m* rebounding, reverberation, echo, repercussion

reper·cutiō -cutĕre -cussī -cussum *vt* to make (*something*) rebound, reverberate, or reflect

reperiō reperīre reppĕrī repertum *vt* to find, find again, discover; to get, procure, obtain, win; to find out, ascertain, learn, realize; to invent, devise

repert·or -ōris *m* discoverer, inventor, author

repert·us -a -um *pp of* **reperio**; *n pl* discoveries, inventions

repetītī·ō -ōnis *f* repetition; (rhet) anaphora, repetition

repetīt·or -ōris *m* claimant

repĕt·ō -ĕre -īvī or **-ĭī -ītum** *vt* to head back to, try to reach again, return to; to aim at again; to fetch back; to attack again; to prosecute again; to demand anew; to demand back, claim, demand in compensation, retake; to trace back, retrace; to trace in thought, think over, recall, recollect; to trace back (*in speech*); to repeat, undertake again, resume, renew; **lex de pecuniis** (or **rebus**) **repetundis** law on extortion, extortion law; **pecuniam repetere** to sue for the recovery of money; **res repetere** to sue for the recovery of property; **reus pecuniarum repetundarum** guilty of extortion

repetund·ae -ārum *f pl* extortion; money extorted; **repetundarum argui** to be charged with extortion; **repetundarum teneri** to be held on an extortion charge

repexus *pp of* **repecto**

replĕō -plēre -plēvī -plētum *vt* to refill, fill up, replenish; to fill to overflowing; to make up for, replace, compensate for; to recruit, bring (*an army*) to full strength

replēt·us -a -um *adj* filled, full; well provided

replicātī·ō -ōnis *f* folding back, rolling back, rolling up; reflex action

replic·ō -āre *vt* to fold back, unfold, turn back

rēp·ō -ĕre -sī *vi* to creep, crawl

re·pōnō -pōnĕre -posŭī -positum or **repostum** *vt* to put back, set back, lay (*e.g., the head*) back; to replace; to restore; to substitute; to lay out, stretch out (*the body*); to lay aside, store, keep, preserve; to lay aside, put away; to renew, repeat; to place, class; to replay, requite;

in sceptra reponere to reinstate in power; **membra reponere** (with *abl* or **in** + *abl*) to stretch out on (*e.g., a bed*); **se in cubitum reponere** to rest on one's elbow, prop oneself up on one's elbow; **spem reponere** (with **in** + *abl*) to put one's hope in or on, count on

report·ō -āre *vt* to bring back; to report; to carry off, gain, obtain; **victoriam reportare** to win a victory

reposc·ō -ĕre *vt* to demand back; to ask for, claim, require, demand

reposĭt·us -a -um *pp of* **repono**; *adj* distant, remote

repost·or -ōris *m* restorer

repostus *pp of* **repono**

repōtĭ·a -ōrum *n pl* second round of drinks

repraesentātĭ·ō -ōnis *f* vivid presentation; cash payment

repraesent·ō -āre *vt* to present again, show, exhibit, display, depict; to pay in cash; to do immediately, accomplish instantly, do on the spot; to rush, speed up (*e.g., plans*); to anticipate; to apply (*medicines*) immediately

repreh·endō or **repr·endō -endĕre -endī -ensum** *vt* to hold back; to restrain, check; to blame, find fault with, rebuke, criticize; (law) to prosecute, convict, condemn; to refute

reprehensĭ·ō -ōnis *f* checking, check; interruption (*of a speech*); blame, rebuke, criticism; refutation

reprehens·ō -āre *vt* to hold back continually; to detain from time to time

reprehens·or -ōris *m* critic

repress·or -ōris *m* restrainer

re·primō -primĕre -pressī -pressum *vt* to hold back, keep back; to restrain, limit, confine, curb, repress, suppress; **se reprimere** to control oneself; **se reprimere** (with **ab** + *abl*) to refrain from

reprōmissĭ·ō -ōnis *f* return promise

reprō·mittō -mittĕre -mīsī -missum *vt* to promise in return

rept·ō -āre *vi* to creep or crawl around

repudiātĭ·ō -ōnis *f* repudiation; refusal, rejection

repudĭ·ō -āre *vt* to repudiate, scorn; to refuse, reject; to jilt; to divorce

repudiōs·us -a -um *adj* objectionable, offensive

repud·ium -ĭī or **-ĭ** *n* repudiation, separation, divorce; **repudium renuntiare** or **repudium remittĕre** (with *dat*) to send a letter of divorce to, divorce

repuerasc·ō -ĕre *vi* to become a child again; to behave childishly

repugn·ans -antis *n* contradiction

repugnanter *adv* reluctantly

repugnantĭ·a -ae *f* incompatibility

repugn·ō -āre *vi* to fight back; (with *dat*) **a** to oppose, offer opposition to, fight against, be against; **b** to disagree with, be inconsistent with, be incompatible with; (with **con-tra** + *acc*) to fight against

repuls·a -ae *f* defeat at the polls; rebuff, cold shoulder; **repulsa con-sulatūs** defeat in running for the consulship; **repulsam ferre** to lose an election

repuls·ans -antis *adj* throbbing; re-echoing

repulsus *pp* of **repello**

repuls·us -ūs *m* reverberation, echo

repung·ō -ĕre *vt* to goad again

repurg·ō -āre *vt* to clean or clear again; to purge away, remove

reputātī·ō -ōnis *f* reconsideration, review

reput·ō -āre *vt* to count back, cal-culate; to think over, reflect upon, reconsider

requi·ēs -ētis *f* rest, relief; relaxa-tion, recreation

requi·escō -escĕre -ēvī -ētum *vt* to put to rest, quiet down, calm down; *vi* to rest, take a rest, come to rest, stop, end; to rest, relax; to find rest, be consoled, find relief; to rest, lie quietly, sleep; (of the dead) to rest, sleep

requiēt·us -a -um *adj* rested up, re-freshed

requirīt·ō -āre *vt* to keep asking for, be on a constant lookout for

re·quirō -quirĕre -quisīvī or -quisiī -quisītum *vt* to look for, search for, hunt for; to look around for, miss; to ask; to ask for, demand, re-quire; (with **ab** or **de** + *abl*) to ask or demand (*something*) from or of

rēs reī or **rēī** *f* thing, matter, affair, object, business, circumstance, event, occurrence, deed, condition, case; reality, truth, fact; property, possessions, estate, effects; benefit, advantage, interest, profit; business affair, transaction; cause, reason, motive, ground; (law) case, suit; (mil) operation, campaign, battle; state, government, politics; histori-cal event; theme, topic, subject mat-ter; **ab re** contrary to interests, dis-advantageous, useless; **contra rem publicam** unconstitutional(ly), contrary to public interests; **eā re** therefore, for that reason; **ex re** according to the circumstances, ac-cording to the situation; **ex re is-tius** for his good; **ex re publicā** constitutionally, for the common good, in the public interest; **ex tuā re** to your advantage; **in re** in fact, in reality; **in rem** for the good; useful, advantageous; **ob eam rem** for that reason; **ob rem** to the pur-pose; **pro re** according to circum-stances; **re** in fact, in practice, in reality, in truth, actually, really; **rem gerere** to conduct a military operation; **rerum potiri** to get control of the government; **rerum scriptor** historian, annalist; **res est mihi tecum** I have some busi-

ness with you; **res sit mihi cum his** let me handle them; **res fru-mentaria** foraging; grain situa-tion, grain supply; **res gestae** exploits, achievements, military achievements; **res judiciaria** ad-ministration of justice, department of justice; **res novae** revolution; **res pecuaria et rustica** livestock; **res Persicae** Persian history, Par-thian history; **res rustica** agricul-ture; **res publica** state, govern-ment, politics, public life, common-wealth, country; **res secundae** prosperous times, prosperity; **res uxoria** marriage; dowry; **summa rerum** world; universe

resăcr·ō -āre *vt* to ask again for; to free from a curse

resaev·iō -īre *vi* to go wild again

resalūt·ō -āre *vt* to greet in return

resān·escō -escĕre -ŭī *vi* to heal up again

re·sarciō -sarcīre — -sartum *vt* to patch up, repair; to make good (*a loss*)

re·scindō -scindĕre -scĭdī -scis-sum *vt* to tear off; to cut down; to tear open; to rescind, repeal, abro-gate; (fig) to tear open, expose

re·sciscō -sciscĕre -scīvī or -sciī -scītum *vt* to find out, learn, ascer-tain

re·scrībō -scrībĕre -scripsī -scriptum *vt* to write back in re-ply; to rewrite, revise; to enlist, en-roll; to repay, pay back; *vi* to write a reply

rescript·um -ī *n* imperial rescript

resĕc·ō -āre -ŭī -tum *vt* to cut back, cut short; to reap; (fig) to trim, cur-tail; **ad vivum resecare** to cut to the quick

resĕcr·ō or **resăcr·ō -āre** *vt* to ask again for; to free from a curse

resectus *pp* of **reseco**

resecūtus *pp* of **resequor**

resēmin·ō -āre *vt* to reproduce

re·sĕquor -sĕquī -secūtus sum *vt* to reply to, answer

resĕr·ō -āre *vt* to unlock, unbar, open; to disclose; to open, begin (*a year*)

reserv·ō -āre *vt* to reserve, hold back; to spare; to hold on to

res·es -ĭdis *adj* remaining, left; lazy, idle, inactive; slow, sluggish; calm

re·sĭdĕō -sĭdēre -sēdī *vi* to remain seated; to stay behind, be left, re-main; to tarry, linger; to stay, re-side

re·sīdō -sīdĕre -sēdī *vi* to sit down, settle back; to sink down, sink, set-tle, subside; to calm down

resĭdŭ·us -a -um *adj* remaining, left; in arrears, outstanding (*mon-ey*); *n* the remainder, rest

resign·ō -āre *vt* to unseal, open; to disclose, reveal; to give up, resign; to annul, cancel; to destroy (*confi-dence*)

resil·iō -īre -ŭī *vi* to spring back,

jump back; to recoil; to contract; to shrink back

resĭm·us -a -um *adj* turned up, snub

rēsīn·a -ae *f* resin

resīnāt·us -a -um *adj* resined, rubbed with resin

resĭp·ĭō -ĕre *vt* to taste of, have the flavor of

resĭp·iscō -iscĕre -īvī or **-ĭī** or **-ŭī** *vi* to come to one's senses

resĭst·ens -entis *adj* firm, tough

re·sistō -sistĕre -stĭtī *vi* to stand still, stop, pause; to stay, stay behind, remain, continue; to resist, put up resistance; to rise again; (with *dat*) **a** to be opposed to, resist; **b** to reply to

re·solvō -solvĕre -solvī -solūtum *vt* to untie, unfasten, undo; to open; to dissolve, melt, thaw; to relax (*the body*); stretch out (*the limbs*); to unravel; to cancel; to dispel; to unnerve, enervate; to release, set free

resonābĭl·is -e *adj* resounding, answering (*echo*)

resŏn·ō -āre *vt* to repeat, reecho, resound with, make ring; *vi* to resound, ring, reecho; (with *dat* or **ad** + *acc*) to resound in answer to

resŏn·us -a -um *adj* resounding, reechoing

resorb·ĕō -ēre *vt* to suck in, swallow again

respect·ō -āre *vt* to look back on; to keep an eye on, care for; to have regard for; to gaze at, look at; *vi* to look back; to look around

respectus *pp* of **respicio**

respect·us -ūs *m* backward glance, looking back; looking around; refuge, asylum; regard, respect, consideration; **respectum habere** (with *dat* or **ad** + *acc*) to have respect for

re·spergō -spergĕre -spersī spersum *vt* to sprinkle, splash, spray; to defile

respersĭ·ō -ōnis *f* sprinkling, splashing

respersus *pp* of **respergo**

re·spiciō -spicĕre -spexī -spectum *vt* to look back at, see behind oneself; to look back for, look around for; to look back upon (*the past, etc.*); to look at, gaze at, look upon, regard, contemplate, consider; to notice; to look after, take care of, see to; to respect; *vi* to look back; to look around; (with **ad** + *acc*) to look at, gaze at

respīrām·en -ĭnis *n* windpipe

respīrātĭ·ō -ōnis *f* respiration, breathing; exhalation; letup, rest, pause (*to catch one's breath*), breathing space

respīrāt·us -ūs *m* respiration

respīr·ō -āre *vt* to breathe, breathe out, exhale; *vi* to breathe, take a breath; to catch one's breath, breathe again, recover (*from fright, etc.*); (of combat, passions, etc.) to slack off, die down, subside; **a con-**

tinuis clādibus respirare to catch one's breathe again after continuous fighting; **ab metu respirare** to breathe again after a shock

resplend·ĕō -ēre *vi* to glitter

re·spondĕō -spondēre -spondī -sponsum *vt* to answer; to say in reply; **ficta respondere** to make up answers; **multa respondere** to give a lengthy reply; **par parī respondere** to answer tit for tat; **verbum verbo respondere** to answer word for word; *vi* to answer, respond, reply; to echo; (law) to answer (*to bail*), appeal (*in court*); (of lawyers) to give an opinion, give legal advice; (of priests, oracles) to give a response; (with *dat*) **a** to answer, reply to; **b** to match, balance, correspond to, be equal to, resemble, measure up to; **amorī amore respondere** to return love for love

responsĭ·ō -ōnis *f* response, answer, reply; refutation; **sibi ipsī responsio** a reply to one's own arguments

responsĭt·ō -āre *vi* to give professional advice

respons·ō -āre *vi* to answer, reply; to reecho; (with *dat*) **a** to answer to, agree with; **b** to resist, defy; **c** to answer back to (*in disobedience or defiance*)

respons·or -ōris *m* answerer

respons·us -a -um *pp* of **respondeo**; *n* answer, response, reply; professional advice, oracular response; **responsum auferre** or **ferre** (with **ab** + *abl*) to receive an answer from; **responsum referre** to deliver an answer

rēspūblĭca reīpūblĭcae *f* state, government, politics, public life, commonwealth, country

respŭ·ō -ĕre -ī *vt* to spit out, cast out, eject, expel; to reject, refuse, dislike, spurn

restāgn·ō -āre *vi* to form pools; to run over, overflow; to be inundated

restaur·ō -āre *vt* to restore, rebuild

restĭcŭl·a -ae *f* thin rope, cord

restinctĭ·ō -ōnis *f* quenching

re·stinguō -stinguĕre -stinxī -stinctum *vt* to quench, extinguish, put out; to snuff out, extinguish, exterminate, destroy

restĭ·ō -ōnis *m* rope maker; (coll) roper (*person who whipped with ropes*)

restipŭlātĭ·ō -ōnis *f* counterclaim

restipŭl·or -ārī -ātus sum *vt* to stipulate in return

rest·is -is *f* rope

restĭt·ō -āre *vi* to stay behind, lag behind, hold back, hang back

restītr·ix -īcis *f* stay-behind (*female*)

re·stitŭō -stitŭĕre -stitŭī -stitūtum *vt* to set up again; to restore, rebuild, reconstruct; to renew, reestablish, revive; to bring back, restore, reinstate; to give back, return, replace; to restore, repair, remedy; to reenact (*a law*); to reverse, revoke, make void, undo, cancel; to make good, compensate for, repair

restitūtī·ō -ōnis *f* restoration; reinstatement, pardon; recall (*from exile*)

restitūt·or -ōris *m* restorer, rebuilder

restitūtus *pp of* **restituo**

re·stō -stāre -stitī *vi* to stand firm, stand one's ground, resist; to stay behind, stay in reserve; to be left, be left over; *v impers* (with *inf* or *ut*) it remains to (*do something*)

restrictē *adv* sparingly; exactly, precisely

restrict·us -a -um *adj* tied back, tight; stingy; moderate; strict, stern

re·stringō -stringĕre -strinxī -strictum *vt* to draw back tightly, tie back, tighten; (of dogs) to show (*the teeth*); (fig) to restrain

resūd·ō -āre *vt & vi* to sweat

resultō -āre *vi* to rebound; to reverberate, resound

re·sūmō -sūmĕre -sumpsī -sumptum *vt* to take up again, resume; to recover (*strength*)

resupīn·ō -āre *vt* to throw (*someone*) on his back, throw over, throw down; (coll) to knock for a loop; to break down (*doors*)

resupīn·us -a -um *adj* bent back, thrown back; supine, lying on the back; leaning backward; proud, haughty (*gait*)

re·surgō -surgĕre -surrexī -surrectum *vi* to rise again, appear again

resuscit·ō -āre *vt* to resuscitate, revive, renew

retardāti·ō -ōnis *f* retarding, delaying

retard·ō -āre *vt* to slow down, retard, hold back, delay, keep back, check, hinder

rēt·e -is *n* net; (fig) trap

re·tegō -tegĕre -texī -tectum *vt* to uncover; to open

retempt·ō -āre *vt* to attempt again, try again, test again

re·tendō -tendĕre -tendī -tentum or **-tensum** *vt* to release from tension, unbend, relax

retenti·ō -ōnis *f* holding back, slowing down; withholding (*of assent*)

retent·ō -āre *vt* to hold back, hold tight; to attempt again, try again, test again

retentus *pp of* **retendo** *and* **retineo**

re·texō -texĕre -texuī -textum *vt* to unravel; to cancel, annul, reverse, undo; to weave anew; to renew, repeat; to correct, revise; to take back, retract (*words*)

rētiār·ius -iī or **-ī** *m* gladiator who tried to entangle his opponent in a net

reticenti·a -ae *f* reticence, silence; (rhet) abrupt pause; **poena reticentiae** punishment for suppressing the truth

retic·ĕō -ēre *vt* to be silent about, suppress, keep secret; *vi* to be silent, keep silence; (with *dat*) to make no answer to

rētĭcŭl·um -ī *n* small net; hair net; network bag, reticule (*for protecting bottles*); racket (*for playing ball*)

retināculra -ōrum *n pl* cable, rope, hawser, tether

retin·ens -entis *adj* (with *genit*) clinging to

retinenti·a -ae *f* recollection, retention

re·tinĕō -tinēre -tinŭī -tentum *vt* to hold back, keep back; to restrain; to keep, retain; to hold in reserve; to keep, preserve, maintain, uphold; to hold, engross (*attention*); to detain, delay

retinn·iō -īre *vi* to ring again, ring out

retōn·ō -āre *vi* to resound

re·torquĕō -torquēre -torsī -tortum *vt* to twist or bend back; to hurl back (*weapons*); **mentem retorquere** to change the mind; **oculos retorquere** (with *ad* + *acc*) to look back wistfully at

retorrid·us -a -um *adj* parched, dried out, withered; wily, old, shrewd

retortus *pp of* **retorqueo**

retractāti·ō -ōnis *f* rehandling, retreatment; hesitation

retract·ō or **retract·ō -āre** *vt* to rehandle, take in hand again, undertake once more, take up once more; to reexamine, review; to revise; *vi* to refuse, decline; to be reluctant

retract·us -a -um *adj* withdrawn, distant, remote

re·trāhō -trahĕre -traxī -tractum *vt* to draw back, withdraw, drag back; to bring to light again, make known again; (fig) to drag away, divert, remove, turn

retrectō *see* **retracto**

retrib·ŭō -ŭĕre -ŭī -ūtum *vt* to give back, restore, repay

retrō *adv* backwards, back, to the rear; behind, on the rear; in the past, formerly, back, past; in return, on the contrary, on the other hand

retrorsum or **retrorsus** *adv* back, backwards, behind; in reversed order

re·trūdō -trūdĕre — -trūsum *vt* to push back; to hide, conceal

retundō retundĕre retŭdī (or **rettūdī**) **retunsum** (or **retūsum**) *vt* to pound back; to dull, blunt; (fig) to deaden, weaken, repress, restrain

retuns·us or **retūs·us -a -um** *adj* blunt, dull; (fig) dull

re·us -ī *m* defendant, plaintiff, the accused; convict, criminal, culprit

reval·escō -ēscĕre -ŭī *vi* to regain one's strength, recover; to become valid again

re·vĕhō -vehĕre -vexī -vectum *vt* to carry back, bring back; **revehi** to ride or drive back, sail back; (fig) to go back (*e.g., to an earlier period*)

re·vellō -vellĕre -vellī -vulsum *vt* to pull out, pull back, tear off, tear out; to tear up (*the ground*), dig up; (fig) to abolish, remove

revēl·ō -āre *vt* to unveil, uncover

re·veniō -venīre -vēnī -ventum *vi* to come again, come back, return

rēvērā *adv* in fact, actually

rēverbĕr·ō -āre *vt* to beat back, repel

reverend·us -a -um *adj* venerable, awe-inspiring

revĕr·ens -entis *adj* reverent, respectful

reverenter *adv* respectfully

reverenti·a -ae *f* awe, respect, reverence

revĕr·ĕor -ērī -ĭtus sum *vt* to revere, respect, stand in awe of

reversi·ō or **revorsi·ō -ōnis** *f* turning back (*before reaching one's destination*); recurrence (*of fever, etc.*)

revert·ō -ĕre -ī or **re·vertor** (or **re·vortor**) **-vertī -versus sum** *vi* to turn back, turn around, come back, return; (in speaking) to return, revert, recur

revictus *pp* of **revinco**

revid·ĕō -ēre *vt* to go back to see, revisit

re·vinciō -vincīre -vinxī -vinctum *vt* to tie back, tie behind, tie up

re·vincō -vincĕre -vīcī -victum *vt* to conquer, crush, repress; to refute, disprove, convict

revinctus *pp* of **revincio**

revir·escō -ēscĕre -ŭī *vi* to grow green again, become green again; to grow young again; to grow again, grow strong again, revive

revīs·ō -ĕre *vt* to go to see again, revisit; to look back to see; *vi* to come or go back; (with **ad** + *acc*) **a** to look at again, look back at; **b** to return to, revisit

re·vīviscō or **re·vīvescō -vīvescĕre -vixī** *vi* to come back to life, be restored to life, revive; (fig) to revive, recover, gain strength

revocābil·is -e *adj* revocable, capable of being recalled

revocām·en -inis *n* recall

revocāti·ō -ōnis *f* calling back, calling away, recall; revoking, retracting (*of a word*)

revŏc·ō -āre *vt* to call back, recall; to recall, call off, withdraw (*troops*); to call back (*an actor, singer*) for an encore; to bring back to life, revive; (law) to arraign again; to recover, regain (*strength, etc.*); to resume (*career, studies*); to revoke, retract;

to check, control; to cancel; (with **ad** + *acc*) to refer, apply, subject, submit (*someone or something*) to

revŏl·ō -āre *vi* to fly back

revolsus see **revulsus**

revolūbil·is -e *adj* able to be rolled back; **non revolubilis** irrevocable (*fate*)

re·volvō -volvĕre -volvī -volūtum *vt* to roll back, unroll, unwind; to retravel (*a road*); to unroll, read over, read again (*a book*); to reexperience; to go over, think over; **revolvi** to revolve, come around again, recur, return

revŏm·ō -ĕre -ŭī *vt* to vomit forth again, disgorge

revor- = **rever-**

revorr·ō -ĕre *vt* to sweep back, scatter again

revulsus *pp* of **revello**

rex rēgis *m* king; (with bad connotations during the republican period) tyrant, dictator; patron; rich man; leader, king (*in children's game*); queen bee

Rhadamanth·us -ī *m* son of Jupiter, brother of Minos, and one of the three judges in the lower world

Rhaet·ī -ōrum *m pl* people of Raetia

Rhaeti·a -ae *f* Alpine country between Germany and Italy

rhapsōdi·a -ae *f* Homeric lay, selection from Homer

Rhe·a -ae *f* Cybele

Rhe·a Silvi·a -ae *f* daughter of Numitor and mother of Romulus and Remus

rhēd- = **raed-**

Rhēg·ĭum -ĭī or **-ī** *n* town on the toe of Italy

rhēn·ō -ōnis *m* fur

Rhēnān·us -a -um *adj* Rhenish

Rhēn·us -ī *m* Rhine

Rhēs·us -ī *m* Thracian king who fought as an ally of Troy

rhēt·or -ŏris *m* rhetorician, teacher of rhetoric; orator

rhētoric·a -ae or **rhētoric·ē -ēs** *f* rhetoric

rhētoric·a -ōrum *n pl* treatise on rhetoric

rhētoricē *adv* rhetorically, in an oratorical manner

rhētoric·us -a -um *adj* rhetorician's, rhetorical; **doctores rhetorici** rhetoric professors; **libri rhetorici** rhetoric textbooks

rhīnocĕr·ōs -ōtis *m* rhinoceros; vessel made of a rhinoceros's tusk

rhō (indecl) *n* seventeenth letter of the Greek alphabet

Rhŏdăn·us -ī *m* Rhone

Rhodiens·is -e or **Rhodi·us -a -um** *adj* Rhodian, of Rhodes; *m pl* Rhodians

Rhodŏp·ē -ēs *f* mountain range in Thrace

Rhodopēi·us -a -um *adj* Thracian

Rhod·os or **Rhod·us -ī** *f* Rhodes (*island off the coast of Asia Minor*)

Rhoetē·us -a -um *adj* Trojan;

Rhoeteus ductor Aeneas: *m* promontory on the Dardanelles near Troy; sea near the promontory of Rhoeteum

rhomb·us -ī *m* magic wheel; turbot (*fish*)

rhomphae·a -ae *f* long javelin

rhythmic·us -a -um *adj* rhythmical; *m* teacher of prose rhythm

rhythm·os or **rhythm·us -ī** *m* rhythm, symmetry

rīc·a -ae *f* veil (*worn by Roman women at sacrifices*)

rīcin·ium -iī or **-ī** *n* short mantle with a cowl

rict·um -ī *n* snout; wide-open mouth

rict·us -ūs *m* snout; wide-open mouth; **risū rictum diducere** to break into a grin; *m pl* jaws, gaping jaws

rīdeō rīdēre rīsī rīsum *vt* to laugh at, ridicule; to smile upon; *vi* to smile, laugh; (with *dat* or **ad** + *acc*) to smile to

rīdibund·us -a -um *adj* laughing

rīdiculāri·us -a -um *adj* laughable, funny; *n pl* jokes

rīdiculē *adv* jokingly, humorously; ridiculously, absurdly

rīdiculōs·us -a -um *adj* funny, amusing; ridiculous

rīdicul·us -a -um *adj* funny, amusing, laughable; ridiculous, silly; *m* joker, clown; *n* joke

rig·ens -entis *adj* stiff, rigid, unbending

rig·eō -ēre *vi* to be still, be numb, stiffen; to be rigid, stand on end, stand erect; to stand stiff, rise

rig·escō -escēre -uī *vi* to grow stiff, become numbed, stiffen, harden; to stand on end

rigidē *adv* rigorously, severely

rigid·us -a -um *adj* rigid, stiff, hard, inflexible; stern, rigid, severe; rough, rude

rig·ō -āre *vt* to wet, moisten, water; to conduct, convey (*water*)

rig·or -ōris *m* stiffness; numbness, cold; hardness; sternness, severity

rigu·us -a -um *adj* irrigating, watering; irrigated, watered

rīm·a -ae *f* crack; **rimas agere** to be cracked

rīm·or -ārī -ātus sum *vt* to lay open, tear open; to pry into, search, tear at, examine; to ransack; **naribus rimari** to sniff at

rīmōs·us -a -um *adj* full of cracks, leaky

ringor ringī rictus sum *vi* to open the mouth wide, to show the teeth; to snarl; (fig) to be snappy, snarl

rīp·a -ae *f* bank, shore

rīpūl·a -ae *f* river bank

risc·us -ī *m* chest, trunk

rīsiōn·ēs -um *f pl* laughs

rīs·or -ōris *m* scoffer, teaser

rīs·us -ūs *m* laugh, smile, laughter; laughingstock; **risum continere** to keep back a laugh, keep from laughing; **risum movere** (with *dat*

of person) to make (*someone*) laugh; **risūs captare** to try to make people laugh, try to get laughs

rīte *adv* according to religious usage; duly, justly, rightly, fitly; in the usual way, customarily

rīt·us -ūs *m* ceremony, rite; custom, habit, way, manner, style; **ritū** (with *genit*) in the manner of, like; **pecudum ritū** like cattle

rīvāl·is -is *m* one who uses the same stream, neighbor; one who uses the same mistress, rival

rīvālit·ās -ātis *f* rivalry in love

rīvūl·us or **rīvōl·us -ī** *m* brook, rivulet

rīv·us -ī *m* brook, stream

rix·a -ae *f* brawl, fight; quarrel, squabble

rix·or -ārī -ātus sum *vi* to brawl, come to blows, fight; to quarrel, squabble

rōbiginōs·us or **rūbiginōs·us -a -um** *adj* rusty; envious

rōbig·ō -inis *f* rust; blight, mildew; film (*on teeth*), tartar

rōbore·us -a -um *adj* oak, of oak

rōbor·ō -āre *vt* to make strong, strengthen

rōb·ur or **rōb·us -oris** *n* hard wood; oak; prison (*at Rome, also called Tullianum*); objects made of hard wood: lance, club, bench; physical strength, power, vigor, toughness; vigor, strength, power, quality (*of mind*); best part, flower, choice, cream, élite; stronghold

rōbust·us -a -um *adj* hardwood; oak; robust, strong, firm, tough (*body*); firm, vigorous, solid (*character*)

rōdō rōdēre rōsī rōsum *vt* to gnaw, gnaw at; to rust, corrode; to say nasty things about, slander, run down

rogāl·is -e *adj* of a pyre

rogāti·ō -ōnis *f* proposal, referendum, bill, resolution; request; (rhet) question; **rogationem ferre** to introduce a bill; **rogationem perferre** to pass a bill; **rogationem suadere** to back, push, speak in favor of a bill; **rogationi intercedere** to veto a bill

rogātiuncul·a -ae *f* inconsequential bill; little question

rogāt·or -ōris *m* proposer (*of a bill to the people*); poll clerk (*who collected and counted votes*); beggar

rogāt·us -ūs *m* request

rogitāti·ō -ōnis *f* proposal

rogit·ō -āre *vt* to keep asking, keep asking for

rog·ō -āre *vt* to ask, ask for, beg, request, solicit, question; to invite; to nominate for election; to bring forward for approval, introduce, propose (*bill or resolution*); (with double *acc*) to ask (*someone for something*), ask (*someone something*); **legem rogare** to introduce a bill; **milites sacramento rogare** to swear in soldiers; **senatorem sententiam rogare** to ask a senator for his opinion, ask a senator how he votes; **sententias rogare** to call the roll (*in the senate*); **populum rogare** to ask the people about a bill, to propose or introduce a bill; **primus sententiam rogari** to have the honor of being the first (*senator*) to be asked his view, be the first to vote

rog·us -ī *m* funeral pile, pyre; (fig) grave, destruction

Rōm·a -ae *f* Rome

Rōmān·us -a -um *adj* Roman; *m pl* Romans

Rōmŭlē·us -a -um *adj* of Romulus

Rōmŭlĭd·ae -ārum *m pl* descendants of Romulus, Romans

Rōmŭl·us -a -um *adj* of Romulus; *m* Romulus (*son of Rhea Silvia and Mars, twin brother of Remus, and founder as well as first king of Rome*)

rōrāri·ī -ōrum *m pl* skirmishers (*light-armed Roman troops who usually initiated an attack and then withdrew*)

rōrĭd·us -a -um *adj* dewy

rōrĭf·er -ěra -ěrum *adj* dew-bringing, dewy

rōr·ō -āre *vt* to drip, trickle, pour drop by drop; to moisten; *vi* to drop dew, scatter dew

rōs rōris *m* dew; moisture; water; teardrop; **ros Arabus** perfume; **ros marinus** or **ros maris** rosemary; **rores pluvii** rain drops; **rores sanguinei** drops of blood

ros·a -ae *f* rose; rose bush; rose bed; wreath of roses

rosār·ium -iī or **-ī** *n* rose garden

roscĭd·us -a -um *adj* dewy; moistened, sprayed

Rosc·ius -iī or **-ī** *m* L. Roscius Otho (*friend of Cicero, whose law in 67 B.C. reserved fourteen rows of seats in the theater for members of equestrian order*); Q. Roscius (*famous Roman actor and friend of Cicero, d. 62 B.C.*); Sextus Roscius (*of Ameria, defended by Cicero in a patricide trial in 80 B.C.*)

rosēt·um -ī *n* rose bed, rose garden

rosě·us -a -um *adj* rosy, rose-colored; of roses

rosmarīn·um -ī *n* rosemary (*spice*)

rostrāt·us -a -um *adj* beaked; (ship) having a pointed bow; **columna rostrata** column adorned with the beaks of conquered vessels to commemorate a naval victory; **corona rostrata** navy medal (*awarded to the first man to board the enemy's ship*)

rostr·um -ī *n* bill, beak; snout, muzzle; curved bow (*of a ship*); *n pl* speaker's stand in the Roman Forum (*so called because it was adorned with the beaks of ships taken from the battle of Antium, 338 B.C.*)

rōsus *pp* of **rodo**

rot·a -ae *f* wheel; potter's wheel; torture wheel; disk; chariot, car

rot·ō -āre *vt* to turn, whirl about; **rotari** to roll around; to revolve

rotŭl·a -ae *f* little wheel

rotundē *adv* smoothly, elegantly

rotund·ō -āre *vt* to make round, round off; to round out, complete

rotund·us -a -um *adj* rolling, revolving; round, circular, spherical; rounded, perfect; well-turned, smooth, polished, balanced (*style*)

rube·faciō -facěre -fēcī -factum *vt* to make red, redden

rubell·us -a -um *adj* reddish

rub·ens -entis *adj* red; blushing

rub·ěō -ēre *vi* to be red, be ruddy; to be bloody; to blush

rub·er -ra -rum *adj* red; ruddy

rub·escō -escěre -ŭī *vi* to grow red, redden; to blush

rubēt·a -ae *f* toad

rubēt·a -ōrum *n pl* bramble bush

rubě·us -a -um *adj* bramble, of brambles

Rubic·ō -ōnis *m* small stream marking the boundary between Italy and Cisalpine Gaul

rubicundŭl·us -a -um *adj* reddish

rubicund·us -a -um *adj* red; ruddy

rubĭd·us -a -um *adj* reddish, red

rūbig- = robig-

rub·or -ōris *m* redness; blush; bashfulness, sense of shame; shame, disgrace

rubric·a -ae *f* red clay; red ochre; red chalk; rubric, law

rub·us -ī *m* bramble bush; blackberry bush; blackberry

ruct·ō -āre or **ruct·or -ārī -ātus sum** *vt & vi* to belch

ruct·us -ūs *m* belch, belching

rud·ens -entis *m* rope; *m pl* rigging

Rudi·ae -ārum *f pl* town in Calabria in S. Italy (*birthplace of Ennius*)

rudiār·ius -iī or **-ī** *m* retired gladiator

rudiment·um -ī *n* first attempt, beginning, commencement; **rudimentum adulescentiae ponere** to pass the novitiate; **rudimentum militare** basic training

Rudīn·us -a -um *adj* of Rudiae

rud·is -e *adj* in the natural state; raw, undeveloped, rough, wild, unformed; inexperienced, unskilled, ignorant, awkward, uncultured, uncivilized; (with *genit* or *abl*, with **ad** + *acc*, or with **in** + *abl*) inexperienced in, ignorant of, awkward at

rud·is -is *f* stick, rod; practice sword

rud·ō -ěre -īvī -ītum *vi* to roar, bellow, bray; to creak

rūd·us -ěris *n* crushed stone; rubble; rubbish; piece of brass or copper

rŭfŭl·us -a -um *adj* reddish

Rŭfŭl·ī -ōrum *m pl* military tribunes appointed by a general (*as opposed to military tribunes elected by the people*)

rūf·us -a -um *adj* red, reddish

rūg·a -ae *f* wrinkle

rūg·ō -āre *vi* to become wrinkled, become creased

rūgōs·us -a -um *adj* wrinkled, shriveled; corrugated

ruīn·a -ae *f* tumbling down, falling down, fall; collapse; debris, ruins; crash; catastrophe, disaster, destruction, defeat; wrecker, destroyer; **ruinam dare** or **trahere** to fall with a crash

ruinōs·us -a -um *adj* going to ruin, ruinous, ruined, tumbling, fallen

rum·ex -icis *f* sorrel

rūmific·ō -āre *vt* to report

Rūmin·a -ae *f* Roman goddess who was worshiped near the fig tree under which the she-wolf had suckled Romulus and Remus

Rūmināl·is -e *adj* **ficus Ruminalis** fig tree of Romulus and Remus

rūmināti·ō -ōnis *f* chewing of the cud; (fig) rumination

rūmin·ō -āre *vt* to chew again; *vi* to chew the cud

rūm·or -ōris *m* shouting, cheering, noise; rumor, hearsay; popular opinion, current opinion; reputation, fame; notoriety; calumny; **adverso rumore esse** to be in bad repute, be unpopular

rumpi·a -ae *f* long javelin

rumpō rumpĕre rūpī ruptum *vt* to break, break down, break open; to burst, burst through; to tear, split; to force, make (*e.g., a path*) by force; to break in on, interrupt, cut short; to break (*a law, treaty*); to break out in, utter (*complaints, etc.*)

rūmuscŭl·ī -ōrum *m pl* gossip

rūn·a -ae *f* dart

runc·ō -āre *vt* to weed, weed out

ru·ō -ĕre -ī -tum *vt* to throw down, hurl to the ground; to level (*e.g., sand dunes*); to destroy, overthrow, lay waste; to throw up, upturn, churn up; *vi* to fall hard, fall in ruins, totter; to run, dash, rush on, hurry; (of rain) to come pouring down; (of the sun) to set rapidly

rūp·ēs -is *f* cliff

rupt·or -ōris *m* breaker, violator

ruptus *pp* of **rumpo**

rūricŏl·a -ae *m* or *f* rustic, peasant, farmer; *m* ox

rūrigĕn·a -ae *m* rustic, peasant, farmer

rūr·ō -āre *vi* to live in the country

rursus or **rursum** or **rūsum** *adv* back, backwards; on the contrary, on the other hand, in turn; again, back again, once more; **rursus rursusque** again and again

rūs rūris *n* the country, countryside, lands, fields; farm, estate; **rure redire** to return from the country; **ruri** or **rure vitam agere** to live in the country; **rus ire** to go into the country; *n pl* countryside

rusc·um -ī *n* or **rusc·us -ī** *f* broom (*of twigs*)

russ·us -a -um *adj* red, russet

rusticān·us -a -um *adj* rustic, country, rural

rusticāti·ō -ōnis *f* country life

rusticē *adv* like a farmer; plainly, simply; unsophisticatedly, boorishly

rusticit·ās -ātis *f* simple country ways, rusticity; boorishness, coarseness

rustic·or -ārī -ātus sum *vi* to live in the country

rusticŭl·us -a -um *adj* somewhat coarse; *m* peasant

rustic·us -a -um *adj* of or in the country, country, rural; plain, simple, unspoiled, unsophisticated; coarse, boorish, rude; *m* farmer, peasant; *f* country girl

rūsum *see* **rursus**

rūt·a -ae *f* rue (*bitter herb*); bitterness, unpleasantness

rūt·a -ōrum *n pl* minerals; **ruta caesa** or **ruta et caesa** (law) everything mined or cut down on an estate, timber and minerals

rutil·ō -āre *vt* to make red, color red, dye red; *vi* to glow red

rutil·us -a -um *adj* red, reddish yellow; strawberry-blond

rutr·um -ī *n* spade

rūtŭl·a -ae *f* a bit of rue

Rutŭl·ī -ōrum *m pl* ancient people of Latium whose capital was Ardea

rutus *pp* of **ruo**

S

Sab·a -ae *f* town in Arabia Felix, famous for its incense

Sabae·us -a -um *adj* Sabaean

Sabāz·ius -iī or **-ī** *m* Bacchus; *n pl* festival in honor of Bacchus

sabbat·a -ōrum *n pl* Sabbath

sabbatārĭ·ī -ōrum *m pl* Sabbath-keepers, Jews

Sabell·us -a -um *adj* Sabellian, Sabine; *m* Sabine (*i.e., Horace*)

Sabīn·us -a -um *adj* & *mf* Sabine; *n* Sabine wine; Horace's Sabine estate

Sabrīn·a -ae *f* Severn River

saburr·a -ae *f* sand, ballast

saburr·ō -āre *vt* to ballast; (coll) to gorge with food

Sac·ae -ārum *m pl* Scythian tribe

saccipēr·ĭum -iī or **-ī** *n* purse pocket

sacc·ō -āre *vt* to filter, strain

saccŭl·us -ī m little bag; purse

sacc·us -ī m sack, bag; wallet; filter, strainer

sacell·um -ī n chapel

sac·er -ra -rum adj sacred, holy, consecrated; devoted to a deity for destruction, accursed; detestable; criminal, infamous; n see sacrum

sacerd·ōs -ōtis m priest; f priestess

sacerdōtāl·is -e adj sacerdotal

sacerdōt·ium -iī or -ī n priesthood

sacrāment·um -ī n guarantee, deposit (sum of money which each of the parties to a law suit deposited and which was forfeited by the loser); civil law suit; dispute; oath; voluntary oath of recruits; military oath; eum obligare militiae sacramento to swear him in; justis sacramentis contendere to argue on equal terms; omnes sacramento adigere or rogare to swear in everyone; sacramentum dicere to sign up, swear in; sacramentum dicere (with dat) to swear allegiance to (a general or emperor)

sacrār·ium -iī or -ī n sacristy; shrine, chapel

sacrāt·us -a -um adj hallowed, consecrated, holy, sacred

sacrif·er -ēra -ērum adj carrying sacred objects

sacrificāl·is -e adj sacrificial

sacrificātī·ō -ōnis f sacrifice, sacrificing

sacrific·ium -iī or -ī n sacrifice

sacrific·ō or sacrufic·ō -āre vt & vi to sacrifice

sacrificŭl·us -ī m sacrificing priest

sacrific·us -a -um adj sacrificial

sacrileg·ium -iī or -ī n sacrilege; temple robbing

sacrilĕg·us -a -um adj sacrilegious; profane, impious, wicked; m temple robber; wicked person; f impious woman

sacr·ō -āre vt to consecrate; to dedicate; to set apart, devote, give; to doom, curse; to hallow, declare inviolable; to hold sacred, worship; to immortalize

sacrōsanct·us -a -um adj sacred, inviolable, sacrosanct

sacrufīcō see sacrifico

sacr·um -ī n holy object, sacred vessel; holy place, temple, sanctuary; religious rite, act of worship, religious service, sacrifice; victim; n pl worship, religion; secret, mystery; sacra facere to sacrifice

saeclum see saeculum

saeculār·is or sēculār·is -e adj centennial

saecŭl·um or sēcŭl·um or saecl·um -ī n generation, lifetime; century; spirit of the age, fashion

saepe adv often

saepenumĕrō or saepe numĕrō adv very often, again and again, oftentimes

saep·ēs or sēp·ēs -is f hedge, fence, enclosure

saepīment·um or sēpīment·um -ī n hedge, fence, enclosure

saep·iō or sēp·iō -īre -sī -tum vt to fence in, hedge in, enclose; to surround, encircle; to guard, fortify, protect, strengthen

saept·um or sept·um -ī n fence, wall, enclosure; stake; sheepfold; voting booth; n pl enclosure; voting booths, polls

saet·a -ae or sēt·a -ae f stiff hair, bristle

saetig·er -ĕra -ĕrum adj bristly; m boar

saetōs·us -a -um adj bristly, hairy

saevē adv fiercely, savagely

saevidĭc·us -a -um adj spoken in anger, savage

saev·iō -īre -iī -itum vi to be fierce, be savage, be furious; (of persons) to be brutal, be violent

saevĭter adv savagely, ferociously, cruelly

saevitĭ·a -ae f rage, fierceness; brutality, savageness, barbarity (of persons)

saev·us -a -um adj raging, fierce, furious, cruel; brutal, savage, barbarous (persons)

sāg·a -ae f fortune-teller (female)

sagācit·ās -ātis f keenness; sagacity, keenness of perception, shrewdness

sagācĭter adv keenly; shrewdly, accurately, acutely, sagaciously

sagāt·us -a -um adj wearing a military coat

sag·ax -ācis adj keen, sharp, acute; intellectually quick, sharp, shrewd; prophetic

sagīn·a -ae f stuffing, cramming, fattening up; food, rations; rich food; fattened animal; fatness (from overeating)

sagīn·ō -āre vt to fatten

sāg·ĭō -īre vi to perceive quickly, catch on quickly

sagitt·a -ae f arrow

Sagitt·a -ae f Sagitta (constellation)

sagittārĭ·us -a -um adj of or for an arrow; m archer, bowman

Sagittār·ius -iī or -ī m Sagittarius (constellation)

sagittĭf·er -ĕra -ĕrum adj arrow-bearing

Sagittĭpōt·ens -entis m Sagittarius (constellation)

sagitt·ō -āre vt to shoot (arrows); vi to shoot arrows

sagm·en -ĭnis n tuft of sacred herbs (plucked in the Capitol by the consul or praetor and worn by the fetiales as a sign of inviolability)

sagŭl·um -ī n short military coat (esp. that of general officers)

sag·um -ī n coarse mantle; military uniform; ad sagum ire or sagum sumere to get into uniform; in sagis esse to be in uniform, be in the armed forces

Saguntīn·us -a -um *adj* & *m* Saguntine

Sagunt·um -ī *m* Saguntum (*city on the E. coast of Spain which Hannibal attacked and which thereby brought on the First Punic War*)

sāl salis *m* salt; salt water, sea water, sea; seasoning, flavor; good taste, elegance; pungency (*of words*), wit, humor; sarcasm; *m pl* witticisms, jokes, sarcastic remarks

salāc·ō -ōnis *m* braggart, show-off

salamandr·a -ae *f* salamander

Salamīni·us -a -um *adj* of Salamis; *m pl* people of Salamis

Salām·īs -īnis *f* island in the Saronic gulf near Athens; city in Cyprus founded by Teucer

salapūt·ium -iī or **-ī** *n* midget

Salāri·a -ae *f* Via Salaria (*from the Porta Collina to the Sabine district*)

salāri·us -a -um *adj* salt, of salt; **annona salaria** revenue from salt mines; *m* salt-fish dealer; *n* salary; allowance; a meal

sal·ax -ācis *adj* lustful; salacious, provocative

salēbr·a -ae *f* jolting; rut; harshness, roughness (*of speech*)

Saliār·is -e *adj* Salian, of the Salii; sumptuous

Saliāt·us -ūs *m* office of Salius, Salian priesthood

salict·um -ī *n* willow grove

salient·ēs -ium *f pl* springs, fountains

salign·us -a -um *adj* willow, of willow

Sali·ī -ōrum *m pl* college of twelve priests dedicated to Mars who went in solemn procession through Rome on the Kalends of March

salill·um -ī *n* small salt cellar

salīn·ae -ārum *f pl* salt pits, salt works; **salinae Romanae** salt works at Ostia (*a state monopoly*)

salīn·um -ī *n* salt cellar

sal·iō -īre -uī or **-iī -tum** *vi* to jump, leap, bound, hop

Salisubsul·ī -ōrum *m pl* dancing priests of Mars

saliunc·a -ae *f* wild nard (*aromatic plant*)

salīv·a -ae *f* saliva; taste, flavor

sal·ix -icis *f* willow tree

Sallust·ius -iī or **-ī** *m* Sallust (*C. Sallustius Crispus, a Roman historian, 86-35 B.C.*)

Salmāc·is -idis *f* fountain in Caria which made all who drank from it soft and effeminate

Salmōn·eus -ĕos *m* son of Aeolus and brother of Sisyphus who imitated lightning and was thrown by Jupiter into Tartarus

Salmōn·is -idis *f* Tyro (*daughter of Salmoneus*)

salsāment·um -ī *n* salted or pickled fish; brine

salsē *adv* facetiously, humorously

Salsipŏt·ens -entis *adj* ruling the sea

sals·us -a -um *adj* salted; briny, salty; facetious, humorous, sharp, witty; *n pl* salty food; witty remarks, satirical writings

saltātī·ō -ōnis *f* dancing, dance

saltāt·or -ōris *m* dancer

saltātōri·us -a -um *adj* dance, for dancing

saltātr·ix -īcis *f* dancing girl, dancer

saltāt·us -ūs *m* dance, religious dance

saltem *adv* at least, in any event, anyhow; **non saltem** not even

salt·ō -āre *vt* & *vi* to dance

saltuōs·us -a -um *adj* wooded, covered with forest

salt·us -ūs *m* wooded pasture, forest; upland; jungle; ravine; valley, glen; (coll) female organ; leap, leaping; **saltum dare** to leap

salūb·er (or **salūb·ris**) **-re** *adj* healthful, healthy, wholesome; (with *dat* or with **ad** + *acc*) healthful for, good for, beneficial to

salūbrit·ās -ātis *f* healthiness, wholesomeness; health, soundness

salūbriter *adv* healthfully; healthily; beneficially

sal·um -ī *n* seas, high seas

sal·ūs -ūtis *f* health; welfare; prosperity, safety; greeting, good wish, best regards; **salutem dicere** (abbreviated **s. d.**) to say hello, send greetings; (at the end of a letter) to say good-bye; **salutem magnam dicere** to send warm greetings; (at the end of a letter) to say good-bye; **salutem plurimam dicere** (abbreviated **s.p.d.**) to send warmest greetings; (at the end of a letter) to give best regards

salūtār·is -e *adj* salutary, healthful, wholesome; beneficial, advantageous, useful; **ars salutaris** art of healing; **salutaris littera** vote of acquittal

salūtāriter *adv* beneficially, profitably, advantageously

salūtātī·ō -ōnis *f* greeting, salutation; formal morning reception or morning call at the house of an important person; callers; **ubi salutatio defluxit** when the morning callers have dispersed

salūtāt·or -ōris *m* or **salūtātr·ix -īcis** *f* morning caller

salūtif·er -ĕra -ĕrum *adj* health-giving

salūtigerŭl·us -a -um *adj* bringing greetings

salūt·ō -āre *vt* to greet, wish well, salute; to send greetings to; to visit, pay respects to, pay a morning call on; to pay reverence to (*gods*); to greet, welcome; (with double *acc*) to salute as, hail as, e.g., **aliquem imperatorem salutare** to hail someone as a victorious general

salvē *adv* well; in good health; **satine salve?** (coll) everything O.K.?

salv·ĕō -ēre *vi* to be well, be in good

health; to be getting along well; **salve, salvete,** or **salveto!** hello!, good morning!, good day!; good-bye!; **te salvere jubeo** I bid you good day

salv·us -a -um or **salv·os -a -um** or **-om** *adj* well, sound, safe, unharmed, unscathed; living, alive; (with substantive in an *abl* absolute) without violation of, without breaking, e.g., **salvā lege** without breaking the law; **salvos sum** (coll) I'm all right, I'm O.K.

sambūc·a -ae *f* triangular stringed instrument, harp

sambūcin·a -ae *f* harpist (*female*)

sambūcistri·a -ae *f* harpist (*female*)

Sam·ē -ēs *f* ancient name of the island of Cephallenia

Sami·us -a -um *adj* of Samos; **Juno Samia** Juno worshiped at Samos; **vir Samius** Pythagoras

Samn·īs -ītis *adj* Samnite; *m* Samnite gladiator; *m pl* Samnites

Samn·ium -iī or **-ī** *n* district of central Italy

Sam·os or **Sam·us -ī** *f* island off the W. coast of Asia Minor, famous for temple to Juno and as the birthplace of Pythagoras

Samothrāc·ēs -um *m pl* Samothracians

Samothrācī·us -a -um *adj* Samothracian; *f* Samothrace (*island in the N. Aegean*)

sānābil·is -e *adj* curable

sānāti·ō -ōnis *f* healing, curing

sanciō sancīre sanxī sanctum *vt* to consecrate, hallow, make inviolable; to ratify; to condemn; (with *abl*) to forbid under penalty of

sanctē *adv* solemnly, reverently, religiously, conscientiously, purely

sanctimōni·a -ae *f* sanctity, sacredness; chastity

sancti·ō -ōnis *f* consecration, confirmation, sanctioning; penalty clause (*that part of the law that provided for penalties against those breaking that law*), sanction

sanctit·ās -ātis *f* sanctity, sacredness, inviolability; integrity, purity, chastity, holiness

sanctitūd·ō -inis *f* sanctity, sacredness

sanct·or -ōris *m* enactor (*of laws*)

sanct·us -a -um *adj* consecrated, hallowed, sacred, inviolable; venerable, august, divine; pure, holy, chaste, virtuous

sandaligerūl·ae -ārum *f pl* maids who brought their mistress's slippers

sandal·ium -iī or **-ī** *n* slipper, sandal

sandapil·a -ae *f* cheap coffin (*for people of the lower classes*)

sand·yx -ȳcis *f* vermilion

sānē *adv* reasonably, sanely, sensibly; certainly, doubtless, truly, very; (ironically) of course, naturally;

(with negatives) really, at all; (in concessions) to be sure, however; (in answers) yes, of course, to be sure; (with imperatives) then; (with **quam**) how very

sanguen see **sanguis**

sanguin·ans -antis *adj* bleeding; (fig) bloodthirsty, savage

sanguināri·us -a -um *adj* bloodthirsty, savage

sanguinĕ·us -a -um *adj* bloody, bloodstained; bloodred

sanguinolent·us -a -um *adj* bloody, bloodstained; bloodred; sanguinary

sangu·is or **sangu·īs -inis** *m* or **sangu·en -inis** *n* blood; blood, consanguinity, descent, family; descendant, offspring; slaughter, murder, bloodshed; forcefulness, life, vigor (*of a speech*); life, strength; **pugnatum plurimo sanguine** fought out in a real massacre; **sanguinem dare** to bleed; **sanguinem effundere** or **profundere** to bleed heavily; **sanguinem haurire** to shed (*someone else's*) blood; **sanguinem mittere** (of a physician) to let blood, bleed

saniēs (*genit* not found) *f* blood (*from a wound*); gore; foam, froth, slaver; venom

sānit·ās -ātis *f* health; sanity; common sense, discretion; solidity, healthy foundation (*for victory, etc.*); soundness, propriety (*of style*)

sann·a -ae *f* mocking grimace, face

sanni·ō -ōnis *m* one who makes faces, clown

sān·ō -āre *vt* to cure, heal; to correct, repair; to allay, quiet, relieve

Sanquāl·is -e *adj* of Sangus (*Sabine deity*); **Sanqualis avis** osprey (*bird*)

sān·us -a -um *adj* sound, hale, healthy; sane, rational, sensible; sober; (with **ab + abl**) free from (*faults, vices*)

sap·a -ae *f* new wine

sāperd·a -ae *m* a fish (*from the Black Sea*)

sapi·ens -entis *adj* wise, sensible, judicious, discreet; *m* sensible person; sage, philosopher; man of discriminating taste, connoisseur

sapienter *adv* wisely, sensibly, prudently

sapienti·a -ae *f* good taste, common sense, prudence, wisdom; science; philosophy

sap·iō -ĕre -īvī or **-iī** *vt* to have the flavor of, taste of; to have the smell of, smell like; to have knowledge of, understand; *vi* to have a sense of taste; to have sense, be sensible, be discreet, be wise; **sero sapiunt** they are wise too late

sāp·ō -ōnis *m* soap

sap·or -ōris *m* taste, flavor; delicacy, dainty; elegance, refinement, sense of taste

Sapph·ō -ūs *f* celebrated Greek lyric poetess of Lesbos

sarcĭn·a **-ae** *f* package, bundle, pack; burden (*of the womb*); sorrow, trouble; *f pl* luggage, gear

sarcinārĭ·us **-a -um** *adj* pack, of luggage; **jumenta sarcinaria** pack animals

sarcĭnāt·or **-ōris** *m* patcher, botcher

sarcĭnāt·us **-a -um** *adj* loaded down, burdened

sarcĭnŭl·ae **-ārum** *f pl* small bundles, little trousseau

sarcĭō **sarcīre sarsī sartum** *vt* to patch, fix, repair

sarcŏphăg·us **-ī** *m* sarcophagus, tomb

sarcŭl·um **-ī** *n* light hoe, garden hoe

Sard·ēs or **Sard·ĭs** **-ĭum** *f pl* Sardis (*capital of Lydia*)

Sardĭān·us **-a -um** *adj* Sardian

Sardĭnĭ·a **-ae** *f* Sardinia

Sardĭnĭens·is **-e** *adj* Sardinian

Sardĭs see **Sardes**

sardŏn·yx **-ychis** *m* sardonyx (*precious stone*)

Sardŏ·us or **Sard·us** **-a -um** *adj & m* Sardianian

sarg·us **-ī** *m* bream (*fish*)

sar·ĭō or **sarr·ĭo** **-īre -īvī** or **-ŭī** *vt* to hoe, weed

sarīs·a **-ae** *f* long Macedonian lance

sarīsophŏr·os **-ī** *m* Macedonian lancer

sarīt·or or **sart·or** **-ōris** *m* hoer, weeder

Sarmăt·ae **-ārum** *m pl* Sarmatians (*barbarous people of S.E. Russia*)

Sarmătĭ·a **-ae** *f* Sarmatia

Sarmătĭc·us **-a -um** *adj* Sarmatian

sarm·en **-ĭnis** or **sarment·um** **-ī** *n* brushwood; *n pl* twigs, fagots

Sarpēd·ōn **-ŏnis** *m* king of Lycia who was killed by Patroclus at Troy

Sarr·a **-ae** *f* Tyre

sarrāc·um or **serrāc·um** **-ī** *n* cart

Sarrān·us **-a -um** *adj* Tyrian

sarrĭō see **sario**

sartăg·ō **-ĭnis** *f* frying pan

sartor see **saritor**

sart·us **-a -um** *pp* of **sarcio**; *adj* (*occurring only with* **tectus**) in good repair; **aedem Castoris sartam tectam tradere** to hand over the temple of Castor in good repair; *n pl* repairs; **sarta tecta exigere** to complete the repairs

sat (indecl) *adj* enough, sufficient, adequate; *n* enough; **sat agere** (with *genit*) to have enough of, have the hands full with

sat *adv* sufficiently, quite; **sat scio** I am quite sure

sat·a **-ae** *f* daughter

sat·a **-ōrum** *n pl* crops

satăg·ō **-ĕre** *vi* to have trouble enough, have one's hands full

satell·es **-ĭtis** *m* or *f* attendant, follower; partisan; accomplice

satĭ·ās **-ātis** *f* sufficiency; overabundance, satiety, satisfied desire

satĭĕt·ās **-atis** *f* sufficiency, adequacy; satiety, weariness, disgust

satin' or **satine** *adv* quite, really

satĭ·ō **-āre** *vt* to satisfy, appease; to fill, glut; to saturate; to cloy

satĭ·ō **-ōnis** *f* sowing, planting; *f pl* sown fields

satis (indecl) *adj* enough, sufficient, adequate; *n* enough; (law) satisfaction, security, guarantee; **satis accipere** to accept a guarantee; **satis dare** (with *dat*) to give a guarantee to; **satis facere** (with *dat*) to satisfy; to pay (*a creditor*); to make amends to (*by word or deed*), apologize to; **satis facere** (with *dat* of person and *acc & inf*) to satisfy (*someone*) with proof that, demonstrate sufficiently to (*someone*) that; **satis superque dictum est** more than enough has been said

satis *adv* enough, sufficiently, adequately, fully; **satis bene** pretty well

satisdatĭ·ō **-ōnis** *f* putting up bail, giving a guarantee

satisfactĭ·ō **-ōnis** *f* amends, satisfaction, apology

satĭus (*comp* of **satis**) *adj* **satius est** (with *inf*) it is better or preferable to

sat·or **-ōris** *m* sower, planter; father; promoter, author

satrapē·a or **satrapī·a** **-ae** *f* satrapy (*office or province of a satrap*)

satrăp·ēs **-is** *m* satrap (*governor of a province of the Persian empire*)

sat·ur **-ŭra -ŭrum** *adj* full, well fed, stuffed; plump; rich, fertile; rich, deep (*colors*); *f* mixture, hotchpotch; medley; satire, satirical poem; **per saturam** at random, pell-mell

saturei·a **-ōrum** *n pl* savory (*aromatic herb used as seasoning*)

saturĭt·ās **-ātis** *f* satiety; plenty, overabundance

Sāturnālĭ·a **-ōrum** *n pl* festival in honor of Saturn, beginning on the 17th of December and lasting several days

Sāturnĭ·a **-ae** *f* Juno (*daughter of Saturn*)

Sāturnīn·us **-ī** *m* L. Appuleius Saturninus (*demagogic tribune in 103 B.C. and 100 B.C.*)

Sāturnĭ·us **-a -um** *adj* Saturnian; **Saturnius numerus** Saturnian meter (*archaic Latin meter based on stress accent*); *m* Jupiter; Pluto

Sāturn·us **-ī** *m* Saturn (*Italic god of agriculture, equated with the Greek god Cronos, ruler of the Golden Age, and father of Jupiter, Neptune, Juno, and Pluto*)

satŭr·ō **-āre** *vt* to fill, satisfy, glut, cloy, saturate; to satisfy, content

sat·us **-a -um** *pp* of **sero**; *m* son; *f* see **sata**; *n pl* see **sata**

sat·us **-ūs** *m* sowing, planting; begetting; race, stock; seed (*of knowledge*)

satyrisc·us **-ī** *m* little satyr

satȳr·us -ī *m* satyr; satyr play (*Greek drama in which satyrs often formed the chorus*)

sauciātǐ·ō -ōnis *f* wounding

saucǐ·ō -āre *vt* to wound

saucǐ·us -a -um *adj* wounded; (fig) smitten, offended, hurt; melted (*snow*)

Sauromāt·ae -ārum *m pl* Sarmatians (*barbaric tribe of S. Russia*)

sāviātǐ·ō or **suāviātǐ·ō -ōnis** *f* kissing

sāviǒl·um or **suāviǒl·um -ī** *n* little kiss

sāvǐ·or -ārī -ātus sum *vt* to kiss

sāv·ǐum or **suāv·ǐum -ǐī** or **-ī** *n* puckered lips; kiss

saxātǐl·is -e *adj* rock, living among rocks; *m* saxatile (*fish*)

saxēt·um -ī *n* rocky place

saxě·us -a -um *adj* rocky, stony; umbra saxea shade of the rocks

saxǐfǐc·us -a -um *adj* petrifying, changing objects into stone

saxōs·us -a -um *adj* rocky, stony

saxǔl·um -ī *n* small rock, little crag

sax·um -ī *n* bolder, rock; Tarpeian Cliff (*W. side of the Capitoline Hill*)

scabellum see **scabillum**

scab·er -ra -rum *adj* itchy; rough, scurfy

scab·ǐēs (*genit* not found) *f* itch; roughness, scurf; (fig) itch

scabill·um or **scabell·um -ī** *n* stool, footstool; castanet tied to the foot

scabǐōs·us -a -um *adj* itchy, mangy; moldy

scab·ō -ěre -ī *vt* to scratch

Scae·a port·a -ae *f* Scaean gate (*W. gate of Troy*)

scaen·a or **scēn·a -ae** *f* stage setting, stage; scene; (fig) public view, publicity; pretense, pretext; tibi scenae serviendum est you must keep yourself in the limelight

scaenāl·is or **scēnāl·is -e** *adj* theatrical, scenic

scaenǐc·us or **scēnǐc·us -a -um** *adj* of the stage, theatrical, scenic; *m* actor

Scaevǒl·a -ae *m* C. Mucius Scaevola (*Roman hero who infiltrated into Porsenna's camp to kill Porsenna, and, on being discovered, burned off his own right hand*)

scaev·us -a -um *adj* left, on the left; perverse; *f* sign or omen appearing on the left

scāl·ae -ārum *f pl* ladder, flight of steps, stairs

scalm·us -ī *m* oarlock; oar; boat

scalpell·um -ī *n* scalpel

scalp·ō -ěre -sī -tum *vt* to carve; to scratch; to tickle

scalpr·um -ī *n* chisel; knife; penknife

scalpurr·ǐō -īre *vi* to scratch

Scamand·er -rī *m* river at Troy, also called Xanthus

scammōně·a -ae *f* scammony (*plant*)

scamn·um -ī *n* bench, stool; throne

scandō scanděre scandī scansum *vt* & *vi* to climb, mount, ascend

scandǔl·a -ae *f* shingle (*for roof*)

scaph·a -ae *f* light boat, skiff

scaph·ǐum -ǐī or **-ī** *n* boat-shaped drinking cup; chamber pot

scapǔl·ae -ārum *f pl* shoulder blades; shoulders, back

scāp·us -ī *m* shaft; yarn beam (*of a loom*)

scarǐf·ō -āre *vt* to scratch open

scar·us -ī *m* scar (*fish*)

scatēbr·a -ae *f* bubbling, gushing, jet

scat·ěō -ēre or **scat·ō -ěre** *vi* to bubble up, gush out, jet; to teem

scatūrǐgin·ēs or **scaturrǐgin·ēs -um** *f pl* springs

scaturr·ǐō -īre *vi* to bubble, gush; to bubble over with enthusiasm

scaur·us -a -um *adj* clubfooted

scaz·ōn -ōntis *m* scazon (*iambic trimeter with a spondee or trochee in the last foot*)

scelerātē *adv* criminally, wickedly

scelerāt·us -a -um *adj* profaned, desecrated; outlawed; criminal, wicked, infamous; *m* villain, criminal

scelěr·ō -āre *vt* to pollute, desecrate

scelerōs·us -a -um *adj* full of wickedness, vicious

scel·us -ěris *n* wicked deed, crime, wickedness; calamity; scoundrel, criminal

scēn- = scaen-

sceptrǐf·er -ěra -ěrum *adj* sceptered

sceptr·um -ī *n* scepter; kingship, dominion, authority; kingdom

sceptǔch·us -ī *m* scepter-bearer (*high officer of state in the East*)

sched·a or **scid·a -ae** *f* sheet, page

schēm·a -ae *f* figure, form, style; figure of speech

Schoenē·is -ǐdis *f* Atalanta

Schoeneǐ·us -a -um *adj* of Schoeneus; *f* Atalanta

Schoen·eus -ěī *m* king of Boeotia and father of Atalanta

schoenobāt·ēs -ae *m* ropewalker

schol·a -ae *f* learned debate, dissertation, lecture; school; sect, followers

scholastǐc·us -a -um *adj* school, scholastic; *m* rhetoric teacher, rhetorician

scida see **scheda**

scǐ·ens -entis *adj* having knowledge; having full knowledge, with one's eyes open; (with *genit*) having knowledge of, familiar or acquainted with, expert in; (with *inf*) knowing how to

scienter *adv* wisely, expertly

scientǐ·a -ae *f* knowledge, skill

scīlǐcet *adv* of course, evidently, certainly; (ironically) naturally, of course, to be sure; (as an explanatory particle) namely, that is to say, in other words

scill·a or **squill·a -ae** f shrimp

scīn = **scisne**, i.e., **scis + ne**

scindō scindĕre scidī scissum vt to cut, split, tear apart or open; to divide, separate; to interrupt

scindŭla see **scandula**

scintill·a -ae f spark

scintill·ō -āre vi to sparkle, flash

scintillŭl·a -ae f little spark

sciō scīre scīvī or **scīī scītum** vt to know; to realize, understand; to have skill in; (with inf) to know how to

Scīpiăd·ēs -ae m a Scipio, one of the Scipio family

Scīpi·ō -ōnis m famous family in the gens Cornelia; P. Cornelius Scipio Africanus Major (conqueror of the Carthaginians in the Second Punic War, 236-184 B.C.); P. Cornelius Scipio Aemilianus Africanus Minor (conqueror of the Carthaginians in the Third Punic War, c. 185-132 B.C.)

scirpĕ·us or **sirpĕ·us -a -um** adj wicker, of wicker; f wickerwork

scirpicŭl·a -ae f wicker basket

scirpicŭl·us -ī m wicker basket

scirp·us or **sirp·us -ī** m bulrush

sciscit·ō -āre or **sciscit·or -ārī -ātus sum** vt to ask, question, interrogate; to consult; (with acc of thing asked about and **ex** or **ab** + abl of person) to ask (something) of (someone), check on (something) with (someone); vi (with **de** + abl) to ask about

sciscō sciscĕre scīvī scītum vt (pol) to approve, adopt, enact, decree; to learn, ascertain

sciss·us -a -um pp of **scindo**; adj split, rent; furrowed (cheeks); shrill, harsh (voice)

scītāment·a -ōrum n pl dainties, delicacies

scītē adv expertly

scīt·or -ārī -ātus sum vt to ask; to consult (oracle); (with acc of thing and **ab** or **ex** + abl) to ask (something) of (someone); vi (with **de** + abl) to ask or inquire about

scītŭl·us -a -um adj neat, trim, smart

scīt·um -ī n statute, decree

scīt·us -a -um adj experienced, skillful; suitable, proper; judicious, sensible, witty (words); smart, sharp (appearance); (with genit) skilled in, expert at

scīt·us -ūs m decree, enactment

sciūr·us -ī m squirrel

scob·is -is f sawdust, scrapings, filings

scomb·er -rī m mackerel

scōp·ae -ārum f pl twigs, shoots; broom

Scop·ās -ae m famous Greek sculptor of Paros (4th cent. B.C.)

scopulōs·us -a -um adj rocky, craggy

scopŭl·us -ī m rock, cliff, crag; promontory

scorpi·ō -ōnis or **scorp·ius** or **scorp·īos -iī** or **-ī** m scorpion; (mil) artillery piece, catapult

Scorpi·ō -ōnis m Scorpion (sign of the zodiac)

scortāt·or -ōris m fornicator, lecher

scortĕ·us -a -um adj leather, of leather

scort·or -ārī -ātus sum vi to associate with prostitutes

scort·um -ī n prostitute; sex fiend

screāt·or -ōris m one who clears his throat noisily, hawker

screāt·us -ūs m clearing the throat, hawking

scre·ō -āre vi to clear the throat, hawk, hem

scrīb·a -ae m clerk, secretary

scriblīt·a -ae f tart

scrībō scrībĕre scripsī scriptum vt to write, draw; to write down; to write out, compose, produce; to enlist (soldiers); (with double acc) to appoint (someone) as

scrīn·ium -iī or **-ī** n bookcase, letter case, portfolio

scripti·ō -ōnis f writing, composition, authorship; wording, text

scriptit·ō -āre vt to keep writing, write regularly

script·or -ōris m writer; scribe, secretary; composer, author; **rerum scriptor** historian

scriptŭl·a -ōrum n pl lines on a game board

scriptūr·a -ae f writing; composing; a writing, written work; tax paid on public pastures; testamentary provision

script·us -a -um pp of **scribo**; n written composition, treatise, work, book; literal meaning, letter; **orationem de scripto dicere** to read off a speech; **scriptum legis** or **scriptum** written ordinance, law

scrīpŭl·um or **scrupŭl·um -ī** n small weight, smallest measure of weight, scruple (one twenty fourth of an uncia)

scrob·is -is m ditch, trench; grave

scrōf·a -ae f breeding sow

scrōfipasc·us -ī m swine keeper, pig breeder

scrupĕ·us -a -um adj stony, rugged, jagged, rough

scrupōs·us -a -um adj full of sharp stones, rugged, jagged, rough

scrupŭlōsē adv precisely, carefully

scrupulōs·us -a -um adj rough, rugged, jagged; precise, careful

scrupŭlum see **scripulum**

scrupŭl·us -ī m small sharp pebble; uneasy feeling, scruple

scrup·us -ī m rough or sharp stone; uneasiness

scrūt·a -ōrum n pl trash, junk

scrūtāt·or -ōris m examiner

scrūt·or -ārī -ātus sum vt to scrutinize, examine

sculp·ō -ĕre -sī -tum vt to carve, chisel, engrave

sculpōnĕ·ae -ārum *f pl* clogs
sculptĭl·is -e *adj* carved, engraved
sculpt·or -ōris *m* sculptor
sculptūr·a -ae *f* carving; sculpture
sculptus *pp* of **sculpo**
scurr·a -ae *m* jester, comedian; man-about-town
scurrīl·is -e *adj* scurrilous
scurrīlĭt·ās -ātis *f* scurrility
scurrīlĭter *adv* jeeringly
scurr·or -ārī -ātus sum *vi* to clown around
scūtāl·e -is *n* thong of a sling
scūtār·ĭus -ĭī or **-ī** *m* shield maker
scūtāt·us -a -um *adj* carrying a shield; *m pl* troops armed with shields
scutell·a -ae *f* saucer, shallow bowl
scutĭc·a -ae *f* whip
scūtĭgerŭl·us -ī *m* shield bearer
scutr·a -ae *f* pan, flat dish
scutŭl·a or **scytāl·a** or **scytăl·ē -ae** *f* platter; eye patch; wooden cylinder; secret letter
scutŭlāt·us -a -um *adj* diamond-shaped; *n pl* checkered clothing
scūtŭl·um -ī *n* small shield
scūt·um -ī *n* oblong shield; (fig) shield, defense, protection
Scyll·a -ae *f* dangerous rock on the Italian side of Straits of Messina, said to have been the daughter of Phorcus and transformed by Circe into a sea monster with howling dogs about her midriff; daughter of Nisus who betrayed her father by cutting off his purple lock of hair
Scyllae·us -a -um *adj* Scyllan
scymn·us -ī *m* cub, whelp
scyph·us -ī *m* goblet, cup
Scyr·os or **Scyr·us -ī** *f* island off Euboea
scytăla see **scutula**
scytălē see **scutula**
Scyth·a or **Scyth·ēs -ae** *m* Scythian; *m pl* Scythians (*general name for the nomadic tribes of the section of Europe and Asia beyond the Black Sea*)
Scythĭ·a -ae *f* Scythia
Scythĭc·us -a -um *adj* Scythian
Scyth·is -ĭdis *f* Scythian woman
sē or **sēsē** (*genit:* **suī**; *dat:* **sibī** or **sibī**; *abl* **sē** or **sēsē**) *pron acc* (reflex) himself, herself, itself, themselves; one another; **ad se** or **apud se** at home; **apud se** in one's senses; **inter se** one another, mutually
sēb·um -ī *n* tallow, grease
sē·cēdō -cēdĕre -cessī -cessum *vi* to go apart, go aside, withdraw; to rebel
sē·cernō -cernĕre -crēvī -crētum *vt* to separate; to dissociate; to distinguish; to reject, set aside
sēcessĭ·ō -ōnis *f* withdrawal; secession
sēcess·us -ūs *m* retirement, retreat; isolated spot
sē·clūdō -clūdĕre -clūsī -clūsum

vt to shut off, shut up; to seclude, bar; to hide
sec·ō -āre -ŭī -tum *vt* to cut, cut off, reap, carve; (in surgery) to cut out, excise, cut off, amputate; to scratch, tear, wound, injure; to cut through, traverse; to cut short, settle, decide; to follow, chase
sēcordĭa see **socordia**
sēcrētĭ·ō -ōnis *f* dividing, separating
sēcrētō *adv* separately, apart; secretly; in private
sēcrēt·us -a -um *pp* of **secerno**; separate; isolated, solitary; secret; (with *genit* or *abl*) deprived of, in need of; *n* secret, mystery; private conversation or interview; isolated place, solitude
sect·a -ae *f* path; way, method, course; school of thought; political party
sectārĭ·us -a -um *adj* gelded; leading
sectāt·or -ōris *m* follower, adherent
sectĭl·is -e *adj* cut, divided
sectĭ·ō -ōnis *f* cutting; auctioning off of confiscated property; right to confiscated property; confiscated property
sect·or -ōris *m* cutter; buyer at a sale of confiscated property, speculator in confiscated estates
sect·or -ārī -ātus sum *vt* to keep following, follow eagerly, run after, keep trailing after; to chase, hunt
sectūr·a -ae *f* digging, excavation; *f pl* diggings, mines
sectus *pp* of **seco**
sēcubĭt·us -ūs *m* sleeping alone
sēcŭb·ō -āre -ŭī *vi* to lie alone, sleep by oneself; to live alone
sēcul- = **saecul-**
secund·a -ōrum *n pl* success, good fortune
secund·ae -ārum *f pl* secondary role (*in a play*); second fiddle
secundān·ī -ōrum *m pl* soldiers of the second legion
secundārĭ·us -a -um *adj* secondary, second-rate, inferior
secundō *adv* secondly
secund·ō -āre *vt* to favor, further, back, support
secundum *adv* after, behind; *prep* (with *acc*) (of space) beside, by, along; (of time) immediately after, after; (in rank) next to, after; (of agreement) according to, in compliance with; in favor of, to the advantage of
secund·us -a -um *adj* following; next, second (*in time*); backing, favorable, supporting; next, second (*in rank*); secondary, subordinate, inferior, second-string; **anno secundo** the next year; **a mensis fine secunda dies** the second-last day of the month; **in secundam aquam** with the current; **secunda mensa** dessert; **secundo flumine** downstream, with the current; **se-**

cundo lumine on the following day; **secundo mari** with the tide; **secundo populo** with the backing of the people; **secundus panis** inferior bread, stale bread; **secundus ventus** tail wind, fair wind; *f pl* see **secundae**; *n pl* see **secunda**

sĕcūrē *adv* securely, safely

secūrĭcŭl·a -ae *f* hatchet

secūrĭf·er -ĕra -ĕrum *adj* carrying an ax, ax-carrying

secūrĭg·er -ĕra -ĕrum *adj* ax-carrying

secūr·is -is *f* ax, hatchet; blow, mortal blow; power of life and death; supreme authority, sovereignty

sĕcūrĭt·ās -ātis *f* freedom from care, unconcern, composure; freedom from danger, security, safety; false sense of security; carelessness

sēcūr·us -a -um *adj* carefree; secure, safe; cheerful; careless; offhand

secus (indecl) *n* sex; **secus muliebre** females; **secus viriles** males

secus *adv* otherwise, differently; **non secus ac** or **non secus quam** not otherwise than, just as, exactly as; **si secus accidet** if it turns out otherwise (*than expected*), if it turns out badly

secūt·or -ōris *m* gladiator (*who fought against an opponent who had a net*)

secūtus *pp* of **sequor**

sed or **set** *conj* but; but also; but in fact

sĕdātē *adv* sedately, calmly

sēdātĭ·ō -ōnis *f* calming

sēdāt·us -a -um *adj* calm, composed

sēdĕcim (indecl) *adj* sixteen

sēdĕcŭl·a -ae *f* little seat, low stool

sedentārĭ·us -a -um *adj* sedentary

sedĕō sedēre sēdī sessum *vi* to sit, remain sitting; (of magistrates, esp. judges) to sit, preside, hold court, be a judge; (of an army) to remain encamped; to keep the field; to settle down in blockade; to be idle, be inactive; (of clothes) to fit; (of places) to be low-lying; to sink, settle; to be firm, be fixed, be established; to stick fast, be stuck; to be determined, be firmly resolved

sĕd·ēs -is *f* seat, chair, throne; residence, home; last home, burial place; base, foundation, bottom

sedīl·e -is *n* seat, chair, bench, stool; *n pl* seats in the theater; rowers' benches

sēdĭtĭ·ō -ōnis *f* sedition, insurrection, mutiny; dissension, quarrel, disagreement; warring (*of elements, etc.*)

sēdĭtĭōsē *adv* seditiously

sēdĭtĭōs·us -a -um *adj* seditious, mutinous; quarrelsome; troubled, disturbed

sēd·ō -āre *vt* to calm, settle, still, allay

sē·dūcō -dūcĕre -dūxī -ductum *vt* to lead aside, draw aside, lead

away, carry off; to put aside; to separate, divide

sēductĭ·ō -ōnis *f* taking sides, siding

sēduct·us -a -um *pp* of **seduco**; distant, remote

sēdŭlĭt·ās -ātis *f* application, earnestness; officiousness

sēdŭlō *adv* diligently; intentionally, on purpose

sēdŭl·us -a -um *adj* diligent, busy; officious

seg·es -ĕtis *f* grain field; crop

Segest·a -ae *f* town in N.W. Sicily

Segestān·us -a -um *adj* of Segesta; *m pl* people of Segesta; *n* territory of Segesta

segmentāt·us -a -um *adj* trimmed with a flounce

segment·um -ī *n* trimming, flounce; brocade

segnĭp·ēs -ĕdis *adj* slow-footed

segn·is -e *adj* slow, inactive; sluggish, lazy

segnĭter *adv* slowly, lazily

segnĭtĭ·a -ae or **segnĭtĭ·ēs** (*genit* not found) *f* slowness, inactivity, laziness

sēgrĕg·ō -āre *vt* to segregate, separate

sējŭgāt·us -a -um *adj* separated

sējŭg·is -is *m* six-horse chariot

sējunctim *adv* separately

sējunctĭ·ō -ōnis *f* separation, division

sē·jungō -jungĕre -junxī -junctum *vt* to separate, disunite, part, sever; (fig) to sever, part, disconnect; to distinguish

sēlectĭ·ō -ōnis *f* selection

sēlectus *pp* of **seligo**

Seleuc·us -ī *m* name of a line of kings of Syria

sēlĭbr·a -ae *f* half pound

sē·lĭgō -lĭgĕre -lēgī -lectum *vt* to pick out, select, choose

sell·a -ae *f* chair, stool; sedan; magistrate's chair

sellārĭŏl·us -a -um *adj* (place) for sitting or lounging

sellār·ĭus -ĭī or **-ĭ** *m* lecherer

sellisternĭ·a -ōrum *n pl* sacred banquets in honor of goddesses

sellŭl·a -ae *f* stool; sedan

sellulār·ĭus -ĭī or **-ĭ** *m* mechanic

sēmanĭmis see **semianimis**

semel *adv* once, one time; but once, once for all; first, the first time; once, ever, at some time, at any time

Semĕl·ē -ēs or **Semĕl·a -ae** *f* daughter of Cadmus and mother of Bacchus by Jupiter

Semelei·us -a -um *adj* of Semele

sēm·en -ĭnis *n* seed, germ; seedling, young plant, shoot; offspring; race, stock; (in physics) particle; instigator, cause

sēmenstris see **semestris**

sēmentĭf·er -ĕra -ĕrum *adj* seedbearing, fruitful

sēmentĭn·us -a -um *adj* of the sowing season

sēment·is -is *f* sowing, planting; young crops

sēmentīv·us -a -um *adj* at seed time, of the sowing season

sēmerm·is -e *adj* half-armed

sēmestr·is or **sēmenstr·is -e** *adj* for six months, half-yearly, semi-annual

sēmēs·us -a -um *adj* half-eaten

sēmet = emphatic form of **se**

sēmiadapert·us -a -um *adj* half-open

sēmianīm·is -e or **sēmianīm·us** or **sēmanīm·us -a -um** *adj* half-dead

sēmiapert·us -a -um *adj* half-open

sēmīb·ōs -ōvis *adj masc* half-ox; **semibos vir** Minotaur

sēmicăp·er -rī *adj masc* half-goat

sēmicremăt·us or **sēmicrēm·us -a -um** *adj* half-burned

sēmicubităl·is -e *adj* half-cubit long

sēmidĕ·us -a -um *adj* semidivine; *m* demigod

sēmidoct·us -a -um *adj* half-educated

sēmierm·is -e or **sēmierm·us -a -um** *adj* half-armed

sēmiēs·us -a -um *adj* half-eaten

sēmifact·us -a -um *adj* half-finished

sēmif·er -ĕra -ĕrum *adj* half-beast; half-savage; *m* centaur

sēmifult·us -a -um *adj* half-propped

sēmigermān·us -a -um *adj* half-German

sēmigrăv·is -e *adj* half-drunk

sēmigr·ō -āre *vi* to go away, depart

sēmihī·ans -antis *adj* half-open

sēmihŏm·ō -ĭnis *m* half man, half beast; subhuman

sēmihōr·a -ae *f* half hour

sēmilăc·er -ĕra -ĕrum *adj* half-mangled

sēmilaut·us -a -um *adj* half-washed

sēmilīb·er -ĕra -ĕrum *adj* half-free

sēmilix·a -ae *m* (term of reproach) sad sack

sēmimarīn·us -a -um *adj* semisubmerged (*in the sea*)

sēmim·ās -āris *adj* gelded, castrated; *m* hermaphrodite

sēmimortū·us -a -um *adj* half-dead

sēminăr·ĭum -ĭī or **-ī** *n* nursery garden; (fig) breeding ground

sēminăt·or -ōris *m* originator, cause, source

sēminĕcis (*genit*; *nom* does not occur) *adj* half-killed, half-dead

sēmin·ĭum -ĭī or **-ī** *n* breeding; stock

sēmin·ō -āre *vt* to sow; to beget, procreate; to produce

sēminūd·us -a -um *adj* half-stripped; half-unarmed

sēmipăgăn·us -ī *m* little clown

sēmiplēn·us -a -um *adj* (garrison) at half strength

sēmiputăt·us -a -um *adj* half-pruned

Semīrăm·is -is or **-ĭdis** *f* famous queen of Assyria, the consort and successor of Ninus

Semīramī·us -a -um *adj* of Semiramis

sēmirās·us -a -um *adj* half-shaven

sēmireduct·us -a -um *adj* bent back halfway

sēmirefect·us -a -um *adj* half-repaired

sēmirŭt·us -a -um *adj* half-ruined, half-demolished

sēm·is -issis *m* half; half an ace (*coin*); one half percent a month or six-percent per annum; **non semissis homo** man not worth a penny, worthless fellow

sēmisĕn·ex -is *m* elderly gent

sēmisepult·us -a -um *adj* half-buried

sēmisomn·is -e or **sēmisomn·us -a -um** *adj* half-asleep

sēmisupīn·us -a -um *adj* half-prone

sēmīt·a -ae *f* path, lane

sēmităl·is -a -um *adj* of byways

sēmitāri·us -a -um *adj* back-alley

sēmiustilāt·us or **sēmiustulāt·us -a -um** *adj* half-burned

sēmīv·ir -īrī *adj* half-man, half-beast; unmanned; unmanly, effeminate; *m* half-man; eunuch

sēmivīv·us -a -um *adj* half-alive, half-dead

sēmod·ius -ĭī or **-ī** *m* half a peck

sēmōt·us -a -um *adj* remote, distant; *n pl* faraway places

sē·movĕō -movēre -mōvī -mōtum *vt* to move apart, separate, remove, put aside

semper *adv* always, ever; regularly, on each occasion

sempitern·us -a -um *adj* everlasting

Semprōnĭus see **Gracchus**

sēmuncĭ·a -ae *f* half ounce (*one twenty-fourth of a Roman pound*); trifle

sēmunciāri·us -a -um *adj* half-ounce; **faenus semunciarium** interest at the rate of one twenty-fourth of the capital (*i.e., about five percent per annum*)

sēmust·us -a -um *adj* half-burned

senācŭl·um -ī *n* open-air meeting place of the senate in the Forum

sēnārĭŏl·us -ī *m* trifling trimeter

sēnārĭ·us -a -um *adj* six-foot (*verse*); *m* iambic trimeter

senāt·or -ōris *m* senator

senātōrĭ·us -a -um *adj* senatorial; in the senate; of a senator

senāt·us -ūs *m* senate; senate session; **senatūs consultum** decree of the senate

Senĕc·a -ae *m* L. Annaeus Seneca (*Stoic philosopher and instructor of Nero,* 4 B.C.-65 A.D.)

senect·us -a -um *adj* aged, old; *f* old age, senility

senect·ūs -ūtis *f* old age; old people

sen·ĕō -ēre *vi* to be old

sen·escō -escĕre -ŭī *vi* to grow old; to decline, become feeble, lose strength; to wane, draw to a close

sen·ex -is *adj* aged, old; *m* old man; *f* old woman

sēn·ī -ae -a *adj* six each, six in a group, six at a time; **seni dēni** sixteen each

senīl·is -e *adj* of old people, of an old man; aged; senile

sēnī·ō -ōnis *m* a six (*on dice*)

seni·or -us (*comp of* **senex**) *adj* older, elder; more mature (*years*); *m* elderly person, an elder (*over forty-five years of age*)

sen·ium -iī or **-ī** *n* feebleness of age, decline, senility; decay; grief, trouble; gloom; crabbiness; old man

sens·a -ōrum *n pl* thoughts, sentiments, ideas

sensicŭl·us -ī *m* short sentence

sensíf·er -ĕra -ĕrum *adj* producing sensation

sensíl·is -e *adj* capable of sensation, sentient

sensim *adv* gropingly; tentatively; carefully, gradually, gently

sens·us -a -um *pp* of **sentiō**; *n pl* see **sensa**

sens·us -ūs *m* sense faculty, capacity for feeling, sensation; feeling, emotion, sentiment; attitude, frame of mind, view; understanding, judgment, intelligence; meaning, intent, sense; sentence; **communes sensūs** commonplaces; universal human feelings

sententi·a -ae *f* opinion, view, judgment; purpose, intention; (law) sentence, verdict; (in the senate) motion, proposal, view; meaning, sense; sentence; maxim; **de sententia** (with *genit*) in accordance with the wishes of; **ex animi (mei) sententia** (in an oath) to the best of (*my*) knowledge and belief; **ex mea sententia** in my opinion, to my liking; **in sententiam alicujus pedibus ire** to vote in favor of someone's proposal; **sententia est** (with *inf*) I intend to; **sententiam dicere** (in the senate) to express a view; **sententiam pronuntiare** or **dicere** to pronounce or give the verdict

sententiŏl·a -ae *f* phrase; maxim

sententiōsē *adv* sententiously

sententiōs·us -a -um sententious, full of meaning

senticēt·um -ī *n* thorny bush

sentin·a -ae *f* bilge water; cesspool; bilge; (fig) dregs, scum, rabble

sentiō sentire sensī sensum *vt* to perceive with the senses, feel, hear, see, smell; to realize; to feel, observe, notice; to experience; to think, judge; *vi* (law) to vote, decide

sent·is -is *m* thorny bush, bramble, brier

sentisc·ō -ĕre *vt* to begin to realize;

to begin to observe, perceive

sent·us -a -um *adj* thorny; untidy (*person*)

seorsum or **seorsus** *adv* apart, separately; (with *abl* or **ab** + *abl*) apart from

sēparābil·is -e *adj* separable

sēparātim *adv* apart, separately

sēparāti·ō -ōnis *f* severing, separation

sēparātius *adv* less closely, more widely

sēparāt·us -a -um *adj* separate, distinct, different

sēpăr·ō -āre *vt* to separate, divide, part; to distinguish

sepelībil·is -e *adj* that may be buried

sepeliō sepelīre sepelīvī or **sepe-lii sepultum** *vt* to bury; (fig) to bury, overwhelm, ruin, destroy, suppress

sēpēs see **saepes**

sēpi·a -ae *f* cuttlefish

sēpimentum see **saepimentum**

sēpiō see **saepio**

sēpiŏl·a -ae *f* little cuttlefish

sē-pōnō -pōnĕre -posŭī -positum *vt* to put aside; to separate, pick out, select; to assign, reserve; to remove, take away, exclude; to distinguish

sēposĭt·us -a -um *adj* remote, distant; select; distinct, private

seps sēpis *m* or *f* snake

sepse = emphatic **sē**

septem (indecl) *adj* seven

Septemb·er -ris *adj & m* September

septemděcim (indecl) *adj* seventeen

septemflŭ·us -a -um *adj* seven-mouthed (*Nile*)

septemgemĭn·us -a -um *adj* sevenfold

septempedāl·is -e *adj* seven-foot, seven-feet-high

septempl·ex -icis *adj* sevenfold

septemtriōnāl·ia -ium *n pl* northern regions, northern part

septemtriōnāl·is -e *adj* northern

septemtriōn·ēs or **septentriōn·ēs -um** *m pl* seven stars near the North Pole belonging to the Great Bear; the seven stars of the Little Bear; northern regions, the North; north wind

septemvirāl·is -e *adj* of the septemvirs, septemviral; *m pl* septemvirs

septemvirāt·us -ūs *m* septemvirate, office of the septemvirs

septemvir·ī -ōrum *m pl* septemvirs (*board of seven officials*)

septēnār·ius -iī or **-ī** *m* heptameter (*verse of seven feet*)

septenděcim or **septemděcim** (indecl) *adj* seventeen

septēn·ī -ae -a *adj* seven each, seven in a group; **septeni dēni** seventeen each, seventeen in a group

septentr- = **septemtr-**

septiens or **septiēs** *adv* seven times

septimān·us -a -um *adj* of or on the seventh; *n pl* soldiers of the seventh legion

septimum *adv* for the seventh time

septim·us or **septum·us -a -um** *adj* seventh

septim·us decim·us -a -um *adj* seventeenth

septingentēsim·us -a -um *adj* seven hundredth

septingent·ī -ae -a *adj* seven hundred

septuāgēsim·us -a -um *adj* seventieth

septuāgintā (indecl) *adj* seventy

septuenn·is -e *adj* seven-year-old

septum see **saeptum**

septun·x -cis *m* seven ounces; seven twelfths

septus *pp* of **saepio**

sepulcrāl·is -e *adj* of a tomb, sepulchral, funeral

sepulcrēt·um -ī *n* grave, tomb

sepulcr·um -ī *n* grave, tomb

sepultūr·a -ae *f* burial

sepultus *pp* of **sepelio**

Sēquān·a -ae *m* Seine

sequ·ax -ācis *adj* following, pursuing; penetrating (*fumes*); eager

sequ·ens -entis *adj* next, following

sequest·er -ris (or **-ra**) **-re** *adj* intermediate; negotiating, mediating; **pace sequestrā** under the protection of a truce; *m* trustee; agent, mediator, go-between

sequius or **sētius** (*comp* of **secus**) *adv* less; worse, more unfavorably; **nihilo setius** or **nilo setius** nevertheless

sequor sequī secūtus sum *vt* to follow, escort, accompany, go with; to chase, pursue; to come after (*in time*); to go after, aim at; to head for (*a place*); *vi* to go after, follow, come next; (*of words*) to come naturally

ser·a -ae *f* bolt, bar (*of door*)

Serāp·is -is or **-īdis** *m* Egyptian god of healing

serēnit·ās -ātis *f* fair weather; serenity; favorableness

serēn·ō -āre *vt* to make fair, clear up, brighten

serēn·us -a -um *adj* clear, bright, fair, cloudless; cheerful, serene; *n* clear sky, fair weather

Sēr·es -um *m pl* Chinese

seresc·ō -ēre *vi* to dry off

sēri·a -ae *f* large jar

sēri·a -ōrum *n pl* serious matters, serious business

Sēric·us -a -um *adj* Chinese; *n pl* silks

seri·ēs (*genit* not found) series, row, succession; train, sequence, order, connection; lineage

sēriō *adv* seriously, in all sincerity

sēri·us -a -um *adj* serious, earnest; *n* serious matter; seriousness, earnestness; *n pl* see **seria**

serm·ō -ōnis *m* conversation, talk; discussion, discourse; common talk,

rumor, gossip; language, diction; prose, everyday language

sermōcin·or -ārī -ātus sum *vi* to talk, converse

sermuncul·us -ī *m* small talk, chitchat

serō serēre seruī sertum *vt* to join, connect; to entwine, wreathe; to compose, combine, contrive

serō serēre -sēvī satum *vt* to sow, plant; (*fig*) to sow the seeds of

sērō *adv* late

serp·ens -entis *m* or *f* creeping thing, snake, serpent, dragon

Serp·ens -entis *m* Serpent, Draco (*constellation*)

serpentigĕn·a -ae *m* dragon offspring

serpentip·ēs -ĕdis *adj* dragonfooted

serperastr·a -ōrum *n pl* splints (*for straightening the crooked legs of children*); officer who keeps his soldiers in check

serpillum see **serpyllum**

serpō serpĕre serpsī serptum *vi* to creep, crawl; to move along slowly, spread slowly

serpyll·um or **serpill·um** or **serpull·um -ī** *n* wild thyme

serr·a -ae *f* saw

serrāt·us -a -um *adj* serrated, notched

serrūl·a -ae *f* small saw

sert·a -ae *f* wreath

sert·a -ōrum *n pl* wreaths, festoons

Sertōr·ius -iī or **-ī** *m* general of Marius who held out in Spain against the partisans of Sulla until he was assassinated by Perperna (*c.* 122-72 B.C.)

sert·us -a -um *pp* of **sero** (to join); *f* see **serta**; *n pl* see **serta**

ser·um -ī *n* whey; serum

sēr·us -a -um *adj* late; too late; **anni seri** ripe years; **ulmus sera** slow-growing elm; *n* late hour; **in serum rem trahere** to drag out the matter until late

serv·a -ae *f* slave (*female*)

servābil·is -e *adj* retrievable

serv·ans -antis *adj* keeping; (with *genit*) observant of

servāt·or -ōris *m* or **servātr·ix -īcis** *f* savior, preserver, deliverer

servīl·is -e *adj* slave, servile

servīliter *adv* slavishly

serv·iō -īre -īvī or **-iī -ītum** *vi* to be a servant or slave; to be obedient; (*of buildings, land*) to be mortgaged; (with *dat*) **a** to be a slave to, be subservient to; **b** to serve; **c** to comply with, conform to, humor; **d** to be devoted to, work at; **e** to serve, be of use to

servit·ium -iī or **-ī** *n* slavery, servitude; slaves

servitūd·ō -inis *f* servitude, slavery

servit·ūs -ūtis *f* slavery; serfdom; slaves; property liability, easement

Serv·ius Tull·ius -iī or **-ī** *m* sixth king of Rome

serv·ō -āre vt to watch over, preserve, protect; to store, reserve; to keep, retain; to observe; to keep to, continue to dwell in

servŏl·a -ae f young slave girl

servolicŏl·a -ae f slave of a slave (female)

servŏl·us -ī m young slave

serv·us or **serv·os -a -um** adj slave, servant; mf slave, servant

sescēnār·is -e adj a year and a half old

sescēnāri·us -a -um adj six-hundred-man (cohort)

sescēn·ī -ae -a adj six hundred each, six hundred in a group

sescentēsim·us -a -um adj six hundredth

sescent·ī -ae -a adj six hundred

sescentiens or **sescentiēs** adv six hundred times

sēsē see **se**

sescunci·us -a -um adj inch and a half thick

sesĕl·is -is f seseli (plant)

sesqui adv more by a half, one and a half times

sesquialt·er -ĕra -ĕrum adj one and a half

sesquihōr·a -ae f an hour and a half

sesquimod·ius -iī or **-ī** m peck and a half

sesquioctāv·us -a -um adj having a ratio of nine to eight

sesquiŏp·us -ĕris n day and a half's work

sesquipedāl·is -e adj foot and a half long or wide

sesquiplāg·a -ae f blow and a half

sesquipl·ex -icis adj one and a half times as much

sesquiterti·us -a -um adj containing one and a third; having a ratio of four to three

sessibŭl·um -ī n chair, seat, easy chair

sessil·is -e adj for sitting on; (plants) growing close to the ground, low-growing

sessi·ō -ōnis f sitting; session; loafing

sessit·ō -āre vi to sit much, keep sitting, rest

sessiuncŭl·a -ae f small group, small circle

sess·or -ōris m spectator; resident

sestert·ium -iī or **-ī** n sesterce

sestert·ius -iī or **-ī** (genit pl: **sestertium**) (abbreviated HS) m sesterce (small silver coin, equal to one fourth of a denarius, i.e., about 8¢, and used as the ordinary Roman unit in accounting); **centena milia sestertia** 100,000 sesterces; **deciens** (i.e., **deciens centena milia**) **sestertium** 1,000,000 sesterces

Sest·os or **Sest·us -ī** f city on the Hellespont

sēt- = **saet-**

Sētī·a -ae f town in Latium famous for its wine

Sētīn·us -a -um adj Setine; n Setine wine

sētius see **sequius**

seu conj or if; or; **seu . . . seu** whether . . . or

sevērē adv seriously; severely, austerely

sevērit·ās -ātis f severity, sternness, strictness

sevēritūd·ō -inis f austerity

sevēr·us -a -um adj serious, grave; severe, strict, austere; ruthless, grim

sēvŏc·ō -āre vt to call aside, call away; to remove, withdraw, separate

sēv·um -ī n tallow, grease

sex (indecl) adj six

sexāgēnāri·us -a -um adj sixty-year-old

sexāgēn·ī -ae -a adj sixty each, sixty in a group

sexāgēsim·us -a -um adj sixtieth

sexāgiens or **sexāgiēs** adv sixty times

sexāgintā (indecl) adj sixty

sexangŭl·us -a -um adj hexagonal

sexcen- = **sescen-**

sexcēnāri·us -a -um adj six-hundred-man (cohort)

sexenn·is -e adj six-year-old, of six years; **sexenni die** in a six-year period

sexenn·ium -iī or **-ī** n six-year period, six years

sexiens or **sexiēs** adv six times

sexprim·ī or **sex prim·ī -ōrum** m pl six-member council (in provincial towns)

sextadecimān·ī -ōrum m pl soldiers of the sixteenth legion

sext·ans -antis m one sixth; small coin (one sixth of an ace); one sixth of a pint

sextār·ius -iī or **-ī** m pint

Sextīl·is -e adj of or belonging to the sixth month of the old Roman year which was afterwards called August in honor of Augustus

sextŭl·a -ae f sixth of an ounce

sextum adv for the sixth time

sext·us -a -um adj sixth

sext·us decim·us -a -um adj sixteenth

sexungŭl·a -ae f six-clawed woman, rapacious woman

sex·us -ūs m sex

sī conj if, if only; **quod sī** but if; **sī forte** if perchance, in the hope that; **sī minus** if not

sibī see **se**

sibil·a -ōrum n pl hisses, hissing

sibil·ō -āre vt to hiss at; vi to hiss

sibil·us -a -um adj & m hissing

Sibyll·a or **Sibull·a -ae** f sibyl, prophetess

Sibyllīn·us -a -um adj sibylline

sīc adv thus, so, in this way; thus, as follows; in these circumstances; in such a way, to such a degree; (in assent) yes

Sicān·ī -ōrum *m pl* ancient people of Italy who migrated to Sicily
Sicānī·a -ae *f* Sicily
Sicān·is -ĭdis *adj* Sicilian
Sicānī·us -a -um *adj* Sicilian; *f* see **Sicania**
Sicān·us -a -um *adj* Sicilian; *m pl* see **Sicani**
sīcār·ĭus -ĭī or **-ī** *m* murderer, assassin; **inter sicarios accusare (defendere)** to prosecute (defend) on a murder charge
siccē *adv* firmly, solidly
siccĭt·ās -ātis *f* dryness; drought; firmness, solidity; dullness (*of style*)
sicc·ō -āre *vt* to dry, dry up, drain; to stanch, heal
siccocŭl·us -a -um *adj* dry-eyed
sicc·us -a -um *adj* dry; thirsty; sober; firm, solid (*body*); solid (*argument*); dry, insipid (*style*)
Sicĭlī·a -ae *f* Sicily
sicilicissĭt·ō -āre *vi* to act like a Sicilian
sīcīlicŭl·a -ae *f* sickle
Siciliens·is -e *adj* Sicilian
sīcĭne *adv* is this how . . . ?
sīcŭbi *adv* if anywhere, wheresoever
sīcŭl·a -ae *f* little dagger
Sicŭl·ī -ōrum *m pl* ancient Italian people who migrated to Sicily
sīcunde *conj* if from some place, if from anywhere
sīcut or **sīcŭtī** *conj* as, just as; (in elliptical clauses) just as, like; (introducing a comparison) as it were, so to speak; (introducing an example) as, as for instance; (of condition) as, in the same condition as; as if, just as if; **sicut . . . ita** although . . . yet
Sicy·ōn -ōnis *f* town in the N. Peloponnesus
Sicyōnī·us -a -um *adj* of Sicyon; *m pl* inhabitants of Sicyon
sīderě·us -a -um *adj* starry; starspangled; heavenly, divine
sīdō sīděre sīdī or **sēdī sessum** *vi* to sit down; to settle; (of birds) to alight, land; to sink; to settle down, subside; (of ships) to be grounded
Sīd·ōn -ōnis *f* city of Phoenicia
Sīdōn·is -ĭdis *adj* Phoenician; *f* Dido; Europa
Sīdōnī·us -a -um *adj* Sidonian, Phoenician; Theban; *m pl* Sidonians
sīd·us -ĕris *n* constellation; star, heavenly body; sky, heaven; light, glory, beauty, pride; season; climate, weather; (in astrology) star, destiny
Sigambr·ī -ōrum *m pl* powerful German tribe
Sīgē·um -ī *n* promontory near Troy where Achilles was said to have been buried
Sīgē·us -a -um *adj* Sigean
sigill·a -ōrum *n pl* figurines; seal (*on a seal ring*)
sigillāt·us -a -um *adj* adorned with little figures

signāt·or -ōris *m* sealer, signer; witness
signāt·us -a -um *adj* sealed, secured
signif·er -ĕra -ĕrum *adj* bearing the constellations, starry; *m* standard-bearer; chief, leader
signifĭc·ans -antis *adj* clear, distinct, expressive
significanter *adv* clearly, graphically
significātĭ·ō -ōnis *f* signal, indication, sign, mark; expression of approval, applause; meaning, sense, signification; emphasis
signifĭc·ō -āre *vt* to show, indicate, point out, express; to intimate; to notify, publish, make known; to portend; to mean, signify
sign·ō -āre *vt* to mark, stamp, impress, imprint; to seal, seal up; to coin; to point out, signify, indicate, express; to adorn, decorate; to distinguish, mark, note
sign·um -ī *n* sign; indication, proof; military standard, banner; password; cohort, maniple; omen, symptom; statue, picture; device on a seal, seal, signet; heavenly sign, constellation; **ab signis discedere** to break ranks, disband; **signa conferre** to engage in close combat; to concentrate troops; **signa constituere** to halt; **signa conversa ferre** to wheel around and attack; **signa ferre** to break camp; **signa movere** to advance; **signa movere in hostem** to advance against the enemy, attack the enemy; **signa proferre** to march forward, advance; **signa servare** to keep the order of battle; **signa sequi** to march in rank; **signa subsequi** to keep the order of battle; **signa transferre** to desert, join the other side; **signis collatis** in regular battle
sīlān·us -ī *m* jet of water
Sīlăr·us -ī *m* river forming the boundary between Lucania and Campania
sil·ens -entis *adj* silent, calm, quiet; *mf pl* the dead
silent·ĭum -ĭī or **-ī** *n* silence; inactivity; **silentium facere** to obtain silence; to keep silence; **silentium significare** to call for silence
Sīlēn·us -ī *m* teacher and constant companion of Bacchus, usually drunk
sil·ĕō -ēre -ŭī *vt* to leave unmentioned, say nothing about; *vi* to be silent, be still; to keep silence; to be hushed; to rest, cease
sil·er -ĕris *n* willow
silesc·ō -ĕre *vi* to become silent, fall silent, become hushed
sil·ex -ĭcis *m* flint, flint stone; cliff, crag; hardheartedness
silicern·ĭum -ĭī or **-ī** *n* funeral feast; (coll) old fossil
silīg·ō -ĭnis *f* winter wheat; wheat flour

sīliqu·a -ae f pod, husk; f pl pulse

sillȳb·us -ī m label giving book's title

sīl·ō -ōnis m (man) button nose, snub nose

silūr·us -ī m sheatfish

sil·us -a -um adj having a turned-up nose, snub-nosed

silv·a or **silŭ·a -ae** f woods, forest; shrubbery, bush, foliage, crop, growth; mass, abundance, quantity, material, supply

Silvān·us -ī m god of woods; m pl woodland gods

silvesc·ō -ěre vi (of a vine) to run wild

silvestr·is -e adj wooded, overgrown with woods; woodland, living in woods; wild, growing wild; rural, pastoral; n pl woodlands

silvicol·a -ae m or f denizen of the forest

silvicultr·ix -īcis adj fem living in the woods

silvifrăg·us -a -um adj forest-smashing (wind)

silvōs·us -a -um adj wooded, woody

sīmi·a -ae f ape

simil·is -e adj similar; (with genit or dat) resembling, like, similar to; **homines inter se similes** men resembling one another; **veri similis** probable; realistic; n comparison, parallel

similiter adv similarly; **similiter atque** or ac just as; **similiter ut si** just as if

similitūd·ō -ǐnis f likeness, resemblance; imitation; analogy; comparison, simile; monotony; (with genit) similarity to; **est homini cum deo similitudo** there is a resemblance between a god and man

sīmiǒl·us -ī m monkey

sǐmǐtū adv at the same time; (with cum + abl) together with

sīm·ǐus -ǐī or **-ī** m ape

Simǒ·īs -entis m river at Troy

Simǒnǐd·ēs -is m famous lyric poet of Ceos (fl 500 B.C.); celebrated iambic poet of Amorgos (7th cent. B.C.)

simpl·ex -ǐcis adj single, simple, unmixed; plain, natural; frank; naive; in single file

simplǐcǐt·ās -ātis f simplicity; candor, frankness

simplǐciter adv simply, plainly; candidly, frankly

simpl·us -a -um adj simple; n simple sum

simpŭl·um -ī n small ladle

simpuv·ǐum -ǐī or **-ī** n libation bowl

simul adv together, at the same time; likewise, also; (with abl or cum + abl) with, together with; **simul atque** or ac or et as soon as; **simul ... simul** both ... and; conj as soon as

simulācr·um -ī n image, likeness, representation; form, shape, phantom, ghost; conception; sign, em-

blem; mere shadow; portraiture, characterization

simulām·en -ǐnis n imitation, copy

simŭl·ans -antis adj imitating; (with genit) imitative of

simulātē adv insincerely, deceitfully

simulātǐ·ō -ōnis f faking, bluffing, bluff, pretense; **simulatione** (with genit) under the pretense of, under the guise of

simulāt·or -ōris m imitator; pretender, phoney

simŭl·ō -āre vt to imitate, copy, represent; to put on the appearance of, simulate

simult·ās -ātis f enmity, rivalry, feud, jealousy, grudge

sīmŭl·us -a -um adj rather snub-nosed

sīm·us -a -um adj snub-nosed, pug-nosed

sīn conj if however, if on the other hand, but if

sināp·i -is n or **sināp·is -is** f mustard

sincērē adv sincerely, honestly, frankly

sincērǐt·ās -ātis f soundness, integrity

sincěr·us -a -um adj sound, whole, clean, untainted; real, genuine

sincǐp·ut -ǐtis or **sincipǐtāment·um -ī** n half a head; cheek, jowl (of a hog); brain

sind·ōn -ǒnis f fine cotton or linen fabric, muslin

sine prep (with abl) without; **flammā sine** flameless

singillātim adv one by one, singly

singlārǐter see **singulariter**

singulār·is -e adj single, alone, one at a time; unique, unparalleled; m pl crack troops

singulārǐter or **singlārǐter** adv singly; particularly

singulārǐ·us -a -um adj single, separate

singulātim adv singly, individually

singŭl·ī -ae -a adj single, one at a time, individual; one each, one apiece; **in singulos dies** on each successive day; every day, daily; m pl individuals

singultim adv sobbingly, gaspingly; falteringly

singult·ǐō -īre vi to hiccup; to throb

singult·ō -āre vt to gasp out, spurt out; vi to sob, gasp; to gurgle

singult·us -ūs m sob, gasp; squirt (of water, etc.); death rattle

singŭl·us -a -um adj one by one, single; each one, one apiece

sinist·er -ra -rum adj left, on the left; (because in Roman augury the augur faced south, having the East on the left) favorable, auspicious, lucky; (because in Greek augury the augur faced north, having the East on his right) unfavorable, inauspicious, unlucky; wrong, perverse, improper; m pl soldiers on the left flank; *f* left, left hand; left side; *n* left side; **a sinistra** on the left

sinisterīt·ās -ātis *f* awkwardness

sinistrē *adv* badly, wrongly, perversely

sinistrorsum or **sinistrorsus** *adv* to the left

sinō sinĕre sīvī or **siī situm** *vt* to allow; **sine modo** only let, if only

Sin·ōn -ōnis *m* Greek soldier through whose treachery the Greeks were able to get the horse into Troy

Sinōp·a -ae or **Sinīp·ē -ēs** *f* Greek colony on the S. coast of the Euxine Sea

Sinuess·a -ae *f* city on the border between Latium and Campania

sīn·um -ī *n* large drinking cup

sinŭ·ō -āre *vt* to wind, curve, arch

sinuōs·us -a -um *adj* winding, sinuous, serpentine

sin·us -ūs *m* curved or bent surface, indentation, curve, fold, hollow; fold of the toga about the breast; pocket, purse; breast, bosom, lap; bay, gulf, lagoon; winding coast; valley, hollow; heart (*e.g., of a city*), interior; intimacy; **in sinu meo est he is dear to me**

sīn·us -ī *m* large drinking cup

sīpar·ium -iī or **-ī** *n* theater curtain; **post siparium** behind the scenes

sīph·ō -ōnis *m* siphon; fire engine

sīphuncŭl·us -ī *m* small pipe

Sipyl·us -ī *m* mountain in Lydia

sīquandō or **sī quandō** *conj* if ever

sīquĭdem *conj* if in fact

siremps or **sirempse** = **si rem ipsam** *adj* the same, e.g., **sirempse legem** the same law

Sīr·ēn -ēnis *f* Siren (*sea nymph who had the power of charming with her song*)

Sīri·us -a -um *adj* of Sirius, of the Dog Star; *m* Sirius, Dog Star

sirp·e -is *n* silphium (*plant*)

sīr·us -ī *m* underground granary

sīs = **sī vīs** please, if you please

sistō sistĕre stitī statum *vt* to cause to stand, make stand, put, place, set; to set up (*monument*); to establish; to stop, check, arrest; to put an end to; to produce in court; **pedem sistere** or **gradum sistere** to halt, stop; **se sistere** to present oneself, appear, come; **sisti non potest** the crisis cannot be met, the case is hopeless; **vadimonium sistere** to answer bail, show up in court; *vi* to stand, rest; to stop, stay; to stand firm, last, endure; to show up in court; (*with dat* or **contra** + *acc*) to stand firm against

sistrāt·us -a -um *adj* with a tambourine

sistr·um -ī *n* rattle, tambourine

Sīsyphĭd·ēs -ae *m* descendant of Sisyphus, i.e., Ulysses

Sīsyph·us -ī *m* son of Aeolus, king of Corinth, whose punishment in

Hades was to roll a rock repeatedly up a hill

sitell·a -ae *f* lottery urn

Sīth·ōn -ōnis *adj* Thracian

Sīthōn·is -ĭdis or **Sīthonĭ·us -a -um** *adj* Thracian; *m pl* Thracians

sitĭculōs·us -a -um *adj* thirsty, dry

sitĭ·ens -entis *adj* thirsting, thirsty; arid, parched; parching; (*with genit*) eager for

sitienter *adv* thirstily, eagerly

sit·ĭō -īre -īvī -ĭī *vt* to thirst for; *vi* to be thirsty

sit·is -is *f* thirst; (*with genit*) thirst for

sitīt·or -ōris *m* thirsty person; **sititor aquae** thirster for water

sittўbus see **sillybus**

sitŭl·a -ae *f* bucket

sit·us -a -um *pp* of **sino**; *adj* lying, situated; founded; (*with* **in** + *abl*) resting on, dependent on

sit·us -ūs *m* position, situation, site; structure; neglect; mustiness; dust, dirt; idleness, inactivity, lack of use

sīve *conj* or if; or; **sive . . . sive** whether . . . or

smaragd·us -ī *m* or *f* emerald

smar·is -ĭdis *f* a small sea fish

smīl·ax -ācis *f* smilax, bindweed (*plant*)

Sminth·eus -ĕī *m* epithet of Apollo

Smyrn·a -ae *f* town in Asia Minor

sobol- = **subol-**

sōbriē *adv* soberly, moderately; sensibly

sōbriĕt·ās -ātis *f* temperance (*in drinking*)

sōbrīn·a -ae *f* cousin (*female, on the mother's side*)

sōbrīn·us -ī *m* cousin (*on the mother's side*)

sōbri·us -a -um *adj* sober; temperate, continent; sensible, reasonable

soccŭl·us -ī *m* small or short sock

socc·us -ī *m* sock; slipper; low shoe worn by actors in comedies; comedy

soc·er or **soc·ĕrus -ĕrī** *m* father-in-law

soci·a -ae *f* associate, companion, ally, partner (*female*)

sociābĭl·is -e *adj* compatible, intimate

sociāl·is -e *adj* allied, confederate; nuptial, conjugal; companionable, sociable

sociālĭter *adv* sociably, in comradeship

socienn·us -ī *m* comrade

sociĕt·ās -ātis *f* companionship, fellowship; association, society, partnership, alliance, confederacy

soci·ō -āre *vt* to unite, associate; to share

sociofraud·us -ī *m* heel, double crosser

soci·us -a -um *adj* joint, allied, confederate; held in common, common; *m* associate, companion, ally, partner; *f* see **socia**

sōcordĭ·a or **sēcordĭ·a -ae** *f* silliness, stupidity; apathy, laziness

sŏcordĭus *adv* too apathetically

sŏc·ors -ordis *adj* silly, stupid; apathetic, lazy, inactive

Sŏcrăt·ēs -is *m* famous Athenian philosopher (469-399 B.C.)

Sŏcratĭc·ī -ōrum *m pl* Socratics, disciples of Socrates

socr·us -ūs *f* mother-in-law

sŏdālĭcĭus -a -um *adj* of companionship; *n* companionship, intimacy; society, secret society

sŏdāl·is -is *m* or *f* comrade, companion, fellow; member (*of a society, priestly college, etc.*); accomplice, conspirator; gallant

sŏdālĭt·ās -ātis *f* companionship, fellowship; society, club, association; secret society

sŏdālĭt- = sŏdalĭc-

sŏdēs = sī audēs if you will, please

sōl sōlis *m* sun; sunlight, sunshine; day

sōlācĭŏl·um -ī *n* bit of comfort

sōlāc·ĭum -ĭī or **-ī** *n* comfort, relief

sōlām·en -ĭnis *n* comfort

sōlār·is -e *adj* sun; **lumen solare** sunlight, sunshine

sōlār·ĭum -ĭī or **-ī** *n* sundial; clock; sunny spot, balcony

sōlāt- = sōlac-

sōlāt·or -ōris *m* comforter

sŏldūrĭ·ī -ōrum *m pl* retainers (*of a chieftain*)

sŏldus see **sŏlidus**

sŏlĕ·a -ae *f* sole; sandal; fetter; sole (*flat fish*)

sŏleār·ĭus -ĭī or **-ī** *m* sandal maker

sŏleāt·us -a -um *adj* wearing sandals

sŏlĕō sŏlēre sŏlĭtus sum *vi* (with *inf*) to be in the habit of, usually, e.g., **solet cenare sero** he usually eats late; (with **cum + abl**) to have intercourse with

sŏlĭdē *adv* for certain; fully, wholly

sŏlĭdĭt·ās -ātis *f* solidity

sŏlĭd·ō -āre *vt* to make firm, make dense; to strengthen

sŏlĭd·us or **sŏld·us -a -um** *adj* solid, firm, dense; whole, entire; genuine, real; trustworthy; firm, resolute; *n* entire sum, total; solid, solid body, mass, substance; solid earth

sōlĭferrĕ·um -ī *n* all-iron spear

sōlĭstĭm·us -a -um *adj* perfect; **tripudium solistimum** perfectly auspicious omen

sōlĭtārĭ·us -a -um *adj* solitary, lonely

sōlĭtūd·ō -ĭnis *f* loneliness; deprivation; wilderness

sōlĭt·us -a -um *adj* usual, customary, characteristic; *n* the usual, the customary; **formosior solito** more handsome than usual, unusually handsome; **magis solito** or **plus solito** more than usual

sŏl·ĭum -ĭī or **-ī** *n* seat, chair; throne; dominion, sway; bathtub; stone coffin, sarcophagus

sōlĭvăg·us -a -um *adj* roaming

alone; single, solitary

sollemn·is -e *adj* annual, periodic; religious, solemn; usual; *n* usage, practice; solemn rite, solemnity, ceremony, feast, sacrifice; festival, games (*in observance of Roman holy days*)

sollemnĭter *adv* solemnly, religiously

soll·ers -ertis *adj* skilled, skillful, expert, clever

sollerter *adv* skillfully, expertly, cleverly

sollertĭ·a -ae *f* skill, ingenuity, shrewdness; clever plan; (with *genit*) skill in

sollicĭtātĭ·ō -ōnis *f* vexation, anxiety; incitement, instigation

sollicĭtē *adv* anxiously, with solicitude; diligently

sollicĭt·ō -āre *vt* to shake, disturb; to disquiet, annoy, molest; to worry, make anxious; to provoke, tempt; to stir up, incite, incite to revolt

sollicĭtūd·ō -ĭnis *f* anxiety, uneasiness

sollicĭt·us -a -um *adj* stirred up, stormy (*sea*); tossed (*by the waves*); troubled, disturbed, disquieted, restless; anxious, solicitous, apprehensive, worried

sollif- = solif-

sollist- = solist-

soloecism·us -ī *m* grammatical mistake, solecism

Sol·ōn -ōnis *m* famous Athenian legislator (*c.* 640-*c.* 560 B.C.)

sōl·or -ārī -ātus sum *vt* to console, comfort; to relieve, mitigate (*fear, worry*)

sōlstĭtĭāl·is -e *adj* of the summer solstice; midsummer's; solar

sōlstĭt·ĭum -ĭī or **-ī** *n* summer solstice; midsummer, summer heat

sŏl·um -ī *n* bottom, ground, floor; soil, land, country; sole (*of foot or shoe*)

sōlum *adv* only, merely, barely; **non solum ... sed etiam** not only ... but also

sōl·us -a -um *adj* only, single, sole, alone; lonely, solitary

sŏlūtē *adv* loosely, freely, without hindrance; negligently; without vigor

sŏlūt·us -a -um *adj* loose, untied, unbandaged; negligent; free; fluent; unrhythmical; uncontrolled; exempt, free; unbiased; unbridled, loose

sŏlūtĭ·ō -ōnis *f* loosening; payment

sŏlvō sŏlvĕre sŏlvī or **sŏlŭī sŏlūtum** *vt* to loosen, untie; to free, release; to dissolve, break up; detach, disengage; to unlock, open; to melt, turn, change; to relax, smooth, soothe; to impair, weaken, destroy; to acquit, absolve; to accomplish, fulfill; to pay, pay off; to solve, explain; to suffer, undergo (*punishment*); to remove, get rid of (*feelings*); *vi* to weigh anchor, set sail

Sŏlȳm·a -ōrum *n pl* Jerusalem

somniculōsē *adv* sleepily, drowsily

somniculōs·us -a -um *adj* sleepy, drowsy

somnif·er -ēra -ērum *adj* sleep-inducing, soporific; deadly (*poison*)

somni·ō -āre *vt* to dream of; to daydream about, imagine; **somnium somniāre** to have a dream

somn·ium -iī or **-ī** *n* dream; daydreaming; nightmare

somn·us -ī *m* sleep; night; sleep of death; indolence

sonābil·is -e *adj* noisy

sonīp·ēs -ēdis *adj* loud-hoofed; *m* steed

sonit·us -ūs *m* sound, noise

sonivi·us -a -um *adj* noisy

son·ō -āre -uī -itum *vt* to speak, sound, express; to mean; to sound like; *vi* to sound, ring, resound, make a noise

son·or -ōris *m* sound, noise, clang

sonōr·us -a -um *adj* sonorous, loud, noisy, clanging

sons sontis *adj* guilty, criminal

sontic·us -a -um *adj* important

son·us -ī *m* sound, noise; tone (*of style*)

sophi·a -ae *f* wisdom

sophist·ēs -ae *m* sophist

Sophŏcl·ēs -is *m* famous Greek writer of tragedies (c. 495-406 B.C.)

Sophoclē·us -a -um *adj* Sophoclean, of Sophocles

soph·us -a -um *adj* wise; *m* wise man, sage

sōp·iō -īre -īvī or **-iī -ītum** *vt* to put to sleep; to stun, knock unconscious; (*fig*) to calm, still, settle, lull

sop·or -ōris *m* deep sleep; stupor; apathy, indifference; sleeping potion

sopōrāt·us -a -um *adj* stupefied; unconscious; buried in sleep; allayed (*grief*); soporific

sopōrif·er -ēra -ērum *adj* sleep-inducing

sopōr·us -a -um *adj* drowsy

Sōract·e -is *n* mountain in Etruria about twenty-six miles from Rome

sōrāc·um -ī *n* hamper

sorb·ĕō -ēre -uī *vt* to suck in, gulp down; to absorb; (*fig*) to swallow (*e.g., hatred*)

sorbill·ō -āre *vt* to sip

sorbilō *adv* drop by drop, bit by bit

sorbitĭ·ō -ōnis *f* drink, pleasant drink

sorb·um -ī *n* Juneberry, service-berry

sorb·us -ī *f* Juneberry tree, service-berry tree

sord·ĕō -ēre *vi* to be dirty, be shabby; to appear worthless

sord·ēs -is *f* dirt, filth; shabbiness, squalor; *f pl* shabby clothes, rags (*often worn as a sign of mourning*); mourning; meanness (*of behavior*); low rank, low condition, vileness; dregs, rabble; vulgarity

sord·escō -escĕre -uī *vi* to become dirty, become soiled

sordidāt·us -a -um *adj* in dirty or shabby clothes (*esp. as a sign of mourning*)

sordidē *adv* vilely, meanly, vulgarly

sordidŭl·us -a -um *adj* rather soiled, rather shabby; (*fig*) low, mean

sordĭd·us -a -um *adj* dirty, filthy, shabby; soiled, stained; dressed in mourning clothes; low (*rank*); vile, vulgar (*behavior*)

sordĭtūd·ō -ĭnis *f* dirt, filth

sōr·ex -icis *m* shrewmouse

sōricīn·us -a -um *adj* squealing like mice

sōrīt·ēs -ae *m* sorites (*logical conclusion drawn from cumulative arguments*)

sor·or -ōris *f* sister; cousin; companion, playmate; **sorores doctae** Muses; **sorores tres** three Fates; **sorores tristes** gloomy Fates

sorōricīd·a -ae *f* murderer of a sister

sorōri·us -a -um *adj* sister's, of a sister; sisterly; **stuprum sororium** incest with a sister

sors sortis *f* lot; casting of lots, decision by lot; prophecy; fate, destiny, lot in life; portion, share; sort, kind, class

sorsum see **seorsum**

sortilĕg·us -a -um *adj* prophetic; *m* soothsayer, fortune-teller

sortĭ·ō -īre or **sort·ior -īrī -ītus sum** *vt* to cast or draw lots for; to allot, assign by lot; appoint by lot; to obtain by lot; to choose, select; to share, divide; to receive, get by chance; *vi* to cast or draw lots

sortītĭ·ō -ōnis *f* drawing lots, determining by lots

sortītō *adv* by lot; by fate

sortīt·us -ūs *m* lottery

Sosi·ī -ōrum *m pl* the Sosii (*two brothers famous as booksellers in Rome at the time of Horace*)

sosp·es -itis *adj* safe and sound; auspicious, lucky

sospit·a -ae *f* preserver (*epithet of Juno*)

sospitāl·is -e *adj* beneficial

sospit·ō -āre *vt* to preserve, protect

sōt·ēr -ēris *m* savior, deliverer, protector

sōtēri·a -ōrum *n pl* party thrown for a person recovering from an illness

spād·ix -īcis *adj* chestnut-brown

spad·ō -ōnis *m* eunuch

spargō spargĕre sparsī sparsum *vt* to scatter, sprinkle, strew; to scatter, disperse; to disseminate, broadcast; to spot, dapple

sparsĭ·ō -ōnis *f* sprinkling

spars·us -a -um *pp* of **spargo**; *adj* freckled, spotty

Spart·a -ae or **Spart·ē -ēs** *f* Sparta (*capital of Laconia, also called Lacedaemon*)

Spartăc·us -ī *m* Thracian gladiator who led a revolt of gladiators against Rome in 73-71 B.C.

Spartān·us -a -um *adj* Spartan
Spartiāt·ēs -ae *m* Spartan
Spartiātic·us or **Spartic·us -a -um** *adj* Spartan
spart·um -ī *n* Spanish broom (*plant, used in making ropes, nets, etc.*)
sparŭl·us -ī *m* bream (*fish*)
spar·us -ī *m* hunting spear
spath·a -ae *f* broad two-edged sword
spatı·or -ārī -ātus sum *vi* to walk, stroll, take a walk; to walk solemnly; to spread out
spatiōsē *adv* extensively; long, for a long time
spatiōs·us -a -um *adj* spacious; broad, large; prolonged
spat·ium -iī or **-ī** *n* room, space, extent; open space, public square; distance (*between two points*); walk, promenade (*place*); interval, period; time, opportunity; measure, quantity (*in metrics*); lap; race track
speci·ēs -ēī *f* sight, view; outward appearance, outline, shape; fine appearance, beauty; deceptive appearance, show, semblance, pretense, pretext; resemblance, likeness; display, splendor; vision, apparition; image, statue; idea, notion; reputation; species, sort; **in speciem** or **per speciem** as a pretext, for the sake of appearances
specill·um -ī *n* probe (*surgical instrument*)
specim·en -ĭnis *n* mark, sign, proof, example; model, ideal
speciō specĕre spexī *vt* to look at, behold
speciōsē *adv* splendidly
speciōs·us -a -um *adj* handsome, good-looking, beautiful; plausible; specious
spectābil·is -e *adj* visible; remarkable
spectācŭl·um or **spectācl·um -ī** *n* sight, spectacle; public performance; stage play; theater
spectām·en -ĭnis *n* sign, proof
spectāti·ō -ōnis *f* observation, view; examining, testing
spectāt·or -ōris *m* observer; spectator; critic, judge
spectātr·ix -īcis *f* on-looker, observer; spectator
spectāt·us -a -um *adj* tried, tested, proved; esteemed
specti·ō -ōnis *f* observing the auspices; right to take the auspices
spect·ō -āre *vt* to observe, watch; to face in the direction of; to consider; to bear in mind; to aim at, tend toward; to examine, test
spectr·um -ī *n* specter, apparition
specŭl·a -ae *f* look-out, watch tower; summit
spēcŭl·a -ae *f* bit of hope
speculābund·us -a -um *adj* on the look-out
speculār·is -e *adj* transparent; *n pl* windowpane, window
speculāt·or -ōris *m* spy; explorer

speculātŏrı·us -a -um *adj* for spying, for reconnaissance; *f* reconnaissance ship
speculātr·ix -īcis *f* spy (*female*)
specŭl·or -ārī -ātus sum *vt* to reconnoiter, observe, watch for
specŭl·um -ī *n* mirror (*made of polished metal*)
spec·us -ūs *m* or *n* cave, cavern; artificial excavation, ditch, canal, channel, pit; hole, cavity (*of a wound, etc.*)
spēlae·um -ī *n* den, cave
spēlunc·a -ae *f* cave
spērābil·is -e *adj* possible (*able to be hoped for*)
spērāt·us -a -um *adj* hoped for, longed for, desired; *f* fiancee, bride-to-be
Sperchē·is -ĭdis *adj* of the Spercheos
Sperchē·os or **Sperchī·us -ī** *m* large river in S. Thessaly
spernō spernĕre sprēvī sprētum *vt* to remove; to scorn, reject
spēr·ō -āre *vt* to hope for, expect, look forward to; to trust, trust in; to anticipate, await with fear
spēs speī *f* hope, expectation; anticipation, apprehension (*of evil*); **praeter spem** beyond all expectation; unexpectedly
Speusipp·us -ī *m* nephew of Plato and his successor as head of the Academy (347-339 B.C.)
sphaer·a -ae *f* sphere, globe, ball
sphaeristēr·ium -iī or **-ī** *n* tennis court
Sphin·x -gis *f* sphinx
spīc·a -ae *f* point; ear (*of grain*); tuft, top, head (*of plants*)
spīcĕ·us -a -um *adj* made of ears of grain
spīcŭl·um -ī *n* point; sting; dart, arrow
spīc·um -ī *n* ear (*of grain*)
spīn·a -ae *f* thorn; thorn bush; prickle (*of animals*); backbone, spine; back; *f pl* subtleties
spīnēt·um -ī *n* thorn hedge, thorny thicket
spīnĕ·us -a -um *adj* made of thorns, thorn
spīnif·er -ĕra -ĕrum *adj* prickly
spīnōs·us -a -um *adj* thorny, prickly; (fig) stinging, irritating (*worries*); confused, obscure (*style*)
spint·ēr -ēris *m* elastic bracelet
spintrī·a -ae *m* male prostitute
spinturnīc·ium -iī or **-ī** *n* bird of ill omen
spīn·us -ī *f* blackthorn, sloe tree
spīr·a -ae *f* coil (*of a serpent*); chin strap
spīrābil·is -e *adj* good to breathe, life-giving (*air*)
spīrācŭl·um -ī *n* pore, vent; breathing space
spīrāment·um -ī *n* pore, vent; breathing space, pause, instant
spīrit·us -ūs *m* breathing, breath; breeze; air; breath of life, life; in-

spiration; spirit, character, courage; pride, arrogance; morale; **spiritum ducere** to take a breath, breathe

spīr·ō -āre vt to exhale, breathe out; to aspire to, aim at; vi to breathe; to be alive; to be favorable; to have poetic inspiration

spissāt·us -a -um adj condensed, concentrated

spissē adv thickly, closely, tightly; slowly

spissesc·ō -ĕre vi to condense, become thick

spissigrād·us -a -um adj slow-paced

spiss·ō -āre vt to condense, concentrate

spiss·us -a -um adj thick, tight, dense; slow, late; difficult

splēn splēnis m spleen

splend·ĕō -ēre vi to be clear and bright, shine, gleam; to be illustrious, be glorious

splendesc·ō -ĕre vi to become clear and bright

splendid·us -a -um adj clear and bright, gleaming, glistening, sparkling; spotless, noble (character); splendid, magnificent; sumptuous; showy; illustrious

splend·or -ōris m brightness, brilliance; clearness; splendor, magnificence; noble

splēniāt·us -a -um adj wearing a patch

splēn·ium -iī or **-ī** n patch (for the face)

spoliātī·ō -ōnis f stripping, plundering; unjust deprivation (of honor or dignity); ousting (from public office)

spoliāt·or -ōris m or **spoliātr·ix -īcis** f despoiler, robber

spoliāt·us -a -um adj stripped, robbed

spoli·ō -āre vt to strip of clothes; to pillage, plunder, rob

spol·ium -iī or **-ī** n hide, skin; spoils, booty, loot

spond·a -ae f bed frame, sofa frame; bed, sofa

spondāl·ium or **spondaul·ium -iī** or **-ī** n ritual hymn accompanied by a flute

spondĕō spondēre spopondī sponsum vt to promise solemnly, pledge, vow; to promise in marriage; vi (law) to give a guarantee, put up bail; (with **pro** + abl) to vouch for

spondē·us -ī m spondee

spondўl·us -ī m mussel

spong·a -ae f sponge; coat of mail

spons·a -ae f fiancée

sponsāl·ia -ium n pl engagement; engagement party

sponsi·ō -ōnis f solemn promise, guarantee; bet; (law) agreement between two parties that the loser pay a certain sum to the other

spons·or -ōris m guarantor, surety

spons·us -a -um pp of **spondeo**; m fiancé, bridegroom; f see **sponsa**; n agreement, engagement

spons·us -ūs m contract

sponte (only abl) f (of persons, mostly with possessive adj) of one's own accord, voluntarily; by oneself, unaided; (of things) of itself, spontaneously; on its own account, for its own sake

sport·a -ae f plaited basket; sieve

sportell·a -ae f little basket, lunch basket

sportŭl·a -ae f little basket (in which gifts of food were given by the patron to his clients); dole, present (of food or money); gift

sprētī·ō -ōnis f scorn, contempt

sprēt·or -ōris m despiser

sprētus pp of **sperno**

spūm·a -ae f foam, froth; lather; scum

spūmāt·us -a -um adj covered with foam

spūmesc·ō -ĕre vi to grow foamy

spūmĕ·us -a -um adj foaming, frothing

spūmif·er -ĕra -ĕrum adj foaming

spūmig·er -ĕra -ĕrum adj foaming

spūm·ō -āre vi to foam, froth

spūmōs·us -a -um adj full of foam, foaming; bombastic (poem)

spuō spuĕre spui spūtum vt to spit, spit out; vi to spit

spurcāt·us -a -um adj foul, filthy

spurcē adv filthily; in filthy language

spurcidic·us -a -um adj foul-mouthed, filthy, smutty, obscene

spurcific·us -a -um adj smutty, obscene

spurcitī·a -ae or **spurciti·ēs -ēī** f filth, smut

spurc·ō -āre vt to make filthy, foul up; to defile

spurc·us -a -um adj (morally) filthy, dirty

spūtātilic·us -a -um adj deserving to be spit at, contemptible, disgusting

spūtāt·or -ōris m spitter

spūt·ō -āre vt to spit, spit out; to avert by spitting

spūt·um -ī n spit

squāl·ĕō -ēre -ŭī vi to be rough, be scaly, be parched, be wrankled; to be coated, be clotted, be stiff; to be covered with filth; to be covered with weeds, be overgrown; to wear mourning clothes, go in mourning

squālidē adv coarsely

squālid·us -a -um adj rough, scaly; stiff, coated with dirt, squalid; in mourning; rough, coarse (speech); cracked, parched (land)

squāl·or -ōris m squalor, dirtiness; desolation; filthy garments (neglected as a sign of mourning)

squal·us -ī m shark

squām·a -ae f scale; scale armor; fish

squāmĕ·us -a -um adj scaly

squāmif·er -ĕra -ĕrum adj scaly

squāmīg·er -ĕra -ĕrum *adj* scaly; *m pl* fish

squāmōs·us -a -um *adj* covered with scales, scaly

squill·a or **scill·a -ae** *f* shrimp

st *interj* sh!

stabiliment·um -ī *n* support

stabil·iō -īre -īvī -ītum *vt* to stabilize; to establish

stabil·is -ē *adj* stable, firm, steady; steadfast, unwavering, immutable

stabilit·ās -ātis *f* stability, firmness, steadiness, durability

stabiliter *adv* firmly

stabŭl·ō -āre *vt* to stable or house (*animals*); *vi* to have a stall

stabŭl·um -ī *n* stable, stall; lair; hut; brothel

stact·a -ae or **stact·ē -ēs** *f* myrrh oil

stad·ium -iī or **-ī** *n* furlong; race track

Stagīr·a -ōrum *n pl* town in Macedonia, the birthplace of Aristotle

Stagīrīt·es -ae *m* Aristotle

stagn·ō -āre *vt* to overflow, inundate; *vi* to form a pool; to be inundated

stagn·um -ī *n* pool, swamp, lake, lagoon; straits; waters

stalagm·ium -iī or **-ī** *n* eardrop, earring (*with pendant*)

stām·en -inis *n* warp (*of a loom*); thread; string (*of an instrument*); fillet (*worn by priests*)

stāminĕ·us -a -um *adj* full of threads, consisting of threads, wrapped in threads

Stat·a -ae *f* surname of Vesta

statāri·us -a -um *adj* standing, stationary; steady, calm; *m pl* actors in a type of comedy; *f* quiet or refined comedy

statēr·a -ae *f* scales; **statera aurificis** goldsmith's scales

staticŭl·us -ī *m* a dance

statim *adv* at once, immediately, on the spot

stati·ō -ōnis *f* standing still; station, post; position; residence; anchorage; *f pl* sentries

Stāt·ius -iī or **-ī** *m* P. Papinius Statius (*poet of the Silver Age of Latin literature, c.* 40-96 A.D.)

statīv·us -a -um *adj* stationary; *n pl* bivouac

stat·or -ōris *m* magistrate's attendant

Stat·or -ōris *m* Stayer (*epithet of Jupiter, who kept the Roman soldiers from retreating*)

statŭ·a -ae *f* statue

statŭm·en -inis *n* rib (*of a hull*)

stat·ŭō -ŭĕre -ŭī -ūtum *vt* to cause to stand, bring to a stop; to set up, erect; to establish (*precedent, etc.*); to set, fix, determine; to decide, settle; to decree; to strengthen, support; to appoint, create; to inflict, pass (*sentence, punishment*); to hold, think, consider; to fix (*a price*); to draw up, arrange (*a battle line*)

stat·us -a -um *pp* of **sisto;** *adj* fixed, set, appointed

stat·us -ūs *m* position, posture; position, situation, condition; social status, rank; form of government; (*mil*) position; **status rei publicae** type of government

statūt·us -a -um *adj* tall

steg·a -ae *f* deck

stell·a -ae *f* star; constellation; **stella comans** comet; **stella diurna** Lucifer; **stella errans** planet

stell·ans -antis *adj* starry

stellāt·us -a -um *adj* set with stars, starry; made into a star

stellif·er -ĕra -ĕrum *adj* star-bearing, starry

stellīg·er -ĕra -ĕrum *adj* star-bearing, starry

stelli·ō -ōnis *m* newt, lizard with spotted back

stemm·a -ātis *n* genealogical tree, pedigree; *n pl* antiquity, history

stercorĕ·us -a -um *adj* full of dung

stercŏr·ō -āre *vt* to manure, fertilize

sterc·us -ŏris *n* manure, dung

steril·is -e *adj* sterile, barren; causing barrenness, blighting; empty, bare; unprofitable; unrequited (*love*); wild (*trees*)

sterilit·ās -ātis *f* sterility, barrenness

stern·ax -ācis *adj* bucking (*horse*)

sternō sternĕre strāvī strātum *vt* to strew, spread; to pave (*roads, etc.*); to knock down, bring low, slay; to raze, level; to flatten, smooth; to calm, calm down; **sterni** to stretch out (*on the ground*)

sternūment·um -ī *n* sneezing, sneeze

sternŭ·ō -ĕre -ī *vt* to give (*e.g., an omen*) by sneezing; *vi* to sneeze; to sputter

Sterŏp·ē -ēs *f* one of the Pleiades

sterquilīni·um -iī or **-ī** or **sterquilīn·um -ī** *n* dung heap; (*term of abuse*) heap of dung

stert·ō -ĕre *vi* to snore

Stēsichŏr·us -ī *m* Greek lyric poet of Himera in Sicily (*c.* 640-*c.* 555 B.C.)

Sthenĕl·us -ī *m* king of Mycenae, son of Perseus, and father of Eurystheus; king of the Ligurians and father of Cycnus who was changed into a swan

stibad·ium -iī or **-ī** *n* semicircular seat

stigm·a -ātis *n* mark, brand; stigma (*of disgrace*)

stigmatī·ās -ae *m* branded slave

stigmōs·us -a -um *adj* branded

still·a -ae *f* drop; mere drop

still·ō -āre *vt* & *vi* to drip

stil·us -ī *m* stylus (*pointed instrument for writing*); writing, composition; style (*of writing or speaking*)

stimulāti·ō -ōnis *f* stimulation, incitement

stimulātr·ix -īcis f inciter (*female*)

stimulē·us -a -um *adj* of goads

stimŭlō -āre *vt* to goad, torment; to spur on, incite, excite

stimŭl·us -ī m or **stimŭl·um -ī** n goad, prick; (mil) pointed stake concealed below the ground; (fig) stimulus, incentive, spur

stingu·ō -ĕre *vt* to quench, extinguish

stīpāti·ō -ōnis f crowd, throng

stīpāt·or -ōris m attendant; m pl retinue

stīpendāri·us -a -um *adj* liable to tax, tributary; m pl tributary peoples; mercenary troops

stīpend·ium -iī or **-ī** n tax, tribute, tariff; (mil) pay; military service; year's service, campaign; **emereri stipendia** to have served out one's term; **emeritis stipendiis** at the end of one's military service, at discharge; **merere stipendia** or **mereri stipendia** to serve, serve in the army

stīp·es -itis m log, trunk; branch, tree; blockhead

stīp·ō -āre *vt* to crowd, cram, pack; to crowd around, accompany in a group

stips stipis f gift, donation, alms

stipŭl·a -ae f stalk, blade; stubble; reed pipe

stipulāti·ō -ōnis f agreement, bargain; (law) formal promise

stipulātiuncŭl·a -ae f insignificant promise, slight stipulation

stipŭl·us -a -um *adj* promised

stipŭl·or -ārī -ātus sum *vt* to stipulate; *vi* to bargain; (law) to make a formal promise

stīri·a -ae f icicle

stirpītus *adv* by the roots

stirp·s or **stirp·ēs** or **stirp·is -is** f stock, stem, stalk, root; plant, shrub; race, lineage; offspring, descendant; character, nature; root, source, foundation, beginning, origin

stīv·a -ae f plow handle

stlattāri·us or **stlātāri·us -a -um** *adj* imported, costly

stlopp·us -ī m slap (*sound produced by slapping an inflated cheek*)

stō stāre stetī statum *vi* to stand, stand still, remain standing; to stand firm, hold one's ground; to stand upright; (of hair) to stand up straight, stand on end; (of eyes) to remain fixed; (of battle) to continue; (of a ship) to be moored, ride at anchor; to be motionless; to be stuck; to depend, rest; to take sides, take part; (with *abl* of price) to come to, cost; (with *abl* or in + *abl*) to depend on, rest with; (with **per** + *acc* of person) to depend on, be due to, be the fault of, thanks to

Stōïc·a -ōrum n pl Stoic philosophy

Stōïcē *adv* like a Stoic

Stōïc·us -a -um *adj* Stoic; m Stoic, Stoic philosopher; n pl see **Stoica**

stol·a -ae f dress (*long outer gar-*ment worn by Roman women and reaching from the neck to the ankles); ceremonial gown (*worn by musicians*)

stolāt·us -a -um *adj* wearing a stola; (fig) proper for a lady, lady-like

stolīdē *adv* stupidly

stolĭd·us -a -um *adj* dull, stupid, stolid, slow

stomăch·or -ārī -ātus sum *vi* to be annoyed, fret, fume, glower

stomachōsius *adv* rather angrily

stomachōs·us -a -um *adj* irritable, resentful

stomăch·us -ī m stomach; taste, appetite; irritation, anger, resentment; **stomachus bonus** good appetite; good humor, patience

storĕ·a or **stori·a -ae** f straw mat, rope mat

strab·ō -ōnis m squinter

strāg·ēs -is f heap, confused mass, pile of debris; havoc, massacre

strāgŭl·us -a -um *adj* covering, serving as a covering; n rug, carpet; bedspread; horse blanket

strām·en -ĭnis n straw

strāment·um -ī n straw; covering, saddle cloth; **stramentum agreste** straw bed

strāminĕ·us -a -um *adj* straw, made of straw

strangŭl·ō -āre *vt* to choke, stifle

strangŭri·a -ae f strangury

stratēgēm·a -ătis n stratagem; trick

stratēg·us -ī m commander, general; master of ceremonies

stratiōtĭc·us -a -um *adj* soldierlike, soldierly, military

strāt·us -a -um *pp* of **sterno**; n quilt, blanket; bed, couch; horse blanket, pack saddle; pavement

strēn·a -ae f good-luck omen

strēnuē *adv* briskly, quickly, actively, strenuously

strēnuit·ās -ātis f briskness, vigor, liveliness

strēnu·ō -āre *vi* to be brisk

strēnu·us -a -um *adj* brisk, vigorous, active; fast (*ship*); restless

strepit·ō -āre *vi* to be noisy, clatter, rustle

strepĭt·us -ūs m noise, din, racket; crash, bang, clank, rumble, rustle, creak, squeak; sound (*of musical instruments*)

strep·ō -ĕre -uī -ĭtum *vt* to shout; *vi* to make a noise (*of any kind*); to rattle, clatter, clang, rumble, rustle, creak, squeak; to roar; to hum, murmur; (of musical instruments) to sound, blare; (of places) to ring, resound, be filled

striăt·a -ae f scallop

strictim *adv* superficially, cursorily

strictūr·a -ae f mass of molten iron

strict·us -a -um *pp* of **stringo**; *adj* close, tight, narrow

strīd·ĕō -ēre -ī or **strīd·ō -ĕre -ī** *vi* to make a high-pitched noise; to hiss, whistle, whizz, shriek, scream; to grate, buzz, rattle

strīd·or -ōris m shrill sound, hiss, shriek, scream, whine; harsh noise, grating, rattle, buzz

strīdŭl·us -a -um adj shrill, strident, hissing, whistling, creaking

strigīl·is -is f scraper

strig·ō -āre vi to stop, halt; to lose strength, give out

strigōs·us -a -um adj lean, thin; bald (style)

stringō stringĕre strinxī strictum vt to strip, clip; to draw (sword); to draw tight, tie tight; to press together, compress; to touch lightly, graze; to border on, touch (places); to affect, touch, move, pain, wound (mind, good name, etc.); to waste, consume

string·or -ōris m twinge, shock

strix strigis f owl, screech owl

stroph·a -ae f trick

Strophăd·es -um f pl island home of the Harpies

strophiăr·ius -iī or **-ī** m brassiere maker

stroph·ium -iī or **-ī** n brassiere; head band, chaplet

Stroph·ius -iī or **-ī** m king of Phocis and father of Pylades

structĭl·is -e adj building, for building

struct·or -ōris m builder, mason, carpenter; carver (at table)

structūr·a -ae f construction; structure

structus pp of **struo**

stru·ēs -is f pile, heap

stru·ix -īcis f pile, heap

strūm·a -ae f tumor, swollen gland

strūmōs·us -a -um adj scrofulous

struō struĕre struxī structum vt to build, build up, erect; to arrange, deploy (troops); to arrange, regulate; to occasion, contrive, plot

strūthĕ·us -a -um adj sparrow's

strūthiocamēl·us -ī m ostrich

Strȳm·ōn -ōnis m river forming the border between Macedonia and Thrace

Strȳmonĭ·us -a -um adj Strymonian, Thracian

stud·eō -ēre -ŭī vt to desire, be eager for; vi to be eager; (with dat) **a** to be eager for, be keen on, be enthusiastic about, take pains with, busy oneself with, apply oneself to; **b** to study; **c** to be a partisan of

studiōsē adv eagerly, enthusiastically, diligently

studiōs·us -a -um adj eager, keen, enthusiastic; studious; (with genit) partial to (a person or cause); (with genit or dat) eager for, keen on, enthusiastic about, devoted to, fond of, desirous of; **litterarum studiosus** studious

stud·ium -iī or **-ī** n eagerness, keenness, enthusiasm; devotion (to a person); party spirit; study; (with genit) eagerness for, enthusiasm for

stultē adv foolishly

stutiloquentĭ·a -ae f or **stultiloqu·ium -iī** or **-ī** n silly talk

stultilŏqu·us -a -um adj talking foolishly

stultitĭ·a -ae f foolishness, silliness

stultivĭd·us -a -um adj foolishlooking

stult·us -a -um adj foolish, silly, stupid

stūp·a -ae f tow, coarse flax, hemp

stupe·faciō -facĕre -fēcī -factum (passive: **stupe·fīō -fīĕrī -factus sum**) vt to stupefy, stun, astonish, knock senseless

stup·eō -ēre -ŭī vt to be amazed at; vi to be knocked senseless, be stunned, be stupefied, be astounded, be amazed; to be stopped in one's tracks

stup·escō -escĕre -ŭī vi to become amazed, become bewildered

stūpĕ·us -a -um adj of tow, hempen

stupidĭt·ās -ātis f stupidity

stupĭd·us -a -um adj amazed, astounded; dull, stupid

stup·or -ōris m numbness, bewilderment, confusion; dullness, stupidity

stupp·a -ae f tow, coarse flax, hemp

stuppĕ·us -a -um adj of tow, hempen

stupr·ō -āre vt to ravish, rape; to defile

stupr·um -ī n immorality; rape; disgrace (esp. from a sex crime)

sturn·us -ī m starling

Stygiāl·is -e adj Stygian

Stygĭ·us -a -um adj Stygian, infernal; deadly

Stymphalĭc·us or **Stymphalĭ·us -a -um** adj Stymphalian

Stymphăl·um -ī n or **Stymphăl·us -ī** m district in Arcadia famous for its vicious birds of prey which were killed by Hercules as one of his twelve labors

Sty·x -gis or **-gos** f chief river in the lower world; river in Arcadia

suādēl·a -ae f persuasion

suādĕō suādēre suāsī suāsum vt to recommend, propose, suggest; to urge, impel, induce; vi (with dat) to advise, urge, suggest to, propose to; **sibi suadere** (with acc & inf) to satisfy oneself that

suās·ĭō -ōnis f recommendation; support, backing (a proposal); persuasive eloquence

suās·or -ōris m adviser; advocate, supporter

suās·um -ī n dye

suāsus pp of **suadeo**

suās·us -ūs m advice

suāveŏl·ens -entis adj fragrant

suāviātĭō see **saviatio**

suāvidĭc·us -a -um adj charming

suāvilŏqu·ens -entis adj charming

suāviloquentĭ·a -ae f charming manner of speech

suāviŏlum see **saviolum**

suāvĭor see **savior**

suāv·is -e adj charming, pleasant, agreeable, attractive

suāvīt·ās -ātis f charm, pleasantness, sweetness, attractiveness

suāviter adv pleasantly, sweetly, charmingly, attractively

suāvitūd·ō -īnis f (term of endearment) honey

suāvium see **savium**

sub prep (with abl) under, beneath, underneath, behind; at the foot of, close to, near (mountain, wall); during, in, within, at, by, in the time of, just before; during the reign of; (with acc) under, along under; up to (walls); approaching, about, just before, just after

subabsurdē adv a bit absurdly

subabsurd·us -a -um adj rather absurd

subaccūs·ō -āre vt to blame, find fault with

subacti·ō -ōnis f working (of the soil); development (of the mind)

subactus pp of **subigo**

subaerāt·us -a -um adj (gold) having an inner layer of bronze

subagrest·is -e adj rather uncouth

subālār·is -e adj carried under the arms

subalb·us -a -um adj whitish

subamār·us -a -um adj somewhat bitter

subaquil·us -a -um adj somewhat dark, brownish

subarroganter adv rather arrogantly

subauscult·ō -āre vt to eavesdrop on; vi to eavesdrop

subbasilicān·us -ī m loafer (person who hangs around the basilicas)

subbib·ō -ēre -ī vt to drink a little

subbland·ior -īrī -ītus sum vi (with dat) to flirt with

subc- = succ-

subdifficil·is -e adj rather difficult

subdiffīd·ō -ēre vi to be a little distrustful

subditīci·us -a -um adj substituted, phoney

subditīv·us -a -um adj substituted, phoney

subditus pp of **subdo**

subdiū adv by day

sub·dō -dēre -dīdī -dītum vt to put under; to subdue; to substitute; to forge, make up; to spread (a rumor) falsely; (with dat) **a** to put or apply (something) to, add (something) to; **b** to subject (someone) to; **se aquis subdere** to plunge into the water

subdoc·eō -ēre vt to instruct (as an assistant teacher)

subdōlē adv rather cunningly

subdōl·us -a -um adj underhand, sly, cunning

subdom·ō -āre vt to tame somewhat

subdubit·ō -āre vi to be rather undecided

sub·dūcō -dūcere -duxī -ductum vt to draw up from below; to pull up, raise, to remove, take away, steal; to haul up, beach (a ship); to

withdraw (troops); to balance (accounts)

subducti·ō -ōnis f drydocking, beaching; calculation, computation

sub·ĕdō -esse -ēdī vt to eat away or wear away at the bottom; **scopulum unda subedit** water wears away the bottom of the cliff

sub·ĕō -īre -īvī or **-iī -itum** vt to enter (a place), enter (the mind); to approach, attack; to undergo (dangers, punishment, etc.); to help, support; to climb; to slip under; to dodge (a blow); vi to come or go up, climb; to follow; to advance, press forward; (with **ad** or **in** + acc) **a** to come up against, attack; **b** to climb (a mountain); **c** to approach, enter

sūb·er -ĕris n cork tree; cork

subf- = suff-

subg- = sugg-

subhorrid·us -a -um adj rather coarse, rather uncouth

sub·iciō -icĕre -jēcī -jectum vt to throw up, fling up; to bring up; to bring up close, expose; to suggest; to add, append; to suborn; to substitute; to forge; (with dat or **sub** + acc) **a** to put, place (something) under; **b** to subject (someone) to (authority, danger, risk); **c** to classify (something) under; **d** to submit (something) to (one's judgment)

subigitāti·ō -ōnis f lewdness; intercourse

subigitātr·ix -īcis f loose woman

subigit·ō -āre vt to lie with

sub·igō -igĕre -ēgī -actum vt to turn up, till, plow; to knead; to whet, sharpen; to rub down; to tame; to train, discipline (the mind); to conquer, subdue, subjugate, reduce; to force, impel, constrain; to incite; to row, propel (a boat)

subimpūd·ens -entis adj rather shameless

subinān·is -e adj rather empty, rather pointless

subinde adv immediately afterwards; from time to time

subinsuls·us -a -um adj rather insipid

subinvid·ĕō -ēre vi (with dat) to envy (someone) a little

subinvīs·us -a -um adj rather disliked, rather unpopular

subinvīt·ō -āre vt to invite unenthusiastically

subīr·ascor -ascī -ātus sum vi to be annoyed; (with dat) to be peeved at

subitāri·us -a -um adj (mil) suddenly called up (to meet an emergency); built in a hurry

subitō adv suddenly, unexpectedly, at once; **subito dicere** to speak ex-tempore

subit·us -a -um adj coming on suddenly, sudden, unexpected; rash (man); emergency (troops); n emergency

subjac·ĕō -ēre -ŭī vi to lie nearby; (with dat) to lie under or close to; **monti subjacere** to lie at the foot of the mountain

subjecti·ō -ōnis f subjection; substitution; forgery

subjectissimē adv most humbly

subject·ō -āre vt to toss up

subject·or -ōris m forger

subject·us -a -um pp of **subicio**; adj (with dat) a located near, bordering on; b subject to; m subject (conquered person)

sub·jungō -jungĕre -junxī -junctum vt (with dat) a to yoke or harness to; b to join to, connect with, add to; c to make subject to

sub·lābor -lābī -lapsus sum vi to sink, fall down, collapse; to glide imperceptibly; to fall back, fail

sublātē adv loftily, in lofty tones

sublāti·ō -ōnis f elevation, raising

sublāt·us -a -um pp of **suffero** and of **tollo**; adj elated

sublect·ō -āre vt to coax, cajole

sub·lĕgō -legĕre -lēgī -lectum vt to gather up, pick up; to pick up stealthily, steal, kidnap; to substitute; to overhear, pick up

sublest·us -a -um adj weak, trifling

sublevāti·ō -ōnis f alleviation, lightening

sublĕv·ō -āre vt to lift up, raise, support

sublic·a -ae f stake, pile (esp. for a bridge)

sublici·us -a -um adj resting upon piles; **pons sublicious** wooden bridge across the Tiber, built by Ancus Marcius

subligācŭl·um -ī n short apron

sublig·ar -āris n apron

sublig·ō -āre vt (with dat) to tie or fasten (e.g., a sword) to or below

sublīmē adv aloft, on high

sublimen adv upwards, on high

sublīm·is -e adj high, raised up, lifted high; lofty, elevated, exalted; raised high, borne aloft, through the sky; aspiring; eminent, distinguished

sublīm·us -a -um adj high, lofty

sublīmit·ās -ātis f loftiness, sublimity

sublingi·ō -ōnis m scullion

sub·līnō -linĕre -lēvī -litum vt to smear secretly; **os sublinere** (with dat) to cheat (someone)

sublūc·ĕō -ēre vi to shine faintly, glimmer

sub·lŭō -luĕre — -lūtum vt to wash underneath; to flow at the foot of (a mountain)

sublustr·is -e adj dimly lighted, throwing some light, glimmering, flickering

subm- = summ-

sub·nascor -nascī -nātus sum vi (with dat) to grow up underneath

sub·nectō -nectĕre -nexŭī -nex-

-um vt to fasten, tie (something) underneath; to confine; (with dat) to fasten or tie (something) below (something else)

subnĕg·ō -āre vt to halfway refuse; (with dat) to halfway refuse (something) to (someone)

subnig·er -ra -rum adj blackish

subnimi·a -ae f robe

subnīs·us or **subnix·us -a -um** adj propped up, resting, leaning; (with dat) a propped up on, resting on, leaning on; b relying on, depending on, confiding in

subnŏt·ō -āre vt to note down, record, register; to observe secretly

subnŭb·a -ae f rival (female)

subnūbil·us -a -um adj somewhat cloudy, overcast

sub·ō -āre vi to be in heat

subobscēn·us -a -um adj somewhat obscene, shady

subobscūr·us -a -um adj rather obscure

subodiōs·us -a -um adj annoying

suboffend·ō -ĕre vi to give some offense

subŏl·et -ēre v impers there is a faint smell; **mihi subolet** I have an inkling, I have a sneaking suspicion, I have a faint idea

subŏl·ēs -is f offspring

subolesc·ō -ĕre vi to grow up instead

subor·ior -īrī vi to rise up in succession, arise, proceed

suborn·ō -āre vt to equip, supply, provide; to employ as a secret agent, incite secretly, suborn

subp- = supp-

subr- = surr-

sub·scrībō -scrībĕre -scripsī -scriptum vt to write underneath; to sign; to write down, record, register; vi to sign an accusation, act as prosecutor; (with dat) a to add (something) to, attach (something) in writing to; b to assent to, agree to; (with **in** + acc) to sign an accusation against, indict, accuse, prosecute

subscripti·ō -ōnis f inscription underneath; signature; (law) subscription; recording (of an offense by the censor); record, register

subscript·or -ōris m signer or joint-signer (of an accusation)

subscriptus pp of **subscribo**

subsc·ūs -ūdis f tenon of a dovetail

subsecīvus see **subsicivus**

subsĕc·ō -āre -ŭī -tum vt to clip, trim, cut off

subsecūtus pp of **subsĕquor**

subsell·ĭum -ĭī or **-ī_n** low seat or bench; seat or bench on a lower level; judge's seat, the bench; tribunal, court; seat in the senate, senator's seat; bleachers (where the poor people sat); **versatus in utrisque subsellis** experienced as judge and lawyer

sub·sentiō -sentīre -sensī *vt* to have some inkling of

sub·sĕquor -sĕquī -secūtus sum *vt* to follow close after, chase, pursue; to back up, support; to imitate; to adhere to, conform to; to come after, succeed (*in time or order*); *vi* to ensue

subserv·ĭō -īre *vi* (with *dat*) **a** to be subject to; **b** to accommodate oneself to, humor; **c** to support, aid

subsicĭv·us -a -um *adj* left over; extra, spare (*time*); extra, overtime (*work*)

subsidiārĭ·us -a -um *adj* (mil) reserve; *m pl* reserves

subsid·ĭum -ĭī or **-ī** *n* aid, support; place of refuge, asylum; protection; (mil) reserves, triarii; military support, relief, aid; **subsidiō esse** (with *dat*) to act as support to; **subsidiō mittere** to send in support

sub·sīdō -sīdĕre -sēdī -sessum *vt* to lie in wait for; *vi* to sit down, crouch down, settle down; to sink, subside, settle; to establish oneself, settle down, establish residence, stay

subsignān·us -a -um *adj* special reserve (*troops*)

subsign·ō -āre *vt* to endorse, subscribe to (*an opinion*); to register, enter, record; to guarantee

subsil·ĭō -īre -ĭī *vi* to jump up

sub·sistō -sistĕre -stitī *vt* to hold out against; *vi* to stand up; to make a stand, take a firm stand; to come to a standstill, stop; to stay behind; (with *dat*) to take a stand against, oppose, fight; **b** to meet (*an expense*)

subsort·ior -īrī -ītus sum *vt* to choose as a substitute by lot; *vi* to choose a substitute by lot; (in a passive sense) to be chosen as a substitute

subsortītĭ·ō -ōnis *f* substitution by lot

substantĭ·a -ae *f* substance, essence; means, wealth, property

sub·sternō -sternĕre -strāvī -strātum *vt* to spread underneath; to cover; (with *dat*) to put at the disposal of, make subservient to; **rem publicam libidini suae substernere** to misuse high office to serve one's lust

substit·ŭō -uĕre -ŭī -ūtum *vt* to submit, present; to substitute; (with *dat* or **in locum** with *genit*) to substitute for or in place of; **animo** or **oculis substituere** to imagine

subst·ō -āre *vi* to stand firm, hold out; (with *dat*) to stand up to

substrātus *pp* of **substerno**

substrict·us -a -um *adj* tight, narrow, small

sub·stringō -stringĕre -strinxī -strictum *vt* to tie up, draw up; to restrain, control; (with *dat*) to press (*something*) close to

substructĭ·ō -ōnis *f* substructure, foundation

sub·strŭō -struĕre -struxī -structum *vt* to lay (*foundation*); **viās glareā substruere** to lay a foundation of gravel on the roads

subsult·ō -āre *vi* to jump up, jump up and down

sub·sum -esse *vi* to be near, be at hand; (with *dat*) **a** to be below or beneath, be under; **b** to be concealed in; **c** to be subject to, subservient to

subsūt·us -a -um *adj* trimmed at the bottom

subtēm·en -ĭnis *n* woof; thread, yarn

subter *adv* below, underneath; *prep* (with *abl*) beneath, below, underneath, under; (with *acc*) underneath, beneath; up to, close to, close beneath

subter·dŭcō -dŭcĕre -duxī -ductum *vt* to withdraw secretly, lead away secretly

subter·fugĭō -fugĕre -fūgī *vt* to evade, avoid; *vi* to run away secretly, get off

subter·lābor -lābī *vt* to glide or flow under; *vi* to slip away, escape

sub·tĕrō -terĕre -trīvī -trītum *vt* to wear away underneath

subterrānĕ·us -ā -um *adj* subterranean, underground

subtex·ō -ĕre -ŭī -tum *vt* to sew on; to veil, cover; (fig) to work up, compose; (with *dat*) **a** to sew onto; **b** to throw (*a covering*) over; **c** to work (*something*) into (*a story or plot*)

subtīl·is -e *adj* woven fine, of fine texture; delicate; subtle; discriminating; precise; plain, direct (*style*)

subtīlit·ās -ātis *f* fineness, minuteness; slenderness; exactness, precision; simplicity (*of style*)

subtīliter *adv* finely, delicately; accurately; plainly, simply

subtim·ĕō -ēre *vt* to be a bit afraid of

sub·trăhō -trahĕre -traxī -tractum *vt* to drag up from beneath, drag out, draw off, withdraw, remove; to avert (*the eyes*); (with *dat*) to drag or draw (*something*) away from

subtrist·is -e *adj* rather sad

subtrītus *pp* of **subtero**

subturpĭcŭl·us -a -um *adj* somewhat disgraceful

subturp·is -e *adj* rather disgraceful

subtus *adv* below, underneath

subtūs·us -a -um *adj* somewhat bruised

subūcŭl·a -ae *f* man's undershirt

sūbŭl·a -ae *f* awl

subulc·us -ī *m* swineherd

Subūr·a -ae *f* rough, noisy district in Rome, N.E. of the Forum between the Esquiline and Quirinal

Subūrān·us -a -um *adj* of the Subura

suburbānĭt·ās -ātis *f* nearness to Rome

suburbān·us -a -um *adj* suburban, near Rome; *m* suburbanite; *n* suburban home

suburb·ium -iī or **-ī** *n* suburb

suburg·ĕŏ -ēre *vt* (with **ad** + *acc*) to keep or turn (*a ship*) close to

subvectī·ŏ -ōnis *f* transportation

subvect·ŏ -āre *vt* to bring up regularly

subvectus *pp* of **suveho**

subvect·us -ūs *m* bringing up, transportation

sub·vĕhŏ -vehĕre -vexī -vectum *vt* to carry or bring up, transport

sub·veniŏ -venīre -vēnī -ventum *vi* (with *dat*) to come up to aid, reinforce, relieve

subvent·ŏ -āre *vi* (with *dat*) to rush to the aid of

subver·ĕor -ērī *vi* to be a bit apprehensive

subvers·ŏ or **subvors·ŏ -āre** *vt* to ruin completely

subvers·or -ōris *m* subverter, repealer

sub·vertŏ or **sub·vortŏ -vertĕre -vertī -versum** *vt* to turn upside down, upset, overthrow, throw over, subvert

subvex·us -a -um *adj* sloping upward

subvŏl·ŏ -āre *vi* to fly up

subvolv·ŏ -ĕre *vt* to roll up

subvor- = **subver-**

subvulturi·us -a -um *adj* vulture-like

succāv·us -a -um *adj* hollow underneath

succēdānĕ·us or **succīdānĕ·us -a -um** *adj* substitute

suc·cēdŏ -cēdĕre -cessī -cessum *vt* to climb; to march on or against, advance to or as far as; *vi* to come up, climb; to come next, follow in succession; to turn out (*successfully*); (with **ad**, **in**, or **sub** + *acc*) to climb, climb up; (with *dat*) **a** to come next to, follow; **b** to succeed in (*an undertaking*); **c** to yield, to submit to; **d** to relieve, take the place of (*e.g.*, *tired troops*); **e** to enter, go below to (*e.g.*, *a shelter*; *grave*); (with **in** or **ad** + *acc*) (fig) to reach, attain (*e.g.*, *high honors*), receive by succession, enter upon (*an inheritance*)

suc·cendŏ -cendĕre -cendī -censum *vt* to set on fire, set fire to; to light (*a fire*); (fig) to inflame

succens·ĕŏ or **suscens·ĕŏ -ēre -ī** *vi* to be angry, be enraged; (with *dat*) to be enraged at

succensus *pp* of **succendo**

succenturiāt·us -a -um *adj* in reserve

succenturi·ŏ -āre *vt* to receive (*someone*) as a substitute into a century or company

succenturi·ŏ -ōnis *m* assistant centurion, substitute for a centurion

successi·ŏ -ōnis *f* succession

success·or -ōris *m* successor

success·us -ūs *m* approach, advance uphill; outcome, success

succīdānĕus see **succedaneus**

succīdī·a -ae *f* leg or side of meat; (fig) extra income

suc·cīdŏ -cīdĕre -cīdī -cīsum *vt* to cut down, cut off, mow down

suc·cīdŏ -cīdĕre -cīdī *vi* to sink, give way; to collapse, fail

succīd·us or **sūcīd·us -a -um** *adj* juicy; (coll) fresh, plump (*girl*)

succidŭ·us -a -um *adj* sinking, falling

suc·cingŏ -cingĕre -cinxī -cinctum *vt* to tuck up; to put on (*e.g.*, *a sword*); to equip, arm, fit out

succingŭl·um -ī *n* belt

succin·ŏ -ĕre *vi* to chime in (*in conversation*)

succīsus *pp* of **succīdo**

succlāmātī·ŏ -ōnis *f* shouting in reply

succlām·ŏ -āre *vt* to shout out after, interrupt with shouts; (with *dat*) to shout out (*words*) at

succontumēliōsē. *adv* rather insolently

suc·crescŏ -crescĕre -crēvī *vi* to grow up; to be replenished; (with *dat*) to attain to

succrisp·us -a -um *adj* rather curled

suc·cumbŏ -cumbĕre -cubŭī -cubitum *vi* to fall or sink back; to yield, succumb, submit

suc·currŏ -currĕre -currī -cursum *vi* (with *dat*) **a** to run up to; **b** to run to help; **c** to occur to, enter the mind of

succ·us or **sūc·us -ī** *m* sap, juice; taste, flavor

success·us -ūs *m* shaking, jolt

succust·ōs -ōdis *m* assistant guard

suc·cutiŏ -cutĕre -cussī -cussum *vt* to toss up

sūcidus see **succidus**

sūcin·us -a -um *adj* & *n* amber

suctus *pp* of **sūgŏ**

sucŭl·a -ae *f* little pig; winch, windlass

sūcus see **succus**

sūdār·ium -iī or **-ī** *n* handkerchief, towel

sūdātōrī·us -a -um *adj* sweat, for sweating; *n* sweat room

sūdātr·ix -īcis *adj* causing sweat

sud·is -is *f* stake, pile; pike (*weapon*); dorsal fin

sūd·ŏ -āre *vt* to sweat, exude; to soak with sweat; (fig) to sweat over; *vi* to sweat; to drip

sūd·or -ōris *m* sweat; moisture; hard work

sūducŭl·um -ī *n* sweat-maker (*i.e.*, *whip*)

sūd·us -a -um *adj* dry; clear, cloudless (*weather*); *n* clear weather, bright sky

su·ĕŏ -ēre *vt* to be accustomed; (with *inf*) be accustomed or used to

su·escŏ -escĕre -ēvī -ētum *vt* to

accustom, familiarize; *vi* to become used; (with *dat*) to get used to

Suess·a -ae *f* town in Latium

suēt·us *pp* of **suesco**; *adj* usual, familiar

Suēv·ī -ōrum *m pl* a people of N.E. Germany

sūf·es -ĕtis *m* chief magistrate at Carthage

suffarcināt·us -a -um *adj* stuffed full

suffarcĭn·ō -āre *vt* to stuff full, cram

suffectus *pp* of **sufficio**

sufferō sufferre sustŭlī sublātum *vt* to suffer, bear, endure

suf·ficiō -ficĕre -fēcī -fectum *vt* to lay the foundation for; to dip, tinge, dye; to appoint to a vacancy; to yield, supply, afford; **consul suffectus** substitute consul (*consul appointed to complete an unexpired term of another consul*); *vi* to suffice, be sufficient; (with *dat* or with **ad** or **in** + *acc*) to suffice for, be adequate to

suf·fīgō -fīgĕre -fīxī -fīxum *vt* to nail up, fasten

suffīm·en -inis *n* incense

suffīment·um -ī *n* incense

suffīxus *pp* of **suffigo**

sufflām·en -inis *n* brake (*on a vehicle*)

sufflāt·us -a -um *adj* puffed up, bloated; (fig) fuming (*with anger*)

suffl·ō -āre *vt* to blow up, inflate; *vi* to blow, puff

suffōc·ō -āre *vt* to choke, strangle

suf·fodiō -fodĕre -fōdī -fossum *vt* to stab, pierce; to dig under (*walls*)

suffrāgātĭ·ō -ōnis *f* voting (*in someone's favor*), support

suffrāgāt·or -ōris *m* supporter (*at the polls*), partisan

suffrāgātōrĭ·us -a -um *adj* partisan

suffrāg·ĭum -ĭī or **-ī** *n* ballot, vote; right to vote, franchise; decision; judgment; applause, approbation; **suffragium ferre** to cast a ballot; **suffragium ferre** (with **de** or **in** + *abl*) to vote on

suffrāg·or -ārī -ātus sum *vi* to cast a favorable vote; (with *dat*) to vote in favor of, support, vote for; **fortunā suffragante** with luck on our side

suffring·ō -ĕre *vt* to break, smash

suf·fugiō -fugĕre -fūgī *vt* to escape, avoid; *vi* (with **in** + *acc*) to run to for cover

suffug·ĭum -ĭī or **-ī** *n* shelter, cover

suf·fulciō -fulcīre -fulsī -fultum *vt* to prop up, underpin, support

suf·fundō -fundĕre -fūdī -fūsum *vt* to pour in, fill; to suffuse, spread; to tinge, color; to infuse; **virgineum ore ruborem suffundere** (with *dat*) to cause (*someone*) to blush

suffūr·or -ārī *vt* to filch

suffusc·us -a -um *adj* darkish, brownish

suffūsus *pp* of **suffundo**

sug·gĕrō -gerĕre -gessī -gestum *vt* to supply, add; to prompt, suggest

suggest·um -ī *m* platform; stage

suggestus *pp* of **suggero**

suggest·us -ūs *m* platform; stage

suggrand·is -e *adj* rather huge

sug·gredior -grĕdī -gressus sum *vt & vi* to approach

sūgillātĭ·ō -ōnis *f* bruise; affront

sūgill·ō -āre *vt* to beat black and blue; to affront, insult

sūgō sūgĕre suxī suctum *vt* to suck

suī see **se**

suill·us -a -um *adj* of swine; **grex suillus** herd of swine

sulc·ō -āre *vt* to furrow, plow; to make a line in (*sand*)

sulc·us -ī *m* furrow; ditch, trench (*for plants*); track (*of a wheel or meteor*); wrinkle; plowing; wake (*of ship*)

sulf·ur -ŭris *n* sulfur

Sull·a -ae *m* Sulla (*Cornelius Sulla Felix, Roman general, dictator, champion of the aristocratic party, and political reformer, 138-78 B.C.*)

Sullān·ī -ōrum *m pl* partisans of Sulla

sullātur·ĭō -īre *vi* to wish to be a Sulla

Sulm·ō -ōnis *m* town about ninety miles east of Rome and birthplace of Ovid

Sulmōnens·is -e *adj* of Sulmo

sulp·ur or **sulf·ur -ŭris** *m* sulfur

sulpurāt·us -a -um *adj* saturated with sulfur; *n pl* matches

sulpurĕ·us -a -um *adj* sulfurous

sultis = **si vultis** if you please, please

sum esse fuī *vi* to be, exist; (with *genit* of possession) to belong to, pertain to, be characteristic of, be the duty of; (with *genit* or *abl* of quality) to be of, be possessed of, have; (with *genit* or *abl* of value) to be valued at, cost; (with *dat*) to belong to; (with **ab** + *abl*) to belong to; (with **ad** + *acc*) to be designed for; (with **ex** + *abl*) to consist of; **est** (with *inf*) it is possible to, it is permissible to; **est** (with **ut**) it is possible that; **sunt quī** there are those who, there are people who, they are of the type that

sūm·en -inis *n* breast, teat, udder; breeding sow

summ·a -ae *f* main thing; chief point, gist, summary; sum, amount, contents, substance; sum of money; **ad summam** generally, on the whole; in short; **summa rerum** the world; supreme power; **summa summarum** the whole universe

summān·ō -āre *vi* to drip a bit

Summān·us -ī *m* Roman god of night lightning

summ·ās -ātis *adj* high-born, aristocratic, noble

summātim *adv* on the surface; generally, summarily

summāt·us -ūs *m* supremacy, supreme power

summē *adv* very, extremely

sum·mergō -mergĕre -mersī -mersum *vt* to sink, submerge, drown

summĕr·us -a -um *adj* pure, straight (*wine*)

sumministr·ō -āre *vt* to supply, furnish

summissē or **summissim** *adv* in a low voice, softly; modestly, humbly

summissi·ō -ōnis *f* lowering, dropping

summiss·us -a -um *adj* lowered, stooping; lowered, soft (*voice*); humble, unassuming; submissive; too submissive, abject

sum·mittō -mittĕre -mīsī -missum *vt* to let down, lower, sink, drop; to let (*hair*) grow long; to lower, reduce, moderate, relax, lessen; to bring down, humble; to rear, put forth, produce; to send secretly; to send as a reinforcement; to send as a substitute; **animum summittere** (with *dat*) to yield to; **se summittere** to bend down, stoop over; to condescend; **se summittere** (with *dat*) to yield to, give in to

summolestē *adv* with some annoyance

summolest·us -a -um *adj* rather annoying

summon·ĕō -ēre -ŭī *vt* to give (*someone*) a gentle reminder, remind privately

summopĕre *adv* with the greatest diligence, completely

summōrōs·us -a -um *adj* rather crabby

sum·movĕō -movēre -mōvī -mōtum *vt* to move up, advance; to clear (*e.g., the court*); to remove; to expel, banish; (mil) to dislodge; (fig) to drive away, forget about (*e.g., worries*)

summ·us -a -um *adj* uppermost, highest; the top of, the surface of; last, latest, the end of; greatest, best, top, consummate; most distinguished; most important; *m* head of the table; *f* see **summa**; *n* top, surface, highest place, head of the table

summum *adv* at most; at latest; **uno aut summum altero proelio** in one or at most in two battles

sūmō sūmĕre sumpsī sumptum *vt* to take up; to put on, dress oneself in, wear; to exact, inflect (*penalty*); to take up, begin, enter upon; to eat, consume; to assume, suppose, take for granted; to cite, adduce, mention; to assume, appropriate; to select; to purchase, buy

sumpti·ō -ōnis *f* assumption

sumptuāri·us -a -um *adj* expense, relating to expenses, sumptuary, against extravagance

sumptuōsē *adv* sumptuously, expensively

sumptuōs·us -a -um *adj* costly, expensive; lavish, wasteful

sumptus *pp* of **sumo**

sumpt·us -ūs *m* cost, expense, charge; **sumptui esse** (with *dat*) to be costly to, be expensive to; **sumptum suum exercere** to earn one's keep; **sumptu tuo** at your expense, out of your pocket

Sūn·ĭum -iī or **-ī** *n* S.E. promontory of Attica

suō suĕre suī sūtum *vt* to sew, stitch, tack together

suōmet = emphatic form of **suo**

suopte = emphatic form of **suo**

suovetauríl·ia -ĭum *n pl* sacrifice of a pig, sheep, and bull

supell·ex -ectĭlis *f* furniture, household utensils; (fig) outfit, qualification

super *adv* on the top, above; besides, moreover; **super esse** to be left over; *prep* (with *abl*) above, over, upon, on; concerning, about; besides, in addition to; at, on (*time*); (with *acc*) over, above, upon; (with numbers) over, more than; besides, over and above

supĕr·a -ōrum *n pl* upper world, sky, Heaven; heavenly bodies

supĕrā *adv* above

superābĭl·is -e *adj* surmountable, climbable; conquerable

super·addō -addĕre — -addĭtum *vt* to add besides, add to boot

supĕr·ans -antis *adj* predominant

superast·ō -āre *vi* (with *dat*) to stand on

superāt·or -ōris *m* conqueror

superbē *adv* arrogantly, haughtily, snobbishly

superbĭ·a -ae *f* arrogance, haughtiness, snobbishness; (justifiable) pride

superbiloquenti·a -ae *f* haughty tone, arrogant speech

superb·ĭō -īre *vi* to be haughty; to be superb, be magnificent; (with *abl*) to take pride in

superb·us -a -um *adj* arrogant, haughty, snobbish; overbearing, tyrannical, despotic; fastidious, disdainful; superb, magnificent

supercil·ĭum -iī or **-ī** *n* eyebrow; frown, will (of *Jupiter*); summit, brow (*of a hill, etc.*); arrogance, superciliousness

superēmin·ĕō -ēre -ŭī *vt* to tower over, top

superfĭci·ēs -ēī *f* top, surface; (law) fixtures, improvements, buildings (*i.e., anything upon the property, but not the land itself*)

super·fīō -fĭĕrī *vi* to be over and above; to be left over

superfix·us -a -um *adj* attached above

superfiŭ·ens -entis *adj* superabundant, running over; (with *abl*) abounding in

superfiŭ·ō -ĕre *vi* to overflow

super·fundō -fundĕre -fūdī -fūsum *vt* (with *abl*) to shower (*something*) with; (with *dat*) to pour (*something*) upon; **superfundī** or **se superfundere** to spread, spread out, extend; **fama superfudit se in Asiam** the report spread to Asia

super·gredior -grĕdī -gressus sum *vt* to walk or step over; to surpass

supĕr·ī -ōrum *m pl* the gods above; men on earth; mortals; upper world

superimmin·ĕō -ēre *vt* to tower above

superimpend·ens -entis *adj* overhanging, towering overhead

superim·pōnō -pōnĕre -posŭī -positum *vt* to place on top, place overhead

superimposit·us -a -um *adj* superimposed

superincĭd·ens -entis *adj* falling from above

superincŭb·ans -antis *adj* lying above or on top

superin·cumbō -cumbĕre -cubŭī *vi* (with *dat*) to lay oneself down upon

superingĕr·ō -ĕre *vt* to pour down

superin·iciō -icĕre — -jectum *vt* to throw on top

superin·sternō -sternĕre -strāvī *vt* to cover

superĭ·or -us (*comp of* **supĕrus**) *adj* higher, upper; the upper part of; past, previous, preceding; older, elder, more advanced; victorious, conquering; superior, stronger; superior, greater; **dē loco superiore dicere** to speak from the tribunal, handle a case in court; to speak from the rostra, deliver a formal address; **ex loco superiore pugnare** to fight from a vantage point

superin·jaciō -jacĕre -jēcī -jectum *or* **-jactum** *vt* to overspread, overwhelm; to overdo, exaggerate

superinjectus *pp of* **superinicio**

superlātĭ·ō -ōnis *f* exaggeration

superlāt·us -a -um *adj* exaggerated

supernē *adv* above, from above

supern·us -a -um *adj* upper; situated high up; supernal, celestial

supĕr·ō -āre *vt* to go over, pass over, rise above; to pass or go past, go beyond; to sail past, double; to outdo, surpass; to overcome, vanquish; *vi* to mount, ascend; to be superior, have the advantage; to be left over, survive; to be superfluous; to be abundant; (with *dat*) to pass over, pass above

superobrŭ·ō -ĕre *vt* to cover completely, smother

superpend·ens -entis *adj* towering overhead

super·pōnō -pōnĕre -posŭī -positum *vt* (with *dat*) to put or place (*something*) upon; (with **in** + *acc*) to put (*someone*) in charge of

superscand·ō -ĕre *vt* to step over, climb over

super·sedĕō -sedĕre -sēdī -sessum *vi* (with *abl*) to refrain from, give up

superstagn·ō -āre *vi* (of a river) to overflow and form swamps

superst·es -itis *adj* standing by as a witness; surviving; posthumous; (with *genit* or *dat*) outliving, surviving; **superstes esse** to live on; **superstes esse** (with *genit* or *dat*) to outlive (*someone or something*)

superstitĭ·ō -ōnis *f* excessive fear; superstition

superstitiōsē *adv* superstitiously

superstitiōs·us -a -um *adj* superstitious; having magical powers

superstĭt·ō -āre *vi* to be remaining, be left

superst·ō -āre *vt* to stand over; *vi* (with *dat*) to stand on, stand over

superstrāt·us -a -um *adj* spread over (*as a covering*)

super·strŭō -strŭĕre -struxī -structum *vt* to build on top

super·sum -esse -fŭī *vi* to be left over, still exist, survive; to abound; to be in excess, be superfluous; to be adequate, suffice; (with *dat*) to outlive, survive (*someone*)

supertĕg·ō -ĕre *vt* to cover, cover over

superurg·ens -entis *adj* putting on pressure, adding pressure

supĕr·us -a -um *adj* upper; of this world, of this life; northern; **ad auras superas redire** to return to the upper air, come back to life; **mare superum** Adriatic Sea; *m pl* see **superi**; *n pl* see **supera**

supervacānĕ·us -a -um *adj* superfluous

supervacŭ·us -a -um *adj* superfluous, needless

supervād·ō -ĕre *vt* to go over, climb over

super·vĕhor -vĕhī -vectus sum *vt* to sail, ride, or drive by or past

super·veniō -venīre -vēnī -ventum *vt* to come upon, come on top of; to overtake; to come over, close over, cover; to surprise; *vi* to arrive suddenly; (with *dat*) to come upon by surprise

supervent·us -ūs *m* sudden arrival, unexpected arrival

supervolĭt·ō -āre *vt* to hover over

supervŏl·ō -āre *vt* to fly over; *vi* to fly across

supīn·ō -āre *vt* to turn up, lay on its back; to turn over (*by plowing*)

supīn·us -a -um *adj* face-up; lying

upwards, turned upwards; sloping, sloping upwards; (streams) flowing upwards (*to their source*); on one's back; lazy, careless, indifferent

suppactus *pp* of **suppingo**

suppaenit·et -ēre *v impers* (with *acc* of person and *genit* of thing regretted), e.g., **illum furoris suppaenitet** he somewhat regrets the outburst

suppalp·or -ārī *vi* (with *dat*) to coax (*someone*) a little

supp·ār -ăris *adj* nearly equal

supparasīt·or -ārī -ātus sum *vi* (with *dat*) to flatter (*someone*) a little like a parasite

suppăr·um -ī *n* or **suppăr·us -ī** *m* linen dress; small sail

suppeditātĭ·ō -ōnis *f* good supply, abundance

suppedĭt·ō -āre *vt* to supply, furnish; *vi* to stand by; to be at hand, be in stock, be available; (with *dat*) to be at hand for; (with **ad** or **in** + *acc*) to be adequate for, suffice for

suppēd·ō -ĕre *vi* to break wind quietly

suppetĭ·ae -ārum *f pl* help, assistance

suppetĭ·or -ārī -ātus sum *vi* (with *dat*) to help, assist

suppĕt·ō -ĕre -īvī or **-ĭī -ītum** *vi* to be at hand, be in stock, be available; (with *dat*) a to be at hand for, be available to; **b** to be equal to, suffice for, be sufficient for; **c** to correspond to

suppĭl·ō -āre *vt* to filch

sup·pingō -pingĕre — -pactum *vt* to fasten underneath

supplant·ō -āre *vt* to trip up

supplēment·um -ī *n* full complement; reinforcements

suppl·ĕō -ēre -ēvī -ētum *vt* to fill up; to make good (*losses, damage, etc.*); (mil) to bring to full strength

suppl·ex -ĭcis *adj* kneeling, on one's knees, in entreaty; humble, submissive; *m* suppliant

supplicātĭ·ō -ōnis *f* public thanksgiving, day of prayer; thanksgiving for victory; day of humiliation

supplĭcĭter *adv* suppliantly, humbly, submissively

supplĭc·ĭum -ĭī or **-ī** *n* kneeling down, bowing down, humble entreaty; public prayer, supplication; (because criminals were beheaded kneeling) execution, death penalty; punishment, torture; suffering, distress, pain

supplĭc·ō -āre *vi* (with *dat*) to go on one's knees to, entreat, beg

sup·plōdō -plōdĕre -plōsī *vt* to stamp (*the foot*)

supplōsĭ·ō -ōnis *f* stamping; **supplosio pedis** stamping of the foot

sup·pōnō -pōnĕre -posŭī -posĭtum *vt* (with *dat*) **a** to put, place, set (*something*) under; **b** to put (*something*) next to, add (*something*) to; **c** to substitute (*something*) for; **potentiam in gratiae locum supponere** to put power in place of influence, substitute power for influence

support·ō -āre *vt* to bring or carry up, transport

supposĭtĭcĭ·us -a -um *adj* spurious

supposĭtĭ·ō -ōnis *f* substitution

suppositus *pp* of **suppono**

suppostr·ix -īcis *f* unfair substituter (*female*)

suppressĭ·ō -ōnis *f* holding back (*of money*), embezzlement

sup·primō -primĕre -pressī -ressum *vt* to press down or under; to sink; to repress, stop; to suppress, keep secret

supprōm·us -ī *m* assistant butler

suppŭd·et -ēre *v impers* to cause (*someone*) a slight feeling of shame; (with *acc* of person and *genit* of cause), e.g., **eorum me suppudet** I am a bit ashamed of them

suppūr·ō -āre *vi* to fester

supp·us -a -um *adj* (animals) facing the ground

suppŭt·ō -āre *vt* to trim up; to count, compute

suprā *adv* on top, above; up above; earlier; beyond, more; **supra quam** more than; *prep* (with *acc*) over, above; beyond; (of time) before; (of amount) over, beyond; in charge of

suprascand·ō -ĕre *vt* to climb over

suprēmum *adv* for the last time

suprēm·us -a -um (*superl* of **superus**) *adj* highest, topmost; the top of; last, latest, final; greatest, supreme, extreme; closing, dying, final; **suprema manus** the finishing touches; **supremus mons** summit of the mountain, mountain top; *n* last moment; *n pl* moment of death; funeral rites, obsequies; testament

sūr·a -ae *f* calf of the leg

surcŭl·us -ī *m* shoot, sprout, twig; slip, graft

surdast·er -ra -rum *adj* somewhat deaf

surdĭt·ās -ātis *f* deafness

surd·us -a -um *adj* deaf; silent, noiseless; unheeding; dull, faint, indistinct

surēn·a -ae *f* grand vizier (*in the Parthian empire*)

surgō surgĕre surrexī surrectum *vi* to get up, rise, stand up; to get up (*from sleep*); to grow up, spring up

surp·ō -ĕre -ŭī *vt* to snatch, wrest; to pilfer

surrancĭd·us or **subrancĭd·us -a -um** *adj* somewhat rancid

surrauc·us or **subrauc·us -a -um** *adj* somewhat hoarse

surrectus *pp* of **surgo**

surrēmig·ō or **subrēmig·ō -āre** *vi* to row along

sur·rēpō or **sub·rēpō -rēpĕre -repsī -reptum** *vt* to creep under, crawl under; *vi* to creep up; (with *dat*) to creep up on, steal upon

surreptīcī·us or **subreptīcī·us -a -um** *adj* surreptitious; stolen

surreptus *pp* of **surrepo** and of **surripio**

sur·rīdĕō or **sub·rīdĕō -rīdēre -rīsī** *vi* to smile

surrīdĭcŭlē or **subrīdĭcŭlē** *adv* rather humorously

sur·rĭgō or **sub·rĭgō -rĭgĕre -rexī -rectum** *vt* to raise, lift up, erect

surring·or or **subring·or -ī** *vi* to grimace, make a face; to be somewhat annoyed

sur·rĭpĭō or **sub·rĭpĭō -rĭpĕre -rĭpŭī -reptum** *vt* to snatch secretly, pilfer; (with *dat*) to pilfer (*something*) from

surrŏg·ō -āre *vt* to propose as a substitute

surrostrān·ī or **subrostrān·ī -ōrum** *m pl* loafers around the rostra

surrub·ĕō or **subrub·ĕō -ēre** *vi* to blush slightly

surrūf·us or **subrūf·us -a -um** *adj* reddish

sur·rŭō or **sub·rŭō -ruĕre -rŭī -rūtum** *vt* to undermine, dig under; to tear down, demolish; (fig) to wreck, stamp out, destroy

surrustic·us or **subrustic·us -a -um** *adj* rather unsophisticated

surrūtus *pp* of **surruo**

sursum or **sursus** *adv* upwards, high up; **sursum deorsum** up and down, to and fro

sūs suis *m* pig, hog, boar; *f* sow

Sūs·a -ōrum *n pl* capital of Persia

suscensĕō see **succenseo**

suscepti·ō -ōnis *f* undertaking

sus·cĭpĭō -cĭpĕre -cēpī -ceptum *vt* to catch (*something before it falls*); to support; to pick up, resume (*conversation*); to bear (*children*); to accept, receive (*under one's protection*); to take up, undertake; to acknowledge, recognize (*a child*) as one's own

suscĭt·ō -āre *vt* to stir up; to erect, build; to awaken; to encourage; (fig) to stir up (*rebellion, love, etc.*)

suspect·ō -āre *vt* to gaze up at; to distrust, suspect

suspect·us -a -um *pp* of **suspicio**; *adj* suspected, mistrusted

suspect·us -ūs *m* respect, esteem

suspend·ĭum -ĭī or **-ī** *n* hanging; hanging oneself

sus·pendō -pendĕre -pendī -pensum *vt* to hang up, hang; to prop up, support; to keep in suspense; to check (*temporarily*); to interrupt; **suspendi** (with **ex** + **abl**) to depend on

suspens·us -a -um *adj* hanging, balanced; raised, poised; in suspense, uncertain, hesitant; (with **ex** + **abl**) dependent upon

suspĭc·ax -ācis *adj* suspicious; mistrusted, causing mistrust, suspicious

su·spĭcĭō -spĭcĕre -spexī -spec- **tum** *vt* to look up at; to look up to, admire; to mistrust, suspect; *vi* to look up; (with **in** + **acc**) to look up at or into

suspīcĭōsē *adv* suspiciously

suspīcĭōs·us -a -um *adj* mistrustful, suspicious; suspicious-looking, suspicious; (with **in** + **acc**) suspicious of

suspĭc·ō -āre or **suspĭc·or -ārī -ātus sum** *vt* to mistrust, suspect; to suppose, believe, surmise

suspīrāt·us -ūs *m* deep breath, sigh

suspīr·ĭum -ĭī or **-ī** *n* deep breath, sigh; **suspirium ducere, repetere**, or **trahere** to draw a deep breath, sigh

suspīr·ō -āre *vt* to sigh for; *vi* to sigh, heave a sigh

susque deque *adv* up and down; **de Octavio susque deque est** it's all one (*i.e., of no consequence*) as far as Octavian is concerned

sustentācŭl·um -ī *n* prop, support

sustentāti·ō -ōnis *f* forbearance, patience

sustent·ō -āre *vt* to hold up, hold upright, support; to sustain (*with food*); to hold (*enemy*); to uphold (*law*); to delay; to postpone

sus·tĭnĕō -tĭnēre -tĭnŭī -tentum *vt* to hold up, support; to hold back, hold in, check; to uphold (*law*); to sustain, support (*with food*); to bear (*trouble*); to hold up, delay, put off

sustoll·ō -ĕre *vt* to lift up, raise; to destroy

susurrāt·or -ōris *m* mutterer, whisperer

susurr·ō -āre *vt & vi* to mutter, murmur, whisper

susurr·us -ī *m* low, gentle noise; murmur, whisper, buzz, hum

sūtēl·ae -ārum *f pl* patches; tricks

sūtĭl·is -e *adj* sewn together, fastened together

sūt·or -ōris *m* shoemaker

sūtōrĭ·us -a -um *adj* shoemaker's; *m* ex-shoemaker

sūtrīn·us -a -um *adj* shoemaker's; *f* shoemaker's shop; shoemaker's trade

sūtūr·a -ae *f* seam; suture

sūt·us -a -um *pp* of **suo**; *n pl* joints

su·us -a -um *adj* his, her, its, their, one's own; due, proper, peculiar; *pron masc pl* one's own people, one's own friends, one's own family; *pron neut pl* one's own property

Sўbar·is -is *f* town in S. Italy noted for its luxurious living

Sўbarīt·a -ae *m* Sybarite

Sўchae·us -ī *m* husband of Dido

sўcophant·a -ae *m* sycophant; blackmailer; cheat; slanderer

sўcophantī·a -ae *f* cunning, deceit

sўcophantĭōsē *adv* deceitfully

sўcophant·or -ārī -ātus sum *vi* to cheat; (with *dat*) to play a trick on

Sўēn·ē -ēs *f* town in S. Egypt

sўllăb·a -ae *f* syllable

sўllabātim *adv* syllable by syllable

symbŏl·a -ae *f* contribution (*of money to a feast*); (coll) blows

symbŏl·us -ī *m* symbol, mark, token

symphōnǐ·a -ae *f* agreement of sound, symphony, harmony

symphōnǐăc·us -a -um *adj* concert, musical; **puerī symphonǐacī** chor- isters; *m pl* musicians

Symplēgăd·es -um *f pl* two islands in the Euxine which floated about and dashed against each other until they were fixed in place as the Ar- go sailed by them

symplegm·a -ătis *m* group (*of per- sons embracing or wrestling*)

synĕdr·us -ī *m* senator (*in Mace- donia*)

syngrăph·a -ae *f* promissory note

syngrăph·us -ī *m* written contract; pass, passport

synŏd·ŭs -ontis *m* bream (*fish*)

synthĕs·is -is *f* dinner service; suit of clothes; dinner clothes

Syph·ax -ācis *m* king of Numidia at the time of the Second Punic War, siding with Carthage (*d₊* 203 B.C.)

Syrācosǐ·us -a -um *adj* Syracusan; *m pl* Syracusans

Syrācūs·ae -ārum *f pl* Syracuse (*chief city in Sicily*)

Syrācūsān·us or **Syrācūsǐ·us -a -um** *adj* Syracusan

Syrǐ·us -a -um *adj* Syrian; *m pl* Syrians; *f* Syria

Syr·us -a -um *adj* Syrian; *m pl* Syr- ians

Syr·inx -ingis *f* nymph who was pursued by Pan and changed into a reed

syrm·a -ae *f* robe with a train (*worn esp. by actors in tragedies*); tragedy

syrt·is -is *f* sand dune; quicksand

Syrt·is -is *f* Gulf of Sidra in N. Africa; Gulf of Cabes; *f pl* the Syr- tes (*lakes and sand dunes of that area as representative of a wild, forbidding place*)

T

tabell·a -ae *f* small board; door sill; game board; writing tablet; ballot; picture, painting; votive tablet

tabellārǐ·us -a -um *adj* (law) regu- lating voting; *m* mailman, courier

tāb·ĕō -ēre *vi* to waste away; to melt away; to stream, run

tabern·a -ae *f* hut, hovel, cottage; booth, stall, shop; inn

tabernācŭl·um -ī *n* tent; **taberna- culum capere** to choose a place for a tent outside the city in which to take the auspices

tabernārǐ·ī -ōrum *m pl* shopkeepers

tāb·ēs -is *f* melting, wasting, decay, dwindling, shrinking; decaying matter, rot; disease, pestilence

tāb·escō -escĕre -ǔī to begin to decay, begin to melt, melt gradu- ally

tābidŭl·us -a -um *adj* wasting, con- suming

tābĭd·us -a -um *adj* wasting, decay- ing, melting; corrupting, infectious

tābĭfǐc·us -a -um *adj* melting, wasting; (fig) gnawing

tabŭl·a -ae *f* plank, board; writing tablet; advertisement; auction; pic- ture, painting; map; votive tablet; *f pl* account books, records, regis- ter, lists

tabŭlār·ǐum -ǐī or **-ǐ** *n* archives, ar- chives building

tabŭlātǐ·ō -ōnis *f* flooring, floor, story

tabŭlāt·us -a -um *adj* boarded; *n* floor, story; layer; row (*of trees*)

tāb·um -ī *n* putrid matter, decay, rot; disease, plague, pestilence

tac·ĕō -ēre -ǔī -ĭtum *vt* to be silent about, pass over in silence; *vi* to be silent, hold one's tongue; to be still, be noiseless

tacitē *adv* silently, secretly

taciturnǐt·ās -ātis *f* silence, taci- turnity

taciturn·us -a -um *adj* silent, taci- turn; noiseless, hushed, quiet

tacĭt·us -a -um *adj* silent, mute; un- mentioned, secret; (law) assumed, implied, tacit; **per tacitum** in si- lence

Tacĭt·us -ī *m* C. Cornelius Tacitus (*Roman historian, c.* 55-*c.* 115 A.D.)

tactĭl·is -e *adj* tangible

tactǐ·ō -ōnis *f* touch, touching; feel- ing, sense of touch

tactus *pp of* tango

tact·us -ūs *m* touch; handling; influ- ence, effect

taed·a -ae *f* pine wood, pitch pine; torch; wedding torch; wedding; pine board

taedet taedēre taedǔit or **taesum est** *v impers* it irks; (with *acc* of person and *genit* of the cause), e.g., **me taedet stultitiae meae** my foolishness irks me, I am annoyed at my foolishness

taedĭf·er -ĕra -ĕrum *adj* torch- bearing

taed·ĭum -ǐī or **-ǐ** *n* irksomeness, te- diousness, weariness, boredom

taenǐ·a -ae *f* band, ribbon

Taenarĭd·ēs -ae *m* Spartan (*esp. Hyacinthus*)

Taenăr·is -ĭdis *adj* Spartan

Taenăr·um -ī or **Taenăr·on -ī** *n* or **Taenăr·us** or **Taenăr·os -ī** *m* or *f* most southerly point of the Peloponnesus (*thought to be the entrance to the lower world*); lower world, Hades

taet·er -ra -rum *adj* foul, revolting, offensive, shocking, loathsome; ugly, hideous; disgraceful; *n* offensiveness, repulsiveness

taetrē *adv* foully, hideously, shockingly

taetricus see **tetricus**

tag·ax -ācis *adj* light-fingered

tālār·is -e *adj* ankle-length; *n pl* angle-length clothes; sandals

tālār·ius -a -um *adj* of dice; **ludus talarius** game of dice

talāssiō or **talassiō** *interj* wedding cry

tāl·ea -ae *f* rod, bar, stake

talent·um -ī *n* talent (*Greek weight, varying from state to state, but equal to about fifty pounds*); sum of money (*consisting of sixty minae*)

tāli·ō -ōnis *f* (law) punishment in kind

tāl·is -e *adj* such, of such kind, of that kind; so great, so excellent, so distinguished

talp·a -ae *m* or *f* mole (*animal*)

Talthyb·ius -iī or **-ī** *m* herald of Agamemnon

tāl·us -ī *m* ankle, anklebone; heel, foot; die (*used in playing dice*)

tam *adv* to such an extent, to such a degree, so, so much; **tam . . . quam** the . . . the; **tam magis . . . quam magis** the more . . . the more

tamār·ix -īcis *f* tamarisk

tamdiū *adv* so long, how long; **tuamdiu quam** or **tuamdiu dum** as long as

tamen *adv* yet, nevertheless, still, all the same; in the same way

Tāmĕs·is -is or **Tāmĕs·a -ae** *m* Thames

tametsī *conj* even if, although

tamquam or **tanquam** *conj* as, just as, as much as; just as if; **tamquam si** just as if

Tanāgr·a -ae *f* town in Boeotia

Tanā·is -is *m* river of Sarmatia (*modern Don*)

Tanāqu·il -ilis *f* wife of the elder Tarquin

tandem *adv* at last, in the end, finally; (*expressing urgency or impatience*) now, tell me, please

tangō tangĕre tetĭgī tactum *vt* to touch; to handle, meddle with; to taste; to come to, reach; to border on; to hit, beat; to wash, anoint; to affect, gall, move to pity; to dupe; to touch upon, mention; to touch, be related to; to undertake

Tantāl·us -a -um *adj* of Tantalus

Tantalĭd·ēs -ae *m* descendant of Tantalus

Tantăl·is -ĭdis *f* descendant of Tantalus (*female*)

Tantăl·us -ī *m* son of Jupiter and father of Pelops who was punished in the lower world with constant hunger and thirst

tantill·us -a -um *adj* so small, so little; *n* a bit

tantisper *adv* just so long (*and no longer*); just for the moment

tantopĕre or **tantō opĕre** *adv* so much, so greatly, to such a degree, so earnestly, so hard

tantŭlum *adv* so little, in the least

tantŭl·us -a -um *adj* so little, so small; *n* so little, such a trifle; **tantulo vendere** to sell for such a trifling amount

tantum *adv* so much, so greatly, to such a degree, so far, so long, so; only, just, but just, hardly, scarcely; **tantum modo** only

tantummŏdo *adv* only

tantundem *adv* just so much, just as far, to the same extent

tant·us -a -um *adj* of such size, so great; so much; so little; so important; *pron neut* so much; so little; so small an amount, so small a number; **tanti** of such value, worth so much, at so high a price; of little account, of such small importance; **tanto** (*with comparatives*) by so much, so much the; **tanto melior!** so much the better!, bravo!, excellent!; **tanto nequior!** so much the worse!

tantusdem -ădem -undem *adj* so great, just as great, just as large

tapēt·a -ae *m* or **tapēt·a -ōrum** or **tapēt·ia -ium** *n pl* carpet; tapestry; coverlet

tardē *adv* slowly

tardesc·ō -ĕre *vi* to become slow; to falter

tardĭp·ēs -ĕdis *adj* limping

tardĭt·ās -ātis *f* tardiness, slowness; dullness, stupidity

tarditūd·ō -ĭnis *f* tardiness, slowness

tardiuscŭl·us -a -um *adj* rather slow, slowish, dragging

tard·ō -āre *vt* to slow down, delay, hinder; *vi* to go slow, take it easy

tard·us -a -um *adj* tardy, slow; lingering; mentally slow, mentally retarded; deliberate; crippling

Tarentīn·us -a -um *adj* Tarentine; *m pl* Tarentines

Tarent·um -ī *n* town on S. coast of Italy, founded by the Spartans around 700 B.C.

tarm·es -ĭtis *m* wood worm, borer

Tarpēi·us -a -um *adj* Tarpeian; **mons Tarpeius** Tarpeian cliff on the Capitoline Hill from which criminals were thrown; *f* Roman girl who treacherously opened the citadel to the Sabine attackers

tarpezīt·a or **trapezīt·a -ae** *m* banker

Tarquiniens·is -e *adj* of the town of Tarquinii

Tarquini·us -a -um *adj* Tarquinian; *m* Tarquinius Priscus (*fifth king of Rome and husband of Tanaquil*); Tarquinius Superbus (*seventh* *and last king of Rome*); *m pl* important Etrurian town

Tarracīn·a -ae *f* or **Terracīn·ae -ārum** *f pl* town in Latium

Tartăr·a -ōrum *n pl* or **Tartăr·us** or **Tartăr·os -ī** *m* Tartarus (*lower level of Hades reserved for criminals*)

Tartărĕ·us -a -um *adj* of Tartarus, infernal

tat or **tatae** *interj* exclamation of surprise

tat·a -ae *m* (coll) daddy

Tat·ius -iī or **-ī** *m* Titus Tatius (*king of the Sabines who later ruled jointly with Romulus until the latter had him killed*)

taure·us -a -um *adj* bull's, of a bull; **terga taurea** bulls' hides; drums; *f* rawhide, whip

Taur·ī -ōrum *m pl* barbarous people living in the peninsula now called the Crimea

Tauric·us -a -um *adj* Tauric

taurīf·er -ĕra -ĕrum *adj* bull-producing (*regions*)

tauriform·is -e *adj* bull-shaped

taurīn·us -a -um *adj* bull's; made of bull's hide; bull-like

taur·us -ī *m* bull

Taur·us -ī *m* Taurus (*constellation*)

taxātĭ·ō -ōnis *f* rating, appraisal

taxill·us -ī *m* small die (*for playing dice*)

tax·ō -āre *vt* to appraise

tax·us -ī *f* yew, yew tree

Tāÿgĕt·ē -ēs *f* one of the Pleiades, the daughter of Atlas and Pleione

Tāÿgĕt·us -ī *m* mountain range in Laconia

tē *acc & abl* of **tu**

-te = suffix for **tu** and **te**

Teān·um -ī *n* town in Campania; town in Apulia

techn·a or **techīn·a -ae** *f* trick

Tecmess·a -ae *f* wife of Ajax the son of Telamon

tectē *adv* cautiously, guardedly

tect·or -ōris *m* plasterer

tectōrĭŏl·um -ī *n* bit of plaster work

tectōrĭ·us -a -um *adj* roofing; plasterer's; painter's; *n* plaster, stucco; fresco painting; beauty preparation

tect·us -a -um *pp* of **tego**; *adj* concealed; secret; guarded (*words*); reserved, secretive (*person*); *n* roof; ceiling; canopy; cover, shelter; house

tēcum = **cum te**

Tegĕ·a -ae *f* town in Arcadia

Tegeae·us -a -um *adj* Tegean, Arcadian; *m* Pan; *f* Arcadian maiden (*i.e., Atalanta*)

Tegeāt·ae -ārum *m pl* Tegeans

teg·es -ĕtis *f* mat

tegill·um -ī *n* hood, cowl

tegim·en or **tegm·en** or **tegŭm·en -ĭnis** *n* cover, covering; vault (*of heaven*)

tegiment·um or **tegment·um** or **tegument·um -ī** *n* cover, covering

tegō tegĕre texī tectum *vt* to cover; to protect, shelter, defend; to hide; to bury; **tegere latus** (with *genit*) to escort (*someone*)

tēgŭl·a -ae *f* tile; *f pl* roof tiles, tiled roof

tegŭmen see **tegimen**

tegumentum see **tegimentum**

tēl·a -ae *f* web; warp (*threads that run lengthwise in the loom*); yarn beam; loom; design, plan

Telăm·ōn -ōnis *m* son of Aeacus, brother of Peleus, king of Salamis, and father of Ajax and Teucer

Telamōnĭăd·ēs -ae *m* son of Telamon (*i.e., Ajax*)

Telamōn·ĭus -iī or **-ī** *m* Ajax

Tēlegŏn·us -ī *m* son of Ulysses and Circe

Tēlemăch·us -ī *m* son of Ulysses and Penelope

Tēlĕph·us -ī *m* king of Mysia, wounded by the spear of Achilles and later cured by its rust

tell·ūs -ūris *f* the earth; ground, earth; land, country

tēl·um -ī *n* missile, weapon; spear, javelin, dart; sword, dagger, ax; shaft

temerārĭ·us -a -um *adj* casual, accidental; rash, thoughtless

temĕre *adv* by chance, without cause; at random; rashly, thoughtlessly; **non temere** not lightly; **nōt** easily; hardly ever; **nullus dies temere intercessit quo non scriberet** hardly a day ever passed without his writing

temerit·ās -ātis *f* chance, accident; rashness, thoughtlessness; *f pl* foolhardy acts

temĕr·ō -āre *vt* to darken, blacken; to violate, disgrace, defile

tēmēt·um -ī *n* alcohol, wine

temnō temnĕre tempsī temptum *vt* to slight, offend

tēm·ō -ōnis *m* pole, tongue (*of a carriage or plow*); wagon

Tempē (indecl) *n pl* scenic valley between Olympus and Ossa in Thessaly

temperāment·um -ī *n* moderation

tempĕr·ans -antis *adj* moderate, temperate

temperanter *adv* moderately

temperantĭ·a -ae *f* self-control, moderation

temperātē *adv* moderately, with due moderation

temperātĭ·ō -ōnis *f* blending, proportion, symmetry; temperament; organization, constitution; control

temperāt·or -ōris *m* controller

temperāt·us -a -um *adj* tempered; self-controlled, temperate

tempĕrī *adv* in time, on time; in due time, at the right time

temperĭ·ēs -ēī *f* blending, tempering; temperature, mild temperature

tempĕr·ō -āre *vt* to compound, combine, blend, temper; to regulate, moderate; to tune; to govern, control, rule; *vi* to be moderate, exercise restraint; (with *abl* or **ab** + *abl*) to abstain from

tempest·ās -ātis *f* time, period, season; stormy weather, storm, tempest

tempestīvē *adv* at the right time, seasonably

tempestīvit·ās -ātis *f* right time, timeliness

tempestīv·us -a -um *adv* timely, seasonable, fit; ripe, mature; in good time, early

templ·um -ī *n* space marked off in the sky or on the earth for observation of omens; open space, quarter; temple, shrine, sanctuary

temporāl·is -e *adj* temporary, transitory

temporāri·us -a -um *adj* temporary; changeable (*character*)

tempŏre or **tempŏrī** *adv* in time, on time; in due time, at the right time

temptābund·us -a -um *adj* making constant attempts, trying

temptāment·um -ī *n* attempt, effort; temptation, trial

temptāmin·a -um *n* *pl* attempts, trials

temptātī·ō -ōnis *f* trial; attack (*of sickness*)

temptāt·or -ōris *m* assailant

tempt·ō or **tent·ō -āre** *vt* to test, feel, probe; to try, attempt; to attack; to try to influence, tamper with, tempt; try to induce; to urge, incite, sound out; to worry, distress, disquiet

temptus *pp* of **temno**

temp·us -ŏris *n* temple (*of the head*); time, period, season; occasion, opportunity; right time, good time, proper period; times, condition, state, position; need, emergency; measure, quantity, cadence (*in metrics*); **ad tempus** punctually; at the right time, at the appointed time; for the time being, for the moment; for the occasion; **ante tempus** before time, too soon, prematurely; **ex tempore** on the spur of the moment; **id tempore** at that time; **in ipso tempore** in the nick of time; **in tempore** at the right moment, just in time; **in tempus** temporarily, for a time; **per tempus** just in time; **pro tempore** as time permits, according to circumstances; **tempori cedere** to yield to circumstances; **tempus in ultimum** to the last extremity

tēmulent·us -a -um *adj* intoxicated

tenācit·ās -ātis *f* tenacity; miserliness

tenāciter *adv* tightly, firmly

ten·ax -ācis *adj* holding tight, gripping, clinging; sticky; firm; obstinate; stingy; (with *genit*) clinging to, holding on to

tendicŭl·ae -ārum *f* *pl* little snare, little noose, little trap

tendō tendĕre tetendī tentum or **tensum** *vt* to stretch, stretch out, hold out, spread, strain; to head for (*a place*); to aim, shoot (*an arrow*); to bend (*a bow*); to tune (*an instrument*); to pitch (*a tent*); *vi* to pitch tents, be encamped; to travel, sail, move, march; to endeavor; to contend, fight; to exert oneself; (with *inf*) to try to, endeavor to; (with **ad** + *acc*) a to tend toward, be inclined toward; **b** to move toward, travel to, aim for; (with **contra** + *acc*) to fight against

tenĕbr·ae -ārum *f* *pl* darkness; night; blindness; dark place, haunts; lower world; unconsciousness; death; obscurity, low station; ignorance

tenebricōs·us -a -um *adj* gloomy; darkened (*senses*); blind (*lust*)

tenebric·us -a -um *adj* dark, gloomy

tenebrōs·us -a -um *adj* dark, gloomy

Tenĕd·os or **Tenĕd·us -ī** *f* island off the coast of Troy

tenellŭl·us -a -um *adj* tender little, dainty little

tenell·us -a -um *adj* dainty

ten·ĕō -ēre -ŭī -tum *vt* to hold, hold tight, keep; to grasp, comprehend; to comprise; to possess, occupy, be master of; to hold back, restrain, repress; to hold, charm, amuse; to have control of, get the better of; to keep, detain; *vi* to hold out, last, keep on

ten·er -ĕra -ĕrum *adj* tender, soft, delicate; young, youthful; impressionable; weak; effeminate; voluptuous

tenerasc·ō -ĕre *vi* to grow weak

tenĕrē *adv* softly

tenerit·ās -ātis *f* weakness

tēnesm·os -ī *m* straining at stool

ten·or -ōris *m* uninterrupted course; **uno tenore** uninterruptedly

tens·a -ae *f* car carrying images of the gods in procession

tens·us -a -um *pp* of **tendo**; *adj* stretched, drawn tight, stretched out

tentīg·ō -ĭnis *f* lust

tentō see **tempto**

tentōr·ium -iī or **-ī** *n* tent

tent·us -a -um *pp* of **tendo** and of **teneo**; *adj* stretched, drawn tight, stretched out

tenuicŭl·us -a -um *adj* poor, paltry

tenŭ·is -e *adj* thin, fine; delicate; precise; shallow (*groove, etc.*); slight, puny, poor, insignificant; plain, simple; small, narrow

tenuit·ās -ātis *f* thinness, fineness; leanness; simplicity; precision; poverty

tenŭiter *adv* thinly; slightly; poorly, indifferently; exactly, minutely; superficially

tenŭ·ō -āre *vt* to make thin; to contract; to dissolve; to lessen, diminish, weaken

ten·us -ōris *n* trap, snare

tenus *prep* (with *abl*, always placed after the noun) as far as, up to, down to; **nomine tenus** or **verbo tenus** as far as the name goes, nominally, in name

Te·os or **Te·us -ī** *f* town on the coast of Asia Minor, the birthplace of Anacreon

tepe·faciō -facĕre -fēcī -factum *vt* to make warm, warm up

tep·ĕō -ēre -ŭī *vi* to be warm, be lukewarm; to glow with love; to be lukewarm, indifferent

tep·escō -escĕre -ŭī *vi* to grow warm; to grow lukewarm, grow indifferent

tepĭdĭus *adv* rather tepidly

tepĭd·us -a -um *adj* warm, lukewarm, tepid

tep·or -ōris *m* warmth; coolness, lack of heat (*in the bath*); lack of fire (*in a speech*)

ter *adv* three times, thrice

terdecĭens or **terdecĭēs** *adv* thirteen times

terebinth·us -ī *f* terebinth, turpentine tree

terĕbr·a -ae *f* borer, drill

terĕbr·ō -āre *vt* to bore, drill, bore out

terēd·ō -ĭnis *f* grub worm

Tēreĭd·ēs -ae *m* Itys (*son of Tereus*)

Terent·ĭus -ĭī or **-ī** *m* Terence (*M. Terentius Afer, Roman comic poet, c. 190-159 B.C.*)

ter·es -ĕtis *adj* smooth, well-rounded; smooth and round, polished, shapely; round, cylindrical; (fig) smooth, elegant, fine

Tĕr·eus -ĕī or **-ĕos** *m* king of Thrace, husband of Procne, and father of Itys

tergemĭn·us -a -um *adj* triple, threefold

tergĕō tergēre tersī tersum or **terg·ō -ēre** *vt* to scour, wipe off, wipe dry, clean, cleanse

tergĭn·um -ī *n* rawhide; scourge

tergĭversātĭ·ō -ōnis *f* refusal; evasion, subterfuge

tergĭvers·or -ārī -ātus sum *vi* to keep turning one's back; to be shifty, be evasive

tergō see **tergeo**

terg·um -ī or **terg·us -ōris** *n* back; ridge; hide, leather; leather objects: bag, shield, drum; (mil) rear; a **tergo** in the rear, from behind; **in tergum** backward

term·es -ĭtis *m* branch

Termināl·ĭa -ĭum or **-ĭōrum** *n pl* festival of Terminus (*the god of boundaries, celebrated on the 23rd of February*)

termināt·ĭō -ōnis *f* decision, determining; arrangement, ending (*of a sentence*)

termin·ō -āre *vt* to mark off with boundaries, bound, limit; to fix, de-

termine, define; (rhet) to end, round out (*a sentence*)

termin·us -ī *m* boundary, limit

Termĭn·us -ī *m* god of boundaries

tern·ī -ae -a *adj* three in a group, three apiece, three each

terō terĕre trīvī trītum *vt* to wear, rub, wear out, crush; to spend, waste; to smooth, grind, sharpen

Terpsichŏr·ē -ēs *f* Muse of dancing; poetry

terr·a -ae *f* the earth; land; earth, ground, soil; country, region, territory

terrāneŏl·a -ae *f* crested lark

terrēn·us -a -um *adj* earthly, terrestrial; earthen, made of earth; *n* land, ground

terr·ĕō -ēre -ŭī -ĭtum *vt* to frighten, scare, terrify; to deter

terrestr·is -e *adj* of the earth, on the earth; land, earth; **proelium terrestre** land battle

terrĕ·us -a -um *adj* sprung from the earth, earth-born

terribĭl·is -e *adj* terrible, frightful

terrĭcŭl·a -ōrum *n pl* scarecrow

terrĭfĭc·ō -āre *vt* to terrify

terrĭfĭc·us -a -um *adj* terrifying, awe-inspiring, alarming

terrĭgĕn·a -ae *m* or *f* earth-born creature

terrĭlŏqu·us -a -um *adj* ominous, alarming

terrĭt·ō -āre *vt* to keep frightening; to intimidate

terrĭtōr·ĭum -ĭī or **-ī** *n* land around a town, territory, suburbs

terr·or -ōris *m* terror, alarm, dread, fright

ters·us -a -um *pp* of **tergeo;** *adj* clean, neat; neat, terse

tertiadecĭmān·ī -ōrum *m pl* soldiers of the thirteenth legion

tertĭān·us -a -um *adj* recurring every second day, tertian; *m pl* soldiers of the third legion; *f* tertian fever

tertĭō *adv* in the third place, thirdly; the third time

tertĭum *adv* for the third time

tertĭ·us -a -um *adj* third

tertĭ·us decĭm·us -a -um *adj* thirteenth

terunc·ĭus -ĭī or **-ī** *m* three twelfths of an ace, quarter ace; **heres ex teruncio** heir to one fourth of the estate

tervenēfĭc·us -ī *m* (term of abuse) three-time killer

tesqu·a -ōrum *n pl* wilderness, wilds

tessell·a -ae *f* cubed mosaic stone

tessellāt·us -a -um *adj* tesselated

tessĕr·a -ae *f* cube; die; watchword, countersign; tally, token; ticket

tesserār·ĭus -ĭī or **-ī** *m* officer of the day

tesserŭl·a -ae *f* small cube; ticket

test·a -ae *f* brick, tile; jug, crock; potsherd; shell fish; shell

testāmentārĭ·us -a -um *adj* pertaining to a will or testament; *m* forger of a will

testāment·um -ī *n* will, testament

testātī·ō -ōnis *f* invoking as witness

testāt·us -a -um *adj* attested, public

testicŭl·us -ī *m* testicle

testificātĭ·ō -ōnis *f* giving evidence, testifying; proof, evidence

testific·or -ārī -ātus sum *vt* to give as evidence, attest; to vouch for; to bring to light; to call to witness

testimōn·ĭum -ĭī or **-ī** *n* testimony, deposition

test·is -is *m* or *f* witness; *m* testicle

test·or -ārī -ātus sum *vt* to give as evidence; to show, prove, vouch for; to call to witness, appeal to; *vi* to be a witness, testify; to make a will

testūdĭnĕ·us -a -um *adj* of a tortoise; made of tortoise shell

testūd·ō -ĭnis *f* tortoise; tortoise shell; lyre, lute; arch, vault; (mil) protective shed (*for besiegers*)

test·um -ī *n* earthenware lid; pot with a lid

tēte = emphatic form of **te**

Tēth·ys -yos *f* wife of Oceanus and mother of the sea nymphs; sea

tetradrachm·um or **tetrachm·um -ī** *n* Greek silver coin (*worth four drachmas*)

tetrarch·ēs -ae *m* tetrarch (*ruler of one fourth of a country*); petty prince

tetrarchĭ·a -ae *f* tetrarchy

tetrĭc·us -a -um *adj* gloomy, sour, crabby

Teuc·er or **Teuc·rus -rī** *m* son of Telamon and brother of Ajax; son of Scamander of Crete, son-in-law of Dardanus, and later king of Troy

Teucrĭ·a -ae *f* Troy

Teucr·us -a -um *adj* Teucrian, Trojan; *m pl* Trojans

Teutŏn·ēs -um or **Teutŏn·ī -ōrum** *m pl* Teutons

texō texĕre texŭī textum *vt* to weave; to plait; to build; to compose

textĭl·is -e *adj* woven; brocaded; *n* fabric

text·or -ōris *m* weaver

textrīn·um -ī *n* weaving

textr·īx -īcis *f* weaver (*female*)

textūr·a -ae *f* texture; web; fabric

text·us -a -um *pp* of **texo**; *n* woven cloth, fabric; web

text·us -ūs *m* texture

Thā·is -ĭdis *f* Athenian courtesan

thalăm·us -ī *m* woman's room; bedroom; marriage bed; marriage

thalassĭc·us -a -um *adj* sea-green

thalassīn·us -a -um *adj* sea-green

Thal·ēs -is or **-ētis** *m* early Ionian philosopher of Miletus, regarded as one of the Seven Sages (*fl* 575 B.C.)

Thalī·a -ae *f* Muse of comedy; sea nymph

thall·us -ī *m* green bough, green stalk

Thaps·os or **Thaps·us -ī** *f* city in Africa where Caesar defeated the Pompeians (46 B.C.)

Thas·os or **Thas·us -ī** *f* island in the Aegean Sea, off the coast of Thrace

Thaumantĭ·as -ădis or **Thaumant·is -ĭdis** *f* Iris (*daughter of Thaumas*)

theātrāl·is -e *adj* theatrical

theātr·um -ī *n* theater

Thēb·ae -ārum *f pl* Thebes (*capital of Boeotia, founded by Cadmus*); Thebes (*city of Upper Egypt*)

Thēbae·us -a -um *adj* & *mf* Theban (*of Egypt*)

Thēbān·us -a -um *adj* & *mf* Theban (*of Boeotia*)

thēc·a -ae *f* case; envelope

Them·is -ĭdis *f* goddess of justice and of prophecy

Themistŏcl·ēs -is or **-ī** *m* Themistocles (*Athenian general and statesman, c.* 528-459 B.C.)

thensaurārĭ·us -a -um *adj* treasure, of treasure

thensaurus see **thesaurus**

Theocrĭt·us -ī *m* founder of Greek pastoral poetry, born at Syracuse (*3rd cent.* B.C.)

theolŏg·us -ī *m* theologian

therm·ae -ārum *f pl* hot springs, hot baths

thermopōl·ĭum -ĭī or **-ī** *n* hot-drink shop

thermopōt·ō -āre *vt* to warm with a drink

Thermopўl·ae -ārum *f pl* famous pass in Thessaly between Mt. Oeta and the sea, defended by Leonidas and his four hundred Spartans (490 B.C.)

thermŭl·ae -ārum *f pl* little hot bath

Thersīt·ēs -ae *m* Greek soldier at Troy notorious for his ugliness

thēsaur·us or **thensaur·us -ī** *m* storehouse; store, treasure, hoard

Thēs·eus -ĕī or **-ĕos** *m* king of Athens, son of Aegeus and Aethra, and husband first of Ariadne and later of Phaedra

Thēsē·us -a -um *adj* of Theseus

Thēsĭd·ae -ārum *m pl* Athenians

Thēsĭd·ēs -ae *m* Hippolytus (*son of Theseus*)

Thespĭăd·es -um *f pl* Muses

Thesp·is -is *m* traditional founder of Greek tragedy

Thespĭ·us -a -um *adj* Thespian; *f pl* town in Boeotia near Mt. Helicon

Thessalĭ·a -ae *f* Thessaly (*most northerly district of Greece*)

Thessalĭc·us -a -um *adj* Thessalian

Thessăl·us -a -um *adj* Thessalian; *m pl* people of Thessaly, Thessalians

Thestorĭd·ēs -ae *m* Calchas (*famous Greek seer who joined the expedition to Troy*)

Thet·is -ĭdis or **-ĭdos** *f* sea nymph, daughter of Nereus and Doris, wife of Peleus, and mother of Achilles

thĭăs·us -ī *m* Bacchic dance; Bacchic troop of dancers

Thisb·ē -ēs *f* girl in Babylon, loved by Pyramus

Tho·ās -antis *m* king of Tauris, slain by Orestes; king of Lemnos and father of Hypsipyle

thŏl·us -ī *m* rotunda

thōr·ax -ācis *m* breastplate

Thrāc·ē or Thrāc·ē -ēs *f* Thrace (*wild country to the N. of the Aegean*)

Thrācĭ·us -a -um *adj* Thracian; *f* Thrace

Thress·a or Threiss·a -ae *f* Thracian woman

Thr·ex -ēcis or Thr·ax -ācis *m* Thracian gladiator

thron·us -ī *m* throne

Thūcўdĭd·ēs -is *m* Thucydides (*famous Greek historian of the Peloponnesian War, c. 456-c. 400 B.C.*)

thunn·us -ī *m* tuna fish

thūr· = tur-

Thūrĭ·ī -ōrum *m pl* city on the Tarentine Gulf in S. Italy

Thūrĭn·us -a -um *adj & m* Thurian

thūs thūris *n* incense, frankincense

Thybris see **Tiberis**

Thўēn·ē -ēs *f* nymph who nursed Bacchus

Thyest·ēs -ae *m* son of Pelops, brother of Atreus, and father of Aegisthus

thymbr·a -ae *f* savory (*plant*)

thym·um -ī *n* thyme

Thўnĭ·a -ae *f* Bithynia (*country in Asia Minor*)

Thўnĭăc·us -a -um *adj* Bithynian

Thўn·us -a -um *adj & m* Bithynian

thynn·us -ī *m* tuna fish

Thўōn·eus -ĕī *m* Bacchus

thyrs·us -ī *m* Bacchic wand twined with vine tendrils and ivy, and crowned with a fir cone

tiār·a -ae *f* or **tiăr·ās -ae** *m* tiara

Tibĕrīn·is -īdis *adj* of the Tiber

Tibĕrīn·us -a -um *adj* of the Tiber; *m* river god of the Tiber

Tibĕr·is or Tibr·is or Thybr·is -is *m* Tiber River

Tibĕr·ĭus -ĭī or -ī *m* Tiberius (*Tiberius Claudius Nero Caesar, successor of Augustus, 42 B.C.-37 A.D., ruling from 14 A.D. to 37 A.D.*)

tībĭ·a -ae *f* shinbone, tibia; flute

tībĭc·en -ĭnis *m* flutist; prop; pillar

tībĭcĭn·a -ae *f* flutist (*female*)

Tibull·us -ī *m* Albius Tibullus (*Roman elegiac poet, c. 54-c. 19 B.C.*)

Tib·ur -ŭris *n* town of Latium on the Anio (*modern Tivoli*)

Tiburt·ēs -um *m pl* Tiburtines

Tiburtīn·us or Tiburn·us -a -um *adj* Tiburtine

Ticĭn·us -ī *m* tributary of the Po

Tigellīn·us -ī *m* notorious favorite of the emperor Nero

tigill·um -ī *n* beam, log

tignārĭ·us -a -um *adj* **faber tignarius** carpenter

tign·um -ī *n* trunk, log, beam, board

tigr·is -is or -ĭdis *f* tigress

Tigr·is -is or -ĭdis *m* large river of W. Asia which joins with the Euphrates

tĭlĭ·a -ae *f* lime tree

Tĭmae·us -ī *m* Greek historian of Sicily (*c. 346-c. 250 B.C.*); Pythagorean philosopher of Locri in S. Italy after whom Plato named one of his dialogues (*5th cent. B.C.*)

Tĭmăgĕn·ēs -is *m* brilliant rhetorician in the time of Augustus

timefact·us -a -um *adj* alarmed, frightened

tim·eō -ēre -ŭī *vt* to fear, be afraid of; *vi* to fear, be afraid

tĭmĭdē *adv* timidly, fearfully

tĭmĭdĭt·ās -ātis *f* timidity, fearfulness, cowardice

tĭmĭd·us -a -um *adj* timid, fearful, cowardly; (*with genit*) fearful of, afraid of

tĭm·or -ōris *m* fear, alarm; dread; a terror

tīnctĭl·is -e *adj* used for dipping

tīnct·us -a -um *pp* of **tingo**

tĭnĕ·a -ae *f* moth; bookworm

tīngō tīngĕre tīnxī tīnctum *vt* to dip, soak; to dye, color; to tinge, imbue

tīnnĭment·um -ī *n* ringing

tīnn·ĭō -īre -īvī -īī -ītum *vt & vi* to ring

tīnnīt·us -ūs *m* ring, ringing, tinkling, jingling

tīnnŭl·us -a -um *adj* ringing, tinkling; shrill

tīntīnnābŭl·um -ī *n* bell, door bell, cattle bell

tīntīnnācŭl·us -a -um *adj* jingling; *m pl* chain gang

tīntĭn·ō -āre *vi* to ring

tīn·us -ī *m* laurustinus (*shrub*)

Tīph·ys -ўos *m* pilot of the Argo

tīppŭl·a -ae *f* water spider

Tīresĭ·ās -ae *m* famous seer at Thebes at the time of the Oedipus

Tīrīdāt·ēs -ae *m* king of Armenia

tīr·ō -ōnis *m* recruit; beginner

tīrōcĭn·ĭum -ĭī or -ī *n* first campaign; inexperience in military life; body of raw recruits; beginning, first try

tīruncŭl·us -ī *m* young beginner

Tīryn·s -this or -thos *f* town in Argolis where Hercules was raised

Tīrynthĭ·us -a -um *adj* Tirynthian

Tīsamĕn·us -ī *m* son of Orestes and king of Argos

Tīsĭphŏn·ē -ēs *f* one of the three Furies who haunted murderers

Tīsĭphŏnē·us -a -um *adj* guilty

Tīt·ān -ānis of Tītān·us -ī *m* Titan; sun; *m pl* giant sons of Uranus and Ge who rebelled against Uranus and put Cronus on the throne

Tītānĭ·us -a -um *adj* of the Titans, Titanic; *f* Latona (*the mother of Apollo and Diana*); Pyrrha (*as descendant of Prometheus*); Circe (*as daughter of Sol*)

Tīthōnī·us -a -um *adj* Tithonian; *f* Aurora

Tīthōn·us -ī *m* son of Laomedon and husband of Aurora from whom he received the gift of immortality without eternal youth

Tit·iēs -ium *m pl* one of the three original tribes of Rome

tītillātī·ō -ōnis *f* tickling

tītill·ō -āre *vt* to tickle

tītivillīt·ium -iī or **-ī** *n* trifle

titubanter *adv* falteringly

titubātī·ō -ōnis *f* staggering

titūb·ō -āre *vi* to stagger, reel, totter; to falter, waver (*in speech*)

tītul·us -ī *m* inscription; label; notice, advertisement; title of honor; renown; pretext

Tity·os -ī *m* giant slain by Apollo for insulting Latona and thrown into Tartarus

Tītyr·us -ī *m* shepherd in Vergil's pastorals, sometimes identified with Virgil himself

Tlēpolēm·us -ī *m* son of Hercules

Tmōl·us or **Timōl·us -ī** *m* mountain in Lydia famous for its wines

tocull·ō -ōnis *m* banker

tōf·us or **tōph·us -ī** *m* tufa (*volcanic rock*) ·

tog·a -ae *f* outer garment of a Roman citizen; **toga candida** white toga (*worn by candidates for office*); **toga picta** brocaded toga (*worn by triumphant generals*); **toga praetexta** crimson-bordered toga (*worn by magistrates and freeborn children*); **toga pulla** dark-grey toga (*worn by mourners*); **toga pūra** or **virīlis** or **lībera** toga of manhood (*worn by young men from about the age of sixteen*)

togāt·us -a -um *adj* wearing a toga; *m* Roman citizen; civilian; humble client; *f* Roman drama (*treating of Roman themes*); prostitute

togŭl·a -ae *f* little toga

tolerābil·is -e *adj* tolerable; patient

tolerābilius *adv* more patiently, fairly patiently

tolĕr·ans -antis *adj* tolerant; (with *genit*) tolerant of, enduring

toleranter *adv* patiently

tolerantī·a -ae *f* toleration, endurance

tolerātī·ō -ōnis *f* toleration, endurance

tolerāt·us -a -um *adj* tolerable, endurable

tolĕr·ō -āre *vt* to tolerate, bear, endure; to support, maintain, sustain

tollēn·ō -ōnis *m* crane, lift, derrick

tollō tollĕre sustŭlī sublātum *vt* to lift, raise; to have (*a child*); to acknowledge (*a child*); to raise, educate; to weigh (*anchor*); to take on, take on board; to remove; to do away with, destroy; to cancel, abolish, abrogate; to lift, steal; to uplift, cheer up, excite; to erect, build up; to waste (*time*); **amicum tollere** to cheer up a friend; **animos**

tollere to boost the morale; **deos tollere** to deny the existence of the gods; **hominem de medio tollere** to make away with or kill a man; **pecunias ex fano tollere** to steal money from a shrine; **signa tollere** to break camp

tolūtim *adv* at a trot

tomācŭl·um or **tomācl·um -ī** *n* sausage

tōment·um -ī *n* stuffing (*for pillows*)

Tom·ī -ōrum *m pl* or **Tom·is -is** *f* town in Moesia on the Black Sea to which Ovid was exiled

Tomīt·ae -ārum *m pl* people of Tomi

Tomītān·us -a -um *adj* of Tomi

Ton·ans -antis *m* Thunderer (*epithet of several gods, esp. Jupiter*)

tondĕō tondēre totondī tonsum *vt* to clip, shear, shave; to prune; to reap, mow; to crop, browse on; (fig) to fleece, rob; **usque ad cutem tondere** to swindle, fleece

tonitrāl·is -e *adj* thunderous

tonitr·us -ūs *m* or **tonitrŭ·um -ī** *n* thunder; *m pl* or *n pl* claps of thunder

ton·ō -āre -ŭī -ĭtum *vt* to thunder out (*words*); *vi* to thunder

tons·a -ae *f* oar blade

tonsil·is -e *adj* clipped

tonsill·ae -ārum *f pl* tonsils

tonsĭt·ō -āre *vt* to shear regularly

tons·or -ōris *m* shearer, barber

tonsōrĭ·us -a -um *adj* shaving; barber's

tonstrīcŭl·a -ae *f* little hairdresser, little barber (*female*)

tonstrīn·a -ae *f* barber shop

tonstr·ix -īcis *f* hairdresser, barber (*female*)

tonsūr·a -ae *f* clipping, shearing; **capillorum tonsura** haircut

tons·us -a -um *pp* of **tondeo**; *f* see **tonsa**

tons·us -ūs *m* haircut; hairdo

tōph·us -ī *m* tufa (*volcanic rock*)

topiārĭ·us -a -um *adj* garden, landscape; *m* gardener, landscaper; *f* landscaping

topic·e -ēs *f* resourcefulness in finding topics for speeches

tor·al -ālis *n* valance

torcŭl·ar -āris or **torcŭl·um -ī** *n* wine press, oil press

toreum·a -ătis *n* embossing, relief

torment·um -ī *n* windlass; catapult, artillery piece; shot; torture rack, torture; (fig) torture; *n pl* artillery

tormĭn·a -um *n pl* colic

torminōs·us -a -um *adj* prone to colic

torn·ō -āre *vt* to form with a lathe, turn on a lathe

torn·us -ī *m* lathe; burin

torōs·us -a -um *adj* brawny, muscular

torpēd·ō -ĭnis *f* numbness, lethargy, listnessness; crampfish, torpedo (*fish*)

torp·ĕō **-ēre** **-ŭī** *vi* to be numb; to be stiff; to be stupefied; to be groggy

torp·escō **-escĕre** **-ŭī** *vi* to grow numb, grow listless

torpĭd·us **-a** **-um** *adj* groggy

torp·or **-ōris** *m* torpor, numbness; grogginess

torquāt·us **-a** **-um** *adj* wearing a necklace

Torquāt·us **-ī** *m* T. Manlius Torquatus (*legendary Roman hero who is said to have slain a gigantic Gaul in single combat and to have worn the Gaul's necklace*)

torquĕō torquēre torsī tortum *vt* to twist, turn, wind, wrench; to whirl, hurl, wind up and hurl; to rack; (*fig*) to torment

torqu·ēs or **torqu·is** **-is** *m* or *f* necklace; collar; festoon

torr·ens **-entis** *adj* burning, seething; rushing, roaring (*stream*); fiery (*speech*); *m* roaring stream, torrent

torrĕō torrēre torrŭī tostum *vt* to roast, bake, burn, scorch; to parch, dry up

torr·escō **-escĕre** **-ŭī** *vi* to become burned or parched

torrĭd·us **-a** **-um** *adj* baked, parched, dried up; frostbitten

torr·is **-is** *m* firebrand

tortē *adv* crookedly

tortĭl·is **-e** *adj* twisted, winding, spiral

tort·ō **-āre** *vt* to twist; **tortarī** to writhe

tort·or **-ōris** *m* torturer, executioner

tortŭōs·us **-a** **-um** *adj* full of turns, winding; (*fig*) tortuous, complicated

tort·us **-a** **-um** *pp* of **torqueō**; *adj* twisted, crooked; gnarled (*oak*); complicated

tort·us **-ūs** *m* twisting, twist, spiral; **tortūs dare** (of a serpent) to form loops

torŭl·us **-ī** *m* tuft (*of hair*)

tor·us **-ī** *m* knot; bulge; muscle; brawn; bed; couch; mattress; mound; boss; flowery expression

torvĭt·ās **-ātis** *f* grimness, wildness

torv·us **-a** **-um** *adj* grim, fierce, stern, savage

tostus *pp* of **torreō**

tot (*indecl*) *adj* so many, as many

totĭdem (*indecl*) *adj* just so many, just as many

totĭens or **totĭēs** *adv* so often, so many times

tōt·us **-a** **-um** *adj* the whole, all, entire; **totus in illis** wholly absorbed in those matters; *n* the whole matter, all; **ex toto** wholly, totally; **in toto** on the whole, in general; **in totum** wholly, totally

toxic·um **-ī** *n* poison

trabāl·is **-e** *adj* of or for beams; **clavus trabalis** spike; **telum trabale** beam-like shaft

trabĕ·a **-ae** *f* ceremonial robe (*woven in stripes and worn by magistrates, augurs, etc.*)

trabeāt·us **-a** **-um** *adj* wearing a ceremonial robe

trab·s **-is** *f* beam, plank; timber; tree; object made of beams: roof, shaft, table, battering ram

tractābĭl·is **-e** *adj* manageable; (weather) fit for navigation

tractāti·ō **-ōnis** *f* handling, management, treatment; discussion, treatment (*of a subject*)

tractāt·us **-ūs** *m* touching, handling, management

tractim *adv* little by little, slowly; at length, in a drawn-out manner

tract·ō **-āre** *vt* to drag around, haul, pull; to touch, handle; to manage, control, wield; to conduct, carry on, transact, practice; to discuss; **se tractare** to behave oneself, conduct oneself

tract·us **-a** **-um** *pp* of **traho**; *adj* flowing, fluent, continuous (*discourse*)

tract·us **-ūs** *m* dragging; drawing out, dragging out, extension (*e.g., of a war*); track, trail; tract, extent, distance; region, district

trāditi·ō **-ōnis** *f* handing over, surrender; transmission

trādĭt·or **-ōris** *m* betrayer, traitor

trādō trādĕre trādĭdī trādĭtum *vt* to hand over, surrender, deliver; to betray; to hand down, bequeath, transmit, pass on; to relate, recount; to teach; **se tradere** (with *dat*) **a** to surrender to; **b** to devote oneself to

trā·dūcō **-dūcĕre** **-duxī** **-ductum** *vt* to lead across, bring over, transfer, to lead in parade, make a show of; to disgrace, degrade; to broadcast, proclaim; to pass, spend

trāducti·ō **-ōnis** *f* transfer, transference; course, passage (*of time*); metonymy

trāduct·or **-ōris** *m* conveyor

trāductus *pp* of **traduco**

trād·ux **-ūcis** *m* vine branch

tragicē *adv* as in tragedy

tragicoŏŏmoedi·a **-ae** *f* melodrama

tragĭc·us **-a** **-um** *adj* of tragedy, tragic; in the tragic style, grand, solemn; of a tragic nature, tragic, moving, terrible; **actor tragicus** tragedian; *m* tragic playwright

tragoedi·a **-ae** *f* tragedy

tragoed·us **-ī** *m* tragic actor, tragedian

trāgŭl·a **-ae** *f* javelin

trag·us **-ī** *m* body odor of the armpits; a fish (*of unknown type*)

trah·ax **-ācis** *adj* greedy

trahĕ·a **-ae** *f* sledge, drag

trahō trahĕre traxī tractum *vt* to draw, drag, trail; to draw out, pull out, extract; to lead, take along, be followed by; to contract, wrinkle; to inhale; to quaff; to take on, assume, acquire, get; to squander, dissipate; to spin, manufacture; to attract, allure, influence; to win over (*to the other side*); to refer, ascribe; to distract; to consider, ponder; to spin out, prolong, protract

Trājān·us -ī *m* Trajan (*M. Ulpius Trajanus, Roman emperor, 97-117 A.D.*)

trājectǐ·ō -ōnis *f* crossing, passage; transposition (*of words*); shift of meaning; exaggeration

trājectus *pp of* **trajicio**

trāject·us -ūs *m* crossing over, passage

trā·jicǐō or **trans·icǐō** or **trans·jicǐō -jicěre -jēcī -jectum** *vt* to have go across, cause to go across, transfer; to ship across, transport; to pass through, break through; to stab through, pierce; (with double *acc*) to bring (*e.g., troops*) across (*river, mountain*); (with **trans** + *acc*) to lead across; (with **in** + *acc*) to lead over into

trālāt- = **translat-**

Trall·ēs -ium *f pl* town in Lydia

trālŏqu·or -ī *vt* to talk over, enumerate, recount

trālūcěō see **transluceo**

trām·a -ae *f* woof, web

trāměō = **transmeo**

trām·es -ǐtis *m* path, track, trail

trāmi- = **transmi-**

trānātō = **transnato**

trān·ō or **transn·ō -āre** *vt* to swim across; to pass through, permeate; *vi* to swim across; to pass through

tranquillē *adv* quietly, calmly

tranquillǐt·ās -ātis *f* tranquillity, stillness, calmness

tranquill·ō -āre *vt* to calm, quiet, tranquillize

tranquill·us -a -um *adj* calm, quiet, tranquil; *n* calm, calmness, peace, quiet, tranquillity; quiet sea

trans *prep* (with *acc*) across, over, beyond

transab·ěō -īre -ǐī *vt* to go through, pierce

transact·or -ōris *m* manager

transactus *pp of* **transigo**

transad·ǐgō -ǐgěre -ēgī -actum *vt* to pierce; to run (*someone*) through; (with double *acc*) to run (*e.g., a sword*) through (*someone*)

Transalpīn·us -a -um *adj* Transalpine, lying beyond the Alps

tran·scendō or **trans·scendō -scenděre -scendī -scensum** *vt* to climb or step over, surmount; to overstep, transgress; *vi* to climb or step across

trans·cīdō -cīděre -cīdī *vt* to flog soundly

tran·scrībō or **trans·scrībō -scrīběre -scripsī -scriptum** *vt* to transcribe, copy off; (law) to transfer, convey; to transfer, remove

trans·currō -currěre -currī or **-cucurrī -cursum** *vt & vi* to run or dash over; to run or dash through; to run or dash by or past

transcurs·us -ūs *m* running through, passage; cursory mention

transd- = **trad-**

transenn·a -ae *f* grating; lattice work, trellis work; lattice window; fowler's net

trans·ěō -īre -ǐī -ǐtum *vt* to pass over, cross; to desert; to pass (*in a race*); to pass over, make no mention of; to treat cursorily; to overstep, pass beyond; to surpass; *vi* to go over, go across, pass over; to pass by, go by; to shift (*to another opinion, forage, etc.*); (of time) to pass, go by; to pass away; (with **ad** + *acc*) a to cross over to (*a place*); **b** to cross over to, desert to; (with **in** + *acc*) to change into, be transformed into; (with **per** + *acc*) to penetrate, permeate, pervade

trans·fěrō -ferre -tŭlī -lātum (or **trālātum**) *vt* to carry or bring across; to transfer by writing, to copy; to shift, transfer; to transform; to postpone; to translate; to use (*words*) figuratively

trans·fīgō -fīgěre -fīxī -fīxum *vt* to pierce, transfix; to run (*someone*) through

transfīgūr·ō -āre *vt* to transform

transfīxus *pp of* **transfīgo**

trans·fodǐō -foděre -fōdī -fossum *vt* to run through, stab, pierce

transform·is -e *adj* transformed, changed in shape

transform·ō -āre *vt* to change in shape, transform

transfossus *pp of* **transfodio**

transfŭg·a -ae *m* or *f* deserter, turncoat

trans·fugǐō -fugěre -fūgī *vi* to desert

transfug·ǐum -ǐī or **-ī** *n* desertion

trans·fundō -funděre -fūdī -fūsum *vt* to transfuse; to pour; (with **in** + *acc*) to pour (*a liquid*) into; (with **ad** + *acc*) (fig) to shift (*affection, allegiance*) to (*another person*)

transfūsǐ·ō -ōnis *f* transmigration

transfūsus *pp of* **transfundo**

trans·gredǐor -grědī -gressus sum *vt* to cross, pass over; to exceed; *vi* to go across; to cross over (*to another party*)

transgressǐ·ō -ōnis *f* crossing, passage; transposition (*of words*)

transgressus *pp of* **transgredior**

transgress·us -ūs *m* crossing

transicǐō see **trajicio**

transiect- = **traject-**

trans·ǐgō -ǐgěre -ēgī -actum *vt* to pierce, run through; to finish, settle, transact, accomplish, perform, conclude; to pass, spend (*time*); *vi* to come to an agreement, reach an understanding

transil·ǐō or **transsil·ǐō -īre -ǔī** *vt* to jump over, jump across; to overstep, exceed; to skip, omit; *vi* to jump across

transit·ans -antis *adj* passing through

transitǐ·ō -ōnis *f* crossing, passage;

switching (*to another party*); contagion, infection; passageway

transitus *pp* of **transeo**

transit·us -ūs *m* crossing, passage; passing; traffic; crossing over, desertion; change, period of change, transition; fading (*of colors*); **in transitu** in passing

translātĭcĭ·us or **trālātĭcĭ·us -a -um** *adj* transmitted, traditional, customary; usual, common

translātĭ·ō or **trālātĭ·ō -ōnis** *f* transfer, shift; transporting; translation; metaphor, figure

translātīv·us -a -um *adj* transferable

translāt·or -ōris *m* middleman (*in a transfer*)

translātus *pp* of **transfero**

translĕg·ō -ĕre *vt* to read through

translūc·ĕō or **trālūc·ĕō -ēre** *vi* to be reflected; to shine through

transmarīn·us -a -um *adj* from beyond the seas, foreign, overseas

transmĕ·ō or **trāmĕ·ō -āre** *vi* to cross, pass

transmigr·ō -āre *vi* to move, migrate, emigrate

transmissĭ·ō -ōnis *f* crossing, passage

transmissus *pp* of **transmitto**

transmiss·us -ūs *m* passing over, crossing, passage

trans·mittō or **trā·mittō -mittĕre mīsī -missum** *vt* to send across; to transmit; to let pass; to hand over, entrust, commit; to pass over, leave unmentioned; to pass through, endure; (with **in** + *acc*) to send (*someone*) across to or into; (with **per** + *acc*) to let (*someone*) pass through; *vi* to cross over, cross, pass (*from one place to another*)

transmontān·ī -ōrum *m pl* people across the mountains

trans·movĕō -movēre -mōvī -mōtum *vt* to move, transfer

transmūt·ō -āre *vt* to change, shift

transnāt·ō or **trānāt·ō -āre** *vt* to swim; *vi* to swim across

transnō see **trano**

Transpadān·us -a -um *adj* Transpadane, beyond or N. of the Po River

transpect·us -ūs *m* view, prospect

transpicĭ·ō or **transspicĭ·ō -ĕre** *vt* to look through

trans·pōnō -pōnĕre -posŭī -positum *vt* to transfer

transport·ō -āre *vt* to transport

transposĭtus *pp* of **transpono**

Transrhēnān·us -a -um *adj* beyond the Rhine, E. of the Rhine

transs- = trans-

Transtiberīn·us -a -um *adj* across the Tiber

transtin·ĕō -ēre *vi* to pass through

transtr·um -ī *n* thwart

transult·ō -āre *vi* to jump across

transūt·us -a -um *adj* pierced through

transvectĭ·ō or **trāvectĭ·ō -ōnis** *f* transportation, crossing

trans·vĕhō or **trā·vĕhō -vĕhĕre vexī -vectum** *vt* to transport; to carry, lead (*in a parade*); **trans·vehi** to ride by (*in a parade*); (of time) to elapse

transverbĕr·ō -āre *vt* to pierce through and through, transfix

transversa *adv* sideways; across one's course

transversārĭ·us -a -um *adj* transverse, lying crosswise

transvers·us or **trāvers·us** or **transvors·us -a -um** *adj* lying across, lying crosswise; inopportune; astray; in the wrong direction; *n* wrong direction, opposite direction; **de transverso** unexpectedly; **ex transverso** unexpectedly; sideways

transvolĭt·ō -āre *vt* to flit through, fly through

transvŏl·ō or **trāvŏl·ō -āre** *vt & vi* to fly over, fly across, fly by, zip by

transvorsus see **transversus**

trapēt·us -ī *m* oil press

trapezīt·a -ae *m* banker

Trapĕz·ūs -untis *f* city in Pontus on the Black Sea

Trasimenn·us or **Trasumenn·us -ī** *m* lake in Etruria where Hannibal defeated the Romans (217 B.C.)

trāv- = transv-

trecēn·ī -ae -a *adj* three hundred each

trecentēsĭm·us -a -um *adj* three hundredth

trecentĭēs *adv* three hundred times

trechedipn·um -ī *n* light garment worn to dinner

tredĕcim (indecl) *adj* thirteen

tremebund·us -a -um *adj* trembling, shivering

treme·facĭō -facĕre -fēcī -factum *vt* to shake, cause to shake

tremend·us -a -um *adj* terrible, frightful

trem·escō or **trem·iscō -escĕre -ŭī** *vt* to tremble at; *vi* to tremble

trem·ō -ĕre -ŭī *vt* to tremble at; *vi* to tremble, shiver, quake

trem·or -ōris *adj* trembling, shaking, shivering; dread

tremŭl·us -a -um *adj* trembling, quivering, tremulous, shivering

trepidanter *adv* tremblingly, nervously

trepidātĭ·ō -ōnis *f* nervousness, alarm

trepĭdē *adv* nervously, in alarm

trepĭd·ō -āre *vt* to start at, be jumpy or nervous at; *vi* to be nervous, be jumpy, be alarmed; (of a flame) to flicker; (of streams) to rush along

trepĭd·us -a -um *adj* nervous, jumpy, agitated, hurried, restless; bubbling; perilous, critical, alarming; **in re trepida** in a ticklish situation

trēs (or **trīs**) **tria** *adj* three; (denoting a small number) a couple of

tress·is -is *m* small coin: mere trifle

tresvirī (*genit:* **triumvirōrum**) *m pl* three-man board, triumvirs

Trēvĕr·ī -ōrum *m pl* people of E. Gaul

triangŭl·us -a -um *adj* triangular; *n* triangle

triāri·ī -ōrum *m pl* soldiers of the third rank in a battle line, reserves

tribuārī·us -a -um *adj* tribal

tribŭl·is -is *m* fellow tribesman

tribŭl·um -ī *n* threshing sledge (*wooden platform with iron teeth underneath*)

tribŭl·us -ī *m* caltrop (*thistle*)

tribūn·al -ālis *n* raised platform; tribunal, judgment seat; (*in camp*) general's platform; cenotaph

tribūnāt·us -ūs *m* tribuneship, rank of tribune

tribūnici·us -a -um *adj* tribunician, tribune's; *m* ex-tribune

tribūn·us -ī *m* tribune; **tribunus aerarius** paymaster; **tribunus militaris** or **tribunus militum** military tribune (*six in each legion, serving under the legatus, and elected by the people or at times appointed by a commander*); **tribunus plebis** tribune of the people (*ten in number, serving the interests of the plebeians*)

trib·ŭō -ŭĕre -ŭī -ūtum *vt* to divide; to distribute, bestow, confer, assign; to give, present; to concede, grant, allow; to ascribe, impute; to devote, spend

trib·us -ūs *m* tribe (*originally three in number and eventually increased to thirty-five*)

tribūtāri·us -a -um *adj* subject to tribute; **tributariae tabellae** letters of credit

tribūtim *adv* by tribes

tribūti·ō -ōnis *f* distribution

tribūt·us -a -um *pp* of **tribuo**; *adj* arranged by tribes; *n* tribute, tax, contribution

tric·ae -ārum *f pl* tricks; nonsense

tricēn·ī -ae -a *adj* thirty each

tric·eps -ipitis *adj* three-headed

tricēsĭm·us -a -um *adj* thirtieth

trichīl·a -ae *f* bower, arbor; summer home

triciens or **triciēs** *adv* thirty times

triclīn·ium -iī or **-ī** *n* dining couch (*running around three sides of a table*); dining room

tric·ō -ōnis *m* practical joker, trickster

tric·or -ārī -ātus sum *vi* to cause trouble; to pull tricks

tricorp·or -ŏris *adj* three-bodied

tricusp·is -ĭdis *adj* three-pronged

trid·ens -entis *adj* three-pronged; *m* trident

Tridentif·er or **Tridentĭg·er -ĕrī** *m* Trident Bearer (*epithet of Neptune*)

tridŭ·um -ī *n* three-day period, three days

trienn·ia -ium *n pl* triennial festi-

val, festival celebrated every three years

trienn·ium -iī or **-ī** *n* three-year period, three years

tri·ens -entis *m* one third; coin (*one third of an ace*); third of a pint

trientābŭl·um -ī *n* land given by the state as an equivalent for one third of the sum which the state owed

trienti·us -a -um *adj* sold for a third

triērarch·us -ī *m* captain of a trireme

triēr·is -is *f* trireme

trietēric·us -a -um *adj* triennial, recurring every three years; *n pl* festival of Bacchus

trietēr·is -ĭdis *f* three-year period; triennial festival

trifāriam *adv* in three places, on three sides

trifau·x -cis *adj* triple-throated

trifĭd·us -a -um *adj* three-forked; split into three parts

triform·is -e *adj* triple

trifĭl·is -e *adj* having three threads or hairs

trifūr -fūris *m* archthief

trifurcĭf·er -ĕrī *m* archvillain, hardened criminal

trigemĭn·us or **tergemĭn·us -a -um** *adj* threefold, triple; *m pl* triplets

trigintā (*indecl*) *adj* thirty

trig·ōn -ōnis *m* ball game

trilĭbr·is -e *adj* three-pound

trilingu·is -e *adj* triple-tongued

tril·ix -īcis *adj* three-ply, triple-stranded

trimestr·is -e *adj* of three months

trimĕtr·us -ī *m* trimeter

trim·us -a -um *adj* three-year-old

Trīnācr·is -ĭdis *adj* Sicilian

Trīnacri·us -a -um *adj* Sicilian; *f* Sicily

trīn·ī -ae -a *adj* threefold, triple; three each

trinōd·is -e *adj* having three knots, triple-knotted

triōbŏl·us -ī *m* three-obol coin, half-drachma piece

Triōn·ēs -um *m pl* Great Bear and Little Bear (*constellation*)

tripartītō *adv* in three parts, into three parts

tripartīt·us or **tripertīt·us -a -um** *adj* divided into three parts, threefold

tripectŏr·us -a -um *adj* triple-bodied, triple-breasted

tripedāl·is -e *adj* three-foot

tripertītus see **tripartitus**

trip·ēs -ĕdis *adj* three-legged

tripl·ex -īcis *adj* threefold, triple; *n* three times as much, threefold portion

tripl·us -a -um *adj* triple, threefold

Triptolĕm·us -a -um *m* son of Celeus the king of Eleusis, favorite of Ceres, inventor of agriculture, and one of the judges in the lower world

tripudi·ō -āre *vi* to dance (*as a religious act*); to do a war dance; to leap, dance, hop about

tripudium -iī or **-ī** *n* solemn religious dance; war dance; dance (*in general*); favorable omen (*when the sacred chickens ate hungrily*)

trip·us -ŏdis *f* tripod (*three-footed vessel*); oracle, Delphic oracle

triquĕtr·us -a -um *adj* triangular; Sicilian

trirēm·is -e *adj* having three banks of oars; *f* trireme

trīs see **tres**

triscurrī·a -ōrum *n pl* broad humor, fantastic nonsense

tristicŭl·us -a -um *adj* somewhat sad

tristific·us -a -um *adj* ominous; saddening

tristimōni·a -ae *f* sadness

trīst·is -e *adj* sad, sorrowful, melancholy, glum, dispirited; bringing sorrow, saddening, dismal; gloomy, sullen; stern, harsh; disagreeable, offensive (*odor*); bitter (*taste*)

tristiti·a -ae *f* sadness, gloom, gloominess, melancholy; severity, sternness

tristiti·ēs -ēī *f* sadness, sorrow, melancholy

trisulc·us -a -um *adj* three-forked

trităv·us -ī *m* great-great-great-grandfather

trītice·us -a -um *adj* wheat, of wheat

trītic·um -ī *n* wheat

Trīt·ōn -ōnis *m* son of Neptune who blows through a shell to calm the seas; lake in Africa where Minerva was said to be born

Trītōniăc·us -a -um *adj* Tritonian

Trītōn·is -idis or **-ĭdos** *f* Minerva

Trītōni·us -a -um *adj* Tritonian; *f* Minerva

trīt·or -ōris *m* grinder

trītūr·a -ae *f* threshing

trīt·us -a -um *pp* of **tero**; *adj* worn, well-worn; beaten (*path*); experienced, expert; common, trite (*language*)

trīt·us -ūs *m* rubbing, friction

triumphāl·is -e *adj* triumphal; having had a triumph; *n pl* triumphal insignia (*without the actual triumph*)

triumph·ō -āre *vt* to triumph over, conquer completely, vanquish; *vi* to make a triumphal procession, celebrate a triumph, triumph

triumph·us or **triump·us -ī** *m* victory parade, triumph; victory, triumph; **triumphum agere** (with **de** or **ex** + *abl*) to celebrate a triumph over

triumv·ir -irī *m* triumvir, commissioner; mayor (*of a provincial town*)

triumvirāl·is -e *adj* triumviral, of the triumvirs

triumvirāt·us -ūs *m* triumvirate, office of triumvir

triumvir·ī -ōrum *m pl* triumvirs, three commissioners, three-man commission (*appointed at various times to serve various purposes*); **triumviri capitales** police commissioners, superintendents of prisons and executions

trivenēfic·a -ae *f* nasty old witch

Trivi·a -ae *f* Diana

triviāl·is *adj* of the crossroads; found everywhere, common, ordinary

triv·ium -iī or **-ī** *n* crossroads, intersection; public street, highway

trivi·us -a -um *adj* of or at the crossroads

Trō·as -ădis *adj* Trojan; *f* Troad, district of Troy; Trojan woman

trochae·us -ī *m* trochee; tribrach (*metrical foot of three short syllables*)

trochlē·a -ae *f* block and tackle

troch·us -ī *m* hoop

Trōi·a or **Trōj·a -ae** *f* Troy

Trōiăd·es -um *f pl* Trojan women

Trōic·us -a -um *adj* Trojan

Trōil·us -ī *m* son of Priam, killed by Achilles

Trōi·us -a -um *adj* Trojan; *f* see **Troia**

Trōjān·us -a -um *adj* Trojan; *m pl* Trojans

Trōjugĕn·a *masc & fem adj* Trojan-born, born at Troy, of Trojan descent, Trojan; *m* Trojan

tropae·um -ī *n* trophy, victory memorial; victory; mark, token, memorial, monument

Trōs Trōis *m* Tros (*king of Phrygia after whom Troy was named*)

trucidāti·ō -ōnis *f* slaughter, massacre, butchery

trucid·ō -āre *vt* to slaughter, massacre, cut down

truculentē or **truculenter** *adv* grimly, fiercely

truculenti·a -ae *f* savagery, ferocity; harshness; inclemency

truculent·us -a -um *adj* savage, grim, fierce, cruel

trud·is -is *f* pointed pole, pike

trūdō trūdĕre trūsī trūsum *vt* to push, thrust, drive, shove; to put forth (*buds*)

trull·a -ae *f* dipper, ladle, scoop; brazier; wash basin

trunc·ō -āre *vt* to lop off, mutilate, maim

trunc·us -a -um *adj* lopped; stripped (*of branches and leaves*), trimmed; maimed, mutilated; imperfect, undeveloped; *m* trunk, tree trunk; trunk, body (*of human being*); chunk of meat; blockhead

trūsit·ō -āre *vt* to keep pushing, keep shoving

trūsus *pp* of **trudo**

trutin·a -ae *f* balance, pair of scales; criterion

trutin·or -ārī -ātus sum *vt* to weigh, balance

trux trucis *adj* savage, grim, fierce, wild

trȳgŏn·us -ī *m* stingray

tū *pron* you (*singular*)

tuātim *adv* in your manner, as is typical of you

tŭb·a -ae *f* bugle, war trumpet

tūb·er -ĕris *n* lump, bump, swelling; truffle (*food*)

tŭb·er -ĕris *f* apple tree; *m* apple

tŭbīc·en -ĭnis *m* bugler, trumpeter

tŭbilustr·ium -ĭī *or* **-ī** *n* festival of bugles or trumpets (*celebrated on March 23rd and May 23rd and including a ritual cleaning of the bugles or trumpets*)

tŭburcĭn·or -ārī -ātus sum *vt* to devour, gobble up

tŭb·us -ī *m* tube, pipe

tŭccēt·um *or* **tūcēt·um -ī** *n* sausage

tŭdĭt·ō -āre *vt* to keep hitting, keep beating

tŭĕor *or* **tŭ·or tŭērī tuĭtus sum** *or* **tūtus sum** *vt* to see, look at, gaze at, watch, observe; to look after, take care of, guard, defend, protect

tŭgŭr·ium -ĭī *or* **-ī** *n* hut, hovel, cottage

tŭitĭ·ō -ōnis *f* guarding, defense; **tuitio sui** self-defense

Tullĭān·um -ī *n* state prison in Rome, reputedly built by Servius Tullius

Tullĭŏl·a -ae *f* little Tullia (*Cicero's daughter*)

Tull·ius -ĭī *or* **-ī** *m* Servius Tullius (*sixth king of Rome*)

tum *adv* then, at that time; next; moreover, besides; **cum . . . tum** both . . . and especially, not only . . . but also, if . . . then surely; **tum cum** at the point when, at the time when, just then when; **tum . . . tum** first . . . then, at one time . . . at another, now . . . now, both . . . and, partly . . . partly

tŭme·faciō -facĕre -fēcī -factum *vt* to make swell; (fig) to inflate

tŭm·ĕō -ēre -ŭī *vi* to be swollen, swell up, be inflated; (of business) to be in ferment, be cooking; (of language) to be bombastic; (of a person) to be excited, be in a dither, be in a rage; to be proud

tŭm·ēscō -ēscĕre -ŭī *vi* to begin to swell, begin to swell up; (of wars) to brew; to grow excited, become enraged, become inflated

tŭmĭd·us -a -um *adj* swollen, swelling; bloated; rising high; proud, inflated, puffed up; arrogant; incensed, enraged, exasperated; bombastic

tŭm·or -ōris *m* tumor, swelling; protuberance, bulging; elevation (*of the ground*); commotion, excitement, anger, rage; vanity, pride, arrogance

tŭmŭl·ō -āre *vt* to bury

tŭmŭlōs·us -a -um *adj* full of hills, hilly, rolling

tŭmultŭārĭ·us -a -um *adj* hurried, confused, disorderly; (mil) emergency, drafted hurriedly to meet an emergency; **exercitus tumultuarius** emergency army; **pugna tumultuaria** irregular fight or battle (*i.e., not fought in regular battle formation*)

tŭmultŭātĭ·ō -ōnis *f* confusion, hustle and bustle, panic

tŭmultŭ·ō -āre *or* **tŭmultŭ·or -ārī -ātus sum** *vi* to make a disturbance; to be in uproar, be topsyturvy

tŭmultŭōse *adv* disorderly, in confusion

tŭmultŭōs·us -a -um *adj* boisterous, uproarious, turbulent, panicky

tŭmult·us -ūs *m* commotion, uproar; insurrection, rebellion, civil war; confusion, agitation (*of the mind*); outbreak (*of crime*)

tŭmŭl·us -ī *m* mound; rising; ground swell; burial mound; **tumulus inanis** cenotaph

tūn = tūne (tū & ne)

tunc *adv* (of time past) then, at that time, on that occasion, just then; (of future time) then, at that time, in that event; (of succession in time) thereupon; (in conclusion) accordingly, consequently, in that case; **tunc . . . cum** then . . . when, just when, just at the time when; only when, whenever; **tunc demum** not until, then only, not till then; **tunc primum** then for the first time; **tunc quando** whenever; **tunc quoque** then too; **tunc vero** then to be sure, exactly then

tundō tundĕre tŭtŭdī tunsum *or* **tūsum** *vt* to beat, pound, hammer, thump; to buffet; to thresh; (fig) to harp on, keep at, importune

tŭnĭc·a -ae *f* tunic (*ordinary sleeved garment worn by both sexes*); skin, peel, husk, coating

tŭnĭcāt·us -a -um *adj* wearing a tunic; in shirt sleeves; coated, covered with skin

tŭnĭcŭl·a -ae *f* short tunic; thin skin or coating

tunsus *pp* of **tundo**

tuor see **tueor**

turb·a -ae *f* turmoil, disorder, uproar, commotion; brawl; crowd, disorderly crowd, mob, gang; multitude; common crowd, the masses; a large number

turbāment·a -ōrum *n pl* means of disturbance

turbāte *adv* in confusion, confusedly

turbātĭ·ō -ōnis *f* confusion, disorder

turbāt·or -ōris *m* ringleader, troublemaker, disturber

turbāt·us -a -um *adj* confused, disorderly; disturbed, annoyed

turbell·ae -ārum *f pl* stir, row; **turbellas facere** to cause a row

turben see **turbo** *m*

turbĭdē *adv* confusedly, in disorder

turbĭd·us -a -um *adj* wild, confused, boisterous; muddy, turbid;

troubled, perplexed; vehement; disheveled (*hair*); stormy (*sky, weather*)

turbĭnĕ·us -a -um *adj* cone-shaped

turb·ō -ĭnis *m* or **turb·en -ĭnis** *n* whirl, twirl, eddy; spinning, revolution; coil; spinning top; reel; spindle; wheel; tornado, whirlwind; wheel of fortune; (fig) whirlwind, storm

turb·ō -āre *vt* to throw into confusion, disturb, agitate; to break, disorganize (*in battle*), cause to break ranks; to confuse, confound; to muddy

turbulentē or **turbulenter** *adv* boisterously, tumultuously, confusedly

turbulent·us -a -um *adj* turbulent, wild, stormy; disturbed, confused; seditious, trouble-making

turd·a -ae *f* or **turd·us -ī** *m* thrush

tūrĕ·us -a -um *adj* of frankincense

turgĕō turgēre tursī *vi* to be swollen, be puffed up; to be bombastic

turgesc·ō -ĕre *vi* to begin to swell, begin to swell up; to begin to blow up (*in anger*)

turgidŭl·us -a -um *adj* poor swollen, swollen little (*eyes*)

turgĭd·us -a -um *adj* swollen, puffed up, inflated; turgid, bombastic

tūrĭbŭl·um -ī *n* censer

tūricrĕm·us -a -um *adj* incense-burning

tūrĭf·er -ĕra -ĕrum *adj* incense-producing

tūrĭlĕg·us -a -um *adj* incense-gathering

turm·a -ae *f* troop, squadron (*of cavalry*); crowd, group

turmāl·is -e *adj* of a squadron; equestrian; *m pl* troopers

turmātim *adv* by troops, by squadrons, squadron by squadron

Turn·us -ī *m* king of the Rutuli, killed by Aeneas

turpĭcŭl·us -a -um *adj* ugly little; somewhat indecent

turpĭfĭcāt·us -a -um *adj* corrupted, debased, degenerate

turpilucricupĭd·us -a -um *adj* (coll) eager to make a fast buck

turp·is -e *adj* ugly, deformed; foul, filthy, nasty; disgraceful, shameless; dirty, obscene, indecent

turpĭter *adv* repulsively; disgracefully, scandalously, shamelessly

turpitūd·ō -ĭnis *f* ugliness, deformity; foulness; disgrace; moral turpitude

turp·ō -āre *vt* to make ugly, disfigure; to soil, dirty, defile, pollute

turrĭg·er -ĕra -ĕrum *adj* turreted; (Cybele) wearing a turreted crown (*representing the earth with its cities*)

turr·is -is *f* turret, tower; howdah (*on an elephant*); (fig) castle, mansion

turrīt·us -a -um *adj* turreted; for-

tified with turrets; crowned with turrets, adorned with a turret crown

turt·ur -ŭris *m* turtledove

tūs tūris *m* incense, frankincense

Tuscŭlān·us -a -um or **Tuscŭlens·is -e** *adj* Tusculan, of Tusculum; *m pl* Tusculans

Tuscŭl·us -a -um *adj* Tusculan; *n* Tusculum (*town in Latium near Alba Longa, about twelve miles from Rome*)

Tusc·us -a -um *adj* Etruscan

tussicŭl·a -ae *f* slight cough

tuss·iō -īre *vi* to cough, have a cough

tuss·is -is *f* cough

tūsus *pp* of **tundo**

tūtām·en -ĭnis or **tūtāment·um -ī** *n* means of defense, defense, protection

tūte = **tū** & **te** emphatic form of **tū**

tūtē *adv* safely

tūtēl·a or **tūtell·a -ae** *f* care, charge, patronage, protection, defense; guardianship; charge, thing protected; guardian, keeper, watcher

tūtĕmet = **tū** & **te** & **met** emphatic form of **tū**

tūt·ō -āre or **tūt·or -ārī -ātus sum** *vt* to guard, protect, defend; to keep safe, watch, preserve; to ward off, avert; (with **ab** + **abl** or with **ad** or **adversus** + *acc*) to protect (*someone*) from, guard (*someone*) against

tūt·or -ōris *m* protector; guardian (*of minors, women, etc.*)

tūt·us -a -um *pp* of **tueor**; *adj* safe, secure; cautious, prudent; *n* safe place, safety, shelter, security; **ex tuto** from a safe place, in safety, safely

tūtō *adv* safely, in safety

tu·us -a -um *adj* your; right for you, proper for you; *pron* yours; **tuā interest** it is of importance to you; **tui** your friends, your people, your family; **tuum est** (with *inf*) it is your duty to, it is up to you to

tuxtax *adv* (word meant to imitate the sound of blows) whack, wham; **tuxtax meo tergo erit** (coll) it's going to go whack, wham, bang over my back

Tȳd·eus -ĕī or **-ĕos** *m* Tydeus (*son of Oeneus, one of the Seven against Thebes, and father of Diomedes*)

Tȳdīd·ēs -ae *m* Diomedes (*son of Tydeus*)

tympanotrīb·a -ae *m* timbrel player, drummer

tympăn·um or **typăn·um -ī** *n* timbrel, drum

Tyndăr·eus -ĕī or **Tyndăr·us -ī** *m* king of Sparta, husband of Leda, father of Castor and Clytemnestra, and reputed father of Pollux and Helen

Tyndarĭd·ēs -ae *m* descendant of Tyndareus

Tyndăr·is -ĭdis *f* descendant of Tyndareus (*female*)

Typhō·ĕus -ĕī or **ĕos** or **Typh·ōn -ōnis** *m* giant who was struck with lightning by Jupiter and buried under Mount Etna

typ·us -ī *m* figure, image (*on the wall*)

tyrannactŏn·us -ī *m* tyrannicide, assassin of a tyrant

tyrannĭcē *adv* tyrannically; arbitrarily, cruelly

tyrannĭcīd·a -ae *m* tyrannicide, assassin of a tyrant

tyrannĭc·us -a -um *adj* tyrannical; arbitrary, cruel

tyrann·is -ĭdis *f* tyranny, despotism

tyrianthīn·a -ōrum *n pl* violet-colored clothes

Tyri·us -a -um *adj* Tyrian, Phoenician; Carthaginian; Theban; crimson (*because of the famous dye produced at Tyre*); *m pl* Tyrians, Carthaginians

Tyr·ō -ūs *f* daughter of Salmoneus and mother of Pelias and Neleus by Poseidon

Tyr·os or **Tyr·us -ī** *f* Tyre (*famous commercial city of Phoenicia*)

tўrotarĭch·os -ī *m* dish of salted fish and cheese

Tyrrhēni·a -ae *f* Etruria

Tyrrhēnĭc·us -a -um *adj* Etrurian, Etruscan

Tyrrhēn·us -a -um *adj* Etrurian, Etruscan; *m pl* Etruscans (*Pelasgian people who migrated to Italy perhaps from Lydia in Asia Minor and settled to the N. of the Tiber*)

Tyrtae·us -ī *m* Spartan poet (*7th cent. B.C.*)

U

ūb·er -ĕris *adj* rich, fruitful, fertile, plentiful, productive; rich, imaginative (*style*); (fig) fruitful, productive; *n* richness, fruitfulness, fertility; fertile soil, fruitful field; breast, teat; udder, dug

ūberius *adv* more fully, more copiously, more fruitfully

ūbert·ās -ātis *f* richness, fertility, productiveness

ūbertim *adv* abundantly, copiously

ubĭ *adv* (interrog) where; **ubi gentium** (coll) where in the world; *conj* where, in which, whereby, with whom, by whom; when, whenever

ubĭcumque *adv* wherever, wheresoever; anywhere, everywhere

Ubĭ·ī -ōrum *m pl* German tribe on the lower Rhine

ubĭnam *adv* where; **ubĭnam gentium** (coll) where in the world

ubĭquāque *adv* everywhere

ubĭque *adv* anywhere, everywhere

ubĭŭbĭ *adv* wherever

ubĭvis *adv* anywhere, everywhere, wherever you please; **ubĭvis gentium** (coll) anywhere in the world

ūd·us -a -um *adj* wet, moist, damp, humid

ulcĕr·ō -āre *vt* to make sore; (fig) to wound

ulcerōs·us -a -um *adj* full of sores, ulcerous

ulcīscor ulciscī ultus sum *vt* to avenge oneself on, take vengeance on, punish; to avenge, requite, repay

ulc·us -ĕris *n* sore, ulcer

ūlīg·ō -ĭnis *f* moisture, dampness

Ulix·ēs -is or **-eī** or **-ei** *m* Ulysses (*king of Ithaca, son of Laertes, husband of Penelope, and father of Telemachus and Telegonus*)

ull·us -a -um *adj* any

ulmĕ·us -a -um *adj* elm, made of elm

ulmitrīb·a -ae *m* (coll) slaphappy (*from being flogged with elm whips*)

ulm·us -ī *f* elm tree; *f pl* elm rods

uln·a -ae *f* elbow; arm; (as measure of length) ell

ulpĭc·um -ī *n* leek

ulterĭ·or -ūs *adj* farther, on the farther side, more remote; further, more, longer, in a higher degree; worse; *m pl* more remote people, those beyond; *n pl* things beyond

ultĭmum *adv* finally, for the last time

ultĭm·us -a -um *adj* farthest, most distant, extreme; earliest; latest, final, last; greatest; lowest; meanest; *n* last thing; end; **ad ultimum** to the end, to the extreme, in the highest degree, to the last degree, utterly; *n pl* extremes; the worst

ultĭ·ō -ōnis *f* vengeance, revenge

ult·or -ōris *m* avenger, punisher, revenger

ultrā *adv* beyond, farther, besides; *prep* (with *acc*) beyond, past; (of number, measure, degree) over, beyond, more than, over and above

ultr·ix ĭcis *adj* avenging

ultrō *adv* to the farther side, beyond; on the other side; besides, moreover, too; of one's own accord, without being asked; without being spoken to; **ultro tributa** expenditure incurred by the government for public works

ultus *pp* of **ulciscor**

ulŭl·a -ae *f* screech owl

ululāt·us -ūs *m* crying, wailing (*esp. of mourners*); war cry

ulŭl·ō -āre *vt* to cry out to; *vi* to shriek, yell; (*of places*) to ring, resound

ulv·a -ae *f* sedge

umbell·a -ae *f* umbrella, parasol

umbilīc·us -ī *m* navel, belly button; midriff; middle, center; projecting end of dowels on which books were rolled; cockle, sea snail

umb·ō -ōnis *m* boss (*of a shield*); shield; elbow

umbr·a -ae *f* shade, shadow; phantom, shade, ghost; mere shadow (*of one's former self, etc.*); shelter, cover; constant companion; grayling, umber (*fish*); **rhetorica umbra** rhetorician's school

umbrācŭl·um -ī *n* bower, arbor; school; umbrella, parasol

umbrātīcŏl·a -ae *m* lounger, loafer (*in the shade*)

umbrātīc·us -a -um *adj* too fond of the shade, lazy

umbrātīl·is -e *adj* remaining in the shade, private, retired; academic

Umbri·a -ae *f* Umbria (*district in central Italy*)

umbrīf·er -ēra -ērum *adj* shady

umbr·ō -āre *vt* to shade, cover

umbrōs·us -a -um *adj* shady

ūmect·ō -āre *vt* to wet, moisten

ūmect·us -a -um *adj* moist, damp

ūm·ĕō -ēre *vi* to be moist, be damp, be wet

umĕr·us -ī *m* shoulder

ūmesc·ō -ĕre *vi* to become moist or wet

ūmidŭl·us -a -um *adj* dampish

ūmid·us -a -um *adj* moist, damp, wet; green (*lumber*); *n* wet place

ūm·or -ōris *m* moisture; liquid, fluid

umquam or **unquam** *adv* ever, at any time

ūnā *adv* together; **ūnā venīre** to come along

ūnanĭm·ans -antis *adj* of one mind, of one accord

ūnanĭmĭt·ās -ātis *f* unanimity

ūnanĭm·us -a -um *adj* unanimous; of one mind, of one heart, harmonious

ūnci·a -ae *f* a twelfth; ounce (*one twelfth of a pound or libra*)

ūnciāri·us -a -um *adj* containing a twelfth; **faenus unciarium** eight and one third percent interest per annum

ūnciātim *adv* little· by little

ūncīnāt·us -a -um *adj* hooked, barbed

ūnciŏl·a -ae *f* a mere twelfth

unctī·ō -ōnis *f* rubdown; (fig) wrestling

unctĭt·ō -āre *vt* to keep rubbing with oil, keep oiling

unctiuscŭl·us -a -um *adj* somewhat too unctuous

unct·or -ōris *m* anointer, rubdown man

unct·um -ī *n* sumptuous dinner; ointment

unctūr·a -ae *f* anointing

unct·us -a -um *pp* of **ungo**; *adj* greasy; resinous; sumptuous; *n* sumptuous dinner; ointment

unc·us -a -um *adj* hooked, crooked, barbed; *m* hook, clamp; grappling iron

und·a -ae *f* water; liquid; wave, billow; (fig) stream, tide, agitated mass

unde *adv* from where, whence; from whom; **unde unde** or **undeunde** from some place or other, somehow or other, by hook or by crook

undecĭens or **undecĭēs** *adv* eleven times

undēcĭm (indecl) *adj* eleven

undecĭm·us -a -um *adj* eleventh

undecumque or **undecunque** *adv* from whatever place, from whatever source

undēn·ō -ae -a *adj* eleven in a group, eleven each, eleven

undēnōnāgintā (indecl) *adj* eighty-nine

undeoctōgintā (indecl) *adj* seventy-nine

undēquadrāgintā (indecl) *adj* thirty-nine

undēquinquāgensĭm·us or **undēquinquāgēsĭm·us -a -um** *adj* forty-ninth

undēquinquāgintā (indecl) *adj* forty-nine

undēsexāgintā (indecl) *adj* fifty-nine

undētrīcensĭm·us or **undētrīcēsĭm·us -a -um** *adj* twenty-ninth

undēvīcēsĭmān·ī -ōrum *m pl* soldiers of the nineteenth legion

undēvīcēsĭm·us -a -um *adj* nineteenth

undēvīgintī (indecl) *adj* nineteen

undĭque *adv* from all directions, on all sides, everywhere; in all respects, completely

undĭsŏn·us -a -um *adj* sea-roaring; **undisoni dei** gods of the roaring waves

und·ō -āre *vi* to move in waves, undulate; to billow; to overflow

undōs·us -a -um *adj* full of waves, billowy

ūnetvīcensĭm·us or **ūnetvīcēsĭm·us -a -um** *adj* twenty-first

ūnetvīcēsĭmān·ī -ōrum *m pl* soldiers of the twenty-first legion

ungō or **unguō ungĕre unxī unctum** *vt* to oil, grease, anoint

ungu·en -ĭnis *n* fat, grease, ointment

unguentār·ĭus -ĭī or **-ī** *m* perfumer

unguentāt·us -a -um *adj* anointed; perfumed, wearing perfume

unguent·um -ī *n* ointment; perfume

unguicŭl·us -ī *m* fingernail; toenail; **a teneris unguiculis** from earliest childhood

ungu·is -is *m* fingernail; toenail; claw, talon, hoof; **ad unguen** to a tee, complete, perfect; **de tenero ungui** from earliest childhood; **transversum unguem** a hair's breadth

ungŭl·a -ae f hoof, claw, talon; (fig) horse

unguō see **ungo**

ūnĭcē adv singularly, solely

ūnĭcŏl·or -ōris adj of one and the same color

ūnĭcorn·is -e adj one-horned

ūnĭ·cus -a -um adj sole, only, single, singular, unique; uncommon, unparalleled, outstanding, unique

ūnĭform·is -e adj uniform

ūnĭgĕn·a -ae masc & fem adj only-begotten, only; of the same parentage

ūnĭmăn·us -a -um adj with one hand, one-handed

ūnĭ·ō -ōnis m single large pearl

ūnĭter adv jointly, conjointly

ūnĭversāl·is -e adj universal

ūnĭversē adv generally, in general

ūnĭversĭt·ās -ātis f aggregate, entirety, whole; whole world, universe

ūnĭvers·us -a -um adj all together, all taken collectively, whole, entire; n the whole; whole world, universe; **in universum** on the whole, in general

ūnoctŭl·us -ī m one-eyed person

ūnomammĭ·a -ae f (coll) single-breasted land (country of the Amazons)

unquam or **umquam** adv ever, at any time

ūn·us -a -um adj one; single, only, sole; one and the same; (indef) a, an, one, some; pron some one, a mere individual; **ad unum** to a man; **unus et alter** one or two; **unus quisque** every one individually, every single one

ūpĭlĭ·ō or **ŏpĭlĭ·ō -ōnis** m shepherd

ŭpŭp·a -ae f hoopoe; hoe, mattock

Ūranĭ·a -ae or **Ūranĭ·ē -ēs** f Muse of astronomy

urbānē adv politely, courteously; with sophistication; wittily, elegantly

urbānĭt·ās -ātis f living in the city, city life; refinement, politeness; sophistication; wit; raillery

urbān·us -a -um adj of the city, of the town, city, town; courteous; sophisticated; witty, facetious, humorous; forward, brash; m city man; city slicker

urbĭcăp·us -ī m conqueror of cities

urbs urbis f city; the city of Rome, the capital

urcĕŏl·us -ī m little pitcher, little pot

urcĕ·us -ī m pitcher, water pot

ūrēd·ō -ĭnis f blight (of plants)

urgĕō urgēre ursī vt to prod on, urge, urge forward; to pressure, put pressure on (someone); to crowd, hem in; to follow up, keep at, stick by; vi to be pressing, be urgent; to be insistent

ūrīn·a -ae f urine

ūrīnāt·or -ōris m diver

ūrīn·ō -āre or **ūrīn·or -ārī -ātus sum** vi to dive

urn·a -ae f pot, jar; water pot; voting urn; urn of fate; cinerary urn; money jar

ūrō ūrĕre ussī ustum vt to burn; to burn up, reduce to ashes, consume; to scorch, parch, dry up; to sting, pain; to nip, frostbite; to rub sore; to corrode; to annoy, gall, burn up, make angry; to inflame (with love), kindle, set on fire

urnŭl·a -ae f small urn

urs·a -ae f she-bear

Urs·a Major (genit: **Urs·ae Major·is**) f Great Bear (constellation)

Urs·a Minor (genit: **Urs·ae Minor·is**) f Little Bear (constellation)

ursīn·us -a -um adj bear, bear's

urs·us -ī m bear

urtĭc·a -ae f nettle; desire, itch

ūr·us -ī m wild ox

Usĭpĕt·ēs -um m pl German tribe on the Rhine

ūsĭtātē adv in the usual way, as usual

ūsĭtāt·us -a -um adj usual, customary, familiar; **usitatum est** (with inf) it is customary to

uspĭam adv anywhere, somewhere; in any matter

usquam adv anywhere, in any place; anywhere, to any place

usque adv all the way, right on, straight on; all the time, continuously; even, as much as; **usque** (with **ab** + abl) all the way from; **usque** (with **ad** + acc) all the way to; **usque quaque** every moment, continually; on all occasions, in everything

ust·or -ōris m cremator

ustŭl·ō -āre vt to burn a little, scorch, singe; to burn up

ustus pp of **uro**

ūsū·capĭō -capĕre -cēpī -captum vt (law) to acquire possession of, acquire ownership of (by long use, by prescription)

ūsūcapĭ·ō -ōnis f (law) acquisition of ownership through long use or long possession

ūsūr·a -ae f use, enjoyment; interest (on capital)

ūsūrārĭ·us -a -um adj for use and enjoyment; paying interest

ūsūrpātĭ·ō -ōnis f use; (with genit) making use of, use of

ūsūrp·ō -āre vt to make use of, use, employ, adopt, practice, exercise; (law) to take possession of, acquire; to seize wrongfully, usurp; to name, call, speak of; to adopt, assume; to perceive (with the senses), observe, experience

ūsus pp of **utor**

ūs·us -ūs m use, enjoyment; practice, employment; experience, skill; usage, custom; familiarity; usefulness, advantage, benefit; occasion, need, necessity; **ex usu esse** or **usui esse** (with *dat*) to be useful to, be beneficial to, be a good thing for; **si usus veniat** if the need should arise, if the opportunity should present itself; **usus adest** a good opportunity comes along; **usus est** (with *abl*) there is need of; **usus et fructus** use and enjoyment; **usu venit** it happens, it occurs

ūsusfructus (*genit*: **ūsūsfructūs**) *m* use and enjoyment

ut or **utī** *adv* how, in what way; *conj* (comparative) as; (adversative) although; (temporal) when, while; (purpose) in order that; (result) that; (concessive) granted that; (introducing examples) as, as for example; (after verbs of fearing) lest, that not; (introducing an explanation or reason) as, as being, inasmuch as; (introducing indirect commands) that

utcumque or **utcunque** *adv* however; whenever; one way or another

ūtensil·is -e *adj* useful; *n pl* utensils, materials

ūt·er -ris *m* bag, skin, bottle

ut·er -ra -rum *adj* which (*of the two*); *pron* which one (*of the two*); one or the other

ut·ercumque -racumque -rumcumque *adj* whichever (*of the two*); *pron* whichever one (*of the two*)

ut·erlibet -ralibet -rumlibet *adj* whichever (*of the two*) you please; *pron* whichever one (*of the two*) you please, either one (*of the two*)

ut·erque -ráque -rumque *adj* each (*of the two*), both; **sermones utriusque linguae** conversations in both languages; *pron* each one (*of the two*), both; **uterque insaniunt** both are insane

uter·us -ī *m* or **uter·um -ī** *n* womb; belly, paunch (*of a man*)

ut·ervis -rāvis -rumvis *adj* whichever (*of the two*) you please, either; *pron* whichever one (*of the two*) you please, either one

utī see **ut**

ūtibil·is -e *adj* useful, practical

Utic·a -ae *f* city in Africa, N.W. of Carthage, where the younger Cato committed suicide

Uticens·is -is *adj* of Utica, Utican

ūtil·is -e *adj* useful, profitable, expedient, practical; (with *dat* or **ad** + *acc*) fit for, useful for, practical in

ūtilit·ās -ātis *f* usefulness, advantage

ūtiliter *adv* usefully, profitably

utinam *conj* (introducing a wish) if only ,would that

utique *adv* anyhow, at least, at any rate

ūtor ūtī ūsus sum *vi* (with *abl*) **a** to use, make use of; **b** to enjoy; **c** to practice, experience; **d** to enjoy the friendship or companionship of

utpōte *conj* as, inasmuch as; **utpote qui** inasmuch as (*he is one*) who, inasmuch as he, because he

ūtrār·ius -iī or **-ī** *m* water carrier, water boy

utrimque or **utrinque** *adv* from or on both sides, on either side; **utrimque constitit fides** on both sides the word of honor held good, both parties kept their word

utrō *adv* to which of the two sides, in which direction

utrobique *adv* on both sides, on either hand

utrōlibet *adv* to either side

utrōque *adv* to both places, in both directions

utrŭbi or **utrŭbī** *adv* at or on which of two sides

utrubique *adv* on both sides, on either hand

utrum *conj* either; whether

utut or **ut ut** *adv* however, in whatever way

ūv·a -ae *f* grape; bunch or cluster of grapes; vine; cluster of bees

ūvesc·ō -ĕre *vi* to become moist; (fig) to get drunk

ūvidŭl·us -a -um *adj* moist

ūvid·us -a -um *adj* wet, moist, damp, humid; drunken

ux·or -ōris *f* wife; mate (*of animals*)

uxorcŭl·a -ae *f* dear little wife

uxōri·us -a -um *adj* of a wife, wifely; very fond of a wife; henpecked

---

V

vac·ans -antis *adj* vacant, unoccupied; at leisure, unemployed; unengaged, single; (with *abl*) lacking, without; *n pl* unoccupied estates

vacātī·ō -ōnis *f* freedom, exemption (*from duty, service, etc.*); exemption from military service; payment for exemption from military service

vacc·a -ae *f* cow

vaccīn·ium -iī or **-ī** *n* hyacinth

vaccŭl·a -ae *f* heifer

vacē·fīō -fĭĕrī -factus sum *vi* to become empty, be emptied

vacill·ō -āre *vi* to stagger, reel; to vacillate, waver; to be untrustworthy

vacivē *adv* at leisure

vacīvit·ās -ātis *f* want, lack

vacīv·us or **vocīv·us -a -um** *adj* empty; free; (with *genit*) free of, void of, free from

vac·ō -āre *vi* to be empty, be vacant,

be unoccupied; to be free, be care-free; to be at leisure, have free time; (with *abl* or *ab* + *abl*) to be free from; (with *dat* or with *ad* or *in* + *acc*) to be free for, have time for; *v impers* there is time, room, leisure; (with *inf*) there is time to or for

vacuāt·us -a -um *adj* empty

vacuē·faciō -facere -fēcī -factum *vt* to empty, clear, free

vacuĭt·ās -ātis *f* freedom, exemption; vacancy (*in an office*)

vacŭ·ō -āre *vt* to empty, clear, free

vacŭ·us -a -um *adj* empty, clear, free; vacant; worthless, useless; single, unmarried; widowed; at leisure; carefree; (with *genit* or *abl* or with *ab* + *abl*) free from, devoid of, without; (with *dat*) free for

vadimōn·ĭum -iī or *-ī* n (law) promise (*to appear in court*), bail (*given as a guarantee of one's appearance in court*); **vadimōnium deserere** to default, fail to show up in court; **vadimōnium differre** to postpone appearance in court, grant a continuance; **vadimōnium facere** to put up bail; **vadimōnium sistere** to appear in court

vād·ō -ĕre *vi* to go, make one's way, advance

vad·or -ārī -ātus sum *vt* to put (*someone*) under bail

vadōs·us -a -um *adj* shallow

vad·um -ī n shallow place, shallow, shoal, ford; body of water, stream, sea; bottom, depths

vae *interj* woe! (with *acc* or *dat*) woe to

vāf·er -ra -rum *adj* sly, cunning; subtle

vafrē *adv* slyly, cunningly

vagē *adv* far and wide

vāgīn·a -ae f sheath, scabbard; sheath (*of ear of grain*), hull, husk; vagina

vāg·ĭō -īre -īvī -iī *vi* (esp. of an infant) to cry; (of swine) to squeal

vāgīt·us -ūs m cry; bleating

vāg·or -ōris m cry, wail (*of an infant*)

vag·or -ārī -ātus sum or **vag·ō -āre** *vi* to wander, range, roam

vag·us -a -um *adj* wandering, ranging, roaming; unsteady, inconstant; vague, uncertain

vah *interj* ah!, oh!

valdē *adv* greatly, intensely; (with *adj* or *adv*) very; (as affirmative reply) yes, certainly; to be sure

valē *interj* good-bye

val·ens -entis *adj* strong, powerful; healthy, hale, well

valenter *adv* strongly; energetically

valentŭl·us -a -um *adj* a strong little

val·ĕō -ēre -ŭī *vi* to be strong, be vigorous; to be powerful, be effective; to avail, prevail, succeed; to be influential; to be valid; to be strong enough, be adequate, be ca-

pable, be able; to be of value, be of worth; to mean, signify; **tē valere jubeo** I bid you farewell, good-by to you; **vale!** or **valete!** good-bye!; **vale dicere** to say good-bye, take leave

valesc·ō -ĕre *vi* to grow strong, acquire strength, thrive

valētūdinār·ĭum -ĭī or *-ī* n hospital

valētūd·ō -ĭnis f state of health; good health; ill health, illness

valg·us -a -um *adj* bowlegged

validē *adv* strongly, vehemently; (in replies) of course, certainly, definitely

valid·us -a -um *adj* strong, powerful, able; healthy, robust; fortified; influential; efficacious

vallār·is -e *adj* (decoration) awarded for scaling a rampart

vall·ēs or **vall·is -is** f valley

vall·ō -āre *vt* to fortify with a rampart, wall in; to protect, defend

vall·um -ī n rampart, palisade, entrenchment; protection

vall·us -ī m stake, pale; rampart with palisades, stockade; tooth (*of a comb*)

valv·ae -ārum f pl folding doors, double doors

vanesc·ō -ĕre *vi* to vanish, fade, disappear

vānĭdĭc·us -a -um *adj* lying, boasting; m liar, boaster

vānĭloquentĭ·a -ae f empty talk

vānĭloquĭdōr·us -ī m liar

vānĭlŏqu·us -a -um *adj* talking nonsense; lying, boasting, bragging

vānĭt·ās -ātis f falsity, unreality, deception, untruth; boasting, lying; vanity, conceit; worthlessness, frivolity, fickleness

vānĭtūd·ō -ĭnis f falsehood

vann·us -ī f fan, winnowing fan

vān·us -a -um *adj* empty, vacant; groundless, pointless; hollow, unreal; lying, false; boastful, conceited, vain; n emptiness, uselessness, deceptive appearance

vapĭdē *adv* poorly, badly

vapĭd·us -a -um *adj* flat, vapid, spoiled, bad; morally corrupt

vap·or -ōris m vapor, steam, smoke; exhalation, warmth, heat

vapōrār·ĭum -ĭī or *-ī* n steam pipe

vapōr·ō -āre *vt* to steam, steam up; to warm, heat; *vi* to steam, smoke

vapp·a -ae f sour wine; spoiled lad, good-for-nothing

vāpulār·is -e *adj* in for a flogging

vāpŭl·ō -āre *vi* to get a beating; (of savings, etc.) (fig) to take a beating

variantĭ·a -ae f diversity, variations

variātĭ·ō -ōnis f variation, difference

vārĭc·ō -āre *vt* to straddle

varicōs·us -a -um *adj* varicose

vārĭc·us -a -um *adj* with legs wide apart

varĭē *adv* variously, in various ways, differently

variĕt·ās -ātis f variety, difference, diversity; vicissitudes; inconstancy

vari·ō -āre vt to diversify, vary, change, make different; to variegate; vi to change color; to vary, differ, change; to differ in opinion; to waver

vari·us -a -um adj colored, variegated, spotted, striped; different, varying, various, changeable; versatile; inconstant, unsteady, untrustworthy

Var·ius -iī or **-ī** m epic and tragic poet and friend of Virgil and Horace (d. c. 12 B.C.)

var·ix -icis f varicose vein

Varr·ō -ōnis m M. Terentius Varro (Roman antiquarian and philologist whose wide erudition earned him the title of the most learned of the Romans, 116-27 B.C.)

vār·us -a -um adj knock-kneed; bent, crooked; opposed, contrary

vas vadis m bail, surety

vās vāsis or **vās·um -ī** (pl: **vās·a -ōrum**) n vessel, dish; utensil, implement; n pl equipment, gear; **va·sa conclamare** (mil) to give the signal to pack the gear

vāsār·ium -iī or **-ī** n allowance for furnishings (given to a provincial governor)

vasculār·ius -iī or **-ī** m metal worker; goldsmith

vascul·um -ī n small vessel

vastāti·ō -ōnis f devastation, ravaging

vastāt·or -ōris m devastator, ravager

vastē adv vastly, widely; coarsely, harshly; violently

vastific·us -a -um adj devastating

vastit·ās -ātis f wasteland; desert; state of desolation, emptiness; devastation, destruction; vastness, immensity; (fig) destroyer

vastiti·ēs -ēī f ruin, destruction

vast·ō -āre vt to make empty, make desolate, vacate, empty; (mil) to lay waste, ravage, devastate, destroy

vast·us -a -um adj empty, deserted, desolate; ravaged, devastated; vast, enormous; uncouth, rude, uncultivated, clumsy

vāt·ēs -is m soothsayer, prophet; bard, poet; f prophetess; poetess

Vātīcān·us -a -um adj Vatican; **mons** or **collis Vaticanus** hill in Rome on the right bank of the Tiber

vāticināti·ō -ōnis f prophesying, prediction, soothsaying

vāticināt·or -ōris m prophet, soothsayer

vāticin·ium -iī or **-ī** n prediction, prophecy

vāticini·us -a -um adj prophetic

vāticin·or -ārī -ātus sum vt to foretell, prophesy; to keep harping on; vi to prophesy; to rant and rave, talk wildly

vatill·um -ī n brazier

-ve conj (enclitic) or; **-ve . . . -ve** either . . . or

vēcordi·a -ae f senselessness; insanity, madness

vēc·ors -ordis adj senseless; foolish; mad

vectīg·al -ālis n tax, toll, tariff; revenue, income (of an individual); honorarium (given to a magistrate)

vectīgāl·is -e adj tax, toll, tariff; paying tribute, subject to taxes, taxable, taxed; **pecunia vectigalis** tax money, tribute

vecti·ō -ōnis f conveyance, transporting

vect·is -is m crowbar, lever; bar, bolt (on a door or gate)

vect·ō -āre vt to carry around; **vectari** to keep riding around

vect·or -ōris m bearer, carrier; rider, passenger

vectōri·us -a -um adj transportation, of transportation; **navigia vectoria** transport ships, transports

vectūr·a -ae f transport, transportation, conveyance; freight costs; fare

vectus pp of **veho**

Vēdiŏv·is or **Vējŏv·is -is** m Anti-Jove (Etruscan divinity of the lower world, identified with Apollo and with the Jupiter of the lower world); Little Jove (identified with the infant Jupiter)

vegĕt·us -a -um adj lively, vigorous, vivacious

vēgrand·is -e adj not huge, small

vehĕm·ens -entis adj vehement, violent, impetuous, ardent; great, tremendous; vigorous, active

vehementer or **vēmenter** adv vehemently, impetuously, violently, eagerly

vehementi·a -ae f vehemence

vehicul·um -ī n vehicle, carriage, cart; vessel, ship

vehō vehĕre vexī vectum vt to carry, convey, transport; **vehi** to ride, sail, be borne along

Vei·ens -entis or **Veientān·us -a -um** adj of Veii

Vei·ī -ōrum m pl old Etrurian city about twelve miles from Rome, captured by Camillus (396 B.C.)

vel adv even, actually; perhaps; for instance; conj or, or perhaps; or rather; **vel . . . vel** either . . . or

Vēlābr·um -ī n low ground between the Capitoline and Palatine

vēlām·en -inis n drape, covering, veil; clothing, robe

vēlāment·um -ī n curtain, veil; n pl olive branches draped with woolen fillets

vēlār·ium -iī or **-ī** n awning (over the open-air theater)

vēlāt·ī -ōrum m pl (mil) reserves

vēl·es -itis m light-armed soldier, skirmisher

vēlīf·er -ēra -ĕrum adj sail, sailing;

carina velifera sail boat, sailing ship

vēlificāti·ō -ōnis *f* sailing

vēlific·ō -āre or vēlific·or -ārī -ātus sum *vt* to sail through; *vi* to sail; (with *dat*) to be under full sail toward, be hell-bent for (*e.g.*, *high office*)

Velīn·us -ī *m* river and lake in the Sabine territory

vēlitār·is -e *adj* of the light-armed troops

vēlitāti·ō -ōnis *f* skirmishing

vēlitēs = *pl* of veles

vēlit·or -ōris *m* skirmisher

vēlivōl·us -a -um *adj* sail-flying (*ship*); sail-covered (*sea*)

vellic·ō -āre *vt* to pluck, pinch, nip; to carp at, rail at

vellō vellĕre vellī (or vulsī) vul-sum (or volsum) *vt* to pluck, pull, tear at, tear away, tear out; to tear up, tear down, destroy

vell·us -ĕris *n* fleece; skin, pelt; wool; *n pl* fleecy clouds

vēl·ō -āre *vt* to veil, wrap, envelop, cover, cover up; to encircle, crown; to cover up, hide, conceal

vēlōcit·ās -ātis *f* speed, velocity

vēlōcitĕr *adv* speedily, swiftly

vēl·ox -ōcis *adj* speedy, swift

vēl·um -ī *n* sail; veil, curtain, awning, covering; vela dare or vela facere to set sail; remis velisque with might and main

velut or velūtī *conj* as, just as, even as; as for example; (to introduce a simile) as, as it were; (in elliptical clauses) like; velut or velut si just as if, just as though, as if, as though

vēmens see vehemens

vēn·a -ae *f* vein, artery; vein of metal; water course; vein (*in wood, stone, etc.*); natural bent or disposition, genius; penis; strength; *f pl* (fig) heart, core

vēnābul·um -ī *n* hunting spear

Venāfrān·us -a -um *adj* of Venafrum

Venāfr·um -ī *n* town in S. central Italy

vēnālicī·us -a -um *adj* for sale; *m* slave dealer; *n pl* merchandise, imports and exports

vēnāl·is -e *adj* for sale; open to bribes; *mf* slave offered for sale

vēnātic·us -a -um *adj* hunting

vēnāti·ō -ōnis *f* hunt, hunting; wild-beast show; game

vēnāt·or -ōris *m* hunter

vēnātōrī·us -a -um *adj* hunter's

vēnātr·ix -īcis *f* huntress

vēnātūr·a -ae *f* hunting

vēnāt·us -ūs *m* hunting

vendibil·is -e *adj* salable; attractive, popular, acceptable, on sale

venditāti·ō -ōnis *f* boasting, showing off

venditi·ō -ōnis *f* sale

vendit·ō -āre *vt* to try to sell; to advertise; to give as a bribe; se

venditāre (with *dat*) to ingratiate oneself with

vendit·or -ōris *m* vendor, seller; recipient of a bribe

vend·ō -ĕre -idī -itum *vt* to put up for sale; to sell, vend; to sell (*some-one*) out, betray; to advertise; to praise, recommend

venēfic·a -ae *f* poisoner; sorceress, witch; (term of abuse) hag, witch

venēfic·ium -iī or -ī *n* poisoning witchcraft, magic

venēfic·us -a -um *adj* poisoning, poisonous; magic; *m* poisoner; sorcerer, magician

venēnāt·us -a -um *adj* poisonous, venomous; filled with poison; magic; bewitched, enchanted; (fig) venomous, bitter

venēnif·er -ĕra -ĕrum *adj* poisonous, venemous

venēn·ō -āre *vt* to poison; (fig) to poison, injure by slander

venēn·um -ī *n* poison; drug, potion; magic charm; sorcery; ruin, destruction

vēn·ĕō -īre -iī -itum *vi* to go up for sale, be sold

venerābil·is -e *adj* venerable

venerābund·us -a -um *adj* reverent, reverential

venerand·us -a -um *adj* venerable

venerāti·ō -ōnis *f* veneration, reverence, great respect

venerāt·or -ōris *m* respecter, adorer; admirer

Venerĕ·us or Venerī·us -a -um *adj* of Venus; of sexual love, venereal; *m* Venus-throw (*best throw in playing dice*); *m pl* attendants in Venus's temple

venĕr·or -ārī -ātus sum *vt* to venerate, revere, worship, pray to; to implore, beg; to pray for

Venĕt·ī -ōrum *m pl* a people in N.E. Italy in the region around modern Venice

Venetĭ·a -ae *f* district of the Veneti

Venetĭc·us -a -um *adj* Venetian

Venĕt·us -a -um *adj* Venetian; bluish; *m* Venetian; a Blue (*i.e., a member of one of the racing factions in Rome which were called Blues, Greens, etc.*)

veni·a -ae *f* kindness, favor, goodwill; permission; pardon, forgiveness; veniam dare (with *dat*) to grant forgiveness to, do a favor to, grant permission to; veniam petĕre to ask for permission; veniā vestrā with your leave

veniō venīre vēnī ventum *vi* to come; (with in + *acc*) a to come into, enter into (*e.g., agreement, friendship*); b to fall into (*e.g., trouble, disgrace*)

vēn·or -ārī -ātus sum *vt* & *vi* to hunt

vent·er -ris *m* stomach, belly; womb; embryo, unborn child; belly, protuberance; appetite, gluttony

ventil·ō -āre *vt* to fan, wave; to display, show off

venti·ō -ōnis *f* coming

ventit·ō -āre *vi* to keep coming, come regularly

ventōs·us -a -um *adj* windy, full of wind; of the wind; wind-like, swift as the wind; conceited; fickle

ventricŭl·us -ī *m* belly; ventricle (*of the heart*)

ventriōs·us -a -um *adj* pot-bellied

ventŭl·us -ī *m* breeze

vent·us -ī *m* wind

vēnŭcŭl·a -ae *f* grape (*of the type well suited for preserving*)

vēnum (*genit not in use; dat: vēnō*) *n* sale, that which is for sale; **vē-num** or **veno dare** to sell, sell as a slave; **venum** or **veno dari** to be sold; **venum** or **veno ire** to go up for sale, be sold

vēnum·dŏ or **vēnun·dŏ -dare -dĕdī -dătum** *vt* to put up for sale, sell

ven·us -ĕris *f* beauty, charm; pleasure of love, sexual indulgence, mating; beloved, love

Ven·us -ĕris *f* Venus (*goddess of love and beauty; planet*); Venus-throw (*highest throw of the dice*)

Venusi·a -ae *f* town in Apulia, the birthplace of Horace

Venusin·us -a -um *adj* of Venusia

venust·ās -ātis *f* beauty, charm, attraction

venustē *adv* prettily, charmingly

venustŭl·us -a -um *adj* cute, pretty, charming little

venust·us -a -um *adj* beautiful, charming, attractive

vēpallid·us -a -um *adj* very pale

veprēcŭl·a -ae *f* little brier bush

vepr·ēs -is *m* thorn bush, bramble bush

vēr vēris *n* spring, springtime; youth

vērātr·um -ī *n* hellebore

vēr·ax -ācis *adj* truthful

verbēn·a -ae *f* vervain; *f pl* sacred branches worn by heralds and priests

verb·er -ĕris *n* scourge, rod, whip; flogging, scourging; thong (*of a sling and similar weapons*); *n pl* strokes, flogging

verberābilissŭm·us -a -um *adj* altogether deserving of a flogging

verberāti·ō -ōnis *f* flogging

verberĕ·us -a -um *adj* deserving of a flogging

verberŏ -āre *vt* to scourge, flog, whip; to batter, beat

verbĕr·ō -ōnis *m* rascal

verbōsē *adv* verbosely

verbōs·us -a -um *adj* verbose, wordy

verb·um -ī *n* word; saying, expression; verb; proverb; mere talk, mere words; formula; **ad verbum** word for word, verbatim; **verba dare** (*with dat*) to cheat (*someone*); **verba facere** to speak, make a speech; **verbi causā** or **verbi gratiā** for instance; **verbo** orally; in a word, briefly; nominally, in name only; in theory; **verbum de verbo, verbum pro verbo, verbum verbo** word for word

Vercingetŏr·ix -igis *m* famous leader of the Arverni in the Gallic War

vercŭl·um -ī *n* (term of endearment) sweet springtime

vērē *adv* really, truly

verēcundē *adv* bashfully, shyly, modestly

verēcundi·a -ae *f* bashfulness, shyness, modesty; respect, awe, reverence; sense of shame, feeling of disgrace, disgrace, shame

verēcund·or -ārī *vi* to be bashful, be shy, feel ashamed

verēcund·us -a -um *adj* bashful, shy, modest, reserved

verēd·us -ī *m* fast hunting horse

verend·us -a -um *adj* venerable; *n pl* the private parts

ver·eor -ērī -ĭtus sum *vt* to revere, have respect for, respect; to fear; *vi* to feel uneasy, be apprehensive, be afraid, be anxious; (*with genit*) to stand in awe of, be afraid of; (*with dat*) to be afraid for; (*with de + abl*) to be apprehensive about; (*with ut*) to be afraid that not; (*with ne*) to be afraid that

veretr·um -ī *n* the private parts

Vergili·ae -ārum *f pl* Pleiads

Vergil·ius or **Virgil·ius -iī** or **-ī** *m* Virgil (*P. Vergilius Maro, famous epic poet of the Augustan Age, 70–19 B.C.*)

verg·ō -ĕre *vt* to turn, incline; *vi* to turn, incline; to decline; to lie, be situated; (*with ad + acc*) a to verge toward; **b** to face, face toward

vēridic·us -a -um *adj* truthful, speaking the truth; truly spoken

vērisimil·is -e *adj* probable, likely; realistic

vērisimilitūd·ō -inis *f* probability, likelihood

vērit·ās -ātis *f* truth, truthfulness; the truth, the real facts; real life, reality; honesty, integrity; correctness (*in etymology or grammar*); **ex veritate** in accordance with the truth

vēriverb·ium -iī or **-ī** *n* truthfulness

vermiculāt·us -a -um *adj* inlaid with wavy lines, vermiculated

vermicŭl·us -ī *m* grub worm

vermin·a -um *n pl* stomach pains

verm·is -is *m* worm

vern·a -ae *m* or *f* slave (*born in the master's house*), home-born slave; native

vernācŭl·us -a -um *adj* of home-born slaves; native, domestic; *m pl* jesters

vernīl·is -e *adj* slavish, servile; pert, smart

vernīlit·ās -ātis *f* slavishness, subservience; pertness

vernīliter *adv* slavishly

vern·ō -āre *vi* to show signs of spring; to burgeon, break into bloom; to be young

vernŭl·a -ae *m* or *f* little home-born slave, young home-born slave; native

vern·us -a -um *adj* spring; **tempus vernum** springtime

vērŏ *adv* in truth, in fact; certainly, to be sure; even; however

Vērōn·a -ae *f* city in N. Italy, the birthplace of Catullus and of Pliny the Elder

Vērōnens·is -e *adj* Veronese

verp·a -ae *f* penis

verp·us -ī *m* circumcised man

verr·ēs -is *m* boar, pig

Verr·ēs -is *m* C. Cornelius Verres (*notorious for outrageous conduct in governing Sicily in 73-70 B.C.*)

verrīn·us -a -um *adj* of a boar, boar, hog, pork

verrō verrēre verrī versum *vt* to pull, drag, drag away, carry off; to sweep, scour, brush; (of the wind) to whip across, sweep (*the land*)

verrūc·a -ae *f* wart (*on the body*); small failing, minor blemish

verrūcōs·us -a -um *adj* full of warts; (fig) faulty, full of blemishes

verrunc·ō -āre *vi* to turn out well

versābil·is -e *adj* shifting, movable

versābund·us -a -um *adj* revolving

versātil·is -e *adj* capable of turning, revolving, movable; versatile

versicŏl·or -ōris *adj* changing color, of various colors

versicŭl·us -ī *m* short line, single line (*of verse or prose*), versicle; *m pl* poor little verses

versificāt·or -ōris *m* versifier

versipell·is -e *adj* changing appearance, of changed appearance; sly; *m* werwolf

vers·ō or **vors·ō -āre** *vt* to keep turning, twist, wind; to roll; to bend, shift; to move about, agitate; to disturb, harass; to handle; to consider

vers·or or **vors·or -ārī -ātus sum** *vi* to live, stay; (with **in** + *abl*) to be involved in, be engaged in, be busy with

versum or **vorsum** *adv* (usually after another adv of direction) back; **rusum vorsum** backward; **sursum versum** up and down

versūr·a or **vorsūr·a -ae** *f* rotation; loan (*of money to pay another debt*); **versuram facere** (with **ab** + *abl*) to get a loan from (*someone to pay another*); **versūrā solvere** to pay off (*another debt*) with borrowed money

versus *pp* of **verro** and of **verto**

vers·us or **vors·us -ūs** *m* turning; furrow; line, row; line, verse; line (*in writing*); turn, step (*in a dance*)

versus or **vorsus** *adv* (with **ad** + *acc*) towards, in the direction of; (with **in** + *acc*) into, in towards;

sī in urbem versus ventūrī erunt if they intend to come into the city; **sursum versus** upwards

versūtē *adv* cunningly

versūtī·ae -ārum *f pl* cunning

versūtilŏqu·us -a -um *adj* smooth-speaking, sly

versūt·us or **vorsūt·us -a -um** *adj* clever, shrewd, ingenious; sly, crafty, cunning, deceitful

vert·ex or **vort·ex -icis** *m* whirlpool, eddy, strong current; whirlwind, tornado; crown or top of the head; head; top, summit (*of mountain*); pole (*of the heavens*); **ex vertice** from above

verticōs·us or **vorticōs·us -a -um** *adj* swirling, full of whirlpools

vertīg·ō -inis *f* turning, whirling; dizziness

vert·ō or **vort·ō vertĕre vertī versum** *vt* to turn, turn around; to invert, tilt; to change, alter, transform; to overturn, overthrow, destroy; to ascribe, impute; to translate; **se vertere** or **verti** (with **in** + *acc*) to change into, change oneself into; **verti** (with **in** + *abl*) **a** to be in (*a place or condition*); **b** to be engaged in, be involved in; *vi* to turn; to change; to turn out; (with **in** + abl) to center upon, depend upon

Vertumn·us -ī *m* god of the changing seasons

ver·ū -ūs *n* spit (*for roasting*); javelin, dart

veruīn·a -ae *f* small javelin

vērum *adv* truly, yes; true but; but in fact; but yet, but even; yet, still; **verum tamen** or **verumtamen** nevertheless, but yet

vēr·us -a -um *adj* true, actual, genuine, real; fair, reasonable; *n* truth, the truth, reality; honor, duty, right; **veri similis** probable; realistic; **veri similitudo** probability

verūt·um -ī *n* dart, javelin

verūt·us -a -um *adj* armed with a dart or a javelin

verv·ex -ēcis *m* wether, castrated hog; (term of abuse) muttonhead

vēsāni·a -ae *f* insanity, madness

vēsāni·ens -entis *adj* furious

vēsān·us -a -um *adj* insane, mad; furious, savage, raging

vesc·or -ī *vi* (with *abl*) to feed on, feast, feast on, enjoy

vesc·us -a -um *adj* nibbled off; little, feeble; corroding, consuming

vēsic·a or **vensic·a -ae** *f* bladder; bombast; objects made of bladder: purse, cap, football, lantern

vēsicŭl·a -ae *f* little bladder; little bag

vesp·a -ae *f* wasp

Vespāsiān·us -ī *m* Vespasian (*T. Flavius Vespasianus Sabinus, Roman emperor, 70-79 A.D., and father of Domitian and Titus*)

vesp·er -ĕris or **-ĕrī** *m* evening; supper; the West; **ad vesperum**

towards evening; **primo vespere** early in the evening; **sub vesperum** towards evening; **tam vesperi** so late in the evening; **vespere** or **vesperi** in the evening

vespĕr·a -ae f evening

vesperasc·ō -ĕre vi to become evening, grow towards evening; to get late

vespertĭlĭ·ō -ōnis m bat

vespertīn·us -a -um adj evening, in the evening; eastern

vesperūg·ō -ĭnis f evening star

vespill·ō -ōnis m undertaker

Vest·a -ae f Roman goddess of the hearth

Vestāl·is -e adj Vestal, of Vesta, Vesta's; f Vestal, Vestal virgin

vest·er or **voster -ra -rum** adj (in addressing more than one person) your; pron yours; **voster** your master; your own stock or lineage

vestibŭl·um -ī n entrance, forecourt; beginning

vestīg·ium -iī or **-ī** n footstep, step; footprint, track; trace, vestige; moment, instant

vestīg·ō -āre vt to track, trace; to check, find out

vestīment·um -ī n garment, clothes

vest·iō -īre -īvī or **-iī -ītum** vt to dress, clothe; to adorn, deck, array, attire; (fig) to dress, clothe

vestīplĭc·a -ae f laundress

vest·is -is f garment, clothing; coverlet, tapestry; blanket; slough, skin (of a snake); **mutare vestem** to change one's clothes; to put on mourning clothes

vestīspĭc·a -ae f wardrobe woman

vestīt·us -ūs m clothes, clothing, dress, apparel, attire; ornament (of speech); **mutare vestitum** to put on mourning clothes; **redire ad suum vestitum** to end the mourning period

vetĕr·a -um n pl tradition, antiquity

veterān·us -a -um adj & m veteran

veter·ascō -ascĕre -āvī vi to grow old

veterāt·or -ōris m old hand, expert; sly old fox

veterātōriē adv cunningly, slyly

veterātōri·us -a -um adj cunning, sly

vetĕr·ēs -um m pl the ancients; ancient authors

veterīn·us -a -um adj of burden; f pl & n pl beasts of burden

veternōs·us -a -um adj lethargic; sleepy, drowsy

vetern·us -ī m lethargy; old age; drowsiness; listlessness

vetĭt·um -ī n prohibition

vet·ō or **vot·ō -āre -uī** or **-āvī -ĭtum** vt to forbid, prohibit, oppose

vetŭl·us -a -um adj poor old

vet·us -ĕris adj old, aged; longstanding; m pl see **veteres**; n pl see **vetera**

vetust·ās -ātis f age; ancient times, antiquity; long duration, great age

vetust·us -a -um adj old, ancient; old-time, old-fashioned, good old (days, etc.); antiquated

vexām·en -ĭnis n shaking, quaking

vexāti·ō -ōnis f shaking, jolting, tossing; distress

vexāt·or -ōris m jostler; harasser; troublemaker

vexillār·ĭus -ĭī or **-ī** m standardbearer, ensign; m pl special reserves

vexill·um -ī n standard, ensign, flag (esp. the red flag hoisted above the general's tent as a signal for battle); troops; **vexillum praeponere** to hoist the red flag (as a signal for battle)

vex·ō -āre vt to shake, toss; to vex, annoy; to harass (troops), attack

vi·a -ae f way, road, street, highway; march, journey; method; right way, right method; **inter vias** on the road

viāl·is -e adj highway

viāri·us -a -um adj for highway maintenance

viāticāt·us -a -um adj provided with traveling money

viātic·us -a -um adj for a trip, for traveling, travel; n travel allowance, provisions for the journey; (mil) soldiers' saving fund

viāt·or -ōris m traveler; passenger; (law) summoner

vīb·ix -īcis f weal, welt (from a blow)

vibr·ō -āre vt to brandish, shake, wave around; to hurl, fling; vi to vibrate, quiver; (of the tongue) to flick

vīburn·um -ī n wayfaring tree, guelder rose

vīcān·us -a -um adj village; m pl villagers

Vic·a Pot·a (genit: **Vic·ae Pot·ae**) f goddess of victory

vicāri·us -a -um adj substituted; m substitute, deputy, proxy; underslave (kept by another slave)

vīcātim adv from street to street; from village to village; in hamlets

vice prep (with genit) on account of; like, after the manner of

vicem adv in turn; prep (with genit) instead of, in place of; on account of; like, after the manner of

vīcēnāri·us -a -um adj of the number twenty

vīcēn·ī -ae -a adj twenty each, twenty in a group

vīcēsimān·ī -ōrum m pl soldiers of the twentieth legion

vīcēsimāri·us -a -um adj derived from the five-percent tax

vīcēsim·us -a -um adj twentieth; f five-percent tax

vici·a -ae f vetch

vīciens or **vīciēs** adv twenty times

vīcīnāl·is -e adj neighboring, nearby

vīcīni·a -ae f neighborhood, nearness, proximity

vīcīnit·ās -ātis f neighborhood, proximity; the neighborhood (i.e., the neighbors)

vīcīn·us -a -um *adj* neighboring, nearby, near; *mf* neighbor; *n* neighborhood

vicis (*genit;* the *nom* does not occur; *acc:* **vicem;** *abl:* **vice**) *f* change, interchange, alteration, succession; return, recompense, retaliation; fortune, misfortune, condition, fate, changes of fate; duty, office, position; function, office; **in vicem** or **invicem** by turns, alternately, mutually; **in vicem** or **invicem** (with *genit*) instead of, in place of; **in vicīs** by turns, alternately, mutually

vicissim or **vicissātim** *adv* in turn, again

vicissitūd·ō -inis *f* change, interchange, alternation

victim·a -ae *f* victim; sacrifice

victimār·ius -iī or **-ī** *m* assistant at sacrifices

victit·ō -āre *vi* to live, subsist; (with *abl*) to live on, subsist on

vict·or -ōris *m* conqueror; (in apposition) **victor exercitus** victorious army

victōriāt·us -ī *m* silver coin stamped with the image of victory

Victōriŏl·a -ae *f* small statue of Victory

victr·īx -īcis *f* or *n* conqueror, victor

victus *pp* of **vinco**

vict·us -ūs *m* living, means of livelihood; way of life

vīcŭl·us -ī *m* hamlet

vīc·us -ī *m* village, hamlet; ward, quarter (*in a town or city*); street, alley (*running through the quarter*)

vidēlicet *adv* clearly, evidently; (in irony) of course, naturally; (in explanations) namely

viden = videsne? do you see?, do you get it?

vidĕō vidēre vīdī vīsum *vt* to see, look at; to know; to consider; to understand, realize; (with **ut**) to see to it that, take care that; **vidērī** to seem, appear, seem right, seem good

vidŭ·a -ae *f* widow; spinster

viduit·ās -ātis *f* bereavement; want, lack; widowhood

vīdŭl·us -ī *m* leather travel bag, suitcase, knapsack

vidŭ·ō -āre *vt* to deprive, bereave; (with *genit* or *abl*) to deprive of, bereave of; **viduata** left a widow

vidŭ·us -a -um *adj* bereft, destitute; unmarried; (with *abl* or **ab** + *abl*) bereft of, destitute of, without; *f* see **vidua**

viēt·or -ōris *m* cooper

viēt·us -a -um *adj* shriveled

vig·ĕō -ēre -ŭī *vi* to thrive, be vigorous, flourish

vig·escō -escĕre -ŭī *vi* to become vigorous, gain strength, become lively

vīgēsĭm·us -a -um *adj* twentieth

vig·il -ĭlis *adj* awake, wakeful; alert, on one's toes; *m* watchman, guard, sentinel

vigil·ans -antis *adj* watchful, alert; disquieting (*worries*)

vigilanter *adv* vigilantly, alertly

vigilanti·a -ae *f* wakefulness; alertness

vigil·ax -ācis *adj* alert; sleep-disturbing, disquieting (*worries*)

vigili·a -ae *f* wakefulness, sleeplessness, insomnia; standing guard; guards, sentinels; vigil; vigilance, alertness

vigil·ō -āre *vt* to spend (*the night*) awake; to make, do, perform, write (*something*) while awake at night; *vi* to remain awake, stay awake; to be alert; (with *dat*) to be attentive to

vīgintī (indecl) *adj* twenty

vīgintivirāt·us -ūs *m* membership on a board of twenty

vīgintivir·ī -ōrum *m pl* twenty-man board or commission

vig·or -ōris *m* vigor, liveliness, energy

vīlic·a -ae *f* foreman's wife, manager's wife

vīlic·ō -āre *vi* to be a foreman, be a manager

vīlic·us -ī *m* foreman, manager (*of an estate*)

vīl·is -e *adj* cheap, inexpensive; cheap, mean, common, worthless

vīlit·ās -ātis *f* lowness of price, cheapness, low price; worthlessness

vīliter *adv* cheaply

vill·a -ae *f* villa, country home, farm

villic- = vilic-

villōs·us -a -um *adj* hairy, shaggy

villŭl·a -ae *f* small villa

vill·um -ī *n* drop of wine

vill·us -ī *m* hair, fleece; nap (*of cloth*)

vīm·en -inis *n* osier; basket

vīment·um -ī *n* osier

Vīmĭnāl·is coll·is (*genit:* **Vīmĭnāl·is coll·is**) *m* one of the seven hills of Rome

vīminĕ·us -a -um *adj* made of osiers

vīn or **vīn' = visne?** do you wish

vīnācĕ·us -a -um *adj* grape, of a grape; *m* a grape seed

Vīnāl·ia -ĭum *n pl* wine festival (*celebrated on the 23rd of April and on the 19th of August*)

vīnāri·us -a -um *adj* wine; *m* wine dealer, vintner; *n pl* wine flasks

vincibĭl·is -e *adj* easily won

vinciō vincīre vinxī vinctum *vt* to bind; to encircle, surround; to restrain; (rhet) to bind together, link together, arrange rhythmically

vincō vincĕre vīcī victum *vt* to conquer, vanquish; to get the better of, beat, defeat, outdo; to surpass, excel; to convince, refute, persuade; to prove, demonstrate; to outlast, outlive; *vi* to be victorious; to prevail, succeed

vinctus *pp* of **vincio**

vincŭl·um or **vincl·um -ī** *n* chain, fetter, cord, band; *n pl* prison

vīndēmi·a -ae *f* vintage

vindēmiāt·or -ōris *m* vintager, grape gatherer

vindēmiŏl·a -ae *f* small vintage; minor sources of income

vind·ex -ĭcis *adj* avenging; *m* (*law*) claimant; defender, protector, champion; deliverer, liberator; avenger, punisher

vindicāti·ō -ōnis *f* (*law*) claim; avenging, punishment

vindĭci·ae -ārum *f pl* legal claim; things or persons claimed; championship, protection; **vindicias dare, dicere,** or **decernere** to hand over the things or persons claimed

vindĭc·ō -āre *vt* to lay a legal claim to; to protect, defend; to appropriate; to demand; to demand unfairly; to claim as one's own; to avenge, punish; **in libertatem vindicare** to claim for freedom, set free, free, liberate, emancipate

vindict·a -ae *f* rod used in the ceremony of setting slaves free; defense, protection; vengeance, revenge, satisfaction

vīnē·a -ae *f* vineyard; vine; (*mil*) shed (*used to defend besiegers against the missiles of the enemy*)

vīnēt·um -ī *n* vineyard

vīnĭt·or -ōris *m* vinedresser

vīnnŭl·us -a -um *adj* charming, pleasant

vīnolenti·a -ae *f* wine drinking, intoxication

vīnolent·us -a -um *adj* intoxicated, drunk

vīnōs·us -a -um *adj* fond of wine

vīn·um -ī *n* wine

vĭŏl·a -ae *f* violet; violet color

violābil·is -e *adj* vulnerable

violār·ium -ĭī or **-ī** *n* bed of violets

violār·ius -ĭī or **-ī** *m* dyer of violet color

violāti·ō -ōnis *f* violation, profanation

violāt·or -ōris *m* violator, profaner, desecrator

vĭŏl·ens -entis *adj* violent, raging, impetuous

violenter *adv* violently, vehemently, impetuously

violenti·a -ae *f* violence, vehemence, impetuosity

violent·us -a -um *adj* violent, vehement, impetuous, boisterous

vĭŏl·ō -āre *vt* to do violence to, outrage, harm or injure by violence; to violate, break

vīpĕr·a -ae *f* viper; adder, snake

vīperĕ·us -a -um *adj* viper's, adder's, snake's

vīperīn·us -a -um *adj* of a viper or snake

vir virī *m* male person; man; real man; hero; husband; manhood, virility; (*mil*) infantryman

virāg·ō -ĭnis *f* female warrior; heroine

virect·a -ōrum *n pl* green places; lawn

vir·ĕŏ -ēre -ŭī *vi* to be green; to be fresh, be vigorous, flourish

vīrēs = *pl* of **vis**

vir·escō -escĕre -ŭī *vt* to grow green

virg·a -ae *f* twig, sprout; graft; rod, switch (*for flogging*); walking stick, cane, staff; magic wand; wand; colored stripe in a garment; branch of a family tree

virgāt·or -ōris *m* flogger

virgāt·us -a -um *adj* made of twigs or osiers; striped

virgēt·um -ī *n* osier thicket

virgĕ·us -a -um *adj* of twigs, of kindling wood

virgĭdēmi·a -ae *f* (coll) harvest of birch rods (*i.e., sound flogging*)

virgināl·is -e *adj* maiden's, girl's, girlish; *n* female organ

virgināri·us -a -um *adj* maiden's, girl's

virginĕ·us -a -um *adj* maidenly, virgin, of virgins

virginĭt·ās -ātis *f* virginity, girlhood

virg·ō -ĭnis *f* virgin, maiden, girl, young woman; young married woman

Virg·ō -ĭnis *f* Virgo (*constellation; aqueduct constructed by M. Vipsanius Agrippa*)

virgŭl·a -ae *f* little twig; wand; **virgula divina** divining rod

virgult·a -ōrum *n pl* thickets, brushwood; slips (*of trees*)

virguncŭl·a -ae *f* lass, young girl

virĭd·ans -antis *adj* growing green, green

viridār·ium -ĭī or **-ī** *n* garden; plantation

virĭd·is -e *adj* green; fresh, young; *n pl* greenery

viridĭt·ās -ātis *f* greenness; freshness

virĭd·or -ārī *vi* to become green

virīl·is -e *adj* male, masculine; adult; manly; **pro virili parte** or **partione** to the best of one's ability; *n pl* manly or heroic deeds

virīlĭt·ās -ātis *f* manhood, virility

virīlĭter *adv* manfully

vīripŏt·ens -entis *adj* almighty

virītim *adv* individually, separately

vīrōs·us -a -um *adj* slimy; strong-smelling, fetid, stinking

virt·ūs -ūtis *f* manliness, manhood, virility; strength; valor, bravery, gallantry; gallant deeds; excellence, worth; virtue, moral perfection, good quality; *f pl* achievements

vīr·us -ī *n* slime; poison; pungency; saltiness

vīs (*genit* not in use) *f* power, strength, force; energy; hostile force, violence, attack, assault; amount, quantity; meaning (*of words*); **vires** *f pl* strength, resources; (*mil*) troops; **per vim** forcibly, violently; **pro viribus** with all one's might

viscāt·us -a -um *adj* limed

viscĕr·a -um *n pl* viscera, internal organs; womb; heart, vitals, bowels; (fig) innermost part, bowels, heart, center; bosom friend, favorite

viscerātĭ·ō -ōnis *f* public distribution of meat

viscō·ō -āre *vt* to make sticky

viscum -ī *n* mistletoe; birdlime

visc·us -ĕris *n* organ (*of the body*); entrails

vīsĭ·ō -ōnis *f* appearance, apparition; notion, idea

vīsĭt·ō -āre *vt* to keep seeing; to visit, go to visit

vīs·ō -ĕre -ī -um *vt* to look at with attention, view; to come or go to look at; to find out; to visit

vīs·um -ī *n* sight, appearance

vīs·us -ūs *m* faculty of sight, sight; thing seen, sight, vision

vīt·a -ae *f* life, way of life; livelihood; course of life, career; biography

vītābĭl·is -e *adj* undesirable, deserving to be shunned

vītābund·us -a -um *adj* avoiding, evading

vītāl·is -e *adj* of life, vital; likely to live, staying alive; *n* means of life; *n pl* vital parts

vītālĭter *adv* vitally

vītātĭ·ō -ōnis *f* avoidance

Vitell·ĭus -ī or **-ī** *m* A. Vitellius (*Roman emperor*, 69 A.D.)

vitell·us -ī *m* little calf; yolk (*of egg*)

vītĕ·us -a -um *adj* of the vine

vītĭcŭl·a -ae *f* little vine

vītĭf·er -ĕra -ĕrum *adj* vine-producing

vītĭgĕn·us -a -um *adj* produced from the vine

vitĭlēn·a -ae *f* procuress

vitĭ·ō -āre *vt* to corrupt, spoil, violate, mar; to falsify

vitĭōsē *adv* faultily, badly, corruptly

vitĭōsĭt·ās -ātis *f* corrupt or bad condition

vitĭōs·us -a -um *adj* faulty, defective, corrupt, bad; vicious

vīt·is -is *f* vine; vine branch; centurion's staff; centurionship

vītĭsāt·or -ōris *m* vine planter

vit·ĭum -ī or **-ī** *n* fault, defect, flaw; sin, offense, vice; flaw in the auspices

vīt·ō -āre *vt* to avoid, evade

vīt·or -ōris *m* basket maker

vitrĕ·us -a -um *adj* glass, of glass; glassy; *n pl* glassware

vītrĭc·us -ī *m* stepfather

vitr·um -ī *n* glass

vitt·a -ae *f* headband, fillet

vittāt·us -a -um *adj* wearing a fillet

vitŭl·a -ae *f* heifer

vitŭlīn·us -a -um *adj* & *f* veal

vītŭl·or -ārī *vi* to celebrate, hold a celebration

vitŭl·us -ī *m* calf, young bull; foal; seal

vitŭperābĭl·is -e *adj* blameworthy

vitŭperātĭ·ō -ōnis *f* blaming, censuring; blame; scandalous conduct,

blameworthiness

vitŭperāt·or -ōris *m* censurer

vitŭpĕr·ō -āre *vt* to spoil (*omen*), render void; to blame

vīvācĭt·ās -ātis *f* will to live

vīvār·ĭum -ī or **-ī** *n* game preserve; fish pond

vīvāt·us -a -um *adj* animated, lively

vīv·ax -ācis *adj* long-lived; longlasting, enduring; quick to learn

vīvescō or **vīviscō vīvescĕre vixī** *vi* to become alive, come to life; to grow lively, get full of life

vīvĭd·us -a -um *adj* teeming with life, full of life; true to life, vivid, realistic; quick, lively (*mind*)

vīvīrād·ix -īcis *f* development of roots

vīviscō see **vivesco**

vīv·ō vīvĕre vixī victum *vi* to be alive, live; to be still alive, survive; to reside; (with *abl* or **de** + *abl*) to live on, subsist on

vīv·us -a -um *adj* alive, living; lively; fresh; natural (*rock*); speaking (*voice*); *n* (com) capital; **ad vivum resecare** to cut to the quick

vix *adv* with difficulty, hardly; scarcely

vixdum *adv* hardly then, scarcely yet

vocābŭl·um -ī *n* designation, name; noun

vōcāl·is -ē *adj* having a voice, gifted with speech or song, singing, speaking; tuneful; *f* vowel

vocām·en -ĭnis *f* designation, name

vocātĭ·ō -ōnis *f* summons (*to court*); invitation (*to dinner*)

vocāt·or -ōris *m* inviter, host

vocāt·us -ūs *m* summons, call

vōcĭferātĭ·ō -ōnis *f* loud cry, yell

vōcĭfĕr·ō -āre or **vōcĭfĕr·or -ārī -ātus sum** *vt* & *vi* to shout, yell

vocĭt·ō -āre *vt* to usually call, name; to shout out again and again

voc·ō -āre *vt* to summon; to call, name; to call upon (*the gods*); to invite; (mil) to challenge; **in dubium vocare** to call in question; **in odium vocare** to bring into disfavor; **in periculum vocare** to lead into danger

vōcŭl·a -ae *f* small or weak voice; soft note, soft tone; whisper, gossip

volaem·um -ī *n* large pear

Volaterr·ae -ārum *f pl* old Etruscan town

Volaterrān·us -a -um *adj* of Volaterrae

volātĭc·us -a -um *adj* flying, winged; transitory, passing; inconstant

volātĭl·is -e *adj* flying, winged; rapid, swift; fleeting, transitory

volāt·us -ūs *m* flight

Volcānāl·ĭa -ĭum *n pl* festival of Vulcan (*celebrated on the 23rd of August*)

Volcān·us or **Vulcān·us -ī** *m* Vulcan (*god of fire and son of Juno and Jupiter*)

vol·ens -entis *adj* willing, permitting; willing, ready; favorable; *m* well-wisher

volg- = **vulg-**

volit·ans -antis *m* winged insect

volit·ō -āre *vi* to flit about, fly about, flutter; to move quickly; to hover, soar

volō velle voluī *vt* to wish, want; to propose, determine; to hold, maintain; to mean; to prefer; *vi* to be willing

volōn·ēs -um *m pl* volunteers (*slaves who enlisted after the battle of Cannae,* 216 B.C.)

volpēs see **vulpes**

Volsc·us -a -um *adj* Vulscan; *m pl* an ancient people in S. Latium

volsell·a -ae *f* tweezers

volsus *pp* of **vello**

volt = older form of **vult** he, she, it wishes

voltis = older form of **vultis** you wish

Voltumn·a -ae *f* Etruscan goddess in whose temple the Etruscan states met

voltus see **vultus**

volūbil·is -e *adj* turning, spinning, revolving, swirling; voluble, rapid, fluent; changeable

volūbilit·ās -ātis *f* whirling motion; roundness; volubility, fluency; mutability

volūbiliter *adv* volubly, rapidly, fluently

volūc·er -ris -re *adj* flying, winged; rapid, speedy; *mf* bird; *f* insect

volūm·en -inis *n* roll, book; chapter, book; whirl, eddy; coil; fold

voluntāri·us -a -um *adj* voluntary; *m pl* volunteers

volunt·ās -ātis *f* will, wish, desire, purpose, aim; goodwill; last will, testament; attitude (*good or bad*); **ad voluntatem** (with *genit*) according to the wishes of; **dē** or **ex voluntate** (with *genit*) at the desire of

volup *adv* to one's satisfaction, agreeably

voluptābil·is -e *adj* agreeable, pleasant

voluptāri·us -a -um *adj* pleasant, agreeable; voluptuous; *m* voluptary

volupt·ās -ātis *f* pleasure, enjoyment, delight; *f pl* sensual pleasures; games, sports, public performances

voluptuōs·us -a -um *adj* pleasant, agreeable

volūtābr·um -ī *n* wallow (*for swine*)

volūtābund·us -a -um *adj* wallowing about

volūtāti·ō -ōnis *f* rolling about, tossing about; wallowing; restlessness

volūt·ō -āre *vt* to roll about, turn over; to engross; to think over; **volutari** to wallow, luxuriate

volūtus *pp* of **volvo**

volv·a or **vulv·a -ae** *f* wrapper, cover; womb; sow's womb (*as a favorite dish*)

volvō volvēre volvī volūtum *vt* to roll, turn about, wind; (e.g., of a river) to roll (*rocks, etc.*) along; to breathe; to unroll, read (*books*); to pour out, utter fluently; to consider, weigh; (of time) to bring on, bring around; to form (*a circle*); to undergo (*troubles*); **volvī** to roll, tumble, revolve; *vi* to revolve; to roll on, elapse

vōm·er or **vōm·is -ĕris** *m* plowshare; penis

vomic·a -ae *f* sore, boil, abscess, ulcer; annoyance

vōmis see **vomer**

vomīti·ō -ōnis *f* vomiting

vom·ō -ĕre -uī -itum *vt & vi* to vomit, throw up

vorāg·ō -inis *f* deep hole, abyss, chasm, depth

vor·ax -ācis *adj* swallowing, devouring; greedy, ravenous

vor·ō -āre *vt* to swallow, devour; (fig) to devour (*by reading*)

vors- = **vers-**

vort- = **vert-**

vōs *pron* you; (reflex) yourselves

vosmet *pron* (emphatic form of **vōs**) you yourselves

voster see **vester**

vōtīv·us -a -um *adj* votive, promised in a vow

votō see **veto**

vōt·um -ī *n* solemn vow (*made to a deity*), vow; votive offering; wish, prayer

vovēō vovēre vōvī vōtum *vt* to vow, promise solemnly, pledge, devote (*to a deity*); to wish, wish for, desire

vox vōcis *f* voice; sound, tone, cry, call; word, utterance, saying, expression; proverb; language; accent

Vulcānus see **Volcanus**

vulgār·is or **volgār·is -e** *adj* common, general, usual

vulgāriter or **volgāriter** *adv* in the common or usual way

vulgāt·or or **volgāt·or -ōris** *m* divulger

vulgāt·us or **volgāt·us -a -um** *adj* common, general; well known; notorious

vulgivāg·us or **volgivāg·us -a -um** *adj* roving; inconstant

vulg·ō or **volg·ō -āre** *vt* to spread, publish, broadcast; to divulge; to prostitute; to level, make common

vulgō or **volgō** *adv* generally, publicly, everywhere

vulg·us or **volg·us -ī** *n* masses, people, public; crowd, herd; rabble, populace

vulnerāti·ō or **volnerāti·ō -ōnis** *f* wounding, wound

vulnĕr·ō or **volnĕr·ō -āre** *vt* to wound; to damage

vulnific·us -a -um *adj* inflicting wounds

vuln·us or **voln·us -ĕris** *n* wound; blow, stroke; blow, disaster

vulpēcŭl·a or **volpēcŭl·a -ae** *f* little fox, sly little fox

vulp·ēs or **volp·ēs -is** *f* fox; craftiness, cunning

vuls·us or **vols·us -a -um** *pp* of vello; *adj* plucked, beardless, effeminate

vulticŭl·us or **volticŭl·us -ī** *m* mere look

vult·um -ī *n* face; looks, expression, features; look, appearance

vultuōs·us or **voltuōs·us -a -um** *adj* full of airs, affected

vult·ur or **volt·ur -ŭris** *m* vulture

Vult·ur or **Volt·ur -ŭris** *m* mountain in Apulia near Venusia

vulturīn·us or **volturnīn·us -a -um** *adj* of a vulture, vulture-like

vultur·ius or **voltur·ius -iī** or **-ī** *m* vulture

Vulturn·us or **Volturn·us -ī** *m* principal river of Campania (*modern Volturno*)

vult·us or **volt·us -ūs** *m* face; looks, expression, features; look, appearance

vulv·a or **volv·a -ae** *f* wrapper, cover; womb; sow's womb (*as a delicacy*)

X

Xanthipp·ē -ēs *f* wife of Socrates

Xanth·us -ī *m* river at Troy, identified with Scamander River

xen·ium -iī or **-ī** *n* gift, present

Xenophăn·ēs -is *m* early Greek philosopher (*c.* 565-470 B.C.)

Xenŏph·ōn -ontis *m* Greek historian and pupil of Socrates (*c.* 430-*c.* 354

B.C.)

xērampelīn·ae -ārum *f pl* dark-colored clothes

Xerx·ēs -is *m* Persian king, defeated at Salamis (*c.* 519-465 B.C.)

xiphi·ās -ae *m* swordfish

xyst·us -ī *m* or **xyst·um -ī** *n* open colonnade or portico, walk, avenue

Z

Zacynth·us or **Zacynth·os -ī** *f* island off W. Greece

Zam·a -ae *f* town in Numidia where Scipio defeated Hannibal and brought the Second Punic War to an end

zāmi·a -ae *f* harm, damage, loss

Zancl·ē -ēs *f* old name of Messana in Sicily

Zēn·ō or **Zēn·ōn -ōnis** *m* founder of Stoic philosophy and a native of Citium in Cyprus (335-263 B.C.); Epicurean philosopher, the teacher of Cicero and Atticus

Zephўr·us -ī *m* zephyr; west wind; wind

Zēth·us -ī *m* son of Jupiter and Antiope and brother of Amphion

zmaragd·us -ī *f* emerald

zōdiăc·us -ī *m* zodiac

Zōïl·us -ī *m* proverbially stern Alexandrine critic of Homer

zōn·a -ae *f* belt, sash, girdle (*worn by women*); money belt; zone

zōnāri·us -a -um *adj* of a belt or girdle; *m* belt maker, girdle maker

zōnŭl·a -ae *f* little girdle

zōthēc·a -ae *f* small room

zōthēcŭl·a -ae *f* small bedroom

ENGLISH–LATIN

A

a *indefinite article, unexpressed in Latin;* **twice — year** bis in anno

aback *adv* **taken — stupefactus,** attonitus, consternatus

abandon *vt* (de)relinquĕre, destituĕre, deserĕre, abjicĕre, omittĕre

abandoned *adj* derelictus, desertus; (*fig*) nefarius, perditus, flagitiosus

abandonment *s* derelictio, destitutio *f*

abase *vt* deprimĕre, comprimĕre, frangĕre, (de)minuĕre

abash *vt* perturbare, confundĕre, pudefacĕre, percellĕre

abashed *adj* pudendus, erubescens

abate *vt* (*to lower*) imminuĕre; (*to slacken*) laxare; (*the price*) remittĕre, detrahĕre; *vi* (*to lessen*) imminuĕre, decrescĕre; (*to decline*) cadĕre, decedĕre; (*of passion*) defervescĕre

abbess *s* abbatissa *f*

abbey *s* abbatia *f*

abbot *s* abbas *m*

abbreviate *vt* abbreviare, contrahĕre, imminuĕre

abbreviation *s* abbreviatio, contractio *f*, compendium *n*

abdicate *vt* abdicare; *vi* se abdicare

abdication *s* abdicatio *f*

abdomen *s* abdomen *n*

abduct *vt* abducĕre, rapĕre

abduction *s* raptio *f*, rapt·us -ūs *m*

aberration *s* error *m*; declinatio *f*

abet *vt* adjuvare, instigare; favēre (*with dat*)

abeyance *s* **to be in — jacēre,** intermitti

abhor *vt* abhorrēre ab (*with abl*), detestari, odio habēre

abhorrence *s* detestatio *f*, odium *n*

abhorrent *adj* perosus; alienus, repugnans, abhorrens

abide *vt* tolerare, subire; *vi* (*to dwell*) habitare, manēre; **to — by stare** in (*with abl*)

abiding *adj* diuturnus, mansurus; constans, fidus

ability *s* facultas, potestas *f*; ingenium *n*; **to the best of one's — summa ope; pro sua parte**

abject *adj* abjectus, vilis; humilis; **—ly** abjecte; humiliter

abjure *vt* abjurare, ejurare

ablative *s* ablativus *m*

able *adj* potens; valens, capax, peritus; ingeniosus; **to be — to posse,** valēre, quire, sufficĕre

ablution *s* ablutio, lavatio *f*

ably *adv* experte; ingeniose

aboard *adv* in *or* super nave; **to go — a ship** navem conscendĕre

abode *s* domicilium *n*; sedes *f*; commoratio, mansio *f*

abolish *vt* abolēre; exstinguĕre, tollĕre, rescindĕre

abolition *s* abolitio, dissolutio *f*

abominable *adj* detestabilis, infandus, execrabilis; odiosus

abominably *adv* execrabiliter; odiose

abominate *vt* abominari, detestari

abomination *s* destestatio *f*

aborigines *s* aborigines, indigenae *m pl*

abortion *s* abortio *f*; abort·us -ūs *m*

abortive *adj* abortivus; (*fig*) irritus, frustratus

abound *vi* abundare, redundare, superesse; **to — in** abundare (*with abl*)

abounding *adj* abundans; copiosus, largus; creber

about *adv* circa, circiter; fere, ferme

about *prep* (*of place*) circa, circum (*with acc*); (*of number*) circa, ad (*with acc*); (*of time*) circa, sub (*with acc*); (*of respect*) de (*with abl*)

above *adv* supra; insuper; **from — desuper, superne**

above *prep* supra, super (*with acc*)

abrasion *s* attrit·us -ūs *m*

abreast *adv* pariter; ex adverso

abridge *vt* contrahĕre; abbreviare; (*fig*) privare

abridgment *s* compendium *n*, epitome *f*

abroad *adv* (*in a foreign land*) peregre; (*of motion, out of doors*) foras; (*of rest, out of doors*) foris; **from — extrinsecus; peregre; to be *or* live abroad** peregrinari; patriā carēre; **to get — (*fig*) divulgari**

abrogate *vt* rescindĕre, abrogare, dissolvĕre

abrupt *adj* praeruptus; (*fig*) subitus, repentinus; (*of style*) abruptus; **—ly** abrupte; raptim

abruptness *s* declivitas, rapiditas, festinatio *f*

abscess *s* abscess·us -ūs *m*; suppuratio *f*; vomica *f*

absence *s* absentia *f*; **in my — me** absente

absent *adj* absens; **to be — abesse**

absent *vt* **to — oneself** se removēre, non comparēre

absentee *s* qui abest *m*; peregrinator *m*

absolute *adj* absolutus, summus, perfectus; (*unlimited*) infinitus; **—ly** absolute; prorsus; penitus, omnino

absolution *s* absolutio *f*; venia, indulgentia *f*

absolve *vt* veniam dare (*with dat*); absolvĕre; dimittĕre; (*from punishment*) condonare

absorb *vt* absorbēre, combibēre; *(fig)* distringěre, tenēre

absorbent *adj* bibulus; absorbens

abstain *vi* abstinēre, se abstinēre

abstinence *s* abstinentia *f*; continentia *f*; jejunium *n*

abstract *vt* abstrahěre; separare, sejungěre, excludere

abstract *adj* abstractus; mente perceptus

abstract *s* compendium *n*; epitome *f*; **in the —** in abstracto

abstracted *adj* abstractus; separatus; contractus; *(in mind)* parum attentus; **—ly** separatim; in abstracto

abstraction *s* separatio *f*; *(idea)* notio *f*

abstruse *adj* abstrusus; reconditus; obscurus, occultus; **—ly** abdite, occulte

absurd *adj* absurdus, insulsus; ridiculus; **—ly** inepte, absurde

absurdity *s* ineptia, insulsitas *f*

abundance *s* abundantia, copia *f*

abundant *adj* abundans; amplus; copiosus, plenus; uber; **to be —** abundare; **—ly** abundanter, copiose; cumulate; *(fruitfully)* feliciter

abuse *s* *(wrong use)* abus·us -ūs *m*; *(insult)* injuria *f*, convicium *n*; contumelia *f*; probra *n pl*, maledicta *n pl*

abuse *vt* *(misuse)* abuti *(with abl)*; *(a woman)* stuprare; *(with words)* maledicěre *(with dat)*; lacerare

abusive *adj* contumeliosus; dicax, maledicus; injuriosus; **—ly** contumeliose; maledice, injuriose

abyss *s* profundum *n*, vorago *f*, gurges *m*; *(fig)* barathrum *n*

academic *adj* scholasticus; academicus

academy *s* Academia *f*; schola *f*, collegium *n*; societas *f*

accede *vi* acceděre, assentire *or* assentiri

accelerate *vt* accelerare, festinare, maturare

acceleration *s* acceleratio *f*

accent *s* accent·us -ūs *m*; sonus *m*; vox *f*; *(mark)* apex *m*

accent *vt* *(in speaking)* acuěre; *(in writing)* fastigare

accentuation *s* accent·us -ūs *m*

accept *vt* accipěre; recipěre

acceptable *adj* acceptus, aptus, gratus; probabilis; **to be —** placěre

acceptably *adv* apte; grate

acceptance *s* acceptio *f*; approbatio *f*

access *s* adit·us -ūs, access·us -ūs *m*; **to have —** admitti

accessible *adj* *(of places)* patens; *(fig)* facilis, affabilis

accession *s* *(addition)* accessio *f*, cumulus *m*; *(to the throne)* regni principium *n*

accessory *adj* adjunctus; *(of crimes)* conscius

accessory *s* affinis, conscius *m*, par-

ticeps *m & f*

accident *s* cas·us -ūs *m*; calamitas *f*

accidental *adj* fortuitus; adventicius; **—ly** casu, forte, fortuito

acclaim *s* acclamatio *f*; clamor *m*

acclaim *vt* acclamare

acclamation *s* acclamatio *f*, clamor, consens·us -ūs, plaus·us -ūs *m*

accommodate *vt* accommodare, aptare; *(with lodgings)* hospitium parare *(with dat)*

accommodation *s* accommodatio *f*; *(convenience)* commoditas *f*; *(lodgings)* hospitium, deversorium *n*

accompaniment *s* concinentia *f*

accompany *vt* comitari; deducěre; *(mus)* concinere *(with dat)*

accomplice *s* particeps, socius, conscius *m*; satelles *m*

accomplish *vt* efficěre, perficěre; peragere, implēre

accomplished *adj* completus; *(fig)* doctus, eruditus; *(eloquent)* disertus

accomplishment *s* exsecutio, peractio *f*; eruditio *f*

accord *s* consens·us, -ūs *m*, concordia *f*; **of one's own —** sua sponte; ultro; **with one —** unanimiter

accord *vt* conceděre, dare, praebēre, praestare; *vi* convenire; inter se congruěre; inter se consentire

accordance *s* **in — with** ex, de *(with abl)*; secundum *(with acc)*; pro *(with abl)*

accordingly *adv* itaque; ita; pariter; sic

according to *prep* de, ex, pro *(with abl)*; secundum *(with acc)*

accost *vt* appellare; compellare; alloqui, affari

account *s* *(financial)* ratio *f*; *(statement)* memoria *f*; *(esteem)* reputatio *f*; *(story)* narratio *f*; **of little —** parvi pretii; vilis; **of no —** nullius pretii; **on — of** ob, propter *(with acc)*; causā *(with genit)*; **on that —** propterea; ideo; **to call to — rationem poscěre; **to give an — rationem redděre; **to take — of** rationem habēre *(with genit)*

account *vt* numerare; *(esteem)* aestimare, habēre, penděre; **to — for** rationem redděre *(with genit)*

accountable *adj* reus

accountant *s* calculator *m*; a rationibus (procurator) *m*

accredited *adj* aestimatus, honoratus

accretion *s* accessio *f*

accrue *vi* accrescěre; advenire; ceděre; *(advantage)* redundare

accumulate *vt* accumulare, coacervare; *vi* crescěre, augēri

accumulation *s* cumulus, acervus, congest·us -ūs *m*; collectio *f*

accuracy *s* cura *f*; subtilitas *f*

accurate *adj* exactus; subtilis; diligens; **—ly** accurate, exacte; subtiliter; diligenter

accursed *adj* exsecratus; scelestus

accusation *s* accusatio *f*; *(charge)* crimen *n*; **to bring an — against** accusare

accusative *s* accusativus *m*

accuse *vt* accusare; criminari; *(to blame)* reprehendĕre; **to — falsely** calumniari, insimulare

accuser *s* accusator, delator *m*; *(in civil suit)* petitor *m*

accustom *vt* assuefacĕre; **to — oneself** assuefieri, consuescĕre; **to be accustomed to** solĕre *(with inf)*

acerbity *s* acerbitas *f*; *(fig)* severitas *f*; rigor *m*

ache *s* dolor *m*

ache *vi* dolĕre; **my head —s** caput mihi dolet

achieve *vt* patrare, conficĕre, perficĕre; *(to win)* consequi

achievement *s* res gesta *f*; facinus *n*

acid *adj* acidus; vinosus

acid *s* acidum *n*

acknowledge *vt* agnoscĕre, recognoscĕre; confitĕri; *(a child)* tollĕre

acknowledgment *s* recognito *f*, confessio *f*; *(receipt for money)* apocha *f*

acme *s* fastigium *n*

acorn *s* glans *f*; balanus *f*

acoustics *s* acustica *n pl*; res auditoria *f*

acquaint *vt* certiorem facĕre; **to — oneself with** noscĕre, cognoscĕre

acquaintance *s* familiaritas, notitia *f*; *(person)* familiaris *m & f*

acquainted *adj* notus; **— with** gnarus *(with genit)*; peritus *(with genit or abl)*; **to become — with** noscĕre, cognoscĕre, pernoscĕre

acquiesce *vi* acquiescĕre, assentire

acquiescence *s* assens·us -ūs *m*

acquire *vt* acquirĕre; adipisci, nancisci

acquisition *s* *(act of acquiring)* conciliatio *f*; quaest·us -ūs *m*; *(thing acquired)* quaesitum *n*

acquisitive *adj* quaestuosus

acquit *vt* absolvĕre, liberare; **to — oneself** se gerĕre

acquittal *s* absolutio *f*

acre *s* jugerum *n*; **— by —** jugeratim

acrid *adj* acer, asper

acrimonious *adj* acerbus; asper, truculentus

acrimony *s* acrimonia *f*; acerbitas, amaritudo *f*; acor *m*

acrobat *s* funambulus *m*

across *adv* transversus

across *prep* trans *(with acc)*

act *s* *(deed, action)* factum, gestum *n*; *(decree)* decretum *n*; *(in a play)* act·us -ūs *m*; **caught in the —** deprehensus; **in the very — in** flagranti

act *vt* *(role, part)* agĕre; *vi* agĕre, facĕre, gerĕre

acting *s* actio, gesticulatio *f*

action *s* actio *f*, act·us -ūs *m*; *(deed)* factum, facinus *n*; *(law)* actio *f*; *(mil)* pugna *f*, proelium *n*; *(of speaker)* gest·us -ūs *m*; **to bring an — against** actionem intendĕre *(with dat)*

active *adj* actuosus; activus; agilis; impiger, vegetus, strenuus, sedulus,

navus; **—ly** impigre; strenue; *(gram)* active

activity *s* agilitas, mobilitas *f*; *(motion)* mot·us -ūs *m*; *(energy)* industria, sedulitas, gnavitas *f*

actor *s* histrio *m*; mimus *m*; *(in comedy)* comoedus *m*; *(in tragedy)* tragoedus *m*

actress *s* mima, scenica *f*

actual *adj* verus, ipse; **—ly** re vera

actuality *s* veritas *f*

acumen *s* acumen *n*; sagacitas *f*; ingenii acies *f*

acute *adj* acutus; acer; *(fig)* sagax, subtilis; **—ly** acute, acriter

acuteness *s* acies *f*; *(of the mind)* acumen *n*, subtilitas *f*

adage *s* proverbium *n*

adamant *adj* obstinatus

adamant *s* adamas *m*

adapt *vt* accommodare, aptare

adaptation *s* accommodatio *f*

adapted *adj* aptus

add *vt* addĕre, apponĕre, adjungĕre; *(in speaking)* superdicĕre; *(in writing)* subjungĕre; *(to reckon)* adscribĕre; **to — up** computare, supputare; **to be added** accedĕre

adder *s* coluber *m*, vipera *f*

addict *vt* **to be addicted** se addicĕre, se tradĕre, se dare

addition *s* additamentum *n*; adjectio, accessio *f*; appendix *f*; incrementum *n*; **in — praeterea, insuper**; **in — to** praeter *(with acc)*

additional *adj* novus, additititus, adjunctus

address *s* alloquium *n*; allocutio, compellatio *f*; *(on letter)* forma directionis, inscriptio *f*; *(speech)* contio, oratio *f*; *(adroitness)* dexteritas, comitas *f*

address *vt* *(to speak to)* alloqui, aggredi, compellare; *(letter)* inscribĕre

adduce *vt* *(witnesses)* producĕre; *(arguments)* afferre

adept *adj* peritus

adequacy *s* sufficientia *f*

adequate *adj* adaequatus, sufficiens, par; **to be — sufficĕre; —ly** satis, apte

adhere *vi* adhaerĕre, cohaerĕre; **to — to inhaerĕre** *(with dat)*; *(fig)* stare in *(with abl)*

adherence *s* adhaesio *f*

adherent *s* assectator, fautor, cliens *m*

adhesion *s* adhaesio *f*

adhesive *adj* tenax

adieu *interj* vale, valete; **to bid —** valedicĕre; valĕre jubĕre

adjacent *adj* confinis, conterminus; vicinus

adjective *s* adjectivum (nomen) *n*

adjectively *adv* adjective; ut appositum; pro apposito

adjoin *vt* adjungĕre; adjacĕre *(with dat)*; *vi* adjacĕre

adjoining *adj* adjacens, confinis

adjourn *vt* comperendinare, differre, prorogare; *vi* deferri

adjournment *s* dilatio *f*

adjudge vt addicĕre, adjudicare

adjudicate vt addicĕre, decernĕre

adjudication s addictio, adjudicatio f; sententia f; arbitrium n

adjunct s adjunctum n, accessio, appendix f

adjuration s obtestatio f; obsecratio f

adjure vt adjurare; obtestari

adjust vt aptare, accommodare; (put in order) componĕre

adjustment s accommodatio, compositio f; (of a robe) structura f

adjutant s optio m

administer vt (to manage) administrare; (medicine, etc.) adhibĕre; (oath) adigĕre; (justice) dispensare, reddĕre

administration s administratio, cura, procuratio f; jurisdictio f; magistrat·us -ūs m.

administrative adj ad administrationem pertinens

administrator s administrator, procurator m

admirable adj admirabilis, mirabilis, admirandus; insignis, egregius

admiral s classis praefectus m

admiration s admiratio f

admire vt admirari; amare

admirer s admirator, mirator, laudator m; amator m

admiringly adv admirans

admissible adj accipiendus, aptus, aequus

admission s admissio, confessio f; adit·us -ūs, access·us -ūs m.

admit vt admittĕre; recipĕre; (to recognize) asciscĕre; noscĕre; **it is admitted** constat

admittedly adv sane

admonish vt monĕre, admonēre, commonēre; hortari

admonition s monitio, admonitio f; monitum n

adolescence s prima adulescentia f

adolescent adj adolescens, adulescens

adolescent s adulescentulus, adulescens m

adopt vt (a minor) adoptare; (an adult) arrogare; (a custom) asciscĕre; (a plan) capĕre, inire

adoption s adoptio, adoptatio f; (of an adult) arrogatio f; (of a custom) assumptio f; **by** — adoptivus

adoptive adj adoptivus

adorable adj adorandus, venerandus

adoration s adoratio f; cult·us -ūs m; (of kings) veneratio f

adore vt adorare, venerari; (fig) admirari, amare

adorn vt ornare, decorare, distinguĕre, illustrare; excolĕre, comare

adornment s exornatio f; ornat·us -ūs m; ornamentum n

Adriatic Sea s Hadria m or Adria m

adrift adv fluctuans; **to be** — fluctuare

adroit adj callidus, dexter, sollers, peritus; **—ly** callide, scite

adroitness s dexteritas, sollertia,

callidias f

adulation s adulatio, assentatio f

adult adj adultus

adult s adultus homo, puber m

adulterate vt adulterare, vitiare, commiscēre

adulteration s adulteratio, commixtio f

adulterer s adulter m; moechus m

adulteress s adultera f; moecha f

adulterous adj stuprosus, adulterinus, incestus

adultery s adulterium, stuprum n; **to commit** — moechari; adulterare

advance vt promovēre; admovēre; (money) praerogare; (a cause) fovēre; (an opinion) exhibēre, praeferre; (to honors) provehēre; vi procedĕre, progredi, incedĕre; (mil) gradum or pedem inferre; signa proferre; (to progress) proficĕre

advance s progress·us -ūs m; (step) pass·us -ūs m; (attack) incursio f; impet·us -ūs m; (money) mutuae pecuniae f pl; **in** — maturius

advanced adj provectus; (of age) grandis

advance guard s primum agmen n

advancement s dignitatis accessio, promotio f; honos m

advantage s (benefit) commodum n, us·us -ūs m, bonum n; (profit) lucrum, emolumentum n; utilitas f, fruct·us -ūs m; **to be of** — prodesse; **to have an** — over praestare (with dat); superior esse (with dat); **to take** — of uti (with abl); (to deceive) decipĕre, fallĕre; **with** — faenerato

advantageous adj fructuosus, utilis; **—ly** utiliter; bene

advent s advent·us -ūs m

adventure s cas·us -ūs m; fors f; facinus n

adventurer s periclitator m; latro m; pirata m

adventurous adj audax

adverb s adverbium n

adverbial adj adverbialis; **—ly** adverbialiter

adversary s adversarius m, hostis m; adversatrix f

adverse adj adversus, infestus; asper; **—ly** male, contrarie, infeliciter

adversity s res adversae f pl; calamitas f

advertise vt communefacĕre; proscribĕre

advertisement s proscriptio f; libellus m; indicium n

advice s consilium n; **to ask** — of consulĕre; **to give** — suadēre (with dat)

advisable adj commodus, utilis

advise vt suadēre (with dat), censēre (with dat), monēre; **to** — **to the contrary** dissuadēre (with dat)

adviser s consultor m

advocate s (law) actor, causidicus m; (fig) patronus m; suasor m; auctor m

aedile s aedilis m

aegis *s* aegis *f*

aerial *adj* aërius, aethereus

affability *s* comitas, affabilitas, facilitas *f*

affable *adj* affabilis, comis, facilis

affably *adv* comiter

affair *s* negotium *n*; res *f*; (*love*) amores *m pl*

affect *vt* afficĕre; commovēre; jactare; ostentare; attingĕre

affectation *s* simulatio, affectatio *f*

affected *adj* simulatus, fictus; (*in style*) putidus; —**ly** putide

affection *s* amor *m*; benevolentia *f*; studium *n*

affectionate *adj* amans, benevolus; —**ly** amanter

affidavit *s* testimonium *n*

affiliate *vt* adoptare; attribuĕre

affinity *s* affinitas *f*; cognatio *f*

affirm *vt* affirmare, asseverare, testificari

affirmation *s* affirmatio *f*

affirmative *adj* affirmans; **I reply in the** — aio; —**ly** affirmative

affix *vt* affigĕre, annectĕre

afflict *vt* affligĕre, afflictare

affliction *s* afflictio, miseria *f*; res adversae *f pl*

affluence *s* abundantia, copia *f*; divitiae *f pl*

affluent *adj* affluens, abundans; dives; —**ly** abundanter

afford *vt* praebēre; (*to yield*) reddĕre, ferre; **I cannot** — res mihi non suppetit ad (*with acc*)

affront *vt* irritare; contumeliā afficĕre; offendĕre

affront *s* contumelia, injuria *f*

afield *adv* foris

afloat *adj* natans; fluctuans; **to be** — natare, fluctuare

afoot *adv* pedestris, pedibus; **to be** — geri

afraid *adj* timidus, pavidus; **to be** — timēre; **to make** — terrefacĕre

afresh *adv* de integro, iterum, de novo

after *prep* post (*with acc*); a, de, e, ex (*with abl*); (*following immediately upon*) sub (*with acc*); (*in rank or degree*) secundum (*with acc*); (*in imitation of*) ad (*with acc*); — **all** tamen; saltem; **a little** — paulo post; **the day** — postridie

after *conj* postquam

afternoon *adj* postmeridianus, pomeridianus

afternoon *s* pomeridianum *n*; **in the** — post meridiem

afterthought *s* posterior cogitatio *f*

afterwards *adv* post, postea; deinde, deinceps, dehinc

again *adv* iterum, rursus, denuo, rursum; deinde; (*hereafter*) posthac; (*likewise, in turn*) invicem, mutuo, vicissim; contra; — **and** — etiam atque etiam; identidem; **once** — denuo; **over** — de novo

against *prep* contra (*with acc*); adversus (*with acc*); (*in a hostile manner*) in (*with acc*); — **the current** adverso flumine; **to be** — adversari

age *s* (*life*) aetas *f*; (*era*) saeculum *n*, aetas *f*; **of the same** — aequaevus, aequalis; **old** — senectus *f*; **to be of** — sui juris esse; **twelve years of** — duodecim annos natus; **under** — impubis

age *vi* senescĕre; maturescĕre

aged *adj* aetate provectus, senilis; (*things*) antiquus

agency *s* actio *f*; (*medium*) opera *f*; (*office*) procuratio *f*; **through the** — of per (*with acc*)

agent *s* actor, auctor *m*; (*in crime*) minister *m*

aggravate *vt* aggravare; (*pain*) augēre; provocare; (*a wound*) ulcerare; **to become aggravated** ingravescĕre

aggravating *adj* molestus

aggravation *s* exaggeratio *f*

aggregate *adj* aggregatus, totus

aggregate *s* summa *f*

aggregation *s* collatio *f*; aggregatum *n*

aggression *s* incursio *f*

aggressive *adj* hostilis, infensus; ferox

aggressor *s* qui bellum infert *m*; qui alterum prior lacessit *m*

aggrieve *vt* dolore afficĕre

aggrieved *adj* iratus

aghast *adj* attonitus, consternatus, stupefactus; **to stand** — obstupescĕre

agile *adj* agilis; pernix

agility *s* agilitas *f*; pernicitas *f*

agitate *vt* agitare; commovēre; perturbare

agitated *adj* tumultuosus; turbulentus; (*fig*) sollicitus

agitation *s* agitatio, commotio *f*; (*of the sea*) jactatio *f*; trepidatio *f*

agitator *s* concitator, turbator *m*

ago *adv* abhinc; **a short time** — haud ita pridem; dudum; **long** — iamdudum, iampridem, antiquitus; **some time** — pridem

agonize *vt* cruciare, excruciare; *vi* discruciari

agonizing *adj* crucians; horribilis

agony *s* dolor *m*; agonia *f*; cruciat·us -ūs *m*

agrarian *adj* agrarius

agree *vi* assentire, assentiri; convenire; (*to make a bargain*) pacisci; (*of facts*) constare, convenire; **to** — **with** assentiri (*with dat*), sentire cum (*with abl*)

agreeable *adj* gratus, acceptus; amabilis; congruens, conveniens; **very** — pergratus

agreeably *adv* grate, jucunde; suaviter

agreement *s* consens·us -ūs *m*; concordia *f*; (*pact*) pactio *f*, pactum *n*; (*bargain*) conditio *f*; (*proportion*) symmetria *f*; reconciliatio *f*

agricultural *adj* rusticus, agrestis

agriculture *s* agricultura *f*; res rustica *f*

agriculturist *s* agricola *m*

ah *interj* ah!, eja!, vah!, vae!

ahead *adv* use verb with prefix *prae-* or *pro-*

aid *s* auxilium, subsidium *n*

aid *vt* succurrĕre (*with dat*), subvenire (*with dat*), adjuvare

aide-de-camp *s* optio *m*

ail *vt* dolēre; *vi* aegrotare

ailing *adj* aegrotus, aeger

ailment *s* aegrotatio *f*; malum *n*; morbus *m*

aim *s* (*mark*) scopus *m*; (*fig*) finis *m*, propositum *n*

aim *vt* intendĕre, tendĕre; *vi* **to —** at affectare, spectare, petĕre, quaerĕre

aimless *adj* vanus, inanis; **—ly** sine ratione

air *s* aër *m*; caelum *n*; (*breeze*) aura *f*; (*attitude*) habit·us -ūs, gest·us -ūs *m*; (*tune*) modus *m*; **in the open —** sub divo *or* sub caelo; **to take the —** deambulare

air *vt* ventilare

airily *adv* hilare

airy *adj* aërius; apertus, patens; ventosus; (*fig*) hilaris

aisle *s* ala *f*

ajar *adj* semiapertus

akin *adj* cognatus, agnatus, consanguineus, propinquus

alabaster *s* alabaster *m*

alacrity *s* alacritas *f*

alarm *s* (*signal*) classicum *n*; (*sudden fright*) trepidatio *f*, pavor *m*; tumult·us -ūs *m*; **to give the —** increpare

alarm *vt* perterrefacĕre, consternĕre, perturbare

alarming *adj* formidolosus

alas *interj* eheu!, heu!

alchemist *s* alchemista *m*

alchemy *s* alchemistica *f*

alcohol *s* spirit·us -ūs vini *m*

alcoholic *adj* alcoolicus

alcove *s* zotheca *f*, cubiculum *n*

ale *s* cerevisia *f*

alert *adj* alacer, promptus, vegetus

alertness *s* alacritas *f*

alias *adv* aliter

alias *s* falsum nomen *n*

alibi *s* (*law*) absentia rei *f*; (*excuse*) species *f*

alien *adj* peregrinus

alien *s* peregrinus *m*; alienigena, advena *m*

alienate *vt* alienare, abalienare, avertĕre, avocare

alienation *s* abalienatio, alienatio *f*

alight *vi* descendĕre; (*from a horse*) desilire; (*of birds*) subsidĕre

alike *adj* aequus, par, similis

alike *adv* pariter, similiter, aeque

alimony *s* alimenta, alimonium *n*

alive *adj* vivus; (*fig*) alacer; **to be —** vivĕre; superesse

all *adj* omnis, cunctus, totus; integer; universus; **— over** undique, passim; **— the better** tanto melius; **— the more** eo plus

all *s* omnia *n pl*; **at — omnino; in — in summa; not at —** haudquaquam; **one's all** proprium *n*

allay *vt* sedare, lenire, mitigare; **to**

be allayed defervescĕre, temperari

allegation *s* affirmatio *f*; insimulatio *f*

allege *vt* affirmare, arguĕre; citare, allegare

allegiance *s* fides, fidelitas *f*; **to swear —** sacramentum dicĕre

allegorical *adj* allegoricus; **—ly** allegorice

allegorize *vi* allegorice scribĕre; allegorice explicare

allegory *s* allegoria *f*

alleviate *vt* levare, allevare, sublevare

alleviation *s* allevamentum *n*, levatio *f*

alley *s* angiport·us -ūs *m*

alliance *s* (*by blood*) consanguinitas *f*; (*by marriage*) affinitas *f*; (*of states*) foedus *n*; societas *f*

allied *adj* foederatus, socius; junctus, propinquus

alligator *s* crocodilus *m*

alliteration *s* alliteratio *f*

allocate *vt* impertire, assignare

allot *vt* distribuĕre, assignare

allotment *s* assignatio, portio *f*; assignatum *n*

allow *vt* concedĕre (*with dat*), permittĕre (*with dat*), sinĕre, pati; **it is allowed** licet; **to — for** indulgēre (*with dat*); **to — of** admittĕre

allowable *adj* licitus

allowance *s* (*permission*) licentia, permissio *f*; (*concession*) venia, indulgentia *f*; (*portion*) portio *f*; salarium *n*; diaria *n pl*; cibaria *n pl*; demensum *n*; **to make — for** ignoscĕre (*with dat*), condonare

alloy *s* mixtura *f*

alloy *vt* miscēre, adulterare, diluĕre

allude *vi* **to —** to attingĕre, designare, denotare, spectare

allure *vt* allicĕre, allectare, pellicĕre

allurement *s* illecebra, blanditia *f*; blandimentum *n*

alluring *adj* blandus; **—ly** blande

allusion *s* parodia *f*; indicium *n*, mentio *f*

allusive *adj* obliquus; **—ly** oblique

alluvial *adj* alluvius

ally *s* socius *m*, socia *f*

ally *vt* sociare

almanac *s* fasti *m pl*

almighty *adj* omnipotens

almond *s* amygdala *f*

almond tree *s* amygdalus *f*

almost *adv* fere, paene, prope, ferme

alms *s* stips *f*

aloft *adv* sublime

alone *adj* solus, unus, solitarius, unicus; **all — persolus; to leave —** deserĕre; **to let — omittĕre,** mittĕre

alone *adv* solum

along *adv* porro, protinus; **all — jamdudum; — with** una cum (*with abl*)

along *prep* per (*with acc*), praeter (*with acc*), secundum (*with acc*)

aloof *adv* procul; **to stand — discedĕre,** abstare

aloud *adv* magna voce; clare

alphabet s alphabetum n; prima elementa n pl

alphabetical adj litterarum ordine

Alpine adj alpinus

already adv jam

also adv etiam, quoque, et, idem, necnon

altar s ara f; altaria n pl

alter vt mutare, commutare; variare; vertĕre

alterable adj mutabilis

alteration s mutatio, commutatio f

altercation s altercatio f, jurgium n

alternate adj alternus; —ly invicem, per vices; alternis

alternate vt & vi alternare, variare

alternation s vicissitudo f

alternative adj alter

alternative s discrimen n, optio f; alternata conditio f

although conj etsi, etiamsi, tametsi, quamquam, licet, cum

altitude s altitudo f

altogether adv omnino; prorsus, plane

altruism s beneficentia f

always adv semper

amalgamate vt miscēre, conjungĕre

amalgamation s mixtio f

amass vt coacervare, cumulare

amateur s artium amator m; tiro m

amaze vt obstupefacĕre

amazed adj attonitus, stupefactus; to be — stupēre; obstupescĕre

amazement s stupor m; in — attonitus, stupefactus

amazing adj mirus, mirandus, mirabilis; —ly mirabiliter

Amazon s Amazon f

Amazonian adj amazonius, amazonicus

ambassador s legatus m

amber s sucinum n; electrum n

ambiguity s ambiguitas f, ambages f pl

ambiguous adj ambiguus, dubius, anceps; —ly ambigue

ambition s ambitio f; studium n

ambitious adj laudis or gloriae cupidus; studiosus; ambitiosus

amble vi ambulare

ambrosia s ambrosia f

ambush s insidiae f pl

ambush vt insidiari (with dat)

ameliorate vt meliorem or melius facĕre, corrigĕre

amenable adj docilis, obediens

amend vt emendare, corrigĕre; vi proficĕre

amendment s emendatio, correctio f

amends s compensatio, satisfactio f; to make — expiare, satisfacĕre, compensare

amenity s amoenitas f; (comfort) commodum n

amethyst s amethystus f

amiable adj amabilis, suavis

amiably adv amabiliter, suaviter

amicable adj amicus; pacatus; benevolus

amicably adv amice; pacate; benevole

amid prep inter (with acc)

amity s amicitia f

ammonia s ammoniaca f

ammunition s belli apparat·us -ūs m; missilium copia f

amnesty s venia, abolitio f

among prep inter (with acc); apud (with acc); ad (with acc); from — e, ex (with abl)

amorous adj amatorius; libidinosus, mulierosus; —ly amatorie; cum amore

amount s summa f, totum n

amount vi to — to crescĕre, exsurgĕre; (fig) esse

amour s amores m pl

amphitheater s amphitheatrum n

ample adj amplus; copiosus; satis

amplification s amplificatio, auctio, dilatatio f

amplify vt amplificare, dilatare

amply adv ample, abunde

amputate vt amputare, secare

amputation s amputatio, sectio f

amuck adv furiose; to run — delirare

amulet s amuletum n

amuse vt oblectare, delectare; to — oneself ludĕre

amusement s delectatio, oblectatio f; delectamentum n; ludibrium n

amusing adj ridiculus; festivus; facetus

an indefinite article, unexpressed in Latin

anachronism s temporum inversio f

analogous adj analogus

analogy s analogia, comparatio f

analysis s analysis f; explicatio f; separatio f

analytical adj analyticus; —ly per analysin

analyze vt in principia resolvĕre; (words) subtiliter enodare

anapest s anapaestus m

anapestic adj anapaesticus

anarchist s civis sediotiosus m

anarchy s anarchia f; rei publicae perturbatio f; licentia f

anathema s anathema n; exsecratio f

anatomical adj anatomicus

anatomy s anatomia, dissectio f

ancestor s proavus m; auctor m; —s majores, priores m pl

ancestral adj avitus; proavitus; patrius

ancestry s genus n; stirps f; origo f

anchor s ancora f; to lie at — in ancoris stare; to weigh — ancoram tollĕre or solvĕre

anchor vt in ancoris tenēre; vi ancoram jacĕre

anchorage s statio f

ancient adj antiquus, vetustus; priscus; pristinus; in — times antiquitus; the —s veteres m pl; barbati m pl

and conj et, ac, atque, -que

anecdote s fabella f

anemic adj exsanguis

anew adv denuo; ab integro

angel s angelus m

angelic *adj* angelicus; *(fig)* egregius, excellens

anger *s* ira *f*; bilis *f*

anger *vt* irritare, exacerbare

angle *s* angulus *m*

angle *vi* hamo piscari

angler *s* piscator *m*

angrily *adv* irate, iracunde

angry *adj* iratus, iracundus, indignans; **to be** — irasci, succensēre, stomachari; **to make** — irritare, exacerbare

anguish *s* angor *m*; dolor *m*; cruciat·us -ūs *m*

anguished *adj* animo fractus

angular *adj* angularis; angulosus

animal *s* animal *n*; *(wild beast)* bestia, fera *f*; *(domestic)* pecus *n*

animal *adj* animalis

animate *vt* animare; *(fig)* excitare

animated *adj* excitatus, vegetus

animation *s* animatio *f*; vigor, ardor, spirit·us -ūs *m*

animosity *s* acerbitas *f*; invidia *f*; odium *n*; inimicitia *f*

ankle *s* talus *m*

annalist *s* annalium scriptor *m*

annals *s* annales, fasti *m pl*

annex *s* appendix *f*

annex *vt* annectēre, adjungēre, addēre, supponēre

annexation *s* adjectio *f*

annihilate *vt* delēre, exstinguēre

annihilation *s* exstinctio *f*; internecio *f*

anniversary *adj* anniversarius; annuus

anniversary *s* festus dies anniversarius *m*

annotate *vt* annotare, commentari

annotation *s* annotatio, nota *f*

announce *vt* nuntiare; *(to report)* renuntiare; *(officially)* denuntiare, pronuntiare; *(laws, etc.)* proscribēre

announcement *s* denuntiatio, pronuntiatio *f*; *(news)* nuntius *m*

announcer *s* nuntius *m*

annoy *vt* incommodare, vexare, male habēre; **to be annoyed** stomachari, offensus esse

annoyance *s* vexatio, molestia *f*; dolor *m*

annoying *adj* molestus, odiosus

annual *adj* anniversarius, annuus; **—ly** quotannis

annuity *s* annua pecunia *f*; annuus redit·us -ūs *m*; *(law)* annuum *n*

annul *vt* rescindēre, tollēre, dissolvēre, abrogare

annulment *s* abolitio *f*; abrogatio *f*

anoint *vt* ung(u)ēre

anointing *s* unctio *f*

anomalous *adj* anomalus; enormis

anomaly *s* anomalia *f*; enormitas *f*

anonymous *adj* sine nomine; **—ly** sine nomine

another *adj* alius; **—'s** alienus; **one after** — alius ex alio; **one** — **inter** se; alius alium; **to** — **place** alio

answer *vt* respondēre *(with dat)*; *(by letter)* rescribēre *(with dat)*; *(to correspond to)* congruēre cum *(with abl)*; *vi* **to** — **for** rationem reddēre *(with genit)*; **to** — **to the name of** vocari

answer *s* responsio *f*, responsum *n*; *(solution)* explicatio *f*

answerable *adj* reus; **to be** — **for** praestare

ant *s* formica *f*

antagonism *s* adversitas, inimicitia *f*

antagonist *s* adversarius *m*; adversatrix *f*; hostis *m*

antarctic *adj* antarcticus

antecedent *adj* antecedens; prior

antecedent *s* antecedens *n*

antechamber *s* atriolum *n*; antithalamus *m*

antedate *vt* diem vero antiquiorem ascribēre *(with dat)*

antelope *s* antilope *f*; dorcas *f*

antepenult *s* syllaba antepenultima *f*

anterior *adj* anterior, prior

anteroom *s* antithalamus *m*; vestibulum *n*

anthem *s* canticum sacrum *n*; hymnus elatior *m*

anthology *s* anthologia *f*; excerpta *n pl*

anticipate *vt* anticipare; *(to expect)* spectare; *(to forestall)* praevenire, praeoccupare; *(mentally)* praesumēre

anticipation *s* anticipatio, praesumptio, anteoccupatio *f*

anticlimax *s* climax inversa *f*

antics *s* joca *n pl*; ineptiae *f pl*

antidote *s* antidotum *n*

antipathy *s* repugnantia, antipathia *f*; fastidium, odium *n*

antiquarian *adj* historicus

antiquarian *s* antiquitatis peritus *m*; antiquarius *m*

antiquated *adj* antiquatus, obsoletus

antique *adj* antiquus, vetus, priscus

antique *s* antiqui artificis opus *n*

antiquity *s* antiquitas, vetustas *f*

antithesis *s* contrarium *n*, contentio *f*

antler *s* cornu *n*

anvil *s* incus *f*

anxiety *s* anxietas, sollicitudo *f*

anxious *adj* anxius, sollicitus; trepidus; avidus; **—ly** anxie, sollicite; trepide; avide

any *adj* ullus; quivis, quilibet; aliquis; — **longer** diutius; — **more** amplius

anybody *pron* aliquis; quivis; quilibet; *(after si, nisi, num, ne)* quis; *(interrog)* ecquis, numquis; *(after negative)* quisquam

anyhow *adv* quoquomodo

anyone *see* **anybody**

anything *pron* aliquid, quicquam, quidpiam, quodvis; *(after si, nisi, num, ne)* quid; *(interrog)* ecquid, numquid; *(after negative)* quicquam; **hardly** — nihil fere

anywhere *adv* ubilibet, alicubi, ubivis

apart *adv* seorsum, separatim; **to be** — distare; **to set** — seponēre; **to stand** — distare

apart from *prep* praeter *(with acc)*

apartment *s* conclave *n*; insula *f*

apathetic *adj* lentus, languidus
apathy *s* apathia, lentitudo *f*, languor *m*
ape *s* simius *m*, simia *f*
ape *vt* imitari
aperture *s* apertura *f*; foramen *n*
apex *s* cacumen *n*; fastigium *n*
aphorism *s* sententia *f*
apiary *s* alvearium *n*
apiece *adv* singuli
aplomb *s* confidentia *f*
apocalypse *s* apocalypsis *f*
apocryphal *adj* apocryphus, commenticius
apogee *s* apogaeum *n*
apologetic *adj* apologeticus; confitens
apologist *s* defensor *m*
apologize *vi* se excusare; veniam petere
apology *s* excusatio, defensio *f*; (*written treatise*) apologia *f*, liber apologeticus *m*; **to make an —** for excusare
apoplectic *adj* apoplecticus
apoplexy *s* apoplexia *f*; apoplexis *f*
apostasy *s* apostasia *f*
apostate *s* apostata *m*
apostle *s* apostolus *m*
apostolic *adj* apostolicus
apostrophe *s* apostrophe *f*; (*gram*) apostrophus *f*
apostrophize *vt* abrupte compellare
apothecary *s* (*druggist*) medicamentarius *m*; (*drugstore*) medicina taberna *f*, pharmacopolium *n*
apotheosis *s* apotheosis *f*
appall *vt* exterrere, percellere
apparatus *s* apparat·us -ūs *m*
apparel *s* vestis *f*, vestit·us -ūs *m*; vestimenta *n pl*
apparel *vt* vestire; adornare
apparent *adj* manifestus, apertus, conspicuus; **to be —** apparere; **—ly** manifeste, aperte, specie, per speciem
apparition *s* spectrum *n*; visum *n*; species *f*
appeal *vi* appellare; provocare; **to — to** (*a magistrate*) appellare; (*the people*) provocare ad (*with acc*); (*the gods*) obsecrare, invocare, testari
appeal *s* (*law*) appellatio *f*; (*entreaty*) obsecratio, testatio *f*; (*to the people*) provocatio *f*
appear *vi* apparere, comparere; se ostendere; (*to seem*) videri; (*to arise*) exoriri, surgere; **to begin to —** patescere
appearance *s* (*becoming visible*) aspect·us -ūs *m*; (*outward show*) species *f*; (*likelihood*) similitudo *f*; (*vision*) visum *n*; **first —** exort·us -ūs *m*; **to all —s** probabilissime; **to make an —** prodire
appease *vt* placare, sedare; mitigare; (*fig*) expiare
appeasement *s* placatio *f*; (*of an enemy*) pacificatio *f*
appellation *s* nomen *n*
appendage *s* appendix, accessio, appendicula *f*
appendix *s* appendix *f*

appetite *s* appetit·us -ūs *m*, cupiditas *f*; **to have an —** esurire
applaud *vt* applaudere; laudare
applause *s* plaus·us -ūs, applaus·us ūs *m*; laus *f*
apple *s* malum, pomum *n*; **— of my eye** ocellus meus *m*
apple tree *s* malus *f*
appliance *s* instrumentum *n*, apparat·us -ūs *m*
applicable *adj* commodus, conveniens
applicant *s* petitor *m*
application *s* petitio *f*; adhibitio, appositio *f*; studium *n*, sedulitas, industria, diligentia *f*; (*med*) fomentum *n*
apply *vt* adhibere, admovere, apponere; aptare, accommodare; (*fig*) applicare; *vi* **to — to** pertinere ad (*with acc*); **to — for** petere
appoint *vt* creare; facere; designare; destinare; constituere
appointment *s* creatio *f*; (*rendezvous*) constitutum *n*; (*order*) mandatum *n*; (*office*) magistrat·us -ūs *m*
apportion *vt* dividere, distribuere
apportionment *s* divisio, distributio *f*
apposition *s* appositio *f*
appraisal *s* aestimatio *f*
appraise *vt* aestimare
appraiser *s* aestimator *m*
appreciable *adj* aestimabilis, haud exiguus
appreciate *vt* aestimare
appreciation *s* aestimatio *f*
apprehend *vt* apprehendere, comprehendere, percipere; (*to seize*) capere; (*to take by surprise*) intercipere; (*to fear*) timere, metuere
apprehension *s* comprehensio *f*; facultas, intelligentia *f*; suspicio *f*; (*seizing*) captura *f*; (*fear*) timor, met·us -ūs *m*
apprehensive *adj* timidus, sollicitus
apprentice *s* discipulus *m*; tiro *m*
apprenticeship *s* identura *f*; tirocinium *n*
apprize *vt* docere
approach *vt* appropinquare (*with dat*), accedere ad (*with acc*), adire; *vi* appropinquare, appetere
approach *s* access·us -ūs, adit·us -ūs *m*; appropinquatio *f*; (*by sea*) appuls·us -ūs *m*
approachable *adj* (*person*) facilis, affabilis; (*place*) patens
approbation *s* approbatio, laus *f*
appropriate *adj* proprius, aptus, idoneus; **—ly** apte, congruenter
appropriate *vt* asciscere, asserere, vindicare; assumere
appropriation *s* vindicatio *f*
approval *s* approbatio *f*
approve *vt* approbare, probare; (*law*) sciscere; *vi* **to — of** probare
approved *adj* probatus, spectatus
approximate *adj* propinquus, proximus; **—ly** prope, propemodum; (*with numbers*) ad (*with acc*)
approximate *vt* appropinquare (*with dat*); accedere ad (*with acc*)

approximation *s* appropinquatio *f*

apricot *s* malum armeniacum *n*

April *s* (mensis) Aprilis *m*

apron *s* praecinctorium *n*; operimentum *n*

apt *adj* aptus, idoneus; *(inclined, prone)* pronus, propensus; **—ly** apte

aptitude *s* habilitas *f*, ingenium *n*

aptness *s* convenientia, congruentia *f*; *(tendency)* proclivitas *f*

aquatic *adj* aquatilis, aquaticus

aqueduct *s* aquaeduct·us -ūs, aquarum duct·us -ūs *m*

aquiline *adj (of the nose)* aduncus

arable *adj* arabilis, culturae idoneus; **— land** arvum *n*

arbiter *s* arbiter *m*

arbitrament *s* arbitrat·us -ūs *m*, arbitrium *n*

arbitrarily *adv* ad arbitrium; ad libdinem; libidinoso

arbitrary *adj* libidinosus; imperiosus, superbus

arbitrate *vt & vi* disceptare

arbitration *s* arbitrium *n*, dijudicatio *f*

arbitrator *s* arbiter *m*; disceptator *m*

arbor *s* umbraculum *n*, pergula *f*

arc *s* arc·us -ūs *m*

arcade *s* portic·us -ūs *f*

arch *s* arc·us -ūs, fornix *m*

arch *adj* astutus, callidus, vafer; nimius

arch *vt* arcuare, fornicare

archaeological *adj* archaeologiae *(genit)*

archaeologist *s* antiquitatis investigator *m*

archaeology *s* rerum antiquarum scientia *f*

archaism *s* locutio obsoleta *f*

archbishop *s* archiepiscopus *m*

archer *s* sagittarius *m*; *(constellation)* Arcitenens *m*

archery *s* ars sagittandi *f*

archetype *s* archetypum *n*

archipelago *s* insulis crebrum mare *n*

architect *s* architectus *m*

architectural *adj* architectonicus

architecture *s* architectura *f*

archives *s* tabulae *f pl*; tabularium *n*

arctic *adj* arcticus

ardent *adj* ardens, fervidus; **—ly** ardenter

ardor *s* ardor, fervor *m*

arduous *adj* arduus

area *s* regio *f*; area *f*; superficies *f*

arena *s* (h)arena *f*

argonaut *s* argonauta *m*

argue *vt* arguěre, probare; *vi* argumentari, disputare, disserěre

argument *s (discussion)* disputatio *f*; controversia *f*; *(theme)* argumentum, thema *n*, ratio *f*

argumentation *s* argumentatio *f*

argumentative *adj* ratiocinativus, litigiosus

aria *s* canticum *n*

arid *adj* aridus, siccus

aright *adv* recte

arise *vi* surgěre, exoriri, exsistěre;

to — from nasci ex *(with abl)*

aristocracy *s (class)* optimates, nobiles *m pl*; *(government)* optimatum dominat·us -ūs *m*

aristocrat *s* optimas *m*

aristocratic *adj* patricius, generosus

arithmetic *s* arithmetica *n pl*

ark *s* arca *f*

arm *s* bracchium *n*; *(of the sea)* sin·us -ūs *m*; fretum *n*; **—s** arma *n pl*; **by force of —s** vi et armis; **to be under —s** in armis esse; **to lay down —s** ab armis disceděre; arma deděre; **to take up —s** armare; arma sumēre

arm *vt* armare; *vi* armari; bellum parare

armada *s* classis magna *f*

armament *s* belli apparat·us -ūs *m*; copiae *f pl*

armchair *s* anconibus fabrefacta sella *f*

armistice *s* indutiae *f pl*

armlet *s* bracchiolum *n*; *(bracelet)* bracchiale *n*

armor *s* armatura *f*, armat·us -ūs *m*; arma *n pl*

armorbearer *s* armiger *m*

armory *s* armamentarium *n*

armpit *s* ala *f*

army *s* exercit·us -ūs *m*; *(in battle)* acies *f*; *(on the march)* agmen *n*

aroma *s* aroma *n*; *(of wine)* flos *m*

aromatic *adj* armomaticus

around *adv* circum, circa; **all —** undique, passim

around *prep* circum *(with acc)*

arouse *vt* suscitare; *(fig)* erigěre; **to — oneself** expergisci

arraign *vt* accusare

arraignment *s* accusatio, actio *f*

arrange *vt* instruěre, struěre, ordinare, disponěre, componěre; *(to agree)* pacisci

arrangement *s* ordo *m*, collocatio *f*; dispositio *f*; pactum *n*

array *s* vestis *f*, vestit·us -ūs *m*; habit·us -ūs *m*; *(mil)* acies *f*

array *vt* vestire; adornare; instruěre

arrears *s* reliqua *n pl*; residuum *n*, residuae pecuniae *f pl*; **to be in —** relinqui

arrest *s* prehensio *f*

arrest *vt (to seize)* prehenděre, deprehenděre, arripěre; *(movement)* tardare, morari; *(attention)* in se convertěre

arrival *s* advent·us -ūs *m*; *(by sea)* appuls·us -ūs *m*

arrive *vi* pervenire, advenire; *(of a ship)* advehi, appelli

arrogance *s* arrogantia, superbia *f*

arrogant *adj* arrogans, superbus; **—ly** arroganter, insolenter, superbe

arrogate *vt* arrogare, assuměre

arrow *s* sagitta, arundo *f*

arsenal *s* armamentarium *n*; navalia *n pl*

arsenic *s* arsenicum *n*

arson *s* incendium dolo malo *n*

art *s* ars *f*; artificium *n*

artery *s* arteria *f*

artful adj artificialis; callidus, subtilis; **—ly** callide, eleganter

article s (object) res f; (ware) merx f; (term) condicio f; (clause) caput n; (gram) articulus m

articulate adj distinctus, dilucidus; **—ly** articulatim, distincte

articulate vt explanare, exprimĕre; articulatim dicĕre

articulation s commissura f; (fig) explanatio f

artifice s artificium n; ars f; dolum n

artificial adj artificiosus; factitius; **—ly** arte

artillery s tormenta n pl

artisan s faber m; artifex, opifex m

artist s artifex m

artistic adj artificiosus, elegans; **—ally** artificiose; affabre

as conj & adv ut; quam; (of time) dum, cum; ita ut; sicut, velut; **— far —** quoad, usque ad, quantum; **— if** quasi, perinde ac si; ita ut si; **— it were** seu, tamquam; **— long — tamdiu**, tantisper dum; **— many — tot**, totidem; quotquot, quodcumque; **— much tantum**; **— often — toties** quoties; **— soon — cum** primum, simul, simul ac, simul atque; **— well — ut**, tamquam; **— yet adhuc**; **not — yet nondum**, necdum

ascend vt & vi ascendĕre

ascendency s auctoritas f

ascent s ascensio f; ascens·us ·ūs m; acclivitas f

ascertain vt confirmare, comperire

ascetic adj asceticus

ascetic s asceta m

asceticism s duritia f

ascribe vt imputare, tribuĕre, ascribĕre

ash s cinis m; (tree) fraxinus f

ashamed adj pudibundus; **I am — of** pudet me (with genit)

ashen adj pallidus

ashore adv (motion) in litus; (rest) in litore

Asiatic adj Asiaticus

aside adv seorsum, oblique; **to call — sevocare**; **to lay** or **set — ponĕre**, seponĕre

aside from prep praeter (with acc)

asinine adj asininus

ask vt rogare, poscĕre; interrogare; requirĕre; vi **to — for** petĕre

askance adv oblique

askew adv traverse

asleep adj dormiens; **to be — dormire**; **to fall — obdormire**, obdormiscĕre

asp s aspis f

asparagus s asparagus m

aspect s aspect·us ·ūs, prospect·us ·ūs m; facies f

aspen s populus tremula f

asperity s acerbitas f

aspersion s opprobrium n, calumniatio f

asphalt s bitumen n

asphyxia s asphyxia f

aspirant s petitor m

aspiration s affectatio, spes f; (pol) ambitio f

aspire vi **to — to** affectare, spectare, petĕre, anniti

aspiring adj appetens; **aspiring to** appetens (with genit)

ass s asinus m; asina f; onager m; (fig) stultus m

assail vt appetĕre; oppugnare, invehi

assailable adj expugnabilis

assailant s oppugnator m

assassin s sicarius m; percussor m

assassinate vt insidiis interficĕre, occidĕre

assassination s caedes f

assault s impet·us ·ūs m; oppugnatio, vis f; **aggravated — (law)** vis f; **sexual — stupratio** f; **to take by — expugnare**

assault vt adoriri, oppugnare; manus inferre (with dat); aggredi; (in speech) invehi in (with acc)

assay vt (metals) spectare; tentare, conari

assay s (of metals) obrussa f; spectatio f

assemblage s congregatio f; coacervatio f

assemble vt congregare, convocare; contrahĕre; vi convenire

assembly s coet·us ·ūs m; convent·us ·ūs m; (pol) comitia n pl; concilium n; (of troops) contio f; synodus f

assent s assens·us ·ūs m

assent vi assentiri, adnuĕre

assert vt asserĕre, affirmare, asseverare; (to vindicate) defendĕre

assertion s affirmatio, asseveratio f; postulatio f

assess vt (to tax) censēre; (to value) aestimare

assessment s cens·us ·ūs m; aestimatio f; vectigal, tributum n

assessor s (judge) consessor m; (of taxes) censor m

assets s bona n pl

assiduous adj, assiduus; **—ly** assidue

assign vt attribuĕre, tribuĕre; (land) assignare; (place) indicare; (time) praestituĕre; (task) delegare; (to allege) suggerĕre, afferre

assignment s assignatio, attributio f; delegatio f

assimilate vt assimulare; (food) concoquĕre; (knowledge) concipĕre

assimilation s assimulatio, appropriatio f

assist vt adesse (with dat), succurrĕre (with dat), juvare, adjuvare

assistance s auxilium n; opem (no nominative) f; **to be of — to** auxilio esse (with dat)

assistant s adjutor m, adjutrix f, administer m

associate adj socius; collegialis

associate s socius, sodalis, consors m

associate vt consociare, adsciscĕre, conjungĕre; vi **to — with** familiariter uti (with abl); se adjungĕre (with dat)

association *s* societas *f*; communitas *f*; consociatio *f*; congregatio *f*

assort *vt* digerĕre, disponĕre; *vi* congruĕre

assortment *s* digestio, dispositio *f*; variae res *f pl*

assuage *vt* allevare, placare, lenire, mitigare

assume *vt* assumĕre, arrogare; induĕre; (*office*) inire

assuming *adj* arrogans

assumption *s* assumptio *f*; arrogantio *f*; (*hypothesis*) sumptio *f*

assurance *s* fiducia *f*; (*guarantee*) fides *f*; (*boldness*) confidentia, audacia *f*

assure *vt* confirmare, affirmare; promittĕre (*with dat*); adhortari; **to be assured** confidĕre

assuredly *adv* certo, profecto

asterisk *s* asteriscus *m*

asthmatic *adj* asthmaticus; **to be — suspirio laborare**

astonish *vt* obstupefacĕre; **to be astonished at** mirari

astonishingly *adv* admirabiliter

astonishment *s* admiratio *f*; stupor *m*

astound *vt* (ob)stupefacĕre

astray *adj* vagus; **to go — errare; to lead — seducĕre**

astride *adj* varicus

astrologer *s* astrologus *m*; Chaldaeus *m*; mathematicus *m*

astrological *adj* astrologicus

astrology *s* astrologia *f*; Chaldaeorum divinatio *f*

astronomer *s* astrologus *m*; astronomus *m*

astronomical *adj* astronomicus

astronomy *s* astrologia, astronomia *f*

astute *adj* callidus

asunder *adv* seorsum, separatim; *use verb with prefix* dis- *or* se-

asylum *s* asylum, perfugium *n*

at *prep* (*of place*) ad (*with acc*), apud (*with acc*), in (*with abl*), *or* locative case; (*of time*) in (*with abl*), ad (*with acc*), *or* abl case

atheism *s* deos esse negare (*used as neuter noun*)

atheist *s* atheos *m*

athlete *s* athleta *m*

athletic *adj* athleticus; lacertosus

atlas *s* orbis terrarum descriptio *f*

atmosphere *s* aër *m*; caelum *n*; inane *n*

atmospheric *adj* aëris (*genit*)

atom *s* atomus *f*; corpus individuum *n*; (*fig*) mica, particula *f*

atomic *adj* atomicus; **— theory** atomorum doctrina *f*

atone *vi* **to — for** piare, expiare

atonement *s* piaculum *n*; expiatio, compensatio *f*

atrocious *adj* atrox, dirus; nefarius, nefandus; immanis; **—ly** nefarie

atrocity *s* atrocitas *f*; atrox facinus *n*

atrophy *s* tabes, atrophia *f*

atrophy *s* tabescĕre, macrescĕre

attach *vt* annectĕre, adjungĕre; applicare; affigĕre; **to be attached to** adhaerēre (*with dat*)

attachment *s* adhaesio *f*; (*emotional*) amor *m*; vinculum *n*; studium *n*

attack *s* impet·us -ūs *m*; oppugnatio *f*; (*of cavalry*) incurs·us -ūs *m*; (*of disease, etc.*) tentatio *f*

attack *vt* adoriri, aggredi, oppugnare; (*with words*) invehi in (*with acc*), insequi; (*of diseases*) corripĕre, invadĕre, tentare

attacker *s* oppugnator, provocator *m*

attain *vt* adipisci, consequi; **to — to** pervenire ad (*with acc*)

attainable *adj* impetrabilis, obtinendus

attempt *s* conat·us -ūs *m*, inceptum *n*; (*risk*) ausum, periculum *n*; **first — tirocinium *n***

attempt *vt* conari, niti, temptare, moliri

attend *vt* (*to accompany*) comitari; (*to escort*) deducĕre; (*to be present at*) adesse (*with dat*), interesse (*with dat*); *vi* **to — on** apparēre (*with dat*); frequentare, assectari; adesse (*with dat*); **to — to** animadvertĕre, procurare; (*to comply with*) obtemperare (*with dat*); invigilare

attendance *s* frequentia *f*; expectatio, adsectatio, cura, diligentia *f*; obsequium *n*; (*retinue*) comitat·us -ūs *m*

attendant *adj* adjunctus

attendant *s* comes *m*; assecla, apparitor *m*; famulus *m*, famula *f*

attention *s* animadversio *f*; animi attentio *f*; (*to duty*) cura, diligentia *f*; **to call — to** indicare; **to pay — to** operam dare (*with dat*), studēre (*with dat*)

attentive *adj* attentus; sedulus; officiosus; **—ly** attente, intento animo; sedulo; officiose

attenuate *vt* attenuare, extenuare

attenuation *s* extenuatio *f*

attest *vt* testari, testificari

attestation *s* testificatio *f*

attic *s* cenaculum *n*

Attic *adj* Atticus; (*fig*) subtilis, elegans

attire *s* ornat·us -ūs *m*; vestis *f*; habit·us -ūs *m*; vestit·us -ūs *m*

attire *vt* vestire; adornare

attitude *s* habit·us -ūs, stat·us -ūs *m*; (*mental*) ratio *f*

attorney *s* cognitor, procurator, advocatus, actor *m*

attorney general *s* advocatus fisci, procurator publicus *m*

attract *vt* trahĕre, attrahĕre; (*fig*) allicĕre

attraction *s* vis attractionis *f*; (*fig*) illecebra *f*, invitamentum *n*

attractive *adj* blandus, suavis, lepidus, venustus; **—ly** blande, suaviter, venuste, lepide

attractiveness *s* lepos *m*, venustas *f*

attribute *s* proprium, attributum *n*

attribute *vt* tribuĕre, attribuĕre; assignare, delegare

attrition *s* attrit·us -ūs *m*

attune *vt* modulari

auburn *adj* fulvus; aureus

auction *s* auctio *f*; (*public*) hasta *f*; to hold an — auctionem facĕre; to sell by — sub hasta vendĕre

auctioneer *s* praeco *m*

audacious *adj* audax; —ly audacter

audacity *s* audacia *f*

audible *adj* quod audiri potest

audibly *adv* clara voce

audience *s* auditores *m pl*; (*bystanders*) corona *f*

audit *s* rationum inspectio *f*

audit *vt* inspicĕre

auditory *adj* auditorius

Augean *adj* Augiae (*genit*)

auger *s* terebra *f*

augment *vt* augēre, ampliare; *vi* augēri, accrescĕre

augur *s* augur *m*

augur *vi* augurari

augury *s* augurium, auspicium *n*; auguratio *f*

august *adj* augustus; magnificus

August *s* (mensis) Sextilis, (mensis) Augustus *m*

Augustan *adj* Augustalis

aunt *s* (*on father's side*) amita *f*; (*on mother's side*) matertera *f*

auspices *s* auspicium *n*; to take — auspicari; without taking — inauspicato

auspicious *adj* auspicatus; faustus, felix; —ly auspicato; feliciter

austere *adj* austerus, severus; —ly austere, severe

austerity *s* austeritas, severitas *f*

authentic *adj* certus; verus; ratus; (*law*) authenticus; fide dignus; genuinus

authenticate *vt* recognoscĕre

authentication *s* auctoritas *f*; legibus confirmatio *f*

authenticity *s* auctoritas, fides *f*

author *s* auctor, scriptor *m*; (*inventor*) conditor *m*; (*of a crime*) caput *n*

authoress *s* auctor *f*

authoritative *adj* imperiosus; fidus; —ly praecise

authority *s* auctoritas, potestas *f*; (*leave*) licentia *f*; jus *n*; imperium *n*; magistrat·us -ūs *m*; to have it on good — bono auctore habere

authorization *s* auctoritate confirmatio *f*; licentia *f*

authorize *vt* potestatem *or* auctoritatem dare (*with dat*), mandare; (*law*) sancire

authorship *s* scriptoris munus *n*; auctoritas *f*

autobiography *s* de vita sua scriptus liber *m*

autocrat *s* dominus *m*

autograph *s* chirographum *n*

autograph *vt* manu propria scribĕre

automatic *adj* necessarius

automaton *s* automaton *n*

autumn *s* autumnus *m*

autumnal *adj* autumnalis

auxiliaries *s* (*mil*) auxilia *n pl*; auxiliarii *m pl*

auxiliary *adj* auxiliaris, auxiliarius

auxiliary *s* adjutor *m*

avail *vt* prodesse (*with dat*); to — oneself of uti (*with abl*); *vi* valēre

avail *s* to be of no — usui non esse

availability *s* utilitas *f*

available *adj* in promptu; utilis

avalanche *s* montis ruina *f*

avarice *s* avaritia *f*; sordes *f*

avaricious *adj* avarus, avidus; —ly avare

avenge *vt* vindicare, ulcisci

avenger *s* ultor *m*, vindex *m & f*

avenging *adj* ultrix, vindex

avenue *s* xystus *m*, xystum *n*

average *s* medium *n*; on the — fere

average *vi* fere esse

averse *adj* aversus; to be — to abhorrēre ab (*with abl*); —ly averse

aversion *s* odium, fastidium *n*; to have an — for fastidire

avert *vt* avertĕre, amovēre, abducĕre

aviary *s* aviarium *n*

avid *adj* avidus

avocation *s* officium *n*, negotia *n pl*

avoid *vt* vitare, fugĕre; (*a blow*) declinare

avoidable *adj* evitabilis

avoidance *s* vitatio *f*; declinatio *f*

avow *vt* asserĕre, profitēri

avowal *s* confessio *f*

avowedly *adv* palam, aperte, ex confesso

await *vt* exspectare

awake *adj* vigil, vigilans; to be — vigilare

awaken *vt* excitare, suscitare, expergefacĕre; *vi* expergisci

award *s* praemium *n*; (*decision*) arbitrium, judicium *n*

award *vt* tribuĕre; (*law*) adjudicare, addicĕre

aware *adj* gnarus, sciens; to be — of scire

away *adv* use verbs with prefix a- *or* ab-; far — procul, longe; to be — abesse; to go — abire

awe *s* reverentia *f*; formido f, met·us -ūs, terror *m*; to stand in — of verēri; venerari

awful *adj* formidulosus, dirus, terribilis; —ly terribiliter, formidulose

awhile *adv* paulisper, aliquamdiu, parumper

awkward *adj* ineptus; rusticus, rudis; inhabilis; (*fig*) molestus; —ly inepte; rustice; dure; inscite

awkwardness *s* ineptia *f*; imperitia, rusticitas *f*

awl *s* subula *f*

awning *s* velarium *n*; inductio *f*

awry *adj* obliquus; pravus

awry *adv* oblique; prave

ax *s* securis *f*

axiom *s* axioma, pronuntiatum *n*, sententia *f*

axis *s* axis *m*

axle *s* axis *m*

azure *adj* caeruleus

B

baa *s* balat·us -ūs *m*
baa *vi* balare
babble *s* garrulitas *f*
babble *vi* blaterare, garrire
babbler *s* blatero, garrulus *m*
babbling *adj* garrulus, loquax
babe *s* infans *m & f*
baboon *s* cynocephalus *m*
baby *s* infans *m & f*
babyish *adj* infantilis
bacchanal *s* bacchans *m*, baccha *f*
bacchanalian *adj* bacchanalis
Bacchic *adj* bacchicus
bachelor *s* caelebs *m*; (*degree*) baccalaureus *m*
back *s* tergum, dorsum *n*; aversum *n*; at one's — a tergo
back *adv* retro, retrorsum; *or use verbs with prefix* re- *or* retro-
back *vt* adjuvare; favēre (*with dat*), obsecundare (*with dat*), adesse (*with dat*); *vi* to — away from defugēre; to — up retrogradi
backboard *s* pluteus *m*
backbone *s* spina *f*
backdoor *s* posticum *n*
backer *s* adjutor, fautor *m*
background *s* recess·us -ūs *m*
backstairs *s* scalae posticae *f pl*
backward *adv* retro; retrorsum; rursus
backward *adj* (*reversed*) supinus; (*slow*) piger, tardus; (*late*) serus; to be — cunctari
backwardness *s* tarditas *f*; pigritia *f*
bacon *s* lardum *n*
bad *adj* malus, parvus, nequam; improbus; aegrotus; (*of weather*) adversus; to go — corrumpi; —ly male, prave; improbe
badge *s* insigne, signum *n*
badger *s* meles *f*
badger *vt* vexare, inquietare, sollicitare
badness *s* malitia, pravitas, nequitia, improbitas *f*
baffle *vt* decipēre, fallēre, eludēre
bag *s* saccus *m*; (*of leather*) uter *m*; (*of network*) reticulum *n*
baggage *s* sarcinae *f pl*; impedimenta *n pl*; scruta *n pl*
bail *s* vadimonium *n*; vas *m*; (*for debt*) praes *m*; to accept — for vadari; to put up — for spondēre pro (*with abl*), fidepromittēre
bailiff *s* (*sergeant of court of justice*) apparitor *m*; (*manager of estate*) villicus *m*
bailiwick *s* jurisdictio *f*
bait *s* esca *f*; (*fig*) incitamentum *n*, illecebra *f*
bait *vt* inescare; (*to tease*) lacessēre
bake *vt* torrēre, coquēre
baker *s* pistor *m*
bakery *s* pistrina *f*, pistrinum *n*
balance *s* libra, trutina, statera *f*; (*equipoise*) aequipondium *n*; (*in bookkeeping*) reliquum *n*; (*fig*) compensatio *f*
balance *vt* librare; compensare; (*accounts*) consolidare, dispungēre; *vi* constare; the account balances ratio constat
balance sheet *s* ratio accepti et expensi *f*
balcony *s* maenianum *n*; podium *n*
bald *adj* calvus, glaber; (*fig*) aridus; —ly (*in style*) jejune
baldness *s* calvitium *n*; (*of style*) ariditas, jejunitas *f*
bale *s* sarcina *f*, fascis *m*
bale *vt* (*e.g., hay*) involvēre; to — out exhaurire
baleful *adj* funestus; perniciosus, noxius
balk *s* (*of wood*) tignum *n*; (*fig*) frustratio *f*
balk *vt* frustrari, eludēre, decipēre
ball *s* globulus *m*; (*for playing*) pila *f*; to play — pilā ludēre
ballad *s* carmen *n*
ballast *s* saburra *f*
ballast *vt* saburrare
ballet *s* pantomimus *m*
ballet dancer *s* pantomimus *m*, pantomima *f*
ballot *s* tabella *f*; suffragium *n*
ballot box *s* cista, cistula *f*
balm *s* balsamum *n*; unguentum *n*; (*fig*) solatium *n*
balmy *adj* balsaminus; suavis, lenis
balsam *s* balsamum *n*
bamboo *s* arundo indica *f*
ban *s* edictum *n*; proscriptio *f*; interdictum *n*
ban *vt* interdicēre (*with dat*), vetare
banana *s* ariena *f*
band *s* vinculum, ligamentum *n*; (*for the head*) redimiculum *n*, infula *f*; (*troop*) caterva *f*, chorus *m*; grex *f*; man·us -ūs *f*; in —s turmatim
band *vi* to — together conjungi, consociari
bandage *s* fascia, ligatura *f*
bandage *vt* ligare, obligare
bandit *s* latro *m*
banditry *s* latrocinium *n*
bandy *vt* jactare; to — words altercari
bane *s* venenum *n*; virus *n*; (*fig*) pestis, pernicies *f*
baneful *adj* pestiferus, perniciosus, exitiosus
bang *s* crepit·us -ūs, sonit·us -ūs *m*
bang *vt* verberare; *vi* sonare, crepare
banish *vt* expellēre, pellēre, relegare, deportare; aquā et igni interdicēre (*with dat*)
banishment *s* (*act*) ejectio, relegatio *f*; interdictio aquae et ignis *f*; (*state*) exilium *n*
banister *s* epimedion *n*
bank *s* (*of a river*) ripa *f*; (*of earth*) agger *m*; (*com*) argentaria *f*, mensa publica *f*

banker s argentarius, mensarius m

banking s argentaria negotiatio f

bank note s tessera mensae publicae f

bankrupt s conturbator, decoctor m; **to be** or **become —** rationes conturbare; decoquĕre; **to go — foro** cedĕre

bankruptcy s rationum conturbatio f; (fig) naufragium patrimonii n

banner s vexillum n

banquet s convivium n, epulae f pl

banter s cavillatio f; jocus m

banter vi cavillari

bantering s cavillatio f

baptism s baptisma n, baptismus m

baptize vt baptizare

bar s vectis f; (of door) obex m; repagulum n; (fig) impedimentum n; (ingot) later m; (in court of justice) cancelli m pl, claustra n pl; (legal profession) forum n; (counter) abacus m; **of the —** forensis; **to practice at the —** causas agĕre

bar vt (door) obserare; (to keep away) obstare (with dat), prohibĕre, intercludĕre

barb s hamus m; aculeus m

barbarian adj barbarus

barbarian s barbarus m

barbaric adj barbaricus

barbarism s barbaria, barbaries f; feritas f; (of language) barbarismus m

barbarity s ferocia, saevitia, immanitas f

barbarous adj barbarus; ferus, immanis; **—ly** barbare; saeve

barbed adj hamatus

barber s tonsor m, tonstrix f

bard s vates m

bare adj nudus; merus; (of style) pressus; **to lay —** nudare, detegĕre

bare vt nudare, denudare; detegĕre, aperire

barefaced adj impudens; **—ly** impudenter

barefoot adj nudis pedibus; discalceatus

bareheaded adj nudo capite

barely adv vix, aegre

bargain s pactio f, pactum n; **to strike a —** pacisci

bargain vi pacisci

barge s linter f

bark s (of tree) cortex m & f, liber m; (of dog) latrat·us -ūs m; (ship) navis, ratis f

bark vi latrare; **to — at** allatrare

barking s latrat·us -ūs m

barley s hordeum n

barley adj hordeacus

barmaid s ministra cauponae f

barn s granarium, horreum n

barometer s barometrum n

barometric adj barometricus

baron s baro m

barracks s castra (stativa) n pl

barrel s cadus m, dolium n, cupa f

barren adj sterilis; macer; jejunus; (fig) angustus

barrenness s sterilitas f

barricade s munimentum n; claustrum n

barricade vt obsaepire, obstruĕre, oppilare

barrier s limes m; cancelli m pl; (fig) claustra n pl

barrister s advocatus m

barter s permutatio f; merx f

barter vt mutare, commutare; vi merces mutare, merces pacisci

base adj humilis, ignobilis, obscurus; inferior; servilis; infamis, vilis, turpis; **—ly** abjecte; turpiter

base s basis f; (mus) sonus gravis m; (fig) fundamentum n; (mil) castra n pl

baseless adj inanis, vanus, falsus

basement s fundamentum n, basis f; imum tabulatum n

baseness s humilitas f; turpitudo f

bashful adj erubescens; pudens; modestus; verecundus; **—ly** timide, verecunde; modeste

bashfulness s pudor m; rubor m; verecundia f

basic adj primus, principalis

basilica s basilica f

basin s (for washing) trulleum n, trulla f; (reservoir) labrum n

basis s fundamentum n

bask vi apricari

basket s corbis f, canistrum n; (for wool) quasillum n; cophinus m

bas-relief s caelamen n; toreuma n

bass s sonus gravissimus m

bast s tilia f

bastard adj spurius

bastard s nothus, spurius m

baste vt lardo perfundĕre

bastion s propugnaculum, castellum n

bat s (bird) vespertilio m; (club) clava f

batch s massa n; numerus m

bath s balneum n; (public) balnea n pl; (tub) alveus m, labrum n; lavatio f; **cold — frigidarium n; hot —** cal(i)darium n

bathe vt lavare; vi balneo uti, lavari, perlui

bathing s lavatio f; natatio f

bathtub s alveus m

batman s calo m

baton s virga f

battalion s cohors f

batter vt percutĕre, obtundĕre, diruĕre, verberare, quassare

battering ram s aries m

battle s proelium n, pugna f; acies f

battle vi pugnare, proeliari

battle array s acies f

battle-ax s bipennis f

battlement s pinna f

bauble s tricae f pl

bawd s lena f

bawdry s lenocinium n

bawl vi vociferari, clamitare

bawling s vociferatio f; indecorus clamor m

bay s (sea) sin·us -ūs m; (tree) laurea, laurus f; **at —** interclusus

bay adj (light-colored) helvus; (dark-colored) spadix; (of bay) laureus

bay *vi* latrare
bayonet *s* pugio *f*
bayonet *vt* pugione fodĕre
bazaar *s* forum rerum venalium *n*
be *vi* esse; exsistĕre; *(condition)* se habēre; **to — absent** abesse; **to — against** adversari; **to — amongst** interesse *(with dat)*; **to — for** *(to side with)* favēre *(with dat)*, stare cum *(with abl)*; **to — present** adesse
beach *s* litus *n*, acta *f*
beach *vt* subducĕre; *vi* vadis impingĕre
beacon *s* ignis in specula *m*; *(lighthouse)* pharus *m*
bead *s* pilula, sphaerula *f*
beagle *s* parvus canis venaticus *m*
beak *s* rostrum *n*
beaked *adj* rostratus
beaker *s* poculum *n*, cantharus *m*
beam *s* *(of wood)* tignum *n*, trabs *f*; *(of light)* radius *m*, jubar *n*; nitor *m*
beam *vi* radiare, refulgēre; *(of a person)* arridēre
beaming *adj* nitens, lucidus
bean *s* faba *f*; phaselus *m & f*
bear *vt* *(to carry)* portare, ferre; *(to endure)* ferre, pati, tolerare; *(to produce)* ferre; *(to beget)* parĕre; **to — away** auferre; **to — out** *(to confirm)* arguĕre; **to — witness to** testari; *vi* **to — down on** appropinquare; **to — upon** *(to refer to)* pertinēre ad *(with acc)*; **to — up** **under** obsistĕre *(with dat)*, sustinēre; **to — with** indulgēre *(with dat)*
bear *s* ursus *m*, ursa *f*
bearable *adj* tolerandus, tolerabilis
beard *s* barba *f*; *(of grain)* arista *f*
bearded *adj* barbatus; intonsus
beardless *adj* inberbis
bearer *s* *(porter)* bajulus *m*; *(of litter)* lecticarius *m*; *(of letter)* tabellarius *m*; *(of news)* nuntius *m*
bearing *s* *(posture)* gest·us -ūs, vult·us -ūs *m*; *(direction)* regio *f*; **to have a — on** pertinēre ad *(with acc)*
beast *s* belua *f*; bestia *f*; *(wild)* fera *f*; *(domestic)* pecus *f*
beast of burden *s* jumentum *n*
beastly *adj* obscenus, foedus, spurcus
beat *vt* *(to punish)* verberare; *(to knock)* pulsare; *(to conquer)* superare, vincĕre; *(the body in grief)* plangĕre; **to — back** repellĕre; **to — down** demoliri; **to — in** perfringĕre; *vi* palpitare; **to — upon** *(of rain)* impluĕre; *(of waves)* illidĕre
beat *s* *(blow)* plaga *f*, ict·us -ūs *m*; *(of the heart)* palpitatio *f*; *(mus)* percussio *f*; *(patrol)* vigiles nocte ambulantes *m pl*
beaten *adj* victus; *(worn)* tritus
beating *s* verberatio *f*; ict·us -ūs *m*; verbera *n pl*; *(defeat)* repulsa *f*; clades *f*; *(of the heart)* palpitatio *f*
beautiful *adj* pulcher; *(shapely)* formosus; **—ly** pulchre, belle
beautify *vt* ornare, decorare

beauty *s* pulchritudo *f*; forma *f*; *(of places)* amoenitas *f*
beaver *s* castor, fiber *m*; *(of helmet)* buccula *f*
because *conj* quod, quia, quoniam; quippe qui
because of *prep* ob *(with acc)*, propter *(with acc)*, gratiā *(with genit)*
beck *s* nut·us -ūs *m*; **at the — and call** ad arbitrium
beckon *vt* nutare, annuĕre
become *vt* decēre; *vi* fieri
becoming *adj* decens; decorus; conveniens; **—ly** decenter; digne; honeste
bed *s* lectus *m*, cubile *n*; *(in a garden)* areŏla *f*; *(of a river)* alveus *m*; **to go to —** cubitum ire; **to make the — **lectum sternĕre
bedding *s* stragulum *n*
bedeck *vt* decorare, ornare
bedevil *vt* *(to enchant)* fascinare
bedfellow *s* tori socius *m*, tori socia *f*
bedlam *s* tumult·us -ūs *m*
bedpost *s* fulcrum *n*
bedraggled *adj* sordidus
bedridden *adj* **to be —** lecto tenēri
bedroom *s* cubiculum *n*
bedtime *s* hora somni *f*
bee *s* apis *f*
beef *s* bubula caro *f*
beehive *s* alveus *m*; alvearium *n*
beekeeper *s* apiarius *m*
beer *s* cerevisia *f*
beet *s* beta *f*
beetle *s* scarabaeus *m*
befall *vt* accidĕre *(with dat)*; contingĕre *(with dat)*; *vi* accidĕre, contingĕre, evenire
befit *vt* decēre, convenire in *(with acc)*
befitting *adj* decens; conveniens, idoneus; **it is —** decet
before *prep* ante *(with acc)*; prae *(with abl)*; pro *(with abl)*; coram *(with abl)*; apud *(with acc)*; **— all things** imprimis; **— long** jamdudum; **— now** antehac
before *conj* antequam, priusquam
beforehand *adv* antea
befriend *vt* favēre *(with dat)*, sublevare, adjuvare
beg *vt* petĕre, poscĕre, orare, obsecrare; *vi* mendicare
beget *vt* gignĕre, procreare, generare
beggar *s* mendicus *m*
begging *s* mendicitas *f*; **to go —** mendicare
begin *vt & vi* incipĕre, incohare, exordiri; **to — with** incipĕre ab *(with abl)*
beginner *s* auctor *m*; inceptor *m*; tiro *m*
beginning *s* inceptio *f*; initium *n*; exordium *n*; origo *f*; principium *n*; **at the — of winter** ineunte hieme
begone *interj* apage!
beguile *vt* fallĕre, fraudare
behalf *s* **on — of** pro *(with abl)*
behave *vi* se gerĕre; **to — towards**

uti (*with abl*); **well behaved** bene moratus

behavior *s* mores *m pl*

behead *vt* detruncare, obtruncare

beheading *s* decollatio *f*

behest *s* jussum *n*

behind *adv* pone, a tergo, post; **to be left—** relinqui

behind *prep* pone (*with acc*); post (*with acc*)

behold *vt* conspicĕre; obtuĕri

behold *interj* eccel, en!

being *s* ens *n*; natura *f*; essentia *f*; homo *m*

bejewelled *adj* gemmatus, gemmeus

belabor *vt* mulcare, verberare

belch *s* ruct·us -ūs *m*

belch *vi* ructare, eructare

belfry *s* campanile *n*

belie *vt* repugnare; (*to refute*) refutare, refellĕre

belief *s* fides *f*; opinio, persuasio *f*

believe *vt* (*thing*) credĕre; (*person*) credĕre (*with dat*); (*to suppose*) existimare, opinari, putare, credĕre, arbitrari; **to make—** simulare

believer *s* credens *m* & *f*; Christianus *m*

bell *s* (*large*) campana *f*; (*small*) tintinnabulum *n*

belle *s* formosa puella *f*

belles lettres *s* litterae *f pl*

belligerent *adj* belliger, belligerans, bellans

bellow *vi* rugire, mugire

bellowing *s* mugit·us -ūs *m*

bellows *s* follis *m*

belly *s* venter *m*; abdomen *n*

bellyache *s* tormina *n pl*

belong *vi* **to—** to esse (*with genit*); inesse (*with dat*); pertinēre ad (*with acc*)

beloved *adj* dilectus, carus; **dearly —** carissimus

below *adj* inferus

below *adv* infra; subter

below *prep* infra (*with acc*); sub (*with abl or acc*)

belt *s* cingulum *n*; (*swordbelt*) balteus *m*; zona *f*

bemoan *vt* deplorare, lamentari

bemused *adj* attonitus

bench *s* scamnum, sedile, subsellium *n*; (*for rowers*) transtrum *n*

bend *vt* flectĕre, curvare; inclinare; (*bow*) intendĕre; (*to persuade*) intendĕre; *vi* se inflectĕre; **to— back** reflectĕre; **to— down** *or* **over** se demittĕre

bend *s* plica *f*; flex·us -ūs *m*; curvamen *n*; (*fig*) inclinatio *f*

bending *s* flexura, curvatura, inclinatio *f*

bending *adj* flexus; inclinans; acclivis; declivis; (*concave*) concavus

beneath *adv* subter

beneath *prep* sub (*with acc or abl*)

benediction *s* benedictio *f*

benefaction *s* beneficium *n*

benefactor *s* largitor *m*; patronus *m*

benefactress *s* patrona *f*

beneficence *s* beneficentia *f*

beneficent *adj* beneficus, benignus, liberalis; **—ly** benefice

beneficial *adj* utilis, commodus; salutaris; **—ly** utiliter

benefit *s* beneficium *n*, gratia *f*; fruct·us -ūs *m*; **to have the—** of frui (*with abl*)

benefit *vt* juvare; prodesse (*with dat*); *vi* proficĕre; lucrari

benevolence *s* benevolentia *f*

benevolent *s* benevolus, beneficus; benignus, liberalis; **—ly** benevole

benign *adj* benignus; **—ly** benigne

bent *adj* curvus, flexus; (*of the mind*) attentus; **— backwards** recurvus; **— forwards** pronus; **— inwards** camur; sinuosus

bent *s* flex·us -ūs *m*, plica *f*; curvatura *f*; (*inclination*) ingenium *n*, inclinatio *f*

benumb *vt* torpore afficĕre

bequeath *vt* legare

bequest *s* legatum *n*

bereave *vt* orbare; privare; spoliare

bereavement *s* orbitas *f*; damnum *n*

bereft *adj* orbus, orbatus, privatus

berry *s* bacca *f*; acinus *m*

berth *s* statio *f*; (*cabin*) diaeta *f*; **to give wide—** to devitare

beseech *vt* obsecrare, implorare, supplicare

beset *vt* circumdare, obsidēre, circumsedēre; urgēre

beside *prep* ad (*with acc*), apud (*with acc*), juxta (*with acc*); **— the point** nihil ad rem; **to be— oneself** delirare

besides *adv* praeterea, ultro, insuper

besides *prep* praeter (*with acc*)

besiege *vt* circumsedēre, obsidēre

besieging *s* obsessio, circumsessio *f*

besmirch *vt* maculare

best *adj* optimus, praestantissimus; **the— part** major pars *f*

best *s* flos *m*; **to do one's—** pro virili parte agĕre; **to have the—** of it praevalēre, valēre; **to make the— of** aequo animo ferre; **to the— of one's ability** pro viribus

bestial *adj* bestialis; immanis

bestir *vt* **to— oneself** expergisci

bestow *vt* tribuĕre, conferre; donare, largiri

bestower *s* largitor, dator *m*

bet *s* pignus, depositum *n*

bet *vt* deponĕre; *vi* pignore contendēre

betide *vi* evenire, accidĕre

betoken *vt* indicare, portendĕre

betray *vt* tradĕre, prodĕre; (*feelings*) arguĕre

betrayer *s* proditor, traditor *m*

betroth *vt* spondēre, despondēre

betrothal *s* sponsalia *n pl*; pactio nuptialis *f*

betrothed *adj* sponsus, pactus

better *adj* melior; potior, praestantior; superior; **it is—** praestat; **to get— convalescĕre; to get the—** of superare, vincĕre

better *adv* melius, potius; praestantius; rectius; satius

better vt meliorem facĕre; corrigĕre; **to — oneself** proficĕre
betters s superiores m pl
between prep inter (with acc); **— whiles** interim
betwixt prep inter (with acc)
bevel vt obliquare
beverage s potio f, pot·us -ūs m
bevy s grex f
bewail vt deplorare, ingemĕre, queri, lamentari
beware vi cavēre; **to — of** cavēre
bewilder vt perturbare, confundĕre
bewilderment s perturbatio f
bewitch vt fascinare; (to charm) demulcēre
beyond adv supra, ultra; ulterius
beyond prep ultra (with acc); (motion) trans (with acc); supra (with acc), extra (with acc); **to go —** excedĕre
bias s inclinatio f; praeponderatio f
bias vt inclinare
Bible s divina scriptura f, biblia n pl
Biblical adj biblicus
bibliography s bibliographia f
bicker vi jurgare, altercari
bickering s altercatio f
bid vt jubēre, mandare, rogare; (to invite) invitare; (at auction) licitari, licēri; **to — farewell** valedicĕre
bid s licitatio f; **to make a —** licēri
bidder s licitator m
bidding s jussum n; (auction) licitatio f
bide vt exspectare, manēre
biennial adj biennalis, bimus
bier s feretrum n, sandapila f
big adj ingens, vastus; grandis, amplus; **— with child** gravida; **— with young** praegnans; **very —** permagnus
bigamist s bimaritus m
bigamy s bigamia f
bigot s nimis obstinatus fautor m
bigoted adj nimis obstinatus
bigotry s contumacia f; nimia obstinatio f
bile s bilis f
bilge water s sentina f
bilious adj biliosus
bilk vt fraudare; frustrari
bill s (of a bird) rostrum n; (proposed law) rogatio f; lex f; plebiscitum n; (com) ratio debiti f; syngrapha f; (notice) libellus m; **to introduce a —** ferre, legem ferre; populum rogare; **to pass a —** legem perferre; **to turn down a —** antiquare
billet s hospitium n
billet vt per hospitia dispargĕre
billion s billio m
billow s fluct·us -ūs m
billowy adj fluctuosus, undabundus
bin s (in wine cellar) loculus m; (for grain) cista f, panarium n
bind vt ligare, nectĕre, stringĕre, vincire; (by obligation) obligare; (books) conglutinare; (wounds) obligare; **to — fast** devincire; **to — together** colligare; **to — up** alligare; (med) astringĕre

binding adj obligatorius; (law) ratus
binding s religatio f; compages f
biographer s vitae scriptor m
biography s vita f
biped s bipes m
birch adj betulinus
birch tree s betula f
bird s avis, volucris f
birdcage s cavea f
birdcall s fistula aucupatoria f
birdlime s viscum n
bird's nest s nidus m
birth s part·us -ūs m; ort·us -ūs m; (race) genus n
birthday s dies natalis m
birthday cake s libum n
birthplace s patria f
birthright s patrimonium n
biscuit s crustulum n
bisect vt dividĕre
bishop s episcopus m
bison s bison m; urus m
bit s (for a horse) frenum n; (small amount) pars f, fragmentum n; (of food) frustum n; **— by —** minutatim
bitch s canis f
bite s mors·us -ūs m; (fig) sarcasmus m
bite vt mordēre; (as pepper, frost, etc.) urēre
biting adj mordax; (fig) asper; mordens
bitter adj amarus; (fig) acerbus; asper; gravis; **—ly** acerbe; aspere
bitterness s amaritas f; (fig) acerbitas f; asperitas f
bitters s absinthium n
bivouac s excubiae f pl
blab s garrulus m
blab vi garrīre, deblaterare
black adj niger; ater; (in looks) trux; (of character) scelestus
black s nigrum n; (negro) Aethiops m; **in — pullatus**
black-and-blue adj lividus
blackberry s morum n
blackbird s merula f
black death s pestis f
blacken vt nigrare; denigrare
blackguard s nebulo m
blacklist s proscriptio f
black magic s magicae artes f pl
blackness s nigritia, nigrities f
blacksmith s ferrarius faber m
bladder s vesica f
blade s (edge) lamina f; (of grass) caulis m, herba f; (of oar) palma f
blamable adj culpabilis; reus
blame vt reprehendĕre, culpare, vituperare
blame s culpa f; reprehensio f
blameless adj integer, innoxius; irreprehensus; **—ly** integre, innocenter
blanch vt candefacĕre; vi exalbescĕre, pallescĕre
bland adj blandus
blandishment s blanditia f, blandimentum n; (charm) lenocinium n
blank adj vacuus, albus, purus; (expression) stolidus

blanket s lodix f; stragulum n

blare s strepit·us -ūs, clangor, stridor m

blare vi stridēre, canēre

blaspheme vi maledicēre, execrari; blasphemare

blasphemous adj maledicus, impius; blasphemus

blasphemy s maledicta n pl, impietas f; blasphemia, blasphematio f

blast s flat·us -ūs m, flamen n

blast vt discutēre, disjicēre; (crops) urēre, robigine afficēre

blaze s flamma f; fulgor m

blaze vi flagrare, ardēre; **to — up** exardescēre

bleach vt dealbare, candefacēre

bleak adj desertus; immitis

blear-eyed adj lippus; **to be — lippire**

bleat vi balare

bleating s balat·us -ūs m

bleed vi sanguinem fundēre

bleeding adj crudus, sanguineus

bleeding s (bloodletting) sanguinis missio f; (flowing of blood) sanguinis profusio f

blemish s macula f, vitium n; labes f

blemish vt maculare, foedare

blend vt commiscēre, immiscēre

bless vt beare; (eccl) benedicēre; (consecrate) consecrare; (with success) secundare

blessed adj beatus; pius; fortunatus; (of emperors) divus

blessing s (thing) bonum, commodum n; (eccl) benedictio f

blight s robigo, uredo f

blight vt urēre; robigine afficēre; (fig) nocēre (with dat)

blind adj caecus; obscurus; (fig) ignarus; **—ly** (rashly) temere

blind vt caecare, occaecare; (fig) occaecare, fallēre

blindfold vt oculos obligare (with dat)

blindfolded adj obligatis oculis

blindness s caecitas f; (fig) temeritas f; stultitia f

blink vi connivēre

bliss s beatitudo f

blissful adj beatus; **—ly** beate

blister s pustula f

blister vt & vi pustulare

blithe adj hilaris, hilarus

bloated adj tumidus, turgidus

block s truncus, stipes m; (of stone) massa f; (of houses) insula f

block vt claudēre; (to impede) obstare (with dat); **to — up** obstruēre

blockade s obsidio f; **to raise a —** obsidionem solvēre

blockade vt obsidēre, claudēre

blockhead s caudex m

blood s sanguis m; (gore) cruor m, sanies f; (fig) (slaughter) caedes f; (lineage) genus n; **bad — simultas** f; **to staunch — sanguinem supprimēre**

bloodless adj exsanguis; (without bloodshed) incruentus

blood-red adj cruentus; sanguineus, sanguinolentus

bloodshed s caedes f

bloodshot adj cruore suffusus

bloodstained adj cruentus, cruentatus, sanguinolentus

bloodsucker s sanguisuga f; hirudo f

bloodthirsty adj sanguinarius; sanguinolentus

blood vessel s vena f

bloody adj cruentus

bloom s flos m

bloom vi florēre, florescēre; vigēre

blooming adj florens; floridus; nitidus

blossom s flos m

blot s macula, litura f; (fig) labes f, dedecus n

blot vt maculare; conspurcare; **to — out** delēre; (to erase) oblitterare

blotch s macula f; pustula f

blotched adj maculosus

blow s (stroke) plaga f, ict·us -ūs m; (with the fist) colaphus m; (fig) plaga f; calamitas f

blow vt (instrument) canēre; (breath) anhelare; **to — out** extinguēre; **to — the nose** emungēre; **to — up** inflare; vi flare; (of a flower) efflorescēre; **to — over** (of a storm) cadēre; (fig) abire

blowing s sufflatio f; flat·us -ūs m; (of the nose) emunctio f

blowup s scandalum n; (scolding) objurgatio f

blubber s adeps balaenarum m

blubber vi lacrimas effundēre

blue adj caeruleus

blueness s caeruleum n

blues s melancholia f

bluff s rupes f; promunturium n

bluff adj rusticus; declivis; ventosus

bluff vt fallēre, decipēre; vi ampullari, gloriari

blunder s (in writing) mendum n; error m, erratum n

blunder vi offendēre, errare

blunderer s homo ineptus m

blunt adj hebes; obtusus; (fig) inurbanus, rusticus; **—ly** plane, liberius

blunt vt hebetare, obtundēre, retundēre

bluntness s hebetudo f; (fig) candor m

blur s macula f

blur vt obscurare

blurt vt **to — out** inconsultum projicēre

blush s rubor m

blush vi erubescēre

bluster vi declamitare; fremēre, strepēre

bluster s jactatio, declamatio f; fremit·us -ūs, strepit·us -ūs m

boar s aper m; verres m

board s (plank) tabula f; (table) mensa f; (food) vict·us -ūs m; (council, etc.) collegium n; consilium n; concilium n; (judicial) quaestio f; (for games) abacus, alveus m

board vt **to — a ship** navem conscendēre; **to — up** contabulare; vi **to — with** devertēre ad (with acc)

boarder s convictor, hospes m

boardinghouse *s* contubernium *n*

boast *vi* se jactare, gloriari

boast *s* jactantia, jactatio, gloriatio, vanitas *f*

boastful *adj* gloriosus; —**ly** gloriose

boasting *s* gloriatio *f*

boat *s* linter *f*; cymba *f*; scapha *f*; navicula *f*

boatman *s* nauta, lintrarius *m*

bode *vt* portendĕre, praesagire

bodiless *adj* incorporalis

bodily *adj* corporeus; corporalis; in persona

bodily *adv* corporaliter

body *s* corpus *n*; (*corpse*) cadaver *n*; truncus *m*; (*person*) homo *m*; (*of troops*) man·us -ūs, caterva *f*; (*of cavalry*) turma *f*; (*of people*) numerus *m*, multitudo *f*; (*heavenly*) astrum *n*

bodyguard *s* stipatores, satellites *m pl*; cohors praetoria *f*

bog *s* palus *f*

boil *vt* fervefacĕre, coquĕre; **to** — **down** decoquĕre; *vi* fervēre, effervescĕre; (*fig*) aestuare

boil *s* furunculus *m*, ulcus *n*

boiler *s* (*vessel*) ahenum, caldarium *n*; (*kettle*) lebes *m*

boisterous *adj* procellosus; violentus, turbidus; —**ly** turbide, turbulente

bold *adj* audax; impavidus; (*rash*) temerarius; (*saucy*) insolens, protervus, impudens; (*language*) liber; (*stout*) intrepidus; —**ly** audacter; temere; fortiter; insolenter

boldness *s* audacia, fidentia *f*; (*in speech*) libertas, impudentia *f*

bolster *s* pulvinar *n*; (*of a bed*) cervical *n*

bolster *vt* supportare, adjuvare; **to** — **up** suffulcire

bolt *s* (*of a door*) pessulus *m*; (*of thunder*) fulmen *n*; (*pin*) clavus *m*; (*missile*) sagitta *f*, telum *n*

bolt *vt* obserare, oppessulare, claudĕre, occludĕre

bomb *s* pyrobolus *m*

bombard *vt* tormentis verberare; (*fig*) lacessĕre

bombardment *s* tormentis verberatio *f*

bombast *s* ampulla *f pl*

bombastic *adj* inflatus, tumidus; **to be** — ampullari

bond *s* vinculum *n*; nodus *m*; copula, catena *f*, jugum *n*; (*document*) syngrapha *f*

bondage *s* servitus *f*, servitium *n*; captivitas *f*

bondsman *s* servus *m*; verna *m*; addictus *m*

bone *s* os *n*; (*of fish*) spina *f*

boneless *adj* exos

bonfire *s* ignes festi *m pl*

bonnet *s* redimiculum *n*

bony *adj* osseus

book *s* liber *m*; volumen *n*; codex *m*;

bookcase *s* foruli *m pl*; librarium *n*; pegma *n*

bookish *adj* libris deditus

bookkeeper *s* calculator *m*; actuarius *m*

bookshelf *s* pluteus *m*

bookstore *s* bibliopolum *n*, libraria taberna *f*

bookworm *s* tinea *f*; (*fig*) librorum helluo *m*

boom *s* (*of a ship*) longurius *m*; (*of a harbor*) obex *m* & *f*, repagulum *n*

boom *vi* resonare

boon *s* bonum, donum *n*

boor *s* rusticus *m*

boorish *adj* agrestis, rusticus; —**ly** rustice

boost *vt* efferre

boot *s* calceus *m*; caliga *f*; (*peasant's*) pero *m*; (*tragic*) cothurnus *m*; **to** — insuper

boot *vi* prodesse; **what boots it?** cui bono?

booth *s* taberna *f*, tabernaculum *n*

booty *s* praeda *f*; spolia *n pl*

border *s* (*edge*) margo *m* & *f*; (*seam*) limbus *m*, fimbria *f*; (*boundary*) finis, terminus *m*

border *vt* tangĕre, attingĕre; circumjacēre; *vi* **to** — **on** adjacēre (*with dat*), attingĕre; imminēre (*with dat*)

bordering *adj* affinis, finitimus

bore *vt* terebrare, perforare; excavare; (*fig*) (*to weary*) obtundĕre, fatigare

bore *s* (*tool*) terebra *f*; (*hole*) foramen *n*; (*fig*) importunus, molestus *m*

borer *s* terebra *f*

born *adj* natus; genitus; **to be** — nasci; (*fig*) oriri

borough *s* municipium *n*

borrow *vt* mutuari; (*fig*) imitari

borrowed *adj* mutuatus, mutuus; alienus

borrowing *s* mutuatio *f*

bosom *s* (*breast*) pectus *n*; sin·us -ūs *m*; (*of female*) mammillae *f pl*; (*fig*) gremium *m*

Bosphorus *s* Bosporus *m*

boss *s* bulla *f*; (*of a shield*) umbo *m*; (*of a book*) umbilicus *m*

boss *vt* (*to order about*) dominari in (*with acc*)

botanical *adj* botanicus

botanist *s* herbarius *m*

botany *s* herbaria *f*

botch *s* bubo, carbunculus *m*; (*bungling work*) scruta *n pl*

botch *vt* male sarcire; male gerĕre

both *adj* ambo; uterque

both *pron* ambo; uterque

both *conj* — . . . **and** et . . . et; cum . . . tum; vel . . . vel

bother *vt* vexare, sollicitare; molestus esse (*with dat*); *vi* **to** — **about** operam dare (*with dat*)

bother *s* negotium *n*; vexatio *f*; sollicitudo *f*

bottle *s* ampulla *f*; lagoena *f*

bottle *vt* in ampullas infundĕre

bottom *s* fundus *m*; (*of a ship*) carina *f*; (*dregs*) faex *f*, sedimentum *n*; (*of a mountain*) radix *f*; **the** — **of** imus; **the** — **of the sea** imum mare *n*

bottom *adj* imus, infimus

bottomless *adj* fundo carens, immensus; profundus

bough *s* ramus *m*

boulder *s* saxum *n*

bounce *vi* resilire, resultare

bound *adj* alligatus, obligatus, obstrictus; **it is — to happen** necesse est accidat; **to be — for** tendĕre ad (*with acc*)

bound *s* salt·us -ūs *m*; (*limit*) modus, terminus *m*; **to set —s** modum facĕre

bound *vt* finire, definire, terminare; *vi* (*to leap*) salire

boundary *s* finis, terminus *m*; (*fortified*) limes *m*

boundless *adj* infinitus, immensus; profundus

bountiful *adj* largus, benignus; **—ly** benigne, large

bounty *s* largitas, benignitas, liberalitas *f*; copia *f*

bouquet *s* corollarium *n*; (*of wine*) flos m

bow *s* arc·us -ūs *m*

bow *s* (*of a ship*) prora *f*; (*greeting*) summissio capitis *f*

bow *vt* flectĕre, inclinare; (*one's head*) demittĕre; *vi* flecti; (*fig*) **to — to** (*to accede to*) obtemperare (*with dat*), obsequi

bowels *s* intestina, viscera *n pl*

bower *s* trichila *f*, umbraculum *n*

bowl *s* cratera, patera *f*; (*for cooking*) catina *f*

bowlegged *adj* valgus

bowman *s* sagittarius *m*

bowstring *s* nervus *m*

box *s* arca, cista *f*; scrinium *n*; (*for medicine*) pyxis *f*; (*tree*) buxus *f*

box *vt* includĕre; pugnis certare cum (*with abl*); **to — the ears of** alapam adhibēre (*with dat*)

boxer *s* pugil *m*

boxing glove *s* caest·us -ūs *m*

boxing match *s* pugilatio *f*

boy *s* puer, puerulus *m*

boyhood *s* pueritia *f*; aetas puerilis *f*

boyish *adj* puerilis; **—ly** pueriliter

brace *s* (*strap*) fascia *f*; (*couple*) par *m*; copula *f*; (*in architecture*) fibula *f*

brace *vt* ligare, alligare; (*to strengthen*) firmare

bracelet *s* armilla *f*

bracket *s* mutulus *m*; **—s** (*in writing*) unci *m pl*

brag *vi* se jactare, gloriari

braggart *s* jactator, salaco *m*

bragging *s* jactantia *f*

braid *s* limbus *m*; (*of hair*) cincinnus *m*

braid *vt* plectĕre, plicare

brain *s* cerebrum *n*; ingenium *n*

brainless *adj* stolidus, inconsultus, socors

brake *s* (*fern*) filix *f*; (*thicket*) dumetum *n*; (*on wheel*) sufflamen *n*

bramble *s* rubus *m*; (*thicket*) rubetum *n*; (*thorny bush*) sentis, vepris *m*

branch *s* (*of tree*) ramus *m*; (*of pedigree*) stemma *n*; (*division*) pars *f*

branch *vi* (*of trees*) germinare; **to**

— out ramos porrigĕre; (*fig*) dividi, scindi, diffundi

brand *s* (*mark*) stigma *n*, nota *f*; (*of fire*) fax *f*, torris *m*; (*type*) genus *n*

brand *vt* inurĕre, notare

branding iron *s* cauter *m*

brandish *vt* vibrare

brandy *s* aqua vitae *f*; vini spirit·us -ūs *m*; spirit·us -ūs gallicus *m*

brass *s* orichalcum, aes *n*

brat *s* infans *m & f*

brave *adj* fortis, animosus, strenuus; **—ly** fortiter, strenue

brave *vt* sustinēre

bravery *s* fortitudo *f*; virtus *f*

bravo *interj* eu!, euge!, bene!, macte!

brawl *s* rixa *f*, jurgium *n*

brawl *vi* rixari, jurgare

brawler *s* rixator, rabula *m*

brawling *adj* contentiosus, jurgans

brawn *s* callum aprugnum *n*; (*muscle*) lacertus, torus *m*

brawny *adj* lacertosus, robustus

bray *vi* (*of asses*) rudĕre; (*of elephants*) barrire; (*to cry out*) emugire

braying *s* tritura *f*; barrit·us -ūs *m*; rugit·us -ūs *m*

brazen *adj* aēnus; (*fig*) impudens

brazier *s* foculus *m*

breach *s* ruptura, ruina *f*; (*of treaty*) violatio *f*; dissidium *n*

bread *s* panis *m*; (*fig*) vict·us -ūs *m*

breadth *s* latitudo *f*

break *vt* frangĕre; rumpĕre; **to — apart** diffringĕre; **to — down** demoliri, destruĕre; **to — in** (*to tame*) domare, subigĕre; **to — in pieces** dirumpĕre; **to — off** abrumpĕre; (*friendship or action*) dirumpĕre; (*a meeting*) interrumpĕre; **to — open** effringĕre; **to — up** interrumpĕre, dissolvĕre; *vi* frangi; rumpi; (*of day*) illucescĕre; (*of strength*) deficĕre; **to — forth** erumpĕre; **to — into** irrumpĕre; invadĕre; **to — off** desinĕre; **to — out** erumpĕre; (*of trouble*) exardescĕre; (*of war*) exoriri; (*of fire*) grassari; **to — through** perrumpĕre; **to — up** dissolvi, dilabi; (*of a meeting*) dimitti; **to — with** dissidere ab (*with abl*)

break *s* interruptio *f*, intervallum *n*; interstitium *n*

breakage *s* fractura *f*

breakdown *s* calamitas *f*; frustratio *f*; (*of health*) debilitas *f*; (*of a machine*) defect·us -ūs *m*

breaker *s* fluct·us -ūs *m*

breakfast *s* prandium *n*

breakfast *vi* prandēre

breakup *s* dissolutio *f*

breast *s* pectus *n*; (*of a woman*) mamma *f*; (*fig*) praecordia *n pl*; **to make a clean — of** confitēri

breastbone *s* sternum *n*; os pectorale *n*

breastplate *s* lorica *f*; thorax *m*

breath *s* spirit·us -ūs *m*, anima *f*; halit·us -ūs *m*; **— of air** aura *f*; **deep —** anhelit·us -ūs *m*; **to catch one's —** obstipescĕre; **to hold**

one's breath animam continēre;
to take one's — away exanimare;
to waste one's — operam perdēre
breathe vt ducēre; spirare; (to whisper) susurrare; **to — out** exspirare; vi spirare, respirare; **to —
upon** inspirare (with dat)
breathing s respiratio f; halit·us
-ūs m; (gram) spirit·us -ūs m
breathless adj exanimis, exanimus;
exanimatus
breeches s bracae f pl
breed s genus n
breed vt parēre, gignēre; (to cause)
producēre; (to engender) procreare,
educare; (to raise) alēre; (horses)
pascēre
breeder s (man) generator m; (stallion) admissarius m; (animal) matrix; (fig) nutrix f
breeding s fetura f; educatio f; **good
— urbanitas, humanitas f
breeze s aura f
breezy adj ventosus
brethren s fratres m pl
brevity s brevitas, breviloquentia f
brew vt coquēre; vi excitari, concitari
bribe s pretium n, merces f
bribe vt corrumpēre, largiri
briber s corruptor, largitor m
bribery s corruptio, corruptela, largitio f; ambit·us -ūs m
brick s later m
brick adj latericius
bricklayer s laterum structor m
bridal adj nuptialis
bride s nupta f
bridegroom s maritus m
bridesmaid s pronuba f
bridge s pons m
bridge vt pontem imponēre (with
dat)
bridle s frenum n
brief adj brevis, concisus; **—ly** breviter, paucis verbis
brief s diploma n; sententiola f; summarium n
brigade s (infantry) legio f; (cavalry) turma f
brigadier s tribunus militum m
brigand s latro, latrunculus m
bright adj clarus; lucidus, splendidus;
nitidus, candidus; (flashing) fulgidus; (smart) argutus; **—ly** lucide,
clare, splendide
brighten vt illustrare, illuminare; vi
lucescēre; splendescēre; clarescēre;
(of a person) in hilaritatem solvi
brightness s nitor, splendor, fulgor,
candor m; (of the sky) serenitas f
brilliance s splendor m; fulgor m;
(of style) nitor m, lumen n
brilliant adj splendidus; nitens; (fig)
praeclarus, insignis, luculentus;
—ly splendide, praeclare, luculenter
brim s ora, margo f, labrum n; **to
fill to the —** explēre
brimful adj ad summum plenus
brimstone s sulfur m
brine s muria f, salsamentum n; (sea)
salum n
bring vt ferre, afferre, inferre; (by

carriage, etc.) advehēre; **to —
about** efficēre, perducēre; **to —
back** referre, reducēre; reportare;
(fig) revocare; (by force) redigēre;
dejicēre; **to — forth** prodēre, depromēre; parēre; (to yield) ferre,
efferre; **to — forward** proferre,
efferre, agēre; **to — in** inferre; invehēre; inducēre; (as a farm, etc.)
reddēre; **to — off** dissuadēre; **to
— on** afferre; adducēre; (fig) objicēre; **to — out** efferre; producēre;
excire; **to — over** perducēre, traducēre; (fig) perducēre, trahēre;
conciliare; **to — to** adducēre; appellēre; (fig) persuadēre; **to — together** conferre; (to assemble) contrahēre; (fig) conciliare; **to — to
pass** efficēre; **to — under** subigēre; **to — up** subducēre; (children) educare; (to vomit) evomēre
brink s margo f; ora f; (fig) extremitas f
brisk adj alacer, agilis, vividus; laetus; **to be —** vigēre; **—ly** alacriter, agiliter
briskness s alacritas f, vigor m
bristle s seta f
bristle vi horrēre
bristly adj setiger, setosus; hirsutus; horridus
Britain s Britannia f
British adj Britannicus
brittle adj fragilis
broach vt in medium proferre
broad adj latus, largus, amplus;
(fig) manifestus, apertus; **—ly** late
broadcast vt divulgare, disseminare
broaden vt dilatare
broadsword s gladius m
brocade s Attalica n pl
broccoli s brassica oleracea Botrytis f
brochure s libellus m
broil s rixa, turba f
broil vt torrēre
broken adj fractus; intermissus; dirutus; (fig) confectus; (of speech)
refractus, infractus, corrupte pronuntiatus
brokenhearted adj abjectus, dejectus
broker s transactor, institor m
bronze s aes n
bronze adj aeneus, a(h)enus, aeratus
brooch s fibula f
brood s proles f; (chicks) pullities f
brood vi (as a hen) incubare; (fig)
to — over agitare, meditari
brook vt ferre, tolerare
broom s genista f; scopae f pl
broth s jus n
brothel s lupanar n, ganea f
brother s frater m
brotherhood s germanitas, fraternitas f; (fig) sodalitium n
brother-in-law s levir m; sororis
maritus m
brotherly adj fraternus
brow s supercilium n; frons f; (of a
hill) dorsum n
browbeat vt terrēre, deprimēre, exagitare, objurgare

brown adj fulvus, fuscus, spadix; (of skin) adustus

browse vi depasci

bruise vt contundĕre, sugillare; infringĕre

bruise s contusio f, contusum n, sugillatio f

brunette s puella subfusca f

brunt s impet·us -ūs m; vehementia f

brush s scopula f; (painter's) penicillus m; (bushy tail) muscarium m; (skirmish) aggressio f

brush vt verrĕre, purgare; **to — aside** neglegĕre, spernĕre; **to — away** amovēre

brutal adj atrox, immanis, inhumanus; **—ly** atrociter, immaniter, inhumane

brutality s atrocitas, ferocitas, saevitia, immanitas f

brute adj brutus; stupidus

brute s belua, bestia f

brutish adj ferinus; stupidus

bubble s bulla f

bubble vi bullire; (to gush up) scatēre

bubbling s bullit·us -ūs m; scatebra f

buccaneer s pirata m

buck s cervus m; (he-goat) hircus m; (male rabbit) cuniculus m

bucket s hama, situla, fidelia f

buckle vt fibulā nectĕre; vi flectĕre

buckle s fibula f, spinther m

buckler s parma f

bucolic adj bucolicus, agrestis

bud s gemma f, germen n; (of a flower) flosculus m

bud vi gemmare, germinare

budding s germinatio f; emplastratio f

budge vt ciēre, movēre; vi movēri, cedĕre

budget s saccus m; publicae pecuniae ratio f

buffalo s urus m

buffet s (sideboard) abacus m; (slap) alapa f; (fig) plaga f

buffet vt jactare

buffoon s scurra m; sannio, balatro m; **to play the —** scurrari

bug s cimex m & f

bugle s buccina f

build vt aedificare, struĕre, condĕre; (road) munire; (hopes) ponĕre; **to — up** exstruĕre

builder s aedificator, structor m

building s (act) aedificatio f; extructio f; (structure) aedificium n

bulb s bulbus m

bulge vi tumēre, tumescĕre; prominēre

bulk s amplitudo, magnitudo f; (mass) moles f; (greater part) major pars f

bulkiness s magnitudo f

bulky adj crassus; ingens; corpulentus; onerosus

bull s taurus m

bulldog s canis Molossus m

bullet s glans f

bulletin s libellus m

bullfrog s rana ocellata f

bullion s aurum infectum n; argentum infectum n; massa f

bully s salaco, thraso m

bully vt procaciter lacessĕre

bulwark s agger m; propugnaculum n; moenia n pl

bump s (swelling) tuber n; (thump) plaga f

bump vt pulsare, pellĕre; vi **to — against** offendĕre

bun s libum n, placenta f

bunch s fasciculus m; (of grapes) racemus m

bundle s fascis, fasciculus m; vesiculus m

bundle vt consarcinare

bungle vt inscite gerĕre; inscite agĕre; vi errare

bungler s homo rudis m

buoy s cortex m

buoy vt **to — up** attollĕre, sublevare

buoyancy s levitas f; (fig) hilaritas f

buoyant adj levis; (fig) hilaris

burden s onus n; (fig) scrupulus m

burden vt onerare; opprimĕre

burdensome adj onerosus, gravis, molestus

bureau s armarium, scrinium n

burglar s fur m

burglary s (domūs) effractura f

burial s (act) sepultura f; (ceremony) funus n

burial place s sepulturae locus m; sepulcrum n

burlesque s ridicula imitatio f

burly adj corpulentus

burn vt urĕre, cremare; (to set on fire) incendĕre; **to — down** deurĕre; **to — out** exurĕre; **to — up** amburĕre, comburĕre; vi flagrare; ardēre; **to — out** extingui; **to — up** conflagrare

burn s adustio f; combustum n

burning s ustio, adustio f; deflagratio f

burning adj ardens; fervens

burrow s cuniculus m

burrow vi defodĕre

bursar s dispensator m

burst s impet·us -ūs m; eruptio f; (noise) fragor m

burst vt rumpĕre, dirumpĕre; **to — open** effrangĕre; vi dirumpi; **to — forth** prorumpĕre; (of tears) prosilire; **to — in** irrumpĕre; **to — out** erumpĕre; **to — out laughing** cachinnum tollĕre

bury vt sepelire; (to hide) abdĕre, condĕre

bush s dumetum n, frutex m; (of hair) caesaries f

bushel s medimnus, modius m

bushy adj (full of bushes) dumosus; (bush-like) fruticosus

busily adv industrie, sedulo, impigre

business s negotium n; (trade, calling) ars f; (employment) occupatio f; (matter) res f; **to mind one's own —** negotium suum agĕre

businessman s negotiator m

buskin s cothurnus m

bust s imago f; effigies f

bustle s festinatio f; trepidatio f

bustle *vi* festinare; trepidare; **to —
about** discurrĕre
busy *adj* occupatus; negotiosus; operosus, impiger; (*meddling*) molestus
busybody *s* ardelio *m*
but *prep* praeter (*with acc*)
but *adv* modo, tantum
but *conj* sed; ast, at; atqui; ceterum;
vero, verum; autem; **— if** quodsi;
sin, sin autem; **— if not** sin aliter, sin minus
butcher *s* lanius *m*; (*fig*) carnifex *m*
butcher *vt* (*animals*) caedĕre; (*people*) trucidare
butcher shop *s* macellum *n*
butchery *s* caedes, trucidatio *f*
butler *s* promus *m*
butt *s* (*mark*) meta *f*; (*cask*) dolium
n; (*mound*) agger *m*; **— of ridicule** ludibrium *n*
butt *vt* arietare; *vi* **to — in** interpellare
butter *s* butyrum *n*
butter *vt* butyro inducĕre
buttercup *s* ranunculus tuberosus *m*
butterfly *s* papilio *m*
buttermilk *s* lactis serum *n*
buttock *s* clunis *m & f*

button *s* bulla *f*
button *vt* nectĕre, confibulare
buttress *s* anterides *f pl*; fulcrum *n*
buttress *vt* suffulcire
buxom *adj* alacer, hilaris, laetus
buy *vt* emĕre, mercari; **to — back**
or **off** redimĕre; **to — up** coemĕre
buyer *s* emptor *m*
buying *s* emptio *f*
buzz *s* bombus *m*; murmur *n*
buzz *vi* bombilare; (*in the ear*) insusurrare
buzzard *s* buteo *m*
by *prep* (*agency*) a, ab (*with abl*);
(*of place*) ad (*with acc*), apud (*with
acc*), juxta (*with acc*), prope (*with
acc*); (*along*) secundum (*with acc*);
(*past*) praeter (*with acc*); (*of time*)
ante (*with acc*); (*in oaths*) per (*with
acc*); **— and —** mox; **— means of**
per (*with acc*); **— oneself** solus
bygone *adj* praeteritus; priscus
bylaw *s* praescriptum *n*; regula *f*
bystander *s* arbiter *m*
byway *s* trames *m*, semita *f*, dever-
ticulum *n*
byword *s* adagium *n*

C

cabal *s* factio *f*; societas clandestina
f
cabbage *s* brassica *f*, caulis *m*
cabin *s* (*cottage*) tugurium *n*; (*on a
ship*) stega *f*
cabinet *s* armarium *n*; scrinium *n*;
cistula *f*; (*in government*) principis
consilium *n*
cable *s* funis, rudens *m*; (*anchor*) an-
corale *n*
cackle *vi* gracillare; (*fig*) deblaterare
cackle *s* glocitatio *f*; (*fig*) gerrae
f pl; clangor *m*
cacophony *s* dissonae voces *f pl*
cactus *s* cactus *f*
cadaver *s* cadaver *n*
cadence *s* numerus *m*
cadet *s* tiro *m*; discipulus militaris *m*
cage *s* cavea *f*, aviarium *n*; septum *n*
cage *vt* includĕre
cajole *vt* inescare, lactare, blandiri
cake *s* libum *n*, placenta *f*
calamitous *adj* calamitosus; funestus; exitiosus
calamity *s* calamitas *f*; clades *f*; malum *n*; res adversae *f pl*
calculate *vt* computare; (*fig*) aestimare, existimare
calculated *adj* aptus, accommodatus
calculation *s* computatio, ratio *f*;
(*fig*) ratiocinatio *f*
calculator *s* computator *m*; ratio-
cinator *m*
caldron *s* ahenum *n*, lebes *m*
calendar *s* fasti *m pl*; calendarium *n*
calends *s* Kalendae *f pl*
calf *s* vitulus *m*; (*of the leg*) sura *f*

caliber *s* (*fig*) ingenium *n*, indoles *f*
call *vt* vocare; (*to name*) appellare;
to — aside sevocare; **to — away**
avocare; (*fig*) devocare; **to — back**
revocare; **to — down** devocare; **to
— forth** evocare, provocare; (*fig*)
exciĕre, elicĕre; **to — in** advocare;
(*money*) cogĕre; **to — off** avocare,
revocare; **to — together** convocare; **to — to mind** recordari; **to
— to witness** testari; **to — up**
excitare, suscitare, elicĕre; *vi* **to —
on** *or* **upon** (*for help*) implorare;
(*to visit*) visĕre
call *s* vocatio *f*; clamor *m*; (*visit*) salutatio *f*; (*requisition*) postulatio *f*;
(*whistle*) fistula *f*
calling *s* (*profession*) ars *f*, artificium *n*
callous *adj* callosus; (*fig*) durus; expers sensūs; **to become —** occal-
lescĕre; obduescĕre
calm *adj* tranquillus, placidus, sedatus, quietus; (*mentally*) aequus;
—ly tranquille, aequo animo, placide
calm *s* tranquillitas *f*, tranquillum *n*
calm *vt* pacare, placare, sedare, mulcĕre; *vi* **to — down** defervescĕre
calmness *s* tranquillitas *f*; serenitas
f
calumny *s* maledictum *n*, obtrectatio
f, opprobria *n pl*
camel *s* camelus *m*
cameo *s* imago ectypa *f*
camouflage *s* dissimulatio *f*
camouflage *vt* dissimulare

camp *s* castra *n pl*; **summer** — aestiva *n pl*; **to strike** — castra movēre; **winter** — hiberna *n pl*

camp *adj* castrensis

camp *vi* castra ponĕre

campaign *s* aestiva *n pl*; stipendium *n*; expeditio *f*

campaign *vi* stipendium merēre; expeditioni interesse

campaigner *s* veteranus *m*

camphor *s* camphora *f*

can *s* hirnea *f*

can *vi* posse; scire; **I — not** nequeo; nescio

canal *s* fossa navigabilis *f*

canary *s* fringilla Canaria *f*

cancel *vt* delēre, expungĕre; abrogare, tollĕre

cancellation *s* deletio, abolitio *f*

cancer *s* cancer *m*

cancerous *adj* cancerosus, canceraticus

candid *adj* candidus, apertus, liber, simplex; —ly candide

candidacy *s* petitio *f*

candidate *s* petitor *m*; candidatus *m*

candied *adj* saccharo conditus

candle *s* candela *f*; (*taper*) cera *f*

candlelight *s* lucerna *f*; **to study by** — lucubrare

candlestick *s* candelabrum *n*

candor *s* candor *m*, simplicitas, ingenuitas *f*

candy *s* saccharum crystallinum *n*

cane *s* baculus *m*; virga *f*; (*reed*) harundo *f*

cane *vt* baculo *or* virgā ferire; verberare

canine *adj* caninus

canister *s* canistrum *n*, pyxis *f*

canker *s* (*of plants*) rubigo, robigo *f*; (*fig*) aerugo *f*

cannibal *s* anthropophagus *m*

cannon *s* tormentum *n*

cannon shot *s* tormenti ict·us -ūs *m*

canoe *s* linter *m*

canon *s* regula, norma *f*; canon *m*

canonical *adj* canonicus

canopy *s* canopeum *n*; aulaea *n pl*

cant *s* fucus *m*

cantata *s* carmen *n*

canteen *s* caupona castrensis *f*

canter *s* lenis atque quadrupedans grad·us -ūs *m*

canter *vi* leniter quadrupedare

canticle *s* canticum *n*

canto *s* liber *m*

canton *s* pagus *m*

canvas *s* linteum crassum *n*, carbasus *f*, carbasa *n pl*

canvass *s* (*legal*) ambitio *f*; (*illegal*) ambit·us -ūs *m*

canvass *vt* circumire, prensare; *vi* ambire

cap *s* pileus *m*; calyptra *f*; (*in rituals*) galerus *m*

capability *s* facultas, habilitas *f*

capable *adj* capax; idoneus, potens, doctus

capably *adv* bene, docte

capacity *s* capacitas, mensura *f*; modus *m*; ingenium *n*

cape *s* promontorium *n*; (*garment*)

humerale *n*, chlamys *f*

caper *vi* saltare, tripudire, assilire; (*of animals*) lascivire

caper *s* salt·us -ūs *m*, exsultatio *f*

capital *adj* praecipuus, princeps; (*law*) capitalis; (*of letters*) uncialis; (*outstanding*) insignis, eximius

capital *s* (*architecture*) capitulum *n*; (*chief city*) caput *n*; (*com*) sors *f*, caput *n*; faenus *m*

capitalist *s* faenerator *m*

capitol *s* capitolium *n*

capitulate *vi* ex pacto urbem tradĕre; se dedĕre

capitulation *s* deditio *f*

capon *s* capus, capo *m*

caprice *s* libido, inconstantia *f*

capricious *adj* levis, inconstans; ventosus, mobilis; —ly leviter, inconstanter, ex libidine

capricorn *s* capricornus *m*

capsize *vt* evertĕre; *vi* everti

capsule *s* capsula *f*

captain *s* (*in infantry*) centurio *m*; (*in cavalry*) praefectus *m*; (*in navy*) navarchus *m*, (*in merchant marine*) magister *m*

caption *s* caput *n*

captious *adj* argutus; morosus; fallax; —ly captiose, morose

captivate *vt* captare, delenire, mulcēre

captive *adj* captivus

captive *s* captivus *m*

captivity *s* captivitas *f*

captor *s* captor *m*; expugnator *m*; victor *m*

capture *s* captura, comprehensio *f*

capture *vt* capĕre, excipĕre

car *s* carrus *m*

carat *s* unciae triens *m*

caravan *s* commeat·us -ūs, comitat·us -ūs *m*

carbon *s* carbonium *n*

carbuncle *s* carbunculus, furunculus *m*

carcass *s* cadaver *n*

card *s* charta *f*; (*ticket*) tessera *f*; (*for combing wool*) pecten *n*

card *vt* pectĕre

cardboard *s* charta crassior *f*

cardinal *adj* principalis, praecipuus

cardinal *s* (*eccl*) cardinalis *m*

care *s* cura, sollicitudo *f*; (*diligence*) diligentia *f*; (*charge*) tutela, curatio, custodia *f*; **to take — of** curare

care *vi* curare; **to — for** (*to look after*) curare; (*to be fond of*) amare

career *s* curriculum *n*; decurs·us -ūs *m*; (*pol*) curs·us -ūs honorum *m*

carefree *adj* securus

careful *adj* (*attentive*) attentus, diligens; (*cautious*) cautus; (*of work*) accuratus; —ly diligenter; caute; accurate, exquisite

careless *adj* neglegens, incautus; (*loose*) dissolutus; —ly neglegenter; incuriose; (*loosely*) solute

carelessness *s* incuria, neglegentia *f*

caress *s* blanditiae *f pl*; complex·us -ūs *m*

caress *vt* blandiri, fovēre

cargo s onus n

caricature s imago in pejus detor-ta f

caricature vt in pejus fingĕre

carnage s caedes, strages f

carnal adj sensualis, carnalis

carnival s feriae f pl

carnivorous adj carnivorus

carol s cant·us -ūs m; carmen n; **Christmas — hymnus de Christi natu m**

carol vi cantare, cantillare

carouse vi comissari, perpotare, per-bacchari

carp s cyprinus m

carp vi **to — at** carpĕre, mordēre, vellicare

carpenter s faber tignarius m

carpentry s ars fabrilis f

carpet s tapes m, tapeta f

carriage s (act) vectura f; (vehicle) vehiculum n; raeda f, petorritum n; (bearing, posture) habit·us -ūs, gest·us -ūs, incess·us -ūs m

carrier s portitor, vector, bajulus m; (of letters) tabularius m

carrion s caro morticina f

carrot s carota f; pastinaca f

carry vt portare, ferre; (by vehicle) vehĕre; gerĕre; (law) perferre; **to — away** auferre; evehĕre; (fig) rapĕre; **to — back** referre; revehĕre; **to — in** importare; invehĕre; **to — off** auferre; rapĕre; **to — on** promovēre; perducĕre; (fig) exercēre; gerĕre; **to — out** efferre, exportare; evehĕre; (fig) exsequi; **to — over** transferre; **to — round** circumferre; **to — through** perferre; vi (of sound) audiri; **to — on** pergĕre; se gerĕre

cart s plaustrum n; curr·us -ūs m; curriculus m; **to put the — before the horse** praeposteris consiliis uti

cart vt plaustro vehĕre; **to — away** auferre

carve vt sculpĕre; caelare, incidĕre; (at table) secare

carver s caelator m; (at table) carptor m; (knife) cultellus m

carving s caelatura f

cascade s praeceps aquae laps·us -ūs m

case s (law) causa, actio f; (matter) res f; (instance) exemplum n; (container) involucrum n; theca f; capsula f; (state) stat·us -ūs m; conditio f; (gram) cas·us -ūs m; **in — si; in that — ergo; since that is the — quae cum ita sint**

cash s pecunia numerata f; nummi m pl; praesens pecunia f

cashier s dispensator m

cash payment s repraesentatio f

cask s cadus m, dolium n

casket s arcula f; pyxis f

cast s (throw) jact·us -ūs m; (mold) typus m; forma f

cast vt jacĕre; (metal) fundĕre; **to — about** circumjacĕre; **to — away** abjicĕre; dejicĕre; **to — down** dejicĕre; (fig) affligĕre; **to — in** in-**jicĕre; to — in one's teeth** repro-brare; **to — off** (the skin) exuĕre; (fig) amovēre, ponĕre; repudiare; **to — out** ejicĕre, expellĕre; **to — over** trajicĕre; **to — upon** super-injicĕre; (fig) aspergĕre; conferre; vi **to — off** ancoram tollĕre

castaway s perditus m; ejectus m

caste s ordo m; **to lose — degene-rare

castigate vt castigare

castigation s castigatio f

castle s castellum n; arx f

castor oil s cicinum oleum n

castrate vt castrare

castration s castratio, castratura f

casual adj fortuitus; (person) negle-gens; **—ly** fortuito, forte, casu

casualty s cas·us -ūs m; occisus m

cat s feles f

cataclysm s cataclysmos m

catacombs s puticuli m pl; catacum-bae f pl

catalogue s catalogus m; index m

cataract s cataracta f, cataractes m; (of the eye) glaucoma n

catastrophe s calamitas f; ruina f; exit·us -ūs m

catch vt capĕre, captare; (by surprise) comprehendĕre; (falling object) suscipĕre; (in a net) illaquēre; (with bait) inescare; (fire) concipĕre; (disease) contrahĕre; vi **to — at** arripĕre; (fig) captare; **to — up** with consequi

catching adj contagiosus; (fig) gratus

categorical adj categoricus; **—ly** categorice, sine exceptione

category s categoria f; numerus m

cater vi obsonari; cibos suppeditare

caterer s obsonator m

caterpillar s eruca f

cathedral s ecclesia cathedralis f

catholic adj catholicus, generalis

cattle s pecus n

cauliflower s brassica oleracea bo-tryitis f

cause s causa, res, materia f; (pol) partes f pl

cause vt facĕre, efficĕre; (feelings) exciēre, movēre

causeless adj sine causa; vanus

causeway s agger m

caustic adj causticus; (fig) mordax, acerbus

caution s cautio f; cura f; prudentia f; monitio f, monitum n

caution vt (ad)monēre

cautious adj cautus, consideratus; circumspectus; providus; **—ly** caute, prudenter; depetentim

cavalcade s pompa f

cavalier s eques m

cavalry s equitat·us -ūs m; equites m pl; copiae equestres f pl

cave s spec·us -ūs m; spelunca f; caverna f; antrum n

cavern s caverna f

cavernous adj cavernosus

caviar s ova acipenseris n pl

cavity s cavum n; caverna f

caw vi crocire, crocitare

cease *vi* desinĕre, desistĕre

ceaseless *adj* assiduus, perpetuus; **—ly** continenter, assidue, perpetuo

ceasing *s* cessatio, intermissio *f*

cedar *s* cedrus *f*

cedar *adj* cedreus, cedrinus

cede *vt* cedĕre, concedĕre

ceiling *s* laquear, lacunar *n*

celebrate *vt* celebrare; laudare, dicĕre

celebrated *adj* celeber; nobilis, notus, praeclarus

celebration *s* celebratio *f*; (*of rites*) sollemne *n*

celebrity *s* celebritas *f*; fama *f*; (*person*) vir illustris *m*

celery *s* heleoselinum *n*

celestial *adj* caelestis, divinus

celibacy *s* caelibat·us -ūs *m*, caelebs vita *f*

celibate *s* caelebs *m*

cell *s* cella *f*

cellar *s* cella *f*, cellarium *n*

cement *s* ferrumen *n*; caementum *n*; (*glue*) gluten *n*

cement *vt* conglutinare; ferruminare; *vi* coalescĕre

cemetery *s* sepulcretum *n*

censer *s* turibulum *n*

censor *s* censor *m*

censorship *s* censura *f*; magisterium morum *n*

censurable *adj* reprehensione dignus; culpandus

censure *s* vituperatio *f*

censure *vt* animadvertĕre, vituperare

census *s* cens·us -ūs *m*; civium enumeratio *f*

centaur *s* centaurus *m*

centenary *adj* centenarius

centenary *s* centesimus annus *m*

center *s* medium *n*; **in the — of the plain** in medio campo

center *vt* in centrum ponĕre; *vi* **to — on** niti (*with abl*)

central *adj* medius, centralis

centralize *vt* (*authority*) ad unum deferre

centurion *s* centurio *m*

century *s* (*pol*) centuria *f*; saeculum *f*

cereal *s* frumentum *n*

ceremonial *adj* caerimonialis, sollemnis; **—ly** sollemniter, rite

ceremonial *s* rit·us -ūs *m*

ceremonious *adj* sollemnis; (*person*) officiosus; **—ly** sollemniter; officiose

ceremony *s* caerimonia *f*, rit·us -ūs *m*; (*pomp*) apparat·us -ūs *m*

certain *adj* (*sure*) certus; (*indefinite*) quidam, nonnullus; **for —** certe, pro certo; **it is —** constat; **—ly** certe; profecto

certainty *s* certum *n*; (*belief*) fides *f*

certificate *s* testimonium *n*

certify *vt* recognoscĕre, confirmare

cessation *s* cessatio, intermissio *f*; **— of hostilities** indutiae *f pl*

chafe *vt* urĕre; (*with the hand*) fricare; (*to excoriate*) atterĕre; (*to vex*) irritare, succensĕre; *vi* stomachari

chaff *s* palea *f*; (*fig*) quisquiliae *f pl*

chagrin *s* dolor *m*; stomachus *m*

chain *s* catena *f*; (*necklace*) troques *m & f*; (*fig*) series *f*

chain *vt* catenis constringĕre; catenas injicĕre (*with dat*)

chair *s* sella, cathedra *f*

chairman *s* praeses *m*

chalice *s* calix *m*

chalk *s* creta *f*; calx *f*

chalk *vt* cretā notare; cretā illinĕre; **to — out** designare

chalky *adj* (*chalk-like*) cretaceus; (*full of chalk*) cretosus

challenge *s* provocatio *f*; (*law*) recusatio *f*

challenge *vt* provocare, lacessĕre; (*law*) rejicĕre; (*to reclaim*) arrogare

challenger *s* provocator *m*

chamber *s* cubiculum *n*, camera *f*, thalamus *m*; pars interior *f*

champ *vt & vi* mandĕre, mordĕre

champion *s* propugnator, defensor *m*; (*of a party*) antesignanus *m*

chance *s* (*accident*) cas·us -ūs, event·us -ūs *m*; fortuna *f*; (*fig*) alea *f*; (*probability*) spes *f*; **by —** casu, forte, fortuito

chance *vt* periclitari; *vi* accidĕre, contingĕre

chance *adj* fortuitus; inexpectatus

chancel *s* cancellus *m*

chancellor *s* cancellarius *m*

change *s* mutatio, commutatio, permutatio *f*; (*variety*) varietas *f*; (*pol*) res novae *f pl*; **small —** nummi *m pl*

change *vt* mutare, commutare, permutare; *vi* mutari, variare; (*of the moon*) renovari

changeable *adj* mutabilis; inconstans; (*of color*) versicolor

changeless *adj* immutabilis

changeling *s* subditus, suppositus *m*

channel *s* canalis *m*; (*of rivers*) alveus *m*; (*arm of the sea*) fretum *n*; (*in architecture*) stria *f*; (*fig*) curs·us -ūs *m*

channel *vt* sulcare, excavare; (*to guide*) ducĕre

chant *s* cant·us -ūs *m*

chant *vt* cantare

chaos *s* chaos *n*; (*fig*) confusio *f*

chaotic *adj* confusus; indigestus

chap *s* fissura *f*; (*person*) homo *m*

chap *vt* scindĕre, diffindĕre; *vi* scindī

chapel *s* aedicula *f*, sacellum *n*

chapter *s* caput *n*

char *vt* amburĕre

character *s* character *m*; mores *m pl*; (*inborn*) indoles, natura *f*; ingenium *n*; (*repute*) existimatio *f*; (*type*) genus *n*; (*letter*) littera *f*; (*in drama*) persona *f*

characteristic *adj* proprius; **—ally** proprie

characteristic *s* proprium *n*, proprietas *f*

characterize *vt* describĕre, notare, designare

charade *s* aenigma syllabicum *n*

charcoal *s* carbo *m*

charge *s* (*law*) crimen *n*; accusatio *f*; (*mil*) impet·us ‑ūs, incurs·us ‑ūs *m*; (*command*) mandatum *n*; (*trust*) cura, custodia *f*; (*office*) munus *n*; (*cost*) impensa *f*, sumpt·us ‑ūs *m*; **to be in — of** praeesse (*with dat*); **to bring a — against** litem intendĕre (*with dat*); **to put in — of** praeficĕre (*with dat*)

charger *s* equus bellator *m*

chariot *s* curr·us ‑ūs *m*; curriculum *n*; (*mil*) essedarium *n*

charioteer *s* auriga *m*

charitable *adj* benignus, beneficus; (*fig*) mitis

charitably *adv* benigne; miti animo

charity *s* caritas *f*; liberalitas *f*

charlatan *s* pharmacopola *m*; ostentator, jactator *m*

charm *s* incantamentum *n*; (*fig*) illecebra, gratia *f*; (*amulet*) amuletum *n*

charm *vt* incantare; (*to delight*) capĕre, captare, delectare; **to — away** recantare

charmer *s* fascinator *m*; (*thing*) deliciae *f pl*

charming *adj* suavis, lepidus, venustus; **—ly** lepide, suaviter, blande, venuste

chart *s* tabula *f*

charter *s* charta *f*, diploma *n*

charter *vt* conducĕre

chase *s* venatio *f*, venat·us ‑ūs *m*

chase *vt* (*to hunt*) persequi, venari; (*to engrave*) caelare; **to — away** abigĕre, pellĕre

chasing *s* caelatura *f*

chasm *s* chasma *n*, hiat·us ‑ūs *m*

chaste *adj* castus, pudicus; (*of language*) purus; **—ly** caste, pudice; pure

chasten *vt* purificare, castigare

chastise *vt* castigare

chastisement *s* castigatio, animadversio *f*

chastiser *s* castigator *m*

chastity *s* pudicitia, castitas *f*, pudor *m*

chat *s* familiaris sermo *m*; **to have a — fabulari, garrire

chat *vi* fabulari, garrire, colloqui

chattel *s* bona *n pl*

chatter *s* clangor *m*; (*idle talk*) garrulitas *f*, loquacitas *f*; (*of the teeth*) crepit·us ‑ūs *m*

chatter *vi* balbutire; (*to talk nonsense*) garrire, effutire; (*of teeth*) crepitare

cheap *adj* vilis; **— as dirt** pervilis; **—ly** bene, vili; viliter

cheapen *vt* pretium minuĕre (*with genit*)

cheapness *s* vilitas *f*

cheat *vt* decipĕre, fraudare

cheat *s* fraus *f*; dolus *m*; (*cheater*) fraudator *m*

check *vt* (*to restrain*) cohibēre, inhibēre; (*to stop*) retardare; (*to bridle*) refrenare; (*accounts*) dispungĕre; (*to verify*) comprobare

check *s* (*hindrance*) coercitio, suppressio *f*; impedimentum *n*; (*reprimand*) reprehensio *f*; (*bridle*) fre‑

num *n*; (*disadvantage*) detrimentum *n*; (*admission ticket*) tessera *f*

checkered *adj* varius

cheek *s* gena *f*

cheekbone *s* maxilla *f*

cheer *s* (*shout*) clamor, plaus·us ‑ūs *m*; hilaritas *f*

cheer *vt* hortari, hilarare, exhilarare; (*to console*) solari

cheerful *adj* hilaris, alacer, laetus; **—ly** hilare, laete; libenter

cheerfulness *s* hilaritas *f*

cheering *s* acclamatio *f*; plaus·us ‑ūs *m*

cheerless *adj* maestus, tristis, illaetabilis

cheese *s* caseus *m*

chemical *adj* chemicus

chemical *s* chemicum *n*

chemise *s* indusium *n*

chemist *s* chemicus, chemiae peritus *m*

chemistry *s* chemia, chymia *f*

cherish *vt* (*to nourish*) alĕre; (*to treat tenderly*) fovēre; (*fig*) colĕre

cherry *s* cerasum *n*

cherry tree *s* cerasus *f*

chest *s* (*of the body*) pectus *n*; (*box*) cista, arca *f*; (*for clothes*) vestiarium *n*; scrinium *n*

chestnut *s* castanea *f*

chew *vt* mandĕre, manducare; **to — the cud** ruminare; (*fig*) meditari

chewing *s* manducatio, ruminatio *f*

chicanery *s* calumnia, praevaricatio *f*

chick *s* pullus *m*; (*term of endearment*) pulla *f*

chicken *s* gallina *f*

chicken-hearted *adj* timidus, ignavus

chicory *s* cichoreum *n*

chide *vt* objurgare; corripĕre

chief *adj* primus; praecipuus, summus; supremus; **—ly** praecipue, imprimis

chief *s* princeps, procer, dux, auctor *m*; caput *n*

chieftain *s* dux *m*

child *s* infans *m* & *f*; puer, filius *m*, puella, filia *f*; (*in the womb*) embryo *m*; **to bear a — parturire; **with — gravida

childbearing *s* part·us ‑ūs *m*

childbirth *s* part·us ‑ūs *m*; Lucinae labores *m pl*

childhood *s* infantia *f*; pueritia *f*; **from — a puero *or* pueris; a primo tempore aetatis, a parvo

childish *adj* puerilis; **—ly** pueriliter

childless *adj* orbus

childlike *adj* puerilis

chill *s* frigusculum, frigus *n*

chill *adj* frigidulus

chill *vt* refrigerare

chilling *adj* algificus; frigidus, gelidus

chilly *adj* alsiosus; frigidulus

chime *s* sonus *m*

chime *vi* canēre, sonare; **to — in** interpellare

chimera *s* chimaera *f*; figmentum *n*

chimney *s* caminus *m*

chin *s* mentum *n*

china s fictilia n pl

chink s rima f; (sound) tinnit·us -ūs m

chink vi tinnire

chip s segmen n, assula f; (for lighting fire) fomes m

chip vt ascio dedolare

chirp s (of birds) pipat·us -ūs m; (of crickets) stridor m

chirp vi (of birds) minurire, pipilare; (of crickets) stridēre

chisel s scalprum, caelum n

chisel vt scalpro caedēre, sculpēre; (fig) decipēre, fraudare

chivalrous adj magnanimus, nobilis

chivalry s equestris dignitas f; (class) equites m pl

chocolate s chocolatum n

choice s electio f, delect·us -ūs m; (power of choosing) optio f; (diversity) varietas f

choice adj electus, exquisitus

choir s chorus m

choke vt suffocare; strangulare; vi suffocari; strangulari

choking s suffocatio f; strangulatio f

choose vt eligĕre, optare; to — to (to prefer to) malle (with inf)

choosing s electio f

chop s frustum n; (of meat) ofella f

chop vt concidĕre; truncare; to — off detruncare; abscidĕre; to — up minutatim concidĕre

choral adj symphoniacus

chord s chorda f, nervus m

chorus s chorus m; symphonia f

Christ s Christus m

christen vt baptizare

Christendom s cuncti Christiani m pl

Christian adj Christianus

Christianity s Christianismus m

Christian name s praenomen in baptismo inditum n

Christmas s festum nativitatis Christi n

chronic adj diuturnus, perpetuus; inveteratus

chronicle s annales m pl; acta publica n pl

chronological adj in — order ordinem temporum respiciens

chronology s temporum ordo m, temporum ratio f

chubby adj crassus, pinguis

chuckle vi cachinnare

church s ecclesia f; templum n

churl s homo rusticus m

churlish adj agrestis, importunus; —ly rustice

cider s hydromelum n

cinder s cinis m, favilla f

cinnamon s cinnamomum n

cipher s (code) nota f; (a nobody) numerus m; (zero) nihil n

circle s circulus, orbis, gyrus m; (around the moon) halo m; vicious — circulus vitiosus m

circle vt circumdare, cingĕre; vi circumire

circuit s circuit·us -ūs, circulus m; to make a — circumire

circuitous adj devius

circular adj orbicus, rotundus

circulate vt spargĕre; (news) disseminare, divulgare; vi circulari

circulation s ambit·us -ūs m; (of blood) circulatio f

circumcise vt circumcidĕre

circumcision s circumcisio f

circumference s peripheria f, ambit·us -ūs, circulus m

circumflex s circumflex·us -ūs m

circumlocution s circumlocutio, periphrasis f; ambages f pl

circumscribe vt finire, terminare, circumscribĕre

circumspect adj prudens, cautus, providus

circumspection s cautio, prudentia f

circumstance s res, conditio f; tempus n; sit·us -ūs m; under the —s quae cum ita sint

circumstantial adj adventicius, fortuitus; enumeratus; (of evidence) conjecturalis; —ly subtiliter

circumvent vt circumvenire, fallĕre, circumscribĕre

circumvention s circumscriptio, fraus f

circus s circus m

cistern s cisterna f, lac·us -ūs m; puteus m

citadel s arx f

citation s citatio, prolatio f; (law) vocatio f

cite vt (law) citare, evocare; (to quote) proferre, memorare

citizen s civis m & f; (of a municipality) municeps m

citizen adj civicus

citizenship s civitas f

city adj urbanus; urbicus

city s urbs f

civic adj civilis, civicus

civil adj civilis; (polite) comis, urbanus; (of war) civilis, intestinus, domesticus

civilian s togatus m; privatus m

civility s urbanitas, comitas f

civilization s cult·us -ūs m; humanitas f

civilize vt excolēre; expolire

clad adj indutus, vestitus, amictus

claim s postulatio, vindicatio f, postulatum n

claim vt postulare, poscĕre, vindicare, arrogare

claimant s petitor, vindicator m

clam s chama f

clamber vi scandĕre, conscendĕre

clammy adj umidus, viscidus, lentus

clamor s clamor m, vociferatio f

clamor vi exclamare, vociferari; — for flagitare

clamp s confibula f; uncus m

clamp vt constringĕre

clan s gens f

clandestine adj clandestinus, furtivus; —ly clam, furtim

clang s clangor m

clang vi clangĕre, strepĕre

clank s strepit·us -ūs m

clank vi crepare

clap s (*of hand*) plaus·us -ūs m; (*of thunder*) fragor m

clap vi plaudĕre, applaudĕre

claptrap s apparat·us -ūs m

clarification s explicatio f, explanatio f

clarify vt deliquare, explanare, explicare

clarion s lituus m

clarity s claritas f; perspicuitas f

clash s concurs·us -ūs m; (*sound*) crepit·us -ūs m; (*fig*) dissonantia f

clash vi concurrĕre; increpare, increpitare; (*fig*) dissidēre, discrepare

clasp s fibula f; (*embrace*) amplex·us -ūs m

clasp vt (*to embrace*) amplecti, complecti; (*to grasp*) comprehendĕre

class s (*pol*) classis f, ordo m; (*kind*) genus n

class vt in classes distribuĕre; **to —— as** in numero habēre

classical adj classicus

classics s scriptores classici m pl

classification s in classes distributio, in genera distributio f

classify vt describĕre, in classes distribuĕre, in genera distribuĕre

clatter s strepit·us -ūs, crepit·us -ūs m

clatter vi crepare, crepitare, strepĕre

clause s (*gram*) membrum, incisum n, articulus m, clausula f; (*law*) caput n

claw s unguis m

claw vt lacerare

clay s argilla, creta f; **made of ——** fictilis

clean adj mundus, purus; (*fig*) purus, castus; **——ly** munde, pure

clean vt mundare, purgare

cleanliness s munditia f

cleanly adj mundus, nitidus

cleanse vt purgare, depurgare, abluĕre, detergēre

clear adj clarus; (*of weather*) serenus; (*bright*) lucidus; (*of liquids*) limpidus; (*transparent*) liquidus; (*of voice*) candidus, acutus, argutus; (*manifest*) conspicuus, manifestus; (*of space*) apertus, patens; (*of language*) dilucidus; (*of conscience*) rectus; (*of the mind*) sagax; **—— of** expers (*with genit*); **it is ——** apparet, liquet; **to keep —— of** evitare; **——ly** clare, plane, aperte, haud dubie

clear vt purgare; (*to acquit*) absolvĕre; (*a doubt*) explanare; (*land, forests*) extricare; (*profit*) lucrari; **to —— away** detergĕre, amovĕre, tollĕre; **to —— out** emundare; **to —— up** enodare, explanare, explicare; vi **to —— up** (*of weather*) disserenascĕre, disserenare

clearance s purgatio f; (*space*) intervallum n

clearness s claritas f; (*of sky*) serenitas f; (*of style*) perspicuitas f

cleavage s discidium n

cleave vt findĕre; vi **to —— to** adhaerēre (*with dat*)

cleaver s dolabra f

cleft s rima, fissura f, hiat·us -ūs m

clemency s clementia f

clement adj clemens, mitis

clench vt comprimĕre

clerk s scriba m

clever adj sollers, ingeniosus, callidus, astutus, versutus; **——ly** sollerter, callide, ingeniose, astute

cleverness s dexteritas, sollertia, astutia f

click s crepit·us -ūs m

click vi crepitare

client s cliens m & f; consultor m

cliff s cautes f, scopulus m, rupes f

climate s caelum n

climax s gradatio f

climb vt & vi ascendĕre, conscendĕre, scandĕre

climb s ascens·us -ūs m

clinch vt confirmare

cling vi adhaerēre; **to —— together** cohaerēre

clink s tinnit·us -ūs m

clink vi tinnire

clip s fibula f

clip vt tondēre, praecidĕre; (*words*) mutilare

clipping s tonsura f; **——s** resegmina n pl

cloak s pallium n; (*for travel*) paenula f; (*in rain*) lacerna f; (*mil*) sagum, paludamentum n

cloak vt dissimulare, praetendĕre, tegĕre

clock s horologium n; (*sundial*) solarium n

clod s glaeba f

clog s (*shoe*) sculponea f; (*fig*) impedimentum n

clog vt impedire

cloister s portic·us -ūs f; monasterium n

close adj (*dense*) densus, spissus; (*tight*) artus, angustus; (*shut*) occlusus, clausus; (*fast*) firmus; (*near*) propinquus; (*secret*) arcanus, obscurus; (*niggardly*) avarus, tenax, parcus; **at —— quarters** comminus; **—— together** confertus, refertus, densus, continuus; **to be —— at hand** adesse, instare; **to keep —— to** adhaerēre (*with dat*); **——ly** prope; (*attentively*) attente, exacte

close vt claudĕre, operire; (*to end*) finire, terminare; **to —— a bargain** pacisci; vi coire; claudi, concludi, terminari; (*in a speech*) perorare

close s finis, terminus m, terminatio, conclusio f; **to bring to a ——** finire; **to draw to a ——** terminari

close adv prope, promime, juxta; **—— to** prope (*with acc*), juxta (*with acc*)

closet s conclave n, cella f; (*for clothes*) vestiarium n

closing adj ultimus

closing s conclusio f, finis m

clot s (*of blood*) cruor, concretus sanguis m

clot vi concrescĕre

cloth s pannus m; (*linen*) linteum n

clothe vt vestire, induĕre; velare

clothes *s* vestit·us -ūs *m*, vestimenta *n pl*, vestis *f*

clothing *s* vestit·us -ūs *m*, vestimenta *n pl*, vestis *f*

cloud *s* nubes *f*

cloud *vt* nubibus velare; (*fig*) obscurare; *vi* nubilare

cloudiness *s* nubilum *n*

cloudless *adj* serenus, purus

cloudy *adj* nubilus; **to grow — nubilare**

clout *s* ict·us -ūs *m*; alapa *f*

cloven *adj* bisulcus, bifidus

clown *s* (*boor*) rusticus *m*; (*buffoon, jester*) scurra *m*

clown *vi* scurrari

clownish *adj* rusticus; scurrilis

cloy *vt* satiare, exsaturare

cloying *adj* putidus

club *s* (*cudgel*) clava *f*, fustis *m*; (*society*) sodalitas *f*, collegium *n*

club *vt* fuste dolare

cluck *vi* glocire; singultire

clue *s* indicium *n*

clump *s* massa *f*; (*of trees*) arbustum *n*, globus *m*

clumsily *adv* rustice, inscite, ineleganter, male, inepte

clumsiness *s* rusticitas, inscitia *f*

clumsy *adj* ineptus, inscitus, rusticus, agrestis; (*of things*) inhabilis

cluster *s* (*of grapes, etc.*) racemus *m*; (*of flowers*) corymbus *m*; (*of people*) corona *f*

cluster *vi* congregari; **to — around stipare**

clutch *s* unguis *m*; comprehensio *f*; **from one's —es** e manibus; **in one's —es** in sua potestate

clutch *vt* arripĕre, prehendĕre

coach *s* curr·us -ūs *m*, raeda *f*; (*trainer*) magister *m*

coagulate *vt* coagulare; *vi* concrescĕre

coagulation *s* coagulatio, concretio *f*

coal *s* carbo *m*

coalesce *vi* coalescĕre, coire

coalition *s* conjunctio, coitio, conspiratio *f*

coal mine *s* fodina carbonaria *f*

coarse *adj* (*of material*) crassus, rudis; (*of manners*) incultus, inurbanus, rusticus; **—ly** crasse; inurbane

coarseness *s* crassitudo *f*; rusticitas *f*

coast *s* ora *f*, litus *n*

coast *vi* praetervehi

coastal *adj* maritimus, litoralis

coat *s* tunica, toga *f*; (*of fur*) pellis *f*

coat *vt* illinĕre, inducĕre, obducĕre

coating *s* corium *n*

coat of arms *s* insignia *n pl*

coat of mail *s* lorica *f*; (*skin*) pellis *f*

coax *vt* cogĕre, mulcĕre, blandiri

coaxing *s* blandimenta *n pl*, blanditiae *f pl*

coaxingly *adv* blande

cobbler *s* sutor *m*

cobweb *s* aranea *f*, araneum *n*

cock *s* gallus *m*

cockroach *s* blatta *f*

cocoa *s* faba Cacao *f*

cocoanut *s* nux palmae indicae *f*

cocoon *s* globulus *m*

coddle *vt* indulgēre (*with dat*)

code *s* notae *f pl*

codify *vt* digerĕre

coerce *vt* coercēre, refrenare, cogĕre

coercion *s* coercitio, vis *f*

coeval *adj* coaevus, aequalis

coexist *vi* simul existĕre

coffee *s* coffea Arabica *f*

coffer *s* arca, cista *f*

coffin *s* arca *f*, sarcophagus *m*

cog *s* dens *m*

cogency *s* vis *f*

cogent *adj* cogens, efficax, gravis

cognate *adj* cognatus

cognizance *s* cognitio *f*

cognizant *adj* conscius, gnarus

cohabit *vi* coire, consuescĕre

cohabitation *s* consuetudo *f*, convict·us -ūs *m*

coheir *s* coheres *m & f*

cohere *vi* cohaerēre; (*fig*) congruĕre

coherence *s* context·us -ūs *m*, convenientia *f*

coherent *adj* cohaerens, congruens; **—ly** constanter

cohesion *s* cohaerentia *f*

cohesive *adj* tenax

cohort *s* cohors *f*

coil *s* spira *f*

coil *vt* glomerare; *vi* glomerari

coin *s* nummus *m*

coin *vt* cudĕre, signare; (*fig*) fingĕre

coinage *s* res nummaria, moneta *f*

coincide *vi* congruĕre, convenire, concurrĕre; eodem tempore fieri

coincidence *s* concursatio *f*, concurs·us -ūs *m*; (*fig*) consens·us -ūs *m*; **by — casu**

coincidental *adj* fortuitus

cold *adj* frigidus, gelidus; **to be — algēre, frigēre; to become — frigescĕre, algescĕre; —ly** (*fig*) frigide, gelide, lente

cold *s* frigus *n*, algor *m*, gelu *n*; (*sickness*) gravedo *f*; **to catch a — gravedinem contrahĕre; to have a — gravedine dolēre**

coldness *s* frigus *n*, algor *m*

colic *s* tormina *n pl*

collapse *s* labes, ruina *f*

collapse *vi* collabi, concidĕre, in se corruĕre

collar *s* (*of garment*) collare *n*; (*for dogs*) millus *m*; jugum *n*

collar *vt* collo comprehendĕre

collarbone *s* jugulum *n*

collate *vt* conferre

collateral *adj* transversus; adjunctus, consentaneus

colleague *s* collega, consors *m*

collect *vt* conferre, colligĕre; (*to assemble*) convocare; (*money*) exigĕre; **to — oneself** mentem colligĕre, animum colligĕre; *vi* colligi, aggregari

collected *adj* praesens

collection *s* collectio, conquisitio, collecta, congeries *f*; (*out of authors*) collectanea *n pl*

collective *adj* communis, collectivus;
—**ly** una, simul, communiter
college *s* collegium *n*
collegiate *adj* collegialis, collegiarius
collide *vi* confligĕre, concurrĕre
collision *s* concursio, conflictio *f*,
concurs·us -ūs *m*
colloquial *adj* quotidianus
collusion *s* collusio, praevaricatio *f*,
dolus *m*
colon *s* colon *n*
colonel *s* legatus *m*
colonial *adj* colonicus
colonist *s* colonus *m*
colonize *vt* coloniam constituĕre in
(*with abl*)
colonnade *s* portic·us -ūs *f*
colony *s* colonia *f*
color *s* color *m*, pigmentum *n*; —**s**
vexillum *n*
color *vt* colorare; (*to dye*) tingĕre, inficĕre; (*fig*) obtegĕre; *vi* erubescĕre
colossal *adj* ingens, immanis
colossus *s* colossus *m*
colt *s* equulus, pullus equinus *m*
column *s* columna *f*; (*mil*) agmen *n*
comb *s* pecten *n*
comb *vt* pectĕre, comĕre
combat *s* pugna *f*, proelium, certamen *n*
combat *vt* pugnare cum (*with abl*); *vi*
pugnare, proeliari
combination *s* conjunctio, junctura
f; (*of persons*) conspiratio, conjuratio *f*
combine *vt* conjungĕre, miscĕre;
temperare; *vi* coire; conspirare
combustible *adj* igni obnoxius
combustion *s* concrematio, ustio *f*
come *vi* venire; (*to arrive*) pervenire;
(*to happen*) fieri; **to — about** evenire; **to — after** sequi; **to —
again** revenire; **to — along** procedĕre; **to — away** abscedĕre; **to
— back** revenire, redire; **to — before** praevenire; **to — by** praeterire; (*to get*) acquirĕre; **to —
down** descendĕre; (*to fall down*) decidĕre; **to — forth** exire; (*fig*)
exoriri; **to — forward** procedĕre;
to — in introire; **to — near** appropinquare, accedĕre; **to — off**
recedĕre, discedĕre; **to — on** pergĕre; **to — out** (*to be published*)
edi, emitti; **to — over** supervenire;
(*the face*) obire; **to — round** (*fig*)
transgredi; **to — to** advenire; (*to
come to one's senses*) ad se redire;
to — to pass evenire, fieri; **to —
together** convenire, coire; **to —
up** subvenire; (*to occur*) accidĕre,
provenire; **to — upon** (*to find*) invenire; (*to attack*) ingruĕre
comedian *s* comoedus *m*; (*playwright*) comicus *m*
comedy *s* comoedia *f*
comely *adj* decens, venustus
comet *s* cometes *m*, stella crinita *f*
comfort *s* consolatio *f*, solatium *n*
comfort *vt* consolari, solari
comfortable *adj* commodus, amoenus
comfortably *adv* commode

comforter *s* consolator *m*
comfortless *adj* solatii expers, incommodus
comic *adj* comicus, facetus
comic *s* scurra *m*
comical *adj* comicus, ridiculus; —**ly**
comice, ridicule
coming *adj* venturus
coming *s* advent·us -ūs *m*
comma *s* comma *n*
command *vt* imperare (*with dat*), jubēre; (*view*) prospectare, despectare
command *s* (*order*) jussum, mandatum, praeceptum *n*, juss·us -ūs *m*;
(*mil*) imperium *n*; (*jurisdiction*)
provincia *f*; — **of language** copia dicendi *f*; **to be in — of** praeesse (*with dat*); **to put someone
in — of** aliquem praeficĕre (*with
dat*)
commander *s* dux, praefectus *m*
commander in chief *s* imperator *m*
commandment *s* mandatum *n*
commemorate *vt* celebrare
commemoration *s* celebratio *f*
commence *vt* incipere, inchoare
commencement *s* initium, exordium, principium *n*
commend *vt* approbare, laudare; (*to
recommend*) commendare; (*to entrust*) committĕre, mandare
commendable *adj* commendabilis,
probabilis, laudabilis
commendation *s* commendatio·*f*
commensurate *adj* adaequans, conveniens
comment *vi* commentari; **to — on**
explicare, enarrare, interpretari
comment *s* sententia *f*, dictum *n*
commentary *s* commentarius *m*,
commentarium *n*
commentator *s* interpres *m*
commerce *s* commercium *n*, mer-
cat·us -ūs *m*, mercatura *f*; **to engage in —** negotiari
commercial *adj* negotialis
commiserate *vi* **to — with** miserēri
commiseration *s* misericordia *f*
commissariat *s* commeat·us -ūs *m*,
res frumentaria *f*
commissary *s* procurator, curator *m*
commission *s* mandatum *n*; (*mil*) legatio *f*
commission *vt* delegare, mandare
commissioner *s* delegatus *m*
commit *vt* (*crime*) admittĕre, patrare, perpetrare; (*to entrust*) committĕre; **to — to memory** ediscĕre
commitment *s* (*obligation*) munus,
officium *n*; (*to jail*) incarceratio *f*
committee *s* consilium *n*
commodity *s* res venalis, merx *f*
common *adj* communis, publicus;
(*ordinary*) vulgaris, quotidianus;
(*well known*) pervulgatus; (*repeated*)
creber; (*inferior*) mediocris; (*gram*)
promiscuus; —**ly** vulgo, fere, plerumque
commoner *s* plebeius *m*; —**s** plebs *f*
commonplace *adj* vulgaris, pervulgatus, tritus
commonwealth *s* respublica *f*

commotion *s* commotio, agitatio *f*, tumult·us -ūs *m*

commune *vi* confabulari

communicate *vt* communicare; *(information)* impertire, nuntiare; *vi* **to — with** communicare *(with dat)*, agĕre cum *(with abl)*

communication *s* communicatio *f*; commercium *n*; *(information)* nuntius *m*

communicative *adj* affabilis, facilis

communion *s* communio, societas *f*

community *s* civitas *f*

commutation *s* mutatio, permutatio *f*

commute *vt* commutare

compact *adj* densus, spissus; *(of style)* pressus; **—ly** dense, spisse, confertim

compact *s* pactum, foedus *n*, pactio *f*

compact *vt* densare

companion *s* comes, socius, sodalis; *(mil)* contubernalis, commilito *m*

companionable *adj* affabilis, facilis

companionship *s* societas, sodalitas, consuetudo *f*; *(mil)* contubernium *n*

company *s* societas, consuetudo *f*; *(gathering)* convent·us -ūs *m*; *(guests)* convivium *n*; *(com)* societas *f*; *(mil)* manipulus *m*; *(theatrical)* grex *f*

comparable *adj* comparabilis

comparative *adj* comparatus, relativus; **—ly** comparate

comparative *s* grad·us -ūs comparativus *m*

compare *vt* comparare, conferre; **compared with** ad *(with acc)*, adversus *(with acc)*

comparison *s* comparatio, collatio *f*; **in — with** prae *(with abl)*, adversus *(with acc)*

compartment *s* loculus *m*, cella, pars *f*

compass *s* ambit·us -ūs *m*; *(limits)* fines *m pl*; *(instrument)* circinus *m*; *(magnetic)* ac·us -ūs magnetica *f*

compass *vt* circumvallare, cingĕre, circumdare; *(to attain)* consequi, patrare

compassion *s* misericordia *f*

compassionate *adj* misericors; **—ly** misericorditer

compatibility *s* congruentia, convenientia *f*

compatible *adj* congruus, conveniens

compatriot *s* civis, popularis *m*

compeer *s* par, aequalis *m*

compel *vt* cogĕre, compellĕre

compendium *s* summarium *n*

compensate *vt* compensare, renumerare; satisfacĕre *(with dat)*

compensation *s* compensatio *f*; poena *f*

compete *vi* contendĕre, petĕre, certare

competence *s* facultas *f*; *(legal capacity)* jus *n*

competent *adj* congruens, idoneus, peritus, capax; *(of authorities)* locuples; **—ly** satis, idonee

competition *s* contentio, aemulatio *f*, certamen *n*

competitor *s* petitor, rivalis, aemulus *m*

compilation *s* collectio *f*, collectanea *n pl*

compile *vt* colligĕre, componĕre

compiler *s* collector, scriptor *m*

complacency *s* amor sui *m*

complacent *adj* qui sibi placet

complain *vi* queri

complaint *s* querela, querimonia *f*; *(law)* crimen *n*; *(med)* morbus *m*

complaisance *s* comitas, accommodatio *f*, obsequium *n*

complaisant *adj* comis, officiosus; **—ly** comiter

complement *s* complementum, supplementum *n*

complete *adj* perfectus, integer, absolutus, plenus; **—ly** plane, prorsus, omnino, absolute, funditus

complete *vt* complēre; *(to accomplish)* perficĕre, conficĕre, peragĕre

completion *s* completio *f*; *(accomplishment)* perfectio *f*; *(end)* finis *m*

complex *adj* multiplex, implicatus, complicatus

complexion *s* color *m*

complexity *s* implicatio, multiplex natura *f*

compliance *s* obtemperatio *f*, obsequium *n*

compliant *adj* obsequens

complicate *vt* impedire

complicated *adj* impeditus, implicatus, complicatus, nodosus

complication *s* implicatio *f*

complicity *s* conscientia *f*

compliment *s* blandimentum *n*, verba honorifica *n pl*; **to pay one's —s to** salutare

compliment *vt* gratulari *(with dat)*; laudare, blandiri

complimentary *adj* blandus, honorificus

comply *vi* **to — with** concedĕre *(with dat)*, cedĕre *(with dat)*, parēre *(with dat)*, obsequi *(with dat)*, morigerari *(with dat)*

component *s* pars *f*, elementum *n*

compose *vt* componĕre; *(verses)* condĕre, pangĕre; *(to calm)* sedare; *(quarrel)* componĕre; **to — oneself** tranquillari

composed *adj* tranquillus, quietus, placidus

composer *s* scriptor, auctor *m*

composite *adj* compositus, multiplex

composition *s* compositio, scriptura *f*; opus *n*

composure *s* tranquillitas *f*, animus aequus *m*

compound *vt* componĕre, miscēre; *(words)* jungĕre

compound *adj* compositus

compound *s* compositio *f*; *(word)* junctum verbum *n*

compound interest *s* anatocismus *m*

comprehend *vt* continēre, amplectari; *(to understand)* capĕre, percipĕre, comprehendĕre, intellegĕre

comprehensible *adj* perspicuus

comprehension *s* intellect·us -ūs *m*, intellegentia *f*

comprehensive *adj* plenus, capax;
—**ly** funditus, omnino
compress *vt* comprimĕre
compression *s* compressio *f*, compress·us -ūs *m*
comprise *vt* continēre
compromise *s* (*unilateral*) accommodatio *f*; (*bilateral*) compromissum *n*
compromise *vt* compromittĕre, implicare; *vi* pacisci
compulsion *s* compulsio, vis, necessitas *f*
compulsory *adj* necessarius, debitus
compunction *s* paenitentia, compunctio *f*
computation *s* ratio, computatio *f*
compute *vt* computare
comrade *s* socius, sodalis *m*; (*mil*) contubernalis *m*
conceal *vt* celare, occultare, abdĕre, dissimulare
concealment *s* occultatio, dissimulatio *f*; (*place*) latebrae *f pl*; **to be in** — latēre
concede *vt* concedĕre
conceit *s* (*haughtiness*) arrogantia, superbia *f*; (*idea*) notio *f*
conceited *adj* arrogans, superbiā tumens
conceive *vt* concipĕre, percipĕre, intellegĕre
concentrate *vt* in unum locum contrahĕre; *vi* **to** — **on** animum intendĕre in (*with acc*)
concentration *s* in unum locum contractio *f*; (*fig*) animi intentio *f*
conception *s* (*in womb*) concept·us -ūs *m*; (*idea*) imago, notio *f*
concern *s* (*affair*) res *f*, negotium *n*; (*importance*) momentum *n*; (*worry*) sollicitudo, cura *f*
concern *vt* pertinēre ad (*with acc*), attinēre ad (*with acc*); (*to worry*) sollicitare; **it —s me** meā interest, meā refert
concerned *adj* sollictus, anxius
concerning *prep* de (*with abl*)
concert *s* (*music*) concent·us -ūs *m*, symphonia *f*; **in** — uno animo, ex composito
concert *vt* (*plan*) inire
concession *s* concessio *f*; (*thing*) concessum *n*; **to make —s** concedĕre
conch *s* concha *f*
conciliate *vt* conciliare
conciliation *s* conciliatio *f*
concise *adj* brevis, concisus; (*style*) densus; —**ly** breviter, concise
conciseness *s* brevitas *f*
conclave *s* conclave, consilium *n*
conclude *vt* (*to end*) conficĕre, perficĕre, terminare, finire; (*to infer*) concludĕre, colligĕre
conclusion *s* (*end*) conclusio *f*; (*decision*) determinatio, sententia *f*; (*of speech*) peroratio *f*; (*of action*) exit·us -ūs *m*; (*inference*) conjectura *f*
conclusive *adj* certus, gravis
concoct *vt* concoquĕre; (*to contrive*) excogitare, conflare
concoction *s* pot·us -ūs *m*; (*fig*) ma

chinatio *f*
concomitant *adj* adjunctus, conjunctus
concord *s* concordia, harmonia *f*; (*mus*) concent·us -ūs *m*
concordat *s* pactum *n*
concourse *s* concurs·us -ūs *m*, concursio *f*
concrete *adj* concretus
concrete *s* concretum *n*, concret·us -ūs *m*
concubinage *s* concubinat·us -ūs *m*
concubine *s* concubina *f*
concupiscence *s* libido *f*
concur *vi* congruĕre, consentire
concurrence *s* consens·us -ūs *m*, consensio *f*
concussion *s* concussio *f*
condemn *vt* damnare, condemnare; **to** — **to death** capitis damnare
condemnation *s* damnatio, condemnatio *f*
condensation *s* densatio, spissatio *f*
condense *vt* (con)densare, spissare; (*words*) premĕre
condescend *vi* dignari, descendĕre, concedĕre, se submittĕre
condescending *adj* comis; —**ly** comiter
condescension *s* comitas *f*
condition *s* (*state*) stat·us -ūs *m*, condicio, res *f*; (*stipulation*) condicio, lex *f*; **on** — **that** ea lege ut
condition *vt* formare, informare
conditional *adj* conditionalis; —**ly** (*law*) conditionaliter; sub condicione
condole *vi* **to** — **with** dolēre cum (*with abl*)
condone *vt* veniam dare (*with dat*), condonare
conducive *adj* utilis, accommodatus
conduct *s* mores *m pl*, vita *f*; (*management*) administratio *f*
conduct *vt* (*to lead*) adducĕre, deducĕre, perducĕre; (*to manage*) gerĕre, administrare
conductor *s* dux, ductor *m*
conduit *s* canalis, aquaeduct·us -ūs *m*
cone *s* conus *m*
confection *s* conditura, cuppedo *f*
confectionery *s* cuppedia *n pl*, conditura *f*
confederacy *s* (*alliance*) foedus *n*, societas *f*
confederate *adj* foederatus
confederate *s* socius, conjuratus *m*
confederate *vi* foedus facĕre
confederation *s* societas *f*
confer *vt* conferre, tribuĕre; *vi* colloqui
conference *s* colloquium *n*
confess *vt* fatēri, confitēri; agnoscĕre, concedĕre
confessedly *adv* ex confesso; manifesto, aperte
confession *s* confessio *f*
confidant *s* familiaris *m & f*, conscius *m*, conscia *f*
confide *vt* committĕre, credĕre, mandare; *vi* **to** — **in** (con)fidĕre (*with dat*)
confidence *s* fides, confidentia, fiducia *f*; **to have** — **in** confidĕre (*with*

dat); **to inspire — in** fidem facĕre (*with dat*)

confident *adj* confidens, fidens; **—ly** confidenter

confidential *adj* fidus; (*secret*) arcanus

configuration *s* forma, figura *f*

confine *s* finis *m*

confine *vt* includĕre; (*to restrain*) coercĕre, cohibēre; (*to limit*) circumscribĕre; **to be confined to bed** lecto tenēri

confinement *s* inclusio *f*; (*imprisonment*) incarceratio, custodia *f*; (*of women*) puerperium *n*

confirm *vt* confirmare; (*to prove*) comprobare; (*to ratify*) sancire

confirmation *s* confirmatio, affirmatio *f*

confiscate *vt* proscribĕre, publicare

confiscation *s* proscriptio, publicatio *f*

conflagration *s* incendium *n*

conflict *s* conflict·us -ūs *m*, contentio, pugna *f*, certamen *n*

conflict *vi* contendĕre; (*differ*) dissentire, discrepare

conflicting *adj* contrarius, adversus

confluence *s* confluens *m*

conform *vt* accommodare; *vi* obsequi, obtemperare

conformation *s* conformatio, figura, forma *f*

conformity *s* convenientia, congruentia *f*; **in — with** secundum (*with acc*)

confound *vt* confundĕre, permiscēre, perturbare; (*to frustrate*) frustrari

confounded *adj* miser, nefandus

confront *vt* obviam ire (*with dat*), se opponĕre (*with dat*)

confrontation *s* comparatio *f*

confuse *vt* confundĕre, perturbare, permiscēre

confused *adj* confusus, perplexus; **—ly** confuse, perplexe

confusion *s* confusio, perturbatio *f*; (*shame*) pudor *m*

congeal *vt* congelare, glaciare; *vi* consistĕre, concrescĕre

congenial *adj* consentaneus, concors

congenital *adj* nativus

congested *adj* refertus, densus; frequentissimus

congestion *s* congeries, frequentia *f*

congratulate *vt* gratulari (*with dat*)

congratulation *s* gratulatio *f*

congratulatory *adj* gratulans, gratulabundus

congregate *vt* congregare, colligĕre; *vi* congregari, convenire

congregation *s* coet·us -ūs *m*, auditores *m pl*

conical *adj* conicus

conjectural *adj* conjecturalis, opinabilis; **—ly** ex conjectura

conjecture *s* conjectura *f*

conjecture *vt* conjectare, conjicĕre

conjugal *adj* conjugalis

conjugate *vt* declinare

conjugation *s* conjugatio *f*

conjunction *s* unio *f*, concurs·us -ūs *m*; (*gram*) conjunctio *f*

conjure *vt* obtestari, incantare, fascinare; *vi* praestigiis uti

conjurer *s* magus, praestigiator *m*

conjuring *s* praestigiae *f pl*

connect *vt* connectĕre, jungĕre, copulare; (*in a series*) serĕre

connected *adj* conjunctus; continuus, continens; (*by marriage*) affinis; **to be closely connected with** inhaerēre (*with dat*); **to be connected with** contingĕre

connection *s* conjunctio, colligatio *f*, nex·us -ūs, context·us -ūs *m*; (*kin*) necessitudo *f*; (*by marriage*) affinitas *f*

connivance *s* indulgentia, dissimulatio *f*

connive *vi* connivēre

connoisseur *s* doctus, peritus, intellegens *m*

conquer *vt* vincĕre, superare; domare

conqueror *s* victor *m*, victrix *f*; domitor *m*

conquest *s* victoria *f*

consanguinity *s* consanguinitas *f*

conscience *s* conscientia *f*; **guilty — ** mala conscientia; **to have no — ** nullam religionem habēre

conscientious *adj* integer, pius, religiosus, diligens; **—ly** diligenter

conscious *adj* conscius, gnarus; **—ly** scienter

consciousness *s* conscientia *f*

conscript *s* tiro *m*

conscript *vt* conscribĕre

conscription *s* delect·us -ūs *m*

consecrate *vt* sacrare, consecrare, dedicare, devovēre

consecration *s* consecratio, dedicatio *f*

consecutive *adj* continuus; **—ly** deinceps, continenter

consent *vi* assentire, consentire

consent *s* consens·us -ūs *m*, consensio *f*; **without my — ** me invito

consequence *s* consequentia; consecutio *f*, event·us -ūs, exit·us -ūs *m*; (*logical*) conclusio *f*; (*importance*) momentum *n*

consequent *adj* consequens, consectarius; **—ly** ergo, igitur, itaque

consequential *adj* consentaneus

conservation *s* conservatio *f*

conservative *adj* reipublicae status conservandi studiosus; **— party** optimates *m pl*

conserve *vt* conservare, servare

consider *vt* considerare, animo agitare, revolvĕre; (*to deem*) aestimare, ducĕre, habēre; (*to respect*) respicĕre

considerable *adj* aliquantus; (*of persons*) eximius, illustris; (*of size*) amplus

considerably *adv* aliquantum; multum; (*with comp*) multo, aliquanto

considerate *adj* prudens, humanus, benignus

consideration *s* consideratio, contemplatio, deliberatio *f*; (*regard*) respect·us -ūs *m*; (*ground, motive*)

ratio *f*; (*importance*) momentum *n*;
without — inconsulte, temere
considering *prep* pro (*with abl*)
consign *vt* committĕre, mandare,
consignare, tradĕre
consignment *s* consignatio *f*
consist *vi* consistĕre; **to** — **of** constare ex (*with abl*)
consistency *s* congruentia, constantia *f*
consistent *adj* constans; consentaneus; —**ly** constanter, congruenter
consolable *adj* consolabilis
consolation *s* consolatio *f*; (*thing*)
solacium *n*
console *vt* consolari
consolidate *vt* corroborare, firmare,
consolidare, stabilire; *vi* solidescĕre
consonant *adj* consonus, consentaneus
consonant *s* consonans littera *f*
consort *s* consors *m* & *f*; (*married*)
conjux *or* conjunx *m* & *f*
consort *vi* **to** — **with** familiariter
uti (*with abl*), se associare cum
(*with abl*)
conspicuous *adj* conspicuus; insignis, manifestus; —**ly** manifeste,
palam
conspiracy *s* conjuratio, conspiratio *f*
conspirator *s* conjuratus *m*
conspire *vi* conjurare, conspirare
constable *s* lictor *m*
constancy *s* constantia, firmitas,
perseverantia *f*
constant *adj* constans, firmus; perpetuus; fidelis; —**ly** constanter,
crebro
constellation *s* sidus, astrum *n*
consternation *s* consternatio, trepidatio *f*, pavor *m*; **to throw into**
— perterrēre
constituent *s* elector, suffragator *m*;
(*part*) elementum *n*
constitute *vt* constituĕre, creare
constitution *s* (*of body*) habit·us -ūs
m, constitutio *f*; (*pol*) civitatis stat-
t·us -ūs *m*, reipublicae leges *f pl*
constitutional *adj* legitimus; (*natural*) naturā insitus; —**ly** legitime
constrain *vt* cogĕre, compellĕre, detinēre
constraint *s* vis, coercitio, necessitas *f*
construct *vt* construĕre
construction *s* constructio, aedificatio *f*; figura, forma *f*; (*meaning*)
sens·us -ūs *m*, interpretatio *f*
constructor *s* structor, fabricator *m*
construe *vt* interpretari; (*gram*) construĕre
consul *s* consul *m*; — **elect** consul
designatus *m*
consular *adj* consularis
consulship *s* consulat·us -ūs *m*; **to
run for the** — consulatum petĕre;
during my — me consule
consult *vt* consulĕre, consultare; *vi*
deliberare
consultation *s* consultatio, deliberatio *f*
consume *vt* consumĕre, absumĕre;

(*food*) edĕre
consumer *s* consumptor *m*
consummate *adj* summus, perfectus
consummate *vt* consummare
consummation *s* consummatio *f*;
(*end*) finis *m*
consumption *s* consumptio *f*; (*disease*) tabes *f*
consumptive *adj* pulmonarius
contact *s* contact·us -ūs *m*, contagio
f; **to come in** — **with** contingĕre
contagion *s* contagium *n*, contagio *f*
contagious *adj* contagiosus, tabificus
contain *vt* continēre; (*to restrain*)
cohibēre
container *s* vas *n*
contaminate *vt* contaminare
contamination *s* contaminatio, labes *f*
contemplate *vt* contemplari, intuēri
contemplation *s* contemplatio, meditatio *f*
contemporaneous *adj* aequalis;
—**ly** simul
contemporary *s* aequalis, aequaevus
m
contempt *s* contemptio *f*, contempt-
us -ūs *m*
contemptible *adj* contemnendus,
abjectus, vilis
contemptibly *adv* contemptim, abjecte
contemptuous *adj* fastidiosus, superbus; —**ly** fastidiose
contend *vt* (*to aver*) affirmare, asseverare; *vi* contendĕre, certare; (*to
struggle*) luctari; (*to dispute*) verbis
certare; **to** — **against** repugnare,
adversari
contending *adj* aversus, contrarius
content *adj* contentus
content *vt* satisfacĕre (*with dat*), placēre (*with dat*), mulcēre
contented *adj* contentus; —**ly** aequo
animo, leniter
contention *s* contentio *f*; certamen
n; controversia *f*
contentious *adj* litigiosus; pugnax
contentment *s* aequus animus *m*
contents *s* quod inest, quae insunt;
(*of book*) argumentum *n*
contest *s* certamen *n*, contentio, certatio *f*
contest *vt* (*to dispute*) resistĕre (*with
dat*), repugnare (*with dat*); (*law*)
lege agĕre de (*with abl*)
contestant *s* petitor, aemulus *m*
context *s* context·us -ūs, sens·us
-ūs *m*
contiguous *adj* contiguus, conterminus, adjunctus
continence *s* continentia, abstinentia *f*
continent *adj* abstinens, continens;
—**ly** abstinenter, continenter
continent *s* continens *f*
continental *adj* in continenti positus; ad continentem pertinens
contingent *s* (*of troops*) numerus *m*,
man·us -ūs *f*
continual *adj* continuus; perpetuus,
assiduus; —**ly** assidue, semper

continuance *s* continuatio, perpetuitas, assiduitas *f*

continuation *s* continuatio *f*

continue *vt* continuare, producĕre; *vi* pergĕre; (*to last*) durare, persistĕre, perstare, (re)manēre

continuity *s* continuitas *f*; (*of speech*) perpetuitas *f*

continuous *adj* continuus, continens, perpetuus; —**ly** continenter

contortion *s* contortio, distortio *f*

contour *s* forma, figura *f*; lineamenta *n pl*

contraband *adj* interdictus, vetitus, illicitus

contract *vt* contrahĕre, astringĕre; (*to shorten*) deminuĕre; (*sickness*) contrahĕre; (*to undertake*) redimĕre; *vi* pacisci; (*to shrink*) contrahi

contract *s* pactum, conventum *n*; (*pol*) foedus *n*

contraction *s* contractio *f*; (*of word*) compendium *n*

contractor *s* redemptor, susceptor *m*

contradict *vt* contradicĕre (*with dat*), obloqui (*with dat*)

contradiction *s* contradictio *f*; (*of things*) repugnantia *f*

contradictory *adj* contrarius, repugnans

contrary *adj* (*opposite*) contrarius, diversus; (*fig*) aversus, repugnans; — **to** contra (*with acc*)

contrary *s* contrarium *n*, contraria pars *f*; **on the** — contra, e contrario

contrast *s* diversitas, dissimilitudo *f*

contrast *vt* comparare, opponĕre; *vi* discrepare

contribute *vt* contribuĕre, conferre; *vi* **to** — **towards** conferre ad (*with acc*)

contribution *s* contributio, collatio *f*; (*money*) stips *f*

contributory *adj* contribuens, adjunctus

contrite *adj* paenitens

contrition *s* paenitentia *f*

contrivance *s* inventio, machinatio *f*; (*thing contrived*) inventum, artificium *n*, machina *f*

contrive *vt* (*to invent*) fingĕre; excogitare, machinari, efficĕre

control *s* (*restraint*) continentia *f*; (*power*) potestas, moderatio, dictio *f*, imperium *n*; **to have** — **over** praeesse (*with dat*)

control *vt* moderari (*with dat*), continĕre, regĕre, coercĕre

controller *s* moderator *m*

controversial *adj* concertatorius

controversy *s* controversia, disceptatio, concertatio *f*

contusion *s* contusio *f*, contusum *n*

conundrum *s* aenigma *n*; (*quibble*) cavillum *n*

convalesce *vi* convalescĕre

convalescence *s* conditio convalescendi *f*

convalescent *adj* convalescens

convene *vt* convocare

convenience *s* commoditas, opportunitas, convenientia *f*; (*thing*) commodum *n*

convenient *adj* commodus, idoneus, opportunus; —**ly** commode, apte, opportune

convention *s* convent·us -ūs *m*; (*custom*) mos *m*

conventional *adj* usitatus, tralaticius, solitus

converge *vi* vergĕre, coire

conversant *adj* peritus, exercitatus; **to be** — **with** versari in (*with abl*)

conversation *s* colloquium *n*, sermo *m*

conversational *adj* in colloquio usitatus

converse *vi* colloqui

converse *s* contrarium *n*, convers·us -ūs *m*

conversely *adv* e contrario, e converso

conversion *s* conversio *f*

convert *vt* convertĕre, commutare; deducĕre

convert *s* neophytus, discipulus *m*

convertible *adj* commutabilis

convex *adj* convexus

convey *vt* portare, vehĕre, convehĕre; (*property*) abalienare; (*fig*) significare

conveyance *s* (*act*) advectio, vectura *f*; (*vehicle*) vehiculum *n*; (*law*) abalienatio, transcriptio *f*

convict *s* convictus, evictus, reus *m*

convict *vt* convincĕre

conviction *s* (*law*) damnatio *f*; (*certainty*) persuasio, fides *f*

convince *vt* persuadēre (*with dat*)

convivial *adj* hilaris, laetus

convocation *s* convocatio *f*

convoke *vt* convocare

convoy *s* praesidium *n*, deductor *m*

convoy *vt* deducĕre

convulse *vt* concutĕre, convellĕre

convulsion *s* convulsio *f*, spasmus *m*

convulsive *adj* spasticus

cook *s* coquus *m*, coqua *f*

cook *vt* & *vi* coquĕre

cool *adj* frigidulus; (*fearless*) sedatus, immotus, impavidus; (*indifferent*) lentus, frigidus; —**ly** frigide; sedate; lente

cool *vt* refrigerare; *vi* refrigerari; (*fig*) defervescĕre

coolness *s* frigus *n*; (*fig*) lentitudo, cautela *f*; animus aequus *m*

coop *s* (*for chickens*) cavea *f*

coop *vt* **to** — **up** includĕre

cooperate *vi* unā agĕre; **to** — **with** adjuvare

cooperation *s* adjumentum *n*, consociatio, opera *f*

cope *vi* **to** — **with** certare cum (*with abl*); **able to** — **with** par (*with dat*)

copious *adj* copiosus, abundans; —**ly** copiose, abundanter

copper *s* aes, cuprum *n*

copper *adj* aëneus, cuprinus

copse *s* dumetum, fruticetum *n*

copy *s* exemplar *n*, imitatio, imago *f*

copy *vt* imitari; (*writing*) transcribĕre, exscribĕre

coquette *s* lupa, lasciva *f*
coquettish *adj* lascivus
coral *adj* coralinus
coral *s* coralium *n*
cord *s* funis, restis *m*
cordial *adj* benignus, comis; —ly
  benigne, comiter, ex animo
cordiality *s* comitas *f*
cordon *s* corona *f*
core *s* (*of fruit*) volva *f*; (*fig*) nucleus
  m
Corinthian *adj* Corinthiacus, Corin-
  thius
cork *s* cortex *m*; (*stopper*) obturamentum *n*
corn *s* (*grain*) frumentum *n*; (*on toes*)
  callus *m*
corner *s* angulus *m*; (*of house*) ver-
  sura *f*; (*of street*) compitum *n*
cornice *s* corona *f*
corollary *s* corollarium *n*
coronation *s* coronae impositio *f*
coronet *s* diadema *n*
corporal *adj* corporeus, corporalis
corporal *s* decurio *m*
corporate *adj* corporatus
corporation *s* collegium *n*; municipium *n*
corporeal *adj* corporeus
corps *s* legio *f*
corpse *s* cadaver *n*
corpulent *adj* corpulentus
corpuscle *s* corpusculum *n*
correct *adj* correctus, rectus, accuratus; —ly recte, bene
correct *vt* corrigĕre, emendare; (*to
  punish*) animadvertĕre, castigare
correction *s* correctio, emendatio *f*;
  (*punishment*) animadversio, castigatio *f*
correctness *s* puritas, accuratio *f*
correlation *s* reciprocitas, mutua
  ratio *f*
correspond *vi* congruĕre; (*by letter*)
  litteras mutuas scribĕre
correspondence *s* congruentia, convenientia *f*; epistolae *f pl*
correspondent *s* epistolarum scriptor *m*
corridor *s* portic·us -ūs *f*, andron,
  xystus *m*
corroborate *vt* confirmare
corrode *vt* erodĕre, edĕre
corrosion *s* rosio *f*
corrosive *adj* corrosivus; (*fig*) mordax
corrupt *vt* corrumpĕre, depravare;
  (*a girl*) stuprare
corrupt *adj* corruptus, putridus; (*fig*)
  pravus, impurus; venalis; —ly corrupte; inceste, turpiter
corrupter *s* corruptor *m*, corruptrix
  f, perditor *m*, perditrix *f*
corruption *s* corruptio, putredo *f*;
  (*fig*) depravatio, pravitas *f*
corselet *s* lorica *f*
corvette *s* celox *f*
cosily *adv* commode
cosmetic *s* medicamen *n*
cost *s* pretium *n*, impensa *f*; — of
  living anona *f*
cost *vi* (con)stare, venire
costliness *s* caritas *f*

costly *adj* carus; (*extravagant*)
  sumptuosus, lautus
costume *s* habit·us -ūs, vestit·us -ūs
  m
cosy *adj* commodus, gratus
cot *s* lectulus *m*; (*mil*) grabatus *m*
cottage *s* casa *f*, tugurium *n*
cotton *s* xylinum *n*
cotton *adj* gossipinus
couch *s* cubile, pulvinar *n*; lectus *m*
cough *s* tussis *f*; to have a bad —
  male tussire
cough *vi* tussire
council *s* concilium *n*
councilor *s* consiliarius *m*
counsel *s* (*advice*) consilium *n*; (*person*) advocatus *m*
counsel *vt* consulĕre, monēre
counselor *s* consiliarius, consiliator *m*
count *s* computatio, ratio *f*; (*of indictment*) caput *n*
count *vt* numerare, computare; (*to
  regard as*) ducĕre, habēre; to — up
  enumerare; *vi* aestimari, habēri; to
  — upon confidĕre (*with dat*)
countenance *s* facies *f*, vult·us -ūs,
  aspect·us -ūs *m*; to put out of —
  confundĕre, perturbare
countenance *vt* favēre (*with dat*),
  indulgēre (*with dat*), adjuvare
counter *s* (*of shop*) abacus *m*; (*in
  games*) calculus *m*
counteract *vt* obsistĕre (*with dat*);
  (*a sickness*) medēri (*with dat*)
counteraction *s* oppositio *f*
counterfeit *vt* imitari, simulare, fingĕre, adulterare
counterfeit *adj* simulatus, spurius,
  ficticius, adulterinus
counterfeit *s* (*money*) nummus adulterinus *m*; simulatio, imitatio *f*
counterfeiter *s* imitator, falsarius *m*
countermand *vt* renuntiare
counterpart *s* res gemella *f*; par *m*,
  f & n
countersign *vt* contrascribĕre
countless *adj* innumerabilis, innumerus
country *s* terra, regio *f*; (*territory*)
  fines *m pl*; (*not city*) rus *n*; (*native*)
  patria *f*
country house *s* villa *f*
countryman *s* civis, popularis *m*
countryside *s* rus *n*, agri *m pl*
couple *s* par *n*; mariti *m pl*; a — of
  duo
couple *vt* copulare, unire; *vi* (*of animals*) coire
courage *s* virtus *f*, animus *m*, fortitudo *f*; to lose — animos dimittĕre; to take — bono animo esse
courageous *adj* fortis, animosus,
  acer; —ly fortiter, acriter
courier *s* cursor, nuntius, tabellarius
  m
course *s* (*movement*) curs·us -ūs *m*;
  (*of life*) ratio *f*; (*of water*) duct·us
  -ūs *m*; (*route*) iter *n*; (*at table*) ferculum *n*; (*order*) series *f*; (*for racing*) circus *m*, stadium *n*; in due —
  mox; in the — of inter (*with acc*);
  of — certe, scilicet
court *s* (*law*) forum, tribunal, judi-

cium *n*, judices *m pl*; *(open area)*
area *f*; *(of house)* atrium *n*; *(palace)*
aula *f*; *(retinue)* comitat·us -ūs *m*
court *vt* colĕre, ambire; *(woman)* petĕre; *(danger)* se offerre *(with dat)*
courteous *adj* comis, urbanus; —**ly**
comiter, urbane
courtesan *s* meretrix *f*
courtesy *s* comitas, urbanitas *f*; *(act)*
officium *n*
courtier *s* aulicus *m*
courtly *adj* aulicus; officiosus
court-martial *s* judicium castrense *n*
courtship *s* amor *m*, ambitio *f*
courtyard *s* aula *f*
cousin *s* consobrinus *m*, consobrina
f, patruelis *m & f*
cove *s* sin·us -ūs *m*
covenant *s* pactum *n*, pactio *f*
covenant *vi* pacisci, stipulari
cover *s* tegmen, integumentum *n*;
(lid) operculum *n*; *(shelter)* tectum
n, *(mil)* praesidium *n*; *(pretense)*
species *f*; **under — of** sub *(with
abl)*, sub specie *(with genit)*
cover *vt* tegĕre, operire; *(to hide)*
celare, velare; **to — up** obtegĕre
coverlet *s* lodix *f*
covet *vt* concupiscĕre, cupĕre, appetĕre
covetous *adj* avidus, appetens, cupidus; —**ly** avide, avare, appetenter
covey *s* grex *m*
cow *vt* domare
coward *s* homo *or* miles ignavus *m*
cowardice *s* ignavia *f*
cowardly *adj* ignavus
cower *vi* sudsidĕre
cowherd *s* bubulcus *m*
cowl *s* cucullus *m*
coy *adj* verecundus, pudens; —**ly** verecunde, pudenter
coyness *s* verecundia *f*, pudor *m*
cozily *adv* commode, jucunde
cozy *adj* commodus, jucundus
crab *s* cancer *m*
crabbed *adj* morosus, difficilis
crack *s* fissura, rima *f*; *(noise)* cre-
pit·us -ūs *m*; **at — of dawn** prima
luce
cracked *adj* rimosus; *(fig)* cerritus,
delirus
cracker *s* crustulum *n*
crackle *vi* crepitare
crackling *s* crepit·us -ūs *m*
cradle *s* cunae *f pl*, cunabula *n pl*
craft *s* *(cunning)* astutia *f*, artes *f pl*,
dolus *m*; *(skill)* ars *f*; *(trade)* ars *f*;
(boat) scapha, cymba *f*, navigium *n*
craftily *adv* callide, astute; dolose
crafty *adj* astutus, callidus, subdolus
craftsman *s* artifex, faber *m*
craftsmanship *s* artificium *n*, ma-
n·us -ūs *f*
cram *vt* farcire; **to — together**
constipare
cramp *s* spasmus *m*
cramp *vt* comprimĕre, coartare
crane *s* *(bird)* grus *m & f*; *(machine)*
tolleno *f*; machina *f*
crank *s* *(machine)* uncus *m*; *(person)*
morosus *m*

crash *s* fragor, strepit·us -ūs *m*, ruina *f*
crash *vi* strepĕre, frangorem dare
crater *s* crater *m*
crave *vt* efflagitare, appetĕre, concupiscĕre, desiderare
craven *adj* ignavus atque abjectus
craving *s* desiderium *n*, appetitio *f*
crawl *vi* repĕre, serpĕre
crayfish *s* commarus *m*
crayon *s* creta *f*
craze *s* libido *f*
craziness *s* imbecillitas, mens aliena-
ta *f*, furor *m*
crazy *adj* imbecillus, demens, cerritus; **to drive — mentem** alienare
(with genit)
creak *vi* stridĕre, crepitare
creaking *s* stridor, crepit·us -ūs *m*
creaking *adj* stridulus
cream *s* flos lactis *m*; *(fig)* flos *m*
crease *s* plica, ruga *f*
crease *vt* corrugare, rugare
create *vt* creare; *(fig)* fingĕre
creation *s* *(act)* creatio *f*; *(world)*
summa rerum *f*, mundus *m*; *(fig)*
opus *n*
creative *adj* creatrix, effectrix
creator *s* creator, opifex, auctor *m*
creature *s* animal *n*; homo *m*;
(lackey) minister *m*
credence *s* fides *f*; **to give — to**
credĕre *(with dat)*
credentials *s* litterae commendaticiae *f pl*; testimonia *n pl*
credibility *s* fides, auctoritas *f*
credible *adj* credibilis; *(of persons)*
locuples
credit *s* *(authority)* auctoritas *f*;
(faith) fides *f*; *(reputation)* existimatio, fama *f*; *(com)* fides *f*; *(recognition)* laus *f*
credit *vt* credĕre *(with dat)*; *(com)* acceptum referre *(with dat)*
creditable *adj* honorificus, honestus,
laudabilis
creditor *s* creditor *m*
credulity *s* credulitas *f*
credulous *adj* credulus; —**ly** credens
creed *s* fides, religio *f*, dogma *n*
creek *s* aestuarium *n*; fluvius *m*
creep *vi* repĕre, serpĕre; *(of flesh)*
horrēre
crescent *s* luna crescens *f*
crescent-shaped *adj* lunatus
crest *s* crista *f*
crested *adj* cristatus
crestfallen *adj* dejectus, demissus
crevice *s* rima, rimula *f*
crew *s* grex *m*; *(of ship)* remiges,
nautae *m pl*
crib *s* *(manger)* praesepe *n*; *(small
bed)* lectulus *m*
cricket *s* gryllus *m*, cicada *f*
crier *s* praeco *m*
crime *s* scelus, delictum, maleficium,
flagitium *n*
Crimea *s* Tauris *f*
criminal *adj* criminosus, scelestus,
flagitiosus; —**ly** nefarie, improbe;
(law) criminaliter
criminal *s* reus, sceleratus *m*
crimp *vt* crispare

crimson *adj* coccineus
crimson *s* coccum *n*
cringe *vi* adulari, assentari
cringing *s* adulatio abjecta *f*
cripple *s* claudus *m*
cripple *vt* claudum facĕre, mutilare, debilitare; (*fig*) frangĕre
crippled *adj* mancus, claudus
crisis *s* discrimen *n*
crisp *adj* crispus, fragilis; (*fig*) alacer
criterion *s* norma *f*, indicium *n*, index *m*
critic *s* judex, censor, existimator *m*; (*literary*) criticus, grammaticus *m*
critical *adj* criticus, intellegens; (*careful*) accuratus; (*blaming*) fastidiosus, censorius; (*crucial*) anceps, periculosus; —**ly** accurate; periculose
criticism *s* ars critica *f*; censura, reprehensio *f*, judicium *n*
criticize *vt* judicare; carpĕre, reprehendĕre, agitare, castigare
croak *vi* coaxare; (*of raven*) crocitare, crocire; (*fig*) queritari
croaking *s* crocitatio *f*; (*fig*) querimonia *f*
croaking *adj* raucus
crock *s* olla *f*
crocodile *s* crocodilus *m*
crook *s* pedum *n*
crook *vt* curvare, flectĕre
crooked *adj* curvatus, flexus; (*fig*) pravus, dolosus; —**ly** prave
crop *s* (*of grain*) messis, seges *f*; (*of bird*) ingluvies *f*
crop *vt* abscidere, tondĕre; (*to harvest*) metĕre; (*to browse*) carpĕre
cross *s* crux *f*; (*figure*) quincunx *m*, decussis *f*; (*fig*) molestia *f*, cruciat·us -ūs *m*
cross *adj* transversus; (*contrary*) adversus; (*peevish*) acerbus, morosus
cross *vt* transire, transgredi; (*river*) trajicĕre; (*mountain*) transcendĕre; (*to thwart*) frustrari, adversari; to — out expungĕre, delēre
cross-examination *s* percontatio, interrogatio *f*
cross-examine *vt* percontari, interrogare
crossing *s* transit·us -ūs, traject·us -ūs *m*; (*of roads*) bivium *n*; (*of three roads*) trivium *n*; (*of four roads*) quadrivium *n*
cross-roads *s* quadrivium *n*
crouch *vi* se submittĕre, subsidĕre
crow *s* (*bird*) cornix *f*; (*of cock*) cant·us -ūs *m*, gallicinium *n*
crow *vi* (*of cocks*) canĕre, cucurire; (*to boast*) jactare, gestire
crowbar *s* vectis *f*
crowd *s* turba, frequentia *f*, concurs·us -ūs *m*; in —s gregatim
crowd *vt* arctare, stipare, premere; *vi* frequentare; to — around stipare, circumfundi
crowded *adj* confertus, frequens, spissus
crowing *s* gallicinium *n*, cant·us -ūs *m*
crown *s* corona *f*, diadema *n*; (*top*)

vertex *m*; (*fig*) apex *m*
crown *vt* coronare; (*with garlands, etc.*) cingĕre; (*fig*) cumulare
crucifix *s* imago Christi cruci affixi *f*
crucifixion *s* crucis supplicium *n*
crucify *vt* in cruce suffigĕre
crude *adj* crudus; rudis, incultus, informis; —**ly** imperfecte; inculte
cruel *adj* crudelis, atrox, saevus; —**ly** crudeliter, saeve, dure
cruelty *s* crudelitas, atrocitas, saevitia *f*
cruet *s* guttus *m*, acetabulum *n*
cruise *vi* circumvectari, navigare
cruise *s* navigatio *f*
crumb *s* mica *f*
crumble *vt* friare, putrefacĕre, comminuĕre, conterĕre; *vi* collabi, friari, corruere
crumbling *adj* puter, friabilis
crumple *vt* corrugare, duplicare
crunch *vt* dentibus frangĕre
crush *vt* contundĕre, conterĕre; (*fig*) opprimĕre, affligere
crush *s* contusio *f*; (*crowd*) turba, frequentia *f*
crust *s* crusta *f*, crustum *n*
crusty *adj* crustosus; (*fig*) cerebrosus, stomachosus
crutch *s* fulcrum *n*
cry *vt* clamare, clamitare; to — out exclamare, vociferari; *vi* (*to shout*) clamare, clamitare; (*to weep*) lacrimare, flēre; (*of infant*) vagire; to — out exclamare; to — out against objurgare
cry *s* clamor *m*; (*of infant*) vagit·us -ūs *m*; (*weeping*) plorat·us -ūs *m*
crying *s* flet·us -ūs, plorat·us -ūs *m*
crypt *s* crypta *f*
crystal *adj* crystallinus, vitreus
crystal *s* crystallum *n*
crystal-clear *adj* pellucidus
cub *s* catulus *m*
cube *s* cubus *m*
cubic *adj* cubicus
cubit *s* cubitum *n*, ulna *f*
cuckoo *s* coccyx, cuculus *m*
cucumber *s* cucumis *m*
cud *s* ruma *f*, rumen *n*; to chew the — ruminare
cudgel *s* fustis *m*
cue *s* (*hint*) nut·us -ūs *m*, signum, indicium *n*
cuff *s* (*blow*) colaphus *m*; (*of sleeves*) extrema manica *f*
cull *vt* carpĕre, legĕre, decerpĕre
culminate *vi* ad summum fastigium venire
culpable *adj* culpandus, nocens
culprit *s* reus *m*, rea *f*
cultivate *vt* colĕre; (*the mind*) excolere; (*friends*) fovēre
cultivation *s* cultura *f*, cult·us -ūs *m*
cultivator *s* cultor, colonus *m*
culture *s* cultura *f*, cult·us -ūs *m*
cumbersome *adj* onerosus, impediens
cunning *adj* sollers, callidus, doctus, peritus; (*in bad sense*) astutus
cunning *s* calliditas, peritia; astutia *f*
cup *s* poculum *n*, calix *m*; (*of flower*) calyx *m*

cupbearer s pocillator m
cupboard s armarium n
Cupid s Cupido, Amor m
cupidity s cupiditas f
cupola s tholus m; turricula rotunda f
cur s canis m; (fig) scelestus m
curable adj medicabilis, sanabilis
curative adj medicabilis
curator s curator m
curb s frenum n; (fig) coercitio f, frenum n
curb vt frenare, infrenare; (fig) coercēre, cohibēre
curdle vt coagulare; vi coagulare, concrescēre
cure s (remedy) remedium n; (process) sanatio f
cure vt medēri (with dat), sanare; (to pickle) salire
curiosity s curiositas f; (thing) miraculum n
curious adj curiosus; (strange) mirus, novus, insolitus; —ly curiose; mirabiliter, mirum in modum
curl vt (hair) crispare, torquēre; vi crispari; (of smoke) volvi
curl s (natural) cirrus m; (artificial) cincinnus m
curly adj crispus
currency s (money) moneta f; (use) us·us -ūs m
current adj vulgaris, usitatus; —ly vulgo
current s flumen n; (of air) afflat·us -ūs m, aura f; **against the —** adverso flumine; **with the —** secundo flumine
curse s execratio, maledictio f, maledictum n; (fig) pestis f
curse vt maledicĕre (with dat), exsecrari; vi exsecratione uti
cursed adj exsecrabilis
corsorily adv breviter, summatim
cursory adj levis, brevis
curt adj abruptus; —ly breviter
curtail vt minuĕre, coartare; decurtare
curtain s velum, aulaeum n
curvature s curvatura f
curve s curvamen n, flex·us -ūs m, curvatura f

curve vt incurvare, flectĕre, inflectĕre, arcuare
curved adj curvatus, curvus; (as a sickle) falcatus
cushion s pulvinar n; (on a seat) sedularia n pl
custard s artolaganus m
custody s custodia, tutela f; (imprisonment) carcer m; **to keep in —** custodire
custom s mos, us·us -ūs m, consuetudo f, institutum, praescriptum n; (duty) portorium, vectigal n
customary adj usitatus, consuetus, tralaticius
customer s emptor m
customs officer s portitor m
cut vt secare; (to fell) caedĕre; (to mow) succidĕre; **to — apart** intercidĕre, dissecare; **to — away** recidĕre, abscindĕre; (to amputate) amputare; **to — down** caedĕre; (to kill) occidĕre; **to — in pieces** concidĕre; **to — off** praecidĕre, abscindĕre; (the head) detruncare; (to intercept) intercludĕre, prohibĕre; (to destroy) exstinguĕre; **to — open** incidĕre; **to — out** exsecare; (out of rock, etc.) excidĕre; **to — short** intercidĕre; (to abridge) praecidĕre; (fig) (to interrupt) interpellare; **to — up** minutatim concidĕre; (enemy) trucidare
cutlass s ensis, gladius m
cutlery s cultri m pl
cutlet s offa f, frustum n
cutthroat s sicarius m
cutting adj (sharp) acutus; (fig) mordax
cutting s (act) sectio, consectio, exsectio f; (thing) segmen n
cuttlefish s loligo, sepia f
cycle s orbis m
cylinder s cylindrus m
cylindrical adj cylindratus
cymbal s cymbalum n
cynic adj cynicus
cynic s cynicus m
cynical adj mordax, difficilis; —ly mordaciter
cynicism s acerbitas f
cypress s cupressus f

D

dab vt illidĕre
dab s massula f
dabble vi **to — in** gustare
dactyl s dactylus m
dactylic adj dactylicus
daffodil s asphodelus, narcissus m
dagger s pugio m, sica f
daily adj diurnus, quotidianus or cottidianus
daily adv quotidie or cottidie, in dies
dainty adj (of persons) fastidiosus, mollis, elegans; (of things) delicatus, exquisitus

dairy s cella lactaria f
daisy s bellis f
dale s vallis f
dalliance s lus·us -ūs m, lascivia f
dally vi morari; (to trifle) nugari, ludificari
dam s moles f, agger m; (of animals) mater f
damage s damnum, incommodum, detrimentum n; (injury) injuria, noxa f
damage vt nocēre (with dat), laedĕre; (reputation) violare

dame s domina, hera, matrona f
damn vt damnare, exsecrari
damnable adj damnabilis, destestabilis
damnably adv damnabiliter, improbe
damnation s damnatio f
damp adj (h)umidus
dampen vt humectare; (fig) infringere, restinguĕre
dampness s uligo f
damsel s puella, virgo f
dance s saltat·us -ūs m, saltatio f
dance vi saltare
dancer s saltator m
dancing s saltatio f, saltat·us -ūs m
dandelion s taraxacum n
dandruff s porrigo f
dandy s homo bellus et lepidus m
danger s periculum n
dangerous adj periculosus; —ly periculose, graviter
dangle vi pendēre, dependēre
dangling adj pendulus
dank adj (h)umidus, uvidus, udus
dappled adj variatus, variegatus
dare vt provocare; vi audēre
daring adj audax; —ly audacter
daring s audacia, audentia f
dark adj obscurus, opacus; (in color) ater, fuscus; (fig) obscurus, ambiguus; atrox; —ly obscure
dark s tenebrae f pl; obscurum n; to keep in the — celare
darken vt obscurare, occaecare; (of colors) infuscare
darkness s obscuritas, opacitas f, tenebrae f pl
darling adj suavis, mellitus, carus, dilectus
darling s deliciae f pl, corculum n
darn vt resarcire
dart s jaculum, spiculum n
dart vt jaculari, jacĕre; vi provolare, emicare, se conjicĕre
dash vt (to splash) aspergĕre; (hopes) frustrari, frangĕre; to — against illidĕre, incutĕre, offendĕre; to — off (to write hurriedly) scriptitare; to — to pieces discutĕre; to — to the ground prosternĕre; vi (to rush) ruĕre, ferri
dash s impet·us -ūs m; curs·us -ūs m; (animation) alacritas f; (small amount) admixtio f
dashing adj acer, alacer, fulgidus, splendidus
data s facta n pl
date s (time) dies m & f, tempus n; (fruit) palmula f; to become out of — exolescĕre; to — adhuc; out of — obsoletus
date vt diem ascribĕre (with dat); vi to — from oriri ab (with abl), originem trahĕre ab (with abl)
date palm s phoenix, palma f
dative s dativus m
daub vt oblinĕre, illinĕre
daughter s filia f
daughter-in-law s nurus f
daunt vt pavefacĕre, perterrēre
dauntless adj impavidus, intrepidus; —ly impavide, intrepide
dawdle vi morari, cessare, cunctari

dawn s aurora, prima lux f, diluculum n; at — prima luce
dawn vi illucescere, dilucescĕre; (fig) to — on occurrĕre (with dat)
day s dies m & f; lux f, sol m; by — interdiu; — by — in dies; every — quotidie, cottidie; from — to — in dies; next — postridie; some — olim; the — after to-morrow perendie; the — before pridie
day adj diurnus, dialis
daybreak s lux prima f; before — antelucio
daylight s lux f, dies m & f
daystar s Lucifer, Phosphorus m
daytime s dies m, tempus diurnum n; in the — interdiu
daze s stupor m
daze vt obstupefacĕre
dazzle vt obcaecare, praestringĕre
dazzling adj fulgidus, splendidus
deacon s diaconus m
dead adj mortuus; defunctus; (fig) torpidus, segnis, iners
dead s manes m pl; — of night media nox f; — of winter summa hiems f
dead adv omnino, totaliter, prorsus
deaden vt hebetare, obtundĕre; vi hebetari, obtundi
deadly adj mortifer, letalis; (fig) capitalis, implacabilis
deaf adj surdus; to be — to non audire
deafen vt exsurdare, obtundĕre
deaf-mute adj surdus idemque mutus
deafness s surditas f
deal s (quantity) numerum m, copia f; (com) negotium n; a good — longer multo diutius; a good — of aliquantus
deal vt partiri, dividĕre, distribuĕre; vi (com) mercari, negotiari; to — with (to treat of) agĕre de (with abl), tractare
dealer s mercator, negotiator, distributor m
dealing s negotiatio, mercatura f; (doing) facta n pl
dean s decanus m
dear adj carus, dulcis, gratus; (costly) carus, preciosus; —ly valde, ardenter; (at high cost) magni, magno
dear interj (dismay) heil; (surprise) ahem!
dearness s caritas f
dearth s inopia, penuria, fames f
death s mors f, obit·us -ūs, interit·us -ūs m; (in violent form) nex f
deathbed s on the — moriens, moribundus
deathless adj immortalis
deathlike adj cadaverosus, luridus
deathly adj pallidus
debase vt depravare, corrumpĕre; (coinage) adulterare; to — one-self se demittĕre, se prosternĕre
debasement s adulteratio f; ignominia f, dedecus n
debatable adj disputabilis, controversiosus, ambiguus

debate *vt* disputare, disceptare; *vi* argumentari, disserēre

debate *s* disceptatio, controversia, altercatio *f*; (*law*) actio *f*

debater *s* disputator *m*

debauch *vt* stuprare, corrumpēre, vitiare; *vi* (*to revel*) debacchari

debauchery *s* ganea *f*, stuprum *n*

debilitate *vt* debilitare

debit *s* expensum *n*

debit *vt* in expensum referre

debt *s* aes alienum *n*; (*fig*) debitum *n*; **to pay off a — aes alienum persolvēre; to run up a — aes alienum contrahēre**

debtor *s* debitor *m*

decade *s* decem anni *m pl*

decadence *s* occas·us ·ūs *m*

decadent *adj* degener

decalogue *s* decalogus *m*

decamp *vi* (*mil*) castra movēre; (*fig*) aufugēre, discedēre

decant *vt* diffundēre

decanter *s* lagoena *f*

decapitate *vt* detruncare

decay *s* tabes, ruina *f*, laps·us ·ūs *m*; (*fig*) defectio *f*

decay *vi* putrescēre, tabescēre, senescēre

decease *s* mors *f*, obit·us ·ūs *m*, decess·us ·ūs *m*

deceased *adj* mortuus, defunctus

deceit *s* fraus *f*, dolus *m*

deceitful *adj* fallax, dolosus, fraudulentus; **—ly** fallaciter, dolose

deceive *vt* decipēre, fallēre, fraudare

December *s* (mensis) December *m*

decency *s* decorum *n*, honestas *f*

decent *adj* honestus, pudicus; **—ly** honeste, pudenter

deception *s* deceptio, fallacia, fraus *f*

deceptive *adj* fallax, fraudulentus, vanus, falsus

decide *vt & vi* (*dispute*) disceptare, dijudicare, decernēre; **to — to — constituēre** (*with inf*), statuēre (*with inf*); **the senate decided** placuit senatui; visum est senatui

decided *adj* firmus, constans; (*of things*) certus; **—ly** certe, plane

deciduous *adj* caducus

decimate *vt* decimare; (*fig*) depopulari

decipher *vt* explicare, expedire, enodare

decision *s* sententia *f*; judicium, arbitrium, decretum *n*; (*of senate*) auctoritas *f*

decisive *adj* certus, firmus; **—ly** praecise

deck *vt* exornare, ornare; (*table*) sternēre

deck *s* pons *m*

declamatory *adj* declamatorius; (*fig*) inflatus

declaration *s* declaratio, professio, affirmatio *f*; (*of war*) denuntiatio *f*

declare *vt* declarare, affirmare, aperire, profitēri; (*war*) denuntiare, indicēre; (*proclamation*) edicēre; *vi* **to — for** favēre (*with dat*)

declension *s* declinatio *f*

declinable *adj* declinabilis, casualis

declination *s* declinatio *f*; (*decay*) defectio *f*

decline *s* (*slope*) declive *n*; (*of strength*) defectio, diminutio *f*

decline *vt* (*to refuse*) recusare, renuēre, abnuēre; (*gram*) declinare, flectēre; (*battle*) detrectare; *vi* vergēre, inclinare; (*to decay, fail*) deficēre, minui, decrescēre; (*of prices*) laxare

decode *vt* enodare

decompose *vt* dissolvēre, resolvēre; *vi* tabescēre, putescēre, dissolvi

decomposition *s* dissolutio *f*

decorate *vt* ornare, decorare

decoration *s* ornatio *f*; (*ornament*) ornamentum *n*; (*distinction*) decus *n*

decorator *s* exornator *m*

decorous *adj* decorus, modestus, pudens; **—ly** decore, modeste, pudenter

decorum *s* decorum, honestum *n*, pudor *m*

decoy *s* illecebra *f*, illicium *n*

decoy *vt* allicēre, inescare; (*fig*) illicēre

decrease *s* deminutio, imminutio *f*

decrease *vt* (de)minuēre, imminuēre, extenuare; *vi* decrescēre, (de)minui

decree *s* decretum, edictum *n*; (*of senate*) consultum *n*, auctoritas *f*; (*of assembly*) scitum *n*

decree *vt* decernēre, edicēre; (*of assembly*) jubēre, sciscēre; **the senate — s** senatui placet, senatui videtur

decrepit *adj* decrepitus, debilis

decry *vt* detrectare, obtrectare, vituperare

dedicate *vt* dedicare, consecrare, devovēre

dedication *s* dedicatio, devotio *f*; (*of a book*) nuncupatio *f*

deduce *vt* deducēre, concludēre

deducible *adj* consectarius

deduct *vt* detrahēre, subtrahēre, demēre

deduction *s* deductio, deminutio *f*; (*inference*) conclusio *f*, consequens *n*

deed *s* factum, facinus *n*; (*law*) syngrapha *f*, instrumentum *n*

deem *vt* judicare, existimare, ducēre, habēre

deep *adj* altus, profundus; (*of sounds*) gravis; (*of color*) satur; (*fig*) abstrusus, gravis; **—ly** alte, profunde; (*inwardly*) penitus; (*fig*) valde, graviter, vehemen-

deep *s* profundum, altum *n*

deepen *vt* defodēre; (*fig*) augēre; *vi* altior fieri; (*fig*) crescēre, densare

deer *s* cervus *m*, cerva *f*; (*fallow deer*) dama *f*

deface *vt* deformare, turpare, foedare

defaced *adj* deformis

defacement *s* deformitas *f*

defamation *s* calumnia *f*, opprobrium *n*

defamatory *adj* probrosus, contumeliosus

defame *vt* diffamare, infamare, calumniari

default *s* culpa *f*, delictum *n*, defect·us -ūs *m*

defeat *s* clades *f*; (*at polls*) repulsa *f*

defeat *vt* vincere, superare; (*to baffle*) frustrari

defect *s* vitium, mendum *n*; (*lack*) defect·us -ūs *m*

defect *vi* (*to desert*) deficĕre

defection *s* defectio *f*

defective *adj* vitiosus, imperfectus, mancus; (*gram*) defectivus

defend *vt* defendere, custodire, tuĕri; (*in court*) patrocinari

defendant *s* reus *m*, rea *f*

defender *s* defensor, propugnator *m*; (*law*) patronus *m*

defense *s* (*act*) defensio *f*; praesidium, munimentum *n*, tutela *f*; (*law*) patrocinium *n*; (*speech*) defensio *f*

defenseless *adj* inermis, infensus; defensoribus nudatus

defensible *adj* excusabilis, justus; inexpugnabilis

defensive *adj* defendens; — **weapons** arma *n pl*

defer *vt* differre; *vi* obsequi

deference *s* observantia, reverentia *f*, obsequium *n*; **out of** — reverenter

defiance *s* provocatio, ferocia *f*

defiant *adj* minax, insolens; —**ly** insolenter

deficiency *s* defectio, inopia, penuria *f*, defect·us -ūs *m*

deficient *adj* inops, mancus; **to be** — deficere, deesse

deficit *s* lacuna *f*

defile *s* fauces *f pl*

defile *vt* contaminare, inquinare; (*fig*) foedare

define *vt* (*meaning*) explicare; (*limits*) (de)finire, circumscribĕre, terminare

definite *adj* definitus, certus; —**ly** certe, certo, prorsus; definite

definition *s* definitio *f*

definitive *adj* definitivus; —**ly** definite, distincte

deflect *vt* deflectĕre, declinare; *vi* deflectĕre, errare

deflection *s* deflexio, declinatio *f*, flex·us -ūs *m*

deflower *vt* stuprare

deform *vt* deformare

deformed *adj* deformatus, deformis, distortus, pravus

deformity *s* deformitas, pravitas *f*

defraud *vt* fraudare, defraudare

defray *vt* praebere, suppeditare

defunct *adj* defunctus, mortuus

defy *vt* provocare, contemnĕre, spernĕre

degeneracy *s* mores corrupti *m pl*

degenerate *adj* degener

degenerate *vi* degenerare

degradation *s* dedecus *n*, ignominia, infamia *f*

degrade *vt* dejicĕre, abdicare; ex loco movēre

degrading *adj* indignus

degree *s* grad·us -ūs, ordo *m*

deification *s* apotheosis *f*

deify *vt* divum habēre, inter deos re-

ferre, consecrare

deign *vt* dignari, curare

deism *s* deismus *m*

deity *s* numen *n*; deus *m*, dea *f*

dejected *adj* afflictus, demissus; —**ly** maeste

dejection *s* animi abjectio, maestitia *f*

delay *s* mora, cunctatio *f*

delay *vt* detinēre, tardare, remorari; *vi* morari, cunctari

delectable *adj* amoenus, jucundus

delegate *s* legatus *m*

delegate *vt* delegare, mandare, committĕre

delegation *s* delegatio, legatio *f*

delete *vt* delēre

deletion *s* litura *f*

deliberate *adj* deliberatus, consideratus, cautus, prudens; (*speech*) lentus; —**ly** deliberate, de industria; lente

deliberate *vi* deliberare, considerare, consulere

deliberation *s* deliberatio, consultatio *f*

delicacy *s* subtilitas, tenuitas *f*; elegantia *f*; (*manner*) lux·us -ūs *m*; (*health*) suavitas *f*; (*food*) cuppedia *f*

delicate *adj* (*tender*) delicatus, tener, mollis, exquisitus; (*of texture*) subtilis; (*in taste*) elegans, fastidiosus; (*in health*) infirmus; —**ly** delicate; eleganter; subtiliter

deli'cious *adj* suavis, dulcis

delight *s* delectatio *f*, gaudium *n*, voluptas *f*

delight *vt* delectare, oblectare; *vi* **to** — **in** delectari (*with abl*)

delightful *adj* suavis, jucundus; —**ly** suaviter, jucunde

delineate *vt* delineare, describĕre, adumbrare

delineation *s* designatio, descriptio *f*

delinquency *s* delictum *n*

delinquent *s* nocens *m & f*, noxius *m*

delirious *adj* delirus, phreneticus

delirium *s* delirium *n*, phrensis *f*

deliver *vt* (*to hand over*) tradĕre, dare; (*to free*) liberare, eripĕre; (*to surrender*) prodĕre; (*speech*) habēre; (*sentence*) dicĕre; (*message*) referre; (*blow*) intendĕre; (*child*) obstetricari

deliverance *s* liberatio *f*

deliverer *s* liberator *m*; nuntius *m*

delivery *s* liberatio *f*; (*of goods*) traditio *f*; (*of speech*) actio, pronuntiatio *f*; (*of child*) part·us -ūs *m*

delude *vt* decipĕre, deludĕre

deluge *s* diluvium *n*, inundatio *f*

deluge *vt* inundare, obruĕre

delusion *s* delusio *f*, error *m*

demagogue *s* plebicola *m*

demand *s* postulatio, petitio *f*, postulatum *n*

demand *vt* postulare, flagitare, poscĕre; exigĕre

demarcation *s* confinium *n*

demean *vt* **to** — **oneself** se demittere

demeanor *s* gest·us -ūs *m*, mores *m pl*

demerit s culpa f, delictum n
demigod s heros m
demise s decess·us ·ūs, obit·us ·ūs m
democracy s civitas popularis f, liber populus m
democrat s homo popularis m
democratic adj popularis; —ally populi voluntate
demolish vt demoliri, disjicěre, diruěre, destruěre
demolition s demolitio, destructio f
demon s daemon m
demonstrable adj demonstrabilis
demonstrably adv clare, manifeste
demonstrate vt (to show) monstrare, ostenděre; (to prove) demonstrare
demonstration s demonstratio f
demonstrative adj demonstrativus; —ly demonstrative
demoralization s depravatio f
demoralize vt depravare, labefactare
demote vt loco movēre
demure adj taciturnus, modestus; —ly modeste, pudice
den s latibulum n
deniable adj infitiandus
denial s negatio, repudiatio f
denomination s nominatio f, nomen n; secta f
denote vt significare
denounce vt denuntiare, deferre
dense adj densus, spissus, confertus; —ly dense, crebro
density s densitas, crassitudo f; (crowd) frequentia f
dent s nota f
dentist s dentium medicus m
denude vt nudare, denudare
denunciation s denuntiatio, accusatio f
deny vt negare, abnegare; (to renounce) renuntiare
depart vi abire, disceděre, proficisci; (to die) obire
departed adj mortuus, defunctus
department s pars, provincia f
departure s abit·us ·ūs, discess·us ·ūs, digress·us ·ūs m; (deviation) digressio f; (death) obit·us ·ūs m
depend vi to — on pendēre ex (with abl), niti (with abl); (to rely on) fiděre (with dat or abl)
dependable adj fidus
dependence s clientela f; (reliance) fiducia f
dependency s provincia f
dependent adj subjectus, obediens, obnoxius
depict vt (de)pingěre; describěre, expriměre
deplete vt deminuěre
depletion s deminutio f
deplorable adj miserabilis, flebilis, plorabilis
deplorably adv misere, pessime
deplore vt deplorare, deflēre
deploy vt (mil) explicare, expedire
deponent adj (gram) deponens
deportment s gest·us ·ūs, habit·us ·ūs m
depose vt (de)movēre

deposit vt deponěre
deposit s depositum n, fiducia f
deposition s depositio f, testimonium n
depositor s depositor m
depot s (com) emporium n; (for military supplies) armamentarium n
deprave vt depravare
depravity s depravatio, turpitudo, pravitas f
deprecate vt deprecari
deprecation s deprecatio f
depreciate vt detrectare, obtrectare
depreciation s detrectatio, obrectatio f; (of price) vilitas f
depredation s spoliatio, direptio f
depress vt depriměre; (fig) infringěre, affligěre
depressed adj depressus, afflictus; (flat) planus; (hollow) cavus
depression s depressio, imminutio f; (fig) tristitia f
depressive adj tristis, affligens
deprivation s privatio, orbatio f; (state) inopia f
deprive vt privare, spoliare
depth s altitudo, profunditas f, profundum n; (bottom) fundus m
deputation s legatio f, legati m pl
deputy s legatus, vicarius m
derange vt (per)turbare, conturbare
deranged adj mente captus
derangement s perturbatio, confusio f; (of mind) mentis alienatio f
dereliction s derelictio, destitutio f
deride vt deridēre, irridēre
derision s ris·us ·ūs m, irrisio f
derisive adj irridens
derivation s derivatio, origo f
derivative adj derivativus, derivatus
derive vt derivare, deducěre; vi proceděre, oriri
derogatory adj inhonestus, indignus
descend vi descenděre, delabi; to — upon (to attack) irrumpěre in (with acc)
descendant s progenies f; —s posteri m pl
descent s descens·us ·ūs m; (slope) declivitas f, clivus m; (lineage) genus n
describe vt describěre, perscriběre; depingěre; narrare
description s descriptio f; narratio f
desecrate vt profanare, polluěre
desecration s profanatio, violatio f
desert s (wilderness) loca deserta n pl, solitudo f
desert s (merit) meritum n, dignitas f
desert vt deserěre, relinquěre; vi transfugěre, deficěre
deserter s desertor m; (mil) transfuga m
desertion s desertio, defectio f; transfugium n
deserve vt merēre, merēri
deserving adj meritus, dignus
design s (drawing) adumbratio f; (plan) consilium, propositum n
design vt designare; (to sketch) adumbrare; (fig) machinari

designate vt designare, nominare, appellare

designation s designatio f; vocabulum, nomen n, titulus m

designer s inventor, auctor, fabricator, machinator m

designing adj callidus

desirable adj optabilis, desiderabilis

desire s appetitio, cupiditas, cupido f; (request) rogat·us -ūs m

desire vt cupĕre, optare, expetĕre; (to request) orare, petĕre

desirous adj cupidus, appetens

desist vi desistĕre; (to cease) desinĕre

desk s scrinium, pulpitum n, mensa scriptoria f

desolate adj desolatus, solitarius; (of persons) afflictus

desolate vt devastare

desolation s vastatio f; (state) solitudo, vastitas f

despair s desperatio f

despair vi desperare

desperado s sicarius m

desperate adj desperatus; (dangerous) periculosus; —ly desperanter; to be —ly in love perdite amare

desperation s desperatio f

despicable adj abjectus, vilis, turpis

despise vt despicĕre, spernĕre, contemnĕre

despite prep contra (with acc)

despite s malevolentia f, odium n

despoil vt nudare, spoliare

despondency s animi abjectio f

despondent adj abjectus, demissus; —ly animo demisso

despot s dominus, tyrannus m

despotic adj tyrannicus; —ally tyrannice

despotism s dominatio f

dessert s secunda mensa f, bellaria n pl

destination s destinatio f, propositum n

destine vt destinare, designare

destiny s fatum n, sors f

destitute adj egens, inops, destitutus; — of expers (with genit)

destitution s inopia, mendicitas f

destroy vt destruĕre, subvertĕre, abolēre, delēre, vastare; to be destroyed interire

destroyer s deletor, vastator m

destruction s eversio, clades f, exitium n

destructive adj exitialis, perniciosus; —ly perniciose

desultory adj inconstans

detach vt sejungĕre, separare, amovēre

detached adj sejunctus; (of houses) solus

detachment s separatio f; (mil) man·us -ūs f; (aloofness) secess·us -ūs m

detail s singula n pl, singulae res f pl

detail vt enumerare

detain vt detinēre, retinēre, retardare

detect vt detegĕre, comperire, patefacĕre

detection s patefacio f, indicium n

detective s inquisitor m

detention s retentio f; (law) mora f

deter vt deterrēre, avertĕre

detergent s smegma m

deterioration s depravatio, corruptio f

determination s constantia, obstinatio f; (intention) propositum n

determine vt (to decide) statuĕre, constituĕre, discernĕre; (to fix) determinare, definire

determined adj certus; (resolute) firmus, obstinatus

detest vt abominari, detestari

detestable adj detestabilis, foedus

dethrone vt regno depellĕre

detonate vi crepare

detonation s fragor m

detour s circuit·us -ūs m

detour vi iter flectĕre, circumagi

detract vt detrahĕre; vi to — from detrectare, obtrectare

detraction s obtrectatio f

detractor s obtrectator m

detriment s detrimentum, damnum n

detrimental adj injuriosus, damnosus; to be — to detrimento esse (with dat)

devastate vt vastare, depopulari

devastation s (act) vastatio, populatio f; (state) vastitas f

develop vt evolvĕre, explicare; (person) alĕre; vi crescĕre; to — into evadĕre in (with acc)

development s explicatio f, progres-s·us -ūs m

deviate vi aberrare, degredi, decedĕre

deviation s aberratio, declinatio, digressio f

device s (contrivance) artificium n, machina f; (plan) consilium n; (emblem) insigne n

devil s diabolus, daemon m; go to the —! abi in malam crucem!

devilish adj diabolicus, daemonicus; (fig) nefandus

devious adj devius; vagus, erraticus

devise vt fingĕre, excogitare, concoquĕre

devoid adj inanis, vacuus, expers; to be — of carēre (with abl)

devolve vi to — upon obtingĕre, pervenire ad (with acc)

devote vt devovēre, consecrare; to — oneself to studēre (with dat), se dedere (with dat)

devoted adj deditus, studiosus; — to studiosus (with genit)

devotee s cultor m

devotion s devotio, addictio f, studium n

devour vt devorare; (fig) haurire

devout adj pius, religiosus; —ly pie, religiose

dew s ros m

dewdrop s gutta roscida f

dewy adj roscidus, roridus

dexterity s sollertia, calliditas f

dexterous adj sollers, callidus, habilis; —ly sollerter, callide, habiliter

diabolical adj nefarius, nefandus

diagnose vt dijudicare, discernĕre

diagnosis s judicium n
diagonal adj diagonalis; **—ly** in transversum
diagram s forma, descriptio f
dial s solarium n
dialect s dialectus f, sermo m
dialectic adj dialecticus
dialogue s sermo m, colloquium n; (written discussion) dialogus m
diameter s diametros f
diamond s adamas m
diaper s striatura f
diaphragm s praecordia n pl
diarrhea s alvi profluvium n
diary s diarium n, commentarii diurni m pl
diatribe s convicium n
dice s tali m pl; (game) alea f
dictate vt dictare, praescribĕre
dictate s praescriptum, praeceptum, jussum n
dictation s dictatio f; dictatum n
dictator s dictator m
dictatorial adj imperiosus, dictatorius
dictatorship s dictatura f
diction s dictio, elocutio f
dictionary s lexicon n, thesaurus linguae m
didactic adj didascalicus
die s alea f
die vi mori, obire, perire; **to — off** demori; **to — out** emori
diet s (food) vict·us -ūs m; (med) diaeta f
diet vi secundum diaetam vivĕre
dietary adj diaeteticus
differ vi differre, discrĕpare, distare; (in opinion) dissentire
difference s differentia, diversitas, dissimilitudo f; (of opinion) discrepantia, dissensio f
different adj diversus, dissimilis, dispar; alius; **—ly** diverse, aliter
difficult adj difficilis, arduus
difficulty s difficultas f, labor m, negotium n; **with —** aegre
diffidence s diffidentia, verecundia f
diffident adj diffidens, verecundus, modestus; **—ly** diffidenter
diffuse adj diffusus; (fig) verbosus; **—ly** effuse, latius
diffuse vt diffundĕre
diffusion s diffusio f
dig vt fodĕre
digest s summarium n
digest vt (to arrange) digerĕre; (food) concoquĕre
digestion s concoctio f
digestive adj pepticus
digging s fossio, fossura f
digit s numerus m
dignified adj gravis, augustus
dignify vt honestare, honorare
dignitary s vir amplissimus m
dignity s dignitas f, honor m
digress vi digredi, aberrare, abire
digression s digressio f, digress·us -ūs m
dike s agger m
dilapidated adj ruinosus, obsoletus
dilate vt dilatare; vi dilatari

dilatory adj cunctabundus, lentus, segnis
dilemma s dilemma n; nodus m, angustiae f pl
diligence s diligentia f
diligent adj diligens, sedulus; **—ly** diligenter, sedulo
dilute vt diluĕre, miscĕre
dilution s temperatio, mixtura f
dim adj hebes, obscurus; **to become —** hebescĕre; **—ly** obscure, obtuse
dim vt hebetare, obscurare; vi hebescĕre
dimension s dimensio, mensura f
diminish vt minuĕre, deminuĕre, extenuare; vi decrescĕre, minui
diminutive adj exiguus, parvulus; (gram) deminutivus
diminutive s (nomen) deminutivum n
dimness s hebetudo, obscuritas, caligo f
dimple s lacuna f, gelasinus m
din s strepit·us -ūs, sonit·us -ūs, fragor m; **to make a —** strepare
dine vi cenare
diner s conviva m
dingy adj fuscus, squalidus
dining room s cenatio f, triclinium n
dinner s cena f
dinner party s convivium n
dint s ict·us -ūs m; **by — of** per (with acc)
dip vt immergĕre, ting(u)ĕre; vi mergi, tingi; (to sink) premi, declinare
dip s devexitas, declinatio f
diploma s diploma n
diplomacy s (function) officium legationis m; (tact) dexteritas f
diplomat s legatus m
diplomatic adj sagax, callidus, astutus
dire adj dirus
direct adj rectus, directus; **—ly** directe, rectā; (immediately) statim
direct vt dirigĕre; (to administer) administrare; (to rule) gubernare; (to order) jubēre; imperare (with dat); (weapon) intendĕre; (letter) inscribĕre; (attention) admovēre
direction s (act) directio f; (quarter) pars, regio f; (management) administratio f; (instruction) mandatum n; (order) praeceptum n
director s rector, magister, gubernator, curator m
directory s (office of director) curatio f, magisterium n; (body of directors) magistri, curatores m pl
dirge s nenia f
dirt s sordes f; (mud) lutum n, limus m
dirtiness s spurcitia f; (fig) obscenitas f
dirty adj spurcus, sordidus; (fig) obscenus
dirty vt foedare, spurcare
disability s impotentia f
disable vt debilitare, enervare
disabled adj inhabilis, debilis, mancus

disabuse vt errorem eripĕre (with dat)

disadvantage s incommodum, detrimentum n

disadvantageous adj incommodus, iniquus

disagree vi discrepare, dissidĕre, dissentire

disagreeable adj injucundus, molestus, insuavis, gravis; (of smells) graveolens; (of persons) difficilis, morosus

disagreeably adv moleste, graviter, ingrate

disagreement s dissensio, discordia f, dissidium n

disappear vi vanescĕre, fugĕre, diffugĕre, abire, perire

disappearance s fuga f, exit·us -ūs m

disappoint vt fallĕre, frustrari

disappointment s frustratio f; incommodum, malum n

disapproval s reprehensio, improbatio f

disapprove vt reprehendĕre, improbare

disarm vt exarmare

disarrange vt (per)turbare, confundĕre

disarray s perturbatio f

disaster s calamitas f, incommodum n

disastrous adj calamitosus, funestus, exitiosus; —ly calamitose

disavow vt diffitēri, infitiari

disavowal s infitiatio f

disband vt dimittĕre; vi dimitti

disbelief s diffidentia, incredulitas f

disbeliever s incredulus m

disburse vt erogare, expendĕre

disbursement s erogatio, solutio f

disc s orbis m

discard vt ponĕre, mittĕre; repudiare

discern vt discernĕre, distinguĕre

discernible adj dignoscendus

discerning adj perspicax, sagax, prudens

discernment s (act) perspicientia f; (faculty) discrimen, judicium n

discharge vt (to unload) exonerare; (to dismiss) dimittĕre; (to perform) perfungi (with abl); (debt) exsolvĕre; (weapon) immittĕre, jacĕre, jaculari; (defendant) absolvĕre

discharge s (unloading) exoneratio f; (shooting) emissio, conjectio f; (dismissal) missio f; (payment) solutio f; (bodily) defluxio f

disciple s discipulus m; (fig) sectator m

discipline s disciplina f

discipline vt assuefacĕre, coercēre

disclaim vt infitiari, diffitēri, negare

disclaimer s infitiatio f

disclose vt aperire, detegĕre, enuntiare

disclosure s patefactio f

discomfit vt fundĕre

discomfort s incommoda n pl, molestiae f pl

disconcerting adj molestus

disconnect vt sejungĕre, disjungĕre

disconsolate adj tristis, afflictus; —ly insolabiliter, triste

discontent s taedium n, molestia, offensio f

discontented adj parum contentus; —ly animo iniquo

discontinue vt intermittĕre; vi desinĕre, desistĕre

discord s discordia, dissensio f; (mus) dissonantia f

discordant adj discors, discrepans; (mus) dissonus

discount vt deducĕre; (to disregard) praetermittĕre

discount s (com) decessio f

discourage vt deterrēre, examinare; to be discouraged animum demittĕre

discouragement s animi abjectio or infractio f

discouraging adj adversus, incommodus

discourse s sermo m, colloquium n; (written) libellus m

discourse vi disserĕre, colloqui, verba facĕre

discourteous adj inurbanus; —ly inurbane

discourtesy s inurbanitas f

discover vt invenire, reperire; (to find out) explorare; (to disclose) patefacĕre

discoverable adj indagabilis, visibilis

discoverer s inventor, repertor m

discovery s inventio f; (things discovered) inventum n

discredit s dedecus n, ignominia f

discredit vt notare, infamare

discreet adj cautus, prudens; —ly consulto, prudenter

discrepancy s discrepantia f

discretion s pudentia, circumspectio f; (tact) judicium n

discretionary adj interminatus, liber

discriminate vt distinguĕre, dijudicare, discernĕre

discriminating adj sagax, discernens

discrimination s distinctio f; judicium, discrimen n

discuss vt agĕre, disputare, disserĕre

discussion s disputatio, disceptatio f

disdain vt fastidire, despicĕre, aspernari

disdain s fastidium n, despect·us -ūs, contempt·us -ūs m

disdainful adj fastidiosus, superciliosus; —ly fastidiose, contemptim

disease s morbus m, malum n

diseased adj aegrotus

disembark vt e navi exponĕre; vi e navi conscendĕre

disenchant vt errorem demĕre (with dat)

disengage vt expedire, eximĕre, avocare

disentangle vt expedire, extricare, explicare

disfavor s invidia f

disfigure vt deformare, turpare, mutilare

disfranchise vt civitatem adimĕre (with dat)

disgorge vt revomĕre, evomĕre

disgrace s dedecus n, infamia f; (thing) flagitium n

disgrace vt dedecorare

disgraceful adj dedecorus, turpis, flagitiosus; —ly turpiter, flagitiose

disguise s (mask) persona f; simulatio f; (pretense) praetext·us –ūs m

disguise vt obtegĕre; (fig) celare, dissimulare

disgust s (loathing) fastidium, taedium n, nausea f

disgust vt fastidium movēre (with dat); **I am disgusted with me** taedet (with genit), me piget (with genit)

disgusting adj taeter, foedus; —ly foede

dish s (flat) patina f; (large) lanx f; (course) ferculum n, dapes f pl

dishearten vt exanimare, percellĕre; **to be disheartened** animum demittĕre

disheveled adj passus, effusus

dishonest adj improbus, perfidus; —ly improbe, dolo malo

dishonesty s improbitas f, dolus malus m, fraus, perfidia f

dishonor s dedecus n, infamia, ignominia f

dishonor vt dedecorare

dishonorable adj inhonestus, turpis

disillusion vt errorem adimĕre (with dat)

disinfect vt purgare

disinherit vt exheredare

disintegrate vi dilabi

disinter vt effodĕre

disinterested adj integer; (of judge) severus; —ly integre, gratuito

disjoin vt segregare, disjungere

disjointed adj incompositus; —ly incomposite

disk s orbis m

dislike s odium, fastidium n, aversatio f

dislike vt aversari, odisse, fastidire

dislocate vt extorquēre, luxare

dislocation s luxatura f

dislodge vt movēre, depellĕre

disloyal adj perfidus; —ly perfide

disloyalty s infidelitas, perfidia f

dismal adj maestus, funestus, miser; —ly maeste, misere

dismantle vt diruĕre, spoliare, nudare

dismay s pavor m, consternatio f

dismay vt terrēre, perterrefacĕre, territare

dismember vt membratim dividĕre, lacerare, discerpĕre

dismemberment s mutilatio f

dismiss vt dimittere; (fear) mittĕre; (to discharge, to cashier) exauctorare

dismissal s missio, dimissio f

dismount vi ex equo desilire

disobedience s inobedientia, contumacia f

disobedient adj contumax

disobey vt non obedire (with dat), non parēre (with dat)

disorder s confusio f; (med) aegrotatio f; (of mind) perturbatio f; (pol) tumult·us –ūs m

disordered adj turbatus; (fig) dissolutus

disorderly adj inordinatus, incompositus, (per)turbatus; (insubordinate) turbulentus

disorganization s dissolutio f

disorganize vt conturbare, confundĕre; **to be disorganized** dilabi

disown vt (statement) diffiteri, infitiari; (heir) abdicare; (thing) repudiare

disparage vt obtrectare, detrectare

disparagement s obtrectatio f

disparaging adj obtrectans

disparate adj dispar

disparity s inaequalitas, discrepantia f

dispassionate adj sedatus, tranquillus, frigidus; —ly sedate, frigide

dispatch vt mittĕre, dimittĕre, legare; (to finish) absolvĕre, perficĕre; (to kill) interficĕre

dispel vt dispellĕre; (worries) ponĕre

dispensary s medicamentaria taberna f

dispensation s distributio, partitio f; (exemption) immunitas, exemptio f

dispense vt distribuĕre, dispertiri; (to release) solvĕre; vi **to — with** indulgēre (with dat), omittĕre, praetermittĕre

dispenser s dispensator m

disperse vt spargĕre, dispergĕre, dissipare; vi dilabi, diffugēre

dispersion s dispersio, dissipatio f

dispirited adj abjectus, demissus, animo fractus

displace vt summovēre; exauctorare

displacement s amotio f

display s (exhibit) ostent·us –ūs m; (ostentation) ostentatio, jactatio f

display vt ostendĕre, ostentare, exhibēre

displease vt displicēre (with dat)

displeased adj offensus; **to be — at** aegre ferre

displeasing adj odiosus, ingratus

displeasure s offensa, offensio f

disposable adj in promptu

disposal s dispositio f; arbitrium n; **at the — of** penes (with acc)

dispose vt disponere, ordinare; (to incline) parare, praeparare; vi **to — of** abalienare, vendĕre; (to get rid of) tollĕre

disposed adj inclinatus; (in bad sense) pronus

disposition s (arrangement) dispositio f; (character) natura, mens f, ingenium n, animus m

dispossess vt ejicĕre, detrudĕre, pellĕre

disproportion s inaequalitas, inconcinnitas f

disproportionate adj inaequalis, impar, inconcinnus; —ly impariter, inaequaliter

disprove vt refutare, confutare, redarguĕre

disputable adj disputabilis, ambiguus

dispute s (debate) disputatio f; (quarreling) altercatio, controversia f; **beyond** — indisputabilis

dispute vt & vi disputare, contendĕre

disqualification s impedimentum n

disqualify vt inhabilem reddĕre, impedire

disquiet vt inquietare, vexare

disregard s incuria, negligentia f

disregard vt negligĕre, omittĕre

disreputable adj infamis

disrepute s infamia f

disrespect s negligentia, insolentia f

disrespectful adj irreverens, insolens; —ly insolenter, irreverenter

disrupt vt dirumpĕre

disruption s diruptio f; (fig) discidium n

dissatisfaction s molestia, offensio f

dissatisfied adj parum contentus

dissatisfy vt parum satisfacĕre

dissect vt dissecare

dissection s incisio f

dissemble vt & vi dissimulare

disseminate vt disseminare, divulgare

dissension s dissensio f, dissidium n

dissent vi dissentire, dissidĕre

dissent s dissensio f

dissertation s disputatio, dissertatio f

dissimilar adj dissimilis, dispar

dissimilarity s dissimilitudo f

dissipate vt dissipare, diffundĕre; vi dissipari, diffundi

dissipation s dissipatio f

dissolute adj dissolutus, corruptus, perditus; —ly immoderate, prodige

dissolution s dissolutio f

dissolve vt dissolvĕre; (to melt) liquefacĕre; (meeting) dimittĕre; vi liquescĕre; (to break up) dissolvi

dissonance s dissonantia f

dissonant adj dissonus

dissuade vt dissuadĕre (with dat), dehortari

dissuasion s dissuasio f

distaff s colus f

distance s distantia f, intervallum n; (fig) frigus n; (long way) longinquitas f; **at a** — procul, longe

distant adj distans, disjunctus, longinquus; (fig) parum familiaris; **to be** — abesse

distaste s fastidium n

distasteful adj (of taste) teter; (fig) molestus, odiosus

distemper s morbus m

distend vt distendĕre

distil vt & vi stillare, destillare

distillation s destillatio f

distinct adj (different) diversus, alius; (clear) distinctus; —ly clare, distincte, certe

distinction s distinctio, discrepantia f, discrimen n; (status) amplitudo f;

(honor) honos m; **there is no** — nil interest

distinctive adj proprius; —ly proprie

distinguish vt distinguĕre, discernĕre; **to** — **oneself** enitĕre

distinguished adj insignis, clarus, notus, eximius

distort vt distorquĕre; (fig) depravare

distortion s distortio f; (fig) depravatio f

distract vt distrahĕre, avocare; (to madden) furiare

distracted adj amens, insanus; —ly amens, mente alienatus

distraction s (cause) invitamentum n; (state) negligentia f; **to** — effictim

distress s afflictio, aegrimonia, aerumna f, dolor, labor m

distress vt afflictare, angĕre

distressed adj anxius, afflictus, sollicitus

distressing adj tristis, gravis, acerbus

distribute vt distribuĕre

distributer s distributor m

distribution s distributio f

district s regio f

distrust s diffidentia f

distrust vt diffidĕre (with dat)

distrustful adj diffidens; —ly diffidenter

disturb vt perturbare; sollicitare, inquietare

disturbance s perturbatio f; confusio f; (pol) mot·us -ūs, tumult·us -ūs m

disturber s turbator, concitator m

disuse s desuetudo f

ditch s fossa f

ditty s cantilena f, canticum n

divan s lectulus m

dive vi mergi

diver s urinator m

diverge vi deflectĕre, declinare, devertĕre; (of views) discrepare

diverse adj alius, varius, diversus

diversification s variatio f

diversify vt variare

diversion s (recreation) oblectamentum n; (of thought) avocatio f; (of river, etc.) derivatio f

diversity s diversitas, varietas f

divert vt avertĕre, divertĕre; (attention) avocare; (to amuse) oblectare

divest vt exuĕre, nudare, privare; **to** — **oneself of** exuĕre, ponĕre

divide vt dividĕre, partiri, distribuĕre; vi discedĕre, se scindĕre

divination s divinatio, vaticinatio f

divine adj divinus; —ly divine

divine s theologus m

divine vt divinare, augurari, vaticinari; (to guess) conjicĕre

diviner s augur, haruspex m

divinity s divinitas f; (god) numen n; divus m, diva f

divisible adj dividuus, divisibilis

division s divisio, partitio f; (part) pars f; (mil) legio f; — **of opinion** dissensio f

divorce *s* divortium *n*
divorce *vt* repudiare, dimittēre
divulge *vt* vulgare, palam facĕre, aperire, patefacĕre
dizziness *s* vertigo *f*
dizzy *adj* vertiginosus
do *vt* agĕre, facĕre, efficĕre; *vi* agĕre; how do you —? quid agis?; to — away with tollĕre, perdĕre
docile *adj* docilis, tractabilis
dock *s* navale *n*; (*law*) cancelli *m pl*
dock *vt* subducĕre
docket *s* lemniscus *m*
dockyard *s* navalia *n pl*
doctor *s* medicus *m*; (*teacher*) doctor *m*
doctor *vt* medicari, curare
doctorate *s* doctoris grad·us -ūs *m*
doctrine *s* doctrina *f*, dogma *n*
document *s* documentum, instrumentum *n*
dodge *s* dolus *m*
dodge *vt* eludĕre; *vi* tergiversari
doe *s* cerva *f*
dog *s* canis *m & f*
dogged *adj* pervicax, pertinax; —ly pertinaciter
doggedness *s* pervicacia *f*
doggerel *s* versus inepti *m pl*
dog kennel *s* canis cubile *n*
dogma *s* dogma, placitum, praeceptum *n*
dogmatic *adj* dogmaticus; arrogans; —ally arroganter
dogmatism *s* arrogantia doctrinae *f*
dog star *s* canicula *f*, Sirius *m*
doing *s* factum, facinus *n*
dole *s* sportula *f*; donatio *f*
dole *vt* to — out parce dare
doleful *adj* lugubris, maestus, flebilis; —ly maeste, flebiliter
doll *s* pupa *f*
dollar *s* thalerus *m*
dolphin *s* delphinus, delphin *m*
dolt *s* caudex, stipes *m*
domain *s* (*estate*) possessio *f*; (*kingdom*) regnum *n*
dome *s* tholus *m*
domestic *adj* domesticus, familiaris; intestinus
domestic *s* famulus, servus, verna *m*, famula, serva *f*
domesticate *vt* domare, assuefacĕre
domicile *s* domicilium *n*, dom·us -ūs *f*
dominant *adj* praevalens
domination *s* dominium *n*
domineer *vi* dominari
domineering *adj* imperiosus
dominion *s* imperium, regnum *n*
don *vt* induĕre
donation *s* donum *n*, stips *f*
donkey *s* asinus, asellus *m*
donor *s* donator *m*, donatrix *f*
doom *s* fatum, exitium *n*
doom *vt* damnare, condemnare
door *s* janua *f*, ostium *n*, fores *f pl*
doorkeeper *s* janitor *m*, janitrix *f*
doorpost *s* postis *f*
doorway *s* ostium *n*
Doric *adj* Doricus
dormant *adj* sopitus; (*hidden*) latens; to lie — jacĕre

dormitory *s* cubiculum, dormitorium *n*
dorsal *adj* dorsualis
dose *s* potio *f*
dot *s* punctum *n*
dot *vt* punctum imponĕre (*with dat*)
dotage *s* senium *n*
dotard *s* senex delirus *m*
dote *vi* to — upon deamare, deperire
doting *adj* deamans, desipiens; —ly perdite amans
double *adj* duplex; (*of pairs*) geminus; (*as much again*) duplus; (*meaning*) ambiguus
double *s* duplum *n*; to march on the — currĕre
double *vt* duplicare; (*cape*) praetervehi; *vi* duplicari; (*to run*) currĕre
doubly *adv* bis, dupliciter
doubt *s* dubitatio *f*, dubium *n*; (*distrust*) suspicio *f*
doubt *vt* dubitare; suspicari
doubtful *adj* (*of persons*) dubius; (*of things*) incertus, ambiguus, anceps; —ly dubie; (*hesitatingly*) dubitanter
doubtless *adv* scilicet, haud dubie, sine dubio
dough *s* farina *f*
doughty *adj* strenuus, fortis
douse *vt* (*to put out*) exstinguĕre; (*to drench*) madefacĕre
dove *s* columba *f*
dowdy *adj* inconcinnus
down *s* pluma *f*; (*of hair*) lanugo *f*; (*of plants*) pappus *m*
down *adv* deorsum; — from de (*with abl*); — to usque ad (*with acc*)
down *prep* de (*with abl*)
down *adj* declivis; tristis; ad inopiam redactus
downcast *adj* (*of eyes or head*) dejectus, demissus; (*fig*) afflictus, maestus
downfall *s* occas·us -ūs *m*, ruina *f*
downhill *adj* declivis
downright *adj* directus, sincerus
downright *adv* prorsus, plane
downstream *adv* secundo flumine
downward *adj* declivis; pronus
downwards *adv* deorsum
downy *adj* plumeus; lanuginosus
dowry *s* dos *f*
doze *vi* dormitare
dozen *s* duodecim
drab *adj* cinereus
draft *s* (*act of drawing*) lineatio *f*; (*drink*) haust·us -ūs *m*; (*of ship*) immersio *f*; (*first copy*) exemplar *n*; (*of air*) aura *f*; (*mil*) dilect·us -ūs *m*; (*money*) syngrapha *f*; (*of net*) jact·us -ūs *m*
draft *vt* conscribĕre
draft horse *s* equus rhedarius *m*
drag *vt* trahĕre, rapĕre; *vi* trahi
drag *s* (*fig*) impedimentum *n*
dragnet *s* tragula *f*
dragon *s* draco, anguis *m*
drain *s* cloaca *f*
drain *vt* siccare; derivare; (*to drink*)

exhaurire, ebibĕre; (*strength*) exhaurire

drainage *s* derivatio, exsiccatio *f*; colluvies cloacarum *f*

draining *s* exsiccatio *f*

drake *s* anas *m*

drama *s* drama *n*, fabula *f*

dramatic *adj* dramaticus, scaenicus

dramatist *s* poeta scaenicus, scriptor fabularum *m*

dramatize *vt* ad scaenam componĕre

drape *vt* induĕre, amicire, velare

drapery *s* aulaeum *n*

drastic *adj* vehemens

draw *vt* (*to pull*) trahĕre, ducĕre; (*picture*) scribĕre, delineare; (*sword*) destringĕre; (*bow*) adducĕre; (*inference*) colligĕre; **to — aside** abducĕre, seducĕre; **to — away** avertĕre, distrahĕre; **to — back** retrahĕre; **to — off** detrahĕre, abducĕre; (*wine*) depromĕre; **to — out** extrahĕre; (*sword, etc.*) educĕre; (*fig*) elicĕre; **to — together** contrahĕre; **to — up** subducĕre; scribĕre; (*troops*) instruĕre, constituĕre; *vi* **to — back** pedem referre, cedĕre; (*fig*) recedĕre; **to — near** appropinquare; **to — off** cedĕre; **to — up to** (*of ships*) appetĕre

drawback *s* impedimentum, incommodum *n*, retardatio *f*

drawbridge *s* pons *m*

drawer *s* (*sliding compartment*) loculus *m*; (*chest*) armarium *n*

drawing *s* descriptio *f*; (*art*) graphice *f*

drawing room *s* exedra *f*

drawl *vi* lentius loqui

dray *s* plaustrum *n*

dread *s* terror, pavor *m*, formido *f*

dread *adj* terribilis, dirus

dread *vt* expavescĕre, formidare

dreadful *adj* terribilis, horribilis, atrox; **—ly** horrendum in modum, atrociter

dream *s* somnium *n*; **in a —** in somno

dream *vt & vi* somniare; (*fig*) dormitare

dreamer *s* (*fig*) nugator *m*

dreamy *adj* somniculosus

drearily *adv* triste, misere

dreariness *s* (*place*) solitudo, vastitas *f*; (*mind*) tristitia *f*

dreary *adj* (*place*) vastus, solus, incultus; (*person*) tristis, miser

dredge *s* everriculum *n*

dregs *s* faex *f*; (*fig*) sentina *f*

drench *vt* madefacĕre, perfundĕre

dress *s* habit·us -ūs, vestit·us -ūs *m*, vestis *f*, vestimenta *n pl*

dress *vt* vestire, induĕre; (*to deck out*) (ex)ornare; (*wounds*) curare; (*to bind up*) obligare; *vi* se induĕre

dressing *s* ornatio *f*; (*of foods*) coctio, coctura *f*; (*med*) fomentum *n*

dressing room *s* procoeton *m*

dribble *vi* stillare

drift *s* propositum *n*; (*purpose*) scopus *m*; (*of sand*) cumulus *m*; (*of snow*) vis *f*

drift *vi* ferri, fluitare

drill *s* (*tool*) terebra *f*; (*mil*) exercitatio *f*

drill *vt* (*to bore*) terebrare; (*mil*) exercēre; (*pupil*) instituĕre

drink *vt* bibĕre, potare; **to — in** absorbēre, haurire; **to — up** epotare; *vi* bibĕre, potare; **to — to** propinare (*with dat*)

drink *s* pot·us -ūs *m*, potio *f*

drinkable *adj* potabilis

drinker *s* potor, potator *m*; (*drunkard*) bibax *m*

drinking *adj* (*given to drink*) bibosus

drinking cup *s* poculum *n*

drip *s* stillicidium *n*

drip *vi* stillare

drive *vt* agĕre, pellĕre, impellĕre; (*to force*) compellĕre, cogĕre; (*a nail, etc.*) infigĕre; **to — away** abigĕre; (*fig*) depellĕre; (*to dislodge*) dejicĕre; **to — back** repellĕre; **to — in** (*sheep, etc.*) cogĕre; (*fig*) compellĕre; **to — off** abigĕre; **to — on** impellĕre; **to — out** expellĕre; **to — out of one's senses** infuriare; **to — up** subigĕre; *vi* (*in carriage*) vehi; **to — off** avehi; **to — on** praetervehi; **to — past** praetervehi

drive *s* (*in carriage*) vectio *f*; (*energy*) impigritas *f*

drivel *s* saliva *f*, sputum *n*; (*nonsense*) ineptiae, nugae *f pl*

drivel *vi* (*fig*) delirare

driver *s* agitator *m*; (*of carriage*) auriga *m*

drizzle *vi* leniter pluĕre

drizzle *s* lenis pluvia *f*

dromedary *s* dromas *m*

drone *s* (*bee*) fucus *m*; (*person*) nebulo *m*; (*buzz*) bombus *m*

drone *vi* fremĕre

droop *vt* demittĕre; *vi* languēre; (*of flowers*) languescĕre, tabescĕre

drooping *adj* languidus

drop *s* gutta, stilla *f*; (*a little bit*) paululum *n*; **— by —** guttatim

drop *vt* stillare; (*to let slip*) omittĕre; (*to lay low*) sternĕre; (*hint*) emittĕre; (*anchor*) jacĕre; (*work*) desistĕre ab (*with abl*); *vi* destillare; (*to fall*) cadĕre; **to — behind** cessare; **to — off to sleep** obdormire; **to — out** excidĕre

drought *s* siccitas, ariditas *f*

drove *s* grex *m*

drown *vt* immergĕre, demergĕre; (*fig*) opprimĕre; **to — out** obscurare; *vi* in aqua perire

drowsily *adv* somniculose

drowsy *adj* somniculosus, somnolentus; (*fig*) ignavus

drudge *s* (*slave*) mediastinus *m*; (*fig*) plagiger *m*

drudgery *s* opera servilis *f*

drug *s* medicamentum *n*

drug *vt* medicare

druggist *s* medicamentarius *m*

drugstore *s* taberna medicina, apotheca *f*

Druids *s* Druidae *m pl*
drum *s* typanum *n*
drum *vi* tympanum pulsare
drummer *s* tympanista *m*
drunk *adj* ebrius
drunkard *s* ebriosus, temulentus *m*
drunken *adj* ebrius, ebriosus
drunkenness *s* ebrietas, temulentia *f*
dry *adj* aridus, siccus; (*thirsty*) siticulosus; (*fig*) jejunus; insulsus
dry *vt* siccare, desiccare, arefacĕre; (*in the sun*) insolare; *vi* arescĕre
dryad *s* dryas *f*
dryly *adv* (*fig*) insulse; (*of jokes*) facete
dryness *s* ariditas, siccitas *f*; (*fig*) aridum sermonis genus *n*
dual *adj* duplex
dub *vt* supernominare
dubious *adj* dubius; —**ly** dubie
duck *s* anas *f*
duck *vt* submergĕre, demergĕre; (*an issue*) evitare; *vi* (*under water*) urinari
duckling *s* anaticula *f*
due *adj* debitus, justus, meritus; **to be** — **to** fieri (*with abl*)
due *adv* rectā; **due east** rectā ad orientem
due *s* debitum *n*
duel *s* certamen *n*
duet *s* bicinium *n*
duke *s* dux *m*
dull *adj* hebes; (*of mind*) tardus, segnes, insulsus; (*of style*) frigidus
dull *vt* hebetare, obtundĕre; stupefacĕre
dullness *s* stupiditas, tarditas *f*
duly *adv* rite; recte
dumb *adj* mutus; **to be** — obmutescĕre
dumbfound *vt* obstupefacĕre
dumb show *s* mimus *m*
dumpling *s* farinae subactae globulus *m*
dumpy *adj* brevis atque obesus

dun *adj* fuscus, furvus
dun *vt* flagitare, exposcĕre
dunce *s* homo stupidus *m*
dung *s* stercus *n*, fimus *m*; (*of birds*) merda *f*
dungeon *s* carcer *m*, ergastulum *n*
dupe *s* homo credulus, homo stolidus *m*
dupe *vt* decipĕre
duplicate *adj* duplex
duplicate *s* duplicitas, fallacia *f*
duplicate *vt* duplicare
duplicity *s* duplicitas *f*
durability *s* firmitudo, stabilitas *f*
durable *adj* firmus, durabilis, stabilis
duration *s* spatium temporis *n*, diuturnitas, perpetuitas *f*
during *prep* per (*with acc*), inter (*with acc*)
dusk *s* crepusculum, obscurum *n*
dusky *adj* obscurus, tenebrosus; fuscus
dust *s* pulvis *m*
dust *vt* detergĕre
dusty *adj* pulverulentus, pulvereus
dutiful *adj* pius, officiosus; —**ly** pie, officiose
duty *s* (*social or moral*) officium *n*; (*task*) munus *n*; (*tax*) vectigal *n*; **to be on** — (*mil*) stationem agĕre
dwarf *s* nanus, pumilio *m*
dwarfish *adj* pumilus
dwell *vi* habitare, inhabitare; **to** — **upon** commorari in (*with abl*)
dweller *s* incola *m & f*, habitator *m*
dwelling place *s* domicilium *n*, sedes, habitatio *f*
dwindle *vi* decrescĕre, imminui
dye *vt* ting(u)ĕre, colorare, inficĕre, fucare
dye *s* tinctura *f*, color *m*
dying *adj* moriens, moribundus; (*last*) ultimus, extremus
dynamics *s* dynamica *f*
dynasty *s* dynastia, dom·us -ūs *f*
dysentery *s* dysenteria *f*

E

each *adj & pron* quisque; (*of two*) uterque; — **other** inter se, invicem
eager *adj* cupidus, avidus, acer, vehemens; —**ly** cupide, avide, acriter, vehementer
eagerness *s* aviditas, cupiditas, alacritas *f*, studium *n*
eagle *s* aquila *f*
ear *s* auris *f*; (*of corn*) spica *f*; **to give** — aurem praebēre
earache *s* aurium dolor *m*
earl *s* comes *m*
early *adj* (*in morning*) matutinus; (*in season*) maturus; (*of early date*) antiquus; (*beginning*) primus, novus
early *adv* (*in morning*) mane; (*too soon*) praemature; (*quickly*, *soon*) cito
earn *vt* lucrari, merēre *or* merēri,

consequi
earnest *adj* intentus, serius, impensus, vehemens; **in** — serio, sedulo, bona fide; —**ly** intente, impense, acriter, graviter
earnestness *s* assiduitas, gravitas *f*, ardor *m*
earnings *s* quaest·us -ūs *m*, lucrum *n*
earring *s* elenchus *m*
earth *s* terra, tellus *f*; (*soil*) solum *n*; (*globe*) orbis (terrarum) *m*
earthen *adj* terrenus; fictilis
earthenware *s* fictilia *n pl*
earthly *adj* terrenus; terrestris; humanus
earthquake *s* terrae mot·us -ūs *m*
earthwork *s* opus terrenum *n*, agger *m*
earthy *adj* terrenus

ease *s* (*leisure*) otium *n*, quies *f*; (*grace*) lepor *m*, facilitas *f*; (*pleasure*) voluptas *f*; **at —** otiosus, vacuus; securus

ease *vt* levare, exonerare, expedire; (*fig*) lenire, mitigare

east *adj* orientalis

east *s* oriens *m*

Easter *s* pascha *f*, sollemnia paschalia *n pl*

eastern *adj* orientalis

eastward *adv* ad orientem

east wind *s* Eurus *m*

easy *adj* facilis; expeditus; (*manner*) facilis, affabilis; (*graceful*) lepidus

eat *vi* vesci (*with abl*), esse; (*fig*) rodĕre; **to — away** peredĕre; (*fig*) corrodĕre; **to — up** comesse, devorare, exesse

eating *s* es·us -ūs *m*

eaves *s* suggrundia *n pl*

eavesdropper *s* auceps, auricularius *m*

ebb *s* recess·us -ūs *m*; **to be at a low —** jacēre

ebb *vi* recedĕre; (*fig*) decrescĕre

eccentric *adj* insolens, inusitatus, abnormis

ecclesiastic *adj* ecclesiasticus

echo *s* echo, imago *f*

echo *vt* repercutĕre, resonare; (*fig*) subsequi; *vi* resonare, resultare

eclipse *s* (*of sun or moon*) obscuratio solis *or* lunae *f*, defect·us -ūs *m*

eclipse *vt* obscurare, obumbrare

eclogue *s* ecloga *f*

economic *adj* economicus

economical *adj* frugi (*indecl*), parcus; **—ly** parce

economics *s* publicarum opum scientia *f*

economize *vi* parcĕre

economy *s* parsimonia, frugalitas *f*; rei familiaris administratio *f*

ecstasy *s* ecstasis, insania *f*, furor *m*

eddy *s* vortex *m*

eddy *vi* volutari

edge *s* (*brink*) margo *m* & *f*; (*of knife, etc.*) acies *f*; (*of forest*) ora *f*

edge *vt* (*garment*) praetexĕre; (*to sharpen*) acuĕre; *vi* **to — closer** appropinquare

edged *adj* acutus

edging *s* limbus *m*

edible *adj* esculentus, edulis

edict *s* edictum, decretum *n*

edification *s* eruditio *f*

edify *vt* docēre

edit *vt* edĕre, recensēre

edition *s* editio *f*

editor *s* editor *m*

educate *vt* educare, erudire

education *s* educatio, eruditio *f*

educator *s* praeceptor, magister *m*

eel *s* anguilla *f*

efface *vt* delēre, obliterare, tollĕre

effect *s* effectum *n*, effect·us -ūs; (*show*) jactatio *f*; **—s bona** *n pl*; **in — re** vera; **without —** irritus

effect *vt* efficĕre, exsequi, facĕre

effective *adj* efficiens, efficax, valens; **—ly** valide, graviter

effectual *adj* efficax, valens, potens,

—ly efficaciter, potenter

effeminacy *s* mollities *f*

effeminate *adj* effeminatus, mollis, muliebris; **—ly** effeminate, muliebriter

effete *adj* effetus

efficacious *adj* efficax; **—ly** efficaciter

efficacy *s* efficacia, vis *f*

efficiency *s* virtus, peritia *f*

efficient *adj* efficiens, aptus, idoneus; efficax; **—ly** perite, bene

effigy *s* effigies *f*

effort *s* labor, conat·us -ūs, nis·us -ūs *m*, opera *f*; **to make an —** eniti

effrontery *s* audacia, impudentia *f*

effusion *s* effusio *f*

effusive *adj* officiosus

egg *s* ovum *n*; **to lay —s** ova parĕre

egotism *s* amor sui *m*

egotist *s* sui amator *m*

egotistical *adj* sibi soli consulens

egress *s* egress·us -ūs, exit·us -ūs *m*

eight *adj* octo; **— times** octies

eighteen *adj* duodeviginti, decem et octo

eighteenth *adj* decimus octavus, duodevicesimus

eighth *adj* octavus

eighth *s* octava pars *f*

eightieth *adj* octogesimus

eighty *adj* octoginta

either *pron* alteruter; uter; alter

either *conj* **— ... or** aut ... aut; vel ... vel

ejaculate *vt* emittĕre

ejaculation *s* clamor *m*

eject *vt* ejicĕre

ejection *s* dejectio *f*

eke *vt* **to eke out a livelihood** victum aegre parare

elaborate *adj* elaboratus; **—ly** elaborate

elaborate *vt* elaborare

elaboration *s* nimia diligentia *f*

elapse *vi* praeterire, abire, labi

elastic *adj* resiliens; (*fig*) mobilis

elate *vt* inflare, superbum reddĕre; **to be elated** efferri

elation *s* gaudium *n*, laetitia *f*, animus elatus *m*

elbow *s* ulna *f*, cubitus *m*

elbow *vt* cubitis depulsare, cubitis trudĕre

elder *adj* major natu

elderly *adj* aetate provectior

eldest *adj* maximus natu

elect *vt* eligĕre, deligĕre, creare

elect *adj* designatus; (*elite*) lectus

election *s* electio *f*, delect·us -ūs *m*; (*pol*) comitia *n pl*

electioneering *s* ambitio *f*

elective *adj* suffragatorius

elector *s* suffragator *m*

electrical *adj* electricus

electricity *s* vis electrica *f*

electrify *vt* electricā *vi* afficĕre; (*fig*) percellĕre

elegance *s* elegantia *f*

elegant *adj* elegans, concinnus; **—ly** eleganter, cum elegantia

elegiac *adj* elegiacus; — **verse** elegi *m pl*

elegy *s* elegia *f*

element *s* elementum *n*; —**s** principia, initia *n pl*; *(fig)* rudimenta *n pl*

elementary *adj* elementarius

elephant *s* elephantus, elephas *m*

elevate *vt* levare, attollere; *(fig)* efferre, inflare

elevated *adj* editus

elevation *s* elatio *f*; *(height)* altitudo *f*; *(hill)* locus superior *m*

eleven *adj* undecim; — **times** undecies

eleventh *adj* undecimus

elf *s* larva *f*, numen pumilum *n*

elicit *vt* elicēre

eligible *adj* eligibilis, idoneus

eliminate *vt* amovēre, tollēre

elision *s* elisio *f*

elite *adj* lectus

elite *s* flos *m*, lecti *m pl*

elk *s* alces *f*

ellipsis *s* ellipsis *f*

elliptical *adj* ellipticus; —**ly** per defectionem

elm *s* ulmus *f*

elocution *s* pronuntiatio *f*

elongate *vt* producere

elope *vi* clam fugēre, aufugēre

elopement *s* fuga clandestina *f*

eloquence *s* eloquentia *f*; *(natural)* facundia *f*

eloquent *adj* eloquens, disertus; —**ly** diserte, eloquenter, graviter

else *adj* alius; **no one** — nemo alius; **who** — quis alius

else *adv* *(besides)* praeterea; *(otherwise)* aliter

elsewhere *adv* alibi; *(motion)* alio

elucidate *vt* illustrare, explicare

elucidation *s* explicatio *f*

elude *vt* eludere, frustrari, evitare

Elysian *adj* Elysius

Elysian fields *s* Elysii campi *m pl*

emaciate *vt* emaciare, macerare

emaciated *adj* macer, macilentus

emaciation *s* macies, tabes *f*

emanate *vi* emanare, oriri

emanation *s* emanatio, exhalatio *f*

emancipate *vt* emancipare, manumittēre; *(fig)* liberare

emancipation *s* *(of slave)* manumissio *f*; *(of son)* emancipatio *f*; *(fig)* liberatio *f*

emasculate *vt* castrare, emasculare; *(fig)* enervare

embalm *vt* condire, pollingēre

embalming *s* pollinctura *f*

embankment *s* agger *m*, moles *f*

embargo *s* retentio navium *f*, interdictum *n*; **to lay an** — **upon a ship** navem retinēre

embark *vt* imponere; *vi* conscendēre; **to** — **upon** *(fig)* ingredi

embarkation *s* conscensio *f*

embarrass *vt* perturbare, confundēre, impedire

embarrassing *adj* incommodus, difficilis

embarrassment *s* conturbatio, implicatio *f*; *(financial)* angustiae *f pl*

embassy *s* legatio *f*, legati *m pl*

embellish *vt* ornare, exornare

embellishment *s* ornamentum, decus *n*, exornatio *f*

embers *s* cinis *m*, favilla *f*

embezzle *vt* peculari

embezzlement *s* peculat·us -ūs *m*

embezzler *s* peculator *m*

embitter *vt* exacerbare

emblazon *vt* insignire

emblem *s* emblema, insigne, signum *n*

emblematic *adj* symbolicus

embody *vt* includēre, repraesentare

emboss *vt* caelare

embrace *s* amplex·us -ūs, complex·us -ūs *m*

embrace *vt* amplecti, complecti; comprehendēre

embroider *vt* acu pingēre

embroidery *s* vestis picta *f*

embroil *vt* permiscēre, implicare

embroilment *s* implicatio *f*

embryo *s* immaturus part·us -ūs *m*

emend *vt* emendare, corrigēre

emendation *s* correctio, emendatio *f*

emerald *s* smaragdus *m*

emerge *vi* emergēre; *(to arise)* exsistēre

emergency *s* tempus, discrimen *n*, cas·us -ūs *m*

emigrant *s* emigrans *m*

emigrate *vi* emigrare

emigration *s* migratio *f*

eminence *s* praestantia, amplitudo *f*; *(rise of ground)* locus editus *m*

eminent *adj* eminens, egregius, praestans; —**ly** eximie, insigniter

emissary *s* emissarius, legatus *m*

emit *vt* emittēre; exhalare

emotion *s* animi mot·us -ūs *m*, commotio *f*

emotional *adj* mobilis

emperor *s* imperator, princeps *m*

emphasis *s* energia, vis *f*, pondus *n*; impressio *f*

emphasize *vt* exprimēre

emphatic *adj* emphaticus, gravis; —**ally** emphatice, graviter

empire *s* imperium, regnum *n*

empirical *adj* empiricus; —**ly** ex experimentis

empiricism *s* empirice *f*

employ *vt* uti *(with abl)*, adhibēre, exercēre, occupare

employer *s* conductor, dominus *m*

employment *s* *(act)* us·us -ūs *m*; *(occupation)* quaest·us -ūs *m*; *(business)* negotium *n*

empower *vt* potestatem facēre *(with dat)*

empress *s* imperatrix *f*

emptiness *s* inanitas *f*; *(fig)* vanitas *f*

empty *adj* vacuus, inanis; *(of street)* desertus; *(fig)* vanus

empty *vt* evacuare; exhaurire; *vi* *(of river)* influēre

empyrean *s* aether *m*

emulate *vt* aemulari, imitari

emulation *s* aemulatio *f*

enable *vt* facultatem facēre *(with dat)*

enact *vt* decernēre, sancire

enactment *s* lex, sanctio *f*, decretum *n*
enamel *s* smaltum, vitrum metallicum *n*
enamel *adj* smaltinus
enamoured *adj* amans; **to be — of** amare, deamare
encamp *vi* castra ponere
encampment *s* castra *n pl*
encase *vt* includere
enchant *vt* fascinare; (*fig*) capere, captare, delectare
enchanter *s* incantator *m*
enchanting *adj* (*fig*) venustus, suavissimus
enchantment *s* incantamentum *n*; (*fig*) illecebrae *f pl*
enchantress *s* maga, cantatrix *f*; venefica *f*
encircle *vt* cingere, circumdare, circumplecti
enclose *vt* includere, saepire
enclosure *s* saeptum *n*
encompass *vt* complecti
encounter *s* (*meeting*) congress·us -ūs *m*; (*fight*) certamen *n*, pugna *f*
encounter *vt* congredi cum (*with abl*), obviam ire (*with dat*), occurrere (*with dat*); (*in battle*) concurrere cum (*with abl*)
encourage *vt* cohortari, confirmare; favēre (*with dat*)
encouragement *s* hortat·us -ūs *m*, confirmatio *f*, favor *m*
encroach *vi* invadere; **to — upon** usurpare, occupare, invadere
encroachment *s* usurpatio *f*
encumber *vt* impedire, onerare, praegravare
encumbrance *s* impedimentum, onus *n*
encyclopedia *s* encyclopaedia *f*
end *s* finis, terminus, exit·us -ūs *m*; (*aim*) propositum *n*; (*of a speech*) peroratio *f*; **in the — denique**; **to put an — to** finem imponere (*with dat*); **to what —?** quo?, quorsum?
end *vt* finire, terminare, conficere; *vi* desinere; (*of time*) exire; (*of events*) evadere
endanger *vt* periclitari
endear *vt* carum reddere, devincire
endearing *adj* carus, blandus
endearment *s* blanditiae *f pl*, blandimenta *n pl*
endeavor *s* conat·us -ūs, nis·us -ūs *m*
endeavor *vi* conari, eniti, laborare, contendere
ending *s* finis, exit·us -ūs *m*
endless *adj* infinitus; perpetuus; **—ly** sine fine, perpetuo
endorse *vt* ratum facere
endow *vt* dotare, donare, instruere
endowed *adj* praeditus
endowment *s* dotatio, dos *f*, donum *n*
endurable *adj* tolerabilis
endurance *s* tolerantia, patientia *f*; (*duration*) duratio *f*
endure *vt* tolerare, pati; *vi* durare; permanēre
enduring *adj* tolerans; durabilis
enemy *s* (*public*) hostis *m*; (*private*)

inimicus, adversarius *m*
energetic *adj* impiger, acer, strenuus, navus; **—ally** acriter, impigre, strenuo
energy *s* vis, vehementia, efficacia *f*, impet·us -ūs *m*
enervate *vt* enervare, debilitare
enforce *vt* exsequi, cogere; (*arguments*) confirmare
enforcement *s* coactio, sanctio *f*
enfranchise *vt* (*slave*) manumittere; civitate donare
enfranchisement *s* (*of slave*) manumissio *f*; civitatis donatio *f*
engage *vt* (*to employ*) adhibēre; (*to reserve*) conducere; (*attention*) occupare; (*to involve*) implicare; (*enemy*) proelium facere cum (*with abl*); *vi* **to — in** suscipere, ingredi; **to engage in battle** proeliari, manum *or* manus conserere
engaged *adj* (*to marry*) sponsus; **to be — in** versari in (*with abl*)
engagement *s* (*to marry*) pactio nuptialis *f*; (*business*) negotium *n*, occupatio *f*; (*mil*) proelium *n*, pugna *f*; (*promise*) pactum *n*, pactio *f*, promissum *n*
engaging *adj* suavis, blandus, amabilis
engender *vt* ingenerare, gignere
engine *s* machina, machinatio *f*
engineer *s* machinator, faber *m*
engineering *s* machinalis scientia *f*; **c vil —** architectura *f*
England *s* Anglia, Britannia *f*
English *adj* Anglicus, Britannicus
Engl shman *s* Anglus, Britannus, Britannicus *m*
engrave *vt* incidere, caelare, insculpere, scalpere
engraver *s* sculptor, caelator *m*
engraving *s* sculptura, caelatura *f*
engross *vt* occupare; **to be engrossed in** totus esse in (*with abl*)
enhance *vt* augēre, amplificare, ornare
enigma *s* aenigma *n*, ambages *f pl*
enigmatic *adj* ambiguus, obscurus; **—ally** ambigue
enjoin *vt* jubēre, injungere
enjoy *vt* frui (*with abl*); uti (*with abl*)
enjoyment *s* fruct·us -ūs *m*, voluptas *f*, gaudium *n*; possessio *f*
enlarge *vt* amplificare, augēre, dilatare; *vi* **to — upon** amplificare, prosequi
enlargement *s* amplificatio, dilatio *f*, auct·us -ūs *m*
enlighten *vt* illustrare, illuminare; erudire
enlightenment *s* eruditio, humanitas *f*
enlist *vt* (*support*) conciliare; (*mil*) conscribere; *vi* sacramentum dicere
enlistment *s* conscriptio *f*
enliven *vt* animare, incitare; exhilarare
enmity *s* inimicitia *f*, odium *n*
ennoble *vt* honestare
ennui *s* taedium *n*
enormity *s* immanitas *f*; atrocitas *f*

enormous *adj* ingens, enormis, immanis; **—ly** immensum, praeter modum

enough *adj* satis; **— trouble** satis laboris

enough *adv* satis; **more than —** satis superque

enrage *vt* infuriare, exasperare, incendĕre

enrapture *vt* rapĕre, captare

enrich *vt* locupletare, ditare

enroll *vt* adscribĕre, inscribĕre; *vi* nomen dare

enshrine *vt* consecrare, dedicare

enshroud *vt* involvĕre, amicire

ensign *s* (*flag*) vexillum *n*; (*officer*) signifer *m*

enslave *vt* in servitutem redigĕre

enslavement *s* servitus *f*

ensnare *vt* illaquĕre, irretire; (*fig*) illicĕre

ensue *vi* sequi, insequi

ensuing *adj* insequens, posterus, proximus

entail *vt* afferre, inferre

entangle *vt* illaquĕre, irretire, impedire, implicare

entanglement *s* implicatio *f*

enter *vi* intrare, inire, ingredi; introire in *or* ad (*with acc*); **to — politics** ad rem publicam accedĕre; *vi* intrare, inire, ingredi, introire; **to — upon** (*to undertake*) suscipĕre, ingredi

enterprise *s* (*undertaking*) inceptum, ausum *n*; (*in bad sense*) facinus *n*; (*quality*) animus alacer, animus promptus *m*

enterprising *adj* acer, promptus

entertain *vt* (*guest*) excipĕre, invitare, adhibēre; (*idea*) admittĕre, habēre; (*to amuse*) oblectare, delectare

entertainer *s* hospes *m*

entertainment *s* (*amusement*) oblectatio *f*, oblectamentum *n*; (*cultural*) acroama *n*; (*by guest*) hospitium *n*

enthrall *vt* captare

enthusiasm *s* studium *n*, fervor, furor, ardor *m*

enthusiastic *adj* fanaticus, ardens, fervidus; **—ally** fanatice, ardenter

entice *vt* allicĕre, elicĕre

enticement *s* illecebra *f*

enticing *adj* blandus

entire *adj* totus, integer, solidus; **—ly** omnino, plane, penitus

entirety *s* integritas, universitas *f*

entitle *vt* (*to name*) appellare, nominare; inscribĕre; (*to give title to*) potestatem dare (*with dat*)

entity *s* ens *n*, res *f*

entomologist *s* entomologicus *m*

entomology *s* entomologia *f*

entrails *s* viscera, exta, intestina *n pl*

entrance *s* adit·us -ūs, introit·us -ūs *m*; ostium *n*; (*act*) introit·us -ūs *m*, ingressio *f*

entrance *vt* rapĕre, consopire, capĕre

entrance hall *s* vestibulum *n*

entrap *vt* illaquĕre, inescare; capĕre

entreat *vt* obsecrare, orare, deprecari

entreaty *s* rogatio, obsecratio *f*, preces *f pl*

entrust *vt* credĕre, mandare, committĕre

entry *s* (*act*) introit·us -ūs *m*, ingressio *f*; (*of house*) vestibulum *n*; adit·us -ūs *m*; (*in accounts*) nomen *n*

entwine *vt* implicare, nectĕre

enumerate *vt* enumerare

enumeration *s* enumeratio, recensio *f*

enunciate *vt* enuntiare, pronuntiare, exprimĕre

enunciation *s* enuntiatio *f*

envelop *vt* involvĕre, amicire, implicare

envelope *s* involucrum *n*

enviable *adj* invidiosus

envious *adj* invidus, lividus

envoy *s* nuntius, legatus, orator *m*

envy *s* invidia *f*

envy *vt* invidēre (*with dat*)

ephemeral *adj* brevis; caducus

epic *adj* epicus, heroicus

epic *s* epos *n*

epicure *s* helluo, homo voluptarius *m*

Epicurean *adj* Epicureus

Epicurean *s* Epicureus *m*; (*hedonist*) voluptarius *m*

epidemic *adj* epidemus, contagiosus

epidemic *s* pestilentia *f*

epidermis *s* summa cutis, epidermis *f*

epigram *s* epigramma *n*

epilepsy *s* morbus comitialis *m*, epilepsia *f*

epilogue *s* epilogus *m*

epiphany *s* epiphania *f*

episode *s* embolium, eventum *n*, excurs·us -ūs *m*

epistle *s* epistola *f*

epistolary *adj* epistolaris

epitaph *s* epitaphium *n*, titulus *m*

epithet *s* epitheton *n*

epitome *s* epitome, epitoma *f*

epoch *s* epocha *f*, saeculum *n*

equal *adj* aequalis, aequus, par; **—ly** aeque, aequaliter, pariter

equal *s* par *m*, *f* & *n*

equal *vt* aequare, adaequare

equality *s* aequalitas *f*, aequum *n*

equalization *s* (act) aequatio, exaequatio *f*; (state) aequalitas *f*

equalize *vt* adaequare, exaequare

equanimity *s* aequus animus *m*

equation *s* aequatio *f*

equator *s* aequinoctialis circulus *m*

equatorial *adj* aequinoctialis

equestrian *adj* equestris

equestrian *s* eques *m*

equidistant *adj* **to be — aequo** intervallo inter se distare

equilibrium *s* aequilibrium *n*

equinox *s* aequinoctium *n*

equip *vt* armare, ornare, instruĕre

equipment *s* arma, instrumenta, armamenta *n pl*, armatura *f*, apparat·us -ūs *m*

equitable *adj* aequus, justus

equitably *adv* aeque, juste

equity *s* aequitas *f*, aequum *n*

equivalent *adj* aequus, par
equivocal *adj* ambiguus, anceps;
— **ly** ambigue
equivocate *vi* tergiversari
era *s* tempus, saeculum *n*
eradicate *vt* eruĕre, exstirpare, eradicare
eradication *s* exstirpatio *f*
erase *vt* delēre, eradēre
erasure *s* litura *f*
ere *conj* priusquam
ere *prep* ante (*with acc*); — **long** brevi, mox; — **now** ante hoc tempus
erect *adj* erectus, arrectus
erect *vt* (*to raise*) erigĕre; (*to build*) exstruĕre; (*statue*) ponĕre
erection *s* erectio, aedificatio, exstructio *f*
erotic *adj* amatorius, eroticus
err *vi* (ab)errare, peccare
errand *s* mandatum *n*
erratic *adj* inconstans
erroneous *adj* falsus, errore implicitus; — **ly** falso, perperam
error *s* error *m*; vitium *n*; delictum, peccatum *n*; (*in writing*) mendum *n*
erudite *adj* eruditus, doctus
erudition *s* eruditio *f*
erupt *vi* erumpĕre
eruption *s* eruptio *f*
escape *s* fuga *f*, effugium *n*
escape *vt* fugĕre, evitare; **to — the notice of** fallĕre; *vi* effugĕre, evadĕre, elabi; (*secretly*) subterfugĕre
escort *s* comitat·us -ūs *m*; (*protection*) praesidium *n*
escort *vt* comitari, deducĕre
especially *adv* praecipue, praesertim, maxime, in primis
essay *s* experimentum *n*, conat·us -ūs *m*; (*treatise*) libellus *m*
essay *vt* conari, tentare
essence *s* essentia, natura *f*
essential *adj* necessarius, proplus; — **ly** naturā, necessario
establish *vt* constituĕre, statuĕre; (*firmly*) stabilire, confirmare; (*to prove*) probare, arguĕre
establishment *s* (*act*) constitutio *f*; (*com*) negotium *n*
estate *s* (*state*) stat·us -ūs *m*, conditio *f*; (*property*) fundus *m*, praedium *n*; (*pol*) ordo *m*, dignitas *f*
esteem *s* aestimatio *f*, honor *m*
esteem *vt* aestimare, putare; (*to respect*) magni facĕre
estimable *adj* aestimandus
estimate *vt* aestimare, censēre
estimate *s* aestimatio *f*, judicium *n*
estimation *s* aestimatio, opinio, sententia *f*, judicium *n*
estimator *s* aestimator, calculator *m*
estrange *vt* abalienare
estrangement *s* alienatio *f*, discidium *n*
estuary *s* aestuarium *n*
eternal *adj* aeternus, sempiternus; — **ly** in aeternum, semper
eternity *s* aeternitas *f*
ether *s* aether *m*
ethereal *adj* aethereus
ethical *adj* moralis

ethics *s* mores *m pl*, ethice *f*; philosophia moralis *f*
etymology *s* etymologia, verborum notatio *f*
eulogize *vt* collaudare
eulogy *s* laudatio *f*, panegyricus *m*
eunuch *s* eunuchus *m*; (*in contempt*) spado *m*
euphony *s* euphonia *f*, sonus dulcis *m*
European *adj* Europaeus
Euxine *s* Euxinus pontus *m*
evacuate *vt* vacuare, vacuefacĕre; (*people*) deducĕre
evacuation *s* discessio *f*; (*of bowels*) egestio *f*
evade *vt* subterfugĕre, eludĕre, devitare
evaporate *vt* exhalare, evaporare; *vi* exhalari
evaporation *s* exhalatio *f*
evasion *s* effugium *n*, tergiversatio *f*
evasive *adj* ambiguus; — **ly** ambigue
eve *s* vesper *m*; (*of feast*) vigiliae *f pl*; **on the —** of sub (*with acc*)
even *adj* aequalis, aequus; (*level*) planus; (*of numbers*) par; — **ly** aequaliter
even *adv* et, etiam, vel; — **if** etsi, etiamsi; **not —** ne ... quidem
evening *s* vesper *m*; **in the —** vespere, vesperi
evening *adj* vespertinus
evening star *s* Hesperus, Vesper *m*
evenness *s* aequalitas, aequabilitas *f*
event *s* cas·us -ūs *m*, factum *n*; (*outcome*) event·us -ūs, exit·us -ūs *m*; **in any —** saltem
eventful *adj* memorabilis
eventual *adj* ultimus; — **ly** aliquando, olim, denique
ever *adv* (*always*) semper; (*at any time*) umquam; (*after si, nisi, num, ne*) quando; **for —** in aeternum
evergreen *adj* sempervivus
everlasting *adj* sempiternus; — **ly** in aeternum
evermore *adv* semper, in aeternum
every *adj* quisque, omnis; — **now and then** interdum; — **other day** alternis diebus
everybody *pron* quisque, nemo non; omnes *m pl*
everyday *adj* quotidianus *or* cottidianus; usitatus
everything *pron* omnia *n pl*
everywhere *adv* ubique, ubivis
evict *vt* expellĕre, dejicĕre, detrudĕre
evidence *s* testimonium, indicium, argumentum *n*; (*witness*) testis *m* & *f*
evidence *vt* testari
evident *adj* apertus, manifestus; **it is —** apparet; — **ly** aperte, manifesto
evil *adj* malus, pravus, improbus
evil *s* malum *n*, improbitas *f*
evildoer *s* maleficus, malefactor *m*
evil-minded *adj* malevolus, malignus
evoke *vt* evocare, excitare, elicĕre
evolution *s* progress·us -ūs *m*, progressio *f*
evolve *vt* evolvĕre, explicare
exact *adj* exactus, subtilis, diligens;

—ly accurate, subtiliter, diligenter;
—ly **as** sic ut
exact vt exigĕre
exaction s exactio f
exactitude s diligentia f
exaggerate vt exaggerare, augēre,
in majus extollĕre
exaggeration s trajectio, superlatio f
exalt vt extollĕre, amplificare, eve-
hēre
exaltation s elatio f
examination s investigatio f; (in
school) probatio f; (of witnesses) interrogatio f
examine vt investigare, inquirĕre,
scrutari; (witnesses) interrogare
examiner s scrutator, investigator m
example s exemplum, exemplar, documentum n; for — exempli gratiā, verbi gratiā
exasperate vt exasperare, exacerbare, irritare
exasperation s ira f
excavate vt excavare, effodĕre
excavation s fossio, excavatio f, cavum n
exceed vt superare, excedĕre
exceedingly adv valde, magnopere
excel vt superare, praestare (with
dat); vi excellĕre
excellence s excellentia, praestantia
f
Excellency s illustrissimus m
excellent adj praestans, egregius,
optimus; —ly egregie, optime
except vt excipĕre
except prep praeter (with acc); nisi
(followed by appropriate case); —
that nisi quod
exception s exceptio f; with the —
of praeter (with acc)
exceptional adj egregius, praestans,
singularis; —ly praeter modum
excess s excess·us -ūs m, intemperantia f
excessive adj immodicus, nimius;
—ly immodice, nimis
exchange s (barter) commutatio f;
(of money) collybus m
exchange vt mutare, permutare
excise vt excidĕre
excision s excisio f
excitable adj irritabilis, fervidus
excite vt excitare, stimulare; (to inflame) incendĕre
excitement s commotio f; perturbatio f; incitamentum n
exclaim vt exclamare; (as a group)
conclamare; vi to — against acclamare (with dat); declamitare in
(with acc)
exclamation s exclamatio f, clamor m
exclude vt excludĕre, prohibēre
exclusion s exclusio f
exclusive adj proprius; — of praeter (with acc); —ly solum
excommunicate vt excommunicare
excommunication s excommunica-
tio f
excrement s excrementum, stercus m
excretion s excrementum n, excre-
tio f

excruciating adj acerbissimus
exculpate vt (ex)purgare, excusare,
absolvĕre
excursion s excursio f, iter n
excusable adj excusabilis
excuse vt excusare; ignoscĕre (with
dat), veniam dare (with dat)
excuse s excusatio f; (pretense) pre-
text·us -ūs m, species f
execute vt (to perform) exsequi, efficĕre; (to punish) necare, securi ferire
execution s effect·us -ūs m, effectio
f; (capital punishment) supplicium n
executioner s carnifex m
executive adj ad administrationem
pertinens
executive s administrator m
executor s curator testamenti m
exemplary adj egregius, eximius
exemplification s expositio f
exemplify vt explicare
exempt vt eximĕre, liberare
exempt adj exemptus, immunis, liber
exemption s exemptio, immunitas,
liberatio f
exercise s exercitatio f, us·us -ūs m;
(mil) exercitium n; (literary) thema n
exercise vt exercēre; uti (with abl)
exert vt adhibēre; to — oneself
viribus eniti
exertion s contentio f, nis·us -ūs m
exhalation s exhalatio f, vapor m
exhale vt exhalare, spargĕre; vi exspirare
exhaust vt exhaurire; (to tire) defati-
gare, conficĕre, debilitare
exhaustion s defatigatio, defectio
virium f
exhibit vt exhibēre, exponĕre, osten-
dēre
exhibition s exhibitio, propositio f;
spectaculum n
exhilarate vt exhilarare
exhilaration s hilaritas f
exhort vt hortari
exhortation s hortatio f, hortamen n
exhume vt exhumare, eruĕre
exigency s necessitas f, angustiae
f pl
exile s (banishment) ex(s)ilium n;
(person) exsul, profugus m
exile vt relegare, in exilium pellĕre,
deportare
exist vi esse, exsistĕre; vivĕre
existence s existentia f; vita f
exit s exit·us -ūs m; ostium n
exonerate vt absolvĕre
exorbitant adj nimius, immodicus
exotic adj externus, peregrinus
expand vt expandĕre, extendĕre, dilatare; vi expandi, extendi, dilatari
expanse s spatium, expansum n
expansion s expansio f, spatium n
expatriate vt expellĕre
expect vt exspectare, sperare
expectancy s spes f
expectation s exspectatio, spes f
expectorate vt exspuĕre, exscreare
expediency s utilitas f
expedient adj utilis, commodus; —ly
apte, commode

expedient s modus m, ratio f
expedite vt expedire, maturare
expedition s (mil) expeditio f; (speed) celeritas f
expeditious adj celer, promptus; —ly celeriter, mature
expel vt expellĕre, ejicĕre
expend vt expendĕre, impendĕre
expenditure s sumpt·us -ūs m, impensa f
expense s impensa f, sumpt·us -ūs m
expensive adj carus, pretiosus; sumptuosus, lautus; —ly sumptuose
experience s experientia, peritia f, us·us -ūs m
experience vt experiri, cognoscĕre, pati
experienced adj peritus, expertus
experiment s experimentum n
experiment vi to — with experiri
experimental adj usu comparatus
expert adj sciens, peritus, callidus; —ly callide, scienter
expertness s calliditas, sollertia f
expiate vt expiare, luĕre
expiation s expiatio f; piaculum f
expiration s exspiratio f, finis, exit·us -ūs m
expire vi exspirare; (of time) exire
explain vt explanare, explicare, exponĕre
explanation s explanatio, explicatio, enodatio, interpretatio f
explicit adj apertus, expressus; —ly aperte, plane
explode vt displodĕre, discutĕre; vi displodi, dirumpi
exploit s res gesta f, factum, faci-nus n
exploit vt uti (with abl), abuti (with abl)
exploration s indagatio, investiga-tio f
explore vt explorare, scrutari, per-scrutari
explorer s explorator m
explosion s fragor m
exponent s interpres m
export vt exportare, evehĕre
exporter s exportator m
exports s merces quae exportantur f pl
expose vt exponĕre; nudare, dete-gĕre, patefacĕre; (to danger) obji-cĕre, offerre
exposition s explicatio, expositio, interpretatio f; (show) spectacu-lum n
expostulation s expostulatio, quere-la f
exposure s (of guilt) deprehensio f; (to cold) expositio f
expound vt exponĕre, interpretari
express adj clarus, expressus; —ly plane
express vt exprimĕre, eloqui, dicĕre; significare
expression s vox f, verbum n; (of face) vult·us -ūs m
expressive adj significans; (fig) lo-quax; — of index (with genit)

expulsion s exactio, ejectio, expul-sio f
expunge vt delēre, oblitterare
expurgate vt expurgare
exquisite adj exquisitus, elegans; —ly eleganter, exquisite
extant adj superstes, exsistens; to be — exstare
extempore adv ex tempore, subito
extemporize vi subito dicĕre, subi-ta dicĕre
extend vt extendĕre, producĕre, pro-pagare; vi extendĕre, porrigi
extension s extensio f; (space) spa-tium n; (of boundaries) prolatio f
extensive adj amplus, latus; —ly late
extent s spatium n; (of a country) tract·us -ūs m, fines m pl; to a great — magna ex parte; to some — aliqua ex parte; to this — hac-tenus
extenuate vt mitigare, minuĕre
extenuation s imminutio f
exterior adj externus, exterior
exterior s species f
exterminate vt exstirpare, extermi-nare, eradicare
extermination s exstirpatio f; inter-necio, occidio f
external adj externus, extraneus; —ly extrinsecus
extinct adj exstinctus, obsoletus; to become — obsolescĕre
extinction s exstinctio f, interit·us -ūs m
extinguish vt exstinguĕre, restin-guĕre
extol vt laudibus efferre
extort vt extorquēre, diripĕre, expri-mĕre
extortion s res repetundae f pl
extortioner s exactor, extortor m
extra adj additus
extra adv insuper, praeterea
extract vt extrahĕre, excerpĕre; (teeth, etc.) evellĕre
extract s (chemical) expressio f; (lit-erary) excerptum n; (synopsis) compendium n
extraction s (act) evulsio f; (birth, origin) stirps, origo f, genus n
extraneous adj extraneus, alienus, adventicius
extraordinarily adv mire, praeter solitum, extra modum
extraordinary adj extraordinarius, insolitus; (outstanding) eximius, mirus
extravagance s intemperantia f; sumpt·us -ūs m
extravagant adj immodicus, nimius; profusus, luxuriosus; (spending) prodigus; —ly immodice, absurde; prodige
extreme adj extremus, ultimus; —ly valde, summe
extreme s extremum, summum n
extremity s extremitas f, extremum n, finis m; (distress) miseria f
extricate vt expedire, extrahĕre, li-berare

exuberance s ubertas, luxuria, redundantia f
exuberant adj uber, luxuriosus; **—ly** ubertim
exude vt exudare; vi emanare
exult vi exsultare, gestire
exultant adj laetabundus, laetus; **—ly** laete
exultation s laetitia f

eye s oculus m; (of needle) foramen n; (of plant) gemma f; **to keep one's —s on** oculos defigěre in (with abl)
eye vt aspicěre, intuēri
eyebrow s supercilium n
eyelash s palebrarum pilus m
eyelid s palpebra f
eyesight s acies, acies oculi f
eyewitness s arbiter m

F

fable s fabula, narratio commenticia f
fabric s fabrica f; (piece of cloth) textile n
fabricate vt fabricare, struěre; (fig) fingěre
fabrication s fabricatio f; (fig) mendacium n
fabulous adj fictus, commenticius; **—ly** ficte
face s facies f, os n, vult·us -ūs m; **— to —** coram
face vt aspicěre, intuēri; se opponěre (with dat), obviam ire (with dat); obire; vi spectare, vergěre; **to — about** (mil) signa convertěre
facet s pars f
facetious adj facetus; **—ly** facete
facilitate vt facilius redděre
facility s facilitas f; opportunitas f
facing adj adversus, spectans
facsimile s imago f, exemplar n
fact s factum, verum n, res f; **as a matter of —** enimvero; **in —** vero, re ipsa; enim, etenim; **the — that** quod
faction s factio f
factory s officina, fabrica f
faculty s facultas, vis f; (of university) ordo m
fade vi marcescěre, deflorescěre, pallescěre
fail vt (to disappoint) relinquěre, deserěre, deficěre; vi succumběre, conciděre, caděre; (com) decoquěre, foro ceděre
fail s **without —** certo, plane, omnino
failing s (deficiency) defect·us ūs m; (fault) culpa f, delictum, vitium n; (disappointment) frustratio f; (ceasing) remissio f
failure s defectio f, defect·us -ūs m; (fault) culpa f, delictum n
faint adj (weary) defessus; (drooping) languidus; (of sight, smell, etc.) hebes; (of sound) surdus; (of color) pallidus; (of courage) timidus; **—ly** languide; timide
faint vi collabi, intermori, (animo) linqui
fainthearted adj timidus, imbellis, ignavus
faintness s (of impression) levitas f; (of body) languor m
fair adj (in appearance) formosus, pulcher; (of complexion) candidus; (of hair) flavus; (of weather) serenus; (of wind) secundus; (impartial) aequus; (of ability) mediocris; **— and square** sine fuco ac fallaciis; **—ly** aeque, juste; (moderately) mediocriter
fair s nundinae f pl
fairness s (of complexion) candor m; (justice) aequitas f
fairy s nympha f
faith s (trust) fides f; religio f; **to have — in** creděre (with dat), confiděre (with dat)
faithful adj fidelis, fidus; **—ly** fideliter
faithfulness s fidelitas, integritas f
faithless adj infidus, infidelis, perfidus; **—ly** perfide
falcon s falco m
fall s cas·us -ūs, laps·us -ūs m; (season) autumnus m
fall vi caděre, conciděre, labi; (to die) occiděre; (to abate) decrescěre; (violently) corruěre; **to — apart** dilabi; **to — at** acciděre ad (with acc); **to — back** reciděre; (to retreat) pedem referre; **to — down** deciděre; conciděre; **to — forwards** prociděre, prolabi; **to — foul of** incurrěre; **to — in(to)** inciděre; **to — in with** (to meet) inciděre; (to agree) congruěre; **to — in love with** amare, adamare; **to — off** (fig) in deterius mutari; **to — out with** (to have a disagreement with) disseděre; dissentire ab (with abl); **to — short of** non contingěre; **to — sick** in morbum inciděre; **to — to** (of inheritances, etc.) obvenire (with dat); **to — under** succumběre; (to be reckoned) pertiněre; (to become subjected to) pati; **to — upon** inciděre ad (with acc); (to assail) inciděre in (with acc), ingruěre in (with acc)
fallacious adj fallax, captiosus; **—ly** fallaciter
fallacy s captio f
fallible adj errori obnoxius
fallow adj (of land) novalis; **to lie —** cessare
false adj falsus, fictus; **—ly** falso
falsehood s mendacium n
falsify vt supponěre, corrumpěre; (documents) vitiare, interliněre

falter *vi* (*to stammer*) haesitare; (*to totter*) titubare

fame *s* fama *f*, nomen *n*

famed *adj* clarus, illustris

familiar *adj* familiaris, notus; intimus; **—ly** familiariter

familiarity *s* familiaritas, consuetudo *f*, us·us ‑ūs *m*

familiarize *vt* assuefacĕre

family *s* familia, dom·us ‑ūs, gens *f*, genus *n*

family *adj* familiaris; (*of home*) domesticus; (*relating to race*) gentilicus

famine *s* fames *f*

famished *adj* famelicus; fame confectus

famous *adj* clarus, celeber, inclitus; **—ly** praeclare, insigniter

fan *s* flabellum *n*; (*admirer*) fautor *m*; (*winnowing*) vannus *f*

fan *vt* ventilare; (*fire*) accendĕre; (*fig*) excitare, inflammare

fanatic *adj* fanaticus; **—ly** fanatice

fanaticism *s* furor religiosus *m*

fancied *adj* opinatus

fanciful *adj* (*capricey*) inconstans, levis; (*imagined*) commenticius

fancy *s* opinio, imaginatio *f*; (*caprice*) libido *f*; (*liking*) prolubium *n*; (*faculty*) phantasia *f*

fancy *vt* imaginari

fang *s* dens *m*

fantastic *adj* vanus; monstruosus

far *adj* longinquus, remotus

far *adv* procul, longe; **as — as** quantum, quatenus; tenus (*with abl*); **by — long, multo; — and near** longe lateque; **— be it from me to say** equidem dicĕre nolim; **— off** procul; **so — hactenus; thus —** hactenus

farce *s* mimus *m*

farcical *adj* mimicus; **—ly** mimice

fare *s* (*food*) cibus, vict·us ‑ūs *m*; (*money*) vectura *f*, portorium *n*

fare *vi* agĕre, se habēre

farewell *interj* vale!; salve!

farm *s* fundus *m*, praedium *n*

farm *vt* (*to till*) arare, colĕre; (*taxes*) redimĕre; **to — out** locare

farmer *s* agricola, colonus *m*; (*of revenues*) publicanus *m*

farming *s* agricultura *f*; res rustica *f*

farsighted *adj* providus

farther *adj* ulterior

farther *adv* longius, ulterius, ultra

farthermost *adj* remotissimus, ultimus

farthest *adj* ultimus, extremus

fasces *n* fasces *m pl*

fascinate *vt* fascinare

fascination *s* fascinatio *f*, fascinum *n*

fashion *s* (*form*) forma, figura *f*; (*manner*) mos, modus, rit·us ‑ūs *m*; (*custom*) consuetudo *f*, us·us ‑ūs *m*

fashion *vt* formare, fabricare, effingĕre *s*

fashionable *adj* elegans, concinnus; **it is — in usu est**

fashionably *adv* ad morem; eleganter

fast *adj* (*swift*) celer; (*firm*) firmus, stabilis; (*tight*) astrictus; (*shut*) occlusus

fast *adv* celeriter; firmiter

fast *s* jejunium *n*

fast *vi* jejunare, cibo abstinēre

fasten *vt* affigĕre, astringĕre; **to — down** defigĕre; **to — to** annectĕre, impingĕre; **to — together** configĕre, colligare; *vi* **to — upon** arripĕre

fastening *s* colligatio *f*, vinculum *n*

fastidious *adj* fastidiosus, delicatus, elegans, morosus; **—ly** fastidiose, morose

fasting *s* jejunium *n*, abstinentia *f*

fat *adj* pinguis, obsesus; (*productive*) fertilis

fat *s* adeps *m & f*, lardum *n*

fatal *adj* fatalis; exitialis, funebris; **—ly** fataliter; funeste

fatality *s* fatum *n*; (*misfortune*) infortunium *n*

fate *s* fatum *n*, sors *f*

fated *adj* fatalis

Fates *s* Parcae *f pl*

father *s* pater *m*; **— of the family** paterfamilias *m*

fatherhood *s* paternitas *f*

father-in-law *s* socer *m*

fatherless *adj* orbus

fatherly *adj* paternus, patrius

fathom *s* ulna *f*

fathom *vt* exputare

fathomless *adj* profundissimus

fatigue *s* (de)fatigatio, lassitudo *f*

fatigue *vt* (de)fatigare, delassare

fatigued *adj* (de)fatigatus, (de)fessus

fatten *vt* saginare, farcire; *vi* pinguescĕre

fattening *s* saginatio *f*

fatty *adj* pinguis

fatuous *adj* fatuus, insulsus

fault *s* culpa *f*, delictum, vitium *n*, error *m*; (*in writing*) mendum *n*; **to find — with** vituperare, carpĕre, incusare

faultless *adj* integer, perfectus; (*corrected*) emendatus

faulty *adj* vitiosus; mendosus

faun *s* faunus *m*

favor *s* favor *m*, gratia *f*; (*goodwill*) benevolentia *f*; (*good turn*) beneficium *n*; (*present*) munus *n*

favor *vt* favēre (*with dat*), secundare

favorable *adj* prosperus, secundus; commodus, idoneus; benignus, propitius

favorably *adv* fauste, feliciter, benigne; opportune

favorite *adj* dilectus, gratus

favorite *s* deliciae *f pl*

favoritism *s* indulgentia *f*; iniquitas *f*

fawn *s* hinnuleus *m*

fawn *vi* **to — on** *or* **upon** adulari

fawning *adj* blandus, adulatorius; **—ly** blande, adulatorie

fawning *s* adulatio *f*

fear *s* timor, met·us ‑ūs *m*, formido *f*

fear *vt & vi* timēre, metuĕre, verēri

fearful *adj* timidus, pavidus; (*terrible*) dirus, terribilis; —**ly** timide

fearless *adj* impavidus, intrepidus; —**ly** impavide, intrepide

feasibility *s* possibilitas *f*

feasible *adj* efficiendus, possibilis

feast *s* (*banquet*) convivium *n*, epulae *f pl*; (*holy day*) dies festus *m*

feast *vt* pascĕre; *vi* epulari, convivari

feat *s* facinus, factum *n*

feather *s* penna *f*; (*downy*) pluma *f*

feather *vt* to — one's nest opes accumulare

feathered *adj* pennatus; plumosus

feathery *adj* plumeus, plumosus

feature *s* lineamentum *n*; (*fig*) proprietas *f*, proprium *n*

February *s* (mensis) Februarius *m*

federal *adj* foederatus; rei publicae (*genit*)

federalize *vt* confoederare

federation *s* confoederatio *f*

fee *s* merces *f*

feeble *adj* infirmus, debilis; to grow — languescĕre

feebly *adv* infirme, languide

feed *vt* (*animals*) pascĕre; (*to nourish*) alĕre; (*fig*) (*of streams, etc.*) servire (*with dat*); *vi* pasci; to — on vesci (*with abl*)

feed *s* pabulum *n*

feel *vt* sentire; (*with hand*) tangĕre, tractare; to — pain dolore affici; to — pity for misereri (*with genit*); *vi* to — happy gaudĕre; to — sad maestus esse

feel *s* tact·us -ūs *m*

feeling *s* (*touch*) tact·us -ūs *m*; (*sensibility*) sens·us -ūs *m*; (*emotion*) affect·us -ūs *m*; (*taste*) judicium *n*; (*pity*) miseratio *f*

feign *vt* fingĕre, dissimulare, mentiri

feint *s* simulatio *f*

felicitation *s* congratulatio *f*

felicitous *adj* felix; —**ly** feliciter

felicity *s* felicitas *f*

feline *adj* felin(e)us

fell *adj* atrox, saevus, crudelis

fell *vt* (*trees*) caedĕre; (*person*) sternĕre

fellow *s* socius, aequalis *m*

felon *s* scelestus, sceleratus *m*

felonious *adj* scelestus, sceleratus

felony *s* scelus *n*

felt *s* coacta *n pl*

female *adj* muliebris

female *s* femina *f*

feminine *adj* muliebris, femineus; (*gram*) femininus

fence *s* saepes *f*, saepimentum *n*

fence *vt* saepire; to — off intersaepire; *vi* batuĕre

fencing *s* ludus gladiatorius *m*

fend *vt* to — off arcēre; *vi* to — for oneself sibi providēre, sibi consulĕre

ferment *s* fermentum *n*; (*fig*) aest·us -ūs *m*

ferment *vt* fermentare; excitare; *vi* fermentari; (*fig*) fervēre

fermentation *s* fermentatio *f*

fern *s* filix *f*

ferocious *adj* ferox, truculentus, saevus, atrox; —**ly** truculente

ferocity *s* ferocitas, saevitia *f*

ferret *vt* to — out eruĕre

ferry *s* traject·us -ūs *m*

ferry *vt* trajicĕre, transvehĕre

ferryboat *s* scapha, cymba *f*

ferryman *s* portitor *m*

fertile *adj* fertilis, fecundus

fertility *s* fertilitas, ubertas *f*

fertilize *vt* fecundare

fervent *adj* fervidus, ardens; —**ly** ardenter, vehementer

fervid *adj* fervidus; —**ly** fervide

fervor *s* fervor, ardor *m*

fester *vi* suppurare, ulcerari

festival *s* dies festus *m*, sollemne *n*

festive *adj* festus

festivity *s* sollemnia *n pl*; (*gaiety*) festivitas *f*

fetch *vt* adducĕre, afferre, arcessĕre

fetid *adj* foetidus, graveolens

feud *s* simultas, inimicitia, lis *f*

fever *s* febris *f*; to have a — febrire

feverish *adj* febriculosus

few *adj* pauci; a — aliquot; in a — words paucis, breviter

fiasco *s* calamitas *f*

fiber *s* fibra *f*

fibrous *adj* fibratus

fickle *adj* inconstans, mobilis, instabilis

fiction *s* fictio *f*, commentum *n*; fabula *f*

fictitious *adj* fictus, commenticius; —**ly** ficte

fiddle *s* fides *f*

fiddle *vi* fide ludĕre

fiddler *s* fidicen *m*

fidelity *s* fidelitas, constantia *f*

fidget *vi* trepidare

fidgety *adj* inquietus

field *s* ager *m*; (*plowed*) arvum *n*; (*mil*) acies *f*, campus *m*; (*grassy*) pratum *n*; (*of grain*) seges *f*; (*sphere*) area *f*, locus, campus *m*

fieldpiece *s* tormentum *n*

fiend *s* inimicus *m*; diabolus *m*

fiendish *adj* diabolicus

fierce *adj* atrox, saevus, vehemens; —**ly** atrociter, saeve, vehementer

fierceness *s* atrocitas, saevitia, ferocitas *f*

fiery *adj* igneus; (*fig*) ardens, fervidus

fife *s* tibia *f*

fifteen *adj* quindecim; — times quindecies

fifteenth *adj* quintus decimus

fifth *adj* quintus; for the — time quintum, quinto

fifth *s* quinta pars *f*

fiftieth *adj* quinquagesimus

fifty *adj* quinquaginta

fig *s* ficus *f*

fight *s* pugna *f*, proelium *n*; (*struggle*) contentio, luctatio *f*

fight *vt* pugnare cum (*with abl*); to — it out decernĕre, depugnare; *vi* pugnare, dimicare; (*in battle*) proeliari; (*with sword*) digladiari; to — hand to hand cominus pugnare

figment *s* commentum *n*

figurative *adj* translatus, assumptus; **—ly** per translationem, tropice

figure *s* figura, forma, imago *f*; (*of speech*) tropus *m*, translatio *f*; (*in art*) signum *n*

figure *vt* figurare, formare; putare, opinari

figured *adj* sigillatus

filament *s* filum *n*, fibra *f*

filbert *s* nux avellana *f*

file *s* (*tool*) lima *f*; (*for papers*) scapus *m*; (*row*) ordo *m*, agmen *n*

file *vt* limare; (*papers*) in scapo condĕre; *vi* **to — off** (*mil*) decurrĕre

filial *adj* pius

filigree *s* diatreta *n pl*

filings *s* scobis *f*

fill *vt* complēre, implēre; (*office*) fungi (*with abl*); **to — out** implēre; **to — up** explēre, complēre, supplēre

fill *s* satietas *f*

fillip *s* talitrum *n*

filly *s* equula *f*

film *s* membranula *f*

filmy *adj* membranaceus; (*fig*) caliginosus

filter *s* colum *n*

filter *vt* percolare; *vi* percolari

filtering *s* percolatio *f*

filth *s* sordes, colluvies *f*, squalor *m*

filthiness *s* foeditas *f*, squalor *m*; (*fig*) obscenitas *f*

filthy *adj* sordidus, spurcus; (*fig*) obscenus

filtration *s* percolatio *f*

fin *s* pinna *f*

final *adj* ultimus, postremus, extremus; **—ly** denique, tandem; postremo

finance *s* (*private*) res familiaris *f*; (*public*) aerarium *n*, ratio aeraria *f*, vectigalia *n pl*

financial *adj* aerarius

find *vt* invenire, reperire; (*to hit upon*) offendĕre; **to — out** comperire, cognoscĕre

fine *adj* (*thin*) subtilis, tenuis; (*of gold*) purus; (*handsome*) bellus, elegans; (*of weather*) serenus; **—ly** subtiliter

fine *s* mul(c)ta *f*, damnum *n*

fine *vt* mul(c)tare

finery *s* ornat·us -ūs *m*

finesse *s* astutia *f*, argutiae *f pl*

finger *s* digitus *m*; (*of glove*) digitale *n*

finger *vt* tractare

finish *vt* conficĕre, perficĕre; (*to put an end to*) terminare; **to — off** conficĕre; peragĕre; *vi* desinĕre

finish *s* finis *m*; (*in art*) perfectio *f*

finite *adj* finitus, circumscriptus

fire *s* ignis *m*; (*conflagration*) incendium *n*; (*of artillery*) conject·us -ūs *m*; (*fig*) fervor, ardor, impet·us -ūs *m*; **by — and sword** ferro ignique; **to be on —** flagrare; **to catch —** flammam concipĕre; **to set on —** incendĕre

fire *vt* accendĕre, incendĕre; (*fig*) in-

flammare; (*missile*) jaculari; (*to dismiss*) dimittĕre

firefly *s* elater noctilucus *m*

fireplace *s* focus, caminus *m*

fireproof *adj* ignibus impervius

fireside *s* focus *m*

firewood *s* lignum *n*

firm *adj* firmus, solidus; constans; **to be — perseverare**; **to stand — perstare**; **—ly** firme, firmiter; solide; constanter

firm *s* societas *f*

firmament *s* firmamentum *n*

firmness *s* firmitas, constantia *f*

first *adj* primus; (*of two*) prior

first *adv* primum; **at — primo**; **— of all** imprimis

firstborn *adj* primogenitus

firstfruits *s* primitiae *f pl*

fiscal *adj* aerarius, fiscalis

fish *s* piscis *m*

fish *vi* piscari; (*fig*) expiscari

fisherman *s* piscator *m*

fishing *s* piscat·us -ūs *m*, piscatio *f*

fish market *s* forum piscarium *n*

fish pond *s* piscina *f*

fishy *adj* piscosus

fissure *s* fissura, rima *f*

fist *s* pugnus *m*

fit *s* (*of anger, etc.*) impet·us -ūs *m*; (*med*) access·us -ūs *m*; convulsio *f*; (*whim*) libido *f*; **by —s and starts** carptim

fit *adj* aptus, idoneus, habilis; (*becoming*) decens; (*ready*) paratus

fit *vt* accommodare; (*to apply*) applicare; (*to furnish*) instruĕre; *vi* (*fig*) convenire

fitful *adj* mutabilis, inconstans

fitness *s* convenientia *f*; (*of persons*) habilitas *f*

fitting *adj* decens, idoneus; **it is — convenit**, decet

five *adj* quinque; **— times** quinquies

fix *vt* (*to repair*) reficĕre; resarcire; (*to fasten*) figĕre, firmare; (*the eyes*) intendĕre; (*time*) dicĕre; *vi* **to — upon** inhaerēre (*with dat*)

fixed *adj* firmus, fixus; certus; **— on** (*intent upon*) intentus (*with dat*)

fixture *s* affixum *n*

fizz *vi* sibilare

flabbiness *s* mollitia *f*

flabby *adj* flaccidus, flaccus; (*drooping*) marcidus

flaccid *adj* flaccidus

flag *s* vexillum *n*

flagrant *adj* impudens, apparens, nefarius

flail *s* pertica, tribula *f*

flake *s* squama *f*; (*of snow*) nix *f*

flaky *adj* squameus

flame *s* flamma *f*

flame *vi* flammare, flagrare; **to — up** scintillare; (*fig*) exardescĕre

flank *s* (*of animal*) ilia *n pl*; (*mil*) lat·us *n*; **on the — a latere**

flank *vt* tegĕre latus (*with genit*)

flap *s* (*of dress*) lacinia *f*

flap *vt* plaudĕre (*with abl*); *vi* (*to hang loosely*) fluitare

flare *s* flamma *f*, fulgor *m*

flare *vi* flagrare, exardescĕre

flash s fulgor m; (of fire) coruscatio f; (of lightning) fulmen n; — **of wit** sales m pl

flash vi fulgēre, coruscare, micare

flask s ampulla, lag. ncula f

flat adj (level) planus, aequus; (not mountainous) campester; (on back) supinus; (on face) pronus; (insipid) vapidus; (fig) frigidus, insulsus; **to fall** — (fig) frigēre

flatness s planities f

flatten vt complanare, planum reddere

flatter vt adulari (with dat), blandiri (with dat), assentari (with dat)

flatterer s adulator, assentator m

flattering adj adulans, blandus, adulatorius

flattery s adulatio f, blanditiae f pl

flaunt vt jactare; vi tumēre, gloriari

flaunting adj lautus, gloriosus

flaunting s jactatio f

flavor s sapor, gustat·us ·ūs m

flavor vt imbuēre, condire

flaw s (defect) vitium n; (chink) rimula f

flawless adj emendatus

flax s linum n

flaxen adj lineus

flay vt deglubare

flea s pulex m

fleck s macula f

fledged adj plumatus

flee vi fugēre; **to** — **away** aufugēre; **to** — **back** refugēre; **to** — **to confugēre** ad or in (with acc)

fleece s vellus n

fleece vt tondēre; (fig) spoliare

fleecy adj laniger

fleet s classis f

fleet adj celer; (winged) volucer; (fig) fugax

fleeting adj fugax; (flowing) fluxus

flesh s caro f; **in the** — vivus

fleshy adj carnosus

flexibility s flexibilitas f; (fig) mollitia f

flexible adj flexibilis, lentus; (fig) exorabilis

flicker vi coruscare

flickering adj tremulus

flight s (flying) volat·us ·ūs m; (escape) fuga f, effugium n; (covey) grex m; (of stairs) scala f; **to put to** — fugare; **to take to** — aufugēre, terga vertēre

flight s jact·us ·ūs m

flint s silex m & f

flinty adj siliceus

flippancy s petulantia f

flippant adj petulans; temere loquens; —**ly** temere ac leviter

flirt s lupus m, lupa f

flirt vi ludēre, lascivire

flirtation s amores m pl

flit vi volitare

float s (raft) rates f; (on fishing line) cortex m

float vt (to launch) demittēre; vi fluitare, (in)natare; (in air) volitare

flock s grex m; **in** —**s** gregatim

flock vi concurrēre, convenire, coire

floe s fragmentum glaciei n

flog vt verberare

flogging s verberatio f, verbera n pl

flood s (deluge) diluvies f; (of river) torrens m; (tide) access·us ·ūs m; (fig) flumen n

floor s (story of building) tabulatum n; (on the ground) solum; (paved) pavimentum n

floor vt (to throw down) sternēre

flooring s contabulatio f

floral adj floreus

florid adj floridus

flotilla s classicula f

flounce s fimbria f

flounder vi volutari; (in speech) haesitare

flour s farina f; (finest) pollen m

flourish vt vibrare; (to sound) canēre; vi florēre, virēre; (mus) praeludēre

flourish s ornamentum n; (of style) calamistri m pl; (mus) praelusio f; (of trumpet) cant·us ·ūs m

flout vt deridēre, contumeliis afficēre, aspernari

flow vi fluēre; (of tide) affluēre, accedēre

flow s fluxio f, laps·us ·ūs m; (of tide) access·us ·ūs m

flower s flos m; (fig) (the best) flos m; (of army) robur n; (of age) adulescentia f

flower vi florescēre

flowery adj floreus; floridus

fluctuate vi fluctuari; (fig) jactare

fluctuation s fluctuatio f; (fig) mutatio f

flue s cuniculus fornacis m

fluency s copia verborum, volubilitas linguae f

fluent adj volubilis; (eloquent) disertus; —**ly** volubiliter

fluid adj fluidus, liquidus

fluid s fluidum n, fluor m

fluke s (of anchor) dens m; (luck) fortuitum n

flurry s commotio f, tumult·us ·ūs m

flurry vt perturbare, inquietare

flush s rubor m

flush vi erubescēre

fluster vt turbare, inquietare

flute s tibia f; (in architecture) stria f

flutist s tibicen m

flutter s volitatio f, tremor m; (fig) trepidatio f

flutter vi (of the heart) palpitare; (of bird) volitare; (with alarm) trepidare

flux s flux·us ·ūs m; **to be in a state of** — fluēre

fly s musca f

fly vi volare; (to flee) fugēre; **to** — **apart** dissilire; **to** — **off** avolare;

to — open dissilire; **to — out** provolare; **to — up** subvolare

flying *adj* volatilis, volucer

foal *s* pullus *m*; *(of asses)* asellus *m*; *(of horses)* equulus *m*

foal *vi* parĕre

foam *s* spuma *f*

foam *vi* spumare; *(to boil)* exaestuare

foamy *adj* spumans; spumeus, spumosus

focus *vt (the mind)* intendĕre

fodder *s* pabulum *n*

fodder *vt* pabulum praebēre *(with dat)*

foe *s (public)* hostis *m; (private)* inimicus *m*

fog *s* caligo, nebula *f*

foggy *adj* caliginosus, nebulosus

foible *s* vitium *n*, error *m*

foil *s (for fencing)* rudis *f; (leaf of metal)* lamina *f; (very thin)* bractea *f; (contrast)* repulsa *f*

foil *vt* eludĕre; repellĕre

fold *s* sin·us -ūs *m*, plica *f; (wrinkle)* ruga *f; (for sheep)* ovile *n; (for cattle)* stabulum *n*

fold *vt* plicare, complicare

foliage *s* frons *f*, folia *n pl*

folio *s* liber maximae formae *m*

folk *s* homines *m pl*

follow *vt* sequi; *(close)* instare *(with dat)*, assectari; *(a calling)* facĕre; *(instructions)* parēre *(with dat); (road)* pergĕre; *(to understand)* intellegĕre; **to — out** exsequi, prosequi; **to — up** subsequi

follower *s* sectator *m; (of teacher)* auditor *m*

following *adj* sequens; posterus, proximus

folly *s* stultitia, insipientia *f*

foment *vt* fovēre

fond *adj* amans, studiosus; ineptus; **to be — of** amare; **—ly** amanter; *(foolishly)* inepte

fondle *vt* mulcēre, fovēre

fondness *s* caritas *f*, studium *n*

food *s* cibus *m*

fool *s* stultus, fatuus *m*; **to make a — of** ludificare; **to play the —** ineptire

fool *vt* ludificari

foolhardy *adj* temerarius

foolish *adj* stultus, fatuus, ineptus, stolidus; **—ly** stulte, inepte

foot *s* pes *m; (of mountain)* radix *f; (of pillar)* basis *f;* **on —** pedester

football *s* pila pedalis *f*

footing *s* locus *m; (condition)* stat·us -ūs *m*

footprint *s* vestigium *n*

foot soldier *s* pedes *m*

footstool *s* scabellum, scamnum *n*

fop *s* bellus homo *m*

foppish *adj* nitidus, delicatus

for *prep (extent of time or space)* render by acc; *(price)* render by genit or abl; *(on behalf of)* pro *(with abl); (cause)* causā *(with genit)*, ob *(with acc)*, propter *(with acc); (after negatives)* prae *(with abl); (toward)* erga *(with acc)*

for *conj* nam; enim

forage *s* pabulum *n*

forage *vi* pabulari, frumentari

foray *s* incursio *f*

forbear *vi* parcĕre *(with dat)*, desistĕre

forbearance *s* patientia, indulgentia *f*

forbid *vt* vetare, prohibēre, interdicĕre

forbidding *adj* insuavis, odiosus

force *s* vis *f; (law)* man·us -ūs *f; (mil)* copiae *f pl*, impet·us -ūs *m;* **in —** validus

force *vt* cogĕre, impellĕre; *(door, etc.)* rumpĕre; **to — down** detrudĕre; **to — out** extrudĕre, extorquēre

forced *adj (unnatural)* arcessitus, quaesitus

forced march *s* magnum *or* maximum iter *n*

forceps *s* forceps *m & f*

forcible *adj* per vim factus; *(of force)* validus; *(violent)* vehemens; *(weighty)* gravis

forcibly *adv* per vim, vi; violenter; graviter

ford *s* vadum *n*

ford *vt* vado transire

fore *adj* anterior, prior

forearm *s* bracchium *n*

forearm *vt* praemunire; **to be forearmed** praecavēre

forebode *vt (to foretell)* portendĕre; *(to be prescient of)* praesagire

foreboding *s* portentum, praesagium *n; (feeling)* praesensio *f*

foreboding *adj* praesagus

forecast *vt* providēre, prospicĕre; praedicĕre

forecast *s* praedictio *f*

forecastle *s* prora *f*

foredoom *vt* praedestinare

forefather *s* atavus *m;* **—s** majores *m pl*

forefinger *s* digitus index *m*

forego *vt* abdicare, dimittĕre

foregoing *adj* prior, proximus

forehead *s* frons *f*

foreign *adj* externus, alienus, peregrinus

foreigner *s* peregrinus, advena *m*

foreknowledge *s* providentia *f*

foreman *s* procurator, villicus *m*

foremost *adj* primus, princeps

forenoon *s* antemeridianum tempus *n;* **in the —** ante meridiem

forensic *adj* forensis

fore part *s* prior pars *f*

forerunner *s* praenuntius, antecursor *m*

foresee *vt* providēre, praevidēre, prospicĕre

foreseeing *adj* providus

foresight *s* providentia, prudentia *f; (precaution)* provisio *f*

forest *adj* silvestris

forest *s* silva *f*

forestall *vt* occupare, anticipare

forestall *vt* praedicĕre, vaticinari

forethought *s* providentia *f*

forewarn *vt* praemonēre

forewarning *s* praemonit·us -ūs *m*

forfeit *s* multa, poena *f*, damnum *n*

forfeit vt mul(c)tari (with abl), amittĕre, perdĕre

forfeiture s damnum n, amissio f

forge vt fabricari, excudĕre; (document) subjicĕre; (signature) imitari; **to — money** adulterinos nummos cudĕre

forge s furnus fabrilis m

forged adj falsus, adulterinus

forger s fabricator m; (of writings) falsarius m; (of money) qui adulterinos nummos cudit

forgery s falsum n

forget vt oblivisci (with genit)

forgetful adj immemor, obliviosus

forgetfulness s oblivio f

forgive vt ignoscĕre (with dat), veniam dare (with dat); condonare

forgiveness s venia f

forgiving adj clemens

fork s furca f; (of roads) bivium n

forked adj bifurcus, bicornis

forlorn adj destitutus, derelictus

form s forma, figura f; **in due —** rite

form vt formare, fingĕre; (to produce) efficĕre

formal adj justus; nimis accuratus; **—ly** frigide ac nimis accurate

formality s rit·us ·ūs m; **with due — rite**

formation s conformatio, forma, figura f; **in —** (mil) instructus

former adj prior; (immediately preceding) superior; antiquus, priscus; **the —** ille; **—ly** antehac, olim, quondam

formidable adj formidabilis

formidably adv formidolose

formless adj informis, rudis

formula s formula f, exemplar n

forsake vt deserĕre, derelinquĕre

forswear vt abjurare, repudiare

fort s castellum n

forth adv foras; (of time) inde; **and so —** et cetera

forthwith adv protinus, statim, extemplo

fortieth adj quadragesimus

fortification s munitio f, munimentum n

fortify vt munire

fortitude s fortitudo f

fortress s arx f, castellum n

fortuitous adj fortuitus; **—ly** fortuito

fortunate adj fortunatus, felix, prosperus; **—ly** feliciter

fortune s fortuna, felicitas f; (estate) opes f pl, res f, divitiae f pl; **to tell —s** hariolari

fortune-teller s fatidicus, sortilegus, astrologus m

forty adj quadraginta

forum s forum n

forward adv porro, prorsus, prorsum

forward adj (person) audax, protervus; anterior

forward vt (letter) perferre; (cause) adjuvare, promovĕre

foster vt alĕre, fovĕre, nutrire

foster brother s collacteus m

foster child s alumnus m, alumna f

foster father s altor, nutritor, educator m

foster mother s altrix, nutrix, educatrix f

foul adj (dirty) foedus, lutulentus, squalidus; (ugly) deformis; (of language) obscenus; (of weather) turbidus; **to fall — of** incurrĕre in (with acc), inruĕre in (with acc); **—ly** foede

foul vt foedare, inquinare

found vt condĕre, fundare, constituere, instituĕre

foundation s fundamentum n, substructio f

founder s conditor, fundator, auctor m

founder vi titubare, submergi

foundling s expositius m, expositia f

fountain s fons m

fountainhead s caput fontis n

four adj quattuor; **— each** quaterni; **— times** quater; **— years** quadriennium n; **on all —s** repens

fourfold adj quadruplex, quadruplus

fourscore adj octoginta

fourteen adj quattuordecim

fourteenth adj quartus decimus

fourth adj quartus; **—ly** quarto

fourth s quadrans n, quarta pars f; **three —s** tres partes f pl

fowl s avis, volucris f; (domestic) gallina f

fox s vulpes f; **an old —** (fig) veterator m

fraction s pars exigua f

fracture s fractura f

fracture vt frangĕre

fragile adj fragilis; (fig) caducus

fragility s fragilitas f

fragment s fragmentum n

fragrance s odor m

fragrant adj suaveolens, odorus; **—ly** suavi odore

frail adj fragilis; caducus, infirmus

frailty s fragilitas, debilitas f; (moral) error m

frame s (of buildings, etc.) compages f; (of body) figura f; (of bed) sponda f; (of mind) habit·us ·ūs m

frame vt fabricari; (to contrive) moliri; (a picture) in forma includĕre; (a document) componĕre

France s Gallia f

franchise s civitas f, suffragium n

frank adj candidus, sincerus, simplex; **—ly** candide, aperte

frankness s libertas, simplicitas, ingenuitas f

frantic adj amens, furiosus, furens; **—ally** furenter

fraternal adj fraternus; **—ly** fraterne

fraternity s fraternitas f; (association) sodalitas f

fratricide s (doer) fratricida m; (deed) fratris parricidium n

fraud s fraus f, dolus m; (person) dolus malus m

fraudulence s fraus f

fraudulent *adj* fraudulentus, dolosus; —ly fraudulenter, dolo malo

fraught *adj* plenus

fray *s* pugna *f*; (*brawl*) rixa *f*

freak *s* (*whim*) libido *f*; monstrum *n*

freckle *s* lentigo *f*

freckled *adj* lentiginosus

free *adj* liber; (*disengaged*) vacuus, otiosus; (*generous*) liberalis; (*from duty*) immunis; (*unencumbered*) expeditus; (*in speech*) liber, candidus; —ly libere; (*of one's own accord*) sponte, ultro; (*frankly*) aperte; (*generously*) large, copiose

free *vt* liberare; (*slave*) manumittěre; (*son*) emancipare

freeborn *adj* ingenuus

freedman *s* libertus *m*

freedom *s* libertas *f*; (*from duty*) immunitas *f*

freehold *s* praedium liberum *n*

freeholder *s* dominus *m*

freeman *s* liber *m*

free will *s* voluntas *f*, liberum arbitrium *n*; **of one's own** — suā sponte, ultro, arbitrio suo

freeze *vt* congelare, glaciare; *vi* consistěre, rigescěre; **it is freezing** gelat

freezing *adj* gelidus

freight *s* onus *n*, vectura *f*

freight *vt* onerare

French *adj* Gallicus; **in** — Gallice; **the** — Galli *m pl*

Frenchman *s* Gallus *m*

frenzied *adj* furens, lymphatus

frenzy *s* furor *m*, insania *f*

frequency *s* crebritas, assiduitas *f*

frequent *adj* creber, frequens; —ly crebro, frequenter, saepe

frequent *vt* frequentare

frequenter *s* frequentator *m*

fresco *s* opus tectorium *n*

fresh *adj* (*new*) recens, novus; (*cool*) frigidulus; (*not tired*) integer; (*forward*) protervus; (*green*) viridis; —ly recenter

freshen *vt* recreare, renovare; *vi* (*of wind*) increbrescěre

freshman *s* tiro *m*

freshman *adj* novicius

freshness *s* novitas, viriditas *f*

fret *vi* dolēre, angi

fretful *adj* morosus, stomachosus; —ly morose, stomachose

fretted *adj* laqueatus

friction *s* frictio *f*, attrit·us -ūs *m*

friend *s* amicus *m*, amica *f*, familiaris *m & f*; (*of a thing*) amator *m*

friendless *adj* amicorum inops, desertus

friendliness *s* benevolentia, comitas, affabilitas *f*

friendly *adj* amicus, benevolus, comis; **in a** — **manner** amice

friendship *s* amicitia *f*

frieze *s* zoophorus *m*

fright *s* pavor, terror *m*

frighten *vt* (per)terrēre; **to** — **away** absterrēre

frightful *adj* terribilis, terrificus; —ly foede

frigid *adj* frigidus; —ly frigide

frigidity *s* frigiditas *f*

frills *s* segmenta *n pl*; (*rhet*) calamistri *m pl*

fringe *s* fimbria *f*, cirrus *m*; (*fig*) limbus *m*

frisk *vt* scrutari; *vi* lascivire, exsilire

fritter *vt* **to** — **away** conterěre, comminuěre, dissipare

frivolity *s* levitas *f*, nugae *f pl*

frivolous *adj* levis, frivolus, inanis; —ly inaniter

fro *adv* **to and** — huc illuc, ultro citroque

frock *s* palla, stola *f*

frog *s* rana *f*

frolic *s* lascivia *f*, ludus *m*

frolic *vi* exsultare, hilarescěre

from *prep* a *or* ab (*with abl*); de (*with abl*); e *or* ex (*with abl*); (*cause*) ob (*with acc*); — **above** desuper; — **abroad** peregre; — **day to day** de die in diem; — **time to time** interdum, passim; — **within** intus; — **without** extrinsecus

front *s* frons *f*; (*mil*) acies *f*, primum agmen *n*; (*fig*) impudentia *f*; **in** — a fronte, adversus; **in** — **of** pro (*with abl*)

front *adj* prior

frontier *s* limes *m*, confinia *n pl*

frost *s* gelu *n*, pruina *f*

frostbitten *adj* praeustus, adustus

frosty *adj* gelidus, glacialis

froth *s* spuma *f*

froth *vi* spumare, spumas agěre

frothy *adj* spumeus, spumosus

frown *s* contractio frontis *f*

frown *vi* frontem contrahěre *or* adducěre

frozen *adj* conglaciatus, gelatus, gelu rigens

frugal *adj* parcus, frugi (*indecl*); —ly frugaliter, parce

frugality *s* parsimonia, frugalitas *f*

fruit *s* fruct·us -ūs *m*, frux *f*; (*of tree*) mala *n pl*; —**s of the earth** fruges *f pl*

fruitful *adj* fructuosus, fecundus, fertilis; —ly fecunde, feraciter

fruitfulness *s* fecunditas, fertilitas, ubertas *f*

fruitless *adj* sterilis; (*fig*) irritus; —ly frustra

fruit tree *s* pomus *f*

frustrate *vt* frustrari; (*to baffle*) decipěre

frustration *s* frustratio *f*

fry *s* (*dish of things fried*) frixa *f*

fry *vt* frigěre

frying pan *s* sartago *f*

fuel *s* fomes *m*, materia *f*

fugitive *adj* fugitivus

fugitive *s* profugus, transfuga, fugitivus *m*; (*from abroad*) extorris *m*

fulcrum *s* (*of a lever*) pressio *f*

fulfil *vt* explēre, exsequi, perficěre

fulfilment *s* exsecutio, peractio, perfectio *f*

full *adj* plenus; (*filled up*) expletus; (*entire*) integer, solidus; (*satiated*) satur; (*of dress*) fusus; —ly plene, funditus, penitus

full moon *s* plenilunium *n*

fumble *vi* haesitare
fume *s* fumus, vapor, halit·us -ūs *m*
fume *vi* irasci
fumigate *vt* fumigare, suffire
fumigation *s* suffit·us -ūs *m*
fun *s* jocus *m*, ludibrium *n*
function *s* munus, officium *n*
function *vi* munus implēre
functionary *s* magistrat·us -ūs *m*
fund *s* copia *f*, pecuniae *f pl*
fundamental *adj* fundamentalis, primus; **—ly** penitus, funditus
funeral *s* funus *n*, exsequiae *f pl*
funeral *adj* funebris
funereal *adj* funereus, lugubris
fungus *s* fungus *m*
funnel *s* infundibulum *n*
funny *adj* ridiculus, jocularis
fur *s* villi *m pl*, pellis *m*
furious *adj* furiosus, furens; **—ly** furiose, furenter
furl *vt* complicare; (*sail*) legēre
furlough *s* commeat·us -ūs *m*; **on —** in commeatu
furnace *s* fornax *f*
furnish *vt* suppeditare, ministrare; ornare, exornare, instruēre

furniture *s* supellex *f*
furrow *s* sulcus *m*
furry *adj* pelle insutus
further *adj* ulterior
further *adv* ultra, longius, ulterius
further *vt* promovēre, provehēre; (*to aid*) adjuvare
furtherance *s* progress·us -ūs *m*
furthermore *adv* insuper, porro, praeterea
furthest *adj* ultimus, extremus
furthest *adv* longissime
furtive *adj* furtivus; **—ly** furtim, furtive
fury *s* furor *m*
fuse *vt* fundēre; *vi* coalescēre
fus’on *s* fusura *f*
fuss *s* strepit·us -ūs, tumult·us -ūs *m*
fuss *vi* sollicitari
fussy *adj* fastidiosus, importunus
futile *adj* futilis, inanis
futility *s* futilitas *f*
future *adj* futurus, posterus
future *s* futura *n pl*, posterum tempus *n*; **in the —** posthac
futurity *s* posteritas *f*

G

gab *s* garrulitas *f*
gab *vi* garrire
gable *s* fastigium *n*
gadfly *s* tabanus, oestrus *m*
gag *s* jocus *m*
gag *vt* os obstruēre (*with dat*)
gaiety *s* hilaritas *f*; nitor, splendor *m*
gaily *adv* hilare, festive
gain *s* quaest·us -ūs *m*, lucrum *n*
gain *vt* consequi, acquirēre, capēre; (*profit*) lucrari; (*victory*) reportare; (*case*) vincēre; **to — possession of** potiri (*with abl*)
gainful *adj* quaestuosus, lucrosus
gainsay *vt* contradicēre (*with dat*)
gait *s* incess·us -ūs *m*
gala *s* dies festus *m*
galaxy *s* orbis lacteus *m*
gale *s* ventus *m*
gall *s* fel *n*, bilis *f*
gall *vt* urēre
gallant *adj* fortis, animosus; (*to ladies*) officiosus; **—ly** fortiter
gallant *s* amator *m*
gallantry *s* virtus, fortitudo *f*; (*to ladies*) urbanitas *f*
galleon *s* navis oneraria *f*
gallery *s* portic·us -ūs *f*; (*open*) peristylium *n*; (*for pictures*) pinacotheca *f*
galley *s* navis longa, triremis *f*; (*kitchen*) culina *f*
Gallic *adj* Gallicus, Gallicanus
galling *adj* mordax
gallon *s* congius *m*
gallop *s* citatissimus curs·us -ūs *m*; **at a —** citato equo, admisso equo
gallop *vi* quadrupedare

gallows *s* patibulum *n*
gamble *vt* **to — away** ludēre, amittēre; *vi* aleā ludēre
gambler *s* aleator, lusor *m*
gambling *s* alea *f*
gambol *s* salt·us -ūs *m*
gambol *vi* lascivire, ludēre
game *s* ludus *m*; (*with dice*) alea *f*; (*quarry*) praeda *f*, ferae *f pl*; **to make — of** ludificari
gander *s* anser *m*
gang *s* grex *m*, caterva *f*
gangster *s* grassator *m*
gangway *s* forus *m*
gap *s* apertura, fissura, lacuna *f*, hiat·us -ūs *m*
gape *vi* hiare, dehiscēre
gaping *adj* hians, hiulcus, oscitans; (*fig*) stupidus
garb *s* vestit·us -ūs, habit·us -ūs *m*
garbage *s* quisquiliae *f pl*
garble *vt* vitiare, corrumpēre
garden *s* hortus *m*
gardener *s* hortulanus, olitor *m*
gardening *s* hortorum cult·us -ūs *m*
gargle *vi* gargarizare
gargling *s* gargarizatio *f*
garland *s* sertum *n*, corona *f*
garlic *s* alium *n*
garment *s* vestimentum *n*, vestit·us -ūs *m*
garner *s* horreum *n*
garnish *vt* decorare, ornare
garret *s* cenaculum *n*
garrison *s* praesidium *n*
garrison *vt* praesidio munire, praesidium collocare in (*with abl*), praesidium imponēre (*with dat*)

garrulity s garrulitas f
garrulous adj garrulus, loquax
garter s periscelis f
gas s spiritus naturales m pl
gash s patens plaga f
gash vt caesim ferire
gasp s anhelit·us -ūs, singult·us -ūs m
gasp vi anhelare, singultare
gastric adj ad stomachum pertinens
gastronomy s gula f
gate s janua f, ostium n; (of town) porta f
gatekeeper s janitor m
gateway s porta f, postis m
gather vt (to assemble) congregare, colligĕre; (fruit, etc.) legĕre; (to pluck) decerpĕre, carpĕre; (in logic) concludĕre; (to suspect) suspicare; vi convenire, concurrĕre
gathering s convent·us -ūs m, congregatio f; collectio f
gaudily adv laute
gaudiness s lautitia f, ornat·us -ūs, nitor m
gaudy adj lautus, speciosus, splendidus
gauge s modulus m
gauge vt metiri
gaunt adj macer
gauntlet s manica f
gauze s coa n pl
gawky adj ineptus, stolidus
gay adj laetus, hilaris, festivus
gaze s conspect·us -ūs m; (fixed look) obtut·us -ūs m
gaze vi intuĕri; to — at intuĕri, adspectare, contemplari
gazelle s dorcas f
gazette s acta diurna n pl
gazetteer s itinerarium n
gear s instrumenta n pl, apparat·us -ūs m
gelatin s glutinum n
gelding s (horse) canterius m
gem s gemma f
gender s genus n
genealogical adj genealogicus
genealogy s genealogia f
general adj generalis; vulgaris, publicus, universus; in — omnino; —ly plerumque, fere; generatim
general s dux, imperator m
generalize vi in summam loqui
generalship s duct·us -ūs m; (skill) consilium n
generate vt generare, gignĕre
generation s generatio f; (age) aetas f, saeculum n
generic adj generalis
generosity s liberalitas, largitas f
generous adj liberalis, largus; —ly large, liberaliter
genesis s origo f
genial adj comis, benignus; —ly comiter, benigne
geniality s comitas, benignitas f
genitals s genitalia n pl, veretrum n
genitive s genitivus m
genius s ingenium n, indoles f; vir ingeniosus m; of — ingeniosus
genteel adj elegans, urbanus; —ly eleganter

gentile adj gentilicus, gentilis
gentile s gentilis m
gentility s nobilitas, elegantia f
gentle adj lenis, mitis, clemens; (gradual) mollis; (thing) lenis
gentleman s vir honestus, homo liberalis m
gentleness s lenitas, clementia f; (tameness) mansuetudo f
gently adv leniter, clementer, placide; (gradually) sensim
gentry s optimates m pl
genuine adj sincerus, purus, verus; —ly sincere, vere
genus s genus n
geographer s geographus m
geographical adj geographicus
geography s geographia f
geological adj geologicus
geologist s geologus m
geology s geologia f
geometrical adj geometricus
geometry s geometria f
germ s germen n
German adj Germanus
germane adj affinis
Germanic adj Germanicus
Germany s Germania f
germinate vi germinare
germination s germinat·us -ūs m
gesticulate vi gestus agĕre, gestu uti
gesture s gest·us -ūs, mot·us -ūs m
get vt nancisci, adipisci, consequi, acquirĕre; (by entreaty) impetrare; to — back recuperare; to — down depromĕre; to — hold of prehendĕre, occupare; to — out delēre, obliterare; to — rid of amovēre, tollĕre; to — the better of superare; to — together colligĕre, cogĕre; congregare; vi (to become) fieri; (to arrive at) pervenire; to — abroad (to spread) palam fieri, emanare; to — along procedĕre; to — away aufugĕre; to — back revertēre or reverti; to — down descendĕre; to — in pervenire; to — off aufugĕre, dimitti; to — on procedĕre, proficisci; (to succeed) bene succedĕre; to — out exire; (e curru) descendĕre; to — over transgredi; to — together congregari; to — up surgĕre; (from sleep) expergisci
ghastly adj luridus; (shocking) foedus
ghost s larva f, phantasma n; umbra f
ghostly adj spiritualis
giant s gigas m
gibberish s barbaricus sermo m
gibbet s furca f, patibulum n
gibe s sanna f
gibe vt illudĕre, subsannare
giblets s gigeria n pl, anseris trunculi m pl
giddiness s vertigo f
giddy adj vertiginosus; (fig) levis, inconsultus
gift s donum n; (talent) ingenium n
gifted adj (endowed) praeditus; ingeniosus
gig s (carriage) cisium n

gigantic *adj* ingens, immanis, praegrandis
giggle *vi* summissim cachinnare
gild *vt* inaurare
gilding *s* (*art*) auratura *f*; (*gilded
   work*) aurum inductum *n*
gill *s* branchia *f*
gilt *adj* auratus
gin *s* junipero infectus spirit·us -ūs
   m
ginger *s* zinziberi *n* (*indecl*)
gingerly *adv* pedetemptim
giraffe *s* camelopardalis *f*
gird *vt* cingĕre; **to — oneself** cingi
girder *s* tignum *n*
girdle *s* cingulum *n*, zona *f*
girdle *vt* cingĕre
girl *s* puella, virgo *f*
girlhood *s* puellaris aetas *f*
girlish *adj* puellaris, virginalis
girth *s* (*of horse*) cingula *f*; amplitudo *f*, ambit·us -ūs *m*
gist *s* cardo *m*
give *vt* dare, donare; (*to deliver*) tradĕre; **to — away** donare; **to —
   back** reddĕre; **to — forth** emittĕre; **to — oneself up to** se addicĕre (*with dat*); **to — out** edĕre,
   emittĕre; nuntiare, proclamare; distribuĕre; **to — over** transferre;
   relinquere; **to — up** tradĕre; (*to
   betray*) prodĕre; (*to abandon*) dimittĕre; *vi* **to — in** (*to yield*)
   cedĕre; **to — way** (*mil*) pedem referre; (*to yield*) cedĕre; (*to comply*)
   obsequi
giver *s* donator *m*
giving *s* datio, largitio *f*
glacial *adj* glacialis
glacier *s* moles conglaciata *f*
glad *adj* laetus, contentus; **to be —
   gaudĕre; —ly** libenter
gladden *vt* laetificare
glade *s* salt·us -ūs *m*
gladiator *s* gladiator *m*
gladness *s* gaudium *n*, laetitia *f*
glamorous *adj* venustus, nitidus;
   to be — nitēre
glamour *s* venustas *f*, nitor *m*
glance *s* aspect·us -ūs *m*
glance *vi* aspicĕre; **to — at** aspicĕre;
   to — off stringĕre
gland *s* glandula *f*
glare *s* fulgor *m*
glare *vi* fulgēre; torvis oculis aspicĕre; **to — at** torvis oculis aspicĕre
   or intuēri
glaring *adj* fulgens; manifestus
glass *s* vitrum *n*; (*for drinking*) calix
   vitreus *m*
glass *adj* vitreus
glassmaker *s* vitrarius *m*
glassware *s* vitrea *n pl*
glaze *vt* vitrum illinĕre (*with dat*),
   polire
gleam *s* fulgor *m*, jubar *n*; (*fig*) aura *f*
gleam *vi* coruscare, micare, fulgēre
gleaming *adj* coruscus, renidens
glean *vt* colligĕre, legĕre
gleaning *s* spicilegium *n*
glee *s* laetitia, hilaritas *f*
gleeful *adj* laetus, hilaris; **—ly** lae-

te, hilare
glen *s* vallis *f*
glib *adj* lubricus, volubilis; **—ly** volubiliter
glide *vi* labi
glimmer *s* lux dubia *f*; **— of hope**
   specula *f*
glimmer *vi* sublucēre
glimpse *s* aspect·us -ūs *m*; **to have
   a — of** despicĕre
glisten *vi* nitēre
glitter *s* fulgor *m*
glitter *vi* fulgēre, micare, coruscare
gloat *vi* oculos pascĕre; **to — over**
   inhiare (*with abl*), oculos pascĕre
   (*with abl*)
globe *s* globus *m*; orbis terrarum *m*
globular *adj* globosus
globule *s* globulus *m*, pilula *f*
gloom *s* tenebrae *f pl*; (*fig*) tristitia *f*
gloomily *adv* maeste
gloomy *adj* tenebrosus, furvus; (*fig*)
   maestus, tristis
glorification *s* laudatio, glorificatio *f*
glorify *vt* celebrare, glorificare, extollere
glorious *adj* gloriosus, illustris; **—ly**
   gloriose
glory *s* gloria, laus *f*
glory *vi* gloriari, se jactare
gloss *s* interpretatio *f*; (*sheen*) nitor
   m
gloss *vt* annotare; **to — over** extenuare, dissimulare
glossary *s* glossarium *n*
glossy *adj* nitidus, expolitus
glove *s* chirotheca *f*
glow *s* ardor, fervor, calor *m*
glow *vi* candēre, ardēre, calēre
glowing *adj* candens, fervens; (*fig*)
   fervidus
glue *s* gluten, glutinum *n*
glue *vt* glutinare
glum *adj* maestus, tristis
glut *s* satietas *f*
glut *vt* satiare, saturare
glutton *s* helluo, homo gulosus, ganeo *m*
gluttonous *adj* gulosus, edax; **—ly**
   gulose
gnarled *adj* nodosus
gnash *vt* **to — one's teeth** dentibus frendĕre
gnat *s* culex *m*
gnaw *vt & vi* rodĕre
gnawing *adj* mordax
go *vi* ire, incedĕre, proficisci; **to —
   about** circumire, perambulari;
   (*fig*) aggredi; **to — abroad** peregrinari; **to — after** sequi, petĕre;
   to — aside discedĕre; **to —
   astray** aberrare, vagari; **to —
   away** abire; **to — back** reverti;
   to — before praeire, antecedĕre;
   to — between intervenire; **to —
   beyond** egredi; (*fig*) excedĕre; **to
   — by** praeterire; (*fig*) (*to follow*)
   sequi; **to — down** descendĕre; (*of
   sun*) occidĕre; **to — for** petĕre;
   to — forth exire; **to — in** introire; **to — into** inire; **to — off**
   abire; (*as gun*) displodi; **to — on**
   (*to continue*) pergĕre; (*to happen*)

fieri; (*to succeed, thrive*) succedĕre;
to — out exire; (*of fire*) extingui;
to — over transgredi; (*fig*) (*a subject*) percurrere; to — round circumire; to — through obire, pertendĕre; to — to adire, accedĕre;
to — towards petere; to — under subire; to — up ascendĕre; to let — dimittĕre; (*to let fall*) omittere

goad *s* pertica *f*, stimulus *m*

goad *vt* instigare; (*fig*) stimulare; (*to exasperate*) exasperare

goal *s* finis *m*; (*at racetrack*) calx *f*

goat *s* caper *m*, capra *f*

gobble *vt* devorare, deglutire

gobbler *s* helluo *m*

goblet *s* poculum *n*, scyphus *m*

goblin *s* larva *f*

god *s* deus, divus *m*

God *s* Deus *m*

goddess *s* dea, diva *f*

godhead *s* deitas *f*, numen *n*

godless *adj* atheus; improbus

godlike *adj* divinus

godliness *s* pietas *f*

gold *adj* aureus

gold *s* aurum *n*

golden *adj* aureus

goldfish *s* hippurus *m*

gold leaf *s* auri breactea *f*

gold mine *s* aurifodina *f*

goldsmith *s* aurifex *m*

good *adj* bonus, probus; (*beneficial*) salutaris; (*kindhearted*) benevolus; (*fit*) aptus, idoneus; — for nothing nequam (*indecl*); to do — prodesse; to make — compensare, restituĕre; to seem — vidēri

good *s* bonum *n*: (*profit*) commodum, lucrum *n*, utilitas *f*; to be — for prodesse (*with dat*); —s bona *n pl*, res *f*; (*for sale*) merx *f*

good *interj* bene!; euge!

good-by *interj* vale!; (*to more than one*) valete!; to say — valēre jubēre

goodly *adj* pulcher; (*quantity*) amplus; a — number of nonnulli

good-natured *adj* comis, benignus, facilis

goodness *s* bonitas *f*; (*moral*) probitas, virtus *f*; (*generosity*) benignitas *f*

goose *s* anser *m*

gooseberry *s* acinus grossulae *m*

gore *s* cruor *m*

gore *vt* cornu perforare, cornu ferire

gorge *s* fauces *f pl*; (*defile*) angustiae *f pl*

gorge *vt* to — oneself se ingurgitare

gorgeous *adj* splendidus, lautus; —ly splendide, laute

gory *adj* cruentus, cruentatus

gospel *s* evangelium *n*

gossamer *s* aranea *f*

gossip *s* (*talk*) nugae, gerrae *f pl*; (*person*) garrulus *m*, garrula *f*, loquax *m* & *f*, lingulaca *f*

gossip *vi* garrire

gouge *vt* evellĕre, eruĕre

gourd *s* cucurbita *f*

gourmand *s* helluo, popino *m*

gout *s* morbus articularis *m*, arthritis *f*; (*in the legs*) podagra *f*; (*in hands*) chiragra *f*

govern *vt* imperare (*with dat*), regĕre, administrare, gubernare

governable *adj* tractabilis

governess *s* magistra, educatrix *f*

government *s* gubernatio, administratio, res publica *f*

governor *s* gubernator, moderator, praefectus *m*; (*of province*) proconsul, legatus *m*; procurator *m*

governorship *s* praefectura *f*

gown *s* (*of Roman citizen*) toga *f*; (*of women*) stola *f*

grace *s* gratia *f*; (*elegance, etc.*) venustas *f*, lepos *m*; (*pardon*) venia *f*; to say — gratias agĕre

grace *vt* exornare; honestare

graceful *adj* gratiosus, venustus, lepidus; —ly venuste, lepide

gracefulness *s* venustas *f*

graceless *adj* deformis, illepidus

Graces *s* Gratiae *f pl* .

gracious *adj* benignus, misericors; —ly benigne, humane

gradation *s* grad·us -ūs *m*; (*in speech*) gradatio *f*

grade *s* grad·us -ūs *m*

gradient *s* proclivitas *f*

gradual *adj* lenis, mollis; per gradus; —ly gradatim, pedetentim

graduate *vt* gradibus distinguĕre; *vi* gradum suscipĕre

graduate *s* qui gradum academicum adeptus est

graft *s* surculus *m*; (*pol*) ambit·us -ūs *m*

graft *vt* inserere

grain *s* granum *n*; (*fig*) particula *f*; against the — (*fig*) Minervā invitā

grammar *s* grammatica *f*

grammarian *s* grammaticus *m*

grammatical *adj* grammaticus

granary *s* horreum *n*, granaria *n pl*

grand *adj* grandis

grandchild *s* nepos *m*, neptis *m* & *f*

granddaughter *s* neptis *f*

grandeur *s* magnificentia, majestas *f*

grandfather *s* avus *m*

grandiloquent *adj* magniloquus

grandmother *s* avia *f*

grandson *s* nepos *m*

granite *s* granites lapis *m*

grant *vt* concedĕre, permittĕre; (*to acknowledge*) fatēri; dare, praebēre

grant *s* concessio *f*

grape *s* uva *f*, acinus *m*

grapevine *s* vitis *f*

graphic *adj* expressus, significans, manifestus; —ally expresse

grapple *vt* compleci; *vi* luctari

grasp *s* complex·us -ūs *m*, comprehensio *f*; pugillum *n*; (*power*) potestas *f*; (*of the hand*) man·us -ūs *f*

grasp *vt* prehendĕre, tenēre, arripĕre; (*fig*) appetĕre, percipĕre, intellegĕre; *vi* to — at captare, appetĕre

grasping *adj* avidus, cupidus

grass *s* gramen *n*, herba *f*

grasshopper s grillus m

grassy adj graminosus, herbosus, herbidus

grate s clathri m pl; (hearth) caminus m

grate vt radĕre, conterĕre; vi stridĕre; **to — upon** offendĕre

grateful adj gratus, juncundus; **—ly** grate

gratification s gratificatio f; (pleasure, delight) voluptas, oblectatio f

gratify vt gratificari (with dat), morigerari (with dat)

gratifying adj gratus

grating s clathri, cancelli m pl; (sound) stridor m

gratis adv gratuito, gratis

gratitude s gratitudo f, gratus animus m

gratuitous adj gratuitus; **—ly** gratuito

gratuity s stips f, munus, praemium n

grave adj gravis, serius; (stern) severus; **—ly** graviter; severe

grave s sepulcrum n, tumulus m

gravedigger s tumulorum fossor m

gravel s glarea f

gravelly adj glareosus

gravestone s monumentum n

gravitate vi vergĕre

gravitation s ponderatio f

gravity s gravitas f, pondus n; (personal) severitas, dignitas f; momentum n

gravy s (broth) jus n; (juice) sucus m

gray adj canus; **to become —** canescĕre

gray-eyed adj caesius

gray-headed adj canus

grayish adj canescens

grayness s canities f

graze vt (cattle) pascĕre; (to touch lightly) perstringĕre, radĕre; vi pasci

grease s adeps m, pinguitudo, arvina f

grease vt ung(u)ĕre

greasy adj pinguis; unctus; (dirty) squalidus

great adj magnus; ingens, amplus, grandis; **as — as** tantus quantus; **—ly** magnopere, valde

great-grandfather s proavus m

greatness s magnitudo f

greaves s ocreae f pl

Grecian adj Graecus

greed s aviditas, avaritia f; voracitas f

greedily adv avide, cupide

greedy adj avarus, cupidus; vorax

Greek adj Graecus

Greek s Graecus m

green adj viridis; (fig) recens; (unripe) crudus, immaturus; **to become —** virescĕre

green s color viridis m; (lawn) locus herbidus m; **—s** olera n pl

greenhouse s viridarium hibernum n

greenish adj subviridis

greenness s viriditas f; (fig) cruditas, immaturitas f

greet vt salutem dicĕre (with dat), salutare

greeting s salutatio f

gregarious adj gregalis

grenade s pyrobolus m

greyhound s vertagus m

gridiron s craticula f

grief s maeror, dolor, luct·us -ūs m; **to come to —** perire

grievance s injuria, querimonia, querela f

grieve vt dolore afficĕre; vi maerēre, dolēre, lugēre

grievous adj gravis, durus, atrox; **—ly** graviter, aegre

griffin s gryps m

grill vt torrēre

grim adj torvus, atrox, truculentus; **—ly** torve, truculente, atrociter

grimace s distortus vult·us -ūs m, oris depravatio f

grimace vi os ducēre

grimy adj niger, squalidus

grin vi distorto vultu ridēre

grin s ris·us -ūs m

grind vt (grain) molĕre; (in mortar) contundĕre; (on whetstone) exacuĕre; **to — the teeth** dentibus frendēre

grindstone s cos f

grip s pugillum n, comprehensio f

grip vt arripĕre, comprehendĕre

grisly adj horrendus, horridus

grist s farina f

gristle s cartilago f

gristly adj cartilagineus, cartilaginosus

grit s harena f

gritty adj harenosus, sabulosus

grizzly adj canus

groan s gemit·us -ūs m

groan vi gemēre

groin s inguen n

groom s agaso, equiso m

groom vt curare

groove s canalis m, stria f

groove vt striare

grope vi praetentare

gropingly adv pedetentim

gross adj crassus, pinguis; turpis, foedus; nimius; **—ly** nimium, valde

grotesque adj distortus

grotto s antrum n

ground s solum n, terra, humus f; (reason) causa, ratio f; (place) locus m; **on the — humi**; **to give —** cedĕre

ground vt fundare; (to teach) instruĕre; (a ship) subducĕre

groundless adj vanus, falsus, fictus; **—ly** temere, de nihilo

group s corona, turba f, globus m

group vt disponĕre; vi **to — around** circulari, stipari

grouse s (bird) tetrao m

grove s lucus m, nemus n

grovel vi serpĕre, se prosternĕre

grow vt colĕre, serĕre; vi crescĕre, augēri; (to become) fieri; **to — out of** (fig) oriri ex (with abl); **to — up** adolescĕre, pubescĕre

grower s cultor m

growl s fremit·us -ūs m

growl vi fremĕre

grown-up *adj* adultus; puber
growth *s* incrementum *n*, auct·us -ūs *m*
grub *s* vermiculus, lombricus *m*
grub *vi* effodĕre
grudge *s* odium *n*, invidia *f*; **to hold a — against** succensēre (*with dat*)
grudgingly *adv* invitus, aegre
gruesome *adj* taeter
gruff *adj* torvus, asper; **—ly** torve, aspere
gruffness *s* asperitas *f*
grumble *vi* murmurare, mussitare
grunt *s* grunnit·us -ūs *m*
grunt *vi* grunnire; (*fig*) fremĕre
guarantee *s* fides *f*; (*money*) sponsio *f*; (*person*) praes, vas, sponsor *m*; (*bail money*) vadimonium *n*
guarantee *vt* praestare, spondēre
guarantor *s* sponsor *m*
guard *s* custodia, tutela *f*; (*mil*) praesidium *n*; (*person*) custos *m* & *f*; **to be on one's —** cavēre
guard *vt* custodire, defendĕre; *vi* **to — against** cavēre
guarded *adj* cautus, circumspectus; **—ly** caute
guardian *s* custos, praeses *m* & *f*, defensor *m*; (*of minor or orphan*) tutor *m*
guardianship *s* custodia, tutela, curatio *f*
guerdon *s* merces *f*
guess *s* conjectura *f*
guess *vt* & *vi* conjicĕre, divinare, opinari
guest *s* hospes *m*; advena *m*; (*at dinner*) conviva *m*
guidance *s* duct·us -ūs *m*, curatio, moderatio *f*
guide *s* dux, ductor *m*
guide *vt* ducĕre, regĕre; (*to control*) moderari
guidebook *s* itinerarium *n*
guild *s* collegium, corpus *n*, sodalitas *f*

guile *s* dolus *m*
guileful *adj* dolosus
guileless *adj* simplex, sincerus
guilt *s* culpa *f*, crimen, vitium *n*
guiltless *adj* innocens, insons
guilty *adj* sons, noxius, nocens, sceleratus
guinea hen *s* meleagris *f*
guise *s* species *f*
guitar *s* cithara Hispanica *f*; **fides** *f pl*; **to play the —** fidibus canĕre
gulf *s* sin·us -ūs *m*; (*abyss*) abyssus *f*, gurges *m*
gull *s* larus marinus, mergus *m*
gullet *s* gula *f*, guttur *n*
gullible *adj* credulus
gulp *vt* absorbēre, glutire, haurire; *vi* singultare
gulp *s* haust·us -ūs, singult·us -ūs *m*
gum *s* (*of mouth*) gingiva *f*; gummi *n* (*indecl*)
gumption *s* alacritas *f*
gun *s* sclopetum *n*; tormentum *n*
gunner *s* tormentarius *m*
gurgle *vi* singultare; (*of stream*) murmurare
gurgling *s* singult·us -ūs *m*; (*of stream*) murmur *n*, murmuratio *f*
gush *vi* micare, scaturire
gush *s* scaturigines *f pl*
gust *s* impet·us -ūs *m*, flamen *n*
gusty *adj* ventosus, procellosus
gut *s* intestinum *n*
gut *vt* exenterare; (*fig*) diripĕre, amburĕre
gutted *adj* (*by fire*) ambustus
gutter *s* canalis *m*; (*rain gutter*) compluvium *n*; (*in fields or upon roofs*) colliciae *f pl*
guttural *adj* gutturalis
guzzle *vi* potare
guzzler *s* potor *m*
gymnasium *s* gymnasium *n*, palaestra *f*
gymnastic *adj* gymnicus
gymnastics *s* palaestra, palaestrica *f*

H

haberdasher *s* linteo *m*
habit *s* consuetudo *f*, mos *m*; (*dress*) habit·us -ūs, vestit·us -ūs *m*
habitation *s* habitatio, dom·us -ūs *f*
habitual *adj* usitatus, inveteratus; **—ly** de more, ex more
habituate *vt* insuescĕre, assuefacĕre
hack *vt* caedĕre; **to — to pieces** concidĕre
hack *s* (*horse*) caballus *m*
hackneyed *adj* tritus, pervulgatus
haddock *s* gadus morhua *m*
hag *f* an·us -ūs *f*
haggard *adj* macer; ferus
haggle *vi* cavillari, licitare
haggler *s* licitator *m*
hail *s* grando *f*
hail *vt* salutare, appellare

hail *vi* **it is hailing** grandinat
hail *interj* salve!; (*to several*) salvete!
hailstone *s* saxea grando *f*
hair *s* capillus, crinis *m*; (*single*) pilus *m*; (*of animals*) saeta *f*, villus *m*
haircloth *s* cilicium *n*
hairdresser *s* concinnator, tonsor *m*
hairless *adj* (*of head*) calvus; (*of body*) glaber, depilis
hairpin *s* crinale *n*
hairy *adj* pilosus, crinitus; (*shaggy*) hirsutus
halberd *s* bipennis *f*
halcyon *s* alcedo, alcyon *f*
halcyon days *s* alcedonia *n pl*
hale *adj* robustus, validus
hale *vt* rapĕre, trahĕre
half *s* dimidia pars *f*, dimidium *n*

half adj dimidius, dimidiatus

half-hour s semihora f

half-moon s luna dimidiata f; (shape) lunula f

half-open adj semiapertus

half year s semestrium n

hall s atrium n; (entrance) vestibulum n

hallo interj heus!, ohe!

hallow vt consecrare

hallucination s error m, somnium n, alucinatio f

halo s corona f

halt vt sistĕre; vi consistĕre; (fig) haesitare; (to limp) claudicare

halt s pausa, mora f; **to come to a — consistĕre**

halter s capistrum n

halting adj claudus

halve vt ex aequo dividĕre

ham s poples m; (smoked, etc.) perna f

hamlet s vicus, viculus m

hammer s malleus m

hammer vt tundĕre, cudĕre

hamper s corbis f

hamper vt impedire, implicare

hamstring s poplitis nervus m

hamstring vt poplitem succidĕre (with dat)

hand s man·us -ūs f; (handwriting) chirographum n; (of dial) gnomon m; at — ad manum, praesto, prae manibus, prope; by — manu; in — junctis manibus; to — cominus; on the other — altera parte; on the right — a dextra; to have a — in interesse (with dat); to take in — suscipĕre

hand vt tradĕre, porrigĕre; to — down tradĕre; to — over referre; (to betray) prodĕre; to — round circumferre

handbill s libellus m

handbook s enchiridion n

handcuffs s manicae f pl

handful s manipulus m

handicraft s artificium n

handiwork s opus, opificium n

handkerchief s sudarium n

handle s manubrium n; (of cup) ansa, ansula f

handle vt tractare

handling s tractatio f

handsome adj pulcher, formosus; —ly pulchre; (liberally) liberaliter

handsomeness s pulchritudo, forma, venustas f

handwriting s man·us -ūs f, chirographum n

handy adj (of things) habilis; (of person) sollers; (at hand) praesto

hang vt suspendĕre; (by a line) appendĕre; (head) demittĕre; vi pendĕre; **hanging down** demissus; **hanging loose** fluens; to — down dependĕre; to — on to haerēre (with dat); to — over imminēre (with dat)

hanging adj pensilis

hanging s (execution) suspendium, n; —s aulaea n pl

hangman s carnifex m

haphazard adj fortuitus

happen vi accidĕre, fieri, evenire, contingĕre; to — upon incidĕre in (with acc)

happily adv beate, feliciter

happiness s felicitas f

happy adj beatus, felix, fortunatus, faustus

harangue s contio f

harangue vt & vi contionari

harass vt vexare, inquietare, exagitare, fatigare

harassing adj molestus

harassment s vexatio f

harbinger s praenuntius, antecursor m

harbor s port·us -ūs m

harbor vt excipĕre

hard adj durus; (difficult) difficilis, arduus; (severe) acer, rigidus, asper; to become — durescĕre

hard adv valde, sedulo, summa vi

harden vt durare; (fig) indurare; vi durescĕre; (fig) obdurescĕre

hardhearted adj durus, crudelis, inhumanus

hardihood s audacia f

hardiness s robur n

hardly adv vix, aegre; — any nullus fere

hardness s duritia f; (fig) iniquitas, acerbitas f; (difficulty) difficultas f

hardship s labor m, difficultas, aerumna f

hardware s ferramenta n pl

hardy adj robustus, durus

hare s lepus m

harem s gynaeceum n

hark interj heus!

harken vi audire; to — to auscultare (with dat)

harlot s meretrix f

harm s injuria f, damnum n; to come to — detrimentum accipĕre

harm vt nocēre (with dat), laedĕre

harmful adj noxius, nocivus, damnosus

harmless adj (person) innocens; (thing) innocuus; —ly innocenter, incolumis

harmonious adj canorus, consonus; (fig) concors, consentiens; —ly consonanter; (fig) concorditer, convenienter

harmonize vt componĕre; vi concinĕre; (fig) consentire

harmony s harmonia f, concent·us -ūs m; (fig) concordia f

harness s equi ornamenta n pl

harness vt ornare, insternĕre

harp s lyra f

harpist s psaltes m

harpoon s jaculum hamatum n

harpoon vt jaculo hamato transfigĕre

harpy s harpyia f

harrow s rastrum n, irpex m

harrow vt occare

harsh adj asper, raucus, discors, stridulus; (in taste) acer; (fig) durus, severus, inclemens; —ly asper, acerbe, severe

harshness s asperitas, acerbitas, severitas f

harvest s messis, seges f
harvest vt metĕre
hash vt comminuĕre
hash s minutal n
haste s festinatio, celeritas f; **in —**
propere; **to make —** properare
hasten vt accelerare, properare,
praecipitare; vi properare, festinare
hastily adv propere, raptim; (without reflection) temere, inconsulte
hastiness s celeritas, temeritas f
hasty adj properus, praeceps, temerarius, inconsultus
hat s pileus, galerus, petasus m
hatch vt (fig) coquĕre, machinari;
(of chickens) ex ovis excludĕre
hatchet s ascia, securis, dolabra f
hate s odium n, invidia f
hate vt odisse
hateful adj odiosus, invisus; **to be —**
to odio esse (with dat); **—ly** odiose
hatred s odium n, invidia f
haughtily adv superbe, arroganter,
insolenter
haughtiness s superbia, arrogantia
f, fastidium n
haughty adj superbus, arrogans, insolens
haul s bolus m
haul vt trahĕre; **to — up** subducĕre
haunch s clunis, coxa f
haunt vt frequentare; (fig) agitare,
inquietare
haunt s locus m; (of animals) lustra
n pl, latebrae f pl
have vt habēre, possidēre, tenēre
haven s port·us -ūs m
havoc s strages f
hawk s accipiter m & f
hawk vt venditare
hawser s retinaculum n
hawthorn s crataegus oxyacantha f
hay s faenum n
hayloft s faenilia n pl
haystack s faeni meta f
hazard s periculum n
hazard vt periclitari
hazardous adj periculosus, anceps;
—ly periculose
haze s nebula f
hazy adj caliginosus, nebulosus
he pron hic, is, ille; (male) mas m
head s caput s; (mental faculty) ingenium n; (fig) princeps; **— first**
praeceps
head adj primus, principalis, capitalis
head vt praeesse (with dat), ducēre; vi
to — for petēre
headache s capitis dolor m
heading s caput n, titulus m
headland s promuntorium n
headless adj truncus
headlong adv praeceps
headquarters s praetorium n
headstrong adj pervicax, contumax
headway s profect·us -ūs m; **to
make —** proficēre
headwind s ventus adversus m
heady adj (of drinks) fervidus, vehemens
heal vt medēri (with dat), sanare; vi
sanescĕre; (of wounds) coalescĕre

healer s medicus m
healing adj salubris, salutaris
health s valetudo, salus f; **to be in
good —** valēre; **to drink to the
— of** propinare (with dat)
healthful adj salutaris, salubris
healthily adv salubriter
healthy adj sanus, integer; (places)
salubris
heap s acervus, cumulus m, congeries
f
heap vt acervare; **to — up** accumulare, exstruĕre
hear vt audire, exaudire; (to learn)
certior fieri, accipĕre, cognoscĕre
hearing s (act) auditio f; (sense) audit·us -ūs m; (law) cognitio f; **hard
of — surdaster**
hearken vi auscultare
hearsay s fama f, rumor m
heart s cor n; (fig) pectus n; (courage)
animus m; **to learn by — ediscĕre**
heartache s cura f, angor m
heartbreak s angor m
heartbroken adj aeger
hearth s focus m
heartily adv sincere, vehementer,
valde
heartiness s studium n, alacritas f
heartless adj crudelis, inhumanus;
—ly crudeliter, inhumane
heartlessness s inhumanitas f
hearty adj sincerus, vehemens, alacer
heat s calor, ardor m; (fig) fervor m
heat vt calefacĕre; vi calescĕre
heath s (plant) erice f; (place) loca
inculta n pl
heathen adj paganus
heathen s paganus m
heather s erice f
heating s calefactio f
heave vt attollĕre, levare; **to — a
sigh** gemitum ducĕre; vi tumēre,
aestuare, fluctuare
heaven s caelum n; (fig) dii, superi
m pl
heavenly adj caelestis, divinus
heavily adv graviter; (slowly) tarde
heaviness s gravitas f; (slowness)
tarditas f
heavy adj gravis, ponderosus; (fig)
tardus, segnis, iners; (sad) maestus
Hebraic adj Hebraicus
Hebrew s Hebraeus m; (language)
Hebraea lingua f
hecatomb s hecatombe f
hectic adj fervidus, febriculosus
hedge s saepes f
hedge vt **to — in** saepire; **to — off**
intersaepire; vi tergiversari
hedgehog s ericius m
heed s cura, opera f; **to take —** cavēre, curare
heed vt curare, observare, respicĕre;
(to obey) parēre (with dat)
heedless adj incautus, temerarius;
— of immemor (with genit)
heedlessness s neglegentia f
heel s calx m & f
heifer s bucula, juvenca f
height s altitudo f; (of person) pro-

ceritas *f*; (*top*) culmen *n*; (*fig*) fastigium *n*

heighten *vt* amplificare, exaggerare, augēre

heinous *adj* atrox, nefarius, foedus; —ly atrociter

heir *s* heres *m*; **sole** *or* **universal** — heres ex asse

heiress *s* heres *f*

heirloom *s* res hereditaria *f*

hell *s* Tartarus *m*, inferi *m pl*

Hellenic *adj* Hellenicus, Graecus

Hellenism *s* Hellenismus *m*

hellish *adj* infernus, diabolicus, nefarius

helm *s* gubernaculum *n*

helmet *s* cassis, galea *f*

helmsman *s* gubernator, rector *m*

help *s* auxilium, subsidium *n*

help *vt* adjuvare (*with acc*), auxiliari (*with dat*), succurrēre (*with dat*), opem ferre (*with dat*)

helper *s* adjutor *m*, adjutrix *f*

helpful *adj* utilis

helpless *adj* inops

helplessness *s* inopia *f*

hem *s* ora *f*, limbus *m*

hem *vt* (*to sew*) suēre; **to** — **in** circumsidēre, obsidēre

hem *interj* hem!, ehem!

hemisphere *s* hemisphaerium *n*

hemlock *s* cicuta *f*

hemp *s* cannabis *f*

hempen *adj* cannabinus

hen *s* gallina *f*

hence *adv* hinc; (*consequently*) igitur, ideo

henceforth *adv* posthac, dehinc

henpecked *adj* uxorius

her *pron* eam, illam, hanc

her *adj* ejus, illius, hujus; — **own** suus, proprius

herald *s* fetialis *m*; (*crier*) praeco *m*

herald *vt* nuntiare, praenuntiare

herb *s* herba *f*; —**s** herbae *f pl*, olus *n*

herd *s* grex *m*; armentum *n*; (*in contempt*) vulgus *n*

herd *vt* **to** — **together** congregare, cogēre; *vi* congregari

herdsman *s* pastor, armentarius *m*

here *adv* hic; — **and there** passim

hereafter *adv* posthac, in reliquum tempus

hereby *adv* ex hoc, ex hac re, hinc

hereditary *adj* hereditarius, patrius

heredity *s* genus *n*; **by** — jure hereditario, per successiones

herein *adv* in hoc, in hac re, hic

heresy *s* haeresis *f*

heretical *adj* haereticus; falsus, pravus

hereupon *adv* hic

herewith *adv* una cum hac re

heritage *s* hereditas *f*

hermaphrodite *s* androgynus, Hermaphroditus *m*

hermit *s* eremita *m*

hermitage *s* eremitae cella *f*

hernia *s* hernia *f*

hero *s* vir *m*; (*demigod*) heros *m*

heroic *adj* fortissimus, magnanimus, heroicus; —**ally** fortissime

heroine *s* virago *f*

heroism *s* virtus, fortitudo *f*

heron *s* ardea *f*

herring *s* harenga *f*

hers *pron* ejus, illius

herself *pron* (*refl*) se; (*intensive*) ipsa; **to** — sibi; **with** — secum

hesitant *adj* dubius, incertus; —**ly** cunctanter, dubitanter

hesitate *vi* dubitare, haesitare

hesitation *s* dubitatio, haesitatio, cunctatio *f*

Hesperian *adj* Hesperius

heterogeneous *adj* diversus

hew *vt* dolare, caedĕre

hey *interj* ohe!

hiatus *s* hiat·us -ūs *m*

hiccup *s* singult·us -ūs *m*

hiccup *vi* singultare

hide *s* pellis *f*, corium *n*

hide *vt* abdēre, abscondēre, celare, occultare; (*to flog*) verberare; *vi* latēre, se abdēre

hideous *adj* foedus, perhorridus, turpis; —**ly** foede, turpiter

hideousness *s* foeditas *f*, horror *m*

hiding *s* occultatio *f*; (*whipping*) verberatio *f*

hiding place *s* latebra *f*

hierarchy *s* hierarchia *f*

high *adj* altus, excelsus, sublimis; (*tall*) procerus; (*of price*) pretiosus, carus; (*of ground*) editus; (*of rank*) amplus; —**ly** (*value*) magni; (*intensity*) vehementer, valde

high *adv* alte, sublimiter; **to aim** — magnas res appetĕre

highborn *adj* generosus, ingenuus, nobilis

high-flown *adj* inflatus, tumidus

highhanded *adj* insolens, superbus; —**ly** insolenter, superbe

highland *s* regio montuosa *f*

highlander *s* montanus *m*

high-minded *adj* (*noble*) magnanimus; (*arrogant*) arrogans, insolens

high priest *s* pontifex maximus *m*

highway *s* via *f*

highwayman *s* latro, grassator *m*

hilarity *s* hilaritas *f*

hill *s* collis, tumulus *m*; (*slope*) clivus *m*

hillock *s* tumulus *m*

hilly *adj* montuosus, clivosus

hilt *s* capulus *m*

him *pron* eum, hunc, illum; **of** — ejus, hujus, illius; **de eo, de hoc, de illo**

himself *pron* (*refl*) se; (*intensive*) ipse; **to** — sibi; **with** — secum

hind *s* cerva *f*

hind *adj* posterior

hinder *vt* obstare (*with dat*); impedire, morari

hindmost *adj* postremus, ultimus, novissimus

hindrance *s* impedimentum *n*

hinge *s* cardo *m*

hinge *vi* **to** — **on** (*fig*) niti (*with abl*)

hint *s* indicium *n*, significatio *f*

hint *vt* & *vi* significare, innuēre, suggerēre

hip *s* coxendix *f*

hippodrome *s* hippodromos *m*
hire *s* conductio, locatio *f*; (*wages*) merces *f*
hire *vt* conducĕre; **to — out** locare; *vi* **to — out** operam suam locare
hired *adj* conductus, conducticius, mercenarius
hireling *s* mercenarius *m*
his *adj* ejus, illius, hujus; **— own** suus, proprius
his *pron* ejus, illius, hujus
hiss *vt & vi* sibilare
hissing *s* sibilus *m*
historian *s* historicus, rerum gestarum scriptor *m*
historical *adj* historicus
history *s* historia, memoria rerum gestarum *f*; **ancient —** antiquitas *f*; **modern —** memoria recentioris aetatis *f*
histrionic *adj* histrionalis
hit *s* ict·us -ūs *m*, plaga *f*; **to be a — bene** succedĕre
hit *vt* icĕre, ferire, percutĕre; *vi* **to — upon** invenire
hitch *s* impedimentum *n*, mora *f*
hitch *vt* (ad)jungĕre
hither *adv* huc
hither *adj* citerior
hitherto *adv* (*of time*) adhuc; (*of place*) huc usque
hive *s* alvus *m*, alvearium *n*
hoard *s* acervus *m*
hoard *vt* coacervare, recondĕre
hoarder *s* accumulator *m*
hoarse *adj* raucus; **to get —** irraucescĕre; **—ly** raucā voce
hoary *adj* canus
hoax *s* fraus, ludificatio *f*
hoax *vt* fallĕre, decipĕre, ludificari
hobble *vi* claudicare
hobby *s* avocamentum *n*
hock *s* poples *m*
hoe *s* sarculum *n*
hoe *vt* sarculare; (*weeds*) pectĕre
hog *s* porcus, sus *m*
hoist *vt* sublevare, tollĕre
hold *vt* tenēre, possidēre, habēre; (*to contain*) capĕre; (*to think*) habēre, existimare, censēre; **to — back** retinēre; **to — forth** porrigĕre, extendĕre; (*to offer*) praebēre; **to — in** inhibēre, cohibēre; **to — off** abstinēre, arcēre; **to — up** (*to lift up*) attollĕre, sustinēre; *vi* **to — back** cunctari; **to — out** (*to last*) durare, permanēre
holder *s* possessor *m*; (*handle*) manubrium *n*
holding *s* possessio *f*
hole *s* foramen *n*; (*fig*) latebra *f*; (*of mice*) cavum *n*
holiday *s* dies festus *m*; **—s** feriae *f pl*
holiness *s* sanctitas *f*
hollow *adj* cavus; (*fig*) vanus, inanis
hollow *s* caverna *f*, cavum *n*; (*depression*) lacuna *f*
hollow *vt* **to — out** cavare, excavare
holly *s* ilex aquifolium *n*
holocaust *s* holocaustum *n*
holy *adj* sanctus

homage *s* obsequium *n*, cult·us -ūs *m*; **to pay —** to colere
home *s* domicilium *n*, dom·us -ūs *f*; **at —** domi; **from —** domo
home *adv* (*motion*) domum; (*place where*) domi
home *adj* domesticus
homeless *adj* tecto carens, profugus
homeliness *s* rusticitas *f*
homely *adj* rusticus, simplex
homemade *adj* domesticus, vernaculus, domi factus
homesickness *s* tecti sui desiderium *n*, nostalgia *f*
homestead *s* sedes *f*, fundus *m*
homeward *adv* domum
homicidal *adj* cruentus, sanguinolentus
homicide *s* (*person*) homicida *m*; (*deed*) homicidium *n*
homily *s* sermo, tractat·us -ūs *m*
homogeneous *adj* pari naturā praeditus
hone *vt* acuĕre
honest *adj* probus, sincerus; **—ly** probe, sincere
honesty *s* probitas, sinceritas *f*
honey *s* mel *n*
honeybee *s* apis mellifera *or* mellifica *f*
honeycomb *s* favus *m*
honeysuckle *s* clymenus *m*
honor *s* honos *m*; (*repute*) fama *f*; (*trust*) fides *f*; (*award*) decus *n*; (*official distinction*) dignitas *f*; **sense of —** pudor *m*
honor *vt* honorare; (*to respect*) colēre
honorable *adj* honestus
honorably *adv* honeste
honorary *adj* honorarius
hood *s* cucullus *m*
hoof *s* ungula *f*
hook *s* hamus, uncus *m*; **by — or by crook** quocumque modo
hook *vt* inuncare; confibulare; (*fig*) capĕre
hooked *adj* hamatus; (*crooked*) curvatus, aduncus
hoop *s* circulus *m*; (*toy*) trochus *m*; (*shout*) clamor *m*
hoop *vi* exclamare
hoot *vt* explodĕre; *vi* obstrepĕre; (*of owls*) canĕre
hop *s* salt·us -ūs *m*
hop *vi* salire, subsultare
hope *s* spes *f*
hope *vt* sperare; **to — for** exspectare
hopeful *adj* bonae spei; **—ly magna cum** spe
hopeless *adj* exspes, desperatus; **—ly** desperanter
hopelessness *s* desperatio *f*
horde *s* turba, caterva *f*, grex *m*
horizon *s* orbis finiens *m*
horizontal *adj* libratus; **—ly** ad libram
horn *s* cornu *n*; (*as trumpet*) buccina *f*
horned *adj* cornutus, corniger
hornet *s* crabro *m*
horoscope *s* horoscopus *m*

horrible *adj* horribilis, foedus; (*excessive*) immoderatus

horribly *adv* horribili modo, foede

horrid *adj* horridus, horrens; **—ly** horride

horrify *vt* horrificare, perterrēre

horror *s* horror *m*; (*deep hatred*) odium *n*

horse *s* equus *m*, equa *f*

horseback *s* on — in equo; ex equo; to fight on — ex equo pugnare; to ride on — in equo vehi

horsehair *s* pilus equinus *m*

horseman *s* eques *m* .

horse race *s* curriculum equorum *n*, certatio equestris *f*

horseradish *s* armoracia *f*

horseshoe *s* solea *f*

horsewhip *s* flagellum *n*, scutica *f*

horsewhip *vt* verberare

horticultural *adj* ad hortorum cultum pertinens

horticulture *s* hortorum cult·us -ūs *m*

hose *s* (*stocking*) tibiale *n*; (*tube*) tubulus *m*

hosiery *s* feminalia *n pl*

hospitable *adj* hospitalis

hospitably *adv* hospitaliter

hospital *s* valetudinarium *n*

hospitality *s* hospitalitas *f*

host *s* (*entertainer*) hospes *m*; (*army*) copiae *f pl*, exercit·us -ūs *m*; (*crowd*) multitudo *f*; (*wafer*) hostia *f*

hostage *s* obses *m & f*

hostess *s* hospita *f*; (*at inn*) caupona *f*

hostile *adj* hostilis, infensus, inimicus; in a — manner hostiliter, infense

hot *adj* calidus *or* caldus; fervidus; (*boiling*) fervens; (*seething*) aestuosus; (*of spices*) acer; (*fig*) ardens; to be — calēre; to become — calescēre; **—ly** acriter, ardenter

hotel *s* hospitium *n*, caupona *f*

hound *s* catulus *m*

hound *vt* instare (*with dat*)

hour *s* hora *f*

hourglass *s* horarium *n*

hourly *adv* in horas

house *s* dom·us -ūs *f*, aedes *f pl*, tectum *n*; (*family*) dom·us -ūs, gens *f*; (*in country*) villa *f*; at the — of apud (*with acc*)

house *vt* domo excipěre; (*things*) condēre

housebreaker *s* fur, effractarius *m*

housebreaking *s* domūs effractura *f*

household *adj* familiaris, domesticus

household *s* familia, dom·us -ūs *f*

householder *s* paterfamilias *m*

household gods *s* Lares *m pl*; Penates *m pl*

housekeeper *s* promus *m*

housekeeping *s* rei familiaris cura *f*

housemaid *s* ancilla, vernacula *f*

housewife *s* materfamilias *f*

hovel *s* tugurium, gurgustium *n*

hover *vi* pendēre, volitare; to — over impendēre (*with dat*)

how *adv* quomodo, quo pacto, qui; (*to what degree*) quam; — many quot;

— much quantum; — often quotiens

however *adv* tamen, nihilominus, autem; quamvis, quamlibet; — great quantuscunque; — many quotquot; — often quotiescunque

howl *s* ululat·us -ūs *m*

howl *vi* ululare, fremēre

hub *s* axis *m*

huckster *s* propola, institor *m*

huddle *vi* congregari

huddle *s* corona *f*

huddled *adj* confertus

hue *s* color *m*

hue and cry *s* conclamatio *f*

huff *s* offensio *f*; in a — offensus

huff *vi* stomachari

hug *s* complex·us -ūs *m*

hug *vt* complecti, amplecti

huge *adj* ingens, immensus, vastus, immanis

hulk *s* alveus *m*; navis oneraria *f*

hull *s* alveus *m*

hum *s* murmur *n*, murmuratio *f*; (*of bees*) bombus *m*

hum *vi* murmurare; (*of bees*) bombilare

human *adj* humanus; — feelings humanitas *f*; **—ly** humane, humaniter, humanitus

human being *s* homo *m & f*

humane *adj* humanus, misericors; **—ly** humaniter, misericorditer, humanitus

humanity *s* humanitas *f*; homines *m pl*

humanize *vt* excolēre

humble *adj* (*obscure*) humilis, obscurus; (*modest*) summissus, modestus; **—ly** summisse

humble *vt* deprimēre, infringēre; to — oneself se summittēre

humid *adj* humidus

humidity *s* humor *m*

humiliate *vt* humiliare, deprimēre

humiliation *s* humiliatio *f*, dedecus *n*

humility *s* animus summissus *m*, modestia, humilitas *f*

humor *s* (*disposition*) ingenium *n*, natura *f*; (*whim*) libido *f*; sense of — facetiae *f pl*, festivitas *f*

humor *vt* obsequi (*with dat*), morigerari (*with dat*), indulgēre (*with dat*)

humorous *adj* facetus, ridiculus, jocularis; **—ly** facete

hump *s* gibber, gibbus *m*

humpbacked *adj* gibber

hunch *s* opinio *f*; to have a — opinari

hundred *adj* centum; — times centie(n)s

hundredfold *adj* centuplex

hundredfold *s* centuplum *n*

hundredth *adj* centesimus

hunger *s* fames *f*

hunger *vi* esurire

hungrily *adv* avide, voraciter, rabide; jejune

hungry *s* esuriens, jejunus; (*fig*) avide; to be — esurire

hunt *s* venatio *f*, venat·us -ūs *m*

hunt *vt* venari, indagare; *vi* to —
for quaerĕre, exquirĕre
hunter *s* venator *m*; (*horse*) equus
venaticus *m*
hunting *s* venatio *f*, venat·us -ūs *m*
hunting *adj* venaticus
huntress *s* venatrix *f*
huntsman *s* venator *m*
hurdle *s* crates *f*; (*obstacle*) obex *m*
& *f*
hurl *vt* jacĕre, conjicĕre, jaculari
hurray *interj* io!, evax!
hurricane *s* procella *f*
hurriedly *adv* raptim, festinanter;
(*carelessly*) negligenter
hurry *vt* rapĕre, accelerare, maturare; *vi* festinare, properare, maturare
hurry *s* festinatio *f*; in a — festinanter
hurt *vt* nocēre (*with dat*), laedĕre;
(*fig*) offendĕre; *vi* dolēre
hurt *s* vulnus *n*; damnum *n*, injuria *f*
hurt *adj* saucius; (*emotionally*) saucius, offensus
husband *s* maritus, vir *m*
husbandry *s* agricultura, res rustica *f*
hush *s* silentium *n*

hush *vt* comprimĕre, pacare; (*a secret*) celare; *vi* tacēre
hush *interj* st!, tace!; (*to several*) tacete!
husk *s* folliculus *m*; (*of beans, etc.*)
siliqua *f*; (*of grain*) gluma *f*
husky *adj* robustus; (*of voice*) raucus
hustle *vt* trudĕre, pulsare; *vi* festinare
hut *s* tugurium *n*, casa *f*
hyacinth *s* hyacinthus *m*
hydra *s* hydra *f*
hyena *s* hyaena *f*
hymen *s* Hymenaeus *m*
hymn *s* carmen *n*, hymnus *m*
hyperbole *s* superlatio *f*
hypercritical *adj* nimis severus
hyphen *s* hyphen *n* (*indecl*)
hypochondriac *s* melancholicus *m*
hypocrisy *s* simulatio, dissimulatio *f*
hypocrite *s* simulator, dissimulator
m
hypocritical *adj* simulatus, fictus
hypothesis *s* hypothesis, sumptio,
conjectura *f*
hypothetical *adj* hypotheticus, sumptus
hysteria *s* deliratio *f*
hysterical *adj* hystericus

I

I *pron* ego; — **myself** egomet, ego
ipse
iambic *adj* iambeus
ice *s* glacies *f*
icicle *s* stiria *f*
icy *adj* glacialis
idea *s* notio, notitia, imago, conceptio *f*
ideal *adj* perfectus, summus, optimus; (*as mere mental image*) mente conceptus, idealis
ideal *s* exemplar *n*
identical *adj* idem
identify *vt* agnoscĕre
idiocy *s* fatuitas, animi imbecillitas *f*
idiom *s* proprietas linguae, consuetudo *f*
idiomatic *adj* proprius linguae
idiosyncrasy *s* proprium *n*
idiot *s* fatuus, excors *m*
idiotic *adj* fatuus, stultus, ineptus
idle *adj* otiosus, vacuus; (*pointless*)
vanus, inanis; (*lazy*) ignavus, iners,
deses; to be — cessare
idle *vt* to — away terĕre; *vi* cessare
idleness *s* otium *n*; ignavia, inertia,
desidia *f*
idler *s* cessator, homo ignavus *m*
idle talk *s* nugae *f pl*
idly *adv* otiose; ignave, segniter; (*in
vain*) vane, frustra
idol *s* simulacrum *n*; (*eccl*) idolum *n*;
(*person*) deliciae *f pl*
idolater *s* simulacrorum cultor *m*
idolatrous *adj* idololatricus
idolatry *s* simulacrorum cult·us -ūs *m*

idolize *vt* venerari
idyl *s* idyllium *n*
if *conj* si; **as** — quasi, tamquam;
and — quodsi; **but** — sin; quodsi;
even — etiamsi; — **not** ni, nisi, si
non; — **only** si modo, dummodo
igneous *adj* igneus
ignite *vt* accendĕre, incendĕre; *vi* exardescĕre, flammam concipĕre
ignoble *adj* ignobilis, obscurus; (*base*)
turpis
ignobly *adv* turpiter
ignominious *adj* ignominiosus, turpis; —**ly** ignominiose, turpiter
ignominy *s* ignominia *f*
ignoramus *s* idiota *m*
ignorance *s* ignoratio, ignorantia *f*
ignorant *adj* ignarus, nescius; (*un-
learned*) indoctus; to be — of ignorare, nescire; —**ly** inscienter, inscite, indocte
ignore *vt* praetermittĕre, neglegĕre
Iliad *s* Ilias *f*
ill *adj* aegrotus, aeger; (*evil*) malus;
to be — aegrotare; to fall — in
morbum incidĕre
ill *adv* male, prave
ill *s* malum *n*
ill-bred *adj* inurbanus, agrestis
illegal *adj* vetitus, illicitus; —**ly** contra leges, illicite
illegitimate *adj* haud legitimus; (*of
birth*) spurius, nothus
illiberal *adj* illiberalis; —**ly** illibera-
liter
illicit *adj* illicitus; —**ly** illicite

illiterate *adj* illitteratus, indoctus, ineruditus

illness *s* morbus *m*, aegritudo, aegrotatio, valetudo *f*

illogical *adj* absurdus; —**ly** absurde

ill-starred *adj* infelix

ill-tempered *adj* iracundus, stomachosus, difficilis

illuminate *vt* illustrare, illuminare

illumination *s* illuminatio *f*, lumina *n pl*

illusion *s* error *m*

illusive *adj* falsus, vanus

illusory *adj* fallax

illustrate *vt* illustrare; (*fig*) explanare

illustration *s* illustratio *f*; (*fig*) exemplum *n*

illustrative *adj* exemplaris

illustrious *adj* illustris, insignis, praeclarus; —**ly** praeclare

image *s* signum, simulacrum *n*; (*likeness*) effigies, imago *f*

imagery *s* figurae *f pl*

imaginary *adj* fictus, commenticius

imagination *s* cogitatio *f*

imaginative *adj* ingeniosus

imagine *vt* imaginari, fingĕre; (*to suppose*) opinari

imbecile *adj* (*weak*) imbecillus; (*of mind*) animo imbecillus, fatuus

imbecile *s* fatuus *m*

imbibe *vt* imbibĕre

imbue *vt* imbuĕre, tingĕre

imitate *vt* imitari

imitation *s* imitatio *f*; (*copy*) imago *f*

imitative *adj* ad imitandum aptus

imitator *s* imitator *m*, imitatrix *f*, aemulator *m*

immaculate *adj* integer, castus

immaterial *adj* incorporalis; (*unimportant*) nullius momenti

immeasurable *adj* immensus, infinitus

immeasurably *adv* infinito

immediate *adj* praesens, proximus; —**ly** statim, confestim, extemplo; —**ly after** sub (*with acc*)

immemorial *adj* antiquissimus; **from time —** ex omni memoria aetatum

immense *adj* immensus; —**ly** vehementer

immensity *s* immensitas *f*

immerge *vt* mergĕre, immergĕre

immersion *s* immersio *f*

imminent *adj* imminens, impendens

immobility *s* immobilitas *f*

immoderate *adj* immodicus; —**ly** immoderate, nimie

immodest *adj* immodestus, impudicus; —**ly** immodeste, inverecunde

immodesty *s* immodestia *f*

immolate *vt* immolare

immolation *s* immolatio *f*

immoral *adj* pravus, improbus, corruptus; —**ly** prave

immorality *s* mores mali *m pl*, turpitudo, improbitas *f*

immortal *adj* immortalis

immortality *s* immortalitas *f*

immortalize *vt* aeternare, ad deos evehĕre

immovable *adj* immobilis, immotus

immunity *s* immunitas, vacatio *f*

immure *vt* includĕre

immutability *s* immutabilitas *f*

immutable *adj* immutabilis

imp *s* larva *f*; (*child*) puer lascivus *m*

impair *vt* imminuĕre, atterĕre, debilitare

impale *vt* infigĕre

impart *vt* impertire, communicare

impartial *adj* aequus, aequabilis, severus; —**ly** severe

impartiality *s* aequitas, aequabilitas *f*

impassable *adj* insuperabilis, impervius

impassive *adj* impassibilis, frigidus, lentus

impatient *adj* impatiens, trepidus; —**ly** impatienter, aegre

impeach *vt* accusare

impeachment *s* accusatio *f*

impede *vt* obstare (*with dat*), impedire, retardare

impediment *s* impedimentum *n*; (*in speech*) haesitatio *f*

impel *vt* impellĕre

impenetrable *adj* impenetrabilis; (*fig*) occultus

impenitence *s* impaenitentia *f*

imperative *adj* necessarius; (*gram*) imperativus

imperceptible *adj* tenuissimus, obscurus

imperceptibly *adv* sensim

imperfect *adj* imperfectus, mancus, vitiosus; —**ly** imperfecte, vitiose

imperfection *s* vitium *n*, defect·us -ūs *m*

imperial *adj* imperatorius, regius; —**ly** regie

imperil *vt* in periculum adducĕre

imperishable *adj* perennis, aeternus, immortalis

impermeable *adj* impervius

impersonal *adj* impersonalis; —**ly** impersonaliter

impersonate *vt* sustinēre partes (*with genit*), imitari

impertinence *s* insolentia, protervitas *f*

impertinent *adj* (*rude*) insolens, protervus; (*not to the point*) ineptus, nihil ad rem; —**ly** insolenter, proterve; inepte

impervious *adj* impervius, impenetrabilis

impetuosity *s* impet·us -ūs *m*, vehementia, violentia *f*

impetuous *adj* vehemens, fervidus, violentus; —**ly** vehementer, fervide, violenter

impetus *s* impet·us -ūs *m*, vis *f*

impiety *s* impietas *f*

impinge *vi* incidĕre

impious *adj* impius, nefarius; —**ly** impie, nefarie

implacable *adj* implacabilis, inexorabilis, durus

implacably *adv* implacabiliter, dure

implant *vt* ingignĕre, inserĕre, ingenerare

implement *s* instrumentum *n*

implement *vt* exsequi

implicate *vt* implicare, impedire

implication *s* indicium *n*; **by — tacite**

implicit *adj* tacitus, totus; **—ly** tacite, omnino

implore *vt* implorare, obsecrare

imply *vt* significare; **to be implied in** inesse in (*with abl*)

impolite *adj* inurbanus; **—ly** inurbane

impoliteness *s* inurbanitas *f*

impolitic *adj* inconsultus

imponderable *adj* ponderis expers

import *vt* importare, invehĕre; (*to mean*) significare, velle

import *s* significatio *f*; **—s** importaticia *n pl*

importance *s* momentum *n*, gravitas *f*

important *adj* magnus, magni momenti, gravis

importunate *adj* importunus; **—ly** importune

importune *vt* fatigare, efflagitare, sollicitare

impose *vt* imponĕre; (*to enjoin*) injungĕre; **to — upon** abuti (*with abl*)

imposition *s* (*tax*) vectigal, tributum *n*; (*excessive burden*) importunitas *f*

impossibility *s* impossibilitas *f*

impossible *adj* impossibilis

imposter *s* fraudator *m*

imposture *s* fraus *f*

impotence *s* imbecillitas, infirmitas *f*

impotent *adj* imbecillus, infirmus

impound *vt* publicare; (*animals*) includĕre

impoverish *vt* in egestatem redigĕre

impractical *adj* inutilis

imprecate *vt* imprecari, exsecrari

imprecation *s* exsecratio *f*, dirae *f pl*

impregnable *adj* inexpugnabilis

impregnate *vt* imbuĕre, gravidam facĕre

impregnation *s* fecundatio *f*

impress *vt* imprimĕre; (*person*) movēre; **to — something on** inculcare aliquid (*with dat*); (*e.g., someone's mind*) infigĕre aliquid (*with dat*)

impression *s* impressio *f*; (*copy*) exemplar *n*; (*mark*) vestigium *n*; (*idea*) opinio, opinatio *f*; **to make an — on** commovere

impressive *adj* gravis; **—ly** graviter

imprint *s* impressio *f*

imprint *vt* imprimĕre, infigĕre

imprison *vt* in vincula conjicĕre

imprisonment *s* custodia *f*

improbable *adj* haud credibilis, parum verisimilis

impromptu *adv* ex tempore

improper *adj* indecorus; **—ly** indecore, perperam

impropriety *s* indecorum *n*

improve *vt* emendare, corrigĕre, excolĕre; *vi* melior fieri, proficĕre

improvement *s* emendatio, correctio *f*, profect·us -ūs *m*

improvident *adj* improvidus, imprudens; **—ly** improvide

improvise *vt* ex tempore dicĕre *or* componĕre

imprudence *s* imprudentia *f*

imprudent *adj* imprudens, inconsultus, temerarius; **—ly** imprudenter, inconsulte, temere

impugn *vt* impugnare, in dubium vocare

impulse *s* impuls·us -ūs *m*

impulsive *adj* vehemens, violentus; **—ly** impulsu

impunity *s* impunitas *f*; **with —** impune

impure *adj* impurus, obscenus, incestus; contaminatus; **—ly** impure, obscene, inceste

impurity *s* impuritas, obscenitas, impudicitia *f*

in *prep* in (*with abl*); (*in the writings of*) apud (*with acc*); (*of time*) render by abl

in *adv* (*motion*) intro; (*rest*) intra, intus

inability *s* impotentia *f*

inaccessible *adj* inaccessus

inaccuracy *s* neglegentia *f*

inaccurate *adj* neglegens, parum accuratus, minime exactus; **—ly** parum accurate

inactive *adj* iners, quietus, ignavus

inactivity *s* inertia, socordia, cessatio *f*

inadequate *adj* impar; **—ly** parum

inadmissible *adj* illicitus

inadvertence *s* imprudentia *f*

inadvertent *adj* imprudens; **—ly** imprudenter

inalienable *adj* proprius

inane *adj* inanis

inanimate *adj* inanimus, inanimatus

inapplicable *adj* to be **— non valēre**

inappropriate *adj* haud idoneus, parum aptus; **—ly** parum apte

inarticulate *adj* indistinctus

inartistic *adj* durus

inasmuch as *conj* quandoquidem

inattentive *adj* haud attentus, neglegens; **—ly** neglegenter

inaudible *adj* to be **— audiri non posse**

inaugurate *vt* inaugurare, consecrare

inauguration *s* inauguratio, consecratio *f*

inauspicious *adj* infaustus; **—ly** malo omine

inborn *adj* ingenitus, innatus

incalculable *adj* inaestimabilis; (*fig*) immensus, incredibilis

incantation *s* carmen, incantamentum *n*

incapable *adj* incapax, inhabilis; **to be — of** non posse (*with inf*)

incapacitate *vt* debilitare

incarcerate *vt* in vincula conjicĕre

incarnate *adj* incarnatus

incarnation *s* incarnatio *f*

incautious *adj* incautus; **—ly** incaute

incendiary *adj* incendiarius

incense s tus n
incense vt ture fumigare; (to anger) irritare, exasperare
incentive s incitamentum n
incessant adj continuus, assiduus; —ly assidue
incest s incest·us -ūs m
incestuous adj incestus
inch s uncia f; — by — unciatim
incident s cas·us -ūs, event·us -ūs m
incidental adj fortuitus; —ly fortuito, casu, forte
incipient adj nascens, primus
incision s incis·us -ūs m, incisura f
incisive adj acer
incite vt incitare, stimulare
incitement s incitamentum n, incitatio f
incivility s rusticitas f
inclemency s inclementia f; (of weather) asperitas f
inclination s (act) inclinatio f; (slope) proclivitas f; (propensity) libido, inclinatio f
incline vt inclinare; vi propendēre
incline s acclivitas f
inclined adj inclinatus, propensus, pronus
include vt includĕre, comprehendĕre
inclusive adj comprehendens
incognito adv clam
incoherent adj interruptus; —ly interrupte
income s redit·us -ūs, fruct·us -ūs m, merces f
incomparable adj incomparabilis, singularis, unicus, eximius
incomparably adv eximie, unice
incompatibility s repugnantia, diversitas f
incompatible adj repugnans, discors
incompetence s jurisdictionis defect·us -ūs m; inscitia f
incompetent adj inscitus, inhabilis
incomplete adj imperfectus
incomprehensible adj haud comprehensibilis
inconceivable adj incredibilis
inconclusive adj anceps
incongruous adj inconveniens, male congruens; —ly parum apte
inconsiderable adj levis, exiguus
inconsiderate adj inconsultus
inconsistency s inconstantia, discrepantia f
inconsistent adj inconstans, absonus, contrarius; to be — with abhorrēre ab (with abl); —ly inconstanter
inconsolable adj inconsolabilis
inconstancy s inconstantia, levitas f
inconstant adj inconstans, levis
incontestable adj non contentendus
incontinence s incontinentia, impudicitia f
incontinent adj incontinens, intemperans, impudicus; —ly incontinenter
incontrovertible adj quod refutari non potest
inconvenience s incommodum n
inconvenience vt incommodare
inconvenient adj incommodus; —ly

incommode
incorporate vt concorporare, inserēre
incorporation s coagmentatio, cooptatio f
incorporeal adj incorporalis
incorrect adj mendosus, vitiosus, falsus; —ly mendose, falso, perperam
incorrigible adj incorrigibilis; (fig) perditus
incorrupt adj incorruptus, integer
incorruptibility s incorruptibilitas f, incorrupti mores m pl
incorruptible adj incorruptibilis, integer
increase s (act) accretio f; incrementum, additamentum n
increase vt augēre, ampliare; vi augēri, crescēre
incredible adj incredibilis
incredibly adv incredibiliter, ultra fidem
incredulity s incredulitas f
incredulous adj incredulus
increment s incrementum n
incriminate vt criminari
incubation s incubatio f
inculcate vt inculcare
inculcation s inculcatio f
incumbent adj it is — on oportet (with acc)
incur vt contrahēre, subire; (guilt) admittēre
incurable adj insanabilis
incursion s incursio f
indebted adj obaeratus; (obliged) obligatus, devinctus, obnoxius
indecency s indecorum n, obscenitas f
indecent adj indecorus, obscenus; —ly indecore, obscene
indecision s haesitatio, dubitatio f
indecisive adj anceps, dubius, incertus
indeclinable adj indeclinabilis
indeed adv vere, profecto, sane; (concessive) quidem; (reply) certe, vero; (interr) itane?, verone?
indefatigable adj indefatigabilis, indefessus
indefensible adj non excusandus; to be — defendi non posse; (mil) tenēri non posse
indefinite adj infinitus, incertus, anceps, obscurus; —ly indefinite
indelible adj indelebilis
indelicacy s indecorum n
indelicate adj putidus, indecorus
indemnify vt compensare; damnum restituĕre (with dat)
indemnity s indemnitas f
independence s libertas f
independent adj sui potens, sui juris, liber; —ly libere, suo arbitrio
indescribable adj inenarrabilis; —ly inenarrabiliter
indestructible adj perennis, perpetuus
indeterminate adj indefinitus
index s index, elenchus m; (of dial) gnomon m
Indian adj Indicus
Indian s Indus m

indicate *vt* indicare, significare

indication *s* indicatio *f*, signum, indicium *n*

indicative *adj* indicativus

indict *vt* accusare; diem dicĕre (*with dat*)

indictment *s* libellus *m*, accusatio *f*

indifference *s* neglegentia, incuria, lentitudo *f*

indifferent *adj* (*apathetic*) remissus, neglegens, lentus; (*mediocre*) mediocris; —**ly** neglegenter, lente; (*without discrimination*) promiscue

indigenous *adj* indigena

indigent *adj* egens, inops

indigestible *adj* crudus

indigestion *s* cruditas *f*

indignant *adj* indignans, indignabundus, iratus; **to be —** indignari; —**ly** indignanter

indignation *s* indignatio *f*, dolor *m*

indignity *s* indignitas, contumelia *f*

indirect *adj* indirectus, obliquus; —**ly** indirecte, oblique

indiscreet *adj* inconsultus; —**ly** inconsulte, temere

indiscretion *s* immodestia *f*; (*act*) culpa *f*

indiscriminate *adj* promiscuus; —**ly** promiscue, sine discrimine

indispensable *adj* omnino necessarius

indisposed *adj* aversus; (*in health*) aegrotus; **to be —** aegrotare

indisputable *adj* manifestus, certus

indissoluble *adj* indissolubilis

indistinct *adj* indistinctus, parum clarus, obscurus; —**ly** indistincte

individual *adj* proprius, singularis, singuli; —**ly** singulatim

individual *s* homo *m* & *f*; —**s** singuli *m pl*

individuality *s* proprium ingenium *n*

indivisible *adj* indivisibilis, individuus

indolence *s* inertia, desidia *f*

indolent *adj* iners, ignavus; —**ly** ignave, segniter

indomitable *adj* indomitus

indorse *vt* ratum facĕre

indubitable *adj* indubitabilis

indubitably *adv* sine dubio

induce *vt* persuadēre (*with dat*), inducĕre

inducement *s* incitamentum *n*, illecebra *f*

indulge *vt* indulgēre (*with dat*), servire (*with dat*)

indulgence *s* indulgentia, venia *f*

indulgent *adj* indulgens, benignus; —**ly** indulgenter, benigne

industrious *adj* industrius, sedulus, strenuus; —**ly** industrie

industry *s* industria, assiduitas *f*

inebriated *adj* ebrius, madidus

ineffable *adj* ineffabilis

ineffective *adj* irritus, inutilis; **to be —** effectu carēre

ineffectual *adj* inefficax; —**ly** frustra, nequiquam

inefficiency *s* inutilitas *f*

inefficient *adj* inscitus, inhabilis

ineligible *adj* non eligibilis

inept *adj* ineptus

inequality *s* inaequalitas *f*

inert *adj* iners, segnis, socors

inertia *s* inertia *f*

inevitable *adj* necessarius

inexact *adj* haud accuratus; (*of persons*) indiligens

inexcusable *adj* inexcusabilis

inexhaustible *adj* inexhaustus

inexorable *adj* inexorabilis, durus

inexperience *s* imperitia, inscitia *f*

inexperienced *adj* imperitus, inexpertus

inexplicable *adj* inexplicabilis, inenodabilis

inexpressible *adj* inenarrabilis

inextricable *adj* inexplicabilis, inextricabilis

infallible *adj* certus, erroris expers

infamous *adj* infamis, turpis, flagitiosus; —**ly** flagitiose

infamy *s* infamia *f*, probrum *n*

infancy *s* infantia *f*

infant *adj* infans; puerilis

infant *s* infans *m* & *f*

infanticide *s* (*person*) infanticida *m*; (*deed*) infanticidium *n*

infantile *adj* infantilis

infantry *s* peditat·us -ūs *m*, pedites *m pl*

infatuate *vt* infatuare

infatuation *s* amentia, dementia *f*

infect *vt* inficĕre; (*fig*) contaminare

infection *s* contagium *n*, contagio *f*

infectious *adj* contagiosus

infer *vt* inferre, conjicĕre

inference *s* conjectura, conclusio *f*

inferior *adj* inferior, deterior, minor

infernal *adj* infernus

infertility *s* sterilitas *f*

infest *vt* infestare, frequentare

infidel *s* infidelis *m* & *f*

infidelity *s* infidelitas, perfidia *f*

infiltrate *vi* se insinuare

infinite *adj* infinitus, immensus; —**ly** infinite; (*very greatly*) infinito

infinitive *s* infinitivus modus *m*

infinity *s* infinitas, infinitio *f*

infirm *adj* infirmus, debilis

infirmary *s* valetudinarium *n*

infirmity *s* infirmitas, imbecillitas *f*

inflame *vt* inflammare, incendĕre, accendĕre

inflammable *adj* ad exardescendum facilis

inflammation *s* inflammatio *f*

inflammatory *adj* turbulentus, ardens

inflate *vt* inflare; **to be inflated** tumēre

inflation *s* inflatio *f*

inflect *vt* inflectĕre, curvare

inflection *s* flex·us -ūs *m*, declinatio *f*

inflexible *adj* rigidus; (*fig*) obstinatus, pertinax

inflexibly *adv* obstinate

inflict *vt* infligĕre, imponĕre

infliction *s* malum *n*, poena *f*

influence *s* gratia, auctoritas *f*, momentum *n*; **to have — on** valēre apud (*with acc*)

influence *vt* movēre, impellĕre

influential *adj* gravis, potens

influenza s catarrh·us -ūs *m*, grave-do *f*

influx s influxio *f*

inform *vt* (*to teach*) instruěre; certiorem facěre; *vi* **to — against** deferre de (*with abl*)

informant s index, delator *m*

information s informatio *f*, indicium *n*, nuntius *m*

informer s delator *m*

infraction s infractio *f*

infrequency s raritas *f*

infrequent *adj* rarus

infringe *vt* infringěre, violare; *vi* **to — upon** occupare, usurpare

infringement s violatio, usurpatio *f*

infuriate *vt* efferare

infuse *vt* infundere; (*fig*) injicěre

infusion s infusio *f*

ingenious *adj* sollers, callidus, ingeniosus; (*of thing*) artificiosus; **—ly** callide, artificiose

ingenuity s ars, sollertia *f*

ingenuous *adj* simplex

inglorious *adj* inglorius, inhonestus; **—ly** sine gloria, in honeste

ingrained *adj* insitus, inveteratus

ingratiate *vt* **to — oneself with** gratiam inire ab (*with abl*)

ingratitude s ingratus animus *m*

ingredient s pars *f*

inhabit *vt* incolěre, habitare

inhabitable *adj* habitabilis

inhabitant s incola *m* & *f*

inhale *vt* haurire; *vi* spiritum ducěre

inharmonious *adj* dissonus, absonus

inherent *adj* inhaerens, insitus; **to be — in** inesse (*with dat*)

inherit *vt* excipere

inheritance s hereditas, successio *f*, patrimonium *n*; **to come into an —** hereditatem adire

inheritor s heres *m* & *f*

inhospitable *adj* inhospitalis

inhospitably *adv* minime hospitaliter

inhospitality s inhospitalitas *f*

inhuman *adj* inhumanus; **—ly** inhumane

inhumanity s inhumanitas *f*

inimical *adj* inimicus

inimitable *adj* inimitabilis

iniquitous *adj* iniquus, improbus

iniquity s iniquitas, injustitia *f*

initial *adj* primus

initiate *vt* initiare, instituěre

initiation s initium *n*

initiative s initium *n*

inject *vt* injicěre, infunděre, immittěre

injection s injectio *f*

injudicious *adj* inconsultus; **—ly** inconsulte, temere

injunction s mandatum, imperatum *n*

injure *vt* nocěre (*with dat*), laeděre

injurious *adj* noxius, damnosus, gravis; **—ly** male

injury s injuria *f*, damnum, detrimentum, malum *n*

injustice s injustitia *f*; (*act*) injuria *f*

ink s atramentum *n*

inkling s (*hint*) rumusculus *m*, obscura significatio *f*

inland *adj* mediterraneus

inlay *vt* inserěre; (*with mosaic*) tessellare

inlet s sin·us -ūs *m*, aestuarium *n*

inmate s incola, inquilinus *m*

inmost *adj* intimus, imus

inn s caupona *f*, deversorium *n*

innate *adj* innatus, insitus

inner *adj* interior

innermost *adj* intimus, imus

innkeeper s caupo *m*

innocence s innocentia *f*; castitas *f*

innocent *adj* insons, innocens, integer, castus; **—ly** innocenter, integre, caste

innocuous *adj* innocuus; **—ly** innocue

innovation s novum *n*, res nova *f*

innovator s rerum novarum auctor *m*

innumerable *adj* innumerabilis

inoffensive *adj* innocens, innoxius

inopportune *adj* inopportunus; **—ly** parum in tempore

inordinate *adj* immoderatus; **—ly** immoderate

inquest s inquisitio *f*; (*law*) quaestio *f*; **to hold an —** quaerěre

inquire *vi* inquirěre, rogare; **to — into** investigare

inquiry s quaestio, investigatio *f*

inquisition s inquisitio *f*

inquisitive *adj* curiosus; **—ly** curiose

inquisitor s quaesitor *m*

inroad s incursio, irruptio *f*

insane *adj* insanus, vecors; **—ly** insane

insanity s insania, dementia *f*

insatiable *adj* insatiabilis, inexplebilis

inscribe *vt* inscriběre, insculpěre, incidere

inscription s inscriptio *f*, titulus *m*

inscrutable *adj* occultus, obscurus

insect s insectum *n*, bestiola *f*

insecure *adj* incertus, intutus, instabilis

insecurity s periculum *n*

insensible *adj* insensilis; (*fig*) durus

inseparable *adj* inseparabilis

insert *vt* inserěre; (*in writing*) ascriběre

insertion s insertio, interpositio *f*

inside *adj* interior

inside *adv* intrinsecus

inside s interior pars *f*, interiora *n pl*

inside *prep* intro (*with acc*)

insidious *adj* insidiosus, subdolus; **—ly** insidiose, subdole

insight s (*knowledge*) cognitio, intellegentia *f*; (*intelligence*) consilium, judicium *n*

insignia s insignia *n pl*

insignificance s exiguitas, levitas *f*

insignificant *adj* exiguus, levis, nullius momenti; (*rank*) humilis

insincere *adj* insincerus, simulatus, fucosus; **—ly** haud sincere, simulate

insincerity s simulatio, fallacia *f*

insinuate vt insinuare; (to hint) significare

insinuation s significatio f

insipid adj insulsus, hebes, frigidus; —ly insulse

insist vt flagitare, exposcĕre; vi instare; to — on urgĕre, postulare

insistence s pertinacia f

insolence s insolentia, arrogantia f

insolent adj insolens, arrogans; —ly insolenter

insoluble adj insolubilis; (fig) inexplicabilis

insolvent adj to be — solvendo non esse

inspect vt inspicĕre, introspicĕre, intuēri; (mil) recensēre

inspection s inspectio, cura f; (mil) recensio f

inspector s curator m

inspiration s (divine) afflat·us -ūs m; instinct·us -ūs m; (prophetic) furor m

inspire vt inspirare, incendĕre, injicĕre

instability s instabilitas f

install vt inaugurare, constituĕre

installation s inauguratio f

instalment s pensio, portio f

instance s exemplum n; at my — me auctore; for — exampli gratiā

instance vt memorare

instant adj instans, praesens; —ly extemplo, statim

instant s momentum n; this — statim, actutum

instantaneous adj praesens; —ly continuo

instead adv potius, magis

instead of prep pro (with abl), loco (with genit)

instigate vt instigare

instigation s incitatio f, stimulus m

instigator s instigator m, instigatrix f

instill vt instillare, imbuĕre, injicĕre

instinct s instinct·us -ūs m, natura f

instinctive adj naturalis; —ly instinctu

institute vt instituĕre, constituĕre, condĕre

institute s institutum n

institution s (act) institutio f; (thing instituted) institutum n

instruct vt (to teach) docēre, instituĕre; (to order) praecipĕre (with dat), mandare

instruction s institutio, eruditio, doctrina f; —s mandata n pl

instructive adj ad docendum aptus

instructor s praeceptor, magister, doctor m, magistra f

instrument s instrumentum n; (mus) organum n; (law) tabula, syngrapha f

instrumental adj aptus, utilis

insubordinate adj seditiosus, male parens

insubordination s inobedientia, intemperantia f

insufferable adj intolerandus, intolerabilis

insufficiency s defect·us -ūs m, inopia f

insufficient adj impar, parum sufficiens; —ly haud satis

insular adj insulanus

insulate vt segregare

insult s probrum n, injuria, contumelia f

insult vt insultare; contumeliam imponĕre (with dat), contumeliā afficĕre

insultingly adv contumeliose

insure vt tutum praestare

insurgent adj rebellis

insurgent s rebellis m

insurmountable adj inexsuperabilis

insurrection s rebellio, seditio f

intact adj integer, intactus, incolumis

intangible adj intactilis

integral adj necessarius

integrity s integritas, innocentia, fides f

intellect s intellect·us -ūs, animus m, mens f, ingenium n

intellectual adj ingeniosus

intelligence s ingenium n, intellegentia f; (information) nuntius m

intelligent adj sapiens, argutus, prudens; —ly intellegenter, sapienter, prudenter

intelligible adj intellegibilis, perspicuus

intelligibly adv intellegibiliter, perspicue

intemperance s intemperantia f

intemperate adj immodicus, intemperatus; —ly intemperanter

intend vt (with inf) intendĕre, in animo habēre; (with object) destinare

intended adj destinatus; (of future spouse) sponsus

intense adj acer, fervidus; (of heat) rapidus; (excessive) nimius; —ly vehementer, valde, nimium

intensify vt augēre

intensity s vehmentia, vis f; (of winter, etc.) rigor m

intent adj intentus, attentus; to be — on animum intendĕre in (with acc); —ly intente

intention s propositum, consilium n; (meaning) significatio f

intentionally adv de industria

inter vt inhumare, sepelire

intercede vi intercedĕre, deprecari, se interponĕre

intercept vt excipĕre, intercipĕre, intercludĕre

intercession s deprecatio f; (of tribune) intercessio f

intercessor s deprecator m

interchange vt permutare, commutare

interchange s permutatio, vicissitudo f

intercourse s commercium n; (social) consuetudo f; (sexual) congress·us -ūs, coit·us -ūs m

interdict vt interdicĕre, prohibēre

interdiction s interdictio f, interdictum n

interest s (attention) studium n; (advantage) utilitas f, us·us -ūs m,

commodum n; (money) faenus n,
usura f; it is of — to me meã interest, meã refert

interested adj — in studiosus (with
genit), attentus (with dat)

interfere vi intercedere, intervenire,
interpellare

interference s intercessio f, dissidium n, intervent·us -ūs m

interim s intervallum n; in the —
interim, interea

interior adj interior

interior s interior pars f

interjection s interjectio f

interlinear adj interscriptus

interlude s embolium n

intermarriage s connubium n

intermarry vi matrimonio inter se
conjungi

intermediary s internuntius m

intermediate adj medius

interment s sepultura, humatio f

interminable adj infinitus

intermission s intermissio, inter-
capedo f

intermittent adj intermittens, interruptus; —ly interdum, aliquando

internal adj intestinus, domesticus;
—ly intus, interne; domi

international adj inter gentes

interpolate vt interpolare

interpolation s interpolatio f

interpret vt interpretari

interpretation s interpretatio f

interpreter s interpres m

interrogate vt interrogare, percontari

interrogation s interrogatio, percontatio f

interrogative adj interrogativus

interrupt vt interrumpĕre, interpellare

interruption s interruptio, interpellatio f

intersect vt intersecare

intersection s quadrivium n

intersperse vt inmiscēre

intertwine vt intertexĕre

interval s intervallum, spatium n

intervene vi (to be between) inter-
jacēre; (to come between) intercedere, intervenire

intervening adj medius

intervention s intercessio f, inter-
vent·us -ūs m

interview s colloquium n, congress·
us -ūs m

interview vt percontari

interweave vt intertexĕre, intexēre

intestinal adj ad intestina pertinens

intestine adj intestinus; (pol) domesticus, civicus

intestines s intestina n pl; (of victim) exta n pl

intimacy s familiaritas, consuetudo f

intimate adj familiaris; intimus;
—ly familiariter; intime

intimate vt indicare, innuĕre, denuntiare

intimation s indicium n, denuntiatio f

intimidate vt minari (with dat), metum injicĕre (with dat), terrēre

intimidation s minae f pl

into prep in (with acc)

intolerable adj intolerabilis, intolerandus

intolerably adv intoleranter

intolerance s intolerantia f; superbia f

intolerant adj intolerans, impatiens

intonation s accent·us -ūs m

intone vt cantare

intoxicate vt ebrium reddĕre

intoxicated adj ebrius

intoxication s ebrietas f

intractable adj intractabilis, indocilis

intrepid adj intrepidus, impavidus;
—ly intrepide

intricacy s perplexitas, implicatio f

intricate adj contortus, implicatus,
perplexus; —ly contorte, perplexe

intrigue s conspiratio f, dolus m, ar-
tificia n pl

intrigue vt fascinare; vi machinari,
dolis contendĕre

intrinsic adj innatus, verus; —ally
vere, per se

introduce vt introducĕre, inducĕre

introduction s (preface) praefatio
f, exordium, prooemium n; (to person) introductio f, adit·us -ūs m

intrude vi se interponĕre, se inculcare, intervenire

intruder s interpellator, advena m;
homo molestus m

intrusion s interpellatio, usurpatio f

intuition s intuit·us -ūs m, cognitio
f, acumen n

intuitive adj intuitivus; —ly mentis
propriã vi ac naturã

inundate vt inundare

inundation s inundatio f, diluvium n

invade vt incurrĕre in (with acc), in-
vadēre

invader s invasor m

invalid adj infirmus, vitiosus; (sick)
aeger, aegrotus

invalid s aegrotus m

invalidate vt irritum facĕre, rescindēre

invaluable adj inaestimabilis

invariable adj constans, immutabilis

invariably adv semper

invasion s incursio, irruptio f

invective s convicium, probrum n

inveigh vi to — against invehi in
(with acc), insectari

invent vt invenire, reperire; (to contrive) excogitare, fingĕre

invention s (act) inventio f; (thing
invented) inventum n

inventive adj sollers, ingeniosus

inventor s inventor, auctor m

inventory s bonorum index m

inverse adj inversus, conversus;
—ly inverso ordine

inversion s inversio, conversio f

invert vt invertēre

invest vt (money) collocare, ponĕre;
(to besiege) obsidēre

investigate vt investigare, indagare; (law) quaerĕre, cognoscĕre

investigation s investigatio f; (law)
cognitio f

investigator s investigator, indagator m; (law) quaesitor m

investment s (of money) collocatio f; (money invested) locata pecunia f; (mil) obsessio f

inveterate adj inveteratus

invigorate vt corroborare, recreare

invincible adj invictus, insuperabilis

inviolable adj inviolatus, sacrosanctus

inviolate adj inviolatus, intactus

invisible adj invisibilis, caecus

invitation s invitatio f

invite vt invitare, adhibēre

inviting adj suavis, gratus, blandus; —ly blande

invocation s invocatio, testatio f

invoice s libellus m

invoke vt vocare, invocare, obtestari

involuntarily adv invite, coacte

involuntary adj non voluntarius, coactus

involve vt implicare, involvēre; (to comprise) continēre

involved adj to be — illigari; to be — in debt aere alieno laborare

invulnerable adj invulnerabilis

inward adj interior; —ly intus, intrinsecus

inwards adv introrsus

Ionian adj Ionicus

irascible adj iracundus

ire s ira f

Ireland s Hibernia f

iris s iris f

Irish adj Hibernicus

irk vt incommodare; **I am irked** taedet me, piget me

irksome adj molestus, odiosus

iron s ferrum n

iron adj ferreus

ironical adj ironicus, deridens; —ly per ironiam

irony s ironia, dissimulatio f

irradiate vt illustrare; vi effulgēre

irrational adj rationis expers, irrationalis, absurdus; —ly absurde

irreconcilable adj implacabilis; (incompatible) repugnans, insociabilis

irrecoverable adj irreparabilis

irrefutable adj certus, invictus

irregular adj irregularis, abnormis; (disorderly) tumultuarius; (gram) anomalus; —ly irregulariter

irregularity s irregularitas f; (of conduct) luxuries, pravitas f; (gram) anomalia f

irrelevant adj non pertinens, alienus; **it is** — nil ad rem pertinet

irreligious adj impius

irremediable adj insanabilis

irreparable adj irreparabilis, irrevocabilis

irreproachable adj irreprehensus, integer

irresistible adj inexsuperabilis, invictus

irresolute adj dubius, incertus animi; (permanent characteristic) parum firmus; —ly dubitanter

irresolution s dubitatio f; animus parum firmus m

irresponsibility s incuria f

irresponsible adj incuriosus

irretrievable adj irreparabilis, irrevocabilis

irreverence s impietas f

irreverent adj impius, inverecundus; —ly impie

irrevocable adj irrevocabilis

irrigate vt irrigare

irrigation s irrigatio, inductio aquae f

irritability s iracundia f

irritable adj irritabilis, iracundus, difficilis

irritate vt irritare; (wound) inflammare

irritation s irritatio, iracundia f, stomachus m

island s insula f

islander s insulanus m

islet s parva insula f

isolate vt sejungēre, secernēre

issue s (result) event·us -ūs, exit·us -ūs m; (question) res f; (offspring) proles f; (of book) editio f; (of money) emissio f

issue vt (to distribute) distribuēre; (orders, etc.) edēre, proponēre, promulgare; (money) erogare; (book) edēre; vi emanare, egredi; (to turn out, result) evenire, evadēre

isthmus s isthmus m

it pron id, hoc

itch s prurigo f, prurit·us -ūs m; (disease) scabies f

itch vi prurire; (fig) gestire

item s res f

itinerant adj circumforaneus, vagus

itinerary s itinerarium n

its pron ejus; —own suus

itself pron (refl) se, sese; (intensive) ipsum

ivory s ebur n

ivory adj eburneus

ivy s hedera f

J

jabber vi blaterare

jackass s asinus m; (fig) stultus m

jacket s tunica f

jaded adj defessus

jagged adj serratus; (of rocks) praeruptus

jail s carcer m

jailer s carcerarius m

jam s baccarum conditura f

jam vt frequentare, stipare; (to obstruct) impedire, obstruēre

jamb s postis m

jangle vi crepitare

January s (mensis) Januarius m

jar *s* olla, amphora *f*, urceus, cadus *m*

jar *vt* vibrare; offendĕre; *vi* discrepare

jargon *s* confusae voces *f pl*

jarring *adj* dissonus, discors

jaundice *s* morbus regius *m*

jaundiced *adj* ictericus, felle suffusus; (*fig*) lividus, morosus

jaunt *s* excursio *f*; to take a — excurrĕre

javelin *s* pilum, jaculum *n*; to hurl a — jaculari

jaw *s* mala, maxilla *f*; —s (*fig*) fauces *f pl*

jawbone *s* maxilla *f*

jay *s* graculus *m*

jealous *adj* invidus, lividus; to be — of invidēre (*with dat*)

jealousy *s* invidia, aemulatio *f*

jeer *s* irrisio *f*, irris·us -ūs *m*

jeer *vt* deridēre, explodĕre; *vi* to — at irridēre, alludĕre

jelly *s* cylon, quilon *n*

jellyfish *s* pulmo, halipleumon *m*

jeopardize *vt* periclitari, in periculum adducĕre

jeopardy *s* periculum *n*

jerk *s* verber, ict·us -ūs, impet·us -ūs *m*

jerk *vt* calcitrare, icĕre

jerky *adj* (*of style*) salebrosus

jest *s* jocus *m*; in — joco, jocose

jest *vi* jocari, ludĕre

jester *s* joculator *m*; (*buffoon*) scurra *m*

jestingly *adv* per jocum

Jesus *s* Jesus *m*

jet *s* scatebra *f*

jetty *s* moles *f*

Jew *s* Judaeus *m*

jewel *s* gemma *f*

jeweled *adj* gemmeus, gemmifer

jeweler *s* gemmarius *m*

jewelry *s* gemmae *f pl*

Jewish *adj* Judaicus

jig *s* tripudium *n*

jilt *vt* repudiare

jingle *vi* tinnire

jingle *s* tinnit·us -ūs *m*

job *s* negotiolum, opus *n*

jockey *s* agaso *m*

jocose *adj* jocosus; —ly jocose

jocular *adj* jocularis, facetus

jog *vi* to — along lente progredi

join *vt* (*to connect*) jungĕre, conjungĕre; (*to come into the company of*) se jungĕre (*with dat*), se jungĕre cum (*with abl*); *vi* conjungi, adjungi, cohaerēre; to — in particeps esse (*with genit*), interesse (*with dat*); to — together inter se conjungi

joint *adj* communis; —ly una, conjunctim, communiter

joint *s* (*of body*) articulus *m*, commissura *f*; (*of plant*) geniculum *n*; (*of any structure*) compages *f*

jointed *adj* geniculatus

joist *s* tignum *n*

joke *s* jocus *m*

joke *vi* jocari, ludĕre

joker *s* joculator *m*

joking *s* jocus *m*; all — aside joco

remoto; —ly per jocum

jolly *adj* hilaris, festivus

jolt *vt* jactare, concutĕre; (*fig*) percellĕre; *vi* jactari

jolting *s* jactatio *f*

jostle *vt* pulsare, agitare, fodicare

jot *s* hilum *n*; not a — minime; to care not a — non flocci facĕre

jot *vt* to — down notare, subscribĕre

journal *s* ephemeris *f*, acta diurna *n pl*

journey *s* iter *n*

journey *vi* iter facĕre; to — abroad peregrinari

journeyman *s* opifex *m*

Jove *s* Jupiter *m*

jovial *adj* hilaris

jowl *s* bucca *f*

joy *s* gaudium *n*, laetitia *f*

joyful *adj* laetus; —ly laete, libenter

joyless *adj* illaetabilis

joyous *adj* hilaris, festivus

jubilant *adj* laetus, gaudio exsultans, gaudio triumphans

jubilation *s* exsultatio *f*

jubilee *s* dies anniversarius *m*, solemne *n*

Judaic *adj* Judaicus

Judaism *s* Judaismus *m*

judge *s* judex, quaesitor, arbiter *m*

judge *vt* judicare; (*to think*) existimare, censēre; (*to value*) aestimare; (*to decide between*) dijudicare

judgment *s* judicium, arbitrium *n*; (*opinion*) sententia *f*, judicium *n*; to pass — on statuĕre de (*with abl*); to pronounce — jus dicĕre

judgment seat *s* tribunal *n*

judicial *adj* judicialis, judicarius; —ly jure, lege

judicious *adj* sapiens, sagax, prudens; —ly sapienter, sagaciter, prudenter

jug *s* urceus *m*

juggle *vi* praestigias agĕre

juggler *s* praestigiator *m*

juice *s* sucus, liquor *m*

juicy *adj* sucidus

July *s* (*mensis*) Quintilis *or* Julius *m*

jumble *s* congeries, confusio *f*

jumble *vt* confundĕre, permiscēre

jump *s* salt·us -ūs *m*

jump *vt* transilire; *vi* salire; to — at (*opportunity*) captare; to — for joy exsultare

junction *s* conjunctio *f*

juncture *s* tempus *n*; at this — hic

June *s* (*mensis*) Junius *m*

jungle *s* salt·us -ūs *m*

junior *adj* junior, minor natu

juniper *s* juniperus *m*

jurisdiction *s* jurisdictio *f*

jurisprudence *s* jurisprudentia *f*

jurist *s* jurisconsultus *m*

juror *s* judex *m*

jury *s* judices *m pl*

just *adj* justus, aequus; (*deserved*) meritus; —ly juste, jure, merito

just *adv* (*only*) modo; (*exactly*) prorsus; (*with adv*) demum, denique; — after *sub* (*with acc*); — as aeque ac, perinde ac, sic ut, haud secus

ac; — **before** sub (*with acc*); —
now modo; — **so** ita prorsus
justice *s* justitia, aequitas *f*; (*just
treatment*) jus *n*; (*person*) praetor
m
justifiable *adj* justus, legitimus, ex-
cusatus

justifiably *adv* jure
justification *s* purgatio, excusatio *f*
justify *vt* purgare, excusare, approbare
jut *vi* prominēre; **to — out** prominēre, eminēre, procurrēre
juvenile *adj* juvenilis, puerilis

K

kale *s* crambe *f*
keel *s* carina *f*
keen *adj* acer, sagax; **—ly** acute,
acriter; sagaciter
keenness *s* (*of scent*) sagacitas *f*; (*of
sight*) acies *f*; (*of pain*) acerbitas *f*;
(*enthusiasm*) studium *n*
keep *vt* tenēre, habēre; (*to preserve*)
servare; (*to celebrate*) agēre, celebrare; (*to guard*) custodire; (*to
obey*) observare; (*to support*) alēre;
(*animals*) pascēre; (*to store*) condēre; **to — apart** distinēre; **to —
away** arcēre; **to — back** retinēre,
cohibēre; (*to conceal*) celare; **to —
company** comitari; **to — from**
prohibēre; **to — in** cohibēre, claudēre; **to — off** arcēre, defendēre;
to — secret celare; **to — together** continēre; **to — under**
compescēre, supprimēre; **to — up**
sustinēre; *vi* remanēre, durare; **to
— away** abstinēre; **to — up with**
subsequi
keep *s* custodia, cura *f*
keeper *s* custos *m*
keeping *s* tutela, custodia, cura *f*;
in — with pro (*with abl*)
keepsake *s* monumentum, pignus *n*
keg *s* cadus *m*, testa *f*
ken *s* conspect·us ·ūs *m*
kennel *s* stabulum *n*
kernel *s* nucleus *m*; (*fig*) medulla *f*
kettle *s* lebes *f*
kettledrum *s* tympanum aeneum *n*
key *s* clavis *f*; (*of a position*) claustra
n pl
keyhole *s* foramen *n*
kick *vt* calce ferire; *vi* calcitrare
kid *s* haedus *m*
kidnap *vt* surripēre
kidnapper *s* plagiarius *m*
kidney *s* ren *m*
kill *vt* interficēre, caedēre, occidēre,
necare; (*time*) perdēre
killer *s* interfector, necator *m*
kiln *s* fornax *f*
kin *s* cognati, consanguinei, neces-
sarii *m pl*
kind *adj* amicus, benignus, benevolus; **—ly** benigne, clementer
kind *s* genus *n*; **what — of** qualis
kindhearted *adj* benignus
kindle *vt* incendēre, accendēre, inflammare
kindly *adj* benignus
kindness *s* benignitas, benevolentia
f; (*deed*) beneficium, officium *n*
kindred *adj* consanguineus, cognatus

kindred *s* consanguinitas, cognatio
f; cognati, propinqui *m pl*
king *s* rex *m*
kingdom *s* regnum *n*
kingfisher *s* alcedo *f*
kingly *adj* regius, regalis
kinsman *s* necessarius, cognatus,
propinquus *m*
kinswoman *s* necessaria, cognata,
propinqua *f*
kiss *s* osculum, basium *n*
kiss *vt* osculari
kissing *s* osculatio *f*
kitchen *s* culina *f*
kite *s* (*bird*) milvus *m*
kitten *s* catulus felinus *m*
knack *s* sollertia, calliditas *f*
knapsack *s* sarcina *f*
knave *s* nebulo, veterator *m*
knavish *adj* nefarius, improbus;
(*mischievous*) malitiosus
knead *vt* subigēre
knee *s* genu *n*
kneel *vi* genibus niti
knell *s* campana funebris *f*
knife *s* culter *m*; (*for surgery*) scalprum *n*
knight *s* eques *m*
knighthood *s* equestris dignitas *f*
knightly *adj* equester
knit *vt* texēre; **to — the brow** frontem contrahēre
knob *s* tuber *n*, nodus *m*; (*of door*)
bulla *f*
knock *vt* **to — down** dejicēre, sternēre; (*fig*) (*at auction*) addicēre; **to
— in** impellēre, infigēre; **to — off**
excutēre, decidēre; **to — out** excutēre; *vi* **to — about** (*to ramble*)
vagari; **to — at** pulsare
knock *s* pulsatio *f*, puls·us ·ūs *m*
knoll *s* tumulus *m*
knot *s* nodus *m*, geniculum *n*; (*of
people*) corona *f*
knot *vt* nodare, nectēre
knotty *adj* nodosus; (*fig*) spinosus
know *vt* scire; (*person*) novisse; **not
to —** ignorare, nescire; **to — how
to** scire (*with inf*)
knowing *adj* callidus, prudens; **—ly**
sciens, de industria, consulto
knowledge *s* scientia, doctrina *f*; (*of
something*) cognitio *f*; (*skill*) peritia *f*; (*learning*) eruditio *f*
known *adj* notus; (*common*) tritus;
to become — enotescēre; **to make
—** divulgare, declarare
knuckle *s* articulus, condylus *m*
kowtow *vi* adulari

L

label s titulus m
labor s labor m; (manual) opera f; (work done) opus n; to be in — laborare utero; woman in — puerpera f
labor vi laborare, eniti; to — under laborare (with abl)
laboratory s officina f
labored adj affectatus
laborer s operarius m
labyrinth s labyrinthus m
labyrinthine adj labyrinthicus; (fig) inextricabilis
lace s opus reticulatum n
lace vt (to tie) nectěre, astringěre; (to beat) verberare
lacerate vt lacerare, laniare
laceration s laceratio f
lack s inopia f, defect·us -ūs m, defectio f
lack vt carēre (with abl), egēre (with abl)
lackey s pedisequus, servus a pedibus m
laconic adj brevis, astrictus; —ally breviter, paucis
lad s puer, adulescens m
ladder s scala f
ladle s ligula, spatha f, cochlear n
lady s domina, matrona f
lag vi cessare, morari, cunctari
lagoon s lacuna f, stagnum n
lair s cubile, latibulum n
laity s laici m pl
lake s lac·us -ūs m
lamb s agnus m, agna f; (meat) agnina f
lame adj claudus; to walk — claudicare; —ly (fig) inconcinne
lameness s clauditas f
lament s lamentum n, lamentatio f
lament vt lamentari, deplorare; vi flēre
lamentable adj lamentabilis, miserabilis
lamentably adv miserabiliter
lamentation s lamentatio f
lamp s lucerna f, lynchnus m
lampoon s satira f, libellus m
lampoon vt famosis carminibus lacessěre
lance s lancea, hasta f
lance vt incidēre
land s (soil) terra, tellus f; (country) regio f; (estate) fundus m, praedium n
land vt in terram exponěre; vi egredi, appellěre
landing place s egress·us -ūs m
landlord s (of inn) caupo m; (of land) dominus m
landmark s lapis, terminus m
landscape s regionis sit·us -ūs m
landslide s terrae laps·us -ūs m
land tax s vectigal n
lane s semita f
language s lingua f; (style or manner of verbal expression) oratio f, sermo m, verba n pl

languid adj languidus; —ly languide
languish vi languěre, languescěre
languishing adj languidus, tabescens
languor s languor m
lanky adj prolixus, exilis
lantern s la(n)terna f
lap s sin·us -ūs m; (fig) gremium n; (in racing) spatium n
lap vt lamběre
lapse s laps·us -ūs m; (error) erratum, peccatum n, error m
lapse vi labi; (of agreement) irritus fieri; (to err) peccare
larceny s furtum n
lard s laridum, lardum n, adeps m & f
large adj magnus, amplus, grandis; to a — extent magna ex parte; —ly plerumque
largess s donativum n, largitio f; to give a — largiri
lark s alauda f
larynx s guttur n
lascivious adj lascivus, salax, libidinosus; —ly lascive, libidinose
lash s verber, flagellum n, scutica f; (mark) vibex m
lash vt (to whip) flagellare; (to fasten) alligare; (fig) castigare
lashing s verberatio f
lass s puella, virgo f
lassitude s lassitudo f
last adj postremus, ultimus; (in line) novissimus; (preceding) proximus; at — demum, tandem; for the — time postremo
last vi durare, perdurare
lasting adj diuturnus, perennis
lastly adv denique, postremo
latch s obex m & f
latch vt oppessulare
late adj serus, tardus; (new) recens; (deceased) demortuus; (said of deceased emperor) divus
late adv sero; too — sero, serius
lately adv modo, recens, nuper
latent adj latens, latitans, occultus
lateral adj lateralis
lather s spuma f
Latin adj Latinus; to speak — Latine loqui; to translate into — Latine redděre; to understand — Latine scire
Latinity s Latinitas f
latitude s latitudo f; (liberty) licentia f
latter adj posterior; the — hic
lattice s cancelli m pl
laudable adj laudabilis
laudably adv laudabiliter
laudatory adj laudativus, honorificus
laugh s ris·us -ūs m
laugh vi ridēre; to — at deridēre; to — with arridēre (with dat)
laughingstock s ludibrium n

laughter s ris·us -ūs m; (loud) cachinnus m, cachinnatio f

launch vt deducĕre; (to hurl) jaculari, contorquĕre; vi **to — forth** or **out** proficisci

laundress s lotrix f

laundry s lavatorium n

laureate adj laureatus

laurel adj laureus

laurel tree s laurus f

lava s liquefacta massa f

lavish adj prodigus; **—ly** prodige

lavish vt prodigĕre, profundĕre

lavishness s prodigalitas, profusio f

law s lex f; (right) jus n; (rule) norma f; (divine) fas n; **to break the — leges** violare; **to pass a — legem** perferre

law-abiding adj bene moratus

law court s judicium n; (building) basilica f

lawful adj legitimus, licitus, fas; **—ly** legitime, lege

lawless adj exlex, illegitimus; **—ly** illegitime, licenter

lawlessness s licentia f

lawn s pratulum n

lawsuit s lis, causa f

lawyer s jurisconsultus, causidicus m

lax adj remissus; (fig) neglegens; **—ly** remisse; neglegens

laxity s remissio f

lay vt ponĕre; (eggs) parĕre; (foundations) jacĕre; (hands) injicĕre; (plans) capĕre, inire; **to — an ambush** insidiari; **to — aside** ponĕre, amovĕre; **to — before** proponĕre; **to — claim to** arrogare, vindicare; **to — down** (office) resignare; (rules) statuĕre; **to — down arms** ab armis discedĕre; **to — hold of** prehendĕre, arripĕre; **to — open** patefacĕre; **to — out** (money) expendĕre; (plans) designare; **to — up** condĕre, reponĕre; **to — waste** vastare

lay s cantilena f

layer s (stratum) corium n; (of a plant) propago f

lazily adv ignave, pigre

laziness s segnities, pigritia f

lazy adv ignavus, piger, iners

lead s plumbum n

lead vt ducĕre; (life) agĕre; **to — about** circumducĕre; **to — away** abducĕre; **to — off** divertĕre; **to — on** conducĕre; vi **to — up to** tendĕre ad (with acc)

leaden adj plumbeus

leader s dux, ductor m; (fig) auctor m

leadership s duct·us -ūs m

leading adj princeps, primus, praecipuus

leaf s folium n; (of vine) pampinus m; (of paper) pagina, scheda f; (of metal) bractea f

leafless adj fronde nudatus

leafy adj frondosus, frondeus

league s foedus n, societas f

leak s rima f, hiat·us -ūs m

leak vi perfluĕre, rimas agĕre

leaky adj rimosus

lean adj macer, macilentus

lean vt inclinare; vi inclinare, niti; **to — back** se reclinare; **to — on** inniti in (with abl), incumbĕre (with dat)

leap s salt·us -ūs m

leap vi salire; **to — for joy** exsultare

leap year s bisextilis annus m

learn vt discĕre, cognoscĕre; (news) accipĕre, audire; **to — by heart** ediscere

learned adj eruditus, doctus; **—ly** docte

learning s (act) discĕre; (knowledge) eruditio f

lease s conductio, locatio f

lease vt conducĕre; **to — out** locare

leash s lorum n

least adj minimus

least adv minime; **at — saltem; not in the — ne** minimum quidem

leather s corium n; (tanned) aluta f

leather adj scorteus

leathery adj lentus

leave vt relinquĕre, deserĕre, destituĕre; (to entrust) mandare, tradĕre; (legacy) legare; **to — behind** relinquere; **to — out** omittĕre, praetermittĕre; vi (to depart) discedĕre, proficisci, abire; **to — off** desinere, desistĕre

leave s permissio f; **— of absence** commeat·us -ūs m; **to ask — veniam** petĕre; **to obtain — impetrare; to take — of** valĕre jubĕre; **with your — pace** tua

leaven s fermentum n

leaven vt fermentare

lecherous adj libidinosus, salax

lecture s lectio, praelectio, acroasis f

lecture vi (to reprove) objurgare; vi praelegere

lecturer s lector, praelector m

ledge s projectura f, limen, dorsum n

ledger s codex (accepti et expensi) m

leech s sanguisuga, hirudo f

leer vi limis oculis spectare

leering adj limus, lascivus

left adj laevus, sinister; **on the — a** sinistra; **to the — ad** sinistram, sinistrorsum

leftover adj reliquus

leftovers s reliquiae f pl

leg s crus n; (of table, etc.) pes m

legacy s legatum n

legal adj legalis, legitimus; judicialis; **—ly** legitime, lege

legalize vt sancire

legate s legatus m

legation s legatio f

legend s fabula f; (inscription) titulus m

legendary adj commenticius, fabulosus

legging s ocrea f

legible adj clarus

legion s legio f

legislate vi leges facĕre

legislation s leges f pl
legislator s legum lator m
legitimate adj legitimus; **—ly** legitime
leisure s otium n; **at —** otiosus, vacuus
leisure adj otiosus, vacuus; **—ly** otiose
leisurely adj lentus
lemon s pomum citreum n
lemonade s aqua limonata f
lend vt commodare; **to — money** pecuniam mutuam dare; (at interest) pecuniam faenerare or faenerari; **to — one's ear** aures praebēre
length s longitudo f; (of time) longinquitas, diuturnitas f; **at — tandem**
lengthen vt extendĕre, protrahĕre, producĕre
lengthwise adv in longitudinem
lengthy adj longus, prolixus
leniency s lenitas, clementia, mansuetudo f
lenient adj lenis, mitis, clemens; **—ly** leniter, clementer
lentil s lens f
leopard s leopardus, pardus m
leper s leprosus m
leprosy s leprae f pl
less adj minor
less adv minus
lessee s conductor m
lessen vt minuĕre; vi decrescĕre, minui
lesson s documentum n; **to give —s** in docēre
lessor s locator m
lest conj ne
let vt (to allow) sinĕre, pati, permittĕre; (to lease) locare; **to — alone** omittĕre; **to — down** (to disappoint) deesse (with dat), destituĕre; **to — fall** a manibus mittĕre; **to — fly** emittĕre, contorquēre; **to — go** (di)mittĕre; **to — in** admittĕre; **to — off** absolvĕre; **to — out** emittĕre; **to — pass** omittĕre; **to — slip** omittĕre
lethargic adj lethargicus
lethargy s lethargus m; (fig) veternus m
letter s (of alphabet) littera f; (epistle) litterae f pl, epistula f; **by — per litteras; to the — ad verbum**
letter carrier s tabellarius m
lettered adj litteratus
lettering s titulus m
lettuce s lactuca f
level adj planus, aequus
level s planities f; (tool) libra, libella f
level vt aequare, adaequare; (to the ground) solo aequare, sternĕre
lever s vectis m
levity s levitas f
levy s delect·us -ūs m
levy vt (troops) conscribĕre; (tax) exigĕre
lewd adj impudicus, incestus
lewdness s impudicitia f

liable adj obnoxius
liar s mendax m & f
libation s libatio f; **to pour a — libare**
libel s calumnia f
libel vt calumniari
libelous adj famosus, probrosus
liberal adj liberalis, munificus; (fig) ingenuus; **—ly** liberaliter
liberality s liberalitas, munificentia f
liberate vt liberare; (slave) manumittĕre
liberation s liberatio f
liberator s liberator m
libertine s homo dissolutus m
liberty s libertas f; licentia f; **at — liber**
librarian s librarius m
library s bibliotheca f
license s (permission) copia, potestas f; (freedom) licentia f
license vt potestatem dare (with dat)
licentious adj dissolutus, impudicus; **—ly** dissolute, impudice
lick vt lambĕre; (daintily) liqurrire
lictor s lictor m
lid s operculum, operimentum n
lie s mendacium n; **to give the — to** redarguĕre; **to tell a — mentiri**
lie vi (to tell a lie or lies) mentiri; (to be lying down) jacēre, cubare; (to be situated) situs esse; **to — down** jacēre; **to — in wait** insidiari; **to — on** or **upon** incubare (with dat), incumbĕre (with dat)
lieu s **in — of** loco (with genit), pro (with abl)
lieutenant s legatus, praefectus m
life s vita, anima f; (fig) vigor m, alacritas f
lifeblood s sanguis m
life history s vita f
lifeless adj inanimus, exanimis; (fig) exsanguis, frigidus; **—ly** (fig) frigide
lifetime s aetas f
lift vt tollĕre, attollĕre, sublevare; **to — up** attollĕre, efferre
ligament s ligamentum, ligamen n
ligature s ligatura f
light s lux f, lumen n; (lamp) lucerna f; **to bring — in** lucem proferre; **to throw — on** lumen adhibēre (with dat)
light adj (bright) lucidus, fulgens; (in weight) levis; (of colors) candidus, dilutus; (easy) facilis; (nimble) agilis; **—ly** leviter
light vt accendĕre, incendĕre; (to illuminate) illuminare; vi flammam concipĕre; **to — on** or **upon** incidĕre (with dat), offendĕre; **to — up** (fig) hilaris fieri
lighten vt (to illumine) illustrare; (weight) allevare, exonerare; vi (in sky) fulgurare
lighthouse s pharus f
lightness s levitas, agilitas f
lightning s fulmen, fulgur n; **struck by — fulmine ictus, de caelo tactus**

like *adj* similis (*with dat*); (*equal*) par (*with dat*), aequus (*with dat*)

like *prep* instar (*with genit*); tamquam, ut, velut

like *vt* amare, diligĕre; **I — this** hoc mihi placet; **I — to do this** me juvat hoc facĕre

likelihood *s* verisimilitudo *f*

likely *adj* verisimilis, probabilis

likely *adv* probabiliter

liken *vt* comparare

likeness *s* similitudo *f*; (*portrait*) imago, effigies *f*

likewise *adv* pariter, similiter, item

liking *s* amor *m*; (*fancy*) libido *f*

lilac *s* syringa vulgaris *f*

lily *s* lilium *n*

lily of the valley *s* convallaria majalis *f*

limb *s* art·us -ūs *m*, membrum *n*

limber *adj* flexilis

lime *s* calx *f*

limestone *s* calx *f*

lime tree *s* tilia *f*

limit *s* finis, terminus, modus *m*

limit *vt* terminare, finire, definire; (*to restrict*) circumscribĕre

limitation *s* determinatio *f*; (*exception*) exceptio *f*

limp *s* claudicatio *f*

limp *vi* claudicare

limp *adj* flaccidus, languidus

limpid *adj* limpidus

linden tree *s* tilia *f*

line *s* (*drawn*) linea *f*; (*row*) series *f*, ordo *m*; (*lineage*) stirps *f*, genus *n*; (*mil*) acies *f*; (*of poetry*) vers·us -ūs *m*; (*cord*) funis *m*

line *vt* (*streets*) saepire

lineage *s* stirps *f*, genus *n*

lineal *adj* linearis; **—ly** rectā lineā

lineament *s* lineamentum *n*

linear *adj* linearis

linen *adj* linteus, lineus

linen *s* linteum, linum *n*

linger *vi* morari, cunctari, cessare

lingering *adj* cunctabundus, tardus; **—ly** cunctanter

lingering *s* cunctatio *f*

linguist *s* linguarum peritus *m*

liniment *s* unguentum *n*, linit·us -ūs *m*

link *s* (*of chain*) anulus *m*; (*bond*) vinculum *m*, nex·us -ūs *m*

link *vt* connectĕre, conjungĕre

linseed *s* lini semen *n*

lint *s* linamentum *n*

lintel *s* limen superum *n*

lion *s* leo *m*

lioness *s* lea, leaena *f*

lip *s* labrum *n*; (*edge*) ora *f*

liquefy *vt* liquefacĕre

liquid *adj* liquidus

liquid *s* liquidum *n*, liquor *m*; **to become —** liquescĕre

liquidate *vt* solvĕre, persolvĕre

liquor *s* liquor *m*

lisp *vi* balbutire

lisping *adj* blaesus

list *s* index *m*, tabula *f*; (*of ship*) inclinatio *f*

list *vt* enumerare; *vi* inclinare

listen *vi* auscultare, audire; **to — to** auscultare, audire

listless *adj* remissus, languidus; **—ly** languide

litany *s* litania *f*

literal *adj* litteralis; **—ly** ad litteram, ad verbum

literary *adj* (*person*) litteratus; **— style** scribendi genus *n*

literature *s* litterae *f pl*

litigant *s* litigator *m*

litigate *vi* litigare

litigation *s* lis *f*

litter *s* (*vehicle*) lectica *f*; (*of straw, etc.*) stramentum *n*; (*brood*) fet·us -ūs, part·us -ūs *m*

litter *vt* sternĕre

little *adj* parvus, exiguus

little *adv* parum, paulum; **a — paulum, aliquantulum; — by — paulatim**

little *s* paulum, aliquantulum *n*

live *vi* vivĕre, vitam agĕre; (*to reside*) habitare; **to — on** vesci (*with abl*)

live *adj* vivus; (*of colors*) vegetus

livelihood *s* vict·us -ūs *m*

lively *adj* vivus, vividus, alacer; (*of colors*) vegetus

liver *s* jecur *n*

livid *adj* lividus; **to be — livēre**

living *adj* vivus, vivens

living *s* (*livelihood, food*) vict·us -ūs *m*

lizard *s* lacerta *f*

load *s* onus *n*

load *vt* onerare

loaf *s* panis *m*

loaf *vi* grassari

loafer *s* grassator *m*

loam *s* lutum *n*

loan *s* mutuum *n*, pecunia mutua *f*

loathe *vt* fastidire

loathing *s* fastidium *n*

loathsome *adj* foedus, taeter

lobby *s* vestibulum *n*

lobe *s* lobus *m*

lobster *s* astacus *m*

local *adj* indigena; loci (*genit*), regionis (*genit*)

locality *s* locus *m*, natura loci *f*

lock *s* (*of hair*) cinnus, floccus *m*; (*of door*) sera *f*

lock *vt* obserare, oppessulare; **to — in** includĕre; **to — out** exludĕre; **to — up** concludĕre

locker *s* loculamentum, armarium *n*

lockjaw *s* tetanus *m*

locust *s* locusta *f*

lodge *s* casa *f*

lodge *vt* (*complaint*) deferre; *vi* (*to stay*) deversari; (*to stick*) inhaerēre

lodger *s* inquilinus *m*

lodging *s* hospitium, deversorium *n*

loft *s* tabulatum, cenaculum *n*

lofty *adj* (*ex*)celsus, sublimis; (*fig*) sublimis, superbus

log *s* tignum *n*, stipes *m*

logic *s* dialectica *n pl*

logical *adj* logicus, dialecticus; **—ly** dialectice, ex ratione

loin *s* lumbus *m*

loiter *vi* cessare, cunctari, grassari

loiterer *s* cessator, grassator *m*

loll *vi* recumběre
lone *adj* solus
loneliness *s* solitudo *f*
lonely *adj* solitarius; desolatus
long *adj* longus; (*of time*) diuturnus; (*lengthened*) productus
long *adv* diu; — **after** multo post; — **ago** jamdudum, jampridem; — **before** multo ante
long *vi* avēre; **to** — **for** desiderare
longevity *s* longaevitas *f*
longing *s* desiderium *n*
longing *adj* avidus; —**ly** avide
longitude *s* longitudo *f*
long-lived *adj* vivax
long-suffering *adj* patiens
long-winded *adj* longus
look *s* aspect·us -ūs, vult·us -ūs *m*; (*appearance*) facies, species *f*
look *vi* vidēre; (*to seem*) vidēri; **to** — **about** circumspicere; **to** — **after** curare; **to** — **around** circumspicēre, respicēre; **to** — **at** intuēri, aspicēre; **to** — **back** respicēre; **to** — **for** quaerěre; **to** — **forward to** exspectare; **to** — **into** inspicēre, introspicěre; (*to examine*) perscrutari; **to** — **on** intuēri; **to** — **out** prospicěre; **to** — **out for** quaerěre; **to** — **towards** spectare; **to** — **up** suspicěre; **to** — **upon** habēre, aestimare
loom *s* tela *f*
loom *vi* in conspectum prodire
loop *s* sin·us -ūs *m*
loophole *s* fenestra *f*; (*fig*) effugium *n*
loose *adj* laxus, solutus, remissus; (*morally*) dissolutus; —**ly** laxe; dissolute
loosen *vt* solvěre, laxare; *vi* solvi
loquacious *adj* loquax, garrulus
lord *s* dominus *m*
Lord *s* Dominus *m*
lord *vi* **to** — **it over** dominari in (*with acc*)
lordly *adj* imperiosus
lordship *s* dominatio *f*, imperium *n*
lore *s* doctrina *f*
lose *vt* amittěre, perděre; **to** — **one's way** aberrare
loss *s* (*act*) amissio *f*; damnum, detrimentum *n*; (*mil*) repulsa *f*
lost *adj* perditus; **to be** — perire
lot *s* pars, portio, sors *f*; **casting of** —**s** sortitio *f*, sortit·us -ūs *m*; **to draw** —**s for** sortiri
lotion *s* lotio *f*
lottery *s* sortitio *f*
loud *adj* magnus; —**ly** magnā voce
lounge *vi* cessare, otiari
lounge *s* lectulus *m*
louse *s* pediculus *m*
lousy *adj* pediculosus; (*fig*) vilis
lout *s* rusticus *m*
loutish *adj* agrestis, rusticus
love *s* amor *m*; **to fall in** — amare, adamare
love *vt* amare, diligěre
love affair *s* amores *m pl*
lovely *adj* venustus, amabilis
love potion *s* philtrum *n*
lover *s* amator, amans *m*

lovesick *adj* amore aeger
loving *adj* amans; —**ly** amanter
low *adj* humilis; (*of price*) vilis; (*of birth*) obscurus; (*of voice*) summissus; (*vile*) turpis; (*downcast*) abjectus
low *adv* humiliter; summissā voce
low *vi* mugire
lowborn *adj* obscurus, degener
lower *vt* demittěre, depriměre; (*price*) imminuěre; *vi* (*of sky*) obscurari
lower *adj* inferior; **of the** — **world** infernus; **the** — **world** inferi *m pl*
lowermost *adj* infimus
lowing *s* mugit·us -ūs *m*
lowlands *s* loca plana, campestria *n pl*, campi *m pl*
lowly *adj* humilis, obscurus
loyal *adj* fidelis, fidus; —**ly** fideliter
loyalty *s* fidelitas, fides *f*
lubricate *vt* unguěre
lucid *adj* lucidus, clarus, perspicuus; (*transparent*) pellucidus
Lucifer *s* Lucifer *m*
luck *s* fortuna *f*; **bad** — fortuna *f*, infortunium *n*; **good** — fortuna *f*, felicitas *f*
luckily *adv* feliciter, fauste
luckless *adj* infelix
lucky *adj* felix, faustus
lucrative *adj* quaestuosus
lucre *s* lucrum *n*, quaest·us -ūs *m*
ludicrous *adj* ridiculus; —**ly** ridicule
luggage *s* sarcinae *f pl*, impedimenta *n pl*
lukewarm *adj* tepidus; (*fig*) segnis, frigidus; —**ly** (*fig*) segniter
lull *s* quies, intermissio *f*
lull *vt* sopire; (*to calm, as a storm*) sedare; (*fig*) demulcēre
lumber *s* scruta *n pl*
luminary *s* lumen *n*
luminous *adj* lucidus, illustris; (*fig*) dilucidus
lump *s* glaeba, massa, congeries *f*; (*on body*) tuber *n*
lump *vt* **to** — **together** coacervare
lumpy *adj* glaebosus, crassus
lunacy *s* alienatio mentis *f*
lunar *adj* lunaris
lunatic *s* insanus *m*
lunch *s* merenda *f*, prandium *n*
lunch *vi* prandēre
luncheon *s* prandium *n*
lung *s* pulmo *m*
lunge *s* ict·us -ūs *m*, plaga *f*
lunge *vi* prosilire
lurch *s* impedimentum *n*; **to leave in the** — deserěre, destituěre
lurch *vi* titubare
lure *s* illecebra, esca *f*
lure *vt* illicěre, inescare
lurk *vi* latēre, latitare
luscious *adj* suavis, praedulcis
lush *adj* luxuriosus
lust *s* libido *f*
lust *vi* concupiscěre
luster *s* splendor, nitor *m*
lustful *adj* libidinosus, salax; —**ly** libidinose, lascive

lustily *adv* valide, strenue
lusty *adj* validus, robustus
lute *s* cithara *f*, fides *f pl*
luxuriance *s* luxuries, ubertas *f*
luxuriant *adj* luxuriosus; (*fig*) luxurians
luxuriate *vi* luxuriare, luxuriari
luxurious *adj* sumptuosus, lautus; —ly sumptuose, laute

luxury *s* luxuria *f*, lux·us -ūs *m*
lye *s* lixivia *f*
lying *adj* mendax, fallax
lying *s* mendacium *n*
lymph *s* lympha *f*
lynx *s* lynx *m* & *f*
lyre *s* lyra *f*, fides *f pl*, barbitos *m*
lyric *adj* lyricus
lyric *s* carmen *n*

M

macaroni *s* collyra *f*
mace *s* fasces *m pl*
mace bearer *s* lictor *m*
macerate *vt* macerare
machination *s* dolus *m*
machine *s* machina *f*
machinery *s* machinamentum *n*, machinatio *f*
mackerel *s* scomber *m*
mad *adj* insanus, vesanus, demens, furiosus; **to be** — furěre, insanire; —ly insane, dementer
madam *s* domina *f*
madden *vt* mentem alienare (*with dat*); (*fig*) furiare
maddening *adj* furiosus
madman *s* homo furiosus *m*, demens *m*
madness *s* insania, dementia *f*, furor *m*
magazine *s* (*journal*) ephemeris *f*; (*storehouse*) horreum, armamentarium *n*
maggot *s* vermis, vermiculus *m*
magic *adj* magicus
magic *s* ars magica *f*
magically *adv* velut magica quadam arte
magician *s* magus *m*
magisterial *adj* ad magistratum pertinens
magistracy *s* magistrat·us -ūs *m*
magistrate *s* magistrat·us -ūs *m*
magnanimity *s* magnanimitas *f*
magnanimous *adj* magnanimus
magnet *s* magnes *m*
magnetic *adj* magneticus
magnetism *s* vis magnetica *f*
magnetize *vt* magnetica vi afficěre
magnificence *s* magnificentia *f*, splendor *m*
magnificent *adj* magnificus, splendidus; —ly magnifice, splendide
magnify *vt* amplificare, exaggerare
magnitude *s* magnitudo *f*
maid *s* ancilla *f*
maiden *s* virgo, puella *f*
maidenhood *s* virginitas *f*
maidenly *adj* puellaris, virginalis
mail *s* (*letters*) epistulae *f pl*; (*armor*) lorica *f*
maim *vt* mutilare
maimed *adj* mancus
main *adj* primus, praecipuus, princeps; — **point** caput *n*; —ly praecipue, maxime
main *s* (*sea*) altum *n*, pelagus *m*

mainland *s* continens *f*
maintain *vt* (*to keep*) tenēre; (*to keep alive*) nutrire, alěre, sustentare; (*to defend*) tuēri, sustinēre; (*to argue*) affirmare
maintenance *s* (*support*) defensio, sustentatio *f*; (*means of living*) vict·us -ūs *m*, alimentum *n*
majestic *adj* augustus, imperatorius; —ally auguste
majesty *s* majestas, dignitas *f*
major *adj* major
major *s* (*mil*) tribunus militum *m*; (*in logic*) major praemissa *f*
majority *s* major pars *f*
make *vt* facěre; (*to form*) fingěre; (*to render*) redděre, facěre; (*to appoint*) creare, facěre, instituěre; **to** — **amends** corrigěre; **to** — **good** resarcire, reparare; **to** — **haste** accelerare, festinare; **to** — **much of** magni facěre; **to** — **over** transferre; **to** — **ready** praeparare; **to** — **up** (*story*) fingěre; (*to compensate*) resarcire; (*one's mind*) decerněre; **to** — **way** ceděre; *vi* **to** — **away with** tollěre, amověre; **to** — **for** petěre
make *s* forma, figura, formatio *f*
maker *s* fabricator *m*; auctor *m*
maladministration *s* administratio mala *f*
malady *s* morbus *m*
male *adj* mas, masculinus
male *s* mas, masculus *m*
malediction *s* dirae *f pl*, exsecratio *f*
malefactor *s* homo maleficus, reus *m*
malevolence *s* malevolentia *f*
malevolent *adj* malevolus
malice *s* malevolentia, invidia *f*
malicious *adj* malevolus, invidiosus, malignus; —ly malevolo animo
malign *vt* obtrectare, vexare
malign *adj* malignus, invidiosus
malignant *adj* malevolus
malleable *adj* ductilis
mallet *s* malleus *m*
malpractice *s* delicta *n pl*
maltreat *vt* vexare, mulcare
man *s* (*human being*) homo *m*; (*male human being*) vir *m*
man *vt* (*ship*) complēre; (*walls*) praesidio firmare
manacle *s* manica *f*, compes *m*
manacle *vt* manicas injicěre (*with dat*)
manage *vt* administrare, curare

manageable *adj* tractabilis
management *s* administratio, cura *f*
manager *s* curator *m*; *(steward)* pro-curator *m*; *(of estate)* villicus *m*
mandate *s* mandatum *n*
mandrake *s* mandragora *f*
mane *s* juba *f*
maneuver *s (mil)* decurs·us -ūs *m*, decursio *f*; *(trick)* dolus *m*, artificium *n*
maneuver *vi (mil)* decurrĕre; *(fig)* machinari
mange *s* scabies *f*
manger *s* praesepe *n*
mangle *vt* lacerare, laniare
mangy *adj* scaber
manhood *s* pubertas *f*; virilitas, fortitudo *f*
mania *s* insania *f*
maniac *s* furiosus *m*
manifest *adj* manifestus, apertus; —ly manifeste, aperte
manifest *vt* declarare, ostendĕre, aperire
manifestation *s* patefactio *f*
manifesto *s* edictum *n*
manifold *adj* multiplex, varius
manipulate *vt* tractare
manipulation *s* tractatio *f*
mankind *s* genus humanum *n*
manliness *s* virtus, fortitudo *f*
manly *adj* virilis
manner *s* modus *m*, ratio *f*; *(custom)* consuetudo *f*, mos *m*; **after the —** of ritu *(with genit)*, more *(with genit)*; **bad —s** rusticitas *f*; **good —s** urbanitas *f*
mannerism *s* affectatio *f*
mannerly *adj* urbanus
mannikin *s* homunculus, homuncio *m*
man-of-war *s* navis longa *f*
manor *s* praedium *n*, fundus *m*
man servant *s* servus, famulus *m*
mansion *s* dom·us -ūs, sedes *f*
manslaughter *s* homicidium *n*
mantle *s* penula, palla *f*
mantle *vt* celare, tegĕre, dissimulare
manual *adj* manualis
manual *s* enchiridion *n*
manufacture *s* fabrica *f*
manufacture *vt* fabricari, fabrefacĕre
manufacturer *s* fabricator, opifex *m*
manure *s* stercus *n*, fimus *m*
manure *vt* stercorare
manuscript *s* codex, liber *m*
many *adj* multi, plerique, complures; **a good —** nonnulli; **as — . . . as** quot . . . tot; **how — quot**; **— ways** multifariam; **so —** tot
many-colored *adj* multicolor
map *s* tabula geographica *f*
map *vt* **to — out** designare, describĕre
maple *adj* acernus
maple tree *s* acer *n*
mar *vt* foedare, vitiare, corrumpĕre
marauder *s* praedator, latro *m*
marauding *s* praedatio *f*, latrocinium *n*
marble *adj* marmoreus

marble *s* marmor *n*
March *s* (mensis) Martius *m*
march *s* iter *n*
march *vt* ducĕre; *vi* iter facĕre, incedĕre, gradi; **to — on** signa proferre; **to — on a town** oppidum aggredi
mare *s* equa *f*
margin *s* margo *m* & *f*
marginal *adj* margini ascriptus
marigold *s* caltha *f*
marine *adj* marinus
marine *s* miles classicus, miles classiarius *m*
mariner *s* nauta *m*
maritime *adj* maritimus
mark *s* nota *f*, signum *n*; *(brand)* stigma *n*; *(impression)* vestigium *n*; *(target)* scopus *m*; *(of wound)* cicatrix *f*; *(fig)* indicium *n*
mark *vt* notare, signare; *(to observe)* animadvertĕre; *(with pencil, etc.)* designare; **to — out** metari
marker *s* index *m*
market *s* macellum *n*, mercat·us -ūs *m*
marketable *adj* venalis
market day *s* nundinae *f pl*
marketing *s* emptio *f*
market place *s* forum *n*
market town *s* emporium *n*
marksman *s* jaculandi peritus *m*
marmalade *s* quilon ex aurantiis confectum *n*
marquee *s* tabernaculum *n*
marriage *s* matrimonium *n*, nuptiae *f pl*
marriageable *adj* nubilis
marriage contract *s* pactio nuptialis *f*
married *adj (of woman)* nupta; *(of man)* maritus
marrow *s* medulla *f*
marry *vt (said of man)* in matrimonium ducĕre, uxorem ducĕre *(with acc)*; *(said of woman)* nubĕre *(with dat)*; **to get married** matrimonio *or* nuptiis conjungi
marsh *s* palus *f*
marshal *s* dux, imperator *m*
marshal *vt* disponĕre
marshy *adj* paluster
mart *s* forum, emporium *n*
martial *adj* bellicosus, ferox, militaris
martyr *s* martyr *m* & *f*
martyrdom *s* martyrium *n*
marvel *s* res mira *f*, mirum *n*
marvel *vi* **to — at** mirari, admirari
marvelous *adj* mirus, mirabilis; —ly mire
masculine *adj* masculus, virilis; *(gram)* masculinus
mash *s* mixtura *f*; *(for cattle)* farrago *f*
mash *vt* commiscĕre; *(to bruise)* contundĕre
mask *s* persona, larva *f*; *(fig)* praetext·us -ūs *m*
mask *vt (fig)* dissimulare
mason *s* lapicida, caementarius *m*
masonry *s* opus caementicium *n*

mass *s* moles *f*; (*of people*) turba *f*; (*eccl*) missa *f*; the —es vulgus *n*

mass *vt* congerĕre, coacervare

massacre *s* caedes, trucidatio *f*

massacre *vt* trucidare

massive *adj* solidus, ingens

mast *s* (*of ship*) malus *m*; (*for cattle*) glans *f*, balanus *m*

master *s* dominus, herus *m*; (*teacher*) magister, praeceptor *m*; (*controller*) arbiter *m*; **to be — of** potens esse (*with genit*), compos esse (*with genit*); **not to be — of** impotens esse (*with genit*)

master *vt* superare, vincĕre; (*to learn*) perdiscĕre; (*passion*) continēre

masterly *adj* (*artist*) artificiosus; imperiosus

masterpiece *s* magnum opus *n*

mastery *s* dominatio *f*, imperium, arbitrium *n*

masticate *vt* mandĕre

mastiff *s* Molossus *m*

mat *s* teges, storea, matta *f*

match *s* (*marriage*) nuptiae *f pl*; (*contest*) certamen *n*; (*an equal*) par, compar *m & f*; **a — for** par (*with dat*); **not a — for** impar (*with dat*)

match *vt* adaequare, exaequare; *vi* quadrare

matchless *adj* incomparabilis

mate *s* socius, collega *m*; conju(n)x *m & f*

mate *vi* conjungi

material *adj* corporeus; (*significant*) haud levis, magni momenti; **—ly** magnopere

material *s* materia, materies *f*

maternal *adj* maternus

maternity *s* conditio matris *f*

mathematical *adj* mathematicus

mathematician *s* mathematicus *m*

mathematics *s* mathematica *f*, numeri *m pl*

matricide *s* (*murder*) matricidium *n*; (*murderer*) matricida *m & f*

matrimony *s* matrimonium *n*

matrix *s* forma *f*

matron *s* matrona *f*

matronly *adj* matronalis

matter *s* (*substance*) materia *f*; (*affair*) res *f*, negotium *n*; pus *n*; **no — nihil** interest

matter *v impers* **it does not — nihil** interest, nihil refert

matting *s* tegetes *f pl*

mattress *s* culcita *f*

mature *adj* maturus, adultus; **—ly** mature

mature *vi* maturescĕre

maturity *s* maturitas, aetas matura *f*

maudlin *adj* flebilis

maul *vt* mulcare, delaniare

mausoleum *s* mausoleum *n*

maw *s* ingluvies *f*

mawkish *adj* putidus; **—ly** putide

maxim *s* axioma, praeceptum *n*, sententia *f*

maximum *adj* quam maximus, quam plurimus

May *s* (*mensis*) Maius *m*

may *vi* posse; **I — licet** mihi

maybe *adv* forsitan

mayor *s* praefectus urbi *m*

maze *s* labyrinthus *m*

me *pron* me; **by — a** me; **to — mihi**; **with — mecum**

mead *s* (*drink*) mulsum *n*

meadow *s* pratum *n*

meager *adj* macer, exilis, jejunus; **—ly** exiliter, jejune

meagerness *s* macies *f*; (*of soil*) exilitas *f*; exigua copia *f*

meal *s* farina *f*; (*food*) cibus *m*; (*dinner*) epulae *f pl*

mean *adj* (*middle*) medius; (*low*) humilis; (*cruel*) crudelis, vilis

mean *s* medium *n*, mediocritas *f*

mean *vt* dicĕre, significare; (*to intend*) velle, cogitare, in animo habēre; (*to refer to*) significare, intellegĕre

meander *vi* sinuoso cursu labi

meaning *s* significatio, vis *f*, sens·us -ūs *m*

meanness *s* humilitas *f*; (*cruelty*) crudelitas *f*

means *s* (*way, method*) ratio, via *f*, consilium *n*; (*wealth*) opes *f pl*; **by all — maxime, omnino; by — of** render by *abl* or per (*with acc*); **by no — nullo** modo, haudquaquam

meanwhile *adv* interea, interim

measles *s* morbilli *m pl*

measurable *adj* mensurabilis

measure *s* mensura *f*, modus *m*; (*course of action*) ratio *f*, consilium *n*; (*law*) rogatio, lex *f*; **in some — aliqua** ex parte

measure *vt* metiri; (*land*) metari; **to — out** admetiri, dimetiri

measurement *s* mensura *f*

meat *s* caro *f*; (*food*) cibus *m*

mechanic *s* opifex, faber *m*

mechanical *adj* mechanicus, machinalis; **—ly** mechanica quadam arte

mechanics *s* mechanica ars, machinalis scientia *f*

mechanism *s* machinatio *f*

medal *s* insigne *n*

medallion *s* numisma sollemne *n*

meddle *vi* se interponĕre

meddler *s* ardelio *m*

mediate *vi* intercedĕre

mediation *s* intercessio *f*

mediator *s* intercessor, conciliator *m*

medical *adj* medicus, medicinalis

medicate *vt* medicare

medicinal *adj* medicus, salutaris

medicine *s* (*science*) medicina *f*; (*remedy*) medicamentum *n*

medieval *adj* medii aevi (*genit, used as adj*)

mediocre *adj* mediocris

mediocrity *s* mediocritas *f*

meditate *vi* meditari, cogitare

meditation *s* meditatio, cogitatio *f*

meditative *adj* cogitabundus

Mediterranean *s* mare internum *or* medium, mare nostrum *n*

medium *s* (*middle*) medium *n*; (*expedient*) modus *m*, ratio *f*; (*agency*) conciliator *m*

medium *adj* mediocris
medley *s* farrago *f*
meek *adj* mitis, demissus; —**ly** summisse
meekness *s* animus demissus *m*
meet *adj* aptus, idoneus; **it is** — convenit
meet *vt* obviam ire (*with dat*), occurrēre (*with dat*); (*fig*) obire; *vi* convenire; **to** — **with** offendēre, excipēre
meeting *s* congressio *f*; (*assembly*) convent·us -ūs *m*
melancholy *s* tristitia, maestitia *f*
melancholy *adj* tristis, maestus
mellow *adj* maturus, mitis; (*from drinking*) temulentus
mellow *vt* maturare, coquēre; *vi* maturescēre
melodious *adj* canorus; —**ly** canore, modulate
melody *s* melos *n*, modus *m*
melt *vt* liquefacēre, dissolvēre; *vi* liquescēre, tabescēre
member *s* membrum *n*; (*fig*) sodalis *m*
membrane *s* membrana *f*
memento *s* monumentum *n*
memoirs *s* commentarii *m pl*
memorable *adj* memorabilis, memoriā dignus
memorandum *s* nota *f*
memorial *s* monumentum *n*
memory *s* memoria *f*; **from** — **ex** memoria, memoriter; **in the** — **of man** post hominum memoriam; **to commit to** — ediscēre, memoriae mandare
menace *s* minae *f pl*
menace *vt* minari, minitari; (*of things*) imminēre (*with dat*)
menacing *adj* minax; (*only of persons*) minitabundus
mend *vt* emendare, corrigēre, restaurare, reparare; (*clothes*) sarcire; *vi* melior fieri
mendicant *s* mendicus *m*, mendica *f*
menial *adj* servilis, sordidus
menial *s* servus, famulus *m*
mental *adj* mente conceptus; —**ly** mente
mention *s* mentio, commemoratio *f*; **to make** — **of** mentionem facēre (*with genit*)
mention *vt* commemorare, nominare; **to not** — silentio praeterire
mercantile *adj* mercatorius
mercenary *adj* mercenarius, venalis
mercenary *s* miles mercenarius *m*
merchandise *s* merces *f pl*
merchant *s* mercator, negotiator *m*
merciful *adj* misericors, clemens; —**ly** misericorditer, clementer
merciless *adj* immisericors, inclemens; —**ly** duriter, inhumane
mercurial *adj* vividus, acer, levis
Mercury *s* Mercurius *m*
mercury *s* argentum vivum *n*
mercy *s* misericordia *f*
mere *adj* merus; —**ly** tantummodo, solum, modo
meretricious *adj* meretricius, fucatus

merge *vt* confundēre; *vi* confundi
meridian *s* meridianus circulus *m*; meridies *m*
merit *s* meritum *n*
merit *vt* merēre, merēri
meritorious *adj* laudabilis
mermaid *s* nympha *f*
merrily *adv* hilare, festive
merry *adj* hilaris, festivus
mesh *s* (*of net*) macula *f*
mess *s* (*dirt*) squalor *m*; (*confusion*) turba, rerum perturbatio *f*
messenger *s* nuntius *m*
metal *adj* metallicus, ferreus, aereus
metal *s* metallum *n*
metallurgy *s* metallurgia, scientia metallorum *f*
metamorphosis *s* transfiguratio *f*
metaphor *s* translatio *f*
metaphorical *adj* translatus; —**ly** per translationem
mete *vt* metiri
meteor *s* fax caelestis *f*
meteorology *s* prognostica *n pl*
meter *s* metrum *n*, numerus *m*
method *s* ratio *f*, modus *m*
methodical *adj* dispositus; (*person*) diligens; —**ly** ratione et viā
meticulous *adj* accuratus; —**ly** accurate
metonymy *s* immutatio *f*
metrical *adj* metricus, numerosus
metropolis *s* caput *n*
mettle *s* animus *m*, virtus, magnanimitas *f*
miasma *s* halit·us -ūs *m*
microscope *s* microscopium *n*
mid *adj* medius
midday *adj* meridianus
midday *s* meridies *m*, meridianum tempus *n*
middle *adj* medius
middle *s* medium *n*; **in the** — **of the road** in media via
midget *s* pumilio *m & f*
midnight *s* media nox *f*
midriff *s* diaphragma *n*, praecordia *n pl*
midst *s* medium *n*; **in the** — **of** inter (*with acc*)
midsummer *s* summa aestas *f*
midway *adv* medius; **he stood** — **between the lines** stabat medius inter acies
midwife *s* obstetrix *f*
midwinter *s* bruma *f*
midwinter *adj* brumalis
mien *s* vult·us -ūs *m*
might *s* vis, potestas, potentia *f*; **with all one's** — summa ope
might *vi* render by imperfect subjunctive
mightily *adv* valde, magnopere
mighty *adj* potens, validus
migrate *vi* migrare, abire
migration *s* peregrinatio *f*
migratory *adj* advena, migrans
mild *adj* mitis, lenis; (*person*) placidus, clemens; —**ly** leniter, clementer
mildew *s* robigo *f*, mucor, sit·us -ūs *m*
mildness *s* clementia, lenitas, mansuetudo *f*

mile *s* mille passuum, milliare *n*
milestone *s* milliarium *n*
militant *adj* ferox
military *adj* militaris
militia *s* milites *m pl*
milk *s* lac *n*
milk *vt* mulgēre
milky *adj* lacteus
Milky Way *s* orbis lacteus *m*, via lactea *f*
mill *s* mola *f*, pistrinum *n*
millennium *s* mille anni *m pl*
miller *s* molitor, pistor *m*
million *adj* decies centena milia (*with genit*)
millionaire *s* homo praedives *m*
millionth *s* pars una ex decies centenis milibus partium *f*
millstone *s* mola *f*
mime *s* mimus *m*
mimic *s* mimus *m*
mimic *vt* imitari
mimicry *s* imitatio *f*
mince *vt* concidēre; **not to — words** plane aperteque loqui
mind *s* mens *f*, animus *m*, ingenium *n*; (*opinion*) sens·us -ūs *m*, sententia *f*; **to call to —** recordari; **to make up one's —** animum inducēre, statuēre, constituēre; **to show presence of —** praesenti animo uti
mind *vt* (*to look after*) curare; (*to regard*) respicēre; (*to object to*) aegre ferre; **to — one's own business** suum negotium agēre
mindful *adj* attentus, diligens; memor
mine *s* fodina *f*, metallum *n*; (*mil*) cuniculus *m*; (*fig*) thesaurus *m*
mine *vt* effodēre
mine *pron* meus
miner *s* (*of metals*) metallicus *m*; fossor *m*
mineral *s* metallum *n*
mineral *adj* metallicus, fossilis
mineralogist *s* metallorum peritus *m*
mineralogy *s* metallorum scientia *f*
mingle *vt* commiscēre, confundēre; *vi* commiscēri, se immiscēre
miniature *s* pictura minuta *f*
minimum *adj* quam minimus
minimum *s* minimum *n*
minion *s* cliens *m & f*
minister *s* minister, administer *m*
minister *vi* ministrare, servire
ministry *s* ministratio *f*, munus, officium *n*
minor *s* pupillus *m*, pupilla *f*
minor *adj* minor
minority *s* minor pars *f*
minstrel *s* fidicen *m*
mint *s* (*plant*) mentha *f*; (*for making money*) moneta *f*
mint *vt* cudēre
minute *s* temporis momentum *n*
minute *adj* (*small*) minutus, exiguus, pusillus; (*exact*) accuratus, subtilis; **—ly** accurate, subtiliter
minx *s* puella procax *f*
miracle *s* miraculum, monstrum *n*
miraculous *adj* miraculosus; **—ly** divinitus

mirage *s* falsa species *f*
mire *s* lutum *n*
mirror *s* speculum *n*
mirth *s* hilaritas, laetitia *f*
mirthful *adj* hilaris
misadventure *s* infortunium *n*
misalliance *s* matrimonium impar *n*
misapply *vt* abuti (*with abl*)
misapprehend *vt* male intellegēre
misapprehension *s* falsa conceptio *f*
misbehave *vi* indecore se gerēre
misbehavior *s* morum pravitas *f*
misbelief *s* fides prava *f*
miscalculate *vi* errare
miscalculation *s* error *m*
miscarriage *s* abort·us -ūs *m*; (*fig*) malus success·us -ūs *m*
miscarry *vi* abortum facēre; (*fig*) male succedēre
miscellaneous *adj* promiscuus
miscellany *s* conjectanea, miscellanea *n pl*
mischance *s* infortunium *n*
mischief *s* incommodum, maleficium *n*; (*of children*) lascivia *f*
mischievous *adj* maleficus, noxius; (*playful*) lascivus
misconceive *vt* male intellegēre
misconception *s* falsa conceptio, falsa opinio *f*
misconduct *s* delictum, peccatum *n*
misconstruction *s* sinistra interpretatio *f*
misconstrue *vt* male interpretari; perverse interpretari
misdeed *s* delictum, peccatum *n*
misdemeanor *s* levius delictum *n*
misdirect *vt* fallēre
miser *s* avarus, sordidus *m*
miserable *adj* miser, infelix, aerumnosus
miserably *adv* misere
miserly *adj* avarus, sordidus
misery *s* miseria, aerumna *f*
misfortune *s* infortunium, incommodum *n*
misgiving *s* sollicitudo *f*
misgovern *vt* male regēre
misguide *vt* seducēre, fallēre
misguided *adj* (*fig*) demens
mishap *s* incommodum *n*
misinform *vt* falsa docēre (*with acc*)
misinterpret *vt* male interpretari
misinterpretation *s* prava interpretatio *f*
misjudge *vt* male judicare
mislay *vt* amittēre
mislead *vt* seducēre, decipēre
mismanage *vt* male gerēre
mismanagement *s* mala administratio *f*
misnomer *s* falsum nomen *n*
misplace *vt* alieno loco ponēre
misprint *s* erratum typographicum, mendum *n*
misquote *vt* falso citare, falso proferre
misquotation *s* falsa prolatio *f*
misrepresent *vt* calumniari
misrepresentation *s* calumnia *f*; falsa descriptio *f*

misrule *s* prava administratio *f*

miss *s* adulescentula, virgo *f*; error *m*

miss *vt* (*to overlook*) omittere, praetermittĕre; (*one's aim*) non ferire, non attingĕre; (*to feel the want of*) desiderare; (*to fail to find*) requirĕre; *vi* (*to fall short*) errare

misshapen *adj* pravus, deformis

missile *s* telum, missile, tormentum *n*

missing *adj* absens; **to be —** deesse

mission *s* legatio, missio *f*

misspell *vt* perperam scribĕre

misspend *vt* prodigĕre, perdere, dissipare

misstate *vt* parum accurate memorare

misstatement *s* falsum, mendacium *n*

mist *s* nebula, caligo *f*

mistake *s* error *m*, erratum *n*; (*written*) mendum *n*; **to make a —** errare, peccare

mistake *vt* habēre pro (*with abl*)

mistaken *adj* falsus; **to be —** falli; **unless I am —** ni fallor

mistletoe *s* viscum *n*

mistress *s* domina, hera *f*; (*sweetheart*) amica *f*; (*paramour*) concubina *f*; (*teacher*) magistra *f*

mistrust *s* diffidentia, suspicio *f*

mistrust *vt* diffidĕre (*with dat*)

mistrustful *adj* diffidens; **—ly** diffidenter

misty *adj* nebulosus, caliginosus; (*fig*) obscurus

misunderstand *vt* perperam intellegere

misunderstanding *s* error *m*; (*disagreement*) offensio *f*, dissidium *n*

misuse *vt* abuti (*with abl*); (*to revile*) conviciari

misuse *s* abus·us ·ūs *m*; (*ill treatment*) injuria *f*

mite *s* (*bit*) parvulus *m*; (*coin*) sextans *m*

miter *s* mitra *f*

mitigate *vt* mitigare, lenire

mitigation *s* mitigatio *f*

mix *vt* miscēre; **to — in** admiscēre; **to — up** commiscēre; (*fig*) confundĕre

mixed *adj* promiscuus, confusus

mixture *s* mixtura, farrago *f*

moan *vi* gemĕre, ingemiscere

moan *s* gemit·us ·ūs *m*

moat *s* fossa *f*

mob *s* turba *f*, vulgus *n*

mob *vt* conviciis insectari, stipare

mobile *adj* mobilis

mobility *s* mobilitas *f*

mock *s* irrisio, derisio *f*

mock *vt* ludĕre, ludificari, irridēre

mock *adj* fictus, fucatus

mockery *s* irrisio *f*, irris·us ·ūs *m*

mode *s* modus *m*, ratio *f*; (*fashion*) us·us ·ūs *m*

model *s* exemplar, exemplum *n*

model *vt* formare, delineare, fingĕre

moderate *adj* moderatus, mediocris, modicus; **—ly** moderate, mediocriter, modice

moderate *vt* moderari, temperare, coercēre

moderation *s* moderatio, temperantia *f*, modus *m*

moderator *s* praeses *m*

modern *adj* recens, hodiernus, novus

modest *adj* (*restrained*) modestus, pudens, verecundus; (*sight*) modicus, mediocris; **—ly** pudenter, verecunde

modesty *s* modestia, pudicitia, verecundia *f*

modification *s* modificatio, mutatio *f*

modify *vt* (im)mutare

modulate *vt* (*voice*) flectĕre; modulari

modulation *s* flexio *f*, flex·us ·ūs *m*

moist *adj* humidus, uvidus, madidus

moisten *vt* (h)umectare, rigare

moisture *s* humor *m*

molar *s* dens genuinus *m*

molasses *s* sacchari faex *f*

mold *s* (*form*) forma, matrix *f*; (*mustiness*) mucor *m*

mold *vt* formare, fingĕre; (*to knead*) subigere; *vi* mucescēre

molder *vi* putrescēre, dilabi

moldiness *s* mucor, sit·us ·ūs *m*

moldy *adj* mucidus, situ corruptus

mole *s* (*animal*) talpa *f*; (*sea wall*) moles *f*, agger *m*; (*on skin*)naevus *m*

molecule *s* particula *f*

molehill *s* **to make a mountain out of a —** e rivo flumina magna facĕre

molest *vt* vexare, sollicitare

molt *vi* plumas ponere

molten *adj* liquefactus

moment *s* (*of time*) punctum temjoris *n*; (*importance*) momentum *n*; **in a —** statim; **of great —** magni ponderis; **this —** ad tempus

momentarily *adv* statim, confestim

momentary *adj* brevis

momentous *adj* gravis, magni momenti (*genit, used adjectively*)

monarch *s* rex, princeps, dominus *m*

monarchical *adj* regius

monarchy *s* regnum *n*

monastery *s* monasterium *n*

monetary *adj* pecuniarius, argentarius, nummarius

money *s* pecunia *f*, nummi *m pl*; **for —** mercede

moneychanger *s* nummularius *m*

moneylender *s* faenerator *m*

mongrel *s* hybrida *m*

mon.tor *s* admonitor *m*

monk *s* monachus *m*

monkey *s* simia *f*

monogram *s* monogramma *n*

monologue *s* oratio *f*

monopolize *vt* monopolium exercēre in (*with acc*)

monopoly *s* monopolium *n*

monosyllabic *adj* monosyllabus

monosyllable *s* monosyllabum *n*

monotonous *adj* semper idem; (*singsong*) canorus

monotony *s* taedium *n*

monster *s* monstrum, portentum *n*, belua *f*

monstrosity *s* monstrum *n*

monstrous *adj* monstrosus, portentosus, prodigiosus; **—ly** monstrose

month s mensis m
monthly adj menstruus
monthly adv singulis mensibus
monument s monumentum n
monumental adj (important) gravis, magnus; (huge) ingens
mood s animi affect·us -ūs, habit·us -ūs m; (gram) modus m
moodiness s morositas f
moody adj morosus, maestus
moon s luna f
moonlight s lunae lumen n; **by —** per lunam
moonstruck adj lunaticus
Moor s Maurus m
moor vt religare, anchoris retinēre
moor s tesca n pl
mop s peniculus m
mop vt detergēre
mope vi maerēre
moral adj (relating to morals) moralis, ethicus; (morally proper) honestus; **—ly** moraliter; honeste
moral s (of story) documentum n
morale s animus m, animi m pl; **— is low** animus jacet, animi deficiunt
morality s boni mores m pl
moralize vi de moribus disserēre
morals s mores m pl
morass s palus f
morbid adj morbidus, morbosus
more adj plus (with genit); plures
more adv plus, magis, amplius; ultra; **— and —** magis magisque; **— than** plus quam; **— than enough** plus satis; **no —** non diutius
moreover adv praeterea, ultro, etenim vero
morning s mane n (indecl); tempus matutinum n; **early in the —** multo mane, bene mane, prima luce; **in the —** mane, matutino tempore; **this —** hodie mane
morning adj matutinus
morning star s Lucifer, phosphorus m
morose adj morosus; **—ly** morose
moroseness s morositas f
morsel s offa f, frustulum n
mortal adj mortalis, (deadly) mortifer, letalis; **—ly** letaliter
mortal s mortalis m & f, homo m & f
mortality s mortalitas f
mortar s mortarium n
mortgage s hypotheca f, pignus n
mortgage vt obligare
mortification s dolor m
mortify vt mortificare, coercēre; (to vex) offendēre
mosaic s tessellatum opus n
mosaic adj tesselatus
mosquito s culex m
moss s muscus m
mossy adj muscosus
most adj plurimus, maximus, plerusque; **for the — part** maximam partem
most adv maxime, plurimum
mostly adv plerumque, fere
mote s corpusculum n
moth s blatta f
mother s mater f

motherhood s matris conditio f
mother-in-law s socr·us -ūs f
motherless adj matre orbus
motherly adj maternus
motion s motio f, mot·us -ūs m; (proposal of bill) rogatio f; **to make a — ferre; to set in —** ciēre
motion vi significare, innuēre
motionless adj immotus, immobilis
motive s causa, ratio f, incitamentum n
motive adj movens, agens
motley adj varius, versicolor
mottled adj maculosus
motto s sententia f, praeceptum n
mound s tumulus, agger m, moles f
mount s mons m; (horse) equus m
mount vt scandĕre, ascendĕre, conscendĕre; vi ascendĕre, conscendĕre, sublime ferri; subvolare
mountain s mons m
mountaineer s montanus m
mountainous adj montuosus, montanus
mounted adj (on horseback) inscensus
mourn vt lugēre, deflēre; vi lugēre, maerēre
mourner s plorator m
mournful adj lugubris, luctuosus, tristis, flebilis, maestus; **—ly** maeste, flebiliter
mourning s luct·us -ūs f; maeror m; (dress) vestis lugubris f; **in —** pullatus, sorditatus; **to go into —** vestitum mutare
mouse s mus m
mousetrap s muscipulum n
mouth s os n; (of beast) faux f; (of river) ostium n; (of bottle) lura f
mouthful s buccella f
mouth piece s interpres m
movable adj mobilis
movables s res f pl, supellex f
move vt movēre; (emotionally) commovēre; (to propose) ferre; vi movēri, se movēre; (to change residence) migrare; **to — on** progredi
movement s mot·us -ūs m
moving adj flebilis, miserabilis
mow vt demetĕre, secare
mower s faenisex m & f
mowing s faenisicium n
much adj multus; **as — ... as** tantus ... quantus; **how —** quantus; **so —** tantus; **too —** nimius; **very — plurimus**
much adv multum, valde; (with comparatives) multo; **too — nimium**; nimis; **very — plurimum**
muck s stercus n
mucous adj mucosus
mud s lutum n, limus m
muddle vt turbare; (fig) perturbare
muddle s confusio, turba f
muddy adj lutosus, lutulentus; (troubled) turbidus
muffle vt involvĕre; **to — up** obvolvēre
muffled adj surdus
mug s poculum n
muggy adj humidus
mulberry s morum n

mulberry tree s morus f
mule s mulus m
muleteer s mulio m
mulish adj obstinatus
multifarious adj varius, multiplex
multiplication s multiplicatio f
multiply vt multiplicare; vi augēri, crescēre
multitude s multitudo, turba f
multitudinous adj creberrimus
mumble vt opprimēre; vi murmurare
munch vt manducare, mandēre
mundane adj mundanus
municipal adj municipalis
municipality s municipium n
munificence s munificentia, largitas f
munificent adj munificus, liberalis;
—**ly** munifice
munitions s belli apparat·us -ūs m
mural adj muralis
murder s caedes, nex f, homicidium n
murder vt necare, trucidare, obtruncare
murderer s homicida m & f, sicarius m
murderous adj (fig) sanguinarius, cruentus
murky adj caliginosus, tenebrosus
murmur s murmur n, fremit·us -ūs m
murmuring s admurmuratio f
muscle s musculus, lacertus, torus m
muscular adj lacertosus, robustus
Muse vi Musa f
muse vi meditari, secum agitare
mushroom s fungus, boletus m
music s musica f; (of instruments and voices) cant·us -ūs, concent·us -ūs m
musical adj (of person) musicus; (of sound) canorus
musician s musicus m; (of stringed instrument) fidicen m; (of wind instrument) tibicen m
muslin s sidon f

must s mustum n
must vi I — go mihi eundum est, me oportet ire, debeo ire, necesse est (ut) eam
mustard s sinapi n
muster vt lustrare; (fig) cogēre, convocare; **to — up courage** animum sumēre; vi convenire, coire
muster s copiarum lustratio f, recens·us -ūs m
musty adj mucidus
mutable adj mutabilis
mute adj mutus
mutilate vt mutilare, truncare
mutilated adj mutilus, truncus
mutilation s mutilatio, laceratio f
mutineer s seditiosus m
mutinous adj seditiosus
mutiny s seditio f, mot·us -ūs m
mutiny vi tumultuari, seditionem facere
mutter vi murmurare, mussitare
mutter s murmuratio f
mutton s ovilla f
mutual adj mutuus; —**ly** mutuo, inter se
muzzle s capistrum n
muzzle vt capistrare
my adj meus; — **own** proprius
myriad adj decem milia (with genit); (innumerable) sescenti
myrrh s myrrha, murrha f
myrtle s myrtus f
myself pron (reflexive) me; **to —** mihi; (intensive) ipse, egomet
mysterious adj arcanus, occultus; —**ly** arcane, occulte
mystery s mysterium, arcanum n; (fig) res occultissima f
mystical adj mysticus; —**ly** mystice
mystification s ambages f pl
mystify vt confundēre, fallēre
myth s mythos m, fabula f
mythical adj fabulosus
mythology s fabulae f pl, mythologia f

N

nab vt prehendēre
nadir s fundus m
nag s (a all) s m
nag vt objurgitare
naiad s naias f
nail s clavus m; (of finger) unguis m
nail vt defigēre
naive adj simplex; —**ly** simpliciter
naked adj nudus, apertus; —**ly** aperte
name s nomen n, appellatio f; (reputation) fama, celebritas f; (term) vocabulum n; **by —** nominatim
name vt nominare, appellare; (to appoint) dicēre
nameless adj nominis expers
namely adv scilicet, videlicet
nap s brevis somnus m; (of cloth) villus m; **to take a —** meridiari, ja-

cēre
nape s — **of the neck** cervix f
napkin s mappa f, mantele n
narcotic adj somnificus
narcotic s medicamentum somnificum n
nard s nardus f, nardum n
narrate vt narrare
narration s narratio, expositio f
narrative s fabula f
narrator s narrator m
narrow adj angustus; (fig) arctus; —**ly** vix, aegre
narrow vt coarctare; vi coarctari
narrow-minded adj animi angusti or parvi (genit, used adjectively)
narrowness s angustiae f pl
nasty adj (foul) foedus; (mean) amarus

natal *adj* natalis
nation *s* gens, natio *f*; (*as political body*) populus *m*; (*state*) res publica *f*
national *adj* publicus, civilis; rei publicae (*genit, used adjectively*)
nationality *s* civitas *f*
native *adj* indigena
native *s* indigena *m & f*
native land *s* patria *f*
native tongue *s* patrius sermo *m*
nativity *s* ort·us -ūs *m*
natural *adj* naturalis; (*innate*) nativus, innatus, insitus; (*fig*) sincerus, simplex; **—ly** naturā; (*unaffectedly*) simpliciter; (*of its own accord*) sponte
naturalization *s* civitatis donatio *f*
naturalize *vt* civitate donare
nature *s* natura, rerum natura *f*; (*character*) ingenium *n*, indoles *f*
naught *pron* nihil; **to set at —** parvi facĕre
naughty *adj* improbus, malus
nausea *s* nausea *f*; (*fig*) fastidium *n*
nauseate *vt* fastidium movēre (*with dat*); **to be nauseated** nauseare, fastidire
nautical *adj* nauticus
naval *adj* navalis, maritimus
nave *s* (*of church*) navis *f*
navel *s* umbilicus *m*
navigable *adj* navigabilis, navium patiens
navigate *vt* gubernare; *vi* navigare
navigation *s* navigatio *f*, res nauticae *f pl*
navigator *s* nauta, gubernator *m*
navy *s* classis *f*, copiae navales *f pl*
nay *adv* non ita
near *prep* prope (*with acc*), ad (*with acc*)
near *adj* propinquus, vicinus; (*of relation*) proximus; **— at hand** propinquus, in promptu
near *adv* prope, juxta
near *vt* appropinquare (*with dat*)
nearly *adv* prope, paene, fere, ferme
nearness *s* propinquitas *f*
nearsighted *adj* myops
neat *adj* mundus, nitidus, concinnus; **—ly** munde, concinne
neatness *s* munditia, concinnitas *f*
nebulous *adj* nebulosus
necessarily *adv* necessario
necessary *adj* necessarius; **it is —** opus est
necessitate *vt* cogĕre
necessity *s* necessitas *f*; (*want*) egestas, necessitudo *f*; (*thing*) res necessaria *f*
neck *s* collum *n*, cervis *f*
necklace *s* monile *n*, torques *m*
necktie *s* collare *n*
nectar *s* nectar *n*
need *s* (*necessity*) opus *n*, necessitas *f*; (*want*) inopia, egestas, penuria *f*; **there is —** of opus est (*with abl*)
need *vt* egēre (*with abl*), indigēre (*with abl*); (*to require*) requirēre
needle *s* ac·us -ūs *f*
needless inutilis, minime necessarius, vanus; **—ly** sine causa

needy *adj* egens, indigens, inops
nefarious *adj* nefarius
negation *s* negatio *f*
negative *adj* negans, negativus; **—ly** negando
negative *s* negatio *f*; **to answer in the —** negare
neglect *vt* neglegĕre, omittĕre; deserĕre
neglect *s* neglegentia, incuria *f*, neglect·us -ūs *m*
neglectful *adj* neglegens
negligence *s* neglegentia, incuria *f*
negligent *adj* neglegens; **—ly** negleganter
negligible *adj* levis, tenuis
negotiable *adj* mercabilis
negotiate *vt* (*a deal*) agĕre; agĕre de (*with abl*); *vi* negotiari
negotiation *s* transactio, actio *f*, pactum *n*
negotiator *s* conciliator, orator *m*
Negro *s* Aethiops *m*
neigh *vi* hinnire
neigh *s* hinnit·us -ūs *m*
neighbor *s* vicinus, finitimus *m*
neighborhood *s* vicinia, vicinitas *f*; proximitas *f*
neighboring *adj* vicinus, finitimus
neighborly *adj* familiaris, comis, benignus
neither *pron* neuter
neither *conj* nec, neque, neve, neu; **neither . . . nor** neque . . . neque
neophyte *s* neophytus *m*
nephew *s* fratris filius, sororis filius *m*
Nereid *s* Nereis *f*
nerve *s* nervus *m*; (*fig*) temeritas, audacia *f*
nervous *adj* trepidus; **—ly** trepide
nervousness *s* diffidentia, sollicitudo *f*
nest *s* nidus *m*
nest *vi* nidificare
nestle *vi* recubare
net *s* rete *n*
net *vt* irretire
netting *s* reticulum *n*
nettle *s* urtica *f*
nettle *vt* (*fig*) vexare
network *s* reticulum, opus reticulatum *n*
neuter *adj* neuter, neutralis
neutral *adj* medius, neuter
neutrality *s* nullam in partem propensio *f*
neutralize *vt* aequare
never *adv* nunquam
nevermore *adv* nunquam posthac
nevertheless *adv* nihilominus, attamen
new *s* novus, recens, integer; **—ly** nuper, modo
newcomer *s* advena *m & f*
news *s* fama *f*; rumor, nuntius *m*
newspaper *s* acta diurna *n pl*
next *adj* proximus; (*of time*) insequens; **— day** postridie
next *adv* dein, deinde, deinceps
nibble *vt* arrodĕre; (*fig*) carpĕre; *vi* rodĕre
nice *adj* (*dainty*) delicatus; (*choice*)

exquisitus; (*exact*) accuratus; (*fine*) bellus; (*effeminate*) mollis; (*amiable*) suavis; (*of weather*) serenus; **—ly** delicate, exquisite, belle; accurate

nicety *s* accuratio, subtilitas, elegantia *f*

niche *s* aedicula *f*

nick *s* incisura *f*; **in the very —of time** in ipso articulo temporis

nick *vt* incidĕre

nickname *s* agnomen *n*

niece *s* fratris filia, sororis filia *f*

niggardly *adj* parcus, avarus

nigh *adj* propinquus

night *s* nox *f*; **by —** nocte, noctu; **to spend the —** pernoctare

nightfall *s* primae tenebrae *f pl*; **at — sub noctem**

nightingale *s* luscinia *f*

nightly *adj* nocturnus

nightly *adv* noctu, de nocte

nightmare *s* incubus *m*

night watch *s* vigilia *f*; (*guard*) vigil *m*

nimble *adj* pernix, agilis

nine *adj* novem; **— times** noviens

nineteen *adj* undeviginti, decem et novem

nineteenth *adj* undevicesimus

ninetieth *adj* nonagesimus

ninety *adj* nonaginta

ninth *adj* nonus

nip *vt* vellicare; (*of frost*) urĕre; **to — off** desecare

nippers *s* forceps *m*

nipple *s* papilla *f*

no *adj* nullus; **— one** nemo *m*

no *adv* non, minime; **to say —** negare

nobility *s* nobilitas *f*; nobiles, optimates *m pl*; (*moral excellence*) honestas *f*

noble *adj* nobilis, generosus; (*morally*) ingenuus, honestus, liberalis

noble *s* optimas *m*

nobleman *s* vir nobilis *m*

nobly *adv* nobiliter, praeclare, generose

nobody *pron* nemo *m*

nocturnal *adj* nocturnus

nod *s* nut·us -ūs *m*

nod *vi* nutare; (*to doze*) dormitare; (*in assent*) annuĕre

noise *s* strepit·us -ūs *m*; (*high-pitched*) stridor *m*; (*loud*) fragor *m*; **to make —** strepĕre, strepitare, increpare

noise *vt* **to — abroad** promulgare, divulgare

noiseless *adj* tacitus; **—ly** tacite

noisily *adv* cum strepitu

noisome *adj* noxius, foedus, taeter

noisy *adj* clamosus

nomad *s* nomas *m & f*

nomadic *adj* vagus, vagabundus

nominal *adj* nominalis; **—ly** nomine, verbo

nominate *vt* nominare, designare

nomination *s* nominatio, designatio *f*; (*of heir*) nuncupatio *f*

nominative *adj* nominativus

nominee *s* nominatus, designatus *m*

none *pron* nemo *m*

nonentity *s* nihilum *n*

nones *s* Nonae *f pl*

nonplus *vt* (*to puzzle*) ad incitas redigĕre

nonsense *s* ineptiae, nugae *f pl*; **to talk —** absurde loqui, garrire

nonsense *interj* gerrae!

nonsensical *adj* ineptus, absurdus

nook *s* angulus *m*

noon *s* meridies *m*; **before — ante meridiem**

noonday *adj* meridianus

no one *pron* nemo *m*

noose *s* laqueus *m*

nor *conj* nec, neque, neve, neu

norm *s* norma *f*

normal *adj* solitus; **—ly** plerumque

north *s* septentriones *m pl*

north *adj* septentrionalis

northern *adj* septentrionalis

northern lights *s* aurora Borealis *f*

north pole *s* arctos *f*

northwards *adv* septentriones versus

north wind *s* aquilo *m*

nose *s* nas·us -ūs *m*, nares *f pl*; **to blow the —** emungĕre

nostril *s* naris *f*

not *adv* non, haud; **— at all** nullo modo, haudquaquam; **— even** ne ... quidem

notable *adj* notabilis, insignis, insignitus

notably *adv* insignite

notary *s* scriba *m*

notation *s* notatio *f*, signum *n*

notch *s* incisura *f*

notch *vt* incidĕre

note *s* (*mark*) nota *f*; (*comment*) adnotatio *f*; (*mus*) sonus *m*, vox *f*; (*com*) chirographum *n*; (*letter*) litterulae *f pl*

note *vt* notare; (*to notice*) animadvertĕre

notebook *s* commentarius *m*, tabulae *f pl*, pugillares *m pl*

noted *adj* insignis, insignitus, notus, praeclarus

noteworthy *adj* notabilis, memorabilis

nothing *pron* nihil, nil, nihilum; **for —** (*free*) gratis, gratuito; (*in vain*) frustra; **good for —** nequam; **— but** nihil nisi; **to think — of** nihili facĕre

notice *s* (*act of noticing*) notatio, animadversio *f*; (*announcement*) denuntiatio *f*; (*sign*) proscriptio *f*, titulus, libellus *m*; **to escape — latĕre**; **to escape the — of** fallĕre; **to give — of** denuntiare

notice *vt* animadvertĕre, observare

noticeable *adj* insignis, conspicuus

noticeably *adv* insigniter

notification *s* denuntiatio, declaratio *f*

notify *vt* certiorem facĕre

notion *s* notio, suspicio *f*

notoriety *s* infamia *f*

notorious *adj* famosus, infamis, notus, manifestus; **—ly** manifeste

notwithstanding *adv* nihilominus

nought *pron* nihil; **to set at —** parvi facĕre

noun *s* nomen *n*

nourish *vt* alĕre, nutrire

nourishment *s* (*act*) alimentum *n*, cibus *m*

novel *adj* novus, inauditus

novel *s* fabula *f*

novelty *s* res nova *f*; novitas *f*

November *s* (mensis) November *m*

novice *s* tiro *m*

now *adv* nunc; (*past*) jam; **— and then** interdum, nonnunquam; **— ...—** modo ... modo

nowhere *adv* nusquam

noxious *adj* noxius

nozzle *s* ansa *f*

nude *adj* nudus

nudge *vt* fodicare

nudity *s* nudatio *f*

nugget *s* massa *f*

nuisance *s* incommodum *n*, molestia *f*

null *adj* irritus

nullify *vt* irritum facĕre

numb *adj* torpidus, torpens; **to become —** torpescĕre; **to be —** torpēre

numb *vt* torpefacĕre; (*fig*) obstupefacĕre

number *s* numerus *m*; **a — of** aliquot; **without —** innumerabilis

number *vt* numerare, enumerare, dinumerare

numberless *adj* innumerus, innumerabilis

numbness *s* torpor *m*; (*fig*) stupor *m*

numerical *adj* numeralis; **—ly** numero, ad numerum

numerous *adj* frequens, creber, multus

numismatics *s* doctrina nummorum *f*

nuptial *adj* nuptialis, conjugalis

nuptials *s* nuptiae *f pl*

nurse *s* nutrix *f*

nurse *vt* (*a baby*) nutrire; (*fig*) fovēre; (*the sick*) ancillari (*with dat*), curare

nursery *s* (*for children*) infantium cubiculum *n*; (*for plants*) plantarium, seminarium *n*

nurture *vt* nutrire, educare

nut *s* nux *f*; **a hard — to crack** (*fig*) quaestio nodosa *f*

nutriment *s* nutrimentum, alimentum *n*

nutrition *s* nutritio *f*, nutrimentum *n*

nutritious *adj* alibilis, salubris

nutshell *s* putamen *n*; **in a —** (*fig*) paucis verbis

nymph *s* nympha *f*

O

oaf *s* stultus, hebes *m*

oak *adj* querceus, quernus

oak *s* querc·us -ūs *f*; (*evergreen*) ilex *f*; (*timber*) robur *n*

oakum *s* stuppa *f*

oar *s* remus *m*; **to pull the —s** remos ducĕre

oarsman *s* remex *m*

oath *s* jusjurandum *n*; (*mil*) sacramentum *n*; **false —** perjurium *n*; **to take an —** jurare; (*mil*) sacramentum dicĕre

oats *s* avena *f*

obdurate *adj* obstinatus, pertinax; **—ly** obstinate, pertinaciter

obedience *s* obedientia *f*, obsequium *n*

obedient *adj* obediens, obsequens; **—ly** obedienter

obeisance *s* obsequium *n*, capitis summissio *f*; **to make — to** flectĕre ante (*with acc*); (*fig*) obsequi (*with dat*)

obelisk *s* obeliscus *m*

obese *adj* obesus

obesity *s* obesitas *f*

obey *vt* parēre (*with dat*), obedire (*with dat*), obtemperare (*with dat*), obsequi (*with dat*)

obituary *s* Libitinae index *m*

object *s* objectum *n*, res *f*; (*aim*) finis *m*, propositum *n*

object *vi* (*to feel annoyance*) gravari;

(*to make objections*) recusare; **to — to** aegre ferre

objection *s* objectio *f*; impedimentum *n*, mora *f*

objectionable *adj* injucundus, improbabilis

objective *s* finis *m*, propositum *n*

objective *adj* externus, objectivus, verus

oblation *s* donum *n*

obligation *s* debitum, officium *n*; **under —** noxius

obligatory *adj* necessarius, debitus

oblige *vt* (*to force*) cogĕre, impellĕre; (*to put under obligation*) obligare, obstringĕre; (*to do a favor for*) morigerari (*with dat*); **to be obliged to** debēre (*with inf*); (*to feel gratitude toward*) gratiam habēre (*with dat*)

obliging *adj* officiosus, comis, blandus; **—ly** officiose, comiter

oblique *adj* obliquus; **—ly** oblique

obliterate *vt* delēre, oblitterare

oblivion *s* oblivio *f*

oblivious *adj* obliviosus, immemor

oblong *adj* oblongus

obloquy *s* vituperatio *f*, maledictum *n*

obnoxious *adj* invisus, noxius

obscene *adj* obscenus; **—ly** obscene

obscenity *s* obscenitas *f*

obscure *adj* obscurus; **—ly** obscure

obscure *vt* obscurare

obscurity *s* obscuritas *f*, tenebrae *f pl*; *(of birth)* humilitas *f*

obsequies *s* exsequiae *f pl*

obsequious *adj* officiosus, morigerus, nimis obsequens

obsequiousness *s* obsequium *n*, assentatio *f*

observable *adj* notabilis

observance *s* observantia *f*; *(rite)* rit·us -ūs *m*

observant *adj* attentus; — **of** diligens *(with genit)*

observation *s* observatio, animadversio *f*; *(remark)* notatio *f*, dictum *n*

observe *vt (to watch)* observare, contemplari, animadvertĕre; *(to keep)* conservare, observare; *(to remark)* dicĕre

observer *s* spectator *m*

obsess *vt* occupare

obsession *s* studium *n*

obsolescent *adj* to be — obsolescĕre

obsolete *adj* obsoletus, antiquatus; **to become** — exolescĕre

obstacle *s* impedimentum *n*; *(barrier)* obex *m*

obstinacy *s* obstinatio *f*, animus obstinatus *m*

obstinate *adj* obstinatus, pertinax; —**ly** obstinate

obstreperous *adj* tumultuosus, clamosus

obstruct *vt* obstare *(with dat)*, obstruĕre, impedire

obstruction *s* obstructio *f*, impedimentum *n*; *(pol)* intercessio *f*

obtain *vt* nancisci, adipisci, consequi; *(by entreaty)* impetrare; *vi* valēre

obtainable *adj* impetrabilis

obtrusive *adj* molestus, importunus

obtuse *adj* obtusus, hebes, stolidus

obviate *vt* praevertĕre

obvious *adj* apertus, manifestus, perspicuus; —**ly** aperte, manifesto

occasion *s* occasio *f*, locus *m*; *(reason)* causa *f*; *(time)* tempus *n*

occasion *vt* locum dare *(with dat)*, movēre

occasionally *adv* interdum

occidental *adj* occidentalis

occult *adj* occultus, arcanus

occupant *s* possessor *m*

occupation *s* possessio *f*; *(engagement)* occupatio *f*; *(employment)* negotium *n*, quaest·us -ūs *m*

occupy *vt* occupare, tenēre; *(to possess)* possidēre; *(space)* complēre

occur *vi* accidĕre, evenire; *(to the mind)* occurrĕre, in mentem venire

occurrence *s* cas·us -ūs, event·us -ūs *m*

ocean *s* oceanus *m*, mare oceanum *n*

oceanic *adj* oceanus, oceanensis

October *s* (mensis) October *m*

ocular *adj* ocularis

oculist *s* ocularius medicus *m*

odd *adj (of number)* impar; *(quaint)* insolitus, novus; —**ly** mirum in modum

oddity *s* raritas *f*, ridiculum *n*

odds *s* **the — are against us** impares summus; **to be at — with** dissidēre ab *(with abl)*

odious *adj* odiosus, invisus

odium *s* invidia *f*

odor *s* odor *m*

odorous *adj* odoratus

Odyssey *s* Odyssea *f*

of *prep (possession) rendered by genit; (origin)* de *(with abl)*, ex *(with abl)*

off *adv* procul; **far —** longe, procul; **well —** bene nummatus

off *prep* de *(with abl)*

offend *vt* offendĕre, laedĕre; *vi* **to — against** violare

offender *s* peccator, reus *m*

offense *s (fault)* offensa, culpa *f*; *(insult)* injuria *f*; *(displeasure)* offensio *f*

offensive *adj (odors, etc.)* odiosus, foedus, gravis; *(language)* malignus, contumeliosus; *(aggressive)* bellum inferens; —**ly** injuriose; odiose

offer *vt* offerre, donare, praebēre; *(violence)* adferre; *(help)* ferre

offer *s* conditio *f*

offhand *adj* incuriosus

offhand *adv* confestim, illico

office *s (place of work)* officina *f*; *(pol)* honos, magistrat·us -ūs *m*; *(duty)* munus, officium *n*

officer *s* magistrat·us -ūs *m*; *(mil)* praefectus *m*

official *adj* publicus

official *s* minister, magistrat·us -ūs *m*

officiate *vi* officio *or* munere fungi, interesse; *(of clergyman)* rem divinam facĕre

officious *adj* officiosus, molestus; —**ly** officiose, moleste

offing *s* **in the —** procul

offset *vt* compensare

offspring *s* proles, progenies *f*

often *adv* saepe; **very —** persaepe

ogre *s* larva *f*, monstrum *n*

oh *interj* ohl, ohe!

oil *s* oleum *n*

oil *vt* ung(u)ĕre

oily *adj* oleosus; *(like oil)* oleaceus

ointment *s* unguentum *n*

old *adj (aged)* senex; *(out of use)* obsoletus; *(worn)* exesus, tritus; *(ancient)* antiquus, priscus; **of** — olim, quondam; **to grow** — senescĕre

old age *s* senectus *f*

old-fashioned *adj* priscus, antiquus

old man *s* senex *m*

old woman *s* an·us -ūs *f*

oligarchy *s* optimates *m pl*

olive *s* olea *f*

olive grove *s* olivetum *n*

Olympiad *s* Olympias *f*

Olympic *adj* Olympicus

omelet *s* laganum de ovis confectum *n*

omen *s* omen, auspicium *n*

ominous *adj* infaustus; —**ly** malis ominibus

omission *s* praetermissio, neglegentia *f*

omit *vt* omittĕre, mittĕre, praetermittĕre

omnipotence *s* omnipotentia, infinita potentia *f*

omnipotent *adj* omnipotens

omnivorous *adj* omnivorus

on *prep* (*place*) in (*with abl*); (*time*) render by abl; (*about, concerning*) de (*with abl*); (*ranged with*) a(b) (*with abl*); (*depending, hanging on*) de (*with abl*); (*near*) ad (*with acc*)

on *adv* porro; (*continually*) usque; **and so** — et cetera, ac deinceps; **to go** — pergĕre

once *adv* (*one time*) semel; (*formerly*) olim, quondam; **at** — statim, illico, ex templo; **for** — aliquando; **— and for all** semel in perpetuum; **— more** iterum; **— upon a time** olim

one *adj* unus

one *pron* unus; unicus; (*a certain person or thing*) quidam; **it is all —** perinde est; **— after another** alternus; **— another** inter se, alius alium; **— by —** singulatim; **— or the other** alteruter; **— or two** unus et alter

one-eyed *adj* luscus

onerous *adj* onerosus, gravis

oneself *pron* (*refl*) se; **to —** sibi; **with —** secum; (*intensive*) ipse

one-sided *adj* inaequalis, iniquus, impar

onion *s* caepa *f*

only *adj* unicus, unus, solus

only *adv* solum, tantum, modo; **not — ... but also** non solum ... sed etiam

only-begotten *adj* unigenitus

onset *s* impet·us -ūs *m*

onslaught *s* incurs·us -ūs *m*

onward *adv* porro

ooze *vi* manare, (de)stillare

opaque *adj* densus, opacus

open *adj* (*not shut*) apertus, patens; (*evident*) manifestus; (*sincere*) candidus, ingenuus; (*public*) publicus, communis; (*of space*) apertus; (*of question, undecided*) integer; **in the — air** sub divo; **to lie —** patēre; **—ly** aperte, palam

open *vt* aperire, patefacĕre; (*to uncover*) retegĕre; (*letter*) resignare; (*book*) evolvĕre; (*to begin*) exordiri; (*with ceremony*) inaugurare; *vi* patescĕre, se pandĕre; (*to gape*) dehiscĕre; (*of wound*) recrudescĕre

open-handed *adj* liberalis, largus

open-hearted *adj* simplex, ingenuus

opening *s* (*act*) apertio *f*; (*aperture*) foramen *n*, hiat·us -ūs *m*; (*opportunity*) locus *m*, occasio *f*

open-minded *adj* docilis

operate *vt* agĕre, gerĕre; *vi* operari

operation *s* effectio *f*; (*business*) negotium *n*; (*med*) sectio *f*

operative *adj* efficax, activus

operator *s* opifex *m*

opiate *s* mendicamentum somnificum *n*

opinion *s* opinio, sententia, mens *f*; (*esteem*) existimatio *f*; **public —** fama *f*

opium *s* opion *n*

opponent *s* adversarius *m*

opportune *adj* opportunus, idoneus, commodus; **—ly** opportune, in tempore

opportunity *s* copia, occasio, opportunitas *f*

oppose *vt* opponĕre, objicĕre; *vi* repugnare, resistĕre, adversari

opposite *adj* adversus, contrarius, diversus

opposite *prep* contra (*with acc*)

opposite *adv* contra, ex adverso

opposition *s* oppositio, repugnantia, discrepantia *f*; (*obstacle*) impedimentum *n*; (*party*) adversa factio *f*

oppress *vt* opprimĕre, vexare, gravare, onerare

oppression *s* gravatio, injuria *f*

oppressive *adj* praegravis, acerbus, molestus; **to become —** ingravescĕre

oppressor *s* tyrannus *m*

opprobrious *adj* turpis, probrosus

opprobrium *s* dedecus, probrum *n*

optical *adj* opticus

option *s* optio *f*

opulence *s* opulentia *f*

opulent *adj* opulens, opulentus

or *conj* vel, aut, —ve; (*in questions*) an; **— else** aut, alioquin; **— not** annon; (*in indirect questions*) necne

oracle *s* oraculum *n*

oracular *adj* fatidicus

oral *adj* verbalis, verbo traditus; **—ly** voce, verbis

orange *s* malum aurantium *n*

oration *s* oratio *f*

orator *s* orator *m*

oratorical *adj* oratorius

oratory *s* ars oratoria, eloquentia, rhetorice *f*

orb *s* orbis, gyrus *m*

orbit *s* orbis *m*; (*in astronomy*) ambit·us -ūs *m*

orchard *s* pomarium *n*

orchestra *s* symphoniaci *m pl*

ordain *vt* (*to appoint*) edicĕre

ordeal *s* discrimen *n*, labor *m*

order *s* (*class, arrangement*) ordo *m*; (*command*) mandatum, jussum, imperatum *n*; (*fraternity*) collegium *n*; **by —** of jussu (*with genit*); **in — dispositus; **in — that** ut; **in — that not** ne; **out of —** incompositus; **to put in —** ordinare, disponĕre

order *vt* (*to command*) imperare (*with dat*), jubēre; (*to demand*) imperare (*with acc*); (*to put in order*) ordinare, disponĕre, digerĕre

orderly *adj* compositus, ordinatus; (*well-behaved*) modestus

orderly *s* accensus *m*; (*mil*) tesserarius *m*

ordinal *adj* ordinalis

ordinance *s* edictum, rescriptum *n*

ordinarily *adv* fere, plerumque

ordinary *adj* usitatus, vulgaris, solitus, quottidianus

ordnance *s* tormenta *n pl*

ore *s* aes *n*

organ s (*of body*) membrum n; (*musical*) organum n

organic *adj* organicus

organism s compages f

organization s ordinatio f, structura f

organize *vt* ordinare, instituĕre

orgy s comissatio f

Orient s oriens m

oriental *adj* Asiaticus

orifice s foramen, os n

origin s origo f, principium n; (*birth*) genus n; (*source*) fons m

original *adj* pristinus, primitivus, primus; (*one's own*) proprius; (*new*) novus, inauditus; **—ly** primum, principio, initio

original s archetypum, exemplar n; (*writing*) autographum n

originality s proprietas ingenii f

originate *vt* instituĕre; *vi* oriri

originator s auctor m

ornament s ornamentum n, ornat·us -ūs m

ornament *vt* ornare, decorare

ornamental *adj* decorus

ornate *adj* ornatus; **—ly** ornate

orphan s orbus m, orba f

orphaned *adj* orbatus

orphanage s orphanotrophium n

oscillate *vi* agitari; (*fig*) dubitare

oscillation s agitatio f; (*fig*) dubitatio f

ostensible *adj* simulatus, fictus

ostensibly *adv* specie, per speciem

ostentation s ostentatio, jactatio f

ostentatious *adj* ambitiosus, gloriosus, jactans; **—ly** ambitiose, jactanter

ostracism s ostracismus m

ostrich s struthiocamelus m

other *adj* (*different*) alius, diversus; (*remaining*) ceterus; **every — day** tertio quoque die; **on the — hand** contra, autem; **the — alter**

otherwise *adv* aliter

otter s lutra f

ought *vi* I **—** debeo, oportet me

ounce s uncia f

our *adj* noster

ours *pron* noster

ourselves *pron* (*reflex*) nos, nosmet; **to —** nobis; (*intensive*) nosmet ipsi

oust *vt* ejicĕre

out *adv* (*outside*) foris; (*motion*) foras; **— of** de (*with abl*), e(x) (*with abl*); (*on account of*) propter (*with acc*); **— of the way** devius

outbreak s eruptio f; (*fig*) seditio f

outburst s eruptio f

outcast s exsul, extorris, profugus m

outcome s event·us -ūs m

outcry s clamor m, acclamatio f, convicium n

outdo *vt* superare

outdoors *adv* foris, sub divo

outer *adj* exterior

outermost *adj* extremus

outfit s apparat·us -ūs m; (*costume*) vestimenta n pl

outflank *vt* circumire, circumvenire

outgrow *vt* excedĕre ex (*with abl*), staturā superare

outing s excursio f

outlandish *adj* externus, barbarus

outlast *vt* diutius durare (*with abl*)

outlaw s proscriptus m

outlaw *vt* aquā et igni interdicĕre (*with dat*), proscribĕre

outlay s sumpt·us -ūs m, impensa f

outlet s exit·us -ūs m

outline *vt* describĕre, adumbrare

outline s adumbratio f

outlive *vt* supervivĕre (*with dat*), superesse (*with dat*)

outlook s prospect·us -ūs m

outlying *adj* externus; (*distant*) remotus

outnumber *vt* multitudine superare

outpost s statio f

outpouring s effusio f

output s fruct·us -ūs m

outrage s injuria f, flagitium n

outrage *vt* flagitio afficĕre, violare

outrageous *adj* flagitiosus, atrox; (*excessive*) immodicus; **—ly** flagitiose; immodice

outright *adv* (*at once*) statim; (*completely*) prorsus, penitus

outrun *vt* praevertĕre, linquĕre

outset s initium, inceptum n

outshine *vt* praelucĕre (*with dat*)

outside s pars exterior, superficies f; (*appearance*) species f; **on the —** extrinsecus

outside *adj* externus

outside *adv* foris, extra; (*motion*) foras; **from —** extrinsecus

outside *prep* extra (*with acc*)

outskirts s suburbium n, ager suburbanus m

outspoken *adj* candidus, liber

outspread *adj* patulus

outstanding *adj* praestans; (*of debts*) residuus

outstretched *adj* extentus, porrectus, passus

outstrip *vt* praevertĕre, cursu superare

outward *adj* externus

outward *adv* extra, extrinsecus

outweigh *vt* praevertĕre (*with dat*), praeponderare

outwit *vt* deludĕre, decipĕre

oval *adj* ovatus

ovation s plaus·us -ūs m; (*triumph*) ovatio f

oven s furnus m, fornax f

over *prep* (*across*) super (*with acc*), trans (*with acc*), per (*with acc*); (*above*) super (*with abl*), supra (*with acc*); (*with numbers*) plus quam

over *adv* supra; (*excess*) nimis; **all — ubique, passim; — and above** insuper; **— and — again** iterum ac saepius, identidem

overall *adj* totus

overawe *vt* (de)terrēre

overbalance *vt* praeponderare

overbearing *adj* superbus, insolens

overboard *adv* ex nave; **to jump —** ex nave desilire

overburden *vt* nimis onerare

overcast *adj* obnubilus

overcharge vt plus aequo exigĕre ab (with abl)
overcoat s paenula, lacerna f
overdo vt exaggerare, in majus extollĕre
overdue adj (money) residuus
overestimate vt majoris aestimare
overflow s inundatio f
overflow vt inundare; vi abundare, redundare
overgrown adj obductus, obsitus; (too big) praegrandis
overhang vt impendĕre
overhaul vt reficĕre
overhead adv desuper, insuper
overhear vt excipĕre, auscultare
overjoyed adj to be — nimio gaudio exsultare
overladen adj praegravatus
overland adj per terram
overlay vt inducĕre, illinĕre
overload vt nimis onerare
overlook vt (not to notice) praetermittĕre; (to pardon) ignoscĕre (with dat); (a view) despectare
overlord s dominus m
overpower vt exsuperare, opprimĕre
overrate vt nimis aestimare
overreach vt circumvenire
overriding adj praecipuus
overripe adj praematurus
overrun vt (per)vagari; (fig) obsidĕre
overseas adj transmarinus
oversee vt praeesse (with dat)
overseer s curator, praeses, custos m
overshadow vt obumbrare; (fig) obscurare

overshoot vt excedĕre, transgredi
oversight s incuria, neglegentia f, error m
oversleep vi diutius dormire
overspread vt obducĕre
overstate vt in majus extollĕre
overstep vt excedĕre, transgredi
overt adj apertus; —ly palam
overtake vt consequi
overtax vt (fig) abuti (with abl)
overthrow s eversio, ruina f, excidium n
overthrow vt subvertĕre, evertĕre, dejicĕre
overture s (mus) exordium n; (proposal) conditio f; to make —s to agĕre cum (with abl)
overturn vt evertĕre, subvertĕre
overweening adj superbus, insolens, arrogans
overwhelm vt obruĕre, opprimĕre
overwork vt to — oneself plus aequo laborare
owe vt debēre
owing to prep propter (with acc)
owl s bubo m, strix f
own adj proprius; one's — suus, proprius
own vt possidēre, tenēre; (to acknowledge) fatēri, confitēri
owner s dominus, possessor m
ownership s possessio f, mancipium, dominium n
ox s bos m
oyster s ostrea f
oyster shell s ostreae testa f

P

pace s (step) pass·us -ūs, grad·us -ūs m; (measure) pass·us -ūs m; (speed) velocitas f, grad·us -ūs m
pace vi incedĕre, gradi; to — up and down spatiari
pacific adj pacificus, tranquillus
pacification s pacificatio f
pacify vt pacare, placare, sedare
pack s (bundle) sarcina f, fasciculus m; (of animals) grex m; (of people) turba f, grex m
pack vt (items of luggage) colligĕre, componĕre; (to fill completely) frequentare, complēre; (to compress) stipare; vi vasa colligĕre
package s sarcina f, fasciculus m
packet s fasciculus m
pack horse s equus clitellarius m
packsaddle s clitellae f pl
pact s pactum n, pactio f; to make a — pacisci
pad s pulvinus, pulvillus m
pad vt suffarcinare
padding s fartura f
paddle s remus m
paddle vi remigare
paddock s saeptum n
pagan s paganus m

page s (of book) pagina, scheda f; puer m
pageant s pompa f, spectaculum n
pail s hama, situla f
pain s dolor m; (fig) angor m; to be in — dolēre; to take —s operam dare
pain vt dolore afficĕre, excruciare; vi dolēre
painful adj gravis, acerbus, molestus; —ly graviter, magno cum dolore
painless adj doloris expers
painstaking adj operosus
paint s pigmentum n; (for face) fucus m
paint vt pingĕre, depingĕre
paintbrush s penicillus m
painter s pictor m
painting s pictura f
pair s par n; (of oxen) jugum n
pair vt conjungĕre, componĕre
palace s regia f, palatium n
palatable adj jucundus, suavis, sapidus
palate s palatum n
palatial adj regius

pale *adj* pallidus; **to be —** pallēre;
   to grow — pallescĕre
pale *s* palus *m*
paling *s* saepes *f*
palisade *s* vallum *n*
pall *s* pallium *n*
pall *vt* satiare; *vi* vapescĕre
pallet *s* grabat·us -ūs *m*
palliative *s* lenimentum *n*
pallid *adj* pallidus
pallor *s* pallor *m*
palm *s* (*of hand*) palma *f*; (*tree*) palma *f*
palpable *adj* tractabilis; (*fig*) apertus, manifestus
palpitate *vi* palpitare
palsied *adj* paralyticus
palsy *s* paralysis *f*
paltry *adj* vilis, minutus
pamper *vt* indulgēre (*with dat*)
pamphlet *s* libellus *m*
pan *s* patina, patella *f*; (*for frying*)
   sartago *f*
pancake *s* laganum *n*
pander *s* leno *m*
pander *vi* lenocinari
panegyric *s* laudatio *f*
panel *s* (*of wall*) abacus *m*; (*of ceiling*) lacunar *n*; (*of jury*) decurio *m*;
   (*of door*) tympanum *n*
paneled *adj* laqueatus
pang *s* dolor *m*
panic *s* pavor *m*
panic-stricken *adj* pavidus
panoply *s* arma *n pl*
panorama *s* conspect·us -ūs *m*
pant *vi* palpitare, anhelare; **to —
   after** (*fig*) gestire
pantheism *s* pantheismus *m*
pantheist *s* pantheista *m*
pantheon *s* Pantheon *n*
panther *s* pantera *f*
panting *adj* anhelus
panting *s* anhelit·us -ūs *m*
pantomime *s* (*play and actor*) mimus *m*
pantry *s* cella penaria *f*
pap *s* papilla, mamilla *f*
paper *s* (*stationery*) charta *f*; (*newspaper*) acta diurna *n pl*; **—s** scripta
   n pl
paper *adj* chartaceus, charteus
papyrus *s* papyrus *f*
par *s* **to be on a — with** par esse
   (*with dat*)
parable *s* parabole *f*
parade *s* (*mil*) decurs·us -ūs *m*; pompa *f*; (*display*) apparat·us -ūs *m*,
   pompa *f*
parade *vt* (*fig*) ostentare, jactare; *vi*
   (*mil*) decurrĕre
paradise *s* paradisus *m*
paradox *s* oxymora verba *n pl*
paragon *s* specimen, exemplar *n*
paragraph *s* caput *n*
parallel *adj* parallelus; (*fig*) consi-
   milis
parallel *vt* exaequare
paralysis *s* paralysis *f*; (*fig*) torpedo *f*
paralytic *adj* paralyticus
paralyze *vt* debilitare, enervare, percellĕre

paramount *adj* supremus
paramour *s* (*man*) moechus, adulter
   m; (*woman*) meretrix, pellex *f*
parapet *s* pluteus *m*
paraphernalia *s* apparat·us -ūs *m*
paraphrase *s* paraphrasis *f*
paraphrase *vt* vertĕre, interpretari
parasite *s* parasitus *m*
parasol *s* umbella *f*, umbraculum *n*
parcel *s* fasciculus *m*; (*plot of land*)
   agellus *m*
parcel *vt* **to — out** partire, disper-
   tire
parch *vt* torrēre
parched *adj* torridus, aridus; **to be
   —** arēre
parchment *s* membrana *f*
pardon *s* venia *f*
pardon *vt* ignoscĕre (*with dat*); (*an
   offense*) condonare
pardonable *adj* ignoscendus, condo-
   nandus
pare *vt* (*vegetables*) deglubĕre; (*the
   nails*) resecare
parent *s* parens *m & f*
parentage *s* genus *n*, stirps *f*
parental *adj* patrius
parenthesis *s* interpositio, interclusio *f*
parity *s* paritas, aequalitas *f*
park *s* horti *m pl*
parlance *s* sermo *m*
parley *s* colloquium *n*
parley *vi* colloqui
parliament *s* senat·us -ūs *m*
parliamentary *adj* senatorius
parlor *s* exedrium *n*
parody *s* ridicula imitatio *f*
parole *s* fides *f*
paroxysm *s* access·us -ūs *m*
parricide *s* (*murder*) parricidium *n*;
   (*murderer*) parricida *m & f*
parrot *s* psittacus *m*
parry *vt* avertĕre, defendĕre
parse *vt* flectĕre
parsimonious *adj* parcus; **—ly**
   parce
parsing *s* partium orationis flexio *f*
parsley *s* apium *n*
part *s* pars *f*; (*in play*) partes *f pl*;
   (*duty*) officium *n*; **for the most —**
   maximam partem; **in — partim;
   on the — of** ab (*with abl*); **to act
   the — of** sustinēre partes (*with
   genit*); **to take — in** interesse
   (*with dat*), particeps esse (*with
   genit*)
part *vt* separare, dividĕre; **to —
   company** discedĕre; *vi* discedĕre,
   abire; (*to go open*) dehiscĕre; **to —
   with** dimittĕre
partial *adj* iniquus; (*incomplete*)
   mancus; **to be — to** favēre (*with dat*);
   —ly aliqua ex parte
partiality *s* iniquitas *f*
participant *s* particeps *m & f*
participate *vi* interesse; **to — in**
   interesse (*with dat*), particeps esse
   (*with genit*)
participation *s* participatio, societas *f*
participle *s* participium *n*
particle *s* particula *f*

particular *adj* (*own*) proprius; (*special*) peculiaris, singularis, praecipuus; (*fussy*) fastidiosus; **—ly** praecipue, praesertim

particularize *vt* exsequi

particulars *s* singula *n pl*

parting *s* discess·us -ūs, digress·us -ūs *m*

partisan *s* fautor *m*

partition *s* partitio *f*; (*between rooms*) paries *m*; (*enclosure*) saeptum *n*

partly *adv* partim, ex parte

partner *s* socius *m*, socia *f*, particeps *m* & *f*; (*in office*) collega *m*; (*in marriage*) conju(n)x, consors *m* & *f*

partnership *s* consociatio, societas, consortio *f*

partridge *s* perdix *m* & *f*

party *s* (*entertainment*) convivium *n*; (*pol*) factio *f*, partes *f pl*; (*detachment*) man·us -ūs *f*; **to join a** **— partes** sequi

pass *s* angustiae *f pl*

pass *vt* (*to go by*) praeterire, transire, transgredi; (*to exceed*) excedēre; (*to approve*) probare; (*time*) agēre, degēre; (*a law*) perferre; **to** **— around** circumferre, tradēre; **to — down** tradēre; **to — sentence** jus dicēre; **to — the test** approbari; *vi* (*of time*) transire, abire, praeterire; **to come to —** evenire, fieri; **to let —** praetermittēre, dimittēre; **to — away** (*to die*) perire, abire; **to — for** habēri, vidēri; **to — on** (*to go forward*) pergēre; (*to die*) perire; **to — out** collabi, intermori; **to — over** transire

passable *adj* (*of road*) pervius; (*fig*) mediocris, tolerabilis

passably *adv* mediocriter, tolerabiliter

passage *s* (*act*) transit·us -ūs *m*; (*by water*) transmissio, trajectio *f*; (*of book*) locus *m*

passenger *s* viator *m*; (*on ship*) vector *m*

passer-by *s* praeteriens *m*

passing *s* obit·us -ūs *m*

passion *s* cupiditas, permotio *f*, fervor *m*; (*anger*) ira *f*; (*lust*) libido *f*

passionate *adj* fervidus, ardens; iracundus; **—ly** ardenter; iracunde

passive *adj* passivus; **—ly** passive

passport *s* diploma *n*

password *s* tessera *f*

past *adj* praeteritus; (*immediately preceding*) proximus, superior

past *s* tempus praeteritum *n*

past *prep* praeter (*with acc*), post (*with acc*)

paste *s* gluten *n*

paste *vt* agglutinare, conglutinare

pasteboard *s* charta crassa *f*

pastime *s* oblectamentum *n*, ludus *m*

pastoral *adj* pastoralis, bucolicus

pastoral *s* poema bucolicum *n*

pastry *s* crustum *n*

pasture *s* past·us -ūs *m*, pascuum *n*, pastio *f*

pasture *vt* pascěre; *vi* (*to graze*) pasci

pat *adj* idoneus

pat *vt* permulcēre, demulcēre

patch *s* assumentum *n*, pannus *m*

patch *vt* resarcire, assuēre

patchwork *s* cento *m*

patent *adj* apertus, manifestus; **—ly** manifesto

patent *s* privilegium *n*

paternal *adj* paternus

paternity *s* paternitas *f*

path *s* semita *f*, trames, callis *m*; (*fig*) via *f*

pathetic *adj* maestus; **—ally** maeste

pathless *adj* invius

pathos *s* pathos *n*, dolor *m*

pathway *s* semita *f*, callis, trames *m*

patience *s* patientia *f*

patient *adj* patiens, tolerans; **—ly** patienter, aequo animo

patient *s* aegrotus *m*, aegrota *f*

patriarch *s* patriarcha *m*

patriarchal *adj* patriarchicus

patrician *adj* patricius

patrician *s* patricius *m*

patrimony *s* patrimonium *n*

patriot *s* amans patriae *m*

patriotic *adj* amans patriae

patriotism *s* amor patriae, amor in patriam *m*

patrol *s* excubiae *f pl*

patrol *vt* circumire; *vi* excubias agēre

patron *s* patronus *m*

patronage *s* patrocinium, praesidium *n*

patroness *s* patrona *f*

patronize *vt* favēre (*with dat*), fovēre

patronymic *s* patronymicum nomen *n*

pattern *s* exemplar, exemplum, specimen *n*

paucity *s* paucitas *f*

paunch *s* ingluvies *f*

pauper *s* pauper *m*

pause *s* pausa, mora *f*; (*mus*) intermissio *f*, intervallum *n*

pause *vi* insistēre, intermittēre

pave *vt* sternēre

pavement *s* pavimentum *n*, stratura *f*

pavilion *s* tentorium *n*

paving stone *s* saxum quadratum *n*

paw *s* ungula *f*, pes *m*

paw *vt* pedibus pulsare

pawn *s* pignus *n*

pawn *vt* pignerare

pawnbroker *s* pignerator *m*

pay *s* merces *f*; (*mil*) stipendium *n*

pay *vt* solvēre; (*in full*) persolvēre, pendēre; (*mil*) stipendium numerare (*with dat*); **to — a compliment** **to** laudare; **to — for** solvēre (*with acc of thing and dat of person*); **to — respects to** salutare; **to — the penalty** poenam dare, poenam luēre; *vi* **it pays** operae pretium est, prodest, lucro est

payable *adj* solvendus

paymaster *s* dispensator *m*; (*mil*) tribunus aerarius *m*

payment *s* (*act*) solutio *f*; (*sum of money*) pensio *f*

pea s pisum, cicer n
peace s pax f; quies f, otium n
peaceful adj tranquillus, placidus, pacatus; —**ly** tranquille, placide, cum bona pace
peacemaker s pacificator m
peace offering s placamen, placamentum, piaculum n
peacetime s otium n
peach s malum Persicum n
peacock s pavo m
peak s (of mountain) cacumen n; vertex, apex m
peal s (of thunder) fragor m; (of bells) concent·us -ūs m
peal vi resonare
pear s pirum n
pearl s margarita f
pearly adj gemmeus
peasant s agricola, colonus m
peasantry s agricolae, agrestes m pl
pebble s lapillus, calculus m
peck s modius m
peck vt rostro impetēre, vellicare
peculation s peculat·us -ūs m
peculiar adj proprius, peculiaris, praecipuus, singularis; —**ly** praecipue
peculiarity s proprietas f
pecuniary adj pecuniarius
pedagogue s paedagogus m; (schoolmaster) magister m
pedant s scholasticus m
pedantic adj putidus, nimis diligens; —**ally** nimis diligenter
pedantry s eruditio insulsa f
peddle vt venditare, circumferre
peddler s venditor, institor m
pedestal s basis f
pedestrian adj pedester
pedestrian s pedes m
pedigree s stemma n, stirps f
pediment s fastigium n
peel s cortex m
peel vt decorticare, glubēre
peep s aspect·us -ūs, tuit·us -ūs m
peep vi inspicēre
peephole s conspicillum n
peer s par m; (of peerage) patricius m
peer vi to — at intuēri
peerless adj unicus, incomparabilis
peevish adj stomachosus, morosus, difficilis; —**ly** stomachose, morose
peg s clavus, paxillus m
pelican s pelicanus, onocrotalus m
pellet s globulus m
pelt s pellis f
pelt vt (to hurl) jacēre; (to beat) verberare, petēre
pen s (to write with) calamus, stylus m; (enclosure) saeptum n; (for sheep) ovile n; (for pigs) suile n
pen vt scribēre, componēre; **to — in** includēre
penal adj poenalis
penalize vt poenā afficēre, mul(c)tare
penalty s poena, mul(c)ta f
penance s satisfactio f
pencil s stilus m, graphis f
pending adj suspensus; (law) sub judice
pending prep inter (with acc)

pendulum s libramentum n
penetrate vt penetrare
penetrating adj acer, perspicax
penetration s acies mentis f, acumen n
peninsula s paeninsula f
penitence s paenitentia f
penitent adj paenitens; —**ly** paenitenter
penitentiary s carcer m
penknife s scalpellum n
penmanship s man·us -ūs f
pennant s vexillum n
penniless adj inops
penny s quadrans m
pension s annua n pl
pensive adj meditabundus
penultimate s paenultima syllaba f
penurious adj parcus, sordidus
penury s egestas, inopia f
people s (nation) populus m; homines m pl; (common people) plebs f; — **say** dicunt
people vt frequentare
pepper s piper n
pepper vt pipere condire; (fig) (with blows) verberare
peppermint s mentha f
perceive vt percipēre, sentire, vidēre, intellegēre
percentage s portio f
perceptible adj percipiendus, manifestus
perceptibly adv sensim
perception s perceptio f, sens·us -ūs m
perch s (for birds) pertica f; (type of fish) perca f
perch vi insidēre
perchance adv forte
percolate vt percolare; vi permanare
percussion s ict·us -ūs, concuss·us -ūs m
perdition s interit·us -ūs m; exitium n
peremptory adj arrogans
perennial adj perennis
perfect adj perfectus, absolutus; (gram) praeteritus; —**ly** perfecte, absolute; (entirely) plane
perfect vt perficēre, absolvēre
perfection s perfectio, absolutio f
perfidious adj perfidus, perfidiosus; —**ly** perfidiose
perfidy s perfidia f
perforate vt perforare, terebrare
perforation s foramen n
perform vt perficēre, peragēre; (duty) fungi (with abl); (to play) agēre
performance s perfunctio, executio f; (work) opus n; (of a play) actio f; (play, drama) fabula f
performer s actor m; (in play) histrio m
perfume s odor m, unguentum n
perfume vt odoribus imbuēre
perhaps adv forte, forsitan, fortasse
peril s periculum n
perilous adj periculosus; —**ly** periculose
period s (gram) periodus f; tempus, spatium n, aetas f; (rhet) circuit·us -ūs m

periodic adj certus; (*style*) periodicus; —**ally** certis temporibus

periphery s peripheria f, ambit·us -ūs m

periphrastic adj per periphrasin dictus

perish vi perire, interire

perishable adj fragilis, caducus, mortalis

peristyle s peristyl(i)um n

perjure vt to — oneself pejerare, perjurare

perjured adj perjurus

perjury s perjurium n; to commit — pejerare, perjurare

permanence s stabilitas, constantia f

permanent adj diuturnus, perpetuus, mansurus; —**ly** perpetuo

permeable adj pervius

permeate vt penetrare; vi permanare

permission s permissio, venia, potestas f

permit vt permittĕre (*with dat*), sinĕre

permutation s permutatio f

pernicious adj perniciosus; —**ly** perniciose

peroration s peroratio f

perpendicular adj perpendicularis, directus

perpendicular s linea perpendicularis f

perpetrate vt facĕre, perficĕre

perpetrator s auctor, reus m

perpetual adj perpetuus, perennis, sempiternus; —**ly** perpetuo

perpetuate vt perpetuare, continuare

perpetuity s perpetuitas f

perplex vt turbare, confundĕre

perplexing adj perplexus, ambiguus

perplexity s perturbatio, dubitatio f

persecute vt persequi, insequi, vexare

persecution s insectatio f

persecutor s insectator m

perseverance s perseverantia, constantia f

persevere vi perseverare, perstare, constare

persevering adj perseverans, constans, tenax; —**ly** perseverante, constanter

persist vi perstare, perseverare

persistence s permansio, pertinacia, perseverantia f

persistent adj pertinax; —**ly** pertinaciter

person s homo m & f, quidam m; (*body*) corpus n; in — ipse

personage s persona f

personal adj privatus, suus; (*gram*) personalis; —**ly** ipse, per se, coram

personality s persona, natura f, ingenium n

personification s prosopopoeia f

personify vt personā induĕre

personnel s membra n pl, socii m pl

perspective s scaenographia f

perspicacious adj perspicax

perspicacity s perspicacitas f

perspiration s sudatio f, sudor m

perspire vi sudare

persuade vt persuadĕre (*with dat*)

persuasion s persuasio f

persuasive adj suasorius; —**ly** persuasibiliter

pert adj procax; —**ly** procaciter

pertain vi pertinēre, attinēre

pertinent adj appositus; to be — ad rem pertinēre; —**ly** apposite

perturb vt turbare, perturbare

perturbation s perturbatio f

perusal s perlectio f

peruse vt perlegĕre, evolvĕre

pervade vt invadĕre, permanare, perfundĕre

perverse adj perversus, pravus; —**ly** perverse

perversion s depravatio f

perversity s perversitas, pravitas f

pervert vt (*words*) detorquĕre; depravare, corrumpĕre

pest s pestis f

pester vt vexare, infestare, sollicitare

pestilence s pestilentia f

pestle s pilum n

pet s corculum n, deliciae f pl

pet vt fovēre, in deliciis habēre

petal s floris folium n

petition s petitio f, preces f pl; (*pol*) libellus m

petition vt supplicare, orare

petitioner s supplex m

petrify vt in lapidem convertĕre; vi lapidescĕre

petticoat s subucula f

pettiness s animus angustus m

petty adj minutus, angustus, levis

petulance s petulantia, protervitas f

petulant adj protervus

phalanx s phalanx f

phantom s simulacrum, phantasma n, species f

pharmacy s ars medicamentaria f; (*drugstore*) taberna medicina, apotheca f

phase s (*of moon*) lunae facies f; (*fig*) vices f pl

pheasant s phasianus m, phasiana f

phenomenal adj singularis

phenomenon s res f; (*remarkable event*) portentum, prodigium n

philanthropic adj humanus

philanthropy s humanitas f

philologist s philologus, grammaticus m

philology s philologia f

philosopher s philosophus, sapiens m

philosophical adj philosophicus; —**ly** philosophice, sapienter; (*calmly*) aequo animo

philosophize vi philosophari

philosophy s philosophia, sapientia f; (*theory*) ratio f

philter s philtrum n

phlegm s pituita f, phelgma n

phlegmatic adj (*fig*) lentus

phosphorus s phosphorus m

phrase s locutio f; (*gram*) incisum n

phraseology s locutio, loquendi ratio f

physical adj physicus; (*natural*) corporis (*genit, used adjectively*); —**ly** naturā

physician *s* medicus *m*
physicist *s* physicus *m*
physics *s* physica *n pl*
physiognomy *s* oris habit·us -ūs *m*
physique *s* vires *f pl*
pick *vt* (*to choose*) eligĕre; (*to pluck*) carpĕre; (*to gather*) decerpĕre; to — off avellĕre; to — out eligĕre; to — up tollĕre
pick *s* (*tool*) dolabra *f*; (*best part*) flos *m*, lecti *m pl*
pickax *s* dolabra *f*
picked *adj* electus, delectus
picket *s* (*mil*) statio *f*
pickle *s* muria *f*
pickle *vt* in aceto condire, in muriā condire
pickled *adj* muriā conditus
picture *s* tabula picta, pictura *f*; (*fig*) descriptio *f*
picture *vt* (*to imagine*) findĕre, ante oculos ponĕre
picture gallery *s* pinacotheca *f*
picturesque *adj* venustus, amoenus
pie *s* crustum *n*
piece *s* pars, portio *f*; (*of food*) frustum *n*; (*of cloth*) pannus *m*; (*broken off*) fragmentum *n*; (*coin*) nummus *m*; (*drama*) fabula *f*; to fall to —s dilabi; to tear to —s dilaniare, lacerare
piece *vt* resarcire; to — together fabricari, consuĕre
piecemeal *adv* frustatim, membratim
pier *s* moles *f*, agger *m*
pierce *vt* perforare; (*with sword, etc.*) transfigĕre, perfodĕre; (*fig*) pungĕre
piercing *adj* acutus, stridulus
piety *s* pietas, religio *f*
pig *s* porcus *m*, sus *m & f*
pigeon *s* columba *f*
pigment *s* pigmentum *n*
pigsty *s* hara *f*, suile *n*
pike *s* (*weapon*) hasta *f*; (*fish*) lupus *m*
pilaster *s* parasta, columella *f*
pile *s* (*heap*) acervus, cumulus *m*; (*for cremation*) rogus *m*; (*for building*) moles *f*; (*nap of cloth*) villus *m*
pile *vt* coacervare, congerĕre; to — up exstruĕre
pilgrim *s* peregrinator *m*
pilgrimage *s* peregrinatio *f*
pill *s* pilula *f*
pillage *s* vastatio, direptio, expilatio, rapina *f*
pillage *vt* vastare, diripĕre, depopulari, expilare, praedari
pillar *s* columna, pila *f*, columen *n*
pillow *s* pulvinus *m*, culcita *f*, cervical *n*
pillowcase *s* cervicalis integumentum *n*
pilot *s* gubernator *m*
pilot *vt* gubernare
pimp *s* leno *m*
pimple *s* pustula *f*
pimply *adj* pustulosus
pin *s* ac·us -ūs, acicula *f*; (*peg*) clavus *m*
pin *vt* acu figĕre; affigĕre
pincers *s* forceps *m & f*

pinch *vt* vellicare; (*as cold*) (*ad*)urĕre; (*to squeeze*) coartare; (*of shoe*) urĕre
pine *s* pinus *f*
pine *vi* to — away tabescĕre, languĕre; to — for desiderare
pineapple *s* (nux) pinea *f*
pink *adj* rosaceus, rubicundus
pinnacle *s* fastigium *n*, summus grad·us -ūs *m*
pint *s* sextarius *m*
pioneer *s* praecursor *m*
pious *adj* pius; (*scrupulous*) religiosus; (*saintly*) sanctus; —ly pie, religiose, sancte
pipe *s* (*tube*) tubus *m*; (*mus*) fistula *f*
pipe *vt* fistulā canĕre
piper *s* tibicen *m*
piquant *adj* salsus, facetus; —ly salse
pique *s* offensio *f*
pique *vt* offendĕre
piracy *s* latrocinium *n*
pirate *s* pirata, praedo *m*
piratical *adj* praedatorius
pit *s* fossa, fovea *f*, puteus *m*; (*in theater*) cavea *f*; (*quarry*) fodina *f*
pitch *s* pix *f*; (*sound*) sonus *m*; (*degree*) grad·us -ūs *m*, fastigium *n*; (*slope*) fastigium *n*; to such a — of eo (*with genit*)
pitch *vt* (*to fling*) conjicĕre; (*camp*) ponĕre; (*tent*) tendĕre
pitcher *s* urceus *m*
pitchfork *s* furca *f*
piteous *adj* miserabilis; —ly miserabiliter, misere
pitfall *s* fovea *f*
pith *s* medulla *f*
pithy *adj* (*fig*) sententiosus
pitiable *adj* miserandus
pitiful *adj* misericors; (*pitiable*) miserabilis, miserandus; —ly misere
pitiless *adj* immisericors, durus; —ly immisericorditer
pittance *s* (*allowance for food*) demensum *n*; (*trifling sum*) mercedula *f*
pity *s* misericordia, miseratio *f*
pity *vt* miserēri (*with genit*); I — him miseret me ejus
pivot *s* axis, paxillus *m*; (*fig*) cardo *m*
placard *s* titulus, libellus *m*
place *s* locus *m*; in — of pro (*with abl*), loco (*with genit*); in the first — primum, primo; out of — intempestivus; to take — fieri, accidĕre
place *vt* ponĕre, locare, collocare
placid *adj* placidus, tranquillus; —ly placide, tranquille
plagiarism *s* furtum litterarium *n*
plagiarist *s* fur litterarius *m*
plagiarize *vt* furari
plague *s* pestilentia *f*; (*fig*) pestis *f*
plague *vt* vexare, exagitare
plain *s* campus *m*, planities *f*; of the — campester
plain *adj* (*clear*) apertus, manifestus, perspicuus; (*unadorned*) inornatus, simplex; (*of one color*) unicolor; (*frank*) sincerus; (*homely*)

invenustus; —ly aperte, manifeste; simpliciter; sincere

plaintiff s petitor m

plaintive adj querulus, flebilis; **—ly** flebiliter

plan s consilium, propositum n; (drawing) descriptio f; (layout) forma f

plan vt (to scheme) excogitare, meditari; (to intend to) in animo habēre (with inf); (to draw) designare, describēre

plane s (tool) runcina f; (level surface) planities f

plane vt runcinare

planet s planeta, stella errans or vaga f

plank s assis m, tabula f

plant s planta, herba f

plant vt serēre, conserēre; (feet) ponēre

plantation s plantarium n

planter s sator m

planting s sat·us -ūs m, consitura f

plaster s tectorium, gypsum n; (med) emplastrum n

plaster vt gypsare, dealbare

plastic adj plasticus, ductilis

plate s (dish) patella f, catillus m; (coating) lamina f; (silver) argentum n

plated adj bracteatus

platform s suggest·us -ūs m, suggestum n

platitude s trita sententia f

Platonic adj Platonis (genit, used adjectively)

platter s patella, lanx f

plausible adj verisimilis

play s ludus m; (drama) fabula f

play vt ludēre; (instrument) canēre (with abl); (game) ludēre (with abl) (role) agēre; **to — a trick on** ludificari

player s (in game) lusor m; (on stage) histrio, actor m; (on wind instrument) tibicen m; (on string instrument) fidicen m

playful adj lascivus, jocosus, ludibundus; (words) facetus; **—ly** per ludum, per jocum

playmate s collusor m

plaything s ludibrium n

playwright s fabularum scriptor m

plea s (law) petitio, exceptio, defensio f; (excuse) excusatio f

plead vi (in court) causam agēre; (to beg) obsecrare, implorare, orare; **to — against** causam dicēre contra (with acc); **to — for** defendēre

pleasant adj amoenus, gratus, jucundus, suavis; **—ly** jucunde, suaviter

pleasantry s jocosa dicacitas f, facetiae f pl

please vt placēre (with dat), delectare; **if you —** si placet; **please!** obsecro!; **sis!, amabo!** (colloquial)

pleasing adj gratus, jucundus

pleasurable adj jucundus

pleasure s voluptas f; **it is my —** libet; **to derive —** voluptatem capēre

plebeian adj plebeius

plebeians s plebs f

pledge s pignus n; (proof) testimonium n

pledge vt (op)pignerare, obligare; **to — one's word** fidem obligare

Pleiads s Pleiades f pl

plenary adj plenus, perfectus

plenipotentiary s legatus m

plentiful adj largus, affluens, uber; **—ly** large, ubertim

plenty s copia, abundantia f

plethora s pletura f

pleurisy s pleuritis f

pliable adj flexibilis, tractabilis, mansuetus

pliant adj lentus

plight s conditio f, stat·us -ūs m, discrimen n

plod vi assidue laborare

plodder s sedulus homo m

plodding adj laboriosus, assiduus, sedulus

plot s (conspiracy) conjuratio f, insidiae f pl; (of drama) argumentum n; (of ground) agellus m

plot vi conjurare, moliri

plow s aratrum n

plow vt arare; **to — up** exarare

plowing s aratio f

plowman s bubulcus, arator m

plowshare s vomer m

pluck s animus m

pluck vt carpēre; **to — off** avellēre, decerpēre; **to — out** evellēre, eripēre; **to — up** eruēre; **to — up courage** animo esse

plug s obturamentum n

plug vt obturare

plum s prunum n

plumage s plumae, pennae f pl

plumber s plumbarius m

plume s crista f

plummet s perpendiculum n

plump adj pinguis, obesus

plum tree s prunus f

plunder s (act) rapina f; (booty) praeda f

plunder vt praedari

plunderer s praedator m

plundering s rapina, praedatio f

plundering adj praedatorius, praedabundus

plunge vt mergēre, submergēre; (sword, etc.) condēre; vi immergi, se mergēre

pluperfect s plus quam perfectum tempus n

plural adj pluralis

plurality s multitudo f, numerus major m

plush adj lautus

ply vt exercēre, urgēre

poach vt (eggs) frigēre; vi illicita venatione uti

poacher s fur m

pocket s sin·us -ūs, sacculus m

pocket vt in sacculis condēre

pocket book s pugillaria n pl

pockmark s cicatrix f

pod s siliqua f

poem s poema, carmen n

poet s poeta, vates m

poetess *s* poetria, poetris *f*
poetic *adj* poeticus; **—ly** poetice
poetics *s* ars poetica *f*
poetry *s* (*art*) poetice *f*; (*poems*) poemata, carmina *n pl*, poesis *f*
poignancy *s* acerbitas *f*
poignant *adj* acerbus, pungens
point *s* punctum *n*; (*pointed end*) acumen *n*, acies *f*; (*of swords, etc.*) mucro *m*; (*fig*) quaestio, res *f*, stat·us -ūs *m*, argumentum *n*; **beside the —** ab re; **from this —** on posthac, hinc; **— of view** sententia *f*; **to the —** ad rem; **up to this —** adhuc, hactenus
point *vt* (*to sharpen*) acuěre; **to — out** monstrare, indicare
pointed *adj* acutus; (*fig*) salsus; (*stinging*) aculeatus; **—ly** acute, aperte
pointer *s* index *m & f*
pointless *adj* (*fig*) insulsus, frigidus; **—ly** insulse
poise *s* (*fig*) urbanitas *f*
poise *vt* ponderare, penděre, librare
poison *s* venenum, virus *n*
poison *vt* venenare, veneno necare; (*fig*) vitiare
poisoning *s* veneficium *n*
poisonous *adj* venenatus, venenosus
poke *vt* (*to jab*) cubito pulsare, fodicare; (*fire*) foděre
polar *adj* arcticus
polarity *s* polaritas *f*
pole *s* asser, contus *m*, pertica *f*; (*of earth*) polus *m*
polemic *s* controversiae *f pl*
pole star *s* stella polaris *f*
police *s* vigiles, custodes *m pl*
policeman *s* vigil *m*
policy *s* ratio *f*, consilium *n*
polish *vt* polire; **to — up** expolire
polish *s* nitor, levor *m*; (*refined manners*) urbanitas *f*; (*literary*) lima *f*
polite *adj* comis, urbanus; **—ly** comiter, urbane
politeness *s* urbanitas, comitas *f*
politic *adj* prudens, astutus
political *adj* civilis, publicus
politician *s* magistrat·us -ūs *m*
politics *s* res publica *f*; **to enter —** ad rem publicam acceděre
poll *s* caput *n*; **—s** comitia *n pl*
poll *vt* suffragiis petěre
polling booth *s* saeptum *n*
poll tax *s* capitum exactio *f*
pollute *vt* polluěre, inquinare, contaminare
pollution *s* (*act*) contaminatio *f*; (*filth*) colluvio, impuritas *f*
polygamy *s* polygamia *f*
polysyllabic *adj* polysyllabus
polytheism *s* multorum deorum cult·us -ūs *m*
pomegranate *s* malum Punicum *n*
pommel *vt* pulsare, verberare
pomp *s* pompa *f*, apparat·us -ūs *m*
pomposity *s* magnificentia *f*
pompous *adj* magnificus, gloriosus; **—ly** magnifice, gloriose
pond *s* stagnum *n*
ponder *vt* in mente agitare, considerare, ponderare

ponderous *adj* ponderosus, praegravis
pontiff *s* pontifex *m*
pontifical *adj* pontificalis
pontificate *s* pontificat·us -ūs *m*
pontoon *s* ponto *m*
pony *s* mannulus, equullus *m*
pool *s* lacuna *f*, stagnum *n*
pool *vt* conferre
poor *adj* (*needy*) pauper, inops, egens; (*inferior*) tenuis, mediocris; (*of soil*) macer; (*pitiable*) miser; (*meager*) exilis; **—ly** parum, mediocriter, misere, tenuiter
pop *s* crepit·us -ūs *m*
pop *vi* crepare; **to — out** exsilire
poplar *s* populus *f*
poppy *s* papaver *n*
populace *s* vulgus *n*, plebs *f*
popular *adj* popularis; **—ly** populariter
popularity *s* populi favor *m*, populi studium *n*
populate *vt* frequentare
population *s* civium numerus, incolarum numerus *m*
populous *adj* frequens
porcelain *s* fictilia *n pl*
porch *s* vestibulum *n*, portic·us -ūs *f*
porcupine *s* hystrix *f*
pore *s* foramen *n*
pore *vi* **to — over** assidue considerare, scrutari
pork *s* porcina *f*
porous *adj* rarus
porpoise *s* porculus marinus *m*
porridge *s* puls *f*
port *s* port·us -ūs *m*
portal *s* porta *f*
portend *vt* praesagire, portenděre, significare
portent *s* monstrum, portentum, prodigium *n*
portentous *adj* monstruosus, prodigiosus
porter *s* janitor, ostiarius *m*; (*carrier*) bajulus *m*
portfolio *s* scrinium *n*
portico *s* portic·us -ūs *f*
portion *s* portio, pars *f*
portion *vt* partire
portly *adj* amplus, opimus
portrait *s* imago, effigies *f*
portray *vt* depingěre, expriměre
pose *s* stat·us -ūs, habit·us -ūs *m*
pose *vi* habitum *or* statum suměre
position *s* positio *f*, sit·us -ūs *m*; (*of body*) gest·us -ūs *m*; (*office*) honos *m*; (*state*) conditio *f*, stat·us -ūs *m*; (*rank*) amplitudo, dignitas *f*
positive *adj* certus; (*gram*) positivus; (*fig*) confidens; **—ly** praecise, certo
possess *vt* possiděre, teněre
possession *s* possessio *f*; (*estate*) bona *n pl*; **in the — of** penes (*with acc*); **to gain — of** potiri (*with abl*), occupare
possessive *adj* quaestuosus, avarus; (*gram*) possessivus
possessor *s* possessor, dominus *m*
possibility *s* facultas *f*
possible *adj* **as quickly as —** quam celerrime; **it is —** fieri po-

test; **it is — for me to** possum (*with inf*)

possibly *adv* fortasse

post *s* (*stake*) postis, cippus *m*; (*station*) statio, sedes stativa *f*; (*position*) munus *n*

post *vt* collocare, ponĕre, constituĕre; **to — a letter** tabellario litteras dare

postage *s* vectura (epistulae) *f*

postdate *vt* diem seriorem scribĕre (*with dat*)

poster *s* libellus *m*

posterior *adj* posterior

posterity *s* posteri, minores *m pl*, posteritas *f*

posthaste *adv* quam celerrime

posthumous *adj* postumus

postman *s* tabellarius *m*

postpone *vt* differre, prorogare

postscript *s* ascriptio *f*

posture *s* stat·us -ūs, habit·us -ūs, gest·us -ūs *m*

pot *s* olla *f*, ahenum *n*

potato *s* solanum tuberosum *n*

potentate *s* tyrannus *m*

potential *adj* futurus

potion *s* potio *f*

potter *s* figulus *m*

pottery *s* fictilia *n pl*

pouch *s* sacculus *m*, pera *f*

poultry *s* aves cohortales *f pl*

pounce *vi* **to — on** insilire (*with dat or in + acc*)

pound *s* libra *f*

pound *vt* contundĕre, conterĕre

pour *vt* fundĕre; **to — in** infundĕre; **to — out** effundĕre; *vi* fundi, fluĕre; **to — down** (*of rain*) ruĕre

pouring *adj* (*of rain*) effusus

pout *vi* stomachari

poverty *s* paupertas, pauperies *f*

powder *s* pulvis *m*

powder *vt* pulvere conspergĕre

power *s* vis, potestas *f*; (*pol*) imperium *n*; (*mil*) copiae *f pl*; (*excessive*) potentia *f*; (*divine*) numen *n*; **to have great —** multum posse, multum valēre

powerful *adj* validus, potens; (*effectual*) efficax; **—ly** valde

powerless *adj* invalidus, impotens; (*vain*) irritus; **to be —** nil valēre

practical *adj* utilis, habilis; **—ly** fere, paene

practice *s* us·us -ūs *m*, experientia, exercitatio *f*; (*custom*) mos *m*, consuetudo *f*

practice *vt* (*to engage in*) exercēre, tractare; (*to rehearse*) meditari

practitioner *s* exercitator *m*; (*medical*) medicus *m*

pragmatic *adj* pragmaticus

prairie *s* campus *m*

praise *s* laus *f*

praise *vt* laudare

praiseworthy *adj* laudabilis, laudandus

prance *vi* exsultare, subsultare; (*of persons*) jactare

prank *s* ludus *m*; (*trick*) jocus, dolus *m*

pray *vt* precari, orare; *vi* precari, orare; **to — for** petĕre, precari;

to — to adorare, supplicare

prayer *s* preces *f pl*

preach *vt & vi* praedicare

preamble *s* prooemium, exordium *n*

precarious *adj* precarius, periculosus, incertus; **—ly** precario

precaution *s* cautio, provisio *f*; **to take —** cavēre, praecavēre

precede *vt* praeire (*with dat*), antecedĕre

precedence *s* prior locus *m*; **to take — over** antecedĕre

precedent *s* exemplum *n*

preceding *adj* prior, superior

precept *s* praeceptum *n*

preceptor *s* praeceptor, magister *m*

precinct *s* termini, limites *m pl*, templum *n*; (*ward*) regio *f*

precious *adj* pretiosus, carus; **— stone** gemma *f*

precipice *s* praeceps *n*; **down a —** in praeceps

precipitate *vt* praecipitare

precipitous *adj* praeceps, praeruptus, declivis

precise *adj* certus, definitus; (*exact*) accuratus, exactus; **—ly** subtiliter, accurate

precision *s* accuratio, cura *f*

preclude *vt* praecludĕre, excludĕre

precocious *adj* praecox

preconceive *vt* praecipĕre, praesentire; **preconceived idea** praejudicium *n*

preconception *s* praeceptio, praejudicata opinio *f*

precursor *s* praenuntius *m*

predatory *adj* praedatorius, praedabundus

predecessor *s* antecessor, decessor *m*

predestine *vt* praedestinare

predicament *s* discrimen *n*, angustiae *f pl*

predicate *vt* praedicare

predicate *s* praedicatum *n*

predict *vt* praedicĕre, augurari

prediction *s* praedictio *f*, praedictum, vaticinium *n*

predilection *s* studium *n*

predispose *vt* inclinare

predisposition *s* inclinatio *f*

predominant *adj* praevalens

predominate *vi* praevalēre

preeminence *s* praestantia, excellentia *f*

preeminent *adj* praecipuus, praestans, excellens; **—ly** praecipue, excellenter

preexist *vi* antea exstare *or* esse

preface *s* praefatio *f*

prefatory *adj* **to make a few — remarks** pauca praefari

prefect *s* praefectus *m*

prefecture *s* praefectura *f*

prefer *vt* praeponĕre, anteponĕre; (*charges*) deferre; **to — to** (*would rather*) malle (*with inf*)

preferable *adj* potior, praestantior

preference *s* favor *m*; **in — to** potius quam; **to give — to** anteponĕre

preferment *s* honos *m*

prefix *s* syllaba praeposita *f*

prefix *vt* praefigĕre, praeponĕre

pregnancy *s* graviditas *f*

pregnant *adj* gravida; *(of language)* pressus

prejudge *vt* praejudicare

prejudice *s* praejudicata opinio *f*, praejudicium *n*

prejudice *vt* to be prejudiced against praejudicatam opinionem habēre in *(with acc)*, invidēre *(with dat)*; to — the people against studia hominum inclinare in *(with acc)*

prejudicial *adj* noxius

preliminary *adj* praevius; to make a few — remarks pauca praefari

prelude *s (mus)* prooemium *n*, praelusio *f*

prelude *vt* praeludĕre

premature *adj* praematurus, immaturus, praeproperus; —ly ante tempus

premeditate *vt* praemeditari

premier *s* princeps *m*

premise *s (major)* propositio *f*; *(minor)* assumptio *f*; —s fundus *m*, praedium *n*

premium *s* praemium *n*; at a — carus

premonition *s* monit·us -ūs *m*, monitum *n*

preoccupation *s* praeoccupatio *f*

preoccupy *vt* praeoccupare

preparation *s* comparatio, praeparatio *f*, apparat·us -ūs *m*; *(rehearsal)* meditatio *f*

prepare *vt* parare, comparare, apparare; *(to rehearse)* meditari; to — to parare *(with inf)*

preponderance *s* praestantia *f*

preposition *s* praepositio *f*

preposterous *adj* praeposterus; —ly praepostere, absurde

prerogative *s* jus *n*

presage *s* praesagium *n*

presage *vt* praesagire, portendĕre, significare

prescience *s* providentia *f*

prescient *adj* providus, sagax

prescribe *vt* praescribĕre, proponĕre

prescription *s* praescriptum *n*; *(of physician)* medicamenti formula *f*

presence *s* praesentia *f*; *(look)* aspect·us -ūs *m*; in my — me praesente; in the — of coram *(with abl)*

present *adj* praesens, hic; for the — in praesens tempus; to be — adesse; —ly mox, illico, statim

present *s* donum, munus *n*

present *vt* donare, offerre; introducĕre; *(in court)* sistĕre; *(to bring forward)* praebēre, offerre; to — itself *or* oneself occurrĕre, obvenire

presentation *s* donatio *f*; *(on stage)* fabula *f*

presentiment *s* praesagitio *f*, praesagium *n*

preservation *s* conservatio *f*

preserve *vt* conservare; *(fruits)* condire

preserver *s* conservator *m*

preside *vi* praesidĕre, praeesse; to — over praesidĕre *(with dat)*, praeesse *(with dat)*

presidency *s* praefectura *f*

president *s* praeses, praefectus *m*

press *s (for wine)* prelum *n*; *(of people)* turba *f*

press *vt* premĕre, comprimĕre; *(fig)* urgēre; to — down deprimĕre; *vi* to — forward anniti; to — on pergĕre, contendĕre

pressing *adj* gravis, urgens

pressure *s* pressio, pressura *f*, pres·s·us -ūs *m*

pressure *vt* urgēre

prestige *s* auctoritas *f*

presumably *adv* sane

presume *vt* sumĕre, credĕre, conjicĕre; *(to take liberties)* sibi arrogare

presumption *s (conjecture)* conjectura *f*; *(arrogance)* arrogantia *f*

presumptuous *adj* arrogans, insolens, audax; —ly insolenter, arroganter

presuppose *vt* praesumĕre

pretend *vt* simulare, dissimulare, fingĕre

pretender *s* simulator, captator *m*

pretense *s* simulatio, species *f*; under — of per speciem *(with genit)*; without — sine fuco

pretension *s (claim)* postulatio *f*; *(display)* ostentatio *f*; to make —s to affectare

preterite *s* tempus praeteritum *n*

preternatural *adj* praeter naturam

pretext *s* species *f*, praetextum *n*; under the — of specie *(with genit)*, sub specie *(with genit)*, sub praetextu *(with genit)*

pretor *s* praetor *m*

pretorian *adj* praetorianus

pretorship *s* praetura *f*

prettily *adv* belle, concinne

pretty *adj* bellus, venustus, lepidus

pretty *adv* satis, admodum; — well mediocriter

prevail *vi (to be prevalent)* esse, obtinēre; *(to win)* vincēre; to — upon persuadēre *(with dat)*

prevalent *adj* (per)vulgatus; to become — increbrescĕre

prevaricate *vi* tergiversari

prevarication *s* praevaricatio, tergiversatio *f*

prevaricator *s* praevaricator, mendax *m*

prevent *vt* impedire, prohibēre

prevention *s* anticipatio, impeditio *f*

preventive *adj* prohibens, anticipans

previous *adj* prior, superior; —ly antea, antehac

prey *s* praeda *f*

prey *vi* to — on praedari, rapĕre; *(fig)* vexare, consumĕre

price *s* pretium *n*; at a high — magni; at a low — parvi

priceless *adj* inaestimabilis

prick *vt* pungĕre; *(fig)* stimulare; to — up the ears aures arrigĕre

prickle *s* aculeus *m*

prickly *adj* spinosus

pride s superbia f; (source of pride) decus n
pride vt to — oneself on jactare
priest s sacerdos m; (of particular god) flamen m
priestess s sacerdos f
priesthood s (office) sacerdotium n; (collectively) sacerdotes m pl
priestly adj sacerdotalis
prig s homo fastidiosus m
prim adj (nimis) diligens
primarily adv praecipue
primary adj primus, principalis; (chief) praecipuus
prime s flos m; to be in one's — florēre, vigēre
prime adj primus, egregius, optimus, exquisitus
primeval adj pristinus, priscus
primitive adj priscus, antiquus, incultus
primordial adj priscus
primrose s primula vulgaris f
prince s regulus, regis filius m; (king) rex, princeps m
princely adj regius, regalis
princess s regia puella, regis filia f
principal adj principalis, praecipuus; —ly praecipue, maxime
principal s caput n, praeses, praefectus, princeps m; (money) caput n, sors f
principality s principat·us -ūs m
principle s principium n; (in philosophy) axioma n; (maxim) institutum n
print s nota impressa f; (of foot) vestigium n
print vt imprimĕre
prior adj prior, potior
priority s primat·us -ūs m
prism s prisma n
prison s carcer m, vincula n pl
prisoner s reus m, rea f; (for debt) nex·us -ūs m
prisoner of war s captivus m
pristine adj pristinus
privacy s solitudo f, secretum n
private adj (secluded) secretus; (person) privatus; (home) domesticus; (one's own) proprius; (mil) gregarius; —ly clam, secreto; (in a private capacity) privatim
private s miles, miles gregarius m
privation s egestas, inopia f
privilege s privilegium n, immunitas f
privy adj privatus, secretus; — to conscius (with genit)
privy s forica, latrina f
prize s (reward) praemium n, palma f; (prey) praeda f
prize vt magni aestimare, magni facĕre
prize fighter s pugil m
probability s veri similitudo, probabilitas f
probable adj verisimilis, probabilis
probably adv probabiliter
probation s probatio f
probe vt scrutari, inspicĕre
probity s probitas, honestas f
problem s quaestio f; to have —s

laborare
problematical adj anceps, incertus
procedure s progress·us -ūs, modus m, ratio f
proceed vi (to go on) pergĕre, procedĕre, incedĕre; to — against persequi; to — from oriri ex (with abl)
proceedings s acta n pl; (law) lis, actio f
proceeds s redit·us -ūs m
process s ratio f; (law) lis, actio f
proclaim vt promulgare, edicĕre, pronuntiare, declarare
proclamation s pronuntiatio f, edictum n
proconsul s proconsul m
proconsular adj proconsularis
proconsulship s proconsulat·us -ūs m
procrastinate vi cunctari, procrastinare
procrastination s procrastinatio f
procreate vt procreare, generare
procreation s procreatio f
proctor s procurator m
procurable adj procurandus
procurator s procurator m
procure vt parare, acquirĕre, nancisci, adipisci
procurement s comparatio f
procurer s leno m
prodigal adj prodigus
prodigal s ganeo m
prodigality s dissipatio, effusio f
prodigious adj prodigiosus, immanis, ingens
prodigy s prodigium, monstrum, portentum n; (fig) miraculum n
produce s fruct·us -ūs m; (of earth) fruges f pl; (in money) redit·us -ūs m
produce vt (to bring forward) proferre, producĕre; (to bring into existence) parĕre, procreare, gignĕre; (to cause) efficĕre, facĕre; (to put on, as a play) docĕre; (crops) ferre
product s (of earth) fruges f pl; opus n
production s productio f
productive adj ferax, fecundus, uber
productivity s feracitas, ubertas f
profanation s violatio f
profane adj profanus, impius; —ly impie
profane vt vilare, profanare, polluĕre
profanity s impietas f, nefas n
profess vt profitēri
professed adj apertus, manifestus
profession s professio f
professional adj ad professionem pertinens; (expert) peritus
professor s doctor m
professorship s doctoris munus n
proffer vt offerre, promittĕre, proponĕre
proficiency s progress·us -ūs m, peritia f
proficient adj habilis, peritus
profile s facies obliqua f; (portrait) imago obliqua f

profit *s* quaest·us -ūs, redit·us -ūs *m*, lucrum *n*

profit *vt* prodesse *(with dat)*; *vi* proficĕre; **to — by** uti *(with abl)*, frui *(with abl)*

profitable *adj* fructuosus, quaestuosus, utilis; **to be — ** prodesse

profitably *adv* utiliter

profitless *adj* inutilis, vanus

profligacy *s* nequitia *f*, perditi mores *m pl*

profligate *adj* perditus, flagitiosus, nequam *(indecl)*

profligate *s* nepos, ganeo *m*

profound *adj* altus, subtilis, abstrusus; **—ly** penitus

profundity *s* altitudo *f*

profuse *adj* profusus, effusus; **—ly** effuse

profusion *s* effusio, profusio, abundantia *f*

progeny *s* progenies, proles *f*

prognosticate *vt* praedicĕre

prognostication *s* praedictio *f*, praedictum *n*

program *s* libellus *m*

progress *s* progress·us -ūs *m*; **to make — ** proficĕre

progress *vi* progredi

progression *s* progress·us -ūs *m*

progressive *adj* proficiens; **—ly** gradatim

prohibit *vt* interdicĕre *(with dat)*, vetare

prohibition *s* interdictum *n*

project *s* propositum, consilium *n*

project *vt* projicĕre; *vi* prominēre, exstare; *(of land)* excurrĕre

projectile *s* missile *n*

projecting *adj* eminens, prominens

projection *s* projectura, eminentia *f*

proletarian *adj* proletarius

proletariat *s* plebs *f*

prolific *adj* fecundus

prolix *adj* longus, verbosus

prolixity *s* verbositas *f*

prologue *s* prologus *m*

prolong *vt* producĕre, prorogare, extendĕre

prolongation *s* proragatio, dilatio *f*

promenade *s* *(walk)* ambulatio *f*; *(place)* xystus *m*

promenade *vi* spatiari, ambulare

prominence *s* eminentia *f*

prominent *adj* prominens, insignis

promiscuous *adj* promiscuus; **—ly** promiscue, sine ullo discrimine

promise *s* promissio *f*, promissum *n*; **to break a — ** fidem fallĕre; **to make a — ** fidem dare

promise *vt* promittĕre, pollicēri; *(in marriage)* despondēre

promising *adj* bonā spe *(abl used adjectively)*

promissory note *s* chirographum *n*

promontory *s* promontorium *n*

promote *vt* *(in rank)* producĕre, provehĕre; *(a cause, etc.)* favēre *(with dat)*, adjuvare

promoter *s* adjutor, fautor *m*

promotion *s* amplior grad·us -ūs *m*, dignitas *f*

prompt *adj* promptus, paratus; **—ly**

statim, extemplo

prompt *vt* subjicĕre, suggerĕre; *(to incite)* impellĕre, commovēre

promulgate *vt* promulgare

promulgation *s* promulgatio *f*

prone *adj* pronus, propensus

prong *s* dens *m*

pronominal *adj* pronominalis

pronoun *s* pronomen *n*

pronounce *vt* *(to declare)* pronuntiare; *(to articulate)* enuntiare, eloqui; *(sentence)* dicĕre, pronuntiare

pronunciation *s* appellatio, elocutio, locutio *f*

proof *s* documentum, argumentum, indicium, signum *n*

proof *adj* tutus, securus; **— against** invictus ab *(with abl)*, adversus *(with acc)*

prop *s* tibicen *m*, fulcrum *n*; *(for vines)* adminiculum *n*

prop *vt* fulcire, sustinēre

propaganda *s* divulgatio *f*

propagate *vt* propagare, vulgare, disseminare

propagation *s* propagatio *f*

propel *vt* impellĕre, propellĕre

propeller *s* impulsor *m*

propensity *s* propensio, inclinatio *f*

proper *adj* *(becoming)* decorus, decens; *(suitable)* aptus, idoneus; **it is — ** decet; **—ly** decore; apte

property *s* *(characteristic)* proprium *n*, proprietas *f*; *(things owned)* res *f*, bona *n pl*, fortuna *f*; **private — ** res familiaris *f*

prophecy *s* praedictum *n*, praedictio, vaticinatio *f*

prophesy *vt* vaticinari, praedicĕre

prophet *s* vates *m & f*, fatidicus *m*; *(Biblical)* propheta *f*

prophetess *s* vates, fatiloqua *f*

prophetic *adj* fatidicus, divinus, vaticinus; **—ally** divinitus

propitiate *vt* propitiare, placare

propitiation *s* propitiatio *f*, placamentum *n*

propitious *adj* felix, faustus; **—ly** fauste

proportion *s* ratio, proportio *f*; **in — ** pro rata parte; **in — to** pro *(with abl)*

proportionately *adv* pro portione

proposal *s* propositio, conditio *f*; *(of senate)* rogatio *f*

propose *vt* ferre, rogare; **to — a toast** propinare *(with dat)*

proposition *s* *(offer)* condicio *f*; *(logic)* propositio *f*, pronuntiatum *n*

propound *vt* proponĕre, exponĕre

proprietor *s* possessor, dominus *m*

propriety *s* decorum *n*, convenientia *f*

propulsion *s* propulsio *f*

prosaic *adj* aridus, jejunus

proscribe *vt* proscribĕre

proscription *s* proscriptio *f*

prose *s* prosa *f*

prosecute *vt* *(to carry out)* exsequi; *(law)* litem intendĕre *(with dat)*, accusare

prosecution *s* exsecutio *f*; *(law)* accusatio *f*

prosecutor *s* accusator, actor *m*

prospect s prospect·us -ūs m; (*hope*) spes f

prospective adj futurus

prosper vt prosperare, secundare; vi prosperā fortunā uti, florēre, vigēre

prosperity s res secundae f pl

prosperous adj prosperus, secundus; —ly prospere, bene

prostitute s scortum n, meretrix f

prostitute vt prostituēre

prostrate vt sternēre, projicēre; (*fig*) affligēre

prostrate adj prostratus, projectus; (*fig*) afflictus, fractus; **to fall —** se projicēre

prostration s (*act*) prostratio f; (*state*) animus fractus m

protect vt tuēri, protegēre, defendēre, custodire

protection s praesidium n, tutela f

protector s defensor, patronus m

protest s obtestatio, denuntiatio f

protest vt affirmare; vi obtestari, reclamare; (*pol*) intercedēre

protestation s affirmatio f

prototype s exemplar n

protract vt protrahēre, differre

protrude vt protrudēre; vi prominēre

protuberance s tuber n, tumor, gibbus m

proud adj superbus, arrogans; **to be — superbire; —ly** superbe, arroganter

prove vt probare, confirmare, evincēre, arguēre; vi (*of person*) se praebēre, se praestare; (*of thing, event, etc.*) evadēre, fieri, exire

proverb s proverbium n

proverbial adj proverbialis, tritus, notus

provide vt (*to furnish*) suppeditare, (com)parare, praebēre; vi **to — for** providēre (*with dat*), consulēre (*with dat*); (*of laws*) jubēre

provided that conj dum, modo, dummodo, eā condicione ut

providence s providentia f

provident adj providus, cautus; —ly caute

providential adj divinus; —ly divinitus

province s provincia f

provincial adj provincialis; (*countrified*) inurbanus, rusticus; (*narrow*) angusti animi (*genit, used adjectively*)

provincialism s dialectos f

provision s (*stipulation*) condicio f; **—s** cibus, vict·us -ūs m, alimentum n; (*mil*) commeat·us -ūs m, res frumentaria f

provisional adj temporarius; —ly ad tempus

proviso s condicio f; **with the — that** eā lege ut

provocation s provocatio, offensio f

provoke vt provocare, irritare, stimulare

provoking adj molestus, odiosus

prow s prora f

prowess s virtus f

prowl vi vagari, grassari

prowler s praedator m

proximity s propinquitas f

proxy s vicarius m

prude s fastidiosa f

prudence s prudentia f

prudent adj prudens; —ly prudenter

prudish adj tetricus

prune s prunum conditum n

prune vt (am)putare, resecare, recidēre

pruning s putatio f

pry vi perscrutor; **to — into** investigare, explorare

prying adj curiosus

pseudonym s falsum nomen n

puberty s pubertas f

public adj publicus, communis; (*known*) vulgatus; —ly palam, aperte

public s homines m pl, vulgus n

publican s publicanus m

publication s publicatio, promulgatio f; (*of book*) editio f; (*book*) liber m

publicity s celebritas, lux f

publish vt publicare, divulgare, patefacēre; (*book*) edēre

publisher s editor m

pucker vt corrugare

pudding s placenta f

puddle s lacuna f, stagnum n

puerile adj puerilis

puerility s puerilitas f

puff s aura f, flamen n

puff vt inflare, sufflare; vi anhelare

puffy adj sufflatus, tumens

pugilist s pugil m

pugnacious adj pugnax

pull vt (*to drag*) trahēre, tractare; **to — apart** distrahēre; **to — away** avellēre; **to — down** detrahēre; (*buildings*) demoliri, destruēre, evertēre; **to — off** avellēre; **to — out** extrahēre; (*hair, etc.*) evellēre; vi **to — at** vellicare; **to — through** pervincēre; (*illness*) convalescēre

pull s (*act*) tract·us -ūs m; (*effort*) nis·us -ūs m; (*influence*) gratia f

pulley s trochlea f

pulmonary adj pulmoneus, pulmonaceus, pulmonarius

pulp s pulpa, caro f

pulpit s suggest·us -ūs m, rostra n pl

pulse s puls·us -ūs m; (*plant*) legumen n; **to feel the — venas** temptare

pulverization s pulveratio f

pulverize vt pulverare, contundēre

pumice s pumex m

pump s antlia f

pump vt haurire, exantlare; **to — with questions** percontari

pumpkin s pepo, melopepo m

pun s verborum lus·us -ūs m, agnominatio f

punch s (*tool*) veruculum n; (*blow*) pugnus, ict·us -ūs m

punch vt pugnum ducēre (*with dat*)

punctilious adj scrupulosus, religiosus

punctual adj promptus, accuratus, diligens; —ly ad tempus, ad horam

punctuality s diligentia f

punctuate vt interpungĕre

punctuation s interpunctio f

punctuation mark s interpunctum n

puncture s punctio f, punctum n

pungent adj pungens, acutus; (caustic, as speech) mordax, aculeatus

Punic adj Punicus

punish vt punire

punishable adj puniendus, poenā dignus

punishment s (act) punitio, castigatio f; (penalty) poena f, supplicium n; **without** — impune

punster s argutator m

puny adj pusillus

pup s catulus m

pupil s pupillus, discipulus m, pupilla, discipula f; (of eye) pupilla, pupula f

puppet s pupa f

puppy s catulus m

purchase s (act) emptio f; (merchandise) merx f

purchase vt emĕre

purchase price s pretium n; (of grain) annona f

purchaser s emptor m

pure adj mundus, purus; (unmixed) merus; (morally) castus, integer; **—ly** pure, integre; (quite) omnino; (solely) solum

purgation s purgatio f

purge vt purgare, mundare

purge s purgatio f; (pol) proscriptio f

purification s purificatio, purgatio f

purify vt purgare; (fig) expiare

purity s puritas, munditia f; (moral) castitas, integritas f

purple s purpura f; **dressed in** — purpuratus

purple adj purpureus

purport s significatio, sententia, vis f

purport vt significare, spectare ad (with acc)

purpose s propositum, consilium n, animus m; (end, aim) finis m; (wish) mens f; **on** — consulto; **to good** — ad rem; **to no** — frustra, nequaquam; **to what** — quo, quorsum

purpose vt in animo habēre, velle

purposely adv consulto, de industria

purr s murmur n

purr vi mumurare

purring s murmuratio f

purse s crumena f, marsupium n

purse vt corrugare, contrahēre

pursuance s continutatio f; **in** — **of** ex (with abl), secundum (with acc)

pursuant adj — **to** ex (with abl), secundum (with acc)

pursue vt (per)sequi, insequi, insectari; (plan, course) insistēre

pursuit s persecutio, insectatio f; (occupation) studium, artificium n, occupatio f

pus s pus n, sanies f

push vt trudēre, urgēre, impellēre; **vi to** — **on** contendēre, iter facēre

push s . ict·us -ūs, puls·us -ūs, im-puls·us -ūs f; (fig) conat·us -ūs m

pushing adj audax, confidens; (energetic) strenuus

pusillanimous adj timidus

put vt ponēre, collocare; **to** — **an end** to finem facēre (with dat); **to** — **aside** ponēre; **to** — **away** seponēre, abdēre, amovēre; (in safety) recondēre; **to** — **back** reponēre; **to** — **down** deponēre; (to suppress) supponēre, sedare; (in writing) scribēre; **to** — **in** inserēre; **to** — **in order** ordinare; **to** — **off** (to postpone) differre; **to** — **on** imponēre; (clothes) se induēre (with abl); (to add) addēre; **to** — **out** ejicēre, extrudēre; (fire) extinguēre; (money) ponēre; **to** — **out of the way** movēre; **to** — **together** componēre, conferre; **to** — **up** erigēre, statuēre; **to** — **up for sale** proponēre, venum dare; vi **to** — **in** (of ships) portum petēre, appellēre; **to** — **out to sea** solvēre; **to** — **up with** tolerare

putrefaction s putredo f

putrefy vi putrescēre, putrefieri

putrid adj puter or putris, putridus

puzzle s quaestio abstrusa f, nodus m, aenigma n

puzzle vt confundēre, perturbare; **to be puzzled** haerēre, dubitare

puzzling adj perplexus, ambiguus

pygmy s nanus, pumilio, pumilus m

pyramid s pyramis f

pyre s rogus m

Pythagorean adj Pythagoraeus

Pythian adj Pythius

Q

quack s (charlatan) circulator, pharmacopola m

quack vi tetrinnire

quadrangle s area f

quadruped s quadrupes m & f

quadruple adj quadruplex, quadruplus

quadruple vt quadruplicare

quaestor s quaestor m

quaestorship s quaestura f

quaff vt ducēre, haurire

quagmire s palus f

quail s coturnix f

quail vi pavēre

quaint adj rarus, insolitus, novus

quake vi tremēre

qualification s (endowment) indoles f; (limitation) exceptio, condicio f

qualified adj (suited) aptus, idoneus, dignus; (competent) peritus, doctus

qualify *vt* aptum *or* idoneum reddĕre, instruĕre; *(to limit)* temperare, mitigare, extenuare

quality *s* proprietas, qualitas *f*; **—s** ingenium *n*, indoles *f*

qualm *s* fastidium *n*; **— of conscience** religio *f*, scrupulus *m*

quandry *s* confusio *f*, angustiae *f pl*

quantity *s* numerus *m*, multitudo, vis, copia *f*; *(in scansion)* quantitas, mensura *f*

quarrel *s* jurgium *n*; *(dispute)* altercatio, controversia *f*; *(violent)* rixa *f*

quarrel *vi* altercari, jurgare, rixari

quarrelsome *adj* jurgiosus, rixosus, pugnax

quarry *s* lapicidinae, lautumiae *f pl*; *(prey)* praeda *f*

quart *s* duo sextarii *m pl*

quarter *s* quarta pars *f*, quadrans *m*; *(side, direction)* pars, regio *f*; *(district)* regio *f*; **at close —s** comminus; **—s** *(dwelling)* tectum *n*, habitatio *f*; *(temporary abode)* hospitium *n*; *(mil)* castra, contubernia stativa *n pl*; *(of moon)* lunae phases *f pl*; **to give — to** parcĕre *(with dat)*

quarter *vt* in quattuor partes dividĕre; *(to receive in one's house)* hospitium praebēre *(with dat)*

quarterly *adj* trimestris

quarterly *adv* quadrifariam, tertio quoque mense

quartermaster *s* castrorum praefectus *m*

quash *vt* *(to subdue)* opprimĕre; *(law)* rescindĕre, abolēre

quatrain *s* tetrastichon *n*

queasy *adj* fastidiosus; **to feel —** nauseare

queen *s* regina *f*

queen bee *s* rex *m*

queer *adj* novus, insolitus, rarus, ineptus

quell *vt* opprimĕre, sedare, domare

quench *vt* exstinguĕre; **to — the thirst** sitim sedare

querulous *adj* querulus, queribundus

query *s* quaestio, interrogatio *f*

query *vt* dubitare; *vi* quaerĕre, quaeritare

quest *s* inquisitio *f*; **to be in — of** quarĕre, requirĕre; **to go in — of** investigare

question *s* interrogatio *f*; *(doubt)* dubitatio *f*, dubium *n*; *(matter)* res, causa *f*; **there is no — that** non

dubium est quin; **to ask a —** quaerĕre, rogare; **to call in —** dubitare; **without —** sine dubio, haud dubie

question *vt* interrogare, percontari; *(to doubt)* dubitare, in dubium vocare; *(to examine)* scrutari

questionable *adj* dubius, incertus

questioning *s* interrogatio, inquisitio *f*

questor *s* quaestor *m*

questorship *s* quaestura *f*

quibble *s* captio, argutiola *f*

quibble *vi* cavillari

quibbler *s* cavillator, sophista *m*

quibbling *s* cavillatio, captio *f*

quick *adj* *(swift)* celer, velox; *(nimble)* agilis; *(mentally)* sagax, astutus, acutus; *(with hands)* facilis; *(of wit)* argutus; **—ly** cito, velociter; *(with haste)* propere, festinanter

quicken *vt* accelerare; *(to enliven)* vivificare, animare; *(to rouse)* excitare

quicksand *s* syrtis *f*

quicksilver *s* argentum vivum *n*

quiet *adj* quietus, tranquillus, placidus; *(silent)* tacitus, taciturnus; **to keep —** quiescĕre; *(to refrain from talking)* silēre, tacēre; **—ly** quiete, tranquille; tacite, per silentium

quiet *s* quies, tranquillitas *f*; *(leisure)* otium *n*; *(silence)* silentium *n*

quiet *vt* tranquillare, pacare, sedare

quill *s* penna *f*, calamus *m*

quilt *s* culcita *f*

quince *s* cydonium *n*

quince tree *s* cydonia *f*

quintessence *s* vis, medulla *f*, flos *m*

quip *s* dictum *n*, facetiae *f pl*

quirk *s* cavillatio, proprium *n*

quit *vt* relinquĕre, deserĕre

quite *adv* omnino, penitus, prorsus, magnopere; **not —** minus, parum; *(not yet)* nondum

quiver *s* pharetra *f*; **wearing a —** pharetratus

quiver *vi* tremĕre, contremiscĕre, trepidare

quivering *s* tremor *m*, trepidatio *f*

Quixotic *adj* ridiculus

quoit *s* discus *m*

quota *s* portio, pars, rata pars *f*

quotation *s* *(act)* prolatio *f*; *(passage)* locus *m*

quote *vt* adducĕre, proferre, commemorare

R

rabbit *s* cuniculus *m*

rabble *s* plebecula, faex populi *f*; *(crowd)* turba *f*

rabid *adj* rabidus; **—ly** rabide

race *s* *(lineage)* genus *n*, stirps *f*; *(nation)* gens *f*; *(contest)* certamen *n*; curs·us -ūs *m*, curriculum *n*

race *vi* certare, cursu contendĕre

race horse *s* equus cursor *m*

racer *s* *(person)* cursor *m*; *(horse)* equus cursor *m*

racetrack *s* circus *m*, curriculum *n*

rack *s* *(shelf)* pluteus *m*; *(for punishment)* equuleus *m*, tormentum *n*

racket *s* *(noise)* strepit·us -ūs *m*

radiance s fulgor, splendor m
radiant adj radians, fulgidus, splendidus
radiate vt emittĕre; vi radiare, fulgēre, nitēre
radiation s radiatio f
radical adj insitus, innatus; (thorough) totus; —ly penitus, omnino
radical s rerum novarum cupidus m
radish s raphanus m
radius s radius m
raffle s alea f
raffle vt to — off aleā vendĕre
raft s ratis f
rafter s trabs f
rag s panniculus, pannus m
rage s furor m, rabies f
rage vi furĕre, saevire
ragged adj pannosus
raid s incursio, invasio f, latrocinium n
raider s praedator, latro m
raid vt praedari
rail s palus, asser transversus, longurius m
rail vt to — off consaepire; vi to — at insectari, conviciari
railing s (fence) saepimentum n; (abuse) convicium, maledictum n
raiment s vestis f, vestit·us -ūs m
rain s pluvia f, imber m
rain vi pluĕre; **it is raining** pluit
rainbow s pluvius arc·us -ūs m
rain cloud s imber m
rainy adj pluvius, pluvialis; pluviosus
raise vt tollĕre, elevare; (to erect) erigĕre; (to build) exstruĕre; (money) cogĕre; (army) conscribĕre; (siege) solvĕre; (to stir up) excitare; (children) educare; (to promote) provehĕre, producĕre; (price) augĕre; (crops) colĕre; (beard) demittĕre; to — up sublevare
raisin s astaphis f
rake s rastellus, irpex m; (person) nebulo, nepos m
rake vt radĕre; to — together corradĕre
rally s convent·us -ūs m, contio f
rally vt in aciem revocare; vi ex fuga convenire; (from sickness) convalescĕre
ram s aries m
ram vt fistucare, paviare; (to cram) infercire
ramble s vagatio f
ramble vi vagari, errare; to — on (in speech) garrire
rambling adj errans; (fig) vagus
ramification s ramus m
rampage vi saevire
rampant adj ferox
rampart s vallum, propugnaculum n
rancid adj rancidus
rancor s simultas f, dolor m
random adj fortuitus; at — temere
range s series f, ordo m; (of mountains) jugum n; (reach) jact·us -ūs m
range vt ordinare, disponĕre; vi pervagari
rank s series f, ordo, grad·us -ūs m, dignitas f

rank vt in numero habēre; vi in numero habēri
rank adj luxuriosus; (extreme) summus, maximus; (of smell) foetidus, gravis, graveolens
rankle vi suppurare, exulcerare
ransack vt diripĕre, spoliare; (to search thoroughly) exquirĕre
ransom s (act) redemptio f; pretium n
ransom vt redimĕre
rant vi ampullari; to — and rave debacchari
rap s (slap) alapa f; (blow) ict·us -ūs m; (at door) pulsatio f; (with knuckles) talitrum n
rap vt (to criticize) exagitare; vi to — at pulsare, ferire
rapacious adj rapax, avidus
rapacity s rapacitas, aviditas f
rape s stuprum n; (act of carrying away) rapt·us -ūs m
rape vt violare, per vim stuprare
rapid adj rapidus, celer, velox; —ly rapide, cito, velociter
rapidity s rapiditas, velocitas f
rapier s verutum n
rapine s rapina f
rapture s exsultatio f, animus exsultans m
rapturous adj mirificus
rare adj rarus, inusitatus; (fig) eximius, singularis; (thin) tenuis; —ly raro
rarefy vt extenuare, rarefacĕre
rarity s raritas, paucitas f; (thing) res rara, res singularis f
rascal s homo nequam, scelestus m
rascally adj scelestus, flagitiosus; nequam (indecl)
rash adj praeceps, temerarius; —ly temere, inconsulte
rash s eruptio pustulae f
rashness s temeritas f
raspberry s morum idaeum n
raspberry bush s rubus idaeus m
rat s sorex, mus m; (person) transfuga m
rate s proportio f; (price) pretium n; (scale) norma f; (tax) vectigal n; — of interest faenus n, usura f
rate vt aestimare
rather adv potius, prius, libentius; (somewhat) aliquantum, paulo, or render by comparative of adjective
ratification s sanctio f
ratify vt ratum facĕre, sancire
rating s aestimatio f
ratio s proportio f
ration s (portion) demensum n; (mil) cibaria n pl
ration vt demetiri
rational adj ratione praeditus, intellegens; —ly ratione, sapienter
rationalize vi ratiocinari
rattle s crepit·us -ūs, strepit·us -ūs m; (toy) crepitaculum n
rattle vt crepitare (with abl); vi increpare, crepitare; to — on inepte garrire
raucous adj raucus
ravage vt vastare, spoliare, populari
ravages s vastatio, direptio f
rave vi furĕre, saevire, bacchari

ravel *vt* involvĕre, implicare

raven *s* corvus *m*, cornix *f*

ravenous *adj* rapax, vorax; **—ly** voraciter

ravine *s* fauces *f pl*

raving *adj* furiosus, furens, insanus

ravish *vt* constuprare

raw *adj* crudus, incoctus; (*of person*) rudis, imperitus; (*of weather*) asper

rawboned *adj* strigosus

ray *s* radius *m*

raze *vt* solo aequare, excidĕre

razor *s* novacula *f*

reach *s* (*grasp, capacity*) capt·us -ūs *m*; (*of weapon*) ict·us -ūs, jact·us -ūs *m*; **out of my —** extra ictum meum

reach *vt* attingĕre; (*of space*) pertinēre ad (*with acc*), extendi ad (*with acc*); (*to come up to*) assequi; (*to arrive at*) pervenire ad (*with acc*); (*to hand*) tradĕre

react *vi* affici; **to — to** ferre

read *vt & vi* legĕre; **to — aloud** recitare

readable *adj* lectu facilis

reader *s* lector *m*; (*lecturer*) praelector *m*

readily *adv* (*willingly*) libenter; (*easily*) facile

readiness *s* facilitas *f*; **in —** in promptu

ready *adj* paratus, promptus, expeditus; (*easy*) facilis; **— money** praesens pecunia *f*; **to be —** praesto esse

real *adj* verus, sincerus; **—ly** re vera; (*surely*) sane, certe

real estate *s* fundus *m*

realistic *adj* verisimilis

reality *s* veritas, res ipsa *f*, verum *n*

realization *s* effectio *f*; (*of ideas*) cognitio, comprehensio *f*

realize *vt* (*to understand*) intellegĕre, vidēre, comprehendĕre; (*to effect*) efficĕre, ad exitum perducĕre; (*to convert into money*) redigĕre

realm *s* regnum *n*

ream *s* (*of paper*) scapus *m*

reap *vt* metĕre, desecare; (*fig*) percipĕre, capĕre

reaper *s* messor *m*

reappear *vi* redire, revenire, resurgĕre

rear *vt* educare, alĕre; *vi* (*of horses*) arrectum se tollĕre

rear *s* tergum *n*; (*mil*) novissimum agmen *n*, novissima acies *f*; **on the — a tergo**; **to bring up the —** agmen cogĕre

rearing *s* educatio *f*

reascend *vt & vi* denuo ascendĕre

reason *s* (*faculty*) mens, ratio, intellegentia *f*; (*cause*) causa *f*; (*moderation*) modus *m*; **by —of** ob (*with acc*), propter (*with acc*), a(b) (*with abl*); **there is no — why** non est cur

reason *vi* ratiocinari; **to — with** disceptare cum (*with abl*)

reasonable *adj* (*fair*) aequus, justus; (*moderate*) modicus; (*judicious*) prudens

reasonably *adv* ratione, juste; modice

reasoning *s* ratiocinatio, ratio *f*; (*discussing*) disceptatio *f*

reassemble *vt* recolligĕre, cogĕre

reassert *vt* iterare

reassume *vt* resumĕre

reassure *vt* confirmare, redintegrare

rebel *s* rebellis *m*

rebel *vi* rebellare, desciscĕre, seditionem commovēre

rebellion *s* rebellio, seditio *f*, rebellium *n*

rebellious *adj* rebellis, seditiosus; (*disobedient*) contumax

rebound *s* result·us -ūs *m*

rebound *vi* resilire, resultare

rebuff *s* repulsa *f*

rebuff *vt* repellĕre, rejicĕre

rebuild *vt* reparare, reficĕre

rebuke *s* reprehensio *f*

rebuke *vt* reprehendĕre, vituperare

rebuttal *s* refutatio *f*

recall *s* revocatio *f*

recall *vt* revocare; **to — to mind** in memoriam redigĕre

recant *vt* retractare, revocare

recantation *s* recept·us -ūs *m*

recapitulate *vt* repetĕre, summatim colligĕre

recapitulation *s* repetitio, enumeratio *f*

recapture *s* recuperatio *f*

recapture *vt* recipĕre, recuperare

recede *vi* recedĕre, refugĕre

receipt *s* (*act*) acceptio *f*; (*note of acceptance*) apocha *f*; (*money*) acceptum *n*

receive *vt* accipĕre, capĕre, excipĕre

receiver *s* receptor *m*

recent *adj* recens; **—ly** nuper

receptacle *s* receptaculum *n*

reception *s* adit·us -ūs *m*, admissio *f*; (*of guest*) hospitium *n*

recess *s* (*place*) recess·us -ūs *m*; (*in wall*) adytum *n*, angulus *m*; (*intermission*) intermissio *f*; (*vacation*) feriae *f pl*

recipe *s* praescriptum, compositio *f*

recipient *s* acceptor *m*

reciprocal *adj* mutuus; **—ly** mutuo, vicissim, inter se

reciprocate *vt* reddĕre

reciprocity *s* reciprocatio *f*

recital *s* narratio, enumeratio, recitatio *f*

recitation *s* recitatio, lectio *f*

reckless *adj* temerarius; **—ly** temere

reckon *vt* numerare, computare, aestimare; *vi* **to — on** confidĕre (*with dat*)

reckoning *s* numeratio *f*; (*account to be given*) ratio *f*

reclaim *vt* reposcĕre, repetĕre

recline *vi* recubare, recumbĕre; (*at table*) accumbĕre

recluse *s* homo solitarius *m*

recognition *s* cognitio, agnitio *f*

recognize *vt* agnoscĕre, recognoscĕre; (*to acknowledge*) noscĕre; (*to admit*) fatēri

recoil *vi* resilire; **to — from rece-**

dēre ab (with abl), refugĕre ab (with abl)

recoil s recessio f

recollect vt recordari

recollection s memoria, recordatio f

recommence vt redintegrare, renovare

recommend vt commendare

recommendation s commendatio, laudatio f; letter of — litterae commendaticiae f pl

recompense s remuneratio f

recompense vt remunerare; (to indemnify) compensare

reconcilable adj placabilis; (of things) conveniens

reconcile vt reconciliare, componĕre; to be reconciled in gratiam restitui

reconciliation s reconciliatio f, in gratiam redit·us -ūs m

reconnoitre vt explorare

reconquer vt revincĕre, recuperare

reconsider vt revolvĕre, retractare

reconstruct vt restituĕre, renovare

reconstruction s renovatio f

record s monumentum n, historia f; —s annales m pl, tabulae f pl

recorder s procurator ab actis m

recount vt referre, enarrare, commemorare

recoup vt recuperare

recourse s refugium n; to have — to (for safety) fugĕre ad (with acc); (to resort to) descendĕre ad (with acc)

recover vt recuperare, recipĕre; vi (from illness) convalescĕre; (to come to one's senses) ad se redire

recoverable adj reparabilis, recuperandus; (of persons) sanabilis

recovery s recuperatio, reparatio f; (from illness) recreatio f

recreate vt recreare

recreation s oblectatio, remissio f, lus·us -ūs m

recriminate vi invicem accusare

recrimination s mutua accusatio f

recruit vt (mil) conscribĕre; (strength) reficĕre

recruit s tiro m

recruiting s delect·us -ūs m

recruiting officer s conquisitor m

rectification s correctio f

rectify vt corrigĕre, emendare

rectitude s probitas f

recumbent adj resupinus

recur vi recurrĕre, redire

recurrence s redit·us -ūs m

recurrent adj assiduus

red adj ruber; (ruddy) rubicundus; to be — rubēre; to grow — rubescĕre

redden vt rubefacĕre, rutilare; vi rubescĕre; (to blush) erubescĕre

reddish adj subrufus, subruber, rubicundulus

redeem vt redimĕre, liberare

redeemer s liberator m

Redeemer s Redemptor m

redemption s redemptio f

redhead s rufus m

red-hot adj candens

redness s rubor m

redolence s fragrantia f

redolent adj fragrans, redolens; to be — redolēre

redouble vt ingeminare

redoubt s propugnaculum n

redoubtable adj formidolosus

redound vi redundare

redress vt restituĕre

redress s satisfactio f; to demand — res repetĕre

reduce vt minuĕre, deminuĕre; (to a condition) redigĕre; (mil) vincĕre, expugnare

reduction s deminutio f; (mil) expugnatio f

redundancy s redundantia f

redundant adj redundans, superfluus

reed s harundo f, calamus m

reef s scopulus m, saxa n pl

reek s fumus, vapor m

reek vi fumare; to — of olēre

reel s fusus m

reel vi (to stagger) titubare

reestablish vt restituĕre

reestablishment s restitutio f

refer vt referre, remittĕre; vi to — to perstringĕre, attingĕre

referee s arbiter m

reference s ratio f; (in book) locus m

refine vt purgare, excolĕre, expolire; (metals) excoquĕre

refined adj politus; (fig) elegans, urbanus, humanus

refinement s (of liquids) purgatio f; (fig) urbanitas, humanitas, elegantia f

reflect vt repercutĕre, reverberare; (fig) afferre; vi to — on considerare, revolvĕre

reflection s repercussio f, repercuss·us -ūs m; (thing reflected) imago f; (fig) consideratio, meditatio, cogitatio f; without — inconsulte

reflective adj cogitabundus

reflexive adj reciprocus

reform vt reficĕre, refingĕre; (to amend) corrigĕre, emendare; vi se corrigĕre

reform s correctio, emendatio f

reformation s correctio f

reformer s corrector, emendator m

refract vt refringĕre

refraction s refractio f

refractory adj contumax, indocilis

refrain s vers·us -ūs intercalaris m

refrain vi to — from abstinēre ab (with abl), parcĕre (with dat); I — from speaking abstineo quin dicam

refresh vt recreare, reficĕre; (the memory) redintegrare

refreshing adj jucundus, dulcis

refreshment s (food) cibus m; (drink) pot·us -ūs m

refuge s refugium, perfugium, asylum n; to take — with confugĕre in (with acc)

refugee s profugus m, ex(s)ul m & f

refulgence s fulgor m

refulgent adj fulgidus

refund vt refundĕre, rependĕre

refusal s recusatio, repulsa f
refuse vt recusare, negare; (*scornfully*) repudire, renuĕre
refutation s refutatio, confutatio f
refute vt refutare, refellĕre, redarguĕre
regain vt recipĕre, recuperare
regal adj regalis, regius; —**ly** regaliter
regale vt excipĕre
regalia s insignia regia n pl
regard s respect·us -ūs m, ratio f; (*care*) cura f; (*esteem*) gratia f
regard vt (*to look at*) respicĕre, intuĕri; (*to concern*) spectare ad (*with acc*); (*to esteem*) aestimare; (*to consider*) habēre
regarding prep de (*with abl*)
regardless adj neglegens, incuriosus
regency s procuratio regni f, interregnum n
regenerate vt regenerare
regeneration s regeneratio f
regent s interrex m
regicide s (*murderer*) regis occisor m; (*murder*) caedes regis f
regime s administratio f
regimen f vict·us -ūs m
regiment s cohors, caterva f
region s regio, plaga f, tract·us -ūs m
register s tabulae f pl, catalogus m, album n
register vt in tabulas referre; (*emotion*) ostendĕre; vi profitēri, nomen dare
registrar s tabularius, actuarius m
registration s perscriptio, in tabulas relatio f
registry s tabularium n
regret s indignatio, paenitentia f, dolor m
regret vt dolēre; **I** — paenitet me (*with genit*), piget me (*with genit*)
regretful adj paenitens
regular adj (*common*) usitatus; (*proper*) justus, rectus; (*consistent*) constans, certus; —**ly** ordine, constanter; juste, recte
regularity s symmetria f; (*consistency*) constantia f
regulate vt ordinare, disponĕre, dirigĕre; (*to control*) moderari
regulation s ordinatio, temperatio, moderatio f; (*rule*) lex f, jussum n
rehabilitate vt restituĕre
rehearsal s meditatio f
rehearse vt meditari
reign s regnum n
reign vi regnare, dominari
reimburse vt rependĕre
reimbursement s pecuniae restitutio f
rein s habena f; **to give full** — **to** habenas immittĕre (*with dat*); **to loosen the** —**s** frenos dare; **to tighten the** —**s** habenas adducĕre
reindeer s reno m
reinforce vt firmare, supplēre
reinforcement s supplementum, subsidium n; —**s** (*mil*) novae copiae f pl
reinstate vt restituĕre

reinstatement s restitutio f
reinvest vt iterum locare
reiterate vt iterare
reiteration s iteratio f
reject vt rejicĕre, repudiare, repellĕre, respuĕre
rejection s rejectio, repulsa f
rejoice vi gaudēre, exsultare
rejoin vt redire ad (*with acc*); vi respondĕre
rejoinder s responsum n
rekindle vt resuscitare
relapse s novus laps·us -ūs m
relate vt referre, memorare, narrare; (*to compare*) conferre; vi **to** — **to** pertinĕre ad (*with acc*)
related adj propinquus, conjunctus; (*by blood*) consanguineus, cognatus; (*by marriage*) affinis
relation s narratio f; (*reference*) ratio f; (*relationship*) cognatio f; (*relative*) cognatus m, cognata f
relationship s (*by blood*) consanguinitas, cognatio f; (*by marriage*) affinitas f; (*connection*) necessitudo, vicinitas, conjunctio f
relative adj attinens; cum ceteris comparatus; —**ly** pro ratione, ex comparatione
relative s cognatus, propinquus m, cognata, propinqua f
relax vt remittĕre, laxare; vi languescĕre
relaxation s remissio, relaxatio, requies f
relaxing adj remissivus
release s liberatio, absolutio, missio f
release vt (*prisoner*) liberare; solvĕre, resolvĕre
relegate vt relegare
relent vi mitescĕre, mollescĕre, flecti
relentless adj immisericors, inexorabilis, atrox; —**ly** atrociter
relevant adj **to be** — **ad rem** attinēre
reliance s fiducia, fides f
reliant adj fretus
relic s reliquiae f pl
relief s (*alleviation*) levatio f, levamentum n; (*comfort*) solatium, lenimen n; (*help*) auxilium n; (*in sculpture*) toreuma n; (*of sentries*) mutatio f
relieve vt levare, allevare, mitigare; (*to aid*) succurrĕre (*with dat*); (*a guard*) succedĕre (*with dat*), excipĕre
religion s religio f, deorum cult·us -ūs m
religious adj religiosus, pius; —**ly** religiose
relinquish vt relinquĕre; (*office*) se abdicare ab (*with abl*)
relish s (*flavor*) sapor m; (*enthusiasm*) studium n; (*seasoning*) condimentum n
relish vt gustare
reluctance s aversatio f; **with** — invite
reluctant adj invitus; —**ly** invite
rely vi **to** — **on** confidĕre (*with dat*), niti (*with abl*)
remain vi manēre, permanēre; (*of things*) restare

remainder *s* reliquum *n*

remains *s* reliquiae *f pl*

remark *vt* dicěre

remark *s* dictum *n*

remarkable *adj* insignis, memorabilis, mirus, egregius

remarkably *adv* insignite, mire, egregie

remediable *adj* sanabilis

remedial *adj* medicabilis; emendatorius

remedy *s* remedium *n*; (*law*) regress-us-ūs *m*

remedy *vt* medēri (*with dat*), sanare, corrigěre

remember *vt* meminisse (*with genit*); reminisci (*with genit*); recordari

remembrance *s* memoria, commemoratio *f*

remind *vt* admonēre, commonefacěre

reminder *s* admonitio *f*, admonitum *n*

reminisce *vi* meditari; **to — about** recordari

reminiscence *s* recordatio *f*

remiss *adj* neglegens

remission *s* venia, remissio *f*

remit *vt* remittěre, condonare

remittance *s* remissio *f*

remnant *s* reliquum, residuum *n*; **—s** reliquiae *f pl*

remodel *vt* reformare, transfigurare

remonstrance *s* objurgatio *f*

remonstrate *vi* reclamare, reclamitare; **to — with** objurgare

remorse *s* paenitentia *f*

remorseless *adj* immisericors

remote *adj* remotus, longinquus, reconditus; **—ly** procul

remoteness *s* longinquitas, distantia *f*

removable *adj* mobilis

removal *s* amotio *f*; (*banishment*) amandatio *f*; (*change of residence*) migratio *f*

remove *vt* amovēre, tollěre, auferre; *vi* migrare

remunerate *vt* remunerari

remuneration *s* remuneratio *f*

rend *vt* lacerare, scinděre; (*to split*) finděre

render *vt* redděre, traděre; (*to translate*) vertěre; (*thanks*) referre

rendering *s* (*translation*) conversio *f*; (*interpretation*) interpretatio *f*

rendezvous *s* constitutum *n*

renegade *s* desertor, transfuga *m*

renew *vt* renovare, instaurare, redintegrare

renewal *s* renovatio, instauratio, repetitio *f*

renounce *vt* renuntiare, repudiare, abdicare; (*an office*) se abdicare (*with abl*)

renovate *vt* renovare, reficěre

renovation *s* renovatio, reparatio *f*

renown *s* fama, gloria *f*

renowned *adj* praeclarus, insignis, celebris

rent *s* (*of lands*) vectigal *n*; (*of houses*) merces, pensio *f*; (*tear*; *fissure*) scissura *f*

rent *vt* (*to let out*) locare; (*to hire*) conducěre

renunciation *s* repudiatio, cessio, abdicatio *f*

reopen *vt* iterum aperire

repair *vt* reparare, reficěre, restituěre; (*clothes*) resarcire

repair *s* refectio *f*; **in bad —** ruinosus

reparation *s* satisfactio *f*

repartee *s* sales *m pl*

repast *s* cena *f*

repay *vt* remunerari; (*money*) reponěre, retribuěre

repayment *s* solutio, remuneratio *f*

repeal *vt* abrogare, rescinděre, tollěre

repeal *s* abrogatio *f*

repeat *vt* iterare, repetěre; (*ceremony*) instaurare

repeatedly *adv* iterum atque iterum, identidem

repel *vt* repellěre; (*fig*) aspernari

repent *vi* **I —** paenitet me

repentance *s* paenitentia *f*

repentant *adj* paenitens

repercussion *s* repercuss-us-ūs *m*

repetition *s* iteratio, repetitio *f*

repine *vi* conquěri

replace *vt* reponěre, restituěre

replant *vt* reserěre

replenish *vt* replēre

replete *adj* repletus, plenus

repletion *s* satietas *f*

reply *vi* respondēre

reply *s* responsum *n*

report *vt* referre, narrare, nuntiare; (*officially*) renuntiare

report *s* (*rumor*) fama *f*, rumor *m*; (*official*) renuntiatio *f*; (*noise*) fragor *m*

repose *vt* poněre, reponěre; *vi* quiescěre

repose *s* quies, requies *f*

repository *s* receptaculum *n*

reprehend *vt* reprehenděre, vituperare

reprehensible *adj* culpā dignus, improbus

represent *vt* repraesentare, expriměre, describěre, proponěre; (*a character*) partes agěre (*with genit*)

representation *s* (*act*) repraesentatio *f*; (*likeness*) imago *f*

representative *s* legatus, vicarius *m*

repress *vt* repriměre, coercēre, cohibēre

repression *s* coercitio, cohibitio *f*

reprieve *s* supplicii dilatio, mora, venia *f*; **to grant a —** supplicium differre, veniam dare

reprieve *vt* veniam dare (*with dat*)

reprimand *s* reprehensio *f*

reprimand *vt* reprehenděre

reprint *vt* denuo impriměre

reprisal *s* ultio *f*; **to make —s on** ulcisci

reproach *s* exprobratio, vituperatio *f*, probrum *n*; (*cause for reproach*) opprobrium *n*

reproach *vt* opprobrare, vituperare, increpitare

reproachful *adj* objurgatorius, contumeliosus; **—ly** contumeliose

reprobate *s* perditus *m*

reproduce vt regenerare, propagare; (likeness) referre

reproduction s regeneratio, propagatio f; (likeness) effigies f

reproof s reprehensio, vituperatio, objuratio f

reprove vt reprehendĕre, objurgare

reptile s serpens, bestia serpens f

republic s civitas popularis, libera civitas f

republican adj popularis

repudiate vt repudiare

repudiation s repudiatio f

repugnance s fastidium n, aversatio f

repugnant adj aversus, repugnans, alienus

repulse s depulsio f; (political defeat) repulsa f

repulse vt repellĕre

repulsion s repulsio f

repulsive adj odiosus, foedus

reputable adj honestus

reputation s fama f, nomen n

repute s fama, opinio f, nomen n

request s petitio, rogatio f; to obtain a — impetrare

request vt rogare, petĕre

require vt postulare, poscĕre; (to need) egĕre (with abl); (to call for) requirĕre

requirement s necessarium n

requisite adj necessarius

requisition s postulatio f, postulatum n

requital s retributio, merces f; (return for a service) gratia f

requite vt compensare, retribuĕre; (for a favor) remunerari

rescind vt rescindĕre, tollĕre

rescue s liberatio, salus f; to come to the — of subvenire (with dat)

rescue vt liberare, servare, eripĕre

research s investigatio f

resemblance s similitudo, imago f, instar n (indecl)

resemble vt similis esse (with genit, esp. of persons, or with dat)

resembling adj similis (with genit, esp. of persons, or with dat)

resent vt aegre ferre

resentful adj iracundus, indignans

resentment s indignatio f, dolor m

reservation s retentio f; (mental) exceptio f; (proviso) condicio f

reserve s (restraint) pudor m, taciturnitas f; (stock) copia f; (mil) subsidium n; in — subsidiarius; without — aperte

reserve vt servare, reservare, reponĕre

reserved adj (of seat) assignatus; (of disposition) taciturnus

reservoir s cisterna f, lac·us -ūs m

reset vt reponĕre

reside vi habitare, commorari; to — in inhabitare

residence s habitatio, sedes f, domicilium n

resident s incola m & f

residue s residuum n

resign vt cedĕre, remittĕre; se abdicare a(b) (with abl); to — oneself animum summittĕre (with dat); vi se abdicare

resignation s (act) abdicatio f; (fig) aequus animus m

resigned adj summissus; to be — aequo animo esse; to be — to aequo animo ferre

resilience s mollitia f

resilient adj resultans, mollis

resin s resina f

resist vt resistĕre (with dat), obstare (with dat), repugnare (with dat)

resistance s repugnantia f; to offer to — obsistĕre (with dat), repugnare (with dat)

resolute adj firmus, constans, fortis; —ly constanter, fortiter

resolution s (determination) constantia f; (decision, decree) decretum n; (of senate) consultum n

resolve s constantia f

resolve vt decernĕre, statuĕre, constituĕre; (to reduce, convert) resolvĕre, dissolvĕre

resonance s resonantia f

resonant adj resonus

resort s locus celeber m; (refuge) refugium n

resort vi to — to (to frequent) frequentare, celebrare; (to have recourse to) confugĕre ad (with acc)

resource s subsidium n; —s facultates, opes, copiae f pl

respect s (regard) respect·us -ūs m; (reference) ratio f; in every — ex omni parte

respect vt (re)verēri, observare

respectability s honestas f

respectable adj honestus, bonus

respectably adv honeste

respectful adj observans, reverens; —ly reverenter

respecting prep de (with abl)

respective adj proprius, suus; —ly mutuo

respiration s spirit·us -ūs m

respite s intermissio, cessatio, requies f

resplendence s nitor, splendor m

resplendent adj resplendens, splendidus; —ly splendide

respond vi respondĕre

respondent s (law) reus m

response s responsum n

responsibility s cura f; it is my — est mihi curae

responsible adj obnoxius, reus

rest s quies, requies f; (support) fulcrum, statumen n; (remainder) reliqua pars f, reliquum n; the — of the men ceteri m pl

rest vt (to lean) reclinare; vi (re)quiescĕre; (to pause) cessare; to — on inniti in (with abl), niti (with abl)

restitution s restitutio f; (restoration) refectio f

restive adj (balky, unruly) contumax; (impatient) impatiens

restless adj inquietus, turbidus, tumultuosus; (agitated) sollicitus; —ly inquiete, turbulenter

restoration s restauratio, refectio, renovatio f

restore vt restituĕre, reddĕre; (to re-

build) restaurare, reficĕre; (*to health*) recurare, recreare; **to — to order** in integrum reducĕre

restrain *vt* cohibēre, coercēre, continēre; (*to prevent*) impedire

restraint *s* temperantia, moderatio *f*

restrict *vt* cohibēre, restringĕre, circumscribĕre, (de)finire

restriction *s* modus, finis *m*, limitatio *f*

result *s* exit·us -ūs, event·us -ūs *m*; eventum *n*; **without —** nequiquam

result *vi* evenire, fieri, evadēre

resume *vt* resumĕre, repetēre

resumption *s* resumptio, continuatio *f*

resurrection *s* resurrectio *f*

resuscitate *vt* resuscitare

retail *vt* divendēre

retailer *s* caupo, propola *m*

retain *vt* retinēre, obtinēre, conservare

retainer *s* (*adherent*) cliens, asectator, satelles *m*; (*fee*) arrabo *m*

retake *vt* recipĕre, recuperare

retaliate *vi* ulcisci

retaliation *s* ultio *f*

retard *vt* retardare

retch *vi* nauseare

retention *s* retentio, conservatio *f*

retentive *adj* tenax

reticence *s* taciturnitas *f*

reticent *adj* taciturnus

retinue *s* comitat·us -ūs *m*

retire *vi* recedēre, regredi; (*from office*) abire; (*for the night*) dormitum ire

retired *adj* (*of place*) remotus, solitarius; (*from work*) emeritus

retirement *s* (*act*) recess·us -ūs *m*, abdicatio *f*; (*state*) otium *n*, solitudo *f*

retiring *adj* modestus

retort *s* responsum *n*

retort *vt* respondēre

retrace *vt* repetēre, iterare

retract *vt* revocare, recantare, renuntiare

retraction *s* retractatio *f*

retreat *vi* recedēre, refugĕre, se recipĕre, pedem referre

retreat *s* (*act*) recess·us -ūs *m*, fuga *f*; (*place*) recess·us -ūs *m*, refugium *n*; (*mil*) recept·us -ūs *m*

retrench *vt* recidĕre

retrenchment *s* recisio *f*

retribution *s* compensatio, poena *f*

retrieve *vt* recuperare, recipĕre

retrogression *s* regress·us -ūs, retrogress·us -ūs *m*

retrospect *s* retrospect·us -ūs *m*; **in — respicienti

retrospective *adj* respiciens; **—ly** retro

return *s* (*coming back*) redit·us -ūs *m*; (*repayment*) remuneratio *f*; (*income, profit*) fruct·us -ūs *m*

return *vt* (*to give back*) reddĕre, restituĕre, referre; *vi* (*to go back*) redire; (*to come back*) revenire, reverti

reunion *s* readunatio *f*, convivium *n*

reunite *vt* iterum conjungĕre; reconciliare; *vi* reconciliari

reveal *vt* retegĕre, recludĕre, **aperire;** (*to unveil*) revelare

revel *s* comissatio, bacchatio *f*; **—s** orgia *n pl*

revel *vi* comissari, debacchari, luxuriare *or* luxuriari

revelation *s* patefactio, revelatio *f*

reveler *s* comissator *m*

revelry *s* comissatio *f*, orgia *n pl*

revenge *vt* ulcisci

revenge *s* ultio, vindicta *f*; **to take — on** se vindicare in (*with acc*)

revengeful *adj* ulciscendi cupidus

revenue *s* redit·us -ūs, fruct·us -ūs *m*, vectigal *n*

reverberate *vi* resonare

reverberation *s* repercuss·us -ūs *m*, resonantia *f*

revere *vt* reverēri, venerari

reverence *s* reverentia, veneratio, religio, pietas *f*

reverend *adj* reverendus

reverent *adj* reverens, pius, religiosus; **—ly** reverenter, religiose

reverential *adj* venerabundus

reverie *s* cogitatio, meditatio *f*

reversal *s* infirmatio *f*

reverse *s* contrarium *m*; (*change*) conversio, commutatio *f*; (*defeat*) clades *f*

reverse *vt* invertĕre, (com)mutare; (*decision*) rescindĕre, abrogare

revert *vi* redire, reverti

review *s* recognitio *f*; (*critique*) censura *f*; (*mil*) recensio, lustratio *f*

review *vt* recensēre, inspicĕre; (*mil*) recensēre, lustrare

reviewer *s* censor, editor *m*

revile *vt* maledicĕre (*with dat*), insectari

revise *vt* corrigĕre, recognoscĕre

revision *s* emendatio *f*; (*of literary work*) recensio, lima *f*

revisit *vt* revisĕre, revisitare

revival *s* redanimatio *f*; (*fig*) renovatio *f*

revive *vt* resuscitare; (*to renew*) renovare; (*to encourage*) animare, instigare, excitare; *vi* reviviscĕre

revocation *s* revocatio *f*

revoke *vt* revocare, renuntiare; (*a law*) rescindĕre

revolt *vt* offendĕre; *vi* rebellare, desciscĕre, deficĕre

revolt *s* rebellio, seditio, defectio *f*

revolting *adj* taeter, foedus

revolution *s* conversio *f*; (*change*) commutatio *f*; (*of planets*) ambit·us -ūs *m*; (*pol*) res novae *f pl*, mot·us -ūs *m*

revolutionary *adj* seditiosus, novarum rerum cupidus

revolutionize *vt* novare

revolve *vt* (*in mind*) meditari, volutare; *vi* revolvi, se (re)volvĕre

revulsion *s* taedium, fastidium *n*; **to cause —** fastidium movēre

reward *s* praemium *n*

reward *vt* remunerare, compensare

rewrite *vt* rescribĕre

rhapsody *s* rhapsodia *f*

rhetoric *s* rhetorica *n pl* or *f*

rhetorical *adj* rhetoricus, oratorius; **to practice** — declamare
rhetorician *s* rhetor *m*
rheumatism *s* dolor artuum *m*
rhinoceros *s* rhinoceros *m*
rhubarb *s* radix Pontica *f*
rhyme *s* homoeteleuton *n*
rhythm *s* numerus, rhythmus *m*
rhythmical *adj* numerosus
rib *s* costa *f*
ribald *adj* obscenus, spurcus
ribaldry *s* obscenitas *f*
ribbed *adj* costatus, striatus
ribbon *s* infula *f*
rice *s* oryza *f*
rich *adj* dives, locuples; (*of soil*) fertilis, uber, opimus; (*food*) pinguis; (*costly*) pretiosus, lautus; **—ly** copiose, pretiose, laute
riches *s* divitiae, opes *f pl*
rickety *adj* instabilis
rid *vt* liberare; **to get — of** dimittere, deponere, exuere
riddle *s* aenigma *n*
ride *vt* **to — a horse** equo vehi; *vi* equitare; vehi; **to — away or off** avehi
ride *s* (*on horseback*) equitatio *f*; (*in carriage*) vectio *f*
rider *s* eques *m*; (*in carriage*) vector *m*; (*attached to documents*) adjectio *f*
ridge *s* jugum, dorsum *n*
ridicule *s* ridiculum, ludibrium *n*, irris·us -ūs *m*
ridicule *vt* irridēre
ridiculous *adj* ridiculus; **—ly** ridicule
riding *s* equitatio *f*
rife *adj* frequens
riffraff *s* plebecula, faex populi *f*
rifle *vt* despoliare, diripēre
rig *vt* adornare; (*ship*) armare, ornare
rigging *s* armamenta *n pl*, rudentes *m pl*
right *adj* rectus; (*just*) aequus, justus; (*opposed to left*) dexter; (*suitable*) idoneus, aptus; (*true*) verus, rectus; **—ly** recte, rite, juste, vere
right *s* (*hand*) dextra *f*; (*law*) jus, fas, aequum *n*; **on the — a dextra
right *vt* emendare, corrigēre; (*to replace*) restituēre; (*to avenge*) vindicare, ulcisci
righteous *adj* justus, pius; **—ly** juste, pie
righteousness *s* justitia, pietas, probitas *f*
rightful *adj* legitimus, justus; **—ly** juste
rigid *adj* rigidus; **—ly** rigide
rigidity *s* rigiditas *f*
rigor *s* severitas, duritia *f*
rigorous *adj* severus, asper; (*hardy*) durus
rill *s* rivulus *m*
rim *s* ora, margo *f*, labrum *f*
rind *s* crusta *f*
ring *s* anulus *m*; (*of people*) corona *f*; (*for fighting*) arena *f*; (*sound*) sonit·us -ūs *m*; (*of bells*) tinnit·us -ūs *m*
ring *vt* **to — a bell** tintinnabulum

tractare; *vi* tinnire, resonare
ringing *s* tinnit·us -ūs *m*
ringleader *s* auctor, dux *m*
rinse *vt* colluēre, eluēre
rinsing *s* colluvies *f*
riot *s* tumult·us -ūs, mot·us -ūs *m*; **to run** — luxuriari
riot *vi* seditionem movēre, tumultuari
rioter *s* seditiosus *m*
riotous *adj* seditiosus, tumultuosus; **— living** luxuria *f*
rip *vt* scindēre; **to — apart** discindēre, diffindēre; (*fig*) discerpēre
ripe *adj* mitis, maturus, tempestivus
ripen *vt* maturare; *vi* maturescēre
ripple *s* flucticulus *m*
ripple *vi* trepidare
rise *vi* oriri, surgēre; (*from sleep*) expergisci; (*to mount*) ascendēre; (*to increase*) crescēre; (*of rioters*) consurgēre; (*of passion*) tumescēre; **to — again** resurgēre, reviviscēre; **to — up** exsurgēre
rise *s* (*ascent*) ascens·us -ūs *m*; (*origin*) origo *f*, ort·us -ūs *m*; (*increase*) incrementum *n*; (*slope*) clivus *m*; **to give — to** parēre
rising *s* (*of sun*) ort·us -ūs *m*; (*insurrection*) mot·us -ūs, tumult·us -ūs *m*
risk *s* periculum *n*; **to run a** — periculum subire, periclitari
risk *vt* in periculum vocare, periclitari
rite *s* rit·us -ūs *m*
ritual *s* rit·us -ūs *m*, caeremonia *f*
rival *s* rivalis, aemulus, competitor *m*
rival *vt* aemulari
rivalry *s* aemulatio *f*, certamen *n*; (*in love*) rivalitas *f*
river *s* flumen *n*, amnis *m*
rivet *s* clavus *m*
rivet *vt* (*eyes, attention*) defigēre
rivulet *s* rivus, rivulus *m*
road *s* via *f*, iter *n*; **on the — in** itinere; **to build a — viam munire
roam *vi* errare, vagari
roar *s* fremit·us -ūs, rugit·us -ūs, strepit·us -ūs *m*
roar *vi* fremēre, rudēre, rugire
roast *vt* torrēre; (*in a pan*) frigēre, assare, coquēre
roast *adj* assus
roast *s* assum *n*
rob *vt* spoliare, compilare, latrocinari
robber *s* latro, fur *m*
robbery *s* latrocinium *n*, spoliatio *f*
robe *s* vestis, palla *f*
robe *vt* vestire
robin *s* sylvia rubecula, rubisca *f*
robust *adj* robustus, validus, lacertosus
rock *s* saxum *n*; (*cliff*) scopulus *m*, rupes *f*
rock *vt* jactare; **to — a cradle** cunas agitare; *vi* vibrare, vacillare
rocket *s* missile *n*
rocky *adj* saxosus, scopulosus
rod *s* virga, ferula *f*
roe *s* caprea *f*; (*of fish*) ova *n pl*
roebuck *s* capreolus *m*
rogue *s* nequam (homo), furcifer *m*
roguish *adj* malus, improbus

roll vt volvĕre, versare; vi volvi; (of tears) labi

roll s (book) volumen n; (of names) catalogus m, album n; (of bread) collyra f

roller s cylindrus m

Roman adj Romanus

Roman s Romanus, Quiris m

romance s fabula, narratio ficta f; (affair) amores m pl

romantic adj fabulosus, commenticius, amatorius

roof s tectum, fastigium n; (of mouth) palatum n

roof vt contegĕre, integĕre

room s (space) spatium n, locus m; (of house) conclave n

roomy adj laxus, spatiosus

roost s pertica f

roost vi cubitare, insidēre

root s radix f; (fig) fons m, origo f; to take — coalescĕre

root vt to become rooted (fig) inveterascĕre; to be rooted inhaerēre; to — out eradicare, exstirpare; vi radices agĕre; (fig) inveterascĕre

rope s funis m, restis f

rose s rosa f

roseate adj roseus

rosy adj roseus, rosaceus

rot vi putrescĕre, tabescĕre

rot s putredo, tabes, caries f

rotate vi volvi, se convertĕre

rotation s ambit·us -ūs m, conversio f; (succession) vicissitudo f; in — ordine

rote s by — memoriter

rotten adj putridus, tabidus, cariosus

rotunda s tholus m

rouge s fucus m

rough adj asper; (of character) agrestis, durus; (of weather) inclemens; (shaggy) hirsutus; —ly aspere, duriter

roughen vt asperare

roughness s asperitas f; (brutality) feritas f

round adj rotundus, globosus; —ly aperte, plane, praecise

round s orbis, circulus m; (series) ambit·us -ūs m

round vt (a corner) circumire, flectĕre; (a cape) superare; to — off concludĕre, complēre

rouse vt excitare, animare

rout s fuga f; (defeat) clades f; (crowd) turba f

rout vt fugare, fundĕre

route s via f, iter n

routine s consuetudo f, ordo, us·us -ūs m

rove vi vagari, errare

rover s ambulator m

row s series f, ordo m; (quarrel) rixa f

row vt remis propellĕre; vi remigare

rower s remex m

rowing s remigatio f, remigium n

royal adj regalis, regius; —ly regaliter, regie

royalty s regia potestas f, regnum n

rub vt fricare; to — away or off detergĕre

rub s fricatio f; (fig) difficultas f

rubbing s attrit·us -ūs, affrict·us -ūs m, fricatio, frictio f

rubbish s rudus n; (fig) quisquiliae f pl

rubble s rudus n

rubric s rubrica f

ruby s rubinus, carbunculus m

rudder s gubernaculum n

ruddy adj rubicundus, rubens, rutilus

rude adj rudis, rusticus, inurbanus; (impertinent) impudicus; —ly rustice, incondite

rudeness s rusticitas, inhumanitas, insolentia f

rudiment s elementum, initium, rudimentum, principium n

rudimentary adj inchoatus, elementarius

rue vt I — me paenitet (with genit)

rueful adj maestus, luctuosus

ruffian s sicarius, grassator m

ruffle vt agitare, turbare; (to irritate) commovēre

ruffle s limbus m

rug s stragulum n

rugged adj asper, praeruptus

ruin s pernicies f, exitium n; ruina f; —s ruinae f pl

ruin vt perdĕre, corrumpĕre; (morally) depravare

ruination s vastatio f

ruinous adj damnosus, exitiosus

rule s (regulation) praeceptum n, lex f; (government) regimen, imperium n, dominatio f; (instrument) regula, norma f

rule vt regĕre, moderari; vi regĕre, dominari

ruler s (person) rector, dominus, rex m; (instrument) regula f

ruling s edictum n

rum s sicera f

rumble s murmur n

rumble vi murmurare, crepitare, mugire

rumbling s murmur n, mugit·us -ūs m

ruminate vi ruminare

rumination s ruminatio f

rummage vi to — through rimari

rumor s rumor m, fama f

rump s clunis f

rumple s (in garment) plica, ruga f

rumple vt corrugare

run vt (to manage) gerĕre, administrare; to — aground impingĕre; to — up (an account) augēre; vi currĕre; (to flow) fluĕre; to — about discurrĕre, cursare; to — after sequi, petĕre, sectari; to — aground offendĕre; to — away aufugĕre; to — away from defugĕre; to — down decurrĕre; (as water) defluĕre; to — for conquirĕre; to — foul of collidi; to — into (to meet) incidĕre in (with acc); to — off aufugĕre; (as water) defluĕre; to — on percurrĕre, continuare; to — out excurrĕre; (of time) exire; (of supplies) deficĕre; to — over (details) percurrĕre; (of fluids) superfluĕre; to — short deficĕre; to — through (to dissipate) dissipare; **to — together** concurrĕre; **to — up** accurrĕre; **to — up against** incurrĕre in (*with acc*)

runaway *s* transfuga *m*

runner *s* cursor *m*

running *s* curs·us -ūs *m*; (*flowing*) flux·us -ūs *m*

rupture *s* hernia *f*; seditio, dissensio *f*

rupture *vt* rumpĕre, abrumpĕre; *vi* rumpi

rural *adj* agrestis, rusticus

ruse *s* dolus *m*, fraus *f*

rush *s* (*plant*) juncus *m*; (*charge*) impet·us -ūs *m*

rush *vt* rapĕre; *vi* ruĕre, ferri; **to — forward** prorumpĕre, se proripĕre;

to — in inruĕre, incurrĕre; **to — out** erumpĕre, evolare

russet *adj* russus, rufus, ravus

rust *s* rubigo, aerugo *f*; (*of iron*) ferrugo *f*

rust *vi* rubiginem contrahĕre

rustic *adj* rusticus, agrestis

rustic *s* rusticus *m*, ruricola *m & f*

rustle *vi* crepitare, increpare

rustle *s* crepit·us -ūs *m*

rusty *adj* rubiginosus, aeruginosus; **to become —** rubigine obduci; (*fig*) desuescĕre

rut *s* (*of wheel*) orbita *f*

ruthless *adj* immisericors, inexorabilis, crudelis; **—ly** incrudeliter

rye *s* secale *n*

S

Sabbath *s* sabbata *n pl*

saber *s* acinaces *m*

sable *adj* pullus, ater, niger

sable *s* (*fur*) pellis zibellina *f*

sack *s* saccus *m*; (*mil*) direptio *f*

sack *vt* (*mil*) vastare, diripĕre

sackcloth *s* cilicium *n*

sacred *adj* sacer, sanctus, sacrosanctus

sacrifice *s* (*act*) sacrificium *n*, immolatio *f*; (*victim*) hostia, victima *f*; (*fig*) jactura *f*

sacrifice *vt* immolare, mactare, sacrificare; (*fig*) devovēre

sacrilege *s* sacrilegium *n*

sacrilegious *adj* sacrilegus

sad *adj* tristis, maestus, miserabilis; **—ly** maeste

sadden *vt* contristare, dolore afficĕre

saddle *s* ephippium *n*

saddle *vt* imponĕre (*with acc of thing and dat of person*); **to — a horse** equum sternĕre

saddlebags *s* clitellae *f pl*

sadness *s* tristitia, maestitia *f*

safe *adj* tutus; (*without hurt*) incolumis; **— and sound** salvus; **—ly** tute

safe-conduct *s* tutela *f*, commeat·us -ūs *m*

safeguard *s* praesidium *n*, tutela *f*

safety *s* salus, incolumitas *f*; **in —** tuto

saffron *adj* croceus

sagacious *adj* sagax; **—ly** sagaciter

sagacity *s* sagacitas *f*

sage *s* (*wise man*) sapiens *m*

sage *adj* sapiens, prudens; **—ly** sapienter

sail *s* velum *n*; **to set —** vela dare

sail *vi* nave vehi, vela facĕre, navigare

sailing *s* navigatio *f*

sailor *s* nauta *m*

saint *s* vir sanctus *m*, femina sancta *f*

saintly *adj* sanctus, pius

sake *s* **for the — of** gratiā (*with genit*), causā (*with genit*), pro (*with abl*)

salad *s* acetaria *n pl*, moretum *n*

salamander *s* salamandra *f*

salary *s* salarium *n*, merces *f*

sale *s* venditio *f*; **for — venalis**; **to put up for —** venum dare

salesman *s* venditor *m*

salient *adj* prominens, saliens

saline *adj* salsus

saliva *s* saliva *f*, sputum *n*

sallow *adj* pallidus, luridus

sally *s* eruptio *f*, impet·us -ūs *m*

sally *vi* eruptionem facĕre, erumpĕre

salmon *s* salmo *m*

saloon *s* caupona *f*

salt *s* sal *m*

salt *vt* salire, sale condire

salting *s* salsura *f*

saltless *adj* insulsus

salt mine *s* salifodina *f*

salt shaker *s* salinum *f*

salt water *s* aqua marina *f*

salubrious *adj* salubris

salutary *adj* salutaris, utilis

salutation *s* salutatio, salus *f*

salute *s* salus, salutatio *f*

salute *vt* salutare

salvage *vt* servare, eripĕre

salvation *s* salus *f*

salve *s* unguentum *n*

same *adj* idem; **at the — time** eodem tempore, simul; **the very —** ipsissimus

sameness *s* identitas *f*

sample *s* exemplum, specimen *n*

sample *vt* libare

sanctify *vt* sanctificare, consecrare

sanctimonious *adj* sanctitatem affectans

sanction *s* comprobatio, auctoritas, confirmatio *f*

sanction *vt* ratum facĕre, sancire

sanctity *s* sanctitas, sanctimonia *f*

sanctuary *s* sanctuarium *n*; (*refuge*) asylum *n*

sand *s* (h)arena *f*

sandal *s* solea, crepida *f*

sandstone *s* tofus, tophus *m*

sandy *adj* (h)arenosus, sabulosus, (h)arenaceus; (*in color*) rufus

sane adj sanus

sanguinary adj sanguinarius, cruentus

sanguine adj sanguineus, alacer

sanitary adj salubris

sanity s sanitas, mens sana f

sap s sucus m

sap vt subruĕre, haurire

sapling s surculus m

Sapphic adj Sapphicus

sapphire s sapphirus f

sarcasm s dicacitas f

sarcastic adj acerbus, mordax; —ally acerbe, amare

sarcophagus s sarcophagus m

sardine s sarda f

sardonic adj amarus

sash s cingillum n, zona f

Satan s Satanas, Satan m

satchel s sacculus m, pera f

satellite s satelles m & f

satiate vt satiare, saturare

satire s satura f

satirical adj acerbus, satiricus

satirist s derisor, saturarum scriptor m

satirize vt notare, perstringĕre

satisfaction s compensatio f; (feeling) voluptas f

satisfactorily adv ex sententia (meā, tuā, etc.)

satisfactory adj idoneus, jucundus, gratus

satisfied adj contentus

satisfy vt satisfacĕre (with dat); (to indemnify) compensare; (desires) explēre

satrap s satrapes m

saturate vt saturare, imbuĕre

satyr s satyrus m

sauce s condimentum n; (of meat) eliquamen n

saucer s patella, scutella f

saucily adv petulanter

saucy adj petulans, procax, protervus

saunter vi vagari, ambulari

sausage s farcimen n

savage adj ferus, efferatus; (cruel) saevus, atrox, immanis; —ly crudeliter, immaniter

save vt servare, conservare; (from danger) liberare, eripĕre; to — up reservare

save prep praeter (with acc)

saving s conservatio f; —s peculium n

savior s servator, liberator m

Saviour s Salvator (mundi) m

savor s sapor, gust·us -ūs m

savor vi sapĕre

savory adj sapidus

saw s (tool) serra f; (saying) proverbium n

saw vt serrā secare; vi serram ducĕre

sawdust s scobis f

say vt dicĕre; that is to — scilicet; to — that . . . not negare

saying s dictum, proverbium n

scab s crusta f

scabbard s vagina f

scaffold s tabulatum n, fala f

scald vt urĕre

scale s (of fish) squama f; (for weighing) libra, trutina f; (mus) diagramma n; (gradation) grad·us -ūs m

scale vt (fish) desquamare; to — a wall murum per scalas ascendĕre

scallop s pecten m

scalp s pericranium n

scaly adj squamosus, squameus

scamp s furcifer m

scamper vi cursare; to — about discurrĕre, cursitare; to — away aufugĕre

scan vt examinare, explorare; (verses) scandĕre

scandal s ignominia f, opprobrium n

scandalize vt offendĕre

scandalous adj probrosus, flagitiosus

scantily adv exigue, anguste

scanty adj tenuis, exiguus, exilis

scapegoat s piaculum n

scar s cicatrix f

scarce adj rarus; —ly vix, aegre

scarcity s paucitas, inopia f

scare vt terrēre, territare

scarecrow s terriculum n

scarf s fascia f, focale n

scarlet s coccum n

scarlet adj coccinus, coccineus

scathing adj acerbus, aculeatus

scatter vt spargĕre, dispergĕre, dissipare; vi dilabi, diffugĕre

scavenger s cloacarius m

scene s prospect·us -ūs m, spectaculum n; (on stage) scaena f; (place) locus m

scenery s (in theater) scaenae apparat·us -ūs m; (of nature) species regionis f

scent s (sense) odorat·us -ūs m; (of dogs) sagacitas f; (fragrance) odor m

scent vt odorari

scented adj odoratus

scepter s sceptrum n

sceptic s scepticus m

sceptical adj dubitans, incredulus

schedule s ratio f

scheme s consilium n

scheme vt & vi moliri, machinari

schism s schisma, discidium n

scholar s litteratus m

scholarly adj litteratus, doctus

scholarship s litterae f pl, eruditio f

scholastic adj scholasticus

scholiast s scholiastes, interpres m

school s ludus m, schola f; (group holding like opinions) secta f

schoolboy s discipulus m

schoolmaster s magister m

schoolroom s schola f

science s scientia, doctrina, disciplina, ars f

scientific adj physicus; —ally physice; (systematically) ratione

scientist s physicus m

scimitar s acinaces m

scion s edit·us -ūs m, progenies f

scissors s forfex f

scoff s irrisio, derisio, cavillatio f

scoff vi cavillari; to — at irridēre, deridēre

scoffer s derisor, irrisor m

scold vt objurgare, increpare; vi desaevire

scolding s objurgatio f

scoop s trulla f

scoop vt to — out excavare

scope s campus m, spatium n

scorch vt adurěre, torrēre

score s nota f; (total) summa f; (twenty) viginti; (reckoning) ratio f

score vt notare

scorn s contemptio f

scorn vt contemněre, sperněre, aspernari

scornful adj fastidiosus; —ly fastidiose, contemptim

scorpion s scorpio, scorpius m

Scot adj Scoticus

Scotchman s Scotus m

Scotland s Scotia f

Scottish adj Scoticus

scoundrel s nebulo, furcifer m

scour vt (to rub clean) (de)tergēre; (to range over) pervagari, percurrēre

scourge s flagellum n; (fig) pestis f

scourge vt verberare

scourging s verberatio f, verbera n pl

scout s explorator, speculator m

scout vt speculari, explorare

scowl vi frontem contrahēre

scowlingly adv fronte contractā

scramble vi to — up scandēre, escendēre

scrap s fragmentum, frustum n

scrape vt radēre, scabēre; to — together corradēre

scrape s difficultas f; (quarrel) rixa f

scraper s radula f

scraping s rasura f; —s ramenta n pl

scratch s levis incisura f

scratch vt radēre, scalpēre

scrawl s scriptio mala f

scrawl vt & vi male scribēre

scream s ululat·us -ūs, clamor m; (of an infant) vagit·us -ūs m

scream vi ululare, clamitare

screech s stridor m

screech vi stridēre

screen s umbraculum n, obex m

screen vt protegēre

screw s cochlea f

screw vt torquēre

scribble vt & vi scriptitare

scribe s scriba m

script s scriptum n; (hand) man·us -ūs f

scrofulous adj strumosus

scroll s volumen n, schedula f

scrub vt defricare, detergēre

scruple s scrupulus m, religio, dubitatio f

scrupulous adj religiosus, anxius; —ly religiose

scrutinize vt scrutari, perscrutari

scrutiny s scrutatio, perscrutatio f

scud vi celeriter aufugēre

scuffle s rixa f

scuffle vi rixari

sculptor s sculptor, scalptor m

sculpture s (art) sculptura f; (work) opus, signum n

sculpture vt sculpēre

scum s spuma f; (fig) sentina f

scurrilous adj scurrilis

scurvy s scorbutus m

scutcheon s scutum n

scythe s falx f

sea s mare, aequor n, pontus m

sea captain s navarchus m

seacoast s ora maritima f

seafaring adj maritimus, nauticus

sea gull s larus m

seal s sigillum, signum n; (animal) phoca f

seal vt signare; (fig) sancire; to — up obsignare

seam s sutura f

seaman s nauta m

seamanship s nauticarum rerum us·us -ūs m, ars navigandi f

sear vt adurēre

search s investigatio, scrutatio f

search vt investigare, explorare; (a person) excutēre; vi to — for quaerēre, exquirēre; to — out explorare

seasick adj nauseabundus; to be — nauseare

season s tempestas f, anni tempus n; (proper time) opportunitas f, tempus n; in — tempestive

season vt condire; (fig) assuefacēre, durare

seasonable adj tempestivus, opportunus

seasoning s condimentum n

seat s sedes, sella f; (dwelling) sedes f, domicilium n

seat vt sede locare; to — oneself considēre

seaweed s alga f

secede vi secedēre

secession s secessio f

seclude vt secludēre, removēre, abdēre

secluded adj remotus, solitarius

seclusion s solitudo f, locus remotus m

second adj secundus, alter; a — time iterum; —ly deinde, tum

second s (person) adjutor m; (of time) punctum temporis n

second vt adesse (with dat), favēre (with dat), adjuvare

secondary adj secundarius, inferior

secondhand adj alienus, tritus

second-rate adj inferior

secrecy s secretum n; (keeping secret) silentium n

secret adj secretus, occultus, arcanus; to keep — celare; —ly clam

secret s secretum n, res arcana f; in — clam

secretary s scriba, amanuensis m

secrete vt celare, occultare, abdēre

secretion s secretio f

sect s secta f

section s pars, sectio f

sector s sector m, regio f

secular adj profanus

secure adj tutus; —ly tuto

secure vt confirmare, munire; (to obtain) parare, nancisci; (to fasten) religare

security *s* salus, incolumitas *f*; (*pledge*) satisdatio *f*, pignus *n*
sedan *s* lectica *f*
sedate *adj* gravis, sedatus; **—ly** graviter, sedate
sedentary *adj* sedentarius
sedge *s* ulva, carex *f*
sediment *s* sedimentum *n*, faex *f*
sedition *s* seditio, rebellio *f*
seditious *adj* seditiosus, turbulentus; **—ly** seditiose
seduce *vt* seducĕre, corrumpĕre, depravare
seducer *s* corruptor *m*
seduction *s* corruptela *f*
seductive *adj* blandus; **—ly** blande
see *vt & vi* vidēre, cernĕre, conspicĕre; (*to understand*) vidēre, intellegĕre, sentire; **to go to —** visĕre; **to — to** curare
seed *s* semen *n*; (*offspring*) progenies *f*; (*of fruit*) acinum *n*
seedling *s* surculus *m*
seek *vt* quaerĕre, petĕre; **to — to** conari (*with inf*), laborare (*with inf*)
seem *vi* vidēri
seeming *adj* speciosus; **—ly** in speciem, ut videtur
seemly *adj* decens, decorus
seep *vi* manare
seer *s* vates *m*
seethe *vi* fervēre, aestuare
segment *s* segmentum *n*
segregate *vt* segregare, secernĕre
segregation *s* separatio *f*
seize *vt* prehendĕre, arripĕre, rapĕre; (*mil*) occupare; (*fig*) afficĕre
seizure *s* comprehensio, occupatio *f*
seldom *adv* raro
select *vt* seligĕre, eligĕre, deligĕre
select *adj* electus, lectus, exquisitus
selection *s* (*act*) selectio *f*; (*things chosen*) electa *n pl*
self-confident *adj* sibi fidens, confidens
self-conscious *adj* pudibundus
self-control *s* continentia, temperantia *f*
self-denial *s* abstinentia *f*
self-evident *adj* manifestus
self-indulgent *adj* intemperans
selfish *adj* avarus
selfishness *s* avaritia *f*
self-respect *s* pudor *m*
sell *vt* vendĕre; *vi* venire
seller *s* venditor *m*
semblance *s* species, similitudo *f*
semicircle *s* hemicyclium *n*
semicircular *adj* semicirculus
senate *s* senat·us -ūs *m*; (*building*) curia *f*
senator *s* senator *m*
senatorial *adj* senatorius
send *vt* mittĕre; (*on public business*) legare; **to — away** dimittĕre; **to — for** arcessĕre; **to — forward** praemittĕre
senile *adj* senilis, aetate provectus
senior *adj* natu major
seniority *s* aetatis praerogativa *f*
sensation *s* sens·us -ūs *m*; (*fig*) mirum *n*
sense *s* (*faculty*; *meaning*) sens·us

-ūs *m*; (*understanding*) prudentia *f*; (*meaning*) vis, significatio *f*
sense *vt* sentire
senseless *adj* absurdus, ineptus; (*unconscious*) omni sensu carens
sensible *adj* sapiens, prudens
sensibly *adv* prudenter, sapienter
sensitive *adj* sensilis, patibilis; (*touchy*) mollis
sensual *adj* voluptarius, libidinosus; **—ly** libidinose
sensualist *s* homo voluptarius *m*
sensuality *s* libido *f*
sentence *s* (*gram*) sententia *f*; (*law*) judicium *n*; **to pass —** judicare
sentence *vt* damnare, condemnare
sententious *adj* sententiosus; **—ly** sententiose
sentiment *s* (*opinion*) sententia, opinio *f*; (*feeling*) sens·us -ūs *m*
sentimental *adj* mollis, effeminatus
sentimentality *s* mollities animi *f*
sentinel *s* custos, vigil *m*
sentry *s* custos, vigil *m*; **sentries** excubiae, stationes, vigiliae *f pl*
separable *adj* separabilis
separate *adj* separatus, disjunctus; **—ly** separatim
separate *vt* separare, disjungĕre, dividēre; *vi* separari, disjungi
separation *s* separatio, disjunctio *f*
September *s* (*mensis*) September *m*
sepulcher *s* sepulcrum *n*
sepulchral *adj* sepulcralis
sequel *s* exit·us -ūs *m*
sequence *s* ordo *m*, series *f*
seraph *s* seraphus *m*
serenade *vt* occentare
serene *adj* serenus, tranquillus; **—ly** serene
serenity *s* serenitas, tranquillitas *f*
serf *s* servus *m*
serfdom *s* servitium *n*, servitus *f*
sergeant *s* optio *m*
series *s* series *f*, ordo *m*
serious *adj* serius, gravis; **—ly** serio
seriousness *s* gravitas *f*, serium *n*
sermon *s* oratio sacra *f*
serpent *s* serpens *f*, anguis *m & f*
servant *s* famulus *m*, famula *f*, servus *m*, serva *f*; (*public servant*) minister *m*
serve *vt* servire (*with dat*); (*food*) apponĕre; (*to be useful to*) prodesse (*with dat*); **to — a sentence** poenam subire; *vi* (*mil*) merēre, militare; (*to suffice*) sufficĕre
service *s* (*favor*) officium *n*; (*mil*) militia *f*, stipendia *n pl*; (*work*) ministerium *n*; **to be of — to** prodesse (*with dat*), bene merēri de (*with abl*)
serviceable *adj* utilis
servile *adj* servilis, humilis
servility *s* humilitas *f*, animus abjectus *m*
servitude *s* servitus *f*
session *s* sessio *f*, convent·us -ūs *m*
set *vt* ponĕre, sistĕre, collocare; (*course*) dirigĕre; (*example*) dare; (*limit*) imponĕre; (*sail*) dare; (*table*) instruĕre; **to — apart** secernĕre, seponĕre; **to — aside** ponĕre; (*fig*)

rescindĕre; **to — down** deponĕre; (*in writing*) perscribĕre; **to — forth** exponĕre; **to — free** liberare; **to — in motion** ciĕre; **to — in order** componĕre; **to — off** (*to adorn*) adornare; **to — on fire** incendĕre, accendĕre; **to — someone over** aliquem praeficĕre (*with dat*); **to — up** statuĕre; *vi* (*of stars, etc.*) occidĕre; **to — in** (*to begin*) incipĕre; **to — out** proficisci

set *adj* (*fixed*) certus, praescriptus

set *s* congeries *f*

setting *s* occas·us -ūs *m*

settle *vt* statuĕre; (*business*) transigĕre; (*colony*) deducĕre; (*argument*) componĕre; (*debts*) solvĕre, expedire; *vi* (*to take up residence*) considĕre; (*to sink*) subsidĕre

settlement *s* constitutio *f*; (*agreement*) pactum *n*; (*colony*) colonia *f*; (*of liquids*) sedimentum *n*

settler *s* colonus *m*

seven *adj* septem; **— times** septies

sevenfold *adj* septemplex

seventeen *adj* septemdecim, decem et septem

seventeenth *adj* septimus decimus

seventh *adj* septimus; **the — time** septimum

seventieth *adj* septuagesimus

seventy *adj* septuaginta

sever *vt* separare; *vi* disjungi

several *adj* aliquot, complures; **—ly** singulatim

severe *adj* severus, gravis, durus; (*of weather*) asper; **—ly** severe, graviter

severity *s* severitas, gravitas *f*

sew *vt* suĕre; **to — up** consuĕre

sewer *s* cloaca *f*

sewing *s* sutura *f*

sex *s* sex·us -ūs *m*

sextant *s* sextans *m*

sexton *s* aedituus *m*

sexual *adj* sexualis

shabbily *adv* sordide, obsolete

shabbiness *s* sordes *f pl*

shabby *adj* sordidus, obsoletus

shackle *vt* compedibus constringĕre

shackles *s* vincula *n pl*, compedes *f pl*

shade *s* umbra *f*; **—s** (*of the dead*) manes *m pl*

shade *vt* opacare, adumbrare

shadow *s* umbra *f*

shadowy *adj* umbrosus, opacus; (*fig*) inanis, vanus

shady *adj* umbrosus, opacus

shaft *s* (*arrow*) sagitta *f*; (*of spear*) hastile *n*; (*of mine*) puteus *m*

shaggy *adj* hirsutus, villosus

shake *vt* quatĕre, concutĕre; (*head*) nutare; *vi* tremĕre; (*to totter*) vacillare

shaking *s* quassatio *f*; (*with cold, fear, etc.*) tremor, horror *m*

shaky *adj* instabilis

shallow *adj* brevis, vadosus; (*fig*) insulsus, levis

sham *s* dolus *m*, simulatio, species *f*

sham *adj* fictus, simulatus

shambles *s* laniena *f*, laniarium *n*

shame *s* pudor *m*; (*disgrace*) dedecus *n*, infamia, ignominia *f*

shame *vt* ruborem incutĕre (*with dat*)

shamefaced *adj* pudens, verecundus

shameful *adj* probrosus, turpis; **—ly** probrose, turpiter

shameless *adj* impudens; **—ly** impudenter

shamrock *s* trifolium *n*

shank *s* crus *n*

shanty *s* tugurium *n*

shape *s* forma, figura, facies *f*

shape *vt* formare, fingĕre

shapeless *adj* informis, deformis

shapely *adj* formosus

share *s* pars, portio *f*; (*of plow*) vomer *m*

share *vt* partire, impertire; particeps esse (*with genit*)

shark *s* p(r)istix *m*

sharp *adj* acutus; (*bitter*) acer, acerbus; (*keen*) acutus, acer, sagax; **—ly** acriter, acute; (*bitterly*) acerbe

sharpen *vt* acuĕre

shatter *vt* quassare, confringĕre; (*fig*) frangĕre

shave *vt* radĕre

shavings *s* ramenta *n pl*

shawl *s* amiculum *n*

she *pron* ea, illa, haec

sheaf *s* manipulus, fascis *m*

shear *vt* tondĕre

shearing *s* tonsura *f*

shears *s* forfices *f pl*

sheath *s* vagina *f*

sheathe *vt* in vaginam recondĕre

shed *vt* fundĕre, effundĕre

shed *s* tugurium *n*; (*mil*) vinea *f*

sheep *s* ovis *f*

sheepfold *s* ovile *n*

sheephook *s* pedum, baculum pastorale *n*

sheepish *adj* pudibundus; **—ly** pudenter

sheepskin *s* pellis ovilla *f*

sheer *adj* merus

sheet *s* linteum *n*; (*of paper*) plagula, scheda *f*; (*of metal*) lamina *f*

shelf *s* pluteus *m*, tabula *f*, pegma *n*

shell *s* concha, crusta *f*; (*husk*) folliculus *m*; (*of nuts, etc.*) putamen *n*

shell *vt* decorticare

shellfish *s* concha *f*

shelter *s* tegmen *n*; (*refuge*) refugium *n*; (*lodgings*) hospitium *n*

shelter *vt* tegĕre, defendĕre; (*refugee*) excipĕre

shepherd *s* pastor, opilio, pecorum custos *m*

shield *s* scutum *n*, parma *f*

shield *vt* tegĕre, protegĕre

shield bearer *s* scutigerulus, armiger *m*

shift *vt* mutare, amovĕre; *vi* (*as the wind*) vertĕre; (*to change position*) se movĕre, mutari

shift *s* (*change*) mutatio *f*

shifty *adj* varius, mobilis

shin *s* tibia *f*, crus *n*

shine *s* nitor *m*

shine *vi* lucĕre, fulgĕre, nitĕre; **to — forth** elucĕre, enitĕre, exsplendescĕre; **to — on** or **upon** affulgĕre (with dat)

shiny adj lucidus, fulgidus, nitidus

ship s navis f, navigium n

ship vt navi invehĕre

shipbuilder s naupegus m

shipbuilding s architectura navalis f

shipmaster s navicularius m

shipwreck s naufragium n; **to suffer — naufragium facĕre**

shipwrecked adj naufragus

shirk vt defugĕre, detrectare

shirt s subucla, camisia f

shiver vi contremiscĕre, horrēre

shoal s caterva f, grex m; (shallow) brevia n pl

shock vt percutĕre, percellĕre; (fig) offendĕre

shock s concussio f, impet·us -ūs m; (fig) offensio f

shocking adj flagitiosus, atrox

shoe s calceus m

shoemaker s sutor m

shoot vt (missile) conjicĕre, jaculari; (person) transfigĕre; vi volare

shoot s surculus m

shooting star s fax caelestis f

shop s taberna, officina f

shopkeeper s tabernarius m

shore s litus n, ora f

short adj brevis; **to run — deficĕre; —ly** brevi, mox

shortage s inopia f

shortcoming s defect·us -ūs m, delictum n

shorten vt coarctare, contrahĕre; vi contrahi, minui

shorthand s notae breviores f pl

shortness s brevitas, exiguitas f; **— of breath** asthma n

short-sighted adj myops; (fig) improvidus, imprudens

short-winded adj anhelus

shot s ict·us -ūs m; (reach, range) jact·us -ūs m

should vi debēre; **I — go** mihi eundum est

shoulder s (h)umerus m; (of animal) armus m

shoulder vt suscipĕre

shout s clamor m, acclamatio f

shout vt & vi clamare, acclamare, vociferari

shove vt trudĕre, pulsare

shovel s pala f, rutrum n

shovel vt pala tollĕre

show vt monstrare; (to display) exhibēre; (to teach) docēre; **to — off** ostendĕre; vi **to — off** se jactare

show s (appearance) species f; (display) ostentatio f; (pretense) simulatio f; (entertainment) spectaculum n

shower s imber m

shower vt fundĕre, effundĕre

showy adj speciosus

shred s segmentum panni n; (scrap) frustum n

shrew s mulier jurgiosa f

shrewd adj acutus, astutus, callidus, sagax; **—ly** acute, callide, sagaciter

shrewdness s calliditas, astutia, sagacitas f

shriek s ululat·us -ūs m, ejulatio f

shriek vi ululare, ejulare

shrill adj peracutus, stridulus

shrimp s cancer pagurus m; (person) pumilio, homulus m

shrine s fanum, delubrum n

shrink vt contrahĕre; vi contrahi; (to withdraw) refugĕre; **to — from** abhorrēre ab (with abl), refugĕre ab (with abl)

shrivel vt corrugare, torrefacĕre; vi corrugari, torrescĕre

shroud s integumentum n; (of ship) rudentes m pl

shroud vt involvĕre, obducĕre

shrub s frutex m

shrubbery s fruticetum n

shrug s (h)umerorum allevatio f

shrug vt **to — the shoulders** (h)umeros contrahĕre or allevare

shudder vi horrēre; **to — at** horrēre

shuffle vt miscēre; vi claudicare

shun vt vitare, devitare, fugĕre

shut vt claudĕre, occludĕre; **to — out** excludĕre; **to — up** concludĕre; vi **to — up** conticescĕre

shutter s claustrum n, foricula f

shy adj timidus, pudibundus; **—ly** timide

shyness s timiditas, verecundia f

sibyl s sibylla f

sick adj (mentally or physically) aeger; (physically) aegrotus; **I am — of** me taedet (with genit), fastidio; **to be — aegrotare**

sicken vt fastidium movēre (with dat); vi in morbum incidĕre, nauseare

sickle s falx f

sickly adj infirmus

sickness s morbus m, aegrotatio f

side s latus n; (direction) pars f; (district) regio f; (faction) partes f pl; (kinship) genus n; **at the — of** a latere (with genit); **on all —s** undique; **on both —s** utrimque; **on one — unā** ex parte; **on that — illinc; on the mother's — materno genere; on this — hinc; on this — of** cis (with acc), citra (with acc); **to be on the — of** stare ab (with abl), sentire cum (with abl)

side adj lateralis, obliquus

side vi **to — with** partes sequi (with genit), stare ab (with abl), sentire cum (with abl)

sideboard s abacus m

sidelong adj obliquus, transversus

sideways adv in obliquum, oblique

siege s obsessio, oppugnatio, obsidio f; **to lay — to** obsidēre

siesta s meridiatio f; **to take a — meridiare**

sieve s cribrum n; (little sieve) cribellum n

sift vt cribrare; (fig) scrutari

sigh s suspirium n

sigh vi suspirare; **to — for** desiderare

sight s (sense) vis·us -ūs m; (act of seeing) aspect·us -ūs m; (range) conspect·us -ūs m; (appearance) species f; (show) spectaculum n; **at**

first — primo aspectu; **to catch**
— **of** conspicĕre; **to lose** — **of** e
conspectu amittĕre

sight *vt* conspicari

sightless *adj* caecus

sightly *adj* decorus, decens

sign *s* signum, indicium *n*; *(mark)*
nota *f*; *(distinction)* insigne *n*; omen,
portentum *n*

sign *vt (e.g., a document)* subscribĕre, signare, consignare

signal *vi* signum dare; *(by a nod)* annuĕre

signal *s* signum *n*; *(mil)* classicum *n*

signal *adj* insignis, egregius

signature *s* signatura *f*, nomen *n*

signer *s* signator *m*

signet *s* sigillum *n*

significance *s (meaning)* significatio, vis *f*, sens·us ·ūs *m*; *(importance)* momentum *n*

significant *adj* gravis, magnus, magni momenti *(genit)*

signify *vt* significare, portendĕre

silence *s* silentium *n*

silence *interj* tace!; *(to more than
one person)* tacete!

silence *vt* comprimĕre; *(by argument)* refutare

silent *adj* tacitus, taciturnus; **to become** — conticescĕre; **to be** —
tacēre; **—ly** tacite

silk *s* sericum *n*, bombyx *m & f*

silk *adj* sericus, bombycinus

silkworm *s* bombyx *m & f*

sill *s* limen inferum *n*

silly *adj* stultus, ineptus

silver *s* argentum *n*

silver *adj* argenteus

silversmith *s* faber argentarius *m*

silvery *adj* argenteus; *(of hair)* canus

similar *adj* similis; **—ly** similiter,
pariter

similarity *s* similitudo *f*

simile *s* translatio, similitudo *f*

simmer *vi* lente fervēre

simper *vi* inepte ridēre

simple *adj* simplex; *(easy)* facilis;
(frank) sincerus; *(silly)* stultus

simpleton *s* stultus, ineptus *m*

simplicity *s* simplicitas *f*

simplify *vt* faciliorem reddĕre

simply *adv* simpliciter; solum, tantummodo

simulate *vt* simulare

simulation *s* simulatio *f*

simultaneous *adj* eodem tempore;
—ly simul, unā, eodem tempore

sin *s* peccatum, delictum *n*

sin *vi* peccare

since *prep* ex *(with abl)*, ab *(with
abl)*, post *(with acc)*; **ever** — usque
ab *(with abl)*

since *adv* abhinc; **long** — jamdudum, jampridem

since *conj (temporal)* ex quo tempore, postquam, cum; *(causal)* quod,
quia, quoniam, cum

sincere *adj* sincerus, candidus; **—ly**
sincere, vere

sinew *s* nervus, lacertus *m*

sinewy *adj* nervosus, lacertosus

sinful *adj* impius, pravus; **—ly** im-

pie, improbe

sing *vt & vi* canĕre, cantare

singe *vt* adurĕre, amburĕre

singer *s* cantator *m*, cantatrix *f*

singing *s* cant·us ·ūs *m*

single *adj* solus, unicus, unus, singularis; *(unmarried)* caelebs; **not a**
— **one** ne unus quidem

single *vt* **to** — **out** eligĕre

singly *adv* singulatim, viritim

singsong *s* canticum *n*

singsong *adj* canorus

singular *adj* unicus, singularis; *(outstanding)* egregius, eximius; **—ly**
singulariter, unice, egregie

sinister *adj* infaustus, malevolus,
iniquus

sink *vt* submergĕre, demergĕre, deprimĕre; *(money)* collocare; *vi* considĕre, subsidĕre; *(in water)* mergi;
(of morale, etc.) cadĕre

sink *s* sentina *f*

sinless *adj* peccati expers

sinner *s* peccator *m*, peccatrix *f*

sinuous *adj* sinuosus

sip *vt* libare, sorbillare, degustare

siphon *s* sipho *m*

sir *s (title)* eques *m*

sir *interj (to a master)* ere!; *(to an
equal)* bone vir!, vir clarissime!

sire *s* genitor *m*

siren *s* siren *f*

sister *s* soror *f*

sister-in-law *s* glos *f*

sisterly *adj* sororius

sit *vi* sedēre; **to** — **beside** assidēre
(with dat); **to** — **down** considĕre;
to — **on** insidēre *(with dat)*; **to** —
up *(to be awake at night)* vigilare

site *s* sit·us ·ūs *m*

situated *adj* situs, positus

situation *s* sit·us ·ūs *m*; *(circumstances)* res, conditio *f*

six *adj* sex; — **times** sexies

sixfold *adj* sextuplus

sixteen *adj* sedecim

sixteenth *adj* sextus decimus

sixth *s* sexta pars *f*

sixtieth *adj* sexagesimus

sixty *adj* sexaginta

size *s* magnitudo, mensura *f*

skein *s* glomus *m*

skeleton *s* sceletos *m*, ossa *n pl*

sketch *s* adumbratio, lineatio *f*

sketch *vt* adumbrare, delineare; *(fig)*
describĕre

skiff *s* scapha *f*

skilful *adj* dexter, peritus, scitus;
(with hands) habilis; **—ly** perite,
scite

skill *s* sollertia, calliditas, peritia *f*

skilled *adj* peritus, doctus

skillet *s* cucumella *f*

skim *vt* despumare; *(fig)* percurrĕre,
stringĕre

skin *s (of men)* cutis *f*; *(of animals)*
pellis *f*; *(prepared)* corium *n*

skin *vt* pellem exuĕre *(with abl)*

skinny *adj* macilentus

skip *vt* praeterire; *vi* subsultare; **to**
— **over** transilire

skirmish *s* concursatio, velitatio *f*

skirmish *vi* velitari

skirmisher s veles m
skirt s instita f; (border) fimbria f
skirt vt tangĕre, legĕre
skull s cranium, caput n
sky s caelum n, aether m; **under the open** — sub divo
slab s tabula, tessera f
slack adj remissus, laxus; (fig) piger, neglegens
slacken vt remittĕre, laxare, minuĕre; vi minui, remitti
slag s scoria f
slain adj occisus
slake vt exstinguĕre, sedare
slander s calumnia, obtrectatio f
slander vt obtrectare (with dat), calumniari
slanderer s obtrectator m
slanderous adj calumniosus, maledicus
slang s vulgaria verba n pl
slant vt acclinare; (fig) detorquĕre
slanting adj obliquus
slap s alapa f
slap vt alapam dare (with dat), palmā ferire
slash s (cut) caesura f; (blow) ict·us ·ūs m; (wound) vulnus n
slash vt caedĕre, incidĕre
slaughter s caedes, trucidatio f
slaughter vt mactare, trucidare
slaughterhouse s laniena f
slave s servus m, serva f
slave dealer s venalicius, manciporum negotiator m
slavery s servitus f, servitium n
slave trade s venalicium n
slavish adj servilis; —ly serviliter
slay vt interficĕre, occidĕre, necare
slayer s necator, homicida m
sledge s traha, trahea f
sleek adj levis, politus, nitidus, pinguis
sleep s somnus m
sleep vi dormire
sleepless adj insomnis, pervigil
sleepy adj somniculosus, semisomnis; (fig) iners
sleet s nivosa grando f
sleeve s manica f
slender adj gracilis, tenuis
slice s segmentum, frustum n, offula f
slice vt secare
slide vi labi
slight adj levis, exiguus, tenuis; —ly leviter, paululum
slight s neglegentia, contemptio f
slight vt neglegĕre, contemnĕre
silly adv astute, callide, vafre
slim adj gracilis
slime s limus m
slimy adj limosus, mucosus, viscosus
sling s funda f; (for arm) fascia f
sling vt jaculari
slink vi to — away furtim se subducĕre
slip s laps·us ·ūs m; (of paper) scheda f; (in grafting) surculus m; (error) peccatum n, culpa f
slip vt (to give furtively) furtim dare; vi labi; **to let** — omittĕre; **to** — **away** elabi
slipper s solea, crepida f

slippery adj lubricus; (deceitful) subdolus
slit s incisura f
slit vt incidĕre, discidĕre
slop s vilis pot·us ·ūs m
slope s declivitas f, clivus m
slope vi proclinari, vergĕre
sloping adj declivis, pronus; (upward) acclivis
sloppy adj lutulentus, sordidus
slot s rima f
sloth s ignavia, pigritia, inertia f
slothful adj piger, segnis, iners; —ly pigre, segniter, ignave
slouch vi languide incedĕre
slough s (of snake) exuviae f pl; (mire) caenum n
slovenly adj sordidus, ignavus
slow adj tardus, lentus; (gentle) lenis; —ly tarde, lente, sensim
sluggard s homo piger m
sluggish adj piger, ignavus, segnis; —ly pigre, segniter
sluice s cataracta f
slumber s somnus, sopor m
slumber vi obdormiscĕre, dormitare
slur s macula f
slur vt inquinare; vi to — **over** extenuare, leviter attingĕre
slut s meretrix f
sly adj astutus, vafer, callidus; **on the** — clam; —ly astute, callide, vafre
smack s (flavor) sapor m; (blow) alapa f
smack vt (to strike) ferire; vi **to** — **of** sapĕre
small adj parvus, exiguus, tenuis
smart adj (clever) sollers, callidus; (elegant) lautus, nitidus; (of pace) velox; —ly callide; nitide
smart s dolor m
smart vi dolĕre
smash s concussio, fractura f
smash vt confringĕre
smattering s cognitio manca, levis scientia f
smear vt illinĕre, oblinĕre
smell s (sense) odorat·us ·ūs m; (odor) odor m
smell vt olfacĕre, odorari; vi olēre; **to** — **of** olēre, redolēre
smelly adj olidus, graveolens
smelt vt (ex)coquĕre, fundĕre
smile s ris·us ·ūs m; **with a** — subridens
smile vi subridēre; **to** — **at** arridēre (with dat)
smirk vi subridēre
smite vt ferire, percutĕre
smith s faber m
smithy s ferramentorum fabrica f
smock s tunica f
smoke s fumus m
smoke vt (to cure by smoking) infumare; vi fumare
smoky adj fumeus, fumidus, fumosus
smooth adj levis; (of skin) glaber; (polished) teres; (calm) placidus; (of talk) blandus; —ly leviter; blande
smooth vt polire, limare
smother vt suffocare, opprimĕre
smudge s sordes f

smudge *vt* inquinare, conspurcare

smug *adj* lautus, nitidus, sui contentus

smuggle *vt* furtim importare, sine portorio importare

smut *s* fuligo *f*

smutty *adj* obscenus; *(blackened)* fumosus

snack *s* portio, morsiuncula *f*

snail *s* cochlea *f*, limax *m* & *f*

snake *s* anguis *m* & *f*, serpens *f*

snap *vt (to break)* frangĕre; **to — the fingers** digitis concrepare; **to — up** corripĕre; *vi* disilire, frangi; **to — at** mordēre

snap *s* crepit·us -ūs *m*

snare *s* laqueus *m*, pedica *f*; *(fig)* insidiae *f pl*

snare *vt* illaquēre, irretire

snarl *vi (as a dog)* ringĕre, hirrire

snatch *vt* rapĕre, corripĕre; **to — away** eripĕre; **to — up** surripĕre

sneak *s* perfidus *m*

sneak *vi* repĕre, serpĕre, latitare

sneer *s* rhonchus *m*, irrisio *f*

sneer *vi* irridēre, deridēre

sneeringly *adv* cum irrisione

sneeze *s* sternutamentum *n*

sneeze *vi* sternuĕre

sniff *vt* odorari, naribus captare

snip *vi* amputare; **to — off** decerpĕre, praecidĕre

snivel *s* mucus *m*

snivel *vi* mucum resorbēre

snob *s* homo arrogans *m*, homo fastidiosus *m*

snobbish *adj* fastidiosus

snore *s* rhonchus *m*

snore *vi* stertēre

snort *s* fermit·us -ūs *m*

snort *vi* fremēre

snout *s* rostrum *n*

snow *s* nix *f*

snow *vi* ningēre; **it is snowing** ningit

snowball *s* glebula nivis *f*

snowdrift *s* niveus agger *m*

snowstorm *s* ningor *m*

snowy *adj* niveus, nivalis; *(full of snow)* nivosus

snub *vt* reprehendĕre, neglegĕre

snub *s* repulsa *f*

snuff *vt* **to — out** exstinguĕre

snug *adj* commodus; **—ly** commode

so *adv* sic, ita, *(before adjectives)* tam; **— far** eatenus, adhuc; **— much** tantum; **— so** mediocriter; **— that** ita ut; **— that not** ne; **— then** quare, quapropter

soak *vt* madefacĕre, macerare; *vi* madēre

soap *s* sapo *m*

soar *vi* in sublime ferri; *(of birds)* subvolare

sob *s* singult·us -ūs *m*

sob *vi* singultare

sober *adj* sobrius; *(fig)* moderatus, modestus; **—ly** sobrie; moderate

sobriety *s* sobrietas *f*; *(fig)* continentia *f*

sociable *adj* sociabilis, facilis, affabilis

social *adj* socialis, civilis, communis

society *s* societas *f*; **high —** optimates *m pl*; **secret —** sodalitas *f*

sock *s* pedale *n*, udo *m*

socket *s (in anatomy)* cavum *n*

sod *s* caespes *m*, glaeba *f*

soda *s (in natural state)* nitrum *n*; *(prepared)* soda *f*

sofa *s* lectulus, grabatus *m*

soft *adj* mollis, tener; *(fig)* delicatus, effeminatus; **—ly** molliter, leniter

soften *vt* mollire, mitigare; *(fig)* lenire, placare; *vi* mollescĕre; *(of fruits)* mitescĕre; *(fig)* mansuescĕre, mitescĕre

softness *s* mollitia, teneritas, lenitas *f*; *(effeminacy)* mollities *f*

soil *s* solum *n*, terra *f*

soil *vt* inquinare, contaminare

sojourn *s* commoratio, mansio *f*

sojourn *vi* commorari

solace *s* solatium *n*

solace *vt* consolari

solar *adj* solaris; solis *(genit)*

soldier *s* miles *m*

soldierly *adj* militaris

soldiery *s* miles *m*

sole *adj* solitarius; **—ly** solum, modo, tantum

sole *s (of foot)* planta *f*; *(of shoe)* solea *f*; *(fish)* solea *f*

solemn *adj* sollemnis; gravis; **—ly** sollemniter; graviter

solemnity *s* sollemne *n*, sollemnitas *f*; gravitas *f*

solemnization *s* celebratio *f*

solemnize *vt* celebrare

solicit *vt* rogare, flagitare

solicitation *s* flagitatio *f*

solicitor *s* flagitator *m*; *(law)* advocatus *m*

solicitous *adj* anxius, trepidus; **—ly** anxie, trepide

solicitude *s* sollicitudo, anxietas *f*

solid *adj* solidus; purus; *(fig)* verus, firmus; **—ly** solide

soliloquize *vi* secum loqui

soliloquy *s* soliloquium *n*

solitary *adj* solitarius; *(of places)* desertus

solitude *s* solitudo *f*

solstice *s* solstitium *n*

soluble *adj* dissolubilis

solution *s* dilutum *n*; *(fig)* solutio, explicatio *f*

solve *vt* solvĕre, explicare

solvency *s* facultas solvendi *f*

some *adj* aliqui; *(a certain)* quidam; nonnulli, aliquot

some *pron* aliqui; nonnulli; *(certain people)* quidam

somebody *pron* aliquis; **— or other** nescio quis

someday *adv* olim

somehow *adv* quodammodo, nescio quomodo, aliquā *(viā)*

someone *pron* aliquis; **— else** alius

something *pron* aliquid; **— else** aliud; **— or other** nescio quid

sometime *adv* aliquando

sometimes *adv* interdum, nonnumquam; **sometimes . . . sometimes** modo . . . modo

somewhat *adv* aliquantum; *(with comparatives)* aliquanto, paulo
somewhere *adv* alicubi; *(with motion)* aliquo; — **else** alibi; *(with motion)* alio
somnolence *s* somni cupiditas *f*
somnolent *adj* semisomnus
son *s* filius *m*
song *s* cant·us –ūs *m*; *(tune)* melos *n*
son-in-law *s* gener *m*
sonorous *adj* sonorus, canorus; —**ly** sonore, canore
soon *adv* brevi tempore, mox; **as — as** simul, simulac, simulatque; **as — as possible** quamprimum; — **after** paulo post
sooner *adv* prius; *(preference)* potius; — **or later** serius ocius
soot *s* fuligo *f*
soothe *vt* permulcēre, mitigare, delenire
soothsayer *s* hariolus, sortilegus *m*
soothsaying *s* vaticinatio *f*
sooty *adj* fumosus
sop *s* offa, offula *f*
sophism *s* sophisma *n* cavillatio *f*
sophist *s* sophistes *m*
sophisticated *adj* urbanus, lepidus
sophistry *s* cavillatio captiosa *f*
soporific *adj* soporifer
sorcerer *s* magus *m*
sorceress *s* maga, saga *f*
sorcery *s* veneficium *n*
sordid *adj* sordidus, foedus; —**ly** sordide
sore *adj* *(aching)* tener; *(grievous)* atrox, durus; —**ly** graviter, vehementer
sore *s* ulcus *n*
sorrow *s* dolor, maeror, luct·us –ūs *m*
sorrow *vi* dolēre, lugēre
sorrowful *adj* luctuosus, tristis, maestus; —**ly** maeste
sorry *adj* *(pitiable)* miser; **I am — about** me paenitet *(with genit)*; **I feel — for** me miseret *(with genit)*, misereo *(with genit)*
sort *s* genus *n*, species *f*; **of that —** ejusmodi
sort *vt* digerēre, ordinare
sot *s* fatuus *m*; *(drunkard)* ebrius, potator *m*
sottish *adj* ebriosus
soul *s* *(principle of life)* anima *f*; *(principle of intellection and sensation)* animus *m*; *(person)* caput *n*
sound *adj* *(healthy)* validus, sanus; *(strong)* robustus; *(entire)* integer; *(in mind)* mentis compos; *(true, genuine)* verus; *(of sleep)* artus; *(valid)* ratus; —**ly** *(of beating)* vehementer, egregie; *(of sleeping)* arte
sound *s* sonus *m*; *(noise)* strepit·us –ūs, sonit·us –ūs *m*; *(of trumpet)* clangor *m*; *(strait)* fretum *n*
sound *vt* *(trumpet)* canēre; *vi* canēre, sonare; *(to seem)* vidēri
soundness *s* sanitas, integritas *f*
soup *s* jus *n*
sour *adj* acidus, acerbus; *(fig)* amarus, morosus; **to turn —** acescēre; *(fig)* coacescēre
source *s* fons *m*; *(of stream)* caput *n*;

(fig) origo *f*, fons *m*
South *s* meridies, auster *m*
southern *adj* australis, meridionalis
southward *adv* in meridiem, meridiem versus
south wind *s* auster, notus *m*
souvenir *s* monumentum *n*
sovereign *adj* supremus
sovereign *s* princeps, rex, regnator *m*
sovereignty *s* dominatio *f*, princi-pat·us –ūs *m*
sow *s* sus *m* & *f*
sow *vt* serēre, seminare; *(a field)* conserēre
space *s* spatium *n*; *(of time)* intervallum *n*
spacious *adj* spatiosus, amplus
spade *s* ligo *m*, pala *f*
span *s* *(extent)* spatium *n*; *(measure)* palmus *m*
spangle *s* bractea *f*
spangle *vt* bracteis ornare
Spaniard *s* Hispanus *m*
Spanish *adj* Hispanicus, Hispaniensis
spar *s* tignum *n*
spar *vi* dimicare; *(fig)* digladiari
spare *vt* parcēre *(with dat)*, parce uti *(with abl)*
spare *adj* parcus, frugalis, exilis
sparing *adj* parcus; —**ly** parce
spark *s* scintilla *f*; *(fig)* igniculus *m*
sparkle *vi* scintillare; *(as wine)* subsilire
sparkling *adj* coruscans
sparrow *s* passer *m*
Spartan *adj* Laconicus, Spartanus
spasm *s* spasmus *m*, convulsio *f*
spasmodically *adv* interdum
spatter *vt* aspergēre, inquinare
spatula *s* spatha *f*
spawn *s* ova *f pl*
spawn *vi* ova gignēre
speak *vt* & *vi* loqui, fari, dicēre; **to — of** dicēre de *(with abl)*; **to — to** alloqui *(with acc)*; **to — with** colloqui cum *(with abl)*
speaker *s* orator *m*
spear *s* hasta *f*
spear *vt* hastā transfigēre
special *adj* specialis, praecipuus; —**ly** specialiter, praecipue
specialty *s* proprietas *f*
species *s* species *f*, genus *n*
specific *adj* certus
specify *vt* enumerare, designare
specimen *s* specimen, exemplum *n*
specious *adj* speciosus
speck *s* macula *f*
speckle *vt* maculis variare
spectacle *s* spectaculum *n*
spectator *s* spectator *m*
specter *s* larva *f*, phantasma *n*
spectral *adj* larvalis
spectrum *s* spectrum *n*
speculate *vi* cogitare, conjecturam facēre; *(com)* foro uti
speculation *s* cogitatio, conjectura *f*; *(com)* alea *f*
speculative *adj* conjecturalis
speculator *s* contemplator *m*; *(com)* aleator *m*

speech s oratio f, sermo m; (faculty) lingua f

speechless adj mutus, elinguis; (fig) obstupefactus

speed s celeritas, velocitas f

speed vt accelerare, maturare; vi properare, festinare

speedily adv cito, celeriter

speedy adj citus, velox, celer

spell s incantamentum, carmen n

spelling s orthographia f

spelt s far n

spend vt impendĕre, consumĕre; (to exhaust) effundĕre; (time) agĕre

spendthrift s nepos, prodigus m

spew vt vomĕre

sphere s sphaera f, globus m; (fig) provincia f

spherical adj sphaericus, sphaeralis, globosus

sphinx s sphinx f

spice s condimentum n

spice vt condire

spicy adj conditus, aromaticus

spider s aranea f

spider web s araneum n

spigot s epistomium n

spike s clavus m

spill vt effundĕre, profundĕre

spin vt (thread) nēre; **to — round** versare, circumagĕre; vi versari

spinach s spinacea oleracea f

spinal adj dorsalis

spine s spina f

spinster s innupta f

spiral adj intortus

spiral s spira, involutio f

spirit s spirit·us -ūs m, anima f; (character) ingenium n; (ghost) anima f; **—s** (of the dead) manes m pl

spirited adj animosus, alacer

spiritless adj piger, ignavus

spiritual adj animi (genit)

spit s veru n; (spittle) sputum n

spit vt & vi sputare, spuĕre

spite s livor m, malevolentia f, odium n

spite vt offendĕre

spiteful adj lividus, malevolus; **—ly** malevole

spittle s sputum n

splash vt aspergĕre

splash s fragor s

splendid adj splendidus; **—ly** splendide

splendor s splendor m

splint s ferula f

splinter s assula f

splinter vt assulatim findĕre

split s fissura f

split vt findĕre; vi findi

spoil vt spoliare; (to mar) corrumpĕre; (to ruin) perdĕre, depravare, vitiare

spoils s spolia n pl, praeda f

spoke s radius m

spokesman s orator m

spondee s spondeus m

sponge s spongia f

spongy adj spongiosus

sponsor s sponsor m

spontaneity s impuls·us -ūs m

spontaneous adj voluntarius; **—ly**

sponte, ultro

spool s fusus m

spoon s cochleare n

spoonful s cochleare n

sport s ludus, lus·us -ūs m; (mockery) ludibrium n, irrisio f

sport vi ludĕre, lascivire

sportive adj jocosus; **—ly** jocose

sportsman s venator m

spot s macula f; (stain) macula, labes f; (place) locus m

spot vt (to speckle) maculis notare; (to stain) inquinare, maculare

spotless adj integer, purus, castus

spotted adj maculosus, maculis distinctus

spouse s conju(n)x m & f

spout s (pipe) canalis m; (of jug) os n; (of water) torrens m

spout vt ejaculari; (speeches) declamare; vi emicare

sprain vt intorquēre, convellĕre

sprawl vi se fundĕre, prostratus jacēre

spray s aspergo f

spray vt aspergĕre

spread vt pandĕre, distendĕre, extendĕre; diffundĕre; (to make known) divulgare; vi patēre; (of news) manare, divulgari; (of disease) evagari

sprig s ramusculus m, virgula f

sprightly adj alacer, vegetus

spring s (season) ver n; (leap) salt·us -ūs m; (of water) fons m, scaturgo f

spring adj vernus

spring vi (to come from) oriri, enasci; (as rivers, etc.) scatēre, effluĕre; (to leap) salire, exsilire

springtime s vernum tempus n

sprinkle vt spargĕre, aspergĕre; vi rorare

sprite s spectrum n

sprout s pullus, surculus m

sprout vi pullulare

spruce adj lautus, nitidus, comptus; **—ly** nitide

spur s calcar n; (fig) incitamentum n

spur vt calcaribus concitare; (fig) urgēre

spurious adj fictus, fucosus, spurius

spurn vt spernĕre, aspernari

spurt vi emicare

sputter vi balbutire

spy s explorator, speculator m

spy vt conspicĕre; vi speculari

squabble s jurgium n, rixa f

squabble vi rixari

squad s manipulus m, decuria f

squadron s (of cavalry) ala, turma f; (of ships) classis f

squalid adj squalidus, sordidus

squall s procella f

squalor s squalor m, sordes f

squander vt dissipare, effundĕre

squanderer s prodigus m

square adj quadratus; (fig) honestus, probus

square s quadratum n, quadra f; (tool) norma f

square vt quadrare; vi convenire, congruĕre

squash vt conterĕre, contundĕre

squat *vi* succumbĕre, recumbĕre, subsidĕre
squat *adj* parvus atque obesus
squeak *vi* stridĕre; (*as a mouse*) din-
trire
squeak *s* stridor *m*
squeamish *adj* fastidiosus; **to feel
— fastidire
squeeze *vt* comprimĕre, premĕre; **to
— out** exprimĕre
squint *vi* strabo esse
squint-eyed *adj* paetus
squire *s* armiger *m*; (*landowner*) dominus *m*
squirrel *s* sciurus *m*
squirt *vt* projicĕre; *vi* emicare
stab *s* ict·us -ūs *m*, puncta *f*
stab *vt* fodĕre, perforare
stability *s* stabilitas *f*
stabilize *vt* stabilire, firmare
stable *adj* stabilis, solidus
stable *s* stabulum *n*; (*for horses*)
equile *n*; (*for cows, oxen*) bubile *n*
stack *s* acervus *m*, strues *f*
stack *vt* coacervare, cumulare
staff *s* baculum *n*, scipio *m*, virga *f*;
(*of a magistrate*) consilium *n*; (*mil*)
contubernales *m pl*
staff officer *s* contubernalis *m*
stag *s* cervus *m*
stage *s* (*in theater*) scaena *f*; (*degree*) grad·us -ūs *m*; (*on journey*)
iter *n*
stagger *vt* obstupefacĕre; *vi* titubare
stagnant *adj* stagnans, torpens; (*fig*)
iners
stagnate *vi* stagnare; (*fig*) refriges-
cĕre
stagnation *s* cessatio *f*, torpor *m*
staid *adj* gravis
stain *s* macula, labes *f*
stain *vt* maculare, contaminare; (*to
dye*) tingĕre
stainless *adj* immaculatus, purus,
integer
stair *s* scala *f*, grad·us -ūs *m*
staircase *s* scalae *f pl*
stake *s* palus *m*; (*wager*) depositum
n; **to be at — agi
stake *vt* deponĕre, appignerare
stale *adj* vetus, obsoletus; (*of bread*)
secundus; (*of wine*) vapidus
stalk *s* (*of plant*) caulis, stipes *m*; (*of
grain*) calamus *m*
stalk *vt* venari; *vi* incedĕre
stall *s* stabulum *n*
stall *vt* sistĕre; *vi* consistĕre
stallion *s* admissarius *m*
stamina *s* patientia *f*
stammer *vi* balbutire, linguā haesitare
stammering *adj* balbus
stammering *s* balbuties *f*
stamp *s* (*mark*) nota *f*; (*with the
foot*) vestigium *n*; (*impression
made*) impressio *f*
stamp *vt* imprimĕre, notare; (*money*)
cudĕre; (*feet*) supplodĕre
stand *s* locus *m*, statio *f*; (*halt*) mora
f; (*platform*) suggest·us -ūs *m*
stand *vt* (*to set upright*) statuĕre,
constituĕre; (*to tolerate*) tolerare,
perferre, sustinēre; *vi* stare; **to —

aloof abstare; **to — by** adesse
(*with dat*); **to — fast** consistĕre;
to — for office petĕre; **to — in
awe of** in metu habēre; **to — in
need of** indigēre (*with abl*); **to —
on end** horrēre; **to — out** exstare,
eminēre, prominēre; **to — still**
consistĕre, subsistĕre
standard *adj* solitus
standard *s* (*mil*) vexillum, signum *n*;
(*measure*) norma, mensura *f*
standard-bearer *s* vexillarius, signifer *m*
standing *s* stat·us -ūs, ordo *m*, conditio *f*; **of long — vetus
standing *adj* perpetuus
standstill *s* **to be at a — haerēre
stanza *s* tetrastichon *n*
staple *adj* praecipuus
star *s* stella *f*, sidus *n*; (*fig*) lumen *n*
starch *s* amylum *n*
starch *vt* amylare
stare *s* obtut·us -ūs *m*, oculorum intentio *f*
stare *vi* stupēre; **to — at** intuēri
stark *adj* rigidus
stark *adv* omnino, penitus
starlight *s* siderum lumen *n*
starling *s* sturnus *m*
starry *adj* sidereus, stellatus
start *s* initium *n*; (*sudden movement*)
salt·us -ūs *m*; (*of journey*) profec-
tio *f*
start *vt* incipĕre, instituĕre; (*game*)
excitare; *vi* (*to begin*) incipĕre,
(ex)ordiri; (*to take fright*) resilire
starting gate *s* carceres *m pl*
startle *vt* terrēre, territare
starvation *s* fames *f*
starve *vt* fame interficĕre; *vi* fame
confici
state *s* stat·us -ūs, locus *m*; (*pol*) civitas, respublica *f*; (*pomp*) magnificentia *f*
state *vt* declarare, dicĕre, affirmare
state *adj* publicus
stately *adj* grandis, lautus, splendidus
statement *s* affirmatio *f*, dictum *n*;
testimonium *n*
statesman *s* vir reipublicae regen-
dae peritus *m*
statesmanship *s* reipublicae regen-
dae ars *f*
station *s* statio *f*, locus *m*
station *vt* locare, disponĕre
stationary *adj* stabilis, statarius,
immotus
stationery *s* res scriptoriae *f pl*
statistics *s* cens·us -ūs *m*
statue *s* statua *f*, signum *n*
stature *s* statura *f*
statute *s* statutum, decretum *n*, lex *f*
staunch *adj* certus, firmus, fidus
staunch *vt* (*blood*) sistĕre
stave *vt* perrumpĕre; **to — off** arcēre
stay *vt* detinēre, sistĕre; (*to curb*)
coercēre; *vi* manēre, commorari
stay *s* (*sojourn*) commoratio, mansio
f; (*delay*) mora *f*; (*prop*) fulcrum *n*
steadfast *adj* constans, firmus, stabilis; **—ly** constanter

steadily *adv* constanter, firme, magis magisque
steadiness *s* stabilitas, constantia *f*
steady. *adj* stabilis, firmus; (*fig*) constans, gravis
steak *s* offa, offula *f*
steal *vt* furari; *vi* furari; **to — away** se subducĕre
stealing *s* furtum *n*
stealthily *adv* furtim
steam *s* vapor *m*
steam *vi* fumare
steed *s* equus bellator *m*
steel *s* chalybs *m*
steep *adj* arduus, praeceps, praeruptus
steep *vt* imbuĕre, madefacĕre
steeple *s* turris *f*
steepness *s* acclivitas, declivitas *f*
steer *s* juvencus *m*
steer *vt* gubernare, dirigĕre
steering *s* gubernatio *f*
stem *s* stipes *m*; (*of ship*) prora *f*
stem *vt* obsistĕre (*with dat*), cohibēre, reprimĕre
stench *s* foetor *m*
step *s* pass·us -ūs, grad·us -ūs *m*; (*plan, measure*) ratio *f*; **flight of —s** scalae *f pl*;— **by —** gradatim, pededentim
step *vi* gradi
stepbrother *s* (*on father's side*) vitrici filius *m*; (*on mother's side*) novercae filius *m*
stepdaughter *s* privigna *f*
stepfather *s* vitricus *m*
stepmother *s* noverca *f*
stepson *s* privignus *m*
sterile *adj* sterilis
sterility *s* sterilitas *f*
sterling *adj* verus, bonus
stern *adj* durus, severus, torvus; **—ly** dure, severe, torve
stern *s* puppis *f*
sternness *s* severitas *f*
stew *s* carnes cum condimentis elixae *f pl*
stew *vt* lento igne coquĕre
steward *s* procurator *m*; (*of estate*) vilicus *m*
stewardship *s* procuratio *f*
stick *s* fustis *m*; (*cane*) baculum *n*
stick *vt* affigĕre; *vi* haerēre, haesitare
sticky *adj* viscosus, viscidus
stiff *adj* rigidus; (*fig*) severus, frigidus; **—ly** rigide
stiffen *vt* rigidum facĕre; (*with starch*) amylare; *vi* obdurescĕre
stifle *vt* suffocare; (*fig*) restinguĕre
stigma *s* stigma *n*, nota *f*
stigmatize *vt* notare
still *adj* quietus, immotus, tranquillus
still *adv* (*adversative*) tamen, nihilominus; (*yet*) adhuc, etiamnum; (*with comparatives*) etiam
still *vt* pacare, sedare
stillborn *adj* abortivus
stillness *s* silentium *n*, taciturnitas *f*
stilts *s* grallae *f pl*
stimulant *s* irritamentum *n*, stimulus *m*
stimulate *vt* stimulare, excitare
stimulus *s* stimulus *m*

sting *s* aculeus *m*; (*fig*) (*of conscience*) angor *m*
sting *vt* pungĕre, mordēre
stinginess *s* avaritia *f*, sordes *f pl*
stingy *adj* avarus, sordidus
stink *s* foetor *m*
stink *vi* foetēre; **to — of** olēre (*with acc*)
stint *s* modus *m*
stint *vt* coercēre
stipend *s* salarium *n*, merces *f*
stipulate *vt* stipulari
stipulation *s* stipulatio, conditio, lex *f*
stir *vt* excitare; *vi* se movēre
stir *s* tumult·us -ūs *m*
stirring *adj* (*of a speech*) ardens
stitch *vt* suĕre
stock *s* (*supply*) copia *f*; (*race*) stirps *f*, genus *n*; (*handle*) lignum *n*
stock *vt* instruĕre; suppeditare
stockade *s* vallum *n*
stockbroker *s* argentarius *m*
stocking *s* tibiale *n*
Stoic *s* Stoicus *m*
stoical *adj* patiens, durus; **—ly** patienter
Stoicism *s* Stoica disciplina *f*
stole *s* stola *f*
stolen *adj* furtivus
stomach *s* stomachus *m*
stomach *vt* tolerare, perferre, pati
stone *s* lapis *m*, saxum *n*
stone *vt* lapidare
stonecutter *s* lapicida, lapidarius *m*
stone quarry *s* lapidicina *f*
stony *adj* (*full of stones*) lapidosus; (*of stone*) saxeus; (*fig*) durus
stool *s* scabellum *n*
stoop *vi* proclinare; (*fig*) se summittĕre
stop *vt* sistĕre, obturare, prohibēre; *vi* subsistĕre; (*to cease*) desistĕre
stop *s* mora, pausa *f*
stopgap *s* tibicen *m*
stoppage *s* obstructio *f*, impedimentum *n*
stopper *s* obturamentum *n*
store *s* (*supply*) copia *f*; (*shop*) taberna *f*
store *vt* condĕre, reponĕre
storehouse *s* promptuarium *n*; (*for grain*) horreum *n*; (*fig*) thesaurus *m*
stork *s* ciconia *f*
storm *s* tempestas, procella *f*
storm *vt* (*mil*) expugnare; *vi* desaevire
stormy *adj* turbidus, procellosus; (*fig*) tumultuosus
story *s* narratio, fabula *f*; (*lie*) mendacium *n*; (*of house*) tabulatum *n*
storyteller *s* narrator *m*; (*liar*) mendax *m*
stout *adj* corpulentus; (*brave*) fortis; (*strong*) firmus, validus; **—ly** fortiter
stove *s* focus, caminus *m*
stow *vt* condĕre, recondĕre; *vi* **to — away** in navi delitescĕre
straddle *vi* varicare
straggle *vi* palari
straggler *s* palans *m*
straight *adj* rectus, directus
straight *adv* directo, rectā

straighten *vt* rectum facĕre; **to —
out** corrigĕre
straightforward *adj* apertus, simplex, directus
straightway *adv* statim
strain *vt* contendĕre; (*muscle*) luxare;
(*to filter*) percolare; *vi* eniti
strain *s* contentio *f*; (*effort*) labor *m*;
(*mus*) modus *m*
strained *adj* (*style*) arcessitus
strainer *s* colum *n*
strait *adj* angustus, artus
strait *s* fretum *n*; **—s** (*fig*) angustiae *f pl*
straiten *vt* contrahĕre, artare
strand *s* litus *n*; (*of hair*) floccus *m*
strand *vt* vadis illidĕre; *vi* impingi
strange *adj* insolitus, novus; mirus;
(*foreign*) peregrinus; **— to say** mi-
rabile dictu; **—ly** mirum in modum
strangeness *s* novitas *f*
stranger *s* advena, peregrinus *m*
strangle *vt* strangulare
strap *s* lorum *n*, strupus *m*
strapping *adj* robustus
stratagem *s* stratagema *n*; (*trickery*)
dolus *m*
strategic *adj* idoneus
strategy *s* consilium *n*
straw *adj* stramineus
straw *s* stramentum *n*; (*for thatch*)
stipula *f*
strawberry *s* fragum *n*
stray *vi* errare, aberrare
streak *s* linea *f*; (*of character*) vena *f*
streak *vt* lineis distinguĕre
stream *s* flumen *n*, amnis *m*
stream *vi* fluĕre, currĕre
streamer *s* vexillum *n*
street *s* via *f*; (*narrow*) vicus *m*
strength *s* robur *n*, vires *f pl*, nervi
m pl
strengthen *vt* roborare, confirmare;
munire
strenuous *adj* strenuus, sedulus;
—ly strenue
stress *s* (*accent*) ict·us -ūs *m*; (*meaning*) vis *f*, pondus *n*; (*effort*) labor *m*
stress *vt* exprimĕre
stretch *vt* tendĕre, extendĕre, distendĕre; **to — oneself** pandiculari;
to — out (*hands*) porrigĕre; (*to
lengthen*) producĕre; *vi* extendi, dis-
tendi; produci; patescĕre
stretch *s* spatium *n*
stretcher *s* lecticula *f*
strew *vt* spargĕre, sternĕre
stricken *adj* saucius, vulneratus
strict *adj* (*severe*) severus, rigidus;
(*accurate*) accuratus, exactus, diligens; **—ly** severe, diligenter; **—ly
speaking** immo
stricture *s* vituperatio *f*
stride *s* grad·us -ūs, pass·us -ūs *m*
stride *vi* varicare
strife *s* jurgium *n*, lis, pugna, discordia *f*
strike *vt* ferire, pulsare, percutĕre;
to — fear into incutĕre in (*with
acc*)
strike *s* cessatio operis *f*; (*blow*)
ict·us -ūs *m*
strikingly *adv* mirum in modum

string *s* filum *n*; (*for bow*) nervus *m*;
(*for musical instrument*) chorda *f*;
(*fig*) series *f*
string *vt* (*bow*) intendĕre
stringent *adj* severus
stringy *adj* fibratus
strip *vt* spoliare; denudare; (*clothes*)
exuĕre
strip *s* (*of cloth*) lacinia *f*; (*of paper*)
scheda *f*; (*of land*) spatium *n*
stripe *s* linea *f*; (*blow*) ict·us -ūs *m*;
(*mark of blow*) vibex *f*; (*on toga*)
clavus *m*
strive *vi* (e)niti, moliri, conari, laborare; **to — for** anniti, sectari
striving *s* contentio *f*, nis·us -ūs *m*
stroke *s* ict·us -ūs *m*, plaga *f*; (*with
pen*) pennae duct·us -ūs *f*; (*of oar*)
puls·us -ūs *m*
stroke *vt* (per)mulcēre
stroll *s* ambulatio *f*
stroll *vi* perambulare, spatiari
strong *adj* robustus, firmus, validus;
(*smell*) gravis; (*powerful*) potens;
(*feeling*) acer; (*language*) vehemens;
—ly valide, graviter, vehementer,
acriter
stronghold *s* arx *f*, castellum *n*
structure *s* structura *f*; (*building*)
aedificium *n*
struggle *s* certamen *n*, pugna *f*;
(*fig*) luctatio *f*
struggle *vi* contendĕre, (ob)niti, luctari
strumpet *s* scortum *n*, meretrix *f*
strut *s* incess·us -ūs *m*
strut *vi* turgēre, tumēre
stubble *s* stipula *f*
stubborn *adj* obstinatus, contumax,
pervicax; **—ly** obstinate, pervica-
citer
stubbornness *s* obstinatus animus
m, obstinatio, pertinacia *f*
stud *s* clavus *m*; equus admissarius *m*
student *s* discipulus *m*
studied *adj* meditatus; (*style*) exquisitus
studious *adj* studiosus discendi;
(*careful*) attentus
study *s* studium *n*; (*room*) bibliotheca *f*
study *vt* studēre (*with dat*); (*to scrutinize*) perscrutari
stuff *s* materia, materies *f*
stuff *vt* farcire; (*with food*) saginare
stuffing *s* (*in cooking*) fartum *n*; (*in
upholstery*) tomentum *n*
stultify *vt* ad irritum redigĕre
stumble *vi* offendĕre; **to — upon**
incidĕre in (*with acc*)
stumbling block *s* offensio *f*
stump *s* truncus, caudex *m*
stun *vt* stupefacĕre; (*fig*) confundĕre,
obstupefacĕre
stunted *adj* curtus
stupefy *vt* obstupefacĕre, perturbare
stupendous *adj* mirus, admirabilis
stupid *adj* stupidus, fatuus; **—ly**
stupide
stupidity *s* stupiditas, fatuitas *f*
stupor *s* stupor, torpor *m*
sturdiness *s* robur *n*, firmitas *f*
sturdy *adj* robustus, validus, firmus

sturgeon s acipenser m
stutter vi balbutire
sty s suile n, hara f
style s (literary) scribendi genus n; (rhetorical) dicendi genus n; (architectural) rit·us -ūs m; (of dress) habit·us -ūs m
style vt appellare, nominare
stylish adj speciosus, affectatus, elegans
suave adj suavis, urbanus
subdivide vt iterum dividēre
subdivision s pars f
subdue vt subjicēre, domare, vincēre
subject adj — to obnoxius (with dat), subjectus (with dat)
subject s homo subditus m; civis m; (topic) materia f, argumentum m; (matter) res f; (gram) subjectum n
subject vt subjicēre, subigēre
subjection s servitus f; patientia f
subjective adj proprius
subjugate vt subigēre, domare
subjunctive s subjunctivus modus m
sublime adj sublimis, excelsus; —ly excelse
sublimity s elatio, sublimitas f
submerge vt demergēre, inundare; vi se demergēre
submission s obsequium, servitium n, reverentia f
submissive adj summissus, obsequiosus; —ly summisse
submit vt (e.g., a proposal) referre; vi se dedēre; to — to obtemperare (with dat)
subordinate vt subjicēre, supponēre
subordinate adj secundus, subjectus, inferior
suborn vt subornare
subscribe vt (to contribute) conferre; vi to — to assentiri (with dat)
subscriber s subscriptor m
subscription s collatio f
subsequent adj sequens, posterior, serior; —ly postea, deinde
subserve vt subvenire (with dat)
subservient adj obsequiosus
subside vi desidēre; (of wind) cadēre; (of passion) defervescēre
subsidiary adj secundus
subsidy s subsidium n, collatio f, vectigal n
subsist vi subsistēre
subsistence s vict·us -ūs m
substance s substantia f; res f; (gist) summa f; (wealth) opes f pl
substantial adj solidus, firmus; (real) verus; (rich) opulentus; (important) magnus; —ly magnā ex parte, re
substantiate vt confirmare
substantive s nomen, substantivum n
substitute s vicarius m
substitute vt supponēre
substitution s substitutio f
subterfuge s effugium n, praetext·us -ūs m
subterranean adj subterraneus
subtle adj subtilis, tenuis; (shrewd) acutus, vafer
subtlety s subtilitas, tenuitas f;

(cleverness) astutia f
subtract vt subtrahēre, detrahēre, deducēre
subtraction s detractio, deductio f
suburb s suburbium n
suburban adj suburbanus
subversion s eversio f
subversive adj seditiosus
subvert vt evertēre
succeed vt succedēre (with dat), insequi, excipēre; vi (of persons) rem bene gerēre; (of activities) prospere evenire, succedēre
success s success·us -ūs, bonus event·us -ūs m, res secundae f pl
successful adj fortunatus, prosper; —ly fortunate, prospere
succession s successio f; (series) series f
successive adj continuus; —ly in ordine, continenter
successor s successor m
succinct adj succinctus, brevis, pressus; —ly presse
succor s subsidium, auxilium n
succor vt succurrēre (with dat), subvenire (with dat)
succulence s sucus m
succulent adj sucosus, suculentus
succumb vi succumbēre
such adj talis; — . . . as talis . . . qualis
suck vt sugēre; to — in sorbēre; — up exsorbēre, ebibēre; vi ubera ducēre
suckle vt nutricari
suction s suct·us -ūs m
sudden adj subitus, repentinus, inexpectatus; —ly subito, repente
sue vt litem intendēre (with dat); vi to — for orare, rogare, petēre
suffer vt pati, tolerare, sustinēre; vi dolēre, affici
sufferable adj tolerabilis, tolerandus
suffering s dolor m
suffice vi sufficēre, satis esse
sufficient adj satis (with genit); —ly satis
suffocate vt suffocare
suffocation s suffocatio f
suffrage s suffragium n
suffuse vt suffundēre
suffusion s suffusio f
sugar s saccharum n
sugar vt saccharo condire
sugar cane s arundo acchari f
suggest vt suggerēre, subjicēre, admonēre
suggestion s suggestio, admonitio f
suicide s suicidium n; to commit — sibi mortem consciscēre
suit s lis, causa f; (clothes) vestit·us -ūs m
suit vt accommodare; convenire (with dat), congruēre (with dat)
suitable adj aptus, idoneus, congruus
suite s comitat·us -ūs m; (apartment) conclave n
suitor s procus m
sulfur s sulfur n
sulk vi aegre ferre
sulky adj morosus

sullen *adj* torvus, tetricus, morosus;
—**ly** morose
sully *vt* inquinare, contaminare
sultry *adj* aestuosus, torridus
sum *s* summa *f*
sum *vt* **to — up** computare; (*to
summarize*) summatim describĕre,
breviter repetĕre
summarily *adj* breviter, summatim
summarize *vt* summatim describĕre
summary *adj* subitus, brevis
summary *s* epitome *f*, summarium *n*
summer *s* aestivus
summer *s* aestas *f*
summit *s* culmen *n*; (*fig*) fastigium *n*
summon *vt* arcessĕre; (*a meeting*)
convocare; **to — up courage** animum erigĕre, animum colligĕre
summons *s* vocatio *f*
sumptuary *adj* sumptuarius
sumptuous *adj* sumptuosus, lautus;
—**ly** sumptuose
sun *s* sol *m*
sunbeam *s* radius *m*
sunburnt *adj* adustus
Sunday *s* Dominica *f*
sunder *vt* separare, sejungĕre
sundial *s* solarium *n*
sundry *adj* diversi, varii
sunlight *s* sol *m*
sunny *adj* apricus
sunrise *s* solis ort·us -ūs *m*
sunset *s* solis occas·us -ūs *m*
sunshine *s* sol *m*
sup *vi* cenare
superabundant *adj* nimius; —**ly**
satis superque
superannuated *adj* emeritus
superb *adj* magnificus; —**ly** magnifice
supercilious *adj* superbus, arrogans
superficial *adj* levis; —**ly** leviter
superfluity *s* redundantia *f*
superfluous *adj* superfluus, supervacaneus
superhuman *adj* divinus, major
quam humanus
superintend *vt* praeesse (*with dat*),
administrare
superintendence *s* cura, curatio *f*
superintendent *s* praefectus, curator *m*
superior *adj* superior, melior; **to be
— to** praestare (*with dat*)
superior *s* praepositus *m*
superiority *s* praestantia *f*
superlative *adj* eximius; (*gram*) su-
perlativus
supernatural *adj* divinus
supernumerary *adj* ascripticius, accensus
supersede *vt* succedĕre (*with dat*)
superstition *s* superstitio *f*
superstitious *adj* superstitiosus
supervise *vt* procurare
supervision *s* cura, curatio *f*
supine *adj* supinus; —**ly** supine
supper *s* cena *f*; **after —** cenatus
supple *adj* flexibilis, flexilis
supplement *s* supplementum *n*, appendix *f*
supplement *vt* amplificare
suppliant *s* supplex *m & f*

supplicate *vt* supplicare
supplication *s* supplicatio, obsecratio *f*
supply *s* copia *f*; **supplies** (*mil*)
commeat·us -ūs *m*
supply *vt* praebēre, suppeditare
support *s* (*prop*) fulcrum *n*; (*help*)
subsidium *n*; (*maintenance*) alimentum *n*
support *vt* (*to hold up*) fulcire, sustinēre; (*to help*) adjuvare; (*to maintain*) alĕre
supportable *adj* tolerabilis
supporter *s* adjutor, fautor *m*
suppose *vt* opinari, putare, credĕre
supposition *s* opinio *f*
supremacy *s* dominat·us -ūs, prin-
cipat·us -ūs *m*, imperium *n*
supreme *adj* supremus, summus;
—**ly** unice, maxime
sure *adj* certus; (*faithful*) fidus;
(*safe*) tutus; —**ly** certe, scilicet,
profecto
surety *s* vas *n*; (*person*) sponsor *m*
surf *s* aest·us -ūs *m*
surface *s* superficies *f*; **the — of
the sea** summum mare *n*
surfeit *s* satietas *f*; (*fig*) taedium *n*
surfeit *vt* saturare; (*fig*) satiare
surge *s* fluct·us -ūs, aest·us -ūs *m*
surge *vi* tumescĕre, surgĕre; **to —
forward** proruĕre
surgeon *s* chirurgus *m*
surgery *s* chirurgia *f*
surgical *adj* chirurgicus
surly *adj* morosus, difficilis
surmise *s* conjectura *f*
surmise *vt* conjicĕre, suspicari
surmount *vt* superare, vincĕre
surmountable *adj* superabilis
surname *s* cognomen *n*
surpass *vt* superare, excedĕre, antecedĕre
surplus *s* reliquum, residuum *n*
surprise *s* (ad)miratio *f*; **to take by
—** deprehendĕre
surprise *vt* admirationem movēre
(*with dat*); (*mil*) opprimĕre; **to be
surprised at** mirari, admirari
surprising *adj* mirus, mirabilis; inexpectatus; —**ly** mire, mirabiliter
surrender *s* (*mil*) deditio *f*; (*law*)
cessio *f*
surrender *vt* dedĕre, tradĕre, cedĕre;
vi se tradĕre, se dedĕre
surreptitious *adj* furtivus, clandestinus; —**ly** furtim, clam
surround *vt* circumdare, circumvenire, cingĕre
surroundings *s* vicinia *f*
survey *s* inspectio, contemplatio *f*;
(*of land*) mensura *f*
survey *vt* inspicĕre, contemplari;
(*land*) permetiri
surveyor *s* agrimensor, metator *m*
survival *s* salus *f*
survive *vt* supervivĕre (*with dat*);
vi superstes esse
survivor *s* superstes *m & f*
susceptible *adj* mollis
suspect *vt* suspicari, suspicĕre; **to
be suspected of** in suspicionem

venire quasi (*with verb in subjunctive*)

suspend *vt* suspendĕre, intermittĕre, differre

suspense *s* dubitatio *f*; **in — suspensus**

suspension *s* suspensio, dilatio *f*

suspicion *s* suspicio *f*; **to throw — on** suspicionem adjungĕre ad (*with acc*)

suspicious *adj* suspicax; (*suspected*) suspectus; **—ly** suspiciose

sustain *vt* sustinĕre, sustentare; (*hardships, etc.*) ferre

sustenance *s* vict·us -ūs *m*

swab *s* peniculus *m*

swab *vt* detergĕre

swaddling clothes *s* fasciae *f pl*, incunabula *n pl*

swagger *vi* se jactare

swaggerer *s* homo gloriosus *m*

swallow *s* (*bird*) hirundo *f*

swallow *vt* vorare, sorbĕre; **to — up** devorare, absorbĕre

swamp *s* palus *f*

swamp *vt* demergĕre

swampy *adj* paludosus

swan *s* cygnus *m*

swank *adj* lautus

swarm *s* examen *n*

swarm *vi* congregari

swarthy *adj* fuscus

swathe *s* fascia *f*

sway *s* dicio, dominatio *f*, imperium *n*

sway *vt* regĕre, movēre; *vi* vacillare

swear *vt* jurare; **to — in** sacramento adigĕre, sacramento rogare; *vi* jurare

sweat *s* sudor *m*

sweat *vi* sudare

sweep *vt* verrĕre; **to — out** everrĕre; *vi* **to — by** (*to dash by*) praetervolare; **to — over** (*to move quickly over*) percurrĕre

sweet *adj* dulcis, suavis; (*fig*) blandus, jucundus; **—ly** suaviter

sweeten *vt* dulcem facĕre; (*fig*) lenire, mulcēre

sweetheart *s* deliciae *f pl*, amica *f*

sweetness *s* dulcedo, suavitas *f*

sweets *s* cuppedia *n pl*

swell *s* aest·us -ūs *m*, unda *f*

swell *vt* inflare, tumefacĕre; *vi* tumēre

swelling *s* tumor *m*

swelter *vi* aestu laborare

swerve *vi* aberrare, vagari

swift *adj* celer, velox; **—ly** celeriter, velociter

swiftness *s* celeritas, velocitas *f*

swim *vi* natare, nare

swimmer *s* natator *m*

swimming *s* natatio *f*; (*of head*) vertigo *f*

swimming pool *s* piscina *f*

swindle *vt* fraudare, circumvenire

swindle *s* fraus *f*

swindler *s* fraudator *m*

swine *s* sus *m & f*

swineherd *s* suarius *m*

swing *s* oscillatio *f*

swing *vt* librare; *vi* oscillare

switch *s* (*stick*) virga, virgula *f*; (*change*) commutatio *f*

switch *vt* (*to flog*) flagellare; (*to change*) (com)mutare

swoon *vi* intermori, collabi

swoop *s* impet·us -ūs *m*

swoop *vi* incurrĕre; **to — down on** involare in (*with acc*)

sword *s* gladius, ensis *m*, ferrum *n*; **with fire and — ferro** ignique

sycamore *s* sycomorus *f*

sycophant *s* sycophanta, assentator *m*

syllable *s* syllaba *f*

syllogism *s* syllogismus *m*, ratiocinatio *f*

symbol *s* signum, symbolum *n*

symbolical *adj* symbolicus; **—ly** symbolice

symmetrical *adj* congruens, concinnus

symmetry *s* symmetria, concinnitas *f*

sympathetic *adj* concors, misericors

sympathize *vi* consentire; **to — with** miserēri (*with genit*)

sympathy *s* consens·us -ūs *m*, misericordia, concordia *f*

symphony *s* symphonia *f*, concent·us -ūs *m*

symptom *s* indicium, signum *n*

synagogue *s* synagoga *f*

syndicate *s* societas *f*

synonym *s* verbum idem declarans *n*

synonymous *adj* idem declarans, idem valens

synopsis *s* breviarium *n*, epitome *f*

syntax *s* syntaxis *f*

system *s* ratio, disciplina *f*

systematic *adj* ordinatus; **—ally** ratione, ordine

T

tab *vt* designare, notare

tabernacle *s* tabernaculum *n*

table *s* mensa *f*; (*list*) index *m*, tabula *f*

tablecloth *s* mantele *n*

table napkin *s* mappa *f*

tablet *s* tabula, tabella *f*, album *n*

tacit *adj* tacitus; **—ly** tacite

taciturn *adj* taciturnus

tack *s* clavulus *m*

tack *vt* **to — on** assuĕre, affigĕre; *vi* (*of ships*) reciprocari

tact *s* judicium *n*, dexteritas *f*

tactful *adj* prudens, dexter; **—ly** prudenter, dextere

tactician *s* rei militaris peritus *m*

tactics *s* res militaris, belli ratio *f*

tadpole *s* ranunculus *m*

tag s appendicula f
tail s cauda f
tailor s vestitor, textor m
taint s contagio f, vitium n
taint vt inficĕre, contaminare; (fig) corrumpĕre
take vt capĕre, sumĕre, accipĕre; to — away demĕre, auferre, adimĕre; to — down (in writing) exscribĕre; to — for habēre pro (with abl); to — hold of prehendĕre; to — in (e.g., a guest) recipĕre; (through deception) decipĕre; to — in hand suscipĕre; to — off exuĕre; to — out eximĕre; (from storage) promĕre; to — up suscipĕre; to — upon oneself sibi sumĕre; vi to — after similis esse (with genit or dat); to — off (to depart) abire; to — to amare, diligĕre
tale s fabula, narratio f
talent s talentum n; (fig) ingenium n
talented adj ingeniosus
talk s sermo m, colloquium n; idle — nugae f pl
talk vi loqui; to — with colloqui cum (with abl)
talkative adj loquax, garrulus
talker s (idle) gerro m
tall adj altus, celsus, procerus
tallow s sebum n
tally s tessera f
tally vi convenire
talon s unguis m
tambourine s tympanum n
tame adj cicur, mansuetus, domitus; —ly mansuete, leniter
tame vt domare, mansuefacĕre
tamer s domitor m
tamper vi to — with (persons) sollicitare; (writings) depravare
tan vt (by sun) adurĕre; (hides) perficĕre
tangible adj tractabilis
tangle s implicatio f, nodus m
tangle vt implicare
tank s lac·us -ūs m
tankard s cantharus m
tantalize vt vexare
tantamount adj par
tap s levis ict·us -ūs m
tap vt leviter ferire; (wine, etc.) relinĕre
tape s taenia f
taper s cereus m
taper vt fastigare; vi fastigari
tapestry s aulaeum, tapete n
taproom s taberna f
tar s pix f
tardily adv tarde, lente
tardiness s tarditas, segnitia f
tardy adj tardus, lentus
target s scopus m
tariff s portorium n
tarnish vt infuscare; vi infuscari
tarry vi commorari, cunctari
tart adj acerbus, amarus
tart s scriblita f, crustulum n
task s pensum, opus n; to take to — objurgare
taste s (sense) gustat·us -ūs m; (flavor) sapor m; (fig) judicium n
taste vt (de)gustare; vi sapĕre

tasteful adj elegans; —ly eleganter
tasteless adj insipidus; (fig) insulsus, inelegans; —ly insulse
tasty adj sapidus, dulcis
tattered adj pannosus
tatters s panni m pl
taunt s convicium n
taunt vt exprobrare
taut adj intentus
tavern s taberna, caupona f
tavern keeper s caupo m
tawdry adj fucatus, vilis
tawny adj fulvus
tax s vectigal, tributum n
tax vt vectigal imponĕre (with dat)
taxable adj vectigalis, stipendiarius
taxation s vectigalia n pl
tax collector s exactor m
teach vt docēre, instituĕre, erudire
teachable adj docilis
teacher s magister, praeceptor m; (of primary school) litterator m; (of secondary school) grammaticus m; (of rhetoric) rhetor m
teaching s institutio, eruditio f
team s jugales m pl; (of animals) jugum n
tear s lacrima f, flet·us -ūs m; (a rent) scissura f
tear vt scindĕre; to — apart discindĕre; to — in pieces dilacerare, dilaniare; to — off abscindĕre; to — open rescindĕre; to — out evellĕre; to — up convellĕre
tease vt vexare, ludĕre
teat s mamma f
technical adj (term) proprius; technicus, artificialis
technique s ars f
technology s officinarum artes f pl
tedious adj molestus; —ly moleste
tedium s taedium n
teem vi scatēre, redundare
teethe vi dentire
teething s dentitio f
tell vt narrare, memorare, referre; (to order) imperare (with dat), jubēre; — me the truth dic mihi verum
teller s numerator m
temerity s temeritas f
temper s temperatio f, animus m, ingenium n; (bad) iracundia f
temper vt temperare; (fig) lenire
temperament s animus m
temperance s temperantia f
temperate adj temperatus, moderatus, sobrius; —ly temperanter, sobrie
temperature s calor m, caloris grad·us -ūs m
tempest s tempestas f
tempestuous adj turbulentus, procellosus
temple s templum n, aedes f; (of forehead) tempus n
temporal adj humanus; profanus
temporarily adv ad tempus
temporary adj brevis
temporize vi tergiversari
tempt vt temptare, illicĕre
temptation s illecebra f
ten adj decem; — times decies

tenable *adj* defensibilis, stabilis
tenacious *adj* tenax, pertinax; **—ly** tenaciter, pertinaciter
tenacity *s* tenacitas, pertinacia *f*
tenancy *s* conductio *f*
tenant *s* conductor, colonus, incola *m*
tend *vt* curare; *vi* tendĕre, spectare
tendency *s* inclinatio *f*
tender *adj* tener, mollis; **—ly** tenere, indulgenter
tender *vt* offerre
tenderness *s* mollitia *f*; *(affection)* indulgentia *f*
tendon *s* nervus *m*
tendril *s* *(of vine)* pampinus *m*; *(of plants)* claviculus *m*
tenement *s* conductum *n*
tenement house *s* insula *f*
tenet *s* dogma *n*
tenfold *adj* decemplex, decuplus
tennis *s* **to play** — pilā ludĕre
tennis court *s* sphaeristerium *n*
tenor *s* tenor, sens·us -ūs *m*
tense *adj* intentus, attentus
tense *s* tempus *n*
tension *s* intentio *f*
tent *s* tentorium, tabernaculum *n*
tentative *adj* tentans
tenth *adj* decimus
tenth *s* decima pars *f*
tenuous *adj* tenuis, rarus
tenure *s* possessio *f*
tepid *adj* tepidus
term *s* *(word)* verbum *n*; *(limit)* terminus *m*; *(condition)* condicio, lex *f*
terminate *vt* terminare, finire; *vi* terminari, desinĕre; *(of words)* cadĕre
termination *s* terminatio *f*, finis, exit·us -ūs *m*
terrace *s* ambulatio *f*
terrestrial *adj* terrestris, terrenus
terrible *adj* terribilis
terribly *adv* horrendum in modum
terrific *adj* terrificus, terrens, formidabilis
terrify *vt* terrēre, perterrēre
territory *s* regio *f*, ager *m*, fines *m pl*
terror *s* terror *m*, formido *f*
terse *adj* brevis, pressus; **—ly** presse
test *s* probatio *f*, experimentum *n*
test *vt* probare, experiri
testament *s* testamentum *n*
testamentary *adj* testamentarius
testator *s* testator *m*
testify *vt* testificari, testari
testimonial *s* laudatio *f*
testimony *s* testimonium *n*
testy *adj* stomachosus, obstinatus, morosus
tether *s* retinaculum *n*
tether *vt* religare
text *s* verba *n pl*
textbook *s* enchiridion *n*
textile *adj* textilis
texture *s* textura *f*
than *adv* quam; atque, ac
thank *vt* gratias agĕre *(with dat)*
thankful *adj* gratus; **—ly** grate
thankless *adj* ingratus; **—ly** ingrate
thanks *s* gratiae, grates *f pl*
thanks *interj* gratias!
thanksgiving *s* grates *f pl*, gratula-

tio *f*; *(public act)* supplicatio *f*
that *adj* ille, is, iste
that *pron demonstrative* ille, is, iste; *pron rel* qui
that *conj* *(purpose, result, command)* ut; *(after verbs of fearing)* ne
thatch *s* stramentum *n*
thatch *vt* stramento tegĕre
thaw *vt* (dis)solvĕre; *vi* tabescĕre
the *article, not expressed in Latin*
the *adv (with comparatives)* **the . . . the** quo . . . eo
theater *s* theatrum *n*
theatrical *adj* scenicus, theatralis
thee *pron* te; **of** — de te; **to** — tibi; **with** — tecum
theft *s* furtum *n*
their *adj* illorum, eorum, istorum; **— own** suus
them *pron* eos, illos, istos; **to** — eis, illis, istis
theme *s* thema, argumentum *n*
themselves *pron reflex* se; **to** — sibi; **with** — secum; *pron intensive* ipsi
then *adv* *(at that time)* tum, tunc; *(after that)* deinde, inde; *(therefore)* igitur, ergo; **now and** — interdum, nonnumquam
thence *adv* inde, illinc; *(therefore)* ex eo, exinde
thenceforth *adv* ex eo tempore, dehinc
theologian *s* theologus *m*
theological *adj* theologicus
theology *s* theologia *f*
theoretical *adj* contemplativus
theory *s* ratio *f*
there *adv* ibi, illic; *(thither)* illuc; **— are** sunt; **— is** est
thereabouts *adv* circa, circiter, fere
thereafter *adv* deinde, postea
thereby *adv* eā re, eo
therefore *adv* itaque, igitur, idcirco, ergo
therefrom *adv* exinde, ex eo
therein *adv* in eo, in ea re
thereupon *adv* exinde, subinde
thesis *s* thesis *f*, propositum *n*
they *pron* ii, illi, isti
thick *adj* densus, spissus; **—ly** dense
thicken *vt* densare, spissare; *vi* concrescĕre
thicket *s* dumetum, fruticetum *n*
thickness *s* crassitudo *f*
thief *s* fur *m*
thievery *s* furtum *n*
thigh *s* femur *n*
thin *adj* tenuis, exilis, rarus; *(lean)* macer; **—ly** tenuiter, rare
thin *vt* attenuare; **to — out** rarefacĕre
thine *adj* tuus
thine *pron* tuus
thing *s* res *f*; **—s** *(possessions)* bona *n pl*; *(clothes)* vestimenta *n pl*
think *vt* cogitare; *(to believe, imagine, etc.)* putare, credĕre, opinari; **to — over** in mente agitare; *vi* **to — highly of** magni habēre
thinker *s* philosophus *m*
thinking *s* cogitatio *f*
thinness *s* tenuitas, raritudo *f*; *(of person)* macies *f*

third adj tertius; —**ly** tertio
third s tertia pars f
thirst s sitis f
thirst vi sitire; **to** — **for** sitire
thirstily adv sitienter
thirsty adj sitiens
thirteen adj tredecim, decem et tres
thirteenth adj tertius decimus
thirtieth adj tricesimus
thirty adj triginta
this adj hic
thistle s carduus m
thither adv illuc, istuc, eo
thong s lorum n
thorn s spina f, aculeus m
thorny adj spinosus; (fig) nodosus
thorough adj germanus, perfectus; —**ly** penitus, funditus
thoroughbred adj generosus, genuinus
thoroughfare s pervium n, via pervia f
though conj quamquam, quamvis
thought s (act and faculty) cogitatio f; (product of thinking) cogitatum n
thoughtful adj cogitabundus; providus; —**ly** anxie, provide
thoughtless adj inconsultus, improvidus; —**ly** temere, inconsulte
thousand adj mille; **a** — **times** millies
thousandth adj millesimus
thraldom s servitus f
thrall s servus m
thrash vt terěre; (fig) verberare
thrashing s verbera n pl
thread s filum n
thread vt inserěre
threadbare adj tritus, obsoletus
threat s minae f pl, minatio f
threaten vt minari (with dat of person); vi impendēre, imminēre
three adj tres; — **times** ter
threefold adj triplex, triplus
three-legged adj tripes
thresh vt terěre
threshing floor s area f
threshold s limen n
thrice adv ter
thrift s frugalitas, parsimonia f
thriftily adv frugaliter
thrifty adj parcus, frugalis
thrill s gaudium n, voluptas f; (of fear) horror m
thrill vt commovēre, percellěre
thrilling adj mirus, mirabilis
thrive vi virēre, vigēre, valēre
thriving adj vegetus, prosperus
throat s jugulum n, guttur n, fauces f pl
throb s palpitatio f, puls·us -ūs m
throb vi palpitare
throes s dolor m
throne s solium n; (fig) regia dignitas f
throng s multitudo, turba, frequentia f
throng vi **to** — **around** stipare
throttle vt strangulare
through prep per (with acc); (on account of) ob (with acc), propter (with acc)
through adv render by compound verb with trans- or per-, e.g., to

read — perlegěre; — **and** — penitus, omnino
throughout adv prorsus, penitus
throughout prep per (with acc)
throw vt jacěre, conjicěre; (esp. weapons) mittěre, jaculari; **to** — **away** abjicěre; **to** — **back** rejicěre; **to** — **down** dejicěre; **to** — **open** patefacěre; **to** — **out** ejicěre; **to** — **together** conjicěre in unum; vi **to** — **up** vomere
throw s jact·us -ūs m
thrush s turdus m
thrust s impet·us -ūs, ict·us -ūs m
thrust vt truděre, impellěre; (with sword) perfoděre
thumb s pollex m
thump s percussio f
thump vt tunděre
thunder s tonitr·us -ūs m
thunder vi tonare
thunderbolt s fulmen n
thunderstruck adj attonitus, obstupefactus
thus adv ita, sic; **and** — itaque
thwart vt obstare (with dat), frustrari
thy adj tuus
tiara s diadema n
tick s (insect) ricinus m; (clicking) levis ict·us -ūs m
ticket s tessera f
tickle vt & vi titillare
tickling s titillatio f
ticklish adj periculosus
tide s aest·us -ūs m
tidings s nuntius m
tie s vinculum n; (relationship) necessitudo f
tie vt (all)ligare; (in a knot) nodare, nectěre
tier s ordo m
tiger s tigris m
tight adj strictus, astrictus, artus; —**ly** arte
tighten vt astringěre, adducěre, contenděre
tile s tegula, imbrex f
till conj dum, donec
till prep usque ad (with acc)
till vt colěre
tillage s agricultura f
tiller s (person) agricola m; (helm) gubernaculum n
tilt vt proclinare
timber s materia f, lignum n
time s tempus n, dies f; (age, period) aetas f; (leisure) otium n; (opportunity) occasio f; (interval) intervallum, spatium n; (of day) hora f; **another** — alias; **at the same** — simul; **for a** — parumper; **for a long** — diu; **for some** — aliquamdiu; **from** — **to** — interdum; **in a short** — brevi; **in** — ad tempus; **on** — tempestive; **what** — **is it?** quota hora est?
timely adj tempestivus, opportunus
timepiece s horarium, horologium n
timid adj timidus
timidity s timiditas f
timorous adj pavidus
tin s stannum, plumbum album n
tin adj stanneus

tincture s color m

tinder s fomes m

tinge vt tingĕre, imbuĕre

tingle vi formicare, verminare

tinkle vi tinnire

tinsel s bractea, bracteola f

tip s cacumen, acumen n, apex m

tip vt praefigĕre; (to incline) invertĕre

tipple vi potare

tippler s potor m

tipsy adj ebriolus, temulentus

tiptoe adv in digitos erectus

tire vt fatigare, lassare; vi defatigari

tired adj fessus, lassus; **I am —** of me taedet (with genit); **— out** defessus

tiresome adj laboriosus; molestus

tissue s text·us -ūs m

titanic adj ingens

tithe s decuma f

title s titulus m; (of book) inscriptio f; (of person) appellatio, dignitas f; (claim) jus n

title page s index m

titter s ris·us -ūs m

to prep commonly rendered by the dative; (motion, except with names of towns, small islands and rus) ad (with acc), in (with acc); **— and fro** huc illuc

toad s bufo m

toast s (bread) panis tosti offula f; (health) propinatio f; **to drink a — to** propinare (with dat)

toast vt torrēre; (in drinking) propinare (with dat)

today adv hodie

today s hodiernus dies m

toe s digitus m

together adv simul, unā

toil s labor m, opera f

toil vi laborare

toilsome adj laboriosus, operosus

token s signum, pignus, indicium n

tolerable adj tolerabilis; mediocris

tolerably adv tolerabiliter; mediocriter

tolerance s patientia f

tolerant adj tolerans, indulgens, patiens; **—ly** indulgenter

tolerate vt tolerare, ferre

toleration s toleratio, indulgentia, patientia f

toll s vectigal n; (at ports) portorium n

toll collector s exactor, portitor m

tomb s sepulcrum n

tombstone s lapis, cippus m

tomorrow adv cras

tomorrow s crastinus dies m; **the day after —** perendie

tone s sonus m, vox f; (in painting) color m

tongs s forceps m & f

tongue s lingua f; (of shoe) ligula f; (pole of carriage) temo m

tonsils s tonsillae f pl

too adv nimis, nimium; (also) quoque, insuper

tool s instrumentum n; (dupe) minister m

tooth s dens m; **— and nail** totis viribus

toothache s dentium dolor m

toothless adj edentulus

toothpick s dentiscalpium n

tooth powder s dentifricium n

top adj summus

top s vertex, apex m; (of tree) cacumen n; (of house) fastigium n; (toy) turbo m; **the — of the mountain** summus mons m

top vt superare

topic s res f, argumentum n

topmost adj summus

topography s regionum descriptio f

topple vt evertĕre; vi titubare

torch s fax f

torment s tormentum n, cruciat·us -ūs m

torment vt (ex)cruciare, torquēre

tormenter s tortor m

torpid adj torpens; **to be —** torpēre

torpor s torpor m

torrent s torrens m

torrid adj torridus

tortoise s testudo f

tortoise shell s testudo f

torture s tormentum n, cruciat·us -ūs m

torture vt torquēre, (ex)cruciare

torturer s cruciator, tortor m

toss s jact·us -ūs m

toss vt jactare; vi jactari

total adj totus, universus; **—ly** omnino, prorsus

totality s summa, universitas f

totter vi vacillare, titubare

touch vt tangĕre, attingĕre; (to stir emotionally) movēre, commovēre, afficĕre; vi inter se contingĕre; **to — on** attingĕre

touch s (con)tact·us -ūs m, tactio f

touching adj mollis, flexanimus

touchstone s (fig) obrussa f

touchy adj stomachosus

tough adj durus, lentus; (fig) strenuus; difficilis

tour s (rounds) circuit·us -ūs m; (abroad) peregrinatio f

tourist s peregrinator m

tournament s certamen n

tow s stuppa f

tow vt remulco trahĕre

toward prep versus (with acc), ad (with acc); (of feelings) erga (with acc), in (with acc); (of time) sub (with acc)

towel s mantele n; sudarium n

tower s turris f

tower vi **to — over** imminēre (with dat)

towering adj excelsus, arduus

towline s remulcum n

town s urbs f; (fortified) oppidum n

town hall s curia f

townsman s oppidanus m

toy s crepundia n pl, oblectamentum n

trace s vestigium n; (for horse) helcium n

trace vt delinēre, describĕre; indagare, investigare; **to — back** repetĕre

track s vestigium n; (path) semita f, calles m

track vt investigare

trackless adj avius, invius

tract s (of land) tract·us -ūs m, regio f; (treatise) tract·us -ūs m

tractable adj tractabilis, docilis, obsequiosus

trade s mercatura f, commercium n; (calling) ars f, quaest·us -ūs m

trade vt commutare; vi negotiari, mercaturas facĕre

trader s mercator m

tradesman s opifex m

tradition s traditio, fama, memoria f, mos majorum m

traditional adj patrius, a majoribus traditus

traduce vt calumniari, infamare

traffic s commercium n; (on street) vehicula n pl

tragedian s (playwright) tragoedus, tragicus poeta m; (actor) tragicus actor m

tragedy s tragoedia f

tragic adj tragicus; (fig) tristis, miserabilis; —ally tragice; miserabiliter

trail vt investigare; (to drag) trahĕre; vi trahi, verrĕre

trail s vestigium n; (path) calles m

train s (line) series f, ordo m; (of robe) instita f; (retinue) comitat·us -ūs m; (of army) impedimenta n pl

train vt educare, instruĕre, assuefacĕre

trainer s lanista, aliptes m

training s disciplina, institutio f; (practice) exercitatio f

trait s mos m

traitor s proditor m

traitorous adj perfidus; —ly perfide

trammel vt impedire, vincire, irretire

tramp s vagabundus, homo vagus m; (of feet) puls·us -ūs m

tramp vi gradi

trample vt calcare, conculcare; vi to — on obterĕre, proterĕre, opprimĕre

trance s stupor m, ecstasis f

tranquil adj tranquillus; —ly tranquille

tranquility s tranquillitas f, tranquillus animus m

tranquilize vt tranquillare

transact vt transigĕre, gerĕre

transaction s negotium n, res f

transcend vt superare, vincĕre

transcendental adj sublimis, divinus

transcribe vt transcribĕre

transcription s transcriptio f

transfer s translatio f; (of property) alienatio f

transfer vt transferre; (property) abalienare

transference s translatio f

transfigure vt transfigurare

transform vt vertĕre, commutare

transformation s commutatio f

transgress vt violare, perfringĕre; vi peccare, delinquĕre

transgression s violatio f, delictum n

transgressor s violator, maleficus m

transient adj transitorius, brevis, fluxus

transition s transitio f, transit·us -ūs m

transitive adj transitivus; —ly transitive

transitory adj transitorius, brevis, fluxus

translate vt vertĕre, transferre

translation s translata n pl

translator s interpres m

transmission s transmissio f

transmit vt transmittĕre

transmutation s transmutatio f

transparent adj pellucidus; (fig) perspicuus

transpire vi perspirare, emanare; (to happen) evenire

transplant vt transferre

transport vt transportare, transvehĕre

transport s vectura f; (ship) navigium vectorium n, navis oneraria f; (rapture) sublimitas f

transportation s vectura f

transpose vt transponĕre

transposition s transpositio, trajectio f

trap s laqueus m, pedica f; (fig) insidiae f pl; to lay a — insidiari

trap vt (to snare) irretire; (fig) inlaqueare

trappings s ornamenta n pl, apparat·us -ūs m; (of horse) phalerae f pl

trash s scruta n pl; (fig) nugae f pl

trashy adj vilis; obscenus

travel vi iter facĕre; to — abroad peregrinari

traveler s viator, peregrinator m

traverse vt transire, peragrare, lustrare

travesty s perversa imitatio f

tray s ferculum n, trulla f

treacherous adj perfidus, dolosus; —ly perfidiose

treachery s perfidia f

tread vt calcare; vi incedĕre

tread s grad·us -ūs, incess·us -ūs m, vestigium n

treason s perduellio, proditio f

treasonable adj perfidus, proditorius

treasure s thesaurus m

treasure vt fovēre, magni aestimare

treasurer s aerarii praefectus m

treasury s aerarium n, fiscus m

treat vt uti (with abl), tractare; (patient) curare; (topic) tractare; (to entertain) invitare

treatise s libellus m, dissertatio f

treatment s tractatio f; (by doctor) curatio f

treaty s foedus, pactum n; to make a — foedus icĕre

treble adj triplex, triplus; (of sound) acutus

treble vt triplicare

tree s arbor f

trellis s clathrus m

tremble vi tremĕre, tremiscĕre

trembling adj tremulus

trembling s trepidatio f

tremendous adj immanis, ingens, vastus; —ly valde, maxime

tremulous adj tremulus, vacillans

trench s fossa f

trespass *vt* violare, offendĕre; *vi* delinquĕre

trespass *s* violatio, culpa *f*

tress *s* crinis, cirrus *m*

trestle *s* fulcimentum *n*

trial *s* tentatio, experientia *f*; (*test*) probatio *f*; (*trouble*) labor *m*; (*law*) judicium *n*, quaestio *f*

triangle *s* triangulum *n*

triangular *adj* triangulus, triquetrus

tribe *s* trib·us -ūs *f*

tribulation *s* tribulatio, afflictio *f*

tribunal *s* (*raised platform*) tribunal *n*; (*court*) judicium *n*

tribune *s* tribunus *m*

tribuneship *s* tribunat·us -ūs *m*

tributary *adj* vectigalis, stipendiarius

tributary *s* amnis in alium influens *m*

tribute *s* tributum, vectigal *n*

trick *s* dolus *m*, artificium *n*, fraus, ars *f*

trick *vt* fallĕre, decipĕre

trickle *s* guttae *f pl*

trickle *vi* stillare, manare

trickster *s* veterator, fraudator *m*

trident *s* tridens *m*

triennial *adj* triennis

trifle *s* res parvi momenti *f*, nugae *f pl*

trifle *vi* nugari

trifling *adj* levis, exiguus, frivolus

trill *s* sonus modulatus *m*

trill *vt* vibrare

trim *adj* nitidus, comptus, bellus

trim *vt* adornare; (*to prune*) putare, tondēre

trinket *s* tricae *f pl*

trip *s* iter *n*

trip *vt* supplantare; *vi* titubare; (*fig*) errare

tripartite *adj* tripartitus

tripe *s* omasum *n*

triple *adj* triplex

triple *vt* triplicare

tripod *s* tripus *m*

trireme *s* triremis *f*

trite *adj* tritus

triumph *s* (*entry of victorious Roman general*) triumphus *m*; (*victory*) victoria *f*

triumph *vi* triumphare; vincĕre; **to — over** devincĕre

triumphal *adj* triumphalis

triumphant *adj* victor; elatus, laetus

trivial *adj* levis, tenuis

triviality *s* nugae *f pl*

troop *s* turma, caterva *f*, grex, globus *m*; **—s** (*mil*) copiae *f pl*

trooper *s* eques *m*

trope *s* tropus *m*

trophy *s* tropaeum *n*

tropical *adj* tropicus

tropics *s* loca fervida *n pl*

trot *vi* tolutim ire

trouble *s* labor, dolor *m*, incommodum *n*, aerumna, molestia *f*

trouble *vt* turbare, vexare, angĕre

troublesome *adj* molestus, operosus

trough *s* alveus *m*

trounce *vt* (*to punish*) castigare; (*to defeat decisively*) devincĕre

troupe *s* grex *m*

trousers *s* bracae *f pl*

trout *s* tru(c)ta *f*

trowel *s* trulla *f*

truant *s* cessator *m*

truce *s* indutiae *f pl*

truck *s* carrus *m*

truculent *adj* truculentus

trudge *vi* repĕre

true *adj* verus; (*genuine*) germanus; (*faithful*) fidus; (*exact*) rectus, justus

truism *s* verbum tritum *n*

truly *adv* vere, profecto

trump *vt* **to — up** effingĕre, ementiri

trumpet *s* tuba, bucina *f*

trumpeter *s* tubicen, bucinator *m*

truncheon *s* fustis *m*

trundle *vt* volvĕre

trunk *s* truncus *m*; (*for luggage*) cista *f*; (*of elephant*) proboscis *f*

trust *s* fiducia, fides *f*

trust *vt* fidĕre (*with dat*), credĕre (*with dat*); (*to entrust*) committĕre

trustee *s* fiduciarius, tutor *m*

trusteeship *s* tutela *f*

trustful *adj* credulus

trusting *adj* fidens; **—ly** fidenter

trustworthiness *s* integritas, fides *f*

trustworthy *adj* fidus; (*of witness*) locuples; (*of an authority*) bonus

trusty *adj* fidus

truth *s* veritas *f*, verum *n*; **in —** vero

truthful *adj* verax; **—ly** veraciter, vere

try *vt* tentare, probare, experiri; (*law*) cognoscĕre; (*to endeavor*) laborare; **to — one's patience** patientiā abuti

trying *adj* molestus, incommodus, gravis

tub *s* labrum, dolium *n*

tube *s* fistula *f*

tuck *vt* **to — up** succingĕre

tuft *s* floccus, cirrus *m*, crista *f*

tug *s* conat·us -ūs, nis·us -ūs *m*; (*ship*) navis tractoria *f*

tug *vt* trahĕre

tuition *s* tutela *f*

tumble *vi* corruĕre, collabi, volvi

tumbler *s* poculum vitreum *n*

tumor *s* tumor, tuber *m*

tumult *s* tumult·us -ūs *m*

tumultuous *adj* tumultuosus, turbulentus; **—ly** tumultuose

tune *s* tonus *m*, moduli *m pl*

tuneful *adj* canorus

tunic *s* tunica *f*

tunnel *s* canalis, cuniculus *m*

turban *s* mitra, tiara *f*

turbid *adj* turbidus, turbulentus

turbulence *s* tumult·us -ūs *m*

turbulent *adj* turbulentus; **—ly** turbulente

turf *s* caespes *m*

turgid *adj* turgidus

turkey *s* meleagris gallopavo *f*

turmoil *s* turba, perturbatio *f*, tumult·us -ūs *m*

turn *s* (*circuit*) circuit·us -ūs *m*; (*revolution*) conversio *f*, circumact·us -ūs *m*; (*change, course*) vicissitudo *f*; (*inclination of mind*) inclinatio *f,* ingenium *n;* **a good —** officium, beneficium *n;* **in —** invicem

turn *vt* vertĕre, convertĕre; *(to twist)* torquēre; *(to bend)* flectĕre; **to — aside** deflectĕre; **to — away** avertĕre; **to — down** *(refuse)* recusare, denegare, respuĕre; **to — into** mutare in *(with acc),* vertĕre in *(with acc);* **to — over** *(to hand over)* tradĕre, transferre; *(property)* alienare; *(in mind)* agitare; **to — one's attention to** animadvertĕre; **to — out** ejicĕre, expellĕre; **to — round** volvĕre, circumagĕre, rotare; **to — up** *(with hoe)* invertĕre; **to — up the nose** nares corrugare; *vi* verti, converti, versari; **to — against** disciscĕre ab *(with abl),* alienari ab *(with abl);* **to — aside** devertĕre, se declinare; **to — away** discedĕre, aversari; **to — back** reverti; **to — into** *(to be changed into)* vertĕre in *(with acc),* mutari in *(with acc);* **to — out** cadĕre, evadĕre, contingĕre, evenire; **to — round** converti; **to — up** intervenire, adesse

turnip *s* rapum *n*
turpitude *s* turpitudo *f*
turret *s* turricula *f*
turtle *s* testudo *f*
turtledove *s* turtur *m*
tusk *s* dens *m*
tutelage *s* tutela *f*
tutor *s* praeceptor, magister *m*
tutor *vt* edocēre
tweezers *s* volsella *f*
twelfth *adj* duodecimus
twelve *adj* duodecim; **— times** duodecies

twentieth *adj* vicesimus
twenty *adj* viginti; **— times** vicies
twice *adv* bis
twig *s* surculus, ramulus *m,* virga, virgula *f*
twilight *s* crepusculum *n;* *(dawn)* diluculum *n*
twin *adj* geminus
twin *s* geminus, gemellus *m*
twine *s* filum *n,* resticula *f*
twine *vt* circumplicare, contorquēre; *vi* circumplecti
twinge *s* dolor *m*
twinkle *vi* micare, coruscare
twinkling *s* *(of eye)* nict·us -ūs *m*
twirl *vt* versare, circumagĕre; *vi* versari
twist *vt* torquēre; *vi* flecti
twit *vt* exprobrare, objurgare
twitch *s* vellicatio *f*
twitch *vt* vellicare; *vi* micare
twitter *vi* minurire
two *adj* duo; **— at a time** bini; **— times** bis
twofold *adj* duplex, duplus
type *s* *(model)* exemplum, exemplar *n;* *(class)* genus *n,* forma, figura *f*
typhoon *s* turbo *m*
typical *adj* solitus, proprius
tyrannical *adj* tyrannicus, superbus; **—ly** tyrannice, superbe
tyrannicide *s* *(act)* tyrannicidium *n;* *(person)* tyranni interfector, tyrannicida *m*
tyrannize *vi* dominari
tyranny *s* tyrannis, dominatio *f*
tyrant *s* tyrannus, dominus superbus *m*
tyro *s* tiro *m*

U

udder *s* uber *n*
ugliness *s* deformitas, foeditas *f*
ugly *adj* deformis, turpis, foedus
ulcer *s* ulcus *n*
ulcerous *adj* ulcerosus
ultimate *adj* ultimus, extremus; **—ly** tandem
umbrage *s* offensio *f;* **to take — at** aegre ferre
umbrella *s* umbella *f*
umpire *s* arbiter, disceptator *m*
unabashed *adj* intrepidus
unabated *adj* integer
unable *adj* impotens, invalidus; **to be — to** non posse, nequire
unaccented *adj* accentu carens
unacceptable *adj* ingratus, odiosus
unaccompanied *adj* incomitatus, solus
unaccomplished *adj* infectus, imperfectus
unaccountable *adj* inexplicabilis, inenodabilis
unaccountably *adv* praeter opinionem, sine causa
unaccustomed *adj* insolitus, insuetus, inexpertus

unacquainted *adj* **— with** ignarus *(with genit),* expers *(with genit)*
unadorned *adj* inornatus, incomptus, simplex
unadulterated *adj* merus, integer
unaffected *adj* simplex, candidus
unafraid *adj* impavidus
unaided *adj* non adjutus, sine ope
unalterable *adj* immutabilis
unaltered *adj* immutatus
unanimous *adj* unanimus, concors; **—ly** concorditer, consensu omnium
unanswerable *adj* irrefragabilis
unappeased *adj* implacatus
unapproachable *adj* inaccessus
unarmed *adj* inermis
unasked *adj* injussus, non vocatus
unassailable *adj* inexpugnabilis
unassuming *adj* modestus, moderatus, demissus
unattached *adj* liber, vacuus
unattainable *adj* arduus
unattempted *adj* inexpertus, inausus, intentatus
unattended *adj* incomitatus, sine comitibus

unattractive adj invenustus
unauthorized adj illicitus
unavailing adj inutilis, irritus
unavenged adj inultus
unavoidable adj inevitabilis
unaware adj inscius, nescius, ignarus
unbearable adj intolerabilis
unbeaten adj invictus
unbecoming adj indecorus, indecens; **it is** — dedecet
unbefitting adj indecorus
unbend vi animum remittĕre
unbending adj inflexibilis, inexorabilis
unbiased adj incorruptus, integer
unbidden adj injussus, ultro
unbleached adj crudus
unblemished adj integer, intactus
unblest adj infortunatus
unborn adj nondum natus
unbroken adj irruptus; integer; (of
horses) indomitus
unbuckle vt refibulare
unburden vt exonerare
unbutton vt refibulare
unceasing adj constans, assiduus;
—ly assidue
uncertain adj incertus, dubius; —ly
incerte, dubie
uncertainty s dubium n, dubitatio f
unchangeable adj immutabilis
unchanged adj immutatus
unchanging adj integer, idem
uncharitable adj immisericors
unchaste adj impudicus, obscenus;
—ly impudice, impure
uncivil adj inurbanus
uncivilized adj incultus
unclasp vt defibulare
uncle s (father's brother) patruus m;
(mother's brother) avunculus m
unclean adj immundus
uncomfortable adj incommodus,
molestus
uncommon adj rarus, insolitus, inusitatus; —ly raro, praeter solitum
unconcerned adj securus, incuriosus
unconditional adj absolutus, sine
exceptione; —ly nullā condicione
unconnected adj disjunctus
unconquerable adj invictus
unconscionable adj iniquus, injustus, absurdus
unconscious adj omni sensu carens;
— of ignarus (with genit), inscius
(with genit)
unconstitutional adj illicitus; —ly
contra leges
uncontrollable adj impotens
unconventional adj insolitus
unconvinced adj non persuasus
unconvincing adj non verisimilis
uncooked adj rudus
uncorrupted adj incorruptus
uncouth adj inurbanus, agrestis
uncover vt detegĕre, recludĕre, nudare
uncritical adj credulus
uncultivated adj incultus; indoctus
uncut adj intonsus
undamaged adj integer, inviolatus
undaunted adj impavidus, intrepidus

undecided adj incertus, dubius, anceps
undefended adj indefensus, nudus
undefiled adj purus, incontaminatus
undefined adj infinitus
undeniable adj haud dubius
under adv subter, infra
under prep (position) sub (with abl);
(motion) sub (with acc); (less than)
intra (with acc), infra (with acc)
underage adj impubes
underestimate vt minoris aestimare
undergarment s subucula f
undergo vt subire, pati
underground adj subterraneus
undergrowth s virgulta n pl
underhanded adj clandestinus, furtivus; —ly clam, furtive
underline vt subnotare
underling s minister, assecla m
undermine vt subruĕre, suffodĕre;
(fig) labefacĕre, labefactare
underneath adv infra, subter
underneath prep (position) infra
(with acc), sub (with abl); (motion)
sub (with acc)
underrate vt minoris aestimare
understand vt intellegĕre, comprehendĕre
understanding adj prudens, sapiens
understanding s mens f, intellectus -ūs m; (agreement) consens·us
-ūs m; (condition) condicio f
undertake vt adire ad (with acc),
suscipĕre; (to begin) incipĕre
undertaker s vespillo, libitinarius m
undertaking s inceptum, coeptum n
undervalue vt minoris aestimare
underworld s inferi m pl
undeserved adj immeritus, injustus;
—ly immerito
undeserving adj indignus
undiminished adj imminutus
undiscernible adj imperceptus, invisus
undisciplined adj immoderatus;
(mil) inexercitatus
undisguised adj apertus
undismayed adj impavidus, intrepidus
undisputed adj certus
undistinguished adj ignobilis, inglorius
undisturbed adj imperturbatus, immotus
undivided adj indivisus
undo vt (knot) expedire; (fig) infectum reddĕre; (to ruin) perdĕre
undone (adj) (not completed) infectus, imperfectus; (ruined) perditus
undoubted adj certus, haud dubius;
—ly haud dubie
undress vt exuĕre; vi vestes exuĕre
undressed adj nudus; (fig) rudis
undue adj nimius, iniquus
undulate vi undare, fluctuare
undulation s undarum agitatio f
unduly adv nimis, plus aequo
undying adj aeternus, sempiternus
unearth vt detegĕre, effodĕre
unearthly adj humano major, divinus
uneasiness s sollicitudo, anxietas f

uneasy *adj* sollicitus, anxius
uneducated *adj* indoctus, illiteratus
unemployed *adj* vacuus, otiosus
unemployment *s* otium *n*, cessatio *f*
unencumbered *adj* expeditus
unending *adj* infinitus, perpetuus
unendurable *adj* intolerandus
unenjoyable *adj* injucundus
unenlightened *adj* ineruditus
unenviable *adj* non invidendus, miser
unequal *adj* inaequalis, dispar, impar; —ly inaequaliter, impariter, inique
unequaled *adj* singularis, eximius
unerring *adj* certus; —ly certe
uneven *adj* inaequalis, iniquus; (*rough*) asper
unexpected *adj* inopinatus, insperatus, improvisus; —ly de improviso
unexplored *adj* inexploratus
unfading *adj* semper recens
unfailing *adj* certus, perpetuus; —ly semper
unfair *adj* iniquus; —ly inique
unfaithful *adj* infidus, perfidus, infidelis; —ly perfide
unfamiliar *adj* ignotus, alienus
unfashionable *adj* obsoletus
unfasten *vt* laxare, resolvere
unfavorable *adj* adversus, iniquus, inopportunus
unfavorably *adv* male, inique
unfed *adj* impastus
unfeeling *adj* durus, crudelis; —ly dure, crudeliter
unfetter *vt* vincula demere (*with dat*)
unfinished *adj* imperfectus; (*crude*) rudis, impolitus
unfit *adj* inhabilis, ineptus, inutilis
unfold *vt* explicare, evolvere; (*story*) enarrare; *vi* dehiscere, patescere
unforeseeing *adj* imprudens, improvidus
unforeseen *adj* improvisus, insperatus
unforgiving *adj* inexorabilis
unfortified *adj* immunitus, nudus
unfortunate *adj* infelix, infortunatus, nefastus; —ly infeliciter
unfounded *adj* vanus, fictus
unfriendly *adj* parum amicus, inimicus, alienus
unfruitful *adj* infructuosus, sterilis, infecundus
unfulfilled *adj* infectus
unfurl *vt* pandere, solvere
unfurnished *adj* imparatus
ungainly *adj* ineptus, inhabilis
ungenerous *adj* illiberalis
ungentlemanly *adj* inurbanus, illepidus
ungird *vt* discingere
ungodly *adj* impius
ungovernable *adj* indomabilis, intractabilis
ungracious *adj* iniquus, asper
ungrateful *adj* ingratus; —ly ingrate
ungrudging *adj* non invitus; —ly sine invidia
unguarded *adj* incustoditus, indefensus; (*of words*) inconsultus
unhandy *adj* inhabilis

unhappily *adv* infeliciter, misere
unhappiness *s* tristitia, miseria, maestitia *f*
unhappy *adj* infelix, infortunatus, miser
unharness *vt* disjungere
unhealthiness *s* valetudo, gravitas *f*
unhealthy *adj* infirmus, morbosus; (*unwholesome*) gravis, insalubris
unheard-of *adj* inauditus
unheeded *adj* neglectus
unhelpful *adj* invitus, difficilis
unhesitating *adj* promptus, confidens; —ly confidenter
unhinge *vt* de cardine detrahere; (*fig*) perturbare
unholy *adj* impius, profanus
unhoped-for *adj* insperatus
unhurt *adj* incolumis, salvus
unicorn *s* monoceros *m*
uniform *adj* constans, aequabilis; —ly constanter, aequabiliter
uniform *s* vestit·us –ūs *m*; (*mil*) sagum *n*
uniformity *s* constantia, aequabilitas *f*
unify *vt* conjungere
unilateral *adj* unilaterus
unimaginative *adj* hebes
unimpaired *adj* integer, intactus
unimpeachable *adj* probatissimus
unimportant *adj* nullius momenti (*genit*), levis
uninformed *adj* indoctus
uninhabitable *adj* non habitabilis, inhabitabilis
uninhabited *adj* desertus
uninjured *adj* incolumis
uninspired *adj* hebes
unintelligible *adj* obscurus
uninteresting *adj* frigidus, jejunus
uninterrupted *adj* continuus, perpetuus
uninviting *adj* injucundus, non alliciens
union *s* (*act*) conjunctio *f*; (*social*) consociatio, societas *f*; (*agreement*) consens·us –ūs *m*; (*marriage*) conjugium *n*
unique *adj* unicus, singularis
unison *s* concent·us –ūs *m*
unit *s* monas *f*, unio *m*
unite *vt* conjungere, consociare; *vi* coalescere, coire; conjurare
unity *s* concordia *f*
universal *adj* universus, universalis; —ly universe, ubique
universe *s* mundus *m*, summa rerum *f*
university *s* academia, universitas *f*
unjust *adj* injustus, iniquus; —ly injuste, inique
unjustifiable *adj* indignus
unkempt *adj* incomptus, neglectus
unkind *adj* inhumanus; —ly inhumane
unknowingly *adv* insciens
unknown *adj* ignotus, incognitus
unlawful *adj* illegitimus, illicitus; —ly contra legem *or* leges
unless *conj* nisi
unlike *adj* dissimilis, dispar, diversus
unlikely *adj* parum verisimilis
unlimited *adj* infinitus, immensus
unload *vt* exonerare

unluckily *adv* infeliciter
unlucky *adj* infelix, infaustus
unmanageable *adj* intractabilis, contumax
unmanly *adj* mollis
unmannerly *adj* male moratus, inurbanus
unmarried *adj (man)* caelebs; *(woman)* innupta
unmask *vt* detegĕre
unmatched *adj* unicus, singularis
unmerciful *adj* immisericors; **—ly** immisericorditer
unmindful *adj* immemor
unmistakable *adj* certissimus
unmistakably *adv* sine dubio
unmoved *adj* immotus
unnatural *adj (event)* monstruosus; *(deed)* immanis, crudelis; **—ly** contra naturam
unnecessarily *adv* ex supervacuo, nimis
unnecessary *adj* haud necessarius, supervacaneus
unnerve *vt* debilitare
unnoticed *adj* praetermissus; **to go — latēre**
unobjectionable *adj* culpae expers, honestus
unoccupied *adj* vacuus; otiosus; *(of land)* apertus
unofficial *adj* privatus
unpack *vt* e cistis eximĕre
unpaid *adj (of money)* debitus; *(of a service)* gratuitus
unpalatable *adj* amarus, insuavis
unparalleled *adj* unicus, singularis
unpardonable *adj* inexcusabilis
unpatriotic *adj* immemor patriae
unpitying *adj* immisericors, inexorabilis
unpleasant *adj* injucundus, incommodus; **—ly** injucunde, incommode
unpolluted *adj* impollutus; *(fig)* integer, intactus
unpopular *adj* invisus, invidiosus
unpracticed *adj* inexpertus, imperitus
unprecedented *adj* novus, inauditus
unprejudiced *adj* aequus
unpremeditated *adj* subitus, ex tempore
unprepared *adj* imparatus
unprincipled *adj* improbus
unproductive *adj* infecundus, infructuosus, sterilis
unprofitable *adj* vanus, inutilis
unprofitably *adv* inutiliter, frustra
unprotected *adj* indefensus
unprovoked *adj* non lacessitus, ultro
unpunished *adj* inpunitus, inultus
unqualified *adj* haud idoneus, inhabilis
unquenchable *adj* inexstinctus
unquestionable *adj* haud dubius, certissimus
unquestionably *adv* certe
unquestioning *adj* credulus
unravel *vt* retexĕre; *(fig)* enodare, explicare
unreasonable *adj* rationis expers, absurdus; iniquus
unreasonably *adv* absurde, inique
unrefined *adj* rudis, crudus, incultus

unrelenting *adj* implacabilis, inexorabilis
unremitting *adj* assiduus, continuus
unrepentant *adj* impaenitens
unrestrained *adj* effrenatus, indomitus, effusus
unrighteous *adj* injustus, iniquus; **—ly** injuste
unripe *adj* immaturus, crudus
unroll *vt* evolvĕre, explicare
unruliness *s* petulantia *f*
unruly *adj* effrenatus, turbulentus
unsafe *adj* intutus, periculosus
unsatisfactory *adj* non idoneus, malus
unsavory *adj* insipidus, insulsus, insuavis
unseasonable *adj* intempestivus, immaturis; incommodus, importunus
unseemly *adj* indecorus, indecens
unseen *adj* invisus
unselfish *adj* suae utilitatis immemor, liberalis; **—ly** liberaliter
unsettle *vt* turbare, sollicitare
unsettled *adj* incertus, inconstans; *(of mind)* sollicitus
unshaken *adj* immotus
unshaved *adj* intonsus
unsheathe *vt* destringĕre, e vagina educĕre
unsightly *adj* turpis, foedus
unskilful *adj* imperitus, inscitus; **—ly** imperite, inscite
unskilled *adj* imperitus, indoctus
unsophisticated *adj* simplex
unsound *adj* infirmus; *(mentally)* insanus; *(ill-founded)* vanus
unsparing *adj* inclemens; *(lavish)* prodigus, largus; **—ly** inclementer; prodige, large
unspeakable *adj* ineffabilis, inenarrabilis
unstable *adj* instabilis; *(fig)* levis, inconstans
unstained *adj* incontaminatus, purus
unsteadily *adv* inconstanter, instabiliter
unsteady *adj* inconstans, instabilis
unsuccessful *adj* infelix, infaustus; **—ly** infeliciter
unsuitable *adj* inhabilis, incommodus, alienus
unsuited *adj* haud idoneus
unsullied *adj* incorruptus
unsuspected *adj* non suspectus
untamed *adj* indomitus, ferus
untasted *adj* ingustatus
untaught *adj* indoctus, rudis
unteachable *adj* indocilis
untenable *adj* infirmus, inanis
unthankful *adj* ingratus
untie *vt* solvĕre
until *conj* dum, donec, quoad
until *prep* usque ad *(with acc)*, in *(with acc)*; **— now** adhuc
untimely *adj* intempestivus, importunus, immaturus
untiring *adj* assiduus, indefessus
untold *adj* innumerus
untouched *adj* intactus, integer; *(fig)* immotus
untrained *adj* inexercitatus

untried *adj* inexpertus, intemptatus

untrodden *adj* non tritus, avius

untroubled *adj* placidus, tranquillus; *(of sleep)* levis

untrue *adj* falsus, mendax; *(disloyal)* infidus

untrustworthy *adj* infidus

unusual *adj* inusitatus, insolitus, insuetus; —**ly** praeter solitum, raro

unutterable *adj* infandus, inenarrabilis

unvarnished *adj* (*fig*) nudus, simplex

unveil *vt* detegĕre, patefacĕre

unversed *adj* imperitus

unwarranted *adj* injustus, iniquus

unwary *adj* imprudens, incautus

unwearied *adj* indefessus, impiger

unwelcome *adj* ingratus, injucundus

unwholesome *adj* insalubris

unwieldy *adj* inhabilis

unwilling *adj* invitus; —**ly** invite

unwind *vt* revolvĕre, retexĕre

unwise *adj* imprudens, insipiens; —**ly** imprudenter, insipienter

unworthy *adj* indignus

unwrap *vt* explicare, evolvĕre

unwritten *adj* non scriptus

unyielding *adj* inflexibilis, obstinatus

unyoke *vt* disjungĕre

up *adv* sursum; — **and down** sursum deorsum

upbringing *s* educatio *f*

upheaval *s* eversio *f*

uphold *vt* servare, sustinēre, sustentare

upkeep *s* impensa *f*

uplift *vt* sublevare

upon *prep* (*position*) super (*with abl*), in (*with abl*); (*motion*) super (*with acc*), in (*with acc*); (*directly after*) e(x) (*with abl*); (*dependence*) e(x) (*with abl*)

upper *adj* superus, superior

uppermost *adj* summus, supremus

upright *adj* erectus; (*of character*) honestus, integer; —**ly** recte; integre

uproar *s* tumult·us -ūs *m*, turba *f*

uproot *vt* eradicare, eruĕre

upset *vt* evertĕre, subvertĕre, percellĕre

upset *adj* perculsus

upstream *adv* adverso flumine

up to *prep* usque ad (*with acc*), ad (*with acc*), tenus (*postpositive, with abl or genit*)

upwards *adv* sursum, sublime; — **of** (*of number*) plus quam

urban *adj* urbanus, oppidanus

urge *vt* urgēre, impellĕre, hortari; **to** — **on** stimulare

urge *s* impuls·us -ūs *m*

urgency *s* gravitas, necessitas *f*

urgent *adj* gravis, instans, vehemens; **to be** — instare; —**ly** vehementer, magnopere, graviter

urn *s* urna *f*

us *pron* nos; **to** — nobis; **with** — nobiscum

usage *s* mos *m*, consuetudo *f*

use *s* us·us -ūs, mos *m*, consuetudo, usura *f*; **no** —**!** frustra!; **to be of** — usui esse, prodesse; **to make** — **of** uti (*with abl*)

use *vt* uti (*with abl*); (*to take advantage of*) abuti (*with abl*); **to** — **something for** aliquid adhibēre (*with dat*); **to** — **up** consumĕre, exhaurire; *vi* **I used to** solebam (*with inf*)

used *adj* usitatus; — **to** (*accustomed to*) assuetus (*with dat*)

useful *adj* utilis, commodus, aptus; —**ly** utiliter, commode, apte

useless *adj* inutilis, inhabilis; (*of things*) inanis; —**ly** inutiliter, frustra

usual *adj* usitatus, solitus, consuetus; —**ly** plerumque, fere, ferme; **I** — **go** soleo ire

usurp *vt* usurpare, occupare

usurper *s* usurpator *m*

usury *s* usura *f*; **to practice** — faenerari

utensils *s* utensilia, vasa *n pl*, supellex *f*

utility *s* utilitas *f*

utilize *vt* uti (*with abl*), adhibēre

utmost *adj* extremus, ultimus, summus; **to do one's** — omnibus viribus contendĕre

utter *adj* totus, extremus, summus; —**ly** omnino, funditus

utter *vt* eloqui, proferre, pronuntiare, edĕre

utterance *s* elocutio, pronuntiatio *f*, dictum *n*

uttermost *adj* extremus, ultimus

V

vacant *adj* vacuus, inanis; **to be** — vacare

vacation *s* vacatio *f*, feriae *f pl*

vacillate *vi* vacillare

vacuum *s* inane *n*

vagabond *s* vagabundus, grassator *m*

vagrant *adj* vagabundus, vagus

vague *adj* vagus, dubius, ambiguus; —**ly** incerte, ambigue

vain *adj* vanus, futilis; superbus, arrogans; **in** — frustra; —**ly** frustra

valet *s* cubicularius *m*

valiant *adj* fortis; —**ly** fortiter

valid *adj* validus, legitimus, ratus; (*argument*) gravis

valley *s* vallis *f*

valor *s* fortitudo *f*

valuable *adj* pretiosus

valuation *s* aestimatio *f*

value *s* pretium *n*, aestimatio *f*

value *vt* aestimare, ducĕre; **to** — **highly** magni aestimare, magni habēre

valueless *adj* vilis, inutilis

vanguard *s* (*mil*) primum agmen *n*

vanish *vi* vanescĕre, diffugĕre

vanity *s* gloria, ostentatio *f*

vanquish *vt* vincĕre, superare

vapor *s* vapor *m*, exhalatio *f*

variable *adj* commutabilis, varius

variation *s* varietas, commutatio, vicissitudo *f*

variety *s* varietas, diversitas, multitudo *f*

various *adj* varii, diversi; **—ly** varie, diverse

vary *vt* variare, mutare; *vi* mutari

vase *s* amphora *f*, vas *n*

vast *adj* vastus, ingens, immensus; **—ly** valde

vastness *s* immensitas *f*

vault *s* fornix, camera *f*; *(leap)* salt·us -ūs *m*

vault *vi* salire

vaunt *vt* jactare; *vi* se jactare

veal *s* caro vitulina *f*

vegetable *s* holus *n*

vegetable *adj* holitarius

vehemence *s* vehementia, vis *f*, impet·us -ūs *m*

vehement *adj* vehemens, violentus, fervidus; **—ly** vehementer, valde

vehicle *s* vehiculum *n*

veil *s* velamen *n*, rica *f*; *(bridal)* flammeum *n*; *(fig)* integumentum *n*

veil *vt* velare, tegĕre

vein *s* vena *f*

velocity *s* velocitas, celeritas *f*

velvet *s* velvetum *n*

vend *vt* vendĕre

veneer *s* ligni bractea *f*; *(fig)* species *f*

venerable *adj* venerabilis

venerate *vt* venerari, colĕre

veneration *s* adoratio *f*, cult·us -ūs *m*

vengeance *s* ultio, poena *f*; **to take — on** vindicare in *(with acc)*, ulcisci

venom *s* venenum, virus *n*

vent *s* spiramentum, foramen *n*

vent *vt* aperire; **to — one's wrath on** iram erumpere in *(with acc)*

ventilate *vt* ventilare

venture *s* ausum *n*

venture *vt* periclitari; audēre

veracious *adj* verax

veracity *s* veracitas *f*

verb *s* verbum *n*

verbal *adj* verbalis; **—ly** verbo tenus

verbatim *adv* ad verbum

verbose *adj* verbosus; **—ly** verbose

verdict *s* sententia *f*; **to deliver a — ** sententiam pronuntiare

verge *s* margo, ora *f*; **to be on the — of** non procul abesse ut

verge *vi* vergĕre

verification *s* affirmatio *f*

verify *vt* ratum facĕre, confirmare

vermin *s* bestiolae *f pl*

versatile *adj* varius, agilis, versatilis

verse *s* vers·us -ūs *m*

versed *adj* peritus, exercitatus

version *s* forma, translatio *f*

vertex *s* vertex, vortex *m*

vertical *adj* rectus, directus; **—ly** ad lineam, ad perpendiculum

very *adj* ipse

very *adv* valde, admodum

vessel *s* vas *n*; *(ship)* navigium *n*

vest *s* subucula *f*

vestal *s* virgo vestalis *f*

vestige *s* vestigium, indicium *n*

vestment *s* vestimentum *n*

veteran *s* *(mil)* veteranus, vexillarius, emeritus *m*; *(fig)* veterator *m*

veterinarian *s* veterinarius *m*

veto *s* intercessio *f*, interdictum *n*

veto *vt* interdicĕre *(with dat)*; *(as tribune)* intercedĕre *(with dat)*

vex *vt* vexare, sollicitare

vexation *s* vexatio, offensio *f*, stomachus *m*

via *prep* per *(with acc)*

vial *s* phiala *f*

vibrate *vi* tremĕre, vibrare

vibration *s* tremor *m*

vicar *s* vicarius *m*

vice *s* vitium *n*, turpitudo *f*

vicinity *s* vicinitas, vicinia *f*

vicious *adj* vitiosus, perditus; *(of temper)* ferox; **—ly** ferociter

vicissitude *s* vicissitudo *f*

victim *s* victima, hostia *f*; *(exploited)* praeda *f*

victimize *vt* circumvenire

victor *s* victor *m*, victrix *f*

victorious *adj* victor; *(of woman)* victrix; **to be —** vincĕre

victory *s* victoria *f*; **to win a — ** victoriam reportare

vie *vi* certare, contendĕre; **to — with** aemulari *(with dat)*

view *s* aspect·us -ūs, conspect·us -ūs *m*; *(from above)* despect·us -ūs *m*; *(opinion)* opinio, sententia *f*, judicium *n*; **in my —** me judice; **to have in —** praevidēre

view *vt* visĕre, conspicĕre, intuēri, inspicĕre

vigil *s* pervigilatio *f*, pervigilium *n*

vigilance *s* vigilantia, diligentia *f*

vigilant *adj* vigilans, diligens, intentus; **—ly** vigilanter, diligenter

vigor *s* vigor, impet·us -ūs *m*, robur *n*

vigorous *adj* strenuus, acer, vegetus; **—ly** strenue, acriter

vile *adj* vilis, abjectus, perditus, flagitiosus

vilify *vt* infamare, calumniari

villa *s* villa *f*

village *s* vicus, pagus *m*

villager *s* vicanus, paganus *m*

villain *s* scelestus, nequam *(indecl)* *m*

villany *s* scelus *n*, improbitas, nequitia *f*

vindicate *vt* vindicare; *(to justify)* purgare; *(person)* defendĕre

vindictive *adj* ultionis cupidus

vine *s* vitis *f*

vinegar *s* acetum *n*

vineyard *s* vinea *f*, vinetum *n*

violate *vt* violare

violation *s* violatio *f*

violator *s* violator *m*

violence *s* violentia, vis *f*, impet·us -ūs *m*; *(cruelty)* saevitia *f*

violent *adj* violentus, vehemens; **—ly** violenter, vehementer

virgin *adj* virginalis

virgin *s* virgo *f*

virile *adj* virilis

virility *s* virilitas *f*

virtually *adv* fere

virtue *s* virtus, probitas *f*; *(power)* vis *f*; **by — of** per *(with acc)*, ex *(with abl)*

virtuous *adj* probus, honestus; *(chaste)* castus, pudicus; **—ly** honeste, caste

virulence *s* vis *f*, virus *n*; *(fig)* acerbitas *f*

visage *s* facies *f*, os *n*

viscous *adj* viscosus, lentus

visible *adj* aspectabilis, conspicuus, manifestus; **to be —** apparēre

visibly *adv* manifesto

vision *s* *(sense)* vis·us -ūs *m*; *(apparition)* visum *n*, viso *f*

visionary *adj* vanus, fictus, inanis

visit *s* salutatio *f*

visit *vt* visēre, visitare

visitor *s* salutator *m*, salutatrix *f*; advena, hospes *m*

visor *s* buccula *f*

vista *s* prospect·us -ūs *m*

visual *adj* oculorum *(genit)*

vital *adj* vitalis; *(essential)* necessarius; **—ly** praecipue

vitality *s* vis *f*, animus *m*

vitiate *vt* vitiare, corrumpĕre

vituperate *vt* vituperare, reprehendĕre

vituperative *adj* maledicus

vivacious *adj* vividus, alacer, hilaris; **—ly** acriter

vivacity *s* alacritas *f*

vivid *adj* vividus, acer; **—ly** acriter

vivify *vt* animare, vivificare

vocabulary *s* verborum copia *f*

vocal *adj* vocalis, canorus

vocation *s* officium, munus *n*

vociferous *adj* clamosus

vogue *s* mos *m*; **to be in —** in honore esse

voice *s* vox *f*, sonus *m*; *(vote)* suffragium *n*

void *s* inane, vacuum *n*

volatile *adj* levis, volaticus

volcanic *adj* flammas eructans

volcano *s* mons ignivomus *m*

volition *s* voluntas *f*

volley *s* conject·us -ūs *m*

voluble *adj* volubilis

volume *s* *(book)* volumen *n*; *(quantity)* copia, multitudo *f*; *(size)* amplitudo *f*

voluminous *adj* copiosus, amplus, magnus

voluntary *adj* voluntarius; *(unpaid)* gratuitus

volunteer *s* voluntarius *m*; *(mil)* miles voluntarius, evocatus *m*

volunteer *vi* sponte nomen dare

voluptuous *adj* voluptarius, voluptuosus, delicatus

vomit *vt* vomĕre, evomĕre

voracious *adj* vorax; **—ly** voraciter

voracity *s* voracitas *f*

vortex *s* vortex *m*

vote *s* suffragium *n*; *(fig)* *(judgment)* sententia *f*

vote *vi* suffragium ferre, suffragium inire; *(of judge)* sententiam ferre; *(of senator)* censēre; **to — against** antiquare; **to — for** suffragari *(with dat)*

votive *adj* votivus

vouch *vi* spondēre; **to — for** testificari, asseverare

voucher *s* *(person)* auctor *m*; *(document)* testimonium *n*

vow *s* votum *n*

vow *vt* *(to promise)* (de)vovēre, spondēre, promittĕre

vowel *s* vocalis littera *f*

voyage *s* navigatio *f*

voyage *vi* navigare

voyager *s* navigator *m*

vulgar *s* vulgaris, communis; *(low)* plebeius, vilis

vulgarity *s* insulsitas *f*

vulnerable *adj* obnoxius

vulture *s* vultur *m*

W

wade *vi* per vada ire; **to — across** vado transire

wag *vt* vibrare, agitare

wage *vt* **to — war** bellum gerĕre

wager *vt* deponĕre; *vi* sponsionem facĕre

wages *s* merces *f*, stipendium *n*

wagon *s* carrus *m*, plaustrum *n*

wail *vi* plorare, plangĕre, ululare

wailing *s* plorat·us -ūs, planct·us -ūs *n*

waist *s* medium corpus *n*

wait *vi* manēre; **to — for** exspectare; **to — on** servire *(with dat)*

wait *s* mora *f*; **to lie in — for** insidiari *(with dat)*

waive *vt* decedĕre de *(with abl)*, remittĕre

wake *vt* exsuscitare, excitare; *vi* expergisci

wake *s* vestigia *n pl*; **in the — of** post *(with acc)*

wakeful *adj* insomnis, vigil

waken *vt* exsuscitare, excitare; *vi* expergisci

walk *s* *(act)* ambulatio *f*; *(place)* ambulacrum *n*, xystus *m*; *(covered)* portic·us -ūs *m*; *(gait)* incess·us -ūs *m*

walk *vi* incedĕre, ambulare, gradi

wall *s* *(of house)* paries *f*; *(of town)* moenia *n pl*, murus *m*

wall *vt* muro cingĕre, moenibus munire

wallow *vi* volutari

walnut *s* juglans *f*

wan *adj* pallidus, exsanguis

wander *vi* vagari, errare; **to — about** pervagari; **to — over** pererrare

wanderer *s* erro, vagus *m*

wandering *s* erratio *f*

wane *vi* decrescĕre, minui, tabescĕre

want s egestas, inopia, indigentia, defectio *f*

want *vt (to wish)* velle; *(to lack)* egēre *(with abl)*, indigēre *(with abl)*, carēre *(with abl)*; *(to miss)* desiderare

wanting *adj (defective)* vitiosus; *(missing)* absens; **to be — deficĕre, deesse**

wanton *adj* protervus, lascivus, petulans; **—ly** lascive, petulanter

war s bellum *n*; **to declare —** bellum indicĕre; **to declare — on** bellum indicĕre *(with dat)*; **to enter —** bellum suscipĕre; **to wage — bellum gerĕre**

war *vi* bellare

war cry s ululat·us ·ūs *m*

ward s *(of town)* regio *f*; *(guard)* custodia *f*; *(minor)* pupillus *m*, pupilla *f*

ward *vt* **to — off** arcēre, avertĕre, defendĕre

warden s custos *m*; *(of prison)* carcerarius *m*

warehouse s apotheca *f*

wares s merx *f*

warfare s bellum *n*, res bellica *f*

war horse s equus bellator *m*

warlike *adj* militaris, bellicosus

warm *adj* calidus; *(fig)* acer; **to be — calēre; —ly** ardenter, acriter

warm *vt* calefacere, tepefacĕre

warmth s calor, fervor *m*

warn *vt* monēre, praemonēre

warning s monitio *f*, monit·us ·ūs *m*; *(object lesson)* exemplum *n*

warrant s auctoritas *f*, mandatum *n*

warrant *vt* praestare, promittĕre

warranty s satisdatio *f*

warrior s bellator, miles *m*, bellatrix *f*

wart s verruca *f*

wary *adj* cautus, providus, circumspectus

wash *vt* lavare; **to — away** abluĕre, diluĕre; **to — out** eluĕre; *vi* lavari

wash s *(clothes)* lintea lavanda *n pl*

washing s lavatio, lotura *f*

wasp s vespa *f*

waste s detrimentum *n*, effusio, dissipatio *f*; *(of time)* jactura *f*

waste *adj* vastus, desertus; **to lay — vastare, (de)populari**

waste *vt* consumĕre, perdĕre, dissipare; *(time)* absumĕre, terĕre; *vi* **to — away** tabescĕre, intabescĕre

wasteful *adj* profusus, prodigus; **—ly** prodige

wasteland s solitudo, vastitas *f*

watch s *(guard)* vigilia *f*; *(sentry)* excubiae *f pl*; **to keep — excubare; to keep — over** invigilare *(with dat)*, custodire

watch *vt (to observe)* observare, spectare, intuēri; *(to guard)* custodire; *vi* **to — out for** exspectare

watchful *adj* vigilans; **—ly** vigilanter

watchman s vigil, excubitor *m*

watchtower s specula *f*

watchword s tessera *f*, signum *n*

water s aqua *f*

water *vt* irrigare; *(animals)* adaquare

waterfall s cataracta *f*

watering place s aquarium *n*

watery *adj* aquaticus, aquosus

wave s unda *f*, fluct·us ·ūs *m*

wave *vt* agitare, vibrare, jactare; *vi* undare, fluctuare

waver *vi* fluctuare, labare, dubitare

wavering *adj* dubius, incertus

wavy *adj* undans, undosus; *(of hair)* crispus

wax s cera *f*

wax *vt* incerare; *vi* crescĕre, augēri

waxen *adj* cereus

way s via *f*, iter *n*; *(manner)* ratio *f*, modus *m*; *(habit)* mos *m*; **all the — from** usque ab *(with abl)*; **all the — to** usque ad *(with abl)*; **to get in the — of** intervenire *(with dat)*; **to give — (of a structure)** labare; *(mil)* pedem referre; **to give — to** indulgēre *(with dat)*; **to stand in the — of** obstare *(with dat)*

wayfarer s viator *m*

waylay *vt* insidiari *(with dat)*

wayward *adj* inconstans, levis, mutabilis

we *pron* nos; **— ourselves** nosmet ipsi

weak *adj* infirmus, debilis, imbecillus; *(argument)* tenuis; *(senses)* hebes; **—ly** infirme

weaken *vt* infirmare, debilitare, enervare; *vi* labare, hebescĕre, infirmus fieri

weakness s infirmitas, debilitas *f*; *(of mind)* imbecillitas *f*; *(flaw)* vitium *n*; *(of arguments)* levitas *f*

wealth s divitiae, opes *f pl*; copia, abundantia *f*

wealthy *adj* dives, opulentus; abundans

wean *vt* ab ubere depellĕre; *(fig)* desuefacĕre

weapon s telum *n*

wear *vt (clothes)* gerĕre; **to — out** terĕre, exedĕre; *vi* durare

weariness s lassitudo *f*

wearisome *adj* molestus

weary *adj* lassus, fessus, fatigatus

weather s caelum *n*, tempestas *f*

weather *vt* **to — a storm** procellam superare

weave *vt* texĕre

web s *(on loom)* tela, textura *f*; *(spider's)* araneum *n*

wed *vt (a woman)* ducĕre; *(a man)* nubĕre *(with dat)*; *vi (of husband)* uxorem ducĕre; *(of bride)* nubĕre

wedge s cuneus *m*

wedlock s matrimonium *n*

weed s herba inutilis *f*

weed *vt* eruncare

week s hebdomas *f*

weekly *adj* hebdomadalis

weep *vi* flēre, lacrimare; **to — for** deplorare

weeping s plorat·us ·ūs *m*, lacrimae *f pl*

weigh *vt* pendĕre, ponderare, trutinari; *(fig)* meditari; **to — down** degravare; *(fig)* opprimĕre; *vi* **to — much** magni ponderis esse

weight s pondus n, gravitas f; (influence) (fig) auctoritas f; (importance) momentum n

weighty adj ponderosus, gravis

welcome s gratulatio, salutatio f

welcome vt salvēre jubēre, excipēre

welcome interj salve!; (to several) salvēte!

weld vt (con)ferruminare

welfare s salus f

well s puteus, fons m

well adj sanus, validus, salvus

well adv bene, recte, probe; **very —** optime

well interj heia!

well-bred adj generosus, liberalis

well-known adj pervulgatus; notus, nobilis

welter s congeries, turba f

west s occidens, occas·us -ūs m

western adj occidentalis

westward adv in occasum, occasum versus

west wind s Zephyrus, Favonius m

wet adj humidus, uvidus, madidus

wet vt madefacĕre, rigare

whale s balaena f, cetus m

wharf s navale n, crepido f

what pron interrog quid, quidnam, ecquid

what adj interrog qui; **— sort of** qualis

whatever pron quisquis

whatever adj quicumque

wheat s triticum n

wheedle vt blandiri, delenire

wheedling adj blandus

wheel s rota f

wheelbarrow s pabo m

whelp s catulus m

when adv quando

when conj cum, ubi, ut

whence adv unde

whenever conj quandocumque, utcumque, quotiens

where adv ubi

where conj quā, ubi

whereas conj quandoquidem

whereby adv re, quā viā, quo, per quod

wherefore adv quare, quamobrem, quapropter

wherein adv in quo, in quibus, ubi

whereof adv cujus, quorum; de quo, de quibus

whereto adv quo, quorsum

whereupon adv quo facto, post quae

wherever conj quacumque, ubicumque

whet vt acuĕre; (fig) exacuĕre

whether conj (in single indirect question) num, -ne, an; **whether . . . or** (in multiple indirect questions) utrum . . . an, -ne . . . an, . . . an; (in disjunctive conditions) sive . . . sive, seu . . . seu; **whether . . . or not** utrum . . . necne

whetstone s cos f

which pron interrog quis; (of two) uter; pron rel qui

which adj interrog qui; (of two) uter; adj rel qui

whichever pron quisquis, quicum-

que; (of two) untercumque

while s tempus, spatium n; **a little — pauli**sper; **a long —** diu; **it is worth —** operae pretium est; **once in a —** interdum

while conj dum, quoad, donec

whim s libido f

whimper vi vagire

whimper s vagit·us -ūs m

whimsical adj levis, mobilis

whine vi miserabiliter vagire

whip s flagellum n, scutica f

whip vt flagellare, verberare

whirl vt torquēre, rotare; vi torquēri, rotari

whirlpool s vertex, gurges m

whirlwind s turbo, typhon m

whisper s susurrus m

whisper vt & vi susurrare

whistle s (pipe) fistula f; (sound) sibilus m; (of wind) stridor m

whistle vi sibilare

white adj albus; (brilliant) candidus; (of hair) canus

whiten vt dealbare, candefacĕre; vi albescĕre, canescĕre

who pron interrog quis; pron rel qui

whoever pron quicumque, quisquis

whole adj totus, cunctus, integer

whole s totum n, summa f; **on the — plerumque**

wholesome adj saluber, salutaris

wholly adv omnino, prorsus

whose pron cujus; quorum

why adv cur, quare, quamobrem

wicked adj improbus, nefarius, impius; **—ly** improbe, nefarie

wickedness s nequitia, improbitas, impietas f, scelus n

wicker adj vimineus

wide adj latus, amplus; **—ly** late

widen vt dilatare, laxare, extendĕre; vi patescĕre, dilatari, laxari

widow s vidua f

widower s viduus m

widowhood s viduitas f

width s latitudo, amplitudo f

wield vt tractare, vibrare

wife s uxor, conju(n)x f

wifely adj uxorius

wig s capillamentum n

wild adj ferus; (of trees, plants, etc.) silvestris; (of land) vastus, incultus; (of disposition) saevus, amens, ferox; **—ly** saeve, ferociter

wilderness s vastitas, solitudo f, loca deserta n pl

wile s fraus f, dolus m

wilful adj pervicax, consultus; **—ly** de industria

will s voluntas f, animus m; (intent) propositum, consilium n; (document) testimonium n; (of gods) nut·us -ūs m; **at — ad libidinem**

will vt velle; (legacy) legare, relinquēre

willing adj libens, promptus; **to be — velle**; **—ly** libenter

willow s salix f

wily adj vafer, astutus

win vt adipisci, nancisci, consequi, (victory) reportare; (friends) sibi conciliare; **to — over** conciliare; *vi* vincĕre, superare

wind *s* ventus *m*

wind *vt* circumvolvĕre, circumvertĕre, glomerare, torquĕre; **to — up** (*to bring to an end*) concludĕre; *vi* sinuare

windfall *s* (*fig*) lucrum insperatum *n*

winding *adj* sinuosus, flexuosus

windmill *s* venti mola *f*

window *s* fenestra *f*

windpipe *s* aspera arteria *f*

windy *adj* ventosus

wine *s* vinum *n*; (*undiluted*) merum *n*; (*sour or cheap*) vappa *f*; (*new*) mustum *n*

wing *s* ala *f*; (*mil*) cornu *n*

winged *adj* alatus, volucer

wink *vi* nictare, connivĕre

winner *s* victor *m*

winning *adj* (*fig*) blandus, amoenus

winnings *s* lucrum *n*

winnow *vt* ventilare

winter *s* hiems *f*; **in the dead of —** media hieme; **to spend the —** hiemare

winter *vi* hiemare, hibernare

winter *adj* hibernus

winter quarters *s* hiberna *n pl*

wintry *adj* hiemalis, hibernus

wipe *vt* detergĕre; **to — away** abstergĕre; **to — out** delēre, abolēre, expungĕre

wire *s* filum aeneum *n*

wisdom *s* sapientia, prudentia *f*

wise *adj* sapiens, prudens; **—ly** sapienter, prudenter

wise *s* modus *m*; **in no —** nequaquam

wish *s* optatum, votum *n*; **best —es** salus *f*

wish *vt* optare, velle, cupĕre; *vi* **to — for** exoptare, expetĕre

wisp *s* manipulus *m*

wistful *adj* desiderii plenus; **—ly** oculis intentis

wit *s* (*intellect*) ingenium *n*, argutiae *f pl*; (*humor*) sales *m pl*, facetiae *f pl*; (*person*) homo facetus *m*; **to be at one's —s' end** delirare; **to — scilicet

witch *s* venefica, saga *f*

witchcraft *s* ars magica *f*, veneficium *n*

with *prep* cum (*with abl*); apud (*with acc*)

withdraw *vt* seducĕre, avocare; (*words*) revocare; *vi* recedĕre, discedĕre

wither *vt* torrēre, corrumpĕre; *vi* marcēre, arescĕre

withered *adj* marcidus

withhold *vt* retinēre, abstinēre, cohibēre

within *adv* intus, intra; (*motion*) intro

within *prep* intro (*with acc*), in (*with abl*); **— a few days** paucis diebus

without *adv* extra, foris; **from —** extrinsecus

without *prep* sine (*with abl*), absque (*with abl*), expers (*with genit*);

to be — carere (*with abl*)

withstand *vt* obsistĕre (*with dat*), resistĕre (*with dat*)

witness *s* testis *m & f*; (*to a signature*) obsignator *m*; **to bear — testificari; **to call to —** testari, antestari

witness *vt* testificari; (*to see*) intuēri, vidēre

witticism *s* sales *m pl*

witty *adj* facetus, salsus, acutus

wizard *s* magus, veneficus *m*

woe *s* dolor, luct·us -ūs *m*; **—s** mala *n pl*

woeful *adj* tristis, luctuosus, miser; **—ly** triste, misere

wolf *s* lupus *m*, lupa *f*

woman *s* mulier, femina *f*

womanhood *s* muliebris stat·us -ūs *m*

womanly *adj* muliebris

womb *s* uterus *m*

wonder *s* admiratio *f*; (*astonishing object*) miraculum, mirum *n*

wonder *vi* (ad)mirari; **to — at** admirari

wonderful *adj* mirabilis, admirandus; **—ly** mirabiliter, mirifice

wont *adj* **to be — to** solēre (*with inf*)

woo *vt* petĕre

wood *s* lignum *n*; (*forest*) silva *f*, nemus *n*

wooded *adj* lignosus, silvestris

wooden *adj* ligneus

woodland *s* silvae *f pl*

woodman *s* lignator *m*

wood nymph *s* Dryas *f*

wooer *s* procus, amator *m*

wool *s* lana *f*

woolen *adj* laneus

word *s* verbum, vocabulum *n*; (*spoken*) vox *f*; (*promise*) fides *f*; (*news*) nuntius *m*; **in a —** denique; **to break one's — fidem fallĕre; **to give one's — fidem dare; **to keep one's — fidem praestare; **— for —** ad verbum

wordy *adj* verbosus

work *s* opera *f*, opus *n*; (*trouble*) labor *m*; (*task*) pensum *n*

work *vt* (*to exercise*) exercēre; (*to till*) colĕre; *vi* laborare, operari

workman *s* (*unskilled*) operarius *m*; (*skilled*) faber, opifex *m*

workmanship *s* opus *n*, ars *f*

workshop *s* officina *f*

world *s* (*universe*) mundus *m*, summa rerum *f*; (*earth*) orbis terrarum *m*; (*nature*) rerum natura *f*; (*mankind*) homines *m pl*

worldly *adj* profanus

worm *s* vermis, vermiculus *m*, tinea *f*

worm-eaten *adj* vermiculosus

worry *s* sollicitudo, cura *f*

worry *vt* vexare, sollicitare; *vi* sollicitari

worse *adj* pejor, deterior; **to grow — ingravescĕre

worsen *vi* ingravescĕre

worship *s* veneratio *f*, cult·us -ūs *m*

worship *vt* venerari, adorare, colĕre

worshiper *s* cultor, venerator *m*

worst *adj* pessimus, deterrimus

worst *vt* vincĕre

worth s (*value*) pretium n; (*merit*) dignitas, virtus f; **to be —** valēre

worthless adj vilis, inutilis; (*of person*) nequam (*indecl*)

worthy adj dignus

wound s vulnus n

wound vt vulnerare; (*fig*) offendĕre, laedĕre

wounded adj saucius

wrap vt involvĕre; **to — up** complicare

wrath s ira, iracundia f

wrathful adj iratus, iracundus; **—ly** iracunde

wreak vt **to — vengeance on** ulcisci, vindicare

wreath s sertum n, corona f

wreathe vt (*to twist*) torquēre; (*to adorn with wreaths*) coronare, nectĕre

wreck s naufragium n

wreck vt frangĕre; (*fig*) perdĕre

wren s regulus m

wrench vt detorquēre, luxare

wrest vt extorquēre, eripĕre

wrestle vi luctari

wrestler s luctator, athleta m

wretch s miser, perditus, nequam (*indecl*) m

wretched adj miser, infelix, abjectus; **—ly** misere, abjecte

wretchedness s miseria, aerumna f

wring vt contorquēre, stringĕre; **to — the neck** gulam frangĕre

wrinkle s ruga f

wrinkle vt corrugare; **to — the forehead** frontem contrahĕre

wrinkled adj rugosus

writ s (*law*) mandatum n

write vt scribĕre, perscribĕre; (*poetry*) componĕre; (*history*) perscribĕre

writer s scriptor, auctor m

writhe vi torquēri

writing s (*act*) scriptio f; (*result*) scriptum n, scriptura f; (*hand*) man·us -ūs f

wrong adj pravus, perversus, falsus; (*unjust*) injustus, iniquus; **—ly** falso, male, perperam; **to be —** errare, falli

wrong s nefas n, injuria f, malum n; **to do —** peccare

wrong vt nocēre (*with dat*), injuriam inferre (*with dat*), laedĕre

wrought adj factus, confectus, fabricatus

wry adj distortus, obliquus

Y

yard s (*court*) area f; (*measure*) tres pedes m pl; **a — long** tripedalis

yawn vi oscitare, hiare; (*to gape open*) dehiscĕre

year s annus m; **every — quotannis; five —s** quinquennium n; **four —s** quadriennium n; **three —s** triennium n; **two — biennium n**

yearly adj annuus, anniversarius

yearly adv quotannis

yearn vi **to — for** desiderare

yeast s fermentum n

yell s ululat·us -ūs m, ejulatio f

yell vi ululare, ejulare

yellow adj flavus, luteus, gilvus, croceus

yelp vt gannire

yes adv ita, immo, sane

yesterday adv heri

yet adv (*contrast, after adversative clause*) tamen, nihilominus; (*time*) adhuc; (*with comparatives*) etiam; **as — adhuc; not — nondum**

yield vt (*to produce*) ferre, parĕre;

praebēre; (*to surrender*) dedĕre, concedĕre; vi cedĕre

yoke s jugum n; (*fig*) servitus f

yoke vt jugum imponĕre (*with dat*), conjungĕre

yonder adv illic

you pron (*thou*) tu; (*ye*) vos; **— yourself** tu ipse

young adj juvenis, adulescens; (*of child*) parvus; (*fig*) novus

younger adj junior, minor natu

youngster s adulescentulus m

your adj tuus; vester

yours pron tuus; vester

yourself pron reflex te; **to — tibi; with —** tecum; *intensive* tu ipse

yourselves pron reflex vos; **to — vobis; with —** vobiscum; *intensive* vos ipsi, vosmet ipsi

youth s (*age*) adulescentia f; (*collectively*) juventus f; (*young man*) juvenis, adulescens m

youthful adj juvenalis, puerilis; **—ly** juveniliter, pueriliter

---

Z

zeal s studium n, ardor, fervor m

zealous adj studiosus, ardens; **—ly** studiose, ardenter m

zenith s vertex m

zephyr s Zephyrus, Favonius m

zero s nihil, nihilum n

zest s (*taste*) sapor, gust·us -ūs m;

(*fig*) gustat·us -ūs, impet·us -ūs m

zigzag adj tortuosus

zodiac s signifer orbis m

zone s zona, regio f

zoology s zoologia, animantium descriptio f